1001 IDEAS
THAT CHANGED THE WAY WE THINK

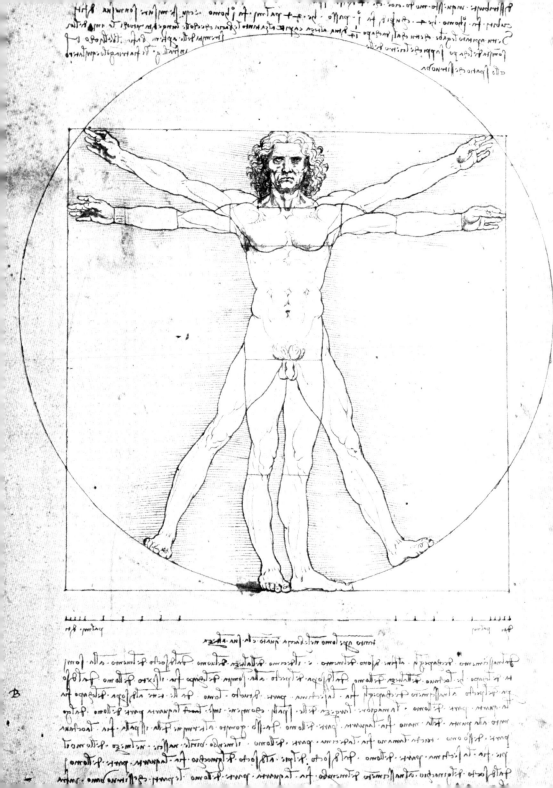

1001IDEAS

THAT CHANGED THE WAY WE THINK

GENERAL EDITOR **ROBERT ARP**

PREFACE BY **ARTHUR CAPLAN**

A Quintessence Book

First published in Great Britain in 2013 by Cassell Illustrated
A division of Octopus Publishing Group Limited
Endeavour House, 189 Shaftesbury Avenue
London, WC2H 8JY
www.octopusbooks.co.uk

An Hachette UK Company
www.hachette.co.uk

Reprinted in 2014

ISBN-13: 978 184403 750 6

QSS.IDES

A CIP catalogue record for this book is available from the British Library.

This book was designed and produced by
Quintessence Editions Ltd.
The Old Brewery, 6 Blundell Street
London, N7 9BH
www.1001beforeyoudie.com

Project Editor Elspeth Beidas
Editors Frank Ritter, Fiona Plowman, Jodie Gaudet
Designers Isabel Eeles, Tea Aganovic, Tom Howey
Picture Researcher Julia Harris-Voss
Production Manager Anna Pauletti

Editorial Director Jane Laing
Publisher Mark Fletcher

Colour reproduction by KHL Chroma Graphics Pte Ltd, Singapore
Printed in China by Midas Printing International Ltd.

Contents

Preface
By Arthur Caplan

These days, it is not uncommon to hear commentators on higher education accuse those who spend time studying the humanities in college or university of being foolish. The idea that a person might take courses in philosophy, psychology, religion, the arts, sociology, or politics strikes many as simply ludicrous. They argue that the whole point of education is to get a job, and that to get a job a person needs to have a practical skill or possess a body of readily applicable knowledge. These goals make the study of "big ideas" in the humanities or social sciences at best ludicrous and at worst pointless.

As you begin to browse through *1001 Ideas That Changed The Way We Think*, one of the most important things that you realize is just how utterly wrong are those people who see the value of education only in terms of the career opportunities it creates. A cursory look through this book soon makes it evident that the discoveries, inventions, and findings that make the most difference in our lives are just as likely to emanate from the humanities and social sciences side of the intellectual landscape as they are from technology, science, and engineering. In fact, the latter are only likely to flourish when firmly embedded in a wider context of big ideas that allow them to do so.

Moreover, the rich history of ideas that can be found in this book reveals an even more important truth—what it is that makes life meaningful is not found simply in an education that prepares one to excel at computer programming, advertising, bioengineering, or business. It is only through an engagement with great ideas that we can find meaning and purpose in our lives. These ideas enable us not only to decide on but also to defend the personal views that we assume regarding important matters. Is there an absolute moral ethic that you should always follow, as Plato claims? What is it that we actually see when looking at art, as John Berger asks? Do you agree with the American Psychiatric Association's diagnostic manual classification of what is "normal" with respect to mental health? Should you live your life wary of the lure of the ephemeral, materialistic trinkets and baubles that are shilled by capitalism, as Jean-Jacques Rousseau urges? The way that you live your life and the way that you choose to present yourself to the world will be far more enriched by reading this book than by spending years in a graduate school of business, law, or accounting. Indeed, the rationale for doing the latter ought only to be grounded by an immersion in the former.

There is yet another reason why the entries in this book merit your attention—they are intellectually challenging, and as a result are fun to think about. Jeremy Bentham's full-throated articulation of utilitarianism provides a fascinating antidote to centuries of morality reliant on divine or royal authority, virtue, and inviolate principles. His thinking is reflected in every cost-benefit and risk-benefit analysis that accompanies nearly all public policy thinking today. Even recent efforts to install happiness as the correct measure of a nation's overall status, as suggested by King Jigme Singye Wangchuck of Bhutan, owe a great deal to Bentham. However, for all his brilliance, Bentham could fail in applying his theories to social reform. His efforts to promote the Panopticon as an alternative to the harsh, often inhumane conditions that dominated prisons and asylums, with their tiny quarters, bars, locks, lack of windows, and chains, were noble. But the notion of being subject to permanent surveillance caused other problems, because a certain amount of personal privacy is often considered requisite for maintaining a person's sense of self and self-esteem.

In looking forward, there are plenty of big ideas reviewed in this book that can help to provide conceptual handrails for what might be in our future. Perhaps one of the most provocative is Garret Hardin's "lifeboat Earth" argument that, in a world of limited resources with a growing population, we cannot let the poor, weak, and disadvantaged consume resources if it means that the ability of all to survive will be imperiled. While his dire forecast of the inevitability of life and death rationing has power, it may be that some of the other ideas examined in these pages will provide us with the tools to generate more resources or reduce population growth. By thinking big, we may be able to make the chances of Hardin's bleak prediction coming true much smaller.

As Bentham knew, a big idea is worth promoting and even testing in the real world. And as will become apparent upon reading this book, a big idea is also worth criticizing, endorsing, dismissing, and amending—but only you will know which seems the most appropriate response to what you find in these pages. Enjoy.

New York, United States

Introduction
By Robert Arp

I am a philosopher by training, so, as philosophers seem naturally to be attracted to ideas of any kind, it makes sense that I would be the editor of a book like this one. The word "philosophy" is derived from the Greek words *philo*, meaning "love" or "desire," and *sophy*, meaning "wisdom" or "knowledge." Philosophy is therefore the "love of wisdom," and an important way to attain knowledge is by exposing yourself to plenty of ideas.

But what exactly is an idea? The English word is a direct cognate of the Latin *idea*, which is derived from the Greek ίδέα. The Greek word ίδέα is itself a derivation of the Greek verb meaning "to see." Ancient Greek philosopher Plato used the word "idea" to refer to "Forms"—unchanging, perfect, ideal things of which everything in the universe was a better or worse copy. There was a Form of human, a Form of cat, a Form of tree, even Forms of justice, beauty, and goodness. The Forms were real, existing things, and a person had to use their mind to reason, think about, and understand them, especially when philosophizing.

Plato's definition of an idea might strike us as strange, because for him ideas were extra-mental things "out there" in reality—not visible to the eye, but knowable by the mind—whereas nowadays we think of ideas as concepts or images that exist, at best, in a person's mind. Nonetheless, Plato's concept of an idea was influential in Western history for many centuries. In the Middle Ages, medieval Christian philosophers and theologians—who borrowed much from the theories of Plato and his prize student, Aristotle—used the term "idea" to refer to an archetype of some thing that existed in the mind of the Christian God. According to this view, before God created the universe and all that it contains, He had the idea of the universe and all that it contains already in mind. It was also around this time that the word "idea" began to be used interchangeably with the Latin words *conceptio* (conception), *conceptus mentis* (mental concept), *notio* (notion), *verbum mentale* (mental word), and *species intelligibilis* (intelligible species).

By the seventeenth century and the birth of what is known as Modern philosophy, "idea" no longer referred to some Platonic concept existing outside of the mind. Rather, it had taken back its original Greek connotation of "to see." For example, René Descartes noted that "Among my thoughts, some are like images of things, and it is to these alone that the name 'idea' properly belongs." He also wrote that "idea is the thing thought upon." By the time that John Locke penned his influential *An Essay Concerning Human Understanding* in 1690, the word "idea" had assumed a purely mental association: "the word 'Idea' stands for whatever is the object of the understanding when a man thinks. I have used it to express whatever is meant by phantasm, notion, species, or whatever it is which the mind can be employed about when thinking."

Locke envisioned ideas to be objects of thought, a definition that was taken up in the twentieth century by the U.S. philosopher and educator Mortimer Adler (who cofounded the Center for the Study of The Great Ideas in Chicago in 1990). However, Adler added the caveat that an idea must be a common object "being considered and discussed by two or more individuals." In his short article "What is an Idea?" (1958), Adler maintained that "freedom and justice, war and peace, government and democracy might be called ideas or objects of thought." He contrasted this "objective" definition of an idea with a "subjective" definition, wherein an idea is understood to be an individual's own conscious thought or perception. Adler's notion of an objective idea was most clearly expressed in his classic work *The Idea of Freedom* (1958) in which he described five different conceptions of freedom and traced the discussion of them among philosophers throughout history.

Today, the word "idea" has several connotations and denotations, many of which are aligned to these historical conceptions. For example, the first two definitions of "idea" that are given in the Merriam-Webster Dictionary are: "a transcendent entity that is a real pattern of which existing things are imperfect representations," and "a standard of perfection (ideal)," both of which have clearly been informed by Plato's Theory of Forms.

In line with Descartes's description of ideas as "images of things," an idea can also be considered a perceptual image, or a picture in a person's mind of something, including a sensation that has been "called to mind" through memory. For example, imagine the Eiffel Tower: the "picture" that this conjures up in your mind is an idea. These mental images do not always have to be fully formed, however: an idea can also be thought of as a more general "mental impression." A good example of an idea in this sense is Einstein's theory of special relativity. Unless you have a clear knowledge of physics, you probably have an inchoate notion in your mind that special relativity has something to do with $E = mc^2$, motion being relative, and objects traveling at the speed of light. You therefore have some idea or impression of special relativity, but it is vague, rudimentary, and obviously not as complete as the idea of special relativity in the mind of a person with a Ph.D. in Astrophysics.

Another understanding of an idea is as a concept. The words "thought" and "idea" are often used interchangeably by people, as are the words "opinion" and "idea." These concepts, thoughts, and opinions are frequently referred to in terms of being understood or formulated, conveying the sense that the ideas behind them are clear in the speaker's mind. Examples of this type of idea include "digestion," "cost-benefit analysis," or "gravity affects all material bodies in the Earth's atmosphere." There is an intimate connection between understanding a concept, being able to formulate a thought, and having knowledge. The most knowledgeable people in certain areas of study often have a solid understanding of the ideas that comprise that field.

An idea can also be read as synonymous with a goal, end, aim, or purpose—"I took a job with the idea of getting some money together," for example. Or it can be a concept in a person's mind that might be so abstract as to not be imaginable in a picture-like form, such as the idea of what constitutes the process of reasoning.

In the following pages, you will find 1,001 of the most important ideas that have ever been imagined, conceived, and articulated throughout the course of recorded history. These are 1,001 ideas that changed the way we think. Various dictionaries all describe thinking as a process that utilizes ideas in some way—to plan, predict, pronounce, produce, and numerous other activities—which is a straightforward and commonly understood notion. It is a simple fact that you cannot do any thinking without ideas! So many ideas have changed people's way of thinking, with their impact ranging from small groups of individuals to entire societies and even the whole world. You would not be reading this book right now were it not for Johannes Gutenberg's ideas of mechanical movable type and the printing press so as to "spread learning to the masses" in the fifteeenth century. And you would not be reading anything at all if the ancient Sumerians had not had the idea to design pictograms and an alphabet some 5,000 years ago.

It is possible to organize and classify ideas in many ways. In an attempt to be sensible and economical, the ideas in this book have been placed in one of the following categories: Philosophy; Religion; Psychology; Science and Technology (including mathematical ideas and inventive ideas); Politics and Society (including education ideas, legal ideas, and economic ideas); and Art and Architecture (including music ideas and literary ideas). In the text for each idea you will find a description of exactly what the idea is; an account of its origin (who or where the idea came from); a quotation that uses, or is about, the idea; and a brief explanation of why the idea is important.

1001 Ideas That Changed The Way We Think is ordered chronologically, but it has not always been easy to establish a definitive date for when each idea first appeared. Generally we have used the earliest recorded instance of the idea, or the date that the first work containing the idea was published. Time periods for each chapter have been simplified into the following historical eras: Ancient World (2,000,000 BCE to 499 CE); The Middle Ages (500 to 1449); Early Modern (1450 to 1779); Late Modern (1780 to 1899); Early Twentieth Century (1900 to 1949); and Contemporary (1950 to present).

You will notice that a good many of the titles of the ideas in this book appear more like an invention, mechanism, device, contraption, or even a process, activity, or system—such as the Kinetoscope (an 1890s machine that magnified looped film for a viewer), the telephone, the map, the magazine, the encyclopedia, or even waterpower, groupthink, nuclear fusion, and breakdancing. It can be hard to divorce these ideas from their aforementioned uses, but the authors have tried to present the idea behind the invention, or the idea that gave birth to a process, or the idea that acted as a catalyst for a system, rather than simply describe what that invention, process, or system does.

You will also notice that there appear to be numerous principles, laws, rules, theories, or hypotheses in this book. In these cases, the principles, laws, and the like are themselves the idea. Examples of this type of idea include the uncertainty principle, the second law of thermodynamics, the greenhouse effect, presumption of innocence, the Ten Commandments, and, one of my personal favorites, Godwin's Law (coined by Mike Godwin in 1990), which states that if an online discussion continues long enough—on any topic whatsoever—someone in the discussion will inevitably make a comparison to Adolph Hitler or the Nazis.

I hope that you find as much joy in reading these 1,001 ideas as I did when the contributors submitted them to me to edit. As a final thought, I will leave you with a quotation from a speech given in 1963 by the United States' thirty-fifth president, John F. Kennedy, that I recall from a class on the U.S. government during my teenage years: "A man may die, nations may rise and fall, but an idea lives on. Ideas have endurance without death."

Index of Ideas by Category

Art and Architecture

Philosophy

Politics and Society

Religion

Psychology

Science and Technology

Ancient World
Pre 500 CE

Archaeologist Steven Mithen has put forward the theory that, around 30,000 years ago, our hominin ancestors' mental modules opened up, and ideas and information began to flow freely between them—a process that he termed "cognitive fluidity." It is likely that the first ideas that humans came up with had a practical application, as in the case of the Levallois Technique for shaping flint tools. Early humans then applied creative thought to develop ideas such as clothing, jewelry, anthropomorphism, and Paleolithic cave art. Later, with the rise of the ancient civilizations of Egypt, Greece, and Rome, countless abstract concepts were formed in areas such as mathematics and philosophy.

← A painting from the tomb of Ramses I (c. 1290 BCE), showing the Egyptian pharaoh with the gods Harsiesis and Anubis. Images like this one were common in Egyptian funerary art.

Human Control of Fire
Homo erectus

Harnessing fire in order to use its
properties as a practical tool

Controlling fire has been a hallmark of human culture
since before the existence of modern Homo sapiens.
Early people obtained fire from natural sources,
later developing a variety of methods to create fire
artificially. The ability to create, control, and use fire
remains essential to human civilization.

The first exposure that early humans had to fire most
likely came from wild fires and forest fires sparked by
lightning. While destructive and potentially deadly, they
provided early access to the tool, although it was not
a force that people could control, much less create at
will. There is evidence to show that as early as 1.6 million
years ago Homo erectus groups had harnessed fire to
some extent, and by 400,000 to 250,000 BCE there is clear
evidence that Homo erectus could control and perhaps

"Fire, though it may be quenched, will not become cool."

Ovid, ancient Roman poet

even create it. By 125,000 BCE, well after the emergence
of modern Homo sapiens, human use, control, and
creation of fire were widespread and common.

Humanity's mastery of fire had an immediate and
profound impact on its evolution. Fire gave people
protection from wild animals, allowed them to
illuminate the darkness, gave warmth to fend off the
cold, enhanced their ability to fashion tools, gave them
the ability to cook food, and served as an effective
deterrent against insects and pests. Fire was so useful
in the preparation of food that humans became the
only animal that could nutritionally thrive by eating
cooked but not raw food. Fire's importance in culture
is so marked that the word itself became a ubiquitous
metaphor used to describe ideas such as romantic love,
conflict, destruction, and intense desire. **MT**

Cannibalism
Unknown

The practice of humans eating the flesh
of other humans

The earliest evidence of cannibalism comes from
butchered bones found in the Grand Dolina cave
in Spain, dating back to c. 800,000 BCE. These bones
suggest that the practice existed among members of
western Europe's first known human species, Homo
antecessor, and similar findings from later periods
show that it continued with the emergence of
Homo sapiens and other hominid species. There are
several theories as to why cannibalism first arose: one
hypothesis suggests that it may have been a result of
food shortages; another that it may have functioned as
a form of predator control, by limiting predators' access
to (and therefore taste for) human bodies.

Cannibalism persisted into modern times in
West and Central Africa, the Pacific Islands, Australia,

"I ate his liver with some fava beans and a nice chianti."

Thomas Harris, *The Silence of the Lambs* (1988)

Sumatra, North America, and South America. In some
cultures, human flesh was regarded as just another
type of meat. In others, it was a delicacy for special
occasions: the Maoris of New Zealand would feast on
enemies slain in battle. In Africa, certain human organs
were cooked in rites of sorcery because witch doctors
believed that victims' strengths and virtues could be
transferred to those who ate their flesh. In Central
America, the Aztecs are thought to have sacrificed
prisoners of war to their gods and then eaten their flesh
themselves. Australian Aborigines ate their deceased
relatives (endocannibalism) as a mark of respect.

The colonization of these regions between the
fifteenth and nineteenth centuries by European
Christians made cannibalism taboo. However, it
occasionally still occurs in extreme circumstances. **GL**

Clothing
Unknown

Garments, fabrics, or other coverings worn by humans over their bodies

The materials that early humans used to create the first clothing were probably those they found around them, such as pliable grasses, plant leaves, and animal skins. Because these materials decompose so easily it is difficult to determine when humans first created clothing. Researchers studying human lice have suggested that clothing could have become widespread as early as 650,000 years ago, while other studies suggest an origin of about 170,000 years ago. These time periods correspond to either the beginning or the end of an Ice Age, indicating that clothing may have first developed as a way of coping with colder climates.

The first items of clothing were most probably fairly crude in their construction, draped around the body and tied with sinew. The development of the needle

"Clothes can suggest, persuade, connote, insinuate, or indeed lie . . ."

Anne Hollander, *Seeing Through Clothes* (1975)

around 35,000 years ago by Homo sapiens allowed the creation of more complex clothing—garments that could be layered and tailored to fit certain parts of the body. It has been hypothesized that this technology may have been what enabled Homo sapiens to flourish as a species over the Neanderthals, who were more adapted to the cold biologically and thus did not have the impetus to refine the cutting and sewing techniques that were needed for warmer clothes.

Although clothing may have been created out of necessity initially, it has since become far more than a means of adaptation to the environment. Throughout history it has been used to protect a wearer from the elements, but also as a way to convey nonverbal information, such as signaling differences in wealth, class, sex, or membership of a particular group. **MT**

Honoring the Dead
Homo heidelbergensis

The practice of paying respect to a deceased person through specific rituals

It is difficult to pinpoint when the idea of honoring the dead began. There is some evidence to show that Homo heidelbergensis (who existed between 600,000 and 400,000 years ago) were the first proto-humans to bury their dead. Whether they honored their dead or ascribed some kind of spiritual aspect to the burial process is unknown, however. There are human burial sites from about 130,000 years ago that show more convincing evidence that those performing the burial intended to remember or honor the deceased, through the position of the body, the inclusion of items such as tools and animal bones with the body, and the addition of decorative elements to the tomb. This suggestion of ritual in the burial process could indicate that it was one of the first forms of religious practice.

"Our dead are never dead to us, until we have forgotten them."

George Eliot, author

In some cultures or traditions, honoring the dead is an ongoing practice in which deceased relatives or ancestors are viewed as having a continued presence among, or influence over, the living. In others, the traditions that honor the dead occur immediately after someone's death, or at various times throughout the year. Honoring the dead is not necessarily a religious tradition, though many religions have specific and extensive rituals for the practice.

Honoring the dead is a near-universal practice that exists across geographical, cultural, and religious boundaries. The shared rituals involved in the custom provide a social bond in societies, and a way to link the deceased with the living. These elements are strongly present in many religious rituals, often forming the basis of individual, and cultural, identities. **MT**

The 60,000-year-old burial tomb of a Neanderthal man in the Chapelle aux Saints cave, France. ➡

Using Sharp Projectiles
Homo heidelbergensis

Creating tools and weapons with sharpened points or tips

⬆ Two examples of Solutrean Points. The Solutrean tool industry existed between *c.* 20,000 and *c.* 16,000 BCE, and was characterized by finely crafted, leaf-shaped blades.

Humanity's first use of sharp projectiles predates history, as three wooden spears found in Schöningen, Germany, show that Homo heidelbergensis had used projectile weapons by at least 400,000 BCE, and perhaps as early as 500,000 BCE. The longest of the three spears measured 7 feet 7 inches (2.3 m) long and all of them had a thicker section toward the front in the style of a modern javelin, which suggests that they were specifically used for throwing rather than thrusting. By 300,000 BCE, Homo neanderthalensis had begun using shaped stone spear points, and by 64,000 BCE stone-tipped arrow heads first appeared in South Africa.

Until the development of sharp projectiles, humans had to rely on blunt weapons, such as rocks, throwing sticks, and their hands and teeth. Sharp projectiles were far superior to blunt weapons as they were not only deadlier, but also could be used from a greater distance. This allowed people to hunt larger, more dangerous game while retaining some measure of security. Sharp projectiles spurred technological development, leading inventors to develop new methods of shaping stones, developing woodworking techniques, and, eventually, mining and casting metals. As further evidence of their importance, groups of wild chimpanzees in Senegal have recently been observed to fashion their own sharpened projectiles from tree branches for use in hunting. The frequency of projectile use was found to be higher among female chimpanzees, leading researchers to speculate that females may have played a key role in the evolution of tool technology among early humans.

Ever since the appearance of sharpened projectiles, human cultures have refined, perfected, and revered them for their simplicity and deadly efficiency. As the primary tools of warfare and survival, they were not replaced until relatively recently in human history when firearms became effective and widely available. **MT**

"It is easy to dodge a spear that comes in front of you, but hard to avoid an arrow shot from behind."

Chinese proverb

Levallois Technique
Neanderthals

Neanderthal craftsmen develop a technique for making better flint tools

Dating back around 250,000 years, the Levallois technique is the name given to a method of knapping flint that was developed by Neanderthals and other proto-humans. The name derives from the Levallois-Perret suburb of Paris, France, where tools forged by this technique were discovered during archaeological digs in the nineteenth century.

The Levallois technique is a more refined version of earlier forms of stone knapping, which involved chipping pieces away from a prepared stone core. It enabled the tool's creator to have much greater control over the shape and size of the final flake. The technique begins with selecting a pebble about the size of a hand. A striking platform is then formed at one end of the stone, and the edges are trimmed by chipping off pieces around the outline of the intended flake. The base of the stone is then struck in order to produce its distinctive dorsal ridge. When the striking platform is struck, the flake releases from the stone with a characteristic plano-convex configuration and all of its edges sharpened by the earlier chipping. The flake is then ready to use as a knife or as the point of an edged projectile weapon.

Populations distributed over a vast geographical region, from Africa to Northern Europe, employed the Levallois technique. It allowed the Neanderthals to perfect their spear-making industry, which in turn aided in the hunting of large animals. Being able to kill larger animals, and therefore feed more individuals while spending less time hunting, aided in the formation of stable people groups, enabling greater sedentism. It also allowed for the production of projectile points for early bow and arrow technology. The fact that the Levallois technique was refined and perfected by the Neanderthals gives the lie to the popular conception of them as crude and apelike brutes. **APT**

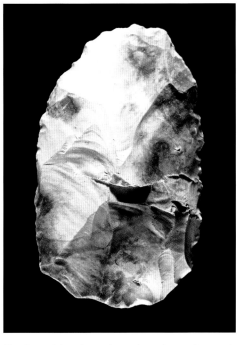

⬆ A flint tool shaped using the Levallois technique, discovered in Montreres, France. The core of a Levallois flake is often described as looking like the shell of a tortoise.

"In terms of cutting tools (whether as knives or projectile points), the Levallois technique produced superior pieces."

Brian Patrick Kooyman, professor of archaeology

Trade
Unknown

Exchanging goods, services, and other items of value

The first exchange of goods or services came about long before written history. There is evidence that long-distance commerce existed as far back as 150,000 years ago, and by the time that humanity emerged from the Neolithic period (10,000–2000 BCE) and began establishing cities and agrarian communities, trading had been firmly established as a vital part of life. The move toward a sedentry, agricultural lifestyle transformed the nature of human society, creating a surplus of food that allowed humans to evolve new occupations such as toolmaking and weaving. These craftspeople in turn created a surplus of their products, which they were then able to trade back for food. Villages began to specialize in making products that were in demand in other areas, and by 3,000 BCE ancient

"Every man thus lives by exchanging, or becomes in some measure a merchant …"

Adam Smith, *Wealth of Nations* (1776)

Mesopotamians had established trade routes with the urban centers of the Indus Valley Civilization, perhaps linking disparate urban areas for the first time.

Trade is an engine that drives economies, facilitates social interactions, spurs political change, and leads to the spread of ideas, languages, goods, cultures, religions, wealth, people, and diseases. Through trading, humans acquired goods from far off lands, shared news of events, and pushed themselves to seek out corners of the world unknown to them in search of new opportunities. Trade has both stabilized relationships between potential enemies and led to conflicts, wars, and the subjugation, murder, and enslavement of millions. Over the course of history, empires have arisen, fallen, and been reborn as basic human desires have driven the need for trade. **MT**

Jewelry
Paleolithic Middle East

Personal adornment, often made from precious or valuable materials

The earliest known jewelry comes from the Paleolithic Middle East, where people used sea snail shells to make beads as early as 135,000 years ago. Jewelry is not an art form confined to Homo sapiens, however, because evidence exists to show that Homo neanderthalensis created and used jewelry in Spain at least 50,000 years ago. It is believed that these early forms of jewelry were most probably worn as a form of protection from evil or as a mark of status or rank.

Over the millennia, humans have fashioned jewelry from bone, stone, wood, shells, feathers, teeth, and other natural materials, with metallic jewelry first appearing around 5000 BCE. By about 3000 BCE the ancient Egyptians had begun crafting gold and silver jewelry, sometimes incorporating glass and precious

"Rich and rare were the gems she wore, And a bright gold ring on her hand she bore …"

Thomas Moore, "Rich and Rare …" (1808)

gems into their designs. The Egyptians believed that every gemstone carried certain mystical powers, which would be transferred to the owner when worn as jewelry. This association of jewelry with the spiritual and mystical extended to burying jewelry with the dead to take with them to the afterlife—a practice that was a common feature of many ancient cultures. Much of the ancient jewelry that is held in archaeological collections today was discovered in tombs.

The development of jewelry provided humankind with both a new form of beautification and another method of communication. It is an art that lets the wearer feel more attractive, powerful, or important, while at the same time conveying a symbolic message that here is a person of wealth, piety, or influence, or even one who is available—or unavailable—for romance. **MT**

Jewelry found at a burial site at the Balzi Rossi Caves in Liguria, Italy, which dates back 25,000 years.

Shamanism

Unknown

A magico-religious tradition built around a practitioner who contacts the spirits

⬆ A wooden figure representing a shaman associated with the Inuit spirit Taqhisim. The shaman relied on the spirits with whom he was associated for help in his duties.

"It was not I who cured. It was the power from the other world, and the visions and ceremonies had only made me like a hole through which the power could come to the two-legged."

Black Elk, Oglala Sioux shaman

Shamanism is the general magico-religious tradition built around the figure of the shaman, and is a phenomenon both ancient (dating back to at least 40,000 BCE) and global. Most of the oldest art in the world—"The Sorcerer" cave painting in France, for example—is shamanistic, and most of the oldest texts in the world—Mesopotamian and biblical texts, for example—allude to shamanistic practices such as necromancy (contacting the spirits of the dead). The word "shaman" is derived from the Tungus word *saman*, which refers to a "priest" or person—either male or female—who, in an altered state (such as a trance or a drug-induced hallucination), contacts the spirit world for help.

Although the specific features of shamanism vary depending on the culture in which it is practiced (Japanese Shinto is different from African shamanism, for example), all shamanistic traditions share four basic characteristics. First, the shaman is seen as the intermediary between the human world and the spirit world. Second, the shaman only becomes such an intermediary by being chosen by the spirits and by performing certain rituals, such as the banging of a drum. Third, in their altered state of mind, the shaman is able to ask the spirits about how to cure certain diseases or to question what the future holds (fortune-telling). And fourth, the shaman is responsible for perpetuating the magico-religious tradition by recounting sacred myths and stories.

Some later religions, such as the Abrahamic ones, opposed shamanistic practices. This was not so much done because of the practices themselves (the shaman figure is very similar to a prophet or priest), but because the shaman was said to attain his knowledge in the wrong ways, through both good and bad spirits. Nevertheless, shamanism still endures today, making it one of the world's oldest religious traditions. **AB**

Anthropomorphism
Unknown

Attributing human characteristics to non-human entities

Anthropomorphism—from the Greek words for "human" (*anthropos*) and "form" (*morphe*)—refers to the ancient activity of attributing human characteristics to non-human beings, such as deities, animals, vegetation, or the elements. Some of the oldest art— the Lion-Man of Hohlenstein Stadel (Germany), for example—depicts animals with human characteristics. Shamanistic traditions, which are connected with this type of art, tend to see spirits in all things, meaning that when they attribute human characteristics to trees— calling them "dryads," for example—they believe that a tree spirit, much like a human spirit, is the principle that helps the tree to grow and act like a human. The same applies to all, or most, of nature.

A subcategory of anthropomorphism is anthropotheism, in which higher non-human entities—the gods or God—are depicted with human characteristics. Plato (*c.* 424–348 BCE) charged the Greek poets with "telling lies about the gods" because they depicted gods such as Zeus acting with petty human motives, and certain biblical passages, such as those describing God's "right hand," have often been seen as examples of anthropotheism.

In psychological terms, anthropomorphism has a number of implications. Ascribing human characteristics to a non-human entity can alter our views of and feelings toward that entity—it can make it seem more worthy of moral care and consideration, for example. The process of anthropomorphism can also be viewed as the mind's way of simplifying complicated entities to enable us to understand them.

Today, anthropomorphism continues to be an important idea in shamanistic religions such as Taoism and Shinto. It also remains a prominent feature in popular culture, from cartoon characters such as Bugs Bunny to respected works of literature such as George Orwell's *Animal Farm* (1945). **AB**

⬆ This lion-headed figurine, found in Hohlenstein Stadel, Germany, is one of the oldest sculptures in the world. It is made of mammoth ivory and dates back to *c.* 28,000 BCE.

"We acquire certain opinions of several animals and think of some as royal, others as silly, others as witty, and others as innocent."

Philostratus, *The Life of Apollonius of Tyana* (*c.* 200)

Paleolithic Cave Art
Unknown

Powerful works of art drawn by prehistoric humans

Paleolithic cave art is a form of art dating back at least 40,000 years and distributed over a vast geographical area, from Europe, to India, to the Americas. Most of the paintings, such as those found in the caves of Lascaux in France, depict large equine animals: horses, cows, aurochs, and deer, as well as outlines of human hands. Curiously, full depictions of humans are absent in European cave art, but prevalent in African cave art. The caves themselves tend to be in places that are not easily accessible.

There are many theories about the origin of cave art. Henri Breuil (1877–1961) theorized that, given the number of large animals depicted in the artworks, it was likely an instance of "hunting magic" intended to increase the numbers of wild game hunted by early humans and

> *"Seeing [the paintings] was startlingly intense … there was so much … I hadn't expected."*
>
> Gregory Curtis, *The Cave Painters* (2006)

Neanderthals. Another theory identifies cave art with early shamanistic rituals, perhaps, in some locations, involving the use of hallucinogenic substances. And some researchers have suggested that cave art may even have been an early form of animation.

Cave art seems to have emerged at the same time as modern Homo sapiens. However, we must not be too quick to attribute its existence to this development. Evidence suggests that at least some of the cave art in Europe was produced by Neanderthals. The art is a powerful visual link to our prehistory. And, as noted by Pablo Picasso, it tells us something about the art and culture of a particularly liberated proto-human culture. It is the art that humans produced when there were no traditions or rules of representation to tell them how art and culture must be produced. **APT**

Mediumship
Unknown

The necromantic communication between a disembodied and an incarnate human

While a shaman (a priest-type figure able to contact the spirit world) seeks to communicate with spirits in general and for many purposes, a medium—a subcategory of a shaman—is usually interested only in facilitating communication between the spirit of a disembodied human and an incarnate one. Shamanism originated in *c.* 40,000 BCE, and it is probable that the practice of mediumship arose at a similar time.

In the ancient Near East, mediums—also called necromancers because they consulted the dead (necro)—were seen as a valuable source of advice. Through them, people could consult the spirits for guidance in important matters. However, in the past century or so, and due largely to the outpouring of death during World Wars I and II, mediumship in the

> *"Saul and two men went to the medium. 'Consult a spirit for me,' he said …"*
>
> The Bible, 1 Samuel 28:8

West became popular not so much as a means of advice but as a way to establish closure with loved ones separated by physical death.

Mediumship is a very old, very influential idea and practice; nevertheless, it has often been viewed in a negative light, by both religion and science. The Abrahamic religions, for example, claim that though the power of a medium is occasionally real and the knowledge attained through such practices is valuable (knowledge per se is good), mediums should not be consulted because their method is not approved by God. Scientists take this even further, often seeing all mediums as frauds because their methods are difficult to test and their effects hard to quantify. A belief in and fascination with mediumship remains strong for many people, however. **AB**

The paintings in the Lascaux caves in France are estimated to be 16,000 years old.

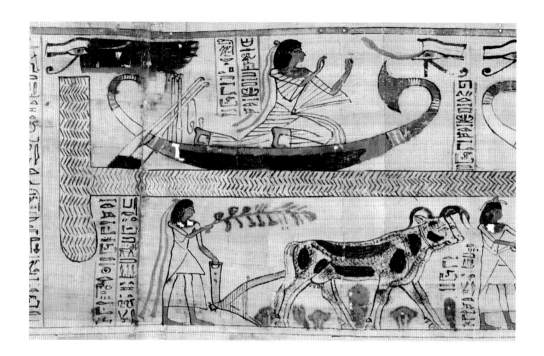

Soul
Unknown

The belief in a non-physical entity with certain essential characteristics

The belief in the existence of souls has been prevalent in humankind for millennia. The concept of a soul is thought to have appeared around the same time as the emergence of shamanism in *c.* 40,000 BCE, which can be seen as the first example of religion. The discovery of ritual items at shamanistic burial sites suggests that those carrying out the burial believed in the afterlife, which in turn implies that they believed individuals to have a non-physical component that survives after death. This non-physical component—or soul—can be defined as the immaterial essence or animating principle of an individual life. It is generally viewed as separate to the body and is often credited with the faculties of thought, action, and emotion.

The oldest religious traditions—shamanistic, polytheistic, and monotheistic—generally agree that the soul grounds the identity of a given thing, and contains in it an organizing life-principle for that entity. Thus, for example, the vegetative life and identity of a rose is grounded in its soul, in the same way that the sentient life and identity of a zebra is grounded in *its* soul. For some religious traditions—shamanism, for example—the type of soul in a rose, zebra, or human is not clearly distinguished, which often leads to the notion that everything with a soul is of equal value. However, other traditions argue that the soul of a human is immortal and rational, and so is more valuable than the soul of a rose or a zebra, both of which are mortal and non-rational.

The near-universal belief that the soul of a human is immortal has led to the near-universal belief in both an underworld that houses the unworthy souls of the dead and a heavenlike place that welcomes the worthy souls. In the underworld the souls are seen in misery, partly because they are without bodies, whereas in the heavenlike place the souls are often depicted enjoying the fruits of the body. **AB**

A dead person's soul travels through the underworld in this ancient Egyptian papyrus (*c.* 1600–1100 BCE).

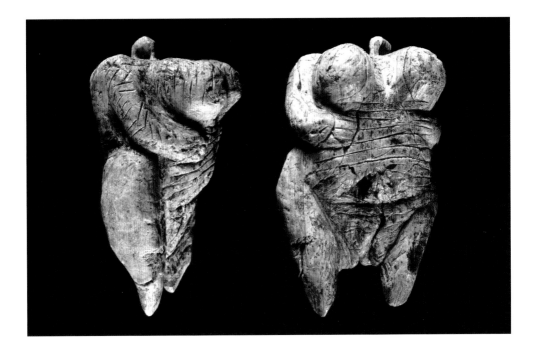

Symbols
Paleolithic Germany

A visual or material representation of a concept

The use of symbols to visually represent an idea dates back to prehistory. Even though the earliest cave paintings were created as long ago as 40,000 BCE, they were simply depictions: outlines of human hands that do not appear to have any symbolic meaning. Perhaps the earliest remaining human creation that could be considered a symbol comes from Hohle Fels cave near Schelklingen, in southern Germany. There, about 35,000 years ago, someone carved a mammoth tusk into a figurine depicting a woman with large breasts, large thighs, and a protruding stomach. The figure is widely believed to be a depiction of a fertility goddess or spirit, a symbolic representation of human reproduction and fecundity.

The first petroglyphs—figures and images engraved into rock—may have appeared about 30,000 years ago, but certainly existed as long as 10,000 to 12,000 years ago. There are many theories to explain the symbolic purpose of the different petroglyphs that have been found across the globe, including conveying time and distances traveled, establishing territorial boundaries, or even representing a form of ritual language. Since then, symbols have been universally used across cultures, and are ubiquitous in modern societies.

You are using symbols as you read this sentence. Your eyes scan the symbols called letters and effortlessly translate those letters into the sounds they represent, which together form words that you understand, allowing you to read. That is the power and importance of symbols: their ability to convey meaning and information beyond their form almost instantaneously. Symbols can cross language and cultural boundaries with ease, relating notices, warnings, advice, and complex messages at a glance. Their usefulness relies on their simplicity, and the ability of a human viewer to see an abstract visual depiction and readily draw meaning from it. **MT**

⬆ The Venus of Hohle Fels, believed to be a fertility symbol, is the oldest known example of figurative art.

Sedentism
Unknown

The process by which nomads settled in permanent locations

Anthropologists and archaeologists agree that the earliest humans were hunters who moved from place to place in search of sustenance. Gradually, however, our ancient ancestors found locations where the climatic conditions were favorable and the natural resources abundant enough to enable them to remain in the same place year-round, year on year. They were the first to adopt the lifestyle now known as sedentism.

The earliest recorded sedentary cultures developed between around 25,000 BCE and 17,000 BCE in Moravia (part of the modern-day Czech Republic) and on the plains of western Russia, where people went hunting and fishing from permanent bases. In around 10,000 BCE the Natufians—who had by then been settled for at least 2,000 years in parts of modern-day

> *"Researchers realized quite early on that sedentism was not . . . straightforward . . ."*
>
> Bill Bryson, *At Home: A Short History of Private Life* (2010)

Israel, Jordan, and Syria—began to cultivate plants, a development that occurred at about the same time as the Jomon in Japan first cultivated rice. By 5000 BCE early Scandinavians had established sedentary sites on which they supplemented barley and other plant produce by raising cattle for milk, meat, and hide.

To the modern mind, it may appear natural to prefer a fixed abode to a life of constant wandering. Nevertheless, this major change in human behavior remains only partially explained: did nomads settle in order to farm, or did they settle because they had started to grow crops and to domesticate animals? The debate continues as to whether sedentism is a consequence of agriculture, or vice versa. Either way, the two developments were crucial to the establishment of modern civilization. **GL**

The Dome Structure
Unknown

Stable architectural structure in the shape of a half sphere

The dome is the most stable of all simple architectural structures, and evidence of dome-shaped dwellings dates back tens of thousands of years. Domes are among the first structures that prehistoric people used as shelter, and they were created using branches, animal hide, and mammoth tusks. The dome is architecturally appealing because it is inherently stable and evenly distributes forces applied to it across the surface of the dome and downward toward the base.

The dome structure can be found across the prehistoric and ancient world. The most common use of domes in ancient civilizations was in structures that were intended to be permanent, including religious buildings and tombs. The architecture of the dome was advanced the most by ancient Roman architects,

> *"Just give me a home, in a great circle dome Where stresses and strains are at ease."*
>
> R. Buckminster Fuller, architect

who developed the use of angled bricks to create "true domes" for temples and other public buildings. The Pantheon in Rome, built in 126 CE, remained the largest dome in the world for more than 1,700 years. Domes are also a key feature of the architecture that developed during the Byzantine era (*c.* 330–1453), and became a dominant characteristic in the architecture of Muslim societies throughout the Middle Ages (*c.* 500–*c.* 1450).

Domes have had a lasting impact on architecture and continue to be prevalent in building designs. Reflecting the ancient use of the dome for important public edifices, many modern governmental buildings feature domes. A contemporary development is the geodesic dome, a structure that combines overlapping circles to form stable interlocking triangles. This allows the architectural construction of complete spheres. **TD**

Money
Ancient Anatolians

The use of currency to pay for goods or services

⬆ A Neo-Hittite relief from the tenth to eighth century BCE, found in Carchemish, Turkey, showing two merchants agreeing on the terms of a trade.

Early human cultures relied primarily on bartering to exchange goods and services. It was not until about 12,000 BCE that the first form of money emerged in ancient Turkey, when people begin using obsidian as a medium of exchange. Although obsidian could be utilized to create stone tools, those trading it did not necessarily use it for tool creation, instead employing it as an object of value. Some time between about 9000 and 6000 BCE, people begin using livestock, such as cattle and sheep, as a form of currency. By about the sixth century BCE, people in western Turkey had created the first form of currency after they melted gold into small coins imprinted with a stamped image. The first true paper money appeared in China in the eleventh century, consisting of banknotes that provided a written promise to pay someone in precious metal on presentation—thereby advancing the concept of currency beyond that of a tangible object of value. Although most currencies throughout history have been tied to the value of a commodity, such as gold or silver, modern systems use fiat money: money that is valuable solely because it is used as such.

Without money, humans would have to barter whenever they wanted to engage in any kind of commerce. Bartering, though widely still in use, can be incredibly unwieldy. If a buyer does not have what a seller needs, or vice versa, no commerce can take place. With money, however, humans introduced a universally agreed-upon object that all parties recognized as valuable. This had a profound impact on human society, creating new links between people through trade, which in turn enabled people to break away from their traditional kin groups. Market economies and strong currencies became the key to thriving cities, underpinning the intellectual, cultural, and technological advances that evolved from these centers of commerce. **MT**

"Money . . . is none of the wheels of trade: it is the oil which renders the motion of the wheels more smooth and easy."

David Hume, *Essays: Moral and Political* (1741–42)

Preserving Food
Mesopotamia

Using natural processes and substances to prolong the length of time for which food is edible

There is archaeological evidence of food preservation in prehistory, dating the practice at least as far back as 12,000 BCE. It is a custom that has occured in virtually all cultures since then. The first method of natural preservation was drying, whereby food was simply left out in the sun, and since then numerous other techniques have been developed. These include refrigeration, freezing, smoking, salting, fermenting, chemical pickling (in which a food is placed in a preservative liquid), fermentation pickling (in which a food is allowed to ferment, producing its own preservative), sugaring, jellying, and (with increasing industrialization from the early nineteenth century onward) canning and bottling. These methods are sometimes employed jointly.

It is difficult to overstate the importance of food preservation to human history as it was what enabled humans to make the important transition from hunting and gathering to settled agricultural communities. The ability to stockpile food freed people from the need to focus solely on hunting and gathering, and enabled them to develop new occupations such as toolmaking. The resulting cultural and technological developments enabled humans to make a huge leap forward in terms of civilization—and also sowed the first seeds of social disruption and inequity. Later, advances in food preservation enabled people to undertake voyages of discovery and conquest. Moreover, food preservation is responsible for creating new flavors and new kinds of food (such as cheese and wine)—and even rendering otherwise inedible foods (such as olives) palatable.

All of these methods of food preservation are still in use today. In the twentieth century, modern chemistry produced a variety of artificial food preservatives, and modern physics produced a new method of food preservation: irradiation. **GB**

⬆ Fish dried naturally by the sun and wind, on sale at a market in Phuket, Thailand. Drying is one of the oldest methods of naturally preserving food.

"Nearly everything we eat today has been treated . . . in order to prolong its life as a safe, transportable, salable, and storable food."

Sue Shephard, *Potted, Pickled, and Canned* (2000)

Mesolithic Sculpted Figurines
Unknown

The development of sculpture and material representations of abstract human ideas

↑ This figurine from *c.* 6000 BCE is one of numerous Mesolithic artifacts discovered at Lepenski Vir, Serbia. The sculpture is thought to have been an object of worship.

"The increased production of female figurines and phallic images of stone... suggest[s] a rise in ritual practices."

Heilbrunn Timeline of Art History, Metropolitan Museum of Art

One of the great developments of the Mesolithic period (*c.* 10,000–4000 BCE) was a proliferation of sculpted figurines of human and animal forms. Although figurative sculpture was not unknown before the start of the period—the Venus of Willendorf, for example, a 4.3-inch (11 cm) limestone figurine discovered in Austria in 1908, dates from around 24,000 BCE—most sculptures had previously been exclusively utilitarian (unadorned pots and drinking vessels).

The earliest such effigies were made in Japan during the Jomon period, which is roughly coextensive with the Mesolithic. Jomon pottery was made without the use of potters' wheels (which date from around 4500 BCE), by coiling thin, rounded strips of wet clay into the requisite shapes and then firing them in low-heat ovens. The word *Jomon* means "cord marks." Jomon pottery began as simple jars and bowls, but later developed into statuettes known as *dogu.*

Around 15,000 *dogu* effigies are known to exist. They are hollow and made of clay in which red ocher is the dominant color. Most of them are between 4 inches and 1 foot (10–30 cm) in height and represent females with hourglass figures, large faces, and wide eyes (several of them appear to be wearing goggles). Some of the women are depicted as pregnant, with protuberant abdomens covered in vermilion patterns. They are thought to have been fertility symbols.

In 1986 the remains of a Mesolithic temple dating from around 10,000 BCE were discovered near Sanliurfa in southeastern Turkey. Inside it were figurines created in the eighth millennium BCE depicting headless humans with outsize genitals, together with effigies of fawns, foxes, pigs, scorpions, snakes, storks, and wolves. Researchers studying these figurines have suggested that, rather than being important cultural or religious symbols as previously supposed, they may in fact simply have been toys. **GL**

Slavery
Unknown

A form of servitude in which one person is the property of another

The practice of slavery is believed to have originated with the development of agriculture in around 10,000 BCE. Agriculture required a labor force, and enslaved prisoners of war provided a cheap and convenient means of creating one.

Slavery was legal throughout the ancient world. Slaves were typically acquired by military conquest or by purchase from foreign lands. Their conditions were not always harsh: in ancient Greece and Rome, slaves could own property and run their own businesses—they had almost all the same liberties as free men, other than the rights to serve in the military and to participate in political affairs. Without slave labor, many civilizations would have been unsustainable. The Roman Empire (27 BCE–*c.* 500) depended on slaves for everything, from building construction to copying manuscripts.

Slavery flourished in Europe until the fourth century CE, after which it was superseded by serfdom. However, slavery re-emerged in the fifteenth century with the opening-up of Africa and the discovery of the New World. During this time, large numbers of Africans were shipped to the West Indies and the Americas by Europeans to work as slaves in mines and on plantations.

Attitudes toward slavery began to change in the eighteenth century, however, and an abolition movement was formed by people campaigning against the cruelty and injustice of the practice. In 1792 Denmark abolished slavery, and over the next hundred years many other nations followed suit.

Nonetheless, it was not the end of slavery. The practice was used extensively during the history of the Soviet Union in the form of the gulags (forced labor camps) and regularly recurs in times of war. In the late twentieth century there emerged a new form of slavery known as debt bondage, in which employers charge workers so much for food and shelter that the exploited people can never fulfill their obligations. **GL**

⬆ An ancient Egyptian carving from *c.* 1332–1323 BCE, showing prisoners being counted; slaves were often gained through military conquest, providing a cheap labor force.

"Slavery they can have anywhere. It is a weed that grows in every soil."
Edmund Burke, statesman

Agriculture
Unknown

Cultivating naturally occurring crops or livestock for use as food or raw materials

The first sustained agricultural efforts occurred around 10,000 BCE in the Fertile Crescent, an area of the modern-day Middle East that includes the Tigris and Euphrates rivers, the Levant, and the Nile River delta. Agriculture also arose independently in China in around 8000 BCE, and in the Americas before 3000 BCE. Early farmers learned to take wild plants, such as rye, chickpeas, and flax, and plant them for harvest, thereby reducing the need to travel to new locations to find food sources. The domestication of animals provided additional sources of food, products, and labor.

Several theories have been put forward as to why humankind made the switch to agriculture. One argument is that it was a means of coping with a crisis of overpopulation after the development of sedentism.

"I had rather be on my farm than be emperor of the world."
George Washington, U.S. president 1789–97

Another theory posits that climate change at the end of an Ice Age led to the spread of forests, segmenting previously open ranges. This encouraged sedentism and territoriality, which led to the protection and propogation of local food resources.

Agriculture forever changed the way in which humanity sourced food. By the Bronze Age (*c.* 3500–1000 BCE), Middle Eastern civilizations obtained the majority of their dietary needs from farmed food supplies. While this reliance upon agricultural production for food has produced sometimes disastrous famines and negative ecological consequences, it has also allowed the human population to expand tremendously. In the twentieth century, advances in farming techniques led to a massive increase in crop yields, spurring a population boom that is still ongoing. **MT**

Alemaking
Unknown

The art of brewing the world's most ancient and popular alcoholic beverage

Many speculate that alemaking began in around 9000 BCE, because this would correspond with the appearance of the first cereal farms. In the East, the ancient Chinese had a kind of rice beer called *kui*, which they began brewing around 7000 BCE; in the West, the ancient Mesopotamians were manufacturing beer at the Godin Tepe settlement at the beginning of the Bronze Age (*c.* 3500–1000 BCE). The oldest literary sources for ale-making are Mesopotamian— *The Epic of Gilgamesh* (*c.* 2000 BCE), *The Hymn to Ninkasi* (*c.* 1800 BCE), and *The Code of Hammurabi* (*c.* 1772 BCE)—all of which indicate that alemaking and drinking were occurrences of daily life.

Beer has a long history and has played a small but important part in human life. The ancient Egyptians

"When you pour out the filtered beer . . . it is like the onrush of Tigris and Euphrates."
The Hymn to Ninkasi (*c.* 1800 BCE)

spoke of the gods and the blessed enjoying "the beer of everlastingness," whereas the Mesopotamians wrote hymns to Ninkasi, the goddess of alcohol, thanking her for the drink. Historians have even theorized that humankind's fondness for beer and other alcoholic beverages was a factor behind the move to an agrarian society from a hunter-gatherer one.

There are roughly four steps to alemaking. First, there is the "mashing," which involves mixing a starch source, such as malted barley, with hot water. Second, the resulting mixture or "wort" is collected in a (copper) kettle, where some of the water is allowed to evaporate and hops are added. Third, the mixture is cooled and yeast is added. Finally, the liquid is stored in a cask or keg and allowed to sit before being imbibed. **AB**

A 7,000-year-old painting in the Spider Cave in Valencia, Spain, showing a figure farming honey.

Dyeing Cloth
Unknown

Changing the colors of fabrics and cloth by adding artificial dyes

Dyes have been a part of human history for millennia, and appear to have been invented independently in numerous different cultures. The earliest known use of dyes reaches back to about 30,000 BCE, when red ocher was used to decorate burial mounds in northern Italy. The oldest evidence for textile dyeing comes from the Neolithic settlement of Çatalhöyük (*c.* 7500–5700 BCE) in modern Turkey. By 3,000 BCE, more advanced dyeing procedures existed in India, where dyes were affixed to fabric with the use of mordants (substances that chemically affix the dye to the fibers of the cloth). Early dyes came exclusively from natural sources, such as plants, roots, tree bark, and insects.

It is unclear whether the first dyed fabrics had a significance beyond being merely decorative, but

"The soul is dyed the color of its thoughts."

Heraclitus, ancient Greek philosopher

over time they became a key indicator of the wearer's wealth and social status. In around 1500 BCE the ancient Phoenicians developed a dye known as Tyrian purple, a color that for centuries was reserved exclusively for the garments of kings, emperors, and high priests. When Alexander the Great conquered Persia in 331 BCE, he found purple robes in the capital's treasury that would have been worth millions of dollars today.

Before the introduction of dyes, humanity was relegated to using the colors that existed in natural fibers. But many colors found in nature were not found in the products humanity could make, and the desire to control and wear these colors was strong. With dyes, an explosion of color entered the world, allowing textile producers to transform otherwise drab fabrics into vibrant, colorful cloths of beauty and value. **MT**

Simple Machines
Unknown

The development of basic devices that modify motion and force to perform work

The ancient Greeks were first to define simple machines—devices that change the magnitude or direction of a force to make a task easier—but most of them had exised for millennia. Historically, there are six types of simple machine: the lever, wheel and axle, pulley, inclined plane, wedge, and screw.

The inclined plane was most probably the first, used by proto-humans to slide heavy weights (though there is no hard evidence to prove this). Next came the wedge, which—by creating a sideways force when pushed into something—enabled the user to split materials such as rocks and wood. The earliest examples of such tools, found in India and Mesopotamia, date to around 7000 BCE. The first documentation of the wheel and axle comes from the Sumerian city-state of Ur, from

"Give me a lever long enough . . . and I shall move the world."

Archimedes, ancient Greek mathematician

around 3500 BCE. Its earliest use was probably in raising water from wells, but it also led to the development of horse-drawn chariots. The pulley, by necessity, followed the wheel—being a wheel with a rope wrapped around it—and it was used to raise and lower objects. It is likely that pulleys were used in the building of the Great Pyramid of Giza in *c.* 2560 BCE. Levers are also believed to have been used in ancient Egypt, but it was Archimedes (*c.* 290–212 BCE) who first described the principle of using one. The screw—which allows a rotary motion to be converted into a forward or backward one—appeared in ancient Greece. Sometimes credited to Archytas (*c.* 428–*c.* 350 BCE), it was used in wine and olive presses. These simple machines enabled us to push beyond our natural capabilities and laid the foundations for innumerable technological advances. **GL**

Human Sacrifice
Mesopotamia

An ancient exchange between a civilization and its god(s)

Human sacrifice involves the killing of one or more humans in order to serve a particular religious or ritualistic purpose. Some of the earliest evidence for the practice of human sacrifice dates from 6,000 BCE, among the Mesopotamian peoples of the ancient Near East. The Mesopotamians were among the first cultures to develop a practice of retainer sacrifice, in which the slaves and servants of royalty and nobility were killed at the time of their master's death. In carrying out this action it was believed that they would continue to serve their master as courtiers, guards, and handmaidens in the afterlife. A similar practice is also known to have existed at this time in ancient Egypt.

Perhaps more commonly, human sacrifice has been employed throughout history as a means of exchange or trade between a community and its god or gods. In this context, human life is offered as a form of appeasement, typically in exchange for the protection of lands or good fortune in war. Greek legend, for example, tells of Agamemnon's intentions to sacrifice his daughter in exchange for success in the Trojan War (c. 1200 BCE). In addition, human sacrifice has been used on a large scale at the completion of religious buildings such as the Great Pyramid of Tenochtitlan in Mexico, for which the Aztecs are documented to have sacrificed between 10,000 and 80,000 prisoners in 1487.

Human sacrifice gradually became less prevalent over time and is extremely uncommon as a practice in the modern world—it is defined in legal terms as "ritual murder." However, the ongoing study of human sacrificial practices and increasing amounts of archaeological information uncovered continue to reveal important insights into the behaviors and customs of our ancestors. In this way, the idea of human sacrifice continues to inform and influence our present-day religious and moral codes. **LWa**

A sixteenth-century Aztec painting of a human's heart being offered to the war god Huitzilopochtli. ↑

Winemaking

Ancient Georgia

Creating a fermented drink from cultivated grapes

Unlike other types of plants that can be used to create alcoholic beverages, grapes do not need additional nutrients to begin fermenting. When yeast is added to grape juice, or is naturally present in the environment, it will transform the naturally occurring sugars into alcohol, thus creating wine.

Although wild grapes and fruits had long been available to early hunter-gatherers, the first evidence of winemaking comes from Neolithic sites in Georgia dated to about 6,000 BCE. Ancient people there first cultivated the naturally growing *Vitis vinifera* grape and fermented the fruit into wine, adding preservatives to allow them to store the drink for longer. Written cuneiform records show that ancient Sumerians in the city-state of Ur had fairly advanced winemaking practices by 2750 BCE, and by 2500 BCE winemaking had spread to western Mediterranean cultures. Wine's place in ancient societies was largely confined to the upper echelons of society, but beginning in c. 500 BCE in classical Greece, wine's popularity exploded and it subsequently became widely available to the masses in addition to the aristocracy. Winemaking technology advanced greatly during the time of the Roman Empire (27 BCE–476), with improvements to the design of the wine press and the development of barrels for storing and shipping.

Ever since its earliest days, wine has proven to be much more than merely a fermented drink. People have used it in religious ceremonies, heralded it for its medicinal qualities, and traded it as a valuable commodity. Before effective water treatments became available, wine gave people a way of drinking water relatively safely, by using diluted wine to kill naturally occurring pathogens. As a popular drink, social lubricant, and object of admiration and value, wine continues to hold a strong place in the modern world, with worldwide production exceeding 6 million gallons (23 million liters) in 2010. **MT**

⬆ An Egyptian wall painting (c. 1400–1390 BCE) demonstrating the method for pressing grapes for wine.

Ghosts
Mesopotamia

The existence of disembodied human souls or spirits

Since the early days of modern civilization in ancient Mesopotamia, around 5000 BCE, people have believed in ghosts. While most religious traditions are unclear on how the human soul or spirit relates to the human body, the distinction between the two—with the human soul being in some sense the "true person"—has rarely been questioned. Although "ghost" and "human soul" are often thought to be synonymous, they are not quite the same. While "human soul" is a positive term, "ghost" is, generally speaking, a negative one, indicating the unnatural state of the disembodied human soul.

From Mesopotamia to Japan, there has been a strong sense that the human soul is not supposed to be disembodied, though it can be, and so there has been a kind of universal horror at the thought of it being

"Now the souls of the dead who had gone below came swarming..."

Homer, *Odyssey* (c. 850 BCE)

disembodied. Gods and angels may function normally without bodies—or at least bodies in our sense—but humans do not. Homer's *Odyssey* (c. 850 BCE) offers a typical example of this when it shows the ghosts in the underworld hungry for blood, since blood and flesh are what make a human. Without blood or—better—bodies, ghosts are foggy-minded and incompetent.

Nevertheless, in shamanistic traditions, ghosts have often been consulted for knowledge or advice through the practice of necromancy. Abrahamic religions consider this an evil practice, presumably because the disembodied soul or ghost, dwelling in the underworld, could only be contacted via spirits of the underworld—demons—and so the whole enterprise would be tied up with demonic or evil activity. For these religions, the ghost condition is meant to be healed. **AB**

Creation Myth
Unknown

A story that explains how humanity, life, and the universe came into existence

Creation myths, offering a traditional explanation for how the universe originated, exist across cultural boundaries and come in myriad forms, detailing the creation of everything from humans to animals to natural phenomena. They offer a range of explanations: stories of creation by a powerful maker (such as the Abrahamic religions), of the world being created from a primordial mother and father (such as the Babylonian myth "Enuma Elish"), origin from an ancient cosmic egg (found in the Hindu tradition), creation by divers who pull the earth out of a body of water (common in Native American folklore), and many others.

As humans evolved into modern Homo sapiens and their capacity to think and reason expanded, their thoughts turned to questions about their origins

"Creation myths are the deepest and most important of all myths."

Marie-Louise Von Franz, *Creation Myths* (1972)

and how the world came to be. It is impossible to know when the first such tale was created as they all originate from prehistoric times and existed only as oral stories. However, the first known myths come from ancient Mesopotamia, dating back to around 5000 BCE. Many of the myths share common themes, images, or motifs, such as the existence of divine beings or spirits. They also reflect humanity's understanding of nature, relating common experiences of birth, destruction, and death as they reflect on how it all came to be.

Before scientific inquiry allowed humanity to shed light on the natural world, creation myths provided both answers and cultural foundations. Societies and religions identified themselves by such stories, and these cultural bonds and shared religious identities remain today as both unifying and destructive forces. **MT**

The "Great Ghost and Attendants" rock painting (c. 3000–2000 BCE) at Canyonlands National Park, Utah.

Miracles
Mesopotamia

Extraordinary occurrences that are attributed to a divine power

Humankind has believed in miracles since the rise of organized religion from *c.* 5000 BCE. Some religious traditions, such as shamanism, do not make a strong distinction between the supernatural and natural, and so the thought of the supernatural doing something irregular is unimportant. Similarly, in a pantheistic religion such as Hinduism, the natural world is viewed as illusionary, making the concept of miracles redundant. However, in theistic or polytheistic religions, in which a god or gods are thought to exist, miracles are to be expected because humans will not be able to understand all of the deity's actions.

Materialists or Naturalists reject the concept of miracles, however, and embrace "methodological naturalism," which demands that no supernatural

"And seeing signs and miracles, he was greatly amazed..."

The Bible, Acts 8:13

agents be considered when investigating a particular unexplained phenomenon. Theists typically respond to this by asking whether we have good reason to believe that God and other supernatural creatures exist. If we do, then the universe is therefore not a closed system and we are rationally justified in believing that miracles can occur—though this, by itself, will not help us to know whether a particular claim to the miraculous is true.

Today, the term "miracle" is often used in the sense of describing something that has happened against all odds, rather than carrying specific religious connotations. Nevertheless, for many modern theists, miracles not only highlight God's concern for humans, but also remind them of an unseen world of angelic and demonic causation that shapes human history. **AB**

Evil
Mesopotamia

The concept of an act carried out with deliberately harmful intent

Ever since people were able to think and understand what was going on in the world, humanity has understood that pain, suffering, and destruction exist. There is no single definition of evil used around the world, though all languages have words to describe what is wanted, moral, or "good," as well as that which is unwanted, immoral, or "bad." In the earliest recorded religion, that of the ancient Mesopotamians which originated in around 5000 BCE, the concept of evil was well known. To the Mesopotamians, evil demons caused strife and suffering, and religious rituals and exorcism were available that could protect people against evil. The idea of being punished for evil deeds in the afterlife originated with the Zoroastrian religion in the second millenium BCE, in which sinners were

"There has to be evil so that good can prove its purity above it."

Siddhartha Gautama (Buddha)

believed to be sent for eternity to the House of Evil and the just were believed to be sent to the House of Song.

"Evil" is a word that typically applies when a person acts with malice. Evil acts are immoral acts, the worst actions in which a person can engage. The idea of evil is, in many cultures, vital to the understanding of right and wrong. It serves as a basis for moral judgments and religious doctrines, and is instrumental in the creation and administration of laws and criminal justice. In some cultures and religious traditions, evil is personified in the form of a spirit or malevolent force, while in others it exists as suffering, or as the result of humanity ignoring divine guidance. Across cultures and perspectives, reflections on the concept of immorality, wickedness, and evil shape how people view the world in terms of morality, the divine, and human nature. **MT**

A relief showing Assyrian warriors impaling prisoners during the siege of Lachish in 701 BCE. ➡

Leisure
Ancient Egypt

Rest and relaxation as an integral feature of the social hierarchy

The idea of leisure is inextricably linked to the emergence of a distinction between work and play. Some of the earliest indications of the existence of leisure can be identified in prehistoric human societies. The shift away from a nomadic, hunter-gatherer existence for prehistoric peoples enabled the development of a more stationary lifestyle based on the growing of crops and rearing of animals. As such, early societies developed practices of land ownership, which ultimately led to the emergence of a social hierarchy. It was within the newly established social elite that the idea of leisure first emerged.

More concrete evidence for the existence of leisure, however, can be found in ancient civilizations such

as that of ancient Egypt. Leisure played an important role in ancient Egyptian society, in which activities such as music, theater, and dance were performed for both religious and entertainment purposes. This blurring of the boundary between leisure and religious, ritualistic, or even political activities is characteristic of the historical development of leisure. A similar role for leisure activities is also seen in later civilizations such as Babylonia and ancient Greece. Sports such as boxing, wrestling, and archery all featured prominently as part of a program of recreation and relaxation.

By the turn of the twentieth century, the idea of leisure had become even more deeply instilled in modern Western society, with a burgeoning economy allowing more time for leisure and the state dedicating funds specifically for the development of public parks and recreation areas. Similarly, an important role is now assigned to the idea of "free" evenings and weekends. However, a significant discrepancy between access to leisure time and activities in the developing and developed worlds provides a key indicator of the inherent inequalities still associated with the idea of leisure today. **LWa**

Ancient Egyptian nobles listen to a harpist in this mural found in the Tomb of Anherkha (c. 1187–1064 BCE).

Arranged Marriage
China

Marriage as a means of preserving cultural and religious harmony or homogeny

The idea of arranging a marital union between two people originated in Far Eastern cultures more than 7000 years ago as a means of ensuring cultural and religious harmony within families and communities. Typically, the arrangement would be made by parents or members of the community, such as religious leaders, who would negotiate a pairing along with any exchange of money or property to be made. Arranged marriage also emerged in the ancient world on the Indian subcontinent and in the Near East and at a similar time in African and South American cultures, demonstrating the pervasiveness of ideas such as homogeny and cultural conservatism throughout human history.

Although significantly more common in Eastern cultures, arranged marriages were also popular in Europe during the sixteenth and seventeenth centuries. Families in the upper classes and nobility would often arrange a union between children deemed to be well suited in terms of both social and financial standing. Similarly, arranged marriages within royal circles have been the norm for centuries, often motivated by the political need to extend or consolidate power. This tradition continues in a contemporary context: the union between Charles, Prince of Wales, and Lady Diana Spencer in the United Kingdom in 1981 reportedly did not originate in unalloyed romantic attachment.

Arranged marriages are still common in countries such as India, Pakistan, and Afghanistan, and global migration has led to its more recent emergence in places such as the United States. Technological advances have led to the creation of matchmaking websites for arranging marriages, and there are now conferences where potential spouses and their families can network. Despite its ancient origins, arranged marriage continues to be relevant in a contemporary world. **LWa**

↑ Detail from an eighteenth-century illustration depicting a Hindu marriage ceremony.

Belly Dancing

Unknown

A dancing style characterized by movements of the hips and abdomen

⬆ A detail from a wall painting found in the tomb of the ancient Egyptian nobleman Nabamun, dating to *c.* 1350 BCE, showing dancers entertaining guests at a banquet.

"It is the most eloquent of female dances, with its haunting lyricism, its fire, its endlessly shifting kaleidoscope of sensual movement."

Wendy Buonaventura, *Serpent of the Nile: Women and Dance in the Arab World* (1989)

The term "belly dance" describes a variety of folk dances that originated in Asia, Egypt, the Middle East, or India. The dancing features complex torso movements, gyrating hips, undulations, and coordinated movements of the hips, chest, arms, and legs. Many, if not most, forms of belly dancing primarily feature a female dancer, although males are also known to perform.

Belly dancing is a folk dance that has been passed down from generation to generation, so it is difficult to determine its exact historical origins. It is possible that this type of dancing originated in prehistoric times in cultures that worshipped mother goddesses and performed ritualistic dancing as part of their religious ceremonies. There is strong evidence to suggest that belly dancing existed in ancient Egypt, with painted images of belly dancers found in tombs dating to *c.* 5000 BCE.

In Western cultures, the term "belly dancing" is largely credited as originating in the World's Fair in Chicago, Illinois, in 1893. Saul Bloom, the fair's entertainment director, coined the term *danse du ventre*, French for "belly dance," to describe the folk dances performed by dancers from Egypt and the Middle East. Prior to the popularization of the term, Western audiences were first exposed to "oriental" folk dances during the Victorian period, as a result of the rise of interest in Ottoman or "oriental" cultures.

To many modern audiences, belly dancing is a mostly erotic exercise in which the female dancer's movements are designed to entice and excite. Belly dancing, unlike many other types of folk dance, is a solo, non-choreographed, improvisational act that draws attention to a woman's abdomen. The movements of the dancers simultaneously venerate fertility and sexuality, which perhaps explains its nearly universal appeal. **MT**

Gymnastics
Ancient Egypt

The practice of exercising the body to develop physical agility and coordination

The term "gymnastics" derives from the Greek *gymnos*, meaning "naked," a reference to the fact that in ancient Greece most male athletes competed in the nude. This linguistic connection, and the fact that gymnastics is one of the oldest Olympic events, has led to the common belief that the sport originated in ancient Greece. However, there is plenty of evidence to show that the practice long predates the Greeks: Egyptian wall paintings dating from roughly 5000 BCE show acrobats performing gymnastics as entertainment for the nobility, and a wall painting of *c.* 2000 BCE depicts a young woman bending backward on all fours in a demonstration of flexibility; Minoan frescos in Crete, dating from around 2700 BCE, show acrobats vaulting off the backs of bulls (likely as part of a religious ceremony); while in China mass gymnastic-like exercises were practiced as part of the art of *Wushu* (a form of martial art) some 2,000 years before the Greek Olympics, which began in 776 BCE at Olympia in southern Greece.

Modern gymnastics is credited to a German, Johann Friedrich Guts Muths (1759–1839). He developed a complete program of exercises intended to improve balance, flexibility, and muscular strength, based on his experience working at a progressive school. Gymnastics spread through Europe in the nineteenth century, primarily for military physical training.

Today, the sport encompasses artistic gymnastics (which requires special equipment such as a balance beam), rhythmic gymnastics (a style that combines elements of ballet and dance with the use of equipment such as a ribbon), trampolining, aerobics, and acrobatics. Gymnastics is an art of body contortion as much as a feat of strength and grace. The greater flexibility that can be developed through training, in addition to the power gained, reveals the true physical potential of the human body. **KBJ**

⬆ A Greek sculpture of a gymnast that dates back to the fourth century BCE. Gymnastics was a central component of ancient Greek education and was mandatory for all students.

"Everything is about your movements and precision and timing, which is what gymnastics is about."

Shawn Johnson, U.S. gymnast

Megalithic Monuments
Unknown

Huge Neolithic and Bronze Age structures of undressed stone

The exact chronology of the spread of enormous stone monuments is unknown, but it is generally agreed that the earliest such structures, dating from around 4500 BCE, were the dolmens of the Mediterranean coast. A dolmen consists of several upright supports beneath a flat stone roof; the whole edifice—originally a burial site—was then covered with earth that has often since been eroded to reveal a stark and imposing megalith.

Later came menhirs, collections of upright stones arranged in circles, semicircles, ellipses, or alignments of several parallel rows. Menhirs occur most commonly in Brittany, France, and their name is derived from the Breton *men* (stone) and *hir* (long). The best-known menhirs, however, are probably those at Avebury and Stonehenge in England.

"Monuments … are effective and enduring means of communication."
E. DeMarrais, J. M. Castillo, and T. Earle, anthropologists

How these vast stones were extracted from the earth, transported, and erected is one of the great unsolved mysteries of the ancient world: the largest sections of Stonehenge are 32 feet (10 m) high, weigh 45 tons, and were quarried 200 miles (320 km) from the site. Their purpose also remains obscure, although the similarity of the symbols found carved on many of the monuments suggests that they were used for religious ceremonies. They may equally have been expressions of triumphalism, however.

At the start of the Bronze Age in northern Europe (*c.* 2000 BCE), the emergent Beaker folk continued the megalith tradition, albeit on a reduced scale, by constructing round barrows (large stone mounds) for single burials. Meanwhile, monuments were also erected in Africa, Asia, the Americas, and Melanesia. **GL**

Heaven and Hell
Unknown

The dwellings of, respectively, the just and blessed, and the unjust and cursed

The idea of an afterlife that consists of a rewarding dwelling in the heavens for the righteous and a cursed dwelling in the underworld for the unrighteous is an extremely ancient and global one. There is evidence that the Mesopotamians (whose culture originated in *c.* 4000 BCE) believed that most of their gods dwelt "above," while the souls of the dead went down to the underworld—a place of intense heat, darkness, and sorrow. Similarly, the ancient Egyptians believed that the dead descended to the underworld, where they were judged for their actions; if they were deemed just, then they could climb the ladder to the heavens, and if unjust, they were devoured by the crocodile-monster Ammit.

There is remarkable harmony of thought between the ancient polytheistic and the monotheistic

"Then I saw a New Heaven and a New Earth … coming down from God …"
The Bible, Revelation 20:14; 21:1, 2

Abrahamic religions in this view of the afterlife as split between "Heaven" and "Hell." However, these terms are often misunderstood, especially in Christianity. According to the Bible, God transcends all locations, and so while God is often spoken of as dwelling in Heaven, Heaven itself is a created, temporary place where the angels and righteous humans dwell. This contrasts with "Hell," a created, temporary place where damned angels and unrighteous humans go. Ultimately, however, the book of Revelation talks about God destroying Hell in a "Lake of Fire," and then "creating a New Heaven and a New Earth"—the New Heaven for the angels, and the New Earth for humans. As the two destinations for the soul when the body dies, Heaven and Hell continue to motivate pan-religious beliefs, actions, and art. **AB**

Rebel angels are cast into Hell in an illustration of Milton's *Paradise Lost* by William Blake (1808). ➜

Calendar
Ancient Egypt

Ordering the years, months, and days according to the sun, moon, and seasons

The term "calendar" derives from the Latin *calendarium* or *calendra*, meaning "account book," and *kalendae*, referring to the new moon and first day of the Roman month. A calendar is a system of ordering "time" in what is ordinarily an annual cycle, divided and subdivided according to the annual revolution of the Earth around the sun, the seasons that this causes, and the positions of the moon. The most common calendrical period (beyond the distinction between day and night) is the lunar month (the full cycle of the phases of the moon), which lasts about 29.5 days. All the major early centers of ancient civilization kept calendars, including Mesopotamia, the Indus and Nile valleys, eastern China, Mesoamerica, and the Andes.

Among the earliest calendars are the Egyptian calendar (traceable as far back as 4000 BCE), the Chinese calendar (mythically said to have been created in 2637 BCE, with historical evidence stemming as far back as the fourteenth century BCE), the Mesoamerican calendar (stemming back perhaps as far as 1000–900 BCE), the Indian calendar (the basic principles of the Vedic calendar can be traced to within the first millennium BCE), and the Japanese calendar (dating from around 660 BCE). A commonly used calendar throughout the world (part of the legacy of European colonialism) is the Gregorian calendar, which was developed from the first century BCE Julian calendar. The Gregorian calendar gets its name from Pope Gregory XIII, who dictated the need for changes to the Julian calendar (itself a reform of the Roman calendar), and has been adopted by many countries since the sixteenth century.

The calendar, as a concept, has been so essential to the organization of civilization, religion, agriculture, politics, social affairs, and other aspects of human society that the story of the calendar is almost as old as the story of civilization itself. **JE**

The Aztec calendar stone (c. 1479) reflects the Aztec view of time and space as wheels within wheels.

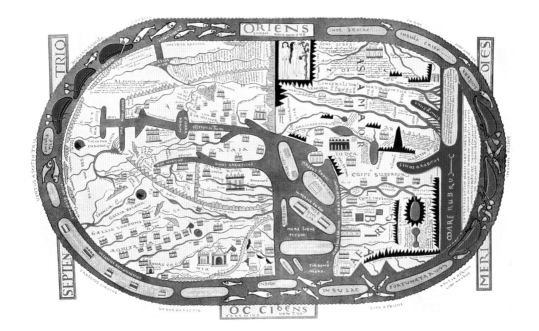

Flat Earth Myth
Ancient Egypt

The ancient but erroneous belief that the Earth is flat

The ancient Egyptians and Mesopotamians were probably the first to believe, in c. 4000 BCE, that the world was a flat circular surface, though this notion was fairly ubiquitous in antiquity—understandably so, given that the science needed to measure the Earth had not yet been discovered. In the West, the best-known instances of a flat, circular surface are from either the Greek poet Homer (fl. c. 850 BCE), who speaks of "the circular surface of the Earth," or the biblical Psalmist, who sings of God sitting "enthroned above the circle of the Earth." In the East, Hindu, Jainist, Buddhist, and Shinto scholars believed likewise, usually speaking of the Earth as floating on water, with the heavens or sky umbrella-like overhead.

The idea of a flat, circular Earth was common in the ancient world, but once the Greeks—arguably starting with Pythagoras (c. 570–c. 495 BCE), though certainly with Ptolemy (c. 100–c. 170 CE) a few centuries later—devised the technology necessary to measure latitude, longitude, and climes, the flat Earth thesis began to diminish (at least in the West). For example, the Christian philosopher Boethius (c. 480–524/25), whose *Consolation of Philosophy* (c. 524) was arguably the most important book (after the Bible) in the Christian West, argued that the Earth was spherical. Why, then, is it sometimes thought that the Christian West, even at the time of Columbus, thought the world flat?

Although the Renaissance and Enlightenment were largely Christian philosophical-scientific projects, some of these thinkers were hostile to the Bible and were eager to dismiss it as myth since, among other things, its poetic utterances about a disk-shaped Earth were scientifically flawed. This kind of enlightened propaganda created in the popular imagination the false, but influential, notion that most in the Christian West thought the world flat. Today, the Flat Earth Society exists for anyone interested in the theory. **AB**

⬆ A world map of the flat Earth, printed by Beatus Rhenanus in the early sixteenth century.

Feng Shui
China

Arranging one's surroundings to encourage harmony and enhance quality of life

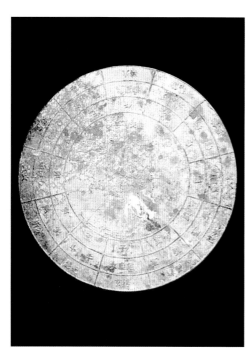

⬆ A bronze feng shui compass from China's Spring and Autumn Period (770–476 BCE). The feng shui compass, or *Lo-Pan*, is used to define the *bagua* (energy map) of any given space.

Feng shui is the Chinese art of arranging and moving the external built environment—anything from buildings and gardens to the furnishings and objects within them—to maximize that environment's harmony and balance, and optimize the flow of energy (known as *qi* or *chi*) through and around it. Feng shui was derived from the Chinese concepts of yin (positive forces) and yang (negative forces), and evidence suggests that it may have been practiced in some form for thousands of years. The earliest believed examples of the practice date back to *c.* 4000 BCE, and include dwellings and graves that have been aligned according to certain astronomic principles.

One early approach to locating *qi* was based on the scheme *Wu Xing*, the five phases, which conceptualizes *qi* as alternating between yin and yang as it progresses through the Earth's five elemental phases—metal, earth, fire, wood, and water. In the *Wu Xing* system, every calendar year and every direction of the compass is allocated its own elemental designation. Therefore, each individual may harmonize their personal *qi* by orienting their home, workplace, and even their grave to directions compatible with their year of birth. Numerous additional rules govern the successful arrangement of patterns of objects, but as a general philosophy of design, orientations appropriate to feng shui are said to promote welfare, increase creativity, facilitate better interpersonal relationships, aid contemplation, and reduce stress.

The principles of feng shui were largely unknown in Europe and the United States until the late nineteenth century. The German Protestant missionary Ernest Eitel (1838–1908) published a study of feng shui in 1878, titled *Feng-shui: The rudiments of natural science in China*, but it was not until perhaps the last quarter of the twentieth century that the wider public became familiar with the ancient Chinese system. **JE**

"Both heaven and earth influence all living beings ... it is in your hands to turn this influence to the best account for your advantage."

Ernest Eitel, *Feng Shui* (1878)

Wind Power
Ancient Egypt

Converting the energy of the wind into a useful source of power

The concept of harnessing the wind to provide power was first put into practice in ancient Egypt in *c.* 3500 BCE, with the introduction of sails to propel boats. Previously, boats were powered by groups of rowers, and thus were limited in how far and how fast they could travel. The development of square sails fashioned from papyrus meant that boats could travel farther and faster, with a smaller crew. This had a significant impact on trade, as it not only sped up the process of transporting goods but also enabled boats to become bigger—by *c.* 1200 BCE, the Phoenicians were using 80-feet-long (24 m) wooden cargo vessels with large cloth sails.

The first example of the wind being used to drive a mechanical device is generally considered to be the windwheel of the Greek mathematician and engineer Heron, or Hero, of Alexandria (*c.* 10–70 CE). In his *Pneumatica*, Heron described his innovations to the hydraulis, a water organ originally designed by Ktesibios of Alexandria (*fl. c.* 270 BCE). The original mechanism forced air through pipes to sound notes depressed on a keyboard. Pressure in an air chamber was kept constant by using water to weigh down on it. Heron improved the valve that released the air into the sounding pipe, and replaced the water with a wind turbine that could be moved to catch the prevailing wind in order to maintain the necessary air pressure.

The origins of perhaps the best-known wind-powered mechanical device, the windmill, are much debated, but there is reliable evidence that it was in widespread use in Persia by the seventh century. Windmills became a common tool for pumping water and grinding corn and grain across Europe and Asia, and remained so until the nineteenth century. In the twentieth century wind power became widespread as a means of generating electricity, and today wind turbines are one of several renewable energy sources that offer an alternative to fossil fuels. **DM**

⬆ A tenth- or eleventh-century BCE papyrus with an illustration from the ancient Egyptian Book of the Dead, showing a deceased person sailing through the underworld.

"The air when set in motion becomes wind (for wind is nothing else but air in motion)…"

Heron of Alexandria, *Pneumatica* (first century CE)

Sundial
Ancient Egypt

Using the shadow cast by the sun to reveal the time of day

Sundials are the oldest known instruments for telling the time of day. The earliest known sundials were ancient Egyptian obelisks created around 3500 BCE, although the oldest surviving example, also Egyptian, was made relatively recently, in c. 800 BCE.

The key component of any sundial is the gnomon, a vertical stick or pillar that casts a shadow that moves as the sun crosses the sky from east to west. Beneath the gnomon is a flat surface, the dial plate, usually marked with numbered lines showing the hours of daylight. It is the shadow of the gnomon on the dial plate that indicates the time of day.

As sundials were adopted more widely across the ancient world, they became increasingly sophisticated: their dial plates were inscribed with different sets of

"Sundials tell 'sun time.' Clocks and watches tell 'clock time.'"

Sundials.co.uk

numbers to reflect the varying lengths of the day in each season. This system assigned twelve hours to every day, so each hour in high summer could be three or four times longer than each hour in midwinter. The earliest example of this type of sundial is attributed to the Greek astronomer Aristarchus of Samos (c. 310–230 BCE).

In the Middle Ages, sundials were taken up with great enthusiasm by Muslims, who marked their dial plates with the times for daily prayers, sometimes to the exclusion of the hours of the day. But after the emergence of clockwork in the fourteenth century, sundials gradually fell from favor. They retained their value, however, being used until the nineteenth century to reset mechanical timepieces. Since 1955, atomic clocks have given the official world time. **GL**

Pictograms and Alphabet
Sumeria

The building blocks for the evolution of written communication

Pictograms—pictorial symbols designed to express meaning—represent the earliest known form of written communication. One of the first pictographic systems, known as cuneiform, emerged in around 3200 BCE among the Sumerian people of the ancient Near East. This intricate script, consisting originally of more than 1,000 symbols, endured for more than 3,000 years and influenced the development of many subsequent pictographic systems in the ancient world.

Despite its importance, however, cuneiform was eventually supplanted by the more efficient Phoenician alphabet (c. 1100 BCE), which consisted of only two dozen distinct characters based on the basic consonant sounds. Transported throughout the Mediterranean by Phoenician merchants, the alphabet was adopted in

"Until writing was invented, man lived in acoustic space: boundless, directionless ..."

Marshall McLuhan, *The Medium Is the Massage* (1967)

ancient Greece, where it was modified to incorporate vowel sounds—thereby creating what is generally considered the world's first complete alphabet.

The ancient Greek alphabet (c. 1000 BCE) is also the earliest ancestor of the Latin alphabet (c. 600 BCE), which is the most common alphabet in use today. In line with the Greek system, the Latin alphabet is based on the use of a distinct number of basic consonant and vowel sounds (known as phonemes). Significantly, this enables the translation of words from one language into another; an innovation that continues to have an important impact on modern communication. However, despite the advantages of alphabetic systems, pictograms are still widely used in the modern world—something you are sure to notice next time you are driving on unfamiliar roads or visiting a public bathroom. **LWa**

A tablet with cuneiform writing from the ancient Sumerian city of Uruk, dating back to c. 3200 BCE.

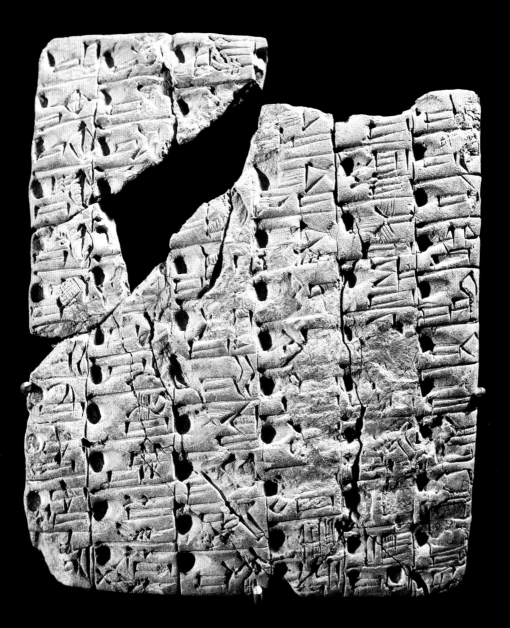

Cremation
Unknown

The practice of disposing of dead bodies by burning them

The practice of cremation—the incineration of a dead body—began in *c.* 3000 BCE, most likely in Europe and the Middle East. Cremation is well known to be a key feature of cultures in India, but its introduction on that subcontinent was relatively recent, dating from 1900 BCE.

From *c.* 1000 BCE the ancient Greeks burned the bodies of soldiers killed in action on foreign soil so that their ashes could be repatriated to their native land. Thus associated with heroes, cremation became regarded as the most fitting conclusion to a life well lived. It remained a status symbol in ancient Rome until the rise of Christianity from the first century CE, which taught that the dead would rise at the end of the world. This persuaded converts to bury their dead, so their bodies would still exist on the day of judgment.

" . . . he is cremated . . . The swan of the soul takes flight, and asks which way to go."

Sri Guru Granth Sahib, Sikh scripture

Cremation thereafter became unfashionable and in some countries forbidden. One of the principal non-religious objections was that it might conceal foul play. Attitudes changed in the late nineteenth century, partly because of the publication in 1874 of *Cremation: The Treatment of the Body After Death*, a book by Queen Victoria's surgeon, Sir Henry Thompson. In Japan, cremation was legalized in 1875; the first U.S. crematorium was opened in 1876; and in 1884, English courts ruled that it was permissible to dispose of human corpses in this way.

Cremation is now firmly reestablished in most countries: in Japan it is almost universal; in Britain and Germany more than 50 percent of dead bodies are cremated. Only the United States bucks the trend: more than 90 percent of Americans are still interred. **GL**

Judgment Day
Ancient Egypt

A day of reckoning on which people are divinely judged on their morality

Judgment day is commonly understood to refer to a day in the future when individuals will be judged on the basis of the morality of their actions by a divine authority. The idea of a day of judgment can be traced back to the ancient Egyptians in the third millennium BCE. The Egyptians believed that upon death a person's soul would enter the underworld and arrive at their personal judgment day in the Hall of Two Truths. From yhere, a good person's soul would proceed to a blissful afterlife, while an evil soul would be sent to the Devourer of the Dead.

The idea of a day of judgment also emerged in later religions, and is still in place in modern belief systems. However, in contrast to the Egyptian story, judgment day is now taken to refer to a specific day

"The Day of Judgment is an important notion: but that Day is always with us."

Alfred North Whitehead, mathematician

on which the whole of humanity will be judged. The earliest eschatology of this kind is found in the Zoroastrian religion, which emerged around 1500 BCE. Here, judgment day serves as the precursor to a perfect state of the world in which all evil has been eradicated.

This notion of a heavenlike world emerging after the final judgment of all peoples is a familiar feature of the major Abrahamic religions. Judaism posits the "End of Days," followed by a Messianic Age of Peace, and much of the Islamic Koran is concerned with the Qiyamah (Last Judgment) and subsequent treatment of the righteous and unrighteous in heaven or hell. The idea of judgment day has also attracted attention from secular society, showing that the concept of a final judgment penetrates not only across different faiths and times, but also deep into the human psyche. **LWa**

Perfume
Indus Valley Civilization

The use of pleasant-smelling substances on the body

⬆ An Assyrian perfume burner from the thirteenth century BCE. A flame placed inside the burner would heat incense in the well at the top, creating a fragrant smoke.

> "... Take unto thee sweet spices, stacte, and onycha, and galbanum; these sweet spices with pure frankincense: of each shall there be a like weight: And thou shalt make it a perfume, a confection after the art of the apothecary, tempered together, pure and holy ..."

The Bible, Exodus 30:34–36

Human beings produce natural odors, some pleasant, some less so. Nature is full of attractive odors—produced by a wide range of herbs and flowers, but also by specific animals—and it did not take people long to commandeer naturally fragrant materials in order to make themselves smell more pleasing. Modern perfumes are created from combinations of various synthetic and natural compounds, oils, and additives, but before these were available, perfume makers collected, combined, and refined natural compounds to create scents for the use of both men and women.

The earliest known evidence of the use of perfume is from the Indus Valley Civilizations, where people stored scents in terracotta pots as early as c. 3000 BCE. Mesopotamian culture had an advanced perfume-making industry by around 2000 BCE, and from c. 700 BCE the ancient Greeks made perfumes available not only to cause the owner to smell good but also to treat specific illnesses, to attract a sexual partner, and even to clarify addled thoughts. In the first century CE the city of Rome alone imported 2,800 tons of frankincense and 550 tons of myrrh each year to meet the people's desire for perfume, and both fragrances became important in religious practices, in the form of incense.

The human sense of smell is a powerful one, capable of forming some of our strongest memories and associations, as well as producing changes in mood, emotion, and other physiological responses. With the creation of perfumes, humanity was able to stimulate and shape the sense of smell to produce a desired response. Perfume became a means, not only of controlling the environment, but also of exercising control over our emotions directly through our senses. The use of perfume in its various guises remains as popular as ever in modern times, with the industry at the beginning of the twenty-first century having a value of about $10 billion. **MT**

Ma'at
Ancient Egypt

A personified principle of rightness and regularity in the universe

Although the first mention of *Ma'at*—the ancient Egyptian principle of truth, justice, and regularity in the universe—is in the Pyramid Texts (*c.* 2375–2345 BCE), the general concept is much older. Like the Persian *Asha*, the Hindu *Rta*, the ancient Chinese *Dao*, and the Stoic *Natura*, *Ma'at* is the divine standard and ordering principle of creation, standing in opposition to both spiritual and physical chaos. The Egyptian concept of chaos, called *Isfet*, is similar to the "waters" of the Mesopotamian and biblical traditions, which God separated and held back in order to create the world. And just as the Bible metaphorically speaks of God's ordering wisdom in the feminine ("Wisdom . . . She . . ."), so too was *Ma'at* often depicted as a goddess who brings order and justice to the universe. In Egyptian mythology, she was viewed as being responsible for regulating the stars and the seasons, as well as the actions of both mortals and gods.

Although a principle as broad as *Ma'at* can be seen everywhere, she was most often viewed on the judgment throne. As the principle of truth and justice, Ma'at acted as the judge or advisor to the judge of the underworld. Her task in this role was to determine whether a soul was just or unjust by weighing the heart of the dead person against a feather. If the scale balanced, then the deceased was allowed to continue on to the afterlife; if the heart was heavier than the feather, then the deceased was deemed not to have followed the principles of *Ma'at* during their life and their heart was eaten by a demon. In politics, the pharaohs were often called "the lords of *Ma'at*" because they were supposed to keep order in society as rulers answerable to the divine. Although the term "*Ma'at*" was probably of limited influence outside of Egypt, the concept—by whatever name—is central to how most societies understand order, especially moral order, and regularity. **AB**

⬆ An ancient Egyptian painting of the goddess Ma'at (*c.* 1600– *c.* 1100 BCE), shown wearing her customary ostrich feather. The ostrich feather was used as a symbol of truth.

"I have not committed sin or injustice . . . I have not transgressed against Ma'at."

Papyrus of Ani (*c.* 1250 BCE)

Numerology
Ancient Egypt

A mystical connection between numbers and the world

Numerology appeals to a divine or mystical connection between the properties of numbers and aspects of human life. Ancient intrigue in the power of numbers can be identified in many early cultures, notably that of ancient Egypt from *c.* 3000 BCE. Depictions of the Egyptian mythological figure of Seshat, the goddess of both mathematics and astrology, have survived in major temples throughout Egypt, offering an insight into the interplay between the mathematical and the mystical in Egyptian culture.

The study of numbers and their relation to the world was also adopted in later cultures and was prominent in early Greek philosophy. The Greek philosopher Pythagoras (*c.* 570–*c.* 495 BCE) was particularly influential in this respect, developing several mathematical

"Numbers are the universal language offered by the deity to humans …"

St. Augustine of Hippo, Christian philosopher

principles that are still in use today. The principles' bases are at least arguably numerological, given the mystical approach to the properties of numbers that Pythagoras employed in their establishment.

Modern numerology draws on many aspects of the ancient mystical treatment of numbers in order to analyze personality types or predict future events. Pythagorean numerology, for example, developed in the 1970s, appeals to the Pythagorean idea that "all is number." Although today this is largely discredited as a pseudoscientific practice, its ancient origins are responsible for certain persistent superstitions. In modern Chinese culture, for example, even numbers are considered luckier than odd, while many Westerners will be familiar with an unaccounted for aversion to the number thirteen. **LWa**

Mathematics
Ancient Egypt

A symbolic representation of abstract numerical ideas

The ability of humanity to formulate and use mathematical concepts probably predates historical records, as questions about measurements, size, and quantities have always been of practical concern, as indeed has been the ability to count. Prehistoric artifacts dating as far back as 30,000 BCE, while not in themselves evidence of grasped mathematical concepts, are some indication that people were making marks or tallies in attempts to count or quantify.

Hieroglyphics dating from about 3000 BCE are evidence that ancient Egyptians were already using numerals, while ancient Egyptian papyruses dating from around 2000 BCE represent some of the earliest known mathematical texts in existence. Nothing survives to document how much the ancient Egyptians

"Mathematics, rightly viewed, possesses not only truth, but supreme beauty."

Bertrand Russell, philosopher

actually understood of mathematical concepts, but early Indian civilizations appear to have used geometric patterns as early as 2600 BCE. Chinese mathematics seems to have arisen independently, with the oldest Chinese mathematical text originating around 300 BCE.

Mathematics is both vital to human progress and impractical at the same time. Every mathematical concept is "only" an abstraction, but as an abstract form of concept, mathematics allows for answers and deductions that are not constrained by the realities of the natural world. Mathematics, therefore, is a discipline, science, and language that creates a bridge between the world of thought or concepts and the everyday reality of human existence. It is a bridge that we traverse constantly to calculate, measure, and solve many of the other problems we face. **MT**

   The Rhind Mathematical Papyrus (*c.* 1650 BCE) is one of the oldest mathematical texts in the world. ➡

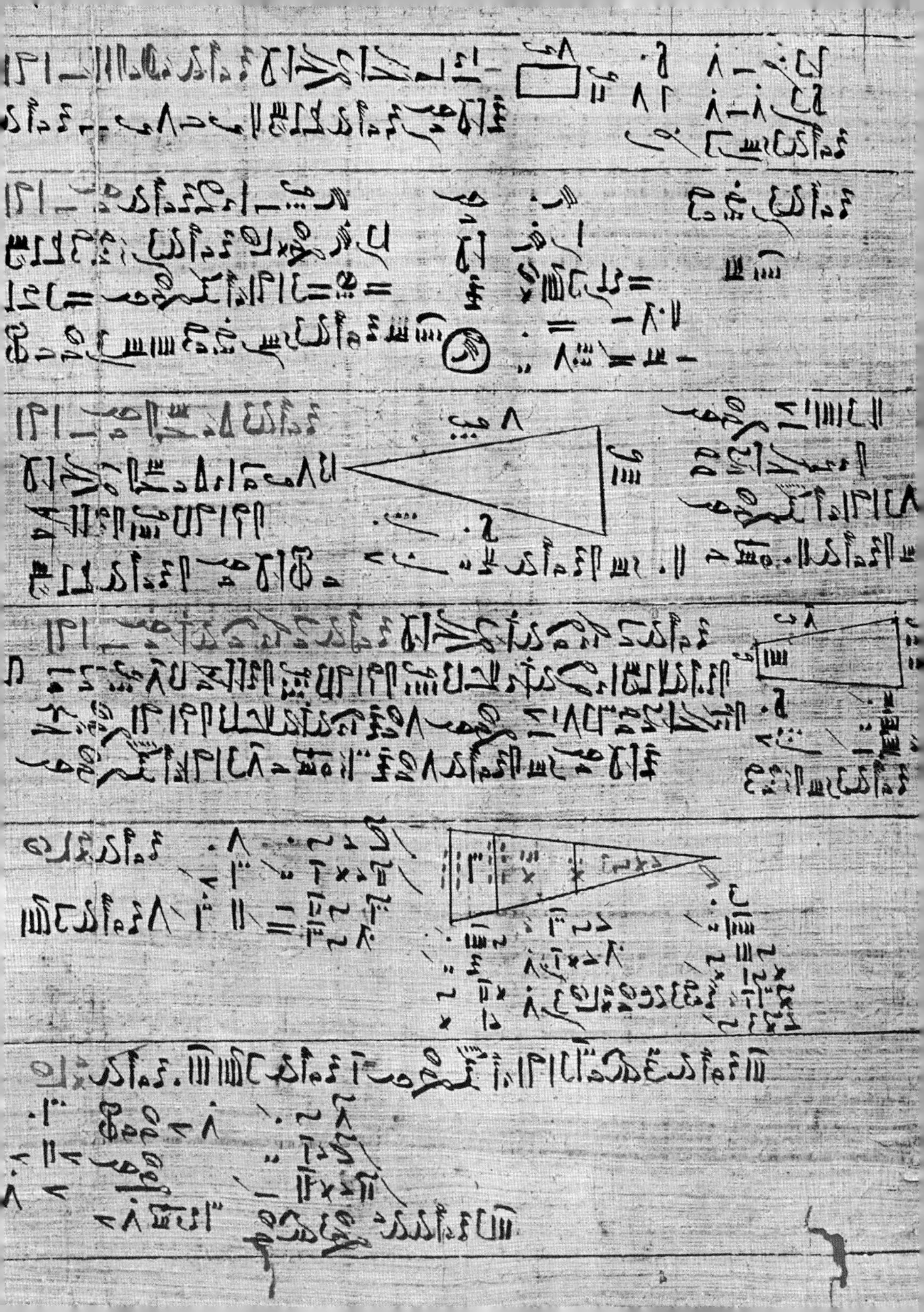

Egyptian Funerary Art
Ancient Egypt

The preservation and honoring of those passing into the afterlife

Egyptian funerary art was motivated by the central religious and cultural belief that life continued after death, which was a feature of ancient Egyptian society from about 3000 BCE. Practices such as mummification, the creation of sarcophagi, and the building of pyramids and tombs were intended to honor and preserve the body of the deceased in order to ease their transition to the afterlife. In addition, a number of carefully selected objects were often buried with the deceased person, comprising either personal possessions or more valuable items depending on their wealth and status during life.

The discovery and investigation of Egyptian funerary art have proven invaluable to archaeologists attempting to piece together the social order and

"For an ancient Egyptian nobleman ... a fine burial ... was his greatest aspiration."

Abeer el-Shahawy, *The Funerary Art of Ancient Egypt* (2005)

structure of ancient Egyptian civilization. Procedures such as the delicate preservation of the deceased's internal organs in Canopic jars during the process of mummification serve to demonstrate the elaborate and complex nature of the belief systems in place as well as the power and significance of the belief in an afterlife that was held throughout Egyptian society.

The best-known surviving examples of Egyptian funerary art are undoubtedly the Great Pyramids found at the Giza Plateau on the outskirts of Cairo in modern Egypt. Now a UNESCO World Heritage site, the Pyramids are today more significant as a popular tourist destination than as the focus of a religious or spiritual belief system. However, they continue to represent a firmly held belief in the afterlife that plays a central role in the lives of many religious believers today. **LWa**

Autopsy
Ancient Egypt

Careful examination of a cadaver to find out the cause of death

The word "autopsy" comes from the Greek *autopsia* (to see with one's own eyes), and refers to the postmortem examination of a body, usually by a physician of some kind, to discover the cause of death. The ancient Egyptians invented the autopsy procedure around 3000 BCE, although their focus was on preparing the body for immortality rather than ascertaining what occurred in the body's final moments. Much later, ancient Greek physicians, particularly Erasistratus and Herophilus in the third century BCE, became the main developers of the technique of cutting open a cadaver for the purpose of advancing knowledge of anatomy. Five hundred years after that, the Roman physician Galen (129–c. 200/c. 216 CE) used personal observation of the interior of the human body to link a person's

"The autopsy has a long and at times ignoble history ..."

The Hospital Autopsy (2010), ed. by J. L. Burton & G. Rutty

symptoms with abnormalities found during the autopsy after their death. His observations marked the beginning of reliable, scientific medical diagnosis.

In the early nineteenth century, an expansion of the medical profession caused a shortage in the legal supply of bodies for the purpose of dissection by students in pursuit of their studies. Corpses were obtained by robbing graves, buying in bodies from workhouse infirmaries, or even by resorting to murder. The best-known case is that of Burke and Hare, who murdered up to thirty people in 1828 in order to sell their bodies to the medical schools of Edinburgh. Modern-day autopsies bring scientific rigor to detective work in homicide cases and are important as a safeguard against the illegal taking of life by corrupt medical practitioners, care workers, and others. **JF**

The Egyptians mummified bodies by embalming them to dry them out and then wrapping them in linen strips.

Soap
Babylonia

The creation of a substance from the salt of a fatty acid that, when dissolved in water, possesses the ability to remove dirt from a variety of surfaces

⬆ Early soaps were used primarily in the creation of textile products such as wool, the manufacture of which is depicted here in a first-century CE fresco from Pompeii.

"If I rub my hands with it, soap foams, exults … The more complaisant it makes them, supple, smooth, docile, the more it slobbers, the more its rage becomes voluminous, pearly …"

Francis Ponge, *Soap* (1967)

No one can be sure when soap was first made, but the earliest evidence is from 2800 BCE: a lining of soaplike material was discovered to be deposited in clay cylinders by archaeologists on an excavation of ancient Babylon. Other digs at Babylonian sites known to be 600 years younger have yielded the earliest known record of how to make soap. Clay tablets inscribed with cuneiform reveal formulas that mix water, cassia oil, and ashes, but do not explain how the soap was used.

The Ebers Papyrus, written in Egypt in *c.* 1550 BCE, not only describes how to combine animal fats and vegetable oils with alkaline salts to create soapy substances, but also explains how this could then be used for washing. All soaps have essentially the same chemical structure: a hydrophilic (water-loving) head on a hydrophobic (water-fearing) hydrocarbon tail. This arrangement enables soap to perform the deceptively simple act of cleaning. First, it interacts with water molecules, reducing surface tension, so they spread better. Then, while its hydrophilic heads attract these molecules, its hydrophobic tails (which are also lipophilic, or fat-loving) embed into grease. When enough tails have lodged into a dirt particle, it is lifted into the water; the grease is effectively washed away.

The first use of soap was for cleaning wool and cotton used in the manufacture of textiles, and it was also used as a medical treatment for skin problems. It was not until the second century CE that soap was referred to in relation to personal cleanliness.

As to the question of how this cherished household helper got its name, Roman legend tells the story of Mount Sapo, a mountain where animals were ritually sacrificed. When the rains washed the animal fats and wood-fire ashes down to the river Tiber, it takes no great leap of imagination to guess what formed when they mixed, *sapo* being Latin for "soap." **JH**

Literature
Sumeria

Communicating ideas, beliefs, and experiences through the written word

What differentiates literature from other forms of writing is not always clear. While technical, descriptive, and scientific works are sometimes included in the broader definition of literature, the term more commonly encompasses only creative, expressive, and narrative works. Through literature, then, a writer uses words to convey ideas, feelings, experiences, and other commonly shared human phenomena, instead of simply relating facts.

Literature could not have existed without the invention of writing, yet writing in itself does not necessarily constitute literature. Writing had existed as early as 3000 BCE in the Bronze Age cultures of ancient Mesopotamia, yet literature did not appear until 400 years later in ancient Sumeria. Prior to the invention of writing, literature only existed in an oral form, passed down between generations as stories and myths. One of the earliest and best known of these stories is the *Epic of Gilgamesh*—a description in the Akkadian language of the odyssey of Gilgamesh, the king of the Mesopotamian city-state Uruk—that was first recorded in writing in around 2000 BCE. Various forms of literature arose independently across ancient civilizations and changed over time, coming to include everything from poetry to drama, narrative fiction, and graphic novels.

Literature exists as anything on a spectrum, from escapist enjoyment or tedious study to a bond that develops between those who read a specific work and share a common identity or purpose. A literary work can express the fears, desires, or feelings of an entire nation, and can hold historical and cultural significance. Literature enables ideas to be transmitted across geographic and temporal boundaries, serving as a link not only between cultures, but also between the past and the present, between generations, civilizations, and peoples. **MT**

Abacus
Sumeria

The oldest ancestor of the modern calculator and computer

First developed by the Sumerians in ancient Mesopotamia in 2500 BCE, an abacus is a device used for counting and making arithmetic calculations. The etymology of the term "abacus"—which comes from Semitic languages in which the noun *abaq* means "dust"—has given rise to the theory that the original abacuses were flat boards covered with sand, on which numbers could be written and then erased.

From its ancient origins, the abacus eventually spread to Greece: a marble tablet, 5 feet (150 cm) long and 2 feet 6 inches (75 cm) wide, from the Greek island of Salamis, made in around 300 BCE, is the oldest counting board that has so far been discovered. The abacus then reached Rome and China. Over time, it developed from a shallow sandbox into its now familiar

> "Learning how to use the abacus can help to improve concentration [and] memory."

Paul Green, *How to Use a Chinese Abacus* (2007)

form: a frame across which are stretched several wires, each with a number of beads that can be slid from end to end of each wire. Each row of beads represents a different value: one row is typically units, another tens, another hundreds.

In around 700 CE, the Hindus developed an innovative numeral system with place values and zeroes that made counting, addition, subtraction, multiplication, and division easier than ever before to carry out in writing. This new idea caught on with the Arabs, who introduced it into Europe in around 1000 CE. From then on, abacuses were used less frequently in the West, although even today they remain common sights in China, Japan, and parts of Western Asia, where the best operators can keep pace with people using pocket calculators. **GL**

Map
Babylonia

A graphical representation of a geographic area

⬆ A Babylonian cuneiform tablet from *c.* 700–500 BCE, containing a map of Mesopotamia. In the center is Babylon, surrounded by Assyria and Elam.

"Journey over all the universe in a map, without the expense and fatigue of traveling, without suffering the inconveniences of heat, cold, hunger, and thirst."

Miguel de Cervantes, *Don Quixote* (1605)

The oldest possible evidence of humanity creating visual depictions of spatial relationships comes from the Lascaux caves in southwestern France, where prehistoric man may have painted images of the stars in the night sky. However, it was not until about 2300 BCE, in ancient Babylon, that clear evidence of what we would easily recognize as a map emerged. Inscribed on clay tablets, Babylonian maps show natural terrain features and cities, as well as cuneiform labels for locations and even directions.

In the first millennium BCE, cartography—the art and practice of mapmaking—advanced considerably in ancient Greece and Rome. The Chinese developed maps as early as the fourth century BCE, and ever since their introduction, humanity has improved on them.

A map is a visual representation of the spatial relationships between features or factors. Usually drawn to scale, maps can represent land features, bodies of water, political boundaries, populations, elevations, cultural differences, and a host of other kinds of information. Maps are often made from the perspective of someone looking down, which allows for two-dimensional representations of three-dimensional spaces. They are often made on flat surfaces such as pieces of walls or paper, though three-dimensional maps, such as globes, are also common, as are flat projections of non-flat areas, such as maps of the world.

Maps are images, and as images they transcend written and verbal language. They are a form of communication that shares information across different cultures and regions, conveying knowledge instantaneously through the medium of symbols. Even if a map is grossly unrealistic and in no way looks or feels like the features it purports to represent, it allows humans to visualize what they might otherwise never be in a position to see in person. **MT**

Dictionary
Mesopotamia

A book that collects together in a standard form all the words of a language

The world's oldest dictionary dates back to about 2300 BCE. The bilingual cuneiform tablet was written during the reign of Sargon of Akkad (c. 2334–c. 2279 BCE), who unified the Sumerian city-states and created the Akkadian Empire of Mesopotamia, and contains Sumerian words and their Akkadian counterparts.

In about 300 BCE, the Chinese developed the first dictionary that organized words of the same language, grouping them as synonyms in nineteen different categories. Multilingual dictionaries and glossaries of specialized terms were common in Europe during the Middle Ages (c. 500–c. 1450), but it was not until Samuel Johnson (1709–84) created *A Dictionary of the English Language* in 1755 that the first modern dictionary made its appearance. Johnson's dictionary, completed after nine years, attempted to encompass all the words of the English language, not merely the obscure ones.

Today there are numerous types of dictionaries that contain explanations of the words of individual languages, and a host of multilingual and specialized dictionaries on almost any topic. Some dictionaries list terms relevant to a particular subject matter or field of study—legal or medical dictionaries are examples—while others contain words from one or more languages with translations.

The first dictionaries were of little importance in societies where oral communication was the norm. Complete dictionaries were needed only after the invention of writing; only became practical after the invention of the printing press; and only became truly necessary after literacy became commonplace. The dictionary codified language and provided a measuring stick that the literate could apply to their own tongue. Referred to by everyone, the dictionary conferred a uniformity in how the written word was used, enabling free and accurate communication—without any spelling mistakes. **MT**

↑ Samuel Johnson's publication of a dictionary in 1755 earned him a degree from the University of Oxford. Johnson illustrated word usage in his dictionary with numerous literary quotations.

"Take care that you never spell a word wrong. Always before you write a word, consider how it is spelled, and, if you do not remember, turn to a dictionary."

Thomas Jefferson, U.S. president 1801–09

Consolation of Philosophy
Ancient Egypt

Determined and careful reasoning can in itself bring comfort to the soul

Humans have utilized their rationality for many things, including philosophical speculation or, broadly speaking, the activity of thinking hard about a problem. In particular, humans have thought hard about suffering and death. Although almost certainly not the first to have thought about these problems, the Egyptians, in *A Dispute over Suicide* (c. 2280 BCE), are among the first to have recorded their speculation. The Mesopotamians, too, wrote semi-philosophical treatises, such as the *Babylonian Theodicy* (c. 1000 BCE).

The best-known instances of such philosophical works are *The Apology* (399 BCE) and *Phaedo* (360 BCE) by Plato (c. 424–c. 348 BCE), but it was the Christian Platonist Boethius (c. 480–c. 524 CE) who coined the phrase "the consolation of philosophy." In his book of

"I . . . decided to write down my wretched complaint . . ."
Boethius, *The Consolation of Philosophy* (524 CE)

the same name, written in 524, Boethius finds himself unjustly imprisoned, awaiting execution. Stripped of all his former glory, power, and influence, he is overcome with despair until Lady Philosophy arrives. Unlike Lady Wisdom in the Book of Proverbs, who simply tells her pupil what's what, Boethius's Lady Philosophy encourages him to think carefully about why he is suffering and why, ultimately, it does not matter.

The consolation Lady Philosophy brings is not occasioned, as secular humanists sometimes imagine it, by a rejection of religion; rather, Boethius chooses between finding no comfort from anything, finding comfort through non-speculation, and finding comfort through philosophical reasoning. The third option implies being able to draw from evidence wherever it might be, including from religious sources. **AB**

Poetry
Sumeria

A literary art form that uses words and their sounds to convey meaning vividly

Humanity was able to use language long before the invention of the written word, and poetry almost certainly existed before writing. When early cultures wanted to relate stories or oral histories, they may have used poetic forms and styles, such as rhyme and meter, to make it easier for listeners to remember what they heard. In a more modern sense, poetry uses words to create works of art. Distinct from prose or literature, poetry relies on the qualities of the words as written, formatted, or structured to not only convey meaning but also to do so in a beautiful or stylistic way.

The first known written poem, the *Epic of Gilgamesh*, came from ancient Sumeria sometime around 2150 BCE. Poetry arose across cultural boundaries, with notable early works coming from Indian, Chinese, and Greek

"Poetry is finer and more philosophical than history . . ."
Aristotle, Greek philosopher and scientist

societies. Over the millennia, poets have incorporated a range of literary devices, such as alliteration and rhyme, as well as written poetry in an array of formats and arrangements. The more recent development of free verse or free-form poetry has given poets the opportunity to create without the formal, structural boundaries of the past.

Humanity created words to describe the natural world, yet these words are not merely descriptors— simply hearing them can create an emotional reaction. Poetry captures the impact that words have on us. Whether structured, rhymed, or free form, poetry seizes the images and emotions that occur in our minds when we hear or read words, and shapes those words into forms that impart more meaning than they might otherwise suggest. **MT**

Flood Myth
Mesopotamia

An ancient deluge sent as punishment against humans

Most ancient civilizations had a flood myth recounting, with remarkable similarity, how God or the gods sent, as punishment, a massive flood to destroy most humans. A Sumerian account from *c.* 2150 BCE is the oldest written record of a flood myth, though the biblical account is the most detailed. In all versions of the myth, the divine becomes angered by the actions of the newly created humans. A flood is then sent to destroy all the humans that have earned divine displeasure, but in every case there is one outstanding man who is warned of the coming doom and told to build a boat in order to survive the ordeal. In most cases, the man brings his family on board, along with a pair of every kind of animal that would be in the flood's destructive path. Once divine wrath has ceased and

"We sent the Flood, but a man survived the catastrophe . . ."
Atrahasis III.8 (Mesopotamian flood myth tablet)

the flood waters recede, the humans give thanks to the divine and then repopulate the destroyed area.

Although some have understood this myth to be the story of an event that affected the whole world, this is not necessarily the best reading. Descriptive phrases such as "and the waters covered all the mountaintops" are probably just hyperbole, suggesting that while the global similarity of the myths makes an original historical event of some kind quite likely, it would probably be best to view it, both textually and scientifically, as a local—perhaps Near Eastern—flood.

Whatever the case, the flood myth has consistently inspired belief in some higher form or another. The flood's consequent rainbow provides a powerful symbol of both God's justice (in punishing evildoers) and love (in sparing the repentant). **AB**

Catastrophism
India

The theory that the Earth has been affected in the past by sudden violent events

Catastrophism is the theory that the Earth's geomorphological features originated with a series of great catastrophes that have occurred throughout history. These catastrophes were originally held to be so great in scale that ordinary processes on Earth could not be responsible, and supernatural forces had to be the cause. Such a theory was prevalent in many early mythologies in their accounts of astounding floods, such as those found in the *Epic of Gilgamesh* (*c.* 2150 BCE), the Book of Genesis, and in Plato's (*c.* 424—*c.* 348 BCE) accounts of the Ogygian flood in his dialogues *Timaeus, Critias,* and *Laws* (all written *c.* 360 BCE).

By the beginning of the nineteenth century, the leading scientific proponent of catastrophism was the French anatomist and paleontologist Georges

"The hearts of the Great Gods moved them to inflict the Flood . . ."
Epic of Gilgamesh (*c.* 2150 BCE)

Cuvier (1769–1832). The kind of catastrophism that he posited was later combined with uniformitarianism (the belief that the Earth's changes occurred gradually over a long period of time), initially via the work of Walter Alvarez (*b.* 1940), a dinosaur paleontologist. The modern synthesis of the two schools of thought recognizes both long processes of geologic change and the occurrence in the Earth's history of massive, era-defining changes (notably, meteor strikes), which no longer need to be explained with reference to supernatural intervention. Early adherents of catastrophism naturally turned to God and superstition to explain phenomena about which they had no information, but the idea was an influential element of the modern understanding of geologic change and processes. **JE**

An Ottoman miniature from the thirteenth century, depicting Noah's Ark.

Immortality
Sumeria

The idea that a being can live forever in body or spirit

There are two basic types of immortality: immortality of the spirit and physical immortality. Immortality of the spirit is the idea that a person, or animal, possesses a soul or a supernatural component that, even after the body dies, goes on to live forever. Physical immortality is the idea that the material body itself is immune to death, or is otherwise unable to die.

Throughout the history of humanity, nearly all people have had some experience with death, either of a person or another creature. That all life is mortal is readily apparent to any observer, yet at the same time humanity has developed the idea of immortality, the notion that existence does not end. Anthropologists have identified a belief in some type of immortality

as being present from the earliest known cultures. In the ancient Sumerian *Epic of Gilgamesh* (c. 2150 BCE), widely regarded as one of the first written narrative tales, Gilgamesh, the king of Uruk, embarks on a quest for immortality. Some religious traditions hold that spiritual immortality is closely linked with the actions people take in their lifetimes; in other traditions, there is no direct relationship between a person's ethical and moral activity and whether that person "earns" the continuance of an immortal spirit or eternal life.

Is death the end? Does our consciousness survive our mortality, or will our spirit continue into eternity? The belief in immortality provides answers to these basic human questions, even if the belief is inaccurate. For believers, the prospect of eternal life, or eternal damnation, often serves as a motivator, providing a reason for engaging in ethical or moral behavior. However, as modern science advances, this consideration may one day become irrelevant—methods for halting the ageing process are becoming increasingly sophisticated, and some scientists theorize that the power of technology could eventually enable the human body to live forever. **MT**

A Sumerian tablet (c. 2500 BCE) showing the tree of life, the fruit of which was said to endow longevity.

Inheritance
Sumeria

The transference of a deceased person's property to a new owner

In a society in which a person can own property, there is always the inevitable question of what happens to that property after the owner dies. The idea of inheritance answers this question, establishing exactly who becomes the new owner of the property formerly owned by the deceased.

There have been a number of inheritance systems throughout history, such as a parent's property passing entirely to the eldest male child, entirely to the youngest child, equally to all male children, equally to all children, disproportionately split between children of different ages, only from fathers to sons, and only from mothers to daughters, among others. Inheritance can encompass more than just property, and may

also include rights or obligations, such as the right to become king, or the obligation to recompense an unpaid a debt.

Perhaps the oldest known reference to inheritance comes from ancient Sumeria. The Sumerian Code of Ur-Nammu (c. 2100–2050 BCE), the oldest known legal code, contained several individual inheritance laws. The later Babylonian Code of Hammurabi, which appearanced in about 1772 BCE, contained well-established inheritance laws that addressed issues such as how to divide the deceased person's property, the rights a wife had to distribute property that was given to her, and when a son could be disinherited.

In one respect, inheritance systems are very pragmatic, answering the question of ownership when an owner dies. However, they can also have a significant impact on family and social relationships. Through inheritance, children know that they will become the owners of wealth, ascend to the throne, or have to answer for parental mistakes. As one generation inherits biological traits from their parents, so too do they inherit social standing, property, and even stigma. **MT**

⬆ An Assyrian tablet from c. 1300 BCE, engraved with legal text that relates to inheritance.

Oracle
China

The power of divinely inspired prophecy and prediction

Oracles in the ancient world were typically religious figures believed to possess prophetic abilities inspired by the gods. The word "oracle" comes from the Latin verb *ōrāre*, meaning "to speak," and indicates the oracle's role in delivering messages from the divine. Oracles are known to have advised some of the most powerful figures in human history, and as such were themselves both powerful and influential individuals.

Belief in the power of oracular prophecy was a feature of many ancient cultures, including those of China and India where the presence of oracles can be traced back to the second millennium BCE. In European history, some of the earliest and best-documented accounts of oracles derive from Greek antiquity. Perhaps the best-known was the oracle at Delphi, who became

"The ancient oracle said that I was the wisest of all the Greeks."
Socrates, quoted in *The Apology* by Plato (399 BCE)

famous in the seventh and sixth centuries BCE for communicating with the Greek god Apollo. The role was customarily filled by a priestess, who would advise politicians, philosophers, and kings on issues of war, duty, and the law. The fact that men of power in the male-dominated Greek society took advice on these issues from a woman demonstrates the high level of faith that was invested in oracular prophecy at the time.

In the modern world, oracles are no longer a common feature of daily life. However, the idea of prophecy is still drawn on in a variety of contemporary contexts. One of the most enduring examples of oracular prophecy can be found in the continued use of the *I Ching*, an ancient Chinese system of divination that is still in use as a means of predicting future events in both Eastern and Western cultures. **LWa**

Astrology
Mesopotamia/China

Humanity's search for deeper meaning in the skies

Astrology is a system of beliefs that appeals to the motions of the celestial bodies in order to explain features of human life or to predict future events. The ancient origins of astrology can be traced back to the Mesopotamians in the second millennium BCE and at a similar time to the peoples of ancient China. The Chinese astrological system is distinctive for its use of animals to symbolize the twelve years of the zodiac, beginning with the year of the Rat and ending with the year of the Pig. Each animal is associated with a set of personality traits ascribed to those born in a given year.

In contrast to this, the astrological systems that developed in ancient India and South Asia were focused more directly on predicting a person's destiny or fate. This alternative focus also appeared in Western

"We are merely the stars' tennis balls, struck and bandied which way please them."
John Webster, *The Duchess of Malfi* (1613)

astrology and persists in its modern manifestation, in which it is believed that events in a person's life can be predicted and explained by the motions of the stars and planets. This form of astrology uses the signs of the tropical zodiac and is well known in the Western world through the medium of horoscopes.

Although this Western form of astrology has been largely discredited as pseudoscientific in the modern world, its influence as an idea is difficult to overestimate. With a significant number of people still regularly consulting horoscopes, it cannot be denied that astrology plays an active, if perhaps minor, role in the day-to-day lives of many. Likewise, elements of ancient astrology can be identified in contemporary Indian, Japanese, and Chinese cultures, within both personal and political spheres. **LWa**

Chinese pottery figures from *c.* 396, representing the horse and tiger signs of the zodiac. ➡

Colonialism
Ancient Egypt and Phoenicia

The process of taking control of the land, resources, and people of a nation by military force

↑ An illustration of a French colonial expedition in Madagascar, 1895. Madagascar was declared a French colony in 1896, and remained one until 1960.

Colonialism is the idea behind a process of political, economic, and often cultural domination by a more powerful nation over a weaker one, usually obtained through military force. The earliest examples of this process can be found among the ancient African empires of Egypt and Phoenicia in the second millennium BCE, which used colonialism as a means of securing trade routes, and later with the expansion of the Greek and Roman empires in the first to fifth centuries CE. The latter of these encompassed a significant portion of modern Europe at its height in the second century CE, and can be credited with introducing numerous technological innovations, such as central heating and improved sanitation, to colonized areas. As such, Roman colonialism had a lasting impact on the development of Europe.

In more recent history, the European colonial period, beginning in the sixteenth century and lasting for approximately 500 years, gave rise to a number of large-scale empires, including those of Spain, Portugal, Britain, and France. Primarily motivated by the prospects of economic gain in the countries of Asia, Africa, and the Americas, the European colonists took control of indigenous resources and trade routes by means of military force. Practices of brutal domination during this period were often justified in terms of "civilizing" the "uncivilized" native populations.

Colonialism in this period was closely connected to the crusading mission of Christian countries, which sought to supplant indigenous religious practices with Christianity. The impact of this religious colonialism can still be seen in the modern world, with many now-independent nations maintaining Christianity as their state religion. Thus, despite the cessation of widespread colonialism in today's geopolitical landscape, the social and cultural impacts of historical colonization continue to shape the lives of many. **LWa**

"The worst thing that colonialism did was to cloud our view of our past . . ."

Barack Obama, *Dreams from My Father* (1995)

Incarnation
Ancient Egypt

The physical embodiment of the divine in animal or human form

Incarnation describes the birth or manifestation of a divine being in sentient form, either as human or animal. The origins of this idea can be traced as far back as ancient Egypt during the second millennium BCE, when the ruling pharaohs were believed to be incarnations of the Egyptian gods Horus and Ra. However, the idea was adopted by many of the world's major religions, and it is arguably still one of the most contentious aspects of religious belief today.

One of the most widely known and believed incarnations in religious history is that of Jesus Christ, who in the Christian doctrine is said to be the son of God. The unity of man and God in this incarnation is of central importance to Christian believers, as it represents the presence of the divine in an otherwise human world. However, both Islam and Judaism categorically reject the idea of Jesus as the incarnation of any form of the divine. Mainstream Islamic believers instead regard Jesus as a prophet, or messenger of God, alongside figures such as Adam, Noah, Abraham, Moses, and Muhammad. Judaism, on the other hand, denies that Jesus was any form of prophet at all. This belief marked an important difference between Jewish and Christian believers after the death of Christ in the first century CE.

In the modern world, the idea of incarnation is still one of great significance for many religious believers. It plays a central role in Buddhist belief systems, where it is considered a feature of the continued cycle of birth and rebirth, which can only be broken by the attainment of enlightenment. Thus, for Buddhists, incarnation is an indication of failure of enlightenment. Moreover, the idea of incarnation continues to divide the major monotheistic religions, and as such it can be viewed as one of the most fundamentally divisive and profound ideas in human history. **LWa**

⬆ An Egyptian stele dedicated to the bull deity Apis, from *c.* 1000 BCE. Apis, the living bull, was worshipped as the earthly incarnation of the god Ptah.

"And the Word became flesh and dwelt among us, and we have seen his glory, glory as of the only son from the Father."

The Bible, John 1:14

Loan
Babylonia

Providing goods, services, or money to a borrower in exchange for future repayment

It is not clear when the first loan occurred, but there is evidence to show that by 2000 BCE, ancient Babylonians were using a system of lending in which temples loaned farmers seeds at the beginning of the planting season. The farmers would then take the seeds, plant the crops, and repay the loan after selling the harvested product. Ancient Greeks and Romans made wider use of loans from the fourth century BCE, with the use of interest charges becoming commonplace. In modern times, and especially since the twentieth century, loans have permeated world economies.

Traditionally, moneylending has generally been viewed negatively as a practice, and moneylenders often appear as villains in literature—such as Shylock in William Shakespeare's *The Merchant of Venice* (c. 1596).

"Neither a borrower nor a lender be, For loan oft loses both itself and friend . . ."
William Shakespeare, *Hamlet* (1603)

The practice of charging interest on a loan has been condemned at various times throughout history by numerous religious traditions, including Hinduism, Buddhism, Judaism, Christianity, and Islam.

Today, loans are ubiquitous around the world. People borrow from lenders, banks borrow from other banks, and governments even borrow from themselves. Loans offer the ability to buy something over time, something that would otherwise be out of the buyer's reach. Without loans, people can purchase only what they can afford with the money they currently possess. The promise of later repayment has built wealth, has allowed consumers to purchase homes and create businesses, has given nations the ability to pay for wars, and has led to countless instances of financial ruin. **MT**

Polygamy
Babylonia

The practice or custom of having more than one wife or husband at the same time

The term "polygamy" includes marriages between a single male and multiple females (polygyny); marriages between a single woman and multiple men (polyandry); and marriages between multiple members of both sexes (polyamory). In biological terms, the propensity for male mammals to have more than one mate at the same time is correlated to the relative size of males and females; as a result, prehistoric humans are generally thought to have been polygamous. The first evidence of polygamy as a social practice, however, perhaps occurs in the Code of Hammurabi, a Babylonian legal text dating to about 1772 BCE. The code stated that unless a man's first wife was infertile or ill, or had engaged in marital misconduct, it remained up to her to allow her husband to marry a second woman.

"A thought is come into my head . . . to marry another wife . . ."
Bernardino Ochino, *A Dialog on Polygamy* (1563)

According to at least one study, more than 90 percent of identified cultures—including both contemporary and historical societies—have recognized at least one form of socially accepted polygamy. Polygyny has tended to be the most prevalent. There are several advantages to polygamy as a form of matrimony: socially, it can be seen as a mark of status, especially when wealthy or powerful males have multiple spouses; economically, it can function as a means of producing readily available family labor and, as a result, more wealth. For those in a polygynous marriage, it can also have a positive effect on maternal and child health. However, while marriage is common throughout the modern world, polygamy is not—even in countries where it is accepted socially or legally. **MT**

An eighteenth-century miniature painting depicting the Mughal emperor Jahangir with his harem. →

Code of Hammurabi
Hammurabi

The idea that subject peoples of many creeds may be united by common laws

Although the Code of Ur-Nammu (2100–2050 BCE) is the oldest surviving written law code, the Code of Hammurabi, drawn up in c. 1772 BCE, is arguably the most complete and best known. Hammurabi (r. 1792–1750 BCE) was the sixth king of Babylon, ruling over a vast territory inhabited by many different peoples. The Code of Hammurabi was a set of transcultural laws designed to establish his authority throughout his kingdom. It comprised 282 individual laws addressing matters of justice in respect to religion, trade, slavery, marriage, and so on.

In the preface to the Code, Hammurabi cites many Mesopotamian gods, most importantly Shamash, the sun god, evoking the ancient idea that justice is connected with divine illumination. Indeed, there

"If a citizen has destroyed the eye of one citizen, they shall destroy his eye."

The Code of Hammurabi 196

are parallels between the Code of Hammurabi's law, which states: "If a citizen has destroyed the eye of one citizen, they shall destroy his eye," and, for example, the Hebrew Bible's Mosaic Law of "an eye for an eye."

The importance of the Code of Hammurabi lies, first, in its mere existence: before Hammurabi, no one had tried to use written laws to unify so many different peoples; second, its impact lies in some of the laws it forwarded. For example, accused persons—usually women—could expect to be cast into a river, either as a trial of their innocence or as a test of their accuser's forgiveness. It seems that procedures like these found their way into the barbaric "trials by water" of women accused of witchcraft in sixteenth and seventeenth-century Europe, which saw "innocent" women swim and "guilty" women sink. **AB**

Human Adoption
Hammurabi

The assumption of responsibility for another person, usually a child

The practice of adoption (taking on the role of parent to anyone who is not one's own offspring) dates from antiquity, but the Code of Hammurabi (c. 1772 BCE), created by Hammurabi (r. 1792–1750 BCE), sixth king of Babylon, was probably the first body of laws to spell out in detail the responsibilities of adopters and the rights of those adopted. It is most usual that an adult adopts a child, but this is not invariably the case. In the course of history, men of almost any age have been adopted in order to preserve a male line of inheritance for political, religious, and economic reasons.

Adoption as it is now widely understood—the commitment of an adult to rear and nurture another person's child—was first enshrined in law in 1851 by the U.S. state of Massachusetts. In Britain, legislation

"Adoption is a redemptive response to tragedy . . . in this broken world."

Katie J. Davis, Christian and author

to permit the practice was passed in 1926, largely to ensure care for children who had been orphaned in World War I, but partly also to cope with an increase in the number of illegitimate births.

In the aftermath of World War II, international adoptions became more common as children of one country were brought up by adults of other, usually more prosperous, nations. Slower to gain acceptance was interracial adoption, which was highly opposed in the United States and elsewhere.

After 1970, the stigma of giving birth out of wedlock was greatly reduced, with the result that fewer children in the adopting countries became available for adoption. The rules governing eligibility to adopt have also changed and now include single parents and, in some countries, same-sex couples. **GL**

◀ A Babylonian stele (c. 1750 BCE) inscribed with the Code of Hammurabi.

Toothbrush

Africa

The use of a specially designed implement to keep the teeth disease free

⬆ A Masai woman in Kenya uses a stick as a toothbrush. Chewing sticks have been used by humans to keep teeth clean for thousands of years.

The idea that the good health of the mouth, and especially that of the teeth, might be maintained by a scrupulous hygienic routine is not nearly as new as many people would imagine. The task of removing food particles from the teeth has long been familiar to humanity; even the Neanderthals picked their teeth, as evidenced by distinctive markings on the teeth of some Neanderthal skulls. Evidence from prehistoric sites also suggests that early man used tools such as wooden chewing sticks, twigs from specific tree species, and even feathers and splinters of bone to remove food from their teeth, although it is unknown whether they suspected that doing so would prevent decay. Today, certain types of chewing sticks, such as *mefaka* in Ethiopia, continue to be recommended, especially for children, as being just as good as the toothbrush for maintaining good dental hygiene.

The earliest known toothbrush has been dated to a site in Africa from around 1600 BCE. By the end of the second millennium BCE, Mesopotamian cultures had a wide range of dental hygiene practices. A number of prescriptions for mouthwashes have been discovered by archaeologists, in addition to directions for using an index finger wrapped in cloths to brush and clean the teeth. A modern variant of this idea is the finger toothbrush, fitted over a forefinger and most often used by parents to clean the teeth of young children.

Many people today have integrated modern dental hygiene techniques into their daily routine, and this, when combined with regular professional care, has greatly reduced the incidence of severe oral diseases in society. Regular dental hygiene is often a problem in developing nations and in poor populations, but improvements in hygienic practices immediately lead to significant improvements in dental health. Regular use of a toothbrush serves as a daily reminder that good hygiene helps maintain optimal health. **MT**

"Every tooth in a man's head is more valuable than a diamond."

Miguel de Cervantes, *Don Quixote* (1605)

Mystical Experience
Ancient Greece

Personal experience of a transcendent reality or state of consciousness

A mystical experience is one in which an individual is aware of transcendent truth at a depth, or in a dimension, that is not experienced in typical consciousness. (The experience is sometimes referred to as a state of altered consciousness.) Such experiences have their origin in mystery religion; the Eleusinian Mysteries, annual initiation ceremonies in the cults of the goddesses Demeter and Persephone, were held out of sight of the authorities from about 1600 BCE at Eleusis, near Athens in ancient Greece. Far from dying out, the mystical ceremonies persisted for 2,000 years, through the era of Hellenic Greece and to the end of the Roman Empire in 476.

In the nineteenth century, U.S. psychologist and philosopher William James (1842–1910) defined a mystical experience as always having four key features: transience, indescribability, instructiveness, and passivity. The mystical experience is unusual in that it takes the subject away from normal perceptions for a limited period of time. When that person returns from the event, he or she has difficulty explaining what has happened, since transcendent reality does not lend itself to language. Despite this difficulty, the experience educates or fundamentally changes the experiencer in some way. A mystical experience cannot be controlled by the subject, and operates in a way that is at least partially separate from the individual's will.

All personal religious experiences are linked to mystical experiences. The implication of the fact that they occur is that there is an unsuspected, different reality lying beyond normal human experience and understanding. Mystical experiences indicate that human reality is not the only reality, and so they confront those who experience them or believe in them with the fundamental limits of human knowledge. Mystical experiences offer proof and first-hand knowledge of human transcendence. **TD**

⬆ A *sadhu* (Hindu holy man) in northern India. *Sadhus* are solely dedicated to achieving the transcendant state of *moksha* (liberation) through meditation and contemplation.

"I could not any more have doubted that HE was there than that I was."

William James, *The Varieties of Religious Experience* (1902)

Abortion
Ancient Egypt

The purposeful termination of a human pregnancy

An abortion results in the termination of a pregnancy by causing the death of a fetus or embryo and/or its removal from a womb. Whereas a miscarriage results in the end of a pregnancy because of naturally occurring factors or from the unintended consequences of intentional actions, an abortion is an act performed specifically to terminate pregnancy.

It is not clear when the first abortion took place. Chinese lore holds that Emperor Shennong gave his concubines mercury to cause them to have abortions as early as about 3000 BCE. The ancient Babylonian Code of Hammurabi (*c.* 1792 BCE) contained prohibitions against causing a woman to miscarry by assaulting her. However, the first concrete evidence of purposeful abortions appears in about 1550 BCE with the Ebers

"I will not give to a woman a pessary to produce abortion."

Hippocratic Oath

Papyrus, an ancient Egyptian medical text that, among descriptions of other medical practices, includes a recipe for a potion that could stop a pregnancy at any stage. By ancient Greek and Roman times (*c.* 500 BCE), abortion had become fairly common, so much so that the plant most often used to induce abortions, silphium, is now believed to be extinct.

Modern medicine has enabled abortions to become more easily available, and also made them considerably safer, yet the moral and ethical implications of the procedure have, ever since its invention, spurred rigorous and widespread debate. Is it morally or ethically permissible to perform abortions? If so, when? And who decides? Such questions, and their answers, continue to vex individuals and societies across the globe. **MT**

Birth Control
Ancient Egypt

Controlling human fertility in order to prevent pregnancy

Birth control is the limiting of human reproduction by any method: total or periodic sexual abstinence, coitus interruptus, contraception, abortion, or sterilization. The practice is ancient, but the term was coined in 1914 by Margaret Sanger (1879–1966), a U.S. nurse, who founded the first U.S. clinic for this purpose and helped to establish the notion of planned parenthood.

The earliest description of birth control can be traced back to about 1550 BCE and the ancient Egyptian Ebers Papyrus, which explains how to mix dates, acacia, and honey into a paste, and smear it over wool for use as a pessary. Another birth control method, the condom, also dates from this period. Condoms were made from animal intestines until 1839, after which vulcanized rubber became their universal material.

"Birth control is the first … step a woman must take toward the goal of her freedom."

Margaret Sanger, U.S. social reformer

Other contraceptive methods that emerged in the nineteenth century include vaginal barriers, such as caps and diaphragms, and stem pessaries. Also introduced was sterilization: vasectomy for men and surgical occlusion of the fallopian tubes for women. From the 1960s, the oral contraceptive pill had a liberating effect on attitudes to sex, which became more detached than ever from concerns about pregnancy.

The reasons for birth control are primarily personal: the mother's health; a combination of sexual desire and reluctance to make a commitment to either a partner or a potential child; concern about the economic consequences of a dependent. There are wider social issues, too: some predict that by 2100 the population of the world could reach 16 billion, a total likely to place a severe strain on resources. **GL**

Anesthesia
Middle East

A method of effectively reducing pain during surgery

The use of anesthetics dates back to around 1500 BCE, when opium poppies were harvested in the Middle East and eastern Mediterranean. The Islamic Empire has many accounts of both oral and inhalant anesthetics being used during surgical operations—mostly sponges soaked in various narcotic preparations and placed over the patient's nose and mouth.

In 1800 the use of nitrous oxide was first recorded by the British chemist Humphry Davy (1778–1829), who observed that he had felt dizzy and even euphoric after inhaling it. It would be another forty years before it found broad clinical acceptance as an anesthetic, but the days when pain was considered an unavoidable ingredient to life, or God's punishment to women in labor, or a way of purifying a wicked heart, were numbered.

"The state should, I think, be called 'anesthesia.' This signifies insensibility."

William T. G. Morton, pioneer of the use of ether

Nitrous oxide may have been discovered by the British scientist Joseph Priestly in 1772, but it was Davy who first suggested it might be used to relieve the pain and shock of surgery if inhaled. In his now-famous paper, "Researches, Chemical and Philosophical, Chiefly Concerning Nitrous Oxide, or Dephlogisticated Nitrous Air and its Respiration" (1800), Davy wrote: "As nitrous oxide in its extensive operation appears capable of destroying physical pain, it may probably be used with advantage during surgical operations . . . " Davy may have become distracted in the years that followed byother work, including the development of the voltaic battery and the invention of a safety lamp for miners (the Davy lamp), but his search for an anesthetic for everyday surgical use was a watershed in the development of modern medicine. **BS**

Regicide
Babylonia

The killing of a monarch in order to transfer power to an alternative authority

The idea of regicide—the deliberate killing of a monarch—is revealed in a long series of unfortunate monarchs, pharaohs, and emperors killed at the hands of their people. From around 1500 BCE, in the annual festival of Sacaea in Babylon, a mock king—a convicted criminal who was allowed to reign for five days, and to enjoy the king's harem—was installed, then tortured and killed. His death, symbolic of that of the king, was offered in sacrifice to the Sumerian god Tammuz.

Regicide has frequently been used as a means of transferring power to another authority. The history of the Roman Empire (27 BCE–476) features a number of cases, such as the murder of the Emperor Caligula in 41 CE by his personal bodyguards, the Praetorian Guard. At least fifty Roman emperors are known to

"I am afraid to think what I have done, Look on't again I dare not."

William Shakespeare, *Macbeth* (1606)

have suffered a similar fate. Common use of the term "regicide" in the sense of "monarch-killer" began in the sixteenth century, when Pope Sixtus V described Queen Elizabeth I as such after the execution of Mary, Queen of Scots in 1587. Less than a century later, after the first English Civil War (1642–46), King Charles I became the subject of the best-known regicide in British history.

The idea of regicide is by no means confined to the annals of the past. Regicides of the twentieth century include the killing in 1934 of Alexander I of Yugoslavia by a member of a revolutionary organization, and the execution in 1958 of Faisal II of Iraq, ordered by Colonel Abdul Karim Qassim. The ideological conflicts represented by regicides such as these, and the plays for power that motivates them, are as significant in the modern world as they were in the past. **LWa**

An illuminated manuscript from the twelfth century, showing the massacre of a king and his servants. ➜

Ne chofe ne
weul ie une
laiffier adur

Exorcism
Babylonia

A ritual to expel the forces of evil from the innocent and possessed

Exorcism is a religious practice that is believed to expel evil spirits, demons, or the devil from a possessed person, object, or place. Demonic possession is an ancient idea, with evidence of practices resembling exorcism occurring as early as the second millennium BCE among the Babylonian people of Mesopotamia. Since then, most of the world's religions have developed exorcism rituals. Though these differ with respect to the methods employed, they are all based on the idea of ridding a possessed person or place of a metaphysical evil.

In the West, the idea of exorcism is most strongly associated with the Roman Catholic Church. Instructions for a Catholic exorcism are given in section thirteen of the *Rituale Romanum*, which details all the services that can be performed by a Catholic priest or deacon, and the ritual has been performed by Catholic exorcists around the world. This practice was particularly common during the fifteenth to eighteenth centuries and was often linked to accusations of witchcraft. Today the Catholic Church allows exorcisms to be performed only by an ordained priest with the permission of a local bishop. However, the Church maintains that instances of genuine exorcism are very rare. Those performing an exorcism are instructed to make a prior assessment of the apparently possessed in order to determine whether they in fact exhibit symptoms of mental disorders, such as schizophrenia, psychosis, or dissociative identity disorder.

From a non-religious, scientific perspective, it is generally believed that all cases of demonic possession can be explained in terms of mental disorders such as those listed above. However, a rise of 50 percent in exorcisms performed during the 1960s and 1970s, exacerbated by the Hollywood movie *The Exorcist* (1973), demonstrates that the ancient beliefs behind the practice are still alive in the modern world. **LWa**

A thirteenth-century bas-relief from the font of Modena Cathedral, Italy, depicting an exorcism.

Zero
Babylonia

The symbol that transformed the understanding and practice of mathematics

The symbol "0" is so widely recognized that it is hard to imagine a world in which there was no clear way of indicating "zero." But that was the case until relatively recently in human history.

The use of a symbol to represent "nothingness" is an ancient idea, but the method of notation for it was not always satisfactory. In the second millennium BCE the Babylonians represented nothing with nothing: they merely left a space. This was open to misinterpretation, so they later took to using two slanted wedges to represent nought and also to sometimes denote placeholders. (A placeholder is a symbol used to indicate that there is nothing in a certain column, as today we write "one hundred" as "100" in numerical form to indicate that there are no tens and no units in the quantity represented.)

In the seventh century CE, the Indian mathematician Brahmagupta (c. 598–665) drew up rules for dealing with zero as a number, not just a placeholder. Hindus adopted this idea in their original binary numbering system, and retained it when they later converted to the decimal system that is now used universally.

The latter notation—including the placeholder—was then taken up by the Arabs, and reached the West in the twelfth century through translations of a treatise on arithmetic by Persian mathematician al-Khwarizmi. The use of zero aroused controversy in the early Christian church, which questioned whether it was right to attribute a value to something that does not exist, and preferred to retain the Roman system (I, V, X, D, C, etc.), in which zero did not feature.

In the modern world, the value of zero remains literally nothing, but its figurative applications are both numerous and useful, particularly in science and mathematics. It is almost ubiquitous, its only notable absence being from the Western calendar, which goes from 1 BCE to 1 CE, with no year zero in between. **GL**

The End of the World
Zoroastrian religion

The belief in an inevitable end to the current world order

The idea of the end of the world is usually not about the end of all that there is, but instead about the end of the present order of the world. The concept originated with the Zoroastrian religion, established in c. 1500 BCE, but the most influential exposition of it in the West is the Book of Revelation, written by John of Patmos (fl. first century CE).

The idea is primarily religious in nature, and the branch of theology concerned with the end of the world is called eschatology. The concept is found in a number of religious traditions, including Hinduism, Norse mythology, Judaism, Islam, and Christianity. These traditions differ in what is supposed to follow the end of the world: either a new beginning inaugurating a new cycle of history (as in Norse mythology) or a

"God will invade . . . when that happens, it is the end of the world."

C. S. Lewis, *The Case for Christianity* (1942)

perfect and unchanging state of affairs on Earth or in Heaven (as in Revelation). They generally associate the end of the world with judgment and redemption, and suppose knowledge of it to be conferred in advance, by prophecy or revelation. That knowledge is then useful in urging people to conduct their behavior with an eye toward their fate when the world actually ends.

Religious forms of eschatology remain common, and tend to receive extensive news coverage when believers claim the end to be near. In modern times, eschatology sometimes appears in secularized forms, as when a particular socioeconomic system—such as full communism for Karl Marx or liberal democracy for Francis Fukuyama—is regarded as the final stage of human history. The end of the world remains a potent idea in literature and the arts. **GB**

Atonement
Ancient Israel

Offering a sacrifice in order to express repentance for wrongdoing

The idea of making amends for a wrongdoing (legal or moral) has been present in every society. The notion has had significant impact through the Hebrew concept of atonement, a feature of the oral origins of the Torah (c. 1500 BCE). Atonement refers to a sacrifice made in repentance to gain forgiveness of sin.

The practice was institutionalized in Hebrew Levitical worship sacrifices, most notably in Yom Kippur, or the Day of Atonement, the holiest day in the Jewish religious year, instituted by Yahweh through Moses. Some commentators say Yom Kippur commemorates Moses's return from Mount Sinai with the second set of stone tablets as an expression of God's forgiveness for the exiles' worshipping the golden calf. In the Hebrew and later Jewish tradition, atonement is associated

"If there be laid on him a kofer [atonement payment, ransom], then he shall give . . ."

Orthodox Jewish Bible, Shemot [Exodus] 21:30

with any sacrifice for the forgiveness of transgressions against God, but not against others. Jesus Christ's crucifixion extended this aspect of atonement into the Christian tradition. Christian theologians associate Christ's death with Levitical sacrifices for sin against God, in particular, the Passover sacrifice.

As the Christian tradition took hold in the West, the concept and language of atonement followed, shaping both theological and philosophical perceptions of moral and religious wrongdoing. Subsequently, the meaning of the word "atonement" was broadened to include any amends offered by one disputant to another. However, the word in English has its root in the older English concept of onement, meaning "reconciled." Thus, to be "at onement" is to have set aside differences or made appeasement. **JW**

Atheism
India

Belief that no God, gods, divine beings, or supernatural phenomena exist

Atheism can be described as a range of ideas about the non-existence of the divine, deities, or gods. In one sense, atheists are those who do not believe that any gods or divine beings exist, or are those who hold no belief in the supernatural. Atheists may also believe that there are no gods, as opposed to holding no beliefs about such existence.

No single originator is credited with having first identified the notion of atheism. However, the Vedas, the oldest scriptures of Hinduism, produced in India between c. 1500 and c. 500 BCE, make the first known references to the rejection of an idea of gods. In the Western world, the ancient Greek poet and philosopher Diagoras of Melos (fl. fifth century BCE) was widely recognized as being the first outspoken atheist, a belief

"Is a man merely a mistake of God's? Or is God merely a mistake of man?"

Friedrich Nietzsche, philosopher

that resulted in him having to flee Athens. The term "atheist" was also broadly applied to early Christians who did not believe in the pagan pantheon of the Roman Empire. However, widespread and public assertions that there were no gods did not become commonplace until after the French Revolution (1787–99). Today, atheism is common in many nations, though rates of non-belief are often difficult to determine precisely.

The idea of gods, the divine, or supernatural agents is often closely related to very basic, driving questions. Who created the universe? How did we come to be here? For the atheist, the answer does not rely upon a supernatural or divine basis. Atheism, though not a uniform set of beliefs or body of doctrine, allows for the possibility that there is no divine, godly answer to our questions. **MT**

Agnosticism
India

Belief that it is impossible to know if the supernatural, including God, exists

Agnosticism holds that the nature of God, gods, or supernatural phenomena is such that humanity can never know if they exist or not. It is a statement about what kind of knowledge a person can possess and about what kind of belief is proper or moral to hold. According to the term's originator, British biologist Thomas Huxley (1825–95), the term describes a method of how people can use their intellect to come to hold, or refuse to hold, any particular belief.

Even though the term "agnosticism" did not come into popular use until Huxley coined it in 1869, the idea has existed for approaching 3,000 years. The earliest known expression of the idea comes from the Hindu Vedas, produced between c. 1500 and 500 BCE, which expressed skepticism at the ability to answer

"Who knows for certain? … None knoweth whence creation has arisen …"

The Rigveda, Hindu scripture

fundamental questions about existence. Ancient Greek philosophers voiced similar opinions about the nature of certainty and knowledge. When Huxley introduced the term, he created it from the Greek roots *a*, for "without," and *gnosis*, for "knowledge." His belief was that the knowledge of God is unattainable, and a rational person can hold no belief about it.

In modern times, people often use "agnostic" to denote those who describe themselves as being unsure about whether a God exists. Yet the existence of the divine is not something agnosticism purports to answer. It expresses skepticism, especially regarding the extent of human comprehension. It is also a statement about the morality of hubris, holding that it is immoral to believe in something that has no basis, or to assert an answer to an unanswerable question. **MT**

The agnostic biologist Thomas Huxley (pictured here in c. 1895) was a champion of Charles Darwin. ➡

Samsara
India

The continuous cycle of reincarnation to which all human beings belong

The concept of *samsara* was first developed in the Vedas, the oldest scriptures of Hinduism, produced in India between *c.* 1500 and *c.* 500 BCE. Though *samsara* is principally associated with Hinduism and Buddhism, the concept features in other religions such as Jainism and Sikhism, and is often referred to in popular culture.

Samsara means "to flow together" and refers to the cycle of rebirth in which an individual is reincarnated in a succession of lives based upon the *karma* (a sort of metaphysical record of a person's moral worth) received for deeds committed during each life. This rebirth is more of a curse than a blessing, though it does offer the opportunity for spiritual cultivation that can bring about release. In Hinduism, this is closely tied to the *varna* (caste) system: living according to your

> "Samsaric pleasures are like salt water, the more we indulge, the more we crave."
>
> Geshe Sonam Rinchen, *Thirty-Seven Practices of Bodhisattvas* (1997)

dharma (duty) can eradicate *karma* and earn rebirth in a higher caste that is more capable of attaining *moksha*, the state in which you realize union with Brahman (ultimate reality) and exit the cycle of rebirth. In Buddhism, *karma* causes a person to be reincarnated as one of six types of beings: humans, gods, demigods, animals, hungry ghosts, and hell-bound beings. Only humans can realize *nirvana*, the state in which ignorance is vanquished and *karma* is eliminated so that you may exit the cycle of rebirth upon death.

The desire to exit *samsara* is the driving force in many Eastern religions. Reincarnation is taken as a base metaphysical assumption throughout Indian religion and it is the primary justification for the *varna* system that has structured Indian society for millennia. **JM**

Caste System
India

The division of society into four hereditary social classes

The caste system, also known as the *varna* system, is a hierarchical social structure prevalent in the Hindu nations of India and Nepal. Its origins trace back to the Vedas, the oldest scriptures of Hinduism, produced in India between *c.* 1500 and *c.* 500 BCE, and it is a central theme in the 700-verse *Bhagavad Gita* (*c.* 100 CE).

The caste system divides Hindu society into four hereditary social classes. Highest are the *Brahmins*, who are priests and teachers. Next come the *Kshatriyas*, who are political leaders and warriors. Third are the *Vaishyas*, who manage agriculture and commerce. The lowest are the *Shudras*, who work as servants for the other three castes. Those who are cast out of the *varna* system are known as "Untouchables" because contact with them was thought to defile the other castes.

> "Now I have no caste, no creed, I am no more what I am!"
>
> Kabir, Indian mystic poet

Hindu texts justify this system based on *karma* and rebirth. A person's actions in this life determine their *gunas* (qualities) in the next: *Brahmins* are characterized by *sattva* (intellect), *Kshatriyas* by *rajas* (action), *Vaishyas* by both *rajas* and *tamas* (devotion), and *Shudras* by *tamas* alone. These *gunas* predispose a person toward certain types of work, and society functions best when people do the jobs to which they are suited. Each *varna* has its own spiritual discipline: *Brahmins* follow *jñana* (knowledge), *Kshatriyas* pursue *karma* (action), *Vaishyas* practice both *karma* and *bhakti* (devotion), while *Shudras* undertake *bhakti*. In the twentieth century, Mahatma Gandhi criticized the social injustice of the caste system, and it was reformed as a result of his protests. **JM**

A *Dharmachakra* (wheel of law) from *c.* 900, which symbolizes the six realms of existence in *samsara*.

Dharma
India

The belief that the universe has an inherent order

⬆ A first-century BCE Indian sculpture of the footprints of Buddha. On the soles of the feet are two *Dharmachakras* (wheels of learning).

"Dharma leads to happiness, but happiness cannot lead to dharma."

Ramayana (500–100 BCE)

The concept of *dharma* dates back to the Vedas, the oldest scriptures of Hinduism, produced in India between *c.* 1500 and *c.* 500 BCE. It is expounded later Hindu texts, such as the epic work *Ramayana* (500–100 BCE) and the 700-verse *Bhagavad Gita* (*c.* 100 CE), and is present in other Asian traditions such as Buddhism, Jainism, and Sikhism.

Dharma comes from the Sanskrit word for "uphold" or "support." In Hinduism, *dharma* refers to the inherent order of things, both in terms of natural laws and social/ethical norms. *Karma* is a causal force that connects all things in the universe. As a result of this force, everything that a person does affects not only his own future, but also the futures of others. All human beings have a responsibility to maintain the natural order, which is manifested in the caste system of Hindu society. A person's actions lead to *karma*, which determines their *gunas* (traits) and *varna* (caste), which in turn dictate the moral obligations that individual has to other people (*dharma*). For example, in the *Bhagavad Gita*, Arjuna's *dharma* as a *kshatriya* (warrior) obligates him to fight in a war even though he does not want to.

In Buddhism, *dharma* refers to not only the natural/moral order, but also to the teachings of the Buddha. *Dharma* determines a person's duties at various stages of life (*ashrama*): in youth, a student's obligation is to learn; in middle age, a householder is expected to promote the good of society; in advanced age, the forest dweller and renunciant are expected to focus on spiritual cultivation.

Dharma is one of the central metaphysical justifications for the caste system in India. The symbolic representation of *dharma*, the *Dharmachakra* or *"dharma* wheel," appears in the center of the flag of India, representing the idea that truth and virtue should be the guiding principles of the nation. **JM**

Meditation
India

Controlling one's own mind to realize a new mode of consciousness

The practice of meditation encompasses a range of techniques that can be used by individuals to cause their mind to experience a different level of consciousness. Meditation can be focused on many different goals, including self-regulation, religious experience, building internal energy sources, and relaxation. Typically, meditation is a practice that involves training the mind to engage in a particular habit of reflections. In some traditions, meditation involves attempting to separate the mind from the other experiences of the body, whereas others emphasize a physical element of meditation by encouraging repetitive action or vocalizations.

Many religious traditions developed practices that were intended to move the individual beyond the experience of the immediate self, and all of these can be considered forms of meditation. The earliest recommendations for the use of meditation can be found in the Vedas, the oldest scriptures of Hinduism, produced in India between c. 1500 and c. 500 BCE, and in ancient Buddhist texts, which promote meditation as essential for a path to enlightenment. In Tibetan Buddhism, meditation is both a path toward inner reflection to know oneself better and a path ultimately to move beyond the limits of the self.

In several traditions, meditation is intended to have a calming effect on the mind, which is why the term is often used nowadays to refer to a range of quiet relaxation techniques that do not necessarily have religious meaning. Even in the modern world, the idea of meditation usually means more than just relaxation, however. Communication with a reality that goes beyond the typically limited experience of consciousness requires that consciousness be transformed in some way. Thus, most religions include a form of prayer that can be considered a kind of meditation. **TD**

⬆ A carving of the Buddha sitting in *dhyani mudra* (meditation pose), at the Gal Vihara temple in Polonnaruwa, Sri Lanka, built during the reign of King Parakramabahu the Great (1153–86).

"Meditation is the dissolution of thoughts in Eternal awareness."

Swami Sivananda, Hindu spiritual teacher

Chakras
India

Energy-collection centers of the body that are essential for physical and mental health

In the traditions of Buddhism and Hinduism, *chakras* are centers of energy that correspond to parts of the body. A non-physical life force is said to travel through the body, and each *chakra* is linked to a part of this force. *Chakras* exist in the body along a central channel and are connected to vital bodily functions, including consciousness, vision, communication, health, digestion, reproduction, and survival. In the most common understanding of the system, each *chakra* is associated with a deity, color, bodily organ or set of organs, and a mantra (a transformative sound or syllable). Bringing the energy of the body in line with the central channel and the *chakras* is possible through meditation, and this process of alignment plays an important role in achieving fulfillment and enlightenment.

"Kundalini [a corporeal energy] will rise and always cleanse the chakras."
Shri Mataji Nirmala Devi, founder of Sahaja Yoga

The idea of *chakras* is an ancient one and it is found in Sanskrit documents and in oral traditions of both Buddhism and Hinduism. "Breath channels," for example, appear in the Hindu Vedas, produced in India between *c.* 1500 and *c.* 500 BCE. The idea of a hierarchy of the *chakras* was introduced later, in eighth-century Buddhist teachings. There is no standard interpretation of *chakras* in either religious tradition, with *chakra* systems varying from teacher to teacher within the same religious tradition.

Chakras are essential if we are to understand the body as a system of energy. Two of the five major world religions are built on the idea that human beings are capable of making peace within themselves as a result of energy systems within the body. The *chakras* are key to unlocking this inner power. **TD**

Karma
India

Every action has consequences that go beyond a mere human lifetime

Karma is a law of causality that first appeared in the Upanishads, the sacred texts that expound the Vedas, the oldest scriptures of Hinduism, produced in India between *c.* 1500 and *c.* 500 BCE. *Karma* is also a key concept in Buddhism and Jainism.

The term *karma* means "action" in Sanskrit, and refers to the idea that every action has a specific set of causes and effects. Ethically, *karma* is a metaphysical record of a person's moral worth. When someone commits an evil act, they acquire *karma*; when someone does good, they acquire merit, which cancels out *karma*. *Karma* is linked to *samsara* (the cycle of reincarnation) because when people die, their *karma* determines the type of rebirth they will have in the next life. In Hinduism, this is closely tied to the *varna* (caste) system: a virtuous life eradicates *karma*

"It is God's inviolable law that karma never fails to produce its effect."
Mahatma Gandhi, Indian nationalist leader

and guarantees rebirth in a higher caste that is more capable of attaining *moksha*, a state of unity between a person's *atman* (true self) and Brahman (ultimate reality). In Buddhism, life is characterized by suffering; the goal of spiritual cultivation is to eradicate *karma* and attain *nirvana*, a state in which all *karma* is nullified and a person can exit the cycle of rebirth. In Jainism, expunging all *karma* leads to *moksha*, a blissful state of liberation from *samsara*. In Hinduism and Buddhism, people receive *karma* only for intentional acts, whereas in Jainism, even unintentional acts can generate *karma*.

Due to the prevalence of Hinduism and Buddhism throughout Asia, *karma* has become a central moral paradigm. The doctrine of *karma* has influenced the spiritual beliefs of numerous traditions, including Sikhism, Falun Gong, and Theosophy. **JM**

A Buddhist *Thangka* painting from Nepal, showing the seven main *chakras* of the body.

Mantra
India

Sounds, syllables, and words as the source of spiritual transformation

One of the primary goals for those who practice Hinduism and Buddhism is to experience a transformation of consciousness through particular acts of the mind and body. A mantra is a vocalized or written repetition of syllables, words, or phrases that helps to focus the mind and body in order to achieve this transformation. In some mantras, the words themselves become an action that can bring about the transformation. The sound or words of a mantra are representative of an ultimate reality that is meaningful beyond the understanding of the person who is pronouncing them. By performing a mantra, a person is able to place their mind and will in line with the ultimate reality.

The most recognizable mantra is the sound or syllable "Om." According to the the the Upanishads—part of the Hindu Vedas, written between c. 1500 and c. 500 BCE—the syllable "Om" represents all of creation. Meditating while uttering this syllable brings the subject closer to realizing the connectedness of all things in the universe. Mantras are also meaningful in the Buddhist tradition, in which they have been expanded beyond vocalized sounds to include written language and characters. As Buddhism spread to China, the writing of mantras became more important as a form of meditation. In either form, vocalized or written, repetition of mantras is a common form of meditating on their fundamental truth.

The idea of a mantra is important for understanding the way that a person's mind can be intentionally and completely focused on a certain task. Mantras are particularly useful in religious practices that strive to push the self beyond its own consciousness. Outside of religious traditions, the term "mantra" has come to refer to any phrase that is commonly repeated, typically one that contains an essential truth or guiding principle. **TD**

A *Mani* stone enscribed with the six-syllabled Buddhist mantra of Avalokiteshvara. ⬆

Zoroastrianism
Zoroaster (Zarathustra)

An ancient Persian religion teaching cosmic dualism

It is not known precisely when the ancient Persian religion of Zoroastrianism first came into existence, although scholars generally agree that it first appeared in the late Bronze Age (1500–800 BCE) as a development of Persian polytheism. The sacredness of the bull, for example, entered into Zoroastrianism (and Hinduism also), as did the strong insistence on ritual purification and the holiness of fire (for this reason Zoroastrians never burn their dead, but rather dispose of corpses by "exposing" them to the birds).

The ancient Persians and Zoroastrians alike also revered *asha* (in Hinduism *rta*), a term that is best understood as truth or universal law, especially moral law. *Asha* was itself upheld by three *ahuras*, or "good deities": Varuna, Mithra, and, the most supreme of all, Mazda, the lord of wisdom.

Claiming to be a true prophet of Mazda, Zoroaster, also known as Zarathustra, whose time of life is disputed, taught a form of cosmic dualism, namely, that there are two supreme, morally opposed gods—Ahura Mazda (good) and Angra Mainyu (bad). Zoroaster believed that Ahura Mazda and his *ahuras* were waging a great war against Angra Mainyu and his *devas* (evil deities), and that humankind, caught in the middle of this war, should choose to ally himself with Ahura Mazda, not only because Mazda is good but also because Mazda will be ultimately victorious.

Zoroastrianism's influence lies firstly in itself, which is to say that it is one of the oldest living religions. Beyond this, Zoroastrianism gave Islam its format of five prayers a day, Tibetan Buddhism its practice of corpse exposure, Mahayana Buddhism its world savior concept (Saoshyant, or Maitreya), and Gnosticism and Manichaeism their belief that the world was made by an evil spirit. Zoroastrianism's apparent influence on Jewish and Christian eschatology, however, has proved difficult to substantiate. **AB**

⬆ The remains of a Zoroastrian Fire Temple in Yazd, Iran. Fire is held sacred in Zoroastrianism.

Angels
Ancient Israel

Conditionally immortal, supernatural spirits existing partway between God and man

An eternal being is one that has no beginning and no end, and in the history of religion only the monotheistic God and the pantheistic Deity can truly be called eternal. However, many religions talk about "gods" and "goddesses"—immortal beings that have a beginning, but no natural end. These gods can be destroyed but they do not die of diseases or old age as humans do.

According to the oral origins of the Hebrew Torah (*c.* 1500 BCE) and the Bible, angels roughly correspond to these gods: they are probably gendered (most of the angels in the Bible are masculine, but some, such as in Zechariah 5:9, are probably feminine). They can be good or bad ("angel" usually means "good angel" whereas "demon" usually means "bad angel"), and they play an important, but often unseen, part in human

> ### "There stood before me an angel of God ... and he said, 'Do not be afraid ...'"
> The Bible, Acts 27:23–24

history (for example, one fallen angel, Satan, took the form of a serpent and brought ruin to man, but another, Gabriel, was a messenger of good news).

Angels are spirits that do not have physical bodies, but they probably have "spiritual bodies" of some sort. Regarding humans, Jesus said, "We will be like the angels," and St. Paul said that we will be given "spiritual bodies," suggesting that the distinction between angels and humans—at least in the next life—is much closer than some, such as the great Italian angelologist Thomas Aquinas (1225–74), have imagined.

Angels have profoundly shaped world culture. The vast majority of the world's population believes in them, with some taking comfort in the belief that "guardian angels" watch over them; others fear the potential of bad angels as agents of evil. **AB**

Adam and Eve
Ancient Israel

The first two humans believed by Christians to have been created by God

According to the oral origins of the Hebrew Torah (*c.* 1500 BCE) and the Bible, Adam and Eve were the first two humans. Genesis 1 discusses the creation of mankind in general; Genesis 2 discusses the creation of man in particular: Adam first, then Eve. According to Genesis 2, God formed Adam from dust (*adamah* means "red earth" in Hebrew) and then breathed life into him. Subsequently, God made Eve from Adam's rib; both are said to be made in God's image.

Generally the consensus has been that the "breath" or "image" of God is the rational nature, soul, or spirit of the first humans. Like the angels, humans as rational souls have the ultimate capacity for rationality (that is, given the proper conditions, can think rationally), have the ultimate capacity for free will, have the

> ### "In the image of God He created them: male and female He created them."
> The Bible, Genesis 1:27

ultimate capacity for emotions, and so on. Adam and Eve are distinguished from the animals by this image, yet their corporeal bodies are similar to that of the beasts. Moreover, while Adam and Eve are described as equal with regard to being rational souls or persons, they are also described as unequal in respect of their responsibility: Adam shares with God the masculine property of headship (that is, Adam is responsible to lead and protect his wife, the feminine).

Given that most adherents of the Abrahamic religions believe that a historical Adam and Eve existed, their importance is obvious: as the first parents, they are the models for what humans were designed to be, and yet, at least according to Christians, represent what humans unfortunately usually become—sinful, unjust, or "fallen," and in need of redemption. **AB**

⬅ A panel from *St. Matthew and the Angel* (1602) by Michelangelo Merisi da Caravaggio.

The Devil
Ancient Israel

If God is a personification of good, the Devil personifies the absence of good, or evil

From the Greek *diabolos*, the word "Devil" is considered synonymous with the Hebrew *satan*, which itself means "adversary"—in particular, an adversary of God. The Devil is a Hebrew idea that originated in *c.* 1500 BCE and appears in the Hebrew Bible, though scholars disagree about exactly where in the text. Jews see no direct link between the serpent that tempted Adam and Eve in the Garden of Eden and the adversary of Job or the tempter of King David. However, for Christians and Muslims, Revelation 12:9 and 20:2 make it clear that the Devil is that same serpent or "dragon." Allowed by God to go about his evil practices, he is "the prince of this world" (John 12:31) or "the god of this world" (2 Corinthians 4:4).

The Devil's princeship or lordship over this earth probably has to do with his apparent status as an

"The Devil has come to you in great wrath, because he knows that his time is short."
The Bible, Revelation 12:12

extremely powerful but "fallen" angel who took his war against God to earth and now holds dominion over many non-believers. Although direct statements about the Devil having been an angel are few in the Bible ("Lucifer" probably has nothing to do with the Devil), there are some that make this fairly clear. Jude 1:6, for example, talks about "angels who neglected their first estate," and Revelation 12:7-9 talks about "the great dragon and his angels" who were cast out of Heaven.

The Devil is unable to tempt many people at once (people wrongly attribute to him an omnipresence that only God has), but his global influence is undeniable. For billions he is a symbol of pure evil (reflected in phrases such as "That's diabolical"), even though, theologically, pure evil cannot exist—evil being a deprivation of natural goodness. **AB**

Reincarnation
Unknown

Every human has been born, has lived, and has died before, and will do so again

The concept of reincarnation is both ancient and widespread. It refers to the belief that human beings have immortal souls that have been, and will be, joined with other bodies, past and future. Thus each individual human has lived before their current birth and they will survive death by being reborn as another. In some cases, for example in Hinduism and Buddhism, the cycle of reincarnation can be escaped by a process of coming to enlightenment or salvation. It has played a central role in Hinduism for thousands of years. In both Hinduism and its offshoot, Buddhism, reincarnation is part of a continuous cycle of birth, death, and rebirth known as *samsara*. The ultimate goal of those religions is to escape *samsara*, a process called *moksha* (or "letting go"). In ancient Greece, reincarnation appears

"Don't grieve. Anything you lose comes round in another form."
Jalal al-Din Rumi, Persian poet and mystic

in the sixth-century BCE work of Pythagoras and the fourth-century BCE philosophy of Plato. Meanwhile, in the Christian New Testament, Jesus Christ overtly claims that John the Baptist was the reincarnation of the Hebrew Prophet Elijah, and at least some sects of Islam (particularly in South Asia) also believe in reincarnation.

From the late nineteenth century, interest in reincarnation—along with all things Eastern—enjoyed an explosion of popularity in Western culture. The writings of teachers, such as Madame Blavatsky of the Theosophical Society and Edgar Cayce, helped to spread the belief that people have lived many lives. General George S. Patton claimed to have been a soldier in many of the world's great armies. And L. Ron Hubbard, the founder of the controversial Church of Scientology, also espoused a belief in reincarnation. **APT**

The *Kalachakra* (Wheel of Time) symbolizes the six stages in the Buddhist cycle of reincarnation. ➡

Avatar
India

The manifestation or incarnation of a deity in human or animal form

⬆ An Indian miniature from the seventeenth century, showing Vishnu in his first avatar as a fish. The story of the fish avatar describes Vishnu rescuing the first man from a great flood.

References to an entity known as an "avatar" are first found in the Vedas, the oldest scriptures of Hinduism, produced in India between *c.* 1500 and *c.* 500 BCE. The later *Bhagavad Gita* (*c.* 100 CE) refers in detail to the process of *avataravada* (the Hindu theory of incarnation), although the term "avatar" itself does not appear in Hindu scripture until later texts. An avatar is probably best described as the incarnation of a deity, but the term also conveys the wider notion that the gods have the ability to take any form and will descend to Earth to counteract a particular evil in the world (the Sanskrit word *avatāra* translates into English as "descent"). The complex Hindu god Vishnu is particularly closely associated with the notion of the avatar, and he is believed to have a number of incarnations.

There are ten principal avatars of Vishnu accepted across all of Hindu scripture. The avatars are said to take a variety of forms, including a fish, tortoise, dwarf, and boar. Two of the most significant manifestations of Vishnu are the human avatars of Rama and Krishna, whose stories are recounted in the central Hindu texts *Ramayana* (500–100 BCE) and *Bhagavata Purana* (*c.* 950). The ninth avatar of Vishnu is believed to be the Buddha, and the tenth avatar, Kalki, who has never yet manifested himself in the world, is predicted to appear at the end of Kali Yuga, the world's current epoch, to restore balance and righteousness to humanity.

As the anticipated coming of the tenth avatar of Vishnu demonstrates, the notion of avatar is still relevant and significant to Hindus today. This belief in a future manifestation of God in human form can similarly be found across many of the world's major religions and within more minor religions and cults. Thus, the idea of *avataravada* or incarnation serves in the contemporary world as a source of hope for a better, and more virtuous, future humankind. **LWa**

"Whatever form pleases His bhaktas, is a form that He readily assumes."

Vedanta Desika, Sri Vaishnava guru

Sewer System
Minoa

A means of safely transferring human waste away from inhabited areas

In the early days of humanity's existence, when people lived as nomadic hunters and gatherers, the need for control of human waste was limited because people rarely stayed in an area long enough, or in large enough numbers, for long-term waste collection issues to arise. Eventually, however, people made the transition from a nomadic life to a sedentry one, which led to the establishment of villages, towns, and, eventually, cities. Inevitably, the collection of large numbers of people staying in the same place resulted either in significant accumulations of waste or contamination of neighboring waterways.

From about 2500 BCE to 1500 BCE, ancient cities in the Indus Valley developed basic sanitation facilities, including toilets cleaned by flushing water, waste receptacles, and drainage systems. It was not until about 1500 BCE, however, that the Minoan civilization of Crete and the eastern Mediterranean created a complete sewer system featuring toilets, terracotta pipes to carry away waste, and large stone sewers to receive it. However, it was the Romans who developed the most complete sewer system of the ancient world. Their main innovation was the use of aqueducts to bring water to the cities, with clean water separated from the dirty water used to flush the large, stone-covered sewers. After the fall of the Roman Empire in 476, the world would not see such effective, technologically advanced sewer management again until the construction of centralized sewage treatment plants in the nineteenth century.

Sewer systems have been key to the development and expansion of large, permanent human settlements. Cities lacking a comprehensive sewer system are prone to outbreaks of diseases and epidemics. With the construction of sewers, however, humans can congregate into huge, relatively clean cities without exposing themselves to serious health risks. **MT**

⬆ The remains of a system of stone drains at the ancient Minoan settlement of Ayia Triada on Crete, Greece. The town and royal villa there were built between 1600 and 1100 BCE.

> *"Sanitary services . . . [are] indispensable for the functioning and growth of cities."*
>
> Martin V. Melosi, *The Sanitary City* (2000)

Messiah
Ancient Israel

A divinely appointed king who will act as a savior for humanity

The Hebrew word *mashiach* and the Greek word *christos* are translated in English as "messiah" and "christ," respectively. The two terms refer to the same concept: a heroic leader or savior king who will rescue the people from their hardship. The Persian king Cyrus the Great, for example, is called a messiah in the Hebrew Bible because he helped the Jews to return to their homeland.

While there are many lesser messiahs or christs mentioned in Jewish and Christian texts, Jews and Christians distinguish these from the Messiah or Christ. According to ancient Israeli prophecy, the Messiah will be a king who rules at the end of history and establishes lasting peace for God fearers. Jesus identified himself

as this messiah, which is why Christians speak of him not simply as "Jesus, a christ," but "Jesus, the Christ," or "Jesus Christ." Jesus, Christians argue, fits the bill as the Messiah because not only was he a king in two senses (the earthly, Davidic sense, and the heavenly, son of God sense) but also he was the greatest savior or hero imaginable: he rescued people from death and separation from God.

The idea of a messiah is a profoundly important one for Jews and Christians—for Jews because the Messiah is yet to come, and for Christians because he has come and will return again at the end of earthly history. Without the hero king, Christians believe that they cannot be reconciled with God because only the Messiah can represent all people (as kings do) and take, sacrificially, their transgressions upon himself.

Not surprisingly, the idea of the messiah has inspired a myriad of "Christ types" in popular culture, such as Aragorn in J. R. R. Tolkein's *The Lord of the Rings* (1954) and Superman (the leader of the Justice League). Conversely, it has also inspired many "anti-christ" figures, such as Johnny Rotten of the Sex Pistols and even Satan. **AB**

A second-century painting showing the Jewish prophet Samuel anointing David as the King of Israel. ⬆

Scapegoat
Ancient Israel

An individual selected to bear the blame that properly belongs to a group

Since the beginning of recorded history, man has made sacrifices to God or the gods. Most commonly, these sacrifices were appeasement sacrifices, used to express man's sorrow to God or the gods for some transgression committed and to ask for reconciliation with, and the restored favor of, the divine figure. From about 1500 BCE, the ancient Israelites were one of many groups to carry out this practice, which they developed in the specific form of a scapegoat—literally, a goat who symbolically bore the sins of the people and was cast away from the camp in order to show God how sorry the people were for their acts of injustice.

The word and understanding of the concept of a scapegoat comes from the ancient Israelites, but they were not unique in the practice of using one. The ancient Greeks, for example, spoke of *phramkoi*, or a person who symbolically bore the problems of the people and was consequently exiled or even killed in order to please the gods and reverse the people's collective misfortune.

Besides differing over the use of an animal or a human, the Israelites and Greeks also disagreed about the quality of the scapegoat. The Israelites usually reserved the best kind of animal for such activities, whereas the Greeks intentionally sought out less desirable persons—slaves and cripples—for the task.

The Christian Bible's depiction of Jesus as "the lamb of God," who died for the sins of the many, is another key example of this broad scapegoat-appeasement-atonement tradition. However, unlike the animal, who cannot literally take away the sins committed by man, or the imperfect human, who never volunteered for the role, Jesus has been seen by Christians as the perfect sacrifice and appeasement of God's justice. The idea of a scapegoat was important in many ancient cultures, and is still very important today, largely because of Christianity. **AB**

⬆ *The Scapegoat* (1854), by William Holman Hunt, was inspired by Hunt's study of Jewish scripture.

Millennialism
Zoroastrian religion

The belief that the world will undergo a radical upheaval at the end of the millennium

In its strict sense, "millennialism" is a term used to refer to the expectation among a collective that the end of days will occur at the millennium, to be followed by a specified period of peace, harmony, and abundance for all. However, millennialism can more broadly be taken to refer to the conviction of any collective that takes an "end of days" approach to the unfolding of history. For example, in the Christian theological tradition, millennialism is accompanied by the belief that God will pass judgment on all of humanity for the purpose of meting out punishment and reward.

However, millennialist convictions have been part of human societies across the world for thousands of years. The concept of millennialism first appeared in the teachings of the Zoroastrian religion, founded

"Cast him [Satan] into the bottomless pit … till the thousand years should be fulfilled …"

The Bible, Revelation 20:3

in around 1500 BCE, and it has since featured in belief systems that include the Baha'i Faith and Mormonism. Often a belief in millennialism has been strong at the time that a new religion is founded, before fading as the religion becomes more established in society.

Millennialism seems to satisfy a deep psychological need in the species to exact retributive justice. It also serves to keep groups focused on the things that matter, and perhaps even serves to strike fear into the hearts of those members of communities or societies who might otherwise commit venal or immoral acts. More importantly, however, millennialism can be interpreted as the ultimate form of revolutionary change. Hence the belief in it is, counterintuitively, a kind of progressive impulse that can be lauded against the impulse to conservatism that marks most of human history. **JS**

Monotheism
Ancient Egypt

The belief that there is one supreme, uncreated God who created everything else

Monotheism is the idea that there is a single supreme God, who, themself uncreated, created all else. The idea dates from around 1350 BCE, when the pharaoh Akhenaten (*d.* 1336 BCE) ruled that Egypt should worship only the sun, instead of having an array of gods.

Today, there are two forms of monotheism: theism, which sees the one supreme God as personal and concerned with their own creation; and deism, which sees God as impersonal and unconcerned. Most monotheists are theists, especially those of the Abrahamic beliefs. According to these traditions, the world's first religion was a form of monotheism, but later on was perverted, fragmenting the personality and powers of God into many separate deities, thus giving rise to polytheism (the belief that there are

"In the beginning, God created the heavens and the earth."

The Bible, Genesis 1:1

many gods). Early on, monotheists did not oppose the belief that other gods existed; rather, they insisted that other gods—usually called angels—were created by God and therefore should not be worshipped. Contemporary theistic monotheism divides into either "one personality, one substance" (Judaism and Islam), or "three personalities, one substance" (Christianity).

Monotheism, in any of its forms, is distinct from both pantheism, which states that there is one God who is all that exists (matter and individual personalities being illusionary), and henotheism, which favors the exclusive worship of one god (like monotheism) but does not deny the existence of other potentially uncreated gods. From its earliest days in the ancient Near East and Egypt to the present day, monotheism has been hugely influential in world religions and philosophies. **AB**

◄ A panel from an altarpiece (*c.* 1449), showing the Archangel Michael weighing souls at the Last Judgment.

Hero
Ancient Greece

A courageous warrior who performs great, usually moral, deeds

⬆ A Roman mosaic depicting Theseus, the heroic founder of Athens, overcoming the minotaur—a half-man, half-bull monster that lived in a labyrinth on Crete.

"Hero" comes from the Greek *heros*, meaning "great warrior." The idea of a hero or great warrior is older than ancient Greek culture, but the Greek variation of the concept is arguably the best known. Scholars believe that the heroic actions described by Homer (*fl. c.* 850 BCE) occurred in the years 1300 to 1150 BCE.

The first heroes in Greek culture, like those in most ancient cultures, were usually gods or demigods who strove against some daunting foe or task. For example, Marduk, a lesser Babylonian god, fought the primordial goddess, Tiamat, to become the world's first dragon slayer; and Hercules, a Greek demigod, endured twelve labors—including slaying the nine-headed Lernaean Hydra and obtaining the girdle of Hippolyta, queen of the Amazons—to achieve the title of "hero."

In every culture, a hero is a warrior who has at least one moral virtue: courage. Marduk and Hercules, for example, both have this virtue, yet their motivation for courageous battle is often the pursuit of some non-moral good, such as glory (Hercules) or power (Marduk). Over time it was recognized that a true hero is not only a courageous warrior but also one whose goals are justice and sacrificial love. Indeed, a true warrior does not necessarily have to be a warrior in the physical sense. In the West, for example, Jesus became a hero not simply because he fought (spiritually) against Satan and Death, but because he fought in the name of righteousness and love.

Many of the West's more recent examples of heroes, such as the Knights of the Round Table or Superman and other members of the Justice League, further develop this idea. In the East, the notion of the hero, such as the Chinese Yue Fei—a military commander who fought 12 battles without a single defeat, before later being imprisoned and strangled—is that of a courageous warrior who self-sacrifices for the good of the group or nation. **AB**

"What makes a hero? Courage, strength, morality, withstanding adversity?"

Fyodor Dostoyevsky, *Notes from Underground* (1864)

Passover
Moses

A biblical event rich in symbolism for both Jews and Christians

Sometime during the Late Bronze Age (1500–800 BCE), the Israelites—God's "chosen people" according to the Bible—were enslaved in Egypt. Scholars have calculated the year of their exit from Egypt, termed the "Exodus," to have been c. 1250 BCE, following the remarkable event of the Passover the same year.

The book of Exodus states that God sent ten "plagues" against the Egyptians, trying, with increasing severity, to convince the pharaoh to release the Israelites. The tenth "plague" was the most severe of all, for this saw God "passing through" the Egyptian people, slaughtering every firstborn male, both human and animal, who was not sheltered behind a specially marked door. All those protected by doors that had been faithfully marked with lamb's blood on God's instruction were "passed over" by Him. When the firstborn of pharaoh himself was killed, the Egyptian king released the Israelites.

The Passover is also called the Feast of Unleavened Bread because, on the night before God passed over the faithful (the night of 14/15 Nisan, sometime in spring), the Israelites had been told to prepare certain foods to sustain them as they hastily left Egypt. A lamb was to be roasted, and unleavened bread (bread without yeast) was to be served. In commemoration of that fateful night, the Passover festival, which lasts between seven and eight days, is still the most celebrated of the Jewish festivals. After the Temple's destruction in 70 CE, however, Jews ceased to partake in sacrificial Paschal lamb (from the Hebrew *Pesach*, meaning Passover).

Christians, too, celebrate the Passover, although for them the liberation celebrated is that of the faithful from sin by the sacrifice of Jesus, "the lamb that was slain." Indeed, according to the Synoptic Gospels (Matthew, Mark, and Luke), it was the Passover that Jesus celebrated on his "Last Supper," making all future Eucharistic celebrations even richer in meaning. **AB**

⬆ Ultra-Orthodox Jewish men in Jerusalem select *matzoth* (unleavened bread) to be eaten during Passover. It is traditionally eaten on the first day of the holiday.

"This is the day that I brought your divisions out of Egypt. Celebrate this day as a lasting ordinance for the generations to come."

The Bible, Exodus 12:17

Dietary Laws

Moses

Religious guidelines for the preparation and consumption of foods

Dietary laws restricting the preparation and consumption of certain foods have been an important feature of many religious traditions. In the Jewish tradition, commands given by God through prophets for a proper diet (notably to Moses at Mount Sinai in the thirteenth century BCE) are a key element in the teachings of the Torah. Building on the Jewish tradition of religious texts, the Christian and Muslim traditions also include dietary laws regulating what believers can consume and how it should be prepared.

In the Jewish tradition, dietary laws are called *kashrut*, and any food that is prepared according to them is considered *kosher*. Dietary laws in Jewish, Christian, and Muslim teachings include both matters of hygiene in food preparation and complete

" . . . whatever doesn't have fins and scales you shall not eat; it is unclean to you."

The Bible, Deuteronomy, 14: 9–10

prohibitions of some foods. Prohibited foods typically include "unclean animals," which usually refers to pork, some kinds of seafood, and dead animals (those not specifically killed for consumption). In both the Jewish and Muslim traditions, additional guidelines are added to the laws defined in religious texts.

Dietary laws also figure in Eastern religious traditions. Hinduism advocates a vegetarian diet, and in particular the avoidance of beef because cows are considered to be sacred. Vegetarianism is also a feature of Jainism, due to its central tenet of nonviolence.

The justification of dietary laws connects religious practices of faith to modern findings about dietary health. Modern analyses describe many connections between the healthiness of food consumption and specific foods that are restricted by these laws. **TD**

The Ten Commandments

Moses

A list of general ethical principles given to humankind by God

The Ten Commandments—also known as the "Decalogue"—are a set of Judeo-Christian ethical principles that God is said to have dictated to Moses at Mount Sinai in the thirteenth century BCE. Unlike the other 603 commandments listed in the first few books of the Bible, the Ten Commandments are special, not only in how they came to be written (directly by God), but also in their timeless content. Roughly, they are: (1) Worship no gods but God, (2) Do not worship idols, (3) Do not blaspheme God's name, (4) Remember the Sabbath, (5) Honor your parents, (6) Do not murder, (7) Do not commit adultery, (8) Do not steal, (9) Do not bear false witness, and (10) Don't covet. In the New Testament of the Bible, Jesus claims that they can be broken down into two:

"In ten phrases, the Ten Commandments express the essentials of life."

Krzysztof Kieslowski, film director

love God first, and love other human beings as oneself. However, arguably, there is just one commandment: Do justice—treat each as it ought to be treated—wherein one ought to treat a superior as a superior (God as God), an equal as an equal (human beings as human beings), and a subordinate as a subordinate.

Whatever the case, none of the Ten Commandments is special for being uniquely known by the ancient Israelites: versions of most are found in most religions. This ubiquity is often explained by the presence of Natural Law, or general principles of justice, that can be known to all and that many believe to have been given by a divine power. This universality of the essential meaning of the Ten Commandments demonstrates their importance as a foundation for how people should live. **AB**

A seventeenth-century painting of Moses with the Ten Commandments, by Jacques de Letin.

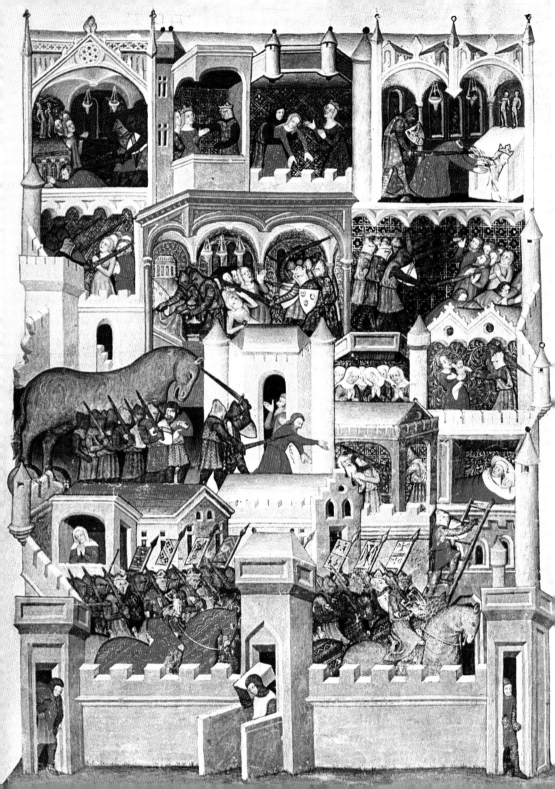

Trojan Horse
Agamemnon

A subversive force that is unwittingly invited in by its target

The origins of the term "trojan horse" can be traced back to the Trojan War (dated by later Greek authors to have taken place in the twelfth or thirteenth century BCE), the legendary conflict between the early Greeks and the people of Troy in western Anatolia. Traditional accounts tell that Paris, son of the Trojan king, abducted Helen, wife of Menelaus of Sparta, whose brother Agamemnon then led a Greek expedition against Troy. The war lasted ten years, until Agamemnon developed a deception plan that used a huge wooden horse to infiltrate a raiding party into Troy. The Trojan Horse was left at the gates of Troy when the Greeks supposedly abandoned their siege. The Trojans were persuaded that the horse was an offering to Athena that would make Troy impregnable and, despite several warnings,

"Do not trust the horse, Trojans. Whatever it is, I fear the Greeks even bearing gifts."

Virgil, *The Aeneid* (*c.* 20 BCE)

it was taken inside the city walls. That night, warriors emerged from the horse and opened the city's gates to the returned Greek army. The Greeks massacred Troy's men and carried off its women, then sacked the city.

A "trojan horse" can refer to any kind of subversion introduced to a host from the outside; today it is most often used to describe malicious computer software. A computer user is induced to install an application that, once activated, makes the computer a "bot" or "zombie," allowing a remote malware developer "backdoor" access to the infected computer. A trojan can subject the host computer to a variety of destructive or undesired activities, such as stealing data, acquiring personal passwords or account numbers, and erasing files. Trojans are frequently used for espionage, blackmail, fraud, and identity theft. **BC**

The Twelve Olympians
Ancient Greece

The most important gods and goddesses in the Greek pantheon

The Twelve Olympians, known in Greek as the *Dodekatheon*, were the most important gods and goddesses in the ancient Greek pantheon. Believed to dwell on Mount Olympus in Greece, they were central to the Greek mythology that developed from around 1000 BCE. According to Hesiod's seventh-century BCE *Theogony*, the first written work on Greek mythology, they were third- and fourth-generation gods, all descending via the union of Kronos and Rhea, and, before that, the union of Ouranos and Gaia. Zeus, Hera, Poseidon, and Demeter are the third-generation gods of the twelve, and Dionysus, Apollo, Artemis, Hermes, Athena, Ares, Aphrodite, and Hephaestus are the fourth generation. All of the fourth-generation Olympians are children of Zeus, who is the king of the twelve.

"The Greek gods . . . did not love humans . . . and did not ask to be loved by them . . ."

Barry B. Powell, *Classical Myth* (1994)

Although the Olympians are best known by their Greek (or, later, Roman) names, most were not of Greek origin. The Greeks belonged to a larger Indo-European (Hittite) culture, which had its own mythology that itself borrowed heavily from even more ancient, largely Mesopotamian, sources. For example, the Hittite storm god was the chief deity and went by the name, "Sius," which is etymologically linked with the Greek "Zeus" . Additionally, the war between the Olympians and the Titans is probably based on an ancient Mesopotamian story, which, in its biblical form, talks about a war between angels and demons in heaven.

Although few worship the Olympians any more, their influence remains. This can be seen in the arts in particular, where many great Western works use, or refer to, the Olympians and their achievements. **AB**

A fourteenth-century illumination depicting the Greek capture of Troy with the Trojan Horse.

Yijing
China

An ancient Chinese text providing a system of divination based on Daoist philosophy

The *Yijing* (*I Ching*) is known in the West as *The Book of Changes*. One of the oldest Chinese texts, it is a system of divination grounded in Chinese geomancy and Daoist philosophy. It was probably written sometime between the third and fifth centuries BCE, though its origins date back to around 1000 BCE.

The *Yijing* is meant to be a guide to help people understand and manage change. The *Dao* (the way of nature) manifests itself through a complementary process of change between the forces of *yin* (negative or dark) and *yang* (positive or bright). If you can determine the interrelationship of *yin* and *yang* at a given time, you can understand how to best harmonize your actions with the *Dao*. The text of the *Yijing* is made up of oracular readings associated with sixty-

> *"Knowing others is intelligence; knowing yourself is true wisdom."*

Yijing (*I Ching* or *The Book of Changes*)

four hexagrams. Each hexagram is composed of two trigrams made up of three lines each. These lines are either solid, representing *yang* (—), or broken, denoting *yin* (- -). A reading is obtained by casting yarrow stalks or flipping coins to determine the *yin/yang* nature of the lines, which combine to form two trigrams, which in turn make a hexagram. The reader then looks up that hexagram in the *Yijing* to determine the proper course of action to take under the circumstances.

The *Yijing* is one of the seminal texts of Daoism, influencing countless East Asian thinkers. It has been studied in Japan since the Tokugawa era (1603–1867), and the flag of South Korea displays the Daoist *taijitu* symbol surrounded by four trigrams. Western scholars, such as Gottfried Wilhelm von Leibniz and Karl Jung, have studied its theories of structural change. **JM**

Halloween
Britain and Ireland

The night when the veil between life and death is thinnest

The most probable origin of Halloween lies in the ancient Celtic festival of Samhain, which is believed to have first taken place around 1000 BCE in Britain and Ireland. Associated with pre-Christian Gaelic festivals and later linked with the Roman festivals of Pomona and Feralia, Samhain was held to mark the end of the harvest and the beginning of the new year on November 1. October 31 was known as "All Hallows' Eve," or "Hallowe'en," and it was believed to be the time when the veil between life and death was thinnest and contact with spirits might be possible. In order to ward off or mislead these shades, turnips and gourds with frightening faces painted or carved on them were displayed, and bonfires were lit. Pumpkins were later substituted for turnips as they were more readily available—a tradition that has persisted to the modern day, though their purpose is now more decorative than apopotraic.

In the Catholic tradition, Halloween falls on the night before All Saints Day, or "Hallowmas" (November 1), a celebration to honor martyrs of the faith. Young men, often costumed as saints, would go from house to house requesting donations for the poor and praying for their souls, a practice known as "souling." When Martin Luther initiated the Protestant Reformation on All Hallow's Eve in 1517 and questioned the legitimacy of saints, he negated All Saints Day, and so for the next 300 years Halloween was primarily celebrated by Catholics and Anglicans (Episcopalians) and ignored or banned by Protestants. However, an influx of Scottish immigrants and Irish Catholic refugees in the nineteenth century led to a resurgence of interest in the holiday in the United States, and by the mid-twentieth century it was a popular fixture across the country. Today Halloween is largely a secular celebration, and its observance has spread worldwide. **PBr**

All-powerful God
Ancient Israel

The view of God as a single being who has total power, benevolence, knowledge, and presence

An all-powerful god is not merely one who knows all and sees all, but one for whom nothing is impossible. The all-powerful deity rules the universe with perfect knowledge (omniscience) and ability (omnipotence), imparting divine justice impartially. Such a god is omnipresent, inherently truthful, and loving: a perfect being that no other can eclipse.

In ancient polytheistic religions, the gods often possessed spectacular, yet limited, abilities, while monolatrous religions recognized many gods but venerated one as supreme. The idea of a single, all-powerful supreme god appears to have originated in ancient Israel sometime around 800 BCE. The Israelite religion was originally polytheistic, and Hebrew scriptures contain references to multiple gods. However, during a period of conflict with their neighbors, the Israelites began to focus their worship on the god Yaweh, who came to be viewed as the main deity. Following defeat by the Assyrians and Babylonians, belief in Yahweh intensified, and by around the eighth century BCE Yahweh had come to be seen as supreme. Today, a majority of the world's population is a member of a religion that holds that such a god exists.

For the believers in an all-powerful being, faith is a necessity and an ever-present Damoclean sword. Nothing you do, think, say, or feel is ever outside of God's awareness, and there is no punishment, nor reward, that is outside the realm of possibility. In a world where God is all-powerful everything is as God intends it to be, and the work of humanity can be nothing but a reflection of God's glory. The belief in such a god and such a world has compelled artists to create, warriors to kill and conquer, the pious to dedicate themselves to spiritual discipline, and the faithful to devote every moment of their lives to the being for which there can be none greater. **MT**

⬆ The Three Shekel Ostracon—believed by many to be a forgery—is an eighth-century BCE pottery fragment bearing a receipt for a donation of three Shekels to the Temple of Yahweh.

"God is that infinite All of which man knows himself to be a finite part. God alone exists truly. Man manifests Him in time, space, and matter."

Leo Tolstoy, author

Ancient Olympic Games
Ancient Greece

A series of athletic competitions held near Olympia in Greece

The ancient Olympic Games were first held in 776 BCE in Greece, though their mythical origins go back much further. There were three other major panhellenic athletics championships held at that time, but the most important was at Elis, near Olympia, which was held as part of a religious festival in honor of Zeus, king of the gods. Although war between Greek city-states was a frequent occurrence, traditionally a truce was declared to allow athletes from all cities to take part. The Olympiad, the four-year period between each Games, was used as a calendar to date other events.

At the first Games, the only event was the *stadion*, a race held over about 600 feet (190 m). Later, there were events such as boxing, wrestling, and equestrianism (including chariot racing). By 720 BCE most athletes

"The winner ... keeps happiness beside him sweeter than honey."

Pindar, "Olympia 1" victory ode (*c.* 500 BCE)

took part naked, a tradition that one story attributes to a runner who lost his shorts during the *stadion*. Participants competed for the honor of their native city-state, but there were no team sports. Non-citizens, slaves, and women were not allowed to take part, though by the sixth century BCE women had their own separate event, the Heraia. The Games continued yearly for almost twelve centuries, until 393 CE when the Christian Roman emperor Theodosius I banned them as part of a purge of pagan ceremonies and rituals.

The Olympic Games first encapsulated the idea that sport could contribute to peace and harmony between nations. The amateur nature of sport was emphasized through the awarding of a simple laurel wreath or olive branch to the winner. The glory of winning—even the joy of taking part—was enough. **JF**

Continual Progress
Ancient Greece

The belief that humankind is in a continual state of self-improvement

The notion that human society should always be in a state of progression is as old as antiquity. All civilizations have, from their inception, held firm to the idea that continual moral, religious, and material improvements are an inevitable consequence of our inquisitive, aspirational natures. The Greek classicist Hesiod (*fl. c.* 700 BCE) spoke of human progression in *Works and Days*. In Aeschylus's fifth-century BCE play *Prometheus Bound*, Prometheus is consigned to eternal punishment by Zeus for giving humans the gift of fire in a heroic attempt to free them from ignorance and enable them to pursue the loftier realms of art, culture, and learning. In *The City of God* in the fifth century CE, St. Augustine of Hippo wrote of the genius of man and of what he saw as assumed stages of our continual development.

"Men through their own search find in the course of time that which is better."

Xenophanes, ancient Greek poet

It was not until the seventeenth century and the French "Quarrel of the Ancients and Moderns," that the idea of contstant progress in Western civilization was first debated.

On one side of the Ancients/Moderns argument were those who felt that contemporary society could never hope to match the achievements of the societies of classical antiquity; on the other, were those, such as the author Bernard le Bovier de Fontenelle (1657–1757), who argued that the seventeenth-century human mind was every bit as rich and imaginative as it was in the time of Aristotle and Homer. Humankind's economic and material progression continued to be assumed in Adam Smith's *The Wealth of Nations* (1776), and again in G. W. F. Hegel's *Philosophy of History* (1831), in which he writes of our "impulse of perfectibility." **BS**

⬅ A fifth-century BCE Greek vase depicting athletes participating in a foot race.

Aqueduct
Assyria

A man-made structure designed to take water from one location to another

Aqueducts were invented in the ancient world as a means to channel water to a desired location. One of the first major examples was built in 691 BCE to carry water some 50 miles (80 km) to the capital of the Assyrian Empire, Nineveh. The Romans developed the idea further, constructing aqueducts capable of carrying large quantities of water above the level of the surrounding land. Some of these are still standing, including the Pont du Gard at Nîmes, France, and the longest Roman aqueduct of them all, 87 miles (140 km) long, built at Carthage in present-day Tunisia. Medieval examples include a system of irrigation channels known as *levadas* that transferred water from the moist north of Madeira through the central mountain range to the dry, more populous south.

"A stream in the sky . . . the most impressive work of art I have ever seen."

Walter Scott, describing the Pontcysyllte Aqueduct

Aqueducts were also used as part of the canal system for transporting goods during Britain's Industrial Revolution (1760–1840). The network featured structures such as the 1,000-foot (305 m) long Pontcysyllte Aqueduct, which was constructed in 1805 to carry the Llangollen canal 126 feet (38 m) above the Dee valley—it is still the highest aqueduct in the world. Aqueducts have continued to be built into the modern day, such as the North Bay Aqueduct, built in 1988 as part of the California State Water Project.

The aqueduct harnesses the natural propensity of water to run along gullies and ditches. The genius of the Assyrians was to build human-made structures to take the water where they wanted it to go, to supply the cities where people wanted to live, rather than being dependent on natural sources. **JF**

All is Water
Thales of Miletus

All matter is composed of water as its basic substance

The ancient Greek philosopher Thales (*c.* 624–546 BCE) posited the idea that "all is water" as one of the first abstract explanations for the origin of matter. Just as the abstract notion of a "building" encompasses everything from homes to arenas and temples, the idea that all is water similarly offers an idea that unifies all matter in the world as a single substance.

In Thales's time it was commonly believed that matter was composed of one of four elements: air, earth, fire, or water. Yet for Thales this theory was incomplete. Through his observations of the world, he concluded that everything has, at least in part, some water in it. The oceans are obviously composed of water, but water is also found in animals, plant life, clouds, and even in rocks, which do not appear to be

"If there is magic on this planet, it is contained in water."

Loran Eisley, anthropologist and philosopher

wet, yet have a degree of moisture to them. For Thales this led to the conclusion that of the four elements, water must be the most important. If water is present everywhere, he reasoned, it must be the fundamental substance present in all things.

Even though the notion that there are only four elements and that water is the most important is no longer given credence, the idea is renowned more for what it did not presume, rather than for its accuracy. Prior to Thales and his aquatic thesis, the ancient Greeks approached questions of origins and explanations in terms of myths and gods. Thales's idea turned such thoughts away from the supernatural, and instead toward an abstract notion that explains everything. In that idea lay the foundation for Greek philosophy, science, and naturalism, and all it bore. **MT**

Thales believed that water could be found in everything, even the rocks surrounding this waterfall. ➡

The Arch

Etrusca

A weight-supporting structure that literally opened up the design of buildings

The first true arches appeared among the Etruscans in around 600 BCE, used in the construction of gates, bridges, and drains. Popularized by the ancient Romans, the arch was later adopted by the Arabs and the medieval architects of northern Europe.

Arches are constructed from a series of wedge-shaped blocks known as voussoirs, which are juxtaposed to form a variety of shapes: the most common design is a semicircle, but arches may also be segmental (less than half a circle), pointed (formed from two intersecting arcs), or other non-circular curves. The shape of arches has long been a prime characteristic of architectural style, with, for example, Romanesque rounded arches giving way to Gothic pointed ones.

The central, uppermost voussoir is known as the keystone. This stone is the crucial component: until it is firmly in place, the arch requires support from below, which is usually provided by temporary wooden struts.

The aesthetic appeal of arches is obvious; their practicality may be less apparent. In fact, arches are structurally more sound than any lintel (horizontal support) because they are made of small blocks rather than a single, large crossbeam. Since downward pressure forces the voussoirs together, arches are capable of bearing much greater loads than lintels, although single arches require buttresses on either side to resist the diagonal forces that would otherwise push the uprights apart and cause the structure to collapse. With a series of arches, however, the thrust of each span counteracts the thrusts of its neighbors, and hence they require only light support: this is the principle applied in Roman aqueducts and many bridges built between the Middle Ages (*c.* 500–*c.* 1450) and the height of the Steam Age in the eighteenth century. Arches are widely used in modern building construction because materials such as steel and concrete reduce the overall weight and further reinforce the stability of the structure. **GL**

Arched windows above the gateway of the Al-Ukhaidir fortress in Iraq, built in 775. ⬆

Φ

Infinity
Anaximander

An indefinitely great number or amount of something

The idea of an endless amount of something is a concept that has perplexed most of intellectual history. In the sixth century BCE the ancient Greek philosopher Anaximander (c. 610–546 BCE) suggested that the four elements that make up the world (air, fire, water, earth) originated from an unlimited primitive substance called *to apeiron*: the infinite. In his *Physics* (350 BCE), Aristotle (384–322 BCE) later argued that there are two ways of understanding infinity—potential and actual—and that an actually infinite quantity is impossible (except for time). There is only an "illimitable potentiality of addition" and an "illimitable potentiality of division," for "it will always be possible to find something beyond the total."

Anaximander's use of infinity as all of reality seems to imply some qualitative notion of significance, rather than an enumeration of discrete quantities. In contrast, Aristotle refers to quantities of parts: "the infinite . . . is not that of which no part is outside, but that of which some part is always outside."

Aristotle's quantitative treatment of infinity became the standard for studying the concept, and his conclusions were well respected until the discovery of calculus demanded a more thorough analysis. Gottfried Leibniz (1646–1716) and Isaac Newton (1642–1727), developing calculus independently of one another, disagreed about the role of infinitesimally small quantities in explaining integrals. Newton used the notion sparingly and developed the Method of Fluxions to avoid them; Leibniz made extensive use of them. Aristotle's challenge to infinite quantities remained until German mathematicians Richard Dedekind (1831–1916) and Georg Cantor (1845–1918) proved the logical possibility of actually infinite sets in the late eighteenth century. Today, various conceptions of infinity remain hotly contested in both philosophy and mathematics. **JW**

↑ A rock carving of the mathematical symbol for infinity, also known as the lemniscate symbol.

Fables
Attributed to Aesop

The idea of presenting criticism or advice indirectly in a simplified, fictional setting

⬆ A bronze statue from between 330 and 100 BCE, that is believed to depict Aesop holding a papyrus scroll. Aesop is traditionally described as being very ugly.

A fable is a narrative, in prose or verse but usually simple and brief, that is intended to convey a moral lesson. Fables frequently involve non-human characters—animals (real or mythic), plants, artifacts, forces of nature, and so on—that are represented as having human attributes. Fables are a common form of folk literature; the best-known fables of the Western world are credited to the legendary figure Aesop, who is supposed to have been a slave in ancient Greece sometime between 620 and 560 BCE.

In the ancient classical world, fables were not considered as fare for children nor as works of literature in their own right. Rather, they were used as vehicles for indirect—and thus carefully polite—criticism and persuasion. For example, Xenophon (*c.* 430–354 BCE), in his *Memorabilia* (*c.* 371 BCE), describes Socrates advising a citizen named Aristarchus to tell his ungrateful relatives—to whom he had provided capital for a business and who are now accusing him of idleness—the fable of the dog and the sheep, concluding, "Tell your flock yonder that like the dog in the fable you are their guardian and overseer."

Interest in fables remained high through classical antiquity, the Middle Ages, and the Renaissance, with collections of fables—typically ascribed to Aesop—serving as the basis for rhetorical textbooks and literary works. Jean de La Fontaine (1621–95) produced *Fables* (1668–1694), which are perhaps the most best-known original fables in modern times.

As literary tastes developed in sophistication, fables increasingly became the province of humorists such as George Ade and children's writers such as Dr. Seuss—although the defamiliarizing effect of fables, with the artistic form being used to stimulate fresh perception of a familiar subject, is still deployed in books such as George Orwell's criticism of Stalinism, *Animal Farm* (1945). **GB**

"Fable is more historical than fact, because fact tells us about one man and fable tells us about a million men."

G. K. Chesterton, "Alfred the Great" (1908)

Biological Warfare
Ancient Assyria

Using living organisms as a weapon to kill, incapacitate, or harm an enemy

Biological weapons are designed to take advantage of the dangerous and deadly properties of natural toxins and pathogens. Because biological weapons have the potential to reproduce themselves—sometimes within a human or animal host—they also have the potential to be incredibly destructive, and thus extremely effective.

The earliest known use of biological weapons occurred in the sixth century BCE, when ancient Assyrian warriors poisoned the wells of their enemies with a species of ergot fungus that naturally grows on rye grain. In 190 BCE, the Carthaginian military commander Hannibal used jars full of venomous snakes as a weapon in naval warfare when he launched them into enemy ships to cause panic. In the fourteenth century CE, Tartar warriors took the corpses of comrades who had died of the plague and launched them into besieged cities. By the time germ theory allowed scientists to more easily identify the cause of diseases, and thus potentially create more effective biological weapons, the international community declared the use of such weapons illegal in the Geneva Protocol of 1925. Nevertheless, the Japanese successfully used biological warfare against the Chinese people during the Sino-Japanese War (1937–45) and World War II (1939–45).

By 2011 biological weapons had been disavowed by at least 165 countries, and today they are primarily seen as potential terrorist weapons. Isolated incidents of biological weapon use have occurred, though their influence has not been significant. Nonetheless, the potential danger that such weapons pose continues to be of significant concern to governments around the world. Most modern governments maintain that they have no offensive biological weapons programs, but studying natural pathogens and biological agents for defensive purposes remains a part of many state defense programs. **MT**

⬆ A ninth-century BCE stone bas-relief from the palace of Ashurnazirpal II in Nimrud, Mesopotamia, showing an Assyrian soldier cutting the rope on a pail above a well in the besieged city.

"The world really is just one village. And our tolerance of disease in any place in the world is at our own peril."

Joshua Lederberg, molecular biologist

Philosophical Hedonism
India

Human actions should be motivated by the pursuit of pleasure

How should we live? We pursue education so that we can get a career, so we can make money, so we can buy things, so we can ... what? Presumably, we do not want a career or money just to have a career or money, but in order to be happy. The idea that the morally good or "right" motivation for acting is the pursuit of pleasure and avoidance of pain is called hedonism.

Hedonism can be traced to the sixth-century BCE Indian philosophy *Cārvāka*, but its most influential form was in the ancient Greek teachings of Aristippus of Cyrene (*c.* 435–356 BCE) and Epicurus (341–270 BCE). Regarding pleasure as the only valuable pursuit, hedonism sets itself apart from other widely accepted moral views, such as that a person has moral duties to do certain things regardless of whether they make them

"[We] do everything for the sake of being free of pain and mental distress."

Epicurus, in a letter to Meneoceus

happy (deontology) and that a person has obligations to do whatever God commands, irrespective of the impact on their own welfare (divine command theory).

However, philosophical hedonism should be distinguished from the mere pursuit of pleasure. While some accuse hedonists of advocating a life of debauchery, philosophical hedonists reject this characterization. Epicurus argued that while every pleasure is good, "it does not follow that every pleasure is a choice worthy without qualification." He extolled traditional virtues of self-sufficiency, prudence, and even a healthy diet, since they too contribute to a lifetime of happiness. Though hedonism was rejected by many influential moral philosophers (such as Thomas Aquinas and Immanuel Kant), it continues to play an influential role in contemporary moral and political thought. **JW**

Daoism
Laozi

The attainment of tranquility by living in harmony with the natural world

Daoism is a Chinese philosophical and religious tradition that originated with Laozi (*fl.* sixth century BCE) and was later expanded on by Zhuangzi (*c.* 369–286 BCE). It is a type of naturalism that encourages human beings to live in harmony with the *Dao*, the natural world that is the basis of all existence. The *Dao* manifests itself as *de*, the particular things that we see in the world, which contain within them certain proportions of *yin* (negative or destructive forces) and *yang* (positive or creative forces). Everything contains some proportion of *yin* and *yang*: for example, we can see things only when there is both light and shadow, and music exists as a combination of notes and rests.

If there is an overabundance of *yin* or *yang*, the *Dao* has a tendency to balance itself by reverting to the

"The sage helps the natural development of all things and does not dare to act."

Laozi, *Daodejing* 64 (sixth century BCE)

opposite extreme. Daoists therefore practice *wu wei*, or "non-interference": rather than acting against nature, a person should instead follow the natural flow of events and turn them to their own advantage (like a surfer moving in harmony with a wave). Politically, this results in a minimalistic approach to government: a good ruler should educate the people so that harsh laws are unnecessary.

Daoism has had an enormous influence upon East Asia, particularly China and Taiwan. Like Confucianism, its core philosophical tenets are deeply ingrained in the culture. Daoist metaphysics influenced Mahayana Buddhism, which led to the creation of Chan (Zen) Buddhism. Core principles of Daoism have been a cornerstone of the martial arts (for example, Bruce Lee's Tao of Jeet Kune Do). **JM**

An illustration (*c.* 1700) of the three sages of T'ai Chi, a martial art derived from Daoism. ➡

Φ

Ju
Laozi

True strength is gained by yielding to force, rather than resisting it

The principle of *ju* (*rou* in Chinese) was first articulated by the sixth-century BCE Chinese Daoist philosopher Laozi in his classic philosophical text, the *Daodejing*. *Ju* can be translated as "suppleness," "yielding strength," or "gentleness," and refers to the ability to adapt dynamically to pressure so as to overcome it.

The *Dao* (the natural world) can be thought of as similar to a rubber band stretched taut between two fingers: any attempt to pull it builds up potential energy that will eventually cause it to snap back to the opposite position. To avoid this reversion, a Daoist should not directly oppose force, but should instead flow with it and turn it to their advantage. Two classic examples illustrate this concept: bamboo and water. In the high winds and freezing rain of an ice storm, the rigid branches of trees will snap off, while the more flexible stalks of bamboo survive by bending under the pressure and then springing back. Water flows around a rock thrown into a pond, yet has the power to slowly erode the stone or shatter it with a crashing wave.

Ju is a core underlying principle in the Japanese and Chinese martial arts, particularly the disciplines of judo and jujutsu (*jiu-jitsu*), which are both named after the concept. It requires exponents to be ready to adapt themselves to whatever maneuver their adversary approaches them with. When a small judo practitioner is shoved by a larger opponent, for example, the practitioner does not shove back, but instead pulls their opponent forward, redirecting the opponent's force and throwing the opponent to the ground. It is only by yielding to their opponent's force that the practitioner is able to triumph. Bruce Lee also made extensive use of *ju* in his philosophy of Jeet Kune Do, encouraging the martial artist to fit in with each opponent by adapting a "way of no way" that eschews set forms. **JM**

A Song Dynasty (960–1279) statue of Laozi, the Chinese master philosopher and father of Daoism. ⬆

Wu Wei
Laozi

Maximum efficiency comes as a result of minimal interference

The concept of *wu wei* was first articulated by the Chinese Daoist philosopher Laozi (*fl.* sixth century BCE) in his *Daodejing*, and then later developed by Zhuangzi (*c.* 369–286 BCE) in the fourth century BCE. *Wu wei* can be translated as "non-interference" or "non-coercive action," and the concept refers to letting things take their natural course with minimal intervention.

Wu wei does not mean total inaction; rather it is a way of maximizing efficiency by minimizing interference. The goal of Daoism is to fit in seamlessly with the workings of the natural world, and *wu wei* is the method through which this harmony is achieved. Zhuangzi gives the example of Cook Ding, who is so skilled as a chef that he is able to butcher a whole ox without dulling the edge of his knife. Just as understanding anatomy helps Cook Ding to carve up his ox, understanding nature helps the Daoist to harmonize his actions with the workings of the natural world. Because the *de* (the particular way that the negative and positive forces of *yin* and *yang* are focused in a given context) is constantly shifting, the Daoist must learn to ride the flow of the Dao in the same way that a kayaker avoids collision by navigating the smoothest path through turbulent waters.

The concept of *wu wei* has been particularly influential in government, environmental philosophy, and the martial arts. Politically, a good ruler should focus upon educating the population rather than trying to exert control: society functions best when the virtues and desires of the people are in harmony with nature. In environmental philosophy, *wu wei* rejects consumerism in favor of minimizing the negative environmental impact that humans have upon the natural world. Martial artists strive to fit in with the movements of their opponents, using each attacker's energy against him rather than opposing it directly. **JM**

⬆ A group of men practicing T'ai Chi in front of the Temple of Heaven in Beijing, China.

Drama

Thespis

A method of performance in which a story is acted out for entertainment

"Drama" refers to a performing art, but the term also encompasses the associated body of literature that the performances are based on. While aspects of theater, such as performance, costumes, and storytelling, were present in all ancient cultures, Thespis, a sixth-century BCE singer of liturgical poems in ancient Greece, is credited by Aristotle (384–322 BCE) with inventing a style in which the singer played the various characters in the story with the aid of differing masks. Thespis staged the first tragedy—and thus the first drama—in c. 534 BCE.

From these origins, drama swiftly developed in the Western world. Aeschylus (c. 525–456 BCE), whose *The Persians* is the earliest surviving play, is credited with introducing a second actor to the performance;

his rival Sophocles (c. 496–406 BCE) is credited with introducing a third. Diverse dramatic traditions continued to flourish in different times and places, with influential dramatists including Christopher Marlowe, William Shakespeare, and Ben Jonson in Elizabethan and Jacobean England; Pierre Corneille, Molière, and Jean Racine in seventeenth-century France; and Henrik Ibsen, August Strindberg, and Anton Chekhov in nineteenth-century Europe. Distinct genres of drama, techniques of performance and direction, conventions in costume and scenery, and methods of incorporating music, dance, and poetry all evolved alongside dramatic literature—even a form of drama eschewing performance altogether (the "closet drama") emerged. In the East, meanwhile, independent dramatic traditions such as *Noh* and *Kabuki* in Japan, Chinese opera, and *Kathakali* in southern India developed.

Through much of history, drama took place in the theater. But in the twentieth and twenty-first centuries, drama was extended from the theater into new media, including radio, cinema, television, and the Internet. This adaptability and widespread prevalance shows the continuing vitality of the art form. **GB**

The third-century BCE theater at Epidaurus, Greece, is still used for dramatic performances today. ⬆

Tragedy
Thespis

A drama about suffering that can offer emotional release for its audience

A tragedy is a drama—or by extension a narrative—culminating in a disastrous end for the protagonist. In a typical tragedy, the protagonist is admirable but flawed; the course of events leading to the conclusion is presented as inevitably resulting from his or her character and situation; and the presentation is serious and solemn, as befits a depiction of the grandeur and misery of the human condition. Thespis (*fl.* sixth century BCE) of ancient Greece is traditionally considered the inventor of tragedy, and thus also the inventor or drama, after staging the first recorded tragedy in c. 534 BCE.

In ancient Greece, tragedy was one of the major genres, and the tragedies of Aeschlyus, Euripides, and Sophocles are still regarded as canonical. Aristotle's discussion of tragedy in the *Poetics* (c. 335 BCE), based on these works, is still influential. The tragedies of the Roman stage, particularly those of Seneca, were more influential in Renaissance Europe, however. Important modern writers of tragedy include Elizabethan playwright William Shakespeare and seventeenth-century French dramatist Jean Racine. Additionally, there have been attempts to replicate the dramatic functions of tragedy in different art forms, including poetry (such as Lord Byron's *Manfred*, 1816–17) and the novel (such as Thomas Hardy's *Jude the Obscure*, 1895).

From the eighteenth century onward, tragedy of this nature was increasingly displaced in the theater in favor of its intellectually less demanding cousins: domestic tragedy, melodrama, and tragicomedy, although there are arguable exceptions, such as the twentieth-century plays of Arthur Miller and Eugene O'Neill. The critic George Steiner argued, in *The Death of Tragedy* (1961), that after Shakespeare and Racine, "the tragic voice in drama is blurred or still." Steiner attributed the dwindling impact of tragedy to the rise of the optimism associated with the Age of Enlightenment. **GB**

 A marble relief from the first century BCE, showing the dramatist Euripides holding a mask of Heracles.

Pythagorean Theorem
Pythagoras

An equation that explains the relationship between the sides in a right-angled triangle

⬆ An Arabian manuscript from 1258, discussing Pythagorean theorem. It was authored by the Persian philosopher, scientist, and mathematician, Nasir al-Din al-Tusi.

Expressed as the equation $A^2 + B^2 = C^2$, the Pythagorean theorem demonstrates the relationship between the sides of all right triangles. In a right triangle, meaning a triangle in which one angle is 90 degrees, the value of the squared length of the longest side of the triangle will always be equal to the sum of the squared lengths of the other two sides.

Even though there are ancient Babylonian tablets that express the Pythagorean theorem in terms of the measurements found in right triangles, the ancient Greek mathematician Pythagoras of Samos (*c.* 570– *c.* 495 BCE) is widely credited with identifying the equation. No original written works by Pythagoras remain to prove this definitively though, and it is impossible to determine if the idea was his alone. However, it is claimed that upon discovering his eponymous mathematical truth, Pythagoras offered a hetacomb to the gods (a public sacrifice of 100 oxen). He and many of his contemporaries believed that mathematics were so connected to the divine that they formed a religious movement around his discovery. However, when he and his followers—who dubbed themselves the Brotherhood of Pythagoreans— moved to Croton, a Greek colony in southern Italy, their controversial beliefs led to public outcry, forcing them to flee for their lives.

The Pythagorean theorem is not merely a deduction about right triangles and the relationship of their sides. It has since become a foundational mathematical theorem, and an indelible part of the modern world. Through it, Pythagoras showed that the abstract notions of numbers and mathematics correspond to humanity's everyday perceptions of the real world. His theorem revealed that nature had a structure, a structure composed of equations, and those equations were something humanity could comprehend, measure, and use. **MT**

"Number is the ruler of forms and ideas, and the cause of gods and demons."

Pythagoras

Pythagorean Tuning
Pythagoras

A tuning system derived from the intervals of the perfect fifth and perfect fourth

Pythagorean tuning was the brainchild of Greek philosopher Pythagoras of Samos (*c.* 570–*c.* 495 BCE), who formalized a theory in which musical intervals could be derived from the simple ratios of string lengths. The tuning system utilizes the intervals of fourth (4:3) and fifth (3:2) to generate the scale. The difference between the two (9:8) makes up the whole tone, and a minor second is the remainder of a fourth minus two whole tones, the Limma 256:243. As a consequence, six Pythagorean whole tones, which would logically make up an octave (2:1), are larger by an interval called the Pythagorean comma (531,441:524,288), a small interval but noticeable to the human ear.

Despite its purely theoretical origin and practical problems—chords including thirds sound out of tune, for example—Pythagorean tuning was favored throughout the medieval period and is still used today in shaping melodies on non-keyboard instruments, such as the violin. To many musicians, the larger Pythagorean whole tone and smaller half tone sound better than the ones of equal temperament (the scale used at keyboards today, in which the octave has been divided into twelve equal parts and which makes it possible to play harmonies in all keys).

The obsession of early music theorists with the size of scale steps has had a key influence on music, inspiring numerous attempts throughout history to create the perfect intonation system: from compromises to create perfect harmonies in a limited number of keys, to contemporary systems utilizing tensions and dissonances for expressive effects, such as the use of the syntonic comma—the difference between a just intonated major third and the Pythagorean third—in the music of U.S. composer Ben Johnston. Other attempts include keyboards with more than one key for certain pitches, to enable the tuning to be adjusted to different harmonies. **PB**

⬆ A woodcut from 1492 showing the biblical figure Jubal as the discoverer of music (top left) and Pythagoras studying the relationships between intervals in different instruments.

"Take but degree away, untune that string, and hark, what discord follows!"

William Shakespeare, *Troilus and Cressida* (1602)

Vegetarianism
Pythagoras

A conscious decision not to eat meat and other animal products

Vegetarianism is the principled refusal to eat meat. The ancient Greek philosopher Pythagoras (*c.* 570–*c.* 495 BCE), who required members of his philosophical society to abstain from eating meat, is often viewed as the first important vegetarian. Before the word "vegetarian" was coined in the 1840s, non meat-eaters were often called "Pythagoreans."

What is wrong with eating meat? Vegetarians have offered various criticisms for the practice, contending that eating meat is cruel (often, from the twentieth century onward, citing the methods of industrial meat production), unethical (often citing recent work in practical ethics, particularly by Peter Singer), unhealthy (often citing the fact that vegetarians tend to be less obese and less likely to die from ischemic heart disease), unnatural (often claiming, wrongly, that prehistoric humans subsisted on a vegetarian diet), environmentally unfriendly (often citing the relative inefficiency of meat production), and in conflict with the tenets of religious faith (sometimes citing reincarnation, as with the ancient Pythagoreans and several modern Hindu sects). There are also different degrees of vegetarianism: for example, ovo vegetarians will eat eggs, lacto vegetarians will eat milk, and ovo-lacto vegetarians will eat eggs and milk, whereas vegans forego all products derived from animals and fruitarians furthermore forego all plant foods that involve killing the plant, eating only fruits, nuts, and seeds. Vegetarianism is typically associated with a similar refusal to use products derived from animals, such as leather and wool.

The modern vegetarian movement is dated to 1847, when the Vegetarian Society was founded in Great Britain. In Western countries, vegetarianism has been increasing since the 1960s, and due to continuing and intensifying ethical and environmental concerns, it is likely to flourish in the future. **GB**

Pythagoras Advocating Vegetarianism (c. 1618–30) by Peter Paul Rubens. ↑

Nirvana
Siddhartha Gautama (Buddha)

The state of enlightenment achieved when *karma* and craving are extinguished

The concept of *nirvana* originated with the historical Buddha, Siddhartha Gautama (*c.* 563–483 BCE), during the sixth century BCE. Though Buddhism is grounded in Hindu philosophy, it is a heterodox approach to spiritual cultivation that eschews some of the core tenets of Hinduism, and the belief in *nirvana* epitomizes this philosophical shift.

The Sanskrit word *nirvana* literally translates as "snuffing out," and refers to the eradication of the *karma* (a force generated by a person's actions) and craving that bind an individual to the cycle of rebirth (*samsara*). One of the central ideas of Buddhism is *anatman*, which is a rejection of the Hindu notion that there is a permanent, essential self (the *atman*, or soul)

that is one with ultimate reality. Because there is no self to whom *karma* can attach, Buddhism explains the transfer of *karma* using a candle metaphor: just as an old candle (one's dying body) begins to peter out, its flame (*karma*) ignites the wick of a second candle (an infant's body). Thus, *karma* is able to transfer without having to attach to a self. *Nirvana* occurs when one has reached enlightenment and eliminated ignorant attachment to false ideals, which snuffs out *karma* and allows one to exit the cycle of rebirth. Theravada Buddhism divides *nirvana* into two stages, the awakening of the *arhat* (enlightened being) and *parinirvana* (the exit from *samsara* upon death), though practitioners in the Mahayana tradition take the *bodhisattva* vow to not enter *nirvana* until all sentient beings have been awakened.

Though *nirvana* signifies a key split from Buddhism's Hindu origins, the concept has influenced Hinduism and is present in the 700-verse scripture the *Bhagavad Gita*, in which Krishna uses the concept of *brahama nirvana* to describe the state of liberation in which *karma* is eradicated and one has achieved union with Brahman (ultimate reality). **JM**

An eighteenth-century painting depicting a reclining Buddha during the transition from this world to *nirvana*.

The Four Noble Truths
Siddhartha Gautama (Buddha)

The Buddhist path to enlightenment lies in freedom from desire

According to traditional biographies, Siddhartha Gautama (*c.* 563–483 BCE) was a prince from northern India who renounced his privileged life to seek spiritual awakening. At first he followed the ascetic tradition of Indian holy men, mortifying the flesh with extreme fasting and other hardships. After seven years of such striving, and now so emaciated as to be barely alive, he came to sit under the Bodhi Tree at Gaya. One evening, he accepted a little nourishing food, relaxed, and felt a profound change overtake him. After sitting through the night, at dawn he achieved a state of perfect understanding, becoming a Buddha (enlightened one).

Siddhartha's insight into the nature of reality was later formulated as the Four Noble Truths of Buddhism. The first truth is that life, as usually lived, is suffering

"Birth is suffering, aging is suffering, illness is suffering, death is suffering."
The Pali Canon of Buddhist scriptures

(*duhkha*)—frustration of desire, losing what we want, having to live with what we do not want. The second truth is that suffering results from clinging to the illusory things of the world with desire or hatred, striving for one or fleeing another. The third truth spells out the solution: the achievement of *nirvana*, the state of enlightenment in which the world can be seen for the delusion that it is. Freedom from illusion will mean freedom from attachment to illusory desires. The final truth sets out the practical path to enlightenment—*dharma*—including right understanding, right speech, right action, and right concentration.

In the context of the traditional Indian belief in reincarnation, *nirvana* is seen as the escape from the endless cycle of death and rebirth. Freedom is found in the realization that even the self is an illusion. **RG**

Music of the Spheres
Pythagoras

The orbits of the planets emit different tones that together create a musical harmony

Attributed to Pythagoras (*c.* 570–*c.* 495 BCE), "music of the spheres" is the idea that acoustical relationships between the planets are governed by their distance from Earth and their rotational speed, just as arithmetic divisions of a string generate different musical intervals. Plato (*c.* 424–*c.* 348 BCE) described it as eight Sirens (one for each body of the solar system) orbiting around a turning spindle, each "hymning" different tones that together form one harmony. Around 900 years later, the philosopher Boethius (*c.* 480–*c.* 524) brought back these ideas with his notion of *Musica mundana* (the music of the world), to which he also added *Musica humana* (the harmony of the human body).

This connection between music, mathematics, and astronomy had a profound impact on history. It resulted

"The melody . . . is made by the impulse and motion of the spheres themselves."
Cicero, *Somnium Scipionis* (*c.* 50 BCE)

in music's inclusion in the *Quadrivium*, the medieval curriculum that included arithmetic, geometry, music, and astronomy, and along with the *Trivium* (grammar, logic, and rhetoric) made up the seven free arts, which are still the basis for higher education today. The term "music of the spheres" also appeared during the eighteenth century in connection with psychoanalysis, in which it was used as a metaphor to explain the relationship between self and the world.

Modern physics has renewed interest in the concept. Using music as a metaphor for string theory, physicist Brian Greene (*b.* 1963) compared resonating particles to the different tones generated by a violin string. Most recently, NASA's Chandra X-ray Observatory detected sound waves from a black hole with a frequency of fifty-seven octaves below middle C. **PB**

An engraving of Apollo presiding over the Music of the Spheres (1496) by Franchino Gaffurio. ➡

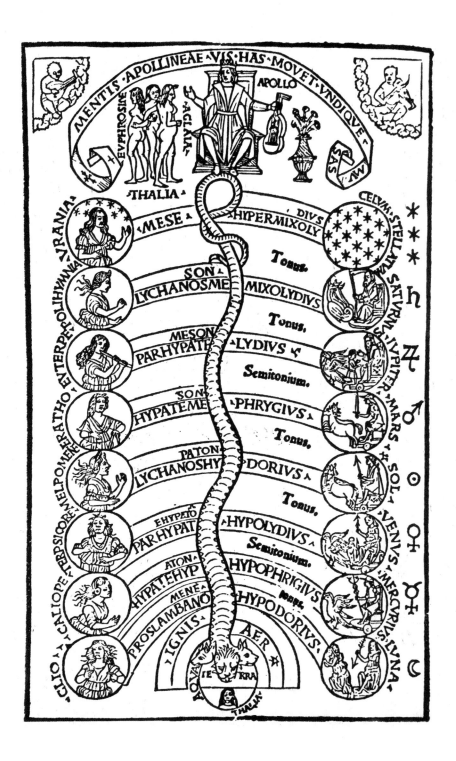

Arhat
Siddhartha Gautama (Buddha)

A being who has attained enlightenment, characterized by the qualities of profound wisdom and compassion

⬆ A painting of an *arhat* sitting and reading by Guanxiu, a celebrated Buddhist monk, painter, poet, and calligrapher of the ninth century.

The notion of the *arhat* was developed by Siddhartha Gautama (*c.* 563–483 BCE), the historical Buddha, during the sixth century BCE. It was expounded in the Lotus, Heart, and Diamond Sutras and remains a core tenet of Buddhist philosophy.

Arhat literally means "holy one" or "worthy one" and refers to a person who has attained enlightenment through diligent practice. The Buddha taught that the world is characterized by *duhkha*, which can be translated as "suffering," "sorrow," or "profound unsatisfactoriness." Our ignorant attachment to false ideals causes us to act selfishly, which results in *karma* (a force generated by a person's actions), which in turn binds us to *samsara*, the cycle of rebirth. However, if we cultivate ourselves with regard to wisdom, compassion, and meditation, we can wipe out the ignorance and see reality as an impermanent process in which all things are fundamentally interdependent. Once awakened to this truth, a person attains enlightenment and eradicates all *karma*, attaining *arhat* status. When *arhats* die, there is no *karma* to bind them to *samsara*, so they enter a state of blissful oblivion, free from the endless torment of reincarnation. *Arhats* are characterized by profound wisdom and compassion, and they typically act as teachers for other Buddhists before they die and forever exit the cycle of rebirth.

In the Theravada tradition, the *arhat* is considered to be the goal of spiritual cultivation. The term is also used in Jainism to represent a spiritual being who embodies purity. Mahayana Buddhism does not embrace the notion that the *arhat* is the final stage; a person who has attained enlightenment is expected to take the *bodhisattva* vow to remain in *samsara* until all sentient beings are awakened. This divergence of opinion remains one of the key differences between the Theravada and Mahayana traditions. **JM**

> *"Can an Arhat have the thought, 'Have I attained the Way of the Arhat?'"*

The Diamond Sutra

Comedy
Ancient Greece

A lighthearted narrative intended to amuse rather than enlighten the audience

A comedy is a drama—or a narrative—intended to amuse or delight. It generally features a happy ending for its protagonist, is typically located in a familiar setting and uses colloquial diction, and often flatters the audience with a sense of superiority to the characters. The tradition of dramatic comedy arose in c. 510 BCE in ancient Greece, around the time that the foundations of democracy were being laid. Political and social satire was a key feature of early comedy, together with slapstick action and scatological and sexual jokes.

In ancient Greece, the greatest comedies were those of Aristophanes (c. 450–c. 388 BCE), whose plays combined philosophical speculation and political satire, and Menander (c. 342–c. 292 BCE), whose "New Comedy" style, involving young lovers and stock characters, was influential on Roman playwrights such as Plautus and Terence, and later on William Shakespeare and Lope de Vega in the sixteenth and seventeenth centuries. In modern drama, comedy has proliferated and diversified with bewildering variety. Important types of comedy are often identified as romantic comedy, with lovers overcoming misunderstandings and obstacles to achieve a happy union; satiric comedy, with criticisms of persons or practices underlying the humor; the comedy of manners, with witty dialogue in a sophisticated milieu; and farce, with sexual innuendo, physical humor, and unsubtle wordplay. These examples are by no means exhaustive. With the advent of cinema, there came screwball comedy; with the advent of television, there came situation comedy. In modern times, comedy also succeeded in colonizing newer art forms, such as novels and essays.

Unlike tragedy, its counterpoint, comedy is still going strong in the twenty-first century, both in drama and elsewhere. It has even inspired new art forms, such as stand-up comedy. **GB**

Freedom of Speech
Ancient Greece

The right to speak freely without fear of reprisals from others

Freedom of speech—the ability to express ideas without fear of violent repercussions—predates many other "natural" human rights, and arguably became a political issue in ancient Athens when discussions about how to structure democracy were underway in c. 508 BCE. Since that time, freedom of speech has been debated and legislated in almost every Western political context for almost every generation. The struggle to keep speech free will likely never cease so long as communication technologies and voice boxes allow people to put their words out into the world.

Democracy relies on a plurality of ideas and the effective communication of those ideas, so the Athenians were invested in making sure that citizens—at that time aristocratic males—had the ability to

> *"Give me the liberty to know, to utter, and to argue freely according to conscience …"*
>
> **John Milton, poet**

speak without fear of reprisal from their dissenting neighbors. The societies that rose and fell subsequent to Athens also encoded freedom of speech to varying degrees. The better laws, such as England's Bill of Rights in 1689 and the United States' Bill of Rights in 1789, declared freedom of speech for all citizens. Efforts to censor voices arguing against standing powers proved dangerous to the wellbeing of the society, and the persistence of the negative consequences of censorship led to the encoding of freedom of speech in the Universal Declaration of Human Rights in 1948.

Today, freedom of speech is a slippery freedom to realize completely, since there are laws against libel, slander, obscenity, and copyright violation. However, in an increasingly connected world, discussions about freedom of speech remain pertinent. **MK**

Democracy
Ancient Greece

A state in which citizens can vote to determine its policies, leaders, and laws

A democratic state is one in which citizens have the ability to vote in order to determine laws, choose elected officials, or otherwise influence governmental activity. This definition includes several types of governments, such as those in which citizens have direct influence over policies, laws, or elections, and those in which voters choose representatives to make such decisions.

Democracy's roots extend to the ancient Greek city of Athens, where in 508 BCE the form of government first appeared under the leadership of Cleisthenes (c. 570–after 508 BCE). Athenian democracy faded near the end of the fourth century BCE, though democratic principles lived on during the Roman Republic (509–27 BCE). After the end of the Republic, it was not until the formation of the first modern democracies that this type of

"Elections belong to the people. It's their decision."

Abraham Lincoln, U.S. president 1861–65

government returned. The Corsican Republic became the first modern democracy in 1755 when it adopted a national constitution based on democratic principles. Though it ceased to exist in 1769, it was followed shortly after by the founding of the United States of America (1776) and the French First Republic (1792).

Prior to democracies, only a select few had the ability to direct the politics and actions of most states. Governments ruled by nobles, the wealthy, clerics, or other small groups of people concentrated their power, while those over whom they ruled had little say or influence over state decisions. With democracy, all eligible members of the community could vote and have at least a small influence on its direction. Since its reintroduction in the late eighteenth century, democracy has continued to spread around the world. **MT**

Eternal Flux
Heraclitus

The concept that the world is in a constant state of change

Eternal flux is a state in which there is always change and nothing remains the same. The first exposition of eternal flux is traditionally attributed to the ancient Greek philosopher Heraclitus (c. 540–480 BCE). Heraclitus was nicknamed "the obscure," and only fragments of his work survive, so it is difficult to be sure about what he had in mind. According to a traditional reading, Heraclitus embraced a radical form of eternal flux: everything is changing at every time. In Plato's dialogue *Cratylus* (c. 360 BCE), Socrates says, "Heraclitus, I believe, says that all things pass and nothing stays . . . he says you could not step twice into the same river." In response, he argued that if the objects of knowledge are constantly changing, then knowledge is impossible. Modern scholars are inclined, though not

"Everything is in a state of flux, including the status quo."

Robert Byrne, author

unanimously, to read Heraclitus as embracing eternal flux in a less radical form: allowing that there is stability but insisting that there is flux underneath it. A river is the same river moment from moment because it is composed of flowing water.

In its radical form, the idea of eternal flux was directly influential on Plato (c. 428–c. 348 BCE), who regarded the ordinary world as in flux and whose Theory of Forms was intended to locate the objects of knowledge in a changeless realm. The idea of a world in constant change recurs throughout history of philosophy, and the obscure Heraclitean fragments lend themselves to various different uses. Notable philosophers who have expressed a debt to Heraclitus's idea of eternal flux include G. W. F. Hegel, Friedrich Nietzsche, and Alfred North Whitehead. **GB**

The *bema* of Pnyx, the speakers' platform for democratic assemblies held in ancient Athens from 508 BCE.

Rational / Irrational Numbers
Ancient Greece

The distinction between numbers that can be written as fractions and those that cannot

The Latin word *ratio* comes from the Greek *logos*, meaning "word" or "reason." But the Latin concept of ratio, a relationship between two numbers of the same kind, is better thought of in terms of "proportion." Ratios are most often expressed as fractions (½; ¾) or as relationships of scale (1:2; 1:120). A rational number is a number that can be written as the ratio of whole numbers. It is either the quotient of the division of two integers of which the denominator is not zero (2 is the quotient of 2/1 and 6/3, for example) or the fraction made by two integers (⅓; ⅖). Every whole integer (-1; 3) or finite or repeating decimal expansion (.5; .3333 . . .) is a rational number.

However, not every number is rational, and this discovery troubled ancient mathematicians. The Pythagoreans of the early fifth century BCE were

"God made the integers; all else is the work of man."

Leopold Kronecker, mathematician

convinced that numbers are divine and that God and his creation must be complete and intelligible. The possibility of $\sqrt{2}$ and π, whose decimal places expand infinitely and in non-repeating patterns, led to scandal. The Greeks called these numbers *a-logos* (not reasonable); Persian mathematician Al-Khowârizmî (780–850) later called ratios either "audible" (expressible) or "inaudible" (inexpressible).

However controversial, these numbers were vital to mathematics and became highly important in discussions of infinity and calculus. The term "irrational" can be traced firmly to 1585, although some cite an earlier date. The key developments, however, occurred in nineteenth-century transfinite mathematics. Richard Dedekind (1831–1916), for example, developed a way of identifying "real" (irrational) numbers, known as the "Dedekind cut." **JW**

Confucian Virtues
Confucius

The ideal society is developed through the cultivation of five moral virtues

Confucianism is a Chinese philosophical tradition that was founded in the sixth century BCE. The chaos of the Zhou dynasty (1122–256 BCE) made Confucius (551–479 BCE) wonder how China could return to the halcyon days of the Shang dynasty (1766–1122 BCE). He argued that moral virtue was the foundation of a good state.

There are many Confucian virtues, but five are typically considered essential: *ren, yi, li, xiao,* and *xin*. *Ren* translates as "benevolence" or "humaneness," and refers to the moral sentiments that make us sensitive to the distress of others and to our moral responsibilities. *Yi* refers to the general ethical principles that guide virtuous action and help resolve moral disputes. *Li* concerns the observance of the customs and rituals that facilitate harmonious social interaction.

"The excellence required to hit the mark in the everyday is of the highest order."

Confucius, *Analects 6.29*

Xiao promotes filial piety, a respect for the hierarchical relationships that govern human life. *Xin* is the virtue of honesty, fidelity, integrity, or trustworthiness. A person should cultivate these five virtues with the goal of becoming a *junzi*, or exemplary person. If a state is ruled by exemplary persons and populated by citizens who strive to cultivate the virtues, it will be harmonious and prosperous. Rulers should lead by example and educate their citizens so that harsh laws are unnecessary.

Confucius is arguably the most influential Chinese thinker of all time. His political philosophy dominated Chinese government until the Cultural Revolution of the twentieth century. Neo-Confucian thought also heavily influenced Japanese philosophy and politics during the samurai era. Today, the Confucian virtue ethic continues to be pervasive throughout East Asia. **JM**

A portrait of the Chinese philosopher Confucius, painted with gouache on paper in *c.* 1770. ➡

至聖孔子

名丘字仲尼山東
兗州府曲阜縣人

Innatism
Ancient Greece

The mind is born with knowledge/ideas, rather than beginning as a "blank slate"

How do we come to know objects as independent (distinct from our minds) and discrete (distinct from one another) entities? One explanation is that we perceive objects as they impress themselves onto our senses. Atomists such as Democritus (c. 460–c. 370 BCE) claimed that objects are clusters of tiny particles, and we perceive them because other atoms bounce from them onto our senses. Another explanation is innatism, that ideas of objects exist in our minds when we are born and are later revealed through reason and experience.

Innatism can be traced to the Pythagoreans in the late sixth century BCE, and Socrates (c. 470–399 BCE) defended the idea by demonstrating that an uneducated child can use the Pythagorean theorem if asked the right questions. In *Meditations on First Philosophy* (1641), René

"We do not learn, and that what we call learning is only a process of recollection."

Plato, *Meno* (fourth century BCE)

Descartes (1596–1650) used wax to show that our senses relay only ideas of properties, and not ideas of objects. After holding wax to a flame, we come to experience different sets of properties at different times; it is no longer the same shape, size, or temperature as before. Yet we still say it is wax—even the same wax!

Innatism has been influential in education and psychology. For example, the "Socratic Method" of teaching developed from the belief that learning is a process of reminding students of their innate knowledge. Despite innatism's popularity, in the seventeenth century, philosopher John Locke argued powerfully that it is more plausible to believe all of our ideas are imprinted on the "blank slate" of our minds by experience; psychologists now work largely under this assumption. **JW**

Intellectual Property
Ancient Greece

Intangible assets owned by their creator in the same way as they own physical property

Intellectual property relates to intangible assets that people create or invent. The concept has existed since classical times when, in about 500 BCE, Greek chefs in southern Italy obtained the exclusive right to prepare a popular dish. Yet it was not until 1474 that the Venetian Republic adopted an intellectual property law that contained most of the provisions found in modern statutes. In addition to recognizing the rights of an inventor, the law provided penalties for infringement, gave incentives for inventors to seek patents, and imposed a time limit on the length of any patent granted. In 1867, the North German Confederation enacted a Constitution that first used the term "intellectual property."

With the creation of intellectual property, the notion of what property is transcended the material or tangible. People could own thoughts, ideas, creations, or artistic works. By extension, providing a way to protect creative endeavors allowed people to pursue them with the knowledge that if their efforts bore fruit, they would reap the benefits in the same manner as if they had toiled at a physical creation. At the same time, limitations on intellectual property rights balanced the creator's right to benefit solely against society's interest in benefiting from a new creation.

Modern intellectual property recognizes several different types, including copyrights for written or artistic works, patents for inventions, trademarks for slogans or symbols, and trade secrets for processes or business practices. In 1967 the World Intellectual Property Organization was established to promote the worldwide protection of intellectual property. It became a specialized agency of the United Nations in December 1974, and today counts more than 180 countries among its members. **MT**

Roman Gods
Ancient Rome

The gods and goddesses worshipped by the people of ancient Rome, each of whom oversaw a different aspect of human life

Ancient Rome, from its origins as a republic to its growth as an empire, existed for nearly 1,000 years, from around 500 BCE until the fall of the western empire in 476 CE. During that time the ancient Romans worshipped a variety of gods, many of whom were incorporated from the religions of cultures that they had conquered.

The Romans believed in a number of different gods, some taken from early Latin tribes and the Etruscan civilization, but many adopted from the ancient Greek colonies of southern Italy. In their adoption of the Greek pantheon, the Romans replaced the Greek names of the gods with Latin ones, for example renaming the Greek messenger god Hermes as the Roman god Mercury, and the Greek god Zeus as the Roman Jupiter, or Jove.

The Romans had a polytheistic religion, with multiple gods that were each responsible for different powers or purposes: Mars was the god of war and Venus was the goddess of love and beauty, for example. The gods were believed to be humanistic in their form, and were described in Roman mythology as being related to each other as a family.

For the Romans, the gods had a very practical, daily impact on their lives. A sea voyage might necessitate honoring the god of the ocean, Neptune, while moving to a new home or preparing for the birth of a child might require sacrifices or rituals to any number of other gods. This day-to-day, almost businesslike, interaction between an individual and the divinity was not so much an exercise in spirituality as much as it was an attempt to control or influence the divine forces in daily life. When Christianity appeared in the Empire in the first century CE, it required a very different set of beliefs and assumptions about the nature of humanity's relationship with the divine, a belief system that the Romans initially greeted with skepticism and overt hostility. **MT**

⬆ A second-century statue of the Roman god Jupiter. Jupiter was the chief deity in Roman mythology, and was also the god of sky and thunder.

"It is convenient there be gods, and, as it is convenient, let us believe that there are."

Ovid, Roman poet

The Golden Ratio

Unknown

A number that is inherent in the formation of aesthetically pleasing art or architecture

The golden ratio is an irrational number that has fascinated physicists, mathematicians, architects, and philosophers ever since its discovery. An irrational number is a number that possesses an infinite number of decimal points and is not repetitive. The number—1.61803398874989484820—was used by the ancient Greeks as the desired ratio of length in relation to width, and provided the foundational formula for the construction of much of that civilization's architecture, such as the Parthenon (447–438 BCE).

The use of the ratio most probably predated ancient Greece, with some scholars suggesting that the ancient Egyptian builders of the pyramids at Giza (2520–2472 BCE) used it to determine the final dimensions of the pyramids. However, it was not until the work of ancient Greek mathematicians in around 500 BCE that the golden ratio was first formally described and studied.

As a number, the golden ratio is usually rounded down to 1.618. Expressed simply, it is achieved if a line is divided into two parts at the point where the longer of the two parts, divided by the smaller part, is equal to the entire length divided by the longer part. For the Greeks, the golden ratio was also the basis of the "golden rectangle," the most aesthetically pleasing of all possible rectangles. This rectangle was given the name "phi" in honor of the Greek sculptor Phidias (c. 480–430 BCE), whose work was greatly influenced by application of the irrational number.

Leonardo da Vinci referred to the golden ratio as the "divine proportion," and applied its principles in some of his paintings, including *The Last Supper* (1495–98). There seems to be no end to its applications. Even in the twenty-first century, plastic surgeons reportedly use it as a template for creating perfect, symmetrical faces, much as Leonardo himself was said to have done in order to construct the beguiling face of Lisa Gherardini, model for the *Mona Lisa* (1503–06). **BS**

The Parthenon (built in 447–438 BCE) in Athens, Greece, was designed according to the golden ratio.

Religious Pluralism
Ancient Rome

Tolerance toward different religious beliefs and practices

In general terms, religious pluralism is an attitude of tolerance toward any and all religions in the world. In political terms, religious pluralism is a state structure permissive of any and all religious beliefs and practices so long as they do not come into conflict with the laws governing the said state. Religious pluralism is enshrined in the First Amendment to the Constitution of the United States (1791), in the Canadian Charter of Rights and Freedoms (1982), and in the United Nations Universal Declaration of Human Rights (1948).

Ancient Rome (c. 500 BCE–c. 500 CE) is often cited as one of the first states that embraced religious pluralism. Being a polytheistic society, Rome was already predisposed to religious pluralism. Although its rules and

procedures for governance and jurisprudence inculcated various tenets of a traditional religion, alternative religions were also tolerated, except in cases in which their practice was perceived as an act of rebellion.

Religious pluralism also existed in Spain during the Umayyad dynasty. After escaping the political and religious turmoil of Damascus in 750 CE, 'Abd al-Rahmān I (731–788) governed the Muslim occupied regions of Spain. Despite occasional clashes between Christians and Muslims, Jewish and Christian populations enjoyed most of the same rights and freedoms as did the Muslim population during al-Rahmān's rule, and throughout the reign of the ensuing dynasty.

Contemporary theorist John Hick (1922–2012) was a strong advocate of religious pluralism. He argued that all truth claims concerning God relate not to the god itself but to one's subjective experience of God. According to Hick, the world is religiously ambiguous; it can be experienced either religiously or non-religiously and according to any number of culturally conditioned religious traditions. The world offers no positive support for any one religion. For this reason, all religions should be tolerated if not embraced. **DM**

⬆ The Temple of All Religions in Kazan, Russia, features architecture from the world's major religions.

Demons
Ancient Greece

Spirits that act in the world as a force of evil and malevolence

A demon is a form of spiritual being that is found in most of the world's religions and is commonly associated with an evil force such as the Devil. The origins of this idea can be traced back to ancient Greece, although the original Greek word for "demon," *daimon*, did not carry with it the negative connotations that it has today. The word *daimon* was instead used to describe spirits of both a malevolent and benevolent nature. However, the subsequent adaptation of the idea by the early Abrahamic religions stripped it of this neutral status, and thus the modern word "demon" refers exclusively to evil or malevolent spirits.

The demons of different religions arise in a variety of forms, often with names designating their distinctive features, such as the Se'irim, or "hairy beings," of the

"Never trust a demon. He has a hundred motives for anything he does . . . "

Neil Gaiman, *The Sandman, Vol.1* (1988)

Hebrew Bible. In many religious traditions, demons are believed to be capable of "possessing" a person, place, or object. This has given rise throughout history to the practice of exorcism, whereby a demonic presence is expelled from the person or place it is inhabiting through a series of rituals performed by a priest or other spiritually qualified person.

Exorcism is still an official practice of the Catholic Church today, and belief in demons continues to be a feature of many religious doctrines across the world. An exception to this is the Baha'i Faith, which treats the development of "demonic" traits in people as a psychological manifestation of their personal failure to follow God. Traditions of the occult such as Wicca, on the other hand, treat demons as real beings but see them as possible to manipulate and control. **LWa**

Eternal Stasis
Parmenides

The idea of a world in which nothing ever changes

Eternal stasis is a state in which there never was, never is, and never will be change. The first exposition of eternal stasis was a work of verse called *On Nature*, by the early fifth-century BCE Greek philosopher Parmenides of Elea. Parmenides argued for a form of monism, the idea that there is only one thing. And what exists, he argued, is unique, ungenerated, indestructible, and incapable of motion or change. Multiplicity and change are illusions.

Parmenides changed the course of Greek cosmology. Before him, the reality of change was assumed; after him, it was a challenge. A few philosophers agreed with him, with Zeno (*c.* 495–430 BCE) notably advancing subtle arguments to show the impossibility of change. Other philosophers rejected his monism: by allowing multiplicity of elements (as with Empedocles) or

"What Is is ungenerated and deathless, whole and uniform, and still and perfect."

Parmenides of Elea, *On Nature* (*c.* 480 BCE)

atoms (as with Democritus), they also allowed change. However, the Parmenidean idea that the changeless is superior to the changeable persisted. It was reflected in Plato's (*c.* 428–*c.* 348 BCE) influential Theory of Forms, according to which objects in the changing world are imperfect approximations of the changeless "Forms." It was also reflected in astronomy, in which the heavens were regarded as changeless until the astronomical revolution of Copernicus, Kepler, and Galileo in the sixteenth and seventeenth centuries.

In philosophy, arguments against the reality of change resurged briefly around the turn of the twentieth century in the work of the British idealists F. H. Bradley and John McTaggart. The idea of a superior realm of the changeless persists, typically in connection with theology, mathematics, and ethics. **GB**

Outer Space
Leucippus

The physical universe beyond the Earth's atmosphere

↑ An illustration from Otto von Guericke's *Experimenta Nova Magdeburgica de Vacuo Spatio* (1672), which included details of his experiments with vacuums.

Outer space is the empty (or virtually empty) space that exists between astronomical bodies; on Earth, it is conventionally regarded as beginning 62 miles (100 km) above sea level. Probably the first thinker to conceive of astronomical bodies as separated by empty space was the ancient Greek philosopher Leucippus (*fl.* early fifth century BCE). The originator of the atomic theory, Leucippus held that all that exists is atoms and the void. His theory stated that the Earth was formed when a group of atoms in the void became isolated, whirled around one another, and separated by shape and size, with the heavier forming a spherical mass. The process was not considered unique, and the atomists argued that there were innumerable such worlds, separated by the void.

The idea of such a vacuum was problematic in ancient Greek philosophy, however, and in the fourth century BCE Aristotle (384–322 BCE) influentially argued against its possibility, contending that it was plagued by inconsistency and absurdity and was unhelpful in explaining physical phenomena. His arguments were taken as decisive throughout the Middle Ages. In the Renaissance, however, thanks to the rediscovery of such texts as the Roman atomist Lucretius's *De Rerum Natura* (*c.* 50 BCE) and to experiments carried out by early physicists, the idea began to be taken seriously again. In 1672, Otto von Guericke argued for the reality of vacuum and explicitly contended that "beyond or above the region of air, there begins a pure space void of every body."

As astronomical discoveries progressed, the estimated size of outer space steadily increased. And exploration of outer space began in the 1950s, with humans traversing the void and landing on the moon in 1969. Such scientific and technological advances have brought with them international laws to ensure that human use of outer space remains peaceful. **GB**

"Space is only 80 miles from every person on Earth—far closer than most people are to their own national capitals."

Daniel Deudney, *Space: The High Frontier in Perspective* (1982)

Nothingness
Parmenides

The concept of something that does not exist

Nothingness—the property or state of being nothing—is anything but a simple idea. The ancient Greek philosopher Parmenides (*fl.* early fifth century BCE) was the first to introduce the idea of nothingness, only to reject it as unthinkable. On that basis, he reached various striking conclusions, particularly monism: the idea that there is only one thing.

After Parmenides, the idea of nothingness—and cognate ideas, such as the void—took several turns. In physics, although the ancient atomists held that the world consisted of atoms in a void, Aristotle (384–322 BCE) argued for the impossibility of a void, and his views were accepted until the idea of empty space was rehabilitated in the Scientific Revolution (*c.* 1550–1700). Whether empty space counts as nothing according to contemporary physics is debatable: even when there is no matter in a region of space, it will still have measurable properties. In Western theology, early Christian theologians developed the idea that God created the world ex nihilo, out of nothing, as opposed to from pre-existing materials; in the eighteenth century, philosopher G. W. Leibniz (1646–1716) posed the question, "Why is there something instead of nothing?" and answered by invoking God. Nothingness was associated with feelings of insignificance and meaninglessness and the fear of death by existentialist philosophers in the twentieth century.

Calculating about nothing posed challenges, which were surmounted by the invention, in ninth-century India, of a positional notation including the number zero. Reasoning about nothing also posed challenges, which were at least partly surmounted by the realization that "nothing" is not a noun but a negative indefinite pronoun: to say "nothing exists" is not to ascribe existence to something named "nothing" but to deny existence to anything. **GB**

⬆ A seventeenth-century engraving of the Greek philosopher Parmenides. Parmenides is best known for his metaphysical and cosmological poem *On Nature* (*c.* 480 BCE).

"King Lear: Speak.
Cordelia: Nothing, my lord.
King Lear: Nothing!
Cordelia: Nothing.
King Lear: Nothing will come of nothing:
speak again."

William Shakespeare, *King Lear* (1606)

The Fountain of Youth
Herodotus

A mythological water source with the power of granting eternal youth

The Fountain of Youth is a mythical spring that is supposed to have the power of prolonging or restoring the youth of those who drink from or bathe in it. Myths of such a fountain are to be found in various cultures, particularly throughout the Middle East. The first recorded mention of it is from the ancient Greek historian Herodotus (c. 484–435 BCE), who recounted a claim that there was such a fountain in Ethiopia.

In the Middle Ages, stories about the Fountain of Youth circulated in the Islamic world and then spread to such European works as *The Travels of Sir John Mandeville* (c. 1356). In the sixteenth century, the Spanish historian Peter Martyr d'Anghiera, who wrote early accounts of the European exploration of the New World, reported a native story of a miraculous fountain

"The only bath in the Fountain of Youth would be … to possess other eyes."

Marcel Proust, *Remembrance of Things Past* (1913–27)

on an island in the Gulf of Honduras, an inlet of the Caribbean Sea. While the explorer Juan Ponce de León was indeed given a charter to discover and settle a legendary island (Beniny or Beimeni), the popular idea that he sought the Fountain of Youth there seems to have been invented by the sixteenth-century historian Gonzalo Fernández de Oviedo, who maliciously added that Ponce de León hoped to cure his impotence. However, the story about his search for the Fountain persists as a historical myth.

Few people take the story of the Fountain of Youth seriously today, but it remains a popular theme in literature and the arts (such as Darren Aronofsky's film *The Fountain*, 2006). It is also inevitable as a metaphor in discussing the modern concerns of prolonging lifespan and reducing the effects of aging. **GB**

Fatalism
Ancient Greece

The belief that events are predestined and nothing can alter their course

Fatalism, the belief that some events are destined to occur regardless of whatever else might occur, originated with thinkers in ancient Greece. A well-known example is the story of Oedipus from Sophocles's ancient play *Oedipus Rex* (c. 429 BCE). In the play, Oedipus seeks revenge for the murder of his former king and his wife's former husband, Laius, only to discover that Laius and his wife abandoned Oedipus as a child to escape an oracle that their son would kill his father and sleep with his mother. Yet, despite all their machinations, the prophecy had come true: Oedipus had killed his father and married his mother.

Fatalism is distinct from determinism. The latter is the view that every event is fully determined by prior events, that is, if some prior events had been different,

"Your life must now run the course that's been set for it."

Kazuo Ishiguro, *Never Let Me Go* (2005)

later events would be different. Fatalism neither implies, nor is implied by, determinism.

The ancient Greek Stoic philosophy is often linked with fatalism, though it is unclear whether it is fatalistic or deterministic. Some Stoics suggested that the universe is organized according to a single divine purpose that will be realized irrespective of what humans intend. Others argued that perfect virtue is found through learning to be guided by nature and becoming free from passions. This emphasis on learning and becoming free suggests that some events are left to individual agents. Scholars debate whether this constitutes a conceptual problem for Stoicism or fatalism. Fatalism, especially in regard to moral attitudes and happiness, remains influential in contemporary thought, notably in military training. **JW**

History
Herodotus

A branch of knowledge that records and explains past events

⬆ The title page of a Latin edition of Herodotus's *The Histories*, printed by Gregorius de Gregoriis in Venice in 1494—over 2,000 years after it was originally written.

Before the invention of writing, history remained an entirely oral phenomenon. The first known written documents, and thus those marking the boundary between the pre-historical period and the historical period, come from ancient Sumeria in approximately 3200 BCE. It was not until much later, however, that the ancient Greeks first looked at history as a field of study, something that could be examined, weighed, evaluated, and used as a tool. Herodotus (c. 484–435 BCE) is widely credited as the first person to create a historical work when, sometime during the fifth century BCE, he wrote *The Histories*.

In *The Histories*, Herodotus gave an account of the wars between the Greeks and the Persian Empire from 499 BCE to 449 BCE; in particular he sought to understand the cause of the conflict by examining the wars, and the events leading up to them, from both sides. Herodotus traveled widely in the region and interviewed numerous people in the course of compiling his work, and his style of narration is very much that of a storyteller. *The Histories* is not entirely impartial and it was dismissed by later Greek thinkers as lies. Nonetheless, it provides an extensive insight into the cultures of the Mediterranean and Middle East during that period and is still used as a leading historical source.

Humankind has likely asked questions about the past since people first became capable of recognizing that the world is not a static reality. By viewing the past as something understandable, humans created a way of expanding their understanding of themselves and the world, and gained a broader view of the concept of time. History allowed people an opportunity to experience, though not firsthand, events that would otherwise be forever unknowable. The understanding that history provides often forms a lens through which people shape their expectations, judgments, emotions, and actions. **MT**

"History is a relentless master. It has no present, only the past rushing into the future."

John F. Kennedy, U.S. president 1961–63

I Know That I Do Not Know
Socrates

The argument that knowledge is never really acquired

The well-known statement, "All I know is that I do not know," is attributed—questionably, according to some scholars—to the ancient Greek philosopher Socrates (c. 470–399 BCE), based on two dialogues written by his disciple Plato (c. 424–c. 348 BCE). In *The Republic* (c. 360 BCE), Socrates concludes a discussion with Thrasymachus on "justice" by saying, "the result of the discussion, as far as I'm concerned, is that I know nothing, for when I don't know what justice is, I'll hardly know whether it is a kind of virtue or not, or whether a person who has it is happy or unhappy." In *The Apology* (399 BCE), Socrates says of a well-respected politician that "he knows nothing, and thinks that he knows; I neither know nor think that I know."

The resulting slogan was adopted by later thinkers and incorporated into the tradition that became known as "Academic Skepticism." Rather than believing that it is impossible to know anything, Academic Skeptics actually claim only that we can know very little about reality—namely, truths of logic and mathematics. This contrasts with Pyrrhonian skepticism, which involves an attitude of doubting every positive judgment, including logic and mathematics.

A serious problem with Socrates's statements is that he seems committed to an incoherent position. If he truly does not know anything, then it is false that he knows that; but if he does know he does not know anything, then it is false that he does not know anything. Thus, the claim "I know that I do not know" is self-defeating (resulting in the statement also being known as the Socratic paradox). In response, many scholars argue that this is an uncharitable reading of Plato. They contend that Socrates's claims are expressed in a particular context, referring only to specific concepts and not to knowledge generally ("justice" in *The Republic*, and "beauty" and "goodness" in *The Apology*). **JW**

⬆ A portrait statue of Socrates from *c.* 200 BCE–100 CE. According to his pupils Plato and Xenophon, Socrates was portly and pug-nosed with fleshy lips, resembling a satyr.

"The result of the discussion, as far as I'm concerned, is that I know nothing…"

Socrates, quoted in Plato's *The Republic* (c. 360 BCE)

The Socratic Method
Socrates

A teaching method that relies on continually asking questions

The Socratic Method is a pedagogical style named after its well-known exemplar. Unlike the great sophist orators of his time and the later Aristotelian and Scholastic teachers, who disseminated information through carefully planned lectures, Socrates (c. 470–399 BCE) engaged his audience individually and personally with a series of questions. These questions were designed to elicit a reflective and mostly skeptical perspective on various philosophical, political, and religious ideas. In a well-known case, depicted in Plato's dialogue *Meno* (c. 380 BCE), Socrates used his method to "teach" an uneducated slave-boy a set of Euclidean propositions, including the Pythagorean theorem. The central assumption underlying Socrates's approach is that knowledge is innate—we do not acquire new information, instead education reminds us of what we already know.

Socrates's Method was overshadowed in the Middle Ages by the popularity of classical orators such as Aristotle and Cicero, leading to an increase of lecture-centered pedagogy known as the Scholastic Model (also called the "banking model," because it assumes knowledge can be "deposited" in a student as money in a bank). A further setback came in the seventeenth century with the rise in prominence of empiricism, the view that we come to the world as "blank slates" and must obtain knowledge through experience. Empiricism implies that innatism is mistaken, and thus challenges the pedagogy based on it.

The question of the effectiveness of the Socratic Method still receives attention from education researchers. Some contend that it constrains learning and fosters aggression. Others respond that, as with all teaching styles, the Socratic Method can be abused, but when used well it can be effective. It is still frequently applied in law schools, as memorably portrayed in the movie *The Paper Chase* (1973). **JW**

A nineteenth-century painting by Gustav Adolph Spangenberg, depicting Socrates and his disciples. ⬆

The Four Elements
Empedocles

The theory that the universe is built out of four natural elements

In his poem *On Nature* (*c.* 450 BCE), Greek poet Empedocles (*c.* 490–430 BCE) called upon a set of gods to represent the elements of his own cosmology. The notion that everything in existence is composed of earth, air, fire, and water, or a combination of these four elements, was borrowed from the ancient Babylonian creation myth, *Enuma Elish* (*c.* 1800 BCE), in which the universe emerges from conflicts between gods, each of whom represent some element or force of nature.

Empedocles was seeking what is now often referred to as a "unified field theory," a theory capable of providing the groundwork for the explanation of any given natural phenomenon. The strategy he inherited from his intellectual predecessors, such as Thales and

Anaximenes (who were themselves influenced by the Babylonian myth), was to attempt to identify the most basic ingredient, or ingredients, of the universe. In the late sixth century BCE, Thales had believed that ingredient to be water. Later, Anaximenes argued that water was too fundamentally different from certain natural phenomena (like fire) for it to be the basic ingredient of the universe. Instead, he proposed that air was the basic ingredient. Empedocles, however, saw no way to explain the vast array of natural phenomena without introducing a total of four basic ingredients: earth, air, fire, and water. These elements were what Empedocles referred to as "the four roots."

Aristotle (384–322 BCE) added a fifth element, aether. Medieval scholars learned of Empedocles's notion of the four elements via Aristotle, and Empedocles's cosmological theory dominated science until the seventeenth century. Although forms of atomism emerged as early as the fifth century BCE, it was not until the work of Sir Isaac Newton (1642–1727) and Robert Boyle (1627–91) gained a hold that the four elements were replaced by the atom (or something pretty close) as the foundation of the universe. **DM**

⬆ A fifteenth-century illustration of Christ surrounded by the four elements.

Classicism
Ancient Greece

A work of art based on principles of symmetry, proportion, and order

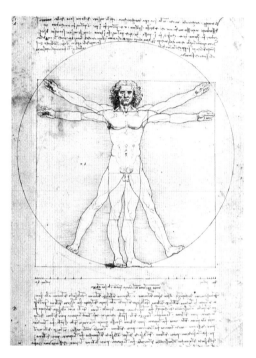

⬆ *Vitruvian Man* (*c.* 1490) by Leonardo da Vinci. The drawing is accompanied by notes based on the work of the Roman architect Vitruvius, who drew heavily on the Classical style.

"Classicism is not the manner of any fixed age or of any fixed country: it is a constant state of the artistic mind. It is a temper of security and satisfaction and patience."

James Joyce, *Ulysses* (1922)

It is common to hear of something in the arts referred to as a "Classical antique" or in "Classical style." The term "Classical" refers to an artwork created in the style of Greece in the fifth century BCE, and should evidence the principles of symmetry, proportion, and order.

For example, after writing his *Canon of Proportion* in *c.* 450 BCE, the Greek sculptor Polykleitos (*fl.* fifth and early fourth century BCE) made a bronze sculpture, the *Doryphorus*, in which he used the human head as the module for the rest of the body's measurements, following a ratio of 1:7 for the height. At much the same time, the architects of the Athenian Parthenon (447–438 BCE) used the mathematical golden ratio, or golden section, to create a system of modules, proportion, and optical corrections that enabled them to implement notions of harmony and perfection into its design. In 350 BCE the ancient Greek philosopher Aristotle (384–322 BCE), in his treatise the *Poetics*, described the structure and form of an ideal tragedy, using Sophocles's play *Oedipus Rex* (*c.* 429 BCE) as his example. And in his *Ten Books on Architecture* (*c.* 15 BCE), the Roman writer Vitruvius (*d.* after *c.* 15 BCE) returned to these Classical Greek precedents to develop his influential taxonomy and pattern book for the art of building.

When the writers, artists, and architects of the Italian Renaissance (fourteenth to sixteenth century) looked around them, believing that "man is the measure of all things," they were inspired by the monuments of Greece and Rome to abandon the soaring Gothic technologies of the Middle Ages and re-embrace the Classical style. Leonardo da Vinci's drawing *Vitruvian Man* (*c.* 1490) was derived from a passage in Vitruvius's book on geometry and human proportions; Brunelleschi's dome (1439–61) for Florence Cathedral took the Roman Pantheon for inspiration; Michelangelo's *David* (1501–04) harked back to Classical ideals. The ancient Classical style still sets a standard for artists and architects today. **PBr**

Man Is the Measure of All Things
Protagoras

A way to argue from disagreement against objectivity

"Man is the measure of all things" is a slogan that plays an important role in a particular style of argument against objective knowledge. The statement is attributed to the ancient Greek philosopher Protagoras (c. 490–420 BCE), a predecessor of Plato and the most prominent of the Sophists (a group of ancient Greek intellectuals); only fragments of his writings survive.

In Plato's dialogue *Theaetetus* (c. 360 BCE), Protagoras is represented as purporting that the truth of claims of perception is relative to the perceiver. Suppose that two people disagree about whether the wind is hot. It feels hot to person A and cold to person B. This is where the "man is the measure of all things" phrase applies: there is no way for the two to transcend their perceptions and check their judgments against reality. The best that can be said is that the wind is hot to person A and cold to person B; there is no saying that the wind is hot or cold without referring to who is perceiving it. The disagreement, therefore, is only apparent.

The resulting doctrine of relativism—the theory that knowledge is subjective according to differences in perception and consideration—also extended to claims about moral and aesthetic qualities, such as justice and beauty. While there is no evidence that Protagoras himself thought relativism was true across the board, Socrates, and later Aristotle, reasoned that his arguments committed him to thinking so and thus were self-refuting.

Similar arguments, from disagreement via the "man is the measure of all things" slogan to various forms of relativism, subjectivism, and skepticism, applied to a dizzying variety of topics, recur throughout the history of philosophy and have been the subject of spirited debate. Outside philosophy, the slogan is also used in connection with the Renaissance's reorientation from the divine to the human. **GB**

⬆ A portrait of the ancient Greek philosopher Protagoras, painted by Jusepe de Ribera in 1637. Ribera's artistic style was heavily influenced by the work of Caravaggio.

"Since then nothing is grasped apart from circumstances, each person must be trusted regarding those received in his own circumstances."

Sextus Empiricus, *Adversus mathematicos VII:62–63* (second or third century CE)

Sophism
Ancient Greece

A school of philosophy associated with moral skepticism and specious reasoning

The term "sophism" has changed greatly throughout history. In ancient Greece "sophist" was first used to refer to wise men, such as writers Homer and Hesiod. Around the fifth century BCE, sophists were depicted as untrustworthy rhetoricians, typically politicians and orators, who applied philosophical reasoning solely to practical matters. Well-known sophists of this era include Protagoras, Gorgias, and Thrasymachus. These sophists rejected the abstract theorizing of the pre-Socratics, and embraced skepticism about traditional philosophical topics. They argued that the human mind is suited only for practical skills, such as politics, public entertainment, and commerce. This practical emphasis made them effective in legal and political proceedings, and they accepted fees to teach their methods.

"Some men weave their sophistry till their own reason is entangled."

Samuel Johnson, writer

Aristophanes ridiculed sophists, regarding them as shysters and braggarts, but his rendering is unreliable because he regarded Socrates as a sophist. Socrates, while he acknowledged the sophists' practical skill, criticized them for invoking groundless distinctions and constructing faulty arguments.

In the Middle Ages, the term "sophism" inherited a more neutral dimension as "sophisma," referring to a puzzling claim needing clarification or disambiguation. Although largely retaining its negative connotation, writings called sophismata flourished at this time, analyzing conceptually problematic claims. Well-known authors of sophismata include Thomas Bradwardine and Richard Kilvington. Despite this brief respite, today sophism retains its predominantly negative connotation, referring to faulty, deceitful reasoning. **JW**

Existential Nihilism
Empedocles

There is no meaning or purpose to life and all existence

Existential nihilism posits that life has no intrinsic value or meaning. Life is simply one phenomenon of many in a universe governed by arbitrary and impartial laws. No one phenomenon is more meaningful or valuable than any other. Thus existential nihilism is an explicit rejection of the sanctity and superiority of life and any value system that is derived therefrom.

The earliest expression of existential nihilism is in the poetry of Empedocles (c. 490–430 BCE). However, its most thorough articulations are in works by Friedrich Nietzsche (1844–1900), Søren Kierkegaard (1813–55), and Jean-Paul Sartre (1905–80). Nietzsche was highly critical of the paradigms and institutions from which moral values are drawn. He berated philosophers for idolizing "Reason," denounced religion, and declared God dead.

"The life of mortals is so mean a thing as to be virtually un-life."

Empedocles

These attacks on conventional foundations of morality reinforce his underlying argument that constant reassessment of the basis of our values is necessary to avoid subverting humanity's creativity.

Sartre argued that because life has no intrinsic meaning, each individual is free to assert and affirm their own meaning through their actions. He declared "existence precedes essence," meaning that life has no meaning until a person acts in a way that bestows meaning upon themself. Furthermore, it is immoral to live life in ignorance of the existential ramifications of one's actions, and especially immoral to do so willingly.

Existential nihilism has left a lasting impression on Western culture. It reinforces the individualism and moral relativism that have become prevalent, especially in North American culture. **DM**

Moral Relativism
Ancient Greece

Objective truth does not exist; all truths depend on opinion

Moral relativism originated with the ancient Greeks in the fifth century BCE. It maintains that there is no objective moral truth and thus that all moral truths depend on the opinion of individuals. Broadly speaking, there are three versions of moral relativism: subjectivism, conventionalism, and divine command theory.

Subjectivism says morality is relative to the opinion of particular human persons. It is often confused with aesthetic preferences ("You like blondes; I like brunettes") and is thought—popularly but wrongly—to be the only way to negotiate tough ethical dilemmas.

Conventionalism says morality is relative to the opinion of a certain group. In its pragmatic form, it says the right thing to do is what keeps society stable. In its utilitarian form, it says the right thing to do is

"It is . . . the abdication of reason that is the source of moral relativism."

Peter Kreeft, professor of philosophy

what maximizes happiness for the most people. It is a type of moral relativism as its principles are socially constructed, not objectively grounded.

Divine command theory says morality is relative to the opinion of a particular god or group of gods. What distinguishes divine command theory from objective moral theories involving God (such as Natural Law theory) is that in divine command theory the god is not identical in nature to objective moral goodness.

Moral relativism usually results from a confusion between the undisputed fact of cultural relativism (different cultures often express different values) and the non sequitur that moral truths themselves are, therefore, relative. Whatever else we might think of moral relativism, its ancient roots and modern followers (especially in the West) make it an important idea. **AB**

Zeno's Arrow
Zeno of Elea

A Greek philosopher demonstrates that movement is an illusion

A pupil of the ancient Greek philosopher Parmenides, Zeno of Elea (c. 495–430 BCE) lived in a Greek colony in Italy. Although his ideas are known to us only through comments in the works of later Greek thinkers, Zeno is well-known for his teasing paradoxes.

The paradox of the arrow is a thought experiment that challenges commonsense notions of time and movement. When an arrow is shot from a bow, it appears obvious that the flying arrow moves. But Zeno denies it is ever in motion. He invites us to look at the arrow at any moment during its flight—as it were, freezing the frame. We will see that, in that instant, the arrow is at rest, statically occupying its place in space, no more no less. But the flight of the arrow is simply a succession of instants. Since in every single instant

"Zeno's arguments . . . cause much disquietude to those who try to solve them."

Aristotle, *Physics* (c. 330 BCE)

the arrow is immobile, there is never an instant when it is in motion. Our impression of the arrow moving is therefore an illusion, according to Zeno.

The implications of Zeno's vision are radical. If time is a series of static, unconnected moments, then in reality the world is unchanging and eternal, without past or future. A sensible person is, of course, loath to accept such notions. One solution to Zeno's arrow paradox seemed obvious to Aristotle. He argued that there were no "instants" of time. As he put it, "Time is not composed of indivisible moments." In other words, time flows continuously, like a stream, from the past into the future, freeing the arrow to fly to its target. But British philosopher Bertrand Russell, in the early twentieth century, accepted Zeno's arrow paradox as "a very plain statement of a very elementary fact." **RG**

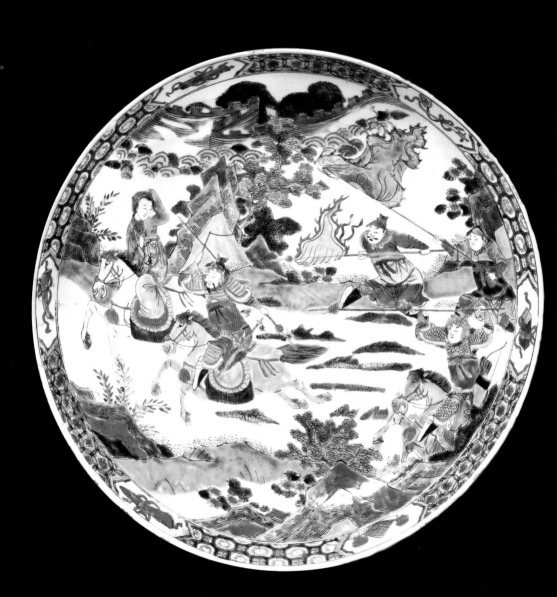

The Art of War
Sunzi

Knowledge, discipline, and deception enable you to win any battle

The *Sunzi Bing Fa* (The Art of War) was probably written during the transition between China's Spring and Autumn Period (722–481 BCE) and its Warring States Period (403–211 BCE). It is a philosophical treatise on how to manage conflict and win battles, believed to be by Chinese military general Sunzi (*fl.* fifth century BCE).

Since war necessitates the loss of lives and resources, every war is a defeat. The greatest victory is to defeat the enemy without ever having to meet them on the battlefield. War should be a last resort, and all peaceable remedies must be exhausted before resorting to violence. However, once a commitment has been made to violence, the goal is to achieve victory as quickly as possible at the minimum cost. A good commander does not resist change, but rather flows

"The supreme art of war is to subdue the enemy without fighting."

Sunzi, *The Art of War*

with the dynamic nature of the situation and turns it to his advantage. This is best achieved through knowledge of the terrain, which allows a commander to place his troops strategically in a position from which he is able to use his forces efficiently against his opponent's weak spots. A commander must know his enemy by gaining as much intelligence as possible before committing to battle. Warfare is ultimately the art of deception: discipline and knowledge will allow a commander to trick his opponents into exposing their weaknesses.

The Art of War is one of the most influential works on warfare ever written. It is required reading for officer candidates in many East Asian countries and is recommended to U.S. military personnel by the Army and Marine Corps. Business executives, lawyers, and coaches frequently use it as a strategy guide. **JM**

Casuistry
Greek Sophists

A form of reasoning that builds upon earlier precedents

Probably originating among ancient Greek teachers of rhetoric and persuasion in the mid fifth century BCE known as Sophists, casuistry, or case-based reasoning, allows a person to see new, untried arguments as analogous to older, successful ones that have set a precedent for ethical decision making. It forms the basis of English common law, which shapes the jurisprudence in many Western nations today. The idea that the law develops incrementally through social conventions is fundamental to this system of moral reasoning.

Religious groups, such as the Jesuits, have also used casuistry as the basis for their examination of individual moral questions, searching for the best precedent in the scriptures dictating moral and social codes. This type of paradigm setting is also used in the medical

"Cages for gnats, and chains to yoke a flea, Dried butterflies, and tomes of casuistry."

Alexander Pope, *The Rape of the Lock* (1712)

and bioethical fields, in which doctors build their system of practice on the success or failure of previous therapies and pharmacology.

In journalism, the term "casuistry" is usually used pejoratively—it is seen as either overgeneralization or a too subtle interpretation of general principles to defend a specific case. The special circumstances of a case may render the analogy to a previous one specious and even damaging.

The danger of biased or poorly made original cases or lack of judgment on the part of the court of public opinion is always a threat to the validity of casuistic moral reasoning. At its worst, it is considered to be the type of moral relativism and situational ethics that allows immoral acts to be used as precedent for further bad actions. **PBr**

⬅ A porcelain dish from China's Kangxi period (1654–1722), decorated with a painting of a battle scene.

Divine Command
Socrates

The idea that our moral obligations come externally from God rather than ourselves

The theory of Divine Command, which predates Christianity, is the idea that all our ethical and moral questions, actions, and concepts are fundamentally dependent upon God, who is assumed to be the originator of all goodness and morality. Thus morality is wholly based upon God's commands, and the degree to which we behave morally is inexorably linked to how faithfully we have followed God's commands in response to any given situation.

The idea of Divine Command has been criticized and debated by philosophers and intellectuals since Socrates (c. 470–399 BCE) asked his famous question: "Is the pious loved by the gods because it is pious, or is it pious because it is loved by the gods?" In other words,

does God command an action because it is right, or is it right because He commands it? Philosophers such as Immanuel Kant (1724–1804) say it is in our own best interests to believe in God, and therefore in the morality that comes from faith, because to try and live with the weight of morality's complexities would be too much for anyone to bear alone. But the theory does contain an obvious dilemma: if God commands us to hurt someone or inflict suffering, then to do so would be the morally correct thing to do. Morality suddenly becomes an arbitrary thing, just as it does in the secular world when it is reduced to obeying unquestioningly the dictates of an authority, and proponents of Divine Command theory thus find themselves facing the proposition that cruelty might be morally permissible, indeed necessary, if it is pleasing to God.

Perhaps it is the argument of the Dominican priest and theologian Thomas Aquinas (1225–74) that offers the best hope of a workable basis for morality. God created us, he wrote, in possession of a likeness of His own inner nature, and that by listening to our inner natures we are able to seek that Narrow Path which helps subdue the immoral "devil on our shoulder." **JS**

A painting (1911) of the twenty-four elders of the Bible bowing before God, by Henry John Stock. ⬆

Satire
Aristophanes

The use of entertaining ridicule to achieve social or political ends

Using humor to expose the failings of others likely dates back to the origin of humor itself. Ancient Egyptian documents contain examples of writing and art that ridicule others in society. But as a literary form, satire refers to the deployment of parody, sarcasm, or irony for the purpose of exposing failings and flaws of individuals or society. Satire often has the social or political purpose of changing its target's behavior.

The Greek playwright Aristophanes (c. 450–c. 388 BCE) is one of the best-known satirists, and was credited by his contemporaries—friends and enemies—with the development of comedic satire into an art form. His first surviving play, *The Acharnians* (c. 425 BCE), is cited as the earliest example of satirical comedy.

Beginning with Aristophanes and moving to the early satirists of the Roman Empire, satire emerged as a powerful political and social tool. Usually produced for mass consumption, satire presented political arguments in the form of entertainment, and was just as effective at influencing public opinion as any other kind of political argument. Two early Roman satirists, Horace (65–8 BCE) and Juvenal (c. 55–c. 127 CE), lend their names to a basic categorization of two types of satire. Horatian satire refers to a mild and humorous form that typically aims to expose absurdity or ridiculousness. Juvenalian satire is a more aggressive form that has less emphasis on humor and more on communicating outrage over perceived injustice or immorality.

Satire is one of the most common forms of political communication in modern politics and popular culture. Ridiculing political opponents is often an effective means of making a political or social point, and can create a lasting impression on an audience. Humorous satire offers entertainment and has become a cultural industry in print, television, and other media; examples include sketch comedies on television, and the increasingly popular "fake news" programs. **TD**

↑ An illustration from an ancient Egyptian papyrus (c. 1100 BCE) parodying scenes of human activity.

Cynicism
Antisthenes

A school of philosophy that rejected personal ambition and possessions in favor of leading a simple existence

⬆ *Diogenes* (*c.* 1860), by the French artist Jean-Léon Gérôme. The dog with him is an emblem of his cynic philosophy, which emphasized an austere existence.

"Cynic, n. A blackguard [who] sees things as they are, not as they ought to be."

Ambrose Bierce, *The Devil's Dictionary* (1906)

When we say that someone is cynical we are most often accusing that person of habitual suspicion of the claims and motivations of their fellow citizens. This colloquial meaning of the term "cynicism" most likely originates in the image of the ancient Greek philosopher Diogenes (*d. c.* 320 BCE) who, according to legend, lived as a vagabond and roamed the streets of Athens carrying a blazing lantern, even in daylight, hoping that it would help in his search for "one good man." There is more to cynicism, however, than derogatory opinions concerning human nature.

Cynicism is an ethical philosophy originating in the teachings of Antisthenes (*c.* 445–*c.* 365), one of the lesser-known students of Socrates. Cynicism teaches that the only true path to happiness is to abandon the trappings of social convention—such as the pursuit of wealth, conformity with etiquette, the desire for fame and power—and to live in agreement with nature. If, says the cynic, one abstains from making judgments based upon popular values, which are therefore false, one can achieve a state of *arete*, Greek for "virtue" or "excellence." Cynicism is therefore not a school of thought in the traditional sense, rather it can be viewed more as a way of life.

The ancient cynics—in particular, Diogenes—are also credited with developing the concept of "cosmopolitanism." Legend relates that, when asked about his political allegiances, Diogenes claimed to be a *kosmopolites*, or "a citizen of the world." This notion of world citizenship would later be taken up by Immanuel Kant (1724–1804) and expanded by Martha Nussbaum (*b.* 1947). Nussbaum argues that legitimate norms of justice govern the relationships between all persons, and not merely the relationships that exist between those who live within arbitrary political regions. This interpretation derives from ancient cynicism. **DM**

Humorism
Polybus

A system of medical diagnosis and treatment based on four bodily fluids

Humorism, or the theory of humors, revolves around the concept that physical health and mental temperament depend on the balance of four bodily fluids, or humors: black bile, yellow bile, phlegm, and blood. Polybus (fl. c. 400 BCE), the son-in-law of Hippocrates, the father of medicine, is sometimes credited with formulating the theory.

According to humorism, each of the four fluids has certain characteristics: blood and yellow bile are hot, yellow bile and black bile are dry, black bile and phlegm are cold, and phlegm and blood are wet. These correspondences were of use in both diagnosis and treatment to restore the balance of humors. For example, a dry fever might be attributed to a surplus of yellow bile and might be treated by inducing vomiting, decreasing the amount of yellow bile, or with cold baths, increasing the amount of phlegm (the cold, wet phlegm balancing out the hot, dry yellow bile). Further correspondences with various natural systems—the seasons, for example—furnished additional resources for the theory. The theory of humors also provided a theory of temperament, which is still familiar in the terms sanguine, choleric, melancholic, and phlegmatic.

Humorism was a dominant belief among physicians in the West for around 2,000 years, with proponents including the Roman physician Galen and the eleventh-century Islamic physician Avicenna. Unsurprisingly, the theory is reflected in art and literature as well, including in Michelangelo's Sistine Chapel and the plays of William Shakespeare and Ben Jonson. With the rise of modern medicine in the seventeenth century, the physiological claims of humorism were gradually rejected. The fourfold categorization of temperament continued to be influential, however, with thinkers from Immanuel Kant to Hans Eysenck discerning a measure of truth in it. **GB**

Atoms
Democritus

The fundamental pieces of the universe and the basic substance of all matter

Atoms make up everything there is. They are the tiniest possible pieces of matter and are found in everything. From this one elemental piece of primary matter, all gases, solids, liquids, and even light comes into existence. This understanding of the world was first expressed by ancient Greek philosopher Democritus (c. 460–c. 370 BCE). According to Democritus, the qualities of various types of atoms—differentiated by shape, weight, or size—explained the different properties that could be observed in different states of matter.

Democritus based his notions of atomic theory almost purely on conjecture and speculation, as he had no way of observing atomic phenomena. Similar ideas about atoms also arose in India around the same time, though it was Democritus who came up with

"Nothing exists except atoms and empty space; everything else is an opinion."
Democritus

the term "atoms." However, it was not until the late eighteenth and early nineteenth century that scientific advances allowed researchers, such as John Dalton (1766–1844), to test Democritus's atomic theory. The work of subsequent scientists led to the contemporary understanding of atoms, their component parts, and subatomic particles.

Even though atomic theory began as little more than philosophical musings, it eventually became a foundational concept of modern science. Not only did atomic theory allow for quantitative, empirical measurements of matter, it allowed researchers to make and test predictions based on their understanding of how matter was composed at the fundamental level, enabling the development of both theoretical and practical scientific applications. **MT**

The End Justifies the Means
Ancient Greece

Achieving a desired outcome can justify prior immoral actions

Many philosophers argue that to do what is right it is necessary to have a morally good reason for acting. Typically, identifying morally good reasons involves appealing to abstract principles (for example, treat everyone as an end and not simply as a means; do unto others as you would have them do unto you). To determine a sufficient principle, some philosophers appeal to pure reason (universal moral truths), while others appeal to consequences of a certain type. One traditional appeal to consequences is based on preference: if outcome Y is preferred, then act X (that produces Y) is permissible; in other words, "the end justifies the means." If the outcome of an act is desirable, the act is justified regardless of what it involves (even if it would seem immoral under other circumstances).

"[A] prince wishing to keep his state is very often forced to do evil . . ."
Niccolo Machiavelli, *The Prince* (1532)

The origin of the phrase "the end justifies the means" can be traced to the ancient literati, for example, the Greek playwright Sophocles (*c.* 496–406 BCE) and Roman poet Ovid (43 BCE–17 CE). Another well-known proponent is Italian statesman Niccolo Machiavelli (1469–1527). His work *The Prince* (1532) is a masterpiece of practical decision making, predicated on one goal: to maintain political position as long as possible. This end may require instances of lying, coercion, and killing, but, if the principle is sound, these acts are justified.

Notably, there is little reason to think desired outcomes have anything to do with moral goodness. For example, genocide and rape may be desired by some. Thus, as a moral principle it is widely considered implausible, and it is often invoked as a criticism of views that appear to imply it. **JW**

Physician-assisted Suicide
Ancient Greece

The morality of a doctor aiding the death of a patient

Physician-assisted suicide occurs when a person is provided with the means by which to bring about their own death by a physician. An early expression of this idea can be found in the Hippocratic Oath of Greek antiquity composed around 400 BCE. New medical practitioners were asked to take the oath on completion of their medical training; contained within it was the following pledge: "I will neither give a deadly drug to anybody if asked for it, nor will I make a suggestion to this effect." It is here then that we first encounter the idea of physician-assisted suicide as an issue lying at the heart of medical ethics.

Physician-assisted suicide differs from euthanasia because the latter involves ending the life of another as opposed to supplying the means by which a

"Do any of you here think it's a crime to help a suffering human end his agony?"
Jack Kevorkian, physician

person can end their own life. However, contemporary debates surrounding both practices often focus on the same issues concerning the value of life and the right to death. During the 1990s the issue of physician-assisted suicide entered the media spotlight when U.S physician Jack Kevorkian claimed to have assisted more than 130 patients to die. Kevorkian was tried four times before being convicted and sentenced to a maximum of twenty-five years in prison. However, the campaign that Kevorkian fronted for the legalisation of physician-assisted suicide is still ongoing and the practice is legal in three U.S. states and several countries in Northern Europe. Despite its ancient origins, it is clear that the issue of physician-assisted suicide continues to be both controversial and relevant in the modern world. **LWa**

◀ A Mesopotamian victory stele from *c.* 2230 BCE, showing Naram-Sin, the king of Akkad, trampling his enemies.

Perspective
Ancient Greece

A technique of depicting three-dimensional reality in two-dimensional space, providing the viewer of the image with a sense of depth

⬆ An oil painting of St. Jerome in his study by the Italian Renaissance artist Antonello da Messina, *c.* 1475, featuring a highly skilled use of perspective.

"No power on earth can keep the picture from being three-dimensional once the first line is drawn or color-plane applied."

Sheldon Cheney, author and art critic

In art, perspective is a technique that allows an artist to create a realistic representation of a three-dimensional scene or object on a two-dimensional surface. Some of the earliest evidence of the use of perspective appears in the art of ancient Greece in approximately 400 BCE. There, the use of perspective was inspired by the production of theater sets, which incorporated panels set at staggered intervals in order to create a sense of depth on stage. The Greek philosophers Anaxagoras (*c.* 500–*c.* 428 BCE) and Democritus (*c.* 460–*c.* 370 BCE), along with the mathematician Euclid (*fl. c.* 300 BCE), drew from these a set of geometrical principles that governed perspective in two-dimensional space.

By the fourteenth century CE, the basic techniques associated with perspective, such as representing distant figures as smaller than near ones, were well known. However, the art of perspective developed dramatically during the Renaissance period, when lifelike representations of people, objects, and places became the norm. The Italian artist Leon Battista Alberti (1404–72) was one of the first to offer systematic rules for the imitation of nature and the use of linear perspective, while Leonardo da Vinci (1452–1519) employed atmospheric perspective, in which light and shade help to create startlingly realistic effects.

In the modern world, perspective techniques that originated in the Renaissance find new applications in a variety of new digital media. Artists in the fields of computer-generated imagery and computer graphics are able to achieve ever more realistic and convincing representations of the world. The principles of perspective may be applied in an unprecedented blurring of the boundaries between virtual and real or non-virtual worlds. In this sense, the idea of perspective can be seen as playing a fundamental role in our modern-day experiences of reality. **LWa**

Materialism
Democritus

The idea that nothing exists independently of the material or physical world

Many ancient thinkers appeal to supernatural or extra-natural entities in order to account for certain features of the natural world. Materialists, however, deny the existence of any non-natural events, entities, or forces. Early materialists include the Greek atomists, Democritus (*c.* 460–*c.* 370 BCE) and Leucippus (*fl.* early fifth century BCE), who argued that the world consists of nothing but atoms in empty space (even the soul was thought to be composed of atoms), and Epicurus (341–270 BCE), who postulated that the atoms move only in an up–down direction.

The significance of materialism is typically found in discussions of philosophical questions, such as how to account for the properties of objects and how to explain consciousness. For example, while Plato (*c.* 424–*c.* 348 BCE) sought to explain why, say, two blue objects look exactly the same by arguing that they participate in pre-existing (*ante rem*) universals, Aristotle (384–322 BCE) argued that all universals are present in existing objects (*in re*), and was thus a materialist about properties. However, both men seem to appeal to an immaterial divine being to explain the origin of physical reality, and to an immaterial soul to explain consciousness. Thus, it was deemed possible to be a materialist about some things and not others.

The comprehensive materialism of the sort defended by the atomists gained popularity in the late nineteenth and early twentieth centuries as advancements in science reduced the apparent need for extra-natural explanations, and pluralism in mathematics challenged the idea of a unique, Platonic reality of mathematical forms. More recently, advancements in our understanding of the brain have undermined older appeals to immaterial substances or properties to explain consciousness, but they have also served to highlight the limitations of materialism. **JW**

Determinism
Leucippus

The view that all events occur as a result of prior events and the laws governing reality

Although determinism does not entail naturalism (the view that there are no extra- or supernatural causes), it is usually defined in terms of natural laws and events. Determinism should be distinguished from fatalism, which is the view that some future events will occur regardless of what happens between the present and that future time. Determinism is fatalistic, in the sense that the current state of events and the laws of nature entail that certain events will occur rather than others. But it is not identical to fatalism, which holds that these events will occur regardless of other occurrences.

The earliest version of determinism is probably best associated with the views of the atomists, Leucippus (early fifth century BCE) and Democritus (*c.* 460–*c.* 370 BCE), although Leucippus seems to allow

> *"A man can do what he wants, but not want what he wants."*

Arthur Schopenhauer, philosopher

that, in rare cases, atoms may "swerve" unaccountably. Determinism was popular with Roman stoics and found support in the physics of Isaac Newton.

Determinism is significant in the history of thought primarily in its relationship to the "free will problem," that is, the question of what sort of freedom is required for morally responsible agency. If responsibility demands that agents be free to choose among a variety of options at the moment of decision making, then determinism is incompatible with moral responsibility. And even the sort of indeterministic luck highlighted by Leucippus's swerving atoms may be incompatible with moral responsibility. However, if responsibility is a matter of internal dispositions toward actions, or "reactive attitudes," determinism may be compatible with moral responsibility. **JW**

Hippocratic Oath
Hippocrates

A seminal statement of the responsibilities of the medical profession

The Hippocratic Oath describes the duties of a physician. It is traditionally attributed to Hippocrates (c. 460–c. 375 BCE), who is credited with initiating the idea of medicine as a profession. In its original form, the oath is contained in the *Hippocratic Corpus*, a body of writing attributed to Hippocrates himself and his students.

The original Hippocratic Oath was sworn to Apollo, his son Asclepius, and Asclepius's daughters Hygieia and Panacea—the Greek mythological figures associated with healing, medicine, health, and cures. It begins with the physician's duties to fellow physicians, only later turning to their duties to patients. Centrally, the oath requires physicians to treat the sick to the best of their abilities and with their best judgment. Further clauses have been interpreted as prohibiting physicians

"I will prevent disease whenever I can, for prevention is preferable to cure."

The Hippocratic Oath (Louis Lasagna version, 1964)

from engaging in abortion, euthanasia, and surgery, although it is sometimes argued that the oath only requires physicians to avoid use of a particular means of abortion, to refrain from poisoning their patients, and to leave surgery to specialists.

Updated and modernized forms of the Hippocratic Oath are in circulation; the Declaration of Geneva (1948) and Louis Lasagna's modern version of the oath (1964) are the best known. There are also various descriptions of the duties of the physician from different ethical and religious traditions, such as the Oath of Maimonides (c. 1793). While some physicians regard statements such as the oath as valuable ethical guides, others consider them to be mere formulaic relics. In any event, physicians continue to wrangle about how to understand and codify their professional duties. **GB**

The University
Plato

An educational institution where the most learned and experienced teach others

The world's first university—a school dedicated to the pursuit of inquiry, thought, and discovery—began in a sacred olive grove outside the city of Athens. Dedicated to Athena, the goddess of wisdom, the academy of Greek philosopher Plato (c. 424–c. 348 BCE) was founded sometime around 387 BCE. The academy was a place of learning where Plato, and later others, would teach students about subjects such as philosophy and politics.

Numerous different academies were subsequently established in the ancient Greek, Roman, and Byzantine worlds. The first modern university, however, is widely recognized to be the University of Bologna. It was founded in 1088, and Holy Roman Emperor Frederick I Barbarossa later granted the school a charter, in 1158,

"There are few earthly things more beautiful than a university."

John Masefield, poet

at the same time giving university academics the right to free travel. At first, religious teachings dominated university education, but by the eighteenth and nineteenth centuries the role of churchmen in society had diminished, and much of the curriculum in many universities came to be focused instead on the study of science and the humanities.

The idea of the university is to create a place where students and teachers can freely acquire information, pursue knowledge, and make new discoveries. While everyone learns in their day-to-day lives, creating a place where higher learning is the sole pursuit has allowed for any number of advancements. There is no field of human endeavor that has not been impacted by advancements made by students or teachers who pursue knowledge in the university. **MT**

Theory
Plato

A summarized process of contemplation and understanding that can be
supported by evidence

⬆ A marble bust of Plato. Plato's work contains discussions
on aesthetics, political philosophy, theology, cosmology,
epistemology, and the philosophy of language.

The modern concept of theory derives from *theoria*, an
ancient Greek notion of contemplation and metaphorical
vision associated with wisdom. *Theoria* is a verb used
to describe a broad range of intellectual activity. Plato
(*c.* 424–*c.* 348 BCE) associated it with every stage of the
intellectual process of understanding, a process that can
be summarized afterward. Philip of Opus (*fl. c.* fourth
century BCE), a follower of Plato, restricted *theoria* to the
activity of looking at the stars, with the aim of acquiring
the divine perspective and thereby achieving tranquility.
Aristotle (384–322 BCE), another of Plato's pupils, limited
it to the act of contemplation.

The notion of obtaining a vision of reality
underwrites the contemporary concept of theory as
an account of some feature of reality that results from
careful investigation. For example, Albert Einstein's
special theory of relativity was formulated after careful
consideration of Galilean relativity and the limitations
of Newtonian physics. Similarly, Charles Darwin's
theory of natural selection was formulated after careful
consideration of the development of organisms in a
variety of environmental contexts.

Like all scientific claims, theories are subject to
new discoveries and may be overturned by more
adequate accounts. For example, although popular for
centuries, Ptolemy's geocentric theory of the cosmos
was overturned by Copernicus's heliocentric one.
And although his theory of falling objects persisted
unchallenged for 200 years and remains eminently
practical, Newtonian gravity was replaced by Einstein's
general theory of relativity. In popular usage, a
"theory" is often treated as an account that has yet
to be tested (synonymous with "hypothesis"), but in
academic circles theories are well-supported but not
infallible visions of reality that help us to explain natural
occurrences and to suggest new investigations. **JW**

*"The ultimate value of life depends
upon ... the power of contemplation."*
Aristotle, philosopher and polymath

Philosophical Realism
Plato

The idea that reality, including abstract reality, exists independently of observers

If a philosopher defends the claim that an object or event exists in some relevant sense, that philosopher is said to be a realist about that object or event. For example, if a philosopher defends the existence of numbers as abstract objects, as does Plato (*c.* 424–*c.* 348 BCE), that philosopher is a realist about numbers and abstract objects. A philosopher who denies the existence of numbers and abstract objects, such as William of Ockham (*c.* 1285–1347/49), is an anti-realist or "nominalist." Traditionally, a nominalist is an anti-realist about abstract objects or universals who asserts that the only things that exist are concrete. However, this causes some confusion when discussing medieval philosophers such as William of Ockham and Peter Abelard, who identify themselves as theists but defend the existence of an immaterial divine being. Thus, in philosophy, the term "nominalism" is commonly used synonymously with anti-realism.

It is important to note that realism need not imply objective existence; an event or object may exist even if it is only subjectively available to a subject or even if it is socially or mentally constructed, as in the case of conceptualism, although some conceptualists reject the nominalist appellation. Thus, realism allows for a wide-ranging interpretation of what may be termed "positive ontological status."

Popular debates over realism about particular objects or events include the existence of God, the nature of moral values, the effects of social and political interactions, and the nature of consciousness. One of the longest-running debates between realists and anti-realists involves the nature of properties. Indeed, a strong contemporary strain of anti-realism challenges the idea that science delivers approximate truths about reality, and contends, instead, that it delivers only a set of powerful fictions about it. **JW**

Universals and Particulars
Plato

"Particular" objects each embody a "universal" quality apparent in many objects

The idea that there are "universals" and "particulars" that might relate to one another in a certain way has plagued intellectuals since Plato (*c.* 424–*c.* 348 BCE) advanced the idea in about 390 BCE. "Particulars" are objects, such as a fire engine or pair of mittens. Fire engines and mittens, however, might both be red and thus share a common or "universal" redness. What is more significant, a particular or the universal it embodies? Is it an orange or its color, a zebra or its stripes, a golf ball or its shape? Universals can quite literally be everywhere, whereas particulars are limited to a specific entity and so are rooted in time and space.

Thinkers who hold to the primacy of universals over particulars claim that they possess a pervasive reality (the color red, or a certain geometric shape) that is

"If particulars are to have meaning, there must be universals."

Plato

quite distinct from the particulars that the universals inhabit. There are not just objects in the world that have stripes; the universality of stripes also exists. Whether universals exist is an ancient argument in metaphysics. In this debate there are nominalists, who deny they exist, and realists, who maintain that they do. Realists in the Platonic tradition claim that universals are real entities that exist independently of particulars, suggesting that we need certain universals for words to have meaning and for sentences to be either true or false. Nominalists, on the other hand, argue that only individuals or particulars are real, and that universals simply do not exist. Nominalism posits that there are relatively few kinds of entities in the universe, and by eliminating unnecessary complexities therefore offers a simpler explanation of the world around us. **JS**

Obeying Laws
Plato

Laws should be adhered to because it is immoral to disobey them

Laws—a set of rules providing a code of conduct for a community—have existed in human societies for thousands of years. Typically, disobeying a law is viewed as a crime and results in a punishment for the perpetrator, thereby providing an incentive to citizens to abide by the laws of their society. Plato (c. 424–c. 348 BCE), however, argued that a person ought to obey the law not merely to avoid punishment, but because they have a moral obligation to do so.

Written in c. 360 BCE, Plato's Crito explains why the condemned Socrates refused to escape from prison and his sentence of death despite the measures taken by his friends to ensure his safe passage. Socrates, who speaks for Plato in the text, offers a number of reasons for why obeying the law is more important than obeying one's own desires or the moral sentiments of the masses. After establishing that it is never morally permissible to do harm, Socrates argues that willfully disobeying the law harms the state by undermining the system of laws it is founded upon. Socrates then argues that it is because of the law that citizens enjoy security, education, and a number of other benefits. Furthermore, in so far as the law regulates marriage, the law is responsible for the very existence of its citizens. For these reasons, the laws are like a person's parents or masters. It is, therefore, unacceptable for anyone to harm the law through disobedience.

Plato's arguments continue to be influential today. What is especially significant is that he draws a distinction between the precepts of law and the precepts of morality, explaining why the distinction is both rational and pragmatic. Today this distinction is referred to as the "separation thesis." Modern thinkers such as Joseph Raz follow Plato when they argue that the legitimacy of law and, by extension, the social institutions it protects are contingent upon maintaining a distinction between law and morality. **DM**

A painting (1787) by Jacques-Louis David, showing Socrates after receiving his death sentence.

The Philosopher King
Plato

The idea that the ruler of a nation should be a learned philosopher

In his Socratic dialogue *The Republic*, written in c. 360 BCE, Plato (c. 424–c. 348 BCE) puts forward his theory of ideal leadership. He argues that, in the best possible world—in which humanity can form a nation or a state that pursues utopian ideals of justice, knowledge, and truth—a nation can only be led by a select type of person. That ruler, called the "philosopher king," must be first and foremost concerned with the pursuit of wisdom, arrived at through philosophy.

In *The Republic*, Plato describes an idealistic state named Kallipolis, ruled by wise guardians, or philosopher kings. For Plato, a philosopher was a person who pursued truth and maintained a detachment from factors irrelevant to that pursuit. A

philosopher king focuses only on that which is truly important. For Plato, this meant that a leader must develop an understanding of fundamental truths, or forms, and not submit to the whims of popular opinion. Just as a ship's captain with knowledge of celestial navigation must not pay attention to the derision of sailors who have no such understanding, so too must the philosopher king maintain the pursuit of justice and wisdom as he pilots the ship of state.

The Republic, along with its ideas of a utopian society and ideal rulers, has been one of the most influential works about political theory and justice in the Western world. The idea of the philosopher king has shaped how people have thought about political leadership and the role of government, and about how ideal leaders should act, think, and govern. However, some critics, such as British philosopher Karl Popper (1902–94), have decried the idea of rulers permitted to ignore the opinions and wishes of the people. The concept of the philosopher king implies no safeguard against tyrannical individuals who impose their own ideals of leadership, and it is therefore antithetical to the idea of an open society. **MT**

⬆ A fragment of Plato's *The Republic* (c. 360 BCE), his great work of philosophy and political theory.

The Great Chain of Being
Plato

The belief that everything in creation, including living things, fits into a hierarchy

In *The Republic* (*c.* 360 BCE), Plato (*c.* 424–*c.* 348 BCE) uses the idea of a single vertical line to represent all of existence. Plato divides the line into quarters: the topmost quarter represents concepts or ideas, such as justice or piety. The next quarter represents mathematical relationships. The third quarter represents tangible things, such as apples, horses, and carts. Finally, in the lowest quarter, are imitations: artistic imagery, reflections, and things of that sort.

Plato's line represents a hierarchy. Ideas, says Plato, are timeless, indestructible, and dependent upon nothing else for their existence; they therefore exist to the fullest extent. Conversely, imitations are finite, and corruptible, and they depend upon other things; they are therefore the lowest sort of beings.

"It is the possession of sensation that leads us … to speak of living things as animals."

Aristotle, *De Anima* (fourth century BCE)

Plato's student Aristotle (384–322 BCE) elaborated on this. He established a hierarchy of living things, ranking those creatures possessing the powers of thought, sensation, self-propulsion, and self-nutrition higher than creatures possessing fewer of these "vital powers." Humans, then, occupy the top, and plant life the bottom.

Medieval thinkers added divine beings to the hierarchy, placing God at the pinnacle and an array of angels and archangels between God and humankind. Thus, what started out as Plato's vertical line came to be known as the "Great Chain of Being."

Contemporary evolution theory has adopted and adapted the idea. What Aristotle calls "vital powers" have undergone serious reconsideration, giving rise to animal and environmental rights movements and the re-evaluation of humanity's role in the universe. **DM**

Justified True Belief
Plato

Knowledge consists of beliefs that are objectively true and can be justified

The most widely accepted account of knowledge is mental assent to a proposition that is true on the basis of evidence sufficient for thinking that proposition is true. "Mental assent" refers to the psychological attitude "belief," and "evidence sufficient for thinking a proposition is true" refers to "justification." Thus, knowledge is justified true belief.

Originating in the dialogue *Theaetetus* (*c.* 360 BCE) by Plato (*c.* 424–*c.* 348 BCE), this account was criticized by Socrates with regard to knowledge derived from the senses. The definition refers only to propositional knowledge ("I know that Mozart was a composer."). It is unclear how it might relate to skill-based knowledge ("I know how to play Mozart's 'Adagio in C.'") or knowledge by acquaintance ("I know [of] Mozart's 'Adagio in C.'").

"If one cannot give and receive an account of a thing, one has no knowledge of [it]."

Plato, *Theaetetus* (*c.* 360 BCE)

An important challenge to this theory of knowledge as justified true belief is the "Gettier problem." It was first offered by Bertrand Russell (1872–1970), but made famous by Edmund Gettier (*b.* 1927). Russell and Gettier constructed examples to show that someone may have a justified true belief without having knowledge. Russell imagined someone, S, who believes truly that it is noon on the basis of looking at a clock. However, S does not know that this clock stopped working exactly twelve hours ago. So, even though it is noon, S has good reason to believe it is noon, and S believes for this reason that it is noon, it seems S does not know it is noon. These "Gettier cases" sparked a number of revisions and additions to the classical theory of knowledge, and the quest for a satisfactory account of knowledge continues. **JW**

Absolute Power Corrupts Absolutely
Plato

The view that possession of absolute power inevitably has a corrupting effect

⬆ A detail from Ambrogio Lorenzetti's fresco *Bad Government and the Effects of Bad Government on the City Life* (1337–39), located in the Palazzo Pubblico, Siena, Italy.

> *"Power tends to corrupt, and absolute power corrupts absolutely . . . There is no worse heresy than that the office sanctifies the holder of it."*
>
> Sir John Dalberg-Acton, letter to Bishop Mandell Creighton (1887)

Probably the most ancient expression of the idea that power has a corruptive effect appears in the parable of the Ring of Gyges in *The Republic* (*c.* 360 BCE) by Plato (*c.* 424–*c.* 348 BCE). In the parable, the otherwise virtuous Gyges indulges in corrupt behavior after finding a magic ring that renders him invisible.

However, the maxim "absolute power corrupts absolutely" originates much later, being a paraphrase of a letter written by Sir John Dalberg-Acton (1834–1902), a British Catholic historian better known as Lord Acton, to Bishop Mandell Creighton in 1887. Acton scolds Creighton in the letter for his suggestion, in previous correspondence, that the pope, king, or any other person holding comparably high station ought to be judged according to standards different to those applied to common men. Acton argues that, quite to the contrary, "Historic responsibility has to make up for the want of legal responsibility. Power tends to corrupt, and absolute power corrupts absolutely."

Acton, however, followed at least two distinguished persons in associating power with corruption: in a speech that was delivered in the British House of Commons in 1770, Prime Minister William Pitt, Earl of Chatham (1708–78), had claimed that, "Unlimited power is apt to corrupt the minds of those who possess it; and this I know, my Lords, that where law ends, tyranny begins!" Acton's observation was also anticipated by French writer, poet, and politician Alphonse Marie Louis de Prat de Lamartine (1790–1869), who, in his essay *France and England: a Vision of the Future* (1848), had claimed "It is not only the slave or serf who is ameliorated in becoming free . . . the master himself did not gain less in every point of view . . . for absolute power corrupts the best natures." Acton, too, believed that few could resist power's corrupting effect, asserting, "Great men are almost always bad men." **DM**

Compulsory Education
Plato

A system of education that begins at birth and identifies society's future leaders

The notion of compulsory education refers to a period of education mandated by law or by some comparable authority. One of the earliest efforts to codify requirements for education is set out in the Talmud, the compendium of Jewish law. The Talmud recommends a form of private education in the family home that emphasizes religious matters in addition to training in whatever the family vocation might be.

Plato (*c.* 424–*c.* 348 BCE) was one of the earliest thinkers to draw up the architecture of a full-blown system of public education. In *The Republic* (*c.* 360 BCE), he describes an education system designed to effect the social stratification that, according to him, is prerequisite for justice to prevail in a state. The education system of his republic begins at birth, when infants are removed from the family and raised by a collective. Educators are tasked with monitoring children in order to identify leadership qualities so that those who have "gold in their souls" (Plato uses this precious metal as a metaphor for leadership potential) can be properly trained to assume elevated offices of state, the highest of which is the office of philosopher king.

In *Laws* (*c.* 360 BCE), a later work, Plato presents a more moderate education system, one that more closely resembles contemporary systems. Infants are not removed from their families and there are no philosopher kings. However, proper social stratification is still the objective. Formal schooling begins at the age of six, when the curriculum focuses on literacy and arithmetic. By age thirteen, music is introduced into the curriculum, and at age eighteen the youth begins his terms of military service. By the age of twenty-one, those students demonstrating the necessary aptitudes are selected for advanced studies that lead to the highest offices of the state. Education systems surprisingly close in character to this ancient model are now the norm in every developed country. **DM**

⬆ A second-century relief from a Roman burial monument, depicting a boy reading to his teacher. Schooling was provided for boys only during Roman times.

"I would teach children music, physics, and philosophy; but most importantly music, for the patterns in music and all the arts are the keys to learning."

Plato, *The Republic* (*c.* 360 BCE)

Idealism
Plato

Experience of the world is all there is, and our minds are the only things that are real

For an idealist philosopher, the human mind is the fulcrum upon which reality rests. Nothing exists unless we perceive it, sense it, or know it. Though there are many different types of philosophical idealism, it can be divided into two basic forms. The first is epistemological idealism, a position that holds that a person's knowledge of the world only exists in the mind. The second is metaphysical idealism, which states that reality itself is dependent on our perceptions and our minds, and that the idea of an independent reality, a physical reality, is nonsensical.

In his work *The Republic* (c. 360 BCE), Greek philosopher Plato (c. 424–c. 348 BCE) relates the Allegory of the Cave—a dialogue between Plato's mentor, Socrates, and Plato's brother, Glaucon—to illustrate the role of

"Those bodies which compose ... the world have not any substance without a mind."
Bishop George Berkeley, philosopher

education in the development of the mind and its gradual understanding of ideal reality. At the allegory's heart is Plato's Theory of Forms: these non-material, abstract entities are, for Plato, the highest level of reality.

Later thinkers, such as Irish philosopher Bishop George Berkeley (1685–1753), reintroduced idealism, saying that the objects we encounter and perceive do not really exist, but only our perceptions of them do. In Berkeley's words, *"Esse est percipi"*: To be is to be perceived.

Idealism had its heyday during the early nineteenth century. It was so popular, and controversial, that it garnered strong reactions and moved other thinkers to create countering positions. As such, it has played an important part in the development of logical positivism, analytic philosophy, and Marxism. **MT**

Allegory of the Cave
Plato

Plato's metaphor for the human condition and the need for education

The Allegory of the Cave appears in Plato's (c. 424–c. 348 BCE) Socratic dialogue, *The Republic* (c. 360 BCE). It begins with an underground cave that is inhabited by prisoners who have been chained there since childhood. The prisoners can only look toward the back of the wall, where flickering shadows stimulate their imaginations and cause them to think that all they imagine is real. However, if a prisoner were to get free and see the cause of the shadows—figures walking in the vicinity of a flickering fire—he would begin to reassess what he thought real. Moreover, if this prisoner were to escape from the cave, he would then be able to see the sun itself, which illuminates everything in the world in the most real way. However, if this free man were to return to the cave to explain his findings to the

"Imagine people living in a cavernous cell down under ground ..."
Plato, *The Republic* (c. 360 BCE)

other prisoners, he no longer would be accustomed to the darkness that they share, and to those ignorant people he would sound like a fool or worse.

This allegory has been highly influential in the history of philosophy for its succinct depiction of Plato's epistemological, ethical, metaphysical, and educational thought. The cave represents our world; we humans are prisoners who imagine such things as sex, power, and money to be the overwhelmingly real and important things of life when, in fact, they are shadows of greater goods that we have the capacity to know. The fire is the inspiration that helps us ascend until we finally come face to face with reality. The liberated prisoner's descent back into the cave represents the ethical duty of the philosopher, who, having discovered the truth, tries to help others seek enlightenment. **AB**

   An illustration of Plato's Allegory of the Cave that appeared in the July 1855 edition of *Magasin Pittoresque.* ➡

Platonic Love

Plato

The type of love between two people that transcends obsessive physicality

Platonic love as it is understood today is a love between two people that is chaste, affectionate, but free of intimacy and sexual desire. The term has its roots with the Greek philosopher Plato (*c.* 424–*c.* 348 BCE), who used it in his philosophical text *The Symposium*, written in *c.* 360 BCE. In the text, Plato dissects a series of speeches made by men at a drinking party, or symposium, held in the Athenian household of the poet Agathon. The speeches, expressed in the form of a dramatic dialogue, are written "in praise of love," and those invited to speak include an aristocrat, a legal expert, a physician, a comic playwright, a statesman, Plato himself in the roles of both host and tragic poet, and Socrates (*c.* 470–399 BCE) , Plato's own teacher and one of the founders of Western philosophical thought.

"We ought to have lived in mental communion, and no more."

Thomas Hardy, *Jude the Obscure* (1895)

It is Socrates's speech that has since been interpreted as introducing the concept of platonic love. Socrates condemns the sort of love that sees a man and a woman obsess over the physical act of love (*eros* in Greek) to the detriment of the pursuit of higher ideals in philosophy, art, and science. He speaks of the ideas of a prophetess and philosopher, Diotima of Mantinea, for whom love is a vehicle through which we can contemplate the divine and possess what she calls the "good." According to Diotima—here "teaching" with Socrates in the role of "naive examinee"—a physically beautiful person should inspire us to seek spiritual things. Her idea of love does not exclude the possibility of physical love, however; the idea that platonic love should exclude physical love altogether is a later, and quite inaccurate, Western construct. **BS**

Formalism in Art

Plato

The concept that a work's artistic value is entirely determined by its form

Plato (*c.* 424–*c.* 348 BCE) believed that the identity, usefulness, and essential meaning of any given thing is bestowed upon it by the idea of that thing, or, rather, its form. According to Plato, the physical constituents of a particular thing are perishable, fleeting, and replaceable, and are therefore irrelevant to its essential nature—Christopher Columbus might replace a plank on the *Pinta*, but that does not, in Plato's view, make it a different ship. Applied to art, Plato's principle argues that it is form alone that bestows meaning upon any given work of art. This philosophy of art has come to be known as "Formalism."

The most thoroughgoing analysis of Plato's principle applied to art can be found in the work of Roman Ingarden (1893–1970). With respect to music, for example, he identifies the various notes and the temporal sequence of each note as defined by the composer—in other words, the form of the music— with the "the musical work" and not, as some might have it, the performance or written score. The performance, says Ingarden, is guided by the form as it is communicated by the score; however, the desired psychological and physiological responses of the audience are contingent upon the temporal arrangement of the notes. After all, one can play all the notes contained in Beethoven's *Symphony No. 5*, but unless they are played in a particular order and are separated by very specific time intervals, the performance will not evoke the same emotion or convey the same meaning—indeed, it will not be Beethoven's *Symphony No. 5*.

Contemporary formalists such as Clement Greenberg (1909–94) embrace Plato's principle, practicing and espousing art that emphasizes the creation and depiction of form over the representation of readily identifiable subjects. **DM**

Space
Plato

The entity in which things come to be and that, with time, is a precondition of all thinking and understanding

According to the treatise *Timaeus* (*c.* 360 BCE) by Plato (*c.* 424–*c.* 348 BCE), space is a receptacle into which all things come into being. It exists eternally, and is not sensed *per se* but is intuited by "a kind of bastard reasoning." However, our conventional understanding of space as an extension in three dimensions is from the Greek mathematician Euclid (*fl. c.* 300 BCE), who wrote a generation after Plato. With the addition of "Cartesian coordinates" (the system that locates a point in space using a set of three numbers), Euclid's conception of space provides the framework for the application of algebra and calculus to classical physics.

The German philosopher Immanuel Kant (1724–1804) suggested that space is one of two "*a priori* conditions of the understanding." That is to say that understanding, and thinking in general, presupposes the existence of space, which, along with time, makes all other concepts and propositions possible. Logical propositions are sequential, and those sequences "unfold" in space. For this reason, space cannot be a projection of the mind; instead, it transcends all cognitive activity and makes thinking possible.

In the twentieth century Albert Einstein (1879–1955) introduced further conceptually challenging and powerful innovations to our understanding of space. His formula for special relativity, $E=mc^2$, couples space with time to show that energy exerted in travel through space inversely affects a person's passage through time (and vice versa). Although a human might feel this effect only during extreme exertions of energy (during travel at or near the speed of light), the effect can be quantified and measured with sophisticated mechanical devices. General relativity, on the other hand, suggests that space possesses shape and that the shape of space is dictated by the presence of mass. **DM**

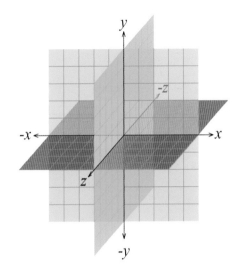

⬆ A diagram of three-dimensional Euclidian space. Every point is determined by three coordinates, relating the point's position on each axis relative to the other two.

"The third type [of existing things] … space … exists always and cannot be destroyed."

Plato, *Timaeus* (*c.* 360 BCE)

Moral Absolutism
Plato

Moral and ethical principles are universal, and all actions are either right or wrong

What makes someone good? What makes our actions right or wrong? For a moral absolutist, there exists a standard of morality that is universally applicable to all human activity. This standard dictates what a person should do in any situation, and any deviation from that is an immoral act. For the moral absolutist, a clear moral code is the measuring stick that determines the moral value of any thought or action. A person's intentions and beliefs, as well as intended or unintended consequences, are irrelevant.

Moral absolutes have probably existed since prehistory. Those found in the Jewish Torah are thought to date from the sixth to fourth centuries BCE. Greek philosopher Plato (*c.* 424–*c.* 348 BCE), in his dialogue *Theaetetus* (*c.* 360 BCE), considered the problem of moral

"Act only ... [if] you can at the same time will that it should become a universal law."

Immanuel Kant, philosopher

relativism: namely, that a relativist cannot claim that there is no universal truth because doing so would require believing at least one universal truth. This criticism of relativism laid the logical foundation for the case for moral absolutism. German philosopher Immanuel Kant (1724–1804) believed that morality was based on absolute rights and ethical principles or duties; lying, for example, was always immoral for Kant.

Moral absolutism was, and is, a way that many people approach questions of morality and ethics. With a moral absolute, judging a person's actions as right or wrong is very often a simple proposition. Yet these concrete dictums can, and have, led to terrible consequences, and the practical effect these absolutes have leads many to question the nature of morality itself, and what it means to be a moral person. **MT**

Geocentrism
Ancient Greece

The theory that the universe orbits around the Earth

Geocentrism, also referred to as the geocentric model or the Ptolemaic model of the universe, holds that the planet Earth is the center of the universe and all celestial bodies orbit or surround it. The observable movements of the moon, the planets, and the stars can all be explained by the existence of celestial spheres that govern their movements. The geocentric model of the universe remained the dominant theory about how the universe operated until the sixteenth century.

Early Greek astronomers believed that the Earth lay at the center of the universe. In the fourth century BCE, philosophers Plato and Aristotle contributed to this model by proposing that the heavenly bodies were affixed in celestial or stellar spheres that rotated around the similarly spherical Earth. In the second century CE,

"[The Earth] alone remained immovable, whilst all things revolve round it."

Pliny the Elder, naturalist and natural philosopher

the Hellenistic philosopher Claudius Ptolemy built upon this model and developed a system that explained planetary movement based on the idea that multiple spheres govern the movement of heavenly bodies.

Today the geocentric model of the universe seems almost ludicrous, but it held influence for a long time because it fit so well with observable data. Early astronomers did not have the luxury of telescopes or instruments that could make accurate measurements; the geocentric model not only explained the motions of the heavens with accuracy, but it also catered to the notion that humanity was the center of the universe. The subsequent heliocentric (sun-centered) model was far more accurate, but geocentrism nevertheless provided early thinkers with a rational explanation of how and why the universe operated. **MT**

The world according to Aristotle, from *De Philosophia Mundi* (twelfth century) by William de Conches. ➡

I

ΑΡΙΣΤΟΤΕΛΟΥΣ ΠΕΡΙ ΟΥΡΑΝΟΥ, ΤΟ Α.

ΠΕΡΙ φύσεως ἐπιστήμης σχεδὸν ἡ πλείστη φαίνεται περί τε σώματα καὶ μεγέθη, καὶ τὰ τούτων οὖσα πάθη, καὶ τὰς κινήσεις. ἔτι δὲ περὶ τὰς ἀρχάς, ὅσαι τῆς τοιαύτης οὐσίας εἰσί· τῶν γὰρ φύσει συνεστώτων, τὰ μὲν ὅτι σώματα καὶ μεγέθη, τὰ δ' ἔχει σῶμα καὶ μέγεθος, τὰ δ' ἀρχαὶ τῶν ἐχόντων εἰσί. συνεχὲς μὲν οὖν ὅτι τὸ διαιρετὸν εἰς ἀεὶ διαιρετά· σῶμα δὲ, ὃ πάντῃ διαιρετόν. μεγέθους δὲ, τὸ μὲν ἐφ' ἕν, γραμμὴ· ὃ δ' ἐπὶ δύο, ἐπίπεδον· ὃ δ' ἐπὶ τρία, σῶμα· καὶ παρὰ ταῦτα οὐκ ἔστιν ἄλλο μέγεθος, διὰ τὸ τὰ τρία πάντα εἶ), καὶ τὸ τρὶς πάντῃ· καθάπερ γάρ φασι καὶ οἱ πυθαγόρειοι, τὸ πᾶν καὶ τὰ πάντα τοῖς τρισὶν ὥρισται· τελευτὴ γὰρ καὶ μέσον καὶ ἀρχὴ τὸν ἀριθμὸν ἔχει τὸν τοῦ παντός· ταῦτα δὲ τὸν τῆς τριάδος. διὸ παρὰ τῆς φύσεως εἰληφότες ὥσπερ νόμους ἐκείνης, καὶ πρὸς τὰς ἁγιστείας τῶν θεῶν χρώμεθα τῷ ἀριθμῷ τούτῳ. ἀποδίδομεν δὲ καὶ τὰς προσηγορίας τὸν τρόπον τοῦτον· τὰ γὰρ δύο, ἄμφω μὲν λέ

The Fifth Element

Aristotle

An unobserved element, ether, is one of five elements that make up the universe

The fifth element, known as aether or ether, was one of the five basic elements of nature in the ancient Greek world. These fundamental elements of fire, water, earth, air, and ether were the foundation of the universe.

To the ancient Greeks, the universe existed as a system of celestial spheres in which the Earth was stationary, located in the center, with all the planets, stars, and other celestial bodies surrounding it in spheres that governed their movements. In his dialogue *Timaeus* (360 BCE), Plato (*c.* 424–*c.* 348 BCE) wrote about the elements and their different types, identifying ether as being the brightest part of the air. Aristotle (384–322 BCE), in his work *On the Heavens* (*c.* 350 BCE), later hypothesized that ether was a fifth element in the spaces between the celestial spheres.

"There is something besides the bodies nearby and around us . . ."

Aristotle, *On the Heavens* (*c.* 350 BCE)

After Aristotle, the classical explanation of the five elements as the fundamental particles of nature dominated Western scientific thought until the Renaissance. Yet ether, the fifth element, was different. Scientists could directly observe each of the other four elements in nature, while ether remained hidden. Aristotle had to make observations about the world and then hypothesize an element that had yet to be observed. Modern science has long dispelled the idea of the elements, but that ether did not exist, and was never observed, did not diminish the importance of the concept. Aristotle's postulation that an as-of-yet unobserved particle explained other observed phenomena anticipated the scientific notion that a hypothesis should be able to predict behavior or observation, a concept central to modern science. **MT**

Hypothesis

Aristotle

An explanation for a phenomenon that can be tested by further investigation

A hypothesis is a type of claim used to explain a phenomenon. As Aristotle (384–322 BCE) uses the word, a hypothesis is the claim in an explanation that states that something is or is not the case, and that we are obliged to demonstrate. Aristotle contrasts hypotheses with "illegitimate postulates," which are claims that are assumed to be true and are used without demonstration, and "definitions," which express the meaning or referent of a term or phrase but do not assert whether there are any instances of the meaning or referent.

Consider an example: Why might an adolescent have acne? In order to investigate, we may form a number of hypotheses: for example: acne is caused by eating too much sugar, by not cleaning well, and by undergoing

"The great tragedy of science—the slaying of a beautiful hypothesis by an ugly fact."

Thomas Huxley, biologist

puberty. In order to see which hypothesis best explains our phenomenon, we must subject each to a series of tests—that is, we must identify certain events that we would observe if the hypothesis were true and then check for them. For example, if our adolescent's acne is due to eating too much sugar, then removing sugar from his diet should cause a marked decrease in acne.

The concept of hypothesis came into modern use through the scientific work of Francis Bacon (1561–1626) and Isaac Newton (1642–1727), although neither expressed much respect for it. Bacon regarded hypotheses as unscientific starting points, and Newton explicitly rejected their use. Nevertheless, in practice, they both made important use of hypotheses, and contemporary scientists recognize them as an essential component in the scientific process. **JW**

The opening page of Aristotle's cosmological treatise *On the Heavens* (c. 350 BCE).

The Chicken and Egg Conundrum
Aristotle

The age-old puzzle that if chickens come from eggs and vice versa, how do you establish which of the two existed first?

⬆ First-century marble bust of Aristotle; it is a copy of a Greek bronze sculpted by Lysippus in the fourth century BCE. Lysippus is said to have created 1,500 bronzes, none of which have survived.

"How wonderful that we have met with a paradox. Now we have some hope of making progress."

Niels Bohr, physicist

When a hen lays a fertilized egg, that hen will keep the egg warm until it hatches a chick. That chick will then grow up to become a hen and lay other eggs, repeating the process as part of an ongoing cycle. But when did this process start? What was first: the chicken or the egg? This infamous question identifies a problem of causality, a paradox in which both chicken and egg cannot exist without the other, yet there must have been a moment when one of them came first.

What existed at the beginning? How did objects, the world, animals, and humans come to be? These are the basic questions that lie at the heart of the chicken and egg conundrum. When the ancient Greek philosopher Aristotle (384–322 BCE) asked the question, he believed that both must have always been in existence. Over the centuries the question remained a challenge to philosophers, though it became less important after English naturalist Charles Darwin (1809–82) introduced the theory of evolution by natural selection and explained the development of any organism as a process of slow progress over time.

In 2010, British researchers released the results of a study that, they claimed, conclusively proved that the chicken came first. While the solution was not universally accepted, and others claim that the egg existed prior to the chicken, the question's importance is not solely one of biological history. The chicken and the egg conundrum prompts us to consider beginnings, and how they relate to our experiences. Some theologians have answered the question by saying that the creation of the universe necessarily means that the chicken came first. Other traditions hold that time does not have a clear beginning and end, and the idea of what came first is nonsensical because all things have existed for eternity. **MT**

Spontaneous Generation
Aristotle

Certain organisms can blossom into life spontaneously from non-living matter

Some of the earliest Western thinkers believed that life forms first emerged from a "primordial slime" that was either activated by the sun and air or fertilized by seeds transmitted by them. Aristotle (384–322 BCE) was the first figure to argue that some life forms emerge spontaneously by means of an elemental principle similar to a seed.

Aristotle stated that reproduction involves an active principle, represented by the male's semen, which acts upon a passive principle, represented by the material substrate of the potential organism provided by the female. The form of the organism is transmitted by the semen to the material, giving rise to the new organism. In spontaneous generation, however, the passive substrate is a mixture of seawater and earth, not a living organism. The active principle is provided by *pneuma*, or "vital heat," found in all things in varying levels. This *pneuma* stimulates a sort of fermentation that eventually gives rise to the new organism.

According to Aristotle, only certain organisms are produced in this way—namely, certain fish, oysters, and eels. These organisms provided Aristotle with empirical evidence that spontaneous generation occurs: that oysters are generated spontaneously, for example, is suggested by the fact that they do not multiply during transportation. Furthermore, the "eggs" that they contain never hatch offspring. Eels, according to Aristotle's observations, did not possess the organs required for procreation, nor did they produce eggs.

Speculation concerning the possibility of spontaneous generation gave rise to a number of biological theories, including the homunculus (little man). It persisted throughout the Middle Ages and was not compellingly, if not definitively, refuted until the nineteenth century, by Louis Pasteur. **DM**

The Third Man Problem
Aristotle

Aristotle's critique of Plato's Theory of Forms

The ancient Greek philosopher Aristotle (384–322 BCE) was both the greatest student and greatest critic of Plato (c. 424–c. 348 BCE). His biggest criticism of Plato's philosophy is encapsulated in the "Third Man Problem."

Plato distinguishes between the essential nature (sometimes referred to as the Form or Idea) of any given thing and the thing itself. He claims that the Idea of a thing is unchanging and exists independently from the thing itself. For example, if a person knows something about canines, they know something about what makes a canine a canine and not, technically speaking, something about a specific dog. Among other reasons, Plato defends this metaphysical claim on the basis that individual things are constantly changing and so we can never truly know anything about them.

> *"Of the ways in which we prove that the Forms exist, none is convincing."*
> Aristotle, *Metaphysics* (c. 350 BCE)

Plato himself acknowledged a certain logical inconsistency in the notion that Ideas exist separately from things themselves: Plato's logic suggests that, by extension, we should postulate a third thing—the Idea of the Idea of our subject. For the same reason we might postulate a fourth Idea, and a fifth, and so on. Aristotle argues that this *reductio ad absurdum* is grounds to reject Plato's claim. He argues that the essential nature of a thing exists in the individual and, at the same time, in all the other members of the species to which the individual belongs.

This disparity of views is at the heart of one of the longest running and most multifaceted debates in Western philosophy: the idealism/realism debate. At stake is nothing short of the foundations of science and the nature of knowledge. **DM**

Perfection
Aristotle

The concept of something that is completely flawless or complete

Perfection, in the sense of being flawless, is derived from discussions by Aristotle (384–322 BCE) of privation, or deficiency. Aristotle stated that "a doctor and a musician are 'perfect' when they have no deficiency in respect of the form of their peculiar excellence." In other words, a "perfect" specimen is flawless in every way with respect to its performance of its profession or its embodiment of its species. This, however, is just one sense of a concept that is key to Aristotle's philosophy.

The word "perfect" is a translation of the Greek *teleion*, a derivative of the polysemous word *telos*. In this context, the relevant meaning of *telos* is "end," or "goal." With this in mind, the English translation "perfect" can be understood to encapsulate the idea of being complete, of having fulfilled a goal. This was

"Have no fear of perfection—you'll never reach it."

Salvador Dalí, artist

important for Aristotle because, as a matter of principle, he believed that all things exist for a reason—that is, they have some *telos*—and that all things naturally strive toward the fulfillment of their *telos*. Therefore, perfection, for Aristotle, is something all things strive for, be they a blade of grass or a human being.

In biology, Aristotle employs this notion to explain (in part) the various stages of an organism's development—each is a step toward the fulfillment of its *telos*. In cosmology, however, Aristotle employs the idea very generally, suggesting that the *telos* of all heavy bodies invariably drives them toward a state of rest around a cosmic center point. That all heavy bodies fall to Earth is evidence that this center point is, in fact, Earth. In this way, perfection is a concept wholly entangled with geocentrism. **DM**

The Scientific Method
Aristotle

The development of a system for pursuing scientific enquiry

In *Posterior Analytics* (c. 350 BCE), Aristotle (384–322 BCE) became the first thinker to attempt an analysis and systematization of the proper procedure for conducting science. For him, science was the search for universal truths concerning the causes of things. He believed that these causes are revealed not through experimentation and empirical observation, but through the rigorous application of sound deductive reasoning.

Experimentation of the sort commonly associated with modern science emerged in the East in the early eleventh century, in the works of Alhazen, Al-Biruni, and Avicenna. Their notion of a cyclical scientific process of observation, hypothesis, and experimentation was transmitted to the Western world via philosopher Roger Bacon in the thirteenth century, whose *Opus Majus*

"The scientific method is a potentiation of common sense."

Peter Medawar, biologist

offered an explanation and critique of what he extolled as a new approach to science (and, ultimately, theology).

Philosopher of science Karl Popper enhanced the scientific method in the twentieth century, when he introduced the notion of falsifiability. According to Popper, properly scientific hypotheses are falsifiable—that is, clear and logically feasible conditions can be articulated under which the hypothesis might be false. This allows the scientist to conduct experiments aimed at bringing about these conditions, thereby either disproving or strengthening the hypothesis. Popper also argued that a condition for the acceptance of a scientific theory must be its ability to produce testable predictions that are not also predicted by another theory. For example, the greatest criticism of string theory is that it has so far failed to produce testable predictions. **DM**

A diagram from Roger Bacon's *Opus Majus* (c. 1268), illustrating his scientific studies of the eye. ➡

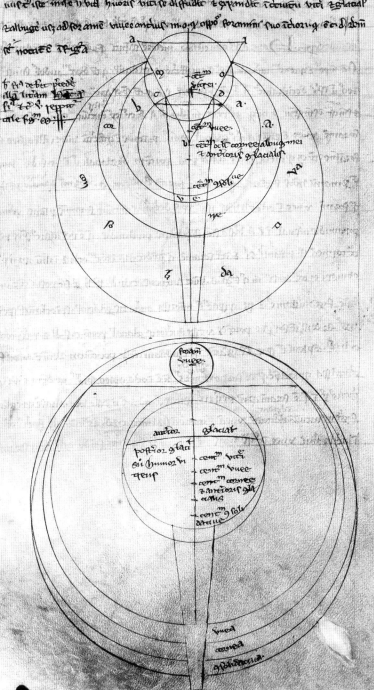

ΑΡΙΣΤΟΤΕΛΟΥΣ
ΤΩΝ ΜΕΤΑ ΤΑ ΦΥΣΙΚΑ
ΑΛΦΑ ΤΟ ΜΕΙΖΟΝ.

ΑΝΤΕΣ ἄνθρωποι τοῦ εἰδέ-
ναι ὀρέγονται φύσει. σημεῖον δ' ἡ τῶν
αἰσθήσεων ἀγάπησις. καὶ γὰρ χω-
ρὶς τῆς χρείας ἀγαπῶνται δι' ἑαυ-
τάς, καὶ μάλιστα τῶν ἄλλων ἡ διὰ
τῶν ὀμμάτων. οὐ γὰρ μόνον ἵνα
πράττωμεν, ἀλλὰ καὶ μηδὲν
μέλλοντες πράττειν, τὸ ὁρᾶν αἱ-
ρούμεθα ἀντὶ πάντων, ὡς εἰπεῖν,

τῶν ἄλλων. αἴτιον δ' ὅτι μάλιστα ποιεῖ γνωρίζειν ἡμᾶς αὕτη τῶν
αἰσθήσεων, καὶ πολλὰς δηλοῖ διαφοράς. φύσει μὲν οὖν αἴσθησιν ἔ-
χοντα γίνεται τὰ ζῷα. ἐκ δὲ τῆς αἰσθήσεως, τοῖς μὲν αὐτῶν οὐκ ἐγγί-
νεται μνήμη, τοῖς δὲ γίνεται. καὶ διὰ τοῦτο τὰ μὲν φρόνιμα, τὰ δὲ
μαθηματικώτερα τῶν μὴ δυναμένων μνημονεύειν ἐστίν. φρόνιμα μὲν, ἄνευ τοῦ μανθάνειν, ὅσα μὴ δύναται τῶν ψόφων ἀκούειν·
οἷον μέλιττα, καὶ εἴ τι τοιοῦτον ἄλλο γένος ζῴων ἐστί. μανθάνει δ',
ὅσα πρὸς τῇ μνήμῃ καὶ ταύτην ἔχει τὴν αἴσθησιν. τὰ μὲν οὖν ἄλ-
λα ταῖς φαντασίαις ζῇ, καὶ ταῖς μνήμαις, ἐμπειρίας δὲ μετέχει μι-

A

The Law of Non-contradiction
Aristotle

Something cannot both exist and not exist at the same time

The rules or "laws" of logic prescribe the acceptable means of manipulating semantic elements in a system. Perhaps the oldest and best-known rule of logic is the Law of Non-contradiction: nothing can both be and not be. It originated with Aristotle (384–322 BCE) as a metaphysical principle, expressed in his *Metaphysics* (*c.* 350 BCE): "The same attribute cannot at the same time belong and not belong to the same subject and in the same respect." As such, the Law sets a boundary for every type of investigation. However, contemporary logicians restrict its application to propositions (for any proposition, p, it is not the case that both p and not-p are true at the same time in the same way).

The universal applicability of the Law has been challenged by a minority of scholars since the late

> ## "Contradictory propositions are not true simultaneously."
> Aristotle, *Metaphysics* (*c.* 350 BCE)

1800s. For example, Friedrich Engels argued that we find contradictions in nature: "Even simple mechanical change of position can only come about through a body being at one and the same moment of time both in one place and in another place." Similarly, Graham Priest argued that intuitions believed to support the Law fail in well-known cases, such as the Liar Paradox (if "This claim is false" is true, then it is also false; if it is false, then it is also true).

However, for the majority of scholars, these criticisms serve only to clarify and strengthen the classical view of the Law's fundamental role in reasoning. For example, in response to the Liar Paradox, some argue that the claim's entailing a contradiction proves that it conveys no coherent meaning. It is as meaningless as "that is a round square." **JW**

Indeterminism
Aristotle

Certain happenings are not caused deterministically by prior events

In the study of causation, there is a debate about how to characterize events that stand in a cause-and-effect relationship. On one hand, laws and prior events may exert complete control over the effects produced by a cause. For example, when one billiard ball strikes another, the angle and velocity of the striking ball, along with gravity, inertia, and the smoothness of the surface, fully determine where the struck ball goes. "Determinism" is the view that all events bear this relation. On the other hand, laws and prior events may exert less than complete control over the effects produced by a cause. For example, for any set of radioactive isotopes, there is no way to predict the exact order in which members will decay, but we are quite sure that all will eventually decay. Physicists

> ## "Nor is there any definite cause for an accident, but only chance."
> Aristotle, *Metaphysics* (*c.* 350 BCE)

attribute this unpredictability to randomness in the quantum law that governs the process. "Indeterminism" is the view that some events are indeterministic.

"Indeterminism" is a recent term, but the idea is old. Aristotle allowed for the possibility of accidents in nature, and Epicurus and Leucippus argued that atoms could act unpredictably. The Stoics later rejected this indeterminism in favor of determinism (or possibly fatalism). Nevertheless, the question of whether any causation is indeterministic remains significant. In physics, there is evidence that some quantum events are indeterministic, yet in every other area of physics events seem to be deterministic. In philosophy, there is disagreement as to whether morally responsible agency requires indeterministic causation. As yet, there is no widely accepted resolution to these problems. **JW**

← The title page of Aristotle's *Metaphysics* (*c.* 350 BCE), the first major work of metaphysic philosophy.

Rest as the Natural State of Things
Aristotle

All objects gravitate toward a state of rest that correlates to the element of which they are composed

⬆ A fifteenth-century French illustration depicts Christ holding a globe containing the four elements of Aristotle's *Physics* (*c.* 350 BCE) at rest: beneath the heavens, fire, air, water, and earth.

"The downward movement of a mass of gold or lead . . . is quicker in proportion to its size."

Aristotle, *On the Heavens* (*c.* 350 BCE)

Before the theory of gravity and Newton's laws of motion, science was dominated by the notion that everything in existence is composed of certain fundamental elements. Ancient Greek philosopher Empedocles (*c.* 490–430 BCE), for example, believed that everything in existence was composed of earth, air, fire, and water, and offered an elaborate account of how these elements mixed and separated to form the planets, stars, and other denizens of the universe. Central to this account were the distinct qualities of each element. Each element, said Empedocles, tended to occupy a position in the universe relative to its density and weight: heavier, denser elements tended to settle in the lowest regions of the cosmos, leaving the lighter, "thinner" elements in the higher regions.

Aristotle (384–322 BCE) generalized the underlying principle of this account when he argued that rest is the natural state of all things. According to Aristotle, all objects tend toward a state of rest that corresponds to the natural state of their predominant element. If, for example, a thing is primarily composed of earth, it will naturally fall toward Earth, where it will come to rest. If it is predominantly composed of fire, it will tend toward a state of rest in the heavens. Following this reasoning, Aristotle argued that heavy bodies fall at a faster rate than lighter bodies, a conclusion that was not definitively refuted until the experiments of Galileo in the sixteenth century.

Historically, the most significant extrapolation of the principle of rest being the natural state of things was Aristotle's conclusion that Earth is the unmoving center of the universe. This arose from the persistent observation that heavy bodies fall toward Earth. Thanks to Claudius Ptolemy in the second century CE, geocentrism became the dominant worldview until well into the seventeenth century. **DM**

Categorical Logic
Aristotle

The first systematic science of the logic of categories

For Aristotle (384–322 BCE), the analysis of the mechanisms of logic at work in language was part (the first part, in fact) of any thoroughgoing science. In his text, *Prior Analytics* (*c.* 350 BCE), the philosopher set out a system of logic that would dominate science for approximately 2,000 years.

Aristotle's logic is a "categorical" system of logic because its deductions concern either categories of things, the characteristics its members possess or do not possess, or the members themselves. The fundamental instrument of Aristotle's system of logic is the syllogism. In its simplest form, a syllogism is an argument composed of three categorical statements, one of which posits a specific thing that must be true given the truth of the other two general statements. The classic example of a syllogism states: "All men are mortal. Socrates is a man. Therefore, Socrates is mortal." Aristotle himself described a syllogism as a "discourse in which, certain things being stated, something other than what is stated follows of necessity from their being so."

A rival system of logical analysis was developed by the Greek Stoic philosopher Chrysippus (*c.* 280–*c.* 206 BCE) in the third century BCE; however, it was Aristotle's ideas that remained dominant. Aristotle's system of logic was at the center of monastic debates concerning the nature of God, and it also enabled monks to determine how many angels could dance on the head of a pin. In biology, this system of categorical logic influenced Aristotle's own initial efforts to define the various species (categories) of living organisms; this influence continued in subsequent efforts to expand and refine the definition of species. It was not until the late nineteenth century that German mathematician Gottlob Frege reinvigorated predicate logic of the sort promoted by the ancient Stoics. **DM**

Equal Temperament
Aristoxenus

A musical tuning system that uses equal intervals in the scale

Attributed to the Greek philosopher Aristoxenus (*f.* 350 BCE), equal temperament (ET) is today the most common musical scale. It is used for the tuning of pianos, guitars, and other instruments that employ a fixed scale. The defining characteristic of ET is that it divides the octave into equal parts.

ET's predecessors—such as just intonation or Pythagorean tuning—divide the tone based upon different ratios of the frequency. Just intonation, for example, fixes D on the frequency ⁹⁄₈ times that of C. If the frequency of C is 262 hertz, then D, being 294.75 hertz, is 32.75 hertz higher than C. However, according to just intonation, F falls on the frequency ⁴⁄₃ times that of C (349.33 hertz), and G falls on the frequency ³⁄₂ times C (393 hertz). Thus the difference between F and G, an

> *"Harpists spend 90% of their lives tuning their harps and 10% playing out of tune."*
>
> Igor Stravinsky, composer

interval that is nominally the same as that between C and D, is approximately 44.6 hertz. This discrepancy between the size of intervals does not occur in ET.

In ET the frequency of each note is precisely $\sqrt[12]{2}$ (approximately 1.05946) times higher than that of the preceding note. This ratio ensures that the interval between each note in the scale is exactly the same. The advantage of this is that compositions can be transposed between keys without having to substitute intervals in the original key with different-sized intervals in the new key. The only way to avoid this while using other temperaments is to retune the instruments. Despite its ancient origins, ET has only recently entered into common usage following advancements in technology that have allowed us to accurately measure audio frequency. **DM**

Hylomorphism
Aristotle

A conceptual framework for the analysis of any given thing or process

According to the theory of hylomorphism of Aristotle (384–322 BCE), every substance (that is, any existing thing) is composed of matter and form. The matter of a thing can be understood as the stuff a thing is made of. However, more than that, it represents everything the substance could be—its "potentiality," as Aristotle described it. The form of a thing, on the other hand, is its shape and more—it represents everything the substance actually is, its "actuality." Like his teacher and mentor Plato (*c.* 424–*c.* 348 BCE), Aristotle believed that the form of thing gives it meaning and identity.

Hylomorphism is central to Aristotle's explanations of the various processes unfolding in the universe. Reproduction, for example, occurs when the animal form, carried in semen, is imposed upon suitable

"By the matter I mean … the bronze, by the form I mean the arrangement of the figure."

Aristotle, *Metaphysics* (*c.* 350 BCE)

material, provided by the female, thereby producing a new substance, the infant animal. For Aristotle, a comprehensive understanding of any given substance or phenomenon requires a thorough appreciation of its form and matter, and its actuality and potentiality, and the nuances and complexities of their unity.

Despite its abstract nature, hylomorphism was extremely influential: it was the underlying conceptual foundation of all sciences from the Middle Ages until the late eighteenth century, when it was replaced by atomism. It has also been employed in contemporary attempts to untangle the persistent enigmas of consciousness. Aristotle's application of hylomorphism to consciousness is referenced by U.S. philosopher Hilary Putnam in his early work on functionalism and continues to influence contemporary philosophy of mind. **DM**

Types of Friendship
Aristotle

All friendships fall within one of three categories of increasing perfection

In general there are, according to Aristotle (384–322 BCE), three different types of things that people like and three corresponding types of friendships. People like things that are useful to them, and so there are friendships based on utility. People like pleasure, and so there are friendships based on pleasure. Finally, some things are inherently likable because they are inherently good, and likewise, there are friendships between good people based solely upon their virtuous characters.

Friendships based on utility arise most often when people become associated for the sake of a mutual benefit. These are the sorts of friendships that exist between business associates or politicians. They are also, says Aristotle, the weakest sorts of friendships because "those who are friends for the sake of utility

"Good men will be friends for their own sake, that is, in virtue of their goodness."

Aristotle, *Nicomachean Ethics* (*c.* 350 BCE)

part when the advantage is at an end." Friendships based on pleasure are most common among the young. They are tenuous, however, because people's pleasures change as they get older.

Perfect friendships are those based on the virtuous character of the participants. Aristotle claims that "perfect friendship is the friendship of men who are good, and alike in virtue." Such friendships arise because it is inherently pleasurable to share the company of good people. They are perfect because they are the most enduring and because the benefits are the same for both participants. Unfortunately, perfect friendships are likely only among the very old. This is because, as Aristotle explains, it takes many years of experience before one's virtues are refined sufficiently to enter into a perfect friendship. **DM**

A detail from the *School of Athens* (1510–11) fresco by Raphael, featuring Aristotle and Plato. ➡

Fallacy
Aristotle

An argument that may be persuasive but contains an error of logic or language

A fallacy is an error in reasoning, but reasoning can be erroneous in a number of ways, so there is no definitive type of fallacy. Aristotle (384–322 BCE) was the first to gather and explain the most common types of errors in reasoning, such as equivocation, begging the question, and false cause. In the subsequent centuries of philosophical debate, new categories of fallacies were identified, and the philosophers William of Ockham (c. 1287–1347) and John Buridan (c. 1300–after 1358) compiled an extensive number of fallacy types, giving them Latin names such as *argumentum ad populum* (appeal to the people) and *argumentum ad baculum* (appeal to the stick, or force).

There are now more than 200 named fallacies, commonly divided between formal and informal.

"… some reasonings are genuine, while others seem to be so but are not …"

Aristotle, *On Sophistical Refutations* (c. 350 BCE)

Formal fallacies are mistakes in the logical form of an argument, independent of its semantic content. For example, in the non-fallacious form called Modus Ponens, a correct deduction can be derived from a conditional premise and a correct antecedent, regardless of the content. However, in the related formal fallacy called "affirming the consequent," a false deduction is derived from the same correct conditional premise and a false antecedent. It follows that not every instance of the deduction would be true, even if the premise statements appeared correct individually.

An informal fallacy occurs when the content or organization of the premises of an argument constitutes an error in reasoning, as when an arguer changes the subject (red herring) or appeals to an inappropriate authority (*argumentum ad verecundiam*). **JW**

Occam's Razor
Unknown

The simplest explanation is usually the correct explanation

"When you have two competing theories that make exactly the same predictions, the simpler one is the better." This is the Principle of Parsimony, the axiom that it is pointless to achieve with more than what can be done with less, or the Principle of Plurality, that many hypotheses should be posited only when absolutely necessary. The idea that the simplest explanation is usually the correct explanation has always been the guiding principle whenever humanity has been faced with a choice, problem, or dilemma. We know a dog barks because we can hear it. We know a grapefruit is sour because we can taste it. And that principle has a name: we call it Occam's razor.

Occam's razor gives precedence to the notion of simplicity and holds that simplicity is equal to perfection. The principle is named after an English philosopher and Franciscan monk, William of Occam (c. 1287–1347), although there is no evidence that he ever used the phrase in any of his extensive writings, despite clearly being predisposed to the concept.

In fact, the principle of Occam's razor was recognized long before Occam's time, not least in ancient Greece. Aristotle (384–322 BCE) wrote, "The more perfect a nature is, the fewer means it requires for its operation." The principle remained significant. Austrian physicist Ernst Mach (1838–1916), who studied the mechanics of projectiles moving at supersonic speeds, said that scientists should use the simplest methods possible in their research. Now, the principle that one should never make more assumptions than are absolutely required underlies all scientific and theoretical modeling. It helps to shake off variables that muddy the waters of enquiry and threaten to introduce ambiguities and inconsistencies. Occam's razor has become part of science's everyday intellectual furniture, its most basic of tools. **BS**

Homunculus
Aristotle

The theory that living creatures, including humankind, begin life as miniature versions of their adult forms, only having to grow in size to reach maturity

The term "homunculus" is derived from the Latin *homo*, meaning "human being," or "person," and the diminutive suffix, *culus*. Although literally defined as "little person," the term usually means a fully formed organism of microscopic proportions.

Homunculi figured prominently in preformationist theories of the development of individual organisms. Generally speaking, preformationism tells us that living organisms begin life as fully formed, but miniature, creatures whose maturity involves little more than growth. Preformationism is often defined in contrast to epigenetic theories, which explain the maturation of an organism as a process through which its infant form changes and develops into its adult form.

Aristotle (384–322 BCE) produced an explanation of animal development that was epigenetic in nature, but he is often associated with the homunculus because of the dominant role he attributes to the male contribution in the reproductive process. Aristotle's epigeneticism persevered for almost 2,000 years but then Nicolaas von Hartsoeker (1656–1725), using an early microscope, concluded that there were miniature men inside human sperm, which he called homunculi. Von Hartsoeker's well-known image of a homunculus occupying the head of a sperm became the banner for the "Spermist" form of preformationism that gained popularity in the late seventeenth century.

Perhaps the most extreme form of preformationism was espoused by Philippus Aureolus Theophrastus Bombastus von Hohenheim (1493–1541), better known as Paracelsus. In his *De Natura Rerum* (*The Nature of Things*, 1537), Paracelsus suggested that, by allowing a man's semen to putrify in the uterus of a horse, and later feeding it with human blood, the result will be a human infant. This being the case, he argued, females are entirely unnecessary in human reproduction. **DM**

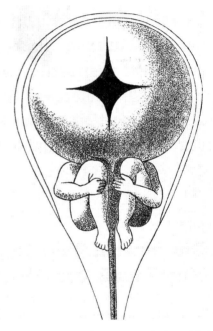

⬆ An illustration by Nicolaas von Hartsoeker (*c.* 1700) depicts an example of the homunculi that his microscopic researches led him to believe existed in the heads of human sperm.

". . . it becomes thencefold a true living infant, having all the members of a child that is born from a woman, but much smaller. This we call a homunculus . . ."

Paracelsus, *De Natura Rerum* (1537)

The Liar's Paradox
Aristotle

A paradoxical proposal that reveals the limitations of universal accounts of truth

The Liar's Paradox is a well-known thought experiment in philosophy that challenges the adequacy of standard bivalent (two-valued) logical systems. The classic "liar's sentence" is: "This sentence is false." The problem is that if we assume that all meaningful claims are either true or false, and there is no middle value, then this sentence, since it seems meaningful, must be true or false. But if it is true, then, according to its content, it is false, and this is contradictory. On the other hand, if it is false, then, according to its content, it is true, which is also contradictory. Thus, it is neither true nor false.

Although there is no widely accepted solution to this paradox, philosophers have expended considerable ink in response. Some suggest that our standard account of truth must be mistaken. This

"A man says that he is lying. Is what he says true or false?"
Eubulides of Miletus, philosopher

account, traced back to Aristotle (384–322 BCE), has it that a claim (P) is true if and only if there is some state of affairs expressed by P; for example, "the cat is on the mat" is true if and only if the cat is on the mat.

The logician Alfred Tarski (1901–83) argues that the Liar's Paradox shows that this universal account of truth cannot be included in the language it governs. Other philosophers, such as Graham Priest, argue that it shows that bivalent systems are inadequate, and that we must appeal to multivalued logics to solve the problem. Still others, including Arthur Prior, Jon Barwise, and John Etchemendy, attempt to resolve it within the boundaries of both the classical account of truth and bivalent logical systems, arguing that the "liar's sentence" is simply false. The Liar's Paradox is still sparking important developments in logic. **JW**

The Four Causes
Aristotle

The idea that all things may be defined in four different but complementary ways

Aristotle (384–322 BCE) maintained that we can define a given thing in four different ways, corresponding to four different "explanatory factors," or "causes." The first cause is the material cause, which has to do with the contents or ingredients of the thing in question. For example, the material cause of a window might be a wooden frame and glass pane; or the material cause of peanut butter might be peanuts, salt, and sugar.

The second cause is the efficient or genetic cause, which has to do with the agency that brings about the thing in question. For example, a solar eclipse is an event caused by the moon coming between the sun and the earth and blocking the sun's light from some part of the earth, or, more simply, pregnancy is caused by sexual activity or artificial insemination.

"We do not have knowledge of a thing until we have grasped its . . . cause."
Aristotle, *Physics* (c. 350 BCE)

The third cause is the formal or essential cause, which has to do with naming the genus and species to which the thing in question belongs (this is arguably the most important, or at least most precise, definition). For example, Aristotle says human beings are "rational animals," where "animal" is the immediate genus, and "rational" the species differentiated from "non-rational."

The fourth or final cause has to do with the purpose, goal, or destiny of the thing in question. For example, the eye is for seeing, or, according to the Westminster Confession of Faith (1646), man was made "to glorify God and enjoy Him forever." While Aristotle was the first to clarify these four causes, the concepts themselves are so fundamental to life in general (and science in particular) that their importance cannot be overemphasized. **AB**

　　A solar or lunar eclipse—as depicted in this manuscript (1410)—illustrates Aristotle's second cause. ➡

تفوذ درا ستقامت وما ماه را با قوس تعدیل اندکست وقد دیک دکسری حرکت اقتد وباعا و
باعا بین حرکت ماه سیدا پیدا یند و اگر اورا رجوعت بکن بودی برنیمه بلای ذلک تد دیر تیانست
بودن خلد فاین ستاره کا ن نخ کا ه ما ما جون رجوعت درپک نیمه اقند باستقامت درنیمه دیک بکذ
واجب جان کردیو کا ستاره در نیمه دورخوابش راجع بودی دیم دوم ستقیم درجوعت قوت را ما
می بوده علوبان را باذلک سبب یقیت که آن آما عد و که بهمرابر کذرد کمز از آن قاعده که زان دیراست
دجن بدی وبیوند که کند ازنیمه باشد

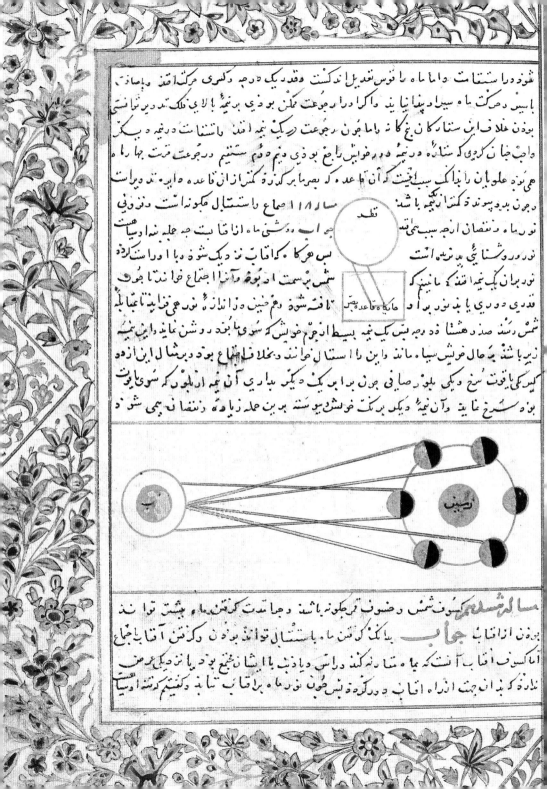

مسله ۱۱۸ اجماع را استقبال هکونداست دن ز دنی
نور ماه دنقصان ارجب سبب نمی لته جواب دوشنی ماه انا انا ثبت جد جله بنداورسیت
نور دروشنایی بذنیه است سبب هوکا جکه آفتاب نز دیک شوه دبا اورا استکرده
نور بیان یک نید انند که ما بینم که شش برست ادبوهم وآنرا اجتماع بذ خواند بود
قدری دودی یا بذ نود براد جین حین دراندازه دم قاعده صص انقشه شوه دم اندازه ندی می نمایته تاعال بلی
شمس دشت صد دهشتا هد ورجه بس یک نیمه بسیط اندهم خویش که سوی با بُعد و روشن نماید واین نیمه
زیبا باشند بحال خویش سیا مانند واین را استقبال خوانند دخلا انا اجماع بود دبر بشال این از ده
کیس کی یاقوت سرخ دیکی بلبوز رصاین جرن بربا یک دیکر بیداری آن نیمه ازلوب که سوی یافت
بود سرخ نماید وآن نیمه ادیک بک بک خویش بوسته بدین جله زیاده دنقصا ن نمی شد د

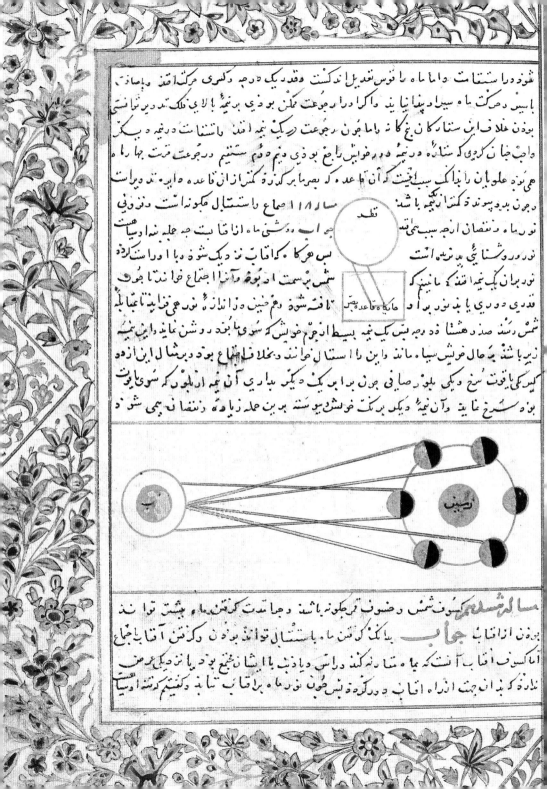

راس

رصین

مساله شمسکه یکنسوف شمس دخسوف قرجلونه باشد وجما ثدت کنقتن ماه پیشت توا اند
بودن اذا نقاب جواب یاکنک کنس ماه باستقبال توانند بودن دکنش آفتاب یاجماع
اناکسف افتاب آنکه بها متمانه کند دراس دیاذنه با ایشان جنبع بود دیا اند دیکر عرص
نلاد که بذ اند جهت انداز افتاب به درکذ ده بس جوں نور ماه براافتاب تابد دکنیم ن تابه واسیا

Hasty Generalization
Aristotle

The notion that generalizations based on unrepresentative samples may be false

A hasty, or false, generalization, *secudum quid* in Latin, is a fallacy in which an arguer draws an inference about a population of objects or events on the basis of an unrepresentative sample. For example, imagine meeting three people upon visiting a new college, all of whom are female. If, on the basis of these meetings, you draw the conclusion that everyone on campus that day is female, you would be making a hasty generalization because it is not clear whether your sample is representative of the college's population.

A sample may be unrepresentative in two ways: it may be too small or it may be biased. In the college example, if there were only twelve people on campus that day, the sample size of 25 percent may be sufficient. But if the population on campus were much larger,

"Given a thimbleful of facts we rush to make generalizations as large as a tub."

Gordon W. Allport, *The Nature of Prejudice* (1954)

say 3,000, it would not. In addition, if you chose your sample randomly, your sample would be unbiased. But if you happened upon a sorority meeting, the sample would be biased toward females.

An early form of this fallacy can be traced to Aristotle's *Prior Analytics* (*c.* 350 BCE), and a discussion is found in William of Ockham's *Summa Logicae* (*c.* 1323). The fallacy plays an important cautionary role in the sciences, which rely heavily on generalizations. For example, medical researchers draw inferences about the effectiveness of potential treatments from samples of people who need the treatment. Researchers try to conduct a series of studies to avoid an overly small sample, and introduce controls (such as a placebo, random selection, and diet) into the experimental process to avoid bias and interference. **JW**

Teleology
Aristotle

The theory that all aspects of the universe were created to fulfill an ultimate purpose

The Greek word *telos* means "purpose," and its contemporary meaning is attributed to Aristotle (384–322 BCE). Teleology is the study of final causes, and the final cause of an event is its *telos*—that for which other events are caused. Until recently, philosophers associated purpose with the direction of events by a creative mind, and there is considerable debate among ancient and contemporary thinkers about whether a purposing mind exists objectively.

For example, ancient atomists deny that nature exhibits purpose, and Socrates is disappointed when he learns that atomists' fully material explanation of movement does not include a "mind or any other principle of order." Aristotle similarly associates *telos* with a mind, citing the artist's mind as the cause that

"Reason forms the starting point, alike in the works of art and . . . nature."

Aristotle, *On the Parts of Animals* (*c.* 350 BCE)

motivates and directs all other causes, and *telos* came to have particular influence through his biology and ethics. In the former, Aristotle categorizes animals according to their most distinctive features and notes that, since nothing generates itself and whatever is in a state of potentiality is nearer or farther from its realization, there must be an organizing principle outside of the organism directing it to its intended actuality. Aristotle extends this essentialism into his ethics, identifying the human *telos* with virtue.

Aristotle's teleology influenced medieval Islamic and Christian thought, especially that of al-Kindi and Thomas Aquinas, both of whom refer to the appearance of purpose in nature in justifying God's existence. Aristotelian teleology remained popular in biology until the arrival of Charles Darwin. **JW**

Nature Abhors a Vacuum
Aristotle

The motions of objects mean that a vacuum is impossible

A central tenet of the physics of Aristotle (384–322 BCE) is that the laws of nature do not permit a void—a space containing absolutely nothing, or a vacuum. This principle came to be referred to as Aristotle's *horror vacui* (fear of emptiness) and is encapsulated in the phrase "Nature abhors a vacuum."

According to Aristotle, the very notion of a void was nonsensical, because the term "void" seemed to be defined as an indefinable nothing. Semantics aside, Aristotle observed that all things in motion eventually come to a halt. Were there a void, said Aristotle, a thing in motion would remain so forever. Furthermore, in a void, objects would not be compelled to move or fall in any particular direction. This, of course, did not correspond to Aristotle's observations of the world, and

"Just as every body is in place, so, too, every place has a body in it."

Aristotle, *Physics* (*c.* 350 BCE)

so he concluded that the universe must be filled and that the motions of things are determined, in part, by their relative densities.

For these reasons (and others) Aristotle taught that the universe was filled with a medium that he called ether, which, in addition to the traditional four elements identified by Empedocles before him, comprised the five elements of the universe. This notion persisted through the Middle Ages and into the seventeenth century. It was among the chief reasons why atomism, which embraces the notion of a void, gained little traction. Around the seventeenth century, a more sophisticated (and vague) conception of this medium came to be referred to as "phlogiston." However, in 1643, the Italian physicist Evangelista Torricelli proved fairly conclusively that a vacuum can indeed exist. **DM**

Cosmopolis
Alexander the Great

The concept of many different peoples living together in the same city

The Greek word *cosmopolis* means "universe city" and refers to a large, important city that is inhabited by people from many different ethnicities.

After the collapse of Classical Greece and the rise of Alexander the Great (356–323 BCE), there occurred a shift from using the word *polis* (city-state) to *cosmopolis*. The cities that formed during Alexander's reign were large, multicultural commercial centers. In no way could they support the original Classical Greek model of city life, in which each individual had a direct role in the politics, economy, social welfare, and spiritual wellbeing of the city. However, the collapse of Alexander's empire after his death marked the rise of Hellenistic Greece, and what is called the Hellenization of the Mediterranean world. Diverse cultures that were once foreign to the

"Different people, different beliefs, different yearnings … different dreams."

Jimmy Carter, U.S. president 1977–81

Greeks now took on Greek-like qualities. More than ever, the *polis* came to be replaced by the *cosmopolis*.

This shift is also clear in philosophy. The Classical Greek philosophers Socrates and Plato had focused on the intimate and important relationship between the citizen and the city, but Hellenistic philosophers, such as Epicurus and Antisthenes, spoke of virtues that should go beyond the city walls to all persons. People now felt a kinship and moral responsibility to everyone, not only their fellow citizens, but at the price of some loss of identity and pride in their particular city.

"Cosmopolis" may now refer to many things: a novel (2003) by Don DeLillo, David Cronenberg's movie adaptation of that novel in 2012, a novel (1892) by Paul Bourget, a city in Washington in the United States, and a musical work by Elias Breeskin, to name a few. **KBJ**

Hellenism
Alexander the Great

An art style more dynamic and ornate than that of the Classical Greek period

The Hellenistic period (323–31 BCE) existed between that of Classical Greece and the rise of the Roman Empire. Hellenistic art and architecture is distinct from both Classical Greek art and Roman art. Hellenistic works are more dynamic, broader, and more ornate than the works of Classical Greek artists.

The beginning of the Hellenistic period dates from the death of Alexander the Great (356–323 BCE), who had carved out one of the ancient world's largest empires. The extent of Alexander's conquest had meant that many parts of the Classical world were exposed to Greek ideas about philosophy, science, art, and architecture. The Classical school of art had been characterized by simple and realistic portrayals, but the new Hellenistic art was more expressive,

"A taste for the small and exquisite was combined with a love of the … grandiose …"

H. Honour & J. Fleming, *A World History of Art* (1984)

often depicting extreme emotions, dramatic settings, and drastic movements. Meanwhile, Hellenistic architecture became more elaborate; dramatic friezes and Corinthian columns featured in buildings that took advantage of larger spaces in order to create a sense of wonder, spectacle, or grandeur.

Where Classical Greek art accurately depicted human anatomy and form, Hellenistic art left a legacy of broader possibilities for artists. After the Greek world was absorbed by Roman expansion, culminating in the battle of Actium in 31 BCE, Roman artists continued the tradition of Hellenistic works and their grander depictions, leaving behind a dramatic legacy. When artists and architects of the Renaissance revisited the Classical period, they often turned to Hellenistic examples and themes for inspiration. **MT**

Eternal Return
Zeno of Citium

The notion of a cyclical universe in which every moment in time is revisited endlessly

If time and space are infinite, the chance is also infinite that the world will exist again exactly as it is. Although the idea of re-creation within the universe dates to even earlier religious and philosophical teachings, the ancient Greek philosopher Zeno of Citium (*c.* 334–*c.* 263 BCE) was first to propose the idea that the universe goes through regular cycles of creation and destruction, and that fate determines whether the universe will infinitely repeat the same course within these cycles.

The idea of an eternal return is the mathematical and philosophical explanation of what must occur in an infinite universe with infinite variation. An infinite universe means that the particular variations that produced the reality in which we live will also produce an infinite series of realities, and occasionally these

"Everything goes, everything comes back; eternally rolls the wheel of being."

Friedrich Nietzsche, philospher

realities will contain everything exactly as it has already occurred. Most religious and philosophical examples of the argument for "eternal return" also include the idea of fate. That is, there is no other way that the universe can exist other than how it exists in the present because it will eternally return to this present.

The philosophy of Friedrich Nietzsche (1844–1900) was greatly influenced by the experience of freedom and fate rooted in the idea of the eternal return. The idea is also the basis for several theories in physics about the cycles of the universe. These include the theory that the Big Bang was one of an infinite series of big bangs that continuously create universes. The idea of an eternal return is also consistent with theoretical models of a "multiverse," in which an infinite number of universes and dimensions exist at the same time. **TD**

Waterpower
Ancient Greece

Using the energy of water as a power source for machines of all kinds

⬆ The Laxey Wheel, 72.5 feet (22.1 m) in diameter, was built in 1854 on the Isle of Man, Britain, to pump water out of nearby mine shafts. It is the largest working waterwheel in the world.

"Water is the driving force of all nature."

Leonardo da Vinci, artist and inventor

Gravitational pull forces water to seek the lowest available point it can find; gravity always causes water to flow. Waterpower, or hydropower, is the harnessing of water's kinetic energy to perform tasks. Water's natural movement has been used to power everything from electrical power stations and sawmills to clocks and Japanese kinetic garden ornaments.

Like all forms of life, humanity has always needed to consume water to survive, although being able to control and direct it is a relatively recent advancement. As early as 7000 BCE, ancient Egyptians learned to fertilize their fields by creating dikes along the Nile river to trap the yearly floodwaters and cause nutritious sediments to settle on their land. However, it was not until the rise of Hellenistic Greece that people found a way to harness water as a source of mechanical power; sometime between the third and first centuries BCE, Hellenic people developed the first waterwheels. These wheels captured the power of flowing water, using it to turn a shaft that in turn caused a millstone to rotate against another stationary one to grind grain.

Hydropower became very important during the early days of the Industrial Revolution (1760–1840) in Britain. In the textile industry, for example, watermills were built to twist thread, drive looms, and finish textiles; in iron manufacturing, water drove trip hammers and powered forges. In the twentieth century, water was harnessed to create hydro-electricity.

Whether water has existed in the landscape in sudden, flooding excess or deadly scarcity, humanity has always depended on its presence. However, when humanity first had the idea of using water's natural properties as a source of mechanical power, the status of one of the great natural forces of the world, one that bestows both hardships and blessings, was changed. Water was transformed into a powerful lever, a force that humanity could direct to do its will. **MT**

A Priori and A Posteriori Knowledge
Ancient Greece

The debate about whether knowledge is obtained by experience or by reason

Philosophy and science are rife with questions about the sources of knowledge. Empiricists argue that experience is the sole source of knowledge. Knowledge obtained by experience is called *a posteriori* (Latin for "to the after," implying after or because of experience). Rationalists argue that some of our knowledge is obtained non-experientially, that is, by pure reason alone. Knowledge obtained non-experientially is called *a priori* (Latin for "to the prior," implying before or independent of experience).

The origin of these terms is controversial and includes Medieval Latin translations of Euclid's *Elements* (*c.* 300 BCE) and the fourteenth-century writings of Albert of Saxony. But there is little doubt that these ideas trace back to Ancient Greek thinkers Plato (*c.* 424–*c.* 348 BCE) and Euclid (third century BCE). The first comprehensive description and defense of *a priori* knowledge was offered by Immanuel Kant (1724–1804) in the eighteenth century. It is Kant's discussion of the subject in his *Critique of Pure Reason* (1781) that provides the framework for the contemporary debate.

It seems clear that much of what we understand about reality comes through experience. And yet, while our experiences are contingent (they could have been otherwise) and local (we have experienced very little of reality), we seem to know things that hold necessarily and universally true. For example, claims such as "2 + 2 = 4," "there are no married bachelors," and "there are no round squares" seem true irrespective of what we have experienced, and thus the source of this knowledge, it would seem, cannot be experiential. Dissenters contend that this is the wrong conclusion and that there is sufficient empirical evidence for explaining the uniqueness of these claims. As yet, there is no widespread agreement in this debate, and it continues to motivate new research in philosophy, psychology, and mathematics. **JW**

⬆ A portrait of the Greek mathematician Euclid. His well-known work, the *Elements* (*c.* 300 BCE), encompassed aspects of mathematics, arithmetic, geometry, and music theory.

> *"Any necessary truth, whether* a priori *or* a posteriori, *could not have turned out otherwise."*
>
> Saul Kripke, philosopher and logician

Anti-Semitism
Manetho

Hostility or discrimination toward Jews as a religious, ethnic, or racial group

German agitator Wilhelm Marr (1819–1904) coined the term "anti-Semitism" in his political diatribe *The Way to Victory of Germanicism over Judaism* (1879). The term suggests derogatory attitudes toward Semitic peoples in general, but it particularly denotes hatred of, or discrimination against, Jewish peoples. Manifestations of anti-Semitism are littered throughout history.

The third-century BCE historian and priest Manetho is credited with disseminating Egyptian anti-Semitism throughout ancient Greece. Manetho held that the Jews are enemies of the human race and that it is necessary to extricate them from human society. The Roman Emperor Tiberius banned Judaism and expelled Jews from Rome. Constantine I imposed numerous prohibitions and regulations on Jewish religious

> *"I am a Jew. Hath not a Jew eyes? … If you prick us, do we not bleed?"*

William Shakespeare, *The Merchant of Venice* (1598)

practices and outlawed conversion to Judaism. Hostility toward Jews persisted into the Middle Ages, especially during the Christian Crusades (1095–1291).

The most extreme expression of anti-Semitism in history was arguably during the rise of the Fascist movement in the 1920s and 1930s. Jewish culture and religion were denigrated, and Jews were accused of rebellions and anti-government conspiracies, and of sabotaging their respective nations. It culminated in the extermination of an estimated six million Jewish people during what is now referred to as the Holocaust. Anti-Semitism persists today in a variety of forms: anti-Jewish sentiment often emerges out of the Israeli–Palestinian conflict, and is also spouted by conspiracy theorists, religiously motivated politicians, and hate-mongers in general. **DM**

Skepticism
Pyrrho of Elis

A denial of the possibility of certainty in knowledge

A central question in the history of ideas is: What, if anything, can we know? One disconcerting answer is that it is unclear that we can know anything at all. This answer characterizes "skepticism," from the Greek *skepsis* (to inquire). Skepticism originated with the Greek philosopher Pyrrhon of Elis (*c*. 360–*c*. 272 BCE), whose ideas were passed on by his assistant Timon and made famous by the Roman philosopher Sextus Empiricus (*c*. 160-210 CE), and later the French philosopher Michel de Montaigne (1533–92).

Empiricus claimed that skepticism is a "mental attitude, which opposes appearances to judgments." By framing skepticism as an attitude of doubting, rather than as a position or view, Empiricus avoided the criticism that skepticism is incoherent (since it would

> *"Skepticism is the chastity of the intellect, and it is shameful to surrender it too soon."*

George Santayana, philosopher

be absurd to say, "We know that we know nothing"). By "opposes appearances to judgments," he meant that skeptics set appearances (the way reality seems) in opposition to judgments (beliefs about the way reality is), and he argued: for any argument that a claim is true, there is an equally powerful reason to be skeptical.

This type of skepticism, known as "Pyrrhonism," was strongly challenged in the seventeenth and eighteenth centuries. René Descartes argued compellingly that there was at least one thing he knew—that he existed. In addition, Isaac Newton and John Locke offered powerful reasons for thinking that practical discoveries in physics are more likely to be true than any skeptical alternatives. Nevertheless, problems with Cartesian epistemology and the fall of Newtonian physics mean that skepticism still influences philosophy today. **JW**

← Detail from the Arch of Titus, Rome, Italy, built to celebrate a victory in the First Roman–Jewish War (66–73 CE).

The Elements
Euclid

The greatest ancient mathematical treatise, Euclid's *Elements* is a collection of definitions, axioms, theorems, and proofs that has informed all logical and scientific endeavor

⬆ The title page of an early translation of Euclid's *Elements* (c. 300 BCE), printed by John Day of London in 1570–71. The mathematical and geometric treatise consists of thirteen books.

> "The discovery of Euclidean geometry, this rule had a deep philosophical and religious significance for many people because it showed that human thinking could get at part of the ultimate truth of reality."

John Barrow, professor of applied mathematics and theoretical physics

Little is known with certainty about the life of the ancient Greek scholar Euclid (*f. c.* 300 BCE). Hundreds of years after him, in the fifth century CE, the Greek philosopher Proclus wrote that Euclid taught at Alexandria when Ptolemy I Soter reigned over Egypt, meaning any time between 322 BCE and 285 BCE. Historians believe that he was older than Archimedes. However despite this paucity of knowledge about him, Euclid's memory lives on thanks to the written works he left behind, most notably the thirteen books that comprise the *Elements* (c. 300 BCE). This book earned Euclid the moniker "the father of geometry," and arguably exercised an influence upon the human mind greater than that of any other work except the Bible.

A variety of mathematical subjects are covered in the *Elements*: Book V investigates ratios and proportions, Books VII to IX deal with number theory (indeed IX is well known for its proof that there is an infinite number of primes) and Books XI to XIII focus on three-dimensional figures. However, the treatise is perhaps best remembered for its investigations into geometry (Books I to IV). Euclid's five postulates effectively read as a constitution for the laws of geometry: a framework to describe the real world.

The first Latin translation of Euclid's *Elements* was by the English philosopher Adelard of Bath in about 1120. It was among the first works printed with the newly invented printing press, and as universities began to multiply, it became the ultimate textbook in Europe. It remained the key text on geometry until 1899, when the German mathematician David Hilbert wrote his acclaimed *Foundations of Geometry*. Moreover, geometry was synonymous with Euclidean geometry until discoveries as late as the second half of the twentieth century. Effectively, through the *Elements*, Euclid's ideas ruled for more than 2,000 years. **JH**

Mathematical Proof
Euclid

The central way in which claims in mathematics are justified

Mathematical proof, traditionally, is the logical derivation of claims (theorems) from axioms (claims assumed to be true or taken for granted), and definitions of the terms occurring in the axioms. Although there were mathematicians who proved theorems before him, Euclid (*f. c.* 300 BCE) is credited as the first to present his proofs in a systematic form. In his seminal work, the *Elements* (*c.* 300 BCE), theorems are proven on the basis of definitions and axioms. Euclid's use of deductive logic to solve mathematical problems underpinned mathematics for more than 2,000 years.

What is the point of mathematical proof? Axioms and definitions are assumed to have various desirable qualities—to be *a priori* (that is, knowable independently of experience), certain, and necessary—which logical derivation is regarded as preserving. So theorems, when correctly proven, are also *a priori*, certain, and necessary. Mathematical proof thus enables the mathematician to erect vast structures on the foundations of the axioms and definitions, confident that they will topple only if the axioms and definitions are poorly expressed or constructed.

However, controversy about mathematical proof abounds, as three well-known examples illustrate. First, although Euclid thought that one of his axioms of geometry, the Parallel Postulate, was necessary, alternative geometries later rejected it. Second, the philosophy of mathematics called intuitionism holds a different view of what counts as a valid logical derivation and thus of what counts as a mathematical proof. Third, in 1976, a computer aided in producing a proof of the four-color theorem in graph theory: because the proof is too lengthy to be checked in its entirety, it is controversial whether it constitutes a proper proof. Still, mathematical proof, as traditionally conceived, continues to be at the center of mathematics. **GB**

Prime Numbers
Euclid

Positive integers that have exactly two positive integer factors

Prime numbers are often known as the building blocks of mathematics. A number is considered prime when it is greater than one and only divisible by one and itself, for example 2, 3, 5, 7, 11, and so on. All other numbers greater than one are called composite numbers.

It is not known when humans first recognized the existence of primes. The Rhind Papyrus from 1650 BCE offers hints that the ancient Egyptians might have had some knowledge of them. This scroll contains much of what we know about Egyptian mathematics, including examples of unit fractions, many of which seem concerned with prime numbers. However, the earliest surviving records that reveal an explicit understanding of prime numbers are from ancient Greece. In his series of thirteen books, the *Elements* (*c.* 300 BCE),

"Primes are the atoms of arithmetic—the hydrogen and oxygen . . . of numbers."

Marcus de Sautoy, professor of mathematics

the scholar Euclid proposed various key facts about prime numbers, including the fundamental theorem of arithmetic (in Book VII) and the first known proof that there are infinitely many primes (in Book IX). This latter discovery has been hailed as the moment that mathematics became an analytic subject.

Thousands of years after Euclid, and despite the focus of some of history's greatest intellects, one aspect of prime numbers remains an infuriating puzzle: they have no obvious pattern and there is no efficient way to find them. However, since the late twentieth century and with the help of computers, prime numbers with millions of digits have been discovered. This might not have mattered much to the world beyond mathematics, but for the fact that cryptographers now use them to create virtually unbreakable codes. **JH**

Squaring the Circle
Euclid

The idea of constructing a square that has exactly the same area as a given circle

The phrase "squaring the circle" refers to attempting an impossible task. The phrase has its roots in the three classical problems of ancient geometry, namely, the doubling of the cube, the trisection of an angle, and the squaring of the circle. All of these eventually proved to be impossible: René Descartes proved the first problem to be impossible in 1637, Pierre Wantzel proved the second to be impossible in 1836, and the third was proved impossible by Ferdinand Lindemann in 1882.

The problems originate in the geometric axioms of Euclid (*fl. c.* 300 BCE), according to which it is possible to construct certain geometric shapes of specified proportions using only a straightedge and a compass. With specific regard to the squaring of the circle, Euclidian geometry tells us that it is possible to

*"To square the circle and who cannot find,
For all his thought, the principle he needs."*

Dante, *The Divine Comedy* (c. 1308–21)

construct a square exactly twice the area of any given square. Furthermore, it is possible to construct a square of exactly the same area as any given polynomial (algebraic expression with two or more terms). Following Euclid, Archimedes (*c.* 290–*c.* 212 BCE) proved it possible to square any segments under a parabola. It then seemed likely that constructing a square the precise area of a given circle would be possible. Looking for the correct procedure to do so occupied numerous geometers in the first and second centuries CE.

Were it possible to square the circle, it must be possible to derive pi using only a straightedge and a compass. However, in 1882 Lindemann proved pi to be a "transcendental" number—it is not the root of any rational number, nor can it be derived algebraically. It therefore cannot be derived by such means. **DM**

Alchemy
Hellenistic Egypt

The belief that chemicals might be manipulated to obtain perfected forms

Alchemy was a pursuit that mixed philosophy, religion, and chemistry in an attempt to manipulate physical objects and properties. Alchemists were proto-scientists who merged the study of the physical world with spiritual and metaphysical principles. They pursued a range of disparate goals, some of the best known being the creation of a universal solvent, development of an elixir of life, and the transformation of less valuable metals into precious gold.

Alchemy probably began in Hellenistic Egypt (*c.* 300 BCE), when the Greek philosophical tradition merged with Egyptian advances in metallurgy, glassmaking, and other crafts. Indian and Chinese thinkers also developed alchemy independently as an attempt to improve health and lengthen lifespan.

"Medicine rests upon four pillars: philosophy, astronomy, alchemy, and ethics."

Paracelsus, physician and alchemist

In Europe, alchemists gained prominence during medieval and Renaissance times, attracting many well-known scientific thinkers. Even Isaac Newton (1642–1726), the pivotal figure of modern physics, pursued alchemy for decades as he attempted to discover some way to transmute chemicals into different forms.

Alchemy faded when it failed to meet modern demands for quantification and skeptical analysis, but its legacy of probing the unknown lingers. Alchemists were part scientist, part physician, part philosopher, and part cleric, exploring mysteries in an attempt to both discover knowledge and gain wisdom. Modern science is largely free of the metaphysical concerns that the alchemists considered paramount, but the desire to explore the unknown and quantify the process rests at the heart of every new discovery. **MT**

Illustration demonstrating coagulation, the seventh and final operation of alchemy.

The Problem of Evil
Epicurus

If God is omnipotent and omnibenevolent, why does evil exist?

For many believers, God is not only all powerful and responsible for the creation of the universe, but also all loving and all knowing. Yet the world is still full of cruelty, human suffering, and evil. How could a being with God's powers allow such suffering to take place?

Questions about the nature of the divine and how a God or gods can be explained in light of reality have been around for millennia. The ancient Greek philosopher Epicurus (341–270 BCE) has been credited with the first formulation of the problem (called the Riddle of Epicurus), though its identification has found no easy solution since. In some religious traditions, such as in ancient Mesopotamia, the destructive elements in the world were attributed to conflicts between gods who each held certain powers. For many monotheistic

"Is God willing to prevent evil, but not able? … Is he able, but not willing?"
Epicurus

religions, multiple proposed solutions have arisen over the years. Many of the Enlightenment philosophers of the seventeenth and eighteenth centuries, such as David Hume, Immanuel Kant, and Gottfried Liebniz, all proposed their own solutions to the dilemma.

The question of evil is a problem that still plagues many theologians and lay believers alike. At the problem's heart is not only a question about the nature of the divine, but also one about the limitations of human understanding. Yet for all the proposed solutions, the problem remains, turning a believer's thoughts not only inward toward reconciliation, but also outward, probing the very nature of the divine. For the believer, it is a question that may never be resolved satisfactorily, while for many nonbelievers it is further proof that such a being is nonexistent. **MT**

Freedom to Choose Otherwise
Epicurus

The notion that moral responsibility implies at least two possible courses of action

Philosophers discuss a variety of types of freedom but the one that captures the most attention is the freedom necessary for moral responsibility, that is, it must have been the case that, upon choosing a particular course of action, it was possible for that person to have chosen an alternative course of action. This possibility is known as "alternate possibilities freedom," or "the freedom to choose otherwise," and stands in contrast to the view that, even if determinism were true, it would be possible to be morally responsible for particular actions. The latter view is known as "compatibilism" because it holds moral responsibility to be compatible with determinism.

Although the question of whether the freedom to choose otherwise is necessary for moral responsibility traces back to Epicurus (341–270 BCE), or at least Lucretius

"To deny … free will is to assert that what a man does do and what he can do coincide."
Peter van Inwagen, analytic philosopher

(c. 99–c. 55 BCE), the most significant advancements occurred in the eighteenth and twentieth centuries. Isaac Newton's mechanistic physics forced modern philosophers to face the possibility that our actions are exhaustively determined by natural processes, and that the freedom to do otherwise is an illusion. Unwilling to relinquish the idea of moral responsibility, philosophers such as David Hume and Immanuel Kant defended versions of compatibilism. But difficulties with compatibilism, highlighted by Roderick Chisholm in 1964 and Peter van Inwagen in 1975, led to new interest in the view that moral responsibility that is incompatible with determinism requires the freedom to choose otherwise. Nevertheless, in 1969 philosopher Harry Frankfurt constructed a counterexample to this view and it continues to influence the debate. **JW**

A pencil drawing, *Justice and Divine Vengeance Chasing Murder* (1804), by Pierre-Paul Proudhon.

Yoga Vasistha
Valmiki

A Hindu scripture that sums up the nature of life: the world of materialism and the body is a dream from which we must wake up in order to pursue spiritual enlightenment

⬆ A miniature painting from the School of Raja sansar Chand (c. 1780) depicts the Hindu sage Bharadvaja and his pupils in an illustration of Valmiki's epic poem, the *Yoga Vasistha*.

"The tree of meditation casts a cool shade in which all desires and cravings come to an end and all the burning distress ceases."

Valmiki, *Yoga Vasistha* (c. 300 BCE)

One of the most exhaustive texts in Sanskrit, the *Yoga Vasistha* is a detailed account of a conversation between the young Sri Rama and his teacher, Vasistha Maharshi, much of which is told in parables. There are 32,000 two-line verses—one verse for every question the pupil was said to have asked his master—which ranks it, at 64,000 lines, second in length only to the voluminous *Mahabharata* (c. 400). Even Krishna himself, in the *Bhagavad Gita* (c. 100 CE), uttered just a mere eighteen verses. Legend says that anyone who manages to finish reading the *Yoga Vasistha* will have their spiritual growth significantly hastened. Authorship of the work is generally attributed to the well-known Sanskrit poet and sage Valmiki, who lived around 300 BCE.

Also known as the *Knowledge Vasistha*, *Maha Ramayana*, or *Vasistha Ramayana*, the text is divided into six sections: dispassion or indifference, longing for liberation, creation, existence, quiescence of mind, and liberation. At its core it is a warning of how illusory our concept of the world really is, that we are in a "dream," and how achieving enlightenment depends upon effectively waking from that dream and then learning to put away worldly desires—to become indifferent to the material things around us and so free ourselves to pursue our own individual growth and spiritual awareness. The *Yoga Vasistha* is always at pains to remind us that everything we see and know, being as it exists within our "dream," is false. The goal is always to awaken. And when we awake, if we eliminate all desire and our mind then enters its "no-mind" state, what is attained is the blissful *Moksha*, the pure extinction of all worldly thought and the complete liberation of the self. More than a treatise on enlightenment, the *Yoga Vasistha* also contains advice on politics, gambling, and even how to sow deception. It incorporates elements of Jainism, yoga, and Mahayana Buddhism. **BS**

The Fifth (Parallel) Postulate
Euclid

The axiom of geometry written by Euclid that was unprovable

The *Elements* of Euclid (*f. c.* 300 BCE) lays down the laws of geometry in five postulates. The first four are relatively intuitive; the fifth (parallel) postulate is not. It states: "If a straight line falling on two straight lines makes the interior angles on the same side less than two right angles, the two straight lines, if produced indefinitely, will meet on that side on which the angles are less than the two right angles." For more than 2,000 years, this formula eluded all attempts to prove it as a theorem. Although it was not as intuitively obvious as the first four postulates, many mathematicians believed that the parallel postulate could be proved using the first four postulates.

However, in 1829, mathematicians stopped trying to prove the fifth postulate, concluding that it was unprovable and should be discarded, and began to explore geometries that did not contain it. The Hungarian mathematician János Bolyai (1802–60) watched his father wrestle with Euclid's fifth axiom. He too became hooked, so much so that his father begged him to give it up. However, Bolyai concluded that a proof was impossible and set about developing a new geometry that ignored it. When he published his geometry in 1831, the great mathematician of the time, Carl Friedrich Gauss (1777–1855) wrote, "To praise it would amount to praising myself. For the entire content . . . coincides almost exactly with my own meditations." Moreover, in 1848 Bolyai discovered that a Russian named Nikolay Ivanovich Lobachevsky had also published virtually the same geometry as early as 1829.

These insights amounted to a radical new way of describing the shape of the physical universe. Gone was the flatness of a Euclidean world in which the parallel postulate holds true; this geometry created a strange, non-Euclidean, curved, space-time world: as Bolyai realized, "a new, another world out of nothing." **JH**

Matrix
Ancient China

Rectangular diagrams that speed up the chore of making advanced calculations

A matrix is any rectangular array of numbers, symbols, or mathematical expressions arranged in rows and columns. The earliest recorded matrix—in a Chinese text, known in English as *The Nine Chapters on the Mathematical Art*, dating from some time between 300 BCE and 200 CE—was used to solve simultaneous equations. The word—which literally means "womb" and is related to *mater* (mother)—was introduced into common English usage in the nineteenth century by Cambridge University mathematician James Sylvester (1814–97), who demonstrated that any matrix could give rise to smaller determinants (or "minors") through the removal of some of the original's elements or entries.

Sylvester's colleague Arthur Cayley (1821–95) then increased the practical applications of matrices

> *"Matrix computations are built upon a hierarchy of linear algebraic operations."*
> G. H. Golub & C. F. Van Loan, *Matrix Computations* (2013)

by demonstrating that they conform to algebraic systems. The significance of this discovery is that their relationship with the normal laws of arithmetic is not always straightforward: some of the rules (such as those of association and distribution) still apply, but in certain cases others, such as the commutative law (numbers may swap position in calculations), may not.

The simplest matrices function as nothing more than shorthand notations for mathematical calculations. Advanced matrices, however, have a wide range of applications, not only in mathematics but also in economics, engineering, physics, and statistics, in which they expedite a range of calculations. Their latest use is in computer graphics, where they have made it possible to represent rotations and other transformations of images. **GL**

Elixir of Life
Ancient China

A potion that promises an eternal existence on Earth for those who drink it

The elixir of life is a hypothetical substance that, if consumed, holds the promise of immortal life. The origins of this idea can be identified in many ancient cultures. In particular, the idea of a potion that could extend life indefinitely was prevalent in East Asia from at least the third century BCE, and Emperor Qin Shi Huang (259–210 BCE) is known, in later life, to have ordered 1,000 men and women to go in search of the elixir. Several emperors of this era are known to have died from drinking substances returned to them from such expeditions. Similarly, the idea of an elixir of life, or *Amrita*, is described in ancient Hindu texts, and in ancient India the search for it never ceased.

The task of discovering or creating the elusive elixir was assigned to alchemists, and the idea that melted

"The water I give him will become in him a spring of water welling up to eternal life."

The Bible, John 4:14

metals, particularly gold and mercury, would provide the basic substance of an elixir was taken up in both Eastern and Western cultures. The enduring nature of these metals was believed to confer itself upon those who consumed them, but the consumption of such metals had highly toxic and fatal effects.

In more recent history, the search for immortality has in general been replaced by a more modest striving for prolonged and healthier life. However, contemporary science has not given up the search entirely. In the twenty-first century, research into microbial culture and probiotics is at the forefront of investigations into the possibility of eternal existence. Thus, the elixir of life may yet reveal itself to humanity's future generations, who would surely question whether the elixir is something we truly desire. **LWa**

Propositional Logic
Chrysippus

A revolutionary system of logic that unlocked our understanding of language

Propositional logic is a system of logic used to characterize the form and function of propositions within language. The first comprehensive system of propositional logic emerged in ancient Athens with Greek philosopher and logician Chrysippus (c. 280–206 BCE). This revolutionary branch of logic concerns the operation of whole propositions or statements, and the relationships between them. Accordingly, within propositional logic a statement, such as "Athens is the capital of Greece," is treated as an indivisible whole. This can then be combined with other statements in order to create a more complex statement such as "Athens is the capital of Greece and the sun is shining in Athens."

The system of propositional logic is in contrast to the traditional syllogistic logic employed by Aristotle

"Logic, I should maintain, must no more admit a unicorn than zoology can."

Bertrand Russell, philosopher

a century earlier, which focused on the operation of individual terms. However, it was not until the mid-nineteenth century that the development of symbolic logic paved the way for a modern axiomatization of propositional logic. As such, the first formulation of contemporary propositional logic can be attributed to philosopher and logician Gottlob Frege (1848–1925).

Perhaps the most striking aspect of Frege's groundbreaking work in propositional logic was his claim that it represented a method of systematic inquiry even more fundamental than that of mathematics. This bold idea has since been the source of significant controversy in the study of logic and has given rise to key developments, including the notions of truth values and truth tables that operate on the premise that all statements must be either true or false. **LWa**

The Archimedes Principle
Archimedes of Syracuse

An explanation for the buoyancy of an object in water

Archimedes (*c.* 290–212 BCE) is arguably the best-known inventor of ancient Greece and perhaps one of the greatest mathematicians of all time. He is remembered for myriad inventions: from a device for raising water called the Archimedes Screw through to catapults that defended his home of Syracuse against invading Romans. The story of how the principle that bears his name was discovered is equally well known.

The Archimedes Principle dictates that a body submerged in a liquid is buoyed up by a force that equals the weight of the liquid it displaces. If the body weighs more than the weight of the water it displaces, it will sink; if it weighs less, it will float. These observations, immortalized in the two volumes of *On Floating Bodies* (*c.* 250 BCE), remain the first known

"There, as he was sitting in the bath . . . He saw at once a way of solving the problem."

Vitruvius, *On Architecture* (first century BCE)

investigations into the laws of buoyancy, making Archimedes the father of the science of hydrostatics.

According to legend, Archimedes stumbled on his principle while doing some detective work for Heiron, the king of Syracuse, who suspected that a goldsmith had stolen his gold while making his crown. The Roman writer and architect Vitruvius recounted in his work *On Architecture* (first century BCE) how Archimedes took the crown to the public baths and "as he was sitting down in the tub, he noticed that the amount of water which flowed over the tub was equal to the amount by which his body was immersed." Running, dripping wet, down the streets of Syracuse, he cried out "Eureka!" (I've found it!). But Galileo and others have questioned the accuracy of Vitruvius's account, which was written 200 years after the actual event. **JM**

Trigonometry
Hipparchus

The branch of mathematics that deals with the functions of angles

Trigonometry—a word derived from the Greek *trigonon* (triangle) and *metron* (measure)—began as the study of geometrical angles and the information that we may infer from them. As it developed, it became essential in astronomy, land surveying, mapmaking, and building design (notably Egypt's pyramids); later it became vital in technologies as varied as radar and atomic energy.

The earliest known trigonometer was the Greek astronomer and mathematician Hipparchus (*c.* 190–*c.* 120 BCE), who developed trigonometric tables primarily in the service of his work in astronomy. Prior to Hipparchus, trigonometry was not a recognized branch of mathematics: for example, Pythagorus (*c.* 570–*c.* 495 BCE) had talked of arithmetic, geometry, harmonics, and astronomy. The earliest surviving

"Mathematical formulas . . . are wiser than we are, wiser even than their discoverers."

Heinrich Hertz, physicist

work on trigonometry, and also the only surviving comprehensive ancient treatise on astronomy, is the *Almagest* (*c.* 150 CE), by Roman astronomer and citizen of Egypt Claudius Ptolemy (*c.* 90–*c.* 168 CE).

In the sixteenth century the emergence of symbolic algebra and the invention of analytic geometry gave trigonometry a vast new range of applications: it became essential in the construction of accurate clocks, navigational equipment, and high-grade musical instruments. In a crucial development, Galileo Galilei used trigonometry to demonstrate that any object falling under the force of gravity moves horizontally as well as vertically. This finding was instrumental in the creation of a new science—ballistics—which made it possible to calculate the range of projectiles (originally focusing on cannonballs). **GL**

The Pyramids of Giza, Egypt, were built in *c.* 2500 BCE using a primitive form of trigonometry. ➡

Yoga Sūtras of Patañjali
Patañjali

A collection of ancient texts providing the foundation for the practice of *Raja Yoga*, in which oneness with universal consciousness is achieved through disciplined meditation

⬆ A nineteenth-century miniature painting from Jodhpur, India, depicts a figure practicing *pranayama*, or "extension of the life force," the yogic discipline of breath control.

Although the practice of yoga predates the author and compiler Patañjali (*f. c.* 150 BCE), it is he who is credited with collecting together what has become the canonical text of *Raja* (Royal) *Yoga*. Originally written in Sanskrit, the text contains 196 *sūtras* (rules) organized into four *padas* (chapters) that communicate the theoretical foundations of the discipline.

Each *sūtra* is a short aphorism stating one, or part, of the philosophical tenets of *Raja Yoga*. As we are told in the *sūtras*, yoga involves training a person's mind through meditation and contemplation to overcome that which is disturbing and unsettling to it. Yogic training, according to the *sūtras*, is divided into eight limbs, each of which prescribes disciplines that must be adopted in various aspects of life in order to achieve *moksha* (liberation), the ultimate goal of yoga.

Moksha occurs when the practitioner of yoga is freed from their sense of self. Patañjali claims that union or integration of the self with the Supreme is the result of the subject restraining the fluctuations of their ego, controlling cognition, and finally annihilating the ego. That is, the practitioner ceases to identify themself as a singular individual and instead identifies with a universal consciousness.

Yoga is one of the six orthodox schools of Hindu philosophy, and, as such, its philosophies and practices are ancient. Indeed, various concepts and cognate uses of the term "yoga" were foundational to many Eastern religions, including Buddhism and Jainism. Although the yoga systems share common roots, there are two predominant schools: the *Raja Yoga* described in the *Yoga Sūtras of Patañjali*, and *Hatha Yoga* taught by Yogi Swatmarama (fifteenth and sixteenth century CE). It is this latter form of yoga, with its greater emphasis on the body's role in meditation, that is more commonly taught in health clubs and yoga studios today. **DM**

"The restraint of the modifications of the mind-stuff is Yoga."

Yoga Sūtras of Patañjali (*c.* 150 BCE)

News Sheet
Ancient Rome

Distributing information rapidly to many people at the same time

Before the invention of writing, the only way to spread news was orally, from person to person or from a speaker to a crowd. It was not until the advent of the Roman Republic that what might be called the first proto-newspaper arose: the Acta Diurna. First appearing in about 131 BCE, the Acta Diurna—Latin for "daily acts"—were public notices about important events in the Republic. The Romans carved news items on stone tablets or metal sheets and posted copies in locations where the public could gather and view them; those able to read would share the information with those of their fellows who could not.

It was not until after the invention of the printing press by Johannes Gutenberg of Mainz, Germany, in 1450 that the first modern newspaper emerged. Published by Johan Carolus in Strasbourg, Germany (now France), in 1605, the Relation aller Fürnemmen und gedenckwürdigen Historien (Account of All Distinguished and Commemorable News) was a book-sized, weekly publication. Soon after its appearance, numerous other newspapers arose in Europe, later spreading to various parts of the world. The first magazine appeared more than a century later, in London in 1731. Named The Gentleman's Magazine, it marked the first use of that term for a publication of varied content. Newsprint remained the prime way in which most people obtained news until it was partly superseded by radio, television, and, later, the Internet and social media.

Newspapers serve to answer our need for new information, for stories about what is going on in the world other than that which we can see for ourselves. They teach, entertain, satisfy our curiosity, and indulge our desire for gossip. The newspaper was also the earliest means of spreading information quickly, cheaply, and efficiently to large numbers of people: it was therefore the first mass medium. **MT**

Bodhisattva
Mahayana Buddhism

Buddhists who dedicate their lives to helping all beings achieve enlightenment

The idea of the bodhisattva developed with the rise of Mahayana Buddhism during the first century BCE. Mahayana means "greater vehicle," and the tradition considers itself superior to Theravada Buddhism because of doctrines such as the bodhisattva ideal.

Bodhisattva means "awakening-being" and refers to Buddhists who have dedicated themselves to helping all beings achieve enlightenment. The Theravada School asserts that the goal of Buddhism is to become an arhat, an enlightened being who has attained nirvana and can exit samsara (the cycle of rebirth). The Mahayana concept of the bodhisattva takes the arhat a step further, asserting that after attaining enlightenment, one can choose to remain in the cycle of rebirth to teach others until all sentient beings have become

> ## "I have made the vow to save all beings. All beings I must set free."
> ### The Buddha

enlightened. This is motivated by bodhicitta, a universal sense of compassion for all beings that is awakened when one realizes enlightenment. Bodhisattvas practice an ethic that involves the "exchange of self and other" (paratmaparivartana) in which they place the welfare of other sentient beings above their own. This is the ultimate expression of anatman (no-self) since it eradicates the distinction between a person's own good and the good of other beings. This sometimes requires them to make use of upaya (skillful means), which are actions that might violate conventional moral precepts but nonetheless promote enlightenment.

The Bodhisattva ideal pervades all Mahayana traditions. Serious practitioners take the bodhisattva vow, swearing to become Buddhas so that they can bring all sentient beings to enlightenment. **JM**

Memento Mori
Ancient Rome

A Latin phrase that reminds us all of the end that inevitably awaits us

Memento mori is a Latin phrase that is usually rendered in English as "Remember: you will die." It most probably originated as a proverb, but according to one popular folk story it was first used in the first century BCE by a Roman slave who, having seen his master ride in triumph through Rome after a military victory, used the expression to remind his master of his mortality.

Whatever the truth of that tale, the term was taken up enthusiastically by the Christian religion, which emphasized divine judgment and the transience of all earthly things. *Memento mori* provided the religion with a moralistic counterpoint to another well-known Latin expression: *nunc est bibendum* ("now is the time for drinking"—in other words, do not defer gratification). *Memento mori* encapsulates the outlook of many people who believe that our actions in this life will be rewarded or punished in the next.

By extension, *memento mori* has come to be used as a generic label for funerary architecture that, in addition to commemorating the deceased, also reminds the living of the transience of earthly existence. Examples of this include relief sculptures on tombs depicting human skulls or angels snuffing out candles. The term is also used for the admonitory captions that may accompany such details: the entrance to a chapel in Évora, Portugal, for example, has above it the inscription "*Nós ossos que aqui estamos pelos vossos esperamos*" (We, the bones that are here, await yours).

In painting, there is a genre of still life that is referred to as *vanitas*, Latin for "vanity." Such compositions include symbols of mortality, most commonly the skull, and were intended as sobering daily reminders of mortality. There is also a long and strong tradition of *memento mori* works in literature, particularly poems. Among the best known of these in English is "Elegy Written in a Country Church Yard," written in the eighteenth century by Thomas Gray. **GL**

A seventeenth-century *memento mori* painting by Philippe de Champaigne. ⬆

Societas Publicanorum
Ancient Rome

The first example of a private corporation with publically traded shares

The British East India Company, founded as a joint-stock company in 1707 from earlier incarnations dating back to 1600 and the time of Elizabeth I, is cited as the earliest predecessor of the modern publically traded corporation. However, recent scholarship suggests that the corporation has roots in the first century BCE, in Roman institutions known as *societas publicanorum*.

The more or less uniform geographical expansion of Roman political power allowed for the creation of large markets aided by certain technological advances. For example, advances in mining technology increased the rate and volume of mineral extraction, and agricultural innovations increased food production. With that increased production came higher revenues from taxation, greater usage of public property, and stronger demand for public works in general. In order to cope with this demand, the Roman authorities effectively outsourced certain administrative responsibilities via contract to a new kind of political institution, the *societas publicanorum*.

Roman law permitted private individuals to form associations (*societas*) comprising various partners (*socii*) for the purpose of bidding on and fulfilling such contracts. These associations were permitted to seek external financing by selling shares (*partes*) in the association. In an arrangement similar to that offered by modern corporations, investors did not share the contractual obligations or liabilities of the association itself. And, just like shares in modern corporations, *partes* could be bought, sold, and traded, which made them a more attractive proposition.

The historical significance of *societas publicanorum* cannot be overstated; not only are they the prototypes for the dominant vehicle for business in modern times, they are also likely the earliest models of private provision of public services—in other words, privatization—itself a common practice almost 2,000 years later. **DM**

↑ A first-century marble relief from Pompeii, Italy, that was used as the sign to a coppersmith's shop.

Universal Language
Ancient Rome

The concept of a single language that can be understood and spoken by everyone in the world

⬆ A Latin engraving on the tombstone of the Roman cavalry soldier Publius Cornelius, who participated in the expedition of Aelius Gallus to Yemen in 26–25 BCE.

The idea of a "universal language" refers to either a hypothetical or historical language spoken by most or all of the world's population. Some mythological or religious traditions posit a time when all people spoke the same language, but there is no evidence for this hypothesis. Latin was one of the first languages to achieve a semblance of universality, thanks to the expansion of the Roman Empire (established in 27 BCE). Latin became (in effect) the official language of government, business, religion, education, and law across much of Western Europe, and remained so until the sixteenth century (due in part to the dominance of Latin in the Roman Catholic Church).

With the decay of the Western Roman Empire in the fifth century, regions that had been unified by the Roman Empire began to fall away from central control, and Latin dialects used in general conversation became, over time, distinct languages (the Romance languages). When trade increased, despite the everyday decline of Latin, the desire for an international trade language increased also, as did attempts to construct a universal language in general. Gottfried Leibniz (1646–1716) was one of several thinkers to make efforts toward what he called a "universally characteristic language." Leibniz was impressed by the way that the Egyptian and Chinese languages used graphic expressions for concepts, and proposed a universal system of writing composed of symbols. Inspired by Leibniz, Giuseppe Peano (1858–1932) developed the Interlingua language in 1903, based on a simplified form of Latin.

The pursuit of a universal language continues today. For example, existing constructed languages—most famously Esperanto but also the less well-known Ido—may still give grounds for a future universal language. Both were designed to be international auxiliary languages, or universal second languages. **JE**

"It would be very difficult to form … this language … but very easy to understand it …"
Gottfried Leibniz, mathematician and philosopher

The Second Coming
Early Christians

The notion that Jesus will return and announce himself once more on Earth

It is a central belief of the Christian faith that one day Jesus Christ, the Son of God, will return and once again make himself known to the peoples of the world. Furthermore, it is believed that Christ's "second coming" will bring heaven on Earth. The belief stems from a number of canonical biblical prophecies that, taken together, support the interpretation that Christ will return.

There is no expectation that the world's transition toward heaven will be smooth, however. The period immediately before Christ's return is anticipated to be marked by the emergence of false prophets and the Antichrist, with Christ and the Antichrist having to battle for the future of humanity. It is evident from the Gospels and the works of Paul (believed to have been written sometime around 50 BCE) that Christ's return was anticipated to be an imminent event. The epoch of the return of Christ is expected to be characterized by the destruction of existing worldly empires, followed by the establishment of a kingdom lasting 1,000 years. The majority of Christian theologians in history have believed that the reappearance of Jesus may occur at any moment, and have therefore advised that Christians should always be ready for it.

In modern times, the idea of the second coming of Christ has proven influential in works of fiction, as has the figure of the Antichrist who opposes him. It inspired the supernatural horror movie series *The Omen*—initially released as a novel by David Seltzer in 1976—and also Stephen King's novel *The Stand* (1978). Individuals claiming to be the second coming have included Sun Myung Moon (of the Unification Church), Jim Jones (instigator of the Jonestown mass suicide in 1978), David Koresh (behind the Waco, Texas, mass suicide in 1993), and Marshall Applewhite (cause of the Heaven's Gate mass suicide in 1997). **JE**

Grace
Early Christians

The belief that we need God's help to live a good life and earn a place in Heaven

Grace, strongly developed in early Christian thought, is the idea that we need God's help in living a good life—which is defined as following God's will—in order that after death we may return to God in Heaven. Grace, in its specifically metaphysical meaning, is understood to be a divine act bestowed from God as a manifestation of His love and kindness. In Christian thought, God's ultimate act of grace is considered to be the sacrifice of His Son, Jesus, for the salvation of humankind.

The life of grace is taken to be characterized by divine favor, and is marked by dedicated active service to God and obedience to His commandments. As Christian doctrine evolved, grace specifically came to mean salvation from sin, with grace being an active means of healing the effects of evil in the lives of

> *"This grace ... conducts all ... to the state of the highest perfection and glory."*
> Augustine of Hippo, theologian

believers. The notion of grace is associated with the Christian belief in original sin—that Adam's sin is visited on all humanity, with the result that all of humankind has "fallen" from grace and would remain in that state without the intervention of, and human belief in, Jesus as the Son of God, a manifestation of the one true God on Earth. It is because the salvation of humanity could not occur without Jesus's self-sacrifice that his act has taken on the meaning of the ultimate act of divine grace in Christian theology. The concept of grace as an undeserved divine action, closely aligned with acceptance of Jesus as the Son of God and a life dedicated to serving God and spreading Christianity, has been a central element of Chrisitianity for centuries, and can perhaps be taken as the central doctrinal element of the Christian faith. **JE**

Plainchant
Early Christians

The idea of unaccompanied singing in unison of Christian liturgies

Although the music itself dates from the first century CE, the so-called Apostolic Age, the term "plainchant," describing unaccompanied singing of Christian liturgies, appeared in the thirteenth century and is derived from the Latin *cantus planus* (plain song). The term is often used in a more restricted sense, however, referring to the Roman Catholic Church's sung liturgy, Gregorian Chant, which is misattributed to Pope Gregory I (540–604). The plainchant repertoire was refined, particularly following the Council of Trent (1545–63), when it was standardized in order to create a common liturgical practice. Centuries later, the Second Vatican Council of 1963 replaced Latin with vernacular languages, and introduced new liturgical music.

The standardization of the Roman Catholic Church's liturgical materials as an aid to expansion was instrumental in the development of musical notation, although this was not recognized as an important consequence in early medieval sources. Dating from the ninth century, the early notation of chant, with neumes representing notes or groups of notes, would gradually develop into the highly precise system of symbols for pitch, rhythm, and dynamics used today. Notation was crucial to the expansion of composition from a single melodic line to polyphony, and in medieval times plainchant melodies were sometimes elaborated into complex polyphonic compositions.

While plainchant has been of enormous importance for the church through the centuries, and remains so, it reached a general audience during the mid-1990s with the release of the album *Chant* by The Benedictine Monks of Santo Domingo de Silos, which sold three million copies in the United States. The popularity of the plainchant-like works of Hildegard von Bingen (1098–1179) has also helped plainchant to become a vehicle for new-age aesthetics, and to generate an interest in other historical female composers. **PB**

　A carving of a man playing the third tone of plainchant on a cithara, *c.* 1118–20, from Cluny Abbey, France. ⬆

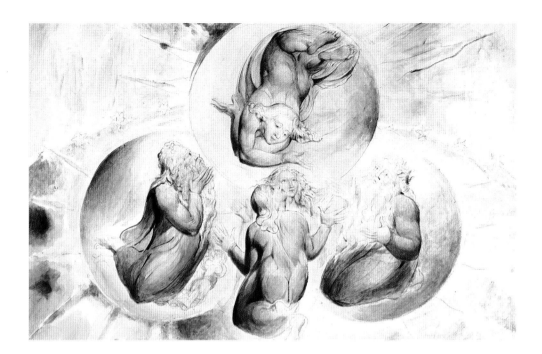

Three Theological Virtues
Early Christians

Three positive character qualities associated with salvation

The Greek philosopher Aristotle (384–322 BCE) defined virtue as "a positive trained disposition." The ancients believed in four cardinal virtues, namely wisdom, justice, temperance, and courage, but held that because all four are aimed at the good of humankind, they are never wholly separable from one another. Using Paul's First Epistle to the Corinthians 13:13 (written c. 55 CE) as their proof text, the Church Fathers added to this list three more virtues, ones especially connected with the nature of God and the perfection of the cardinal virtues. These were faith, hope, and love.

Believers would say that faith has to do with holding on to what they know to be right, despite emotions to the contrary. Faith is the emotive thrust that keeps them trusting in God—who they have good reason to believe exists and is good—even when He feels absent. The virtue of faith helps them to act rationally, even when it is hard to do so.

Hope is the rational desire to be with God and attain true happiness therein. Insofar as reason helps believers to discern God's existence and good character, hope is the proper desire to want to be with God. Hope—a rational desire that is grounded in rational possibilities—may be contrasted with "wish," which is no more than an irrational desire for some impossible future happiness.

Love—that is, agape love—disposes believers to sacrifice themselves for others in a manner that perfects justice, but never contradicts it. Justice requires a person to treat others correctly—to provide for the basic needs of one's family, for example—but love goes beyond this; it might, for example, oblige a father to lay down his very life for his family. The three theological virtues have played an enormous role in Western, especially Christian, thinking about rationality and character development, and their importance shows no sign of abating. **AB**

Terrorism
Jewish Zealots

The pursuit of religious, political, or ideological goals through creation of fear

Terrorism, the idea of deliberately creating terror by targeting attacks on people and/or buildings for a variety of purposes, originated in around 70 CE in the practices of the Jewish Sicarii—known for their use of a short sword (*sica*)—who killed wealthy Jewish collaborators during the period of Roman rule over the Jewish people. Later examples of terrorist groups include the Assassins, a Shiite group in eleventh- and twelfth-century Persia, who killed in order to oppose efforts by Sunni practitioners to suppress their religious beliefs; and, in eleventh-century India, a group called the Thugs who killed to nourish the goddess Kali with blood, threatening Indian society until the colonial era.

The concept of state terrorism is more controversial, leading to disagreements over the appropriateness of

> *"How can you have a war on terrorism when war itself is terrorism?"*
>
> Howard Zinn, historian and social activist

attributing the label "terrorism" to actions or campaigns coordinated by nation-states pursuing particular goals under conditions in which only guerrilla warfare is possible. State terrorism (assuming scholarly consensus that such campaigns can be called terrorism) is also an important topic of analysis, characterizing many actions taken by right-wing dictatorships (such as in Germany under Hitler or Indonesia under Suharto), left-wing totalitarian states (such as in the U.S.S.R. under Stalin or during the Cultural Revolution in China under Mao), and under contemporary "liberal-democratic" capitalist states (sometimes indirectly, such as U.S. support of right-wing client-state dictatorships, such as Pinochet's Chile or in Guatemala following the 1954 coup, or sometimes directly, such as the contemporary U.S. tactic of extrajudicial killings through drone strikes). **JE**

Encyclopedia
Pliny the Elder

A comprehensive collection of knowledge, often found in book form

Roman naturalist and writer Gaius Plinius Secundus, or Pliny the Elder (23–79 CE), compiled the world's first encyclopedia some time around 77 CE when he wrote *Naturalis Historia*, or *Natural History*. This ambitious work was an attempt to bring together knowledge on every subject in the natural world, from zoology and astronomy to classical art. While Pliny's work was as comprehensive as he could make it, it was organized into chapters that addressed individual fields of study and not in individual entries on specific topics. European, Muslim, and Chinese scholars created more encyclopedias in the centuries that followed, but it was not until the early eighteenth century that the first modern versions of the encyclopedia emerged. Numerous encyclopedias or compendiums appeared

> *"To me the charm of an encyclopedia is that it knows—and I needn't."*
>
> Francis Yeats-Brown, British army officer and writer

that, like Pliny's work, contained information on myriad topics and subject areas, while at the same organizing that knowledge into an easier to use format. Individually tailored entries, accompanied by drawings, diagrams, and cross-references that linked them to related material, became the standard for all encyclopedias.

What is the sum total of human knowledge? This is the core question that encyclopedias seek to answer. Whether they cover a particular discipline or try to capture the breadth of understanding, encyclopedias offer the reader the promise of being able to know the answer to any question simply by reaching for the proper volume. As technology advanced and book searches became replaced by keystrokes, the ability to have all knowledge at the tips of your fingers became almost instantaneously attainable. **MT**

Social Welfare
Emperor Trajan

Services provided by a state's government to benefit its citizens

Social welfare is the idea that the government of a state is responsible for providing a minimal level of well being for its citizens. While charity is an ethical and religious principle intended to guide behavior, social welfare is a political principle promoting a broader social responsibility to help those in need. The first widespread social welfare programs were instituted in the Roman Empire, and the Emperor Trajan (53–117 CE) established the first and most extensive of these.

Justifications for social welfare programs have included religious beliefs, ethical requirements, and political calculations. Most major world religions teach the importance of care for the poor, and historically governments able to provide a level of subsistence for their populations have been better able to avoid

"Power has only one duty—to secure the social welfare of the People."

Benjamin Disraeli, British prime minister 1874–80

some of the problems of poverty that lead to social instability. The Islamic Caliph Umar (579–644) identified a public aspect to the moral obligation or Pillar of Islam requiring charity, and established taxes to pay for public services. In another well-known historical example of social welfare, the Song Dynasty in China (960–1279) implemented government assistance in the form of healthcare and public housing.

Today, every democracy in the world implements some form of social welfare program, and most citizens of those countries believe that it is important to provide resources for those unable to provide for themselves. Such programs are often controversial, however, provoking debates about who deserves assistance, how much assistance should be given, and what percentage of public resources should be used for them. **TD**

Perfect Number
Nichomachus

A natural number equal to the sum of all its divisors except itself

The concept of a "perfect number," a positive integer equal to the sum of its positive proper divisors minus itself, stems back to the Neo-Pythagorean philosopher and mathematician Nicomachus of Gerasa (*c.* 60–*c.* 120 CE), who authored the *Introduction to Arithmetic*, the standard text on arithmetic for 1,000 years. The first such perfect number is six (sum of $1 + 2 + 3$), with the three next such numbers being 28 ($1 + 2 + 4 + 7 + 14$), 496, and 8,128. These four perfect numbers were known to Nichomachus, who identified 8,128 as a perfect number as early as 100 CE. Nichomachus classified all numbers as "deficient," "perfect," or "superabundant," depending on whether the sum of their divisors was less than, equal to, or greater than the number itself.

"[Nature seems] to have been determined and ordered in accordance with number."

Nicomachus, *Introduction to Arithmetic* (*c.* 100 CE)

The study of numbers was of fundamental (and commonly spiritual) importance to Pythagorean and Neo-Pythagorean thinkers—Nichomachus himself wrote a two-volume work titled *The Theology of Numbers* on the mystic properties of numbers (only fragments of which survive). The work led to a number of early mathematical discoveries, including that of the first four perfect numbers.

Perfect numbers have proven elusive; as of 2007, only forty-four have been found. A formula covering identified perfect numbers—all positive thus far—combines what is known as the Euclid-Euler theorem ($2^{(n-1)} \times (2n-1)$), with a Mersenne prime inserted for n (a Mersenne prime is a number generated by the formula $(2^n)-1$, named for the French monk Father Marin Mersenne, 1588–1648). **JE**

Gnosticism
Valentinus

The belief that gnosis (esoteric or intuitive knowledge) can lead to the soul's salvation

Gnosticism, from the Greek *gnosis* (knowledge), is a contemporary term that refers to a number of schools of spiritual thought, each emphasizing the attainment of revealed knowledge of the divine as the means for spiritual salvation and transcendence of the physical world. While gnostic tendencies may be found in a number of world religions, the term "gnosticism" is often used to refer to a set of "gnostic" Christian schools in the second to third century CE, the period of early Christianity before orthodoxy had become enforced. A key leader of the Gnostic movement was Valentinus (c. 100–c. 160 CE), who founded an influential sect in the second century in Rome.

Valentinian gnosticism presupposes a central being, Bythos, from whom emanate three pairs of aeons, or

> "... God invisibly cooperates with what has been modeled to lend it credence."
>
> Valentinus

beings, that represent cosmological opposites (such as male and female); from these three pairs emanate others, making an overall total of thirty aeons. All the aeons together constitute the realm of spiritual being (the *pleroma*). But the last aeon, Sophia, sinned through having an offspring, Achamoth, who created a rival world (*kenoma*, Greek for "vacuum"); a rival imitator creator "deity," the Demiurge (identified with the God of the Old Testament), generates the physical universe. Gnostic Christianity, though relating to both the Old Testament and the figure of Christ, incorporates elements of pagan gnosticism and Platonism. Knowledge of Valentinus and gnosticism increased with the discovery in 1945 of the Nag Hammadi library, a number of preserved early gnostic Christian texts, discovered buried in Nag Hammadi in upper Egypt. **JE**

Easter
Melito of Sardis

A period of celebration commemorating the death and resurrection of Jesus Christ

The Easter feast, celebrating the death and the resurrection of Jesus Christ, is among the most important Christian feasts. Easter was first mentioned in a mid-second century Paschal homily believed to be written by Melito of Sardis (*d. c.* 180) for reading aloud on the morning of Pascha, an earlier name for the feast. Originally, Easter was observed with Jewish Passover, but after the first Council of Nicaea in 325 it was declared that Easter should be observed on Sunday, held to be the day of the resurrection of Christ. The date was movable, being the first Sunday after the first full moon after the spring equinox.

Two of the most common symbols of Easter are the egg and the rabbit, and the egg symbolizes new life breaking through the seeming death of the

> "Easter is the demonstration of God that life is essentially spiritual and timeless."
>
> Rev. Charles M. Crowe, pastor

eggshell, represented by its hardness. This symbolic interpretation of the egg likely predated Christianity, but was adapted to represent Christ's return from death and coming forth from the tomb. The Easter rabbit is also likely to hark back to cultures predating Christianity, for which the appearance of the rabbit in the landscape symbolized the coming of spring (itself symbolized by the animal's renowned fertility). The rabbit has been adapted by many Christian cultures, but has not taken on any specific Christian meaning comparable to that of the egg.

In Germany the egg and rabbit Easter symbols were united in the notion of an egg-laying hare, one that, after importation into the United States in the eighteenth century, came to lay the chocolate eggs now loved by children the world over. **JE**

Christ Carrying the Cross (c. 1500) by Hieronymus Bosch. ➡

Free Rein Defense

Irenaeus

The Christian argument that the existence of evil is consistent with natural laws

⬆ A portrait (c. 202) of St. Irenaeus, bishop of Lyons. His main work, *Against Heresies* (c. 180)—and, indeed, all his other writings—was devoted to refuting gnosticism.

"For when strength was made perfect in weakness, it exhibited the benignity of God, and His most admirable power."

Irenaeus, *Against Heresies* (c. 180)

For theologians, the concept of evil is a challenge to the propositions that God is omniscient, omnipotent, and omnibenevolent. The problem, or theodicy, is this: given God's omniscience, God must know that evil exists in the world. This being the case, God must be either incapable of preventing evil, and therefore not omnipotent, or God is permissive of evil, and therefore not omnibenevolent. Stated plainly, the existence of evil is a problem because evil itself challenges the conventional monotheistic concept of God.

Two distinct approaches to this problem have emerged: one inspired by Augustine of Hippo (354–430), the other inspired by Irenaeus, bishop of Lugdunum, now Lyons (c. 140–200). The Free Rein Defense, or FRD, is most closely aligned to the Irenaean approach. Irenaean theodicy upholds the utility of evil in humankind's development as moral agents. The FRD proposes that the universe must operate in accordance with certain natural laws (such as the laws of classical physics) because, were this not the case, cause and effect would break down; it would be impossible to predict (even vaguely) the effect of any given cause; and effective action would be impossible. In other words, if the laws that govern the universe were not given free rein to unfold as they may, human beings along with every other denizen of the universe would be little more than God's puppets, and concepts such as free will, intention, piety, sin, and even good and evil would be nonsensical. For this reason, the defense continues, God allows the complex chains of causes and effects to unfold unimpeded. As a consequence, however, the natural laws ultimately and inevitably give rise to evil and suffering. Today the FRD and its underlying principles have come under severe attack, especially from secular culture, informed by existential nihilism, insisting that life's meaning must be created by humankind. **DM**

Creatio Ex Nihilo
Irenaeus

The belief that an all-powerful god created the universe out of nothing

Standing in contrast to proposals that the universe was created out of preexisting chaos, the Christian doctrine of *creatio ex nihilo*—that God directly created the universe from nothing—originated at the time in early Christian history when no established church doctrine had yet been consolidated. The doctrine found an able expositor and defender in Irenaeus, bishop of Lugdunum, now Lyons (*c.* 140–200).

Irenaeus developed the doctrine of *creatio ex nihilo* specifically to counter popular gnostic teachings that the material world was not the direct work of God, but instead was the work of a lesser god who fashioned it from preexisting matter. The gnostic idea of the world followed the Platonic view, which itself set up a dualism between ultimate reality (that of God) and the empirical world—the latter, according to the gnostics, being inferior, illusionary, and an obstacle and distraction that prevents us from attaining knowledge about or inhabitation of the "real world."

The gnostics, following Platonic dualism, viewed the empirical world as evil, essentially because it stood between the believer and God. In contrast, Irenaeus upheld that, first, the created world is real, rather than a false veneer hiding the real, hidden world; second, it is created directly by the true God rather than being the work of a lesser, subordinate deity; and, third, it is created from nothing rather than from preexisting and chaotic, imperfect matter. Irenaeus, then, fundamentally attributes all that exists to a single, perfect entity, and in so doing attempts to eradicate the notion that creation can be evil. The notion of *creatio ex nihilo* underwrites Christian cosmology, setting the stage for numerous other Christian beliefs about creation, while simultaneously underwriting the Judeo-Christian metaphysical view that there is only one God, who is fundamentally superior to and beyond all else in creation. **JE**

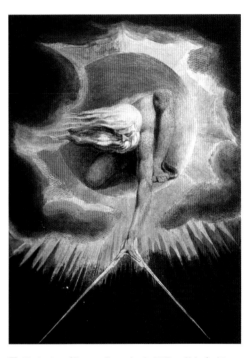

⬆ *The Ancient of Days*, an illustration by William Blake for his book *Europe: A Prophecy* (1794). The book was engraved on eighteen plates, and survives in just nine known copies.

"God the Creator ... created all things, since He is the only God ... alone containing all things, and Himself commanding all things into existence."

Irenaeus, *Against Heresies* (*c.* 180)

Original Sin
Irenaeus

The concept that Adam's sin with Eve in the Garden of Eden has tainted all of humankind

The notion of "original sin," hereditary guilt passed from Adam throughout the lineage of humankind, is not explicitly developed in the Old Testament, though it is consistent with a number of passages throughout Genesis and the Old Testament in general. Such a notion was initially developed in the works of Irenaeus (c. 140–200), who taught that evil came into the material world through Adam's sin. Irenaeus developed this doctrine in order to combat the gnostic sects in their belief that the world of matter was both inherently evil and the product of a lesser deity, rather than the creation of a true, good God (which contains evil as a consequence of humankind's disobedience).

While the doctrine of original sin was initially developed by Irenaeus, its precise articulation was

> *"Original sin ... appears to be a hereditary depravity and corruption of our nature ..."*
>
> John Calvin, theologian

developed by Tertullian (c. 155–220), St. Cyprian (200–258), and St. Ambrose (339–397). They taught what might be the core of the doctrine of original sin, namely that sin that originated in Adam passed down through human generations. St. Augustine (354–430) and St. Anselm (c. 1033–1109) advanced the doctrine, which became canonically central to orthodox Catholic and Christian faith. "Original sin" provides a justification for the existence of the Church (the Church would be needed to promote the true way in a fallen world) in addition to a motivating factor for joining it (humankind needs the intervention of the Church to find salvation). The doctrine of original sin, long in development, is a fundamental element of the Christian faith and has proven key to securing the importance of the Church in the lives of believers. **JE**

Vitalism
Galen

The belief that some special "living" quality exists beyond the parts of animate life

Vitalism is a broadly metaphysical doctrine that conceives of a living being as being distinguished from nonliving beings by virtue of some "essence" that is particular to life and which exists above and beyond the sum of that living being's inanimate parts.

The Greek medical practitioner Galen (c. 130–c. 210) held that spirit (*pneuma*) was the essential principle of life and took three forms—animal spirit (*pneuma physicon*), which occurred in the brain; vital spirit (*pneuma zoticon*), which occurred in the heart; and natural spirit (*pneuma physicon*), which resided in the liver. Galen's ideas remained influential for as long as 1,400 years after his death.

An earlier form of vitalism had been proposed by Aristotle (384–322 BCE), and his works *On the Soul* and

> *"After death ... I will no longer move, no longer sense, nor speak, nor feel, nor care."*
>
> Aristotle, philosopher

On the Generation of Animals (both c. 350 BCE) became canonical vitalist treatises. Aristotle held that the soul (the psyche) is what attributes organizational unity and purposeful activity to a living entity. Later thinkers to offer a more advanced version of the theory included the philosopher and biologist Hans Driesch (1867–1941). Driesch also articulated a philosophy highlighting what he took to be an essential, autonomous, and nonspatial psychoid or mindlike essence behind living things, referring to his experiments with sea urchin embryos, in which separated cells developed into whole organisms.

Galen was responsible for particular conceptual errors that persisted long after him, and vitalism as a theory of life has few adherents within contemporary biology. Nevertheless, there is no question that both had enormous influence on Western thinking. **JE**

The left-hand panel of a diptych (c. 1479) by Hugo van der Goes, showing the fall and redemption of Man.

Bloodletting
Galen

The theory that the sick may be healed by relieving their bodies of excess blood

Bloodletting is the practice in medicine of withdrawing blood from patients to prevent or cure illness or disease. While the ancient Egyptians and Greeks were among the first to practice medical bloodletting, it was the Greek physician Galen (c. 130–c. 210) who produced a systematic bloodletting treatment in the second century—a development that would result in much loss of life over the following centuries.

In accordance with the Hippocratic school of medicine, Galen regarded health as a matter of balancing the four humors—blood, phlegm, yellow bile, and black bile. Of these, he was particularly interested in blood, which he demonstrated to flow through the arteries of living animals. He believed that

illness was often due to a superabundance of blood and therefore recommended bloodletting by venesection (opening a vein by incision or puncture) to remedy it, in part because venesection is a controllable procedure. He offered guidelines about when, where, and how to bleed, depending on the patient's condition and the disease's course. Later methods of bloodletting included blood cupping (cutting the skin and then using heated cups to withdraw the blood by means of suction as they cool) and the use of leeches (especially the species *Hirudo medicinalis*), for which sucking blood from host mammals is a natural behavior.

Convinced of his findings, Galen eventually completed three books expounding his views on bloodletting. His systematization of Greek medicine was so powerful and persuasive that his views dominated Western medicine for the next 1,500 years. It was only in the Renaissance that scholars, such as Andreas Vesalius, began to challenge his authority. Nevertheless, the practice of bloodletting continued, amid increasing controversy, until the end of the nineteenth century. Except for a few rare conditions, it is now generally regarded as ineffective or harmful. **GB**

An illustration of bloodletting and skin disease treatment from a medical treatise of 1519.

The Holy Trinity
Tertullian

The belief that God consists of three persons combined in one substance

Until the first half of the first century CE, Jewish monotheism typically understood God to have one "character" or "personality." However, the appearance of Jesus in the first century CE challenged this, as by performing a number of acts (such as forgiving sins) that the ancient Jews believed were the prerogative of God alone, Jesus seemed to claim for himself some kind of identity with God. Yet despite making these claims, Jesus, at the same time, also clearly understood his identity to be different from that of God the Father. The nature of God's identity was complicated even further when Jesus said that the Father would send "the Holy Spirit"—apparently another aspect of God— to aid Christians in their spiritual growth.

During the first four centuries after Jesus's death, Christians argued about how, precisely, the claims of God's unity and yet plurality could be reconciled. The early Christians were deeply concerned with rational intelligibility, and while they could accept that the exercise of reason might point to a mystery that is understood rationally only by God, they could not accept logical contradiction. Various "heretical" ideas were suggested, including modalism (which claims that the Father, Son, and Holy Spirit are mere modes or appearances of the one God) and Arianism (which claims that the Son was created by the Father). However, one of the early church fathers, Tertullian (c. 160–c. 225) was the first to speak of both God being one "substance," and the Father, Son, and Holy Spirit being distinct "persons" or "personalities" of that substance.

A century later, at the Council of Nicene, the rough formula of "three persons in one substance" became the accepted orthodox key to understanding the unity and plurality of the Godhead. Given the pervasiveness of Christianity, the idea that God is tri-personal is now the dominant conception of monotheism across the globe. **AB**

⬆ *The Trinity*, a sixteenth-century oil painting by Jacopo Robusti Tintoretto.

Metanoia
Tertullian

A change of mind powerful enough to alter a person's outlook and behavior

The term "metanoia" is derived from the Greek prefix *meta*—meaning "over," "after," or "with"—and *nous*, meaning "intellect" or "mind." Translating literally, metanoia means a change of one's mind or purpose. The term is generally used in two different contexts, both of which retain this literal meaning. In the Bible, the term is most often translated as "repent," and the term also figures prominently in the psychological works of Carl Jung (1875–1961).

The Christian scholar Tertullian (*c*. 160–*c*. 225) argued that, in the context of Christian theology, metanoia is best translated as "change of mind." In this specific context, the change of mind may be taken to refer to the change from nonbeliever to believer. Furthermore, this particular kind of change of mind is expected to

> *"Do you not realize that the kindness of God is meant to lead you to repentance?"*
>
> The Bible, Romans 2:4

entail a wholesale change in the person's behavior and disposition; the person who experiences metanoia is expected not only to embrace a pious attitude but also to act accordingly. Hence the word "repent" refers to renunciation of sin in both thought and act.

In Jungian psychology, metanoia occurs during the so-called "middle-life" phase of human personal development. According to Jung, late in the third decade of life, people experience an urgent need to reassess their values, and this leads them to a phase of intense introversion. Jung calls this process "metanoia" because it involves the comprehensive breaking-down and rebuilding of each person's worldview and value system. The process of metanoia, says Jung, results in greater self-realization. Today, it underlies therapy that seeks emotional healing by inducing breakdown. **DM**

Fideism
Tertullian

The view that faith in God is sensible, even if reason cannot confirm His existence

The relation of faith and reason has long plagued Christian belief, given the dual intellectual heritage of Western civilization in both Athens, home to the Western origins of reason, and Jerusalem, home to the Western origins of faith. Fideism, the philosophy that faith is (relatively) independent of reason—that reason is not necessary to justify belief in God—is commonly held to extend as far back as Tertullian (*c*. 160–*c*. 225), who emphasized a theme of Paul's First Letter to the Corinthians, that the truth of Christianity can only be discovered through revelation.

Fideism has influenced, to varying degrees, significant figures in the history of philosophy, including Blaise Pascal (1623–62), Søren Kierkegaard (1813–55), William James (1842–1910), and Ludwig

> *"Who then will blame Christians for not being able to give reasons for their beliefs?"*
>
> Blaise Pascal, Christian philospher

Wittgenstein (1889–1951). Pascal's defense of his faith includes a critique of the use of apologist arguments in attempts to get others to attain belief. Kierkegaard argued that belief requires a committed leap of faith, which itself is distinct from evidence or reasons. James, a U.S. pragmatist who also studied psychology and religion, put forward a set of criteria under which it is rational to believe without proof. Wittgenstein interpreted religion as a self-contained and expressive occurrence with its own internal logic, and within its own self-referential criteria; consequently it is independent from reason and external critique. While the extent to which the four philosophers in question, and Tertullian himself, are actually fideists is debatable, fideism itself has long provided a common defense of faith in the absence of evidence of God. **JE**

Midrash
Rabbi Judah ha-Nasi

The considered and shared interpretation of biblical stories

↑ A fourteenth-century illuminated Jewish manuscript from France, showing a child being given a lesson in the teachings of the Torah.

"At times the truth shines so brilliantly that we perceive it as clear as day. Our nature and habit then draw a veil over our perception, and we return to a darkness almost as dense as before."

Maimonides, rabbi and philosopher

In the Jewish tradition, "Midrash" is a method of interpreting biblical stories for the purposes of clarification, completion, and resolving complex or contradictory passages. From the time of the Torah's origins, rabbis were required to communicate stories from it in a way that was comprehensible to people and useful for them. These teachings were communicated primarily through an oral tradition until c. 200, when Rabbi Judah ha-Nasi (135–219) recorded a set of interpretations known as the Mishna. Commentaries on the Mishna by other rabbis over the following three centuries were compiled as the Gemara; these, coupled with the Mishna, comprise the Talmud.

Midrash is required when communicating biblical stories because the lessons of the stories are not always immediately apparent. Some biblical principles may seem to contradict other biblical principles, or conflict with contemporary legal or moral teachings from other sources. So, in order that believers can understand the meaning of the text, it is necessary that they find a teacher who is able to explain its content by making connections, clarifying lessons, and relating the text to a broader moral and literary context.

These biblical explanations tend to be transmitted orally, but the oral tradition of interpretations may also be collected and recorded as supplemental pretext for understanding the primary biblical source. Accordingly, the term "Midrash" may be used to refer to the entire compilation of teachings about the Bible.

The existence of Midrash admits to the necessity of interpretation when it comes to religious texts. In the Jewish tradition, educated teachers who are able to apply expertise in language and tradition give these interpretations and record them for others. These interpretations themselves become texts to be studied, and promote the idea that religious texts are a part of an ongoing conversation among believers. **TD**

Manichaeism
Mani

A dualistic religious philosophy dividing the world between good and evil principles

The prophet Mani (c. 216–276), born in southern Babylonia, was the founder of Manichaeism, one of the most influential religions in the ancient world. Central to the religion is the belief that good and evil cannot have originated from the same source. Evil and good are perceived as independent of each other, and humanity can only escape evil by recognizing this dual reality and following the precepts of the good.

The realm of evil is interpreted to be the same as the realm of matter, which itself is in direct opposition to the realm of God. Existence commenced with the two primal principles of darkness and light, each in its own realm, and began when darkness waged a war on light. Manichaeism may be distinguished from many forms of gnosticism, in which matter is also seen as evil, by its belief that dualism is an inherent part of the nature of existence, with darkness and evil having an independent existence from the good.

For a while Manichaeism constituted a serious challenge to Christianity. Following the death of Mani, the doctrine spread through Syria into the West, and eastward into central Asia. Its message, that the good must be actively pursued and the tendencies of darkness must be opposed, inspired its followers to reject the world of matter, which meant the physical body, too. The message presented by Manichaeist missionaries was quite uncharacteristic of and distinct from the many forms of gnosticism with which it coexisted.

While Manichaeism was ultimately to be supplanted by Christianity, Mani's worldview and teachings survived as a subject of interest to thinkers such as the French Protestant philosopher Pierre Bayle (1647–1706), Scottish empiricist philosopher David Hume (1711–76), and French essayist and philosopher Voltaire (1694–1778), marking it as a significant philosophical system in Western philosophy. **JE**

⬆ A Manichaen miniature showing Manichaen priests. The approximately 1,000-year-old fragment was found during an archaeological expedition in Idikut Shahri, Turkestan.

"Those who follow me . . . and put their hope in God Ohrmizd . . . are the ones that are saved and find salvation from this cycle of rebirths and attain eternal redemption."

Mani, *An Apocryphal Epistle to Mar Ammo*

Christian Universalism
Origen

The belief in the eventual salvation of all souls, and that Hell is only temporary

Is it God's plan to achieve salvation for all humanity, or is the opportunity for salvation only accepted by some? The early Christian theologian Origen (185–254) believed that instructive suffering in the afterlife eventually induces all souls, even the Devil, to accept Jesus and God. This universalism was later declared heretical, and the Church (both Catholic and Protestant) taught the faithless to expect eternal suffering in Hell. However, some seventeenth-century German Anabaptists and English Ranters rediscovered universalism, and in 1820 Friedrich Schleiermacher (1768–1834) became the first modern theologian to defend the doctrine.

Universalism also flourished in the United States, with the founding of the Universalist Church of America in 1793. Major figures in the movement included John

"Once [eternal damnation] exists, [eternal bliss] can exist no longer."

Friedrich Schleiermacher, theologian

Murray (1741–1815), who spread the doctrine amid opposition from orthodox Christians who believed it would lead to immorality, and Hoseau Ballou (1771–1852), who stressed the importance of reason in religious thinking and argued that punishment for sin is restricted to earthly life only.

Typical arguments for universalism proceed from God's love for humanity and righteousness against evil. If God's love for humanity prevails, eternal torment is impossible; only suffering for some ultimate good makes sense. Heavenly bliss is lessened by awareness of hellish torment. God's redemptive love also implies His persuasive inducement of every soul's free choice of faith eventually. And God's perfect goodness could not accept permanent evil, for how can God ultimately prevail as long as Hell persists? **JSh**

Porphyrian Tree
Porphyry

A classification system that categorized all knowledge in a tiered diagram

The Porphyrian tree, also called the *Arbor poryphyriana* or the *scala praedicamentalis*, is an ancient classification system that diagrams any concept into a five-tiered hierarchy of existence. At each tier in the hierarchy, a concept can be either one of two things, such as material or immaterial, sensitive or insensitive, and rational or irrational. When applied to an idea, the Porphyrian tree creates a visual depiction of the concept in three vertical columns. The central column depicts each of the five tiers, with the columns on either side representing the two possible choices. Its vertical appearance with appendages or branches is somewhat treelike, hence the name.

In his work the *Categories*, ancient Greek philosopher Aristotle (384–322 BCE) created a categorization system that fit all human ideas, emotions, or knowledge into one of ten categories. In about 268, Neoplatonic philosopher Porphyry (c. 234–c. 305) wrote his *Introduction*, or *Isagoge*, in which he reorganized those categories into his eponymous binary categorization system. After sixth-century philosopher Boethius translated Porphyry's work into Latin, it quickly gained a place as the standard logic text in Western culture. The *Introduction* became necessary reading for anyone studying philosophy, and did not fall out of favor until the late nineteenth century. It was translated into many languages and became one of the best-known works of philosophy ever written.

With the Porphyrian tree, humanity had a way to categorize every idea into a single applicable visual depiction. The tree created a taxonomy of thought, grouping similar concepts while quickly revealing any differences between them. Though no longer in use, the grouping and categorization of phenomena into a treelike visual format is used in everything from logic to grammar and zoology. **MT**

Santa Claus
St. Nicholas

A legendary figure who is the traditional patron of Christmas, well known for being a bringer of gifts for children

The figure of Santa Claus, the benevolent old fellow who travels around the world on Christmas Eve night giving presents to good children (and, if their parents are to be believed, coal to bad ones), stems from the legend surrounding St. Nicholas, Roman Catholic bishop of Myra (270–346) in Lycia (now Turkey). Precise details of the saint's life are not known, but he had a reputation for generosity and kindness. He is believed to have provided dowries of gold for three poor girls, and to have restored to life three children who had been cut up by a butcher and put in a tub of brine. Over time, the legend of the dowries, combined with elements of the Norse god Odin and Nordic folktales of a magician who punished naughty children and rewarded good children with presents, led to the characterization of St. Nicholas as the figure that we know today. The saint's name was corrupted into Santa Claus in English-speaking countries.

Santa is invariably pictured as a large, old, and white-bearded man, wearing a red coat with a white collar and cuffs, with a matching red hat and black belt and boots; this depiction of him originated with images drawn by cartoonist Thomas Nast for *Harper's Weekly* in 1863. A tradition that began in 1822 with Clement Clarke Moore's poem, "A Visit from St. Nicholas," has Santa Claus living in the North Pole (the region believed to have been inhabited by Odin). Santa is also said to live in the company of elves (in Norse mythology, elves are ancestral spirits), who spend the year preceding Christmas Eve making toys.

The popularity of Santa Claus in the celebration of Christmas shows no sign of abating. He is the subject of numerous Christmas films, songs, and Christmas-themed commercials. On the Internet, the North American Aerospace Defense Command makes a point of "tracking" Santa annually. **JE**

⬆ A seventeenth-century oil painting of St. Nicholas, from the Greek School. St. Nicholas is the patron saint of Greece, and of children, sailors, unmarried girls, merchants, and pawnbrokers.

"Alas! How dreary would be the world if there was no Santa Claus!"

Francis P. Church, publisher and editor

Christmas
Ancient Rome

The Christian commemoration of the birth of Jesus Christ

⬆ A miniature depiction of the Nativity, showing the baby Jesus, Mary, Joseph, and an angel, is enclosed by an initial letter "G" in an Italian choral manuscript of the fourteenth century.

"The supernatural birth of Christ, his miracles, his resurrection, and ascension remain eternal truths, whatever doubts may be cast on their reality as historical facts."

David Friedrich Strauss, theologian

The birth of Jesus Christ has been celebrated in December since the second century CE, but it was not until 354 that Bishop Liberius of Rome finally declared December 25 to be the event's official date. "Christmas," the English term for the celebration, means "Christ's Mass," the mass for the celebration of Christ's birth.

There are two main theories regarding its celebration specifically on December 25: first, that the date of Christmas was set in opposition to the Roman Feast of the Invincible Sun, which was celebrated on the 25th, the original date of the winter solstice; and second, that the birth date of Christ was calculated to be exactly nine months after March 25, the date on which early Christians believed he was conceived.Whatever its origin, the observance on December 25 had spread throughout the majority of Christendom by the end of the fourth century. Christmas became a public holiday in Rome in the early sixth century on the order of Emperor Justinian.

Most Protestant sects retained the celebration after the sixteenth-century Protestant Reformation, although Puritans tried to stop the celebration of Christmas in the seventeenth century. The restoration of the English monarchy in 1660 led to a reformed, more secular celebration.

The Christmas tree is a relatively recent innovation, having originated in Germany as late as the sixteenth century when fir trees were decorated with fruits, candles, and tinsel. Christmas greeting cards originated in the nineteenth century in England, while Christmas presents may have originated with a New Year exchange of gifts in pagan Rome. The figure of Santa Claus was an amalgamation of features of a Christian saint, Nicholas of Myra, with elements of the Germanic god Thor, whose home is in the polar regions. Christmas is one of the most important celebrations in the Christian world, and its effect on the Western cultural calendar has been profound. **JE**

Canonization of the Bible
Christian Church Fathers

The official sanctioning of the writings of the Old and New Testaments

The first 200 years of Christianity's development were marked by a determined attempt to develop an orthodox canon of texts. The Roman Catholic church fathers were obliged to consider many competing and often contradictory schools of thought, all of them forcefully claiming their interpretations of various scriptures to be the truth. The collection of texts that now makes up the New Testament was determined over the course of a number of councils (notably, the Councils, or Synods, of Carthage in the third, fourth, and fifth centuries). Significantly, the philosopher and theologian Augustine of Hippo (354–430) had an active hand in the development of what was to become the officially sanctioned Christian canon. The official biblical canon was declared at the Council of Carthage held in 397, and inevitably its decisions to include certain scriptures and exclude others were considered highly controversial.

Despite declaring the official canon, the Roman Catholic Church did not draw permanent official canonical boundaries until the Protestant Reformation in the sixteenth century. The German monk and theologian Martin Luther (1483–1546) published a distinctive new canon, today the official canon of the Lutheran church, which notably removed the books Hebrews, James, Jude, and Revelation from the biblical canon. These texts were excluded because they contradicted essential Protestant doctrines, including *sola gratia* (the belief that salvation occurs through divine grace alone) and *sola fide* (the belief that salvation comes through faith alone, rather than through good works). The creation of a biblical canon was simultaneously a key element of the unification and consolidation of the power of orthodox Christianity and a key mechanism by which heterodox scriptures, traditions, and movements were excluded. **JE**

⬆ An early twentieth-century German engraving shows Christ holding Genesis, the first book of the Old Testament, and Apocalypsis (Revelation), the last book of the New Testament.

"The whole canon of the Scriptures, however, in which we say that consideration is to be applied, is contained in these books . . . because of the authority which is deservedly accredited to them."

St. Augustine of Hippo, *Christian Instruction* (*c.* 397 CE)

The Confessions
Augustine of Hippo

A foundational work in the field of Christian apologetics

Written around 397, the *Confessions* of Augustine of Hippo (354–430) is a foundational work of Christian apologetics; it also comprises perhaps the world's first autobiography, being an essentially confessional account of an individual's return to God from a life of (largely sexual) sin. Augustine's perspective, in which Neo-Platonic philosophies and ideals are merged into an early Christian framework, is that Christ, being God made man, is the bridge between sinful humanity and a perfect God.

Much of the *Confessions* is a personal story of conversion, with the final books, or parts, containing philosophical reflections on topics within philosophy and theology. For Augustine, "sin" is equated with the pursuit of temporal pleasures, while redemption and a

"But my sin was this, that I looked for pleasure, beauty, and truth not in Him . . ."

Augustine of Hippo, *Confessions* (397)

return toward God can be accomplished through the free exercise of the will in pursuing "eternal" goods, such as wisdom and obedience to God. Later in his life, Augustine increasingly emphasized the role of God's grace, accessible to humanity through the agency of Christ, in increasing the capacity of the will to choose God and refuse sinful temptations.

The *Confessions* was deeply influential in Western theology and philosophy, as well as in the development of what became canonical Christian beliefs and interpretations. The work has also had a profound effect on common orthodox Christian beliefs, particularly the association of temporal pleasures with sin, and of virtue with a rejection of temporal (carnal) pleasures—exemplified by the celibacy of its clergy required by some branches of Roman Catholicism. **JE**

Just War
Augustine of Hippo

Waging war is morally justified if it meets specific moral, religious, or political criteria

Is war ever moral, just, or ethically defensible? Rules and limitations on warfare are as old as warfare itself, but it was the philosopher and theologian Augustine of Hippo (354–430) who paved the conceptual way for countless future conflicts when he identified the notion of a "just" or morally justifiable war.

While earlier thinkers, such as Aristotle and Cicero, also wrote about the morality and rules of warfare, Augustine was the first person in the Christian tradition to present the concept of a "just war." Augustine believed that those acting on the authority of God could justly engage in a war, even though it would naturally lead to killing, violence, and destruction that otherwise would be immoral. In accepting the concept of just war, Augustine was taking a moral position that

"A just war is in the long run far better for a man's soul than . . . prosperous peace."

Theodore Roosevelt, U.S. president 1901–09

was in stark opposition to the pacifist teachings of many Church leaders.

Augustine argued that legitimate authorities could morally engage in warfare in some situations, but the task of identifying the specific conditions of a just war was left to later thinkers, such as St. Thomas Aquinas (1225–74). The conditions originally included acting from a legitimate authority, acting with the right intention, and having a just cause, though they have since been expanded upon and refined by others.

After Augustine, leaders no longer had to choose between the normative restrictions of pacifism and the morally neutral approach of realism. The concept of just war implied that organized, intentional, widespread conflict—with all its horrors—could be a force for good, and waging it a moral act. **MT**

⬅ The frontispiece to an eleventh-century edition of *Confessions* by St. Augustine, first published in 397.

c. 400

Against Original Sin
Pelagius

The unorthodox view that Christian believers are untainted by Adam's sin

The Christian doctrine of original sin holds that Adam's sin in the Garden of Eden is passed down through human generations, and thus human beings are inherently sinful and need divine grace to regain God's favor. However, the Christian monk Pelagius (354–420) taught that human will is entirely free and therefore as capable of choosing good as evil. Divine grace, for Pelagius, is thus merely an aid in choosing goodness, and is not necessary for salvation, which can be accomplished by will alone.

Pelagius's arguments led him to a series of radical conclusions. He argued that Adam's sin was personal, and it would be unjust of God to hold all humanity accountable. Since all are born without sin, baptism has no purpose, and all children who die without the

> *"That we are able to do good is of God, but that we actually do it is of ourselves."*
>
> Pelagius

Sacrament go to heaven. Moreover, Jesus's sacrifice, cornerstone of Christian belief, had no substantive effect; his function is to set an example of how to live.

Pelagius's arguments against original sin effectively challenged the core of what came to be orthodox Christianity. Orthodox apologists decried Pelagius's work once it became known, and he was put on trial for heresy at the Synod of Diospolis in 415. However, he denied or offered orthodox interpretations of his works and was found innocent of heresy. After a series of further political controversies, the Emperor Honorius expelled Pelagian leaders from Rome in 418. Pelagius's works provided a substantive challenge to orthodox Christian beliefs, but the challenge was resolved primarily by the coercive power of the church, and so is largely forgotten today. **JE**

c. 400

Kama Sutra
Vātsyāyana

A Hindu manual offering advice on life, love, and lovemaking

The *Kama Sutra* is an ancient Sanskrit text that details teachings on the subject of seeking pleasure in life, and predominantly features recommendations for intimate and sexual pleasure. The text, compiled in the early fifth century by the Hindu philosopher Vātsyāyana, is intended to provide advice for living a good life, finding and practicing love, and making the self and a partner happy.

According to traditional Hindu teachings, life has three main goals. These goals include living virtuously, attaining prosperity, and realizing pleasure. The *Kama Sutra* is explicitly aimed at the third of these goals, even though the first two goals are considered to be more important for living well. Written as a manual, the *Kama Sutra* details the ways in which the goal of

> *"As variety is necessary in love, so love is to be produced by means of variety."*
>
> Vātsyāyana, *Kama Sutra* (c. 400)

realizing pleasure should be pursued, with the highest pleasures in life coming from sexual relationships and practices. The *Kama Sutra* is also a manual for pursuing love more broadly, and contains advice on marriage, the duties of spouses, and how to interact with past lovers.

Sexual liberation is often considered a modern idea, but the *Kama Sutra* proves that openly thinking and writing about sex is as old as recorded history. The *Kama Sutra* promotes the idea that pleasure is a fundamentally good human experience, and provides permission and advice for making pleasure better. At the intersection of religious tradition and sexual urges, the *Kama Sutra* encourages us to be mindful of the pleasure that we should be bringing to others and to ourselves. **TD**

Erotic carvings at the Temple of Khajuraho, India, built between 950 and 1050. ▶

Intellect and Will
Augustine of Hippo

Two qualities that offer the means toward redemption from sin

The philosopher and theologian Augustine of Hippo (354–430) developed an influential theory of intellect and the will largely in response to the apparent contradiction in Christian belief in a God who simultaneously created and governs the world yet who is not responsible for evil. Augustine proposed that intellect and will are simultaneously the source of "sin" and the means toward redemption. For Augustine, the will is perpetually free and thus capable of the choice of either sin or redemption in Christ; while human nature encompasses sensory capabilities and desires, it also contains intellect and will.

For Augustine, evil involves the pursuit of temporal things, such as carnal pleasure, instead of eternal things, such as wisdom and reunion with God through Christ.

"Mind is mind and hand is body. The mind orders the mind to will."

Augustine of Hippo, *Confessions* (397)

The senses perceive elements of the external world and translate data to the intellect, which identifies its potential options; the free will then makes its choice. Augustine's later works have greater emphasis on the need for "grace" to aid the will in choosing against sin.

Augustine's views on the nature of humanity and the place of intellect and free will were of critical importance until the Enlightenment in the seventeenth and eighteenth centuries. During that period, instead of humanity being characterized by three elements—a divine yet fallen soul (which sets humanity above and apart from nature), reason capable of knowing truth, and free will—humanity was understood as being fully natural, with only limited reason (and thus intellect), and without free will (although the degree of lack of freedom was subject to argument). **JE**

The Free Will Defense
Augustine of Hippo

God allows evil because to prevent it would deny humanity the means to act freely

One argument against God's existence is the "problem of evil," where "evil" is understood to refer to suffering and injustice. If a being is all-powerful, it can eliminate any evil that exists; if it is all-knowing, it will know about any evil that exists or is about to exist; and if it is all-good, it will, presumably, want to eliminate all the evil it can. Since there is evil in the world, it follows that it is impossible that God exists. This argument had special significance for early Christians attempting to defend their fledgling religion from a variety of intellectual competitors, including Manicheans and gnostics. Augustine of Hippo (354–430) offered perhaps the earliest rebuttal with his "Free Will Defense."

According to Augustine, evil has two sources: free individuals, who voluntarily choose to harm others, and

"[The will's] failings are justly punished, being not necessary, but voluntary."

Augustine of Hippo, *City of God* (early fifth century)

God, who justly punishes sinners. He rejects the claim that God would want to eliminate all evil because it assumes that God has no good reason for allowing creatures to act freely. If God wants creatures to respond freely to His overtures of grace, it would be impossible to prevent them from acting against His wishes, since doing so would override their freedom. Furthermore, in accordance with Augustine's understanding of original sin, all humans voluntarily sin against God, and thereby deserve punishment (because God is just).

The Free Will Defense belongs to a family of arguments known as theodicy, which attempt to absolve God of wrongdoing for allowing evil. The efficacy of the defense continues to be contested by philosophers such as Alvin Plantinga, William Rowe, and Stephen Wykstra, and the discussion remains popular. **JW**

aquesta carauana es
de sarra panar

los munts de selone
on nex lo stany
Fluu Casth

singuy   uchion   aacuy   camul

The Middle Ages
500–1449

Historians once referred to much of this period in Western civilization as the Dark Ages, a moniker that was applied not only because of the apparent economic and cultural stagnation during this time, but also because of the perceived dearth of ideas. Historians today agree that there were numerous innovative ideas that emerged from the Middle Ages and, in fact, many of them were crucial for developments in areas such as mathematics, cosmology, the philosophy of the person, and natural rights. Can God create a boulder too heavy for Himself to lift? The answer to this question posed by Dionysius the Areopagite in *c.* 500 is incredibly important to the Judeo-Islamic-Christian idea of God—and debate over it still occurs today.

A Catalan atlas from *c.* 1375, showing merchants travelling to Cathay. It was around this period that merchants first began organizing themselves into guilds.

Paradox of Omnipotence
Pseudo-Dionysius the Areopagite

Could God create a boulder that is too heavy for Him to lift Himself?

⬆ Marble statue of Atlas kneeling with the celestial sphere on his shoulder, known as "Farnese Atlas." It is a Roman copy of the second century CE, after a Greek original.

"For, the denial of Himself, is a falling from truth ... and the falling from the truth is a falling from the existent ... Almighty God cannot fall from the existent."

Pseudo-Dionysius

The "paradox of omnipotence" is a family of verbal paradoxes intended to establish the boundaries of the concept of an omnipotent being, or God. The general form of the paradox proposes that, if a being can perform any act (a trait that is itself part of the definition of omnipotence), then that being should be able to create a task it cannot achieve; it follows that it cannot perform all possible tasks. Simultaneously, if such a being cannot create a task it cannot perform, then a task must exist that it cannot perform.

The first form of the argument is traced to Pseudo-Dionysius the Areopagite (*fl. c.* 500), a Christian theologian so named because his work was at first erroneously attributed to Dionysius the Areopagite, an Athenian mentioned in the Bible who was converted by a speech of St. Paul. Pseudo-Dionysius the Areopagite was primarily concerned with the question of whether it was possible or not for God to "deny himself."

A popular version of the omnipotence paradox is often referred to as the "paradox of the stone," which may be expressed as, "Could God create a boulder that is too heavy to lift himself?" Answers to such formulations of the paradox tend to center on how "omnipotence" itself should be defined. For example, "omnipotence" may not mean that God can do anything whatsoever, but rather that God can do anything possible within God's own nature. God's power is thus limited by an inability to perform logical absurdities, such as making a square a circle. When two concepts are logically incompatible, it is not possible by definition for God to perform them. As a logical impossibility, the creation of a boulder that is too heavy to lift thus falls outside the definition of omnipotence. The paradox of the stone is among the most popular expressions of the paradox of omnipotence, and is among the most ancient types of critique of the Judeo-Christian God. **JE**

Human Flight

Emperor Kao Yang

The search for a method to enable humans to fly

Ancient myths and legends are full of tales of humans having the ability to fly, and the impulse to do so has likely been a part of human history since people first looked at the birds and imagined having the power of flight. The earliest known record of a human taking flight comes from China, where Emperor Kao Yang (*r.* 550–559) is said to have sentenced captive enemies to death by strapping them to large kites and sending them aloft; their relatives were allowed to control the ropes and at least one such unfortunate is said to have survived. Prior to that, Kao Yang would have bamboo wings strapped to the arms of captives and have them thrown from the tops of towers; all are said to have perished. By the time Marco Polo reached China in the thirteenth century, a fairly common practice before a ship set sail was to send a man aloft on a kite and assess his flight; if the man shot straight up into the sky, it was deemed that the voyage would be successful.

By 1250 English philosopher Francis Bacon had described a theoretical mechanical flying machine, and Italian inventor and polymath Leonardo da Vinci went on to create several flying-machine designs. Then, in 1783, two Frenchmen, François Laurent d'Arlandes and Jean-François Pilâtre, took the first flight in a lighter-than-air hot-air balloon. A mere 120 years later, in 1903, Orville and Wilbur Wright became the first to fly in a powered aircraft.

The idea of flight, even when it was still only that, has captivated humanity like no other. Ancient tales of flying carpets, winged dragons, and soaring creatures of all types testify to the strength of the fantasy, and the realization of the dream did little to lessen its appeal. Aircraft-borne flight is now a commonplace occurrence, a method of travel readily available and capable of bridging all corners of the globe, yet being able to fly unaided remains a fantasy capable of spurring inspiration and daydreams. **MT**

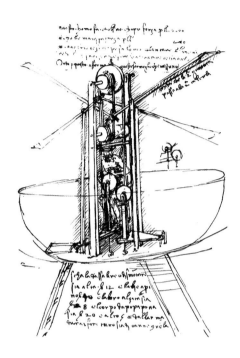

⬆ Drawing of a flying machine (*c.* 1490–1516) by Leonardo da Vinci. Da Vinci designed a number of such devices, but there is no evidence that he ever attempted to build any of them.

"Once you have tasted flight, you will forever walk the earth with your eyes turned skyward, for there you have been, and there you will always long to return."

Leonardo da Vinci, artist and inventor

ΟΑΝΤΩΝΙΟCΑΡΧΙΕΠΙ
CΚΟΠΟC

Ladder of Divine Ascent
John Climacus

The method by which monks and hermits can achieve holiness

Traditional Byzantine churches are often decorated with depictions of the "Soul-saving and Heavenward Ladder," otherwise known as the "Ladder of Divine Ascent." The artworks are associated with a literary work authored by John Climacus, a seventh-century monk at the monastery on Mount Sinai in Egypt. His book, *The Ladder of Divine Ascent,* describes thirty stages of spiritual development that lead the believer to theosis or salvation, the goal of spiritual struggle.

The thirty stages of spiritual development are symbolized by a ladder, and the thirty chapters of Climacus's book each correspond to a step on the ladder. Groups of steps represent either virtues that must be attained or vices that must be avoided, to be replaced by virtues, if the striver is to be successful.

"Do not be surprised that you fall … do not give up, but stand your ground."

John Climacus

Climacus's work was intended for his fellow monks and holy men, and its thirty steps were intended to be followed one after the other in sequence. His readers are cautioned to be vigilant—at every step there are evil powers seeking to pull the striver from the ladder. Upon reaching step thirty at the top of the ladder, which is titled Faith, Hope, and Charity, the monk can expect to receive from Christ the crown of glory.

While there are traces of the ideas of earlier ascetic writers in Climacus's work, the views he expresses are ultimately his own. His proposal that salvation may be reached by climbing a ladder while fending off agents of evil was greatly influential on later Greek ascetic writers, and was popular in Slavic countries for centuries. *The Ladder of Divine Ascent* remains one of the classics of ascetic Christian literature. **JE**

Jihad
Muhammad

A struggle undertaken by Muslims to uphold the cause of God

The term "jihad" is an Arabic word meaning "to endeavor, to strive, to struggle," and is generally used to mark an effort toward a commendable aim. It occurs forty-one times in the Koran, which was revealed to Muhammad from *c.* 610. In the context of religion, jihad can mean the struggle against personal sin or evil inclinations, efforts to improve society morally, or the act of spreading Islam in general. Jihad can be peaceful (spreading Islam through writing, for example) or through force (the "jihad of the sword"). In mystical Islam, the more peaceful modes of jihad are emphasized; inner spiritual struggle is the "greater jihad," while the jihad of the sword is considered the "lesser jihad."

The term "jihad" is thus not synonymous with the concept of a "holy war," but denotes a much wider

"To fight against the infidels is Jihad; but to fight against your evil self is greater Jihad."

Abu Bakr, companion of Muhammad

range of goals and the means by which those ends are pursued. However, about two-thirds of the instances of the term *jahada* in the Koran do reference warfare. The ultimate aim of this warfare is subordination of unbelievers to Islam, understood in the political way of extending Islamic geopolitical rule over the globe, not in the forced conversion of conquered peoples. Moreover, Koranic passages on jihad suggest that the command to fight unbelievers was not unconditional, but contingent upon being provoked by them or threatened by aggression. An understanding of the complexity of jihad as a religious imperative is essential to understanding the responses of practitioners of Islam to the expansion of capitalism into the Middle East, and that of Western state powers all over the globe. **JE**

⬅ A twelfth-century illustration of "The Heavenly Ladder," contained in an instruction book for monks.

The Five Pillars of Islam
Muhammad

Five basic duties that should be carried out by every Muslim

The Five Pillars of Islam are attributed to Muhammad (*c.* 570–*c.* 632), who is said to have received them from the angel Gabriel. Recorded after Muhammad's death, they are accorded the status of *hadith* (a saying or act that Muhammad is confirmed to have said or done).

The first and most important pillar is the *shahada*, or Islamic creed. All Muslims are required to profess, "There is no god but God, and Muhammad is his prophet." The creed ideologically separates Muslims from non-Muslims, firstly by separating monotheists from non-monotheists and secondly by separating monotheists who believe Muhammad was God's prophet from those who do not (such as Jews and Christians). The second pillar is the *salat*, or Islamic prayer. Probably appropriating the notion from Persian

"Verily, the prayer is enjoined on the believers at fixed hours."

The Koran, An Nisa 4:103

Zoroastrianism, Islam requires all believers to pray five times a day (dawn, noon, afternoon, evening, and night). The third pillar is *zakat*, or the practice of alms-giving. Well-off Muslims are expected to give 2.5 percent of their wealth to the poor, particularly poor Muslims (*zakat* is often built into taxation systems in Islamic-controlled countries). The fourth pillar is *sawm*, or fasting, especially during the month of Ramadan (abstaining from food and drink from dawn till dusk). The fifth and final pillar is *hajj*, which is pilgrimage to Mecca—to be undertaken at least once by every Muslim who is able-bodied and wealthy enough. Although some sects of Islam, such as the Twelvers and Ismailis, have additional duties required of true Muslims, all Muslims agree on the Five Pillars, which guarantees their influence. **AB**

Kōan
Chan Buddhism, Tang Dynasty

The notion that study of the paradoxical can promote enlightenment

The term *kōan* literally refers to a "public record" of the teachings used by Zen masters to help awaken their disciples. Kōan began as the study of *gongan* as developed in the Chinese Chan school of Buddhism sometime during the Tang dynasty (618–907). When Chan was transplanted to Japan in the twelfth century and became Zen, *gongan* became known as kōan.

Kōan typically take the form of puzzling questions, statements, or tales that serve as objects of meditation. Examples such as "What is the sound of one hand clapping?" or "If you meet the Buddha on the road, kill him!" may appear nonsensical or paradoxical. One kōan goes so far as to relay the story of the Zen master Nansen chopping a living cat in half to resolve a dispute between two monks who were arguing

"We're lost where the mind can't find us, utterly lost."

Ikkyu, Zen Buddhist monk and poet

over the animal. Ultimately, a kōan is designed to expose the flaws in a student's objective, discursive methods of reasoning, thereby pushing the student to a new mental schema characterized by a heightened awareness that is closer to enlightenment. Rinzai Zen master Hakuin argued that the purpose of a kōan is to awaken a "great doubt" (*daigi*) in a student about the paradigm he or she uses to interpret the world, which ultimately results in a "great death" (*daishi*) in which the old beliefs fall away and the kōan is resolved by a new level of understanding. Kōan study is thus a type of metacognition, since it pushes one to be mindful of the way one thinks about and experiences the world. Kōan study was once practiced universally in Zen schools, although the Rinzai sect now emphasizes it to a much greater degree than the Sōtō school. **JM**

Islamic State
Muhammad

The concept of a divinely guided Islamic government with Allah as head of state

The idea that a state can be organized and governed along purely Islamic principles originated with Muhammad (*c.* 570–*c.* 632) himself, who in 622 established the first *khilāfa* or caliphate (an Islamic religious community headed by a religious leader). An Islamic state is ideological in nature, and those citizens governed by it are divided into two distinct groups: those who believe in and follow Islam, and those who do not. Today, states following the *khilāfa* model include Mauritania since 1958, Iran since its Islamic Revolution in 1979, Pakistan, Afghanistan, and Saudi Arabia. Not all Muslims, however, approve of Islamic states, with some clerics arguing that they violate one of the guiding principles of Islam: that divinity and politics should never become entwined. Such clerics

"Not to accept Sharia … such [an Islamic] society breaks its contract with God."
Abul Ala Mawdudi, theologian and Muslim revivalist

are in the minority, however; most Muslims hold the view that it is sinful not to believe in the Islamic state.

The drafting and enacting of government legislation within an Islamic state rests solely with those who adhere to Islam. Muslims may not copy polytheists (those with a belief in more than one god) in either dress or behavior, or support them in any way that may give them prominence over Muslims. Islamic states derive their legitimacy from Allah Himself, who is sovereign over all and whose law of Sharia is supreme. Sharia provides the Islamic state with the framework it requires to develop a civil society and the organizations and institutions that comprise it, and to shape the common objectives of government: administration, law enforcement, defense, and the material wellbeing of its citizens. **BS**

Shintōism
Japan

A religion founded on the idea that all things have an inherent spirituality

Shintōism, the indigenous religion of Japan, was first documented in the historical records *Nihon Shoki* and *Kojiki* in the eighth century CE. Its beliefs and practices were formalized during the Nara and Heian periods (710–1185) and are still popular throughout Japan.

Shintō literally means "way of the *kami*," the latter term referring to the divine spirits said to inhabit Japan. *Kami* can manifest as natural forces, animistic presences in holy sites, or highly developed living human beings. Because all things in nature, including people, were created by the gods Izanagi and Izanami, they manifest an inherent divinity that can be cultivated and appreciated. The emperors of Japan trace their lineage back to the first in their line, Jimmu Tennō, who was descended directly from the sun-goddess

"A major part of the world's goodness lies in its often unspeakable beauty."
Yukitaka Yamamoto, shrine guardian priest

Amaterasu. Shintō shrines are typically constructed to commemorate a departed person or a natural feature that exhibits *kami*. Ethically, Shintō practitioners strive to purify themselves by cultivating virtues such as *michi* (integrity), *harai* (purity), *makoto* (sincerity), *wa* (harmony), *akai* (cheerfulness), *kansha* (thankfulness), *kenshin* (spiritual surrender), and *meiyo* (honor). Rites are performed at shrines to purge practitioners of *kegare* (uncleanness) and *tsumi* (iniquity).

Most Japanese citizens consider themselves to be Shintō, even though only a minority regularly practice the religion. The *Jinja Honchō* oversees more than 80,000 shrines in Japan, the holiest of which is *Ise Jingū*. Shintō beliefs are so pervasive that they have influenced every aspect of Japanese culture, art, and philosophy, including Japanese Buddhism. **JM**

A sixteenth-century illustration of a Shinto shrine located in the city of Ise, Japan. ➡

c. 726

Iconoclasm
Emperor Leo III

The belief that images hinder relationships with God, so they should be destroyed

Iconoclasm can be described as the willful destruction of works of art, particularly those representing aspects of religious beliefs or personages associated with them. The destruction is motivated by the idea that such images block a direct relationship between the faithful and God because they are liable to become objects of adoration in themselves.

There exist a number of simplifications and misunderstandings regarding iconoclasm. It may be regarded as only an act of pure destruction or vandalism (such as the actual smashing of images), or destruction grounded in hatred for or fear of such images, or as the monolithic expression of the will of all believers of a religion. Iconoclasm is more complex and multifaceted than these depictions would allow. In Christianity, biblical prohibitions against worshipping false idols and false gods have given massive support to iconoclastic movements throughout history, especially in territories conquered by Christian armies.

The Byzantine Iconoclasm refers to a period of the Byzantine Empire during which the emperor, Leo III the Isaurian (c. 685–741), banned religious images; his edict resulted in a large-scale campaign in which religious images and artifacts were widely destroyed. The First Iconoclasm, initiated by Leo III, lasted from 726 to 787, after which there was a lull before his successor, Leo V the Armenian (775–820), alarmed that God appeared to be signaling his displeasure with the empire by allowing continuing military failure, instituted the Second Iconoclasm, which lasted from 814 to 842.

Iconoclasm has persisted through the ages and within different cultures. Perhaps the most notorious example of recent times occurred in 2001, when members of the Taliban in Afghanistan used explosives to destroy the two Buddhas of Bamiyan (sixth and seventh century), which were the largest standing statues of Buddha in the world at that time. **JE**

A twelfth-century monastery in Cappadocia, Turkey, where Christians in favor of icons took refuge. ↑

Perpetual Motion

Bavaria

A movement that could continue indefinitely without an external source of energy

Laws of physics dictate that a "perpetual motion machine" able to produce as many or more outputs (in terms of energy or productivity) than its inputs is an impossibility. Even so, throughout history, numerous attempts at creating a machine capable of perpetual motion—motion that would continue effectively forever without external power or energy—have been made. But as far as we know, all have failed.

The first such attempt was the Bavarian "magic wheel," invented in the eighth century and consisting of a spinning wheel that was powered magnetically. The magic wheel was supposed to be capable of spinning indefinitely, but it could not overcome the opposing force of friction.

While other attempts to create a machine capable of perpetual motion were equally as unsuccessful, they were the cause of scientific inquiry that in a few cases led to inventions still significant today. The mathematician Blaise Pascal (1623–62), for example, tried to create a successful perpetual motion machine, and by accident hit upon what would become the roulette wheel.

In 1775, finally exasperated by so many failed attempts, the Parisian Royal Academy of Sciences declared that it would admit no further proposals for perpetual motion machines. Strangely enough, this official declaration of failure produced a significant rise in attempts to create a perpetual motion machine. The nineteenth-century invention of electric generators was to have a similar invigorating effect.

Of the attempts still seen today, some are based on the model of the "overbalanced wheel," first drawn in 1235 by the artist Villard de Honnecourt. In hopes of overcoming the force of gravity, such designs attempt to attain perpetual motion through the carefully controlled movement of interacting, shifting weights intended to spin the wheel indefinitely. **JE**

⬆ A design for a magnetic perpetual motion machine (c. 1670) by John Wilkins, the bishop of Chester.

Feudalism
Europe

A system for structuring society, based on land ownership by lords

Feudalism was an economic system characteristic of Europe from the ninth century until the fifteenth century and primarily characterized by the ownership of lands by lords, who also exercised governmental powers. Landless peasants, known as serfs, were permitted to work the land for themselves, for which "privilege" their productive "surplus" was coercively extracted and paid to the lords, either as rent or in the form of forced labor on the lords' private lands. The lords, in turn, were obligated to provide protection from marauders and justice whenever a serf should make a claim, and to guarantee serfs access to common lands. The lords were often themselves subject to a king or queen, to whom they owed loyalty; in the event of war they were obliged to provide serfs for military service.

"Landlords, like all other men, love to reap where they never sowed."

Adam Smith, *The Wealth of Nations* (1776)

The term "feudalism" is derived from the term "fief," which was land "given" under certain conditions (a series of obligations, privileges, and duties) by a lord to their vassal in return for the vassal's loyalty and acceptance of obligations to the lord. A number of factors contributed toward the decline of feudalism, including the Black Death in the mid-fourteenth century (which severely decreased the population of Europe), peasant revolts, the development of an increasingly powerful merchant class, and the increasing ability of kings to enlist mercenary armies rather than rely on their lords for conscripts. Feudalism, with its relatively uncomplicated and easily understood relations between kings, lords, and serfs, has greatly influenced the fantasy genre in novels, movies and television, and video games. **JE**

Bushidō
Japanese warrior class

A set of ideals, rules, and ethical principles followed by the samurai in Japan

In Japanese, the word *bushidō* translates as "the way of the warrior." This code of conduct guided the Japanese warrior class, the samurai, who, from about 800, provided armed support for rich landowners excluded from the imperial court by the Fujiwara clan. The ideals of Bushidō informed not only the samurais' actions in combat, but also their day-to-day lives. Bushidō taught the samurai how to cultivate their martial spirit and become proficient with various weapons, and directed that a samurai's personal honor demanded that he be ready to lay down his life in loyalty to his feudal lord.

However, it was not until the ascendance of the Kamakura shogunate (1192–1333) that Bushidō became a driving force behind the actions of leading Japanese historical figures. By the time of the Tokugawa period

"The way of the samurai is found in death …. Be determined and advance."

Yamamoto Tsunetomo, samurai

(1600–1868), the tenets of Bushidō had been formally recognized and codified into law. The samurai class was abolished during the Meiji restoration of the mid to late nineteenth century, but the Bushidō code lived on, albeit in a different form.

By the time of World War II, the samurai class no longer existed, but its principles of loyalty, duty, honor, and sacrifice had strong adherents in the Japanese military. In postwar years, many of the tenets of Bushidō remained firmly rooted in Japanese culture and society as the nation made its transition into a major industrial and commercial power. The Bushidō principles expounded by the samurais of old remain strong in contemporary Japanese society today and can be seen in many aspects of Japanese life, not least in Bushidō martial arts such as judo and karate. **MT**

Romanesque Architecture
Europe

An architectural style that draws inspiration from the buildings of ancient Rome, characterized by semicircular arches

⬆ The Palatine Chapel in Aachen Cathedral, Germany, built in *c.* 800. The chapel holds the remains of Charlemagne and was the site of coronations for 600 years.

"After about the first millennium, Italy was the cradle of Romanesque architecture, which spread throughout Europe, much of it extending the structural daring with minimal visual elaboration."

Harry Seidler, architect

The idea that architecture should once again draw inspiration from the style of the Romans, with its round-arched windows and doorways, dates from around the year 800 and the palace of Emperor Charlemagne (742–814) at Aachen, Germany. Today, the only part of that palace still to be seen is the Palatine Chapel, now incorporated into Aachen Cathedral. The chapel also features the barrel and groin vaults characteristic of Roman buildings and exemplifies the deliberate adoption of Roman forms by Carolignian architects.

When Romanesque architecture fully became the major medieval style of Western European architecture between 950 and 1150, its characteristics were drawn from proto-Romanesque structures, which had dominated over the preceding two centuries. Architectural historians consider the years from 950 to 1050 as a period in which the style was still developing, with the monuments most characteristic of Romanesque architecture emerging between 1050 and 1150. Romanesque architecture was deeply influenced by feudalism and monasticism, which together provided the grounds for stability within medieval culture.

Romanesque buildings varied widely while sharing common characteristics, with architects in different regions finding different solutions to problems related to structure. Historians, taking account of complicated regional variations and the characterization of the proto-Romanesque period, continue to debate the exact start of the period of Romanesque architecture, but the style certainly concluded in the twelfth century with the transition into the Gothic period.

Much later, during the Gothic Revival of the nineteenth century, Romanesque architecture was also to receive a partial rebirth. For example, London's Natural History Museum, designed by Alfred Waterhouse, is a Romanesque revival structure. **JE**

Restaurant
Austrian monks

The concept of an establishment designed solely for serving food

The idea of an establishment dedicated to serving food dates back as far as ancient Rome and Sung dynasty China, while many historians credit eighteenth-century France for originating the truly modern restaurant (the name derives from the French word *restaurer*, meaning "to restore"). The oldest true restaurant in Europe, however, is said to be the Stiftskeller St. Peter, which is housed within the walls of St. Peter's Archabbey in Salzburg, Austria. Mentioned in a document as far back as 803, it is believed to be the oldest continuously operating restaurant in the world. Today, diners there may enjoy their food to the accompaniment of daily live performances of the music of Mozart.

The predecessors of what we would call restaurants, establishments in which food, alcohol, and other beverages were permitted to be sold, tended to be inns (mostly for the benefit of travelers rather than local people) and street kitchens. The earliest French "restaurants" were highly regulated places selling what were called *restaurants*, meat-based consommés specifically intended to "restore" an individual's strength. The first French restaurant of this type was likely that of a Parisian seller of *bouillon* (broth) named Boulanger, who established his restaurant in 1765. Such places were first developed into what has become the modern restaurant industry during the French Revolution (1789–99), when the tight grip that the guilds had on the supply of certain foods was loosened, and at the same time a larger consumer base for restaurants was established.

More than 200 years later, the restaurant has become a staple of human culture. With a rise in affluence comes a desire to pass to others the chores of buying and preparing food, and in a world increasingly fascinated by fine dining it is unlikely that the idea of the restaurant will ever fall out of fashion. **JE**

Transubstantiation
Paschasius Radbertus

The belief that Holy Communion wafers and wine change into Christ's body and blood

The Eucharist—a ceremony that functions as a re-enactment of the Last Supper, in which participants drink a sip of consecrated wine and eat a small piece of consecrated bread—was central to Christianity from the religion's beginnings. The concept of transubstantiation, however—the belief that the bread and wine taken during the Eucharist change miraculously into the body and blood of Jesus Christ at the moment of consecration by the priest—did not appear until the ninth century.

In 831 the Benedictine abbot Paschasius Radbertus (*c.* 785–860) wrote a treatise titled "On the Body and Blood of the Lord." In it, he asserted that "the substance of bread and wine is efficaciously changed within into the flesh and blood of Christ, in such a way that after

"Jesus took bread, and blessed it . . . and said, Take, eat; this is my body."
The Bible, Mark 26:26

the consecration the true flesh and blood of Christ is truly believed [to be present]." Radbertus's view was initially met with some resistance—notably from Ratramnus, a monk from the same abbey who wrote his own work titled "On the Body and Blood of the Lord" (*c.* 850)—but by 1079 it had been declared an official doctrine by a council held in Rome under Pope Gregory VII. The term "transubstantiation" was coined around the same time by Hildebert de Lavardin (*c.* 1055–1133), archbishop of Tours.

As a doctrine of faith, transubstantiation is fascinating for both its creativity and its undeniable oddity (to modern sensibilities at least). The sacrament of the Eucharist is designed to foster connectedness with God; through transubstantiation, God effectively becomes present in the mouths of all believers. **JS**

HÞÆT PE GARDE

na ingear dagum. þeod cyninga
þrym ge frunon huða æþelingas elle
fremedon. oft scyld sceþing sceaþe
þreatum moneзū mæзþum meodo setl
of teah eзsode eopl syððan ærest peaþ
fea sceaft funden he þæs frofre зeba
þeox under polcnum peorð myndum þah
oð þ him æзhpylc þara ymb sittendra
ofer hron rade hyran scolde зomban
зyldan þþæs зod cyninз. ðæm eafera pæs
æfter cenned зeonз inзeardum þone зod
sende folce tofrofre fyren ðearfe on
зeat þhie ær druзon aldor ase. lanзe
hpile him þæs lif frea puldres pealdend
porold are for зeaf beopulf pæs bren
blæd pide sprane scyldes . . .

Beowulf
England

The first European literary work not to be composed in Greek or Latin

The story of Beowulf is believed to have originated in the fifth century, existing first as an oral tale before being transcribed into a written work sometime between the eighth and eleventh centuries. The story made its way to the modern world through a single surviving manuscript that was likely written hundreds of years after the story was first told. It attracted little attention until the nineteenth century, when initial interest in the work focused on its historical insights into the lives of the early Anglo-Saxon people. The story's value as a work of merit as English literature was recognized only when the author J. R. R. Tolkien (1892–1973) published a paper about its importance in 1936.

Many of the most heralded works of English literature, such as those by Geoffrey Chaucer, William

"Let him . . . win glory before death . . . that is best at last for the departed warrior."

Beowulf (c. 850)

Shakespeare, and John Keats, came and went before anyone took note of Beowulf's existence, much less gave it enough thought for it to have any impact at all. However, the epic poem not only gives insights into pre-Norman Conquest English culture, but is the first European literary work not composed in Greek or Latin. Beowulf sheds light on the the the heroic ideals of the Germanic Anglo-Saxon people and its theme has come to influence poets, artists, and writers around the world.

Beowulf tells the tale of a Scandinavian warrior, the eponymous hero, who defends a Danish king's home from a monstrous intruder. After defeating the monster and its mother, Beowulf returns home to become a king over his own people, later dying after fighting a dragon. It is written in Old English, the Germanic language from which modern English descends. **MT**

Gunpowder
China

A man-made explosive consisting of potassium nitrate, carbon, and sulfur

Although the exact date of gunpowder's origination remains a mystery, by the year 850 Chinese alchemists had identified the basic formula for the explosive. Discovered by accident during a search for the elixir of life, gunpowder was composed of a combination of potassium nitrate, carbon, and sulfur. Gunpowder explodes when exposed to a suitable heat source, releasing a tremendous amount of heat in addition to rapidly expanding gases, and those explosive properties were harnessed in the development of pyrotechnics, rock blasting, and firearms.

By 904, military forces of the Song dynasty (960–1279) were using gunpowder in battles against the Mongols. It appeared in the Middle East sometime in the middle of the thirteenth century, and its use

"By chance they discovered a strange mixture that burned and exploded . . ."

Clive Ponting, Gunpowder: An Explosive History (2006)

spread to Europe shortly thereafter. By the time the Ottomans were using siege guns at Constantinople in 1453, gunpowder and the weapons based upon it had become an integral part of the practice of warfare.

The influence of gunpowder over the course of human history has been overwhelming. While modern weapons use different formulations of gunpowder, the explosive powder changed warfare forever. Its destructive characteristics influenced everything from the development and shape of military fortifications to naval architecture and civil engineering. The invention also transformed the idea of what a warrior or soldier should be. No longer did a person have to be bigger, stronger, or more courageous than an enemy. Instead, all that was needed was a firearm, a good eye, and the ability to pull a trigger. **MT**

◀ The first page of the sole surviving medieval manuscript of Beowulf (c. 850).

Polyphony
Europe

A type of music that consists of two or more independent melodic voices

In the Western tradition, polyphony is usually distinguished from counterpoint or contrapuntal music, as exemplified by Bach's fugues. The formal style of polyphony that originated in about 900 was largely associated with religious themes, but it is likely that polyphony as a style of informal musical presentation long predates such highly stylized musical forms of European cultural expression. "Polyphony" is actually a term with a variety of uses in the context of music and music theory. It can refer to the functional capacity of certain instruments, such as some keyboards, to play more than one note at a time, but it more often refers to a musical presentation involving two or more distinct but simultaneously played tones or even chanted melodies.

" . . . polyphony was for the most part confined to special occasions . . ."

Studies in the Performance of Late Medieval Music (1983)

The layering and texturing of melody can be seen as representative of the human condition insofar as the tapestry of human life and its meaning is difficult to communicate as single strands. Polyphony maps onto the human mind in a way similar to the phenomenon of motivation: something that is complex and fragmentary forms a coherent whole that insists on being heard. Polyphony can be seen as a contribution to pluralism, to the appreciation of valuable complementary differences.

The joy and fervor with which music is frequently approached by practitioners is undoubtedly increased by their adding a polyphonic instrument to their repertoire. Polyphony engages the senses, and its complex tonal presentation certainly brings incomparable aesthetic benefits for the listener. **JS**

Vaccination
China

The administration of a safe material to promote immunity to a harmful organism

It was in Asia that humankind first realized that the likelihood of a person developing a dangerous disease could be reduced through a form of exposure to the disease that was safer than direct infection. In India, crushed, dried pustules of victims of smallpox were fed to children to help them develop antibodies to the disease. In China, around 1000, medical practitioners blew powdered smallpox pustule crusts into the nostrils of patients, which was a more effective means of encouraging the development of immunity. However, as long as actual smallpox pustules were used, there was a high risk of patients falling prey to the disease rather than developing immunity to it.

The practice of inoculation spread to Africa, Turkey, Europe, and the Americas, but it was English physicist and scientist Edward Jenner (1749–1823) who pioneered a safe smallpox vaccination. In 1796 he carried out an experiment on an eight-year-old, James Phipps, inserting pus taken from a cowpox pustule into an incision on the boy's arm. Jenner then proved that Phipps was immune to smallpox. A year later, Jenner submitted his findings to the Royal Society but was told he required more proof. He continued his experiments and self-published his paper in 1798. He was met with ridicule, but eventually the practice became widespread.

In 1885 French chemist and microbiologist Louis Pasteur (1822–95) developed a rabies vaccine. Vaccine research and development then progressed rapidly right through to the mid-twentieth century, leading to vaccines for chickenpox, diphtheria, tetanus, anthrax, cholera, plague, typhoid, tuberculosis, mumps, measles, polio, influenza, hepatitis A and B, and meningitis. At the same time, legislation began to be introduced to regulate vaccine production and enforce vaccination. The eventual eradication of smallpox was a direct result of this systematic program. **CK**

Guild

Europe

The banding together of merchants or craftspeople to present a united front against outside competitors who might threaten their livelihoods

The guild is commonly thought of as a medieval and early modern European institution, although similar organizations in different cultures have also been described as guilds. A guild is usually a self-organized group of merchants or crafters that works to promote the economic and professional interests of members of that group. During the Middle Ages (from the fifth until the fifteenth century), guilds developed gradually from religious organizations that conducted charitable and social activities, so it is difficult to date them precisely. In England, merchant guilds were active from the beginning of the eleventh century, and craft guilds from before the end of the twelfth century.

Both merchant and craft guilds were characterized by attempts to establish monopolies. Merchant guilds held the exclusive rights to trade within a town and controlled mercantile infrastructure, such as weights and measures; they often became the governing body of their towns. Craft guilds attempted both to monopolize their craft—requiring craftspeople to join the guild, establishing tariffs against outside competition, and so forth—and to regulate its practitioners. The hierarchy of apprentice, journeyman, and master is characteristic of the medieval craft guild. But such guilds also established quality standards, labor practices, and price schedules, working to ensure a good standard of living for their members.

The guild system began to decline in the sixteenth century due to the emergence of new economic systems. Attempts to revive it, such as the guild socialism movement of the early twentieth century, have not been successful. The system persists to a degree today in specialized and traditional crafts, in professions such as law, medicine, screenwriting, and realty, and in ceremonial groups such as the livery companies of London. **GB**

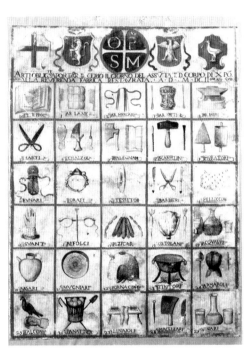

⬆ An illustration from 1602, showing the insignia of various guilds in Umbria, Italy. Such emblems were often incorporated into the signs of the shops that plied the relevant trade.

"The spirit of the medieval Western guild is most simply expressed in the proposition, guild policy is livelihood policy."

Max Weber, *General Economic History* (1927)

Courtly Love
Europe

A rethinking of the ideas of Christian love, marriage, and virtue

⬆ An illustration for Giovanni Boccaccio's epic poem *The Teseida* (1340–41), showing the scribe dedicating the work to an unknown young woman.

"[Courtly love is] love of a highly specialized sort, whose characteristics may be enumerated as Humility, Courtesy, Adultery, and the Religion of Love."

C. S. Lewis, *The Allegory of Love* (1936)

Whereas the religious coloring of the Middle Ages necessitated a strict commitment to nonadulterous relationships and marital fidelity in all aspects of life, the Age of Chivalry, commencing around 1000 in the late Middle Ages, saw a distinct change in attitudes among nobles toward marriage and affection. The chivalric code embraced extramarital yet discreet affairs that were highly ritualized and entirely secret. This transformed relationships between men and women of noble birth, creating conditions for intimate relationships that were impossible in the obligatory and often stifling roles assigned to married persons.

Between the eleventh and thirteenth centuries, the primary theme of courtly love, known to the French as *fin amour*, was made famous by troubadours, or traveling lyric poets. These poets, who were sometimes musicians also, helped to record the principles of courtly love for posterity, and even shape them contemporaneously, raising the idea of courtly relationship to sublime heights.

Courtly love is probably most responsible for the detachment of love from marriage as an institution, which as a social fact has made its way into secular culture and transformed modern sensibilities about the nature of the relationship between married couples. Husband and wife are no longer expected simply to bow to the standard accepted social conventions about obedience and raising a family, all of which can take place in arranged marriages. Instead, romantic love, in which each lover commits in a worshipful way to the other in a manner historically associated with religious conviction, has become the focus and expectation of intimate relationships between a man and woman. The new intimacy between couples ushered in by courtly love served as a foundational element of the modern distinction between public and private spheres of interest. **JS**

Consubstantiation
Berengarius of Tours

The belief that the body and blood of Christ coexists with blessed bread and wine

The doctrine of consubstantiation is a view of Holy Communion in which the body and blood of Jesus Christ coexists together with the bread and wine. All are present, nothing has been lost; Jesus's body and blood, and the bread and wine, are one. It is a difficult theology to entertain, particularly as there is no biblical text to support it. But neither was there a clear biblical foundation for the Catholic concept of transubstantiation—that the bread and wine change their metaphysical makeup when blessed at the Mass and become, in their entirety, the actual body and blood of Christ. Transubstantiation, however, had been the Church's teaching for centuries, and the theology of the Mass was at the very center of the Catholic universe. There could be no coexisting of doctrines there.

In 1047, Berengarius of Tours (c. 999–1088), archbishop of Angers, proposed consubstantiation in an attempt to explain why the bread and wine seem to remain bread and wine even after they have been consecrated by the priest. According to Berengarius, "the consecrated Bread, retaining its substance, is the Body of Christ, that is, not losing anything which it was, but assuming something which it was not." In saying "not losing anything which it was," Berengarius was clearly rejecting the long-held teaching of transubstantiation, and his interpretation was condemned at church councils in 1050, 1059, 1078, and 1079. He clung to his proposal with passion, however, calling Pope St. Leo IX ignorant for refusing to accept it. Only his powerful connections prevented his being burned as a heretic.

The idea of consubstantiation persisted in the Church for centuries, however, and was given fresh impetus centuries later by the monk and theologian Martin Luther (1483–1546), despite always being considered fundamentally heretical in churches of not only Catholic but also Protestant persuasion. **JS**

⬆ A detail from an altarfront in Torslunde, Denmark, dating to 1561, showing Martin Luther offering communion to worshippers at a baptism.

"The concept of consubstantiation attempts to express in a tangible way (for the believer) the notion of the infinite in the finite without reducing the two terms to a common denominator."

Brian Schroeder, *Altared Ground* (1996)

Gothic Ideal
Abbot Suger

An architectural style that emphasized height and soaring lines

In architecture, sculpture, painting, illuminated manuscripts, and the decorative arts, the Gothic ideal reigned supreme in Europe from the twelfth to the sixteenth century. But the late medieval "gothic" style was originally so named pejoratively by Neoclassicists who looked back to the Greco-Roman era for their ideal. The architectural motifs first found in Saint-Denis Royal Abbey Church in Paris, rebuilt in *c.* 1140 under Abbot Suger (1081–1151), and in the great cathedrals, including pointed arches, flying buttresses, ribbed vaults, and stained-glass windows, were seen as barbaric and excessive when compared to the clean lines of an ancient Greek temple such as the Parthenon.

In the eighteenth century the Gothic Revival style appeared in Europe and England and was seen as

"The principle of the Gothic architecture is infinity made imaginable."

Samuel Taylor Coleridge, poet and philosopher

appropriate for both government buildings, such as the British Houses of Parliament, and homes, most famously Strawberry Hill, just outside London. Gothic motifs were popular in architecture, furniture, ceramics, and jewelry. At the same time, the "gothic" novel appeared as an outgrowth of the Romantic movement. Often set in medieval castles and populated with heroes and damsels in distress, these works of horror, suspense, and mystery often had supernatural plot points and characters, usually as villains. This genre is exemplified by English author Mary Shelley's *Frankenstein; or, The Modern Prometheus* (1818). American Gothic, such as Washington Irving's *The Legend of Sleepy Hollow* (1820), and Southern Gothic, such as the contemporary *Southern Vampire Mysteries* series by Charlaine Harris, are further variations on the theme. **PBr**

Flying Buttress
France

An architectural support that revolutionized architecture

The flying buttress is a type of architectural flanking, arched support system that came of age in the Gothic era, from the twelfth century, most notably in high-roofed churches. The buttress is referred to as "flying" because it is in part unsupported; it can be understood as "flying" from its masonry block support to the wall in the form of an arch. High roofs created extreme forces capable of pushing the walls outward unless they were redirected toward the ground. Without flying buttresses countering these forces, the high walls would collapse. While the Cathedral of Notre-Dame in Paris is a well-known example of a church featuring flying buttresses, prototypes of the general engineering principles of the flying buttress are found much earlier, in some Roman and even Byzantine architecture.

"While the daybreak was whitening the flying buttresses [he saw] a figure walking."

Victor Hugo, *The Hunchback of Notre-Dame* (1831)

One advantage of employing flying buttresses was that fewer materials were needed to create walls, and heavier and far larger stained-glass windows could be introduced into churches, thereby providing greater beauty upon which the eyes of worshippers could gaze, indeed drawing the eyes of worshippers upward toward the heavens in more immediate contemplation of God. The buttresses themselves became not mere practical supports but objects upon which sculptors could introduce ever more intricate designs and figures. The flying buttress greatly expanded the potential for societies with limited, rudimentary engineering to create vast structures. Architects were empowered to urge believers to greater religious conviction and love of the infinite power of the Creator than they ever could have inspired with buildings of lesser scale. **JS**

Bourges Cathedral in France, built between *c.* 1200 and *c.* 1300, is a masterpiece of Gothic art.

The Ontological Argument for God
St. Anselm

An argument put forward by a Christian cleric to provide logical proof for the existence of God

⬆ A copper engraving of the Benedictine monk St. Anselm, made in 1584 by the French Franciscan priest and explorer André de Thévet. The colorization was added later.

"God cannot be conceived not to exist. God is that, than which nothing greater can be conceived. That which can be conceived not to exist is not God."

St. Anselm, *Proslogion* (1077–78)

The original and most rigorous formulation of the ontological argument for the existence of God is credited to St. Anselm (1033–1109). In Anselm's argument, the existence of God is taken to be a necessary conclusion based on examining the concept of God.

One formulation of the argument goes as follows: Premise 1 (P1): God is that being than which none greater can be conceived. Premise 2 (P2): It is possible God exists only in the mind. Premise 3 (P3): If so, then there could be a being greater than God, namely, one who exists in reality. Premise 4: P3 is contradictory of P1, and as P3 is premised on P2 and as P1 is more certain than P2, we should reject P2. It may be concluded that God exists in the mind and in reality.

This argument has been subjected to a number of sophisticated treatments, both for and against, by philosophers from a variety of traditions. In *Meditations on First Philosophy* (1641), René Descartes offered a version of the ontological proof in his effort to secure human knowledge from the skeptics. Immanuel Kant famously argued that the argument is not properly formulated because existence is not a predicate. Most recently, Alvin Plantinga offered an updated version of the argument, although it is less compelling than St. Anselm's original.

One of the most interesting things about the ontological argument for the existence of God is just how flimsy it is. That the move from analysis of a concept to assertion of ontological commitment should ever have been thought convincing is itself testimony to the desperate zeal with which the human mind approaches metaphysical issues such as God's existence. Yet the argument also indicates how creative the human mind can be when confronted with a problem as heady as trying to prove the existence of a transcendent, higher power. **JS**

Scholasticism
St. Anselm

A method of learning that places a strong emphasis on conceptual analysis

The theological rigor of the mostly monastic thinkers in the first half of the Middle Ages gave way in the second half to Christian academic intellectuals who deployed the methods of dialectical reasoning and conceptual analysis used by Greek philosophers to address problems now associated with philosophy proper. These academicians are known as scholastics, or "school men," because they were engaged at European universities.

The scholastics first worked to reconcile the positions of various respected Christian thinkers with ancient philosophers such as Aristotle and Plato, before moving to the defense and explication of orthodox Christian positions against a world of plural viewpoints and opinions. Individuals such as St. Anselm (1033–1109), St. Thomas Aquinas (1225–74), Duns Scotus (c. 1266–1308), and William of Ockham (c. 1287–1347) adopted a set of metaphysical and religious premises against which to view and consider all philosophical claims. These scholastics concerned themselves largely with problems such as freedom of will, nominalism and realism, and the existence of God.

The philosophical approach and body of work of the scholastics remain a rich source of ideas for those who reflect on ontology and the nature of reality. The scholastics provided Western philosophy with a set of provocative theses, against which many modern thinkers have rebelled, producing notable philosophical works in their own right. For example, much of the work of René Descartes can be viewed as a reaction to the methods and conclusions of the scholastics, and was explicitly such. But perhaps the most profound contribution the scholastics made to intellectual history was a concerted effort at reviving the conceptual analysis found in ancient philosophy, and in some cases they even surpassed the ancients in their efforts. **JS**

Wabi-sabi
Fujiwara no Shunzei

There is beauty in the impermanence and imperfection of things

Wabi-sabi is a Japanese aesthetic paradigm that is prevalent throughout all forms of Japanese art. It is a compound term that consists of two related concepts: *wabi* and *sabi*. Though *wabi-sabi* gained prominence with the flourishing of the tea ceremony in the early Tokugawa period (1603–1867), its origins can be traced back to the earliest use of *sabi* by twelfth-century court poet, Fujiwara no Shunzei (1114–1204).

By itself, *wabi* refers to the idea that beauty is found in simplicity. Understatement is always more powerful than overstatement, which is evident in the subtlety of color and lines, and in the use of empty space in Japanese architecture and art. Minor imperfections actually make an object more beautiful than a flawless specimen. *Sabi* includes the aesthetic

> *"Loneliness—The essential color of a beauty not to be defined."*
> #### Jakuren, Buddhist priest and poet

of desolation (particularly in landscapes) and an aged, worn appearance in handcrafted objects. This not only epitomizes the Zen notion of emptiness, but also the idea of impermanence. Objects with a rustic patina are considered to have matured with experience. The concept that combines the two, *wabi-sabi*, celebrates the incomplete and transient nature of things. The sixteenth-century Kizaemon tea bowl is one of the great examples of this aesthetic: its worn, asymmetrical appearance heightens the appeal of its desolate charm. Classic works of Japanese architecture, such as the Silver Pavilion or the dry landscape garden of Ryoanji, both in Kyoto, illustrate the minimalistic beauty of *wabi-sabi*.

Wabi-sabi is the single most important concept in Japanese aesthetics. Heavily influenced by Zen, it governs all Japanese art forms. **JM**

Holy Grail
Chrétien de Troyes

A mystical cup that was thought by Christians to have healing properties

The Holy Grail is first mentioned in the Arthurian romance *Perceval, Le Conte du Graal* (c. 1181) by Chrétien de Troyes (c. 1135–c. 1183). The Grail itself is simply a beautifully decorated chalice, or cup, used to hold the Mass wafer, which Catholics receive as the literal, transubstantiated body of Christ. In the story, the wafer sustains the injured Fisher King, who lives by this bread alone. In its earliest conception, therefore, the Holy Grail is best thought of as a romantic medieval appropriation of the Eucharist, which brings health to those who partake of it.

The thirteenth-century poet Robert de Boron added to the Grail legend by describing it as the combination of the chalice Jesus used at the Last Supper and the blood of Jesus that Joseph of Arimathea saved

"Then looked they and saw a man come out of the holy vessel . . ."

Sir Thomas Malory, *Le Morte d'Arthur* (1485)

during the crucifixion. In this way, Joseph of Arimathea became the first of the Grail guardians, and it was his task to keep the Grail safe until it could help in healing the faithful. In later Arthurian romances, the "Grail Quest" is undertaken by King Arthur's knights as a means to help restore Camelot—the near paradisiacal kingdom on Earth—which is being torn apart by sin.

Although the Holy Grail has gradually become more than a simple metaphor for the Eucharist, it still retains the strong Christian notion that Jesus's sacrifice makes possible redemption not only as the healing of moral brokenness (the forgiveness of sins) but also the healing of nonmoral brokenness (the restoration of broken bodies, dying lands, and so on). The legend of the Holy Grail depicts humanity's quest for redemption, but also hints at what that redemption might look like. **AB**

Zen
Myōan Eisai

The concept that enlightenment may be realized through quiet meditation

Zen is a religious and philosophical tradition established by Myōan Eisai (1141–1215), who studied Chan Buddhism in China and founded Japan's first Zen temple in 1191. The Chan School traces its own origins to Bodhidharma, the legendary Indian monk who brought Mahayana Buddhism to China and founded the Xiaolin temple. Mahayana Buddhism began to incorporate elements of Daoism, which led to the simplified, experience-driven approach of first Chan, and then Zen.

Like Indian Mahayana Buddhism, Zen asserts that suffering in the world comes as a result of our ignorant attachment to false ideals, particularly the concept of a permanent self. The true nature of reality is *engi*, or interdependent arising, in which everything is part of a dynamic, interrelated web of being. All things are

"Zen . . . turns one's humdrum life . . . into one of art, full of genuine inner creativity."

D. T. Suzuki, author and lecturer

impermanent and nothing exists apart from the natural and social context in which it is embedded. Through meditative practices, a person can experience the truth of *engi* and gain *satori* (enlightenment), which is characterized by *mushin*, a state of "no-mind" that perceives things as they truly are without abstraction. Zen training involves the cultivation of two main virtues: *chie* (wisdom about the true nature of reality) and *jihi* (compassion for all sentient beings). The two most dominant schools of Zen are Sōtō, which focuses upon seated meditation, and Rinzai, which emphasizes the contemplation of *kōans*, or paradoxical riddles. The cultivation of *mushin* results in a type of hyperpraxia in which a person's performance of any task is greatly enhanced, and many artists since the samurai era have studied Zen to augment their abilities. **JM**

Theistic Satanism
Europe

The view of Satan as a godlike being that is deserving of worship as a hero

Atheistic Satanists—such as Anton LaVey (1930–97)—claim that Satan is not a real being but rather a symbol of absolute individualism. In contrast, proponents of theistic Satanism agree with the Abrahamic religions that Satan is a real being; however, unlike those religions, they believe that he is worthy of worship.

The origins of Satanism are hard to trace, but the concept is believed to have first appeared in Europe around the twelfth and thirteenth centuries. Part of the difficulty in dating the practice is due to the fact that many people in history have been accused of forms of Satanism—such as those put on trial for witchcraft during the sixteenth and seventeenth centuries—but it is generally thought unlikely that many of them actually participated in Devil worship.

"Better to reign in Hell than serve in Heaven!"

John Milton, *Paradise Lost* (1667)

Satanism became a popular theme in literature from the eighteenth century onward, and in 1891 Joris-Karl Huysmans offered a detailed description of the Black Mass in his novel *Là-bas* (Down There). Traditionally, the Black Mass is a central rite of Satanism, and the ceremony is usually said to combine an inverted form of the Chrisitan Eucharist with elements of magic.

Today, theistic Satanism is generally understood to be an explicit Satanist religion in which believers enter into pacts with demons, celebrate the Black Mass, offer animal sacrifices, and so on. This explicit Satanist religion is multidenominational with widely varying characteristics, but all agree that Satan is right to rebel against God, who is understood—partly in response to poets such as John Milton and theologians such as John Calvin—to be an arbitrary tyrant. **AB**

Robin Hood
England

The legendary outlaw who robbed from the rich to give to the poor

According to popular legends, Robin Hood was a skilled archer who, along with his "merry men" (including Little John and Friar Tuck), lived in Sherwood Forest. Together, they carried out robberies of the rich and then gave their plunder to the poor. Although the government at the time generally condemned Robin and his men as treasonous criminals (centuries later Guy Fawkes was spoken of as a "Robin Hood"), storytellers and poets have portrayed him as a heroic outlaw.

We do not know for certain if a man named Robin Hood ever lived, although the evidence to suggest as much is compelling. Some of the earliest references to this man are from English legal documents from the first half of the thirteenth century, leading many to believe that Robin Hood was a historical figure, and

"He was a good outlawe, and dyde pore men moch god."

A Gest of Robyn Hode (*c.* 1500)

indeed an outlaw. He must have been a unique outlaw, because shortly after this time legends quickly grew up around him and his exploits. Although in no way consistently told, they were immortalized in songs and poetry by well-known English writers, such as William Langland and William Shakespeare.

The legend and legacy of Robin Hood are not so much about politics—a peasant revolt against a corrupt government—as they are about ethics. Robin Hood is a legendary figure because he appeared to embody an ethical dilemma: a person who committed an injustice (robbing) to commit an act of love (giving to the poor). However, today he is admired worldwide as a figure who did not unjustly take (rob), but rather justly took (reclaimed) for the weak what was unjustly taken from them in the first place by the strong. **AB**

The Witches' Sabbath (1797) by Francisco de Goya. The goat in the center is the Devil in its beastlike form.

Fibonacci Numbers
Leonardo Bigollo (Fibonacci)

A number sequence in which each number equals the sum of the previous two

Fibonacci numbers are a sequence of numbers in which the third number, and every number after that, is the sum of the previous two numbers (0, 1, 1, 2, 3, 5, 8, 13, 21, 34 . . .). The sequence can begin with 0 and 1, with the third number 1, the fourth 2, and so on; or 1 and 1, where the third number is 2, the fourth is 3, and so forth.

The sequence was named after the Italian mathematician Leonardo Pisano Bigollo (c. 1170–1240), also known as Fibonacci, who was one of the finest mathematicians of the Middle Ages. He introduced the sequence to the Western world in his *Book of Squares* in 1202, although the sequence had appeared much earlier in Indian Sanskrit oral traditions dating back as far as 200 BCE. In the *Book of Squares*, Fibonacci likened his sequence of increasing numbers to a community

"There are no numbers in mathematics as ubiquitous as the Fibonacci numbers."

The Fabulous Fibonacci Numbers (2007)

of rabbits, and used it to calculate how many rabbits could be produced over a year if a person began with just two rabbits, with each female being able to reproduce at the age of only one month, doing so immediately, and then giving birth once a month later to a male and a female, each female of which then goes on her own reproductive journey.

The sequence can also be seen in biology, with the number of petals on daisies aligning with Fibonacci numbers: black-eyed daisies have thirteen petals, Shasta daisies twenty-one, and field daisies thirty-four. If you ever want to draw a mathematically correct pine cone, just draw five spirals going one way and eight going the other. And have you ever wondered why it is so difficult to find a four-leafed clover? Because four is not a Fibonacci number. **BS**

Trial by Jury
England

A legal proceeding in which the verdict is determined by members of the community

Although there were trials by jury in ancient Athens and ancient Rome, current legal systems that use trial by jury usually descend from or are influenced by the English common law, which traces a codified right to trial by jury to the provisions of the Magna Carta, an agreement forced on King John of England in 1215 by his barons. Article 39 of the Magna Carta provided that "no free man" could be imprisoned, outlawed, or exiled without "the lawful judgment of his peers."

Trial by jury is a legal procedure in which members of a jury, or jurors, are responsible for deciding the facts of the case: for example, whether the defendant is guilty in a criminal trial. Jurisdictions vary in their use of trial by jury; it is generally more common in criminal cases than in civil cases.

"A court is only as sound as its jury, and a jury is only as sound as the men who make it up."

Harper Lee, To Kill a Mockingbird (1960)

Jurors are typically selected at random from a pool of citizens, so the jury is presumed to be impartial. Those who support trial by jury argue that it provides a check on the power of the government, allows the voice of the community to be heard in the legal system, and displays that the power of the state is under the people's control. Critics, however, object that juries can be—and have been—swayed by personal feeling or community prejudice. They also object that juries are not capable of understanding scientific and statistical evidence, both of which are becoming increasingly deployed in court. The chief modern alternative to trial by jury is found in the system of civil law, in which a judge, or a panel of judges, is responsible for deciding the facts of the case (sometimes in collaboration with a jury). **GB**

Magna Carta
England

A charter limiting the king of England's powers and specifying citizens' rights

The Magna Carta—Latin for "great charter"—is a document signed in June of 1215 by King John of England (1166–1216). The charter limited the power of the English king and guaranteed, in part, that citizens would not be subject to the whims of the sovereign, but must be dealt with under the terms of English law that had existed prior to the Norman conquest in 1066.

King John's rule in early thirteenth-century England had not been going well by the time his barons forced him to sign the Magna Carta and give up some of his powers. Under the feudal system, the barons had an obligation to pay the king taxes and to support him by providing troops during times of conflict. When the king lost his territories in France and started raising taxes without consulting the barons, they, along with

"To no one will we sell, to no one will we refuse or delay right or justice."

Magna Carta (1215)

Archbishop Stephen Langton, rebelled and forced the king to sign the Magna Carta after capturing London.

By limiting the power of the English throne and recognizing citizens' rights, the Magna Carta became one of the first steps toward the establishment of English constitutional law. English settlers later took that history of constitutional law with them when they moved to New England, and the principles found in the Magna Carta were instrumental in both the writing of the Declaration of Independence (1776) and the formation of the U. S. Constitution (1787). Even though most of the individual rights guaranteed by the Magna Carta were later repealed, and the powers of English sovereigns during the Middle Ages were, for all practical purposes, total, its symbolic importance has played a guiding role in the development of modern democracy. **MT**

Theosophy
Unknown

A system of esoteric philosophy concerning the nature of divinity

In common use as a synonym for theology as long ago as the third century BCE, it was not until the thirteenth century CE that theosophy was categorized as being something very different from mainline theology and classical philosophy. In his *Summa Philosophiae* published in 1225 the author, scientist, and Bishop of Lincoln Robert Grosseteste (1175–1253) described theosophists as "authors inspired by holy books"—a very different calling to that of theologians, who were charged with the task of teaching spiritual truths.

Theosophy comes from the Greek *theosophia*, meaning "divine wisdom." It encourages a person to question established beliefs and to think critically, and is committed to a set of religious and philosophical ideas striving to show how these ideas are common to all religions. Its goal for the individual is enlightenment and self-actualization through reincarnation and karma. It is not, however, a standalone religion and it does not have a religious-style hierarchy. There are no clergy, and informal study sessions take the place of formal congregational gatherings.

The Theosophical Society was founded in New York City in 1875, and began combining Eastern religious traditions with Western esoteric beliefs in an attempt to achieve what its co-founder—Helena Blavatsky (1831–91), the Russian-born scholar of ancient wisdom literature—termed a "synthesis" of beliefs, called the Perennial Religion. Critics, however, claimed that all Blavatsky had learned she had simply read from books, not acquired personally from teachers and monks as she professed.

Theosophy today continues to foster understanding between competing faiths, and above all asks for selfless service from its adherents. As theosophical author Charles Webster Leadbeater once said: "In this path growth is achieved only by him who desires it not for his own sake, but for the sake of service." **BS**

Mental Asylum
Europe

An institution dedicated to offering care and treatment for those suffering from mental illness

Also known as the psychiatric institution, lunatic asylum, mental hospital, madhouse, or, colloquially, the nuthouse, a mental asylum is a place where people receive care and treatment for an acute or chronic mental illness. Perhaps the world's oldest existing mental asylum, Bethlem Royal Hospital in London, England, has been operating for more than 600 years. It was founded by Christians in 1247 as a simple shelter for homeless people, but gradually its activities came to be focused specifically on helping the "mad."

While places to house and protect the insane existed for centuries after that, a significant transition from lunatic asylum to mental hospital coincided with the rise of institutionalized psychiatry in the nineteenth century. Prior to this, madness was treated as a purely domestic problem—it was up to families and their parish authorities to care for the mentally ill. Private madhouses did exist for those who were considered extremely violent or who were unable to be cared for by relatives, but such places were only affordable to the wealthy. Consequently, the insane were often sent to workhouses or correctional institutions. Public or charitable asylums began popping up in the seventeenth and eighteenth centuries in England, but they were few and far between, and often at full capacity as a result.

With the rise of institutionalized psychiatry came national funding for hospitals, accessibility for all social classes, and mandatory moral treatment of all patients. The nineteenth century saw the development of treatments that no longer relied on restraints or coercive methods, and in the twentieth century came the rise of physical and drug therapies. Today, rather than locking away the mentally ill, asylums offer treatments to enable the ill to learn to function better within society. **KBJ**

⬆ An engraving by William Hogarth, of the final image in his eight-painting series *A Rake's Progress* (1735). This concluding scene is set in Bethlem Royal Hospital mental asylum.

"We do not have to visit a madhouse to find disordered minds ..."

Johann Wolfgang von Goethe, writer

Eyeglasses
Unknown

Objects worn over the eyes that use lenses to correct deficiencies in the wearer's vision

⬆ *Virgil With Spectacles*, a painting by Tom Rink. Mostly worn by monks and scholars, early forms of eyeglasses were held in front of the eyes or balanced on the nose.

"I always think about what it means to wear eyeglasses ... I think about all the people before eyeglasses were invented. It must have been weird because everyone was seeing in different ways according to how bad their eyes were."

Andy Warhol, artist

People have been using magnification devices to assist with seeing things since at least Roman times. Seneca the Younger (c. 4 BCE–65 CE) allegedly used a glass globe filled with water in an attempt to magnify text in his later years. By 1000, reading stones, similar to what we know as magnifying glasses, were in use, though they were unwieldy and not wearable. Although it is not exactly clear who invented them, eyeglasses existed by at least 1268, when English philosopher Roger Bacon (c. 1220–94) first wrote about them.

Eyeglasses offered a practical, portable means of correcting vision. Early spectacles were made from quartz lenses, but later advances in glassmaking allowed inventors to pair the optics with lighter frames that could be more easily worn. It was not until 1604, however, that an explanation for why eyeglasses worked was put forward. In a treatise on optics, German mathematician Johannes Kepler explained that vision was a process of refraction within the eye, and that people with blurred vision had an optical defect which meant that light rays were focused either in front of or just behind their retina—a problem that lenses corrected by redirecting the light. By the 1780s, Benjamin Franklin, a printer by trade, had created bifocals, allowing those with more than one vision problem to rely on a single set of glasses.

The earliest eyeglasses were used primarily to enable people to continue reading after they developed hyperopia, or farsightedness, as they aged. Early scholars likely relied on eyeglasses to maintain their ability to read and write and to contribute to the development of new ideas. As eyeglasses became more common and cheaper to produce, they allowed millions of people to engage in pursuits that their vision problems would otherwise have prevented. Moreover, they became one of the first widely available medical devices that used technology to overcome physical problems. **MT**

Doctrine of Double Effect

St. Thomas Aquinas

A set of ethical criteria for carrying out an act that would usually be morally wrong

Also referred to as the principle of double effect, the doctrine of double effect is a conceptual distinction made by Catholic theologians in the Middle Ages to explain and justify a very specific aspect of the rules of engagement of war, although it has since been used in analyzing a variety of contemporary moral problems, including euthanasia and abortion.

The Christian theologian and philosopher St. Thomas Aquinas (1225–74) is credited with introducing the doctrine of double effect into Catholic thinking in his unfinished work *Summa Theologica* (1265–74). Aquinas argued that killing an aggressor is permissible if a person does not intend to kill the aggressor and only intends to defend themself. This, in part, established the primacy of self-defense as the only justification for going to war. A more generalized interpretation of the doctrine is that it permits acting in such a way as to bring about foreseeable but unintended harms, provided that there is a greater intended good as the end result. In such instances, the harmful effect is seen to be something like a side effect of the action (with the primary aim of the action being the good result that is to come in the end), although agents are still required to minimize the foreseeable harms where and when possible.

The doctrine of double effect helped to establish the framework for justified warfare among agreeing nations in the West for more than 1,500 years. More importantly, it serves as a crucial non-absolutist position whereby agents must scrutinize and minimize potential harms that could result from their actions, giving additional autonomy to people to make decisions in situations that are not amenable to simple solutions. In short, the doctrine of double effect recognizes and reflects the inadequacy of simple, formulaic rules for determining justified actions in complex situations. **JS**

⬆ An old manuscript of the *Summa Theologica* (1265–74) by St. Thomas Aquinas. Aquinas's work was intended as a manual for beginners in theology.

"Nothing hinders one act from having two effects, only one of which is intended . . ."

St. Thomas Aquinas, *Summa Theologica* (1265–74)

Five Proofs of God's Existence
St. Thomas Aquinas

Intellectual arguments for the existence of God, based on reason and observation

Of the many attempts to prove the existence of God, arguably the best are the five proofs, or five ways, that were offered by St. Thomas Aquinas (1225–74) in his unfinished work *Summa Theologica* (1265–74). They are: motion (motion cannot begin on its own and so there must have been a first mover); causation (the sequence of causes that created the universe must have a first cause); contingency of creation (all things depend upon other things for their creation, so there must be a being that caused the initial creation); degrees of perfection (there are differing degrees of beauty in the universe, so there must be a perfect standard—God—to which all things are compared); and intelligent design (the universe follows laws that appear to have order, which implies the existence of a Great Designer).

"It is better to … deliver … contemplated truths than merely to contemplate."

St. Thomas Aquinas, *Summa Theologica* (1265–74)

Technically more of an attempt to clarify the ways in which people conceptualize the creator as described in Christianity, the five proofs are generally seen as earnest arguments for the reality of God. Thus, like many other philosophical claims, the five proofs have taken on a significance different to the one intended by their author. After all, Aquinas, being a Roman Catholic, already knew of God's existence through faith.

The adequacy, or inadequacy, of the five proofs brings up the provocative issue of the relationship between the divine and rationality. Indeed, the five proofs highlight the strained relationship between that which is known *a posteriori* (through experience) and that which is known *a priori* (through reason), which then calls into question the priority of philosophical inquiry over scientific inquiry, and vice versa. **JS**

God and Causation
St. Thomas Aquinas

The view that God does not work directly in the world, but through secondary causes

In his unfinished work *Summa Theologica* (1265–74), philosopher, priest, and theologian St. Thomas Aquinas (1225–74) refers to God as the "Primary Cause" of all of creation, which God then sustains through his presence. The inhabitants of God's creation—including humankind—are his "Secondary Causes." The idea of "causation" is not always as linear as the example of creator followed by creation suggests. The "chicken and the egg" causality dilemma (which came first, the chicken or the egg?) means different things to different people. A literal reading of Genesis makes it clear that the chicken (God) came first; but in evolution it is the egg that first appeared.

According to René Descartes (1596–1650), a primary cause is able to "cause itself" and is not dependent

"All intermediate causes are inferior in power to the first cause …"

St. Thomas Aquinas, *Summa Theologica* (1265–74)

upon anything before it for its existence. For Aquinas, creation was the radical "causing" of the universe—it was not a change to the universe, or to space or time; it was not an altering of existing materials. If anything had already existed to aid in or be added to the causing of the universe, then God would not have been the maker of it. As the initiator of the first, primary cause, God is responsible for the means by which all subsequent secondary causes are enabled and sustained. These secondary causes are truly causal, and are variable and arbitrary according to the whims and vagaries of its agents, whether they are humans, or the laws of nature, or the mechanics of physics. For Aquinas, humans cause their own actions and God influences the actions of humans, and neither impinges upon the freedom of the other. **BS**

St. Thomas Aquinas receiving the Holy Spirit (in the shape of a dove), by Andrea di Bartolo (c. 1368–1428).

C. 1280 ▲

Mechanical Clock
Unknown

A mechanical device that enabled the accurate measurement of time

The mechanical clock—a self-sufficient device that is able to measure time without requiring an external power source once it has been set up for a cycle of its limited period of operation—appeared in Europe in the thirteenth century, although no examples have survived to offer a precise date. However, from around 1280, increasingly frequent mentions of mechanical clocks in church records indicate that religious communities, in particular, were beginning to rely on mechanical clocks to keep them to their schedule of meals, services, and private prayer.

Since prehistoric times, humankind has devised a variety of ways to measure the passage of time, including the sundial, hourglass, and water clock. However, it was not until the invention of a mechanical

> "By putting forward the hands of the clock you shall not advance the hour."

Victor Hugo, poet, novelist, and dramatist

balancing mechanism, known as an escapement, that mechanical clocks became a practical proposition. Chinese engineer Su Song (1020–1101) produced an escapement in the eleventh century, but because his clock relied on water movement for its power it could not be defined as a completely mechanical clock.

Early mechanical clocks used the regular motion of pendulums to move gears and measure time. They may have been inaccurate by as much as half an hour per day; today, it would take an atomic clock 138 million years to lose or gain less than a second. Even so, the mechanical clock commodified time by encapsulating it into a measurable, divisible product. Clocks gave scientists the ability to measure time in breathtakingly brief moments, and formed entire industries and economies that rested on its progress. **MT**

C. 1280 ▨

Kabbalah
Jewish religion

A Jewish tradition of mystical interpretation of the Torah

Kabbalah (meaning roughly "tradition") is the dominant form of Jewish mystical theology. Although its devotees trace Kabbalah to Moses, or even to Adam, scholars largely agree that it developed in the eleventh and twelfth centuries. In around 1280, the Spanish rabbi Moses de León (1250–1305) published the *Zohar*, which became the foundational work of Kabbalah. The *Zohar* underwent a reinterpretation in the sixteenth century by Isaac Luria (1534–72), and Luria's Kabbalism is sometimes distinguished from that of the *Zohar*.

Kabbalah distinguishes between God as he is in himself and as he is manifested. As he is in himself, God is beyond comprehension. God becomes manifest by means of a process of emanation, through ten powers or potencies known as the Sefirot. It is through the

> "The kabbalah that appeared more than 800 years ago . . . is still present . . ."

Joseph Dan, *Kabbalah: A Very Short Introduction* (2006)

Sefirot that God reveals himself and through which he sustains the universe's existence. Elements in the human psyche correspond to the Sefirot, and therefore moral or immoral behavior affects the harmony or disharmony of the universe. Humans are thus central to the system of the universe. Kabbalah also provides esoteric readings of the Torah and surrounding texts.

Within Judaism itself, Kabbalah's popularity varies. It was tainted by the fall of a false messiah in the seventeenth century, and in the nineteenth century it was often rejected as importing pagan teachings or as superstitious nonsense. But certain sects revere it as sacred, and elements of Kabbalah have become widely adopted in Judaism. Outside Judaism, Kabbalah sometimes attracts curious non-Jews, especially when incorporated in mystical or New Age traditions. **GB**

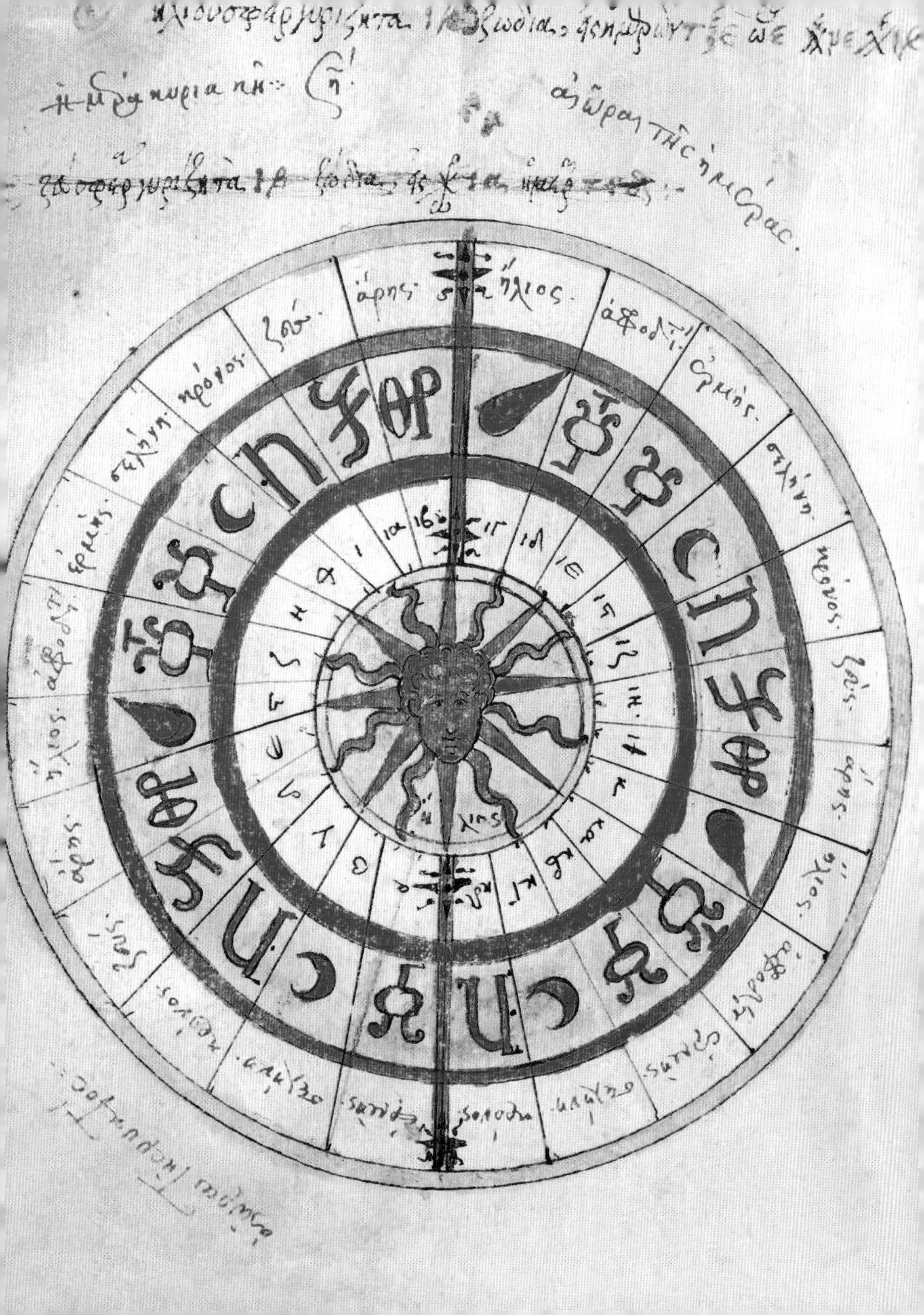
ἄρης
ἥλιος
ἀφροδίτη
ἑρμῆς
σελήνη
κρόνος
ζεύς

Nunchi
Korea

The subtle art and ability of listening to and gauging others' moods

Nunchi is a Korean term that describes the ability to listen to and understand the mood of others, to see into their *kibun* (state of mind) and respond accordingly. In the West, this ability is seen as possessing little more than "good instincts," but in a society in which people are taught from childhood not to make their true feelings known, *nunchi* is an indispensible aid in communicating with those around you. The origins of the concept lie in Confucianism, a revised version of which, known as Neo-Confucianism, became prominent in Korea from the early fifteenth century.

Best translated as "the sense of eye," *nunchi* is an important tool in navigating Korea's high context culture, in which words and word choices are seen as less important in conveying complex messages than

"Nunchi *is used to discover another's unspoken 'hidden agenda'. . ."*
Theresa Youn-ja Shim, *Changing Korea* (2008)

in the West. In Korea, communication is less verbally explicit. For example, when a Korean asks somebody "Are you thirsty?" what they are more likely to mean is "I am thirsty, would you like to have a drink?" And so the proper response, if one is attuned to their *nunchi*, is not to say yes or no—that might upset the other person's *kibun*—but simply to reply "What would you like to drink?" *Nunchi* is a kind of sixth sense, the art of seeking out visual and verbal clues, in order to decipher them and thus understand what is really being said.

Those who are not Korean need not despair. Anyone can develop *nunchi* through keen observation, pausing before answering a question, by talking to someone who is Korean, or by simply going to Korea and immersing themselves in the verbal and visual subtleties of everyday Korean life. **JMa**

The Book of the City of Ladies
Christine de Pizan

An early defense of the virtues and achievements of women

The Book of the City of Ladies (1405) is generally considered the first feminist novel written by a Western woman. Its author, Christine de Pizan (1364–*c*. 1430), lived in Venice and wrote in excess of forty literary works in her lifetime. Widowed at the age of twenty-five, her writings provided her with an income that helped in the raising of her three children. She did not write from a position of privilege.

In *City of Ladies*, Pizan creates a mythical city in which she installs three allegorical foremothers named Justice, Rectitude, and Reason, who preside over a populace where women are appreciated and respected. The author then begins a dialogue with the three women who, together, lift her out of the "slough of despond" into which the rampant misogyny of her time has

"Neither the loftiness nor the lowliness of a person lies in the body according to the sex."
Christine de Pizan, *The Book of the City of Ladies* (1405)

placed her. The book was in part a response to the misogynistic writings of popular French male author Jean de Meun (*c*. 1240–*c*. 1305), who depicted women as vicious and immoral. However, Pizan's treatise was far more than defensive in nature. She took great care to demonstrate the positive effect that women had on mediating the affairs of their troublesome menfolk, and encouraged women to use rhetoric as a means to assert themselves and to resolve social and family conflicts.

The women in Pizan's city are strong and articulate. They are scholars, prophets, inventors, painters, strong wives, and proud daughters, and together they offer up a portrait of womanhood that goes a long way toward correcting the skewed and paternalistic views of many male historians. They also provide a rare window into medieval womanhood. **BS**

An illustration from a French edition (*c*. 1411–12) of Christine de Pizan's *The Book of the City of Ladies* (1405). ➡

Linear Perspective in Painting
Leon Battista Alberti

A system that enabled artists to create the illusion of space and distance on a flat surface

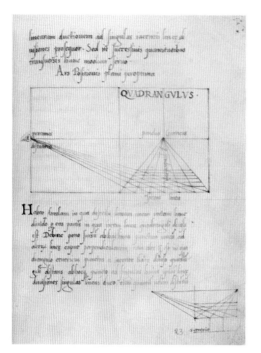

⬆ An illustration and accompanying description from *On Painting* (1435) by Leon Battista Alberti, demonstrating his technique for creating perspective in an artwork.

"Beauty—the adjustment of all parts proportionately so that one cannot add or subtract or change without impairing the harmony of the whole."

Leon Battista Alberti

Linear perspective occurs when, in a two-dimensional image such as a painting, converging lines meet at a single vanishing point, with all objects in the scene becoming smaller and smaller the farther away they are in the background of the image, according to a set scale. This idea was first written about by the Italian architect, author, and priest Leon Battista Alberti (1404–72) in his book *On Painting* (1435), generally considered to be the world's first modern treatise on how to accurately represent three-dimensional images on a two-dimensional surface, such as a wall or canvas.

The problem of perspective had been looming for a while. After hundreds of years of overtly religious art devoted mostly to heavenly figures, artists in the Renaissance changed their focus to the world around them. Buildings, towns, and everyday objects began to appear in pictures, and all of a sudden it became prudent for an artist who was interested in realistically depicting the world to try to figure out how to paint landscapes and streetscapes so that the paintings resembled what the viewer actually saw in real life.

Most artists working in Europe after 1435 were aware of Alberti's seminal work. Beginning with a "stage" area in the picture's foreground, he then drew a kind of receding grid on which all the other elements in the painting would be arranged, using the viewer's height as a guide. This was not the first time a creative artist had identified and tried to make sense of perspective, however. The architect Filippo Brunelleschi (1377–1446) had suggested a solution some years earlier, but the particulars of his approach were never properly understood. Alberti's grid showed a proper understanding of perspective and how to achieve it. His work had a profound impact on Renaissance painting (*c.* 1450–1600), and his principles still form the basis of linear perspective today. **BS**

Printing Press

Johannes Gutenberg

A machine that allowed for easy reproduction of printed materials

Invented in the 1440s, the printing press of Johannes Gutenberg (1398–1468) is widely regarded as one of the most important and influential inventions in history. Gutenberg's printing press used customizable forms to transfer the same text or images to different pieces of paper or other material. The press allowed people to create identical copies of books and other written materials quickly, cheaply, and efficiently.

While Chinese inventor Pi Sheng (990–1051) is credited with inventing movable type in the eleventh century, it was Gutenberg who refined the process of using block printing and movable type to mechanize printing and enable mass production. Using his knowledge and experience as a professional goldsmith, he developed a method of creating individual lead letters that could be assembled quickly into blocks of text, then melted down for recasting when sufficient copies had been made. When combined with a screw-type press, paper that by then was readily available, and a remarkable ease of use, Gutenberg's movable type transformed the means by which ideas were spread in the community.

Prior to the press, written materials had to be copied individually by hand in a painstaking, laborious process. After its introduction, even bound books could be mass-produced. (The first book printed by Gutenberg was the Bible.) Within a few decades of its appearance, the printing press was being used in every country in Western Europe, and the number of books being produced each year skyrocketed. It is estimated that in the fifteenth century fewer than 25 million books were made in Europe. By the sixteenth century that number had ballooned to more than 200 million. The printing press's widespread adoption not only led to a surge in literacy rates, but also made it easier for scientists, philosophers, and other thinkers to share and spread their ideas. **MT**

⬆ An engraving (1754) of German printer Johannes Gutenberg in his workshop, checking a page while printing his first Bible on his newly invented printing press.

"It shall scatter the darkness of ignorance, and cause a light . . . to shine amongst men."

Johannes Gutenberg

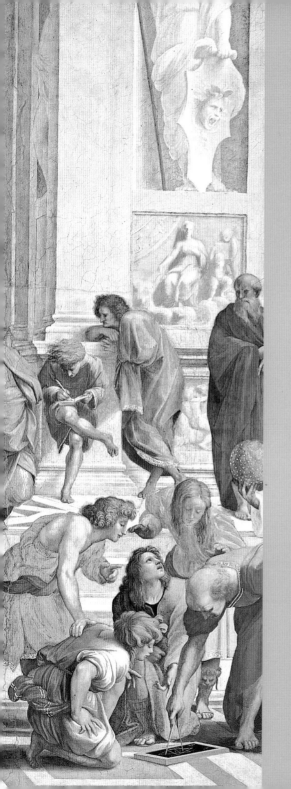

Early Modern
1450–1779

This was an exciting time in history, when the globe was first circumnavigated and the wonders of nature were beginning to be understood from a scientific perspective. Significant philosophical ideas from this period include those found in Niccolo Machiavelli's political treatise *The Prince*, René Descartes's statement that "I think, therefore I am," and John Locke's argument that the mind at birth is a blank slate. Important practical ideas include those behind the internal combustion engine and mechanical programming, the precursor to computer programming. Galileo turned all of Western science— and history—on its head with the idea that the natural state of something is to be in motion, ending the nearly 2,000-year reign of Aristotelian physics.

← *The School of Athens* (1509–11), a fresco by Renaissance artist Raphael, makes clever use of perspective to depict the ancient Greek philsopher Plato and his student Aristotle.

Homophony
Europe

A musical texture in which multiple parts move together in harmony

Homophony in music is a texture in which two or more parts move in harmony (based primarily on chords). Homophony is distinct from polyphony, which involves combinations of melodies that are relatively independent. Homophony is typically characterized by one part (often the highest) predominating, with little rhythmic difference between parts. In polyphony, by contrast, rhythmic distinctiveness will reinforce the autonomy of the melody.

Music of the Middle Ages (from 400 to about 1450) began with the development of monophony, which is essentially music with a single part or melodic line. This was manifested in the sacred music of the Roman Catholic Church, characterized primarily by vocal chants that were sung without accompaniment and

"What most people mean … [by] harmony … [is] the texture is homophonic."

Worlds of Music (2006), gen. ed. Jeff Todd Titon

in unison. The gradual development of counterpoint led to the later integration of polyphony into music of this period. Homophony developed after this, in the Renaissance (*c.* 1450–1600), and involved pieces that could be performed by both singers and different instruments. As a term, however, homophony did not appear in English until its use by composer and music historian Charles Burney (1726–1814) in his *General History of Music* (1776).

Since the middle of the Baroque period (*c.* 1600–1760), music theorists have considered four voices in homophonic arrangement as the basic texture of Western music. The rise of homophony also led to the development of new melodic forms such as the sonata, which was popular in the Classical (*c.* 1730–1820) and Romantic (*c.* 1815–1910) periods. **JE**

Renaissance Music
Europe

A stylistic period in music history, lasting from roughly 1450 to 1600

The Renaissance is an era in art and intellectual history that spans from *c.* 1450 to *c.* 1600. Traditional accounts of the period emphasize the "discovery of man," a renewed interest in antiquity and science, and a reaction to the perceived notion of the "barbaric" medieval culture.

In contrast to practitioners of the visual arts and architecture, it was not possible for musicians of the period to be inspired by actual music from antiquity. Instead, antiquity's influence came through theoretical writings by Plato and others on the relationship between music and text: music's role was to emphasize the meaning of the text, making a direct impact on the soul. Thus, vocal music was privileged over instrumental during the period. A stylistic consequence was that word-painting—letting the melodic patterns

"The Renaissance was … the green end of one of civilization's hardest winters."

John Fowles, *The French Lieutenant's Woman* (1969)

directly illustrate the emotion or imitate the action of a text—became a prevalent stylistic device both in secular and sacred music.

Thanks to the development of music printing during the sixteenth century, music could be more widely distributed. Instrumental music developed in a specialized fashion, both with performers devoting their time to one instrument and with instrumental ensembles consisting of similar instruments of different sizes. This practice carries on today in highly specialized orchestras that include homogenous instrument sections. The polyphonic compositional practices of composers in Italy and Northern Europe that shaped the Renaissance's highly complex vocal works, such as those of Luigi da Palestrina and Josquin des Prez, are still taught to music students at universities. **PB**

Public Library
Malatesta Novello

A collection of books that can be accessed freely by the general public

⤒ The reading room in the Biblioteca Malatestiana in Cesena, Italy, the world's first public library. The interior of the library has not changed since it first opened in 1452.

A public library requires not only books and manuscripts on shelves, but also a public body to own them and a literate population to read them. This combination of circumstances first occurred in Renaissance Italy, although libraries themselves are a far older idea.

The world's first libraries, containing archives of clay tablets, were founded in Sumerian temples in around 2600 BCE. The Egyptians built a major reference library at Alexandria in around 300 BCE, while rich Romans established their own private libraries in the first century BCE. Christian and Buddhist monks kept rooms of manuscripts, while reference libraries first appeared in Islamic cities during the ninth century. These libraries were known as "Halls of Science" and they were endowed by Islamic sects to promote their beliefs and to disseminate secular knowledge. All these libraries were privately owned and were used only by the few enthusiasts and scholars able to read. It was not until 1452 that the world's first publically owned library opened in Cesena in central Italy. Commissioned by Malatesta Novello (1418–56), lord of Cesena, and known as the Biblioteca Malatestiana, the library belonged to the city of Cesena. It contained 340 manuscripts on subjects as varied as the classics, medicine, and science, which the literate public could read on one of fifty-eight desks.

The idea of a library funded by pubic monies and open to the general public soon spread throughout Europe, with the royal National Library of France, founded in 1368, opening its doors to the public in 1692. Public libraries were established in U.S. cities during the nineteenth century, while an act of parliament in 1850 allowed British towns and cities to set up free public libraries paid for by local taxes. Public libraries became an important feature of local communities, giving anyone with the motivation the opportunity to improve their knowledge. **SA**

"I have always imagined that Paradise will be a kind of library."

Jorge Luis Borges, writer

Oration on the Dignity of Man
Giovanni Pico della Mirandola

A speech that embodied the key concepts of the Renaissance

Often referred to as the "Manifesto of the Renaissance," the "Oration on the Dignity of Man" was a speech written (but never given) in 1486 by Giovanni Pico della Mirandola (1463–94), just twenty-three years of age and already one of the greatest philosophers and humanists of his day. Mirandola abandoned the study of canon law in 1480 in preference for philosophy after the death of his mother. The Oration was intended as an introduction to his *900 Conclusions*, a selection of theological theses drawn from numerous sources.

The speech was "pure Renaissance," embodying all of the precepts that made the Renaissance (c.1450–1600) what it was—a belief in human primacy and humankind's ability to reshape the environment, invent anything, or be anything. If a man could properly cultivate all that is rational he would, Mirandola said, "reveal himself a heavenly being." Mirandola emphasized humankind's dominance over creation, and how humans had been endowed with gifts from God that distinguish them from all other creatures. He saw humans as the summit of God's creativity, but did not lord Christianity over other faiths, citing several intellectuals and philosophers from other religions to support his idea that all humans are equally capable of pondering the mysteries of existence. He also encouraged his listeners to follow their own paths and not be intimidated by church doctrines or hierarchies, and offered to pay the travel expenses for any scholar prepared to travel to Rome and debate his ideas with him in a public forum.

Following the publication of *900 Conclusions*, a number of Mirandola's theses were denounced as heretical by Pope Innocent VIII and Mirandola was briefly imprisoned. He intended the oration to be a precursor to an authoritative compendium on the intellectual, practical, and philosophical achievements of humankind, but the book was never completed due to his untimely death. **BS**

↑ A detail of *Adoration of the Magi* (*c.* 1475–76), by Florentine painter Sandro Botticelli, shows Giovanni Pico della Mirandola (in red hat) with the scholar Agnolo Poliziano (holding sword).

"This is what Moses commands us … admonishing, urging, and exhorting us to prepare ourselves, while we may, by means of philosophy, a road to future heavenly glory."

Mirandola, "Oration on the Dignity of Man" (1486)

Sikhism
Guru Nanak

A religion that combines action—doing good deeds—with belief in God

Sikhism was founded in the Punjab region of Pakistan in 1499 by Guru Nanak (1469–1539), who, according to tradition, became interested in spiritual things at the age of five. However, another twenty-five years were to pass before he experienced an extraordinary, life-changing vision. In 1499, three days after his clothes were found by a stream and he was assumed by his family to have drowned, he miraculously reappeared, but refused to speak of what had happened to him. The next day, he declared: "There is neither Hindu nor Mussulman [Muslim], so whose path shall I follow? I shall follow God's path. God is neither Hindu nor Mussulman and the path which I follow is God's." With these words, Sikhism was born.

The Punjabi word *Sikh* translates as "learner," and early followers of the tradition were those in search of spiritual guidance. After the death of Guru Nanak, Sikhism was led by a succession of nine other gurus, all of whom are believed to have been inhabited by the same spirit. Upon the death of the tenth, Guru Gobind Singh (1666–1708), this spirit was transferred to the sacred scripture of Sikhism, the *Guru Granth Sahib* (The Granth as the Guru). From that point on, the *Guru Granth Sahib* was considered to be the sole guru.

Sikhism is a monotheistic religion. Adherents believe that there is only one God, without form and without gender. All people have direct access to God, and all are equal. We should live good, honest, and pure lives within our communities. Ritualistic observances have no relevance—they are empty gestures—and there is no place for superstitious traditions or practices. We spend our lives in an endless cycle of birth, life, and rebirth, and the quality of our lives is determined by how we have lived previously—the law of karma. Today, there are around 20 million Sikhs in the world, the majority of whom live in the Punjab province in India. **BS**

A sixteenth-century Indian miniature painting depicts Guru Nanak listening to a sitar player. ⬆

Coffeehouse
Ottoman Empire

A public space for political debate, stories, gossip, and games—and for drinking coffee

The coffeehouse was originally established to sell coffee to the public, but it quickly became more than that, turning into a place for friends and neighbors to meet and discuss the issues of the day. Samuel Johnson defined it in his *Dictionary* (1755) as: "A house of entertainment where coffee is sold, and guests are supplied with newspapers." Consuming coffee thus became a social experience, and the site where it was served became an important gathering place.

Coffeehouses were established as soon as coffee was introduced to the Ottoman Empire in the early sixteenth century, and later spread to Europe in the seventeenth century. The merchants and entrepreneurs who introduced coffee served it in public shops, and

these shops offered places for customers to stay while they drank their purchase. These social spaces became a venue for the free exchange of ideas, where people could discuss politics, share stories, and play games. Authorities recognized the freedom of discussion offered by these new public spaces as dangerous and frequently took actions to suppress it, including in Mecca in the early sixteenth century and London in the mid-seventeenth century.

Nothing quite like the coffeehouse had ever existed before, and its provision of a space where social and business life could be mixed in pleasant surroundings proved immensely popular. The coffeehouse became an influential public forum, with a legacy that touched everything from the stock market and philosophy to science and literature. It was also seen as a great "social leveler," as it was open to all men, regardless of social status, as long as they could afford the price of a cup of coffee. With modern coffeeshop chains, such as Starbucks, now ubiquitous and an estimated 1.6 billion cups of coffee drunk worldwide every day, the popularity of the coffeehouse shows no sign of abating. **TD**

↑ A Turkish miniature from 1582, showing a coffee wagon in a carnival procession.

Φ

In Praise of Folly
Desiderius Erasmus

A satirical essay about self-importance and lack of spirituality becomes one of the most influential texts of the Renaissance

⬆ A portrait of Desiderius Erasmus, painted in 1517 by the Flemish artist Quentin Massys. Massys also later produced a medal featuring Erasmus's likeness.

In 1509, the humanist scholar Desiderius Erasmus of Rotterdam (1469–1536) wrote an essay he called *In Praise of Folly* (*Moriae Encomium*). After its publication in 1511, it became one of the most popular and influential texts of the Renaissance (*c*. 1450–1600): read by popes, widely translated, and vigorously discussed. Erasmus believed it to be of only minor importance, and he filled it with wordplay and inside jokes to his friend Sir Thomas More. However, this ostensibly light, amusing satire would go on to add fuel to the fire of the Protestant Reformation in the sixteenth century.

The essay personifies the character of Folly as a goddess, the offspring of a nymph, Freshness, and the god of wealth, Plutus. As readers might expect from an entity attended by Inebriation, Ignorance, Misoponia (laziness), Anoia (madness), and Lethe (dead sleep), Folly has a high opinion of herself, declaring that life would be dull and distasteful without her. Folly eventually moves from praising her degenerate friends to satirizing the excesses, superstitions, and needlessly obscure practices of the Roman Catholic clergy. The piece ends with an unadorned statement of Christian ideals.

Erasmus was a Renaissance humanist and also a faithful Catholic, and *In Praise of Folly* reflects the gradual shift in Western Europe away from a medieval worldview centered on the Roman Catholic Church to an investment in the spiritual and intellectual self-sufficiency of the individual. An earlier work by Erasmus had outlined the same ideas of religious obscurism and excess, but *In Praise of Folly*'s ironic, playful tone communicated his message more flavorfully to an increasingly literate public. Though Erasmus distanced himself from the politics of the Protestant Reformation, his work promoted and spread the ideals of a humanist Europe throughout the Western world. **MK**

"Clap your hands, live, and drink lustily, my most excellent disciples of Folly."

Desiderius Erasmus, *In Praise of Folly* (1511)

The Prince
Niccolò Machiavelli

A political philosophy viewing politics as the cynical pursuit of power

The first truly modern political scientist, Niccolò Machiavelli (1469–1527), published in 1513 a slim text he titled *The Prince* (Il Principe). It was a guide on acquiring power, creating a state, and then keeping that state. In it, he drew from his experiences as a foreign secretary for the government of Florence, and also the teachings of history, to postulate that politics followed its own rules. Scandalized by the seeming moral depravity of such a system, readers of *The Prince* quickly made his name synonymous with political strategies characterized by cunning, bad faith, and duplicity. All the same, Machiavelli's work would usher in an attitude of political realism that facilitated all subsequent descriptions of national and international power.

The Prince emphasizes Machiavelli's belief that realism, not abstract moral idealism, is the necessary approach to political matters. He recognizes that most political leaders are not inherently extraordinarily virtuous in a Christian sense, but instead have a particular aspiration for glory. In order to take advantage of his temperament and to develop his full potential, then, a political leader ought to take risks, even if those risks included re-creating the "mores and orders" that define a social order. Machiavelli's bold departure from the political philosophy of the day created an eager audience for his book, and it almost immediately began influencing world political practices.

In the generations after him, political realists of the stature of Francis Bacon, David Hume, John Locke, and Adam Smith all cited Machiavelli's approach as a direct influence on their thinking, as did founding fathers of the American Revolution Thomas Jefferson, John Adams, and Benjamin Franklin. Machiavelli's work does not always lead to positive political revolution, however; twentieth-century mobsters John Gotti and Roy DeMeo have deemed *The Prince* a "Mafia Bible." **MK**

The State
Niccolò Machiavelli

The supreme political power in a certain geographic area

Though nations have existed throughout history, the modern idea of the state is largely attributed to Niccolò Machiavelli (1469–1527), who, in his 1513 work *The Prince*, spoke of *lo stato* (the state) as the only organization that not only wields ultimate authority, but also whose interests trump all others, even those of individuals, the Church, or morality itself. Later political theorists, such as Max Weber (1864–1920), would refine the idea of the state as a government that only used its violent authority legally, or for legitimate or acceptable purposes. Today, almost every corner of the Earth is claimed as belonging to a particular state, including the surrounding coastal waters and airspace. States can be governed through any political form, from dictatorships to republican democracies.

> *"L'État, c'est moi."*
> *(The state, it is I.)*
>
> King Louis XIV of France

The state does not exist in a physical form, yet its power is ever present, permeating every part of daily life. The state has the power to control you, yet you cannot touch it. It has the ability to wage war, though it never gives an order. It has the power to detain, incarcerate, and execute without being able to lift a finger because it has no digits. Though Machiavelli's work is often criticized for its support of questionable or immoral tactics to further the state's interests, the idea of a final, ultimate power is the basic concept upon which all modern governments, and nations, are built. Behind all the balances, limitations, and checks on government authority, the final power in any nation always rests with the state and those who pursue its interests, and, ultimately, their ability to use violence. **MT**

🏛

◪

Utopia
Sir Thomas More

A seemingly perfect society, usually constructed in a deliberate manner

The word "utopia" first appeared in a book of the same name published in 1516 by Sir Thomas More (1478–1535). It was created from the Greek for "not" and "place"; its literal translation is "nowhere." More, a Renaissance humanist, philosopher, statesman, and advisor to King Henry VIII, originally titled the book *Libellus ... de optimo reipublicae statu, deque nova insula Utopia* (Concerning the Highest State of the Republic and the New Island Utopia). In it he argues for the creation of a society ruled by reason, communal power, and property, with the caveat that this kind of world is not easily achieved.

While Sir Thomas More coined the word, the concept of utopia predates him. Many people—some in earnest, some in jest, and some in speculation—have written accounts of what a "perfect" society would look like.

> ### "Nations will be happy, when ... kings become philosophers."
> Sir Thomas More, *Utopia* (1516)

Old and new examples of utopian societies are found in Plato's *The Republic* (360 BCE), Francis Bacon's *New Atlantis* (1624), and H. G. Wells's *A Modern Utopia* (1905). Utopias work better on paper than they do in practice, and few of the political and religious communities that have attempted to observe utopian ideals have succeeded. Frequently, once the author or leader of a utopian society dies, the structure of the society crumbles.

Alongside utopia exists the concept of dystopia, an idea that has been more prevalent in popular culture than utopia in the past two centuries. Well-known accounts of dystopias can be found in Aldous Huxley's *Brave New World* (1932) and *Nineteen Eighty-Four* by George Orwell (1949). Dystopian societies are utopias gone wrong because of a distortion of one of the well-intended founding precepts of the utopia. **MK**

Anti-clericalism
Martin Luther

The belief that churchmen stand in the way of both God and the exercise of reason

Anti-clerical movements were and remain deeply concerned with preserving religion's relevance. The sixteenth-century Protestant Reformation, arguably a pivotal moment in the political, social, artistic, and religious development of the Western world, is a vivid example of how anti-clericalism was able to reform culture and religion simultaneously.

The protests against the Roman Catholic Church, *Ninety-five Theses on the Power and Efficacy of Indulgences*, that Martin Luther (1483–1546) nailed to the door of Wittenberg's All Saints' Church in 1517 contained attacks against Catholicism's doctrines, rituals, and ecclesiastical structure, and he gave special attention to clergy members who convinced congregations that without the direct intervention

> ### "Every man must do two things alone ... his own believing and his own dying."
> Martin Luther

of a priest, and the payment that inevitably followed such intervention, a parishioner would be unable to communicate with God, much less get into Heaven. Luther's articulation of this concern fueled work by Enlightenment philosophers such as Voltaire who, though uninterested in reforming the prevailing religious practices, argued the efficacy of reason above all else. Churchmen, then, since they did not typically cultivate faculties of reason, impeded societal progress.

Anti-clericalism and its proponents cleared a path for humanism, science, and reason to flourish, which in turn encouraged attitudes of religious tolerance. Humanist thinking situated the power to access God within each individual, rather than in the office of a priest, which weakened organized religion's hold on secular and personal affairs. **MK**

◄ Woodcut on the title page of the first edition of Sir Thomas More's *Utopia* (1516).

Reformation Art
Martin Luther

A critical attitude to religious art that appeared as part of the Reformation

⬆ *The Judgement of Paris* (c. 1528) by Lucas Cranach the Elder. The painting shows Paris awarding a golden apple (here transformed into a glass orb) to the fairest of three goddesses.

The Roman Catholic Church's love of religious iconography was challenged in 1517 when Martin Luther (1483–1546) posted his *Ninety-five Theses on the Power and Efficacy of Indulgences* on the door of All Saints' Church, Wittenberg. Luther abhorred what he felt was the idolatry inherent in the highly decorated and elaborate style of art found in religious architecture, paintings, and sculpture, and his list of reforms included wording against preachers "laying up earthly treasures." Early Reformation art was to include visual satires of the papacy, mass-produced on the new Gutenberg printing presses and distributed throughout Europe. (Luther himself used the technology to print his illustrated tracts.)

Following Luther, the Northern Protestants sought new subject matter and modes of expression in the arts. Roman Catholic subjects, such as the martyrdom of St. Lawrence (who was slowly roasted to death on a grill), were replaced by subjects such as Christ teaching or blessing children, as seen in the works of German painter Lucas Cranach the Elder (1472–1553). These artworks offered a more realistic depiction of biblical scenes, generally portraying the characters as ordinary people in real settings, rather than idealizing them and using symbolism. There was a widespread stripping away of ornamentation and depictions of saints in the churches. In Germany and elsewhere, the release of former papal land holdings to local barons led to a decline in religious art; instead, the barons commissioned portraits of themselves and their possessions, as well as landscapes and still lifes.

During the Counter-Reformation (1545–1648), initiated by the Roman Catholic Church to combat Protestantism, Catholic artists such as El Greco returned to depicting subjects such as the suffering of martyrs and confession and penance—sacraments discounted by the Protestants—for display before the faithful. **PBr**

"They are not temporal treasures, for the latter are not lightly spent, but rather gathered by many of the preachers."

Martin Luther, *Ninety-five Theses* (1517)

Mannerism
Italy

An art style characterized by distortion of elements such as scale and perspective

The High Renaissance, from the late fifteenth century to the early sixteenth century, was a period of unequaled beauty in the world of art, but it began to wither with the deaths of Leonaro da Vinci in 1519 and Raphael in 1520, and the sacking of Rome in 1527. Across Europe the momentum of the High Renaissance seemed to stall. Art, of course, would continue, but it was the era of the "Late Renaissance" now, the decades between the death of Raphael and the beginning of the Baroque period in c. 1600. It was in this period that Mannerism, as it would come to be called four centuries later, made its appearance.

Mannerism—with its harmonious religious themes, subdued naturalism, and emphasis on complexity—developed in either Florence or Rome, depending upon which accounts you choose to believe. For the first time, artists were able to draw on archaeological excavations to portray classical civilizations accurately, instead of relying on their own imaginations. However, imaginations certainly were unleashed after decades of conformity. Colors were more mixed and vibrant, disconcerting themes combining Christianity and mythology appeared, and the composition of nudes departed from long-held ideas on what constitutes correct posture.

Mannerism lasted about eighty years—much longer than the High Renaissance period it replaced. Notable Mannerists during this time included Giorgio Vasari, Daniele da Volterra, Francesco Salviati, Domenico Beccafumi, Federico Zuccari, Pellegrino Tibaldi, and Bronzino. Typical of the bizarre nature of Mannerism was the work of Giuseppe Arcimboldo (c. 1527–93), whose portrait of Rudolph II showed a man composed entirely of fruit, flowers, and vegetables. Some would later claim him a forerunner of Surrealism. Most admirers of "high" art, however, were pleased to see Mannerism pass into history. **BS**

↑ *Vertumnus—Rudolf II* (c. 1590) by Giuseppe Arcimboldo, showing Holy Roman Emperor Rudolph II as Vertumnus, the Roman god of seasons who presided over gardens and orchards.

"Mannerism . . . was an art of intellectual contortionism; urban artists measured themselves against the daunting example of Michelangelo and found shelter in caricature and exaggeration."

The New Yorker (1987)

Anabaptist Faith
Conrad Grebel

The belief that baptism should only be for people old enough to choose it

Anabaptism is characterized by its adherence to adult, in preference to infant, baptism. Originally a radical offshoot of Protestantism, its tenets are observed today in Amish, Brethren, Hutterite, and Mennonite communities. British and American Puritan Baptists are not direct descendents of the Anabaptist movement, but they were influenced by its presence. The ideas of the Anabaptists had a tendency to heavily influence whatever social order was around them.

The Reformation movement was in full swing in Switzerland when a group of dissatisfied reformers united under an influential merchant and councilman, Conrad Grebel (c. 1498–1526). They performed the first adult baptism, outside of Zürich in 1525. They believed, like a number of other reformers, that infants cannot

"That is the best baptism that leaves the man cleanest inside."

H. Ward Beecher, *Proverbs from Plymouth Pulpit* (1887)

be punished for any sin until they can reasonably grasp concepts of good and evil, so therefore they ought not to be baptized until they are able to come to the sacrament of their own free will. With this belief as a touchstone, Anabaptists attempted to find a place to settle in Europe, but because of the vehemence of their proselytizing they were ousted from town after town. Many early Anabaptist leaders died while in prison.

Anabaptists did not only believe in adult baptism and civil intransigence. They also insisted that church and state should be kept separate from one another, and that coercive measures used in maintaining order, such as physical violence, ought to be foresworn. These tenets continue to guide the spiritual descendents of the European Anabaptists today and are traceable in the U.S. Constitution (1787) and Bill of Rights (1791). **MK**

Church of England
King Henry VIII of England

The officially established Christian church in England

After the second-century arrival of Christianity to British shores, Roman Catholicism was the only state-endorsed religion in the British Isles. The agitation of the Protestant Reformation and a king resentful of the papacy's limits on his power, however, exchanged Roman Catholicism for a brand of Christianity that is tied intimately to the place it is practiced: the Church of England.

As Martin Luther and his fellow Protestants argued against Roman Catholic excess and exclusivity on the continent, King Henry VIII of England (1491–1547) sought an annulment of his marriage to Catherine of Aragon but found himself repeatedly refused by the reigning pope, Clement VII. Incensed, Henry forced a number of acts through the British Parliament in 1534, formally

"The King ... shall be ... the only supreme head in earth of the Church of England."

Act of Supremacy (1534)

separating the English Church from Rome and making the English monarch the head of the English Church. In the course of the years that followed, the Church of England alternated between near Catholicism and Protestant beliefs and practices because of the changeable nature of the monarchy.

While the Church of England has retained many of its Catholic trappings, it developed a number of unique texts that reverberate in the language and popular imagination to this day, including the *Book of Common Prayer*, which contains phrases such as "till death do us part" and "ashes to ashes, dust to dust." The Church of England's music became a staple of the Western canon, inspiring the works of seminal composers such as Edward Elgar, Ralph Vaughan Williams, Gustav Holst, Benjamin Britten, and Leonard Bernstein. **MK**

A portrait of Henry VIII aged forty-nine, painted in 1540 by Hans Holbein the Younger.

·NO ·ÆTATIS·   ·SVÆ·XLIX

Calvinism
John Calvin

A Protestant belief that God's grace and human salvation are predetermined

The teachings of John Calvin (1509–64), a key figure of the Protestant Reformation, are held as some of the most important of the Reformed tradition in Protestantism. In 1536 Calvin first published his book *Institutions of the Christian Religion*, a work that, along with his other teachings, helped to shape the Reformed movement away from many of the positions expounded by Martin Luther. Though he derived much of his work from the example set by Luther, the churches that adhered to his teachings became known as Calvinist.

Calvinism centers around five religious doctrines. The first tenet, "total depravity," is that humanity is sinful and without hope of salvation outside of the intervention of God. The second tenet, "unconditional

> *"God preordained ... a part of the human race ... to eternal salvation ..."*
>
> John Calvin

election," holds that God is unconditionally sovereign and has predetermined everything. The third, "irresistible grace," says that God had chosen certain people to receive salvation even before the creation of the universe. Fourth, "limited atonement," claims that Christ's death was meant only for those elected to receive salvation. Fifth, "preservation of the saints," holds that anyone who chooses to be saved will always remain in that state and none will lose their salvation.

The impact of Calvinism was seen mostly in Scotland, Ireland, England, France, and colonial North America. Many early settlers to the United States were Calvinists, such as the English Puritans, French Huguenots, and Scotch-Irish Presbyterians. Calvinist ideals, such as the belief in a strong work ethic, courage, and adherence to capitalistic free markets, have shaped beliefs far beyond those who occupy the pews of their churches. **MT**

Heliocentrism
Nicolaus Copernicus

The theory that Earth is not the center of the universe

Heliocentrism, the model of the cosmos in which the sun is the central point upon which all other bodies revolve, was proposed in the third century BCE by Greek astronomer Aristarchus of Samos. However, his theory never gained favor because the positions of the stars remained static, which they would not, the logic went, if the Earth were continuously changing its position. Claudius Ptolemy offered a solution to this inconsistency in the second century CE, by arguing that the Earth was the center of the solar system. This geocentric model held sway for the next 1,400 years.

In 1543, Nicolaus Copernicus (1473–1543) of Poland published *De Revoluntionibus Orbium Coelestium Libri VI* (Six Books Concerning the Revolutions of the Heavenly

> *"At rest, however, in the middle of everything, is the sun."*
>
> Nicolaus Copernicus

Orbs), which argued in favor of the heliocentric system. Copernicus was a Roman Catholic cleric and he carefully downplayed any heretical overtones in his argument; the volumes remained unpublished until he died and they were prefaced by a disclaimer stating that the theories were useful for computation, even if they proved untrue. As a result, his work went largely unnoticed for almost one hundred years.

Italian physicist and astronomer Galileo Galilei (1564–1642) revived the argument for heliocentrism when observations through his telescope suggested that the Earth did indeed revolve around the sun. Galileo's views were deemed heretical, and in 1616 he was forbidden by the Vatican to "hold or defend" his heliocentric model. The "Galileo Affair," though, had the unforeseen result of spreading the idea of heliocentrism, and it rapidly became accepted as scientific truth. **MK**

An illustration of the Copernican system, from Andreas Cellarius's *Harmonia Macrocosmica* (1660). ➡

Capoeira
Brazil

Brazilian martial art that combines elements of music and dance

The rich culture of Brazil has given rise to many different arts, but none is more loaded in meaning or mired in human misery than capoeira. The likely origin of the name, from a native Tupi word referring to areas of low vegetation in the Brazilian interior, gives some indication as to its history.

Portugal colonized Brazil in the early sixteenth century, importing slaves from Africa after 1534 to overcome the shortage of native workers to harvest and process sugarcane. The slaves lived in large farms known as *engenhos*, where conditions were harsh and inhumane. Some managed to escape, and in their hope of survival developed a way of living and a culture that was the start of capoeira. Collecting in remote settlements known as *quilombos*, where they were out of the reach of colonial troops, the escaped slaves developed capoeira from a survival technique into an unarmed martial art that helped to keep them free.

During the 1700s, when slaves were brought into the cities, some *quilombo* dwellers moved with them, bringing the culture of capoeira. The colonial government tried to suppress it, arresting capoeira practitioners who found work as bodyguards, hitmen, and mercenaries. In 1890 the new republican government of Brazil banned the practice outright.

In 1932, Mestra Bimba (1899–1974), a fighter from Salvador in the north, founded a capoeira school, renaming the skill Luta Regional Bahia (Regional Fight from Bahia) in order to evade the ban. Capoeira was taught to the cultural elite and lost its criminal links before being removed from the penal code in 1940.

Today, capoeira is a worldwide phenomenon, a Brazilian martial art form that symbolizes resistance to oppression. Theatrical and acrobatic, capoeira still contains subtle and disguised elements of its savage colonial origins. Trickery is paramount, and a capoeirista never takes his eyes off his opponent. **SA**

Men Perform Capoeira, or the *Dance of War*, an engraving after Johann Moritz Rugendas (1835). ↑

Unitarianism

Peter Gonesius

The denial of a triumvirate Godhead and identification of Christ as a prophet only

Unitarianism is a religious movement that takes its name from its foundational tenet of understanding God as one person alone instead of the three beings of the Father, the Son, and the Holy Spirit, coexisting consubstantially as one. Most Christian denominations, then, do not fall in line with Unitarian principles, since they maintain that Jesus Christ is a manifestation of God, not simply a prophet, as Unitarians believe. Unitarianism also, quite significantly, promotes reason as a means of interpreting scripture and religion.

Peter Gonesius (c. 1525–73), a Polish student, first spoke out against the Doctrine of the Trinity, the three divine beings coexisting as one, in 1556. His agitation sparked a nine-year debate that culminated in the creation of the Polish Brethren, Unitarianism's forebears. When members of the Polish Brethren were ordered to convert back to Roman Catholicism or leave Poland, they dispersed to Transylvania and Holland, where they adopted the title "Unitarian." After the Enlightenment's elevation of reason, Unitarianism caught on in England and the United States, too. Unitarian churches sprang up in major U.S. and British cities, and Unitarians occupied influential seats in major universities such as Harvard, where they challenged the prevailing Puritan theology. Unitarians continue to interrogate the religious universe, and in the twentieth century they adopted many of the underpinning ideas of religious humanism, which is religious belief centered on human needs, abilities, and interests.

Unitarian rejection of the Trinity is accompanied by a liberal perspective on God, tempered by forays into science, philosophy, and reason. Unitarians maintain that science and religion do not, in fact, contradict one another. Instead, science and religion ought to be seen as complementary, illuminating one another's otherwise inscrutable facets. **MK**

↑ A nineteenth-century engraving by J. Smith of a Unitarian Chapel in Liverpool, England.

Equals Sign
Robert Recorde

The shorthand use of two parallel lines that revolutionized mathematics

In 1557, Welshman Robert Recorde (*c.* 1510–58) grew weary of writing "is equal to" in his treatise on advanced mathematics and introduction to algebra, *The Whetstone of Witte*. The shorthand symbol that he devised is the two parallel lines familiar to those with the most rudimentary of mathematical knowledge: the equals sign. This symbol, and the concept of equality of two discrete expressions that it represents, makes otherwise abstract mathematical ideas clear and the discovery of unknown quantities in algebra possible.

The ancient Egyptian Rhind Papyrus (*c.* 1650 BCE) contains the first recorded linear equation, but scholars are uncertain if the ancient Egyptians' concepts of equivalence and balance were the same as those developed by mathematicians such as Recorde in the

"To avoid the tedious repetition of … is equalle to: I will … use, a paire of paralleles."
Robert Recorde

sixteenth century. In any case, the equals sign took many years to find a common place in mathematical texts; seventeenth-century mathematicians were partial to æ, representing the Latin *aequalis* (equal).

The state of being equal, indicated by the presence of the equals sign, is an indispensable concept in basic mathematics and algebra. In fact, an equation could be argued to be the most basic notion in all of mathematical thinking: figures on either side of an equals sign are of the same value. Both sides of the equation can be simultaneously manipulated (by dividing, subtracting, or adding, for example) with the intent of "solving" the unknowns in the equation. Most laws of physics and economics upon which daily life revolves are expressed most cleanly through equations such as, Newton's First Law of Gravitation. **MK**

Baroque Architecture
Italy

A late sixteenth-century architectural style of dynamism, fluid curves, and ornament

Baroque architecture arose in Italy in around 1570 as an element of the Counter-Reformation (1545–1648). Seeking to win back congregations depleted by decades of Protestant reform, the Roman Catholic Church appealed to the faithful by creating churches that invoked a sense of awe.

Baroque buildings are known for their flamboyant appearance, typified by graceful curves, wild scrolls, and oval forms. Often, their exteriors sport ornate wrought ironwork, snaking columns, and elaborate stone carvings. The interiors are opulent, with large, colorful frescoes, gilded wooden fittings and statuary, planes of stucco sculptures, and faux marble finishes. The careful use of lighting, along with illusory effects such as trompe l'oeil, gives them an almost theatrical appearance.

"[The Baroque era] is one of the architectural peak periods in Western civilization."
Harry Seidler, architect

In 1656 Pope Alexander VII commissioned the Italian architect and sculptor Gian Lorenzo Bernini (1598–1680) to renovate St. Peter's Square in Rome. Bernini worked on the project for eleven years. He resolved a spatial problem caused by the erroneous alignment of pre-existing architectural elements by creating an oval piazza surrounded by a colonnade of 284 marble columns, crowned by 140 statues of the saints. Other Italian architects, such as Francesco Borromini (1599–1667) and Guarino Guarini (1624–83), created Baroque structures of similar elegance and grandeur.

The Baroque style was introduced to Latin America by colonizers of the New World, and Jesuit missionaries came to favor the style. Latin American Baroque architecture became even more extravagant and boldly ornamented than its European antecedent. **CK**

  The Baldacchino in Saint Peter's Basilica, Rome, designed by Gian Lorenzo Bernini in 1633. ➔

Imaginary Numbers
Rafael Bombelli

Numbers with a square that is less than or equal to zero

Imaginary numbers are not actually imaginary at all, but are numbers whose square is less than or equal to zero (the "imaginary" in the term is a vestige from the time when mathematicians had not yet defined a number system to accommodate numbers whose square is less than or equal to zero). Despite the speculative connotation, imaginary numbers are significant in understanding real-world quantities and phenomena. Scholars have argued that fractions, negative numbers, and "zero" are as seemingly irrational as imaginary numbers, and yet are still represented in everyday life.

Greek mathematician and engineer Heron of Alexandria (c. 10–70 CE) is credited with the concept of imaginary numbers, but it was Rafael Bombelli (c. 1526–72) who first codified and thoroughly described their

"The imaginary number is a fine and wonderful resource of the human spirit ..."

Gottfried Leibniz, mathematician and philosopher

properties in his treatise *L'Algebra* (1572). He defined an imaginary number as the square root of minus one and gave it the symbol *i*. Subsequently, mathematicians and theorists seized on imaginary numbers in understanding physical phenomena, such as magnetic fields, electric circuits, and the origins of the universe.

Mathematicians admit that imaginary numbers are difficult to understand. However, if one thinks about imaginary numbers, unlike real numbers, as not providing formulas but relationships and consider them an "upgrade" to conventional mathematical systems, the possibilities expand for what imaginary numbers can do. Quantum mechanics, for example, relies upon a dimension that can be imparted only by imaginary numbers, so understanding them is crucial to comprehending the origins of the universe. **MK**

Ballet
Balthasar de Beaujoyeulx

A formalized, dramatic form of dance performed to music in a decorated setting

The word "ballet" is a French adaptation of the Italian word *balleto*, used to describe theatrical dances held at court during the early fifteenth century, directed by dancing masters such as Domenico da Piacenza (c. 1400–c. 1470). When, in 1533, Catherine de' Medici (1519–89) married the future King of France, Henry II (1519–59), she took choreographer and musician Balthasar de Beaujoyeulx (d. c. 1587) with her to France, where he staged entertainments for the French court. In 1581, he staged the *Ballet Comique de la Reine* (The Dramatic Ballet of the Queen) at the Palais du Petit Bourbon of the Louvre in Paris, and it came to be recognized as the first *ballet de cour*. The five-hour-long performance depicted the ancient Greek myth of Circe with dance, music, and verse, using choreography to

"[The Ballet Comique *was] a political, philosophical, and ethical mirror of its day."*

Carol Lee, *Ballet in Western Culture* (2002)

tell the story. A year later, a book was made containing engravings portraying the spectacle, and copies were given to Europe's aristocracy: ballet became a way to publicize royal power, culture, and wealth.

Ballet developed under the patronage of King Louis XIV (1638–1715), when in 1681 he established the first professional ballet school, the Académie Royale de Danse, which later became the Paris Opera Ballet. By 1700, terms such as *chassé* and pirouette were in use to describe ballet movements, and ballet companies had been founded throughout Europe. It was not until the nineteenth century that *en pointe* technique—in which dancers dance on the tips of their feet, wearing specially reinforced shoes to distribute their body weight away from their toes—became integral to ballet aesthetics. **CK**

Two Dancers on a Stage (c. 1874) by Edgar Degas. This is one of many images Degas painted of the ballet.

Infinity of Inhabited Worlds
Giordano Bruno

The theory that, because the universe is infinite and expanding, logically the universe must contain an infinite number of inhabited worlds

⬆ A bronze relief from 1887, by the Italian sculptor Ettore Ferrari, showing Giordano Bruno being burned at the stake by the Venetian Inquisition for his heretical theories.

"The universe is then one, infinite, immobile ... It is not capable of comprehension and therefore is endless and limitless, and to that extent infinite and indeterminable, and consequently immobile."

Giordano Bruno

The theory concerning the infinity of inhabited worlds posits that the universe is infinite, and therefore the number of worlds occupying it is also infinite. Philosopher, astronomer, and mathematician Giordano Bruno (1548–1600) published this theory in 1584 to the shock of a society deeply committed to the principles of Aristotle and Socrates in comprehending the structure of the universe.

Bruno's heretical ideas about cosmology were not limited to the physical realm. Had they been restricted to the material world, his departure from established beliefs might not have compelled the Roman Catholic Church to burn him at the stake. An excommunicated priest, Bruno was intrigued by possible ways to understand reality more intimately, and was therefore interested in all aspects of science and thought. He lectured widely on Copernicus's then-controversial theory of a heliocentric solar system, and speculated that the observable cosmos was not static but infinite and always expanding. In his lectures and writings, he was critical of the physics of Aristotle and promoted a heretical relationship between philosophy and religion. All this left no place in his thinking for Christian tenets of divine creation and the Last Judgment.

Form and matter are "one," says Bruno, anticipating the direction of modern science, but greatly upsetting the church fathers, who jailed him and put him on trial for the "heretical" content of his publications and lectures. Despite Bruno's protests that his claims were intended to be philosophical rather than religious, the Catholic Inquisitors pressed him for a retraction. The philosopher refused and was subsequently burned alive. Bruno's ideas persist, however, in his unwillingness to limit the universe to a geometric structure and his advocacy of an indivisible "one" that unites all matter; both are forerunners of quantum mechanics. **MK**

Ballroom Dancing
Jehan Tabourot

A style of formal dancing, originally practiced only by members of high society

Ballroom dancing was once a form of social dancing for privileged people, as distinct from the folk dances of the poor. However, it has long outgrown that distinction. The term itself derives from a "ball" or formal dance, from the Latin *ballare*, to dance. In 1588, the French cleric Jehan Tabourot (1519–95), writing under the name Thoinot Arbeau, published *Orchésographie*, a study of formal French dances including the slow *pavane*, five-step *galliard*, and solemn *basse*, or low dance. He provided information about dance etiquette and how dancers and musicians should interact, as well as musical examples in which the dance steps were placed next to individual notes, a major innovation in dance notation.

In 1669, Louis XIV of France (1638–1715) established the Académie Royale de Musique et de Danse, which laid down specific rules for every dance. New dances were added to the acceptable canon, including the minuet in 1650; Louis XIV himself danced the minuet in public, signaling his approval of the style.

In 1819, Carl Maria von Weber (1786–1826) wrote *Invitation to the Dance*, a piano piece he described as a "rondeau brillante." Although it was a concert work, it inspired the waltz, a dance that shocked society by bringing male and female dancers into close contact.

Modern competitive ballroom dancing is classified into five International Standard dances—the waltz, tango, Viennese waltz, foxtrot, and quickstep—and five International Latin dances—the samba, cha-cha-cha, rumba, paso doble, and jive. In North America, nine Smooth or Rhythm dances are preferred: the quickstep, samba, paso doble, and jive are replaced by East Coast swing, the bolero, and the mambo. What was once a diversion of high society is now mass entertainment, a staple on our television screens, the stuff of films, and an enjoyable and sociable pastime for millions. **SA**

Continental Drift
Abraham Ortelius

The proposal that the continents, once joined, move across the Earth's surface

In the third edition of his book *Thesaurus Geographicus*, published in 1596, Dutch mapmaker Abraham Ortelius (1527–98) presented a remarkable new theory. Aided by the growing sophistication of world maps showing continents with coastlines that seemed to mirror each other, he suggested that the continent of the Americas had, as a result of earthquakes and other seismic activity, been "torn away from Europe and Africa." However, the study of landforms and how they are shaped was still very much an emerging science at the end of the sixteenth century, which meant that Ortelius's theories could not be debated thoroughly.

It would be another 316 years before the term "continental drift" would enter the lexicon of science. The term was coined by the German meteorologist

> *"The vestiges of the rupture reveal themselves [in] a map of the world."*
> #### Abraham Ortelius

Alfred Wegener (1880–1930) as part of his "reinvention" and expansion of a two-part theory. First, millions of years ago, an ancient land, Pangaea (Greek for "all lands"), began to break apart into two individual, continent-sized landmasses, which he called Laurasia and Gondwanaland; second, they in turn broke up into the continents we have today.

Wegener's conclusions were not well received by his fellow academics, almost all of whom still held to the belief that the continents always had been fixed. His paper, which failed to contain any explanation, much less physical evidence, as to how the continents could possibly have moved so far, did little to alter opinion. It would be another eight years before Wegener was able to provide an explanation, when he presented his theory on plate tectonics. **BS**

Divine Right of Kings
King James I of England

The belief that royalty was sanctioned to rule by God Himself

The theory of the divine right of kings posits that because God has conferred the right to rule on a monarch, that individual cannot be subject to the authority of any other earth-bound entity, including the will of the people he or she governs, other aristocrats, governmental bodies, or even the mightily powerful church. God alone grants a monarch the right to wear a crown, and He alone has the ability to judge, so human attempts to censure or depose a monarch are not only treasonous, but sacrilegious.

This idea emerged in medieval Europe, and because it is a reinterpretation of ancient Roman law, it is difficult to pin down precisely who first encoded it. However, by 1597, James I, then king of Scotland and soon to become king of England, had written

"I will govern according to the common weal, but not . . . to the common will."

King James I of England

The True Law of Free Monarchies, in which he argues for an absolutist monarchy. It is no coincidence that James I was also Protestant and, like many proponents of the divine right of kings, looking to further elude the influence of the Roman Catholic Church. However, at the same time, many political thinkers—among them John Locke and John Milton—were protesting the tyranny of monarchs' absolute power, contending that to confer such immense political strength on a single person was simply replacing one oppressor, the Roman Catholic Church, with another, the king.

The debates over the divine right of kings ushered in considerations not only of the separation of church and state but, as Thomas Jefferson famously wrote in the United States Declaration of Independence (1776), the philosophy that "all men are created equal." **MK**

Opera
Jacopo Peri

A sung, staged performance of a drama, often with orchestral accompaniment

Opera began as a recreation of Greek antique drama. The Florentine Camerata—a group of intellectuals, musicians, and poets in Florence at the end of the sixteenth century—started the art form that would rapidly spread through Europe. The first known opera was *Dafne* (1598) by Jacopo Peri (1561–1633), set to a libretto based on Ovid's *Metamorphoses*. The remaining fragments of this work for a small ensemble reveal the art form as we know it today: arias sung by soloists, choruses, and sections of narrative consisting of sung recitatives. The first major opera that still remains in the repertoire is Claudio Monteverdi's *L'Orfeo* (1607).

Composers through the centuries have found ways to adapt the genre to contemporary musical styles and topics. Operas never gave up mythical and allegorical

"If music . . . is an imitation of history, opera . . . is an imitation of human willfulness . . ."

W. H. Auden, *The Dyer's Hand and Other Essays* (1962)

topics—adaptations of Shakespeare's dramas by Henry Purcell and others, Nordic myths in Wagner's *Ring Cycle*, or cosmic allegories in Stockhausen's seven-opera cycle *Licht*—but realism never made strong gains. Even a work such as John Adams's *Nixon in China* can be seen in allegorical terms, illustrating how myths can be created in contemporary events.

Traditional opera was aimed at the upper classes and courts, but popular forms developed (operetta in the nineteenth century and musicals in the twentieth) and these have held solid cultural positions. Like opera, operettas and musicals have dealt with myths such as Orpheus in the Underworld, fiction such as Victor Hugo's *Les Misérables* (1862), and contemporary topics, such as AIDS (*Rent*, 1994), the Cold War (*Chess*, 1984), and the sexual revolution (*Hair*, 1967). **PB**

In the Loge (1879) by Mary Stevenson Cassatt shows a woman watching a performance in Paris. ➡

Electricity
William Gilbert

A fundamental form of energy that results from the interaction of charged particles

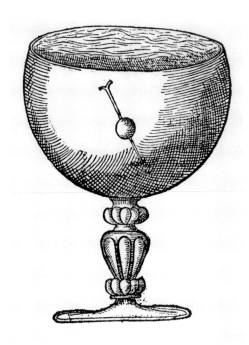

⬆ An illustration from *De Magnete* (1600) by William Gilbert depicts how a magnetized needle pushed through a ball of cork and submerged in water will point to the magnetic pole.

"Is it a fact—or have I dreamt it—that, by means of electricity, the world of matter has become a great nerve, vibrating thousands of miles in a breathless point of time?"

Nathaniel Hawthorne, *The House of the Seven Gables* (1851)

English physician, physicist, and natural philosopher William Gilbert (1544–1603) coined the term "electricity" to describe phenomena arising from the presence and flow of an electric charge. In his book *De Magnete, Magneticisque Corporibus, et de Magno Magnete Tellure* (On the Magnet and Magnetic Bodies, and on the Great Magnet the Earth), published in 1600, Gilbert drew the English term from the Greek word *electron* and the Latin word *electricus*, meaning amber, as the ancients were known to have produced an electrical phenomenon by rubbing a piece of amber. What those ancients, and Gilbert after them, had observed was caused by charges producing electromagnetic fields that have an effect on other charges. The electric charge, in turn, arises from properties and interactions of subatomic particles.

Observations of naturally occurring electricity are recorded in texts of ancient Egypt, Arabia, Greece, and Rome, but quantifying and harnessing the power of electricity did not commence until the seventeenth and eighteenth centuries. By 1821, Michael Faraday had designed the electric motor, and in 1827 Georg Ohm successfully analyzed the properties of the electrical circuit. What followed was a burst of scientific discussion and clever innovation.

Pioneering inventors and scientists, such as Nikola Tesla, Thomas Edison, Joseph Swan, George Westinghouse, Alexander Graham Bell, and Lord Kelvin, adapted scientific discoveries to the tasks and necessities of daily life. Advances in medicine, electric lighting, stoves, home computers, washing machines, radios, televisions, and electrically driven transport were all the result of their labors. Without the demand for electric products, and the convenience of life supported by electricity, the Second Industrial Revolution (c. 1860–1914) would never have occurred, and life as we live it (and light it) would be very different. **MK**

Baroque Music

Europe

A stylistic period in music history, originating in Italy and lasting 150 years

The term "Baroque" is thought to derive from the Portuguese *barroco*, a deformed pearl, implying an imbalance and imperfection in form and style, in contrast to the well-balanced and reserved ideals of antiquity. The first use of the term in reference to the arts is believed to have been in a derogatory review of Rameau's opera *Hippolyte et Aricie* (1733). More generally, however, "Baroque" came to describe the lavish visual art style of *c.* 1600 until 1750—exemplified by Peter Paul Rubens, Gian Lorenzo Bernini, and Rembrandt—in which both the emotional and the rational response to an artwork were emphasized.

In music, the Baroque period coincided with the introduction of tonality, the major and minor modes used today, and with a simplification of musical texture through monody, featuring one melodic line with *basso continuo*—that is, chordal accompaniment and a prominent bassline. The Baroque also gave birth to the genre of opera. During the eighteenth century, the Baroque style became more complex, polyphonic, and ornamented in various genres, including opera, sacred music, and chamber music, culminating in the mature works of George Frideric Handel and Johann Sebastian Bach.

Baroque music, especially the works of Bach, Handel, and Vivaldi, remains prominent on today's concert programs, but the era had another important impact. It initiated the "common practice" period, which lasted from roughly 1600 to 1900 and was defined by shared basic notions of harmonic and rhythmic syntax, despite the different aesthetic ideals behind many of the compositions. Several common-practice stylistic traits remain evident in many twentieth- and twenty-first-century genres, such as musical theater, jazz, and rock. Even the basic ensemble of harmonic accompaniment, keyboard, and a bass instrument is still (with the addition of drums) dominant in popular music. **PB**

⬆ A portrait of George Frideric Handel by T. Hudson, painted in 1749. Handel's best-known work is his oratorio *Messiah*, which was composed in 1741.

"Always sad where it might be tender, this singular brand of music was Baroque . . ."

Anonymous, *Mercure de France* (May 1734)

Metaphysical Poetry
Europe

Poetry as a serious meditation in the form of a witty extended metaphor

⬆ An anonymous portrait of the metaphysical poet John Donne, from c. 1595. Donne is often considered to be the greatest love poet in the English language.

"Metaphysical" was originally a pejorative term used by English critics John Dryden (1631–1700) and Samuel Johnson (1709–84) to describe a broad school of seventeenth-century British and Continental poets who wrote in a lyric style, using psychological analysis, and paradox, and whose juxtaposition of unrelated concepts was intended to shock the reader and force them to carefully consider the meaning behind the poem. Their use of the "conceit," an extended metaphor, allowed them to construct elaborate and intricate poems on topics ranging from sexuality to contemporary politics.

The most influential Metaphysical poet, Englishman John Donne (1572–1631), wrote his nineteen *Holy Sonnets*, including "Death, Be Not Proud," after his beloved wife died in childbirth. His spiritual meditations on the meaning of death and the place of God and love in human life include important psychological insights into how grieving may be comforted. Another important poet in the style is Englishman Andrew Marvell (1621–78), whose poem, "To His Coy Mistress," is a *carpe diem* conceit on the futility of remaining virginal in light of the shortness of human life: "The grave's a fine and private place, But none I think do there embrace." Other notable Metaphysical poets include Henry Vaughan, John Cleveland, and Abraham Cowley, as well as, to a lesser extent, George Herbert and Richard Crashaw.

Twentieth-century scholars, such as T. S. Eliot in his essay "The Metaphysical Poets" (1921), looked back favorably on the Metaphysical poets for their ingenuity and clever use of language and humor. Their subjects were very different from the traditionally slight ones of the period. Instead, they used reason to examine complex political, religious, scientific, and ethical questions. Today, their works are minutely analyzed and vaunted as models for modern poetry. **PBr**

"[Donne] affects the Metaphysics . . . in his amorous verses, where nature only should reign; and perplexes the minds of the fair sex with nice speculations of philosophy, when he should engage their hearts."

John Dryden, critic

Laws of Falling Bodies

Galileo Galilei

The theory that falling objects move under the influence of gravity alone

In the fourth century BCE, Aristotle maintained that an object falls with a speed proportionate to its weight. This idea was accepted until the sixteenth century, when in 1576 Italian mathematician Giuseppe Moletti reported that bodies of the same material but of different weight arrived at the earth at the same time. In 1586, Flemish mathematician Simone Stevin demonstrated that two objects of different weight fall with exactly the same acceleration. Then, in 1597, Italian philosopher Jacopo Mazzoni observed large and small fragments descending at the same rate.

In an apocryphal tale, Italian physicist and astronomer Galileo Galilei (1564–1642) dropped iron balls of unequal weight from the Leaning Tower of Pisa. In fact, Galileo determined the rate at which bodies accelerate as they fall by rolling balls down a sloping board in 1604. Galileo is credited with the definitive experiments on falling bodies because the contributions of others were not scientific; they did not measure time as Galileo did, and they did not use mathematics to establish their theories.

The fact that a lump of lead will fall faster than a leaf seemingly contradicts the rule that all bodies fall at the same rate. However, the two objects fall at different rates because of air resistance. This was demonstrated by U.S. astronaut David Scott (b. 1932) in an experiment on the moon, which has no atmosphere; a hammer and a feather were dropped from the same height and both struck the surface of the moon simultaneously.

Galileo also used experimental observation and mathematical reasoning to explain one-dimensional motion with constant acceleration, the acceleration due to gravity, the behavior of projectiles, the speed of light, the nature of infinity, the physics of music, and the strength of materials. His theories were instrumental in paving the way for the laws of motion and gravity formulated by Sir Isaac Newton (1642–1726). **BC**

' *They were seen to fall evenly.*'

28

⬆ A sketch showing Galileo conducting his experiments from the Leaning Tower of Pisa. Although an infamous story, this was not actually the method that he used to prove his theory.

"In a medium totally devoid of resistance all bodies would fall with the same speed."

Galileo Galilei

International Law
Hugo Grotius

A body of rules subscribed to by all nations for peaceful resolution of disputes

International law comprises the rules widely accepted and agreed upon for regulating the interactions of nations. Dutch philosopher and jurist Hugo Grotius (1583–1645) established its foundations on philosophies of natural justice. As nations were increasingly brought into contact with one another by improved transportation, thinkers wanted to establish a structure for dealing with disputes that would be understandable and acceptable to all the peoples involved.

Grotius's involvement in encoding standards of international justice began with a legal case arising from the seizure by Dutch merchants of a Portuguese vessel in the Singapore Strait in 1603. The Netherlands and Portugal were at war, and a Dutch merchant, without his government's or his company's permission,

"Insofar as international law is observed, it provides us with stability and order."

J. William Fulbright, U.S. senator

had taken advantage by capturing the Portuguese cargo, which he then distributed to his company's shareholders. The Portuguese were incensed, as were many of the Mennonite (and thus pacifist) Dutch shareholders. The scandal, and the ethical and legal debate that followed, inspired Grotius's seminal tract *On the Right of Capture*, completed in 1605 but only published centuries later, in 1864.

Eventually, entities such as the European Court of Human Rights and the International Criminal Court were formed to enforce violations of international law. Importantly, the nations subject to the International Criminal Court and the Court of Human Rights also consent to be subject to its governance. In this way, the sovereignty of the nation itself is protected while still allowing for accountability to the rest of the world. **MK**

Don Quixote
Miguel de Cervantes

The first modern novel, and one of the most rewarding fictions of all time

Don Quixote is one of the most widely read classics of Western literature. It was published in two volumes, in 1605 and 1615, by Spanish novelist, poet, and playwright Miguel de Cervantes Saavedre (1547–1616), who wrote it as a comic satire of the chivalric romances that were in vogue in his country at the time. The novel describes the misadventures of its protagonist, Alonso Quixano—an aging minor nobleman who takes the nobler name of Don Quixote—as he sets out on his horse, Rosinante, with his peasant squire, Sancho Panza, on a knight errant's heroic quest.

Don Quixote is regarded as the first modern novel because, for the first time, the protagonists' evolving characterizations, rather than their actions, are of principal interest. Earlier romances simply related

"And maddest of all, to see life as it is and not as it should be."

Miguel de Cervantes, *Don Quixote* (1605)

events, but Cervantes looked beyond narrative to explore what could be learned from juxtaposing his characters' personalities, especially those of the idealistic Don Quixote and the cynical, world-weary Sancho Panza. Their dialogue produces comedy and tragedy in equal measure, and yet it is never obvious what Cervantes wants his readers to think, or be persuaded to conclude, about the real world.

The character of Don Quixote has become an archetype for the pursuit of idealistic goals; the word "quixotic" immortalizes this characterization. The phrase "tilting at windmills" has its origins in an episode of the novel in which the Don attacks a row of windmills, believing them to be gigantic demonic knights; the phrase has come to mean a tendency to pursue unattainable objectives. **BC**

A nineteenth-century oil painting of Don Quixote and his squire Sancho, by Alexandre Gabriel Decamps. ➡

Rosicrucianism
Christian Rosenkreuz

A secret society dedicated to using arcane knowledge for humankind's benefit

Rosicrucianism refers to the study or membership of a secret society called the Rosicrucian Order, or the Order of the Red Cross. According to the order's mythology, it was founded in Germany by the perhaps fictional Christian Rosenkreuz. Its philosophy is based on "esoteric truths of the ancient past" that offer insight into both the physical world and the spiritual realm. Other secret societies, including Freemasonry, took inspiration from Rosicrucianism.

The first manifesto outlining the Rosicrucian Order was anonymous and appeared in 1607; another surfaced in 1616. Both documents align the order with the Protestant movement and promote a "universal reformation of mankind" while relating a fantastical tale of the 106-year-old Christian Rosenkreuz and his trip

"Summa Scientia Nihil Scire—The height of knowledge is to know nothing."

Christian Rosenkreuz

to the Middle East to gain wisdom. Upon returning to Germany, Rosenkreuz discovers that he is unable to disclose any of his secrets to European leaders, so he collects a small group of friends—no more than eight, it is said—and founds the order. The members, all doctors and sworn bachelors, must swear to heal the sick without payment, to maintain the secrecy of the fellowship, and to replace themselves before they die.

Intellectual Europeans were intrigued by Rosicrucianism's mystical and alchemical elements. The order gave rise to the precursor to the Royal Society, comprising scientists who held regular meetings to share empirical knowledge they had gained through experimentation. In addition, esoteric fraternities, such as the Freemasons, were formed throughout Europe and the United States to strengthen social alliances. **MK**

Telescope
The Netherlands

The notion of an instrument capable of revealing the universe to humanity

The world's first telescope was constructed in the Netherlands in 1608. The news of its invention reached Italian physicist and astronomer Galileo Galilei (1564–1642), and in order to further his study of the heavens he built one of his own the following year; he produced another of superior design the year after that. Although Galileo's telescopes were crude by twenty-first-century standards, they enabled him to make observations of the valleys and mountains of the moon, the four moons of Jupiter, and the phases of the planet Venus, none of which had been examined before. Sir Isaac Newton (1642–1726) followed Galileo's example with his reflecting telescope of 1668, and telescopes powerful enough to scrutinize the Milky Way galaxy were in circulation by the eighteenth century.

"Measure what is measurable, and make measurable what is not so."

Galileo Galilei

The pantheon of telescopes now includes not only reflecting telescopes but also refracting telescopes, plus versions called Schmidt telescopes that incorporate both reflecting and refracting technology. Multimirror telescopes are used to make observations deep into the universe, while solar telescopes are designed specifically for investigations of the sun. Telescopes are themselves no longer earthbound; with the added capabilities of camera and broadcast technology, scientists have been able to send telescopes aboard spacecraft to capture images that would not be accessible from Earth. The huge Hubble Space Telescope, launched into orbit around Earth in 1990, is also able to take images of cosmic objects. The images, unlike those of earthbound telescopes, are not subject to distortion by Earth's atmosphere. **MK**

Logarithm
John Napier

A mathematical concept that reduces calculation times and accelerates scientific progress

⬆ The title page of the 1614 edition of *Mirifici Logarithmorum Canonis Descriptio*. The book discussed theorems in spherical trigonometry and introduced natural logarithms.

"[The logarithm is] an admirable artifice which, by reducing to a few days the labor of many months, doubles the life of the astronomer, and spares him the errors and disgust inseparable from long calculations."

Pierre-Simon Laplace, mathematician

In *Mirifici Logarithmorum Canonis Descriptio* (Description of the Wonderful Rule of Logarithms), published in 1614, Scottish mathematician John Napier (1550–1617) introduced a concept that was to explode the possibilities of research in physics, mathematics, geography, and astronomy: the logarithm.

Napier's name for his new mathematical figure belies its purpose: *logos* in Greek can be understood as "proportion," and *arithmos* as "number." Logarithms, then, are numbers that indicate ratios. Logarithms allow mathematicians, scientists, engineers, and navigators to perform mathematical calculations more efficiently; instead of completing manifold monotonous multiplication calculations, a researcher could employ logarithmic tables and slide rules to solve a mathematical question quickly. Mathematicians such as Nicholas Mercator, John Speidell, and Leonhard Euler expanded upon Napier's concepts to develop the logarithmic form and rules that are still employed throughout the world in the present day.

The applications of the logarithm are far-reaching and critical. Logarithms simplify mathematics in fields such as astronomy, surveying, navigation, and physics, and so scientific discovery and innovation advanced more quickly than they might have without their aid. Researchers and practitioners continue to express ideas in logarithmic scales. For example, musical tones and intervals are expressed in logarithms, and Hick's Law, which proposes a logarithmic relation between the time people take in making a choice and the number of choices they are presented with, is founded upon algorithms. Even though they might not be conscious of the exact calculations, humans use logarithmic reasoning in considering risk assessment: which issues they ought to be concerned with, and which are relative longshots. Logarithms also appear in studies of entropy, statistics, and information theory. **MK**

False Tidal Theory
Galileo Galilei

The theory that the Earth's daily rotation and annual orbit around the sun cause the tides

False Tidal Theory posits that the Earth's "dual motion," its once-daily spin on its axis combined with its annual journey around the sun, is responsible for bodies of water rising and falling in the form of tides. Eminent scientist Galileo Galilei (1564–1642) first proposed this theory in 1616 in an attempt to marry mathematics, astronomy, and physics, at the same time proving the Copernican model of a solar system in which the Earth and other bodies orbit the sun.

Galileo's inspiration for this theory of causation came when he was riding a barge carrying fresh water from Padua to Venice, Italy. Whenever the barge switched direction or changed its speed, he noted, the freshwater in the barrels sloshed in response. He then posited that, even though we cannot perceive it, the Earth is moving at different speeds and directions because it spins on its axis and around the sun. Other leading scientists of the day, including Johannes Kepler (1571–1630), argued for a tidal theory based on the gravitational effects of the moon, but Galileo pointed out that they had no empirical evidence for this, and that such ideas seemed suspiciously occult. When he eventually encoded his tidal theory in *Dialogue Concerning the Two Chief World Systems* (1632), Roman Catholic inquisitors judged Galileo's defense of the Copernican system, including the tidal evidence, to be blasphemous, and he was placed under house arrest and his book banned from publication.

Kepler's theory won the day, and nowadays we all readily attribute the rise and fall of the tides to the pull of the moon. However, Galileo's dogged loyalty to his mistaken theory inspired successive scientists—Albert Einstein among them—to continue seeking a relationship between mathematics, astronomy, and physics, arguably leading to advances in quantum mechanics. While Galileo's conclusion was wrong, his method opened up new possibilities. **MK**

↑ A portrait of Galileo Galilei by the Russian artist Ivan Petrovich Keler-Viliandi, painted in 1858. Galileo originally studied medicine before moving to philosophy and mathematics.

"[Galileo's] aim was to substitute for a petrified and barren system of ideas the unbiased and strenuous quest for a deeper and more consistent comprehension of the physical and astronomical facts."

Albert Einstein, theoretical physicist

Naturalism
Francis Bacon

The belief that the universe's workings may be understood by studying natural causes

Naturalism is the belief that we can acquire knowledge of how the world works by studying natural phenomena, not supernatural causes. Everything in the universe, from the existence of life to the motions of the planets and interactions between objects, is said to be governed and ruled by natural laws that humanity can investigate and understand. Naturalism is a belief that only natural phenomena exist, both in existence and in how knowledge is obtained.

Questions about how the universe came to be, and why events happen as they do, are likely as old as humanity itself. Thinkers such as Thales of Miletus proposed naturalistic solutions to such fundamental questions as early as the sixth century BCE. During the Renaissance (c. 1450–1600), naturalistic explanations

"The subtlety of nature is greater ... than the subtlety of the senses and understanding ..."

Francis Bacon, *Novum Organum Scientiarum* (1620)

became more prominent. In 1620, English philosopher Francis Bacon (1561–1626) published *Novum Organum Scientiarum* (New Instrument of Science), in which he proposed a method of learning called inductive reasoning, where conclusions are drawn from observed data, instead of implied from presumed principles. Inductive reasoning, and the investigative method on which it is based, became essential to scientific inquiry.

The natural world is, for the most part, one that is knowable, measurable, quantifiable, and predictable. Naturalism presumes that the world as we see it is what it is. In contrast, belief in supernatural phenomena stands in the way of understanding the world; humanity cannot exert control over supernatural phenomena or influence them, and, even worse, it can provide no explanation or reason for their actions. **MT**

Thanksgiving
U.S. Pilgrims

A traditional celebration to mark an auspicious event

Religious celebrations of gratitude took place among many settlers in the Americas in the 1600s. In the United States, the traditional celebration of Thanksgiving on the fourth Thursday in November is associated with the Pilgrim settlers of the Plymouth colony in present-day Massachusetts. The most common account of the first Thanksgiving links the celebration to 1621, when the Pilgrims joined with indigenous people to give thanks for a particularly good harvest after a difficult year within the settlement. Several other settlements in the Americas around this time also have claims for celebrating early Thanksgiving.

The idea of the Thanksgiving event had its origins in England during the Protestant Reformation, when reformers were anxious to replace Catholic public

"I do therefore invite my fellow citizens ... to ... observe the last Thursday of November."

Abraham Lincoln, U.S. president 1861–65

holidays with feast days of their own. A tradition began of celebrating fortuitous events with a special thanksgiving meal; conversely, adverse events were marked by a day of fasting. It was hoped that giving thanks to God might bring further good fortune, while fasting might prevent additional disasters.

Even though several of the symbols and traditions of Thanksgiving are taken from the story of the Pilgrims at the Plymouth colony, the holiday is now a celebration of a spirit of gratefulness rather than a commemoration of a particular day or event. As a religious celebration, Thanksgiving is intended to remind those who celebrate it of God as the provider of all good things. Thanksgiving in the United States is also celebrated with a secular appreciation of the work ethic and perseverance of the early U.S. colonists. **TD**

The First Thanksgiving by Jean Leon Gerome Ferris, painted between c. 1912 and c. 1915. ➔

Propaganda
Pope Gregory XV

The distribution by missionaries of Roman Catholic information or ideas, presented in ways surreptitiously designed to change people in their thinking or behavior

⬆ *Portrait of Pope Gregory XV and Ludovico Ludovisi* (seventeenth century) by Domenichino (Domenico Zampieri). Ludovisi, the pope's nephew, was made cardinal to assist his aging uncle.

"Propaganda is a much maligned and often misunderstood word. The layman uses it to mean something inferior or even despicable. The word propaganda always has a bitter after-taste."

Josef Goebbels, Nazi Minister for Propaganda and Enlightenment

Few words in the English language are used as pejoratively as "propaganda." The word conjures up black arts of misinformation and manipulation, with a perverted intention to mislead and deceive. Yet the original purpose of propaganda was more benign, even though its existence was viewed in a hostile way right from the beginning.

The Protestant Reformation after 1517 seriously weakened the Roman Catholic Church. In the course of reforming Catholic practices and stamping out dissent, Pope Gregory XV (1554–1623) decided that his Church needed a single body to fight Protestantism. On June 22, 1622 he set up the Sacra Congregatio de Propaganda Fide (the Sacred Congregation for the Propagation of the Faith). This new body trained missionaries—or propagandists—to revive the Catholic faith in Europe and strengthen it in the European colonies across the Atlantic. Because the missionaries wanted people to accept the Church's doctrines voluntarily, no force was permitted. Accordingly, the missionaries would resort to covert or hidden ways to persuade people to change their religious views. Not surprisingly, propaganda, as an instrument of the Catholic Church, was disliked by its Protestant opponents, and hostility to its overall concept has continued to the present day.

The word "propaganda" began as a term for any organization that set out to spread a particular doctrine or set of beliefs. It soon came to describe the doctrine itself, and, after that, the techniques used to change opinions in order to spread the doctrine. Propaganda can take many forms, both covert and overt, but in reality it is neither good nor bad in itself. Propaganda is merely a process of manipulation of a person's behavior or views for someone else's benefit. The only way to judge propaganda, therefore, is to determine whether or not it is successful. **SA**

Slide Rule
William Oughtred

A manual analog computer designed to speed up lengthy calculations

It was the introduction of logorithm by John Napier (1550–1617) in 1614 that made the slide rule possible. Like the logorithm, the slide rule is used to simplify tedious mathematical operations. The first adjustable logarithmic slide rule, a circular design, was created in 1622 by British mathematician William Oughtred (1574–1660). A typical slide rule today looks much as it did in Oughtred's time: either circular or linear, with scales for mathematical computations: multiplication, division, roots, logarithms, and trigonometry.

Slide rules continued to undergo development as technology improved and demand for detailed calculations increased. For example, improvements were made by manufacturer Matthew Boulton (1728–1809) and by engineer James Watt (1736–1819) for the purpose of designing steam engines, and in 1814 the physician Peter Roget (1779–1869), the Roget of thesaurus fame, invented a slide rule for calculating powers and roots of numbers. In certain fields, such as aviation, customized slide rules were required to facilitate specialized mathematical operations. The slide rule so greatly simplified what had previously taken a great deal of time to calculate longhand that it is now referred to as an analog computer.

The advent of the scientific calculator made the slide rule obsolete, but slide rules offer the advantage of not relying on electricity or batteries, and they display all the operations of a calculation alongside the result. Calculating on slide rules is slower than on calculators or computers, and the precision of a result can be off by as much as three significant digits, which can lead to serious error. All the same, aviators and sailors continue to carry slide rules in case of instrument failure. The existence of the online International Slide Rule Museum attests to the ongoing significance and utility of the instrument. **MK**

Deism
Lord Herbert of Cherbury

Belief in the existence of a creator who does not intervene in the universe

Deism is a religious philosophy that eschews supernatural, religious dogma, and the idea of revelatory religious texts that are inerrant (totally free from error of any kind). Instead, the deist believes that a human's ability to reason is proof in itself of a divine creator, though one that may merely govern, and not interact, with the created universe.

Many of the tenets of deism existed in the classical world, and deistic principles have been present in a variety of cultures in Europe prior to the seventeenth century. In England, the term "deist" first appeared in print in *The Anatomy of Melancholy* (1621) by Robert Burton. English philosopher Lord Herbert of Cherbury (1583–1648) is often cited as one of the first proponents of English deism after his publication of *De Veritate*

> *"Religion is a matter which lies solely between man and his God."*
>
> **Thomas Jefferson, U.S. founding father**

in 1624. The philosophy attracted many influential thinkers of the Enlightenment, including Jean-Jacques Rousseau, Voltaire, and a host of the founding fathers of the United States, such as Benjamin Franklin, Thomas Paine, Thomas Jefferson, and George Washington.

Classical deism declined after thinkers such as John Locke and David Hume began attacking the underlying foundations of the belief system, and by the nineteenth century few people claimed to be deists. The lack of emphasis on a personal relationship with the divine led many believers to divert to other religious movements, while others turned to atheism. The idea, however, of a moderate position between the extremes of atheism and dogmatic religion is still influential, allowing many to believe in a divine creator while accepting anti-theistic scientific notions. **MT**

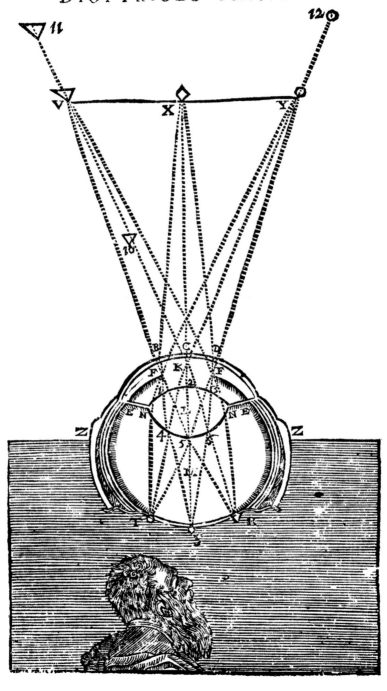

△

Φ

Contact Lens
René Descartes

The theory of using a water-filled vial resting on the eye to correct faulty vision

In 1508 Leonardo da Vinci (1452–1519) composed a journal, *Codex of the Eye, Manual D*, in which he described how the perception of the eye alters when opened in water. Da Vinci was not interested in how to correct faulty vision, however; what concerned him was how the eye alters its optics to maintain clarity of vision when viewing an object at varying distances. For the artist, the eye was key to everything, but it never occurred to him, apparently, that a lens could be placed over the eye to correct faulty vision.

This idea would have to wait another 128 years. In 1636, French thinker and father of modern philosophy René Descartes (1596–1650) pondered whether, if a person were to fill a glass tube with water and then place that tube over the eye's cornea, it might have

"I take out … a double convex lens ….
My eye immediately becomes presbyopic."

Thomas Young, *On Mechanisms of the Eye* (1800)

the effect of correcting that person's vision. Descartes's idea was innovative but impractical, as the glass tube he proposed would be too thick to allow blinking.

In 1801 English scientist and founder of physiological optics Thomas Young (1773–1829) coined the term "astigmatism" and constructed a rudimentary set of contact lenses following Descartes's design principle. However, it would not be until 1887 that the first functioning set of contact lenses was made and fitted, in Zurich, Switzerland, by the German-born ophthalmologist Adolf Fick (1829–1901). Made from heavy blown glass, Fick's lenses ranged in diameter from 19 mm to 21 mm and were shaped after first taking casts of rabbit eyes and those of deceased humans. Instead of resting directly on the cornea, these lenses were placed on the eye around it. **BS**

Epistemological Turn
René Descartes

A philosophical change of approach, from "What do we know?" to "How do we know it?"

What is called the "epistemological turn" was a philosophical change in focus and point of departure that occurred in the seventeenth century with the emergence of modern philosophy. Questions about what a person can *know* to exist (epistemology) began to be seen as more fundamental than those concerning what *does* exist (ontology). The approach that had been dominant throughout philosophy's medieval period then appeared to be "putting the cart before the horse," since thinkers had taken for granted the existence of certain things—God, angels, and the soul—without seriously investigating why they believed in them.

The epistemological turn started with rationalist philosopher René Descartes (1596–1650) and his procedure of doubting everything that is not known

"[The world …] Must vanish on the instant
if the mind but change its theme."

William Butler Yeats, "Blood and the Moon" (1928)

with absolutely certainty—first described in works such as *Discourse on the Method* (1637), and developed in the work of philosophers such as George Berkeley (1685–1753), David Hume (1711–76), and especially Immanuel Kant (1724–1804). The knower is now the original point of departure for the investigation, and also secures the objectivity of possible objects. That is not to say that the apple on the tree is only real because I see it; rather, it is to say that the apple is red and appears on the tree because my mind can take that sensory data and assemble that picture for me. One important result of the epistemological turn has been that people must now examine their beliefs about themselves, the world, and reality—as well as the justification for those beliefs—before making existential claims about such things. **KBJ**

◄ An illustration of how vision works, from a 1692 edition of René Descartes's *Opera Philosophica* (1662).

Rationalism
René Descartes

The belief that the nature of the world is best discovered by the exercise of reason

Rationalism, from the Latin *ratio*, meaning "reason," is a philosophical viewpoint that sees reason as playing the main role in obtaining knowledge; we come to understand the world through our powers of reasoning and logic. The core canons of rationalism are three: we have *a priori* knowledge, that is, ideas independent of experience; we have innate ideas present at birth; and there exist laws of logical necessity, meaning that there are ideas that cannot be thought otherwise. Rationalism is often contrasted with empiricism, which sees experience as the origin of all knowledge.

Rationalism dominated the seventeenth century, and is often described as beginning with Galileo Galilei (1564–1642) and ending with Gottfried Leibniz (1646–1716). The theory was set out most fully in *Discourse on*

"I rejected as false all the reasons which I had formerly accepted as demonstrative."
René Descartes, *Discourse on the Method* (1637)

the Method (1637) by philosopher René Descartes (1596–1650). Many of its core ideas were foundational for the Enlightenment of the eighteenth century, and for many philosophies today. The birth and rise of rationalism occurred along with several important historical events and discoveries that ushered in the modern world. These include the decay of the medieval church system, the separation of church and state in many countries as a result of oppression, the discovery of the New World through navigation using magnetic compass, the speed and span of conquest made possible by gunpowder and guns, and the implementation of scientific method.

Rationalism demonstrated to humankind that it was born with the tools and abilities to solve the mysteries of the universe. With or without God, the world was humankind's to know. **KBJ**

Substance Dualism
René Descartes

The idea that soul is distinct from body, and mental substances from bodily ones

In metaphysics, a "substance" usually refers to that which stands under, or grounds, something else. Typically, a substance is the owner and unifier of its properties, both essential and accidental, and it has within itself an impulse to develop or actualize its capacities or potential properties. Substances are often considered nonphysical living things as they are able to maintain exact similarity throughout change (unlike "property things," such as cars or piles of sand).

Aristotle (384–322 BCE) and St. Thomas Aquinas (1225–74) identified substances with souls, maintaining that substances such as God, humans, animals, and trees all have souls, though the properties in each soul type vary. For example, God has an uncreated, eternal, rational soul/substance; a human has a created,

"[Body and mind] may be made to exist in separation . . . by the omnipotence of God."
René Descartes, *Discourse on the Method* (1637)

conditionally immortal, rational soul/substance; an animal has a created, mortal, sentient soul/substance; and a tree has a created, mortal, vegetative soul/substance. Most religions and philosophies subscribe to some form of substance dualism, positing a real distinction between substance (soul or spirit) and physicality or matter.

Aristotle taught that the soul forms the body it possesses, making the interaction between the two entities fairly intelligible. Yet, rationalist philosopher René Descartes (1596–1650), in *Discourse on the Method* (1637), taught that there are only mental substances (rational souls) and physical substances (matter), and that these share no such intimate connection. This has resulted in the so-called "mind/body problem," which continues to plague philosophy students today. **AB**

The title page of *Discourse on the Method* (1637), by French rationalist philosopher René Descartes. ➡

DISCOVRS
DE LA METHODE

POVR BIEN CONDVIRE SA RAISON,
ET CHERCHER LA VERITE' DANS LES SCIENCES.

PLVS
LA DIOPTRIQVE
ET LES METEORES,

Qui font des effais de cette METHODE.

PAR RENE' DESCARTES.

Reueuë, & corrigée en cette derniere Edition.

À PARIS;

Chez MICHEL BOBIN & NICOLAS LE GRAS, au troifiéme
Pilier de la Grand Salle du Palais, à l'Efperance,
& à L, Couronnée.

M. DC. LXVIII.

The Mind/Body Problem
René Descartes

A proposed answer to philosophical questions concerning the nature of the mind and how it communicates with the body

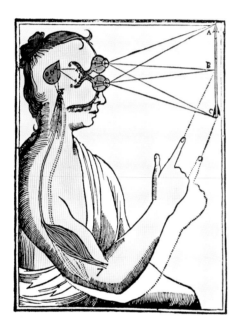

⬆ An illustration from *De Homine Figuris* (Treatise of Man) by René Descartes, published posthumously in 1662. It is regarded as the first textbook of physiology.

What is the relationship between mental and physical events? How does the mind, an incorporeal and nonextended substance, communicate with the body, which is a corporeal and extended thing? These are the central questions of the mind/body problem, one of the oldest metaphysical problems in philosophy.

The most popular version of the mind/body problem appears in *Discourse on the Method* (1637), by rationalist philosopher René Descartes (1596–1650), under the label of Cartesian Dualism; however, it has roots in the philosophies of ancient Greece (Plato and Aristotle), and of medieval scholars such as Augustine, for whom the notion of soul takes the place of mind. The problem persists in modern philosophies of mind.

Descartes believed that the nonmaterial mind inhabited and expressed itself in a mechanically operated body, like a ghost in a machine. He was concerned with exactly how two unlike things could communicate, and to answer this he conceived of an interaction point that he called the "pineal gland." Interactions are bi-directional in nature: sense perception and physical sensations are felt by the body and relayed to the mind, but awareness of and reactions to these things are supplied by the mind. So, "I think" and "I am" are products of the conscious mind, while "Ouch, I stubbed my toe!" and "I am cold" are supplied by the body, conveyed through the pineal gland. But, can physical things be cleanly divided from mental things? Not really. Other attempted solutions to, or ways to avoid, this problem include various forms of dualism, materialism, monism, and epiphenomenalism.

Inquiries prompted by the mind/body problem have led to psychology, physiology, neurobiology, and neuroscience. The problem informs how we conceive of our embodied selves and our corresponding concepts of freedom, identity, and selfhood. **KBJ**

"... it is certain that I, [that is, my mind, by which I am what I am], is entirely and truly distinct from my body, and may exist without it."

René Descartes, *Discourse on the Method* (1637)

Masters of Nature
René Descartes

The argument that the purpose of science is to enable humans to control nature

According to both Francis Bacon (1561–1626) and René Descartes (1596–1650), the purpose of natural philosophy—science—is to allow humans to gain power over nature and harness it for their needs. To be a master, or possessor, of nature (the universe) is to view science as a practical enterprise for human life and prosperity. Descartes's *Discourse on the Method* (1637) was intended to provide humans with the knowledge needed to effectively attack, alter, and control nature.

Prior to the seventeenth century, this kind of thinking would have been seen as absurd and even impious because the study of science was expected to encourage contemplation; science was a form of spiritual discipline. By contemplating science, a person arrived at a sense of the higher moral order and purpose in the world, and achieved a union with the creation of the Greek gods and later the Christian God. Humans were only one element of the design, not the master of it all. However, Bacon and Descartes saw this approach as unfruitful, since science was producing nothing that improved the conditions for humans. To focus purely on moral purposes created a sterile, unproductive, and distorted kind of knowledge. They concluded that this notion of the universe as a moral framework should be set aside to make room for the human quest for efficient domination of nature.

Theirs was a victory of power and knowledge over mystery and wonder. With nature understood as a soulless machine whose causes and laws could be fully understood and utilized by humans, science could become a practical discipline that assisted humans in making the world a better place. Humans could be moral agents when using scientific discoveries for the betterment of all, as they did with medicine or meteorology, and at the same time be masters of their domain rather than its uncomprehending slaves. **KBJ**

Fermat's Last Theorem
Pierre de Fermat

A math problem that defied the world's finest minds for more than 300 years

Fermat's Last Theorem, also referred to as Fermat's Conjecture, postulates that no three positive integers a, b, and c can be suitable for the equation $a^n+b^n=c^n$ where n has a value greater than two. Before it was finally solved after 358 years, the Last Theorem was the world's most difficult math problem, with some of the greatest mathematicians attempting a solution.

In 1637, Pierre de Fermat (c. 1607–65), a French lawyer and amateur mathematician, scribbled in his copy of Diophantus's *Arithmetica* (third century) that he had "a truly marvelous proof" of $a^n+b^n=c^n$ that "this margin is too narrow to contain." While Fermat never wrote out a complete proof, he did leave a proof for the special case of $n=4$. This meant that subsequent mathematicians were left to prove the theorem for cases when n would

> *"Pierre de Fermat created the most profound riddle in the history of mathematics."*
>
> Simon Singh, *Fermat's Last Theorem* (1997)

represent a prime number. Proofs for three, five, and seven were published in the next 200 years, but it was not until the mid-nineteenth century that Ernst Kummer (1810–93) proved the theorem for regular prime integers. All of n would not be solved until 1995.

In their struggle to solve Fermat's Last Theorem, mathematicians were forced to expand upon existing mathematical structures, and algebraic number theory was thereby advanced and the modularity theorem proved. British mathematician Andrew Wiles (b. 1953) at last provided proof for Fermat's Last Theorem to great acclaim in 1995, and the impact of his feat reverberated across popular culture and academic circles. References to Fermat's Last Theorem have appeared in the TV show *Star Trek: The Next Generation* (1987–94), and Stieg Larsson's novel *The Girl Who Played with Fire* (2006). **MK**

Evil Genius
René Descartes

Everything we think we know was created by an evil genius and is, in reality, false

Suppose, posited French rationalist philosopher René Descartes (1596–1650), that everything you have ever perceived, all your knowledge, memories, observations, and sensory experiences, were false. Your entire existence has been the result of a powerful, malevolent being known as the "evil genius." This evil genius has created everything you know just to deceive you and convince you of something that is not true.

Descartes wrote about the evil genius in his work *Meditations on First Philosophy* (1641), in which he attempts to show that the notions of science and God's existence can not only rationally coexist, but also provide a rational basis for knowledge itself. The idea of the evil genius prompted him to doubt everything he knew, and everything he had ever known. Thus, he

"If you would be a real seeker after truth . . . doubt, as far as possible, all things."

René Descartes, *Meditations on First Philosophy* (1641)

attempted to rid himself of all prejudices and historical hindrances imparted to him from the past. Facing the possibility of such systematic and pervasive doubt, the work of a powerful, malevolent spirit, what could Descartes say he truly knew?

Descartes's hypothesis of the evil deceiver laid the foundation for what would become known eponymously as Cartesian skepticism, or Cartesian doubt. This universal doubt laid the foundation for modern philosophy, with its focus on using logic and reason independently of the influence of the material world. Instead of studying the classical philosophic texts of the Greeks and Romans in order to understand the world, Cartesian philosophers employed their own reasoning capabilities to test the limits of knowledge and experience, searching for truth. **MT**

"I Think, Therefore I Am"
René Descartes

We can be certain of our existence once we understand that we are capable of thinking

In the quest to determine what is real, true, and good, we can begin with the basic knowledge that we exist. We reach this conclusion because we are able to understand our own thoughts, and know that in order to think them we must exist.

In his work *Meditations on First Philosophy* (1641), rationalist philosopher René Descartes (1596–1650) asked what, if anything, can we ever really know? If we assume that all our sensory perceptions—and the beliefs based upon them—are flawed and potentially erroneous, how can we come to any conclusion about the world? For Descartes, the answer lay with thought itself. In order to have any thoughts at all, a person must exist. Even if all our senses, memories, and everything we accept as true turn out to be false, as the result

"I am, then, in the strict sense, only a thing that thinks."

René Descartes, *Meditations on First Philosophy* (1641)

of some universal deception, we can still be assured of our own existence because we are able to ask the question in the first place. In summary, *Cogito ergo sum*: "I think, therefore I am."

Descartes is widely viewed as the foundational figure of modern Western philosophy. From his methodological doubt, Descartes built a system of epistemology—the study of knowledge—that would shape philosophy for centuries to come. Many of those who followed Descartes—David Hume, Baruch Spinoza, John Locke, Immanuel Kant—were influenced by his work. His insistence on using reason on its own, without the influence of perceptions, to obtain knowledge, and on the objectivity that that requires had a lasting impact, both on those who agreed with his approach and those who reacted against it. **MT**

◀ A watercolor by William Blake (1808), showing Satan training the rebel angels.

Isolationism
Tokugawa Shogunate

A policy by which a nation sets itself apart from the rest of the world

Isolationism is a political doctrine designed to isolate a nation diplomatically, militarily, economically, and culturally from the world around it. A country with an isolationist government will be mindful of protecting its own economic base from foreign competition through the use of tariffs and other forms of protectionism; it will often refuse to enter into trade and other economic agreements, will fundamentally oppose becoming a part of any political or military alliance, and will generally seek to maintain peace and security within its borders by avoiding being drawn into foreign conflicts or disputes—primarily by adhering to policies of nonintervention. One of the most striking twentieth-century examples of an isolationist approach to foreign affairs may be seen in the determination of the United States government—at least initially—to stay out of the war in Europe in 1939 and 1940. But isolationism is by no means a modern political phenomenon; the history of nations wishing to remain apart from the world around them goes back many hundreds of years.

One of the world's most feudal and inward-looking regimes was the Tokugawa shogunate, also known as Tokugawa bakufu, which ruled Japan from 1600 to 1868. From 1641 to 1832 the shogunate enforced a policy that it called *kaikin*, meaning restriction or "locked country." The policy was isolationism at its most extreme: any Japanese man or woman who left the country, and any foreigner who dared enter it, risked the penalty of death. There were exceptions: limited trade with China was permitted, and a Dutch factory in Nagasaki was permitted to trade under strict supervision. Exceptions aside, the policy remained in effect until the four U.S. warships of Commodore Matthew Perry's "Black Ship" fleet arrived at Edo (Tokyo) Bay in July 1853. The shogunate opened Japan to trade to avoid war with a technologically superior power. **JS**

An engraving from *c.* 1901 showing a Dutch trader speaking to Ieyasu, founder of the Tokugawa shogunate.

Quakerism

George Fox

The belief that God exists in all of us and finds expression in the conscience

Quakerism is a Protestant religious movement that is committed to belief in a direct relationship between the believer and God. Practitioners aspire to live in accordance with the "inward light." Quakerism also goes by the name of Society of Friends, or Friends Church, and it rejects all encoded ecclesiastical forms, such as clergy or creeds. Quaker worship is characterized by its unstructured nature, and leaders of the religion encourage believers to focus on their private lives with the intention of achieving spiritual and emotional purity.

In the mid-seventeenth century, before the name "Quaker" came into use, small groups of English Protestants who did not identify with existing Puritan groups began to gather, organize, and evangelize. They were led by charismatic preachers, notably George Fox (1624–91), who began preaching in 1647 and created a Quaker membership structure that persisted for many generations. Numbers grew both in England and New England, and soon Quaker communities were flourishing on the U.S. East Coast, most notably in what is now Pennsylvania, where William Penn (1644–1718) attempted to govern the entire state according to Quakerism's principles of pacifism and religious tolerance. Although Penn did not turn out to be a strong governor, the influence of Quakerism remained politically potent in the following centuries, with Quakers on both sides of the Atlantic fighting to abolish the slave trade, advocating social justice and prison reform, and seeking pacifist resolutions to disputes.

Quaker influence persists in Western culture, especially in education and trade. Colleges such as Bryn Mawr College, Cornell University, and Johns Hopkins University were founded by Quakers, and Barclays and Lloyds are both Quaker banks. There is also the Quaker Oats brand, but this name and image is not actually connected to the religious organization. **MK**

⬆ A nineteenth-century lithograph by Edward Henry Wehnert, showing George Fox preaching.

LEVIATHAN

Or

THE MATTER, FORME
and Power of A COMMON-
WEALTH ECCLESIASTICALL
and CIVIL

By THOMAS HOBBES
of MALMESEVRY.

Leviathan

Thomas Hobbes

A government with absolute authority is necessary to ensure humanity's survival

According to *Leviathan* (1651) by English philosopher Thomas Hobbes (1588–1679), humanity is naturally selfish, egotistical, hedonistic, and bent on pursuing self-destructive interests. The natural tendency of humanity inevitably leads to conflict and warfare, but it also has the contradictory impulse to better itself and pursue happiness. In order to temper and balance these intrinsic, competing natures, Hobbes believed that an authority must exist, both to curb people's natural destructive urges and to allow them to prosper. That "Leviathan" state—monarchy, democracy, or other form of government—must possess a monopoly on that from which ultimate authority derives: violence.

Hobbes published *Leviathan* after living as an exile in Paris during the tumultuous years of the English Civil

"The condition of Man ... is a condition of Warre of every one against every one."

Thomas Hobbes, *Leviathan* (1651)

War (1642–51). As a royalist, Hobbes wrote *Leviathan* largely as a way of showing his royalist beliefs and support for the monarchy. At the time, however, his views were seen by many as antithetical to the traditional notion that a monarch's rule is based upon divine grant, rather than a social contract between the ruler and the ruled to help keep peace in a civil society.

While the notion that humanity is inherently destructive, and needs an absolute authority to govern it, is not universally agreed upon, the ideas that Hobbes expressed in *Leviathan* had a significant impact on many philosophers, politicians, economists, and social theorists. Utilitarianism similarly presumes humanity's hedonism, while the works of Adam Smith and many other economists recognize the benefits of striking a balance between contradictory interests. **MT**

Knowledge Is Power

Thomas Hobbes

Knowledge contributes to the material prosperity and peace of humankind

The idea that knowledge is power implies that, armed with information, an individual is likely to have greater influence on others, and therefore power. Some would argue that all power derives from knowledge.

Although the phrase "knowledge is power" has been attributed to English philosopher and scientist Francis Bacon (1561–1626), it does not occur in any of his works. However, it appears in *De Homine* (Concerning Man, 1658) by English philosopher Thomas Hobbes (1588–1679). Hobbes worked for Bacon as a young man, and the phrase may stem from their discussions.

Hobbes outlined his political philosophy of knowledge being power in an earlier work, *Leviathan* (1651), subtitled *The Matter, Form, and Power of a Commonwealth, Ecclesiastical and Civil*. He posited

"Natural power is the eminence of the faculties of body or mind."

Thomas Hobbes, *Leviathan* (1651)

that history is knowledge of fact, while science is knowledge of consequences. A royalist sympathizer, Hobbes was writing against the backdrop of the English Civil War (1642–51). Although his works tackle questions of political philosophy, he was concerned with persuading the public to submit to sovereign power in order to maintain a commonwealth.

Hobbes's doctrine—that a legitimate state government is created when many people transfer power to one or a few, who in return secure their well being and security—was both lauded and criticized. His detractors regarded his philosophy as secular, he faced accusations of heresy, and from 1666 he was forbidden to publish any works relating to human conduct in England. Nevertheless, Hobbes's works were the foundation of social contract theory. **CK**

◀ The title page of *Leviathan* by Thomas Hobbes, first published in London in 1651.

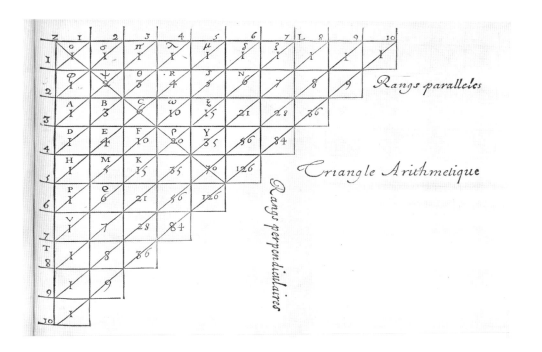

1653

Pascal's Triangle
Blaise Pascal

A triangular array of binomial coefficients used to advance probability theory

In mathematics, what is known as Pascal's triangle is a tabular presentation of numbers arranged in staggered rows. The triangular arrangement gives the coefficients in binomial expression, such as $(x+y)^n$, so the number in each subsequent row is obtained by adding the two entries diagonally above.

The Pascal's triangle concept has its roots in Pythagorean arithmetic and Arabic algebra. Although it was described originally by Chinese mathematician Jia Xian (c. 1010–70), it is named after the French mathematician, physicist, and philosopher Blaise Pascal (1623–62), who was the first to discover the importance of the patterns it contained. Pascal described the triangular table of numbers in his treatise *Traité du*

triangle arithmétique (Treatise on the Arithmetical Triangle), written in 1653 and published posthumously in 1665. The triangle shows many patterns. For example, drawing parallel "shallow diagonals" and then adding together the numbers on each line results in the Fibonacci numbers 1, 1, 2, 3, 5, 8, 13, 21, and so on. (After the second number, 1, each number in the sequence is the sum of the two previous numbers.) Pascal used the triangle to solve problems in probability theory.

Pascal's triangle demonstrates various mathematical properties. His work led to the discovery by English physicist and mathematician Isaac Newton (1643–1727) of the binomial theorem for fractional and negative indices, and to both Newton and German mathematician and philosopher Gottfried Wilhelm Leibniz (1646–1716) developing a mathematical theorem for infinitesimal calculus. In the twentieth century, Polish mathematician Wacław Sierpiński (1882–1969) demonstrated that if all the positions in the triangle containing odd numbers are shaded black, and all the positions containing even numbers shaded white, a geometric fractal that is similar to a mosaic pattern and known as the "Sierpiński gasket" emerges. **CK**

An illustration of Pascal's triangle in Blaise Pascal's book *Traité du triangle arithmétique* (1665).

(86)

XLII.

The outward and inward Senſes.

Senſus externi & interni.

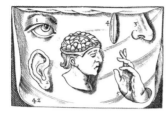

There are five outward Senſes ;
The Eye 1.
ſeeth colours,
what is white or black,
green or blew,
red or yellow.
The Ear 2.
heareth Sounds,
both natural,
Voices and Words ;
and artificial,
muſical Tunes.

Senſus externi
ſunt quinque ;
Oculus 1.
videt Colores,
quid album vel atrum,
viride vel cœruleum,
rubrum aut luteum,ſit.
Auris 2.
audit Sonos,
tum naturales,
Voces & Verba ;
tum artificiales,
Tonos Muſicos.

The

(87)

The Noſe 3.
ſenteth ſmels
and ſtinks.
The Tongue 4.
with the roof of the mauth
taſteth ſabours, what is
ſweet or bitter, keen or bi=
ſom or harſh.   (ting
The Hand 5.
by touching diſcerneth
the quantity
and quality of things,
the hot and cold,
the moiſt and dry,
the hard and ſoft,
the ſmouth and rough,
the heavy and light.
The inward Senſes
are three.
The Common-ſenſe 7.
under the forepart of the
apprehendeth   (head,
things taken from the
outward Senſes.
The Phantaſie 6.
under the crown of the head
judgeth of thoſe things,
thinketh and dreameth.
The Memory 8.
under the hinder part of the
layeth up every thing (head
and fetcheth them out :
it loſeth ſome,
and this is forgetfulneſs.
Sleep,
is the Reſt of the Senſes.

Naſus 3.
olfacit Odores,
& Fœtores.
Lingua 4. cum Palato
guſtat Sapores,
quid dulce aut amarum,
acre aut acidun,
acerbum aut auſterum.
Manus 5.
dignoſcit tangendo
rerum Quantitatem
& Qualitatem,
calidum & frigidum,
humidum & ſiccum,
durum & molle,
lave & aſperum,
grave & leve.
Senſu interni
ſunt tres.
Senſus communis 7.
ſub ſincipite,
apprehendit
à Senſibus externis
perceptas res.
Phantaſia 6.
ſub vertice,
dijudicat res iſtas,
cogitat,ſomniat.
Memoria 8.
ſub occipitio,
ſingula recondit
& repromit :
quædam deperdit,
& hoc eſt Oblivio.
Somnus,
eſt Senſuum requies.

G 4   Anima

1658

Orbis Pictus

John Amos Comenius

The first book to be written primarily for children

For centuries, children were regarded as adults. They were trained for adult life and were sent to work as soon as possible, although no doubt they enjoyed listening to folktales, fables, myths, and literature created for adults. Czech teacher, educator, and writer John Amos Comenius (1592–1670) was the first person to successfully publish a book written specifically for children, the illustrated Orbis Pictus (Visible World), released in 1658. Resembling an encyclopedia, the work was designed to teach children Latin by means of pictures and short, memorable sentences in both Latin and the child's mother tongue. Orbis Pictus was first published in Germany in Latin and German, and English, Italian, French, Czech, and Hungarian editions soon followed. For a century it was the most popular textbook in Europe. Orbis Pictus is the precursor of contemporary audiovisual aids to language learning.

In the late seventeenth century, English philosopher John Locke (1632–1704) argued that at birth the mind of a child was a tabula rasa (blank slate) waiting to be written upon by educators. His assertion changed the concept of childhood, giving rise to books of moral instruction aimed at children. English publisher John Newbery (1713–67) produced A Pretty Little Pocket Book in 1744, which was the first book written for children's enjoyment and for education. By the nineteenth century, there existed fairy stories, novels, and poems that children could read purely for pleasure.

Today, there is debate regarding the definition of children's literature, given that an adult may read and enjoy a children's book, and, to a lesser extent, vice versa—as evidenced by numerous successful crossover works. Historians have also pointed out that a discernable children's literature requires a recognizable childhood, in which case children's literature dates from the eighteenth century, when the concept of "childhood" was recognized in philosophy. **CK**

↑ An entry in Orbis Pictus (1658) that relates to the organs of the five senses.

Chemical Substance
Robert Boyle

A material (in any state—solid, liquid, or gas) that has a definite chemical composition

The Greek philosopher Democritus (c. 460–c. 370 BCE) proposed that everything is made of invisible substances, unbreakable "atoms" of different kinds, whose various combinations are responsible for all natural things. Using alchemical techniques, seventeenth-century scientists could isolate chemicals with stable properties, but these would change dramatically when mixed with other chemicals. Early chemists saw these chemical substances as the basic parts of matter, but some philosophical scientists, including Robert Boyle (1627–91), suggested that the Greek atomists had been right: the basic chemical substances were made of even smaller atoms clinging together in certain combinations. Boyle's book *The Sceptical Chymist: or Chymico-Physical Doubts*

"To liberate the chemical energy of coal, another substance is required . . . oxygen."
Wilhelm Ostwald, chemist

& Paradoxes (1661) inaugurated modern chemistry. Mathematical laws for chemistry were established after Antoine Lavoisier (1743–94) proposed the conservation of mass in 1783 and John Dalton (1766–1844) announced his theory of atomic weights in 1805. By the mid-nineteenth century, chemists had isolated dozens of "elements" that could not be further reduced by laboratory methods. The periodic table of these was proposed by Dmitri Mendeleev (1834–1907) in 1869.

A chemical substance is composed of two or more elemental atoms, in a definite ratio, which are bonded together to form a stable composition with specific properties. A chemical substance can be broken apart (by analysis) and rearranged in new compositions (by synthesis), and in turn these processes involve the release or addition of energy. **JSh**

Magazine
Johann Rist

A regular publication that contains articles of common subject matter and interest

The world's first magazine is generally considered to be *Erbauliche Monaths-Unterredungen* (Edifying Monthly Discussions), published in German in 1663 by Johann Rist (1606–67), a theologian and poet from Hamburg. It lasted until 1668, by which time it had been joined by the French periodical *Journal des Sçavans* (Scholars' Journal), the first academic journal. These early publications were specialist in nature, and generally contained summaries on developments in art, literature, philosophy, and science. This enabled knowledge of academic advances to spread much more quickly, particularly with regard to works published in unfamiliar languages. Moreover, the emphasis on new discoveries led to an intellectual shift away from established authorities and the classics.

"Ephemerality is the little magazine's generic fate . . ."
Frederick C. Crews, *The New York Review* (1978)

It was not until 1731, however, that a general interest magazine—and the word itself—first appeared. Edward Cave (1691–1754) was the son of a cobbler and had been expelled from Rugby School for stealing from the headmaster. He conceived the idea of producing a regular periodical that would cover topics of interest to the general reader. He called this innovation a "magazine," a word describing a military storehouse of material that was derived from the Arabic *makhazin*, meaning "storehouses." Edited under the pen name Sylvanus Urban, Cave produced the first edition of *The Gentleman's Magazine* in London in January 1731 as a monthly digest of news and commentary on topics as wide as commodity prices and Latin poetry. The new magazine was a great success and was published almost without interruption until 1922. **SA**

Illustrations from *The Gentleman's Magazine*, February 1785. ➡

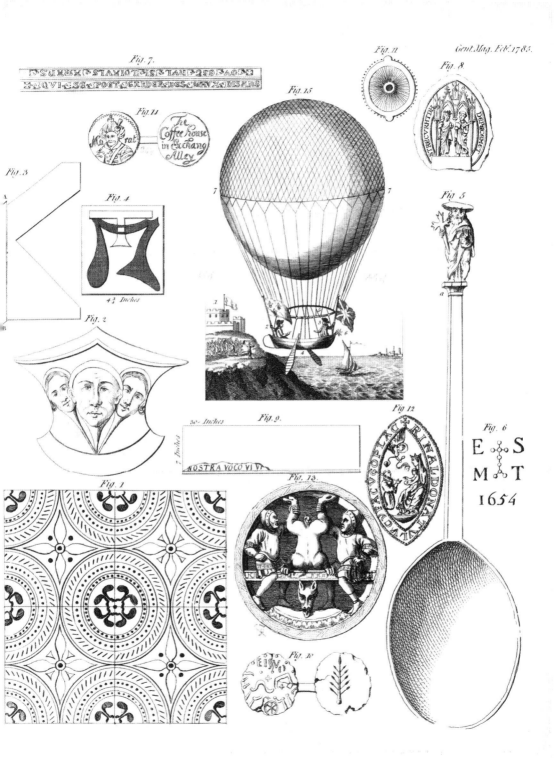

Fig. 7.

Fig. 11

Gent.Mag. Feb.1785.

Fig. 8.

Fig.14

The Coffee house in Exchang Alley

Fig. 15

Fig .3

Fig. 4

7   7

4¾ Inches

Fig. 5

a

Fig. 2

Fig 12

Fig. 6

E ✠ S
M ✠ T
1654

Fig. 9.

30 Inches

7 Inches

NOSTRA VOCO VI VI

Fig. 1

Fig. 13.

Fig. 10.

Biological Cell
Robert Hooke

A microscopic unit that is the basic unit of structure and function in all living organisms

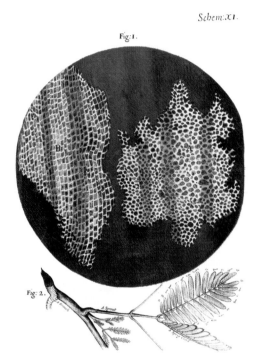

An illustration of cork wood cells as seen under a microscope, from Robert Hooke's book *Micrographia* (1667), believed to be the first major book on microscopy.

All living things are composed of biological cells. Cells contain hereditary information and derive from pre-existing cells. All cells are similar in chemical composition in organisms of a similar species. Animals, plants, and fungi consist of eukaryotic cells, which have an outer membrane and a nucleus that contains DNA. Prokaryotic cells, simple cells found in bacteria, lack a nucleus. Animal cells obtain energy via food; plant cells obtain energy from the sun by the process of photosynthesis.

The idea of the biological cell emerged in 1665, when English naturalist Robert Hooke (1635–1703) was looking at thin slices of cork bark through a compound microscope. Hooke noticed what he called "small rooms" butting up against one another in a pattern that reminded him of an aerial view of monks' chambers at an abbey. In *Micrographia* (1665), his work related to his microscopic observations, Hooke named them "cells," after the Latin word *cellula*, meaning "small room."

Hooke's investigation led to the development of cell theory, which evolved from the combined efforts of microscopists such as Dutchman Antonie Philips van Leeuwenhoek, who discovered blood cells in 1684. Scottish botanist Robert Brown observed the first nucleus in plant cells in 1833. By 1839, German physiologist Theodor Schwann and German biologist Matthias Schleiden recognized that cells are the elementary particles of organisms in plants and animals, and that some organisms are unicellular and others multicellular. German pathologist Rudolf Virchow confirmed the principle of cell division, essential in growth and reproduction, in 1855.

Cell theory signified an important conceptual advance in biology, laying the groundwork for major scientific breakthroughs in the twentieth century, such as the discovery of DNA by James Watson and Francis Crick in 1953. **CK**

"It is the cells which create and maintain in us . . . our will to live and survive."
Albert Claude, Nobel lecture (1974)

Decimal System
John Wilkins

The first proposal for universal measurements, based on tens

The decimal system is a numeral system that employs the number ten as the base and uses ten different numerals: the digits from one to nine inclusive, and zero. A decimal point, signified by a dot—as in 0.45, for example—is used to represent decimal fractions.

Many ancient cultures calculated using numerals based on ten (the number of fingers of both hands), but the outline for modern European decimal notation was introduced in 1668 by an English scientist and natural philosopher, Bishop John Wilkins (1614–72), when the Royal Society of London published his book *An Essay towards a Real Character, and a Philosophical Language*. Wilkins proposed an innovative plan for a system that was based on a single "universal measure" and was designed to measure all things. Adopting an international standard would help "all those different Nations who traffick together" by facilitating commercial trade. Wilkins outlined what was required for such a system and advocated that it should be based on accurately measuring the Earth or time. He devised a decimal system with a standard unit that was almost one meter long, and that was to be used with decimal multiples and submultiples. He also suggested decimal units to measure area, volume, and weight.

Wilkin's proposal was debated for decades. The first practical application of his idea was implemented in the eighteenth century when it became politically desirable to adopt a common system of weights and measures. France introduced the metric system in 1799, and by the early nineteenth century this had been adopted by the international scientific community.

The modern metric system, known as the International System of Units (SI, from the French *Le Système Internationale d'unités*), was established in 1960. Practical and easy to use, the SI contains some of the elements that Wilkins proposed and is the most widely used system of measurement in the world. **CK**

⬆ A French artwork from 1799, demonstrating metric measurements, including the liter, kilogram, meter, stere (unit of volume), Franc (decimalized currency), and are (unit of area).

> " . . . to which purpose, it were most desirable to find out some natural Standard, or universal Measure, which hath been esteemed by Learned men as one of the desiderata in Philosophy."

John Wilkins, *An Essay towards a Real Character, and a Philosophical Language* (1668)

Phlogiston Theory
Johann Joachim Becher

The theory that burning required the release of the hypothetical element phlogiston

In the late seventeenth and mid-eighteenth centuries, chemical theorists used the phlogiston theory to explain burning and rusting. They believed that every combustible substance contained the element phlogiston, and the liberation of this hypothetical elastic fluid caused burning. The ash or residue that remains after burning was believed to be a dephlogisticated substance.

German alchemist and physician Johann Joachim Becher (1635–82) initiated the theory of combustion that came to be associated with phlogiston. In his book *Physica subterranea*, published in 1669, he suggested that instead of the classical elements of earth, air, water, and fire, bodies were made from three forms of earth: *terra lapidea* (vitreous), *terra mercurialis* (mercurial), and

> *"We are not able to ascertain the weight of phlogiston, or . . . the oxygenous principle."*

Joseph Priestley, theologian

terra pinguis (fatty). He thought combustible substances were rich in *terra pinguis*, a combustible earth liberated when a substance burned. For him, wood was a combination of *terra pinguis* and wood ashes.

Becher's theories of combustion influenced German chemist Georg Ernst Stahl (1660–1734), who gave the hypothetical substance *terra pinguis* the name "phlogiston," derived from the Greek word *phlogizein*, meaning "set alight." He believed there was a link between the processes of burning and rusting. Stahl was correct in that each process depends on a chemical reaction with oxygen known as oxidization. However, problems arose because rusty iron weighs more than unrusted iron and ash weighs less than the original burned object. Phlogiston was disproved by French chemist Antoine-Laurent Lavoisier (1743–94). **CK**

Pascal's Wager
Blaise Pascal

An argument for belief in God based on the practical benefit for the believer

Pascal's Wager is a logical argument to show that the potential benefits of believing in the Christian God outweigh the potential risks of not doing so. The argument appears in the posthumously published *Pensées* (1670) of French mathematician, scientist, and philosopher Blaise Pascal (1623–62). Pascal assumes that either the Christian God exists or does not, and that each person can decide whether to believe in him or not. If God does not exist, either believing in him or not believing in him will result in the same outcome, though the believer may have a happier life than the nonbeliever because the believer can gain comfort from the religion. If God does exist, then believing in him grants the possibility for eternal life, while not believing in him will result in eternal damnation.

> *"If you gain, you gain all . . . Wager then, without hesitation, that He exists."*

Blaise Pascal

Previous thinkers, such as St. Thomas Aquinas and René Descartes, had attempted to prove God's existence through rational, logical proofs, but Pascal took another tack. His focus on the best possible outcome, though it echoed some classical writings, eschewed the previous metaphysical justifications for Christianity, and instead adopted a practical measurement based on the potential outcomes.

Pascal's Wager is both a logical argument and an exercise in what would come to be known as decision theory. It makes no attempt at convincing potential believers of the existence of God. Instead, the wager offers a pragmatic approach. Pascal's argument paves the way for other belief systems, such as existentialism, which focus less on metaphysical or spiritual questions in lieu of potential practical benefits. **MT**

Mathematical Function
Gottfried Wilhelm Leibniz

The mathematic concept that a function is a relation between two variables

In mathematics, a function is a relationship between values. Each of its input values gives back one output value. Often it is denoted as $f(x)$, where x is the value given to it. For example, where the number x relates to its square x^2, the output of function f corresponds to input x and is written $f(x)$. So if the input variable, or argument, is -4 then the output is 16, written as $f(-4) = 16$. The function concept is fundamental in modern mathematics and essential in science, where it is used for formulating physical relationships.

Italian physicist, mathematician, and astronomer Galileo Galilei (1564–1642) was the first to articulate the dependency of one quantity on another in mathematics. However, it was German mathematician and philosopher Gottfried Wilhelm Leibniz (1646–1716)

"... other kinds of lines which, in a given figure, perform some function."

Gottfried Wilhelm Leibniz

who introduced the word "function" into mathematics. In his manuscript *Methodus tangentium inversa, seu de functionibus* (The Inverse Method of Tangents, or On Functions, 1673), Leibniz used "function" to describe any quantity varying from point to point on a curve, such as the length of the tangent.

In 1692 and 1694, Leibniz published articles in which he named any parts of straight lines as "functions." In 1694, in a piece for the scientific journal *Acta Eruditorum* (Acts of the Scholars), Swiss mathematician Jacob Bernoulli (1654–1705) used the word "function" to have the same sense. The notation $f(x)$ was introduced in 1734 by Swiss mathematician and physicist Leonhard Euler (1707–83). German mathematician Peter Dirichlet (1805–59) came up with the modern definition of "function" in 1837. **CK**

Microbiology
Antonie van Leeuwenhoek

A branch of science that focuses on the study of microorganisms

Microbiology is a science that involves the study of tiny life-forms known as "microorganisms" or "microbes," including archaea, algae, bacteria, molds, protozoa, viruses, and yeasts. Microbiology has grown to include bacteriology, immunology, mycology, parasitology, and virology. It has multiple applications and is employed in the study of genetics and disease, as well as in industry.

In 1674 Dutch scientist Antonie van Leeuwenhoek (1632–1723) was the first to see bacteria and protozoa when he noticed "animalcules," or minute organisms, while closely observing water through a single-lens microscope of his own design. Van Leeuwenhoek was apparently inspired to take up microscopy after seeing a copy of English scientist Robert Hooke's *Micrographia* (1665), in which the term "cell" was first

"I see some of [the organisms] open their mouths and move the organs or parts."

Antonie van Leeuwenhoek

coined to describe what came to be recognized as the basic unit of all living things.

In 1676 van Leeuwenhoek wrote to the Royal Society in London to announce his discovery of "animalcules." Initially, the society members doubted him, but, in 1680, the Royal Society verified van Leeuwenhoek's discoveries and appointed him as a fellow. He went on to discover red blood cells and then spermatozoa, coming to the radical conclusion that fertilization occurs when a spermatozoon penetrates an egg.

The discovery of microorganisms was revolutionary, later proving particularly important with regard to their relationship with decay and disease. The work of French chemist and microbiologist Louis Pasteur (1822–95) in this field led to the germ theory of disease and the development of vaccines and pasteurization. **CK**

A twentieth-century portrait of Antonie van Leeuwenhoek, the "father of microbiology," by Ned M. Seidler. ➡

fig: A   D

fig: B C

fig: E:

fig: G

fig: F

Evangelicalism
Philipp Jakob Spener

A Protestant movement upholding the sole authority of the Bible in matters of doctrine

⬆ A copper engraving from 1683 of Philipp Jakob Spener, by German engraver Philipp Kilian. Spener became interested in reforming Lutheran practice while studying in Strassburg.

Evangelicalism is a Christian movement that emphasizes the piety of the individual, and their relationship with God and the Savior. Evangelicals believe that the individual is saved by faith in the death of Christ, which atoned for humanity's sin, and that humanity is sinful because of the fall of Adam in the Garden of Eden. Practitioners need to be "born again" by a process of personal conversion that saves them from eternal damnation through redemption, after which they are promised heavenly salvation. Evangelicals de-emphasize ritual: they view good works and the sacraments as being merely symbolic, and do not believe that ordination imparts any supernatural gifts. They look to the Bible as the sole authority in matters of theological doctrine.

Evangelicalism grew out of the ideas of German Lutheran reformer Philipp Jakob Spener (1635–1705). His influential book, *Pia Desideria* (Pious Desires, 1675), attacked the clergy, advocated biblical study for both individuals and groups, and urged the cultivation of inner piety. His friend, German Lutheran August Hermann Francke (1663–1727), laid practical foundations of the movement by organizing a *collegium philobiblicum* (assembly of Bible lovers), devoted to scholarly studies of the scriptures. Francke's ideas were spread via his students at the University of Halle.

The term "Evangelicalism" came into general use in England during the time that a series of revivals under the founder of Methodism, John Wesley (1703–91), and the itinerant English evangelical George Whitefield (1715–70) took place. In North America, the revival was spearheaded by U.S. theologian Jonathan Edwards (1703–58). By the early nineteenth century, Evangelical Protestantism was the most popular expression of Christianity in the United States; in the United Kingdom, evangelicals were strongly associated with missionary work and social reform. **CK**

> "What they take to be faith is by no means that true faith which is awakened through the Word of God, by the illumination, witness, and sealing of the Holy Spirit, but is a human fancy."

Philipp Jakob Spener, *Pia Desideria*
(Pious Desires, 1675)

Feminist Biblical Exegesis
Various

Critical analysis of the Judeo-Christian scriptures from a feminist perspective

Feminist biblical exegesis is concerned with the representation of women in the Bible. It often challenges long-accepted interpretations of the texts put forward by male scholars working in patriarchal societies. Feminist criticism of the Bible examines the social construction of gender and what that means for the depiction of female figures in the Bible. It attempts to reinterpret problematic verses and narratives, and addresses issues of misogynistic narratives.

The roots of feminist biblical exegesis lie in the seventeenth century, in the writings of Protestant female theological writers, such as Quakerism founder Margaret Fell (1614–1702), Philadelphian prophetesses Jane Lead (1624–1704) and Ann Bathurst (c. 1638–c. 1704), Quaker Elizabeth Bathurst (d. 1690), writer Mary Astell (1668–1731), and visionary M. Marsin (a. 1694–1701). They advocated the equality of the sexes in marriage, society, and religion, arguing that their radical belief in universalism was as instituted by God at creation. For centuries the Virgin Mary in the Bible had been considered a counter figure to Eve as an instrument of salvation, and the idea was reintroduced as the writers attempted to advocate the rights of women and find scriptural precedent for female preachers.

Mary Astell's ideas regarding women, and the religious education of women in particular, were ridiculed by contemporaries, but she has become known as the "first English feminist." And as the feminist movement grew from the late nineteenth century, so feminist biblical exegesis became more popular. In 1895 and 1898, Elizabeth Cady Stanton (1815–1902) and a committee of twenty-six women published the best-selling but controversial two-part *The Woman's Bible*, partly as a response to women's exclusion from biblical scholarship and partly as a challenge to the traditional religious orthodoxy that woman should be subservient to man. **CK**

⬆ A restored thirteenth-century stained glass of the Virgin Mary, from the Church of St. Mary Magdalene in Chewton Mendip, United Kingdom.

"If all Men are born free, how is it that all Women are born Slaves?"

Mary Astell, *Some Reflections on Marriage* (1700)

Pantheism
Baruch Spinoza

The view that God and the universe are one, infinite, eternal, and knowable to mankind

The classic statement of pantheism, by philosopher Baruch Spinoza (1632–77), is *Ethica, ordine geometrico demonstrata* (Ethics, Demonstrated in a Geometrical Manner, 1677), although the term "pantheism" itself was not coined until after Spinoza's death. In the *Ethics*, Spinoza argues, "Whatsoever is, is in God, and without God nothing can be, or be conceived . . . God is the indwelling and not the transient cause of all things." To paraphrase, God is the only substance, the only thing that exists in itself. Everything else exists only in God.

Spinoza rejects the idea that God is a person; it is a mistake, he argues, to think that God acts freely, plans the fate of the world, or is moved by prayer. He also rejects the idea that God is external to and distinct from the universe, famously using the phrase *Deus, sive Natura* (God, or Nature). Both of these positions are characteristic of later versions of pantheism and have also been detected in precursors of Spinoza, such as the Stoic philosophers of ancient Greece and Rome, and in non-Western traditions, especially philosophical Taoism. Pantheism is often also associated with a religious reverence for the natural world, although this is not true in Spinoza's case.

Historically, pantheism has been controversial—often regarded as tantamount to atheism—but also influential. The highwater mark for pantheism was in the late eighteenth and nineteenth centuries, when it attracted thinkers such as English poet and philosopher Samuel Taylor Coleridge (1772–1834), U.S. poet and essayist Ralph Waldo Emerson (1803–82), and German philosopher G. W. F. Hegel (1770–1831). Part of pantheism's appeal then was that it seemed to provide a middle route between theism and atheism—in effect it promised religion unadulterated by superstition, and science while still recognizing spirituality. Less in the public eye today, it continues to influence philosophical and religious thought. **GB**

Paradisical Landscape with the Creation of Man (1594), painted by Jan Brueghel the Elder.

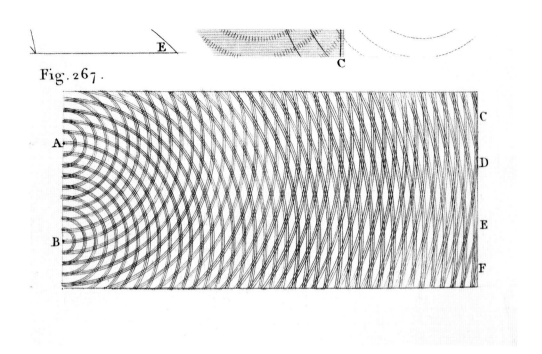

Fig. 267.

1678

Wave Theory of Light
Christiaan Huygens

The concept that light is emitted in all directions as a series of waves

The wave theory of light refraction and reflection, formulated in 1676 and 1677 by Dutch mathematician, astronomer, physicist, and horologist Christiaan Huygens (1629–95), was based on a new concept of light as wavelike. The theory postulates that the velocity of light in any substance is inversely in proportion to its refractive index.

In 1678 Huygens completed his *Traité de la lumière* (Treatise on Light). He read portions of the treatise to the French Royal Académie des sciences (Academy of Sciences) in 1678 and published it in 1690. Huygens posited that the more light was bent, or refracted, by a substance, or ether, the slower it would move while traversing across that substance. Suggesting

that a substance consisted of minute, uniform elastic particles compressed close together, Huygens was able to explain refraction and reflection on this basis.

However, Huygens's wave theory of light was different from that proposed by the English physicist, mathematician, astronomer, natural philosopher, alchemist, and theologian Sir Isaac Newton (1642–1727) in *Opticks* (1704), his book about optics and light refraction. Newton's theory was premised on a proposal by Pierre Gassendi (1592–1655) that light traveled as a shower of particles, referred to as "corpuscles." Because Newton was a great scientist and had many zealous supporters, Huygens's theory was dismissed and neglected until the nineteenth century.

Huygens's theory was vindicated by experiments conducted by English scientist Thomas Young (1773–1829) in 1801, and French engineer Augustin Fresnel (1788–1827) in 1816. The Huygens-Fresnel principle is named after these two men, and it is a recognized basis for understanding and predicting the wave propagation of light. When technology advanced sufficiently to measure the speed of light accurately, Huygens's theory was proved correct. **CK**

⬆ A diagram showing the principle of the interference of light, published by Thomas Young in 1806.

Infinitesimal Calculus

Sir Isaac Newton and Gottfried Wilhelm Leibniz

A mathematical theorem designed to calculate motion and change

⬆ A seventeenth-century portrait of Isaac Newton. Newton's *Principia* (1687) was one of the most important works in the history of modern science.

"And what are these Fluxions? The Velocities of evanescent Increments? And what are these same evanescent Increments? They are neither finite Quantities nor Quantities infinitely small, nor yet nothing."

George Berkeley, *The Analyst* (1734)

Infinitesimal calculus is a mathematical theorem used to find the slope of curves, areas under curves, minima and maxima, and other geometric and analytic values. It consists of differential calculus and integral calculus, which are used for the techniques of differentiation and integration respectively. Infinitesimal calculus has numerous applications, including astronomy, physics, electricity, acoustics, and even economics.

The invention of the techniques used to apply the infinitesimal calculus theorem is attributed to two men who came up with the idea independently: English physicist and mathematician Isaac Newton (1643–1727), and German mathematician and philosopher Gottfried Wilhelm Leibniz (1646–1716). Leibniz published his research in the journal *Acta Eruditorum* in 1684 and Newton in his treatise *Principia* in 1687, though Newton actually began work on the theory first. Their new mathematical system attempted to calculate motion and change. However, the two variants described change differently. For Newton, change was a variable quantity over time: for Leibniz it was the difference ranging over a sequence of infinitely close values.

Although the utility of infinitesimal calculus to explain physical phenomena was recognized, the fact that the mathematical theorem used infinity in calculations caused disquiet. In 1734 the Anglo-Irish Anglican bishop, philosopher, and scientist George Berkeley (1685–1753) published a pamphlet, *The Analyst; or, A Discourse Addressed to an Infidel Mathematician*, which pointed out flaws in the theorem. German-Jewish mathematician Abraham Robinson (1918–74) addressed the flaws in 1960 by developing a rigorous mathematical system of nonstandard analysis in which infinitesimal and infinite numbers are incorporated into mathematics. His theory of tiny numbers, known as "hyperreal numbers," simplifies approximation estimates. **CK**

Identity of Indiscernibles
Gottfried Wilhelm Leibniz

The concept that separate objects or entities cannot have all their properties in common

Known as Leibniz's Law, "the identity of indiscernibles" is a principle of analytic ontology. It states that it is impossible for two numerically distinct objects to have all of the same properties. This is typically understood to mean that no two objects have exactly the same properties: no two distinct things resemble each other exactly. Conversely, the principle of "the indiscernibility of identicals" (which is also known as Leibniz's Law) asserts that if A is identical to B, then every property that A has is a property of B, and vice versa.

The first explicit formulation of the principle was outlined in 1686 by German mathematician and philosopher Gottfried Wilhelm Leibniz (1646–1716) in his *Discours de métaphysique* (Discourse on Metaphysics), published in the nineteenth century. He used the principle in his arguments regarding various metaphysical doctrines, including the impossibility of Newtonian absolute space. In a well-known correspondence with English philosopher and cleric Samuel Clarke (1675–1729), Leibniz advocated his theory of relational space, in which space is composed of relations between objects, so implying that space cannot exist in the absence of matter. Clarke, himself a supporter of Isaac Newton, published the letters in 1717, the year after Leibniz died, under the title *A Collection of Papers, Which passed between the late Learned Mr. Leibnitz, and Dr. Clarke, In the Years 1715 and 1716*. The publication subsequently became one of the most widely read philosophical books in the eighteenth century.

The identity of indiscernibles is recognized as proposing solutions to philosophical inquiries regarding the nature of space and time. It has become generally accepted as metaphysical principle, although philosophers have continued to debate its validity. **CK**

⬆ An anonymous portrait of Gottfried Wilhelm Leibniz from 1710. Leibniz worked in several fields, including mathematics, philosophy, politics, and logic.

"To suppose two things indiscernible, is to suppose the same thing under two Names."

Gottfried Wilhelm Leibniz, *A Collection of Papers, Which passed between the late Learned Mr. Leibnitz, and Dr. Clarke, In the Years 1715 and 1716* (1717)

Motion as the Natural State of Things
Sir Isaac Newton

The theory that everything in the universe is always moving

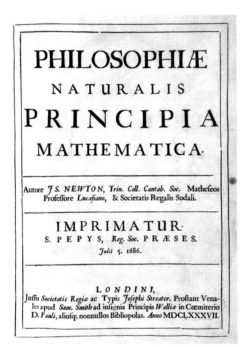

⬆ The title page of a first edition of Sir Isaac Newton's *Philosophiae Naturalis Principia Mathematica* (Mathematical Principles of Natural Philosophy), published in 1687.

"Time is defined so that motion looks simple."

Misner, Thorne, and Wheeler, *Gravitation* (1973)

Motion, at its simplest, is defined as a change in the arrangement of a physical system. The claim that everything in the universe is moving seems to contradict empirical evidence, yet it is a claim that has warranted investigation by some of humankind's greatest minds, from Aristotle to Albert Einstein. Motion, it turns out, despite its ubiquity, is a complex, often inscrutable, phenomenon.

Aristotle (384–322 BCE) began the systematic exploration of physical motion, but it was not until the publication by Sir Isaac Newton (1643–1727) of *Philosophiae Naturalis Principia Mathematica* (Mathematical Principles of Natural Philosophy) in 1687 that observations about motion were codified into "laws." In the preface to this work, Newton connects motion to all natural phenomena: "We offer this work as mathematical principles of philosophy [of rational mechanics]. For all the difficulty of philosophy seems to consist in this—from the phenomena of motions to investigate the forces of Nature, and then from these forces to demonstrate the other phenomena."

Newton goes on to establish that humans are ill-equipped to recognize any object truly at rest, as they are subject to inertia, preventing them from feeling motions of a mass to which they are connected, and neither do humans possess an unchanging frame of reference allowing them to see that they are moving. In making such claims, Newton argues that motion is the "natural state of things."

From Newton's foundation of motion as the natural state of things, classical mechanics, describing the motion of large bodies (planets and humans), was developed, as was quantum mechanics, describing the motion of atomic and subatomic bodies (neutrons, protons, electrons, and quarks). Because motion applies to all matter and energy, the implications of its further exploration cannot be underestimated. **MK**

Gravity
Sir Isaac Newton

The force that attracts a body toward any other physical body having mass

According to the Law of Universal Gravity, formulated by English physicist and mathematician Sir Isaac Newton (1643–1727), every two material objects attract each other with a force proportional to the product of their masses, and inversely proportional to the square of the distance between them. Gravity is a natural phenomenon: it keeps the Earth in orbit around the sun, the moon in orbit around the Earth, and accounts for other, equally significant, phenomena, such as the rise and fall of sea levels to create tides.

There have been theories about gravitation since ancient times. Italian physicist, mathematician, and astronomer Galileo Galilei (1564–1642) was among the first to examine the process of free and restricted fall. However, it was Newton who showed how a universal force, gravity, applied to all objects in all parts of the universe. Newton's Law of Universal Gravity, expressed in his *Philosophiae Naturalis Principia Mathematica* (Mathematical Principles of Natural Philosophy, 1687), overturned previous classical theories and heralded the modern quantitative science of gravitation.

The applications of Newton's Law have been many and diverse. Newton himself used it in *Principia Mathematica* to demonstrate that comets move in parabolic orbits under the gravitational attraction of the sun. In the nineteenth century, astronomers used the Law to predict the existence of the planet Neptune. Years later, however, Newton's theory was shown to have discrepancies when it failed to account for the orbit of Mercury.

In 1915, German theoretical physicist Albert Einstein (1879–1955) resolved the discrepancies with his General Theory of Relativity, which provides a unified description of gravity as a geometric property of space and time, or spacetime. Nevertheless, Newton's theory unaltered remains perfectly adequate as a means of describing gravity for most applications. **CK**

↑ An engraving from *c.* 1880, offering an artist's impression of Sir Isaac Newton thinking about gravity after seeing an apple fall in the orchard at his home.

"Rational Mechanics will be the science of motions resulting from any forces whatsoever, and of the forces required to produce any motions, accurately proposed and demonstrated."

Sir Isaac Newton, *Principia Mathematica* (1687)

Tabula Rasa
John Locke

People are born with minds that hold no preconceived notions

The Latin term *tabula rasa* refers to a blank slate, or literally a tablet from which all markings have been erased. In philosophy, "tabula rasa" expresses the idea that humans have an uninformed mind at birth and acquire beliefs only through experience, sensation, and reflection. While the mind is capable of learning and developing its own thoughts, or creating more complex thoughts from simpler ones, no thoughts are inherent. All people, in this respect, are born equal.

In 1689, John Locke (1632–1704) published *An Essay Concerning Human Understanding*, in which he stated that the mind is like slate scraped free of all markings, a tabula rasa. Prior to Locke, thinkers such as Aristotle wrote about similar concepts as early as 350 BCE. Locke himself was influenced by the work of Arabic writer

"Let us suppose the mind to be, as we say, white paper, void of all characters."

John Locke, *An Essay*... (1689)

and philosopher Ibn Tufail (*c.* 1105–85), who wrote a story of a child isolated on an island who developed from the state of a blank slate into an adult. Tabula rasa informed the empiricist school of philosophy, one that posits all knowledge derives from experience.

The idea of a person existing as a blank sheet of paper waiting to be filled with ideas is a powerful one. The assumption that knowledge is acquired, and that people are free to create their own beliefs and make their own choices, allows for the justification of social phenomena, such as legal systems that hold people accountable for their actions, and political structures that recognize legal equality regardless of status. Yet we also know that genetic and environmental factors influence our ideas, and what we acquire versus what we are born with is still debated today. **MT**

Empiricism
John Locke

The notion that what is perceived by the senses forms the foundation of knowledge

In contrast with the notion that knowledge begins as tradition and innate ideas, empiricism stresses the role of experience and evidence, especially sensory experience, in forming ideas. Empiricists argue that tradition and innate ideas arise from previous sensory experience, and that perceptions of the physical world are supported by experience. For example, if the sky is presented visually to an individual as blue, that individual registers the experience and appearance, while forming the belief that the sky is blue. However, this view of the world encounters problems with knowledge that cannot be attained in such a way, for example mathematical knowledge.

English philosopher John Locke (1632–1704) believed that the mind begins as a *tabula rasa* (blank

"It matters not what men's fancies are, it is the knowledge of things that is ... prized."

John Locke, *An Essay*... (1689)

slate) and that humans do not have innate ideas. This idea was influenced by the Greek philosopher Aristotle (384–322 BCE), and expounded in Locke's *An Essay Concerning Human Understanding* (1689). Locke's empiricism was opposed to the rationalist (Cartesian) philosophy of French philosopher and mathematician René Descartes (1596–1650).

Locke's essay was criticized by contemporary philosophers. However, the work is regarded as one of the foundations of empiricism in modern philosophy and laid the groundwork for subsequent British empiricists, notably David Hume (1711–76). Eventually, empiricism eclipsed Cartesianism, although in the 1920s logical empiricists attempted to synthesize the theories of British empiricists with the scientific methodology of logic and mathematics. **CK**

Allegories of Taste, Hearing, and Touch (1404) by Jan Brueghel the Elder. ➜

Religious Tolerance
John Locke

No one should be denied equal rights on account of their religion

⬆ Sir Godfrey Kneller's portrait of John Locke, 1697. Kneller was the leading portraitist in England during the late seventeenth and early eighteenth centuries.

The idea of religious tolerance is to allow religious freedom—in civil terms, to leave the adherents of a particular religion unmolested in private and in public. In a political sense, it means granting equal rights to individuals regardless of their religious beliefs.

In 1689, English philosopher and physician John Locke (1632–1704) advocated religious tolerance in his *Epistola de Tolerantia* (A Letter Concerning Toleration). He wrote the letter, addressed to an anonymous "Honoured Sir," while in exile in Holland, which was a secular state that permitted religious differences. The recipient of Locke's letter was his friend, the Dutch theologian Philipp van Limborch (1633–1712), who published it. At that time, there were fears that Roman Catholicism might take over England. Locke was involved in helping draft the English Bill of Rights of 1689, but it did not go as far as he wanted regarding religious tolerance. The same year, Parliament passed the Toleration Act, which granted freedom of worship to Nonconformists, such as Baptists and Congregationalists, but not to Catholics and Unitarians. Locke suggested that religious tolerance might resolve the problems experienced by both government and religious leaders, and that there should be a separation between church and state.

Locke's letter caused a controversy among members of the Anglican High Church. Clergyman and writer Thomas Long thought that the letter was part of a Jesuit plot aimed at enabling the Catholic Church to achieve dominance by causing chaos. There followed a protracted published correspondence between Locke and clergyman and academic Jonas Proast (c. 1640–1710), who asserted that the state had the right to use force to make dissenters reflect on the merits of Anglicanism. Locke's ideas came to form the basis of modern views on the toleration of religious differences. **CK**

> *"No man can be a Christian ... without that faith which works ... by love."*
>
> John Locke, *A Letter Concerning Toleration* (1689)

Primary and Secondary Qualities
John Locke

Our perception of objects depends partly on them and partly on our own senses

By making changes to our senses (eyesight, hearing, smell, taste, and touch), different ideas are produced in our minds. For example, a mug previously seen as white will look yellowish to a person who has developed jaundice; and if a person were to exchange eardrums for a bat's echo-location system, the mental images of objects that it would produce would be quite unfamiliar. And yet, we do not typically believe that objects change just because the instruments used to perceive them change. These examples suggest that, contrary to what we naturally think, much of what we perceive depends on our sensory organs and not on the way the world actually is.

In *An Essay Concerning Human Understanding* (1689), the English philosopher and physician John Locke (1632–1704) names the properties of objects (such as shape, sound, volume, and scent) as "qualities," with each having the "power to produce ideas in our minds." Locke distinguishes two types of qualities: those that do not depend on our senses (number, shape, volume, velocity) and those that do (color, sound, scent, taste, texture). The former he calls "primary qualities," by which he means powers in objects to produce ideas in our minds, and the latter he calls "secondary qualities," by which he means powers in ourselves to produce ideas in our minds. This distinction allows Locke to explain variations in sense perceptions among perceivers, and in the same perceiver under different circumstances. It also enables him to explain discrepancies in memories.

The distinction between primary and secondary qualities is part of Locke's empiricist epistemology (study of knowledge) and is central to what became known as the Representation Theory of Perception. Vestiges of Locke's epistemology, now thought to be discredited in parts, still play a role in contemporary psychological explanations of perception. **JW**

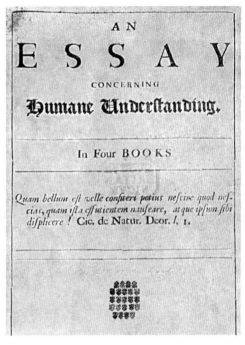

⬆ The title page to John Locke's *An Essay Concerning Human Understanding* (1689). The first explicit formulation of an empiricist philosophy, the *Essay* has been hugely influential.

"...[T]he Ideas of primary Qualities of Bodies, are Resemblances of them, and their Patterns do really exist in the Bodies themselves; but the Ideas, produced in us by these Secondary Qualities, have no resemblance to them at all."

John Locke, *An Essay Concerning Human Understanding* (1689)

Nature of Personal Identity
John Locke

The only constant in personal identity is continually renewed consciousness

The English philosopher and physician John Locke (1632–1704) was the first thinker to theorize that personal identity, or the self, depends on consciousness rather than material substance or the soul. Locke argued that a person's consciousness of their present thoughts and actions is what conceives the self, which extends to past consciousness using memory. Although consciousness can be lost by forgetfulness, the soul or substance remains the same.

Locke explored the theory in *An Essay Concerning Human Understanding* (1689). He asserted that personal identity cannot be founded in substance because a person's body changes throughout life while the person remains the same. To illustrate this, he used the example of a man who has had his finger cut off. The man is not

"[Identity lies] not in the identity of substance, but ... in the identity of consciousness ..."

John Locke, *An Essay ...* (1689)

conscious of anything that occurs to the cut-off finger, so his consciousness does not lie in substance. Locke argued that no two things of the same kind can exist at the same time, so personal identity is founded on the repeated act of consciousness. He also argued that only an individual can know their own consciousness; others cannot judge that person because they can never know the person's consciousness.

Locke's theory was revolutionary at the time. Ever since, philosophers have attempted to theorize what constitutes the self. Scottish philosopher David Hume (1711–76) went on to examine the issue in *A Treatise of Human Nature* (1739), arguing that the notion of self is a fiction. In modern times, Canadian academic James Giles, has proposed a no-self theory that eliminates the concept of personal identity altogether. **CK**

Liberalism
Various

The notion that society is best left to look after itself, with minimal state intervention

Humans have long believed that a single person, or small group of people, has the insight necessary to make the lives of people in a society better than they can accomplish for themselves. In many instances this belief led to large numbers living in poverty, or even being exterminated for the sake of the "general welfare." After the Enlightenment, however, a liberal tradition (from the Latin *liber*, or "free") took shape from the philosophical views of John Locke (1632–1704), Jean-Jacques Rousseau (1712–78), and Adam Smith (1723–90).

Liberalism is a description of the role of government in a society, and is contrasted with socialism and monarchy. The idea is that if individuals are free to pursue their interests—with government supplying only protection from fraud and coercion—they will

"No one ought to harm another in his life, health, liberty, or possessions."

John Locke, *Second Treatise of Civil Government* (1690)

efficiently provide many of the things everyone wants. This "invisible hand" theory of production and its implied freedom of expression are credited with the sharp increase in quality of life in the West since the Industrial Revolution (1760–1840).

Anti-liberalists argue that people will pursue things that are not objectively valuable, such as fast food, pornography, drugs, and money, and some conclude that significant government intervention is necessary. Liberals such as Ludwig von Mises (1881–1973) disagree, saying that there are no objective "judgments of value, but [only] the valuations actually manifested by people in buying or not buying." Liberalism runs against anyone who attempts to enlist the power of government to promote values, to raise taxes, or to prohibit "harmful" products, such as cigarettes and alcohol. **JW**

   A View of the House of Commons, engraved by B. Cole in the eighteenth century. ➜

Φ

Parallelism
Gottfried Wilhelm Leibniz

The notion that mental events and physical events are perfectly coordinated by God

In the philosophy of mind, parallelism is the theory that events in the world occur because of the action of God. The mind and the body are understood as two systems running in parallel, and not affecting each other causally. If a person has an intention (in the mind) that he or she acts upon (with the body), according to the theory of parallelism it is God who causes that event, an action that is appropriate to the intention, to occur.

Parallelism is most associated with the German mathematician and philosopher Gottfried Wilhelm Leibniz (1646–1716), who outlined the theory in a series of works: *Specimen dynamicum* (A specimen of dynamics, 1695), *Essais de Théodicée sur la bonté de Dieu, la liberté de l'homme et l'origine du mal* (Essays

of Theodicy on the Goodness of God, the Freedom of Man and the Origin of Evil, 1710), and *Monadologia* (Monadology, 1714). Leibniz asserted that there exists a perfect correlation between mind and body that was ensured by God at the beginning of time in a "pre-established harmony." Consequently, nothing in the universe influences anything else. The theory is in keeping with his doctrine of monadology, in which the world is made up of incorporeal mindlike entities that he called "monads." Leibniz believed that God created the mind (a single monad) and the body (a collection of monads) in perfect harmony. Thus, their mental and physical states would always correspond in an appropriate fashion.

The theory of parallelism never became popular among philosophers. It has encountered criticism because it conflicts with the empirical procedures of modern science (experience seems to provide ample evidence that the mind and body affect each other). However, some religious believers uphold the theory because it affords their God—who is concerned with the happiness of his subjects—the honor they believe is due to Him as the ruler of the universe. **CK**

A detail from the Triptych of St. Aignan in the Treasury at Chartres Cathedral, showing the Hands of God. ⬆

Voodoo
African slaves in Saint-Domingue

An occult combination of the ideas of shamanistic religion and Catholicism

Voodoo is a Caribbean religion mixing the shamanistic practices of West African Vodun with some elements of Roman Catholicism. Vodun, as practiced in West Africa, has a large pantheon of gods or spirits, including the remote Creator-God (*Bondye*), the actor-gods (*loa*), and the ancestral spirits (*vudu*). As with all shamanistic traditions, Vodun is concerned with both honoring beneficial spirits (who can be communicated with via the shaman, or *bokor*) and suppressing or appeasing the harmful spirits (who are conjured up by the evil shaman, or witch doctor).

When European slavers, in this case the French, came to West Africa and hauled away large groups of Vodun practitioners at the end of the seventeenth century, these parishioners were obliged to practice Catholicism, as stated in King Louis IV's *Code Noir* (1685), which defined the conditions of French slaves. As a result, Vodun practitioners in Saint-Domingue began to call themselves Catholics and adopted many Catholic rituals while privately continuing to practice a modified form of Vodun, called Voodoo.

Voodoo identifies *Bondye* with the biblical Yahweh, but devotes most of its worship to the *loa* actor-gods who are a combination of lesser African deities and Catholic saints. In keeping with its shamanistic roots, Voodoo emphasizes communication with beneficial spirits. This, among other ways, can be achieved when the shaman, through music, dance, and drugs, becomes possessed by the desired spirit.

Voodoo has been influential for two reasons. First, although not a pure African religion, it is probably the most widely known African religion. And second, it introduced to the world of pop culture things such as Voodoo dolls (dolls in the likeness of a human which, when activated, are thought to affect the actual human) and zombies ("the living corpses" that are raised up by the spirit-possessed shaman). **AB**

⬆ A twentieth-century painting of a Voodoo ritual.

Biblical Textual Criticism
Various theologians

The study of Judeo-Christian manuscripts in order to determine the authentic text of the Bible

⬆ Cover of the oldest complete codex of the Hebrew Bible, dating from *c.* 1010. The Hebrew Bible is organized into three main sections: the Torah, the Nevi'im, and the Ketuvim.

Early Jews often destroyed or buried their religious texts, and early Christians usually wrote theirs on papyrus, a material that is easily eroded, meaning that little of the original material for the Bible remains. The earliest copies of the Old and New Testaments date to the fourth century, when parchment was introduced. As copies were made by generations of scribes, errors were introduced. Some were involuntary mistakes, and some were perhaps the result of attempts to elucidate a passage that the person transcribing did not understand; others were intentional, maybe to favor an opinion or doctrine.

Biblical textual criticism attempts to restore the Bible as near as possible to the original text by studying ancient Judeo-Christian manuscripts, such as the Dead Sea Scrolls (*c.* 150 BCE–70 CE) and the Codex Vaticanus (*c.* 325–350), and reconstructing the text in its original form upon leaving the hands of its author. Where there are several variants, textual critics opt for that which best agrees with the context and most closely conforms to the style of the author. Biblical textual criticism was developed around the start of the eighteenth century with the work of theologians John Mill (*c.* 1645–1707), Johann Albrecht Bengel (1687–1752), Johann Jakob Wettstein (1693–1754), Johann Salomo Semler (1725–91), and Johann Jakob Griesbach (1745– 1812).

The Catholic Church endorsed biblical textual criticism in 1943 when Pope Pius XII called for new translations of the Bible from the original languages as the basis for all Catholic vernacular translations, rather than merely the Latin Vulgate of St. Jerome. This initiated a period of Catholic study regarding the authorship, dating, and genealogy of Judeo-Christian manuscripts. As the texts to be examined increases with discoveries of manuscripts, so the debate on what constitutes a definitive text continues. **CK**

"[Textual criticism] is also quite rightly employed in the case of the Sacred Books."

Pope Pius XII, *Inspired by the Holy Spirit* (1943)

Newton's Color Wheel

Sir Isaac Newton

A device developed by Newton to demonstrate that light is composed of seven colors

The Newton color wheel is a disk of seven colored segments: red, orange, yellow, green, blue, indigo, and violet. When the disk is spun quickly, the colors blur together and the eye cannot distinguish between the individual bands of color and perceives white. The wheel is named after its inventor, English physicist Isaac Newton (1642–1727), and first appeared in his well-known work *Opticks* (1704). He discovered that when a ray of white light is bent, or refracted, through a prism, it separates into a continuous gradation of seven colors, or spectral hues. Newton created a two-dimensional circular model merging the red and violet colors at each end of the band of colors to form a hue circle, or color wheel. The size of each segment differed according to his calculations of its wavelength and of its corresponding width in the spectrum. When mixing pigments of opposite colors on the wheel—the complementary colors—Newton found that "some faint anonymous color" resulted. He was unable to mix pigments of opposite hues on the wheel to make white because pigments are based on subtractive color, unlike light, which is additive color. He surmised that complementary colors cancel out each other's hue.

His concept was demonstrated more thoroughly in the nineteenth century by physicists and color theorists, such as Ogden Rood (1831–1902). Rood's book *Modern Chromatics* (1879) includes the Rood color wheel. He emphasized that artists needed a knowledge of complementary hues in order to be able to reveal applied colors in their natural brilliance. A version of Newton's color wheel without the indigo hue was adopted by painters to describe complementary colors that cancel each other's hue to produce an achromatic mixture of white, gray, or black. Newton's color wheel was used in the study of mixing color. Knowledge of how complementary colors work together led to art movements such as Pointillism in *c.* 1886. **CK**

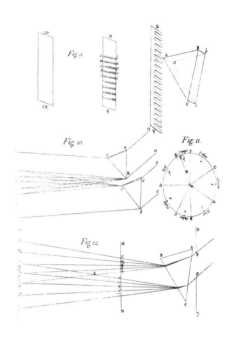

⬆ In these diagrams from *Opticks* (1704), Isaac Newton illustrated the color wheel (center right) and showed how a prism refracts white light into seven spectral hues.

"All colors are the friends of their neighbors and the lovers of their opposites."

Marc Chagall, artist

Pi
William Jones

A mathematical constant that is the ratio of a circle's circumference to its diameter

The mathematical constant pi has been represented by the Greek letter "π" since the mid-eighteenth century, but it is sometimes still written as "pi." Pi is irrational, meaning it is not equal to the ratio of any two whole numbers. It is equal to approximately 3.14159, and an approximation such as 22/7 is often used for everyday calculations. Pi is used for mathematical problems involving the lengths of arcs, curves, and solid volumes. It is also employed in physics and engineering.

Pi has been used by mathematicians since ancient times: the Babylonians used 3.125 to approximate pi in *c.* 2000 BCE. By the seventeenth century, new methods of mathematical analysis provided better ways of calculating pi, and British mathematicians William Oughtred (1575–1660), Isaac Barrow (1630–77),

"The digits of pi march to infinity in a predestined yet unfathomable code."
Richard Preston, *The New Yorker* (1992)

and David Gregory (1659–1708) all used π as a symbol to describe the circumference of a circle. In 1706, Welsh mathematician William Jones (1675–1749)—in his *Synopsis Palmariorum Matheseos* (A New Introduction to the Mathematics)—defined π as the ratio of a circle's circumference to its diameter. Swiss mathematician and physicist Leonhard Euler (1707–83) adopted the symbol in around 1736, and π finally came into common usage.

In 1748, Euler's book *Introductio in analysis infinitorum* (Introduction to the Analysis of Infinities) included an important equation known as "Euler's Identity," which incorporated π and related it to the chief symbols in mathematics at that time. In 1910, Indian mathematician Srinivasa Ramanujan (1887–1920) developed ways of calculating pi, and, in 1934, the pi symbol π was adopted internationally. **CK**

To Be Is To Be Perceived
George Berkeley

The concept that something exists only if it can be perceived by a perceiver

In philosophy, "to be is to be perceived" is the idea that there are only two elements involved in perception: the perceiver and what is perceived. Such a view discounts material objects, advocating that only the ideas that people perceive directly are real.

The phrase *esse est percipi (aut percipere)*—to be is to be perceived (or to perceive)—was coined by Anglo-Irish philosopher Bishop George Berkeley (1685–1753). Known for his immaterialism—the apparent denial of the reality of any external world—he was unconvinced by the philosophical ideas of René Descartes (1596–1650) and John Locke (1632–1704), regarding what he saw as their representationalist theories on perception. The two men distinguished between the material and the ideas by which people perceive it, which Berkeley thought led to skepticism and atheism.

Berkeley wanted to show that the world exists even if no one is looking at it, because for him the world was a collection of ideas perceived by God's mind. He attacked representalism in his *Treatise Concerning the Principles of Human Knowledge* (1710), attempting to refute Locke's belief that general terms signify abstract ideas. For Berkeley, the mind knows ideas, not objects. There are three types of ideas: sensation, thought, and imagination. When various ideas are associated, they are considered to be one thing, which is given a name to signify it. Berkeley did not deny the existence of an ordinary object, such as a chair, which he asserted is perceived by visual ideas regarding form and shape, tangible ideas regarding texture, and so on. He advocated that there is a physical world containing such ordinary objects, rather than a material world. The physical world is dependent on the mind because it consists of ideas that exist because they are perceived. Today, Berkeley is regarded as the father of idealism because he saw reality as a mental construction. **CK**

Optimism
Gottfried Wilhelm Leibniz

The theory that we live in the best of all possible worlds, which includes a belief that the universe is improving and that good will ultimately triumph over evil

In philosophy, the concept of optimism arose in the eighteenth century. Philosophical optimists assert that we live in the best of all possible worlds created by God, who consistently chooses the best for a good reason, and does so freely. The theory is that there must be sufficient reason for everything in the world. In this worldview, Adam sinned of his own free will in the Garden of Eden by eating the apple, but God knew that Adam would sin, and so the rest of the world was built around the consequences of that sinful action. Although humans are imperfect and predisposed to evil, they are still able to identify true good and so correct their errors. Evil is thus necessary to bring out the goodness in humanity.

Optimism is most associated with the German mathematician and philosopher Gottfried Wilhelm Leibniz (1646–1716). He coined the phrase "the best of all possible worlds" in his work *Essais de Théodicée sur la bonté de Dieu, la liberté de l'homme et l'origine du mal* (Essays of Theodicy on the Goodness of God, the Freedom of Man and the Origin of Evil, 1710), in which he attempted to explain the problem of evil and how it does not conflict with God's goodness. Some atheists had argued that, because evil is incompatible with God, the existence of evil is proof that God does not exist. Leibniz was trying to demonstrate that the presence of evil in the world was still compatible with an omniscient, omnipotent, and good God.

Leibniz's idea of optimism inspired French writer Voltaire (1694–1778) to write *Candide, ou l'Optimisme* (Candide: or, Optimism, 1759). The novel satirizes Leibniz and tells the story of a young man, Candide, who is indoctrinated with Leibnizian optimism by his mentor, Doctor Pangloss. However, Candide experiences great hardship. The novel gave rise to the term "Panglossian" to describe someone who is overly optimistic. **CK**

E S S A I S
DE
THÉODICÉE
SUR LA
BONTÉ DE DIEU,
LA
LIBERTÉ DE L'HOMME
ET
L'ORIGINE DU MAL.

A AMSTERDAM,
Chez ISAAC TROYEL, Libraire.
M D C C X.

⬆ The title page of Gottfried Wilhelm Leibniz's *Essays of Theodicy on the Goodness of God, the Freedom of Man and the Origin of Evil* (1710).

"If there were no best among all possible worlds, God would not have created one."

Gottfried Wilhelm Leibniz, *Essays of Theodicy on the Goodness of God, the Freedom of Man and the Origin of Evil* (1710)

Steam Power
Thomas Newcomen

Harnessing the properties of steam to power mechanical devices

The notion that steam, produced by heating water, might be channeled to provide driving force was first demonstrated by Hero of Alexandria in the first century CE. His device, called the aeolipile, was a hollow globe that spun by force of escaping steam jets. The use of steam, fed under pressure into the confined space of a cylinder to expand the air within it and force a piston to move, was no more than a sophisticated development of the idea of the aeolipile. The difference was that the aeolipile was little more than an interesting toy, whereas the steam-powered piston would become the mighty driving force of the Industrial Revolution.

In 1698, English engineer Thomas Savery (c. 1650–1715) built a steam-powered pump to extract water from mine shafts. The device, which became known

"Those who admire modern civilization usually identify it with the steam engine."

George Bernard Shaw, *Man and Superman* (1903)

as the "Miner's Friend," not only used the expansion of steam to force forward a piston, which in turn pumped water from the mine, but also condensed the steam in the cylinder with internal cold-water sprinklers to create a vacuum. As well as drawing back the piston, the vacuum was harnessed to extract additional water from the mine via a valve in the cylinder. However, the rudimentary pressurized boiler was liable to explode.

The first truly successful engine for driving a pump and removing water from mines was the atmospheric steam engine, invented by English ironmonger Thomas Newcomen (1664–1729). This created a vacuum inside a cylinder that pulled down a piston; a lever transferred that force to a pump shaft that descended into the mine. Newcomen installed his first atmospheric steam engine at a mine in Staffordshire in 1712. **CK**

Monadology
Gottfried Wilhelm Leibniz

The view that reality is made up of monads, or hypothetical, intelligent, whole entities

Monadology is the name for any system sharing the concept of a monad. In philosophy, monads are indestructible, soul-like, self-sufficient substances that reflect the world's order. They make up the universe but lack spatial exten§sion and are immaterial. A monad cannot be split because it is a unified whole without parts; in the material world atoms can be split into smaller particles because they are formed of parts.

Although ancient Greek philosophers used the term "monad," it was popularized in the eighteenth century by German philosopher and mathematician Gottfried Wilhelm Leibniz (1646–1716). He wanted to reconcile the theories of the philosophers Baruch Spinoza (1632–77) and René Descartes (1596–1650) regarding the nature of matter. Leibniz began using the term "monad" in 1675

"The monad … is nothing but a simple substance, which enters into compounds."

Gottfried Wilhelm Leibniz, *Monadology* (1714)

and by 1690 conceived monadism. He published his doctrine in his work *Monadologia* (Monadology, 1714). Leibniz asserted that "all matter is interlinked and each body feels the effects of everything that happens in the universe." He argued that a living thing is a body that has a monad as its soul, and that objects in the material world are collections of monads. Leibniz believed that the universe works metaphysically, referencing God, rather than materially, referencing nature.

Various philosophers have used Leibniz's concept of the monad to describe an unseen force. In modern times, the intellectual structure of monadology has been applied to physics because it provides a model for subjectivity and the role of the perceiver. It has led to the rise of quantum monadology as scientists investigate the nature of consciousness and time. **CK**

Rococo
France

A playful architectural, literary, and artistic style

Rococo is a lighthearted style of art, architecture, literature, landscape design, and music that emerged in France after the death of King Louis XIV (1638–1715). It achieved its greatest expression in the decorative arts and architecture, reaching its peak in the 1770s. Rococo was a reaction to the pomp and grandeur of Baroque, and the word "Rococo" is a fusion of the French word *rocaille* (a style of ornamentation with pebbles and shells) and *barocco* (the Italian for Baroque.) Originally, Rococo was a pejorative term, coined when the style was going out of fashion in favor of Neoclassicism.

As the French court distanced itself from Louis XIV's excesses, court artists developed the playful style that became known as Rococo. In France, Rococo's leading exponents were the artists Jean-Antoine Watteau

"The serpentine line ... waving and winding ... leads the eye in a pleasing manner ..."

William Hogarth, *The Analysis of Beauty* (1753)

(1684–1721), François Boucher (1703–70), and Jean-Honoré Fragonard (1732–1806). Published engravings of their work caused interest in Rococo to spread through Europe, influencing painters such as the Italian Giambattista Tiepolo (1696–1770) and Englishman Thomas Gainsborough (1727–88). Architects introduced Rococo's sinuous S-shaped curves into interiors of delicate white stucco adornments. In literature, also, the narrative structure of novels such as *The Life and Opinions of Tristram Shandy, Gentleman* (1759–67), by Laurence Sterne (1713–68), adopted Rococo's free, expressive style. In the early 1760s, Rococo was criticized by leading figures in France for its superficial content and romantic subject matter. Rococo became associated with the degeneracy of the *ancién regime* in France, and it fell out of fashion across Europe. **CK**

Freemasonry
England

A secret fraternal organization with roots in deism

Freemasonry is a secret fraternal order with a structure based on ancient religious orders and chivalric brotherhoods. The order is organized into Grand Lodges, or Orients, in charge of constituent Lodges. Officers in a Lodge are titled worshipful master, senior and junior warden, and tiler. Ordinary freemasons can be an apprentice, fellow of the craft, or a master mason. Members are adult males, who are required to believe in the existence of a supreme being and the immortality of the soul. Freemasonry bears many of the trappings and teachings of a religion, and masons have "to obey the moral law." Masons recognize each other using secret signs, words, and handshakes.

The term "freemason" dates to the fourteenth century and means a mason of superior skill. Later it

"A Mason is to be a peaceable subject to the civil powers, wherever he resides or works ..."

The Constitutions of the Free Masons (1723)

came to describe someone who enjoyed the privileges of belonging to a trade guild. The modern term "freemasonry" came into use in the mid-eighteenth century to refer to the secret society that dates to the constitution of the Grand Lodge of England, which was founded in London on June 24, 1717.

By the 1730s, freemasonry had spread to North America (the earliest known Grand Lodge was in Pennsylvania) and to Europe (the Grand Orient de France was established in 1733). Freemasonry now exists in various forms throughout the world. Where freemasonry is influential, there has been criticism that members systematically prefer other members for job appointments, to the detriment of civic equality and public interest. Freemasonry has also been criticized by religious institutions for its deistic aspects. **CK**

Stages of History
Giambattista Vico

Human society develops in cycles with gains inevitably giving way to corruption

The theory of the stages of history was formed by Italian political philosopher, rhetorician, and historian Giambattista Vico (1668–1744), and was outlined in his book *Scienza Nuova* (The New Science, 1725). The idea is that human history passes through connected stages, together identified by a pattern of growth and decay. Vico suggests that society goes through a "bestial" stage in which it is ruled by a belief in the supernatural; then an "age of heroes," in which society is divided into ruling and underling classes among which defensive alliances are formed; and finally, an "age of men," in which there is class conflict. The lower class achieves equal rights, but only as the result of corruption, and so society may then fall back into an earlier stage of the cycle. At this point, the process starts again.

"The nature of peoples is first crude, then severe, then benign [and] finally dissolute."

Giambattista Vico

A Catholic, Vico believed that providence had a guiding hand in events, righting matters when necessary to help humanity to survive the successive cycles. Vico's stance was against the Cartesian school of thought that prevailed at the time, which he believed failed to take into account the importance of language, myth, and history in interpreting the past.

Vico's book had little impact at the time of publication but was later read by German Romantic theorists, including Johann Wolfgang von Goethe (1749–1832), who were drawn to his vision of human history. *The New Science* went on to inspire various thinkers and artists, notably German economist and historian Karl Marx (1818–83), whose economic interpretation of history was influenced by it, although Marx differed in his view of the benefits of religion. **CK**

Mechanical Programmability
Basile Bouchon

The automation of complicated instructions for machines

In many complicated industrial operations, the setting-up of the machines involved can take as much time as is needed for the machines to perform. With mechanical programmability, the means of controlling the actions of numerous interacting components, and quickly changing their operations, may be set up in advance. For the worker, activating mechanical programs is far easier than setting up machine operations from scratch.

Mechanical programmability is said to have begun in the ninth century, with the invention of a musical organ, powered by water, that automatically played interchangeable cylinders with pins (similar to those of musical boxes). However, the automation of mechanical processes arose in the eighteenth century. In 1725, French textile worker Basile Bouchon

"Punched card accounting was the first serious attempt to convert data ..."

George A. Fierheller, industry leader

invented what is considered to be the first industrial application of a semiautomated machine. He worked at a silk center in Lyon and devised a way of controlling a loom with a perforated paper loop that established the pattern to be reproduced in the cloth. His invention automated the setting-up process of a drawloom, whereby operators lifted the warp threads using cords.

Unfortunately, the number of needles used was insufficient to allow larger designs to be weaved. Also, one tear in the perforated paper loop made the loop unusable. However, in 1728, Bouchon's assistant, Jean-Baptiste Falcon, improved the design; he expanded the number of cords that could be handled by arranging the holes in rows, and replaced the paper roll with rectangular perforated cardboard cards joined in a loop, which made it easier to change the program. **CK**

A model of the mechanically programmed loom designed by Jean-Baptiste Falcon in 1728. ➡

Euler's Number (*e*)
Leonhard Euler

A mathematical constant that lies at the foundation of the natural logarithm

Euler's Number, also known as the number *e*, is a mathematical constant, approximately equal to 2.71828, which is the base of the natural logarithm. A logarithm turns complicated sums involving multiplication into simpler ones involving addition, and complicated sums involving division into simpler ones involving subtraction. The number *e* is important in mathematics and has numerous applications in probability theory, derangements, and asymptotics. The exponential function is used to calculate compound interest for example, and the number *e* is used to perform differential and integral calculus.

Swiss mathematician and physicist Leonhard Euler (1707–83) introduced the number *e* as the basis for natural logarithms in a letter he wrote in 1731. The

> *"Both mechanics and analysis are . . . augmented more than just a little."*

Leonhard Euler, *Mechanica* (1736)

first time the number *e* was used as a constant in a published work was in 1736 in Euler's *Mechanica*. He later linked the number's logarithmic function with its exponential function in his book *Introductio in analysis infinitorum* (Introduction to the Analysis of Infinities, 1748), in which he advanced the use of infinitesimals and infinite quantities in mathematical analysis. Euler's appreciation of the importance of introducing uniform analytic methods into mechanics helped mathematicians to solve problems in a clear way.

In 2010, a computation performed by Japanese systems engineer and academic Shigeru Kondo (b. 1955) listed the number of known decimal digits of the number *e* as 1,000,000,000,000. The computation took Kondo 224 hours—more than nine days—and he then took another 219 hours to verify it. **CK**

Bell Curve
Abraham de Moivre

A form of statistical representation that identifies the norm, or golden mean

The "bell curve" is a means of portraying probability distribution; its main purpose is to show how most features follow natural patterns, hovering around an average occurence and declining exponentially as they move away from the norm. This, when plotted on a graph, results in a bell shape, referred to as the "de Moivre distribution," named after Abraham de Moivre (1667–1754), who proposed its formula in 1733.

A century later, in 1833, German mathematician Carl Friedrich Gauss (1777–1855) theorized that, statistically, probabilities would congregate about a norm. His theory was seized upon by ideologists, who wanted to show that harmonies gathered in neat and proper order around a measured, golden mean; they longed for a verifiable ideal to which social, political, and

> *"The bell curve . . . is more than a technical description. It shapes our thought."*

Ulrich Beck, *World at Risk* (2009)

economic aims could aspire. The post-Enlightenment influence of Gauss's idea was huge: large, unpredictable deviations (outliers) are rare and came to be more or less dismissed as enthusiasm for the smooth curve of the bell grew. In a world that humanity had begun to manage by means of description, it offered a significant improvement in the ordering of knowledge.

Sadly, outliers do, sometimes, throw predictability askew, as seen in the economic crash of 2008. Divergence from the mean does not necessarily imply error. What ought to occur is no predictor of what will occur, and mediocrity is not the goal of natural or social evolution: divergence is normal. Unpredictable change is what we have to live with, and, in this respect, outside mathematical theory, the bell curve has been more of a liability than a blessing to understanding. **LW**

Graph Theory
Leonhard Euler

An abstract representation of mathematical objects with linked related coordinates

Graph theory is a branch of mathematics concerned with networks of points connected by lines—it does not relate to graphs used to represent statistical data, such as bar graphs or pie charts. The field of graph theory originated in 1736, when the Swiss mathematician Leonhard Euler (1707–83) published his solution to the Königsberg bridge problem in the Russian journal *Commentarii Academiae Scientiarum Imperialis Petropolitanae*. The problem, an old puzzle, asked whether it was possible to find a route through the city of Königsberg that entailed crossing each of its seven bridges only once. By considering the problem abstractly and using points and connecting lines to represent the land and bridges, Euler proved by means of a graph that it was impossible.

"The origins of graph theory are humble, even frivolous ..."

Graph Theory 1736–1936 (1976)

Graphs provided a simple means of representing the relationships between objects, and often the act of presenting a problem pictorially in this way could be all that was needed to find a solution. The term "graph" itself was coined in the nineteenth century by British mathematician James Joseph Sylvester (1814–97), who was interested in diagrams representing molecules.

Graph theory has since evolved into an extensive and popular branch of mathematics, with applications in computer science and the physical, biological, and social sciences. In 1936, exactly 200 years after Euler solved the problem of the Königsberg bridges, Hungarian mathematician Dénes König published the first ever book on graph theory, *Theorie der endlichen und unendlichen Graphen* (Theories of Finite and Infinite Graphs). **JF**

Is / Ought Fallacy
David Hume

A moral imperative ("ought") cannot derive from a statement of fact ("is")

The is/ought fallacy occurs when a conclusion reached expresses what ought to be, but is inferred from premises that state only what is so. Thus, can "is statements," the kind typically expressing facts, imply "ought statements," the type associated with morality? Most argue that the two are not interchangeable: in the statement A ought to be B, therefore C, C cannot be logically verified from the "ought" that connects A and B. Alice asks the Cheshire Cat, "Which way ought I to go from here?", but that is a bit odd since directions are factual things—they are "is" statements (the correct way), not moral prescriptions (the right way or good way). Things we ought to do are often culturally prescribed morals or duties, and therefore have no business in the realm of logic or science.

"If it was so, it might be; and if it were so, it would be; but as it isn't, it ain't. That's logic."

Lewis Carroll, *Alice's Adventures in Wonderland* (1865)

The fallacy was articulated by David Hume (1711– 76) and is often also called Hume's Law, or Hume's Guillotine. In *A Treatise of Human Nature* (1739), Hume noted the significant difference between factual or descriptive statements (the rose is red) and prescriptive or normative states (the rose ought to be pretty), and warned that we must exercise caution with such inferences when not told how the "ought" is derived from the "is" of the statement.

Hume's point was that no ethical conclusion could be validly inferred from any set of factual premises. He was alerting people to the slippery tongues of religious fanatics and con artists. So, if anything, Hume taught us to be on guard with language—to listen carefully to what others say, beware of shenanigans, and be ourselves careful to mean what we say. **KBJ**

Spiritualism
Emanuel Swedenborg

The belief that spirits of the dead can communicate with the living

⬆ A musical instrument is seen supposedly rising into the air at a seance in c. 1920. Many images showing "proof" of ghostly happenings were created using clever tricks of photography.

Belief in the possibility of communicating with the departed has been observed in various cultures for centuries. The belief system or religion known as spiritualism postulates that the spirits of the dead reside in a spirit world and can communicate with the living. Spiritualists seeking to make contact with the dead usually enlist the help of a medium, a person believed to possess a special ability to contact spirits directly. Spiritualists and mediums hold formal communication sessions, called seances, to speak with spirits.

Modern spiritualism stems from the work of Swedish scientist, Christian mystic, philosopher, and theologian Emanuel Swedenborg (1688–1772). In 1744, he had his first vision of Christ and so began his spiritual awakening. Swedenborg went on to have dreams and visions, during which he spoke to spirits and visited the spirit world. Swedenborg believed he was chosen to reveal the spiritual meaning of the Bible, which he attempted to do in a series of theological works, the first of which is *Arcana Coelestia* (Heavenly Arcana, written between 1749 and 1756).

After Swedenborg died, the first Swedenborgian societies appeared, founded by followers dedicated to the study of his teachings. Although Swedenborg did not advise people to seek contact with spirits, many people were inspired to do so by his writings. The practice of seeking contact with the dead through the aid of a medium spread. By the mid-nineteenth century, spiritualism was popular in the United States, France, and Britain, and the National Spiritualist Association was founded in 1893. Such was spiritualism's popularity that the Vatican condemned spiritualistic practices in 1898, claiming that attempts to contact the dead were blasphemous and related to the occult.

Spiritualist churches now exist worldwide. Services are generally conducted by a medium, and spiritualists meet to seek their spirit guide. **CK**

"By spirits man has communication with the world of spirits, and by angels, with heaven. Without communication . . . man can by no means live."

Emanuel Swedenborg, *Arcana Coelestia* (1749–56)

The Man-Machine
Julien Offray de La Mettrie

An extreme materialist view of human beings as having only a body and no soul

The idea of humans as machines arose in the eighteenth century. French philosopher and mathematician René Descartes (1596–1650) had suggested that the human body has material properties and works like a machine but that the mind, or soul, was not material and does not follow the laws of nature. The idea of the man-machine rejected this Cartesian view, regarding the dualism of body and mind, and denied the existence of the soul as a substance separate from matter.

The concept of the man-machine was put forward by French physician and philosopher Julien Offray de La Mettrie (1709–51) in his materialist manifesto *L'homme machine* (Man as Machine), first published anonymously in Holland in 1747 but dated 1748. La Mettrie's argument was informed by his clinical expertise and he approached philosophy from a medical standpoint. His provocative work challenged religious orthodoxy by dismissing the idea of humans having an animal or human soul. La Mettrie argued that they do not have free will but rather are automatons whose actions are determined by bodily states. He attacked the hypothesis of monadism proposed by German philosopher and mathematician Gottfried Wilhelm Leibniz (1646–1716) and his supporters as "incomprehensible," writing: "They have spiritualized matter rather than materializing the soul. How can we define a being whose nature is utterly unknown to us?"

La Mettrie's book caused a scandal and copies were burned in public. His philosophy was considered too radical by his contemporaries, and even other French philosophers turned against him, denouncing him as a lunatic. La Mettrie was forced to seek asylum in Berlin at the court of the Prussian King Frederick II, where he spent the rest of his life. La Mettrie's philosophy has undergone a resurgence of interest since the twentieth century with the advent of neuroscience and the study of cognitive systems. **CK**

⬆ A portrait of French philosopher Julien Offray de La Mettrie (1757), engraved in copper by Georg Friedrich Schmidt after Maurice Quentin de Latour.

"We think we are, and in fact we are, good men, only as we are gay or brave; everything depends on the way our machine is running."

Julien Offray de La Mettrie, *Man as Machine* (1748)

Thalassotherapy

Richard Russell

The notion that sea bathing is beneficial in treating physical and mental conditions

Thalassotherapy is a therapy based on the belief that bathing in the sea is beneficial to health. Practitioners believe that the trace elements of calcium, iodide, magnesium, potassium, and sodium found in seawater are absorbed through the skin. The minerals are thought to boost blood and lymph circulation, thus accelerating the metabolism and eliminating toxins. Thalassotherapy is carried out in both the sea and in spas that use hot seawater; sometimes marine mud or seaweed are applied. The therapy is aimed at arthritis, depression, eczema, muscular pain, psoriasis, and rheumatism.

Sea bathing dates back to ancient times, but English physician Richard Russell (1687–1759) was the first to document the medical benefits of seawater. A resident of Lewes in Sussex, England, he went to Brighton to

> "I have seen many patients relieved, and some cured, by the . . . use of sea water."

Richard Russell, *Glandular Diseases* (1752)

test his theories in 1747. Three years later, he published a dissertation in Latin, *De tabe glandurali sive de usu aquae marinae in morbis glandularum*, which advocated the use of seawater to cure enlarged lymphatic glands. This appeared in English in 1752 as "Glandular Diseases, or a Dissertation on the Use of Sea Water in the Affections of the Glands: Particularly the Scurvy, Jaundice, King's-evil, Leprosy, and the Glandular Consumption."

Russell's seawater cure was so popular that it initiated the development of seaside resorts, with wealthy Londoners flocking to towns on England's south coast, such as Brighton. The practice spread to the continent, and a French physician, Joseph La Bonnardière (1829–87), invented the term "thalassotherapy" in 1865, drawing on the Greek words *thalassa* (sea) and *therapeia* (treatment). **CK**

Separation of Powers

Montesquieu

The division of a government's powers into branches, each with its own responsibilities

How does a society, through its government, protect political liberty? For Charles-Louis de Secondat, Baron de Montesquieu (1689–1755), the answer lay with dividing its powers to prevent a concentration of authority that would lead to encroachments on freedom. In his treatise, *Défense de l'Esprit des lois* (The Spirit of Laws, 1748), Montesquieu coined the phrase "separation of powers" to describe a political system wherein three different government branches—the legislative, the judicial, and the executive—each had their own function. The legislative branch creates laws and provides for funding, the executive implements the government's policies, and the judicial branch presides over conflicts. Montesquieu believed that each should have the ability to restrain the other.

> "Liberty [is] intolerable to . . . nations who have not been accustomed to enjoy it."

Charles-Louis de Secondat, Baron de Montesquieu

A French nobleman and lawyer, Montesquieu carefully examined both historical and contemporary governments, looking at how they operated, what they lacked, and what they were able to produce. Today, there is no system of democracy that exists without some type of separation of powers. While governments around the world separate powers in different manners, and have various systems of checks and balances to restrain each branch, the notion that governmental authority must be split to ensure personal liberty and safety is a foundational one in modern political theory. The separation of powers became a cornerstone principle in the creation of the United States of America, and, although not all states use the three-branch system, the idea is almost universally present in modern political structures. **MT**

A male patient undergoes thalassotherapy for arthritis in 1949.

Verificationism
David Hume

The concept that we can discuss only what we can measure

The concept of verificationism holds that it must be possible to determine whether a statement or idea is true or false, and that a question must be answerable for it to deserve consideration. When the concept originated is uncertain, but it was evident in the writings of the Scottish philosopher David Hume (1711–76), and later in those of Immanuel Kant, Gottfried Wilhelm Leibniz, Ludwig Wittgenstein, and even Albert Einstein. Hume suggested that for concepts to be accepted, they must first be verified by sensory experiences. In his *Enquiry Concerning Human Understanding* (1748), he considers the verifiability of divinity and metaphysics. He writes: "Does it contain any experimental reasoning concerning matter of fact, and existence? No. Commit it, then, to the flames."

"The philosopher . . . is not directly concerned with . . . physical properties."

A. J. Ayer, philosopher

Verificationism claims that we are not born with any "innate" knowledge, and that mankind must acquire knowledge through direct observation. In his heavily criticized but widely read work *Language, Truth and Logic* (1952), the philosopher A. J. Ayer (1910–89) suggested the use of verificationism to sift serious statements from gibberish. According to Ayer, "A proposition is verifiable in the strong sense if and only if its truth could be conclusively established by experience."

Verificationism was usurped by logical positivism in an attempt to render meaningless aesthetics, ethics, metaphysical inquiry, and even religious belief. If God cannot be verified, why bother to think of Him? But in the end, verificationism was doomed by a paradox of its own making: its own inherent self-contradictions. Verificationism turned out to be unverifiable because it was neither analytically nor empirically testable. **BS**

Deobandi
Shah Waliullah

A movement advocating that Muslims' first loyalty is to their religion

"Deobandi" is a term used to describe a revivalist movement in Sunni Islam. The movement is named for the city of Deoband in India, which is home to the leading madrassa (Muslim theological school) in the country, Darul Uloom (House of Learning).

Deobandi was inspired by the mid-eighteenth-century teachings of Indian sociologist, historian, and Islamic reformer Shah Waliullah (1703–62). At a time when Muslim power was waning, Waliullah worked to revive Islamic rule. His approach in explaining Islamic social theory originated in the Koran. He wrote about numerous Islamic topics, including *hadith* (the study of traditions), *fiqh* (jurisprudence), *tafsir* (Koranic exegesis), *kalam* (scholastic theology), and *falsafah* (philosophy).

"I am a student of the Qur'an without any intermediary."

Shah Waliullah

His ideas of Islamic economics and society were seen as revolutionary at the time. Some academics regard Waliullah as the first person to conceive the idea of Pan-Islam because he advocated a common system of jurisprudence, the establishment of national governments with just rulers, and an internationalism in keeping with what he regarded as the purpose of the sharia of the Islamic prophet Muhammad.

Inspired by Waliullah's teachings, the Darul Uloom madrassa was founded in 1867, nine years after the First War of Indian Independence and at the height of British colonial rule in the Delhi region of northern India. The Talib rulers in Afghanistan who overthrew the Soviets in 1991 trained at the madrassa, and some commentators regard Deobandi as having given rise to the Taliban movement in Afghanistan. In 2008, Deobandi leaders held a conference denouncing terrorism. **CK**

Romanticism
Johann Georg Hamann

An artistic movement that saw human nature as wild, emotional, and individual

Romanticism in the arts in Europe and North America began in the mid-eighteenth century and peaked in the early nineteenth century. The movement emphasized individualism, sublime nature, heightened emotions, creative power, the supernatural, and the imagination, and celebrated the inner world and genius of the artist. The movement's longing for wild, untamed nature came partly as a response to the arrival of the Industrial Revolution (1760–1840), and the widespread anxiety caused by social dislocation and increasing mechanization.

In artistic terms the movement was a reaction against the order, balance, and idealized harmony that characterized the Enlightenment and Neoclassicism in the eighteenth century. The German literary movement

"Our frame is hidden from us, because we ... are wrought in the depths of the earth."

Johann Georg Hamann, *Socratic Memorabilia* (1759)

Sturm und Drang (Storm and Stress) emphasized human passion, the mystical, and wild nature, and its thinking was profoundly influenced by German philosopher Johann Georg Hamann (1730–88) and his critique of Enlightenment rationalism.

Romanticism spread throughout Europe and North America in literature, art, architecture, and music. Among prominent Romantic writers are the German writer Johann Wolfgang von Goethe and the English poets William Blake and William Wordsworth. Romantic artists include Swiss painter Fuseli, German painter Caspar David Friedrich, French painter Eugène Delacroix, U.S. painter Thomas Cole, and English painter J.M.W. Turner. Romantic composers include Frédéric Chopin from Poland, Hungarian Franz Liszt, and Italian Giuseppe Verdi. **CK**

Classical Music
Joseph Haydn

A European musical movement inspired by ancient Greek and Roman ideals

The classical period of music in Europe took place between about 1750 and 1820. The music is characterized by its use of homophony, a single melodic structure supported by accompaniment, and multiple changes of key and tempo in a single piece. The best-known composers of the period include Joseph Haydn (1732–1809), Wolfgang Amadeus Mozart (1756–91), and Ludwig van Beethoven (1770–1827).

When the great Baroque composer Johan Sebastian Bach died in 1750, Haydn, widely recognized as the first classical composer, was eighteen years old. Many European artists had begun to embrace the ideals of Neoclassicism, a movement espousing a newfound respect for the works of the ancient Greek and Roman artists. Classical composers created music that reflected

"I was cut off from the world ... and I was forced to become original."

Joseph Haydn

the ideals of symmetry, harmony, and balance that they found in classical art. The movement eschewed Baroque and Rococo displays of musical virtuosity and grandiose compositions for simpler, more elegant works. The classical period saw the invention of the sonata, and also a rise in the prominence of other forms, such as the concerto and symphony.

Beethoven is often credited as the last classical composer (or the first of the Romantic era). Today, people often use the term "classical" to refer to a range of chamber music periods, but the music from the true classical period of 1750 to 1820 is perhaps the most popular form. Classical era works are a staple of modern orchestras, symphony performances are rigorously studied, and the music features regularly in movies, television programs, and commercials. **MT**

▣ *The Wayfarer Above a Sea of Fog* (c. 1818), by Caspar David Friedrich, captures the Romantic love of wild nature.

Biblical Source Criticism

Jean Astruc

The study of ancient Judeo-Christian manuscripts to evaluate biblical texts

Sometimes called biblical documentary criticism or biblical literary criticism, biblical source criticism involves studying Judeo-Christian manuscripts to determine whether books and passages in the Bible stem from one author or multiple sources. When investigating a source, scholars try to establish its date, where it was written, why it was written, and whether it was redacted (changed for a specific purpose), in order to arrive at the document's original form.

Source criticism began with a book by French scholar Jean Astruc (1684–1766), *Conjectures on the Original Documents that Moses Appears to Have Used in Composing the Book of Genesis* (1753), in which Astruc investigated the mosaic of manuscript sources that led to the Book of Genesis. His methods were developed

"In the beginning was the Word, and the Word was with God, and the Word was God."

The Bible, John 1:1

by German scholar Julius Wellhausen (1844–1918), who is known for his *Prolegomena to the History of Israel* (1883), which argues that the Torah, or Pentateuch, originated from redactions of four texts dating centuries after Moses, who was traditionally credited as the author.

Thanks to these authors, it is now accepted that the Pentateuch comes from four sources: Yahwist, written in *c.* 950 BCE in southern Israel; Elohist, written in *c.* 850 BCE in northern Israel; Deuteronomist, written in *c.* 600 BCE in Jerusalem during a period of religious reform; and Priestly, written in *c.* 500 BCE by Jewish priests in exile in Babylon. The same methodology, applied to the New Testament, led to the discovery that Mark was the first Synoptic Gospel written. Matthew and Luke both depend on Mark's Gospel, along with the lost collection of sayings Q (*quelle*, German for "source"). **CK**

Compatibilism

David Hume

The argument that determinism and free will need not rule each other out

Also known as soft determinism, compatibilism holds that for humankind determinism and a form of freedom can exist at the same time, without being logically contradictory or inconsistent. Determinism is the view that every event—including human thought, behavior, decision making, and action—has a cause that not only explains it, but also has been determined to occur by previous events. So, you really had no choice but to read this book—a series of prior events and your own desires and motivations deterministically brought you to the point where you are now, reading this book. Compatibilists accept determinism, but also claim that people are free in the sense that, when they do act on their determined motivations, there are no external impediments blocking them from performing or carrying out the act. So, that you are actually able to read this book without something or someone preventing you from reading it means that you are free.

One of the most influential proponents of this view was David Hume (1711–76), particularly in *Of Suicide* (1755), though earlier forms of the concept had been expressed by the Stoics and Thomas Hobbes (1588–1679). Arthur Schopenhauer (1788–1860), whose philosophical work was largely focused on motives and will, later wrote that a person is often free to act on a motive if nothing is impeding the act, but the nature or source of that motive is determined and not in the control of the subject. So, while you may be free to walk into a restaurant because the door is open, the hungry feeling itself or even the timing of it is not in your control—it is your biology.

Some have argued that human genetics demonstrates compatibilism since a great deal of our anatomy, physiology, and psychology is determined by our genes. Determination made me tell you that, but at least I was free to act on that determination. **KBJ**

Critique of Inequality

Jean-Jacques Rousseau

The argument that inequality stems from living in societies and from unjust laws that are created by these societies

When the Genevan philosopher Jean-Jacques Rousseau (1712–78) was asked, "What is the origin of the inequality among men, and is it justified by natural law?" he responded with what many consider a philosophical masterpiece, his *Discourse on the Origin of Inequality* (1755). In it, he argued that "natural man" is good, but failures in the social contract governing the relationship between people lead to inequality.

Rousseau founded his critique on the assumption that people in their natural state are free from jealousy, but the exposure to other people's abilities and achievements that comes from living in society causes jealousy and vice to emerge. Society, then, makes people want to set themselves above others. The concept of property, too, poses a significant problem, because a government and laws are then needed to protect people's possessions. Government thus ends up further promoting inequality, because it is mostly of advantage to the rich.

Rousseau argued that a new social order was needed to banish inequality. He went on to write a sequel to *Discourse on the Origin of Inequality*, called *The Social Contract* (1762), in which he made a case for thinking about society as an artificial person governed by a collective will. This, Rousseau asserted, would enable men to receive independence from "actual law," which protects the societal status quo, and enjoy "true law," which confers political freedom upon an individual. Current "actual law" gives people no choice but to submit all of their rights to a society that only divides them further from one another. Rousseau's ideal of a government founded upon the consent of the governed underlies political philosophies such as Marxism and Socialism, as well as, in modified form, representative democracies such as that of the United States. **MK**

⬆ A cartoon from the French Revolution (1787–99) titled "The Peasant weighed down by the nobility and the clergy," depicting the inequality in society that was faced by many.

"You are undone if you once forget that the fruits of the earth belong to us all."

Jean-Jacques Rousseau, *Discourse on the Origin of Inequality* (1755)

Artificial Preservation of Food
William Cullen

The development of technology dedicated to arresting the natural spoilage of food

While people had been fermenting and drying food since time immemorial, it was not until Scottish physician and agriculturalist William Cullen (1710–90) proposed a device to refrigerate foods, thereby slowing spoilage, that a man-made object alone worked against the laws of nature to preserve food. Refrigeration did not become a common method of food storage until almost 200 years after Cullen first demonstrated it in 1756, but its development was a clear victory in the battle against microorganisms that rob food of its looks, nutritional content, and edibility.

Cullen's first refrigeration system was made by using a pump to create a partial vacuum over a container of diethyl ether, which, when boiled, absorbed heat from the air around it. This, in turn, created cool air and even produced ice. Perhaps because of the complicated nature of the system, people did not see a practical use for refrigeration at first, but efforts continued to create artificial cooling systems. Benjamin Franklin (1706–90), among many other scientists, persisted in conducting experiments to that end. At first, only large food-producing operations, such as slaughterhouses and breweries, used refrigeration, but then trucking companies began to install cooling systems in the vehicles that they used for transporting perishable items, and by the 1920s refrigerators were available as consumer products.

Refrigeration makes possible the shipping of food to geographic locations where that food cannot be grown or processed, thereby expanding the potential variety and nutritional content of the populace's diet. Coupled with improved health care, a balanced diet allows for a better quality, longer lifespan—and this would be difficult to accomplish without the refrigerator. In addition, refrigerators facilitate longer working hours, since food can be purchased or prepared ahead of time and reheated as needed. **MK**

A supplier awaits a telephone call requesting a delivery of ice for a refrigerator or ice box, 1915. ↑

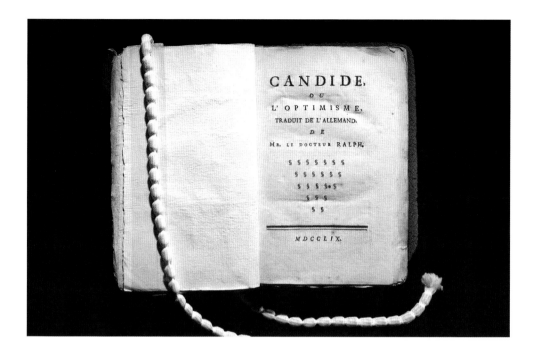

Cultivate Your Garden
Voltaire

Philosophical disillusionment may be countered by work and friendships

To "cultivate your garden" is, according to the satirical novel *Candide* (1759) by Voltaire (1694–1778), the secret to happiness. The book's main character, Candide, rejects the relentless optimism of his tutor, Doctor Pangloss, who argues that "all is for the best in this best of all possible worlds." Candide and his companions discover otherwise when they venture into the world, which is filled with disappointment and misfortune, much of it modeled on real events, such as the Seven Years' War (1756–63) and the Lisbon earthquake of 1755. Yet, peace and happiness are found when Candide and his friends settle on a farm and cultivate a garden.

Voltaire's inspiration for the novel was his own dissatisfaction with the metaphysical optimism that pervaded the philosophical landscape of his time. He especially takes issue with German philosopher Gottfied Wilhelm Leibniz (1646–1716) and his rosy outlook on a world that Voltaire recognized was full of tragedy, misery, and folly. Through *Candide*, Voltaire suggests that, instead of finding solace in abstract hopes, people ought to "cultivate their gardens," or embrace a pragmatic worldview built on intentional work and bolstered by strong human relationships.

Candide and its irreverent philosophy, as well as its cuttingly humorous tone, threatened institutions and philosophers long after its publication, and the novel has been banned hundreds of times over hundreds of years for being "filthy" and "obscene." Even so, it has been canonized in Western literature, and its black humor and portrayal of people trapped in meaningless existences have influenced the work of anti-establishment authors such as Joseph Heller, Thomas Pynchon, Kurt Vonnegut, and Samuel Beckett. *Candide*'s rejection of metaphysical meaning, when combined with its exaggerated portrayal of folly, makes it the forerunner of theatrical works such as Beckett's *Waiting for Godot* (1952). **MK**

⬆ A first edition of *Candide* (1759) by French writer Voltaire, held at the Taylor Institute in Oxford, United Kingdom.

Man Is Born Free

Jean-Jacques Rousseau

The concept that freedom is the natural state of humankind, but that freedom is lost through the corrupting and alienating effects of an overly materialistic society

D U

CONTRACT SOCIAL;

O U,

P R I N C I P E S

D U

DROIT POLITIQUE.

Par J. J. R O U S S E A U,
CITOYEN DE GENEVE.

—— *fœderis æquas*
Dicamus leges.
Æncid. xt

Á AMSTERDAM,
Chez M A R C M I C H E L R E Y.
M D C C L X I I.

⬆ This frontispiece of one of the 1762 editions of Jean-Jacques Rousseau's *Social Contract* also features the work's subtitle, "Principles of Political Right."

"Nature never deceives us; it is we who deceive ourselves."

Jean-Jacques Rousseau

The first words of the hugely influential *Social Contract* (1762) by French philosopher Jean-Jacques Rousseau (1712–78) are haunting: "Man is born free, and everywhere he is in chains. Those who think themselves the masters of others are indeed greater slaves than they." In a "natural" state, Rousseau argues, people are happy, healthy, altruistic, and good. When society is imposed upon them, though, the effects are corrupting and alienating; a man is pitted against his neighbor, a woman against her friend, as all compete for power through prestige and material wealth.

Rousseau's work is founded on a philosophy of anthropology, arguing that, at early stages of societal development, human societies are at their moral best. He asserts that "uncorrupted morals" can be observed in human cultures that are less technologically and socially sophisticated than the eighteenth-century Western world. He uses as an example Caribbean culture, suggesting that, even though they live in a hot climate, which "always seems to inflame the passions," Caribbean people are able to conduct themselves with admirable morality, largely because they are devoid of the societal and material trappings of more technologically and philosophically "advanced" cultures.

Even though he was reacting against philosophers such as Thomas Hobbes (1588–1679), who said that a man "in a state of nature . . . has no idea of goodness he must be naturally wicked; that he is vicious because he does not know virtue," Rousseau created an equally reductive image, that of a "noble savage," which would persist alongside his conception of people being born free of the restrictions society eventually imposes upon them. The latter notion was foundational in the creation of the United States Declaration of Independence of 1776, and also in the eventual abolition of slavery throughout the world. **MK**

Bayes' Theorem
Thomas Bayes

A mathematical formula for calculating the probabality of an event reoccurring

Bayes' Theorem, a probability theory and mathematical formula, is credited to English mathematician Thomas Bayes (1701–61); it was published posthumously in *An Essay towards Solving a Problem in the Doctrine of Chances* (1763). The theorem is used to calculate the probability that something is true or will be true given a prior set of circumstances. For example, let us say that a man wakes up in the morning and the moment after the sun rises he hears a rooster crow. If this happens once or twice he might simply take note of it; but if it happens repeatedly for twenty-five or thirty-five days, or even months or years, it is highly likely that he will form a link between the events: the probability of the rooster crowing the moment after the sun rises is true (it is very likely to carry on happening in the future).

The formula looks like this: $Pr(A|B) = Pr(B|A) \times Pr(A) / Pr(B)$. On the left side of the equation is the conditional probability, or what we want to know—the probability of event A (the rooster crowing) if event B (the sun rising) happens or is true. The part of the formula on the right of the equation gives us the tools for finding the conditional probability. It involves assigning numerical values to the three components; basically, it gives numerical weight to how commonly or often A occurs, B occurs, and A and B occur together. The higher the numbers are for A, for B, and for A and B together, the more probable or likely A occurs, given B.

Bayes' Theorem is important because constantly trying to calculate conditional probabilities is a natural response on the part of humankind to existing in a largely ungovernable material world. People wake up with a very strong expectation that daylight will appear, that gravity is still in place, that their cars will start, and other similar inductive inferences, and they form these beliefs because of consistent, repeated occurrences and relationships. **KBJ**

Neoclassicism
Johann Joachim Winckelmann

An artistic movement that returned to the classical style of ancient Greece and Rome

The discovery of the Roman cities of Herculaneum in 1738 and Pompeii in 1748 helped revive an interest in all things classical at a time when the elaborate Rococo style was starting its downward spiral out of fashion. One work, *The History of Art in Antiquity* (1764), by German scholar Johann Joachim Winckelmann (1717–68), was especially influential in convincing artists to work in the manner of the Greeks, which he believed would give their art an archetypal purity of form based in geometric proportion and symmetry.

Classical mythology and the Homeric epics were popular subjects, and rendering the dress and decorative features correctly was an important part of this style in painting, sculpture, and printmaking. Artists copied designs from pattern books that

> *"The only way for us to become great … lies in the imitation of the Greeks."*
>
> Johann Joachim Winckelmann

were themselves renderings of newly discovered antiquities. The austerity of the Roman style suited the revolutionary themes prevalent in France during this period and many artists, most notably the painter Jacques-Louis David (1748–1825), married the imagined strength of ancient Republican virtues with a reformer's uncompromising zeal. A strong line quality, the imitation of drapery and poses found in Greek and Roman sculpture, and a flattening of color and formality of composition are all hallmarks of this style.

Simultaneously there was also a strong trend toward Romanticism in this period, and while the two movements had differing goals and stylistic features, they did coexist. Some artists even produced works in both genres depending on the subject or the patron for whom they worked. **PBr**

Solar Power
Horace-Bénédict de Saussure

Harnessing the power of the sun to provide energy

The sun has shone on the Earth since the creation of the universe, freely expending its immense power. It was frustrating for humankind that there was no way to harness it, but that situation changed in 1767, when the energy of the sun was captured for the first time.

Horace-Bénédict de Saussure (1740–99) was a Swiss physicist, geologist, and early Alpine explorer. In 1767, after several false starts, he managed to create a solar oven—the first device in the Western world to use the energy of the sun to create heat. It consisted of an insulated box covered by three layers of glass that absorbed and therefore trapped thermal radiation from the sun. The highest temperature he obtained in the device was 230°F (110°C), a temperature that did

"I'd put my money on the sun and solar energy. What a source of power!"

Thomas Edison to Henry Ford, 1931

not vary greatly when the box was carried down from Mount Crammont's summit to the Plains of Cournier, 4,852 feet (1,479 m) below. Carrying the oven down the mountain provided proof that the external air temperature, low at the peak but high on the plain, played no significant part in the result.

Today, extensive arrays of solar panels create free electrons attracted to positively charged electrodes to convert solar radiation into electricity, a process known as the photovoltaic effect. Other systems use polished lenses or mirrors to focus sunlight into concentrated beams that emit photoelectrons, which are then converted into electric current. As the world's finite energy resources are depleted, the relatively infinite power of the sun is now coming into its own. **SA**

Sign Language for the Deaf
Charles-Michel de l'Épée

Using a vocabulary of gestures rather than sounds to communicate

It is unknown when the first sign languages for the hard of hearing developed, but Charles-Michel de l'Épée (1712–89), who founded the world's first free school for the deaf in pre-Revolutionary France in 1771, is often regarded as a seminal figure. While he did not invent a completely original sign language, he learned the signs that his students used; these belonged to what is termed "Old French Sign Language," a collection of signs that, in his time, was used by about 200 Parisians. De l'Épée emphasized their use in instruction, and attempted to systematize a sign language based on them. Moreover, he made his successful instructional methods widely available, encouraging his peers to focus on spreading the use of sign languages; indeed, one of his students cofounded the first school

"As long as we have deaf people on earth, we will have signs."

George Veditz, advocate for deaf rights

for the deaf in the United States and laid the foundation of American Sign Language.

Before sign languages for the deaf were developed, signs, although commonly used, were usually improvisatory and relatively unorganized. In certain communities where deafness was prevalent, "village sign languages" developed: a well-known example was identified in Martha's Vineyard, Massachusetts, from the early eighteenth to the mid-twentieth century. However, without a universal form of communication, deaf people were typically unable to receive much education, to travel beyond their communities, and to communicate outside their families. Even now, sign language is not universally adopted in the education of the deaf, and various controversies about its use persist. **GB**

A postcard depicting the alphabet in sign language, from c. 1930. ➡

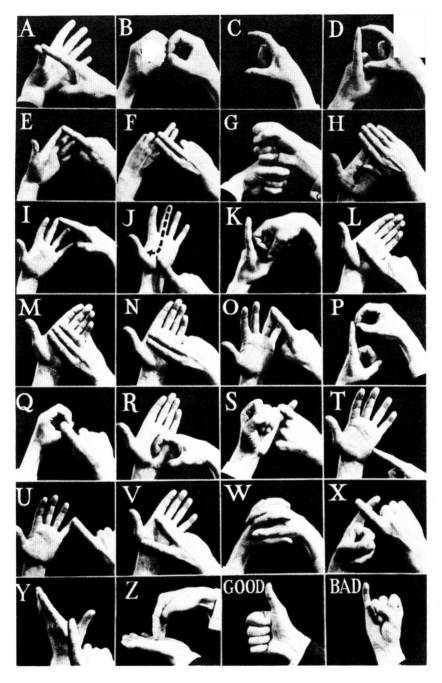

MANUAL ALPHABET (English System)

Abolitionism

England

The belief that no part of society has the right to enslave human beings

⬆ A detail of the celebratory oil painting *Proclamation of the Abolition of Slavery in the French Colonies, April 23, 1848*, made in the following year by François Auguste Biard.

"The state of slavery is of such a nature that it is incapable of being introduced on any reasons, moral or political, but only by positive law, which preserves its force long after the reasons, occasions, and time itself from whence it was created, is erased from memory."

Lord Mansfield, Somersett's Case (1772)

Any aim to end the enslavement of one group of human beings by another is referred to as abolitionism, although the term is generally associated with the effort made to end slavery of Africans in Europe and in North and South America during the seventeenth- and eighteenth-century Enlightenment era.

In England, the most telling legal event was Somersett's Case (1772), in which it was ruled that slavery was unsupported by law in England and Wales. Commitments to abolition waxed and waned during the nineteenth century, but the principles of equality and egalitarianism held sway long enough to convince, or perhaps force, governments in the Americas to follow suit over time. Indeed, during its various conflicts with the United States, the British government encouraged slaves to abandon their owners by offering to emancipate them from the colonies, and many slaves took the British up on their offer of free transport and political freedom. Slavery established the ideological framework for the American Civil War (1861–65), with pro-slavery southern states pitted against the abolitionists of the north; slavery in the United States was only ended in 1865 by the passage of the Thirteenth Amendment to the Constitution. The last nation to abolish slavery was Mauritania in 1981.

Abolitionism offered unqualified commitment to equity in the treatment of all human beings. The idea behind the abolitionist program, that all humans are to be treated as equal, has led to the subordination of the aristocratic, meritocratic ethos by the egalitarian ethos of contemporary liberalism, and to the widespread recognition of the inherent dignity of all human beings. Abolitionism proved to be one of the primary catalysts for self-reflective questioning of the imperialist attitude of the great empires of the nineteenth and twentieth centuries, which led to acceptance of the principle of national self-determination for former colonies. **JS**

Animal Magnetism

Franz Anton Mesmer

The theory that well-balanced magnetic fluids or fields are the key to human health

German physician Franz Anton Mesmer (1734–1815) had a theory that all things had magnetic fluid in them, with a natural energetic transference occurring between living and nonliving things in the universe, the energy in question being largely derived from the stars. Mesmer held that the magnetic fluids or fields in humans could be manipulated for healing or other purposes. Imbalances in the invisible magnetic fluid were held to cause disease, which could be psychological (such as anxiety or phobias) or physical (including spasms, seizures, and pain).

The term "animal magnetism" refers to the universal principle that everything contains this magnetic fluid, and also to the therapeutic system by which people alter the state of their magnetic fluids, rebalancing or even transferring the magnetic fluid, either through touch or by holding hands passively over the body.

In 1774, Mesmer produced an "artificial tide" in a patient. She was given a preparation containing iron, and magnets were attached all over her body. A mysterious fluid seemed to stream through her body, and her symptoms were relieved for several hours. But Mesmer's best-known patient was eighteen-year-old Maria Theresia Paradis, who had been blind since the age of four. During 1776 and 1777, Mesmer treated her with magnets for nearly a year, and her sight seemed to be restored. However, after some time had passed, her blindness returned. A committee at the Vienna University investigated Mesmer and declared him a charlatan, saying that rather than curing her he simply made her believe she was cured.

Mesmer's animal magnetism and practices drew attention to the fact that psychological treatment undoubtedly had a direct influence on the body and its ailments. Treatment with magnets is still being practiced in continental Europe today, and in the United States you can buy the "ionized" Q-Ray bracelet. **KBJ**

⬆ Franz Anton Mesmer calls upon the power of the moon to produce an animal magnetic effect in a patient, in a satirical engraving titled "Mesmer and His Tub," published in 1784.

"The action and virtue of animal magnetism, thus characterized, may be communicated to other animate or inanimate bodies."

Franz Anton Mesmer

Trade Union
Europe

An organization created to improve conditions in the workplace

While trade unions are thought to have roots in the guilds of medieval Europe, they reached popularity around 1775, not long after the beginning of the Industrial Revolution in Europe. At this time, women, children, farm helpers, and immigrants were joining the workforce in large numbers, and workers were beginning to organize spontaneous protests and strikes concerning their treatment and conditions of employment in mills, mines, and factories.

Trade unions had mixed success in representing their members in the eighteenth century. Employers had to choose between giving in to union demands that might involve costs to them, or losing production. Typically their response to demands from unskilled workers was dismissive, but skilled workers fared

"Labor unions are the leading force for democratization and progress."

Noam Chomsky, linguist and historian

better because they were less easily replaced. Even so, membership of a trade union, and the unions themselves, was generally illegal or unsupported by the law in the eighteenth and nineteenth centuries, and members even faced the threat of execution in some countries. Reform came slowly. The labor of children under the age of ten was not outlawed until the Factory Act of 1878, and it was not until the late nineteenth century that some trade unions were legitimized and began to acquire political power.

Trade unions changed our views of both human rights in the workplace and the meaning of labor. Previously, workers were often abused, treated like dispensable property, and paid wages too low to support a family. The consumer has benefited, too, in being able to learn the real cost or value of goods. **KBJ**

Nationalism
United States

The feeling of loyalty to a nation, often resulting in the belief that it is superior

Nationalism, often associated with patriotism, is based on an identification with, and loyalty and devotion to, the body of individuals who comprise a nation. People are also described as nationalist if they consider their nation to be the best and seek to promote the culture and interests of their national community to the detriment of other nations or groups. Enlisting in the army to fight for the freedoms of your fellow citizens, or just simply thinking that you live in the best place on earth, are forms of nationalism. It is essentially an ideology, but one that varies from right to left of the political spectrum.

While nationalism has been practiced for centuries by many different cultures, its modern form can be traced to the United States Declaration

"To wish for the greatness of one's fatherland is to wish evil to one's neighbors."

Voltaire, *Philosophical Dictionary* (1764)

of Independence in 1776, the American and French revolutions in the eighteenth century, and the unification movements of Germany and Italy in the nineteenth century—all of which signify people unifying for self-determination and independence.

In negative terms, nationalism restricts the movement of people and money, and the territorial rights to certain resources. It has also played a role in many wars. In the case of Adolf Hitler and the Nazis, nationalism was associated with genocide justified by claims of racial, cultural, and genetic superiority.

World War II (1939–45) radically changed the political landscape in many ways, not least in the recognition that pride in one's nation needs to be kept in check. As the Bible says in Proverbs 16:18, "Pride goes before destruction, and a haughty spirit before a fall." **KBJ**

In CONGRESS, July 4, 1776

The unanimous Declaration of the thirteen united States of America.

When in the Course of human events, it becomes necessary for one people to dissolve the political bands which have connected them with another, and to assume among the powers of the earth, the separate and equal station to which the Laws of Nature and of Nature's God entitle them, a decent respect to the opinions of mankind requires that they should declare the causes which impel them to the separation.

We hold these truths to be self-evident, that all men are created equal, that they are endowed by their Creator with certain unalienable Rights, that among these are Life, Liberty and the pursuit of Happiness.— That to secure these rights, Governments are instituted among Men, deriving their just powers from the consent of the governed,— That whenever any Form of Government becomes destructive of these ends, it is the Right of the People to alter or to abolish it, and to institute new Government, laying its foundation on such principles and organizing its powers in such form, as to them shall seem most likely to effect their Safety and Happiness. Prudence, indeed, will dictate that Governments long established should not be changed for light and transient causes; and accordingly all experience hath shewn, that mankind are more disposed to suffer, while evils are sufferable, than to right themselves by abolishing the forms to which they are accustomed. But when a long train of abuses and usurpations, pursuing invariably the same Object evinces a design to reduce them under absolute Despotism, it is their right, it is their duty, to throw off such Government, and to provide new Guards for their future security.— Such has been the patient sufferance of these Colonies; and such is now the necessity which constrains them to alter their former Systems of Government. The history of the present King of Great Britain is a history of repeated injuries and usurpations, all having in direct object the establishment of an absolute Tyranny over these States. To prove this, let Facts be submitted to a candid world.

He has refused his Assent to Laws, the most wholesome and necessary for the public good.

He has forbidden his Governors to pass Laws of immediate and pressing importance, unless suspended in their operation till his Assent should be obtained; and when so suspended, he has utterly neglected to attend to them.

He has refused to pass other Laws for the accommodation of large districts of people, unless those people would relinquish the right of Representation in the Legislature, a right inestimable to them and formidable to tyrants only.

He has called together legislative bodies at places unusual, uncomfortable, and distant from the depository of their public Records, for the sole purpose of fatiguing them into compliance with his measures.

He has dissolved Representative Houses repeatedly, for opposing with manly firmness his invasions on the rights of the people.

He has refused for a long time, after such dissolutions, to cause others to be elected; whereby the Legislative powers, incapable of Annihilation, have returned to the People at large for their exercise; the State remaining in the mean time exposed to all the dangers of invasion from without, and convulsions within.

He has endeavoured to prevent the population of these States; for that purpose obstructing the Laws for Naturalization of Foreigners; refusing to pass others to encourage their migrations hither, and raising the conditions of new Appropriations of Lands.

He has obstructed the Administration of Justice, by refusing his Assent to Laws for establishing Judiciary powers.

He has made Judges dependent on his Will alone, for the tenure of their offices, and the amount and payment of their salaries.

He has erected a multitude of New Offices, and sent hither swarms of Officers to harrass our people, and eat out their substance.

He has kept among us, in times of peace, Standing Armies without the Consent of our legislatures.

He has affected to render the Military independent of and superior to the Civil power.

He has combined with others to subject us to a jurisdiction foreign to our constitution, and unacknowledged by our laws; giving his Assent to their Acts of pretended Legislation:

For Quartering large bodies of armed troops among us:

For protecting them, by a mock Trial, from punishment for any Murders which they should commit on the Inhabitants of these States:

For cutting off our Trade with all parts of the world:

For imposing Taxes on us without our Consent:

For depriving us in many cases, of the benefits of Trial by Jury:

For transporting us beyond Seas to be tried for pretended offences

For abolishing the free System of English Laws in a neighbouring Province, establishing therein an Arbitrary government, and enlarging its Boundaries so as to render it at once an example and fit instrument for introducing the same absolute rule into these Colonies:

For taking away our Charters, abolishing our most valuable Laws, and altering fundamentally the Forms of our Governments:

For suspending our own Legislatures, and declaring themselves invested with power to legislate for us in all cases whatsoever.

He has abdicated Government here, by declaring us out of his Protection and waging War against us.

He has plundered our seas, ravaged our Coasts, burnt our towns, and destroyed the lives of our people.

He is at this time transporting large Armies of foreign Mercenaries to compleat the works of death, desolation and tyranny, already begun with circumstances of Cruelty & perfidy scarcely paralleled in the most barbarous ages, and totally unworthy the Head of a civilized nation.

He has constrained our fellow Citizens taken Captive on the high Seas to bear Arms against their Country, to become the executioners of their friends and Brethren, or to fall themselves by their Hands.

He has excited domestic insurrections amongst us, and has endeavoured to bring on the inhabitants of our frontiers, the merciless Indian Savages, whose known rule of warfare, is an undistinguished destruction of all ages, sexes and conditions.

In every stage of these Oppressions We have Petitioned for Redress in the most humble terms: Our repeated Petitions have been answered only by repeated injury. A Prince whose character is thus marked by every act which may define a Tyrant, is unfit to be the ruler of a free people.

Nor have We been wanting in attentions to our Brittish brethren. We have warned them from time to time of attempts by their legislature to extend an unwarrantable jurisdiction over us. We have reminded them of the circumstances of our emigration and settlement here. We have appealed to their native justice and magnanimity, and we have conjured them by the ties of our common kindred to disavow these usurpations, which, would inevitably interrupt our connections and correspondence. They too have been deaf to the voice of justice and of consanguinity. We must, therefore, acquiesce in the necessity, which denounces our Separation, and hold them, as we hold the rest of mankind, Enemies in War, in Peace Friends.

We, therefore, the Representatives of the united States of America, in General Congress, Assembled, appealing to the Supreme Judge of the world for the rectitude of our intentions, do, in the Name, and by Authority of the good People of these Colonies, solemnly publish and declare, That these United Colonies are, and of Right ought to be Free and Independent States; that they are Absolved from all Allegiance to the British Crown, and that all political connection between them and the State of Great Britain, is and ought to be totally dissolved; and that as Free and Independent States, they have full Power to levy War, conclude Peace, contract Alliances, establish Commerce, and to do all other Acts and Things which Independent States may of right do.— And for the support of this Declaration, with a firm reliance on the protection of divine Providence, we mutually pledge to each other our Lives, our Fortunes and our sacred Honor.

John Hancock

Button Gwinnett
Lyman Hall
Geo Walton.

Wm Hooper
Joseph Hewes,
John Penn

Edward Rutledge.
Thos Heyward Junr.
Thomas Lynch Junr.
Arthur Middleton

Samuel Chase
Wm Paca
Thos Stone
Charles Carroll of Carrollton

George Wythe
Richard Henry Lee
Th Jefferson
Benja Harrison
Thos Nelson jr.
Francis Lightfoot Lee
Carter Braxton

Robt Morris
Benjamin Rush
Benja Franklin
John Morton
Geo Clymer
Jas. Smith.
Geo. Taylor
James Wilson
Geo. Ross
Caesar Rodney
Geo Read
Tho M:Kean

Wm Floyd
Phil. Livingston
Frans Lewis
Lewis Morris

Richd Stockton
Jno Witherspoon
Fras. Hopkinson
John Hart
Abra Clark

Josiah Bartlett
Wm Whipple
Saml Adams
John Adams
Robt Treat Paine
Elbridge Gerry
Step Hopkins
William Ellery
Roger Sherman
Sam Huntington
Wm Williams
Oliver Wolcott
Matthew Thornton

The Pursuit of Happiness
Thomas Jefferson

All people have an undeniable right to pursue a life of happiness

In the second sentence of the United States Declaration of Independence, written by Thomas Jefferson (1743–1826) in 1776 and signed on July 4 of the same year, the pursuit of happiness—along with life and liberty—is identified as an unalienable right to which all people are entitled. The declaration listed grievances of the U.S. colonists against King George III of England, detailing in part how his actions had deprived the colonists of their human rights—including their right to pursue lives of happiness.

In 1689, English philosopher John Locke (1632–1704) had published *Two Treatises of Government*, in which he wrote that governments exist under an umbrella of natural law, a law that guarantees everyone a right to life, liberty, and estate. When Jefferson wrote the

> *"… these United Colonies are, and of Right ought to be Free and Independent States …"*
>
> The Declaration of Independence (1776)

Declaration of Independence, he used Locke's idea, along with others, to convey the notion that a society, and the government that rules it, must protect those inherent rights. Yet when he wrote the Declaration of Independence, Jefferson chose to use the word "happiness" instead of "estate."

Jefferson believed in government as a means of ensuring that people are free, happy, and able to pursue their own personal desires. The concept of individualized rights, and that of a government whose primary purpose is to protect those rights instead of itself, is at the heart of democracies around the world. The Declaration of Independence, although not a law in itself, was an expression of shared values established in a moral framework, one that the citizens of the United States strived to live up to. **MT**

The Invisible Hand
Adam Smith

Human affairs are guided by a natural force toward optimal outcomes

A phrase coined by Scottish moral philosopher and economist Adam Smith (1723–90) in *The Wealth of Nations* (1776), the "invisible hand" is thought by some to be a metaphor for the self-regulating behavior of the marketplace, and by others to be the hand of God or natural human moral sense. In all cases, it is a "natural force" of social freedom and economic justice that guides participants in free market capitalism to trade resources in a mutually beneficial manner.

When people come together in a society, there is often a struggle before they find ways to adapt, cooperate, and thrive. However, individual freedom and natural self-interest need not produce chaos if the natural force of the "invisible hand" guides human economic and social commerce; the result may be

> *"It is not from the benevolence of the butcher … that we expect our dinner."*
>
> Adam Smith, *The Wealth of Nations* (1776)

order and harmony. In a free market, people trade resources, some scarce, and this enables individuals to be better off than if each produced for himself alone. As people bargain and trade, the resources of their society naturally become part of the ends and purposes they value highly. Thus, with the "invisible hand" guiding events, there is no need for regulations to ensure that each participant sees benefit.

Smith was radical in regarding social and economic order as organic products of human nature and freedom. The prospering marketplace had no need for control by kings or governments, but would grow best with open competition and free exchange. In this way, Smith's idea of the "invisible hand" and the writings that pertained to it actually referred to human social psychology as much as to economics. **KBJ**

◄ The U.S. Declaration of Independence, signed in 1776 by Thomas Jefferson and others.

Biblical Redaction Criticism
Hermann Reimarus

The view that Jesus's sayings must be distinguished from those of the apostles

Biblical redaction criticism is an area of Bible study that examines how its authors and editors processed and assembled their final literary output, all with a view to discovering what those individuals hoped to achieve.

Modern Biblical redaction criticism began with the German philosopher Hermann Reimarus (1694–1768) and his analysis of the historical figure of Jesus in *Von dem Zwecke Jesu und seiner Jünger* (On the Intention of Jesus and His Teaching, 1778), which was published a decade after his death. Reimarus distinguished what the gospel writers said about Jesus from what Jesus said himself. For example, Reimarus suggested that the disciples fabricated the story of the Resurrection.

Reimarus's work caused an uproar on its publication, but it encouraged others to make a critical study of

"The apostles were . . . teachers and consequently present their own views."
Hermann Reimarus, *On the Intention of Jesus . . .* (1778)

the New Testament. German theologian David Strauss (1808–74) caused controversy with his *Das Leben Jesu kritisch bearbeitet* (The Life of Jesus, Critically Examined, 1835), which asserted that the gospels had been altered and that the miracles mentioned were mythical in character. Strauss also suggested that the writers of the gospels of Matthew and Luke had used the gospel of Mark as a source.

German theologian Wilhelm Wrede (1859–1906) attempted to demonstrate the historical unreliability of the gospel of Mark, and also the influence that the apostle Paul had on Christianity and the idea of salvation. Redaction criticism has since been applied to other areas of scripture, but detractors assert that its methods cast doubt on the Bible both as an inspired work and as a trustworthy historical document. **CK**

Totem Poles
Pacific Northwest Native Americans

The symbolic display of cultural information through large carvings

The word "totem" is derived from the Ojibwe word *odoodem*, meaning "his kinship group." Native American totem poles are ambiguous structures, vertical carvings with intricate designs whose meaning is often unclear. While the age of many totem poles is uncertain, the Western red cedar most often used in their construction barely lasts for a hundred years. European explorers first encountered them in 1778, but their history predates that. They may be the product of a long history of monumental carving, starting perhaps with house posts and funerary memorials and then enlarging into symbols of family or clan prestige. Produced by illiterate societies, no documentation exists of their age, but it is clear that these structures were proud symbols of their creators.

"Some [are] reminders of quarrels, murders, debts, and other unpleasant occurrences."
Ishmael Reed, *From Totems to Hip-Hop* (2002)

The importation of iron and steel tools from Europe and Asia during the 1800s enabled totem makers to carve far larger and more complex poles. The Haida people of the islands of Haida Gwaii, off the coast of British Columbia, probably originated these carvings, which then spread down the coast into what is now Washington State. (Totem poles do not exist in the American southwest or northern Alaska, as no tall trees can grow in these inhospitably hot and cold climates.)

The designs of totem poles vary according to the intent of their creators. Some recount legends and family histories; others refer to cultural beliefs or shamanic powers. Certain poles were mortuary structures; others were "shame poles," on which an individual who had failed in some way had their likeness carved upside down. They were never objects of worship. **SA**

Totem poles are read from bottom to top, and can depict people, animals, and spirits.

Late Modern
1780–1899

Ideas that emerged during this period regularly assumed a material form in the parts and processes of the Industrial Revolution. Karl Marx and Friedrich Engels responded to this industrialization—and its attendant capitalism—with their own revolutionary ideas concerning socialism and communism. Charles Darwin's ideas about evolution provided a natural explanation for the existence and diversity of living things, and Auguste Comte's ideas about naturalism and positivism offered a natural explanation for the workings of the whole universe, leading Friedrich Nietzsche to argue in 1882 that "God is dead." By the dawn of the twentieth century, the technological, political, scientific, and religious landscape looked very different indeed.

◁ *The Gare St. Lazare* (detail, 1877), by Claude Monet, offers an Impressionist view of the steam engine, the driving force behind the Industrial Revolution.

Kant's Copernican Turn
Immanuel Kant

Reality should conform to the categories of the mind, not the reverse

"It always remains a scandal of philosophy and universal human reason that the existence of things outside us . . . should have to be assumed merely on faith, and if it occurs to anyone to doubt it, we should be unable to answer him with a satisfactory proof." So stated German philosopher Immanuel Kant (1724–1804) in his *Critique of Pure Reason* (1781), overturning decades of Enlightenment philosophy. Traditional philosophy had failed, said Kant, because it could not produce an argument that there is a world that is external to us.

Kant lived and died in what was then Königsberg in East Prussia and is now Kalingrad in Russia. In his entire life, he famously never traveled more than 10 miles (16 km) from the city. He became a scholar, working as a private tutor in order to support his philosophical

"[Let us proceed] by assuming that the objects must conform to our cognition."

Immanuel Kant, *Critique of Pure Reason* (1781)

investigations. Kant argued that we shape our experience of things through our mind but we never have direct experience of these things. He was trying to end philosophical speculations whereby objects outside our experience were used to support what he saw as useless theories. He called this massive change a "Copernican Revolution in reverse." Copernicus (1473–1543) had overturned astronomy by confirming that the Earth moved round the sun and was not the static center of our universe, but Kant proposed a revolution that placed the mind at the center of all things.

Kant's Copernican Turn, as the idea has been termed, has had a long-lasting effect on philosophy, influencing nineteenth-century philosophers such as G. W. F. Hegel, and twentieth-century phenomenologists such as Edmund Husserl and Martin Heidegger. **SA**

Transcendental Idealism
Immanuel Kant

Knowledge of the world begins with perception, not the senses

Transcendental idealism was a philosophical doctrine of the late eighteenth century that naturally grew out of the German Enlightenment and German Idealism. Its best-known and initial systematic treatment was carried out by Immanuel Kant (1724–1804) in his *Critique of Pure Reason* (1781), but transcendental idealism went on to influence all major areas of philosophy: logic, ethics, social and political philosophy, and aesthetics.

In this context, the term "transcendental" means independent of experience, and "idealism" means dependent on the existence of ideas and the mind; the doctrine investigates the knowledge of objects that are "in me but not me." The transcendental idealist believes that what we discover about objects depends on how they appear to us as perceivers. In this way,

"Experience [does not] teach us that something . . . cannot be otherwise."

Immanuel Kant, *Critique of Pure Reason* (1781)

Kant secured the priority of the mind over the external world and at the same time preserved the validity of scientific investigation.

Kant was trying to reconcile elements of empiricism and rationalism to correct the errors that prevented metaphysics from possibly becoming a real science. He felt that a synthesis of the two could account for both the sense data received for the acquisition of knowledge and the need for the mind to be pre-equipped to process such data, produce judgments, and detect relationships of necessity and causality, as well as reasoning of a higher order. Kant's transcendental idealism is really an early form of cognitive psychology, and its investigation into perception and reason changed the way we view the relationship between the mind and the world. **KBJ**

Analytic-Synthetic Distinction
Immanuel Kant

Judgments require close analysis of the content of propositions

In philosophy, the analytic-synthetic distinction is a conceptual distinction between two kinds of propositions or judgments. A proposition is analytic when the predicate concept is contained in the subject concept (as in the law of identity, A=A) or when it is true by definition ("all triangles have three sides"). A proposition is synthetic when the predicate concept is not contained in the subject concept, but lies beyond it ("all bachelors are unhappy"), or the truth of the proposition is known by the meaning of the words and something about the world around us ("car exhaust contributes to smog").

German philosopher Immanuel Kant (1724–1804) first introduced the terms "analytic" and "synthetic" in his well-known work *Critique of Pure Reason* (1781).

". . . [predicate] B, though connected with concept A, lies quite outside it."

Immanuel Kant, *Critique of Pure Reason* (1781)

He saw this as a logical and semantic distinction applying to judgments: what makes a proposition true or false? Analytic propositions do not expand our concept of the subject; they do not add to our knowledge. They are considered true by virtue of the law of noncontradiction: the judgment that "a triangle has four sides" is false by virtue of the fact that "four sides" cannot be predicated of a "triangle" (TRI-angle). A synthetic proposition is known to be true by its connection with some intuition or prior knowledge, and so its truth or falsity is not so easy. A maple tree can be both leafy and not leafy without contradiction. Kant's analytic-synthetic distinction changed the way that we view the act of judgment, as complex conscious cognitions, the capacity for which is a central cognitive function of the human mind. **KBJ**

Latin Square
Leonhard Euler

A matrix of symbols in which each symbol appears once in each row and each column

Familiar to aficionados of Sudoku puzzles, the Latin square was first mentioned in a paper, *Recherches sur une nouvelle espèce de quarrés magiques* (Investigations on a New Type of Magic Aquare, 1782), by the Swiss mathematician and physicist Leonhard Euler (1707–83).

A Latin square is an n x n matrix composed using n different symbols that occur once in each row and once in each column. This is a three-symbol set:

$$\alpha \qquad \beta \qquad \gamma$$
$$\beta \qquad \gamma \qquad \alpha$$
$$\gamma \qquad \alpha \qquad \beta$$

For every added symbol used to generate the matrix there is a substantial increase in the total of different matrices that may be constructed. For example, given a set containing one symbol, only one

"Euler introduced Latin and Greek letters to help him analyze magic squares . . ."

Leonard Euler: Life, Work and Legacy (2007)

matrix can be constructed. Given a set containing two symbols, two matrices might be constructed. A set of three symbols, however, can yield twelve matrices, such as the one above. Given nine symbols, five and a half octillion unique matrices can be constructed, including those used for the popular Sudoku puzzles.

Latin squares are used in the design of scientific experiments. A scientist testing five versions of an experimental drug can divide his test subjects into five groups and randomly pair one version to each group for testing during the first phase of the experiment. The Latin square can then be used to schedule four more phases so that each version of the drug is tested upon each group of test subjects without duplication. Latin squares also have several applications in the field of telecommunications. **DM**

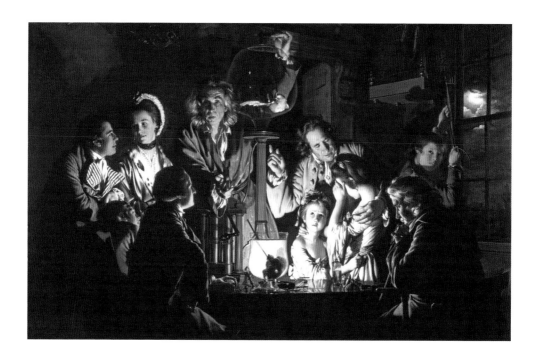

Enlightenment
Immanuel Kant

The free use of intellect to solve problems without recourse to authority

In 1784, German philosopher Immanuel Kant (1724–1804) published the essay, "Answering the Question: What is Enlightenment?" in *Berlin Monthly*. He was writing toward the end of the Age of Enlightenment, and his essay is the definitive commentary on the meaning of that period of intellectual history.

Kant argues that enlightenment is an intellectual coming of age in which humankind liberates itself from the chains of ignorance. The motto of the Age of Enlightenment, *sapere aude*, or "dare to be wise," indicates a willingness to challenge the paternalistic authority of both monarchic government and the church. Kant compares enlightenment to the state of a minor who has finally reached adulthood and become emancipated from parental authority by embracing autonomy (the ability to make free and rational decisions). He argues that the ignorance of humankind is self-imposed: like an immature adult who is reluctant to leave the comfort of his parents' home, many people cling to authority because of intellectual laziness. If we could educate all the members of society to judge on the basis of reason instead of dogma, people could be transformed into free-thinking individuals, which would bring an end to despotism and oppression.

Although a political revolution might offer a temporary reprieve from tyranny, Kant claims that it is only the cultivation of our minds that can bring about lasting change in society. Through the public use of reason, we can put forward and critique new ideas and thereby make intellectual progress.

Kant's understanding of enlightenment has been highly influential in political theory concerning the importance of intellectual freedom in both academics and civil rights. This includes the separation of church and state, since citizens should not be subject to the "spiritual despotism" of a paternalistic government. **JM**

This painting (1768) by Joesph Wright of Derby conveys the Enlightenment fascination with science. ⬆

1784

Black Hole
John Michell

Entities in space that are so dense that no light can escape their gravitational pull

In his work on the effect of gravity on light (1784), English geologist John Michell (1724–93) was the first to suggest the existence of black holes, referring to them as "dark stars." Karl Schwarzschild (1873–1916) is also credited with developing the concept. However, U.S. physicist John Wheeler (1911–2008) coined the term around 1968, and his vast amount of research pioneered the modern study of black holes.

A black hole is a place in outer space where the force of gravity is so extreme that nothing inside it can escape, not even a ray of light. The reference to a hole suggests that the entity is empty, but the complete opposite is true. In fact, a black hole consists of a great amount of matter packed into a very small space. What may be termed a hole is created by the extreme force of gravity sucking all surrounding matter toward that extremely dense center.

Because light cannot escape from black holes, they are invisible. To find one, astronomers need a telescope with special tools that analyze the behavior and patterns of stars; those stars closest to a black hole act differently and thus betray the black hole's presence.

Black holes exist in various sizes, but they all have a large mass. Some are as small as an atom and have the mass of a large mountain; there are "stellar" black holes that have a mass twenty times that of the sun; and the largest are called "supermassive," which have a mass of more than a million suns combined. There is scientific proof that all large galaxies have a supermassive black hole at their center; at the center of the Milky Way lies Sagittarius A, with a mass of about 4 million suns.

Researching black holes has resulted in a better understanding of the real universe. And if they were present at the Big Bang, they would have impacted the expansion rate of the universe and the abundance of elements found in it, and so they might hold the key to understanding how the universe began. **KBJ**

⬆ A computerized image of a black hole, surrounded by its white accretion disk of superheated material.

IMMANUEL KANT.

London Published April 1812 by Adlard & Jones.

First Categorical Imperative
Immanuel Kant

The moral principle that one's behavior should accord with universalizable maxims

German philosopher Immanuel Kant (1724–1804) founded deontology, or "duty ethics," a moral theory grounded in pure reason rather than virtues, self-interest, or compassion. In his *Groundwork of the Metaphysics of Morals* (1785), Kant argues that we can determine our moral duties through an appeal to the categorical imperative. Here, "categorical" means unambiguously explicit, while "imperative" means command, thus a "categorical imperative" refers to a universal moral law.

Kant's categorical imperative has three formulations. The first formulation encourages a person to act as if the maxim (rule) for their action were willed as a universal law for all rational beings. For example, if a person is considering whether or not to tell a lie, they must evaluate two maxims: "lie whenever you like" and

> *"Act only in accordance with that maxim [you could accept as] a universal law."*
>
> Immanuel Kant, *Groundwork . . .* (1785)

"always tell the truth." They must then universalize these laws to see if everyone can consistently follow them. If they universalize the liar's maxim, they get a world of liars in which nobody would believe their lie, so there is a contradiction between the world they need to exist for the lie to work (a world of trusting, truth tellers in which they are the only liar) and the world that would exist if everyone lied (a world of dishonest skeptics). Truth telling can be universalized without contradiction, so there must be a universal moral duty to tell the truth. Moral laws must be reversible: if truth telling is a maxim that all people must follow, then I must follow it too.

Since its inception, Kantian deontology has been one of the most dominant theories in ethics. The categorical imperative is routinely used in applied ethics to test the fairness of laws and policies. **JM**

Second Categorical Imperative
Immanuel Kant

Treat people as ends in themselves, not merely as a means to your own ends

Immanuel Kant (1724–1804), the founder of the moral theory of deontology, was dissatisfied with prevailing theories of ethics that emphasized the agent's character, moral sentiment, and ego. He sought to give ethics universality and precision through an appeal to the categorical imperative, which refers to the moral duties that all rational beings ought to respect.

The second formulation of Kant's categorical imperative states that a person should always treat rational beings as ends in themselves, never as a means to the end of their own satisfaction. Rational beings view themselves as ends, as beings with intrinsic value, which is to say that a person has moral worth independent of whether or not other people find them instrumentally useful. It is wrong for a person to use

> *"So act that you use humanity . . . as an end and never merely as a means."*
>
> Immanuel Kant, *Groundwork . . .* (1785)

a rational being simply as a means, an object whose sole purpose is to make another person happy. This formulation is often referred to as "respect for persons" because, when we view persons as ends rather than means, we respect their status as fellow rational beings. If someone wants to use a person instrumentally, they must first obtain their consent. For example, forcing someone to paint someone else's house would be wrong, but paying someone to do so is just.

Respect for persons has become a cornerstone of applied ethics, directly influencing key notions such as respect for autonomy (the ability to make free and rational decisions about a person's own life) and voluntary informed consent (the idea that a person must be fully informed of risks and benefits before entering into a contract or authorizing a medical procedure). **JM**

◄ A print of a portrait of Immanuel Kant, published in London in 1812.

Uniformitarianism
James Hutton

An assumption about the natural laws and processes that create Earth's landscape

James Hutton (1726–97) was a Scottish doctor, naturalist, and geologist. In a paper, *Theory of the Earth*, presented to the Royal Society of Edinburgh in 1785, he asserted that "the solid parts of the present land appear, in general, to have been composed of the productions of the sea, and of other materials now found upon these shores." He proposed that land formation took place under the sea as sediments accumulated on the seabed. The land was then lifted up above the sea, tilted, and eroded, and then returned below the sea again where further layers of deposits were added. This cycle of formation, elevation, erosion, and submersion was repeated countless times over countless years. Hutton found evidence for this theory in rock unconformities—breaks in the

> *"[Geological forces] never acted with different degrees of energy [from now]."*
>
> James Hutton, *Theory of the Earth* (1785)

geological record—in the Cairngorm Mountains and along the Berwick coast in Scotland.

For many centuries, how and when Earth was formed, rocks were created, and the landscape shaped were all unknowns. Was Earth as created in Genesis, or was it much older? Such questions remained unanswered until Hutton proposed his theory. The ideas took time to be established but were confirmed in the multivolume *Principles of Geology*, published from 1830 to 1833 by Charles Lyell (1797–1875). Lyell stated that Earth was shaped entirely by slow-moving forces that act over a long period of time and continue to act to this day. Reviewing this book, the English polymath William Whewell (1794–1866) coined the term "uniformitarianism" to describe this process, a process in which "the present is the key to the past." **SA**

Geological Deep Time
James Hutton

The concept that Earth's history extends into an "abyss of time"

The concept of deep time originated with two men of the Scottish Enlightenment, doctor and geologist James Hutton (1726–97) and mathematician John Playfair (1748–1819). Hutton's *Theory of the Earth* (written and presented to the Royal Society of Edinburgh in 1785, then published in the society's *Transactions* in 1788) introduced deep time, and there are observations of it in the works of Charles Lyell and Charles Darwin.

The span of human history is a tiny blip when compared to the Earth's 4.54 billion-year geological timescale, and to recognize that fact is to internalize the notion of deep time. What must be recognized is the difference between relative age (that measured by relationship) and numerical age (that measured by date). Traditionally, the concept of deep time has been

> *"The result . . . is that we find no vestige of a beginning—no prospect of an end."*
>
> James Hutton, *Theory of the Earth* (1785)

applied in geology and paleontology, but it is also useful in attempts to discover the age of the universe.

Deep time is measured using the geologic timescale, a system of chronological measurement relating to rock layers and stratification. The time units used are the supereon, eon, era, period, epoch, and age. Special fossils found in rocks, called index fossils, are essential for creating relative timescales. They are called index fossils because they are found only in rocks of a limited timespan, of a certain sedimentary level, and so they help in the dating of other things found in that same sedimentary layer. With the discovery of radioactivity, geologists could discover the age of minerals when they crystalized in rocks. The geologic timescale is itself not confirmed; it fluxes constantly as more data is uncovered and dates are catalogued. **KBJ**

1787

Panopticon
Jeremy Bentham

A design for a prison that enabled around-the-clock surveillance of inmates

The panopticon was a proposed model prison designed in 1787 by English utilitarian philosopher and legal reform theorist Jeremy Bentham (1748–1832). The design element that made it highly novel was that it allowed around-the-clock surveillance of the prisoners. The word "panopticon" means "all-seeing," and the ones who could "see all" were the inspectors who conducted the surveillance, never the inmates of the prison. Prisoners could not tell at any given time whether they were being watched, and it was this insecurity and anguish that would be a crucial instrument of discipline. Bentham also saw his design as applicable for hospitals, schools, sanitariums, workhouses, and lunatic asylums.

At the center of Bentham's design was a tower structure surmounted by an inspection house. Here, staff, guards, and managers were stationed to scrutinize the cells set into the surrounding perimeter. Bentham believed that the model prison would be more cost-effective than others because it could be run by fewer staff—just the thought of being watched would be enough to keep prisoners behaving well. Additionally, the prison could provide its own income: inmates sentenced to hard labor could walk on a treadmill or turn a capstan to power looms or other machines.

The panopticon prison never came to fruition in Bentham's lifetime, although similar structures were built in the nineteenth century. However, the principles behind his idea had a lasting impact. Much later, French philosopher Michel Foucault (1926–84) wrote that it was a metaphor for modern disciplinary society, one that observes and normalizes people in a form of social quarantine. Bentham's design created a conscious, visible, and ever-present mark of power, in which heavy locks, bars, and chains were no longer necessary for domination—the prisoners' paranoia and psychological angst kept them under control. **KBJ**

The Presidio Modelo was a "model prison" of Panopticon design, built in Cuba between 1926 and 1928. ⬆

1789

Utilitarianism
Jeremy Bentham

What is morally good is that which promotes the greatest good for the greatest number

According to utilitarianism, it is the outcome of any action that determines whether it is a moral or immoral act. Any act that promotes the greatest good for the greatest number of people is considered moral, regardless of whether it conforms to any other notion of morality, ethics, or religious doctrine.

Prior to the development of utilitarianism during the seventeenth- and eighteenth-century Enlightenment, thinkers had recognized the value of human happiness and used it as a measuring stick of ethics and morality. However, it was not until the publication in 1789 of *An Introduction to the Principles of Morals and Legislation* by English utilitarian philosopher Jeremy Bentham (1748–1832) that utilitarianism fully bloomed as an

ethical theory. For Bentham, maximizing human pleasure, or happiness, and minimizing pain could be achieved through mathematical calculations that were applicable in any ethical judgment.

However, it was in Bentham's godson, John Stuart Mill (1806–73), that utilitarianism found its most ardent voice. For Mill, some pleasures were qualitatively superior to others. Eschewing Bentham's qualitative assessment, Mill believed in a spectrum of pleasures, and he made it clear that simply maximizing base pleasures was not the ultimate goal of utilitarianism.

Utilitarianism has had a wide-reaching impact on any number of human endeavors beyond moral philosophizing. In political circles, utilitarian arguments are commonly employed to support or refute governmental policies and actions, and economists have applied utilitarian principles widely in developing methods for maximizing prosperity. Although the school of thought is not without its critics, its introduction as an ethical theory demonstrated that morality need not be based upon principles handed down from authority, but rather upon the measurable outcomes that actions produce. **MT**

⬆ A portrait of Jeremy Bentham, painted in *c.* 1829 by Henry William Pickersgill.

DÉCLARATION
DES DROITS DE L'HOMME
ET DU CITOYEN,
Décretés par l'Assemblée Nationale dans les séances des 20, 21, 23, 24 et 26 août 1789, acceptés par le Roi

PRÉAMBULE

LES représentans du peuple François, constitués en assemblée nationale, considérant que l'ignorance, l'oubli ou le mépris des droits de l'homme sont les seules causes des malheurs publics et de la corruption des gouvernemens ont résolu d'exposer dans une déclaration solemnelle, les droits naturels, inaliénables et sacrés de l'homme, afin que cette déclaration, constamment présente à tous les membres du corps social, leur rappelle sans cesse leurs droits et leurs devoirs; afin que les actes du pouvoir législatif et ceux du pouvoir exécutif, pouvant être à chaque instant comparés avec le but de toute institution politique, en soient plus respectés; afin que les réclamations des citoyens, fondées désormais sur des principes simples et incontestables, tournent toujours au maintien de la constitution et du bonheur de tous.

EN conséquence, l'assemblée nationale reconnoit et déclare, en présence et sous les auspices de l'Être suprême les droits suivans de l'homme et du citoyen.

ARTICLE PREMIER
LES hommes naissent et demeurent libres et égaux en droits; les distinctions sociales ne peuvent être fondées que sur l'utilité commune.

II.
LE but de toute association politique est la conservation des droits naturels et imprescriptibles de l'homme; ces droits sont la liberté, la propriété, la sûreté, et la résistance à l'oppression.

III.
LE principe de toute souveraineté réside essentiellement dans la nation, nul corps, nul individu ne peut exercer d'autorité qui n'en émane expressement.

IV.
LA liberté consiste à pouvoir faire tout ce qui ne nuit pas à autrui Ainsi, l'exercice des droits naturels de chaque homme, n'a de bornes que celles qui assurent aux autres membres de la société la jouissance de ces mêmes droits; ces bornes ne peuvent être déterminées que par la loi.

V.
LA loi n'a le droit de défendre que les actions nuisibles à la société. Tout ce qui n'est pas défendu par la loi ne peut être empêché, et nul ne peut être contraint à faire ce qu'elle n'ordonne pas.

VI.
LA loi est l'expression de la volonté générale; tous les citoyens ont droit de concourir personnellement, ou par leurs représentans, à sa formation; elle doit être la même pour tous, soit qu'elle protége, soit qu'elle punisse. Tous les citoyens étant égaux à ses yeux, sont également admissibles à toutes dignités, places et emplois publics, selon leur capacité, et sans autres distinction que celles de leurs vertus et de leurs talens

VII.
NUL homme ne peut être accusé, arreté, ni détenu que dans les cas déterminés par la loi, et selon les formes qu'elle a prescrites, ceux qui sollicitent, expédient, exécutent ou font exécuter des ordres arbitraires; doivent être punis; mais tout citoyen appelé ou saisi en vertu de la loi, doit obéir à l'instant, il se rend coupable par la résistance.

VIII.
LA loi ne doit établir que des peines strictement et évidemment nécessaires, et nul ne peut être puni qu'en vertu d'une loi établie et promulguée antérieurement au délit, et légalement appliquée.

IX.
TOUT homme étant présumé innocent jusqu'à ce qu'il ait été déclaré coupable, s'il est jugé indispensable de l'arrêter, toute rigueur qui ne serait pas nécessaire pour s'assurer de sa personne doit être sévérement réprimée par la loi.

X.
NUL ne doit être inquiété pour ses opinions, mêmes religieuses pourvu que leur manifestation ne trouble pas l'ordre public établi par la loi.

XI.
LA libre communication des pensées et des opinions est un des droits les plus précieux de l'homme: tout citoyen peut donc parler, écrire, imprimer librement, sauf à répondre de l'abus de cette liberté dans les cas déterminés par la loi.

XII.
LA garantie des droits de l'homme et du citoyen nécessite une force publique: cette force est donc instituée pour l'avantage de tous, et non pour l'utilité particulière de ceux à qui elle est confiée.

XIII.
POUR l'entretien de la force publique, et pour les dépenses d'administration, une contribution commune est indispensable; elle doit être également répartie entre les citoyens en raison de leurs facultés.

XIV.
LES citoyens ont le droit de constater par eux même ou par leurs représentans, la nécessité de la contribution publique, de la consentir librement, d'en suivre l'emploi, et d'en déterminer la quotité, l'assiette, le recouvrement et la durée.

XV.
LA société a le droit de demander compte à tout agent public de son administration.

XVI.
TOUTE société, dans laquelle la garantie des droits n'est pas assurée, ni la séparation des pouvoirs déterminée, n'a point de constitution

XVII.
LES propriétés étant un droit inviolable et sacré, nul ne peut en être privé, si ce n'est lorsque la nécessité publique, légalement constatée, l'exige évidemment, et sous la condition d'une juste et préalable indemnité.

AUX REPRESENTANS DU PEUPLE FRANCOIS

Declaration of Rights

Jérôme Champion de Cicé

An argument that there are universal human rights that confer equality before the law

On August 26, 1789, the French Constituent Assembly adopted the last article of the Declaration of the Rights of Man and the Citizen, a key moment of the French Revolution (1787–99) and a crucial first step toward writing the constitution for post-Revolutionary France. It was authored by clergyman Jérôme Champion de Cicé (1735–1810).

The document featured seventeen articles containing provisions about individuals and the nation. It abolished feudal rights, clearly defining individual and collective rights as universal: life, liberty, property, security, and resistance to oppression. These rights are valid at all times, everywhere, and are natural rather than bestowed. The Declaration also recognized equality before the law, and this effectively eliminated

> "Men are born free and remain free and equal in rights."
>
> Jérôme Champion de Cicé, Declaration, Article 1 (1789)

any special rights or exceptions awarded to the nobility and clergy. It restricted the powers of the monarchy, overturning the divine right of kings, and stated that all citizens had the right to participate in the legislative process, with the government containing only elected officials. However, political rights pertained only to "active" citizens: those at least twenty-five years of age, who paid taxes equal to three days of work, and who owned property. This meant that only white men had these rights; women, children, and foreigners did not.

The Declaration inspired similar rights-based documents of liberal democracy in many European and Latin American countries. It changed the way we view the relationship between the state and its citizens, and brought about global legal reform. **KBJ**

Chemical Elements

Antoine Lavoisier

The distinct, indivisible substances that make up the material world

A chemical element is a pure substance that cannot be broken down to simpler substances or changed into another substance by chemical means. Elements are the chemical building blocks for matter; each chemical element has one type of atom, and each is distinguished by its atomic number (the number of protons around its nucleus).

Talk of elements started with the ancient Greeks. Aristotle wrote that they were entities that composed other things but were themselves indivisible. For the Greeks, there were four elements: earth, air, fire, and water. The fundamental nature of a chemical element was recognized in 1661 by the English chemist Robert Boyle (1627–91), but it was not until 1789, with the publication of the *Elementary Treatise of Chemistry* by

> "I now mean by elements ... certain primitive ... or perfectly unmingled bodies."
>
> Robert Boyle, chemist

French chemist Antoine Lavoisier (1743–94), that the first true modern list of elements existed. Lavoisier's list was created following a careful study of decomposition and recombination reactions, and contained just thirty-three elements. By 1869, when Russian chemist Dmitri Mendeleev (1834–1907) created the periodic table to summarize the properties of elements and to illustrate chemical behavior and recurring trends, the total number of known elements had increased to sixty-six.

To date, 118 elements have been identified. Their discovery has led to a more profound understanding of our physical world in its composition, mechanics, and evolution. All objects contain chemical elements, and more than thirty have key functions in keeping plants, animals, and people alive and healthy—they are indeed the foundation of life itself. **KBJ**

← *The Declaration of the Rights of Man and the Citizen* (1789), painted by Jean-Jacques-François Le Barbier.

Feminism
Olympe de Gouges/Mary Wollstonecraft

A movement arguing that women should possess the same legal and social rights as men

⬆ A watercolor portrait of French revolutionist and feminist Olympe de Gouges (1784). In 1791 de Gouges published her *Declaration of the Rights of Woman and the Female Citizen.*

"I love my man as my fellow; but his scepter, real, or usurped, extends not to me, unless the reason of an individual demands my homage; and even then the submission is to reason, and not to man."

Mary Wollstonecraft

The term "feminism" refers to a series of social and political movements that have sought to address various longstanding prejudices concerning the rights of women, their perception by society, and their access to social resources. The movement has thus petitioned, in various ways, for the right to equal intellectual, economic, and legal status. Feminism has undergone many paradigm shifts, and even now the meaning of the term continues to metamorphose.

At least since humanity's move from mobile, hunter-gatherer societies to settled, agrarian ones, the interests of men have generally been given priority in society, especially by religions. However, sparked by the French Revolution in the 1790s, women began to articulate the view that there was a strong case for their equal treatment.

During the "pamphlet wars" of the 1790s (a series of exchanges between reformers and those seeking to resist the application of "French principles" to Britain), two women, Olympe de Gouges (1748–93) in France, and Mary Wollstonecraft (1759–97) in England, published challenges to the view that women were second-class citizens. While they accepted some inequalities that later waves of feminism would reject out of hand, they opened up a public debate that remains of critical importance today.

The ideas of feminism have challenged and changed many aspects of society, from female political involvement to reproductive rights. Feminism has been adopted in different ways by groups as radically diverse as Muslims and Native Americans, but their common theme is the desire to question the structure of societies and assumptions about what women are, and what they ought to be. Nevertheless, equality for women is still a distant vision for the vast majority. **LW**

Dandyism
Europe

The notion of looking superb as being more important than being superb

Celebrity status used to be connected to power, and those in power would dress in ways that made their status unmistakable. In Europe, powerful aristocrats would seek to maintain their position within restricted social circles by wearing the right haute couture and displaying the right manners, but generally they did not seek wider attention. From the 1790s onward, however, the arrival of new bourgeois wealth brought a wave of men able to boast nothing more in the way of status than a disposable income. Eager for the attention of the wealthy upper class, and with the leisure to focus on themselves, they sought the spotlight with dress and manners designed to catch the eye. Such well-dressed and well-groomed men of the late eighteenth and early nineteenth centuries discovered that dandyism could facilitate their entry into aristocratic society.

The dandy gained a foothold in England and Scotland, then France and the United States, after the wars of the late eighteenth century created conditions that favored a wider culture newly accessible to aristocratic-looking men. Perhaps the best-known dandy was George "Beau" Brummell (1778–1840), a middle-class young man who learned the nicer points of sartorial splendor at Eton College, Oxford University, and later the prestigious Tenth Royal Hussars. He became an intimate of the Prince Regent, later King George IV (1762–1830), until they quarreled in 1813.

The dandy would avoid the traditional aristocratic burden of responsibility for society while displaying an aloof concern for looking good. If there was serious purpose behind the show, it was to couple disdain for emerging democratic culture with an air of nihilism, or aesthetic hedonism. Dandyism later became an entryway into society for men of little wealth but great artistic talent, such as writer and poet Oscar Wilde (1854–1900). **JSh**

The Third Critique
Immanuel Kant

The theory that experiencing the sublime creates tension between mental faculties

The Critique of the Power of Judgment, also known as *The Third Critique*, was published in 1790 by German philosopher Immanuel Kant (1724–1804). An influential work on aesthetics, it contains a greatly expanded treatment of the sublime. For Kant, the sublime is experience of absolute grandeur, pertaining to the supersensible and moral nature of humans. It is one of two types of aesthetic experience, the other being experience of the beautiful. Speaking of the sublime, he distinguishes two kinds: the mathematical (such as the immeasurable powers of God), and the dynamical, (for example, the powerful force of a tsunami).

Experience of the sublime is that of formlessness, limitlessness, and incomprehensiveness; the sublime resists representation. When confronted with it, our

> *"Attempting to imagine what it cannot, [the mind] has pain in the failure ..."*
>
> **Immanuel Kant,** *The Third Critique* (1790)

mind cannot find a way to organize it, to make it make sense. But instead of being simply frustrated or upset by this inability, the sublime brings about alternating feelings of displeasure and pleasure. These feelings are the result of psychological tension between the mind's faculties of imagination, understanding, and reason. The displeasure stems from the failure to grasp something through the senses and understand it, and the pleasure is an enthusiasm for the supersensible flight of fancy. The faculty of reason contains ideas of absolute freedom and totality, so it is the only one capable of making sense of the experience. *The Third Critique* altered cognitive aesthetics. Kant's notion of the sublime changed the way we think about aesthetic experiences, the feelings we have when faced by art or nature, and the judgments at which we arrive. **KBJ**

Against Revolution

Edmund Burke

The notion that gradual reform is better than revolution for bringing about change

Published in 1790 by Irish political theorist and philosopher Edmund Burke (1729–97), *Reflections on the Revolution in France* remains to this day the best-known intellectual attack on the French Revolution. The work provoked a huge response, most notably from English-American political activist Thomas Paine (1737–1809), who initiated an exchange of pamphlets.

In the work, Burke called for military defeat of revolutionary France and the reinstatement of the old aristocratic society. While he disliked the divine right of kings and the idea that people had no right to challenge an oppressive government, he argued for tradition, social status, prejudice in some forms, and private property—each citizen should have a clear idea of where they belong in their nation's social hierarchy.

"To give freedom is still more easy . . . it only requires to let go the rein."

Edmund Burke, *Reflections on the Revolution . . .* (1790)

Burke favored gradual constitutional reforms rather than revolution, and emphasized how mob rule could threaten individual rights, freedoms, and society as a whole. He argued that the French based their revolution on overly abstract principles; structuring government on abstract ideas such as liberty and equality rather than effective command and order could lead to abuse and tyranny. Many of Burke's predictions came true; he foresaw a popular army general becoming master of the assembly, and, two years after Burke died, Napoleon seized the assembly and created a military dictatorship that was corrupt and violent.

Reflections expresses classical liberal and conservative political views. Right or wrong, the book offers an excellent analysis of how a revolution can murder itself by its own principles. **KBJ**

Presumption of Innocence

William Garrow

The legal principle that an accused person is innocent until proven guilty

Of all the legal apparatus that surrounds a criminal trial, one aspect stands out above all others. When the accused stands in the dock, he or she is presumed innocent until proven guilty. It is up to the prosecution to make the case that the defendant is guilty, it is not up to the defendant to have to prove his or her innocence. This age-old principle dates back to Roman times, although it was first named by an English juror, William Garrow (1760–1840), in the eighteenth century.

William Garrow became a barrister in 1783. He specialized as a criminal defense counsel, later becoming attorney general for England and Wales in 1813 and a judge in 1817. Quite early in his career, in 1791, he coined the phrase "innocent until proven guilty" and insisted that the prosecution case must be properly tested in court. The principle itself had origins in the sixth-century legal Digest or compendium of Roman law compiled for Emperor Justinian, which stated, "The burden of proof lies with who declares, not who denies," drawing on the earlier work of the third-century Roman jurist Julius Paulus. For the principle to work, three related rules presume that in respect of the facts, the state as prosecution has the entire burden of proof; that the defendant has no burden of proof and does not even have to testify, call witnesses, or present any evidence; and that the judge and jury are not allowed to draw any negative inferences from the fact that the defendant has been charged and is in court.

The presumption of innocence has international appeal. It appears in Islamic Sharia law, and also in European common law and the civil law systems of countries such as Italy and France. Many countries have explicitly included it in their constitutions and legal codes. The course of justice would be radically different without it. **SA**

Equal Education for Women
Mary Wollstonecraft

The argument that women will achieve equality with men, both in the workplace and in their marriages, only by receiving an education appropriate to their station in society

In *A Vindication of the Rights of Women*, published in 1792, writer and philosopher Mary Wollstonecraft (1759–97) argues that women should have the same rights to an education suited to their places in society as men do. Wollstonecraft believed that educating women would not only further the interests of women, but would also strengthen marriages, home life, and society as a whole. She argued that stable marriages occur when spouses are equals and share the marriage as equal partners. She also wrote that men and women have a sexual nature, and the strength of the marriage is dependent on both partners remaining faithful.

Wollstonecraft wrote *A Vindication of the Rights of Women* in England during the time of the French Revolution (1787–99), and many of her opinions were radical for the time. Although she wrote about a wide variety of subjects, ranging from child education to politics and history, *A Vindication of the Rights of Women* is widely seen as one of the first works of what would later become feminism. She wrote the book to argue against the notions that women were destined only to be wives to their husbands and were suited only for limited domestic purposes. Hers was a decidedly radical opinion for the time as many people, especially men, viewed women as little more than chattels.

A Vindication of the Rights of Women was well received in its time, but revelations about Wollstonecraft's illegitimate daughter, unorthodox personal life, and suicide attempts caused the work to be viewed with suspicion for more than a hundred years. It was not until the twentieth century that Wollstonecraft's life and work became better understood. It served as inspiration for many feminists, including Virginia Woolf (1882–1941), even though feminists today do not regard education on its own to be sufficient to provide equality between the sexes. **MT**

⬆ A portrait of Mary Wollstonecraft painted by John Keenan in *c.* 1793. Mary Wollstonecraft's daughter, Mary Shelley (*née* Mary Wollstonecraft Godwin) went on to write *Frankenstein* (1818).

"Virtue can only flourish amongst equals."

Mary Wollstonecraft

The Age of Reason
Thomas Paine

A critique of institutionalized religion that advocated deism instead

In 1794, 1795, and 1807, the English-American political activist Thomas Paine (1737–1809) published a three-part pamphlet series, *The Age of Reason; Being an Investigation of True and Fabulous Theology*. It was well received in the United States but not in Britain, where there was growing fear of radical political views following the French Revolution (1787–99). Paine wrote the first two parts while he was imprisoned in France during the Reign of Terror (1793–94). The views contained were not new to the educated, but, using an engaging, satirical, "no holds barred" style, he was able to access a larger audience. The low cost of his pamphlets also helped.

A deist manifesto, *The Age of Reason* gives the central tenets of deism as, first, God created the world but does not constantly intervene or interact with us directly,

"Give to every other human being every right that you claim for yourself."
Thomas Paine, *The Age of Reason* (1794)

and, second, the existence of God can be proved on the basis of reason and observing the natural world. Paine, rejecting the possibility of miracles, argued that nature was the only form of divine revelation, since it was obvious that God had established a uniform and eternal order throughout his creation.

Paine also rejected Christianity, calling it a human invention, and criticized attempts by what he viewed as a corrupt Christian Church to gain political power. He also denied that the Bible was the word of God, referring to it as just an ordinary piece of literature. Paine's attempts to spread deism and attacks on the Christian Church made him many enemies. But his pamphlets were designed to bring politics to the people in a clear and simple style, and this changed political discourse. **KBJ**

The Morality of Terror
Maximilien de Robespierre

Persecution by the state is justifiable if directed toward virtuous ends

On February 5, 1794, during the infamous Reign of Terror in France (1793–94), Maximilien de Robespierre (1758–94) wrote *Report on the Principles of Political Morality*, an impassioned defense of the Revolution. He argued that the Republic could be saved from its enemies by the virtue of its citizens, and that terror was virtuous and fully justified because it helped maintain the principles of the Revolution and the Republic. The violence occurring during the Terror was necessary in order to achieve higher political goals. In the event, 16,594 people were executed in France during the Terror, with the ironic inclusion of Robespierre himself.

Robespierre believed that terror had a deep moral purpose, beyond winning any war. He envisioned a society in which people sought the happiness of their

"Virtue ... without terror is destructive; terror ... without virtue is impotent."
Robespierre, *Report on the Principles ...* (1794)

fellow citizens—the peaceful enjoyment of liberty, equality, and natural justice—rather than material benefits. Declaring that "the blade of the law shall hover over the guilty," he vowed to use the political power he had gained during the Terror to hound out and eliminate all opponents of the Revolution and create what he called a "Republic of Virtue." In reality, terror seems to have been resorted to out of the fear and weakness of the controlling Jacobin party.

For the first time in history, the use of terror was an official, fully endorsed government policy. Robespierre's *Report* is a horrifying example of how a noble idea, such as virtue, can be twisted out of all recognition to become a logical justification for tyranny and violence. It is a perfect example of how genuinely good intentions can result in evil. **KBJ**

An illustration of Robespierre—the original proponent of the Terror—being led to the guillotine in 1794.

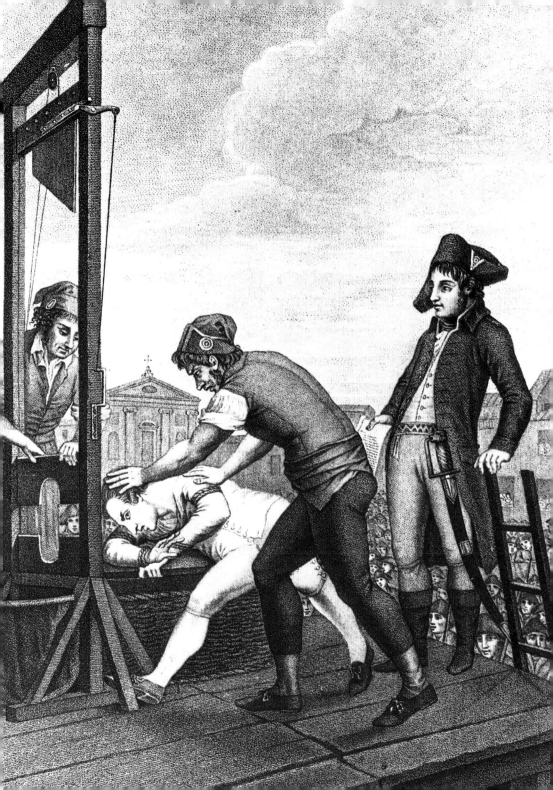

Gradualism
James Hutton

The theory that changes occur, or ought to occur, slowly and incrementally

Scottish geologist and farmer James Hutton (1726–97) is credited with originating the idea of gradualism in 1795, and his notion of gradual change revolutionized the sciences of geology and biology. It has also influenced the fields of politics and linguistics.

In natural sciences, gradualism is a theory that change is the cumulative product of slow but steady processes. In geology, Hutton argued that landforms such as canyons, or even layers of soil, were the result of slow, steady changes over very long periods of time. The theory contrasts with that of catastrophism, which held that the changes originated in short-lived events.

In biology, naturalist Charles Darwin (1809–82) embraced gradualism in his theory of evolution, which states that mutations occur gradually over time to

"This is no time . . . to take the tranquilizing drug of gradualism."
Martin Luther King Jr., "I Have a Dream" speech (1963)

become naturally selected helpful traits. Individual organisms possessing a small variation that suits them slightly better to their environment are more likely to survive and reproduce than those without the slightly helpful trait. Generations of the more fortunate individuals survive and reproduce, while those without the trait die out, with the result that the population of that organism changes gradually over time.

In politics and society, it is believed that gradual changes to policy, law, and practices are preferred to the violent or abrupt changes resulting from revolution and uprisings. Political gradualism is contrasted with reformism, which urges swift and radical changes. In the United States, gradualism was proposed in the 1950s to eliminate racial segregation, but many reformists felt this was merely a way of avoiding the issue. **KBJ**

Doppelganger
Jean Paul

The notion of a coexisting identical being, double, or negative version of a person

The word "doppelganger" was adopted by German writer Johann Paul Richter (1763–1825, pseudonym Jean Paul), who used it in his work *Siebenkäs* (1796–97). The term, which began appearing in English around 1851, literally means "double walker," or, more simply, a double of a living person.

In German folklore, a doppelganger is a sinister or evil paranormal entity, not a ghost or spirit of the dead but a kind of apparition that is the negative or opposite of its human counterpart. There are doppelganger-like descriptions in Egyptian, Norse, and Finnish mythologies, also. In folklore, seeing your double was an omen of imminent death or horrible things.

A doppelganger is also a literary device referring to a character in a story that is a copy or impersonator

". . . the 'double' was originally an insurance against destruction to the ego . . . "
Sigmund Freud, "The 'Uncanny'" (1919)

of another character. Soap operas classically use this device in their plots. These "fake" doubles often have intentions and emotions different to those of their "real" counterparts and cause great psychological anxiety for the person they haunt. Today, a literary doppelganger is less likely to have evil intentions; it may simply be a look-alike of someone, the cause of a moment's "double take" on the part of an observer.

The idea of a doppelganger has greatly impacted literature, movies, and television, providing some of the greatest plots, twists, and characters. It has influenced *Dr. Jekyll and Mr. Hyde* (1886), *Twin Peaks* (1990–91), *Fight Club* (1999), *Mulholland Drive* (2001), and *Black Swan* (2010). The notion is easily abused, and can lead at times to cliché, but when used imaginatively it can underpin intense, cliff-hanging drama. **KBJ**

Gambler's Fallacy
Pierre-Simon Laplace

The false assumption that probability is affected by past events

If, when using a fair coin, heads are flipped five times in a row, the Gambler's Fallacy suggests that the next toss will be tails because it is "due"; the chance of tails coming up on the next toss is therefore seen as greater than half. This is bad reasoning because the results of previous tosses have no bearing on future tosses.

The fallacy is also known as the Monte Carlo Fallacy because of an incident that happened there at a roulette table in 1913, when black fell twenty-six times in a row. While this is a rare occurrence, it is among the possibilities, as is any other sequence of red or black. Needless to say, gamblers at that table lost millions that day because they reasoned, incorrectly, that red was due to be next, or next after that. The fallacy also occurs in the erroneous thought that gambling is an

"[Gambler's fallacy relies on the] idea that essentially chance events have memories."

J. D. Mullen and B. M. Roth, *Decision Making* (1991)

inherently fair process, in which any losses incurred inevitably will be corrected by a winning streak.

French mathematician Pierre-Simon Laplace (1749–1827) first noted the fallacy behavior in his *Philosophical Essay on Probabilities* (1796), in which he wrote about expectant fathers trying to predict the probability of having sons. The men imagined the ratio of boys to girls born each month to be fifty/fifty, and that if neighboring villages had high male birth rates it implied that births in their own village had a high probability of being female. Also, fathers who had several children of the same sex believed that the next one would be of the opposite sex—it being "due."

The Gambler's Fallacy warns that there is no Lady Luck or "invisible hand" in charge of your game. Walk away with your money and dignity now. **KBJ**

Homeopathy
Samuel Hahnemann

The theory that tiny amounts of harmful substances prompt the body to cure itself

German physician Samuel Hahnemann (1755–1843) was so disturbed by the use of bloodletting, leeching, and purging in common medical procedure that he gave up his own practice and became a researcher. In 1796 he identified the founding principle of homeopathy: that a substance which produces symptoms in a healthy person will cure similar symptoms in a person who is sick. Hahnemann refined his theory with two other principles: first, that the less you use of a substance, the more potent it becomes, and, second, that a sickness is always unique to the person who is suffering it.

The idea of homeopathy closely echoes the Hippocratic idea that "like cures like." Hahnemann came across a version of this "law of similars" in 1790 while translating William Cullen's *A Treatise of Materia*

"The physician's high and only mission is to restore the sick to health ..."

Samuel Hahnemann, *Organon of Medicine* (1833)

Medica (1789) into German. Homeopaths claim that the principle is the same as that underlying vaccination: just as a vaccine provokes a reaction from the individual's immune system that in the future protects against that person from actual disease, so the homeopathic remedy, it is said, provokes the body into healing.

It is hardly surprising that homeopathy was embraced in the early nineteenth century: medical procedures, just as Hahnemann claimed, often did more harm than good. Today, homeopathy's impact is evidenced by the existence of a multimillion-dollar industry in alternative medicine. And the persistence of the idea that there is more to human healing than conventional medicine allows for remains a challenge: are we more than the sum of our parts, or does it just make us feel good to think we are? **LW**

Willmar Schwabe's "Improved chemist's shop with 134 remedies in bottles, A, B and D" (1889). ➜

TAB. B.

Homöopathische Central-Apotheke
von
Dr. Willmar Schwabe
in
Leipzig.

Verbesserte Apotheke mit 134 Medicamenten in Flaschen A, B und D.

66. Ipecacuanha. D. 2.

118. Staphisagria D. 3.

64. Ignatia. D. 3.

Flac. A. 25 Gr.   Flac. D. 5 Gr.   Flac. B. 15 Gr.

Assembly Line
Eli Whitney

Manufacturing items in a sequential manner, using interchangeable components

In 1797, the U.S. government solicited contracts from private firms to produce 40,000 Model 1795 .69 caliber flintlock muskets. U.S. inventor Eli Whitney (1765–1825) proposed to supply 10,000 muskets over two years by assembling machined parts that conformed precisely to a model or jig. Prior to the mechanization of the assembly line, craftsmen made unique products by hand. The interchangeable parts produced by Whitney's unconventional method would allow unskilled workmen to assemble the muskets at a faster, and thus cheaper, rate than was traditionally possible.

Although Whitney was probably the first to exploit the assembly line concept for business purposes, other theorists and inventors had done seminal work. In his book *The Wealth of Nations* (1776), Scottish philosopher

"The tools ... shall fashion the work and give to every part its just proportion."

Eli Whitney

and economist Adam Smith had discussed the idea of division of labor for the manufacture of pins; and French gunsmith Honoré Blanc, influenced by the French artillerists' Gribeauval system of cannon and shell standardization, had used gauges and filing jigs to achieve engineering tolerances in the manufacture of interchangeable musket parts. Whitney's assembly line not only speeded up manufacture but also made it easier to replace parts of damaged or defective muskets.

Modern mass-production assembly lines rely upon the judicious arrangement of machines, equipment, and workers to achieve a continuous flow of work pieces. All movements of materials are simplified to eliminate cross flow or backtracking. In the early twentieth century, the Ford Motor Company adopted the assembly line to mass-produce the Model T. **BC**

Malthusian Law
Thomas Malthus

The theory that population growth will naturally ensure the persistence of poverty

British political economist Thomas Malthus (1766–1834) doubted that human progress was as inevitable as the utopians of his era proclaimed. In *An Essay on the Principle of Population* (1798), he explained that, while progress required more material wealth for everyone, he could not see how agricultural production could keep pace with rapid population growth.

Malthus observed that agriculture could grow arithmetically so that 100 units of food could be (say) 150 units in forty years, and 200 units in eighty years. Assuming no depletion of soil and water, doubling total food in three generations would be an impressive technological feat. However, if the typical family has four children, then a generation of 100 people is replaced by a generation of 200, followed

"Population, when unchecked ... increases in a geometrical ratio."

Thomas Malthus

(geometrically) by 400 people in around eighty years. Thus, 100 units of food for 100 people today eventually translates to 200 units of food for 400 people, so the later individuals get half as much food as before.

Since food is never distributed equally, Malthusian law predicts much malnourishment and death from famine. The law explains why, despite increases in food production of more than 50 percent over the past two generations, 2 billion people today go hungry.

Malthus's work inspired the evolutionary theory of Charles Darwin (1809–82), that competition for food among an oversupply of animals would naturally select the unfit for elimination, causing a species to evolve over time. Malthusian law has not been refuted, but humanity could evade its implications through family planning and birth control. **JSh**

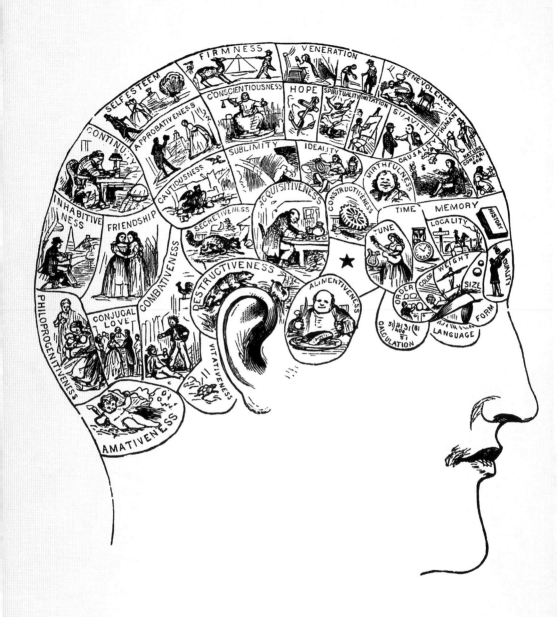

Phrenological Chart of the Faculties.

Phrenology
Franz Joseph Gall

The belief that a person's mental attributes may be determined by assessing their skull

Developed around 1800 by German physiologist and neuroanatomist Franz Joseph Gall (1758–1828), phrenology was originally called craniscopy; today it is considered a pseudoscience. Drawing on the science of character, theory of the brain and mind, and faculty psychology (in which different faculties of the brain perform different tasks), phrenology sought to link a person's character with the shape of their skull.

Phrenology was extremely popular in England in the early nineteenth century, with some employers even asking a phrenologist to determine whether a prospective employee was an honest and hardworking person. However, by the 1850s the "science" had lost credibility as it had become apparent that few practicing it could deal with contradictory evidence.

"I never knew I had an inventive talent until Phrenology told me so."

Thomas Edison, inventor

The logic of Gall's phrenology ran as follows: first, the brain is an organ of the mind and it controls propensities, feelings, and faculties; second, the mind is composed of many distinct, innate faculties (including moral and intellectual ones); third, because these faculties are all distinct, they must each have a different place or organ in the brain; fourth, the size of an organ is a measure of its power, and its actions depend on its organization; fifth, the shape of the brain is determined by the development of its various organs. Thus, by "reading" the dents, dips, and protrusions of the skull, particular character traits, intellectual abilities, and natural propensities may be identified and quantified.

Gall's ideas influenced today's neuropsychology, which studies the structure and function of the brain as it relates to processes and behaviors, and psychiatry. **KBJ**

Separation of Church and State
Thomas Jefferson

The view that the church should keep out of the state's business, and vice versa

The closeness of relationship between the political apparatus of a nation state and its organized religious body or bodies is one that varies from nation to nation, depending on the law system in place and the populace's prevalent views on religion in society. The degree of separation of church and state is typically detailed in a country's constitution.

From ancient Greece through medieval times, church and state were generally mixed. Crimes were described as being against the state and the gods; kings had additional priestly titles, or their throne was granted by divine right; and Catholic popes could depose kings and compel regal government. However, during the Protestant Reformation, Martin Luther (1483–1546) advocated the "doctrine of two kingdoms," which

"The government of the United States is not ... founded on the Christian religion."

George Washington, U.S. president 1789–97

divided God's rule into a worldly kingdom governed by laws, and a spiritual kingdom governed by grace. The doctrine is described as one of the earliest conceptions of a separation of church and state.

In North America, the most influential separationist was U.S. founding father Thomas Jefferson (1743–1826). The First Amendment to the United States Constitution (1791) asserted that the government must respect an individual's freedom of religion, and not create laws to establish a national religion. This separation of church and state changed the way that people perceived the role of religion in society, especially concerning government, law, morality, and individual freedom. Historically, the separation of church and state has benefited the advancement of science, since many scientific discoveries run counter to religious belief. **KBJ**

A phrenology illustration from the *People's Cyclopedia of Universal Knowledge* (1883).

1802

The Watchmaker Analogy
William Paley

As a watch implies a watchmaker, the natural world implies the existence of God

Western conceptions of God are shaped by a variety of human experiences, such as the powerful sense of awe inspired by a glowing sunset, a towering mountain range, or even the complexity of a mammalian cell when viewed under a microscope. Such experiences have led many thinkers to believe that the objects and events that inspire these feelings are intentional, that is, they have been designed. Since design implies a personal agent, these experiences seem, to many, grounds for believing that an extra-natural intelligent being crafted the cosmos. This inference is known as the "teleological (goal-directed) argument" for God's existence, which can be traced to Xenophon's *Memorabilia* (*c.* 371 BCE) and Plato's *Timaeus* (*c.* 360 BCE).

British philosopher and Anglican bishop William Paley (1743–1805) formulated a well-known version of this argument, known as "The Watchmaker Analogy," in his *Natural Theology* (1802). Paley contrasts the experience of finding an ordinary stone with finding a watch, and then asks whether it is reasonable to regard their possible origins as being the same. He answers with a resounding "no"; everything about the watch points to the existence of an intelligent craftsman, whereas the features of the stone suggest nothing at all about its origins. This distinction between design and chance leads Paley to conclude that atheism is as absurd as the idea that the watch is the product of chance: he asserts that "every indication of contrivance, every manifestation of design, which existed in the watch, exists in the works of nature."

Arguments such as this one continue to play an important role in discussions of the limits of science and its relationship with religion. The contemporary Intelligent Design movement that began with Phillip E. Johnson's *Darwin on Trial* (1991) and Michael J. Behe's *Darwin's Black Box* (1997) is a development in the tradition that Paley helped to advance. **JW**

According to the watchmaker analogy, feats of nature such as Mount Everest are evidence of God. ⬆

1809

Heavier-Than-Air Flight
George Cayley

The theory that machines might be able to fly by utilizing lift and thrust

Every bird demonstrates its capability of heavier-than-air flight by, in part, employing a lifting body—its wings—to create air pressure differentials. When a wing travels through the air, the air pressure above it is less than the air pressure below it; as a consequence, the air below pushes the wing higher, enabling whatever is attached to the wing, or wings, to fly. The concept of heavier-than-air flight is no more than that: to soar like a bird, attached to wings that lift.

From an early nineteenth-century perspective, rigid-frame kites had been invented in China as early as 2800 BCE, while human flight had been possible only since 1783, as a passenger floating under a hot-air balloon. Early thinkers, such as Leonardo da Vinci (1452–1519), had

studied the flight of birds, and had even designed craft that might replicate their abilities. However, no real progress was made toward practically achieving heavier-than-air flight until English engineer George Cayley (1773–1857) began studying the aerodynamics necessary in 1791, when he started experimenting with hang gliders. Cayley built a working model of a glider and designed a glider to carry a person, as well as publishing a treatise, *On Aerial Navigation*, in 1809. Humankind finally flew in 1853, when Cayley's coachman completed the first manned glider flight in a full-scale model of Cayley's design. Fifty years later, in December 1903, Orville (1871–1948) and Wilbur (1867–1912) Wright became legendary overnight when they flew the first powered, heavier-than-air flying machine.

Without heavier-than-air flight, the world would seem a much larger place than it does today. Within fifty years of the Wright brothers' flight, aircraft could fly faster than sound and travel across continents. A short time after that, aircraft were traveling into space. Military aircraft have changed warfare, while same-day intercontinental travel is now available to anyone sufficiently well-off to purchase a ticket. **MT**

⬆ A photograph from 1894 (colored later), showing aviation pioneer Otto Lilienthal flying a hang glider.

Lamarckian Evolution
Jean-Baptiste Lamarck

A theory concerning the evolution of living creatures that held that adaptive behaviors of parents resulted in physical characteristics in their offspring

⬆ According to Jean-Baptiste Lamarck's theory of evolution, a given giraffe could, over a lifetime of straining to reach high branches, develop an elongated neck.

English naturalist Charles Darwin (1809–82) was not the first to use the term "evolution," or to propose that today's species are different from those living long ago. French naturalist Jean-Baptiste Lamarck (1744–1829), after contributing to biology and taxonomy, ambitiously suggested that vital forces within life guide it toward greater complexity, resulting in the evolutionary "progress" observable in higher life forms. Lamarck's *Philosophie Zoologique* (1809) added another older idea, that useful acquired features of parents can be reproductively inherited by their offspring. Lamarck accounted for giraffes' long necks by saying that the slightly stretched necks of some individuals were passed on to their offspring in the form of slightly longer necks; the offspring in turn would keep stretching their necks during their lifetimes before having their own longer-necked offspring; thus each generation has longer and longer necks.

The Lamarckian theory would mean that parents' sperm and eggs are modified somehow by their achievements, but no evidence has supported this. In 1883 August Weismann (1834–1914) became the first Darwinian biologist to reject this theory of the inheritance of acquired characteristics, arguing that germ cells are produced in the body without any contribution from other somatic (body) cells formed during the parent's lifetime. Yet, despite growing evidence favoring the modern evolutionary synthesis propelled by Weismann and Gregor Mendel (1822–84), scientists' confidence in nonrandom evolutionary progress sustained a preference for Lamarck.

New research in epigenetics confirms ways in which environmental factors can indirectly manipulate the timing and extent of genes' activity. Epigenetics has aroused interest in neo-Lamarckian effects, but Larmarckian ideas of inheritance remain refuted. **JSh**

> *"Lamarckian types of theory ... are traditionally rejected—and rightly so—because no good evidence for them has ever been found."*
>
> Richard Dawkins, biologist

Tonality
Alexandre-Étienne Choron

A way of organizing pitch that continues to dominate most forms of Western music

In 1810 French musicologist Alexandre-Étienne Choron (1771–1834) defined tonality in the way it is used today, as an organization of harmonic triads around a focal major or minor triad, the Tonic, with the Subdominant on the fourth scale degree, driving to the Dominant on the fifth, followed by a resolution to the Tonic. A variety of metaphors, such as "gravitational pull," have subsequently been used to describe the perceptual forces at play in this arrangement.

The three chords of the Tonic, Subdominant, and Dominant provide a rudimentary harmonization of most tunes constructed from a diatonic scale. Since the early seventeenth century they have come to replace an older melodic/harmonic approach based on the twelve church modes. Today, the concept of tonality includes a complex syntax of chords surrounding a referential Tonic chord.

"Tonality" has been used in wider, less useful, senses, too, to describe pitch organizations around a referential pitch center, such as the scale system in North Indian classical music, and even to describe the organization of highly atonal music (such as "twelve-tone tonality," the technique devised by the composer George Perle).

Notes that do not belong to a chord, or chords that do not belong to the key, create tension and require resolution; this was explored in the chromatic music of J. S. Bach in the eighteenth century and that of Richard Wagner in the nineteenth, culminating in Wagner's operas *Tristan and Isolde* (1865) and *Parsifal* (1882). During the first decades of the twentieth century, a notion arose that the constant increase in complexity would result in a total breakdown of the system in favor of atonality. However, tonality continues to dominate music today, particularly in many genres of popular music, but also in neo-romantic music. **PB**

Absolute Music
Germany

The notion that instrumental music has no purpose or content outside of itself

A German philosophical idea of the nineteenth century, "absolute" music refers to instrumental music that is "untainted" by words and extra-musical ideas; it is a pure art form. One of the first advocates for this concept was writer and composer E. T. A. Hoffman (1776–1822), as expressed in his review of Beethoven's Fifth Symphony in 1810. Richard Wagner (1813–83) later challenged this idea, arguing that poetry, dance, and music created a complete artwork, the *Gesamtkunstwerk*.

Defenders of absolute music, including German music critic Eduard Hanslick (1825–1904), pointed to the instrumental music of Johannes Brahms (1833–97) as the ideal. Hanslick argued that there is no strict causation between a particular musical phrase and its emotional effect, and that the same musical phrase set

"Music cannot imitate nature: a musical storm always sounds like the wrath of Zeus."

W. H. Auden, *The Dyer's Hand and other Essays* (1962)

to diametrically different poetry could be considered equally appropriate. Music has no purpose beyond itself. Hanslick never denied that a piece of music could engender extra-musical thoughts and feelings, but maintained that these emotions were not intrinsically linked to the music itself, only the individual listener.

The notion of absolute music represents a valid aesthetic problem: if music's content is just "tonally moving forms," as Hanslick termed it, why are there often agreements between different listeners as to the expressive properties of a composition? With the advent of silent cinema, music written to fit standardized dramatic situations—love scene, chase, agonized reflection—created a more or less fixed vocabulary of musical gestures. Perhaps there is a purpose for music after all: to provide support for moving images. **PB**

Ce Bouquet, ne peut être trop beau pour notre Père.

Repas d'un St Simonien.

Dame St Simonienne prechant la Doctrine.

St Simonienne Jardinière.

St Simonienne Cordonnier.

St Simonienne revenant de la chasse.

St Simonienne Forgeron.

St Simonienne Couvreur.

St Simonienne appelant les Adeptes au travail.

St Simonienne Docteur en Droit.

St Simonienne étudiant la Sagesse.

Chez BERRIEUX, Md d'Estampes, rue St Jacques Nº 25.

Utopian Socialism
Henri de Saint-Simon

A vision of a just, happy society without poverty or the need for social controls

Utopian socialists describe a society with four features: it maximizes wellbeing for all; it satisfies standards of ethics and justice; it requires egalitarian cooperation; and all peoples can freely join. Utopian socialism emphasizes ethical cooperation and equal opportunity as the route to maximal wellbeing, and expects that all people will gladly join. If human nature is mainly good, then little civil control is needed in small-scale communalism, and freedom can be optimized. If human nature turns out to be a mixture of good and bad, then large-scale socialist government is recommended, and perhaps a single world government.

Widespread adoption of Enlightenment ideas and mass democracy by 1800 gave encouragement to consideration of ideal democratic societies able to

> "The utopian socialists saw themselves as social scientists…"
>
> **Vincent Geoghegan, *Utopianism and Marxism* (2008)**

eliminate feudalism and poverty, reduce wealth and caste distinctions, and re-think economic systems. Sociologist and political economist Henri de Saint-Simon (1760–1825) shocked Europe with *L'Industrie* (1816) and subsequent works, in which he proposed government guarantees of economic productivity to all who want to work, and the elimination of nonproductive classes, such as aristocrats, bureaucrats, and clergy. His collaborator, Auguste Comte (1798–1857), advanced scientific principles in social organization. Socialist Robert Owen followed, along with Charles Fourier and Pierre-Joseph Proudhon. Karl Marx and Friedrich Engels were indebted to this tradition, but their Communist Manifesto of 1848 identified utopian socialism as better than capitalism, yet less realistic than revolutionary communism. **JSh**

Pessimism
Arthur Schopenhauer

Life consists of a doomed and ultimately meaningless striving for power

In their worldview, optimists expect higher values to prevail in the long run; realists or cynics expect few long-term successes; pessimists expect everything of value to disappoint and perish. All three apply objective ethical standards to praise or condemn reality. Forms of pessimism had existed as far back as ancient Greece, but it was not until the work of nineteenth-century German philosopher Arthur Schopenhauer (1788–1860) that modern pessimism was born.

In 1819 Schopenhauer published his theory that will, or the drive to power, is the ultimate reality. Inspired by ancient Hindu Upanishads and Buddhism, he perceived will to be behind everything that is biologically alive. Our ethical duty is to love and aid each other, since our achievement is worthy, but we

> "It would be better if there were nothing … there is more pain than pleasure on earth."
>
> **Arthur Schopenhauer**

also see that nothing lasts for long and death destroys each of us. The godless cosmos is nothing but ceaseless unsatisfiable striving that may be eternal but never amounts to anything. Schopenhauer goes further than Stoicism or Buddhism, counseling people to stop having children, embrace resignation, extinguish their will to live, and hasten death. Schopenhauer influenced dramatist Richard Wagner, philosophers Friedrich Nietzsche and Ludwig Wittgenstein, and author Jorge Luis Borges.

Contemporary atheists agree that the universe is meaningless and nothing good is eternal, yet they value life for its own sake, following scientific rationalists such as August Comte and Herbert Spencer in expecting endless biological and technological progress. Few deny that this life is worthwhile. **JSh**

← Occupations of women (*c.* 1830), as envisaged by the utopian socialist Saint-Simonianism movement.

Braille
Louis Braille

Using touch to read combinations of dots representing letters and numbers

Louis Braille (1809–52), the inventor of the braille writing system for the visually impaired, became blind at a young age after suffering an accident. As a child at the Royal Institute for Blind Youth in Paris, Braille learned to read by running his hands over raised letters. In 1821, after learning about a military code known as night writing, one that employed raised dots to represent sounds to allow soldiers to read in the dark, Braille began to develop his system of using raised dots to represent letters instead of sounds.

Braille's system substitutes tactile letters for visual ones. Today, braille can be written through the use of specially made typewriters that imprint paper with combinations of raised dots, or computers and printers that do the same; otherwise, users can emboss dots in paper by hand with the aid of a special stylus and slate. People who cannot see clearly use their fingers to touch the sequences of raised dots and interpret them as individual letters or numbers. Like other forms of writing, braille is a method of representing letters, rather than a language in itself. It can be used to represent any language, including musical notation.

Prior to the invention of braille, visually impaired people had very few options when accessing literature. Conventional lettering could be raised for use as a tactile writing system, but creating new works of raised letters was unwieldy and complicated. With braille, reading and writing became much simpler for those with visual impairments, potentially allowing them to experience the entire written world.

After the introduction of braille, literacy rates among visually impaired people skyrocketed, especially after braille typewriters, and later printers, became readily available. Visually impaired people were even enabled to use computers when refreshable braille displays, which usually raise dots through holes in a flat surface, were introduced in the 1980s. **MT**

The braille system of writing uses a code of sixty-three characters. ⬆

Photography
Joseph-Nicéphore Niépce

The concept of capturing a permanent visual record of a fleeting moment in time

The world's first photograph was produced in 1822 by French inventor Joseph-Nicéphore Niépce (1765–1833). Using bitumen of Judea, a light-sensitive type of asphalt that hardens on exposure to light, he succeeded in obtaining a photographic copy of an engraving superimposed on glass. In 1826, using a camera, he took the world's first permanently fixed photograph, a view from his workroom captured on a pewter plate. Light passing through the camera's lens was converted into a two-dimensional, static, and durable image.

His collaborator, Louis-Jacques-Mande Daguerre (1787–1851), perfected the stable daguerreotype in 1837. Ambrotypes (on glass plates) and tintypes (on metal plates) were replaced by the film photography of George Eastman (1854–1932) in the 1880s. Kodak introduced cheap color photography in the 1930s, which was followed by Polaroid's instant photography (1960s), and digital cameras using charge-coupled devices (1980s).

As in painting, the choice of subject, perspective, context, framing, focus, and color tone all make photography a creative artistic medium. The positioning of human actors and the dramatic arrangement of action captured by the photographer permit a photograph to tell a compelling story, as in theater. The static scene can suggest a realism and a truth more objective than an eyewitnessed account. At the intersection of aesthetics, ethics, and epistemology, photography is the place where the beautiful, the good, and the true can temporarily unite. A beautiful photograph can lend goodness to its subject; a disturbing one can arouse a sense of injustice; and a justly taken image can be the truth. However, a photograph can mask its own agenda, and no other art form, perhaps excepting the novel, can serve ideology as effectively.

Today, photography is ubiquitous and inexpensive. However, with the advent of photo-editing computer software, the photograph can easily be made to lie. **JSh**

↑ Niépce captured this view, one of the earliest surviving photographs, from his window in 1826.

Dark Night Sky Paradox
Heinrich Wilhelm Olbers

The question of why the universe's billions of stars do not brighten the night sky

⬆ Olbers answered his paradox by suggesting that light from stars, such as these ones in the globular cluster Messier 10, is gradually absorbed while traveling through space.

"Were the succession of stars endless, then the background of the sky would present us a uniform luminosity."

Edgar Allen Poe, "Eureka" (1848)

Experience and common sense suggest that when night descends, the sky gets dark except for the moon and the bright pinpoints of light that we recognize as stars. However, this apparently straightforward phenomenon actually poses significant problems for scientific theories of an infinite universe. German physician and astronomer Heinrich Wilhelm Olbers (1758–1840) pointed out the paradoxical nature of night in 1823, arguing that if the universe really is endless and uniformly populated with stars, then, no matter from where the observation is being made, the night sky should be completely bright.

The name Olbers tends always to be used in referring to the "dark night sky paradox" as Olbers' Paradox. However, British astronomer and cosmologist Edward Robert Harrison (1919–2007), in his widely accepted account of Olbers' Paradox titled *Darkness at Night: A Riddle of the Universe* (1987), makes the case that Olbers was derivative in his description of the problem and actually contributed nothing of importance to the paradox bearing his name. Harrison asserts that German astronomer Johannes Kepler (1571–1630) advanced it far earlier, in 1610, in an argument against the theory of infinite stars in an infinite universe. Later work on this scientific conundrum was conducted in the eighteenth century by Edmond Halley (1656–1742)—after whom the comet was named—and Frenchman Jean-Phillippe Loys de Chéseaux (1718–51), the latter being the first to state the paradox in its present form.

Regardless, mathematical physicist Lord Kelvin (1824–1907), in a barely noted paper of 1901, proposed a satisfactory resolution to the paradox. Olbers' Paradox is proof that the universe, rather than being static, is constantly expanding. The light from the stars in the far reaches of the universe, he claims, has not yet reached Earth, and that is why the sky is dark in between the stars that we observe. **MK**

Greenhouse Effect

Joseph Fourier

The theory that the atmosphere traps infrared radiation from the Earth

The discovery of the "greenhouse effect" is attributed to the French physicist Joseph Fourier (1768–1830), who published his first article on the subject in 1824. Citing the researches of fellow physicist Horace-Bénédict de Saussure (1740–99) with "hot boxes"—miniature greenhouses covered with several panes of transparent glass to trap heat from the sun—Fourier concluded that atmospheric gases could trap heat in the same way as glass panes—a comparison that suggested the term greenhouse effect.

Life on Earth depends on maintaining an average surface temperature comfortably between the boiling and freezing points of water. The planet is heated by absorbing solar radiation, but it also gives it off in the form of invisible infrared radiation. Every region of the planet would heat up during the day but rapidly cool to subzero temperatures at night were it not for gases in the atmosphere forming an insulating blanket that absorbs escaping heat and redirects it back to the planet's surface. The so-called greenhouse effect is what keeps our temperature in a comfortable range.

The discovery of which gases in the atmosphere were responsible for this process was made by Irish physicist John Tyndall (1820–93) in 1859. Tyndall found that carbon dioxide and water were strong absorbers of radiant energy (unlike the main atmospheric gases, nitrogen and oxygen) and that even in relatively small quantities they could account for the heat trapped by the atmosphere. He also believed that changes in the various components of the atmosphere could result in changes to the Earth's climate.

Today, Tyndall's theory is at the center of fierce debate. Many scientists believe that human activity since the Industrial Revolution (1760–1840) has created an increase in "greenhouse gases," causing not only higher average temperatures but also climate changes that could have severe consequences for life on Earth. **GD**

⬆ A diagram demonstrating the absorbtion and reflection of solar radiation that is involved in the greenhouse effect, enabling the Earth to remain at a comfortable temperature.

"Recent warming coincides with rapid growth of human-made greenhouse gases. The observed rapid warming gives urgency to discussions about how to slow greenhouse gas emissions."

James Hansen, Earth and environmental sciences professor

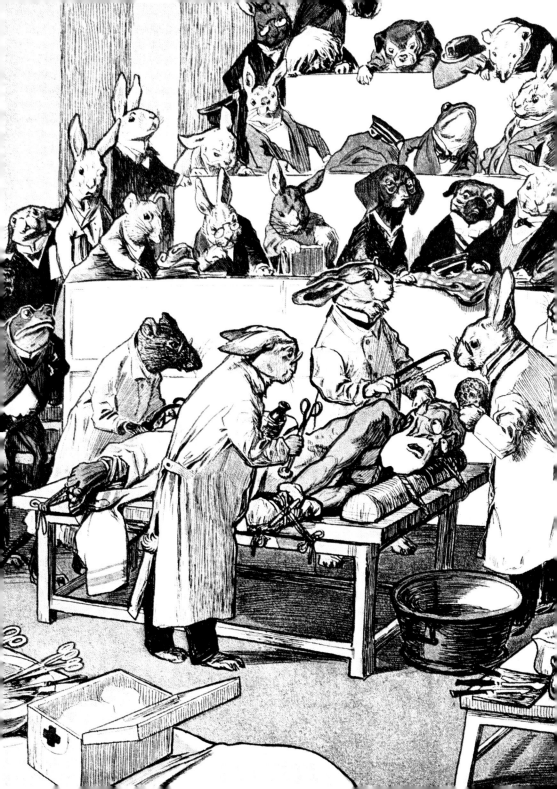

Animal Rights

Lewis Gompertz

The belief that animals deserve at least some of the ethical rights of humans

Whether humankind owes a moral, ethical, or legal duty to animals has probably been discussed since people first began domesticating and using animals. Some early thinkers, such as the Greek philosopher Pythagoras (c. 570–c. 495 BCE), believed that animals deserve to be treated respectfully, and some religious traditions, such as Jainism, hold that humans should never engage in violence against any type of animal.

The first animal protection law was created in 1635 in Ireland, and subsequent laws in various nations prohibited various acts as cruel or inhumane. But the idea that animals have inherent rights did not appear until 1824, when English animal rights advocate Lewis Gompertz (1783/4–1861) published *Moral Inquiries on the Situation of Man and of Brutes*. Gompertz posited

"Arguments … cannot shatter this hard fact: in suffering the animals are our equals."

Peter Singer, moral philosopher

that animals, like humans, are entitled to liberty and to legally protected rights. More recently, in 1970, animal ethics philosopher and animal welfare campaigner Richard Ryder (b. 1940) coined the term "speciesism," calling attention to the fact that human ill-treatment of animals does not differ from any other form of bigoted behavior that seeks to deprive others of rights. (Another form of speciesism would consist of human beings insisting that some species, lions for example, are entitled to more rights than, say, mice.)

Why should humans have rights and other animals not? That is the basic question at the heart of the idea of animal rights. For proponents and opponents alike, the idea of animal rights challenges our ideas of humanity, and why humans should, or should not, provide protection for other animals. **MT**

Second Thermodynamic Law

Nicolas Léonard Sadi Carnot

Every physical reaction generates heat, and is therefore irreversible

French military engineer Nicolas Léonard Sadi Carnot (1796–1832) laid the foundations of the Second Law of Thermodynamics in his book *Reflections on the Motive Power of Fire* (1824). Carnot was postulating an ideal heat engine (one that converts thermal energy to mechanical work) to show how such a machine could achieve maximum efficiency. But he realized that no actual engine could ever attain the reversibility of motion of the ideal, since all actual processes inevitably generate heat, relative to the external environment. Carnot had recognized a fundamental paradox: the laws of physics are reversible, but this law was not.

English physicist James Joule (1818–89), fascinated by electricity and working to improve the efficiency of his industry, decided in 1834 that heat and mechanical

"[Any theory against the second law will] collapse in deepest humiliation."

A. Eddington, *The Nature of the Physical World* (1927)

work are essentially related. An exchange of letters with Belfast-born mathematician and physicist William Thomson (Lord Kelvin, 1824–1907) led the latter to coin the term "thermodynamics" in 1849. Meanwhile, German physicist Rudolf Clausius (1822–88), after reading Carnot, spent fifteen years formulating his Mechanical Theory of Heat. In 1854, he reformulated the second law: "The entropy of the universe tends to a maximum."

Physicists still ponder the probable paradox of the second law. Engineers continue to develop technologies in areas such as communications, electronics, and industrial development, trying to meet the apparently insatiable human hunger for energy and the comforts it affords. However, Carnot's ideal heat engine remains as distant a prospect as ever. **LW**

⬅ A satirical artwork from 1921, that reverses the role of humans and animals in vivisection.

1830

Mormonism
Joseph Smith, Jr.

A primitivist Christian ideology based on a revelation of its founder and on the Bible

The founder of Mormonism, Joseph Smith, Jr. (1805–44), was a treasure hunter and diviner who saw visions. He revealed that, in the course of one of his revelations, an ancient prophet, Moroni, directed him to the burial place of two golden plates inscribed with the history of a previously unknown tribe of Native American Israelites. A transcription of the history of these people provided the basis of Mormonism's most revered text, *The Book of Mormon*, which Smith published in 1830. *The Book of Mormon*, the Bible, and two other texts containing extensive contributions from Smith comprise Mormonism's four standard works. Many passages in *The Book of Mormon* echo sections of the Old and New Testaments.

Smith's revelation occurred in the 1820s, during the Protestant revival movement known as the Second Great Awakening, which was part of a general attempt to renew the Christian foundations of what was seen as an ailing or corrupt version of the faith. Smith's family, already deeply influenced by the movement, provided a fertile base for his visions. Despite his lack of wealth or connections, Smith was charismatic and had a powerful ability to attract followers and convince them of the validity of his claims, however unlikely they might have seemed. Inevitably, he alienated some, and he may even have committed acts of fraud, but those who believed in him did so unreservedly. Mormonism became a cause of martyrs and pioneers. It taught a return to fundamental conservative principles: family, community, and hard work, with commitment, material and spiritual, to the Church of Latter Day Saints.

Mormonism is to Christianity what Christianity is to Judaism: it emerged out of the former religion but it has its own focus. As an ideological movement, it illustrates how the personality of one individual can invoke a response leading to an entirely new religion. **LW**

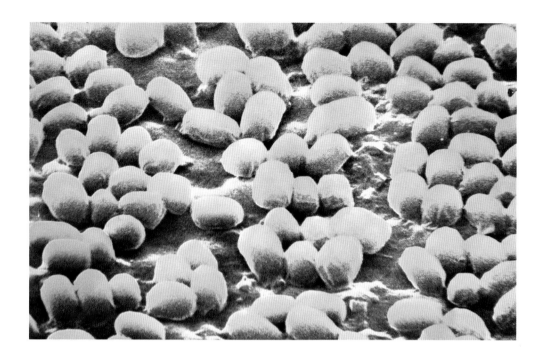

c. 1830

Germ Theory of Disease

Agostino Bassi

The theory that microscopic organisms are the cause of some diseases

The germ theory of disease, now widely accepted in medicine, postulates that organisms invisible to the naked eye, known as microorganisms, can infect the human body and become the cause of diseases. At the time it was first suggested in the nineteenth century, the theory flew in the face of long-held claims by physicians that bad air, or "miasmas," caused epidemics, or even that diseases were divine retribution for ungodly behavior.

In 1677 Anton van Leeuwenhoek (1632–1723) was experimenting with a microscope when he first discovered microorganisms. The breakthrough of associating these with infection and disease occurred in around 1830 when Italian entomologist Agostino

Bassi (1773–1856) showed that muscardine, an infectious disease affecting silkworms, was caused by a living entity, a fungus later named *Beauveria bassiana* in recognition of his work. In 1844 Bassi asserted that microorganisms caused human diseases, too.

In the 1860s, French chemist and microbiologist Louis Pasteur (1822–95) confirmed Bassi's theory that other microorganisms were linked to disease, also showing that microbes were responsible for decomposition. In 1876, German physician Robert Koch (1843–1910) proved that bacteria are the cause of diseases such as anthrax and tuberculosis.

While merely identifying the cause of a disease does not necessarily suggest a cure, the germ theory of disease transformed medicine from an art to a science. Discovering physical, identifiable, causes for specific diseases led to new understanding not only of how to treat illnesses, but also of how to prevent their spread. Germ theory led to a fuller understanding of the importance of clean water, care in personal hygiene, and hygienic food preparation. The development of pharmaceuticals targeted at specific harmful microorganisms would soon follow. **MT**

⬆ A colored scanning electron micrograph of anthrax bacteria spores (*Bacillus anthracis*).

Φ

Positivism
Auguste Comte

Only that which can be empirically verified or proved logically or mathematically exists

↑ An engraved portrait of French philosopher and founder of positivism Auguste Comte, from c. 1840. Comte is also known as the founder of the science of sociology.

"By the very nature of the human mind, every branch of our knowledge is necessarily obliged to pass successively through three different theoretical states."

Auguste Comte

The word "positivism" is an English transliteration of Auguste Comte's (1798–1857) French term *positivisme*. Developed from 1830 to 1845, *Positivisme* was Comte's reaction against contemporary German philosophy, which was highly speculative and metaphysical. He thought that the development of the physical sciences, with their emphasis on observation and experimentation, required that philosophy should base itself on a similar premise, rather than relying on ancient thought or the ideas of earlier philosophers. At the same time as Comte was developing *positivisme* in France, intellectuals such as John Stuart Mill (1806–73) and Hubert Spencer (1820–1903) were thinking along the same lines in Britain. Influences on the early positivists included the Enlightenment thinkers John Locke (1632–1704), David Hume (1711–76), and Immanuel Kant (1724–1804).

Positivists maintain as a historical law that every science has three successive stages—the theological, the metaphysical, and the positive—and that the positive stage, which confines itself to the study of experimental facts, represents the perfection of human knowledge. A second and third wave of positivism in the late nineteenth and early twentieth centuries developed these ideas still further, with the movement splitting into two groups, one led by Paul-Emile Littré (1801–81), the other by Pierre Laffitte (1823–1903).

Positivism carried with it important implications for philosophical and religious thought. With its absolute insistence on empirical verification and the primacy of the senses, positivism rejected the idea of a personal God, replacing it with a humanist perspective that Comte and the early positivists promoted as a religion in its own right. It also spawned a number of new theoretical subject disciplines, including sociology, while new slants were provided on ancient disciplines, such as logic and the theory of knowledge. **JF**

Transcendentalism and Self Reliance
Ralph Waldo Emerson

The purity of the individual is gained through identification with nature

The Transcendentalism taught by U.S. essayist, lecturer, and poet Ralph Waldo Emerson (1803–82) consists of an open-minded experience of the natural world that goes beyond just being human to becoming an awareness of participation in existence, as expressed in the maxim, "I am a part or particle of God." In 1830, Emerson gave a lecture containing his philosophy of Self Reliance—we must learn how best to provide ourselves with the essentials, and also learn what these are. Taken together, the two ideas promoted an examination of each strand of a person's life; anything unnecessary was to be excised so that reality revealed itself. The philosophy applied as much to its form of expression as to the way of living it recommended.

U.S. poet and philosopher Henry David Thoreau (1817–62), deeply influenced by his friend and mentor, extended Emerson's philosophy through his practical experiment in living at Walden Pond, Massachusetts. Like Plato, Thoreau sought to show that the means by which human needs are met are often far from ideal.

In a sense, both Transcendentalism and Self Reliance were reactions to the onward march of pioneerism, the philosophy of "we shall overcome" directed at the land (and the indigenous peoples) of North America. Transcendentalism rejected this deep confidence in the materials and manners of so-called "civilization." Instead, it sought to demonstrate how an appreciation of place was an appreciation of self, since the external and internal worlds were reflections of one another.

Emerson's Transcendentalism was acknowledged by Friedrich Nietzche in *The Gay Science* (1882), and it shaped the work of William James and John Dewey. Relying on one's hands and wits, paring back requirements to cover needs, Transcendentalism has been compared recently with Eastern thought and traditions that seek to link actions, abilities, and perspective in order to alter both the individual and the whole of existence. **LW**

↑ Having first lectured on the individualistic belief system of Transcendentalism, Ralph Waldo Emerson presented his ideas in the essay "Nature," published anonymously in 1836.

> *"Not the sun or the summer alone, but every hour and season yields its tribute of delight; for every hour and change corresponds to and authorizes a different state of the mind, from breathless noon to grimmest midnight."*

Ralph Waldo Emerson, "Nature" (1836)

Inflation
Andrew Jackson

A steep increase in money circulation, then prices, in relation to the supply of goods

Inflation has been around ever since money and the value it represents were dissassociated. The abolition of the Second Bank of America in 1830 by the seventh U.S. president, Andrew Jackson (1767–1845), led to a spiral of increased speculation that ended in the Panic of 1837. Yet the term "inflation" only started to appear during the American Civil War (1861–65), in reference to currency depreciation, when the rate in the Confederacy soared to 9,000 percent.

Inflation has two stages: money is printed in large amounts over a short period of time, and prices increase. Although the nominal value of the money stays the same, the amount each unit can buy decreases. Things cost more. Central banks attempt to keep inflation between 2 and 3 percent, but during

"Inflation had risen to the unimaginable figure of just over 100,000 percent…"

Jung Chang, *Wild Swans* (1991)

a recession or depression, printing money resembles economic growth. In wartime, the pressure to conscript labor, increase the price of goods, and divert capital from civilian to military programs is even greater.

The delay between monetary inflation and price inflation can be deliberately extended: it lasted for two decades after World War II (1939–45) in the United States, when the country spent most of its hoard of gold. Except for profiteers, suppliers, and the rich, no one benefits during inflationary periods. They shatter the illusion that money is a secure form of asset protection. Political discomfort, then anger, then social unrest or even war often follow. Inflationary periods underline just how tenuous our hold on material security really is under systems that depend for their continuance on the idea of continuous growth. **LW**

Hegelianism
Georg W. F. Hegel

A philosophical movement based on the work of German Idealist Georg W. F. Hegel

One of the German Idealists, Georg Wilhelm Friedrich Hegel (1770–1831) sparked a movement that was interpreted in radically different ways by those whom he inspired. Philosophy was "its own time, raised to the level of thought," and Hegelianism both placed thought in its historical context and investigated the transcendental nature of reality. It held that contradictions demanded resolution at a higher level of intellectual complexity, with the infinite (or Absolute Spirit) characterized by "becoming," rather than "being." Attempts to reconcile this mysticism with a geneology of political progress created deep tensions.

After Hegel died in 1831, interpreters of his work divided into three camps. The right read him as a defender of their religious and political conservatism

"Dialectics, logic, history, law, aesthetics… assumed a new aspect, thanks to… Hegel."

George Plekhanov, *The Meaning of Hegel* (1891)

and saw in his work an inevitability to history: the unfolding of events was a logical necessity. The left, in contrast, understood Hegelianism as a directive to social and cultural revolution. The center focused on Hegel's theoretical significance, particularly in logic.

The right spawned schools of thought that advocated purely rational solutions and this, combined with criticism of Judaism as the paradigm of a "positive" (irrationally submissive) religion, paved the way for the spread of anti-Semitism. The left, as Karl Popper argued, spawned the legitimization of totalitarianism. The center influenced theories in fields as diverse as law and the study of beauty. Hegelianism had a historical, philosophical, social, and religious influence, but it was as a justification for political movements of every persuasion that it really came into its own. **BC**

Think Tank
First Duke of Wellington

The notion of an independent, expert, policy-oriented research organization

Although the first known use of the term "think tank" was in 1959 in an article, "Facts and Impressions from the Groves of Academe," in reference to the Center for Behavioral Sciences at Palo Alto, the concept originated much earlier. In 1831, Arthur Wellesley (1769–1852), First Duke of Wellington, initiated the founding of the Naval and Military Museum—thought to be the first think tank—which was renamed the United Service Institution in 1839. The institution was granted royal patronage in 1860, and, as a result of its promotion of informed debate, its influence began to be felt on British defense policy. The institute was expanded in the 1960s for independent study of national defense.

In the United States, businessman Robert S. Brookings (1850–1930) founded the Institute for

"Think tanks are increasingly prominent . . . in the policy processes of many countries."

Think Tanks Across Nations (1998)

Government Research in 1916. Reorganized as the Brookings Institution in 1927, its role was to bring nonpartisan expertise to policy questions of the day. In 1965 it became a major center for policy innovation in welfare, health care, education, housing, and taxation.

Ostensibly, think tanks are nonpartisan and function as extensions of state power, gaining and losing influence with changes in governments and shifts in ideological climate. Sometimes think tanks can function more independently, questioning and monitoring state strategies and structures. Think tanks conduct interdisciplinary research for governmental clients, while commercial projects include developing and testing new technologies and products. Funding sources include endowments, contracts, private donations, and sales of reports. **BC**

Ready-made Clothing
George Opdyke

The innovation of mass-producing clothing to sell to the public

U.S. entrepreneur George Opdyke (1805–80) may or may not have invented the ready-made garment industry—the selling of finished factory or production line clothing in standard sizes—but he was certainly responsible for bringing it into mainstream society. The invention by Elias Howe (1819–67) of the power-driven sewing machine was still another fifteen years away, and Opdyke lived in an era of hand-sewn clothing, but neither factor stopped the Louisiana-based merchant from developing a small-scale production line of ready-made clothes in 1831. The South's slave population required cheap, ready-to-wear clothing, and his store on Hudson Street, New Orleans, helped to provide it.

Opdyke had taken a riverboat down the Ohio and Mississippi rivers to New Orleans in 1827 after

"In early life [Opdyke] went to New Orleans and learned the trade of a tailor."

Harpers Weekly (December 21, 1861)

operating a dry-goods store in what was then the frontier trading post town of Cleveland. Upon arrival, he found that manufacturers were selling clothes at a profit of 100 percent, and he knew that he had found his vocation. He gathered around him a coterie of tailors and seamstresses and gave his new business a name: Opdyke Manufacturing. In his first year he made 6,000 dollars, and his future was assured.

However, today's dominance of ready-made clothing was not achieved instantly. In 1850, almost 80 percent of all clothing worn in the United States was still hand-made, partly because the industry was kept on life support as tailors worldwide faced the threat of automation and job losses. Indeed, in 1841, a group of French tailors destroyed a factory of automated looms in Paris in a desperate effort to protect their livelihood. **BS**

A photographic portrait of George Opdyke, taken between 1855 and 1865. ➡

Motion Pictures
Simon von Stampfer and Joseph Antoine Ferdinand Plateau

The process of viewing a rapid succession of still images depicting a moving subject step by step, in such a way that the eye is tricked into seeing actual movement

⬆ Six stroboscopic disks, of the kind used in a Phenakistoscope. The disk was attached to a handle and then spun, creating the impression of a moving picture.

"The cinema is an invention without a future."

Louis Lumière, filmmaker

At least two men can claim to have been the first to invent the visual trick that is a "motion picture." In 1832, Austrian inventor Simon von Stampfer (1792–1864) read how British physicist Michael Faraday (1791–1867) had experimented with rapidly rotating objects to create the illusion of movement. Impressed, he devised some experiments himself, and these led him to develop his version of a moving picture. The Stampfer Disk, presented to the public in December 1832, actually consisted of two disks, one with slits around its edge and the other with pictures showing stages of movement. When the slit disk turned in front of the picture disk, the pictures seemed to merge and join into the now-familiar sensation of seamless motion.

However, Stampfer was not alone. In Belgium, in the same year, Joseph Antoine Ferdinand Plateau (1801–83), also inspired by Faraday, revealed an almost identical mechanism that he termed a Phenakistoscope. Plateau's fascination with "persistence of vision" theory, the idea that the after-image on the retina persists for a short time, led him to experiment with staring at the sun. A decade later, Plateau was completely blind. Meanwhile, back in 1833, Stampfer was getting ready to receive imperial privilege for his discoveries.

More than sixty years passed before their motion picture devices were progressed into what we now call cinema. Connecting together single photographic frames, the French Lumière brothers, Auguste (1862–1954) and Louis (1864–1948) were first, in 1895, to project moving, photographic pictures to a paying audience of more than one. U.S. inventor Thomas Edison (1847–1941) produced the first commercially successful projector in 1896. Their inventions radically changed how we see the world, because now our ideas are almost totally subject to the way the world is presented to us. **LW**

Knot Theory
Carl Friedrich Gauss

A means of describing the internal structure of knots in mathematical terms

In 1771, the French musician Alexandre-Théophile Vandermonde (1735–96) recognized that pinpointing the position of a one-dimensional, nonintersecting line in space would deepen mathematical understanding. But the world had to wait until 1833 for German mathematician Carl Friedrich Gauss (1777–1855) to develop a mathematical model that described the universal nature of loops that cannot be undone.

Knots occupy three-dimensional space, but they also link a line within that space that is always, in mathematical studies, joined to itself. Describing the position of this linked curve in numerical terms is a hugely complex problem: it requires a "geometry of position," a notation to show how a looped and twisted three-dimensional object is located, both relative to itself and in relation to the space surrounding it. For this, Gauss defined the linking integral, a whole number that describes how many loops or links a knot has.

People have been braiding and tying knots, using them to remember things and making patterns out of them, almost since the evolution of opposable thumbs. Developing a theory that described these twists and loops was a phenomenal challenge. Ultimately, knot theory is knowledge for its own sake, a kind of Zen appreciation of a *koan* (paradox) or problem, numerically defined. Perhaps, more than any other idea, it shows that sometimes solving a puzzle requires no further justification than its inherent merit. However, since its development, the theory has proved useful as a basis for understanding how DNA behaves and the arrangement and position of other polymers in space. It will also help in the development of quantum computers when our thirst for more powerful information processors outweighs the capacity of current silicon-based systems. **LW**

Electrolysis
Michael Faraday

The generation of a nonspontaneous chemical reaction using electrical current

One of the most influential scientists of all time, Englishman Michael Faraday (1791–1867) was fascinated by electricity, magnetism, and the nature of energy and matter. In 1833, Faraday discovered how to reverse the natural process by which electromagnetic bonds are formed. He formulated two laws to illustrate how electrochemistry holds matter together, and described how to manipulate this pattern so that a new arrangement comes about.

Electrolysis requires a liquid medium, the electrolyte, through which a direct electrical current can be passed. The current splits the bonds that hold ions in their molecular positions at the anode, or positive end, of the reaction and causes them to enter into new molecular relationships at the cathode, or negative end. The

"Nothing is too wonderful to be true, if it be consistent with the laws of Nature."

Michael Faraday

ratio and rate of transfer depend on the nature of the solution, the amount of power used, and the material at the anode, but the process is universal.

Controlling and reversing electrochemical reactions extended humanity's sense of power over the environment. If we could manipulate such fundamental forces, we were not merely Earth's inheritors, we were its masters. Being able to manipulate the very structure of matter at a molecular level enabled us to separate elements from naturally occuring compounds; this massively improved our ability to exploit natural sources of metals, and drove forward industrial and technological expansion. Electrolysis refined our ability to take charge of human progress. It also opened the eyes of the scientific world to the particular nature of matter and the forces that bond it together. **LW**

Weber-Fechner Law
Ernst Weber and Gustav Fechner

The magnitude of a sensation is proportional to the intensity of the stimulus causing it

If you are in a dark room you can easily tell when someone lights a single candle, but if you are in a room with 1,000 burning candles you notice no difference in light if someone lights one more. The Weber-Fechner law explains why this is true. The law states that people only notice a difference in sensation when there is a proportionate increase in the intensity of the stimulus relative to the original intensity.

In 1834, German physiologist Ernst Weber (1795–1878) noted that a person holding a light object will easily notice when someone adds a small amount of weight to it, but someone holding a heavier object will not notice a small increase. He developed a law that stated there was a linear relationship between the level of stimuli and our perception of a just-noticeable difference in

" . . . Weber's law also underlies the octave tonal structure of music perception . . ."

György Buzsáki, *Rhythms of the Brain* (2006)

sensation. In 1860, Weber's student Gustav Fechner (1801–87) improved on the law when he found that it was not a linear relationship, but rather a logarithmic one. As stimuli become more intense, it becomes harder and harder to notice a difference because your body requires a much greater amount of additional stimuli.

The Weber-Fechner law paved the way for psychophysics: the study of how sensations relate to stimuli, or how physical stimuli affect our perceptions. With the discovery of the law, we could measure how, and when, our senses caused us to perceive something new. We could also begin to answer the question that had troubled philosophers for so long: at what point does the physical process of sensation transform into the mental phenomena of experience and perception? In other words: where do mind and body meet? **MT**

Supply and Demand
Antoine Cournot

The use of a combination of mathematics and economic principles to predict trends

The first person to understand and attempt to describe that most innate of all economic principles, the law of supply and demand, was not an economist but the French mathematician and philosopher Antoine Cournot (1801–77). Generations before it became commonplace to use mathematical models for the purpose of predicting trends and behavior in the marketplace, Cournot—in his misunderstood, largely overlooked, but nevertheless seminal work *Researches into the Mathematical Principles of the Theory of Wealth* (1838)—did something remarkable: he constructed the first formula for predicting how the rule of supply and demand might affect the price of an item or service.

The world was slow to realize the importance of Cournot's idea, and he became embittered and disillusioned. He rewrote *Researches* in 1863 to make it more "readable," yet still it went unnoticed, which led to him becoming increasingly reclusive and melancholy. Remarkably, without ever having encountered Cournot's work, the English economist William Jevons (1835–82), in his *Theory of Political Economy* (1871), presented ideas that Cournot had pioneered earlier. It was not until 1890, when the great neoclassical economist Alfred Marshall (1842–1924) expanded upon Cournot's formula in his own monumental work, *Principles of Economics*, that it was brought into the mainstream and given the recognition it deserved.

Cournot used concepts such as function and probability to describe economic theories, and drew lines of supply and demand on graphs three decades before the practice became routine. It was a great pity that the significance of his breakthrough was largely unappreciated in his lifetime, for he had more or less invented the modern discipline of econometrics, the ability to measure economic theory and apply it to realistic, everyday situations. **BS**

Cell Theory
Matthias Jakob Schleiden

All living matter—from microorganisms to mammals—is made up of cellular structures that interact through electrical and chemical activity

The invention and refinement of the microscope opened the cellular world to scientists hungry to discover more about how life was organized and of what it was composed. After Dutchman Antonie van Leeuwenhoek (1632–1723) discovered microorganisms moving under his lens, it was not long before Robert Hooke (1635–1702), an English physicist who was also a distinguished microscopist, used the word "cells" to describe the divided units he observed in the structure of a piece of cork. However, the official formulation of cell theory is credited to two later individuals. First, in 1839, German botanist Matthias Jakob Schleiden (1804–81) suggested that every structural element of plants is composed of cells or their products. The following year, a similar conclusion was reached by German zoologist Theodor Schwann (1810–82) in relation to animals. All living existence had been proved to have a common denominator, and cell theory was born.

Schleiden saw that living organisms have a common architecture: they are all made up of extremely variable but nevertheless identical basic organic arrangements that communicate systematically through electrical and chemical activity. This, the basis of cell theory, amounted to the first formal description of both the structure and the operation of universal features of life.

Cell theory led to the development of an entire discipline within biology dedicated to understanding how these units functioned and maintained themselves, and also how they divided or replicated, and exchanged information. The cell became recognized as the fundamental unit of life, and disease became defined as the altered functioning of cellular activity. As important a leap in scientific understanding as the discovery of DNA, cell theory opened up possibilities in the fields of evolutionary theory, medicine, and microbiology. **LW**

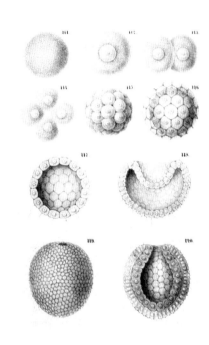

⬆ An illustration by Ernst Haeckel depicts stages in the embryonic development of vertebrates, from cell doubling (top row) to formation of separate germ layers (bottom right).

"The principal result of my investigation is that a uniform developmental principle controls the individual elementary units of all organisms."

Theodor Schwann, zoologist

National Nativism
United States

The belief that new immigrants are a threat to their longer-established countrymen

Nativism is an ideological or political point of view in which the interests of an established society are zealously preferred and perpetuated over the interests of newly arrived immigrants. It is pervasive, universal, and persists to this day. On a national level, however, it first came to prominence in around 1840 in the United States as a response to successive waves of migrants arriving on the eastern shores of the New World from Europe; it intensified when 100,000 Irish Catholics fled their nation's potato famine in 1847.

A controversial political party that emerged at this time was the Know-Nothing Party, made up of people who wanted to keep immigrants from setting foot in the New World and who would, failing that, do all they could to prevent them from participating in

"Immigrants are ... paupers, and diseased, and become a charge upon the Town ..."

Cholera warning, Burlington, Vermont (1849)

society once they did. The adherents to this ideology of irrational prejudices were given a name: nativists.

Nativism had various guises: It was middle-class elitism that looked down on socially and intellectually "inferior" immigrants; it was a fear that immigrant votes would distort the body politic; and it was also a fear of competition in the workplace. But mostly it was a raft of anti-Catholic sentiments, embedded in a deeply Protestant nation and directed against an imagined papal plot, long expected to surface and attempt to subvert the new U.S. republic. A young Abraham Lincoln (1809–65) denounced the movement, saying he would prefer to live in Russia where "despotism is out in the open" rather than live in his own country where "all men are created equal except for Negroes, foreigners, and Catholics." **BS**

Property Is Theft
Pierre-Joseph Proudhon

The notion that any claim to ownership is incompatible with communal justice

From the Genevan philosopher Jean-Jacques Rousseau (1712–78) onward, socialists have maintained that the idea of private property ownership flagrantly flouts the natural rights of community members who, they argue, should enjoy the material benefits of the environment in which they live. Thus, any cultural norm that takes away those rights does a disservice to the community. French politician and philosopher Pierre-Joseph Proudhon (1809–65) went further: private ownership is not only a negative infringment, it is a positive crime.

Proudhon's political outlook can be traced, to some degree, to his own impoverished background. After enduring a harrowing upbringing of poverty and long periods of unemployment as an adult, Proudhon was eventually awarded a bursary to support his studies in

"[The individual] is always subordinate to the right ... the community has over all."

Pierre-Joseph Proudhon

Paris. It was there that he developed the idea, in his first major work, *What Is Property?* (1840), that property is theft. Like Karl Marx, he foresaw possession and power becoming concentrated within an elite of diminishing size, until revolution redressed the balance. Unlike Marx, however, he saw ultimate redress as being the entire dissolution of the state. Historic disenfranchisement would be corrected, he believed, when human beings, freed by anarchy, could rely on their natural harmoniousness and work things out for themselves.

Proudhon's ideas are helpful in understanding the unfolding dichotomy in the world between libertarian or rights-based notions of unfettered ownership and the growing dissent expressed by disaffected members of society for whom such notions are merely excuses used by a wealthy elite to defend their power. **LW**

◄ An anti-immigration cartoon from 1888 depicts "a possible curiosity of the twentieth century. The last Yankee."

1840

Anarchism
Pierre-Joseph Proudhon

The belief that government infringes the rights of individuals or of the collective

Anarchism—the belief that any form of political coercion, including government, is illegitimate and inefficient, and therefore should be opposed—emerged as a developed political philosophy only in the nineteenth century, with the consolidation of the modern state. Many consider French politician, philosopher, economist, and socialist Pierre-Joseph Proudhon (1809–65) to be the first self-described anarchist. In *What Is Property?* (1840), he urged the replacement of government with a social organization based on voluntary contractual agreement.

Appropriately, there is no party line in anarchism. Anarchists differ in their analysis of the wrongness of government: philosophical anarchists regard it as illegitimate; ideal anarchists regard it as inefficient compared to the anarchist alternative (individualism, communism, or something in between); and revolutionary anarchists regard it as so immoral and harmful that it deserves violent resistance and overthrow. These are not mutually exclusive attitudes, of course. Anarchists also differ in their views on the ideal system of society and distribution of property: communitarian anarchists hold various views—such as mutualism, collectivism, communism, and syndicalism—acknowledging the legitimacy and importance of voluntary, noncoercive, nonhierarchical social organization and rejecting, in varying degrees, the idea of private property, while libertarian anarchists insist on the sovereignty and primacy of the individual and private property. Variants abound: there are also green, Christian, and feminist anarchisms, to name a few.

Despite the continuing intellectual vitality of anarchism, its prospects for effecting a substantial political change are generally considered to have waned in the wake of World War I (1914–18) and the Russian Revolution of 1917. **GB**

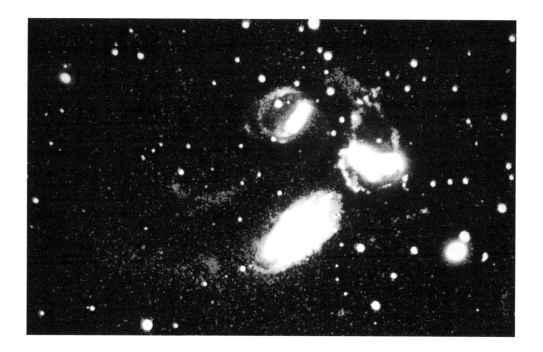

1842

The Doppler Effect
Christian Doppler

The theory that movement measurably compresses or stretches energy waves

When an object that is emitting waves, such as sound waves, is moving, the wavelength ahead of the object is shortened, relative to its actual frequency. You might say that the forward motion crushes the waves together; at the same time, relatively, the waves behind the moving source are stretched out. This change in wave pattern is what is meant by the Doppler effect, or the Doppler shift, and is familiar from the altering sound of a race car or police siren as it passes.

Austrian physicist Christian Doppler (1803–53) first described the effect in relation to astronomy in *On the Colored Light of the Binary Stars and Some Other Stars of the Heavens* (1842). Doppler was determined, after enduring an at times humiliating journey through academia, to demonstrate his ability to apply his genius to natural phenomena. He named the effect while seeking to explain differences in the colors of double stars. His principle was swiftly demonstrated in relation to any type of wave—sound, light, water—emanating from a moving source. It also applies to an observer moving relative to the medium through which the wave is transmitted, and to situations in which the medium itself is the method of transmission.

The Doppler effect now helps with predictions in such diverse fields as meteorology, navigation, and medical diagnosis. As Doppler himself predicted, as soon as instruments developed sufficiently to take measurements, scientists could determine the directional motion of stars. This alerted them to "the red shift," whereby light from a star, as observed from the Earth, shifts toward the red end of the spectrum (with a lower frequency or longer wavelength) if the Earth and star are receding from each other. In other words, they discovered that we are in an expanding universe. It follows that things were once very much closer. The Doppler effect thus contributed to a seismic shift in universal understanding. **LW**

⬆ An image illustrating the different red shift values of Stephan's Quartet group of galaxies and NGC 7320.

1843

Cartoon
John Leech

A lighthearted illustration with the purpose of provoking discussion

The word "cartoon" comes from the world of fine art and refers to a board used to sketch out rough ideas for paintings or sculptures before a final version is attempted. However, it was not until the establishment of modern print media that the cartoon as a piece of humorous art became properly recognized. All cartoons have developed from a tradition of individual pictures presented to amuse the viewer, certainly, but also to provoke a reaction in that viewer.

On July 15, 1843, the sketch "Substance and Shadow," by English artist John Leech (1817–64), appeared in Britain's *Punch* magazine. This marked the first use of the word "cartoon" to refer to a satirical representation of fictional characters whose figures and features

depicted types (namely poverty and greed in Leech's first offering). The first popular fictional cartoon character, designed simply to entertain, had appeared much earlier, in 1809, and this had presaged the enduring appeal of a cartoon with a storyline. A bony, elderly gentleman, Dr. Syntax, had a penchant for traveling and an unfortunate propensity for mishaps. His creator, Thomas Rowlandson (1756–1827), developed an entire fictional history for Dr. Syntax, generating a hunger for merchandise (prints and postcards), and sowing the seeds for much profitable franchising since.

The idea of the cartoon has been influential on two fronts. First, it has been popular as straightforward, humorous entertainment, generating the pantheon of characters that have become a mainstay of children's television; second, the cartoon has had adult possibilities, for social and political commentary and nonlibellous satire, but also for adult sexual fantasy. From innocuous child icons to images of evil, cartoons now span and imitate the entire range of human possibility. Not being human, they have limitless abilities; being insensitive, they can be made to explore the heights and depths of human imagining. **LW**

Commercial Air Travel
William Henson and John Stringfellow

Profiting through providing air transport for the general public

Italian artist and inventor Leonardo da Vinci (1452–1519) had made drawings of flying machines with flapping wings, and Frenchmen Jean-François Pilâtre de Rozier (1754–85) and François Laurent d'Arlandes (1742–1809) had made the first ascent in a hot-air balloon in 1783. However, it was British inventor William S. Henson (1812–88) and his friend and fellow engineer, John Stringfellow (1799–1883), who first investigated in earnest the possibility of a profitable flying business. From their observations of bird flight, they concluded that a fixed-wing design propelled by a sufficiently robust power plant offered a promising combination.

In 1843, a full sixty years before Wilbur (1867–1912) and Orville (1871–1948) Wright made their inaugural

flight in such an aircraft in 1903, the pair set up the Ariel Transit Company with the idea of attracting the investment necessary to build their first prototype. Unfortunately, their extravagant advertising campaign scared off investors, and even the engineer Sir George Cayley (1773–1857), Henson's mentor and inspiration, refused to back them unless they could demonstrate a working model of their Ariel Steam Carriage, patented in 1842. The Ariel never flew, the scheme collapsed, and Henson emigrated. But the public had been introduced to the possibility of exotic destinations being only a commercial flight away.

It is impossible to overestimate the impact of commercial air travel on the character of modern industrialized society. The holiday destinations of the world have changed visitors and hosts alike, and tourism has brought new possibilities for cross-cultural mobility, but the exploitation of lands and peoples has raised new questions. The industry never approached the heights of profitability that its early investors and inventors envisaged, but it undoubtedly changed the way we think of distance, and how we weigh the costs and consequences of our leisure pursuits. **LW**

↑ A lithograph of the Aerial Steam Carriage (1842); far from flying over pyramids, it never flew at all.

Ring Theory
William Rowan Hamilton

The study of "rings," or structures in abstract algebra, that relate integrally (in terms of whole numbers) if they are commutative, but not if noncommutative

⬆ The largely self-taught Irish mathematician Sir William Rowan Hamilton, here photographed in 1857, had been made professor of astronomy at Trinity College, Dublin, in 1827.

"The mathematical quaternion partakes of both these elements; in technical language it may be said to be 'time plus space,' or 'space plus time': and in this sense it has, or at least involves a reference to, four dimensions."

William Hamilton, quoted in R. P. Graves's
Life of Sir William Rowan Hamilton (1882)

Ring theory, in simple terms, is the study of mathematical sets in which addition and multiplication are possible. There are really two ring theories: "commutative" ring theory, in which the order of the elements added or multiplied does not affect the mathematical outcome, and the more complex "noncommutative" ring theory. The latter was developed from the theory of quaternions of Irish physicist, astronomer, and mathematician Sir William Rowan Hamilton (1805–65). Hamilton remarked, ". . . there dawned on me the notion that we must admit, in some sense, a fourth dimension of space."

The motivation behind the search for an integrated theory of rings lies in the depth of the problems they represent. In mathematics, rings are sets, in which two operations, addition and multiplication, fulfill conditions for various axioms. Study of the mathematical properties of rings is ancient, but by the seventeenth century, abstract numerical problems were attracting much interest. Fermat's Last Theorem, the most fiendishly difficult of all, developed by Frenchman Pierre de Fermat (1601–65), was tackled by Richard Dedekind in the 1880s, and out of his work arose the first comprehensive theory of algebraic numbers. This theory, which included the idea that sets could be treated as integers, was the generalization that first allowed commutative ring theory to evolve. Meanwhile, Hamilton's "quaternion," discovered in 1843, had broken down the commutative property of multiplication and opened the way for noncommutative ring theory.

Following their development as abstract problem solvers, both types of ring theory have helped to further scientific understanding, both in mathematics and, practically, in physics. The theories have altered how we conceive of the relationships between numbers, and this has had profound implications in our understanding of the structure of the universe. **LW**

Enlightened Despot
Wilhelm Roscher

The notion of an absolute monarch influenced by the Enlightenment

Monarchs, from the eighteenth century onward, who pursued legal, social, and educational reforms inspired by the Age of Enlightenment became known as "enlightened despots." The theory held that leaders thus inspired had the authority, sense of duty, and character to institute administrative, economic, and agricultural reform; to increase separation of the powers of the church and state; and to develop health and educational systems. On the other hand, reformation of the monarchical system itself was ruled out, and there was no move to disrupt the existing social order.

During the second half of the eighteenth century, European ideas about how to govern began to shift under the influence of the Enlightenment. These ideas, including strong arguments for increasing equality and religious toleration, and for involving wider sectors of the population in political decision making, threatened the status quo and, it was argued, the stability of the state. In response, German economist Wilhelm Roscher (1817–94) put forward his concept of enlightened despotism in 1843 (although his term, coined in 1847, was "enlightened absolutism"). Roscher saw in his idea the final stage of a tripartite process of monarchical emancipation. He argued that reform could take place without dismantling the state, and intellectual progress could take place through the existing order.

Today, the oxymoronic or seemingly contradictory idea that a monarch could be enlightened and a despot at the same time creates confusion, and to some extent the idea created just the same tension at its inception. Present-day dictatorial regimes use justifications that echo those of the first apologists. Their leaders and supporters may genuinely consider themselves to be social reformers, ruling in the interests of all, but their efforts are subject to human fallibility and the dictates of pragmatism. The despots were no different. **LW**

Emergentism
John Stuart Mill

The concept that an entity might have a property possessed by none of its parts

British philosopher John Stuart Mill (1806–73) first introduced the theory of emergentism in his book *System of Logic* (1843). According to Mill, a property of something is "emergent" if it is in some sense more than the sum of its parts. Emergentism is often contrasted with reductionism, the theory that the simplest components of matter are the only real properties. Emergentism offers a layered view of nature, in which new properties emerge with each new layer of physical complexity.

Mill described two ways in which causes can collaborate to produce an effect. Nonemergent properties can be predicted from our knowledge of each individual cause alone—for example, if one force propels an object to the north and another equal

"The higher quality emerges from the lower level of existence . . ."

C. Lloyd Morgan, ethologist and psychologist

force propels it to the east, the resulting motion will be northeasterly. But with emergent properties, the conjunction of causes produces something that cannot be predicted from knowledge of how each cause operates individually. Mill cites the properties of chemical compounds, which may not be anticipated solely on the basis of their components' properties.

Some critics have argued that advances in chemistry have cast doubt on this argument. But the contemporary importance of emergentism lies more in its implications for our understanding of the mind than in accounting for chemical reactions. As a philosophy of mind, emergentism occupies a middle ground between materialism, which reduces the mind to brain activity, and dualism, which treats the mind as wholly independent of the brain. **GD**

1843

Leap of Faith

Søren Kierkegaard

The concept that, to attain faith, we must go beyond the limits of the rational

The Danish Existentialist philosopher Søren Kierkegaard (1813–55) first articulated the idea of the leap of faith in his pseudonymous books *Fear and Trembling* (1843), *Philosophical Fragments* (1844), and *Concluding Unscientific Postscript to Philosophical Fragments* (1848).

Kierkegaard argued that self-cultivation is a process in which a person leaps progressively between three different stages. In the first, aesthetic stage, a person is motivated by egoism and hedonism, but the transience of such self-gratification makes it ultimately unfulfilling, and many are prompted to look elsewhere for a sense of significance. The second, ethical stage is characterized by a concern for others that becomes progressively grounded in the universal principles of philosophical moral discourse. Although the social and rational basis of the ethical life is more satisfying than that of the aesthetic, it still produces anxiety and despair because a person can never fully live up to their duties. The final, religious stage involves a leap of faith in which a person suspends ethical and rational considerations to embrace God. Kierkegaard uses the biblical story of Abraham and Isaac to illustrate this leap: Abraham must set aside universal moral prohibitions against killing his son, embrace the will of God, and thus become a "knight of faith." In the religious stage, a person's morals are based upon *imitatio Christi*, or an emulation of the virtues of Christ.

Kierkegaard's understanding of faith has had an outstanding impact on philosophy and theology, influencing thinkers such as Karl Barth, Karl Jaspers, Paul Tillich, and Dietrich Bonhoeffer. The term "leap of faith" has entered common parlance, but it is typically misused to indicate something done on the basis of blind faith. A person can only make a true leap of faith after passing through the aesthetic and ethical stages; they should not simply take everything on faith without first struggling to experience and understand the world. **JM**

An angel halts Abraham, Kierkegaard's "knight of faith," in *The Sacrifice of Isaac* (1650), by Laurent de la Hyre. ⬆

1845

Manifest Destiny
John L. O'Sullivan

The belief that Americans had a God-given destiny to establish a great nation

The phrase "manifest destiny" came to express a mid-nineteenth-century idea of the people of the United States of America that they had a divinely conferred duty to settle all the land lying between the country's Atlantic and Pacific coasts. Settling the continent, according to those who believed in the notion, was the U.S. people's anointed purpose, made manifest because of the exceptional nature of the people concerned, with their unique culture and political ideals of democracy and liberty.

In the mid- to late-nineteenth century, the United States went through a period of rapid expansion as the nation extended beyond the borders of the Louisiana Purchase and into the far west. The nation

had long been set on expansion, yet the actual phrase "manifest destiny" did not appear until the summer of 1845, when the editor of *Democratic Review* magazine, John L. O'Sullivan (1813–95), wrote an article discussing the nation's right to annex Texas. O'Sullivan presented the idea that the United States was no common nation, but rather a nation with a special destiny given by the divine, one that would lead it to span the continent. The notion quickly gained popularity with politicians, public officials, and average citizens alike.

The idea of taming a wild land and making it habitable, and of building a new nation from the wilderness, captivated generations of Americans. The land was already inhabited, but the idea of manifest destiny was not intended to refer to long-established indigenous peoples. As settlers of European origin expanded westward, their idea of manifest destiny could be realized only through the destruction or relocation of aboriginal populations. Today, the idea of U.S. exceptionalism, that the nation is special among all others and has a duty to promote democratic ideals, is still a driving force in many aspects of U.S. politics and culture. **MT**

Illusionism
Jean Eugène Robert-Houdin

Entertaining theater audiences by confounding their natural expectations with seemingly impossible tricks, from apparent mind reading to superhuman feats of endurance

⬆ A nineteenth-century poster advertising a performance by Jean Eugène Robert-Houdin in Paris. His professional career as an illusionist only lasted around eleven years.

Most historians agree that credit for first bringing illusionism, or stage magic, to a theater audience should go to Frenchman Jean Eugène Robert-Houdin (1805–71). There are other potential candidates—Scotsman John Henry Anderson (1814–74) among them—but, even if they preceded him, none could rival Robert-Houdin for originality and variety. His first performance, in 1845, was poorly given and unfavorably received, but he persevered until his illusions even attracted the attention of King Louis-Philippe; the king was given a private performance in 1847, just months before he was deposed by revolution in 1848.

One of Robert-Houdin's illusions made it seem as though his son was balancing horizontally, unsupported, on one elbow. Robert-Houdin explained the feat to his audience as being the effect on the boy's body of ether, a liquid whose properties were just beginning to be discovered. Robert-Houdin made full use of scientific discoveries still unfamiliar to his audience; for example, a child would be asked to lift a small box, but then the illusionist used electromagnetism to make it impossible for a man to do the same thing. Robert-Houdin's illusions were so brilliant that in 1856 Napoleon III asked him to deflect potential rebellion in Algeria by outdoing the faux-magic of marabouts (Muslim religious teachers).

Illusionism transformed simple entertainment into a sophisticated demonstration of the apparently supernatural. Today, journeying from street to screen, it continuously renews the idea that the impossible can happen, while recognizing that escapism is a fundamental human hunger. People will happily pay to be baffled, shocked, and amused, and have their expectations challenged. Illusionism is popular because it awakes audiences to the unknown within the known, despite their natural skepticism. **LW**

> *"Magic is the only honest profession. A magician promises to deceive you, and he does."*
>
> Karl Germain, magician and lawyer

🏛

🔺

Might Makes Right
Adin Ballou

Being strong is the best way to secure what you want

The phrase "might makes right" contains three ideas, two of which oppose each other. The first idea is the use of a pithy sentence to summarize a concept. The second is the perjorative use of the phrase, implying that force, wielded unworthily by an authority over unwilling subjects, is unjustified. The third describes social, political, or even biological relations, and concludes from those descriptions that acts in the interest of dominance and power are justifiable.

The first person to use the phrase in English was the U.S. utopian anarchist Adin Ballou (1803–90), in his work *Christian Non-Resistance: In All Its Important Bearings, Illustrated and Defended* (1846). Ballou was conditioned by his perspective of history, his extreme pacifism, and his conviction that the road to happiness lay beyond any humanly imposed law. However, his dictum summed up a much older idea. The ancient Greek historian Thucydides (*c.* 460–*c.* 404 BCE) had observed that "the strong do what they can, and the weak suffer what they must," but the sage had prefaced this with the comment, "Right, as the world goes, is only in question between equals in power."

The neat phraseology of "might makes right" has become something of a meme, and pithy ways of wording ideas succinctly have been an increasing feature of human communication ever since it was coined. The idea itself influenced two separate positions, one dichotomously opposed to Ballou's meaning. Ballou emphasized (as did Thucydides) the injustice of imposed authority. Ballou put the phrase in inverted commas to illustrate that authorities who exercise their programs for governance by force have no legitimacy. The alternative interpretation of the idea refers to its use as a statement of historical description and the fallacy, thereby, that it justifies certain political systems, such as totalitarianism. **LW**

Hand-washing in Hospitals
Ignaz Semmelweis

Good personal hygiene in medical staff prevents the transmission of disease

In 1847, Hungarian obstetrician Professor Ignaz Semmelweis (1818–65) declared that there was a connection between the unhygienic habits of (male) clinicians and the high mortality rate among women they were attending. The official response to his idea illustrated just how difficult acceptance of a challenging observation can be when it threatens the self-image of an institution.

In mid-nineteenth-century Europe, far more women having babies in hospitals were dying of puerperal sepsis, a bacterial infection, when attended by hospital doctors than when not attended by them. Semmelweis focused on the hygiene habits of the doctors themselves. In contrast to midwives, the doctors refused to consider themselves as potential

> *"… cadaveric material is the cause of … mortality in the First Obstetrical Clinic …"*
>
> Ignaz Semmelweis

transmitters of disease, and this was reflected in their negligence regarding hand-washing. Semmelweis published his theory, but was not applauded. Instead, the Viennese medical establishment villified him utterly, rejected his findings, and denied him reappointment to his post. He died, tragically, in an asylum.

Semmelweis's idea has had both an obvious and an indirect effect on our thinking. Eventually, it did change behavior relating to medical hygiene, vastly reducing suffering and mortality in hospitals. But it also showed how a powerful profession could refuse point-blank to accept its own negative role in a situation. This reflected a much broader habitual response among those in power to findings that undermine or challenge their self-image. It is a social phenomenon that continues to demand attention today. **LW**

Topology
Johann Benedict Listing

The study of the properties preserved in geometrically distorted shapes

Swiss genius Leonhard Euler (1707–83) was the first to consider the problem of the Königsberg Bridges as a geometric puzzle; his memoir on the subject effectively gave rise to topology. The problem—to cross seven bridges in a single journey, without recrossing any—was reduced by Euler to a graph of lines and points. This demonstrated that numbers and shapes were related in ways not previously considered: where distance, for example, was irrelevant, but quality was not. Topology is, therefore, the geometry of a process of reducing, distorting, or bending shapes whose fundamental geometric properties remain intact.

If Euler laid the foundation stone, the first to set the field's descriptive boundaries was Czech-German Johann Benedict Listing (1802–82). His publication of

"If it's just turning the crank it's algebra, but if it's got an idea in it, it's topology."

Solomon Lefschetz, mathematician

the *Vorstudien zur Topologie* (Introductory Studies in Topology, 1847) laid out the first systematic treatment of the subject. German mathematicians Augustus Möbius (1790–1868) and Bernhard Reimann (1826–66) were also important influences on the development of this field, but Listing described the Möbius strip (a continuous one-sided surface) four years before Möbius himself and so deserves credit as topology's originator.

The initial importance of the discovery was that it showed that numbers and shapes could be related qualitatively, rather than only through the quantitative geometrical relations that ordinary geometry treats. This different kind of geometry weds shape to space through a new set of conditions and it is in this respect that it is innovative, opening up dynamic possibilites, such as the discovery of new forms of matter. **LW**

Communism
Karl Marx and Friedrich Engels

An economic system and political philosophy advocating social ownership

Communism is an ideology and a theory that sees the trajectory of human history as an inevitable progression from inequality to equality, via revolution. The goal of this progression is a classless, stateless society in which people willingly contribute toward the wellbeing of all. This contribution will involve holding both human and natural resources to be common goods. Distributing the products of work according to need will ensure that status, envy, greed, and even war pass away, and harmony will ensue.

Karl Marx (1818–83) and Freidrich Engels (1820–95) are jointly credited with authorship of *The Communist Manifesto* (1848), the pamplet in which the theory was first outlined. Its publication sparked a massive political reaction, although the ideal of an egalitarian

"Communism may be summed up in one sentence: abolish all private property."

Karl Marx, philosopher and economist

society with all resources held in common ownership has existed throughout recorded history. Heavily influenced by the philosophical work of Georg Wilhelm Friedrich Hegel (1770–1831), communism offered both an explanation of inequality and a battle plan.

It is impossible to imagine how differently human history would have unfolded if communism had not radicalized political theory. The "Communist Threat" set ideological battle lines between liberal, industrialized, capitalist nations of the "First World" and authoritarian, semi-industrialized, socialist nations of the "Second World." Some argue that it even crystallized its fiercest detractors toward fascism. Nevertheless, the ideology maintains a firm grip, not least because there will always be those who sense in the aims of communism an abiding hunger for a fairer world. **LW**

A Russian Communist poster from 1920, bearing the message "Knowledge breaks the chains of slavery." ➡

ЗНАНИЕ
РАЗОРВЕТ ЦЕПИ РАБСТВА.

Pre-Raphaelitism
England

An artistic movement that sought to emulate the style of Italian artists before Raphael

⬆ *The Beloved* (1865–66) by Dante Gabriel Rossetti, one of the founding members of the Pre-Raphaelite Brotherhood. The painting shows the brilliance of color favored by the group.

The term "Pre-Raphaelite" comes from the title of a group of artists, both literary and visual, who founded, in 1848, the Pre-Raphaelite Brotherhood. Led by Dante Gabriel Rossetti (1828–82), William Holman Hunt (1827–1910), and John Everett Millais (1829–96), its inspiration largely sprang from the ideas of English artist and critic John Ruskin (1819–1900). The original movement sought to challenge the artistic and literary conventions of the day, subverting the rules by using value criteria based on feeling rather than intellect. The results shocked and challenged the Victorian public's perception of what art ought to be. The second movement counterpointed the first, since one of its aims was to revive an interest in traditional arts and crafts, which were primarily functionalist in nature.

Ruskin's writing questioned the entire pantheon of social norms and this spurred the Pre-Raphaelites to look beyond conventional Victorian society for their inspiration. They reacted against the "Mannerist" artistic genre and instead focused more on naturalistic accuracy, sometimes of fantastical subjects. Their work hankered back to an earlier era, represented by the Italian Rennaissance artist Raphael (1483–1520) and his predecessors. They considered the artistic process to include the entire activity of the person, and that an artist ought not to be limited to a single medium. Writers were encouraged to paint, for example, and liberal modes of self-expression, including sexual expression, were encouraged.

The themes of Pre-Raphaelitism were enormously more complex than this brief summary can convey and yet the group was, in a sense, the "hippie revolution" of its day. From the intuitionism and mysticism of W. B. Yeats (1865–1939) to the determined realism of Anthony Burgess (1917–93), art, literature, and the debates on norms and conventions have all been fired into life by the Pre-Raphaelites. **LW**

"All great art is the work of the whole living creature, body and soul, and chiefly of the soul."

John Ruskin, artist and critic

Civil Disobedience
Henry David Thoreau

The active refusal by an individual to follow certain rules, laws, or policies of government

Any person who believes a government is acting unjustly has a duty to oppose those actions by protesting and resisting them, according to U.S. writer Henry David Thoreau (1817–62). These acts of civil disobedience are designed to both educate others about the injustice and to bring about change. Civil disobedience stems from an individual's belief that the actions of the state are immoral or unjustified.

In 1849 Thoreau wrote "Resistance to Civil Government," an essay later published as *On the Duty of Civil Disobedience*. In that work he coined the term "civil disobedience" to describe his refusal to pay taxes to support what he perceived as unjust U.S. government policy. In his study of history, Thoreau observed that many people who change society for the better are seen initially as enemies, and that those who follow their consciences are often at odds with society at the time, yet are later regarded as the most influential of reformers and heroes. Governments, even democracies, he argued, cannot be relied upon to promote what is good or what is right because they are primarily corrupt organizations. Thoreau believed that individuals have a duty to follow the dictates of their consciences and oppose unjust laws by actively refusing to obey, instead of merely voting, speaking against, or hoping for change.

The tenets of mass nonviolence that Thoreau outlined were instrumental in the successful use of civil disobedience in the twentieth century, in both Mahatma Gandhi's (1869–1948) Indian independence movement and Martin Luther King, Jr.'s (1929–68) civil rights campaign. Prior to that, the Egyptian Revolution of 1919 was widely seen as the first successful use of civil disobedience by a population to achieve a political goal, and the tactics employed by these movements are commonly used today. **MT**

⬆ Henry David Thoreau, photographed in 1847. The activist spent a night in jail for civil disobedience in July 1846: he refused to pay his tax to a government that endorsed slavery.

"Disobedience is the true foundation of liberty. The obedient must be slaves."

Henry David Thoreau

1850

Modern Olympic Games
William Penny Brookes

An international sports competition held every four years in different venues

English physician and botanist William Penny Brookes (1809–95) believed that extending opportunities for physical and intellectual betterment could do much to address the ill-effects of poverty. To this end, he developed a competition based on the ancient Olympics, and in Much Wenlock, England, in October 1850, he held the first "Wenlock Olympian Games." This laid the foundation for a revival of the ancient Greek Olympiad, a four-yearly event in which international athletes from an ever-increasing range of summer and winter sports compete.

While Brookes provided the initial inspiration for the Games, it is French aristocrat Baron Pierre de Coubertin (1863–1937), himself invited by Brookes to attend a Wenlock Olympian Games in 1889, whom the International Olympic Committee recognize as its founder. Coubertin later sought to play down the impact of the Wenlock Games on his own efforts to revive the Olympiad, although the photographs of his stay with Brookes attest to the influence of that visit. The first international games took place in Athens in 1896, with 245 participants from fourteen countries in nine sports and forty-three events.

While the philosophy of harmony that guided the original Greek competition still resonates in its modern equivalent, its main influence has been on how we think about who competes in sport. Brookes's original idea of inclusivity regardless of class or status has been extended to include women, athletes of color, and those with disabilities. Unfortunately, the modern Olympiad's reputation has been somewhat tarred by accusations of bribery in the context of selecting a new capital city to host the event every four years, and by the prevalence of illegal performance-enhancing drug use, particularly since the introduction of a ban in 1968. While this has made some observers cynical, most embrace the ideals that the Olympics represents. **LW**

Competitors prepare for the men's 100 meters race at the 1896 Olympic Games in Athens. ↑

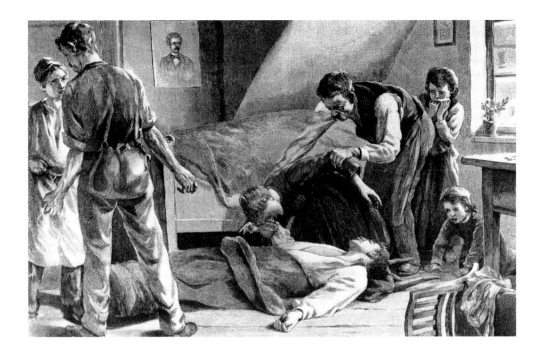

1850

AD&D Insurance
Franklin Health Assurance Company

A form of life insurance that covers death or dismemberment from an accident

Referred to in the industry as AD&D, accidental death and dismemberment insurance is a form of coverage that pays a predetermined sum of money to a named beneficiary in the event that the insured person loses his or her life, or a body part in an accident. In the contemporary context, AD&D insurance is most often secured by laborers or persons otherwise employed in a high-risk occupation. The insurance is a safeguard against lost wages or the insured's inability to work due to an accident. AD&D was originally conceived, however, as protection against the perils of travel.

The first AD&D policy was issued in 1850 by the Franklin Health Assurance Company of Boston, Massachusetts. Franklin Health Assurance offered accident coverage to steamboat and railroad passengers against any accident that may occur on their voyage. Numerous firms followed suit and eventually broadened the scope of their coverage to insure against lost wages due to accidents of all sorts.

Over time the plethora of firms offering policies of this sort consolidated through attrition and, in the 1920s and 1930s, alternative means of administering health coverage emerged. In 1929 the precursor to the Blue Cross (a federation of health insurance organizations and companies) was developed at Baylor University in Dallas, Texas, as a means of providing insurance that would pay for hospital expenses for those enrolled in the plan. Since then the Blue Cross (and Blue Shield) system has grown into one of the primary vehicles for health care coverage in the United States. The success of the private accident and health insurance industry that grew up around AD&D insurance is arguably the reason why the United States government has long resisted intervention in health care, despite the establishment of public health care systems in other developed nations. **DM**

⬆ The body of a construction worker fatally injured in a fall from scaffolding is brought home to his family.

De Morgan's Laws
Augustus de Morgan

The principle in logic that "and" and "or" are dual

De Morgan's laws are a pair of rules in propositional logic and Boolean algebra that are named for the British mathematician and logician Augustus De Morgan (1806–71), who first formalized them in 1850. Although the rules are fairly intuitive and may even seem trivial—indeed, logicians have used them since at least the fourth century BCE—De Morgan was the first to incorporate them into a system of formal logic.

De Morgan's laws are a pair of rules of inference that allow us to turn conjunctions ("and" statements) into disjunctions ("or" statements) and vice versa, via negation. Essentially, they can be expressed as follows: (1) The negation of a conjunction is the disjunction of the negations and (2) The negation of a disjunction is the conjunction of the negations.

> "… logical truth depends upon the structure of the sentence …"

Augustus de Morgan, *Formal Logic* (1847)

Consider, for example, the following conjunction: "Pam is perky and Quincy is quick." The negation of this conjunction is "It is not the case that Pam is perky and Quincy is quick." De Morgan's first law tells us that this statement is logically equivalent to "Either it's not the case that Pam is perky or it's not the case that Quincy is quick." Similarly, consider the following disjunction: "Either Pam is perky or Quincy is quick." The negation of this disjunction is "It is not the case that either Pam is perky or Quincy is quick," which the second of De Morgan's laws tells us is logically equivalent to "It's not the case that Pam is perky and it's not the case that Quincy is quick." Today, the laws are used to simplify electric circuits and logical expressions that are used in computer programs. **GD**

Program Music
Franz Liszt

A musical work whose form and content derive from an extra-musical source

"Program music" is a phrase coined by composer Franz Liszt (1811–86) in the early 1850s, along with the term "symphonic poem." Liszt believed that developments in harmony and orchestration during the nineteenth century necessitated a break with the formal patterns for organizing a composition that had been advanced a century earlier, as the development of content and form must go together—as he put it, "New wine demands new bottles." He also believed that music could benefit from a relationship with the other arts: it could be a "program" inspired by a story, play, or poem, rather than just abstract constructions in sound.

Liszt was not the first to bring extra-musical aspects into music or to make radical changes to compositional practice; there are many earlier works that imitated or alluded to events or characters within a traditional form. Examples include Jean-Philippe Rameau's *The Hen* (1728), Ludwig Beethoven's *Symphony No. 6* (1808), or Hector Berlioz's *Symphonie Fantastique* (1830). Liszt's works were not directly representational, meaning that they did not mimic precise events through sound effects, rather they were suggestive. As he described it, "Music embodies feeling without forcing it to contend and combine with thought, as it is forced in most arts, and especially in the art of words." Liszt opened the door to individualized formal developments, rather than predefined models, a trend that continues to the present day.

During Liszt's lifetime, controversies had already begun about whether music has a content outside of the sound itself—a perhaps unsolvable aesthetic discussion that remains relevant today. Not least are these discussions apparent with the prevalence of representational film music, in which music often is supposed to amplify or mirror the narrative on screen, often with a preconceived and universal vocabulary of musical gestures. **PB**

Rational Dress
Elizabeth Smith Miller

A style of women's dress that focused on comfort and practicality, characterized by the wearing of knickerbockers or bloomers in place of a skirt

In the 1850s women routinely wore up to 14 pounds (6.4 kg) of undergarments, and from the very beginnings of the emancipation movement in the United States and Britain women's fashion was prominent alongside the struggle for better wages, property rights, education, and marriage reform. It was Elizabeth Smith Miller (1822–1911), the daughter of abolitionists Gerrit Smith and Ann Fitzhugh, who initiated the rebellion against restrictive clothing, by wearing Turkish pantaloons—trousers worn under a knee-length skirt tucked in around the ankles.

When Amelia Bloomer (1818–94), Miller's fellow suffragette and editor of the temperance magazine *The Lily*, saw the new dress code, she approved of it immediately. The style became popularized through her magazine, and the pants were later dubbed "bloomers." Bloomers offered a practical alternative to tightly strung corsets and layers of skirts, but only a small percentage of the female population ever wore them. In 1856 came the more fashionable crinoline, which also liberated women from the abundance of petticoats, but it still proved a hazard to women as many were burned to death when their impossibly wide skirts brushed over open fireplaces. Outcries over the harm done by corsets and heavy skirts continued in the 1870s, but it was not until 1881 that the Rational Dress Society established itself in London, promising to oppose "any fashion in dress that either deforms the figure, impedes the movements of the body, or in any way tends to injure the health."

A key development in the widespread acceptance of rational dress was the rise in popularity of the bicycle at the end of the nineteenth century. The design of early bicycles meant that they were all but impossible to ride in long skirts, and pants therefore became respectable for women as a form of "sporting" dress. **BS**

⬆ An illustration from c. 1850 displays the new style of rational dress for women. The bloomer suit maintained Victorian decency while allowing women to move more freely.

"I became so thoroughly disgusted with the long skirt, that the dissatisfaction—the growth of years—suddenly ripened into the decision that this shackle should no longer be endured. The resolution was at once put into practice."

Elizabeth Smith Miller

You Are What You Eat
Ludwig Feuerbach

All human processes are the product of the food that we ingest

In 1850, Jacob Moleschott (1822–93), a Dutch dietician and physiologist, published *The Theory of Food: For the People*, a popular book on nutrition. Describing the physiological bases of hunger and thirst, the processes of digestion and assimilation, and the nutritional properties of various foods, it was widely praised for its eloquence and clarity. However, an even greater sensation than the book itself was a review of it written by Moleschott's friend and former teacher, the German philosopher Ludwig Feuerbach (1804–72).

A materialist who regarded physical processes as the only reality, Feuerbach found support for his views in Moleschott's depiction of human beings as bodily organisms produced and sustained through eating and drinking. Even our thoughts, beliefs, and

> *"Only sustenance is substance. Sustenance is the identity of spirit and nature."*
>
> Ludwig Feuerbach

emotions depend on the work of our digestive system. "No thought without phosphorus," Moleschott wrote, explaining how the brain could not be formed without the ingestion of phosphorus-bearing fat. Feuerbach summarized Moleschott's account of the origin of our mental life by saying, "Food becomes blood, blood becomes heart and brain, the stuff of thoughts and attitudes . . . *Man ist, was man ißt.*" This German pun loses some of its bite in translation, but it has nonetheless become a familiar saying—"you are what you eat."

Feuerbach intended his quip to mean that there is literally nothing more to human beings than the matter we ingest and the transformations it undergoes. Since then, however, it has come to have the looser meaning that what we eat is a major factor in our state of mind and health, becoming a slogan for healthy eating. **GD**

Devolution
Benedict Morel

The notion that a species can evolve backward into a more "primitive" form

Devolution is the belief that an organism or a species can, over time, lose its biological complexity and "de-evolve" (or evolve backward) into a more primitive form of life. The theory was developed by the French psychiatrist Benedict Morel (1809–73), whose theory of "degeneration" in the 1850s represented his search for a biological explanation for the onset of mental illness. Morel wrote of a progressive degeneration, from neurosis to mental alienation and on to imbecility, then finally sterility. He also claimed that behavior such as the excessive consumption of alcohol or drug taking would result in the degeneration of the offspring of those involved, offspring that could, over generations if the pattern were repeated, begin to revert to a more "primitive" biological form.

Morel believed that species must inevitably evolve in a Darwinian sense, a thought that presupposes some kind of future hierarchical structure that organisms are destined to achieve. However, he also believed that species could regress. Biologists have, after all, found countless examples of decreasing complexity in the fossil record, particularly in the jaw bones of fish, mammals, and reptiles, although strictly speaking from a biologist's perspective devolution cannot exist. All change, whether regressive or not, is evolutionary— it is always a progression forward, regardless of its resultant level of complexity. Ninety-nine percent of all species that have ever existed on Earth are now extinct, a fact that makes a mockery of the concept of teleology in nature—that species evolve because they tend to adapt to their changing environments and therefore survive.

Perhaps Morel was right. With so many species no longer with us, clearly the idea of ever-increasing complexity, and the ability to adapt and survive that should accompany it, is far from a sure thing. **JF**

Chance Favors the Prepared Mind
Louis Pasteur

We are more likely to make the most of an opportunity if we have thought about or studied the issue beforehand

A very large number of scientific advances have been made as a result of chance: the antibiotic effect of penicillin, the low toxicity of warfarin, the anaesthetic properties of nitrous oxide, even the hallucinogenic effects of LSD; the list is endless. But many, if not all of these, would not have been recognized had not the scientists working on them already, through hard work and careful observation, been prepared to take advantage of them when the opportunity arose. Furthermore, in order to change the world and the way that people think, a scientist has to do more than simply achieve a breakthrough, whether by effort or good luck. He or she has to prove that the breakthrough is not a fluke, and to persuade fellow scientists to follow it up and ordinary people to believe in it.

The English author Sir Horace Walpole (1717–97) coined the term "serendipity" in 1754 for those happy accidents that bring about major advances in individual prosperity, not to mention the medical and physical sciences. But it was French chemist and microbiologist Louis Pasteur (1822–95) who recognized that such accidents benefit only those who are ready for the opportunity that comes their way. In a lecture given at Lille University in 1854, Pasteur stated, "In the field of observation, chance favors only the prepared mind." Preferring observation to theory, Pasteur made many important discoveries, including the process known as fermentation, by which bacteria (beneficial and harmful) grow in organic substances. Until his thorough study of yeasts revealed this, it was believed that bacteria arrived by spontaneous generation. It was only a step from this discovery to the long battle against harmful microbes that cause diseases such as typhoid, cholera, and tuberculosis. The special heating process that destroys microbes in milk was first carried out in 1862, and bears his name: pasteurization. **JF**

⬆ French chemist and microbiologist Louis Pasteur performs an experiment in his laboratory. Pasteur's scientific accomplishments earned him France's highest decoration, the Legion of Honor.

"Preparation is essential. It brings the necessary ideas to mind at the same time, so that they can be combined in a novel way. When the combination happens, it leads to a sequence of insights and to the 'Aha!' experience of discovery."

Mark Stefik and Barbara Stefik, *Breakthrough* (2004)

The Simple Life
Henry David Thoreau

Simplifying one's lifestyle as a means of improving spiritual wellbeing

⬆ A detail from Ferdinand Brütt's painting of a summer's day (1904) evokes Henry David Thoreau's idea of "the simple life," which for him involved living in natural surroundings.

"Be content with what you have; rejoice in the way things are. When you realize there is nothing lacking, the whole world belongs to you."

Laozi, Daoist philosopher

Prescriptions for simple living date back to ancient times and are found in such traditions as Daoism, primitive Christianity, and ancient Greek and Roman philosophy. The eighteenth-century Swiss philosopher Jean-Jacques Rousseau (1712–78) also praised the life of rustic simplicity at a time when enthusiasm for sophisticated modern life was running high. The thinker most closely associated with the virtues of simple living, however, is the U.S. transcendentalist philosopher Henry David Thoreau (1817–62), whose two-year experiment with the simple life on the shores of Walden Pond, near Concord, Massachusetts, was memorialized in his classic book *Walden*, published in 1854. As a transcendentalist, Thoreau affirmed the inherent goodness of people and nature, but believed that human beings were at their best when they were most "self-reliant" and independent of the corrupting influence of society and its institutions.

For Thoreau, the simple life meant a retreat from the consumerism and materialism of the modern world in order to regain a lost closeness to nature and to foster self-reflection. For many people today, the practice of voluntary simplicity promises a reduction of worry and stress, a more eco-friendly lifestyle, and a better balance between work and leisure.

The first step in simple living is usually to decrease one's possessions and consumption. Proponents of simple living recommend being content with the satisfaction of one's needs, rather than devoting oneself to the pursuit of an ever-increasing catalog of wants. Many also choose to grow their own food. For those who want to take "baby steps" in the direction of a simpler life, "downsizing" entails a gradual shift of emphasis away from economic success and toward activities designed to bring greater personal fulfillment. The simple life, in this view, is the good life. **GD**

Gradgrind's Education
Charles Dickens

A fictional educational philosophy critiquing utilitarian attitudes toward education

In 1854, English novelist Charles Dickens (1812–70) published his tenth novel, *Hard Times*, a searing indictment of the moral, political, and social ideologies that he held responsible for perpetuating the hard times experienced by the poor in mid-nineteenth-century England. Set in the fictional industrial city of Coketown amid smokestacks and factories, *Hard Times* tells the story of Thomas Gradgrind, his family and associates, and others with whom his life intersects. Gradgrind, a retired merchant who has become a school headmaster, espouses a philosophy of rational, calculating self-interest and exclusive focus on cold facts and numbers. Events in the novel eventually prompt Gradgrind to renounce his philosophy, which is portrayed as an unintended source of misery for those around him.

The failures of Gradgrind's educational philosophy are meant to offer an object lesson in the folly of a "utilitarian" outlook that dismisses the worth of anything that cannot be economically quantified or measured, such as the experience of wonder and the exercise of the imagination. "With a rule and a pair of scales, and the multiplication table always in his pocket," Gradgrind is said to be "ready to weigh and measure any parcel of human nature, and tell you exactly what it comes to. It is a mere question of figures, a case of simple arithmetic." His single-minded focus on facts and figures at the expense of more imaginative pursuits has left him unable to appreciate that the most unquantifiable aspects of human existence, the lively "sentiments and affections" on which he heaps such disdain, are the ones that make life worth living.

Gradgrind's name has entered the vernacular as a synonym for a soulless devotion to facts and figures and, in particular, for a pedagogical theory that favors the learning of facts to the neglect of cultivation of the arts and humanities. **GD**

HARD TIMES.

⬆ An illustration from Charles Dickens's novel shows the utilitarian educationist Thomas Gradgrind after finding his children, Louisa and Tom, who have sneaked off to Sleary's circus.

"A man of realities. A man of facts and calculations. A man who proceeds upon the principle that two and two are four, and nothing over, and who is not to be talked into allowing for anything over."

Charles Dickens, *Hard Times* (1854)

The Immaculate Conception
Pope Pius IX

A Catholic doctrine teaching that Mary, the mother of Christ, was born free of sin

According to Roman Catholicism, all humans are born with the stain of an original sin inherited from our first ancestors, whose reckless disobedience of God—first in the Garden of Eden when Adam and Eve ate fruit from the Tree of Knowledge of Good and Evil—inflicted lasting damage on human nature itself. This original sin is the reason we are weak in our ability to resist moral temptation and prone to vices, such as lust and greed. To overcome the effects of original sin and become eligible for eternal life with Christ, we need God's sanctifying grace, which is normally conferred at baptism. The sole exception to this universally sinful human condition is the mother of Jesus, the Virgin Mary.

Unique among human beings, Mary was conceived "immaculately," that is, without the stain of original sin.

"Mary . . . a virgin whom grace has made inviolate, free of every stain of sin."

St. Ambrose

The sanctifying grace that others receive at baptism was granted to her from the moment her soul was created. This dogma, known as the Immaculate Conception, has been an official tenet of the Church since it was first formally proclaimed by Pope Pius IX in 1854, although it had been a popular belief since the fifth century. Nonetheless, it had been a bone of contention among Catholic theologians, many insisting that sanctifying grace could be conferred only after conception. A decisive consideration in favor of the dogma, according to Pope Pius IX, however, was what he called "a profound sensus fidelium," the consensus among the faithful as reflected in their devotion to Mary. The Immaculate Conception should not be confused with other Catholic dogmas: the virginal conception of Jesus and Mary's perpetual (or lifelong) virginity. **GD**

Entropy
Rudolf Clausius

A measure of the unavailability of a system's thermal energy for conversion into work

Entropy is a concept in classical thermodynamics, which is the study of how heat is converted into usable energy. Entropy is the measure of how much of a system's thermal energy (heat) is unavailable for doing useful work or how evenly that energy is distributed in the system. The more even the distribution, the less energy is available. German physicist Rudolf Clausius (1822–88) produced the first mathematical formulation of entropy in 1854. However, it was not until 1865 that he coined the term "entropy," which comes from the Greek *entropía*, meaning "transformation content."

For an illustration of entropy, consider what happens when an ice cube is placed in a glass of water. Initially, the energy in the glass is very unevenly distributed, with the warmer water molecules possessing more

"Entropy shakes its angry fist at you for being clever enough to organize the world."

Brandon Sanderson, science fiction writer

energy than the colder ice. Consequently, the system is in a state of low entropy, with much of its energy available for the work of melting the ice. But once the system has achieved equilibrium, with the ice melted and thermal energy distributed randomly throughout the glass, the system is in a state of high entropy and its energy is unavailable for work.

This example also illustrates the second law of thermodynamics, which states that the entropy of any isolated system, one that exchanges neither matter nor energy with the outside world, always tends to increase. Without outside energy inputs, every system tends toward greater equilibrium, randomness, and disorder. Since the universe as a whole is an isolated system, it is steadily approaching a state of maximum entropy, at which point all its available energy will be spent. **GD**

◄ A painting depicting the Immaculate Conception by José Antolinez (c. 1650–75).

Biblical Psychological Criticism
Franz Delitzsch

A field of biblical criticism analyzing the psychological dimensions of Judeo-Christian scripture

⬆ A portrait of the German Lutheran theologian Franz Delitzsch. As well as biblical psychology, his work covered Jewish antiquities, a history of Jewish poetry, and Christian apologetics.

Biblical psychological criticism is a field of study that applies psychological and psychoanalytical insight to the origins, authorship, content, translation, and interpretation of the Bible. Psychological criticism also aims to examine the history of the Bible's personal and cultural effects. It attempts to psychoanalyze the authors of scripture and the characters mentioned in the biblical texts, and to clarify the writers' intentions. Psychological criticism also inquires into the relationship of the reader with the scriptures and how that affects the personal world of an individual and becomes relevant in their life.

Psychological inquiry of the scriptures began before the birth of modern psychology. Biblical psychological criticism started with *A System of Biblical Psychology* (1855) by German theologian Franz Delitzsch (1813–90). He examined works by writers such as Tertullian (c. 160–225), St. Augustine of Hippo (354–430), and St. Thomas Aquinas (1225–74) in a survey to assess what he defined as a "psychological literature" that stretched from the writers of the early Christian church to contemporary theologians. Delitzsch suggested that biblical psychology was a science and "one of the oldest sciences of the church."

Delitzsch's *A System of Biblical Psychology* was not received favorably at the time. However, as psychology evolved to mean more than the study of the soul, or psyche, and developed into a discipline that involved the study of the mind, so biblical psychological criticism also evolved with it, influenced by the work and writings of pioneering psychiatrists Sigmund Freud and Carl Jung on the conscious and unconscious activities of the soul. Biblical psychological criticism gained currency in the 1960s via the works of U.S. academics such as Frederick Charles Grant and Wayne G. Rollins, and German theologian Gerd Theissen. **CK**

"When we approach scripture we come with the same baggage. It is not possible to come in any other way."

Wayne G. Rollins, *Jung and the Bible* (1983)

1856

Limited Liability Corporation
British Government

A company that has a separate legal identity from the people who own and run it

The abbreviation "Ltd." (Limited), frequently seen after the name of a business, identifies it as a limited liability corporation, a particular type of company that has a legal identity separate from both its managers and shareholders. Limited liability sets a limit on how far investors or partners can be held liable for a company's debts and unfulfilled obligations should the business fail. That limit is typically set at the value of their original investment, so that shareholders risk only what they have already put into the company. Consequently, if the company is successfully sued, only the company itself, not its owners or investors, will be liable to pay any resulting judgment. This feature distinguishes limited liability corporations from businesses with a sole proprietor and general partnerships, in which the owners are liable for all the company's debts.

In England, limited liability has been granted to some associations, such as monasteries and some trade guilds, since the fifteenth century. However, joint stock companies—businesses owned by shareholders— were not allowed to incorporate as limited liability corporations in the United Kingdom until Parliament passed the Limited Liability Act of 1855. The Joint Stock Companies Act of 1856 established a simple procedure whereby any group of seven people or more could register a limited liability corporation. Since then, this form of corporation has spread throughout the world and been adopted by the vast majority of businesses operating in market economies.

It is difficult to exaggerate the importance of this innovation, for it effectively made the company equivalent to a person under the law. By limiting shareholder liability, this new status helped companies to raise enough capital to form the large enterprises required by the emerging industrial economies and thereby enabled the growth of modern capitalism. **GD**

⬆ The Houses of Parliament in London, England, where the Limited Liability Act was passed in 1855. This historic legislation met the need for larger amounts of capital investment in industry.

"Corporation: An ingenious device for obtaining profit without individual responsibility."

Ambrose Bierce, journalist and satirist

The Great Controversy
Ellen G. White

The religious belief that all humanity is caught in a battle between good and evil

Throughout recorded history, religious teachers have depicted humanity as caught in a fierce battle between the forces of good and evil. The Seventh-day Adventist Church offers one perspective on this battle, derived from a reading of the Bible. In 1858, Ellen G. White, one of the founders of the Seventh-day Adventist Church, wrote *The Great Controversy*, recounting the history of "the great controversy between Christ and Satan," from its beginnings before the creation of the world right up to its end-time when the world will be destroyed.

In this account, sin first came into existence when Satan, originally an angel created to enjoy fellowship with God in Heaven, became filled with pride and grew discontent with living under God's laws. Aspiring to autonomy and equality with God, he led a rebellion

"… that old serpent, called the Devil, and Satan … was cast out into the earth."

The Bible, Revelation 12:9

that resulted in his expulsion from Heaven. The field of battle then shifted to Earth, where Satan infected Adam and Eve with his same pride, persuaded them to disobey God, and thereby wrested from them the dominion over the Earth that God had granted them. Establishing himself as the new "prince of this world," he continued his rebellion from his new earthly base of operation. His eventual downfall was later assured, however, by the selfless sacrifice of Christ on the cross.

For Seventh-day Adventists, this controversy involves God's character, sovereignty, and law over the universe. Satan objects to God's law, denouncing it as arbitrary and burdensome. His rebellion impugns God's character, construing it as defective, and challenges God's right to govern the universe. The battle is ongoing and touches every life. **GD**

Gray's Anatomy
Henry Gray

An inexpensive and accessible anatomy textbook for medical students

The compilation of a single, accessible, and inexpensive work of reference about human anatomy that could be used by everyone seems an obvious idea, yet it was only comparatively recently that it came to fruition. The work of a single-minded and creative doctor, *Gray's Anatomy* made its first appearance in 1858 and has remained the standard text ever since.

Henry Gray (1827–61) trained as a medical student at St. George's Hospital in London. In 1853 he was appointed lecturer in anatomy at St. George's Medical School. Two years later, Gray, who was only twenty-eight at the time, recognized that no single anatomy textbook existed that he could recommend to his students. He asked his colleague Henry Vandyke Carter (1831–97), a skilled medical illustrator, to help

"As a practical work … Gray's Anatomy *has always been recognized and appreciated."*

Preface to the twentieth edition of *Gray's Anatomy* (1918)

him compile such a book. They worked together for eighteen months before the finished text was published in 1858. Known then as *Anatomy: Descriptive and Surgical*, the book was 750 pages long and contained 363 figures. It was an immediate hit. Gray, however, did not live to see its long success; in 1861 he died of smallpox while treating his nephew.

Gray's Anatomy was organized in a systemic way, with separate sections for the entire skeletal system, nervous system, and so on. Over the years, the book increased in length, so that by the thirty-eighth edition in 1995, it had 2,092 large-format pages. The contents were then reorganized for the thirty-ninth edition into regional anatomies according to where in the body the structures are located. The fortieth edition, in both print and online editions, appeared in 2008. **SA**

Engraving of the muscles of the neck from *Gray's Anatomy* (1897). ➡

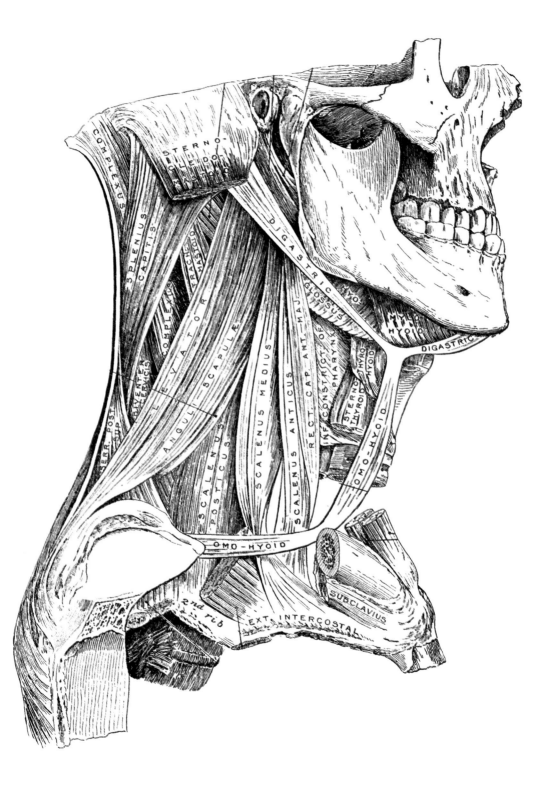

Natural Selection
Charles Darwin

The gradual process by which populations evolve to have certain biological traits

In his studies of the natural world, English scientist Charles Darwin (1809–82) observed that in any population of living organisms there is inevitable variation between individuals. When those variations allow an organism a better chance of surviving and reproducing, that organism, and its inherent traits, will be naturally selected to continue on into future generations due to its suitability for survival. Over time, the accumulated small traits naturally selected by the environment will lead to the evolution of new species.

In 1859 Darwin published *On the Origin of Species*, which caused a tectonic shift in the view of life on Earth. Darwin was not the first to observe that life changed over time, or to propose that environmental conditions could influence an organism's ability to adapt. In fact,

"... the origin of species—that mystery of mysteries, as it has been called ..."

Charles Darwin, *On the Origin of Species* (1859)

Alfred Russell Wallace (1823–1913), a contemporary of Darwin, independently arrived at many of the same conclusions. However, Darwin's extensive research and evidence in support of his theory ensured his claim as the discoverer of evolution by natural selection.

Since its introduction, evolution by natural selection has become the bedrock theory of the life sciences. In the simple calculation of organisms surviving based on natural traits, it removed the notion of a prearranged natural world that had been widely assumed throughout Western history. The idea that all organisms—even humanity itself—evolved from more primitive forms had profound implications for both scientists and society at large. Even today there are those who vehemently oppose the idea of natural selection, largely because of the conclusions it entails. **MT**

On Liberty
John Stuart Mill

Individual freedoms should only be limited to prevent harm to others

Philosopher and statesman John Stuart Mill (1806–73) published *On Liberty* in 1859 as part of his theory of utilitarianism. While Mill's later *Utilitarianism* (1861–63) states that the right thing to do is what promotes the greatest good for the greatest number of people, *On Liberty* delineates the appropriate limitations of a government in enforcing this principle.

Mill argues that politics is necessarily a struggle between liberty (maximizing personal freedom) and authority (maximizing safety). Too much emphasis upon the former produces anarchy, while too much of the latter results in tyranny. The balance between these two extremes is struck by following the harm principle: liberty to pursue one's own happiness is a fundamental good for all human beings and can

"Over one's mind and over one's body the individual is sovereign."

John Stuart Mill

only be infringed upon if the exercise of one's liberty harms other persons. A state is not justified in making paternalistic laws that restrict citizens' freedoms for their own good. For example, while the state can ban drink driving because it harms others, it should not outlaw alcohol simply because the drug might harm its user. If the state is to err, it should do so on the side of liberty rather than authority. Mill argues that three types of liberty should always be protected by a just state: (1) freedom of consciousness, including beliefs and speech; (2) freedom of tastes and pursuits; and (3) the freedom to unite for any noninjurious purpose.

On Liberty is one of the most important treatises in the history of political philosophy. The harm principle is a cornerstone of liberal democracy and continues to be used by both lawmakers and political theorists. **JM**

← Charles Darwin (pictured in 1902), who laid the foundations of evolutionary theory.

Last Universal Ancestor
Charles Darwin

The organism from which all organisms now living on Earth descend

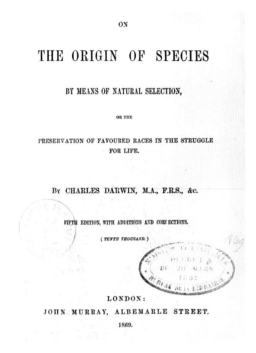

ON

THE ORIGIN OF SPECIES

BY MEANS OF NATURAL SELECTION,

OR THE

PRESERVATION OF FAVOURED RACES IN THE STRUGGLE
FOR LIFE.

BY CHARLES DARWIN, M.A., F.R.S., &c.

FIFTH EDITION, WITH ADDITIONS AND CORRECTIONS.

(TENTH THOUSAND.)

LONDON:
JOHN MURRAY, ALBEMARLE STREET.
1869.

⬆ The title page of the expanded fifth edition of Charles Darwin's *On the Origin of Species*, published in 1869—exactly a decade after the first edition.

"There is a grandeur in this view of life, with its several powers, having been originally breathed into a few forms or into one."

Charles Darwin, *On the Origin of Species* (1859)

Contemporary evolutionary biology attests that all organisms on Earth share a common ancestor, known as the "last universal ancestor," estimated to have lived 3.5 to 3.8 billion years ago. Charles Darwin (1809–82) first introduced the theory that all life descended from a single ancestor in his book *On the Origins of Species* (1859), basing his argument for common descent on evidence drawn from the presence of homologous structures in different species and embryonic development.

In order to understand the idea of homologous structures, compare the arm of a human being, the forelimb (flipper) of a seal, and the wing of a bat. Although each has a very different function, they closely resemble one other in their relative position and assembly. These similarities suggest that these three structures all evolved from a single prototype belonging to a shared ancestor of the three organisms. Other homologies found across a wide range of species led Darwin to the conclusion that all or most animals shared a common descent. He also noticed that the embryos of disparate species shared a similar structure, making it impossible to distinguish them in the earliest stages of their development, thus indicating a common ancestry.

Although Darwin's observations were limited by the science of his time and seemed at best only to support a common descent for all animals and, through a different independent lineage, for all plants, he believed that we could extrapolate to the much stronger conclusion of a universal ancestor for all living organisms, based on similarities "in their chemical composition, their germinal vesicles, their cellular structure, and their laws of growth and reproduction." More recently, comparative analyses of the DNA of different species have offered new insights and confirmation of Darwin's hypothesis of a universal common ancestor, which scientists now believe to have been a small, single-cell organism. **GD**

Riemann Hypothesis
Bernhard Riemann

A theory explaining the apparently random pattern of prime numbers

In 1859, Bernhard Riemann (1826–66), an obscure German mathematician, introduced a bold hypothesis in his paper "On the Number of Prime Numbers Less Than a Given Magnitude." As the title indicates, his hypothesis offers a formula for calculating how many prime numbers appear in any block of numbers. To this day, the Riemann Hypothesis has been neither proven nor refuted, despite a century and a half of painstaking research and a $1 million prize awaiting the first person to solve it.

A full explanation of the Riemann Hypothesis requires an account of the mathematical entities that it employs, called "the zeros of the Riemann zeta function," of which the Riemann Hypothesis says, "All the non-trivial zeros of the Riemann zeta function have real part one half." An adequate explanation of these mysterious "zeros" would involve a book-length exposition, but it is possible at least to get a general grasp of the mathematical problem that these entities are recruited to address.

The Riemann Hypothesis concerns the distribution of prime numbers. The set of primes is infinite—however high you count, there are always more up ahead. However, as one proceeds along the number line, the occurrence of primes becomes more and more infrequent. More prime numbers lie between 1 and 100 than between, say, 9,001 and 9,100. But there is an irregularity to how the primes thin out that complicates any attempt to calculate just how many primes to expect in any block of numbers. There already exists an established formula for the average density of primes, but it was Riemann who first proposed an exact formula for calculating the deviation from average density, too. Still unproven, the Riemann Hypothesis remains, in the words of author John Derbyshire, "the great white whale of mathematical research." **GD**

⬆ A portrait of the German mathematician Bernhard Reimann, created in the 1860s. Reimann made significant contributions to analysis, number theory, and differential geometry.

"However timid and listless he may have appeared to casual observers, Reimann's mathematics has the fearless sweep and energy of one of Napoleon's campaigns."

John Derbyshire, writer

Sexual Selection
Charles Darwin

Animal species evolve certain traits in order to attract mates

If species evolve based on their ability to adapt to their environments, how can some animals have developed extreme—and seemingly nonadaptive—traits, such as vibrant feather displays or large and ungainly sets of antlers? The answer, according to Charles Darwin (1809–82), lies in sexual selection. Regardless of how suited to an environment an organism is, that organism will not be able to reproduce unless it can find a mate. If those potential mates only choose partners with certain qualities, then only those individuals that display such qualities will be able to reproduce, while the others will die without successfully producing offspring.

In his seminal book *On the Origin of Species* (1859), Darwin laid the groundwork for the understanding of evolution by natural selection, also explaining

> *"Sexual selection is, therefore, less rigorous than natural selection."*

Charles Darwin, *On the Origin of Species* (1859)

that an organism must necessarily be able to attract a mate in order to reproduce and pass on whatever beneficial characteristics it may have. He explained that individuals, typically males, of the same species commonly display characteristics or traits that only exist to allow the male to attract and mate with a female. This explains why animals develop traits that do not necessarily allow them to better adapt to an environment, and also competition between males of the same species over the ability to mate with a female.

With sexual selection Darwin showed that evolution is not simply a process of adaptation to the environment. Sexual and social pressures also have a great impact on how a species evolves, even to the point of making an individual organism less likely to survive. **MT**

Abduction
Charles Sanders Peirce

The ability to derive conclusions from information and observable facts

The U.S. philosopher and logician Charles Sanders Peirce (1839–1914) first began writing on what he called his abduction theory in the 1860s, and continued to expand and refine it over the next five decades. Abduction is a form of inference that uses information describing something to draw a hypothesis that offers a plausible explanation for what has been observed or has occurred. In the words of its originator: "Abduction is the process of forming an explanatory hypothesis. It is the only logical operation which introduces any new idea."

Peirce believed that there were three different types of reasoning. There was deduction or necessary reasoning, deriving a conclusion B from A where B is a formal consequence of A. Inference was having

> *"Bad reasoning as well as good reasoning is possible . . ."*

Charles Sanders Peirce

good reason to believe a conclusion on the basis of a premise. Abduction, however, was a kind of guesswork, "very little hampered by the rules of logic"; an initial phase of inquiry in a situation where premises do not necessarily guarantee correct conclusions.

A classic example of abductive theory is this: you are driving home from work and notice a blue car is behind you. After making several turns the blue car continues to be behind you, and is still there after several more changes of direction. After doing a U-turn because you had forgotten something in your office that you need at home, you notice the same blue car is still behind you. Having already ruled out the possibility of coincidence, and in the absence of any more plausible explanations, you reluctantly conceive the hypothesis that the blue car is following you deliberately. **JMa**

◄ The male peacock's showy display of plumage is an example of traits arising from sexual selection.

Industrial Design
Christopher Dresser

The combination of principles of design with industrialized manufacturing processes to create an entirely new aesthetic

⬆ A watering can designed by Christopher Dresser in 1876, manufactured by Richard Perry, Son & Company. Much of Dresser's most influential work was produced around this time.

"One of Dresser's great strengths as a designer was his ability to understand the properties of materials and the processes of production . . . "

Robert Edwards, art critic

Although industrialization came with the transition to new manufacturing processes from about 1760, the idea of design had existed for centuries prior to this. Some would argue that the first ever industrial designer was Leonardo da Vinci, as evidenced in his "Book of Patterns of Machine Elements" in the fifteenth century. The word "design" itself, however, was not defined in the *Oxford Dictionary* until 1588, as "a plan or scheme devised by a person for something that is to be realized . . ." It was the civil servant and inventor Henry Cole (1808–82) who made the case for functional design in 1849 with his publication of the short-lived *Journal of Design*, and also for a Great Exhibition in London to showcase the world's manifold new industrial creations, made possible by innovations such as cast iron, industrial carpentry, and automated looms.

The first modern, commercially successful attempt at combining art and technology to improve the aesthetics of everyday objects, however, belongs to the great nineteenth-century Scottish designer Christopher Dresser (1834–1904). After studying as a botanist and authoring three well-received books on the subject, he turned his attention to design in 1860 after failing to gain the chair of botany at the University of London. His success in applying design principles to consumer products, such as wallpapers, ceramics, stained glass, and metalware, was so immediate that he was quoted in 1871 as saying, "as an ornamentalist I have much the largest practice in the kingdom."

Industrial design has had a great impact on everyday life; in its quest to design products for utility, comfort, and beauty, professional industrial design has given the world iconic objects ranging from the Barcelona chair and the KitchenAid mixer to the iPod. Design is now art, and art, design—form and function limited only by the boundaries of our imagination. **BS**

Renaissance Man / Woman
Jacob Burckhardt

Individuals with wide-ranging talents and interests as shown by the Renaissance era

In modern societies, anyone with many diverse interests may be loosely described as a Renaissance man or woman. While the European Renaissance is well known as an era marked by the appearance of such men as Leonardo da Vinci, Copernicus, and Galileo, the period itself only became known as the Renaissance after French historian Jules Michelet described it as such in the mid-nineteenth century. The characterization of the Renaissance man was first explicitly described a few years later in a work published in 1860 by Swiss historian Jacob Burckhardt (1818–97), *The Civilization of the Renaissance in Italy*. Burckhardt described fifteenth-century Italy as particularly notable for the rise of the "many-sided" man, who was knowledgeable or adept at languages, natural history, and other scientific subjects while also involved in politics and the arts.

This idealized sense of the Renaissance man as a multitalented individual is retained in its modern meaning. Burckhardt notes that the Italian Renaissance was imbued with the ideals of humanism, which placed a high value on an individual developing their capacities as fully as possible. In keeping with these ideals, Burckhardt observes that upper-class women were often given the same education as men. Nevertheless, he concedes that, despite their education, few women were afforded the same opportunities to practice their talents and skills in the many fields open to men.

Our modern understanding of Renaissance men and women is greatly indebted to Burckhardt's insight into the culture of individualism that encouraged creativity over conformity. As that individualism spread throughout Europe and has since become widely and firmly established in modern societies, many of the greatest achievements in the arts and sciences are owed to those who are rightfully called Renaissance men and women. **TJ**

Darwinism
Thomas Huxley

A movement in support of Charles Darwin's theory of evolution

In the 1860s, naturalist Charles Darwin (1809–82) was busy developing his theory of evolution and searching out corroborative evidence for it. He had better things to do than defend his ideas from his opponents, and it was not his concern to pull his ideas together to form an overarching super-theory. Both tasks were undertaken by English biologist Thomas Huxley (1825–95), who dubbed himself "Darwin's bulldog" for his advocacy of Darwin's ideas. Indeed, in the lectures he gave in London in the 1860s, Huxley may well have extended the scope of Darwin's ideas further than the biologist himself intended. In Huxley's hands, Darwin's work became a movement with a life of its own: Darwinism.

The Darwinist view that the theory of evolution had destroyed the idea of a divine creator encouraged the

"As for your doctrines, I am prepared to go to the Stake if requisite . . ."

Thomas Huxley, in a letter to Charles Darwin (1859)

public perception that agnosticism, and later atheism, was the logical conclusion to be drawn from Darwin's work. Darwin himself had delayed publication of *On the Origin of Species* (1859) in fear of such controversy, and the dispute over the theory of evolution's implications became more entrenched and bitter as a result of Huxley's championing of Darwin's work.

Atheist scientists, such as the British biologist Richard Dawkins (*b.* 1941), have become well known in recent years for their intolerance of religion of all kinds, and their firm view that Darwinist ideas have made religious belief untenable. However, by no means all scientists agree. In the face of this debate, the U.S. National Academy of Sciences recommended in 1981 that religion and science should not be presented in the same context, to avoid misunderstanding. **JF**

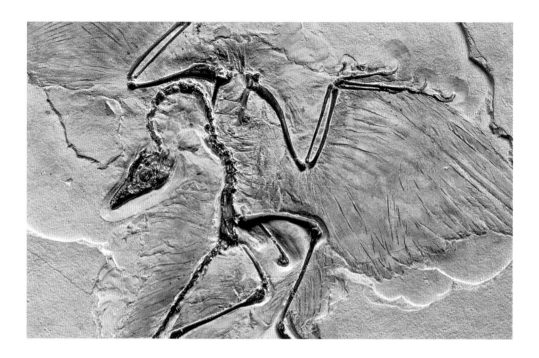

The Missing Link
Charles Lyell

A critical gap in the fossil record showing the evolutionary link between ape and man

The British geologist, and close friend of Charles Darwin, Charles Lyell (1797–1875) popularized the term "missing link" in reference to hypothetical fossil remains that exhibit traits of both an ancestor and a descendent, and thus provide evidence of a clear evolutionary line of heredity. Today, the term—which is more of a popular one than a scientific one—is often used by critics claiming that these missing fossils suggest that evolution is unsound theory.

In 1863, Lyell published *Geological Evidences of the Antiquity of Man*, the book that would introduce the concept of the "missing link." As a geologist, Lyell had been investigating what he knew to be layers of sedimentary rock deposited at different times, and he had noticed that there was a distinct difference in the appearance of fossils found in adjacent sedimentary layers. He brought in the term "missing link" to explain that sudden unexplained transition. Coincidentally, 1863 was the year in which someone first used the phrase to criticize the theory of evolution. In that year, a Scottish doctor, John Crawford, said that in order for evolution to be true, there must be some fossil evidence to show how "man came from a monkey."

In the evolutionary process, organisms evolve across generations and through long periods of time. The time intervals involved give rise to the expectation that animals existing as intermediary stages in between two related species will show shared traits of both. The idea of missing links in the fossil record has captivated people since its introduction, especially those who are troubled by evolution's assertions. But as a scientific notion, the idea of the missing link is largely useless. All organisms that point the way toward the evolution of new species can be considered transitional, and thus each is a missing link in the vast chain of evolving species. Verification of the theory of evolution does not hinge on the identification of missing-link fossils. **MT**

1863

Bahá'i Faith

Bahá'u'lláh

A religious ideology stressing unity in God, science, and the human striving for peace

The Bahá'i Faith was founded in the nineteenth century. Its basis is unity in worship of a single god, and its vision is for harmony between all people, and, eventually, unity between all paths. The religion anticipates an eventual convergence of the paths of science and religion, sexual equality (although this does not imply acceptance of homosexuality), and increasing respect for the environment. Bahá'i stresses the unity of all creation, in addition to the oneness of God, of the human family, and of religion itself.

The Persian founder of the Bahá'í Faith, Bahá'u'lláh (1817–92), was born Mírzá Husayn-`Alí Núrí, the son of a visier who, along with Bahá'u'lláh's mother, died before he came of age. When the orphaned boy was old enough to enter government, he refused to do so, instead seeking more wisdom. The decision was to mean almost unimaginable suffering, although perhaps it was this that enabled Bahá'u'lláh, in the notorious dungeon of Síyáh-Chál in Tehran, to reach a state of consciousness that led him to found the faith. In 1863, he announced, in the Garden of Rivdán, Baghdad, that he was the one about whom the Báb (the Gate, a manifestation of God) had prophesied. The foundation of the Bahá'i Faith began with Bahá'u'lláh spending twelve days in that garden, at the start of a long exile.

Enduring further long imprisonment, torture, and the loss of his beloved son, Bahá'u'lláh developed the clarity and determination to develop his ideas and write them out as teachings. The Bahá'i emphasis on equality, tolerance, integration rather than segregation, and freedom from prejudice opened the way to a humane and inclusive understanding of religion. Seeking common ground between reason and religion, economy and spirituality, Bahá'i challenged the inequalities and injustices of the social and political systems of Bahá'u'lláh's day. The religion still challenges exclusive religious orthodoxies today. **LW**

⬆ The Bahá'i Shrine and Gardens in Haifa, Israel, are the international headquarters for the Bahá'i Faith.

Gettysburg Address

Abraham Lincoln

A reaffirmation of a founding principle of the United States: that all humans are born equal

⬆ A painting of Abraham Lincoln giving his Gettysburg Address by J. L. G. Ferris (c. 1900), a U.S. artist best known for his series of seventy-eight scenes from U.S. history.

". . . we here highly resolve that these dead shall not have died in vain—that this nation, under God, shall have a new birth of freedom—and that government of the people, by the people, for the people, shall not perish from the earth."

Abraham Lincoln

The Battle of Gettysburg took place during July 1–3, 1863, and resulted in the retreat of General Robert E. Lee's Army of Northern Virginia from its incursion into Union territory. On November 19, months after the battle, President Abraham Lincoln (1809–65) attended a ceremony dedicating a national cemetery at the Gettysburg battlefield site. The Gettysburg Address is the speech he gave to the assembled crowd at the ceremony, and it is widely celebrated as one of the most important and influential political speeches in the history of the United States.

When President Lincoln delivered his address, he was second on the bill to Edward Everett (1794–1865), a famed orator who gave a two-hour-long speech to the assembled crowd. Lincoln's speech was incomparably shorter, lasting no longer than two to three minutes, and encompassing about 250 words. Yet in that speech, the president reflected the ideals expressed in the Declaration of Independence (1776), the founding document of the American nation. His simple, eloquent expression of the notion that the nation was founded for equality, and for the good of all people, not once referred to slavery, the Confederacy, the Union, or any of the political issues of the day.

It is unclear what the reaction to Lincoln's speech was at the time, and less than two years after giving it the president was dead and the civil war over. However, the impact of the Gettysburg Address lived on as a model of political rhetoric, oratorical simplicity, and political ideology. The speech turned the nation's political attention toward the unifying ideal that all people are born equal—an ideal that is almost universally assumed today. The Gettysburg Address is credited as being largely responsible for the introduction of that ideal into U.S. political discourse, and it remains an important political reference point today. **MT**

In Praise of Cosmetics
Charles Baudelaire

No woman is so beautiful that her beauty would not be enhanced by cosmetics

For much of the history of humanity, the wearing of cosmetics by women has been viewed, in the West at least, as something associated with harlots and stage performers (with those two professions once being considered almost equally disreputable). As an early nineteenth-century song once asserted, it is nature itself that "embellishes beauty," so what need would a virtuous woman have for makeup?

The French poet and essayist Charles Baudelaire (1821–67) was raised in this culture of "naturalized beauty" and never really questioned it in his early years. But then, in the 1860s, the man who coined the word "modernity" began to question what Romantic artists and writers referred to as the "supremacy of nature." In his book, *The Painter of Modern Life* (1863), he turned his attention to the nature of beauty in the chapter titled "In Praise of Cosmetics."

Baudelaire had always felt especially drawn to the opposite sex, and was conscious of how society's notion of beauty was changing in an increasingly industrialized world. His essay on beauty was a little too whimsical to be taken absolutely seriously, but it was nonetheless a triumphant defense of the notion that makeup can make the beautiful even more beautiful. "External finery," Baudelaire wrote, is "one of the signs of the primitive nobility of the human soul." Every fashion is "charming," and every woman is bound by "a kind of duty" to appear magical, to astonish, and to charm her fellows. Accordingly, nature could now be imaginatively surpassed by applying black eyeliner, which "gives the eye a more decisive appearance," and rouge, which "sets fire to the cheekbone."

Baudelaire's emphasis on the beauty of artifice over nature marked a significant departure from the Romanticism of the first half of the century, reflecting the rise of decadence and Aestheticism, to many of whose practitioners he was a hero. **BS**

⬆ Charles Baudelaire, here photographed in 1862, believed that "everything beautiful and noble is the result of reason and calculation," with nature being only brutal and instinctive.

"I am perfectly happy for those whose owlish gravity prevents them from seeking beauty in its most minute manifestations to laugh at these reflections of mine . . ."

Charles Baudelaire, "In Praise of Cosmetics" (1863)

Pasteurization
Louis Pasteur

Heating food kills harmful microorganisms that could otherwise cause illness

During his investigations into the microscopic world, chemist and microbiologist Louis Pasteur (1822–95) developed a process by which some foods could be heated—at a particular temperature and for a specified length of time—to destroy any potentially dangerous microorganisms. The process, eponymously named pasteurization, produces food free of many of the most common pathogens. Today, the pasteurization process is widely used around the world in the preparation of numerous beverages and foods, including milk, beer, wine, cheese, seafood, and yogurt.

Historical records show that heating wine to prevent it from spoiling was known in China by at least the twelfth century, and in Japan by the sixteenth. But it was only in 1856 that Pasteur discovered that, while

"Gentlemen, it is the microbes who will have the last word."

Louis Pasteur

microbiotic yeast turned juice into alcohol through the fermentation process, other microbes caused the alcohol to spoil. In 1864, Pasteur developed his process of heating liquids to specific temperatures for specific times in order to prevent spoilage.

Without pasteurization, many foods would have extremely short shelf-lives and would pose a significantly higher health risk to consumers. The introduction of pasteurization greatly reduced the number of cases of tuberculosis, diphtheria, scarlet fever, and other bacteriological diseases. It also led to more efficient food storage and transportation, and facilitated the mass production of safe, reliable foodstuffs. Modern pasteurization techniques, such as exposing food to ionizing radiation, are improvements on Pasteur's methods, but his are still widely used today. **MT**

Anarcho-syndicalism
France

A movement blending traditional anarchist sentiments with Marxist pragmatism

The emergence of anarcho-syndicalism is not easily attributed to a particular individual or place, but French politician and socialist Pierre-Joseph Proudhon (1809–65) was probably the first to put on paper its fundamental theories. Anarcho-syndicalism appeared with the anarchist movements that emerged from the Workingmen's Association of 1864 and the Paris Commune. It lies between traditional, social anarchists, who believe that the only way to end capitalism is through organizing the working class, and individual anarchists, who instinctively oppose all forms of organization and authority. Anarcho-syndicalists believe the state to be profoundly anti-proletarian, and see the working class as a kind of "elementary school for Socialism," a necessary component in the

"To be governed is to be watched, inspected, spied upon, directed ... "

Pierre-Joseph Proudhon, politician and socialist

establishing of an anarchist society; in this aspect the movement is aligned politically with Karl Marx.

By the end of the nineteenth century, anarcho-syndicalist unions were established throughout Europe and in the United States and Argentina, and they continued to evolve. In France, adherents of what would become known as "revolutionary-syndicalism" wanted nothing less than the complete destruction of capitalism and all economic monopolies, although they were ambivalent about what political structures might come along to fill the void. In Spain, anarcho-syndicalists formed the National Confederation of Labor party in 1910, which aligned itself with the poor and the landless and by 1936 had in excess of a million members. Thus, anarcho-syndicalism found itself immersed in Spain's "legitimate" politics. **BS**

⬅ *Louis Pasteur's Portrait* (1885), by Finnish artist Albert Edelfeldt, depicts the microbiologist in his laboratory.

Survival of the Fittest
Herbert Spencer

Those who survive do so because they are adapted to their specific circumstances

In coining this memorable phrase, English philosopher and biologist Herbert Spencer (1820–1903) produced one of the most tenacious, and most misunderstood, buzzwords of the modern era. The word "fittest" is often popularly understood to mean "strongest" or "best" in an athletic sense, rather than following the fundamental observation of naturalist Charles Darwin (1809–82) that adaptation to changing circumstance is the key to evolution. Both Darwin and Spencer used the word to mean "best fitted" or "best equipped" to survive in local circumstances.

The idea of a struggle for existence was first mooted by British scholar Thomas Malthus (1776–1834) fifty years before Spencer and Darwin published

their work. Spencer's first essay, "The Development Thesis," published in 1852, seven years before Darwin's *On the Origin of Species* (1859), discusses the scientific principle that complex organisms are originally simple. In *Principles of Biology* (1864), having read Darwin's work, Spencer suggested the phrase "survival of the fittest" as an alternative to "natural selection"; Darwin introduced it into the fifth edition of *On the Origin of Species* in 1869. Spencer also compared biological evolution with what he saw as a similar evolutionary trajectory in society, an idea that came to be known as Social Darwinism.

The phrase "survival of the fittest" was widely accepted, but in addition to popularizing Darwin's evolutionary ideas, it fostered the philosophy that human weakness, both in individuals and societies, was a failing to be despised (although Spencer himself specifically recognized the importance of compassion in human relations). It also fed nineteenth-century racism by encouraging Europeans to see themselves as having evolved into a superior race. The phrase is still popularly used today to describe anything that can be related to Darwinian theories of natural selection. **JF**

The aye-aye (*Daubentonia madagascariensis*) is perfectly adapted for extricating food insects from wood. ⬆

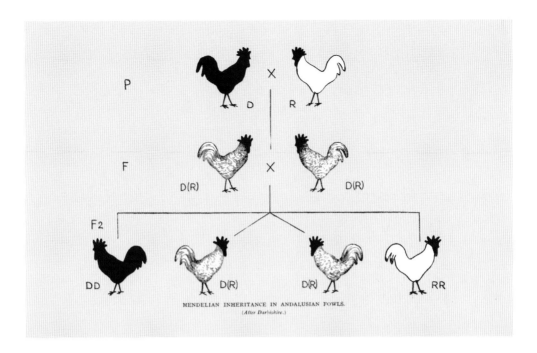

MENDELIAN INHERITANCE IN ANDALUSIAN FOWLS.
(After Darbishire.)

Mendelian Inheritance
Gregor Mendel

How hereditary characteristics are passed from parent organisms to their offspring

The Mendelian theory of inheritance describes the way in which a characteristic can be passed from a parent to his or her children by means of genes. Each parent has two genes (alleles) for inherited characteristics (such as blue eyes or small feet), only one of which carries that parent's own characteristics. When sexual reproduction occurs, one of these genes is passed to the offspring by each parent. Genes are said to be either "dominant" or "recessive." The dominant gene will generally reproduce its characteristic in the offspring. Dominant genes in a particular family may turn up in the offspring of almost every generation, while a recessive gene may be carried unused through many generations before it plays its role again, creating

a "throwback" to a remote ancestor. This pattern of gene utilization explains how recognizable likenesses occur between family members, and between successive generations in a single family.

In the mid-nineteenth century, scientists were still uncertain of the mechanism by which hereditary characteristics were passed from one generation to the other. In general, people believed that all parental characteristics were melded together, so that two individual characteristics would become mixed or diluted, as observed in the skin color of people of mixed race. Silesian scientist Gregor Mendel (1822–84) discovered that, instead, the alleles of specific characteristics sort themselves independently of each other to produce the gametes (germ cells) of offspring. His work, presented in two separate lectures in 1865 to the Natural Science Society in Brünn, Germany, was not, at first, recognized for the breakthrough it was. Instead, Mendel's discoveries had to be "rediscovered" in the early twentieth century. Scientists have since worked out numerous modifications to Mendel's theory of inheritance, but Mendel was the one who set the science of genetics in motion. **JF**

↑ A diagram demonstrating Mendelian inheritance of color in Analusian fowls.

Light
James Clerk Maxwell

The discovery that illumination is caused by electromagnetic radiation

Light is electromagnetic radiation; visible light is electromagnetic radiation that is visible to the human eye. As visual creatures, humans have always known light. Systematic investigation of light extends back to ancient Greece but accelerated with the emergence of modern science. In the 1860s, the Scottish physicist James Clerk Maxwell (1831–79) identified light with electromagnetic radiation. Maxwell's identification was based on his theory of electromagnetism (published in 1865), which united the forces of electricity and magnetism. On its basis, he predicted the existence of electromagnetic radiation and calculated that its speed ought to be about the same as the measured speed of light. He concluded, "Light consists in the tranverse undulations of the same medium [the ether] which

> ". . . the most fruitful [work] that physics has experienced since the time of Newton."
>
> **Albert Einstein on Maxwell's work (1931)**

is the cause of electric and magnetic phenomena." By the late 1870s, Maxwell's identification of light and electromagnetic radiation was widely accepted. The identification was important technologically, especially in enabling the use of nonvisible electromagnetic radiation, from radio waves, microwaves, and infrared light to ultraviolet light, x-rays, and gamma rays.

Later work extended Maxwell's theory, but the idea of the ether was dismissed by the Michelson–Morley experiment in 1905. The idea that light consisted of waves was complicated by the advent of quantum theory, which resolved the debate over whether light consisted of waves (as Maxwell thought) or of particles by showing that neither model alone was satisfactory. The result, emerging in the 1940s, was quantum electrodynamics, the current theory of light. **GB**

Radio Waves
James Clerk Maxwell

A prediction of the lowest frequencies on the electromagnetic spectrum

Radio waves have the lowest frequency and longest wavelength on the electromagnetic spectrum. In the natural world, radio waves are emitted by stars, but they can be created artificially using radio transmitters. Radio waves vary in length from 1 millimeter to 19 miles (30 km). They were first predicted mathematically by Scottish theoretical physicist James Clerk Maxwell (1831–79) as part of his electromagnetic theory in 1865, and were demonstrated in the laboratory twenty years later by German physicist Heinrich Hertz (1857–94), who gave his name to the unit of measurement (kilohertz, abbreviated as khz) of their frequencies. Radio waves fall between 10 and 300,000 khz in frequency.

There are four main types of radio wave: long wave, used for earth to space transmissions and cell

> "In the new era, thought itself will be transmitted by radio."
>
> **Guglielmo Marconi, *New York Times* (October 11, 1931)**

phones; medium wave, used for most ordinary radio broadcasts; VHF (very high frequency), used for FM radio, civilian aircraft, and taxi frequencies; and UHF (ultra high frequency), used for police and some military aircraft radios, and television transmissions. Microwave radiation may also be included in the list, coming above UHF in frequency/length.

Radio waves were and remain the foundation of broadcasting and other types of communication technology, including television, radar, and cell phone as well as radio itself. The higher frequencies can be used for re-transmission via satellite to users out of direct contact because of the Earth's curvature. In addition to being widely employed for communications, radio waves are used for medical procedures, such as noninvasive surgical treatments and MRI imaging. **JF**

Electromagnetic Theory
James Clerk Maxwell

A new understanding of electrical and magnetic fields as two aspects of a single continuum based on wavelength and frequency

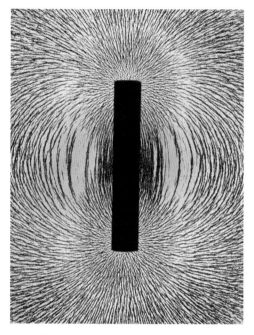

⬆ Metal filings form a magnetic field pattern around either pole of a magnet. Magnetic fields force moving electrically charged particles in a circular or helical path.

"The unification of electricity, magnetism, and light represented the crowning achievement of classical physics in the nineteenth century."

Mauro Dardo, *Nobel Laureates and Twentieth Century Physics* (2004)

Scottish theoretical physicist James Clerk Maxwell (1831–79) understood electromagnetism in terms of work produced earlier in the nineteenth century, by André-Marie Ampère (1775–1836) and Michael Faraday (1791–1867), on electric currents in relation to the magnetic field. In a key paper, "A Dynamical Theory of the Electromagnetic Field," published in 1865 in *Philosophical Transactions of the Royal Society*, Maxwell showed mathematically that electricity and magnetism are two aspects of the same phenomenon, before publishing a landmark work based on his own and others' discoveries, *A Treatise on Electricity and Magnetism*, in 1873. Here, he proposed that electromagnetism consisted of a spectrum, and predicted different frequencies of radiation, from high-frequency ultraviolet light down to long radio waves.

Experimental proof that Maxwell's theory was more than just a clever piece of mathematics was provided a few years after Maxwell's death by German physicist Heinrich Hertz (1857–94). However, Maxwell's idea that a substance known as ether was involved in electromagnetic processes later fell out of favor as a result of Albert Einstein's special theory of relativity, which ruled out ether as a necessary prerequisite for the behavior of electromagnetic radiation.

For the next fifty years, Maxwell's electromagnetic theory dominated theoretical physics, along with Isaac Newton's mechanics, and many practical applications were found for both electric currents and magnets. The theory was seminal to the work of Einstein, who recognized how it had changed scientific and popular perceptions of reality itself. He commented: "Before the electromagnetic theory was put forward, people conceived of physical reality as material points. After Maxwell, they conceived reality as represented by continuous fields, not mechanically explicable." **JF**

🏛

Speed Limit
Great Britain

A law limiting the maximum speed at which a vehicle can be driven

In 1865, the British government passed the Locomotive Act (also known as the Red Flag Act), which set a speed limit of 4 mph (6 km/h) for steam-powered vehicles in the countryside and 2 mph (3 km/h) in towns. One reason for its introduction was concern about damage that the large, heavy locomotives were causing to the roads; it was argued that by reducing their speed, their impact on the road would be lessened. The other main argument for a speed limit was public safety—hence why the Act also stipulated that all self-propelled vehicles must be preceded by a red flag held by a pedestrian, as a warning to horse-drawn vehicles and pedestrians. Unsurprisingly, the Act received a great deal of support from those with horse and railroad interests, and its implementation did much to hinder the early development of road transport in Great Britain.

The first comparable U.S. law was introduced in Connecticut in 1901, with a limit of 12 mph (19 km/h). With the arrival of the internal combustion engine, the red flag was dispensed with and speed limits were raised, first to 14 mph (23 km/h), then to 20 mph (32 km/h). In 1934, after a short unregulated period, a standard limit of 30 mph (48 km/h) was introduced into U.K. urban areas.

This urban limit is now the norm for most countries. In Europe the Italian *autostrada* has a maximum limit of 81 mph (130 km/h), the same as the advisory speed limit on the German *autobahn*. Limits in Japan are low in comparison, with the urban limit at 25 mph (40 m/h), rising to 50 mph (80 km/h) on expressways and 62 mph (100 km/h) on some highways. U.S. speed limits are set by state authorities and vary from one territory to another.

The introduction of speed limits proved to be the first step in a whole raft of legislation governing road safety. Acceptance of restrictions marked a new realization that consideration for other road users should be a matter of law, not just moral obligation. **JF**

Recapitulation Theory
Ernst Haeckel

A theory that embryos literally mimic evolutionary stages as they develop

The phrase "ontogeny recapitulates phylogeny," coined in 1866 by the German physician-turned-naturalist Ernst Haeckel (1834–1919), was popularized by biologists who believed that ontogeny, the development of a human being from embryo to adulthood, involved a recapitulation (run-through) of phylogeny, the entire history of humanity's evolutionary development. To paraphrase, ontogeny is the growth, development, and changing shape of the embryo, and phylogeny the evolutionary development of the embryo's species.

Haeckel believed that every organism's ontogeny was a reflection of its phylogeny: that a chick embryo, for example, when in its early stages of development, resembled that of a fish, complete with gills, fishlike tail, and all of a fish's associated characteristics. During

"In the case of the . . . libido, the phylogenetic origin is . . . obvious"
Sigmund Freud, psychoanalyst

further development it changed again, each time reflecting the evolutionary process that resulted in chicks: from a fish it altered to become a reptile, and eventually it became a chick. Humans, too, according to Haeckel, begin in the womb as fish before changing into a reptile, then in our specific case a mammal, before finally beginning to take on human form. Every stage in the development of an individual person resembles a fully-formed adult that appeared at some point in its own evolutionary history.

Studies in experimental morphology conclusively show that no such correspondence between species has ever existed. Haeckel's efforts to have his theories accepted were not helped when it was revealed that he had altered drawings to emphasize similarities in embryos that could not possibly have existed. **JMa**

Maxwell's Demon
James Clerk Maxwell

An experiment designed to contradict the second law of thermodynamics

In 1867, Scottish theoretical physicist James Clerk Maxwell (1831–79) created a thought experiment to show that it would be philosophically possible to contradict the second law of thermodynamics, which says that closed systems (those isolated from outside stimuli) always tend toward equilibrium (maximum entropy), so that when a hot liquid and a cold liquid are mixed, for example, the result will be a lukewarm liquid in which all molecules are at the same temperature.

Imagine a box, divided in two by a wall, that contains a mixture of "hot" (fast-moving) and "cold" (slow-moving) gas molecules. An imaginary creature (nicknamed Maxwell's demon) crouches by a door in the wall, opening and closing it to ensure that cold molecules end up on one side of the wall and hot

"The Second Law of Thermodynamics has only a statistical certainty."

Letter from Maxwell to Peter Guthrie Tait, physicist

molecules on the other. A heat engine could be run by allowing the hot molecules to run through into the cold side. Similarly, energy could be created by getting all the molecules into one side of the box, then operating a turbine in the doorway, over which the gas would flow from the "full" to the "empty" side of the box.

Recently, Maxwell's demon has acquired applications in information theory. In a Japanese experiment, a particle was moved to a higher energy state by observing the particle's path and encouraging it in that direction rather than back toward a low-energy state. The possibilities of this are exciting, even if we are still a long way from generating significant amounts of energy using this method. The experiment suggests that philosophical reflection can be as important as scientific empiricism. **JF**

Traffic Light
J. P. Knight

A road signal for directing vehicular traffic by means of colored lights

The first use of lights to control traffic occurred in 1868 in a London street, where a revolving gas lamp with red and green glass was set up to help police constables direct horse-drawn traffic on a busy junction. The lamp, the concept of railroad engineer John Peake Knight (1828–86), exploded in January 1869, injuring its attendant constable, and the idea came to nothing.

In Detroit in 1920, early in the age of the automobile, William L. Potts (1883–1947), a police officer, invented a system of lights much closer to the traffic lights we know today. His idea was to adapt the red, green, and amber lights used on railroads to control traffic on the highway, particularly at urban intersections. Within a year, the Detroit authorities had installed fifteen. Around the same time, the Ohio inventor Garrett A.

"[Early traffic signals] were commonly assisted by gongs, whistles, and bells."

M. G. Lay, *Ways of the World* (1992)

Morgan (1877–1963) came up with a semaphore-type traffic signal in Cleveland. His patent for the device was bought by General Electric Corporation and used as the basis for their traffic light monopoly.

Today most traffic lights use the code of red for "stop," green for "go," and amber for "proceed with caution." In many countries, "running the red" is a criminal offense, but in others traffic lights are not seen as legally binding and are widely ignored. Urban myths regarding traffic lights include the untrue idea that in China red means "go," as it would be politically incorrect for it to mean "stop." The traffic light concept has even found applications outside of its original road safety purpose: the European Union has introduced a code system for food nutritional values based on the traffic light colors. **JF**

Traffic lights being manufactured in Shreveport, Louisiana, 1947.

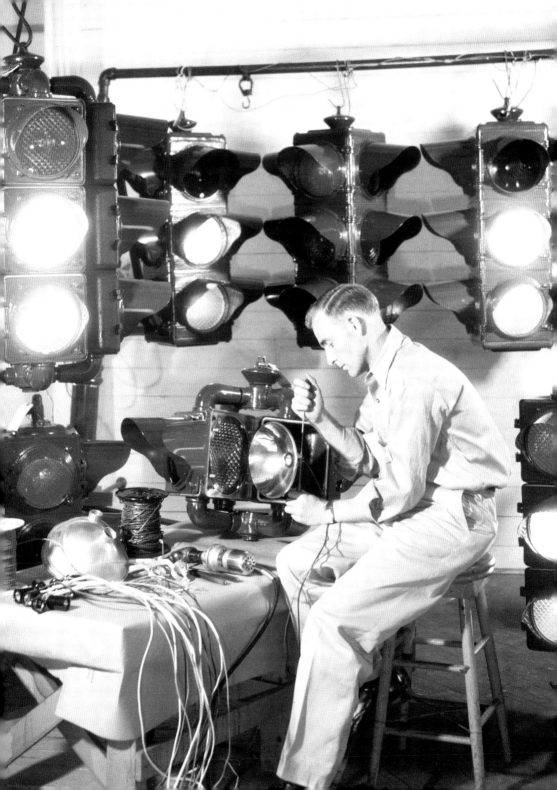

1869

Nature Versus Nurture
Francis Galton

The question of whether characteristics are inherited (nature) or fostered (nurture)

English polymath Francis Galton (1822–1911) was born into a rich and influential family that included naturalist Charles Darwin (1809–82), his cousin. He initially studied mathematics at Cambridge University but became interested in psychology, along with anthropology, geography, statistics, and many other subjects.

In one study, *Hereditary Genius* (1869), he considered the implications of his cousin's theories on sociology and psychology. He favored the position that all characteristics, including intelligence, are inherited through natural selection, though he later came to believe that the nurturing environment had an important influence. His work also led him to develop the pseudo-science of eugenics.

Much of the important evidence in the nature versus nurture debate has come from the study of twins, including both nonidentical (fraternal or dizygotic) twins (who, when raised together, possess different natures but share the same nurture), and identical or monzygotic twins (who, when separated at birth or very soon after, experience different nurture but possess the same initial natural inheritance). The results of such studies have highlighted some remarkable instances of natural inheritance, such as the development of Type 2 diabetes in separated identical twins at almost the same time in their mid-life, and have also cataloged the psychological effects of a variety of environmental factors.

Today, the debate initiated by Galton is still very much alive. At one extreme, Nativists such as John Bowlby and Noam Chomsky believe that most or even all psychological characteristics, including those that develop later in life, are governed by the body's genetic code. On the Empiricist side of the argument, theorists such as Albert Bandura and B. F. Skinner see the human mind at birth as resembling a blank slate, onto which character is engraved by later experiences. **JF**

An illustration depicting some of the factors at play in the nature versus nurture debate.

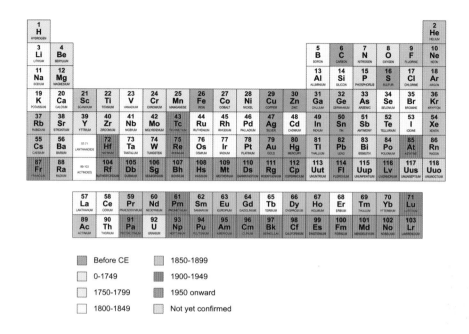

Before CE		1850-1899
0-1749		1900-1949
1750-1799		1950 onward
1800-1849		Not yet confirmed

1869

Periodic Table of the Elements
Dmitri Mendeleev

A chart of the relationship between the elements and their atomic numbers

During the nineteenth century, scientists worked out, by observing the properties of elements, that elements were related in some way. Dmitri Mendeleev (1834–1907), professor of general chemistry at the University of St. Petersburg, was the first to propose relationships between elements based on their atomic structure. In the course of writing *The Principles of Chemistry* (1869), he kept record cards showing each known element's atomic weight and properties. As he explained later, "This soon convinced me that the properties of elements are in periodic dependence upon their atomic weights." Mendeleev illustrated his insights with a table in which he boldly left gaps for elements that he believed existed but had not yet been discovered.

Mendeleev's periodic table was initially met with a degree of skepticism, but in due course scientists filled in the gaps he had left with newly discovered elements whose properties he had predicted from comparison swith those already known.

Early in the twentieth century, chemists also recognized that an element's atomic number—the number of protons (and therefore electrons) in its nucleus—is more significant than its atomic weight (which includes both protons and neutrons) when it comes to deducing an element's properties. Modern versions of the periodic table therefore list similar elements vertically, transposing the rows and columns of Mendeleev's original chart.

The periodic table revolutionized how chemists thought about the relationships between elements. It convinced scientists that the way elements behaved was not simply random, and encouraged them to seek out new elements to fill the identified gaps. The table also highlighted the importance of the size of an atom's nucleus, at a time when the internal structure of the atom, thought to be the smallest particle of matter, was only just beginning to be studied. **JF**

Propaganda by Deed
Mikhail Bakunin

The promotion of a political agenda by using physical violence against enemies

↑ A portrait of Russian revolutionary and anarchist Mikhail Bakunin, taken in c. 1865 by French photographer Nadar (Gaspard Felix Tournachon).

"We must spread our principles, not with words but with deeds, . . . the most popular, the most potent, . . . the most irresistible form of propaganda."

Mikhail Bakunin, *Letters to a Frenchman on the Present Crisis* (1870)

Propaganda by deed (sometimes translated from French as "Propaganda of the deed") may mean an action involving terrorism as a means of self-expression, or the use of extremist terror as a tactic for mobilizing political support. The phrase was invented by the French Marxist Paul Brousse (1844–1912), in the article "Propagande par le fait" (Propaganda by Deed), published in the August 1877 issue of *Bulletin de la Fédération Jurassienne* (Bulletin of the Jura Federation), which Brousse himself edited.

However, the idea encapsulated by the phrase was not new. Mikhail Bakunin (1814–76), a much-traveled Russian anarchist and revolutionary, who was based in Switzerland at the same time as Brousse, had advocated such an approach in his own writings during the Paris Commune seven years earlier. (It could even be said that Maximilien de Robespierre and the Directory used the massacre of the French aristocracy under the guillotine as a kind of action propaganda.)

The highly influential notion of propaganda by deed has driven terrorist acts of all kinds and for all sorts of causes, including political assassinations in Europe between 1880 and 1914, guerrilla warfare in Ireland during the Easter Rising of 1916, Chinese communism under Mao Zedung in the 1940s, black and liberal South African resistance to apartheid in the 1950s and 1960s, IRA bombings in Ulster during the Troubles, and, more recently, the twenty-first-century atrocities perpetrated by al-Qaeda. The essential qualification for such action propaganda is that the terrorist act is carried out publicly, advertising and glorifying its authors, rather than in secret, with the perpetrators hiding their involvement and hoping to escape detection, as would be expected of other criminal behavior. What is terrifying—or, to its perpetrators, attractive—about such propaganda is precisely its originality: the unexpectedness of its pride in organized violence. **JF**

Aryanism
George William Cox

The notion of a blue-eyed, blond-haired super-race destined to unite and rule the world

The concept of Aryanism—not to be confused with Arianism, the early Christian heresy—was first developed by British historian George William Cox (1827–1902) in his book, *The Mythology of the Aryan Nations*, published in London in 1870. The term "Aryan" was derived from an Indo-European root word meaning "noble." Aryans were thought to be the descendants of a noble super-race of pure racial origin from an imagined rural golden age. Its destiny was to unite and rule the world. The Aryanist movement still exists on the political right wing today.

Aryanism underwent further development in Nazi Germany in the 1930s, when it was used to justify the regime's oppression of Jews and East Europeans. According to Hitler, Aryans were to be identified with the blue-eyed and blond-haired people typically found in northern Europe, including Germany. Their destiny was to gain hegemony over non-Aryans, who would be treated as subject peoples. Ironically, this notion actually hindered Hitler's initial war strategy in 1939 and 1940, when he made a number of peace overtures to the British, whom he treated as fellow Aryans. Only after these were firmly rejected by Winston Churchill in 1940 did Hitler concentrate on Aryanism within the Greater Germany of the Third Reich.

The concept of a super-race influenced European thinking for much of the later nineteenth and early twentieth centuries and spawned a number of more or less horrific social and political experiments. These included Nazi efforts to "improve" European genetic inheritance by both fostering "Aryan" elements through the *Lebensborn* program of selective parental assistance and rooting out perceived racial and mental defects via the pseudo-science of eugenics. The logical conclusion of Aryanism was the Holocaust, which demonstrated to members of every race both the dangers and the moral turpitude of the concept. **JF**

↑ Images like this one of a mother and her baby in the German countryside were used by the Nazis during the Third Reich as examples of the perfect Aryan family.

"Aryanism . . . [was] oriented toward a lost perfection and implied an ill-defined hope of the restoration of that unity within modernity."

Christopher M. Hutton, *Race and the Third Reich* (2005)

Papal Infallibility
First Vatican Council

A Roman Catholic doctrine that God protects the pope from error whenever, in the role of mouthpiece of the Church, he speaks about faith or morality

⬆ An oil painting of Pope Pius VII giving an audience in the Vatican's Sistine Chapel (1814), by Jean-Auguste-Dominique Ingres; the pope was, in fact, being held prisoner by Napoleon.

"Should anyone ... reject this definition [of papal infallibility]: let him be anathema."

First Vatican Council (1870)

The question of papal infallibility has caused much debate among both Roman Catholic and non-Catholic Christians since the First Vatican Council voted for the measure by a vast majority (433 to two) in 1870. The declaration was probably occasioned by the Church's need to combat liberal, secular movements that were sweeping Europe at that time.

Papal infallibility combines acceptance of the authority of Christ over faith and moral practice with the belief that Christ's authority was given to St. Peter, as leader of the Church, and subsequently handed on to his successors in the papacy via a process known as apostolic succession. A further logical element is that it is seen as necessary for the pope to be infallible, since he might otherwise lead the Church into error, with catastrophic consequences. The Vatican Council did not expect popes to use the provision to promulgate new doctrines, only to confirm those that were part and parcel of the faith. It viewed papal infallibility as having been part of the fabric of Roman Christianity since 519 when the bishop of Rome was first accepted as guardian of apostolic truth.

Contrary to popular myth, papal infallibility has not, in fact, been used very often. In only two instances—the doctrine of the immaculate conception of Mary (1854) and the doctrine of the corporeal assumption of Mary (1950)—has it been formally invoked by the pope speaking *ex cathedra*, that is, when acting as pastor and teacher to all Christians. However, the notion created a deep and enduring divide between Roman Catholics and all other Christians. For example, conservative Protestants believe that only the Bible is free of error, while human interpretations of the Bible are not. Accordingly, they cannot accept that the pope could ever be infallible. The issue has hindered efforts to bring about Christian unity. **JF**

Antidisestablishmentarianism
Great Britain

Opposition to the removal of state support and status from the Anglican church

In England in the sixteenth century, as part of Henry VIII's Reformation, the Anglican Church became an established church with the monarch at its head. For centuries after that, a succession of reformers questioned establishmentarianism, the recognition of the Anglican Church as a national institution.

However, in the nineteenth century, the British government proposed to disestablish the church, giving it the kind of independent status enjoyed by churches in other European countries and in the United States. Disestablishment of the (Anglican) Church of Ireland took place in 1871, but popular (antidisestablishmentarianist) opposition to identical proposals in England and Wales ensured that in those countries it continued to be an established church, as it is today. Although the principle of a secular state, in which religion and government are clearly separated, has become the norm in most non-Islamic countries, the debate about whether or not the Anglican Church should be disestablished is still very much alive. Many agnostics, atheists, and Anglicans support disestablishment, but others cling instinctively to the traditional link between the church and state.

The word itself is somewhat quaint and is now used mainly as a joke. Its semantic creation is unusual: antidisestablishmentarianism is formed by the linking of three sections to form one word, which is much more common in German than English. It is also one of the longest words in the English language, if not *the* longest, recognized as such in 1923. The opposition movement described thus is obviously a very contrary sort of body, existing in opposition to something that is in opposition to something else. The word is often used for any body of opinion that seems to resist new ideas for the sake of it, in the spirit of the original natural conservatism that spawned it. **JF**

The Birth of Tragedy
Friedrich Nietzsche

A theory of drama that the tragedy of ancient Greece was the highest form of art

German philosopher Friedrich Nietzsche (1844–1900) published his theory of drama, *The Birth of Tragedy from the Spirit of Music*, in 1872, when he was professor of classical philology at Basel in Switzerland. Nietzsche was impressed by the ancient Greeks' ability to transcend pessimism and derive pleasure and meaning through their own performances of tragedy. The Greeks believed that drama provoked enjoyment and an uplifted spirit on the part of the viewer when watching human angst and suffering on stage. Tragedy emerged in Athens in the sixth century BCE and was enacted in open-air theaters during the better part of a day.

In Greek mythology, Apollo and Dionysus are both sons of Zeus. In *The Birth of Tragedy*, Nietzsche discusses how tragedy was born from a fusion of views of life,

"The satyr chorus of the dithyramb is the saving deed of Greek art …"
Friedrich Nietzsche, *The Birth of Tragedy* (1872)

both Apollonian (culture and reason) and Dionysian (wine, ecstasy, and intoxication). In the contemporary world this has become a struggle between civilized and primitive man, between collectivism and individualism. Nietzsche is clearly on the side of the primitive, of the individual, and he dismissively describes Greek art in pre-Dionysus times as naive. The Greeks themselves never considered Apollo and Dionysus to be rivals.

In Nietzsche's account, the protagonist of tragedy tries to make sense of his reasoned, Apollonian lifestyle in the face of a chorus of Dionysus-led exhortations. For Nietzsche, Dionysian man magnifies man; he is the precursor of the "Superman," an ideal, fully-realized human. Nietzsche hoped that his book would make the viewer of tragedy want to revive his Dionysian nature, and reconnect with his "Primordial Unity." **BS**

Φ

Pragmatism
Charles Sanders Peirce

An idea or proposition is likely to be true if it conveys practical benefit

Today, philosophy and empirical science can be seen as two distinct worlds: those of theory and practice. In the late nineteenth century, a group of U.S. thinkers sought to merge these worlds by developing the school of pragmatism. The thinkers regarded an idea as worthwhile if people gained some practical benefits from it. Thus, the actual meaning of any idea rests upon those practical benefits, and any idea that fails to produce such effects deserves to be discarded.

In 1872, a group of Harvard graduates decided to form the Metaphysical Club, an informal philosophical discussion group of about a dozen members. The group lasted less than a year but is widely credited with originating the pragmatic school of philosophy. William James (1842–1910), one of the members, is thought to

"The pragmatist clings to facts and concreteness, observes truth at its work . . ."

William James, *Pragmatism* (1907)

have introduced the idea to the world in a lecture of 1898. However, James insisted the term originated with Charles Sanders Peirce (1839–1914), another member of the group, who coined it in the early 1870s.

The unofficial motto of the state of Missouri is "Show me," a phrase that is quite suited to the sensibility of the pragmatists. To the pragmatist, the worth of an idea, and even its claim to truth, comes from empirical progress, from deriving a concrete use. This attitude initially met with a high level of interest, resulting in pragmatist movements in social science, applied public administration, and even urban development. However, after the early adopters and proponents eventually died, the idea fell out of favor with many academics, although it did gain some renewed interest in the later part of the twentieth century. **MT**

Comparative Psychology
Douglas Spalding

Studying animal behavior can illuminate human psychological processes also

The first person to carry out empirical research on animal intelligence was English biologist Douglas Spalding (1841–77), who experimented with chicks to find out which behavioral traits were innate and which learned. He published his early work in an article for *Macmillan's Magazine* in 1873. Meanwhile, naturalist Charles Darwin (1809–82) and his friend George Romanes (1848–94) were writing on the evolutionary relationship between animals and humans.

Most comparative psychology studies since then have focused on learning, including conditioning and association. One approach has been concerned with traits that many species, including humans, have in common, mainly focusing on shared instinctual processes and the way in which these influence

"We see that living beings need many things in conjunction . . ."

Lucretius, *On the Nature of the Universe* (first century BCE)

learning. This line of study can be undertaken under artificial conditions in the laboratory. Another approach, looking at the way in which evolutionary processes select for particular behavior adaptations, is more suited to field studies in the natural habitat. Scientists have also compared the behavior of modern animals with that of their ancient ancestors, or related species that have become extinct.

Comparative psychology gave rise to a shift in the way that we perceive both animal intelligence and the mental processes that cause animal behavior. Rather than assuming an innate superiority in human mental processes, scientists now study the similarities and differences in how humans and animals learn, and in the behaviors associated with their mental abilities, in order to better understand human psychology. **JF**

1873

Product Placement
Jules Verne

The surreptitious advertising of brands in a normally advertisement-free context

Perhaps surprisingly, given its prevalence in modern entertainment, product placement is anything but a late twentieth-century phenomenon. Instead, the practice originated in the late nineteenth century, when shipping magnates beat a path to the door of world-renowned French author Jules Verne (1828–1905), begging him to mention their companies in his new novel, *Around the World in Eighty Days*, published in 1873; he was happy to do so—for a price.

Subsequent product placement has been associated more with movies and television than with literature. In 1896, French movie makers the Lumière brothers and Swiss businessman François-Henri Lavanchy-Clarke entered into an arrangement to promote a product, Sunlight Soap, in the Lumière's new short film, *Parade of the Eighth Battalion*; in the movie, the logo of the product is seen briefly on a wheelbarrow. Hershey's chocolate bars are mentioned in William A. Wellman's *Wings* (1927), and a young boy desperate to become an explorer is seen reading a copy of *National Geographic* in Frank Capra's *It's a Wonderful Life* (1946). Product placements will always be with us, whether it be subtle—Steve McQueen pursuing bad buys through San Francisco in his Ford Mustang GT in *Bullitt* (1968)—or shamelessly garish—the Compaq computers used in *Alien vs. Predator* (2004).

Some products need only be hinted at to affect sales. In *The Italian Job* (2003), a bottle of champagne was passed around a group of thieves celebrating a recent heist. No brand was mentioned nor label seen, but the bottle's shape was so distinctive that the target audience immediately recognized it. Product placement has been criticized for blurring the distinction between art and advertising, but its existence should not surprise us. After all, television was never only about entertainment—its purpose has always been to sell stuff. **JMa**

1874

Impressionism in Art
France

Art designed to give an impression of its subject, not a realistic representation

The artistic movement dubbed "Impressionism" was formally launched in 1874 by a group of thirty Parisian artists led by Claude Monet (1840–1926), Edgar Degas (1834–1917), and Camille Pissarro (1830–1903), at a private exhibition mounted by the Cooperative and Anonymous Society of Painters, Sculptors, and Engravers. Other prominent artists, such as Paul Cézanne, Pierre-Auguste Renoir, and Berthe Morisot, joined the group later. The movement represented a reaction against the realist style of painting that characterized French painting and sculpture at the time. It was also a deliberate challenge to the Académie des Beaux-Arts, which dictated the artistic standards acceptable in France, including the subjects that artists should paint. The Academie refused to exhibit the work of artists who did not conform to its strictures.

The term "impressionism" was coined by the journalist Louis Leroy, writing in the satirical magazine *Le Charivari*, after seeing Monet's painting *Impression, Soleil Levant* (Impression: Sunrise) at the exhibition in 1874. Initially the word was used by critics to describe the movement derogatively, but the name was accepted by both proponents and denigrators of the style. Actually, Impressionism covers a wide range of styles, some of them more representative than others.

The Impressionists held seven more shows, the last of which was in 1886. By that time the group had begun to dissolve, as each painter focused on his own work. But despite the fleeting nature of the movement's existence, its impact would be long-lived. Before the Impressionist revolution, the visual arts were in a straitjacket of technique and subject matter. Impressionism relied on direct impressions on the senses, without the distraction of faithful representation, for its impact upon those who viewed it. It encouraged artists to extend the range of acceptable subjects, and changed the way that people thought about art. **JF**

↑ Claude Monet's *Impression: Sunrise* (1872), the painting that named a movement across the arts.

Set Theory
Georg Cantor

A theory that mathematical numbers or functions may be arranged into sets without considering their individual properties

⬆ Georg Cantor, photographed in c. 1910; wrongheaded criticism of his work caused him much depression in later life, but his set theory was to originate a new branch of mathematics.

German mathematician Georg Cantor (1845–1918) is credited with the invention of set theory in his paper "On a Characteristic Property of All Real Algebraic Numbers" (1874). In the following years he carried out further work on the theory and its application to other aspects of mathematics, such as infinity and the correspondence between groups of numbers, or equivalence.

Set theory is the study of sets, and of the relation that connects the elements of a set to the set itself. The most revolutionary aspect of Cantor's theory was that it considered orders of different infinities, and particularly those that he termed "transfinities"; at the time, all infinities were seen as the same size. Cantor also included both real and irrational numbers in the sets that he proposed, although influential mathematicians, such as Leopold Kronecker (1823–91), did not believe in the existence of irrational numbers. Set theory became the subject of immediate and long-lasting controversy, which hampered Cantor's career and put a strain on his mental health. A number of paradoxes that appeared to undermine the theory also caused many to doubt the validity of his ideas. Cantor suffered a breakdown in 1884 when his appointment to the University of Berlin was opposed, but by 1885 he had recovered and he continued to publish on set theory, overseeing its gradual acceptance into mainstream mathematics by the beginning of the twentieth century.

Set theory completely revolutionized the way that mathematicians think about numbers and functions and their relationships, and underpins much of modern mathematics. It also has some useful applications in real life, such as the simple Venn diagram and the way in which we categorize disparate human beings according to the properties that define them as part of the group—for example, New York Giants supporters or members of the Royal Society. **JF**

"A set is a many that allows itself to be thought of as one."

Georg Cantor, quoted in *Infinity and the Mind* by Rudy Rucker (1983)

Property Dualism
Thomas Huxley

The theory that substances can have two kinds of property: physical and mental

Property dualism is a philosophical compromise between substance dualism and materialism, combining the more plausible aspects of both while avoiding their main problems. Property dualists agree with materialists that all substances are physical, but they hold that physical substances can have both physical and mental states. An example of a physical state is being 6 feet (1.8 m) tall; an example of a mental state is being in pain, or in love. While pain may be caused by the firing of neurons in the brain, and the sensation of being in love by hormones released into the blood, philosophically these mental states do not consist only of the physical events.

French mathematician and philosopher René Descartes (1596–1650) noted that mental and material states co-exist in human beings, and proposed that the mind and brain exist separately, each in its own right (a theory known as substance dualism). But Thomas Huxley (1825–95) proposed that the conscious mind is an epiphenomenon (a secondary phenomenon), an aspect of what he called automatism. In an article titled "On the Hypothesis that Animals are Automata, and its History" (1874), he likened it to the whistle on a steam locomotive: the action of the engine is absolutely necessary for the whistle to exist, but the whistle itself contributes nothing to the work of the engine, emerging from it as a discrete phenomenon.

Nineteenth-century epiphenomenology had great influence on behaviorists, but eventually went out of fashion in the mid-twentieth century. However, more recently property dualism has enjoyed new popularity with those who favor a materialist view of the human brain and consciousness but reject reductive physicalism. It also has important links with the experimental study of the psychology of higher mental processes. **JF**

The Hedonistic Paradox
Henry Sidgwick

The philosophy that happiness cannot be attained by actively pursuing it

The Hedonistic Paradox is a sobering principle that asserts that anyone who seeks happiness for their own sake will always be denied it; that the way to happiness is not to be found in the selfish pursuit of gratifying the self, but only truly comes as a by-product of helping others. This "paradox of happiness" was first noted by the English philosopher Henry Sidgwick (1838–1900) in his book *The Methods of Ethics*, published in 1874. Sidgwick understood, as did the Epicurean Greeks of the third century BCE, that the pursuit of happiness had within it some inherent problems: that "if you don't achieve what is sought, then you lose by frustration; if you do achieve what is sought, you lose by boredom." Whichever way you go, happiness appears an elusive thing. The Epicureans always sought the optimum,

> "The principle of Egoistic Hedonism … is practically self-limiting."
>
> Henry Sidgwick

rather than the maximum, degree of pleasure, a state they called *ataraxia*—peace of mind. Drink too much wine, and all one is left with is a hangover.

The failure to obtain pleasure by seeking it is well documented in literature. Aristotle asked, "How then is it that no one is continuously pleased? Is it that we grow weary?" The utilitarian philosopher John Stuart Mill said, "Ask yourself whether you are happy, and you cease to be so." The Austrian psychiatrist Viktor Frankl claimed happiness to be ephemeral and elusive, and even when captured was an "unintended side effect of one's personal dedication to a greater cause." Søren Kierkegaard warned that we always run right past it, such is the rate of our furious pursuit, while the great Brazilian novelist Joao Guimaraes Rosa said happiness could only be found "in little moments of inattention." **BS**

Subatomic Particles

George Stoney

The postulation of the existence of unseen particles that are smaller than atoms

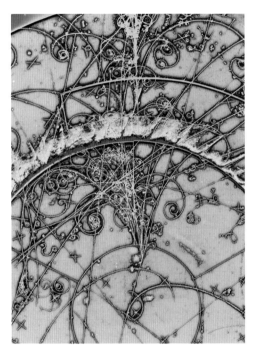

⬆ A colored bubble chamber photograph showing tracks left by subatomic particles from a particle accelerator at CERN, the European particle physics laboratory at Geneva, Switzerland.

"Could anything at first sight seem more impractical than a body which is so small that its mass is an insignificant fraction of the mass of an atom of hydrogen?"

J. J. Thomson, physicist

The discovery in the nineteenth century that the mass of the universe consists wholly of unseen, subatomic particles (particles smaller than atoms) was to occur in an incremental rather than instantaneous way. The discovery process actually took more than a hundred years and was dependent upon the invention of tools that would enable subatomic particles to be found.

In 1800 came the discovery of infrared radiation by the German-born British astronomer William Herschel (1738–1822), and in the following year the German chemist Johann Ritter (1776–1810) observed that silver chloride went from white to black when placed at the dark end of the sun's spectrum, thus proving the existence of ultraviolet radiation. The veil drawn over the world of subatomic particles was thus lifted a little, but it was not until the end of the century that humankind learned more. The electron was detected in 1897, the alpha particle in 1899, and the gamma ray (high-energy photon) in 1900. Some subatomic particles would hold out longer still. The proton avoided detection until 1919, and the neutron was only discovered in 1932.

Although it was British physicist J. J. (Joseph John) Thomson (1856–1940) who first detected the electron in 1897, its existence had already been postulated in 1874 by Irish physicist George Stoney (1826–1911). Stoney calculated the magnitude of electrons in the course of his research on the electrolysis of water and the kinetic theory of gases. He would actually coin the term "electron" in 1891. It was Stoney who took the first speculative leap forward in the recognition of this entirely unseen world when he proclaimed the electron as being the "fundamental unit quantity of electricity." He was certain that electricity must be comprised of indivisible particles of atoms of equal size, and he went on to provide the first ever estimates of their electrical composition. **JMa**

Dictatorship of the Proletariat
Karl Marx

A political state in which the working class has control of political power

Prussian-German philosopher, historian, and revolutionary socialist Karl Marx (1818–83) first coined the phrase "dictatorship of the proletariat" in a series of articles published in London in 1850. His main development of the idea was couched in an attack, published in 1875 and titled "Critique of the Gotha Program," on the principles of the German Workers Party. In the document Marx actually refers to the "revolutionary dictatorship of the proletariat." The Critique was clearly written in acknowledgment of the rise of the proletarian Paris Commune, which had ruled that city for a brief time in 1871.

Although Marx used the word "dictatorship," it is unclear whether he meant the word in the sense of a group holding absolute power, or merely in the older sense of *dictatura*, a term used in the ancient Roman republic to mean possession of political power, or simply "rule." The distinction made between a dictatorship and a democratically elected representative government is a modern development.

In classical Marxist theory, the dictatorship of the proletariat is seen as a necessary phase of transition after a socialist revolution, bridging the gap between class rule by the capitalist bourgeoisie and the abolition of all class distinctions that Marx believed would naturally occur in a socialist (or communist) society. But when Russian Marxist-Leninists came to plan their revolution in the 1890s, the idea of dictatorship of the proletariat gave way to a belief that the proletariat should be led by those who could correctly interpret communist ideas; opponents of communism would have no say in government. Thus, Russian communist rule turned out to be the dictatorship of a political party, rather than of a class as Marx had envisaged. Perceptions of Marxism are heavily colored by the version adopted by the Soviet Union, so it is the Soviet version of the concept that most people remember. **JF**

↑ Karl Marx wrote his "Critique of the Gotha Program" in the later years of his life, during which he was beset by what he called "chronic mental depression."

"Capital is an historical necessity, but, so too, its grave digger, the socialist proletariat."

Rosa Luxemburg, "The Junius Pamphlet" (1916)

1876

Telephone

Alexander Graham Bell

A machine enabling people to talk directly to each other over long distances

Humans are social animals, but the natural desire to be able to speak to individuals who are geographically distant was frustrated until 1876, when what seemed an impossible dream became a reality. Yet the birth of what was understood as the "speaking telegraph" was by no means without controversy because many individuals claimed a role in its invention.

The telephone (the name is derived from the Greek for "distant voice") developed from the electrical telegraph, an early nineteenth-century invention by Samuel Morse (1791–1872) and others. This device used electrical signals conveyed along wires to transmit individual letters that together formed a message. Useful though it was, the telegraph lacked the immediacy and depth of nuance of human speech, but in the second half of the century inventors developed acoustic telegraphy, capable of transmitting multiple messages along a single wire at the same time by using different channels or audio frequencies. From this development it was but a simple step to create a working telephone with a mouthpiece that converted the sound of the human voice into electrical signals, and a receiver that converted the signals back into sound. For the first time, people could offer information, or friendship, to others no matter how distant they were.

Who invented the telephone is still debated, as many different people were working in competition with each other at the time. The man who is usually credited is Scottish-born inventor Alexander Graham Bell (1847–1922), whose Patent 174,465 was the first to be issued by the U.S. Patent Office in Washington, D.C., on March 7, 1876. Returning to his laboratory in Boston, Bell finally managed to get his telephone to work three days later, on March 10. He uttered the immortal words, "Mr. Watson, come here. I want to see you," into the transmitter, and his assistant, listening to the receiver in an adjoining room, heard the words clearly. **SA**

On March 11, 1876, Alexander Graham Bell publicly demonstrated his remarkable invention.

Phonograph
Thomas Edison

A means of reproducing recorded sound, otherwise known as the gramophone

Since the beginning of the universe, it had been true that every sound, once it had faded, was gone forever. Musical performances, however magnificent, were lost, and no one could keep a record of a loved one's voice; only listeners' memories kept sounds from oblivion.

In 1877, U.S. inventor and businessman Thomas Edison (1847–1931) helped to bring that situation to an end by inventing a machine to transcribe messages for use in telegraphy. His mechanic, John Kruesi (1843–99), built a working model for him during the late summer or autumn of that year, and in December he showed the machine to staff of *Scientific American*, which published an article on it. Edison filed for a patent in the same month, which was granted in February 1878.

Further development of the gramophone was left to others, including Scottish-born inventor Alexander Graham Bell (1847–1922) who, with Charles Tainter (1854–1940), designed a prototype using a wax cylinder incised by a floating stylus. Bell and Tainter suggested a joint development of the idea with Edison, but the latter refused, preferring to market his own version of the phonograph, via a new company founded in 1887.

The phonograph was used for speech recordings and as a dictaphone. By the early part of the twentieth century, however, the rotating cylinder had given way to the disk, or record, which produced better quality recordings of music. The rest of the century saw new versions of the gramophone, with 78 rpm (revolutions per minute), 45 rpm, and 33⅓ rpm models, culminating in the digital technology of the compact disk player.

Edison's invention represented the first method of recording sound for playing back at a later time, a truly revolutionary device, and one that changed both the experience of sound, particularly musical sound, and the expectation of its hearers. The phonograph could restore to life, as U.S. journalist Ambrose Bierce put it, "dead noises." **JF**

↑ Thomas Edison, photographed with a commercial descendant of his 1877 cylinder phonograph.

Animation
Charles-Émile Reynaud

Images are made to seem to move when viewed using a remarkable machine

The invention of photography in 1822, and that of the phonograph in 1877, revealed for the first time that sights and sounds could be captured exactly for later enjoyment. Humanity was becoming aware that, with ingenuity, no aspect of the physical world need be lost. With hindsight, it was only a matter of time before the movement of objects in space would be captured, too.

The animation of images had some early precursors, such as the magic lantern, in which a light shone through a translucent oil painting was projected onto a wall. However, projected animation was introduced by French science teacher Charles-Émile Reynaud (1844–1918) with his invention in 1877 of the praxinoscope, in which a strip of pictures was placed around the inner surface of a spinning cylinder. The praxinoscope was

"Animation can explain whatever the mind of man can conceive."
Walt Disney, animator and movie producer

more functional than its technological predecessor, the zoetrope. Rather than watching the images through the zoetrope's narrow viewing slits, the user watched an inner circle of mirrors as they reflected the inner surface of the spinning cylinder. The rapid succession of images would appear to be moving, in a way that was clearer than the zoetrope had accomplished.

In 1888, Reynaud created a large-scale system based on the praxinoscope, called the Théâtre Optique. This was able to project the moving images of the praxinoscope onto a screen. The inventor first demonstrated his system in 1892, for the Musée Grévin in Paris. Reynaud had produced three short movies, and the triple-bill showing, which he called the *Pantomimes Lumineuses*, was the world's first instance of projected animated cartoon movies. **JE**

Social Darwinism
Joseph Fisher

An extension of Darwin's theory of evolution to social and economic relations

The term "social Darwinism" was first used by a Joseph Fisher in an article, "A History of Landholding in Ireland," published in 1877, and was popularized by the historian Richard Hofstadter (1916–70) in his book *Social Darwinism in American Thought* (1944). Always a term of disapprobation, it has over the years been linked, generally scornfully, with economic free marketeering, Mormon social philosophy, and Malthusian socioeconomic theory, among other ideas. In the nineteenth century, it was appropriated by Europeans wanting to use Darwin's theories of evolutionary struggle to explain the rise to prominence of the white or Caucasian race over African and Asian races.

In the late nineteenth century, this pseudo-science gained credence across much of the Western world. It

"There is hardly a good thing in [the world] that is not the result of successful strife."
Edwin Lawrence Godkin, *The Nation* magazine (1877)

drove the "civilizing" mission of European imperialists as they invaded "backward" areas of the world, appropriated native people's land and possessions, and imposed colonial rule. Along with the idea of eugenics invented by Francis Galton in 1883, itself an offshoot of social Darwinism, it informed German policies in South-West Africa in the early years of the twentieth century, and ultimately fed directly into Nazi Aryanism.

In its day, social Darwinism commanded almost universal acceptance and enthusiasm, although the Catholic Church decried its espousal of inequality and lack of compassion. Even after scientists were able to show that the genetic differences between racial groupings are no greater than those between different individuals who belong to the same race, the prejudices it had engendered remained. **JF**

⬅ A poster advertises Charles-Émile Reynaud's *Pantomimes Lumineuses* at the Musée Grévin, Paris (c. 1900).

Φ

Pragmatic Theory of Truth
Charles Sanders Peirce

A belief is likely to be true if holding it is of use to the believer

⬆ An anonymous Northern European painting (*c.* 1630) depicts Truth as a female figure holding scales; her mirror, reflecting the vanities of the world, serves as a pragmatic arbiter of truth.

The pragmatic theory of truth holds that the truth or validity of a belief depends on how useful that belief is, or what the outcome of holding that belief would be. One of the earliest and most influential defenders of this theory was the U.S. pragmatist Charles Sanders Peirce (1839–1914), who defended a version of the theory in various issues of *Popular Science Monthly* magazine and in a subsequent book, *How to Make Our Ideas Clear*, all published in 1878.

In *How to Make Our Ideas Clear*, Peirce distinguished between scientific beliefs that can be tested using the experimental methods of science, and metaphysical beliefs that cannot be tested using these methods. Peirce identified a true belief to be the sort of belief on which ideal investigators using scientific methods would eventually converge, given sufficient time. By this definition, many traditional metaphysical (or religious) beliefs would turn out to be neither true nor false, and therefore "meaningless."

The U.S. second-generation pragmatist William James (1842–1910) broadened Peirce's definition by proposing that a belief was true if it was "expedient" for the person believing it. This allowed for the possibility that metaphysical and religious claims could be true, but it also suggested that truth was relative to a particular individual, particular time, or particular place, rather than absolute.

The pragmatic theory is rarely defended today in the forms envisioned by Peirce or James, but it is an important precursor to modern theories that identify a belief's truth with its conditions of verification—what experience would show this belief to be true?—or with warranted assertability conditions—under what conditions would a person be justified in asserting this belief? Some modern thinkers with a strong pragmatist bent include Michael Dummett, Richard Rorty, Hilary Putnam, and Jürgen Habermas. **BSh**

> *"The opinion which is fated to be ultimately agreed to by all who investigate, is what we mean by the truth, and the object represented in this opinion is the real."*

Charles Sanders Peirce, *Popular Science Monthly* (1878)

Predicate Logic

Gottlob Frege

A method of reasoning that led to the creation of modern logic

German mathematician, logician, and philosopher Friedrich Ludwig Gottlob Frege (1848–1925) began his career specializing in the geometric representation of imaginary forms on a flat plane. However, it was not long before his thoughts began to turn increasingly toward logic and its relationship to mathematics. Frege felt that mathematics and logic were fundamentally entwined, and that mathematics, in the end, reduces to pure logic. As a result of his efforts, he virtually invented, in 1878, the concept of predicate logic; it was the single biggest leap forward in the philosophy and approach to logic since the work of Aristotle.

Predicate logic is the idea that new information can be gleaned from two or more preceding pieces of information. In its simplest form, predicate logic can be seen in the following three sentences:

1) All donkeys are mammals

2) Harvey is a donkey

3) Harvey is a mammal.

The argument is purely logical because the structure, the choice of wording, of the first two statements (called the "logical structure") is designed to convince the listener to accept a proposition.

Frege did not use the phrase "predicate logic" (it was introduced much later) to describe what he was struggling toward: a new system of logical notation, a "language" for the expression of logical theory. It was a language with its own syntax and semantics, which he applied, in turn, to constructing a new platform of principles so exacting that they could be used for propositions never before considered by logicians. Frege recorded his new approach to logic in his landmark book, *Begriffsschrift* (Concept Notation, 1879), little read prior to 1950, partly because of its author's eccentric and extensive notations. Nevertheless, the use of symbols and formulas in logic today is due in no small part to Frege's pioneering work. **BS**

⬆ A digitally colored photograph of Gottlob Frege, *c.* 1920, who said, "Every good mathematician is at least half a philosopher, and every good philosopher at least half a mathematician."

"I hope I may claim in the present work to have made it probable that the laws of arithmetic are analytic judgments . . . arithmetic thus becomes simply a development of logic."

Gottlob Frege

Psychology Laboratory
Wilhelm Wundt

The University of Leipzig opens the world's first facility for studying psychology

In 1862, German physiologist and psychologist Wilhelm Wundt (1832–1920), the "Father of Experimental Psychology," offered the first-ever course in scientific psychology, at the University of Heidelberg. In 1879, now at the University of Leipzig, he established the world's first "psychology laboratory," an academic environment devoted to the research and study of experimental psychology. It was an initiative that marked the beginning of modern psychology (although the laboratory would not become "official" until 1885, when the university at last recognized it).

Across the Atlantic in Massachusetts, the U.S. psychologist William James (1842–1910) had managed to create a psychology laboratory twelve months before

Wundt, at Harvard University Medical School, but James is generally not credited with being first because he used his laboratory purely for teaching purposes, rather than for experimentation. Wundt owed much to the University of Leipzig's administrators, who permitted him to use an empty room to store the equipment he had been using in his lectures, and it was in that room that he first started his series of experiments.

Ever since the publication in 1862 of his book *Contributions Toward a Theory of Sense Perception*, Wundt—the first person in history to be called a psychologist—was determined that psychology would break free from being simply a branch of philosophy and become an independent discipline, a new science that would construct its own set of doctrines through the trial and error of rigorous empirical experimentation. He also determined early on that not all the work would take place within the laboratory. Wundt's new science would bring in religion, the social sciences, language, the study of historical records, and the recording of field observations, all of which would contribute toward what Wundt called a sort of "scientific metaphysics." **BS**

Wilhelm Wundt (seated) is photographed with fellow psychologists at Leipzig University in c. 1910. ⬆

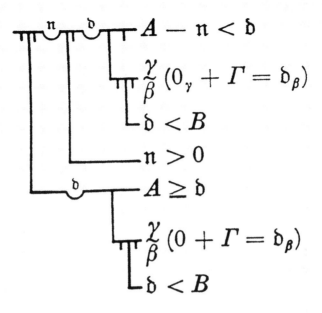

1879

Φ

Symbolic Logic
Gottlob Frege

A formal logical system that uses symbols to represent relationships between propositions

Symbolic logic has its roots in earlier logical systems, such as the syllogistic logic created by Aristotle in the fourth century BCE, yet those earlier systems invariably used words and languages to formulate arguments. In contrast, symbolic logic is a formalized language of arguments and reasoning for making and analyzing claims. It is formalized in the sense that it uses different symbols to represent declarative statements, such as "birds are animals," and other symbols to represent operations or functions, such as "and," "or," "if," and "then." Like all of mathematics, its use is not dependent upon the user's language.

In the eighteenth century German philosopher Gottfried Leibniz (1646–1716) made an attempt at creating a symbolic system of logical reasoning. In the nineteenth century, English mathematician, philosopher, and logician George Boole (1815–64) published influential works on mathematical and algebraic logic. Yet it is German mathematician, logician, and philosopher Friedrich Ludwig Gottlob Frege (1848–1925) who is widely regarded as the inventor of modern symbolic logic after the publication of *Begriffsschrift* (Concept Notation) in 1879.

Both mathematics and philosophy are dependent on the use of logic. The dream for many philosophers had long been to create a logical notation system that would quickly reveal the validity or invalidity of an argument simply by looking at it and understanding the symbols, just as mathematicians do when looking at a mathematical equation. With the introduction of symbolic logic, philosophers could delve into the logical structure hidden behind classical arguments, allowing them to solve some of the more troubling philosophical conundrums, such as St. Anselm's ontological argument for the existence of God. More pragmatically, symbolic logic would also become the basis for computer programming. **MT**

⬆ Gottlob Frege's original notation for his system of first-order logic, conceived in 1879.

Volapük

Johann Martin Schleyer

A universal language invented in the hope of unifying humankind

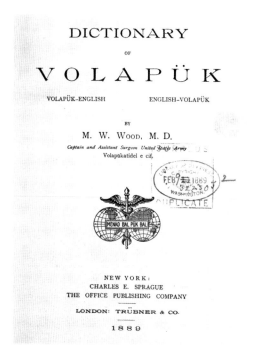

DICTIONARY

OF

VOLAPÜK

VOLAPÜK-ENGLISH ENGLISH-VOLAPÜK

BY

M. W. WOOD, M. D.

Captain and Assistant Surgeon United States Army
Volapükatidel e cif,

FEB 9 1889

NEW YORK:
CHARLES E. SPRAGUE
THE OFFICE PUBLISHING COMPANY

LONDON: TRÜBNER & CO.

1889

↑ The cover of a Volapük dictionary published by Marshall William Wood in 1889, by which time the language was already falling from favor. Nevertheless, it remains available today.

"With respect to money, weights and measures, time zones, laws and language, the brothers and sisters of the human race should move toward unity."

Johann Martin Schleyer

Volapük was a language invented in 1879 by German priest Johann Martin Schleyer (1831–1912). Schleyer claimed that God had appeared to him in a dream and told him to construct a universal language that would be easy to learn. His goal, he said, was to establish a means of communication "capable of expressing thought with the greatest clearness and accuracy," with adjectives, verbs, and adverbs regularly formed, and words written as pronounced, thus minimizing difficulties in spelling.

Schleyer wanted to create a phonetic alphabet and decided to form words composed of only one syllable, words that would be clearly audible. The result, however, was that few Volapük words suggested anything recognizable as words known to speakers of English, German, or Latin, despite their roots being drawn from the existing Roman alphabet and other primary European languages. "Vol", for example, came from "universal," and "pük" from "language." The letters "Q" and "W" were not used, and the letter "R" was barely seen anywhere because Schleyer believed that pronouncing it would be difficult for speakers of Mandarin and Cantonese. "Animal" was "nim," and "rhetoric" was "pükofav."

Despite the scientific and literary communities showing little interest, the new language gained a wide following throughout the 1880s, with Volapük societies and periodicals emerging across Europe. The first gathering designed to promote the language convened in Vienna in 1882, and three Volapük congresses would later meet, in 1884, 1887, and 1889. But by the end of the decade, interest was waning. It did not help that, in 1889, Schleyer refused to accept the legitimacy of the newly elected president of the Volapük Academy, the French professor Auguste Kerckhoffs (1835–1903). By the mid-1890s, the movement had all but collapsed. **BS**

Historian's Fallacy
Matthew Arnold

Writing history as though the participants could know what lay ahead of them

The idea behind the "historian's fallacy" was introduced by British poet and critic Matthew Arnold (1822–88) in his work *The Study of Poetry*, published in 1880. Referring to the study of historical antecedents in national literary styles, Arnold pointed out the logical error of using hindsight to attribute a sense of causality or foreknowledge of important historical events to the people who lived through them, when in reality they may not have had overall perspective. In the twentieth century, U.S. academic David Hackett Fischer (b. 1935) took up Arnold's theme in his book, *Historians' Fallacies: Toward a Logic of Historical Thought* (1970). The originator of the actual phrase "historian's fallacy," Fischer admonished fellow historians to remember that the people of the past had no knowledge of the future.

Historians falling prey to the fallacy, also known as "retrospective determinism," use information unavailable to historic individuals to judge their decisions, often unfairly. They might argue, for example, that if the designers of the *Titanic* had known the type of hull damage that an iceberg strike would cause, they would not have made the walls on the lower levels stop short of the ceilings, enabling seawater rapidly to flood the ship. Similarly, if the firemen and police had understood that the buildings of the World Trade Center would collapse so catastrophically quickly in 2001, they would not have entered them.

In contrast, a historian might adopt a "view from nowhere" and strive for objectivity by ignoring their own knowledge of subsequent events and using only what the historic individuals would have known. As the traditional saying goes, "Hindsight is 20/20," giving those who came later a false advantage over the people who lived through the original events, who had little possibility of knowing what the greater consequences of their actions would be at the time when they were making their decisions. **PBr**

⬆ A portrait of British poet and culture critic Matthew Arnold, taken in about 1883. In *The Study of Poetry* (1880), he described the historian's fallacy as a "natural" error.

"No man is free from the logic of his own rational assumptions . . ."

David Hackett Fischer, *Historians' Fallacies* (1970)

1880

🏛

War Is Good

Helmuth von Moltke

War reinforces the virtues of society and makes better people of the participants

It was in a letter of 1880 to the international law expert Johann Kaspar Bluntschli (1808–81) that German Field Marshal Helmuth von Moltke (1800–91), chief of staff of the Prussian army for three decades, explicitly asserted the idea that "war is good" in the modern era. Von Moltke, who is also known for his contribution to the evolution of military strategy, believed that war was important for the advancement of morality. "Without war," he argued, "the world would sink into a swamp of materialism." Von Moltke believed that the practice of waging war could be moral (in the sense that there was a ethical way to fight a war), and also that war itself was an exercise of morality.

Von Moltke's idea that war is good came from his belief that loyalty and courage are among the highest virtues of humankind, and that virtue can only be achieved through practice. War offers an opportunity for sacrifice according to a sense of duty, one that is not available during a time of peace. Thus, the idea that war is good rests on the notion that war is the only route by which human nobility and character can reach its highest form. Wars are often the source of glory for those who fight in them, and for good reason societies generally celebrate the acts of valor and virtue that have been demonstrated by warriors in battle.

Von Moltke argued that without war people within a society become lazy. A good society contains within it people who are ready to sacrifice themselves for the greater good. War provides proof that there is a greater good worth fighting for, and it also gives people the opportunity to exercise the virtues that are associated with self-sacrifice. Von Moltke's doctrine of "war is good" goes some way to explaining why wars, and those who fight in them, are celebrated by many societies. **PB**

Helmuth von Moltke, center clean shaven, pictured with his staff in 1871. ⬆

1880

The Grand Inquisitor
Fyodor Dostoyevsky

An examination into whether the church has an infantilizing effect on believers

The chapter titled "The Grand Inquisitor" is set within *The Brothers Karamazov* (1880), the great philosophical novel on God, morality, and free will by Fyodor Dostoyevsky (1821–81). Told in the form of a parable, the chapter both advances the novel and engages the reader in a self-contained investigation of how much or how little humanity really does want to be free.

The parable concerns Alyosha, a young novice monk, whose brother, Ivan, tells him of the time Jesus Christ appeared in Seville, Spain, during the Inquisition (1478–1834). Christ is recognized as the Messiah and is worshipped and adored, but despite healing the sick and performing other miracles he is arrested and led to the Grand Inquisitor. The church leader informs Christ that his presence in Spain is interfering with the church's mission; the church and its entrenched hierarchy were doing very well without him. Christ is at first sentenced to be burned at the stake, but is then released and told never to return.

The Inquisitor denounces Jesus, claiming that he was wrong to reject the temptations placed before him by the devil during his time in the wilderness. Refusing his first two temptations—to turn stones into bread, and to throw himself off a high point in Jerusalem so that the angels would lift him up—was bad enough, but refusing the third—to receive the kingdoms of the earth to rule over—was an error. Christ should have accepted that one because people cannot manage the "gift" of free will. Rejecting the devil's temptations, the Inquisitor says, guarantees human beings free will, a burden they are ill-equipped to carry. People want security, not freedom; trying to follow Christ will only give them a lifetime of angst.

The Inquisitor says it is the church's job to remove the burden of freedom and replace it with certainty. Readers are left to wonder whether they, too, have come to let the church think for them. **BS**

⬆ *The Grand Inquisitor* (1985) by Ilya Glazunov, an illustration for Dostoyevsky's *The Brothers Karamazov* (1880).

Impressionism in Music
France

A French school of composition reflecting Impressionism in the visual arts, which emphasized atmosphere and mood over emotion and story

⬆ French composer Ernest Chausson turns pages for friend and fellow musician Claude Debussy, at the Chausson family's house in Luzancy (Seine-et-Marne), August 1893.

"You do me a great honor by calling me a pupil of Claude Monet."

Claude Debussy, composer

The painting *Impression: Sunrise* (1872) by Claude Monet (1840–1926) suggested to a critic the name of one of the most influential artistic movements in history. "Impressionism" implied a contourless and incomplete style of painting, as opposed to the prevalent highly detailed approach. A century earlier, Scottish philosopher David Hume (1711–76) had defined "impression" and "idea," two basic types of perceptions: impression is the lively yet vague one "when we hear, or see, or feel, or love, or hate, or desire, or will."

Applied to music from around 1880—particularly that of Emmanuel Chabrier (1841–94) and Claude Debussy (1862–1918)—the term connects to the visual arts. In Debussy's orchestral music, his innovative orchestration techniques create a lush and somewhat blurred effect, evoking an intimate and mysterious atmosphere. Many titles of Debussy's works, such as *La Mer* (The Sea, 1905) and *Nuages* (Clouds, 1899), related to impressionistic motifs from the visual arts. Others, such as the Javanese-inspired *Pagodes* (Pagodas), conveyed impressions of exotic places. The early Impressionists also partly abandoned major/minor mode tonality in favor of a freer approach incorporating medieval church modes and other scales.

Consideration of the orchestra as a palette of sound colors would have profound impact on later composers, including Igor Stravinsky and Olivier Messiaen, and also on composers of movie scores, including John Williams. Impressionistic techniques lend themselves particularly well to the movie medium, in which music often supports the image, and vice versa, emphasizing orchestral colors rather than melodic themes. Impressionism's influence was also striking in jazz, especially in the use of modal scales for improvisation from the 1950s onward, but also in the Debussy-like lyricism in the music of pianists such as Bill Evans. **PB**

Universal Healthcare
Otto von Bismarck

A welfare state should step in to help workers in ill-health and old age

The establishment of the world's first welfare state originated not in philanthropy but in hard-nosed self-interest. In 1881 the German chancellor, Otto von Bismarck (1815–98), was aware of the growing power of Germany's social democrats, which he viewed as a threat to the monarchy and his own entrenched authority. What he needed was a measure that would swing the populace in favor of the conservatives, led by himself. Conscious of the need to placate his party members, and not himself wholly convinced about the need to establish laws to protect workers at their place of employment, von Bismarck nonetheless opened the debate with a speech to parliament in November 1881.

The term he chose to describe his new social agenda, Practical Christianity, consisted of what he called "sickness funds," which covered approximately one in ten German workers, mostly those in industries such as metalworks, shipyards, railways, and power generation plants. The benefits included sick pay, a death payment, free pharmaceuticals, and certain services in hospitals and clinics. What was once only a vague principle had at last become something concrete, to be paid for through government revenues.

The world's first welfare state was announced in 1883 with the introduction of the Health Insurance Bill, followed by the Accident Insurance Bill a year later. Health reform may well have been the German Chancellor's least favorite piece of social legislation, but its significance as a step forward in the development of various universal healthcare schemes around the world cannot be overestimated. Von Bismarck had set an unstoppable juggernaut in motion. It was all made possible by Europe's rapid industrialization, which could generate the revenues necessary to facilitate, and later expand, healthcare reform. **BS**

The Death of God
Friedrich Nietzsche

Objective moral principles do not exist, and so God, their source, does not exist

German philosopher Friedrich Nietzsche (1844–1900), in his book *The Gay Science* (1882), declared, through the mouth of a madman, the death of God. Nietzsche used this literary, polemic tool because he intended to show that if God were truly dead, then his madman was in fact a true prophet and the wisest of all men.

Nietzsche's attack started with his belief that there are no objective moral principles, and ended with him saying that, since these principles were always seen as the most important descriptors of God, God, therefore, must not exist. Nietzsche felt that when people saw that there were no objective moral principles, they would, poetically speaking, murder God and begin to move into a post-Christian era. Indeed, in the years following Nietzsche's death, the West became

"God is dead. God remains dead. And we have killed him. Yet his shadow still looms."

Friedrich Nietzsche, *The Gay Science* (1882)

gradually less theistic. In fact, even some Jewish and Christian theologians (so-called "theothanatologists") followed Nietzsche, trying to find room for religion without God and objective truth.

Despite its massive influence, Nietzsche's declaration was not much more than that. As an argument it was weak because he moved from an empirical fact, that different cultures exhibit different particular laws, to the hasty conclusion that no general moral principles or laws exist. Rational persons might disagree about the morality of abortion, but no rational person would disagree that simply killing a child for fun is always and absolutely wrong. And if objective moral principles, such as "It is always wrong to kill a child for fun," exist, then it is certainly possible that an absolutely good God exists as well. **AB**

1883

Genetic Determinism
August Weismann

Genetics might account for the complexity of life, rather than environment alone

German evolutionary biologist August Weismann (1834–1914), delivering a lecture titled "On Inheritance" in 1883, was the first to propose that the development of life on Earth was as much the product of genetics as of the environment. He argued that it was the genetic makeup of organisms, their genotypes, not merely the environment, that helped to determine their structures, patterns, shapes, and colors, as well as their features, observable characteristics, and physical traits (phenotypes); even their behavior was genetically determined. Taking into consideration the natural selection theory of Charles Darwin (1809–82), Weismann taught the concept of "germinal selection," which holds that genes are the source of

our morphology, our agents of change. It was an idea that went unchallenged for more than a hundred years.

Genetic determinism was an advanced theory for its time, but the sequencing of the human genome, completed in February 2001, sounded the death knell for Weismann's bold idea. The paucity of discovered genes (30,000 compared to an anticipated 100,000) led to the shocking realization among biologists that only 300 genes, for example, distinguished a human being from a mouse.

In the light of this evidence, genetic determinism fails to account for human complexity. But while it may well have been shown to be a failed scientific paradigm, there is still to this day no commonly accepted alternative. What can be put in its place? Scientists still do not know what prompts cells to change, and still have no theory to make sense of the many contradictions presented by the Human Genome Project (HGP). The HGP proved that there is an overwhelming similarity of genomes across species, and confirmed what some scientists had suspected for decades: that our genes alone cannot explain the vast complexity of life on Earth. **BS**

A strand of DNA, which contains the genetic code for the development and function of living organisms.

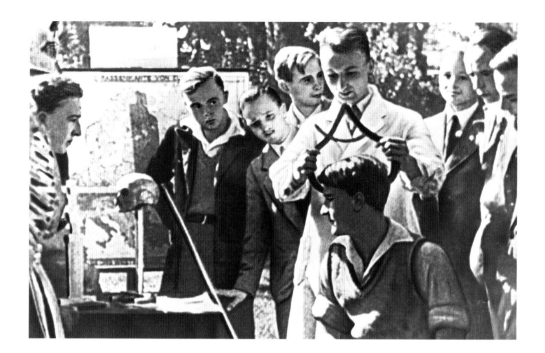

1883

Eugenics
Francis Galton

Crafting a higher form of humanity through genetic manipulation

In 1883, British anthropologist Francis Galton (1822–1911), cousin to naturalist Charles Darwin (1809–82), coined the phrase "eugenics" (from the Greek *eugenes* meaning "well born, of good stock") to describe the human quest for betterment through selective reproduction. "Eugenics," he said, "is the science of improvement of the human race germ plasm through better breeding, [the] study of agencies under social control that may improve or impair the racial qualities of future generations, whether physically or mentally."

Galton felt that humankind's natural evolutionary processes were being hindered by philanthropic gestures to a genetically inferior underclass that perpetuated the inefficient "weak links" in heredity and got in the way of natural selection. Galton's answer to this was to introduce an artificial means of selection to help circumvent this derailing of the natural order. Eugenics spread around the world and gained new adherents, particularly in the United States with the establishment of the Station for Experimental Evolution in 1904 and the Eugenic Record Office in 1910.

One primary manifestation of a belief in eugenics was racism. In the early twentieth century in the United States, "race consciousness" was heightened by eugenics; procreation suddenly became a public issue, with eugenics-inspired legislation concerning segregation, the forbidding of certain marriages, and sexual sterilization. Eugenics also inspired increased rates of abortion in support of social ideals.

The association of the Nazi Party in Germany with the darker principles of eugenics proved to be the pseudo-science's death knell. By the mid-1940s, eugenics across the world had been all but abandoned. The dream, however, has persisted. With the mapping of the human genome and the advent of genetic engineering, eugenics, dressed up and reimagined, is about to enter a new and uncertain future. **BS**

⬆ A Nazi measures heads in search of Aryan characteristics in the Soviet movie *Ordinary Fascism* (1965).

Pointillism
Georges Seurat

A painting style that abandoned brushstrokes for tiny, luminescent dots

It took two years for the French painter Georges Seurat (1859–91) to complet his acclaimed work *A Sunday Afternoon on the Island of La Grande Jatte* in 1884. In that time he would often visit the little island at the entrance to Paris in the middle of the Seine, sketching the people who frequented it so to make his work as authentic in detail and form as possible. He experimented with new pigments, such as zinc chromate, which produced deep yellows for the island's sun-dappled grass. More innovatory, instead of using long brushstrokes, Seurat chose to compose his painting using tiny dots of color. When viewed from a distance, the individual, uniformly sized dots combined to produce an image in wholly different colors, far more vivid than could ever be achieved with traditional

"Some say they see poetry in my paintings; I see only science."

Georges Seurat

brushstrokes. By combining colors optically, rather than mixing his pigments, he had invented a new form of painting, known initially as divisionism. Seurat himself named his method "chromoluminarism," the ability to achieve maximum luminosity from color. In the late 1880s, however, art critics who thought they knew better began to call it pointillism; and the name stuck.

La Grande Jatte was a large painting, 6½ x 9¾ feet (2 x 3 m) in size, and was the first ever to be composed entirely in the pointillist tradition. When displayed at an Impressionist exhibition in 1886 it caused a sensation, a challenge to the great Impressionists Pierre-Auguste Renoir and Claude Monet, and launched a new direction in art: Neo-impressionism. Paul Signac, a contemporary of Seurat, described pointillism as "a means of expressing the optical mixture of tints and tones." **BS**

Intentionality
Franz Brentano

The characteristic of consciousness whereby it is conscious of something

Historically, the term "intentionality" was used for the first time in the tenth century by Anselmus Genavae (c. 1033–1109), archbishop of Canterbury, in an ontological argument about the existence of God. It was later used by St. Thomas Aquinas (c. 1224–74) in the thirteenth century when he tried to describe the process by which all living things thrust themselves out into the world. Its modern usage, however, dates to the German philosopher and psychologist Franz Brentano (1838–1917), who defined it in his book, *Psychology from an Empirical Standpoint* (1884), as a characteristic present in every conscious act.

The word itself was medieval and derived from the Latin word *intendere*, meaning to be directed toward a goal or thing. The concept of intentionality

"Only some, not all, mental states and events have Intentionality."

John R. Searle, *Intentionality* (1983)

relates to the "aboutness" of things—for example, the sentence that cats are animals is about cats (and also about animals). Something that is about (or represents) something else is said to "have intentionality," or (in the case of conscious states, such as believing, desiring, thinking, hoping, perceiving, and fearing) is said to be an "intentional mental state."

"Intentionality" should not be confused with the common meaning of the word "intention." It is not an indicator of one's imminent thoughts or actions, but rather of the way in which our brains are capable of understanding our environment through the process of sensory input and perception. Intentionality is a tool that today's sociologists, psychologists, and anthropologists have used to explain how all sentient creatures perceive the world around them. **BS**

A Sunday Afternoon on the Island of La Grande Jatte (1884, detail) by Georges Seurat.

Subjectivist Fallacy
Friedrich Nietzsche

Whether people believe in something is irrelevant to whether or not it is true

The subjectivist fallacy is a recently identified fallacy in the history of ideas. One older instance of it is found in *Beyond Good and Evil* (1885) by Friedrich Nietzsche (1844–1900), but its earliest identification in literature is unclear. One possibility is that it arose along with the U.S. pragmatist response to problems facing the modernist project. As those ideas filtered into literary criticism and legal studies, it is possible that relativism influenced culture more broadly, culminating in an increase in the fallacy's frequency.

Also known as the "relativist fallacy," the subjectivist fallacy is an error in reasoning in which an arguer assumes that, because it is possible to disagree about the truth of a claim, either it is irrational to hold that claim or any attitude toward that claim is rational. For

> *"Talk of subordinate theories . . . is meaningful but only relative[ly] . . ."*
>
> **W. V. O. Quine, *Ontological Relativity* (1969)**

example, if one person asserts that abortion is immoral and someone else responds, "Well, not everyone agrees, so that can't be right," the latter has committed the subjectivist fallacy. Similarly, if someone claims that communism is immoral and someone else responds, "Well, you have a right to your opinion, but there are differing perspectives on the subject," the latter has committed this fallacy.

According to the law of noncontradiction, no proposition can be both true and false at the same time; thus, the fact that people may hold different opinions about the truth of a claim is irrelevant to the truth of that claim. The relevant questions are whether there is any evidence on which to form a judgment, and if so, whether that evidence is strong enough to justify belief in that claim. **JW**

Dr. Jekyll and Mr. Hyde
Robert Louis Stevenson

A monumental tale contrasting good and evil, respectability and lust

Is it a detective story, fable, religious allegory, gothic novel? Literary critics have long discussed what genre, or mix of genres, *Strange Case of Dr. Jekyll and Mr. Hyde* (1886) by Scottish novelist Robert Louis Stevenson (1850–94) might belong to, but, regardless of its tag, this classic tale of one man's struggle with the darker side of his nature is justly acclaimed.

The 1880s was a golden decade for the author, with the release of *Treasure Island* in 1883 followed by *Kidnapped* in 1886. But *Dr. Jekyll and Mr. Hyde* had a darker purpose and seemed to capture an increasing sense of pessimism, at least in artistic circles, about where the British Empire stood ethically after decades of rampant colonialism and the technological progress and hubris that had helped to make it possible.

> *"Sir, if that was my master, why had he a mask upon his face?"*
>
> **Robert L. Stevenson, *Dr. Jekyll and Mr. Hyde* (1886)**

The second draft of the book (Stevenson burned the first draft, written at a feverish pace after waking from a dream, because its theme so disturbed his wife) concerns a good and decent Londoner beset by an internal struggle of his own making. The erudite, outwardly respectable Dr. Henry Jekyll, who for the better part of his life has tried to suppress myriad evil urges, invents a potion able to separate the good and bad aspects of his character, but which brings forth from Jekyll's innermost being the murderous Mr. Edward Hyde, with gruesome consequences. Over time, Jekyll's character loses its battle to keep Hyde in check, and Hyde grows in influence and power until Jekyll becomes reliant on the potion simply to survive. The book is a classic study of the duality in us all, of our outward respectability and inward yearnings. **BS**

Dr. Jekyll feels the effect of his potion in a dramatic depiction by U.S. illustrator Howard Pyle (1895). ➜

Masochism
Richard, Baron von Krafft-Ebing

Sexual arousal resulting from subjection to the will of another, even to receiving pain

The term "masochism" was brought into common usage by Austro-German psychiatrist Richard, Baron von Krafft-Ebing (1840–1902) in his book *Sexual Psychopathy: A Clinical-Forensic Study* (1886), although it existed beforehand. Fernanda Savage, translator of the novella *Venus in Furs* (1870) by Austrian writer Chevalier Leopold von Sacher-Masoch (1836–95), referred to Sacher-Masoch as "the poet of the anomaly now generally known as masochism. By this is meant the desire on the part of the individual affected of desiring himself completely and unconditionally subject to the will of a person of the opposite sex, and being treated by this person as by a master, to be humiliated, abused, and tormented, even to the verge of death." Sacher-Masoch's own relationships with women paralleled

"Nothing sexual is depraved. Only cruelty is depraved, and that's another matter."

Marilyn French, *The Women's Room* (1977)

the one depicted in his book, in which a man signs a contract with a woman to make him her "slave."

Masochism is sometimes seen in conjunction with sadism, with the participants alternating the giving and receiving of pain. The "master" dominates the "slave," usually in a rigidly controlled environment designed to protect the masochist, even while he or she is subjected to sometimes violent objectification.

One of the best-known books of the erotic genre, *The Story of O* (1954) by French author Anne Desclos under the pen name Pauline Réage, relates the story of a young woman initiated into the lifestyle. The popularity of works such as E. L. James's *Fifty Shades of Grey* trilogy (2011) indicates a trend toward a normalization and acceptance of this more extreme type of interpersonal relationship. **PBr**

Sadism
Richard, Baron von Krafft-Ebing

Sexual pleasure or satisfaction derived from inflicting pain on another

The idea that some individuals may derive sexual pleasure from acts other than intercourse was one of the areas of human behavior scrutinized by the new science of psychology in the nineteenth century. In his book *Sexual Psychopathy: A Clinical-Forensic Study* (1886), Austro-German psychiatrist Richard, Baron von Krafft-Ebing (1840–1902) examined writings, novels, and plays of French nobleman Donatien Alphonse François, Marquis de Sade (1740–1814), in which the aristocrat detailed the pleasure he had derived from inflicting pain on others. As a result of von Krafft-Ebing's study, the term "sadism" passed into common usage.

De Sade's debauched lifestyle included the exploitation of prostitutes, hired servants, and other innocents. He was eventually imprisoned for his crimes

"When she's abandoned her moral center … she is never more beautiful to me."

Marquis de Sade, writer

and also spent time in a mental institution, during which time he continued to write and where one of his plays was performed by the inmates. A play by German author Peter Weiss (1916–82), *The Persecution and Assassination of Jean-Paul Marat as Performed by the Inmates of the Asylum of Charenton Under the Direction of the Marquis de Sade* (1962), alludes to the fact that during the French Revolution (1787–99), when Sade was freed for a time, he became part of the Revolutionary government and admired Marat, one of its leaders.

Sadists generally prefer an unwilling victim and so, although masochists enjoy being abused, sadists do not always choose them for the practice. Sadism is found in varying degrees, from satisfaction derived from the public humiliation of an enemy to actual criminal behavior culminating in rape and/or murder. **PBr**

A caricature of Leopold von Sacher-Masoch (1890), from whose name the word "masochism" derives.

🏛

Marginal Revenue Productivity
John Bates Clark

Examining how much firms can afford to pay an employee or contractor for their labor

Businesses based on the capitalist model need to know whether their workforce is the correct size and appropriately paid in terms of the health of the business. In the nineteenth century, various economists took a mathematical approach to the question. The issue became important in the British industrial economy after the repeal in 1846 of the Corn Laws, which had kept the price of bread, and therefore wages, artificially high.

John Bates Clark (1847–1938) presented the marginal revenue productivity theory of wages in his book *The Philosophy of Wealth* (1886). The theory argues that a firm can afford to pay for a unit of labor only if it contributes at least the cost of buying it to the firm's income. The term "marginal revenue" (MR) describes the change in revenue that results from the addition

"… the distribution of income to society is controlled by a natural law …"

John Bates Clark, *Distribution of Wealth* (1889)

of a unit of input where other factors remain equal. According to the law of diminishing returns, at a certain point investment ceases to yield an optimum return, and the return decreases for every extra unit of input.

Wages are mainly determined by the law of supply and demand, but the theory of marginal revenue productivity (MRP) also introduces the efficiency or productivity of the worker into the equation. The productivity of a worker—the amount of product he or she can turn out, and therefore the profit made by the employing firm, known as marginal physical product (MPP)—makes that worker worth more to the company, which allows the firm to pay the worker a higher wage. The economic equation used— $MR \times MPP = MRP$ —reveals the point up to which it is in a firm's interest to take on more workers. **JF**

Voluntarism
Ferdinand Tönnies

The sociological view that the will takes precedence over emotion and intellect

The term "voluntarism" was coined by German sociologist Ferdinand Tönnies (1855–1936) in his work *Gemeinschaft und Gesellschaft* (Community and Civil Society, 1887). Generally, it refers to the primacy of the will over intellect or emotion. Tönnies used the concept to refer to the ways in which people freely associate with one another, and specifically to the significance of both natural will (*Wesenwille*) and "rational" will (*Kürwille*).

For Tönnies, these expressions of the will are evidenced in two corresponding dimensions of social life. *Gemeinschaft* refers to "community," which includes the natural bonds of family and embedded cultural identities, such as those stemming from religion and vocation. *Gesellschaft* refers to "society," and involves relationships and commitments derived from the

"The wills of human beings interact in many different ways …"

Ferdinand Tönnies, *Community and Civil Society* (1887)

pursuit of personal interests and the achievement of goals external to a person's more fundamental communal identity. The mandates and expectations involved in "community" are expressions of the natural will and are thus regulated from within the community. The means and ends involved in "society" are formulated by self-interest expressed through public opinion and regulated through mutual legislation.

This distinction between two types of will continued to influence the social sciences in the twentieth century. As socio-economic development caused communities to grow, the tension between social engagement as an end in itself and social engagement as merely a means to ends external to that engagement grew. Tönnies's voluntaristic insights apply to the oft-perceived divide between organic and artificial dimensions of society. **JD**

◀ A team of horses and their handlers transport a locomotive by road in c. 1860.

Master Morality and Slave Morality
Friedrich Nietzsche

A definition of morality as being either proactive or reactive

⬆ A sixteenth-century painting of Odysseus and Circe, by Bartholomaeus Spranger. Greek heroes such as Odysseus epitomize Nietzsche's concept of the "Noble Man."

A central theme of *On the Genealogy of Morality*, published in 1887 by German existential philosopher Friedrich Nietzsche (1844–1900), is that there are two fundamentally different kinds of morality. There is "master morality," which exists in the so-called "Noble Man," who determines morality for himself and does not require any outside approval as to its rightness; and there is "slave morality," which is the morality of the oppressed.

Slave morality is negative and reactive; it sees the forces that are arrayed against it and replies, "No." The master morality of the Noble Man, on the other hand, takes little heed of what is outside it or beyond it, and is concerned primarily with how to live in the present. Few things disturb the Noble Man, whose lifestyle affords him the luxury of self-indulgence, together with ambivalence about the tribulations of "weaker," more numerous humans, born to suffer as they try in vain to make sense of slave morality. The Noble Man is the creator of his morality; the slave, conversely, merely responds to it.

For Nietzsche, resentment of the Noble Man is the source of the subversive natures of "weak" slave moralists, whom he regarded as evil. The hero of Greek poet Homer (eighth century BCE) was the epitome of a strong-willed Noble Man, and the ancient civilizations of Greece and Rome were founded on the principles of classic master morality. Nietzsche believed that the standard moral systems of his time were an expression of slave morality—particularly utilitarianism and Christianity, which both promoted the good of the community, not the individual, as an aid to survival. For Nietzsche, ideals such as equality and democracy were the opposite of what humans truly valued; instead, he argued that the strong have always preyed upon the weak, and societies do not exist for the good of all. **BS**

"These two moralities are not simple inversions of one another."
Friedrich Nietzsche

The Secret Doctrine
Helena Blavatsky

A late nineteenth-century synthesis of science, religion, and philosophy

The Secret Doctrine was published in two volumes in 1888 by Russian-born Helena Blavatsky (1831–91), self-proclaimed clairvoyant, master of theosophy, and cofounder, in 1875, of the Theosophical Society in New York. The first volume, *Cosmogenesis*, told how the universe and all sentient beings came to exist; the second, *Anthropogenesis*, gave a series of explanations for the evolution of mankind that were at considerable variance with virtually all other scientific theories at the time.

The book contains a number of fundamental propositions: there is an omnipresent, eternal, immutable principle that transcends human thought; there are numberless universes and endless planes of existence; there is an obligatory pilgrimage that all souls must make in accordance with karmic principles; living beings can be found everywhere, from inside subatomic particles to the grandest of universes and all of them possess consciousness; and human races have come from seven quite separate evolutionary beginnings, each occurring in a different region of Earth, on landmasses that no longer exist—there is, for example, an Atlantean race, and also a race originating in "The Imperishable Sacred Land," which is located somewhere near the North Pole.

The absurdity of Blavatsky's book is now self-evident, but at the time it was not entirely ridiculed. Its publication coincided with an increased interest in both the occult and in esoteric pursuits such as gnosticism, astrology, and Christian mysticism. Despite its impressive length, it contains no fresh insights into the nature of God; it is a collection of previously published religious texts laced with Blavatsky's own questionable, subjective, unsubstantiated interpretations. Blavatsky claimed theosophy was ancient and universal, which begs the question why it was left until 1888 for her to reveal it to a presumably grateful world. **BS**

⬆ Helena Blavatsky, photographed at Ithaca, New York, in 1875, the year she cofounded the Theosophical Society with military officer, journalist, and lawyer Henry Steel Olcott.

"Magic being what it is, the most difficult of all sciences . . . its acquisition is practically beyond the reach of the majority of white-skinned people."
Helena Blavatsky

Φ

What Does Not Kill You Makes You Stronger
Friedrich Nietzsche

Hardship provides a necessary opportunity for the cultivation of superlative human beings

⬆ German philosopher and poet Friedrich Nietzsche in about 1870. He was interested in the enhancement of individual and cultural health, and his philosophies have inspired many.

The idea that "what does not kill you makes you stronger" was first articulated by German existential philosopher Friedrich Nietzsche (1844–1900) in his work, *Twilight of the Idols* (1888). The idea is mentioned in passing as an aphorism, but it is representative of the virtue ethic that Nietzsche developed throughout his writings.

Nietzsche's philosophy is a character ethic focused on the cultivation of the *Übermensch* (superlative human being). All things in the world are manifestations of "will to power," which is the natural tendency of things to strive toward empowerment and excellence. The *Übermensch* is the culmination of this process, a living work of art that represents the epitome of human accomplishment. Nietzsche rejects utilitarianism and deontology because these theories proscribe certain acts as universally wrong while saying nothing about what one must do to become an excellent human being. Suffering, for example, though temporarily painful, often helps in the cultivation of a superlative character, which is why it cannot be condemned as necessarily evil—if it does not destroy us, it has the potential to make us stronger. For Nietzsche, self-cultivation is a process of constantly assessing, demolishing, and rebuilding the self, and anything that assists in this process, no matter how painful in the short term, is a boon. The idea is embodied in the notion of *amor fati* (love of fate): if a person wishes to affirm the quality of their character, they must acknowledge the value of all of the things that made it, both the pleasurable and the painful, the good and the bad.

Although "What does not kill you . . ." has become a well-known aphorism, it is not commonly attributed to its author. Nietzsche believed that all philosophy is autobiography, and his views on this issue were probably motivated by the personal tragedies and ill-health that he had to endure during his lifetime. **JM**

"From the Military School of Life—Whatever does not kill me makes me stronger."

Friedrich Nietzsche, *Twilight of the Idols* (1888)

Vector Spaces
Giuseppe Peano

A mathematical concept that views things as vector spaces and fields, not objects

Italian mathematician Giuseppe Peano (1858–1932), a founder of mathematical logic and set theory, defined the vector space in his work *Geometrical Calculation According to the Ausdehnungslhere of H. Grassmann*, published in 1888. Mathematically, a set of vectors form a vector space provided that it meets several conditions, such as closure under addition, the associative law, the commutative law, and the distributive laws.

As an abstract way of extending Euclidean geometry's application to physical space, the vector space permits the scientist to assign numbers to given states of things at a certain time, and to calculate the results of forces acting on those things into the future. For example, suppose the things are physical particles: when multiple forces simultaneously act on a particle at a point, each represented by a vector, the resulting combined force is easily calculated because forces combine as vectors add. A collection of points forming a field with infinite degrees of freedom can be acted upon by numerous simultaneous forces, and the subsequent behavior of the field can be predicted.

After calculus, no mathematical technique is more useful across science than vector spaces and the linear algebra used with them. Modern theoretical physics—from classical mechanics, fluid theory, electromagnetic field theory, solid state physics, and particle physics, all the way to special and general relativity and quantum physics—relies extensively on them. English theoretical physicist Paul Dirac (1902–84) found vector spaces crucial for handling the principle of superposition and other problems in quantum mechanics. Even disciplines such as neuroscience make use of vector spaces. In 1989, U.S. philosopher Paul Churchland (b. 1942) suggested that mental states represented as sentences should be replaced by a neural network theory in which brain states are handled by vector spaces for the flow of neural representations. **JSh**

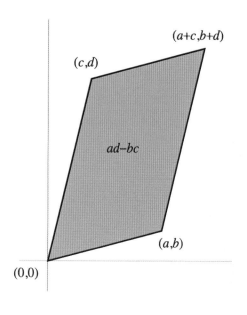

⬆ A quadrilateral formed by two vectors (a,b) and (c,d). Vectors may be added together and multiplied (scaled) by numbers called scalars.

"Now any mathematical quantities which can be added to give new quantities of the same nature may be represented by vectors in a suitable vector space with a sufficiently large number of dimensions."

Paul Dirac, physicist

Cultural Relativism

Franz Boas

Beliefs, customs, and ethics are relative to an individual in his or her own social context

The phrase "cultural relativism" may not have been coined until the social theorist Alain Locke (1886–1954) used it in 1924 to comment on the book *Culture and Ethnology* (1917) by anthropologist Robert Lowie (1883–1957), but the idea was already decades old. It was Franz Boas (1858–1942), the German–American founder of modern anthropology, who first developed the concept, beginning with his essay "On Alternating Sounds" (1889). Boas regarded individual societies, with all their associated cultural peculiarities, in the same way that naturalist Charles Darwin (1809–82) saw all of the species in the Galapagos Islands, not as any one species being superior to any other, but as all having adapted to their own circumstances. Boas then applied this thought to the science of anthropology, and arrived at the principle of cultural relativism. All cultures were unique, he argued, a product of their own individual histories—not just of ethnicity or environment. These views may seem orthodox to us now, but they were deduced at a time when racism and bigotry in the United States were threatening to cripple anthropology itself, with the discipline almost daring its detractors to label it "pre-scientific." The fact that Boas was able to rescue it from this milieu is nothing short of miraculous.

Boas abandoned the idea that understanding people meant merely to study what they ate and drank, or their tastes in music and religion, realizing that a person's beliefs should be seen in the terms of their own culture, not through the prism of our own culture. By using the cephalic index (which measured the width-to-breadth ratio of people's heads), Boas set out to prove that head sizes of immigrants had altered in only a generation and were not fixed. Boas dented the arguments of anthropology's racists, such as Samuel Morton (1799–1851) who had claimed that some races were immutable and had a separate creation—a common justification for slavery. **BS**

Apache leader Geronimo meets U.S. General George Crook in a cross-cultural council in 1886. ↑

1889

Ghost Dance
Wovoka

A Native American ritual dance that, it was believed, would drive away white people

A ritual designed to regenerate the earth and unify Native American tribes, the Ghost Dance reached its peak in the final decade of the nineteenth century, when the slaughter of buffalo herds, acquisition of traditional tribal lands, and systematic killing and corralling into reservations of Native Americans was reaching its gruesome height.

In 1889, the dance was introduced into the Northern Paiute tribe, inhabitants of areas in present-day eastern California and western Nevada, by a Northern Paiute spiritual leader, Wovoka (c. 1856–1932). Since his youth, Wovoka had been revered as a powerful medicine man; he was able, so the stories went, to control the weather, bring an end to a drought or flood, and even

catch a bullet (which later led to the wearing by the Lakota Sioux of "bullet-proof" Ghost shirts that, it was hoped, would protect them in battle). In January 1889, Wovoka had a prophetic vision about the resurrection of his tribe's dead, the extinction of the white invaders, and the restoration of Native American prosperity. Trying to keep alive his people's diminishing hopes for their future, Wovoka taught that salvation would come if his people remained upright and virtuous, at the same time regularly performing the Ghost Dance.

The dance, which itself was a form of round dance, was performed in strict five-day gatherings. The ceremony rapidly spread from the Northern Paiute homelands across Oklahoma and the Great Plains. It was adopted by every tribe that it touched—Arapaho, Apache, Pawnee, Sioux, and Cheyenne, as well as other, smaller tribes. Wovoka's message was not a call to arms, however. The spiritual leader was imploring his people, so desperate to gain revenge for a litany of wrongs and oppression, to achieve their objectives through dance. The mysterious ceremony seemed threatening to the European colonizers, who barely understood its religious significance. **BS**

⬆ An illustration of Sioux Native Americans performing the Ghost Dance in c. 1891.

Expressionism in Art
Vincent van Gogh

An art movement that emphasized the importance of self-expression

The Dutch Postimpressionist painter Vincent van Gogh (1853–90) saw the world differently from most of the Impressionist painters who surrounded him. Instead of capturing the light and colors of the natural landscape as a dispassionate observer, as the Impressionists had done, van Gogh looked inside his troubled psyche and discovered a new style of self-expression. Van Gogh's art provided a mirror for his angst-ridden soul and, years later, it would lead to the formalization of an entirely new kind of painting. Van Gogh once wrote in a letter to his brother, Theo, "Instead of trying to reproduce exactly what I see before my eyes, I use color more arbitrarily to express myself forcibly."

Van Gogh's *The Starry Night* (1889) depicts the view from his sanatorium window at night, but its swirling

> *"My art is self-confession. Through it, I seek to clarify my relationship to the world."*
>
> Edvard Munch, artist

sky and luminous stars are no faithful representation of what he saw; exaggerated and distorted, they suggest his inner reality. *The Starry Night* is now seen as a pivotal painting in the march toward Expressionism

Four years later came *The Scream* (1893) by Norwegian painter Edvard Munch (1863–1944), another icon of Expressionism. The painting depicted Munch himself, pausing while crossing a bridge and crying out in desperation from the blur of his anxiety-informed world. Like *The Starry Night*, the painting has the ingredients of Expressionism—the use of strong, nonnaturalistic colors and distorted lines—many years before the Expressionist movement had its "official" beginnings with the German artistic group Die Brücke (The Bridge), who met together for the first time in Dresden in 1905. **JMa**

The Binding Problem
William James

The question of how the brain binds data supplied by the senses and memory

The U.S. pragmatist philosopher William James (1842–1910) formulated early versions of the binding problem in two works: *The Principles of Psychology* (1890) and *A Pluralistic Universe* (1909). As explained by James, the binding problem concerns the mechanisms by which human minds are capable of experiencing various sensory stimuli as being part of a single, unified "consciousness." This consciousness, traditionally thought of as the "soul," seems to serve as a receptacle for experiences such as hearing a noise, seeing blue, and remembering childhood.

Current research on the binding problem did not get underway until around 1980, when psychologist Anne Treisman (b. 1935) proposed the feature-integration theory of attention, which purported to

> *"No possible number of entities . . . can sum themselves together."*
>
> William James, *The Principles of Psychology* (1890)

explain how the sensory experiences of the various features of an object could be psychologically "integrated" into an experience of a single object. At around the same time, the biophysicist Christoph von der Malsburg (b. 1942) wrote an article investigating the neural processes allowing the brain to represent the relations between discrete visual stimuli, such as colors or shapes, which are picked up by different neurons.

Neurologists, psychologists, and philosophers of mind have continued to research the binding problem, with somewhat different emphases. Some researchers have focused on specific neural functions, such as the processing of visual information, while others have focused on "big picture" questions, such as the emergence of a "unified" consciousness from a large number of seemingly discrete brain processes. **BSh**

← Vincent van Gogh's *The Starry Night* (detail, 1889) externalizes the artist's inner turmoil.

Psychoanalysis
Sigmund Freud

Human behavior is dictated by unconscious and often irrational desires

Psychoanalysis, pioneered in the 1890s by Austrian neurologist Sigmund Freud (1856–1939), is both a method of treating people with mental illness and a theory about why people act the way they do. Psychoanalytic theory holds that unconscious, irrational drives cause human behaviors, and that many desires are repressed, having been formed during childhood and later become hidden in the human subconscious. People can overcome their psychological problems by understanding what their minds have repressed and by accepting their unconscious desires .

Freud developed psychoanalysis as he studied people with "nervous ailments," such as "hysteria." He developed a comprehensive method of understanding human behavior and personality, and their root

"The interpretation of dreams is the royal road to a knowledge of the unconscious."

Sigmund Freud

mental and emotional causes, while also developing a therapeutic method that psychologists could use to treat people suffering from such conditions. Freud's methodology and ideas became so renowned that his name is still largely synonymous with psychoanalysis.

As one of the first scientific methodologies aimed at dealing with mental illness, psychoanalysis paved the way for a much broader understanding of the human mind. While many of Freud's psychoanalytic theories have been criticized and dismissed by modern psychologists and medical professionals, his work provided new insights into human nature itself. Psychoanalysis showed that what we think about ourselves can be greatly influenced by forces outside our control, and that our strongest beliefs about ourselves may not be reflective of reality. **MT**

Freudian Slip
Sigmund Freud

Everyday slips of the tongue provide insights into the workings of the mind

In 1890, in a letter to his friend, the physician Wilhelm Fliess, Austrian neurologist Sigmund Freud (1856–1939) listed numerous examples that he had noticed of a curious tendency by people to utter errors in speech, due perhaps to inattention, incomplete data, or a strong prior-response pattern. In his book *The Psychopathology of Everyday Life* (1901), Freud later referred to these errors in German as *Fehlleistungen* (faulty actions). He theorized that what we now call "Freudian slips" might represent the surfacing of an unconscious thought or wish; they were perhaps symptoms, he said, of the ongoing struggle between our conscious view of reality and those things we repress in our unconscious: they are verbal mistakes that reveal repressed beliefs. Freud's English translator

"My hypothesis is that this displacement . . . is not left to arbitrary psychical choice . . ."

Sigmund Freud

called them "parapraxes," from the Greek meaning "another action." Such slips of the tongue, or linguistic *faux pas*, were random expressions of unconscious processes in otherwise normal individuals.

For Freud, every little error contained potentiality, whether making a wrong turn while driving a car, dialing a wrong phone number, or misspelling an unfamiliar word. "In the same way that psychoanalysis makes use of dream interpretation," he once said, "it also profits by the study of numerous little slips and mistakes which people make." So is it possible that a Freudian slip is nothing more than a mistake or a lapse in concentration? After all, even Freud once told a student who asked him if there were an underlying psychological need to smoke a cigar: "Sometimes, a cigar . . . is just a cigar." **JMa**

Sigmund Freud as a young man, photographed with his fiancée, Martha Bernays; they married in 1886.

News from Nowhere
William Morris

A utopian novel inspired by the socialism and social science of Karl Marx

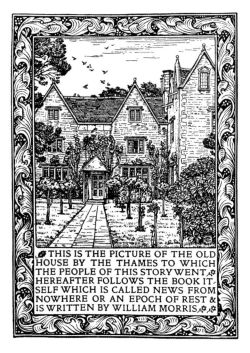

THIS IS THE PICTURE OF THE OLD HOUSE BY THE THAMES TO WHICH THE PEOPLE OF THIS STORY WENT. HEREAFTER FOLLOWS THE BOOK ITSELF WHICH IS CALLED NEWS FROM NOWHERE OR AN EPOCH OF REST & IS WRITTEN BY WILLIAM MORRIS.

⬆ The frontispiece of William Morris's *News from Nowhere* (1890) featured an engraving by W. H. Hooper of Kelmscott Manor, Oxfordshire, Morris's home from 1871 until his death in 1896.

"A map of the world that does not include Utopia is not worth even glancing at ... Progress is the realization of Utopias."

Oscar Wilde, *The Soul of Man under Socialism* (1891)

News from Nowhere or An Epoch of Rest is a utopian romance set in a future Britain, written in the light of Marxist ideals as interpreted by Arts and Crafts artist and socialist thinker William Morris (1834–96). The book was published in 1890.

The word "utopia," coined by Sir Thomas Moore (1478–1535), has a double meaning, being derived from the Greek *eu-tropos* (a good place) and *ou-tropos* (no place). This etymology underlines the question demanded by all such descriptions of society: can any utopia ever really exist?

Originally published as a serial in *Commonweal*, a newspaper of the Socialist League, *News from Nowhere* tells the story of a Victorian man, William Guest, who is transported to a future world. Journeying along the River Thames, he meets a variety of individuals and groups who are living according to Morris's interpretation of the Marxist ideal. Capitalism has been abolished in favor of a cooperative socialist society in which private property, the class system, marriage, formal education, poverty, and most crimes do not exist. In the community of the future, everyone is happily engaged in activities necessary for the continued functioning of society. Work is consciously done for the benefit of all and for that reason it is fulfilling and creative.

Central to Morris's depiction of Britain in the twenty-first century is the concept of returning to a pastoral, pre-industrialized age, in which factory towns such as Manchester have ceased to exist and state control has disappeared. *News from Nowhere* was written as a response to *Looking Backward: 2000–1887* (1888), a science fiction novel by U.S. author Edward Bellamy (1850–98). Bellamy's work is set in a technologically advanced future in which human labor has been reduced by increased mechanization and the state works to make life easier. **PBr**

Subsidiarity
Pope Leo XIII

The belief that government should only do what individuals or private groups cannot

Although the idea of subsidiarity only entered the popular lexicon in the twentieth century, it was already old and well developed in Western political thought well before that time. The term "subsidiarity," derived from the Latin *subsidium*, means "support, help, or assistance." The concept asserts that a matter, situation, or problem ought to be handled by the lowest or least centralized authority capable of handling it effectively. The principle of subsidiarity was first formally presented in the *Rerum Novarum* (1891) of Pope Leo XIII (1810–1903). This encyclical on capital and labor was primarily concerned with working conditions and was an attempt to articulate a middle course between laissez-faire capitalism and the various forms of communism.

The principle of subsidiarity was further developed in the *Quadragesimo Anno* encyclical of Pope Pius XI (1857–1939) in 1931, written in response to the rise of totalitarianism, and it was also influential in the Solidarity (Solidarność) movement in Poland that emerged in the 1980s, led by Lech Wałęsa. Subsidiarity is now best known as a foundational principle of European Union (EU) law, which means that the EU may only make laws or otherwise act in cases in which the action of individual member countries proves insufficient to settle a matter satisfactorily. Subsidiarity was formally established in EU law by the Treaty of Maastricht, signed by the twelve member states in 1992 and enforced in 1993.

Subsidiarity is now an organizing principle of decentralization within the EU, and represents a careful and influential attempt to balance the maintenance of the autonomy of member units with a recognition of their practical imperfections when it comes to achieving certain ends. The concept has also found applications in the fields of political science, cybernetics, management, and the military. **JE**

S. S. LE PAPE LÉON XIII

⬆ An edition of the daily Parisian newspaper *Le Petit Journal*, featuring Pope Leo XIII on the front cover. It is dated August 15, 1891, shortly after Pope Leo XIII issued his *Rerum Novarum*.

"[Subsidiarity] is a fundamental principle of social philosophy, fixed and unchangeable, that one should not withdraw from individuals and commit to the community what they can accomplish by their own enterprise and industry."

Pope Pius XI, *Quadragesimo Anno* encyclical (1931)

Kinetoscope
William Dickson

An object that enabled a single viewer to enjoy a show of moving images

Following the invention of the camera by Thomas Edison (1847–1931), he and his employed assistant, inventor William Dickson (1860–1935), started work on the kinetoscope, a machine that allowed a single viewer to watch through a magnifying viewfinder as up to 50 feet (15 m) of moving looped film ran through the machine, providing the illusion of moving images. Edison conceptualized the invention, while Dickson was responsible for its practical development. The prototype was completed in 1891. From 1893, viewers could watch footage of circus-style tricks for a nickel in Edison's specially built Black Maria film studio, or kinetographic theater. The studio was also used to make the photographic strips; it was built on a revolving platform to catch the correct amount of sunlight from the retractable roof.

Similar technology went into Edison's kinetograph, an early motion-picture camera. The motion picture was improved upon by the Lumière brothers in 1895; they named their version the cinématographe. It combined a camera, printer, and projector, and was far more lightweight than Edison's kinetograph. Another distinction of the cinématographe was the Lumières' decision to utilize intermittent movement in the design, whereas Edison had attempted to perfect continuous movement. In the event, Edison's company, unable to succeed in producing a workable motion-picture projector on its own, purchased Thomas Armat's phantascope instead in 1896, renaming it the vitascope. The Vitascope went on to become the first commercially successful motion-picture projector in the United States.

Edison's idea, made real by William Dickson and improved by the Lumière brothers, gave rise to the technology that has underwritten a number of our contemporary technologies. Without them our world would be a dramatically different place. **JE**

A man watching a film on a kinetoscope, through a peephole window at the top of the device. ↑

Artistic Symbolism
Paul Gauguin

Art that features symbols to express the artist's inner world, dreams, and spirituality

In March 1891, an article by French Symbolist poet and art critic Albert Aurier (1865–92) appeared in the periodical *Le Mercure de France*. Titled "Le Symbolisme en Peinture—Paul Gauguin," it described the psychologically complex but visually simplified and non-naturalistic painting style of the French artist Paul Gauguin (1848–1903) as "artistic Symbolism."

Symbolism in the arts was already long established, having been inaugurated by the poetry of Charles Baudelaire (1821–67). The Symbolist movement in the visual arts had been inspired by the French Symbolist writers and poets of the 1880s, who believed that words paralleled nature rather than imitated it. Artistic or pictorial Symbolism was a reaction against realism, which attempted a exact and direct representation of nature. The Symbolist artists saw subjective expression as a more valid approach to representation than objective reproduction of exact forms. Their works contained elements of dreams and the imagination, presented to the viewer through recognizable symbols. The artists used line, broad strokes of color, and simplified form to reflect and emphasize their inner emotional lives.

Gauguin and Spaniard Pablo Picasso (1881–1973) were outstanding artists of the movement. Gauguin traveled to the South Sea Islands and produced numerous Symbolist works there, including the painting *Where Do We Come From? What Are We? Where Are We Going?* (1897–98), which demonstrates the standard elements of his visual style: darkly outlined forms, flat areas of bright color, and an idiosyncratic use of personal symbols. Gauguin likened his paintings to Symbolist poems as defying easy explanation. The visually simplified but psychologically dense works of Picasso's "Blue Period" (1901–04), also featuring dark outlines but with a narrow palette of blue and blue-green, are also examples of the Symbolist style. **PBr**

Sense and Reference
Gottlob Frege

A theory that distinguishes between the sense and reference of signs in language

The German philosopher and mathematician Gottlob Frege (1848–1925), in his paper "Über Sinn und Bedeutung" (On Sense and Reference, 1892), explained how the words "sense" and "reference" represent two different aspects of a term's meaning. Sense usually refers to how we perceive an object or the degree of information we are given about it, while reference is the indicated object itself. Frege, however, objected to the notion that the meaning of a term is nothing more than its constituent reference, and postulated that a proper name is also composed of what he called its sense, in that it possesses an aspect which differentiates it from another object that has the same name. An example would be, "The leader of the United States' Democratic Party in 2011" and "the president of the United States in

"The sense of a proper name is grasped by everyone who knows the language ..."

Gottlob Frege, philosopher

2011": the two statements are not alike in sense, but the reference, Barack Obama, remains the same.

Frege was interested in establishing whether there is only a relationship between objects, or whether that relationship extends to include the names and signs we attribute to them. People may have differing recollections of sense, such as a feeling or a mood, that are associated with their memory of an object. For example, two people may look at the moon through a telescope but have differing recollections of what they saw, depending upon how obscured their view was and other random variables. Then there is the problem of common names, such as the morning star. For anyone looking at this star, their sense of it will be incorrect if they are ignorant of the fact that the morning and evening star are one in the same. **BS**

Universal Suffrage
New Zealand

All adult citizens have the right to vote, regardless of sex, race, and social status

The idea of universal suffrage, that all adult citizens ought to have the right to vote irrespective of race, sex, belief, wealth, and social status, gained credence with the rise of representative governments in parts of Europe, the United States, and independent Latin American nations. In some countries, the idea of universal suffrage seemed to be an organic extension of representative government, but in many others the concept of universal suffrage was far from intuitive. Consequently, the implementation of universal suffrage often lagged significantly behind the extent to which it had spread in theory.

While some early constitutions guaranteed suffrage to all men (but not women), the founders of most of the first representative systems of government

"The struggle for woman suffrage [is] no white woman's struggle ..."

Carrie Chapman Catt, woman's suffrage leader

intended representative government to benefit propertied men specifically; in some countries, such as the United States, and even more specifically, it was to benefit white propertied men. Such emphasis placed significant barriers (factual or legal) between the institutions of government and women, the poor, and people who were not white.

Universal suffrage, a powerful idea that most now accept as common sense, was long in the making. Votes for women arrived late in the Old World, and were ratified only in 1920 in the United States overall. The first country in which suffrage was extended irrespective of gender was New Zealand, in 1893. Gradually following suit were Australia in 1901, Finland in 1907, and Norway in 1913. Without universal suffrage, the political landscape would look very different today. **JE**

British suffragettes campaign for women's rights and the vote in London, 1908. ➡

Anomie
Émile Durkheim

The theory that a dysfunctional labor market could lead to social decay

Sociology's concept of anomie, first mentioned by French philosopher Jean-Marie Guyau (1854–88) in his book *The Non-religion of the Future* (1885), was used to describe, in broad terms, a society operating without any fixed laws. The phrase was later popularized by the French sociologist Émile Durkheim (1858–1917) in *The Division of Labor in Society* (1893). Here, its definition was broadened to refer to the increasing failure of guild labor collectives to meet the needs of an evolving middle class; inertia was retarding their ability to change and adapt in the industrialized world.

However, Durkheim took the idea one step further, claiming that anomie could progress beyond guild collectives and labor markets and enter society proper. Then all social norms could become confused

"The state of mind of the individual who has been pulled up from his moral roots."
Robert MacIver, sociologist

or unclear, a state he referred to as "normlessness." Anomie begins, according to Durkheim, with economic deregulation. If left unchecked, it can create a situation in which social norms no longer determine the functioning of a society. In the case of the individual, this "normlessness" or sense of alienation could lead to self-harm, which Durkheim would later describe in his book *Suicide* (1897).

The U.S. sociologist Robert MacIver (1882–1970) later characterized individuals beset with anomie as having their sense of attachment to society "broken down." Durkheim himself asserted in *Suicide* that anomie was capable of creating what he labeled a "permanent disease of industrial society" and the "negation of morality," in which state we could not moderate our desires or limit our needs and passions. **BS**

Minimum Wage
New Zealand

A legally enforced minimum amount that any worker can expect to be paid per hour

The idea of a minimum wage was first campaigned for in the 1890s by a group of sweatshop workers (known as "sweaters") who protested bitterly at the conditions in their Australian workplace. It was in New Zealand, though, that a law recognizing workers' rights was first introduced in 1894, and only in 1896 did Australia attend to the matter by establishing wage boards. The United Kingdom set up its own, similar system in 1909, and boards were adopted by Massachusetts in 1912. However, it was not until 1938 that the United States established the Fair Labor Standards Act for all workers.

Setting the lowest legal hourly wage payable to any worker served two purposes: it reduced the chances of civil unrest, and it also worked against poverty and created tolerable living conditions for workers in low-paid jobs. In that sense, the legislation was enacted in tacit recognition of the universality of the human right to fair treatment at work. The actual minimum rate is decided either through collective bargaining or by a judgment from government. It varies according to geography, economic conditions, and the workforce's degree of political power, among other factors.

Globalization has somewhat undermined the political impact of minimum-wage legislation because purely profit-driven industries now move factories from strict to less strict jurisdictions. Opinion has polarized between those who advocate a fair wage as a minimum standard and those who see intervention in the market place as detrimental meddling. Detractors claim that a minimum wage drives up costs and threatens business closures, which in turn cause unemployment rates to rise. Proponents hold that, by protecting a minimum standard of living, the legislation enables those who want to improve their situations to do so. This springs workers from the poverty trap and leads toward the creation of a better educated workforce. **LW**

X-rays
Wilhelm Röntgen

A type of electromagnetic radiation, used in medicine to pass through soft tissue and provide an image of a hard structure within, such as part of the skeleton

Wilhelm Röntgen (1845–1923) was professor of physics at the University of Würzburg, Germany, when, in 1895, he was passing electron beams, known at the time as cathode rays, through a gas container at very low pressure. He discovered that under the right conditions—involving a darkroom, a darkened discharge tube, a fluorescent screen, and a paper plate treated with barium platinocyanide—some materials appeared to become partially transparent, allowing an image to be created on a photographic plate. Denser materials appeared more clearly on the image than lighter ones; in one image, the hand of Röntgen's wife revealed her bones and a ring in black, with a light grey shadow for the surrounding flesh. Röntgen named the new phenomenon the X-ray, meaning "unknown ray." It was many years before scientists learned how the process worked, and neither were the dangers of high-dosage X-rays at first understood.

Substances such as metals and calcium in bones absorb radiation more readily than soft tissue, and so the X-ray quickly became a useful tool for medical examinations. Using X-ray technology, doctors could look for a broken bone or swallowed hard object, and check for cancerous lumps or even lesions caused by tuberculosis. X-rays revolutionized the way in which doctors considered the diagnosis process itself, and opened up many new avenues of scientific exploration.

Röntgen's discovery laid the foundation for such diagnostic technology as ultrasound and electromagnetic scanners, which look inside the body rather than making deductions from what can be seen on the outside. Throughout the twentieth century, medical practitioners came to rely more and more on technological aids to back up, or even inform, their diagnoses, rather than using experience and the observation of symptoms to arrive at them. **JF**

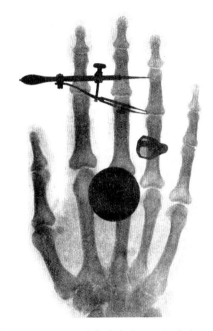

⬆ An X-ray of the hand of Wilhelm Röntgen's wife, Anna, taken in 1896. Anna's ring, a pair of compasses, and a circular object absorb the X-rays more than skin or bone, being made of metal.

"Treat the patient, not the X-ray."

James M. Hunter, quoted in Arnold Melnick,
Melnick on Writing (2012)

Art Nouveau
Siegfried Bing

An artistic style characterized by free form, sinuous line, and organic motifs

The Salon de l'Art Nouveau, opened in 1895 by art dealer Siegfried (aka Samuel) Bing (1838–1905) in Paris, was the first showcase for the "new" art style sweeping both Europe and the United States from 1890 onward. Before Art Nouveau, the late nineteenth century had been characterized by a balancing act between the strict order and historicism of the Neoclassicists and the emotional and visual chaos of the Romantics. Looking to the natural world but moving beyond it for free-flowing, organic form allowed the practitioners of the "new art" to create graceful works that built on traditional styles but also transformed them.

Some critics trace the visual style back to Celtic manuscript illumination with its interlacing knot patterns, others to the Rococo love of the curvilinear

". . . the curve undulating, flowing, and interplaying with others . . ."

Nikolaus Pevsner, *Pioneers of Modern Design* (1936)

and extreme elaboration. Precursors include the works of English Aesthetic movement illustrator Aubrey Beardsley (1862–98), Arts and Crafts designer William Morris (1834–96), and ukiyo-e Japanese printmakers, such as Katsushika Hokusai (c. 1760–1849).

In his book *Pioneers of Modern Design* (1936), Nikolaus Pevsner (1902–83) suggests that Art Nouveau was the transitional style to the modern era. It certainly incorporated many of the philosophical and societal trends of the period from 1890 to 1910. Whether it was a reflection of artists wanting to break free of societal norms or a quest for aesthetic purity removed from moral judgments, the explorations of Art Nouveau touched everything from graphic design to furniture and began the modern era, foreshadowing later modern trends such as abstraction and Surrealism. **PBr**

Daylight Saving Time (DST)
George Vernon Hudson

A proposal to create more hours of daylight by altering clocks

English-born New Zealand entomologist and astronomer George Vernon Hudson (1867–1946) began collecting insects at the age of nine. In Wellington, New Zealand, he found employment as a shift worker, which left him just enough daylight hours to continue building his insect collection. There was, however, only one problem: in Hudson's opinion, there were not quite enough daylight hours available for the proper and measured pursuit of his beloved insects. Something had to be done, so in October 1895 he presented a paper to the Wellington Philosophical Society suggesting that it might be prudent to consider a seasonal adjustment in time.

Hudson proposed changing clocks at the equinox, two hours forward in October, and two hours back in

"Everyone appreciates the long light evenings [and] laments their shrinkage."

William Willett, *The Waste of Daylight* (1907)

March. Although his idea had already been anticipated by the U.S. inventor Benjamin Franklin (1706–90), who proposed the concept in his essay "An Economical Project for Diminishing the Cost of Light" (1784), Franklin's paper was really more a lighthearted satire than any concrete proposal, and it is generally thought that Hudson's idea represented the first real attempt to make Daylight Saving Time (DST) a reality. Hudson's paper, unfortunately, was greeted with disdain. "Wholly unscientific and impractical," said some; "completely out of the question," said others, to be considering altering a system that had been working perfectly.

DST was eventually adopted in Germany during World War I (1914–18) to save fuel expended in the powering of artificial lighting. It is now in use in more than seventy countries throughout the world. **BS**

An Art Nouveau poster designed in 1898 by Henri Privat-Livemont, advertising Absinthe Robette.

Multiverse
William James

The concept that our universe is one of many, all of them expanding infinitely

The "multiverse" is a term for all that is real and exists, and has been postulated in astronomy, philosophy, cosmology, and even science fiction ever since it was first coined in 1895 by the U.S. philosopher and psychologist William James (1842–1910), in his essay "Is Life Worth Living?" However, James was referring to the multiplicity of moral choices that humans face, and for him the multiverse was not a concept of cosmology.

The term was nevertheless picked up by astronomers and today it is used to describe the existence of multiple universes, the totality of all physical reality. The multiverse hypothesis puts forward the possibility that the universe we see around us, and that stretches infinitely beyond the boundary of what we are capable of observing, is only one of countless universes, all independent of one another. Together, these encompass all that exists—because they are infinite, there can be nothing beyond, other than, or containing them.

Mathematical models in the field of theoretical physics are increasingly coming down in support of the multiverse theory. The models include string theory and the theory of eternal inflation, the latter of which holds that the expansion of the universe will never end and will inevitably lead to—and has been leading to ever since the Big Bang—a multiplicity of universes. Recent observations in the realm of subatomic reality also indicate the likelihood of a multiverse. But not everyone is convinced. South African cosmologist George Ellis (b. 1939), writing in *Scientific American* in August 2011, said: "All in all the case for the multiverse is inconclusive," and is "more a concept than a theory."

Empirical evidence for the multiverse will forever elude us, because all that we can measure and observe is ensconced well within the universe that we inhabit. The multiverse is likely to remain nothing more than a tantalizing conundrum. **BS**

A conceptual artwork showing multiple universes forming from black holes following the Big Bang.

1895

Crowd Psychology
Gustave Le Bon

The creation of a branch of social psychology, focused on crowd behavior

Theory on the behavior of crowds, going back as far as Plato, originally assumed that crowd behavior was that of an unthinking mob. Substantive study of crowds in the social sciences was reinvigorated by *The Origins of Contemporary France* (1875/1893), by the conservative historian Hippolyte Taine (1828–93). But it was in *The Psychology of Crowds* (1895) that French sociologist Gustave Le Bon (1841–1931) first mined the writings of existing theorists on crowd behavior to create the new discipline of crowd psychology.

Le Bon listed three primary elements of crowd behavior, including, first, a unity of collective identification, giving a sense of limitless power; second, the creation of a sensitivity to emotional appeals

due to that unity; and third, collective intelligence in the crowd dropping to that of the lowest common denominator. Crowds, said Le Bon, are easily subject to collective hallucinations, suggestions originated by individuals in the crowd that are thoughtlessly and contagiously adopted throughout the whole.

Le Bon's theory of crowd psychology received little significant challenge until the later works of sociologists such as George Rudé (1910–93) and E. P. Thompson (1924–93). Thompson's studies of the actual behavior of crowds focused primarily on the social context and demands of crowds, while Rudé looked at the composition of existing crowds. Their studies challenged views of the crowd as essentially primal and irrational, and instead showed crowds as often being composed of relatively better-off members of communities who are responding to specific threats to their communities, at the same time acting on cultural assumptions that are widely shared.

The study of the psychology and behavior of crowds had long been merely speculation before Le Bon, whose influential studies integrated the study of crowd behavior into formal social science. **JE**

↑ College students collectively raise their arms and shout at a job-hunting ceremony in Tokyo, 2011.

Nobel Prize
Alfred Nobel

An annual series of awards in five categories designed to reward human excellence and make the world a better place, underwritten by vast profits generated by war

⬆ Alfred Nobel's wealth derived primarily from his work on explosives. In addition to dynamite, he invented and patented gelignite, and ballistite, improved by the British as cordite.

"The whole of my remaining realizable estate shall … constitute a fund, the interest on which shall be annually distributed in the form of prizes to those who, during the preceding year, shall have conferred the greatest benefit upon mankind."

Alfred Nobel's Last Will and Testament (1895)

"When two armies of equal strength can annihilate each other in an instant, then all civilized nations will retreat and disband their troops." So said Swedish chemist, engineer, and inventor Alfred Nobel (1833–96), the man who gave the world dynamite, just one of his 355 patents. Nobel was deluded in thinking that his dynamite could bring an end to warfare, but he also— to "relieve his conscience", as Albert Einstein would later say—bequeathed the fortune he had made from making dynamite and other activities to the world in support of the ideals of the Nobel Foundation.

When Alfred's brother Ludvig died in 1888, a Paris newspaper erroneously published the obituary it had prepared for Alfred under the heading "The Merchant of Death Is Dead." The armaments manufacturer, stung by the denunciation, became determined to leave a legacy for good. In his final will, Nobel allocated monies from his vast empire to be divided annually among five recipients whose work had been distinguished in the categories of physics, chemistry, physiology and/or medicine, literature, and "one part to the person who shall have done the most or the best work for fraternity between nations, for the abolition or reduction of standing armies and for the holding and promotion of peace congresses"—the Nobel Peace Prize. It would be five years after his death before the first awards were given, due to the organizational and bureaucratic difficulties involved.

There have been a few errors along the way. In 1926 the Nobel Prize in Medicine went to Danish scientist Johannes Fibiger (1867–1928) for his "discovery" that roundworms led to cancer (they do not). But in a world where more than 300 various "peace prizes" are awarded every year, it is still the Nobel Peace Prize that continues to hold aloft the brightest hope for good in a changing and often fractured world. **BS**

The Baldwin Effect
James Mark Baldwin

The theory that adaptations of behavior can affect evolutionary change

In his paper titled "A New Factor in Evolution" (1896), U.S. philosopher and psychologist James Mark Baldwin (1861–1934) proposed that individually acquired characteristics might indeed become hereditary through reinforcement by relevant genetic dispositions in a given species. This view helped to create a bridge between neo-Darwinian and neo-Lamarckian schools in consideration of natural selection.

The standard explanation of natural selection refers to random mutations producing physical traits advantageous for survival and procreation. Baldwin proposed that capacities for behaviors entirely contingent on particularities of the organism's environment were also a factor. If, for example, an organism were able to develop effective cooperative relationships, and such relationships were necessary for the survival of the species as a whole, then its ability to engage in cooperative activity would add a selective pressure for genetic predispositions in other organisms. Those organisms that were able to express this advantageous behavior would pass on their "new" capacities, to the eventual extent that such capacities could become embedded as instinctual in the species.

Shifts in a society's natural infrastructure, or even its cultural values, may also provide selection pressures that make certain behavioral capacities beneficial. One of the more prevalent criticisms of this notion is that, as such factors become more complex and socially contingent, there is not sufficient time for the advantageous capacities relating to them to become selected in a species. This leads to broader discussions concerning the extent to which the adaptations of organisms evidencing the Baldwin Effect are hereditary or non-hereditary—and thus how distinct Baldwin's account of natural selection, with the Baldwin Effect addition, is from Darwin's "standard" model. **JD**

Fascism
Gaetano Mosca and Maurice Barrès

An authoritarian, totalitarian political ideology exalting national and/or racial identity

At the end of the nineteenth century, European nations faced an unsettled sense of purpose and a perceived crisis of civilization that prompted a reevaluation of political organization. In his work *The Ruling Class* (1896), Italian lawyer and political scientist Gaetano Mosca (1858–1941) asserted that, while governments claim to represent the majority, society is almost invariably ruled by an organized minority of elite political actors. This insight promoted an elitism that, while still applicable within democracy, led to an increased empowerment of nationalistic leaders in Italy. Concurrently, the writings of French novelist and politician Maurice Barrès (1862–1923) promoted ethnic nationalism and authoritarianism as the hope of reestablishing identity, stability, and power to France. Barrès's work also

"The individual is nothing, society is everything ..."

Maurice Barrès, novelist and politician

discussed the charismatic embodiment of a nation's spirit in its leadership, common in fascist rulers.

Fascism emphasizes the supremacy of the state and the subordination of individuals to a national identity and purpose. Often, this occurs alongside a sense of victimization, grievance, or a perceived cultural decline. Fascist regimes mobilize social and economic development around the purpose of rebuilding strength and identity. The totalitarian and authoritarian stance of fascism entails that its methods for pursuing national strength consistently involve displays of power and violent suppression of political opponents. Three of the most prominent European fascist regimes of the twentieth century were led by Benito Mussolini in Italy, Adolf Hitler in Germany, and Francisco Franco in Spain. **JD**

Form Follows Function
Louis Sullivan

What happens inside a building should be manifested by its exterior structure

In his article "The Tall Building Artistically Considered," published in *Lippincott's* magazine (No. 57) in 1896, U.S. architect Louis Sullivan (1856–1924) wrote the following: "It is the pervading law that all things organic, and inorganic, of all things physical and metaphysical, of all things human and all things superhuman, of all true manifestations of the head, the heart, of the soul, that the life is recognizable in its expression, that form ever follows function. This is the law."

Sullivan's original intent, especially in designs such as the Carson Pirie Scott store (1899, 1903–4) in Chicago, was that the purpose of a building should be manifested by its exterior structure and ornament. For Sullivan, ornament should not merely imitate past styles, but be a new amalgam of geometry and nature.

"Form and function should be one, joined in a spiritual union."

Frank Lloyd Wright, architect

The truncated phrase "form follows function" was incorrectly co-opted by Austrian Adolf Loos (1870–1933) in 1908, and used to justify the International Modernist aesthetic (post World War II), which stripped buildings of their ornament, reducing them to flat, linear boxes.

U.S. architect Frank Lloyd Wright (1867–1959) would second Sullivan's intention in his own architectural practice with his "total design" conceptions for domestic and business buildings. For example, in Fallingwater (Kaufmann Residence), the siting over a waterfall and the opening and closing of certain doors and windows help to circulate cool air throughout the structure. Wright morphed organic shapes to geometric forms in projects as diverse as his long, low Prairie-style homes and his cast-concrete, Mayan-inspired, "California Romanza" Hollyhock House. **PBr**

Christian Fundamentalism
United States

A movement arguing that the Bible is the literal and factually inerrant word of God

By the late nineteenth century, many U.S. Protestants were growing uncomfortable with ideas held by modernist Christian theologians, who held that the Bible was a collected work written by many authors, and one that contained information of an allegorical or poetic, rather than literal, nature. Largely in response to the modernists, and to scientific discoveries that were pushing Christian thinkers to adopt a less supernatural theological view, conservative Protestants embraced what they saw as the fundamental Christian beliefs of the Niagara Bible Conference of 1897.

By 1915, a series of booklets, titled *The Fundamentals*, had been published about these conservative ideas, giving the movement its name. No single person is associated with originating the concept, but its

"The world . . . needs to be turned upside down in order to be right side up."

Billy Sunday, evangelist

adherents believed, among other things, that the Bible was literally true, that salvation was only possible through a belief that Jesus Christ died for the sins of mankind, and that only fundamentalists held an accurate view of Christianity, and that Jesus's imminent return to Earth was readily apparent.

Christian fundamentalism has had a large impact on modern U.S. religious, political, and social institutions. Though there is no one denomination or unifying doctrine, fundamentalists view the inerrancy of the Bible as paramount, and hold it their duty to defend it against all competing ideas. Fundamentalist Christians are largely responsible for the modern Creationism movement, and, beginning predominantly in the 1970s, have played a major role in shaping the modern U.S. conservative political movement. **MT**

Frank Lloyd Wright's Fallingwater House (1938), with cantilevered concrete echoing natural rock.

Montessori Education
Maria Montessori

An educational approach emphasizing independent learning through activity and personal discovery, rather than being taught verbally in the classroom

⬆ Italian educational reformer Maria Montessori, who evolved the Montessori method of teaching children, is pictured during a visit to the Gatehouse School in London, England, in 1951.

"Education is a natural process carried out by the child and is not acquired by listening to words but by experiences in the environment."

Maria Montessori

Italian educator Maria Montessori (1870–1952) began developing her educational philosophy and methodology in 1897 and opened her first classroom in Rome in 1907. With a deep integration of child psychology and pedagogy, Montessori built her approach around accommodating and enhancing a child's natural mental and sociological development. Rather than resort to rote, dictated learning, Montessori education aims to provide a prepared environment within which students have the freedom to engage and learn according to their natural tendencies.

A central feature of Montessori education is the enabling of student choice among educational activities in a mixed-age classroom setting. This setting is prepared with simplicity, cleanliness, and order, and with materials and opportunities that fit with students' "planes of development." The planes of development are Montessori's categories of progressive human growth, including birth to six years, six to twelve years, twelve to eighteen years, and eighteen to twenty-four years. Montessori education aims to tailor pedagogy to these planes of development, always emphasizing free exploration within a prepared environment.

The constructivist or "discovery" framework of Montessori education is one of its most distinctive and challenging features. By empowering students to choose their own path through the educational landscape, learning is developed through a student's trial and error, experimentation, and activity, alongside the teacher's creation of an engaging environment. This approach resists the desire to standardize education, delineate a uniform curriculum, and create tests and measurements of information bases. Constructivist philosophies of education such as Montessori's retain a certain independence from the "one size fits all" mentality of some other educational systems. **JD**

Connectionism
Edward L. Thorndike

An attempt to explain human behavior using artificial neural networks

Connectionism is a theory that states that behavioral responses to certain stimuli are established by a process of trial and error that affects neural connections between those stimuli and the most satisfying responses to them. It is applied in psychology, neuroscience, and linguistics to stimulate cognitive processes, such as perception, memory, learning, and motor skills. The crux of connectionism is that the mind operates through a variety of simple and uniform units that form parts of a great network. For example, in the brain, the units are neurons and the connections between them are synapses.

Connectionism was formerly known as parallel distributed processing (PDP), a concept that was prefigured in the works of the earliest psychologists. The first proponent of connectionism as it is now understood is generally agreed to have been U.S. psychologist Edward L. Thorndike (1874–1949), who discussed it in his doctoral thesis of 1898 (later published in 1911 as *Animal Intelligence*). His work was developed by two Americans, neurophysiologist Warren McCulloch (1898–1969) and mathematician Walter Pitts (1923–69), whose influential treatise of 1943 likened the brain to a computing machine and each of its component neurons to a simple digital processor.

Although some critics claim that connectionism is reductionist, the theory has been applied in the field of artificial intelligence and used in the construction of robots, which require the following eight functions: processing units; a stimulus to activate them; a means of output; connections between the units; a means of spreading the process (propagation); a method of converting inputs into new forms; a capacity to learn (remember what has happened and act on the basis of experience); and an environment in which all these activities can occur. **GL**

Space Rocket
Konstantin Tsiolkovsky

The development of a theory for using rocket engines in space

It was on a visit to Paris in the 1880s, while still a provincial school teacher in rural Russia, that Konstantin Tsiolkovsky (1857–1935) looked at the Eiffel Tower and imagined constructing a platform 24,854 miles (40,000 km) high, from the top of which objects could be launched into geosynchronous orbit around the Earth. It was Tsiolkovsky who proposed the first ever theory of rocket propulsion in 1898, and even suggested the use of liquid propellants, an idea finally realized in 1926 by the U.S. physicist and inventor Robert Goddard, who became the first man to launch a liquid-fueled rocket. In 1903 Tsiolkovsky became the first to argue that the exhaust velocity of a rocket's escaping gases would determine its range and speed—the so-called Tsiolkovsky rocket equation, and

> *"Tsiolkovsky's … projects did not attract the attention they deserved."*
>
> G. A. Tokaty, aerodynamicist

in the 1920s he advocated manned platforms in Earth's orbit to be used as staging posts for interplanetary journeys. He even foresaw the development of the multistage rocket.

Tsiolkovsky also wrote science fiction. Unable to confine his enthusiasm for space flight to textbooks and journals, he effusively wrote in 1911: "To place one's feet on the soil of asteroids, to lift a stone from the moon with your hand, to construct moving stations in ether space, to organize inhabited rings around Earth, moon and sun, to observe Mars at the distance of several tens of miles, to descend to its satellites or even to its own surface—what could be more insane!" Yuri Gagarin may have been the first Soviet citizen and the first human being in space, but it was the largely unheralded ideas of Tsiolkovsky that got him there. **BS**

1898

Theory of Radioactivity
Henri Becquerel/Pierre and Marie Curie

The scientific study of particle emissions from atoms with nuclear instability

From the end of the nineteenth century, the theory of radioactivity developed into one of the most important fields of scientific study in history. In November of 1895, Wilhelm Röntgen discovered x-rays, and months later Henri Becquerel's (1852–1908) related studies of phosphorescence led him to posit spontaneous radiation as the explanation of the effects of uranium on photographic plates. As other natural elements were discovered to have similar properties of radiation, Marie Curie (1867–1934) coined the term "radioactivity" in 1898 to name the emerging theory of radiation. In 1903, Becquerel, Pierre Curie (1859–1906), and Marie Curie won the Nobel Prize in Physics for their discoveries.

Radioactive decay involves the loss of energy by an unstable atom. This emission was classified early

"Radioactivity ... is not to be hated and feared, but accepted and controlled."

Ralph Eugene Lapp, physicist

on based on the size and strength of rays observed. Further discoveries revealed that radioactivity was found to occur in terms of particles, such as neutron, proton, and electron emissions, and also in terms of the transitional decay of a nucleus that does not result in transmutation into a new element. The most common example of this latter form is the release of gamma rays, which occur along with other forms of particle decay.

Radioactivity was further explicated by the work of Ernest Rutherford, who is mainly responsible for understanding atomic structure. The models and postulates provided by atomic theory and the application of radioactive discoveries led to major advances and inventions in the twentieth century, including the harnessing of nuclear energy for power and medical treatments such as chemotherapy. **JD**

1899

Juvenile Courts
Illinois Legislature

A court devoted to administering justice solely to children and adolescents

Societies have long recognized the problem of juvenile misbehavior, while at the same time grappling with the problem of imposing legal consequences on problematic youths. In 1772 BCE the Babylonian Code of Hammurabi recognized that some crimes were particular to juveniles. Similar recognitions also existed in Jewish, Roman, and Islamic law, and by the fifth century CE, Roman law held that a child under the age of seven could not be held criminally liable. In the eleventh century, English common law recognized the principle of *parens patriae* (Latin for "parent of the nation"), which reflected the idea that the state could act as a substitute parent for a child in need of guidance or justice. However, it was only in 1899 that the city of Chicago, Illinois, created the first juvenile court to

"The children now love luxury; they have bad manners, contempt for authority ..."

Socrates, quoted by Plato

preside over cases in which a person under the age of sixteen had violated a state law or city ordinance.

A child is not a fully developed person, and the idea that a juvenile can form the requisite criminal intent to be held responsible for a crime has grown more complicated as humanity's understanding of child development has increased. Juvenile courts understand the importance of justice in a society, while at the same time recognizing that children need guidance and cannot be held as culpable as adults.

As juveniles become more involved in violent crimes, the juvenile justice system has faced growing scrutiny. Juvenile murders account for a relatively small number of murders, but they attract greater media attention. The juvenile justice system therefore faces ongoing challenges. **MT**

Marie Curie photographed in her laboratory in 1896, two years before her discovery of radioactivity. 1780–1899 **599**

Conspicuous Consumption
Thorstein Veblen

The purchase of goods and services for the sake of publicly exhibiting wealth or status

⬆ The overt display of luxury goods and services by the ruling classes in the late nineteenth century led Thorstein Veblen to formulate his economic theory of conspicuous consumption.

In his influential book *The Theory of the Leisure Class: An Economic Study in the Evolution of Institutions* published in 1899, Thorstein Veblen (1857–1929) identified a distinctive feature of the newly established upper class of the late nineteenth century and the rising middle class of the twentieth century: their accumulation of luxury goods and services for the expressed purpose of displaying prestige, wealth, and social status. Veblen, a U.S. economist and social scientist, viewed this phenomenon as a negative symptom of the new rich that would inhibit social adaptation to the necessities of the industrial age.

The intention for exhibition embodied in the idea of conspicuous consumption is in contrast to the securing of goods and services for their intrinsic value or their originally established purpose. Focusing on the "conspicuous" aspect of the term, conspicuous consumption can conceivably occur among members of any socio-economic class, from the richest to the poorest. Acquiring status indicators can happen in any social setting. Focusing on the "consumption" aspect of the term, conspicuous consumption relates to the purchase and display of goods beyond what is necessary, and applies primarily to the middle and upper classes, who then set patterns of social behavior and consumption that are imitated by others. In this respect, it is closely tied to consumerism.

One ramification of Veblen's insights into conspicuous consumption relates to the idea of a "luxury tax." Such a tax increases costs on goods and services that primarily serve as declarations of affluence, in order to raise revenue and redistribute wealth with little loss to consumers who purchase for the sake of status and not utility. It may also gradually reduce conspicuous consumption of such "positional goods," or "Veblen goods," which bear the namesake because demand for them increases as price increases. **JD**

> *"Conspicuous consumption of valuable goods is a means of reputability to the gentleman of leisure."*

Thorstein Veblen

Stream of Consciousness
William James

The theory that human conscience is an unending stream of continuous thought

Although the concept of the mind possessing a streaming consciousness can be found in early Buddhist texts, the first modern approach to the phenomenon was put forward by William James (1842–1910), one of the United States first recognized psychologists in his 1,200-word masterwork *The Principles of Psychology* in 1899. In this book James speaks of consciousness as being "unbroken" and states that there are no "gaps," or as he liked to say no "intrusive alien substances," that come along to distinguish or break up one period of consciousness from the next. For consciousness to be interrupted by gaps or intrusions, James thought, is like "expecting the eye to feel a gap of silence because it does not hear, or the ear to feel a gap of darkness because it does not see. So much," he said, "for the gaps that are unfelt."

Consciousness, rather than being "chopped up," was likened instead by James to a river or stream, a process that is ever-flowing even in the event of a sudden interruption, such as an explosion or losing one's footing and falling over. These sorts of things—a clap of thunder or the sound of a gunshot—are about as disconnected from our present thoughts as "a joint in bamboo is a break in the wood." The thunder clap is as intrinsically a part of our continuing, unbroken consciousness as the joint is a part of the bamboo in which it grows. James believed that our cognitive experiences overlap one another and are linked by what he called "fringes," subconscious tabs, which act as clasps that are necessary in binding our conscious thoughts together, and prevent us from living in a chaotic inner world of random, unrelated experiences.

James's theory influenced literature and became a narrative device to depict the multitudinous thoughts and feelings that pass through an individual's mind. James Joyce's *Ulysses* (1922) is one of the best-known examples of the stream of consciousness technique. **BS**

⬆ William James, who is generally accepted as the father of U.S. psychology, has influenced generations of thinkers with his masterwork *The Principles of Psychology* (1899).

"Like a bird's life, the stream of consciousness seems to be made up of an alternation of flights and perchings ..."

William James, *The Principles of Psychology* (1899)

Dream Interpretation
Sigmund Freud

The process of assigning meaning to dreams in order to unlock the unconscious

Dreams—imagined episodes or series of events that come to people's minds while they are asleep—have always defied interpretation. Ancient civilizations may have believed that dreams were prophetic: there are dreams that foretell the future in the Babylonian *Epic of Gilgamesh* (*c.* 2150 BCE), Homer's *Iliad* (seventh century BCE), and throughout the Old Testament of the Bible. However, it is uncertain whether the authors of these works were writing what they believed or merely conforming to literary conventions. Other cultures believed that dreams were supernatural visitations, which sought to explain matters that seemed incomprehensible while awake. The currency of such ideas declined during the Common Era, as it became generally accepted that dreams were manifestations—often in distorted form—of matters that had preoccupied the dreamer before falling asleep.

In 1899, Sigmund Freud (1856–1939), the founder of psychoanalysis, published *The Interpretation of Dreams*, in which he claimed that dreams are expressions of feelings and wishes that are repressed during wakefulness. (The idea that Freud stated in this work that all such thoughts are about sex, although widely credited, has no basis in the text.) The psychologist Carl Jung (1875–1961) then proposed that dreams could either be what Freud described or else expressions of what the dreamers most dreaded: sorting out which dream was which was one of the keys to self-knowledge.

More recently, some scientists have proposed that the function of dreams is purely biological—brainwaves activated by chemical activity in the body—and that no meaning should be attached to the images or messages that they may seem to contain. Dreams are products of the imagination; so, too, are some if not all interpretations thereof. **GL**

Henry Rousseau's painting *The Dream* (1910) is thought to portray the dream process. ⬆

1899

Duck-rabbit Illusion

Joseph Jastrow

An optical illusion used as a psychological test of human perception

Is it a duck, or is it a rabbit? Sketched by an unknown artist and first published in the Münich-based weekly satirical magazine *Fliegende Blätter* (Flying Leaves) on October 23, 1892 (and in the U.S. *Harper's Weekly* a month later), the duck-rabbit drawing was first used in 1899 to test how we perceive our environment by the U.S. psychologist Joseph Jastrow (1863–1944), who referred to it as a piece of "ingenious conceit."

The Jastrow version of the duck-rabbit illusion is technically more of an ambiguity than the original, more a reversible or "bistable" figure than a true illusion. But whatever you call it, it is one of the best-known images devised for testing a person's perceptive acumen, along with the Schroeder staircase, which simultaneously looks equally convincing the right way up and upside-down, and the Necker cube, which spontaneously reverses in perspective as it is viewed.

How does the duck-rabbit illusion work in terms of research? When scrutinized in a controlled situation, the eye tends to be led to the lines that compose the image, rather than to the image itself. It is the lines that we see and try to interpret, the image being the "lure." The lines are then seen alternately as representing a duck and/or a rabbit. It is a psychological tool, used to measure how we make sense of our environment by organizing incoming sensory stimuli.

Can interpretation of the image be used as a measure of intelligence? Is our speed at recognizing both images, our ability to flip our own perception easily from duck to rabbit, and vice versa, a measure of our own creativity? Studies have shown that test participants who are able to see both interpretations quickly tend to be more creative than those who initially struggle to make sense of the image; once the latter group "see" the image, they find it difficult to hold to any one interpretation. The duck becomes the rabbit, and the rabbit, the duck. **BS**

Consumerism

Thorstein Veblen

The economic view that the acquisition and consumption of goods is beneficial to society

While the desire for goods and services beyond mere necessity is a prevalent reality throughout history, Thorstein Veblen's (1857–1929) discussion in *The Theory of the Leisure Class* (1899) occurs in direct relation to the results of the Industrial Revolution. As automation and organization of labor increased productivity in the late nineteenth century, consumer goods became more available. Veblen saw an increasing demand for goods stemming from improved means and greater availability among the developing middle and upper classes in Europe, all of which led him to identify a societal trend toward consumption of goods as an end in itself.

Consumerism is closely tied to Veblen's notion of "conspicuous consumption," in which goods and services are acquired more as a display of wealth and status than

"Are these things really better than the things I already have?"

Chuck Palahniuk, novelist

for their utility. Consumerism goes further, proposing that it is good for members of a society to engage in continual expenditure and consumption, not merely to establish their class status but also to fuel the engines of the economy that contribute to consumer goods.

The impact of consumerism on Western societies has led to the development of strong businesses and massive economies, but also to an increased reliance on credit and debt. Marketing and brand promotion became major factors in economic growth largely because of the spread of conspicuous consumption. A common criticism of consumerism is its potential to lead to a devaluing of simplicity, utility, and institutions traditionally seen as holding intrinsic worth, in exchange for the continued accumulation of material goods for temporary satisfaction and perceived social status. **JD**

Hilbert's Axioms

David Hilbert

A set of assumptions proposed as the foundation of geometry

In his *Grundlagen der Geometrie* (The Foundations of Geometry), published in 1899, David Hilbert (1862–1943) developed twenty axioms intended to more adequately express Euclidian geometry. Euclid's original five axioms had long been viewed as incomplete and insufficiently rigorous. Hilbert's system begins with six primitive, undefined elements: three terms (point, straight line, plane) and three relations (betweenness—relating points; containment—relating points and straight lines, points and planes, and straight lines and planes; and congruence—relating line segments and angles). Hilbert organizes his twenty axioms into five groups. The eight Axioms of Incidence refer to the occurrence and relation of points, lines, and planes in terms of "containment." The four Axioms of

"… a game played according to certain rules with meaningless marks on paper."

David Hilbert on mathematics

Order discuss them primarily in light of the concept of "betweenness." The six Axioms of Congruence refer to the equivalence relations of the basic terms, while the Axiom Parallels define the concept of a parallel line in Euclidian geometry. Finally, Hilbert concludes with two Axioms of Continuity, also known individually as "Archimedes's Axiom" and "Linear Completeness."

Hilbert's Axioms evidenced an appreciation for clarity, organization, and rigor that shaped mathematics in the twentieth century. Furthermore, they are indicative of what would become known as "Hilbert's Program," the attempt to formulate mathematics on a system of axioms that is provably consistent. Ultimately, Hilbert's approach also prompted another monumental discovery: Gödel's proof that no formal axiomatic system can substantiate its own completeness. **JD**

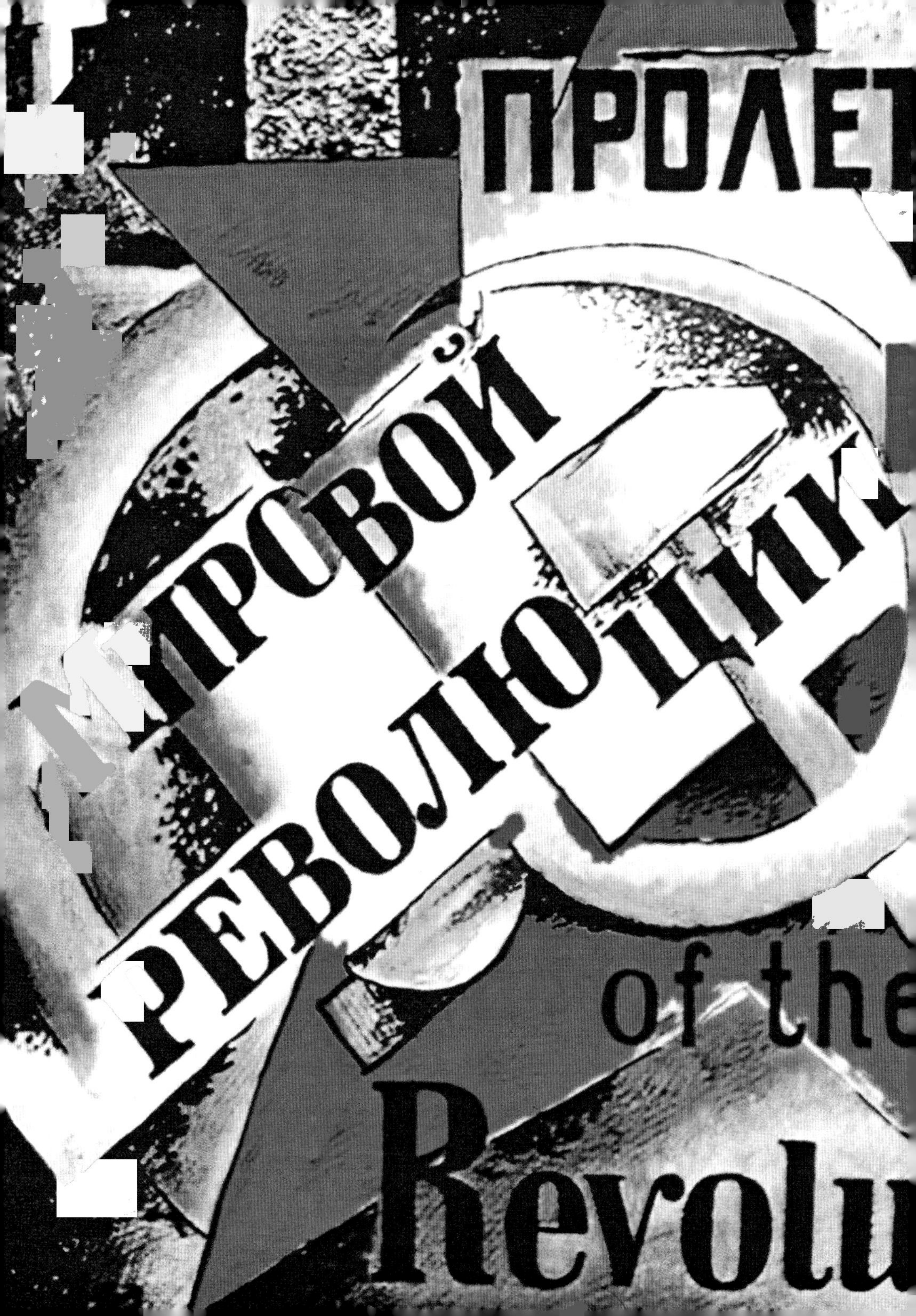

ПРОЛЕТ

МИРОВОЙ

РЕВОЛЮЦИИ

of the

Revolu

Early 20th Century
1900–1949

After the first airplane flight in 1903, inventors' drawing boards were filled with ideas associated with machines; in the world of physics, meanwhile, blackboards were covered with groundbreaking ideas about the workings of the universe, such as general relativity, the Big Bang theory, and nuclear fusion. War has frequently facilitated the adoption of novel ideas and the two world wars that occurred during this period were no exception, bringing with them numerous technological developments and medical advances. World War II also saw the devastating consequences of political ideas such as fascism and the Holocaust, which led to a global articulation of moral principles in the form of the Universal Declaration of Human Rights in 1948.

◄ A detail from a Russian communist poster from 1921. The October Revolution of 1917, in which the Communist Party took power, was greatly influenced by Leninism.

Le Nº Paraît le 15 du Mois

50 CENTIMES NET

RIONS!

1re ANNÉE   AVRIL 1908   Nº 1

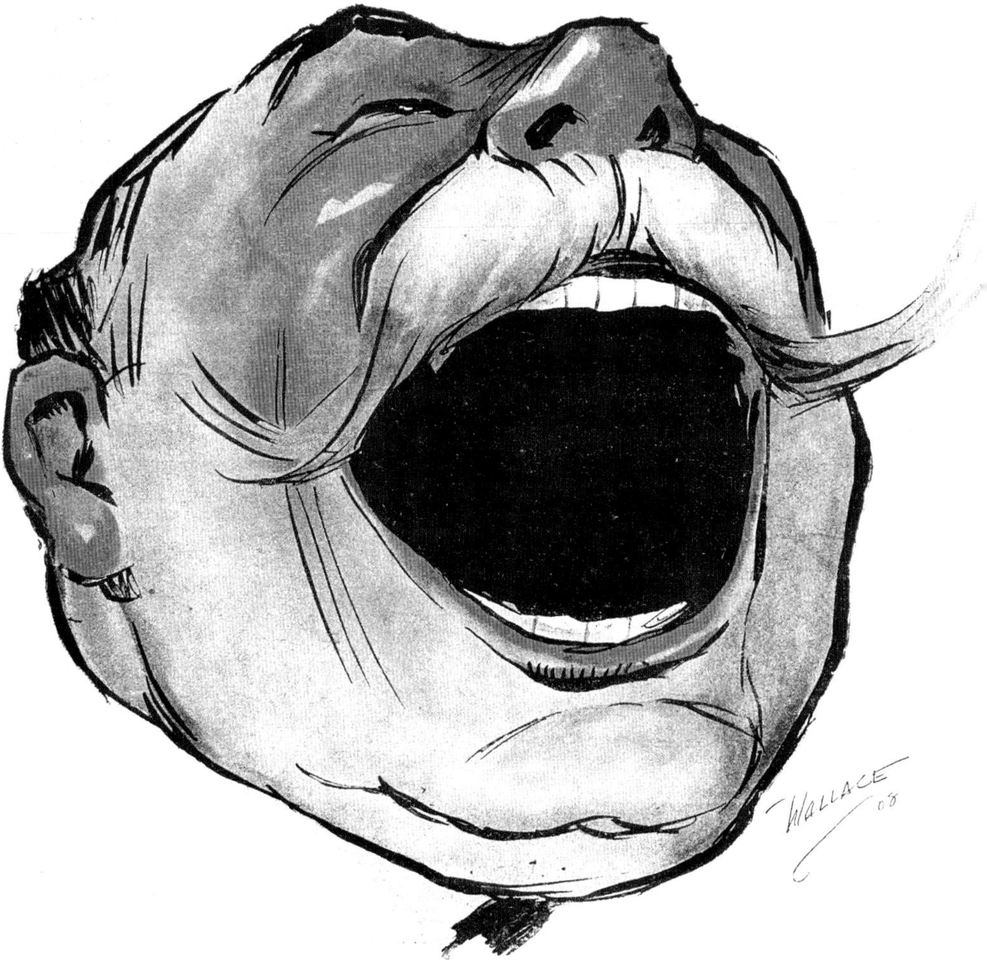

ABONNEMENTS :
Paris : 6 fr.; Départ. : 7 fr.; Étranger : 9 fr

HACHETTE ET CIE. — PARIS

The Uses of Laughter
Henri Bergson

A seminal work discussing the nature and value of laughter

In 1900 French philosopher Henri Bergson (1859–1941) wrote a book titled *Laughter: An Essay on the Meaning of Comic*. It was divided into three chapters: The Comic in General; The Comic Element in Situations and the Comic Element in Words; and The Comic in Character. Throughout the work, Bergson discusses the aspects of human life that set the stage for laughter and its social function.

One of the main features of Bergson's approach to laughter is his examination of the "mechanical." A key premise of his discussion is that human beings have uniquely entered into a habitual, predictable, and mechanical way of living that contrasts with élan vital—the vibrancy of living in its fundamental sense. For Bergson, laughter is a way of seeing the mechanical

> "The comic spirit has a logic of its own, even in its wildest eccentricities."

Henri Bergson, *Laughter* (1900)

in human life. It acts as a reminder of human rigidity, and of our blindness to our own vanity and obtuseness, and serves to unite us in that recognition.

It is Bergson's focus on the uses of laughter, especially in terms of its social function, that provided a unique influence on future studies. These functions include laughter as a kind of "release valve," through which the rules and duties that help humans suppress more threatening urges can safely give way to expression of emotion in comedy and drama. In this sense, it is a response to artificiality in society. Furthermore, Bergson's work reveals how laughter serves as a corrective opportunity, when we laugh at someone's inability to adjust to the standards of society. In the end, these uses of laughter revolve around returning authentic life to stagnant or unengaged living. **JD**

Phenomenology
Edmund Husserl

Defining what constitutes consciousness and how it is used to interpret our world

The phenomenological approach to psychology, developed by Austrian mathematician and philosopher Edmund Husserl (1859–1938) in the early decades of the 1900s can be explained via the following example. Suppose a person sees the image of a dog. Phenomenology says that the act of looking upon the dog qualifies as a genuine experience, regardless of whether the "seeing" might take place in the context of a dream, or is otherwise somehow imagined. Phenomenologists have no interest in analyzing whether or not the experience was real, and do not concern themselves with the dog's actual existence or nonexistence, rather focusing only on the subject believing that they had seen it. The experience is seen as the *qualia*, a Latin term that refers to primary

> "Experiencing is consciousness that intuits something and values it to be actual."

Edmund Husserl

conscious experiences that cannot be misinterpreted, such as a headache. Phenomenologists seek to identify phenomena through the prism of people's perceptions, free of hypothesis and preconception.

In his books *Logical Investigations* (1900) and *Ideas* (1913), Husserl elaborated on concepts that eventually led him to develop this new branch of psychology. He stressed that to properly study a person's consciousness it would be necessary to distinguish between the conscious act and the object to which the act is directed. He stressed the importance of intentionality, the process by which we direct our experience to the things that are in the world. This is the core of Husserlian phenomenology: that our experiences are directed toward things only via our thoughts, ideas, and concepts. **JMa**

⬅ An expressive portrait of laughter adorns a cover of French magazine *Rions!* (Let's Laugh!, 1908).

Russell's Paradox
Ernst Zermelo

A logical paradox that pointed to a contradiction in set theory, demonstrating a fundamental limitation of such a system

⬆ Ernst Zermelo, photographed in 1900, whose work on axiomatic set theory had overwhelming implications on the foundations of mathematics.

"The paradox raises the frightening prospect that the whole of mathematics is based on shaky foundations, and that no proof can be trusted."

Helen Joyce, mathematician

In 1901 the British philosopher and logician Bertrand Russell (1872–1970) published an inconsistency within mathematical set theory that came to be called Russell's Paradox, and became the first to attempt a solution. However, in 1900 it was the German logician and mathematician Ernst Zermelo (1871–1953) who independently was the first to recognize it, although he did not publish the idea and it remained known only to his fellow academics at the University of Göttingen.

Russell's Paradox is a contradiction within set theory, a set being either numbers or physical objects. For example, a set containing the numbers 5, 6, and 7 would be written (5,6,7). Logically, a set is capable of containing itself, but think of what we will call Set A—it has within it all those sets that do not contain themselves. Can A contain itself? If we say "yes" we hit a contradiction because, as we have just said, every set in A cannot contain itself. Yet claiming it does not contain itself does not work either.

A popular, "common" interpretation, leaving aside complex theorems such as the one above, goes as follows: "There is a barber in a small village and all the men in that village either shaved themselves or were shaved by the barber. The barber, however, only shaved those who did not shave themselves. So . . . did the barber shave himself?" If the barber shaved himself, the statement cannot be true because he only shaves men who do not shave themselves. But if he did not shave himself then he has to go to the barber (himself) to get shaved.

What Zermelo and Russell had accomplished was to throw doubt on the then growing idea that mathematics was reducible to pure logic. How could mathematical proofs possibly be trusted, with the set theories that underlie so much of mathematics now appearing to be incomplete and, worse, contradictory? **JMa**

Planck's Law
Max Planck

An equation that sought to measure the amount of radiation emitted by "blackbodies"

First presented by the German physicist Max Planck (1858–1947) in a lecture to a meeting of the German Physical Society in October 1900, Planck's Law remains one of the great cornerstones of thermodynamics, created to calculate the intensity of radiation emitted in a fixed direction from a so-called "blackbody" (an object that absorbs all of the electromagnetic energy that falls upon it), and how that intensity can vary according to the body's temperature.

Planck had been working on what he called his "blackbody radiation problem" for years, but his equation would have been impossible to achieve were it not for the work of his fellow physicists Otto Lummer (1860–1925) and Ernst Pringsheim (1859–1917) and their experiments in infrared bolometry (the measuring of radiant energy) at Berlin's Imperial Physico-Technical Institute in the 1890s.

At the end of the nineteenth century most physicists sought to gain an understanding of blackbody radiation by heating a hollow object, drilling a small hole in its side, and then measuring emitted radiation levels. Planck chose not to measure radiation levels directly but instead calculated the average release and distribution of entropy (the amount of energy not available for "work").

Planck's Law has held together as a theory ever since, although in recent times there seem to be some random exceptions in the world of the very small. In 2009 researchers at the University of California in Los Angeles found carbon nanotubes just 100 atoms in width refusing to emit the quantities of radiation that Planck suggested they should. Then, in September 2012, researchers at the Vienna University of Technology observed the heating and cooling of silica fibers followed the principles of more general rules, rather than those of Planck's mostly immutable equation. **JMa**

Structuralism
Wilhelm Wundt

The search for insights into our perceptions and cognitive processes

Wilhelm Wundt (1832–1920) taught the first courses in physiological psychology in Heidelberg, Germany, in 1867. He wrote the world's first psychology textbook, *Principles of Physiological Psychology* (1873–74) and established the world's first "psychological laboratory," the Institute for Experimental Psychology, at Leipzig in 1879. He was also the first person to be given the title "psychologist" and defined psychology's first paradigm, which was later given the name "structuralism."

Structuralism was an attempt to break down mental processes into their most basic constituent parts, to study them as a chemist would study chemical compounds, and grew out of Wundt's attempt to introspectively study the unconscious mind by studying the sensory perceptions of patients through

> *"Wundt believed that consciousness could be broken down to its basic elements."*
>
> Saul McLeod, *Simply Psychology* (2007)

the manipulation of external stimuli. It was a search for an objective, rational method of examining our perceptions while taking into account the crisis and rapidly evolving societal forces in late twentieth-century Europe. This new form of analysis cast a wide net, with the quest for a greater understanding also taking in the field of linguistics and the work of Ferdinand de Saussure (1857–1913).

Psychologist William James criticized structuralism at a time when various disciplines were competing for dominance in the new science of psychology, claiming it had "plenty of school but no thought." Structuralism declined in popularity in the late 1920s with the death of Wundt's most devoted former pupil, Edward Titchener, and it was replaced by humanism, behaviorism. and psychoanalysis. **BS**

Pacifism
Émile Arnaud

The absolute rejection of war and violence in any form

Pacifism is the belief that killing cannot have any justification, and that there can be no such thing as a "just war." The term was first used by French lawyer and founder of the Ligue Internationale de la Paix et de la Liberté (International League for Peace and Freedom) Émile Arnaud (1864–1921), who codified his beliefs in *Code de la Paix* in 1901. Subsequently, the idea of pacifism became influential, characterizing peace activists and movements during the twentieth century.

The idea of pacifism is formulated as a protest against pragmatic arguments justifying war. Even self-defense, a common justification for the use of violence, is unacceptable to the absolute stance against violence taken by a pacifist. Pacifism advances the idea that violence is the product of a "cycle of violence," and

"There are many causes I would die for. There is not a single cause I would kill for."

Mahatma Gandhi, civil rights activist

that using violence to respond to violence will produce only more violence. Accordingly, pacifism proposes that only radical resistance to any form of violence will break this cycle. Historically, pacifism has its roots in the teachings of notable religious figures, including Buddha and Jesus.

As a moral strategy, pacifism proposes to avoid the guilt associated with committing acts of violence in the name of violence. Pacifist movements have also proven to be a successful political strategy, since pacifism has been a notable element of some movements for social change in the twentieth century. Mahatma Ghandi successfully used pacifist strategies to secure Indian independence, and Martin Luther King, Jr. advanced a pacifist version of civil disobedience in the civil rights movement in the United States. **TD**

Laparoscopic Surgery
Georg Kelling

The development of a minimally invasive form of surgery

Laparoscopic surgery, also known as keyhole surgery, is performed by entering the skin via small incisions or a body cavity. The first laparoscopic procedure was conducted in 1901 by Georg Kelling (1866–1945), who carried out what he referred to as a "celioscopy" on a dog. Kelling's method involved inflating the abdominal cavity of the animal and then inserting a thin cytoscope (an optical device used in diagnostics of the bladder) through the abdominal wall to enable examination of the area without damaging any of the internal organs. The first laparoscopic procedure on humans—which used a similar methodology—was performed by Hans Christian Jacobaeus (1879–1937) in 1910.

Although laparoscopic surgical techniques were gradually refined over the decades that followed,

"The method is based on the fact that … the abdominal wall is extremely flexible …"

Georg Kelling

laparoscopy did not become fully popularized until the advent in the late 1980s of a computer chip television camera that could be attached to the laparoscope (a fiber-optic viewing tube), enabling the surgeon to closely monitor and view the procedure. Originally, the medical community held many reservations about the safety of laparoscopic procedures. However, the reduced risk to patients due to hemorrhaging caused them to grow in popularity, particularly in gynecology for outpatient procedures such as tubal ligation.

Laparoscopic surgery has revolutionized surgery, and it is now common for laparoscopic techniques to be used for numerous procedures. Because laparoscopic surgery is less invasive, patients often experience less pain, spend less time in hospital, and have a lower risk of complications due to surgery. **NM**

Pavlov's Dog
Ivan Pavlov

A study of conditioning in dogs that formed the basis of behavioral psychology

Pavlov's Dog refers to the well-known experiments conducted by Russian physiologist Ivan Pavlov (1849–1936) from 1901. Pavlov discovered that dogs could be conditioned to salivate when a bell rang. This kind of learning, now known as "classical conditioning," has had profound effects on the world of psychology, specifically in behaviorism. Pavlov's work demonstrated that an animal could learn to behave unintentionally in a particular way. The dog's salivation in relation to the bell is an unintended response, but it is nevertheless a learned response. Psychologists studying behaviorism have continued to discover that humans, too, can be conditioned to respond to stimuli, without even realizing it.

Pavlov's experiments began with attempts to learn about the physiology of dogs and how they salivate. He and his assistants would bring in meat or meat powder to the dogs and observe their salivation behaviors. These experiments had nothing, initially, to do with conditioning. However, Pavlov and his assistant, Ivan Filippovitch Tolochinov, noticed that the dogs they were observing would begin to salivate as soon as someone in a white lab coat entered the room. At first this was simply an annoyance but Pavlov realized that the dogs had learned, unintentionally, to associate the scientists with food and would salivate even when there was no food present. Pavlov observed that an initially neutral stimulus, such as a bell or a white coat, could become associated with an unconditioned stimulus such as food, and after a period of experiencing both together the formerly neutral stimulus would cause a conditioned response, such as salivation.

Pavlov's theory is now used in areas such as marketing, politics, and education. Any field that seeks to cause a change in behavior is one that uses classical conditioning. **NM**

Ivan Pavlov (right, with beard) and his research staff with one of their laboratory dogs in c. 1925.

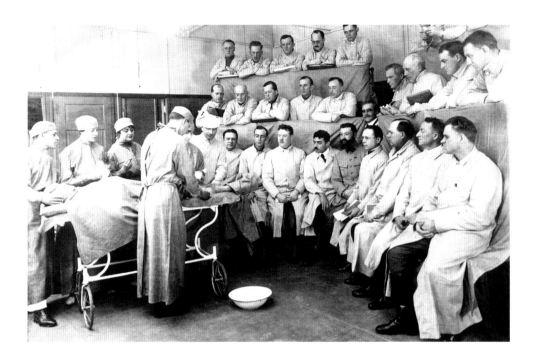

Organ Transplantation
Alexis Carrel

The development of a technique to enable organs to be transplanted

Doctors had dreamed for millennia about the possibility of transplanting organs from one body to another as a means by which to save lives. The surgical procedure, which involves either taking an organ from a donor, who may be living or dead, or from the patient's own body, has only recently become a viable medical procedure. Through the use of drugs that help suppress the body's natural tendency to reject foreign organs, doctors can implant donor organs or tissue into a patient who needs the organ for improved quality of life or survival.

French surgeon Alexis Carrel (1873–1944) carried out pioneering work in organ transplantation and successfully transplanted different organs in dogs from 1902. His success depended on his development of a method of suturing blood vessels, a technique crucial to transplant surgery. Through his work, he was also one of the first to identify the problem of organ rejection. Carrel, with Charles A. Lindberg (1902–74), invented the perfusion pump, which was an essential step toward making organ transplantation possible. The first truly successful organ transplant, however, was performed by Joseph Murray and J. Hartwell Harrison: a kidney transplant between identical twins, in 1954. Today with drugs such as cyclosporine, which suppress the immune rejection response, organ transplantation is often successful.

Currently the only organs that can be transplanted are the heart, kidneys, liver, lungs, pancreas, intestine, and thymus. Organ transplantation is a field that is rapidly improving in technique and possibility. Stem cell research is increasing the possibility of using a donor's own cells to grow new organs for transplantation. For the moment, however, the consistently improving viability of organ transplantation has resulted in a steadily increasing demand for organs. Unfortunately, there is also a shortage of donors and people die every day waiting to receive an organ transplant. **NM**

Alexis Carrel demonstrates before a group of French surgeons at a teaching hospital during World War I.

Φ

The Correspondence Theory of Truth
G. E. Moore

A philosophical way of understanding the nature of truth and falsehood—the "truth" is whatever corresponds to reality

⬆ Together with Bertrand Russell, G. E. Moore led the move away from idealism in British philosophy and founded the analytic tradition.

"The view that truth is the quality of belief in facts … is a form of the correspondence theory, i.e., of the theory that truth means the correspondence of our ideas with reality."

Bertrand Russell, "On the Nature of Truth" (1906)

The correspondence theory of truth holds that truth consists of a relation to a mind-independent reality. While the theory has a long history, its modern origins can be traced to two essays by British philosophers: "Truth and Falsity" by G. E. Moore (1873–1958) in 1902 and "On the Nature of Truth" by Bertrand Russell (1872–1970) in 1906. The pair were friends and influenced each other's thinking.

The idea that truth consists in agreement with reality is an intuitive one, and precursors to the correspondence theory can be found in thinkers as diverse as Aristotle, St. Thomas Aquinas, and John Stuart Mill. It is often associated with metaphysical realism, which holds that the fundamental features of reality are independent of human perception. Russell and Moore's influential version of the correspondence theory proposed that a belief was true if it corresponded to a fact, and false otherwise. This was in explicit contrast to the theories of truth proposed by some idealist philosophers of the day, who had argued that "truth" was a matter of human experience fitting together in the right way, and that all actual beliefs were only "partially true" or "partially false." In later years, Russell defended the closely related thesis of logical atomism, which held that the external world itself was constituted by the discrete, atomic facts of the type that made beliefs true or false.

Moore and Russell's explicit formulation and defense of the correspondence theory sparked an interest in truth across a number of disciplines, including philosophy, logic, and linguistics. Many contemporary scholars still endorse versions of the correspondence theory, although they disagree about the nature of truth bearers (are they sentences, beliefs, or something else?) and the particular relation to the world that makes these truth bearers true or false. **BSh**

Leninism
Vladimir Lenin

The advocation of a Marxist revolution led by a "vanguard" party

Leninism, named after its originator Vladimir Lenin (1870–1924), is a political theory emerging from Marxism that advocates the creation of a socialist state. Leninism proscribes revolution, specifically revolution by a vanguard party (a group of revolutionaries that goes first) to help educate and lead the proletariat (working class) in achieving social and economic freedom from the bourgeoisie (upper class). The end goal of Leninism is the establishment of a direct-democracy rule by the proletariat. Intended specifically as a rejection of the capitalistic practices of the Russian Empire, Leninism was initially a practical theory of revolution, rather than a philosophy, comprised of the "how tos" of revolution. Lenin put forward his ideas in the political pamphlet *What Is to Be Done?*, which was published in 1902.

The term "Leninism" was not coined until two years before Lenin's death. His theory emerged from his attempts to bring Marxist philosophy to Russia by overthrowing the existing government. Lenin's success during the October Revolution of 1917 enabled him to establish a "Dictatorship of the Proletariat." Dictatorship, in this case, meant democratic rule by the working class. As a Marxist, Lenin believed that the working class was repressed, and he advocated a shift of power from the wealthy to the workers who provide the wealth.

Leninism has had profound implications and remains controversial. It led to Lenin's establishment of the Russian Socialist Federative Soviet Republic in 1917, which eventually absorbed numerous surrounding countries and became the Union of Soviet Socialist Republics (USSR). The rule of Joseph Stalin, after Lenin, was marked by the Great Purge (1934–38) and the execution of hundreds of thousands of innocents. However, Leninism remains among its advocates the best means by which to educate and empower the people to rise up against repression. **NM**

Constructivism
John Dewey

A theory of learning that encourages human inquisitiveness and curiosity

Constructivism is a theory of learning with roots embedded in the world of psychology. It tells us we are "constructors of information," that our desire to learn is an active thing—a constructive, logical process that grows as a result of our own experiences and subsequent reflections as we build up our subjective comprehension of the world around us.

The person generally credited with identifying and codifying this approach to learning is the U.S. philosopher and educational reformer John Dewey (1859–1952), who set out his views in a series of essays titled "Thought and its Subject-Matter," published in 1903 in *Studies in Logical Theory*. As an educator, Dewey created an atmosphere of "experiential learning," the act of deriving meaning and knowledge directly from

> *"Education is growth; education is not preparation for life but is life itself."*
>
> John Dewey

real-life experiences, encouraging his students to think, reflect, explore, and question for themselves in a free and open environment.

By the late 1930s, Dewey's approach had started to develop into two schools of thought: social constructivism, the product of Russian psychologist Lev Vygotsky (1896–1934), who emphasized the social and cultural contexts in learning; and cognitive constructivism, the "four stages of learning principle," pioneered by the Swiss psychologist Jean Piaget (1896–1980). Constructivism replaced other "information-processing" approaches to learning that had failed to appreciate the role of the learner, who was considered a mere receptacle of "hardwired" facts, and by the 1980s it had emerged triumphant as the leading theory on how humans learn. **BS**

Nudism

Paul Zimmermann

A way of life, in harmony with nature, expressed through social nudity

It is difficult to pinpoint the origins of nudism, or naturism, as it is often called. However, the first official nudist club, Freilichtpark (Free Light Park), was opened by Paul Zimmermann in an area of secluded woodland north of Hamburg, Germany, in 1903. It attracted visitors from around the world, and nudism gained a large following in Europe, particularly in Germany. The International Naturist Federation was formed in France in 1953 to further the cause.

Nudism was first spoken of as a means of improving physical health and lifestyle in the late 1700s, although its precise definition varies widely both historically and from country to country. Nudism encompasses an individual preferring to be naked in his or her own home,

or the militant nudism of public nudity activists. There is also social nudity: nudists who meet together at special social events, nudist resorts or beaches, and "nudist colonies," although this term is now somewhat outdated and not used by nudists due to various negative connotations. Cruise lines also offer naturist cruises.

Although not as popular as they once were, there are still a number of events in which nudists can participate openly on the world stage. The International Naturist Federation has designated the first Sunday in June the World Day of Naturism. Every year in May, everyone—nudists and non-nudists alike—is asked to participate in the World Naked Gardening Day. The World Naked Bike Ride is a clothing-optional event that began in 2004 (although many other random naked cycle rides had occurred prior to that). What began as twenty-eight rides in twenty-eight cities across the world has since mushroomed to more than eighty cities in almost twenty different countries. Arguments over the pros and cons of public nudity abound, yet surprisingly very little evidence has been forthcoming to demonstrate that the practice has any negative effect on the moral fabric of society. **BS**

Cycling is a popular recreational outdoor activity for nudists.

1904

Protestant Work Ethic

Max Weber

A concept advocating the importance of work for its own sake

As a theological, sociological, economic, and historical concept the Protestant work ethic emphasizes the importance of working not only for the acquisition of material goods, but also for its own sake. It emphasizes the idea that hard work produces its own reward. As a religiously based notion, it was, initially, grounded in the idea that being frugal and working hard acted as evidence for one's Christian salvation. All hard work, regardless of whether or not it is in an ordained profession, such as being a priest, is considered godly, while sloth and idleness are considered sinful.

German sociologist and political economist Max Weber (1864–1920) developed his Protestant ethic idea in two journal articles, published in 1904–05, which were later combined in his book *The Protestant Ethic and the Spirit of Capitalism*. Weber argued that the advent of capitalism is in large part due to the freedom of work provided by the Protestant work ethic. The ethic itself was the result of combining the spiritual teachings of German theologian Martin Luther (1483–1546) with the philosophies of British theologian John Calvin (1509–64). Luther believed that a man's work was his spiritual calling, and Calvin argued that all men must work, even the rich, because idleness itself was sinful. All work became good work as long as it was diligent and not indulgent in sin. As a result, it was godly to receive reward and pay for that hard work, as the work itself was sanctified by virtue of being hard work.

It is argued by many philosophers, economists, and social theorists that the Protestant work ethic not only defined and caused the spread of capitalism, but also that the economic success of the United States is a direct result of the Protestant work ethic adopted by the early Puritan settlers. Work ceased to be something the people did in order to survive, and workers began to produce as much as possible, regardless of surplus. **NM**

⬆ City workers pour out of London Bridge Station, London, in February 1962.

Poincaré Conjecture
Henri Poincaré

A theorem about the characterization of the three-dimensional sphere

⬆ Russian mathematician Grigori Perelman was awarded, but declined, the Fields Medal—often described as the Nobel prize of mathematics—for his proof of Poincaré's Conjecture in 2006.

"Fifty years ago I was working on Poincaré's Conjecture and thus hold a longstanding appreciation for this beautiful and difficult problem. The final solution by Grigori Perelman is a great event in the history of mathematics."

Steven Smale, mathematician and Fields medallist

In 1904 the French mathematician Henri Poincaré (1854–1912) posed what has since become one of the world's great mathematical dilemmas, one that would take more than one hundred years to be answered. It was so confounding that it became one of the Millennium Prize Problems, one of a select grouping of hypotheses and theories that the Clay Mathematics Institute in the U.S. state of Rhode Island offered a one million dollar prize to anyone who could solve it. The question: Is there a test for recognizing when a shape is a three-dimensional sphere by performing measurements inside the sphere?

In order to help understand the dilemma, imagine an orange and a rubber band. If the rubber band is stretched around the orange, it is possible to "shrink" it down to a single point on the orange by continually moving it in on itself, without it coming away from the surface. The orange's surface is, according to Poincaré, "simply connected" and allows for the contraction of the rubber band. Yet, if we try the same thing with a donut, and we try to place a rubber band around it and then try and reduce it, it is impossible to achieve— either the donut or the rubber band will break in the attempt. Poincaré called the orange, or anything that is three-dimensional and lacks boundaries, a closed three-manifold. Poincaré knew that simple connectivity was enough to define a sphere, but wondered if it would be enough to define spheres in higher dimensions.

Poincaré's question was answered in 2003 by the Russian mathematician Grigori Perelman (b. 1966) using the Ricci flow, a geometric flow in differential geometry. Perelman refused the one million dollar prize money and the Fields Medal, mathematics' highest honor, in 2006. Although he was still listed as a researcher at St. Petersburg University, Perelman had apparently left academia and abandoned mathematics. **JMa**

Biblical Socio-scientific Criticism
Max Weber

Analysis of the Bible using social-scientific methodology

Biblical socio-scientific criticism (also known as social-scientific criticism, socio-historical criticism, and social-world criticism) is a multidisciplinary area of biblical study, which draws on the social sciences, in particular cultural anthropology and sociology. It uses social-scientific methods to analyze empirical data and the communities behind biblical documents in order to examine the social and cultural dimensions in which the Bible texts were produced. Socio-scientific criticism aims to enable the understanding of the writers and their purpose, as well as their audience. For example, biblical socio-scientific criticism takes into account social factors in the early Palestinian society in its examination of the origins of Christianity.

Biblical socio-scientific criticism has its roots in the nineteenth century when the German sociologist, philosopher, and political economist Max Weber (1864–1920) wrote two journal articles, published in 1904–05, that later became the founding text of sociology, *The Protestant Ethic and the Spirit of Capitalism*. Weber wrote several books on religion, including *Ancient Judaism* (1917–19), in which he asserted that the apostles did not convert many Jews to Christianity because they could not break the well-structured communities of the Jews.

German theologian Ernst Troeltsch (1865–1923) expanded sociological examination of the Bible in *The Social Teaching of the Christian Churches* (1911), in which he theorized about the institutionalization of groups and how sects emerged. Biblical socio-scientific criticism emerged in its modern form in the 1970s when U.S. theologian Robin Scroggs (1930–2005) published *The Earliest Christian Communities as a Sectarian Movement* (1975) and *The Sociological Interpretation of the New Testament* (1977), which developed key themes in the social context of early Christianity. By the 1980s, biblical socio-scientific criticism had become a mainstream form of analysis of Judeo-Christian scripture. **CK**

⬆ Biblical socio-scientific criticism examines the social and cultural dimensions of scripture, including descriptions of actual geographical locations, such as the Garden of Gethsemane.

"With the salvation doctrine of Christianity as its core, the Pauline mission, in achieving emancipation from the self-created ghetto, found a linkage to a Jewish . . . doctrine derived from the religious experience of the exiled people."

Max Weber, *Ancient Judaism* (1917–19)

Special Relativity
Albert Einstein

A physical theory of measurement that explains motion in the universe

Special relativity is a physical theory of measurement developed by Albert Einstein (1879–1955) in 1905. He realized that the speed of light was so constant that the motion of everything, including time, was relative to and warped around it. The theory tells us two things: 1) The laws of physics hold true for all frames of reference; and 2) The speed of light is measured as constant in all frames of reference. What is profound is Einstein's realization that no matter a person's location or how fast he or she is moving, the speed of light remains constant, regardless of the frame of reference.

Special relativity requires the acceptance of a profoundly counterintuitive idea. Usually, we think of speed as relative to a frame of reference. For example, if I am traveling on a train at 10 miles per hour (16 kph)

"The whole of science is nothing more than a refinement of everyday thinking."

Albert Einstein

and I throw a ball at 5 miles per hour (8 kph) in the direction I am moving, the ball, relative to me, will travel at 5 miles per hour. However, to a person on the ground observing the train and the ball, the ball will be moving at the train's speed plus the speed at which I threw it—15 miles per hour (24 kph). The speed of light, however, does not work in this way. No matter the frame of reference, it moves at the same speed. If I used a flashlight instead of a ball on the same train, the light would travel at the same speed from both my perspective and that of the observer on the ground.

Einstein's theory has influenced everything from the way we measure the speed of objects out in space to the use of global positioning systems (GPS) for cell phones. The world changed how it understood the laws of physics because of special relativity. **NM**

The Theory of Descriptions
Bertrand Russell

A philosophical theory about how we make meaning in language

The theory of descriptions, developed by Bertrand Russell (1872–1970) in his paper "On Denoting" in 1905, helps us to understand what makes a statement true or false. It explains that definite descriptions (such as "the dog is brown") are not sentences that necessarily refer to an object. The theory explains that definite descriptions have a logical structure. That structure can be symbolized, therefore, and we can figure out how they make meaning, which for logicians means we can say the sentence is true or false, as opposed to just nonsense.

The problem that Russell was trying to fix was a problem of "meaning." Before his idea, we assumed that definite descriptions refer to something, or else they are meaningless. Philosophers argued that statements such as "The current king of France is bald" are meaningless

"The world is full of magical things patiently waiting for our wits to grow sharper."

Bertrand Russell

because they refer to nothing—there is no king of France—therefore we cannot say they are true or false. Yet the sentence does seem to communicate something meaningful. Russell argued that we should consider the sentence like an "if-then" statement: There is a person who, if he is the king of France, then he is bald. There is no king of France, so we can say, "No, there is no person who meets that qualifier," and so the sentence, "The present king of France is bald," is false.

Today philosophers, linguists, and mathematicians still argue about Russell's theory, because, although it solves some problems, it creates new ones. If we say that "The present king of France is bald" is false, it sounds like we are saying that there is a king of France. How we answer that question structures everything else we know about language, thought, and truth. **NM**

Permanent Revolution
Leon Trotsky

How socialist revolutions could occur in societies that were less advanced

Although the phrase "permanent revolution" was first used by Karl Marx (1818–83) in his book *The Holy Family* (1844), decades passed before it eventually became linked to the philosophy of the Communist revolutionary theorist Leon Trotsky (1879–1940), who believed there should be a proletarian revolution occurring somewhere in the world all the time. Trotsky formed this idea in a series of essays in 1905 that he later published in his book *Results and Prospects* (1906).He paid no acknowledgment to Marx and Friedrich Engels for inventing and promulgating the term that had been used sparingly at best in the intervening decades.

In the wake of the Russian Revolution in 1917, Trotsky saw the need to export the Bolshevik revolutionary model abroad rather than focusing solely on perfecting

> *" . . . a permanent revolution in a newer and broader sense of the word."*
>
> **Leon Trotsky**

the revolution inside Russia's own borders, the stated aim of Joseph Stalin's "Socialism in One Country" approach. Trotsky considered the success of revolutions elsewhere vital to the success of the new Russia, because a hostile, rampant capitalist world could one day threaten the stability even of their ideal worker's state.

Trotsky wanted to send representatives abroad to assist other revolutionary movements in what he called "backward countries," a policy he considered Russia's ideological responsibility. He believed that workers in colonial and semi-colonial nations needed to achieve emancipation and to establish their own proletarian dictatorships, but felt them to be incapable of bringing any such revolt to a successful conclusion. Trotsky argued for a permanent revolution, ever continuing and expanding until transforming every nation on Earth. **BS**

Tantric Sex
Pierre Arnold Bernard

Increasing sexual pleasure through (misinterpreting) ancient Eastern texts

Tantric sex is a form of physical, mental, and spiritual discipline aimed at increasing sexual arousal, prolonging coitus, and producing multiple or sustained orgasms. Although the adjective is intended to suggest a connection with Indian religions, scholars suggest that tantric sex as it is marketed in the West is a misinterpretation of tantrism. A central figure in fomenting the misinterpretation was Pierre Arnold Bernard (1875–1955)—nicknamed "The Omnipotent Oom"—who founded the Tantrik Order in 1906.

In their native context, tantras are esoteric religious texts of certain sects of Hinduism and Buddhism, focusing on ways of appropriating and channeling the energy of the divine, including visualization, reciting mantras, and yoga. Sex is not a major component.

> *" . . . the use of the term 'tantric' [in 'tantric sex'] . . . is entirely misplaced."*
>
> **David Gordon White, *Kiss of the Yogini* (2006)**

However, it was often taken as such by Westerners, who tended to regard tantrism as reflecting the depravity of a decadent East. Bernard's contribution was to operate a series of studios in the United States offering yoga to the public and secret tantric rites—reportedly involving prolonged coitus—to the initiated. Although his operation was derailed by scandal, his interpretation of tantric sex was influential. With the sexual revolution of the 1960s and the New Age movement of the 1970s, tantric sex was particularly in the public eye. In 1996, Nik Douglas revived Bernard's Tantrik Order as "The New Tantric Order in America."

While the authenticity of tantric sex is dubious, it would be ungenerous to begrudge its devotees the pleasure they find in it. The association of sex with the mysterious East is likely to continue to be appealing. **GB**

　　A painting from Nepal shows the Buddhist guru Padmasambhava in a tantric pose. ▶

Satyagraha
Mahatma Gandhi

Social or political reform through nonviolent protest and a conversion to truth

Satyagraha can be translated as "insistence on truth." A nonviolent philosophy of social change, satyagraha requires that the oppressed seek the conversion of the oppressor to the truth. Similar to "passive resistance," those who follow a path of satyagraha do not use violence as a means by which to stop violence. However, it can be argued that it is different to passive resistance in that its followers seek a whole acceptance of the truth, particularly of the wrong that has been committed. Followers of satyagraha refuse to submit to the evils and repression that others would do to them, firmly loving the oppressor while requiring that the oppressor acknowledge and stop the violence and evil.

Satyagraha was a philosophy developed by Mahatma Gandhi (1869–1948) in 1906 while he

> *"Victory attained by violence is tantamount to a defeat, for it is momentary."*
>
> **Mahatma Gandhi**

was struggling for Indian rights as a lawyer in Johannesburg, South Africa, and that he later used in the Indian independence movement. Gandhi argued that satyagraha was a weapon of the strong that allows for no violence and always insists upon the truth. Unlike many other forms of civil disobedience, success in satyagraha is not only defined as a change in social organization or stigma, but also as a conversion of the oppressor to the truth (that the harm he or she is doing is wrong). For this reason, critics argue that Gandhi's efforts have been profoundly unsuccessful.

Satyagraha has had a profound impact on human struggle, however, including on Martin Luther King, Jr.'s philosophy of love and resistance. The U.S. civil rights movement was in many ways the successful result of and an example of satyagraha in practice. **NM**

Coherence Theory of Truth
H. H. Joachim and F. H. Bradley

Theory that truth depends on coherence with a set of propositions or beliefs

This theory holds that truth consists of coherence with a specified set of propositions or beliefs. Suggestions of the view can be found in the work of thinkers such as Baruch Spinoza and Immanuel Kant. However, the first in-depth defenses of the view are provided by two British idealist philosophers: H. H. Joachim (1868–1938), who in 1906 wrote *The Nature of Truth: An Essay*, and F. H. Bradley (1846–1924), whose essay "On Coherence and Truth" was published in 1909.

The coherence theory is a competitor of the correspondence theory of truth, which holds that truth consists of agreement with the external world. Many of the original proponents of the coherence theory of truth, including Joachim and Bradley, were idealists who believed that there was no such thing as a mind-

> *"We are like sailors who have to rebuild their ship on the open sea …"*
>
> **Otto Neurath, "Protocol Sentences" (1932)**

independent external world, and that everything was in some sense "mental." The coherence theory fits naturally with this view, since it identifies true beliefs with those that "fit" together within the integrated, systematic whole. The theory was also defended by the logical positivist Otto Neurath, who argued that it fit with the scientific practice of evaluating new hypotheses and evidence by seeing how they "cohere with" previously accepted theories.

While coherence theories of truth still have prominent defenders, they are not as widely accepted as they once were. Possible reasons for this may be the widespread rejection of idealism by academic philosophers and that contemporary anti-realists often adopt deflationary theories of truth, which claim that there is no deep "nature" of truth. **BSh**

⬅ Gandhi in South Africa in *c.* 1903. He developed his philosophy of satyagraha while working there as a lawyer.   1900–1949   **627**

Pareto Efficiency
Vilfredo Pareto

An economic model in which no one can be better off without making another worse off

Pareto efficiency (also known as Pareto optimality) is a hypothetical state of affairs in economic theory in which no one can be made better off without making at least one individual worse off. The concept is taken from the work of the Italian economist and sociologist Vilfredo Pareto (1848–1923), who used the idea in his studies of economic efficiency and income distribution. An allocation of resources is Pareto efficient if no other allocation of resources exists in which someone is better off and everyone is at least as well off. Pareto developed the concept in his *Manual of Political Economy*, which was first published in 1906.

Pareto efficiency has been an influential idea in economics and it has also had applications in engineering and the social sciences. In economics,

"When it is useful to them, men can believe a theory of which they know nothing…"
Vilfredo Pareto

it has been long assumed that the operations of market actors untouched by government intervention would tend toward Pareto optimality. However, it is now recognized that markets inherently suffer from a number of market failures, tendencies toward imperfect competition, information asymmetries, and other faults that would inhibit the organic development of Pareto efficient outcomes.

Despite the shortcomings of its use in certain tendencies of neoclassical economics, the concept of Pareto efficiency has proven vastly influential in economic thought. Pareto's legacy to economics has been profound and he has become acknowledged as the Newton of Economics, for having united economics in mathematical form. All modern economics is based on the idea of Pareto efficiency. **JE**

Racialism / Racism
Leon Trotsky

The belief that people can be divided into a hierarchy of biological categories

Racism is the idea that there are distinct biological groups called "races," some of which are superior to others. There is much controversy as to the definition of racism and its origin. Although human history is riddled with instances of one group claiming to be better than another, racism specifically requires the belief that groups can be divided into biological categories. Racism, then, in the strictest sense, is not only the idea that one group, culture, or nation is better than another, but alsospecifically that one group, due to its race, is better than another. The issue is also complicated by the inability to actually distinguish groups of people by "race" in any legitimate scientific sense.

"Racialism," a precursor term to racism, first appeared in the *Oxford English Dictionary* in 1907. It

"Racism is a vapid and bombastic variety of chauvinism in alliance with phrenology."
Leon Trotsky

was defined as "belief in the superiority of a particular race." The term "racism" was first used in response to Adolf Hitler and the rise of Nazi Germany. Critical of the Third Reich in the early 1930s, Leon Trotsky (1879–1940) argued that Hitler used racism as a means by which to rationalize repressing the working class and consolidating power for himself.

Racism is now best understood as the classification of others by race for the purpose of subjugation, and it continues to be used as a way to justify bigotry, intolerance, and genocide. In many countries, legislation against racial discrimination exists. Although racism remains pervasive, the general agreement by the scientific community that there are no actual biological or sociological categories of race is slowly undermining justification for oppression based on race. **NM**

Steiner Education
Rudolph Steiner

A humanist approach to education that stresses the role of the imagination

Austrian-born Rudolph Steiner (1861–1925) was many things—philosopher, architect, political reformer, and literary critic—but he is best remembered as the driving force behind the establishment of his own distinct brand of education. The founder of anthroposophy, the idea that there is a spiritual world that is able to be accessed and comprehended through personal development, he integrated this belief into his philosophy on the education of the whole child. Steiner wrote his first book, *The Education of the Child*, in 1907 in which he considered children to be three-fold beings: body, spirit, and soul. He emphasized the importance of imagination, the visual arts, and participating in festivals and ceremonies in order to connect the child more fully with nature and the wider cosmos.

"To truly know the world look deeply within your own being."
Rudolph Steiner

The first Steiner/Waldorf school opened for the children of employees of the Waldorf-Astoria Cigarette Company in Stuttgart, Germany, in 1919. There are currently over 600 schools in sixty countries worldwide, teaching more than 125,000 students. Today's curriculum is tailored to the various phases of a child's development. In a child's early years activities such as clay modeling are favored, along with basic mathematics and an introduction to reading and writing. There are no text books until the age of eleven or twelve; instead children are encouraged to produce their own texts based on their own experiences. Subjects comprise the usual core disciplines, but may also include weaving and toy making. Learning at primary level takes place in a noncompetitive environment, and the use of electronic devices is discouraged. **BS**

Atonality
Arnold Schoenberg

A form of pitch organization without reference to tonal centers

The term "atonal music" has several different but interrelated meanings, including music free of the boundaries of major/minor tonality or music free of any other form of pitch centricity. The term began to be applied to compositions written by Austrian composer Arnold Schoenberg (1874–1951) and the Second Viennese School, beginning with his second string quartet in 1907. He and his students, Alban Berg and Anton Webern, pioneered important atonal works that are still in the repertoire, including Schoenberg's *Pierrot Lunaire* (1912) for voice and chamber ensemble.

Atonality became a driving force for experimentation during the twentieth century at a time when composers were searching for new approaches. The methods they pursued were manifold, including using microtones

"One must be convinced of the infallibility of one's own fantasy ..."
Arnold Schoenberg

(scale steps smaller than half tones) and randomly generated notes, and applying different mathematical formulas to pitch generation. Electro-acoustic music that utilizes sound objects rather than clearly defined pitches could also be considered an extension of atonal composition.

Atonal techniques also made their way into popular culture. In movie music, atonality became a powerful element not only in suspenseful, violent, or dramatic scenes but also in reflective scenes to suggest some kind of ambiguity. Both approaches are present in Alex North's movie scores, such as *Viva Zapata!* (1952). Avant-garde jazz and rock artists and groups, such as U.S. saxophonist John Coltrane and the British rock group Henry Cow, have also used atonality, thus extending the boundaries of their genres. **PB**

Cubism
Pablo Picasso and Georges Braque

A style of visual art distinctive for its use of geometric shapes, angles, and lines

A radical style of visual art pioneered by Pablo Picasso (1881–1973) and Georges Braque (1882–1963), Cubism attempted to capture reality as a composite of elementary shapes and angles as if seen from multiple perspectives at once. Art critic Louis Vauxcelles had scornfully described a series of Braque's paintings exhibited in 1908 as "full of cubes," but the beginnings of the style were already evident in Picasso's painting *Les Demoiselles d'Avignon* (1907).

With two of its female faces resembling tribal masks, the painting showed the influence of African art. The women's bodies form angular shapes that appear as part of the flat background. The Cubists rejected the idea of perspective that had long been the basis of visual art. They were inspired by Paul Cézanne's idea

"Let them eat their fill of their square pears on their triangular tables!"

Marc Chagall, artist

that a painting is after all a work of art—a conscious attempt to reconstruct a scene viewed from a particular perspective. Abandoning such conventions, Cézanne's Postimpressionist paintings used dense layers of color to convey depth and movement. The early Cubists took these ideas much further, literally following Cézanne's advice that nature should be depicted "in terms of the cylinder, the sphere, the cone, all in perspective."

From 1910 Picasso and Braques had taken this interest in geometric patterns to a more abstract level, and Picasso took it further still when he invented the collage technique. By 1912 Cubism was in decline, but with its insistence on unveiling the many disparate elements and perspectives that construct any image, this short-lived movement had a profoundly subversive and liberating influence on all modern art. **TJ**

Expressionism in Music
Arnold Schoenberg

A school of music, often atonal in style, that focused on evoking heightened emotions

Expressionism originated in the visual arts, with the German group Die Brücke (The Bridge) in 1905, and was later extended to music. Although not stylistically homogenous, the movement's program provides stylistic clues that apply across the visual arts, literature, cinema, and music: fragmentation rather than unity, no imitation of nature, and an emphasis on the individualized, subjective artist.

In music, the early atonal works of Arnold Schoenberg (1874–1951), from about 1908, most clearly manifested these characteristics. They were highly original pieces, avoiding standard melodic and harmonic constructs and repetitions, and in the case of texted compositions, they dealt with human emotion rather than lyrical description. Schoenberg's

"Music is at once the product of feeling and knowledge."

Alban Berg, composer

Erwartung (Expectation, 1909), for example, a drama for one voice connects musical expressionism with a surreal, psychoanalytically laden libretto: a woman who wanders in the forest searching for her lover, eventually finds his bloodstained corpse. Schoenberg described his intention as to "represent in slow motion everything that occurs during a single second of maximum spiritual excitement, stretching it out to half an hour."

The Nazi seizure of power, followed by the Degenerate Art Exhibition in Munich in 1937 (in which many expressionistic works were displayed), ended the movement in Germany, although it continued to develop in art and cinema. In music, it regained popularity in the 1950s. Hungarian composer György Ligeti (1923–2006), in particular, used expressionistic stylistic traits and reinvigorated Expressionism. **PB**

◄ Picasso's seminal cubist painting *Les Demoiselles d'Avignon* (1907) deeply shocked the art world.

Modern Christian Apologetics
G. K. Chesterton

A branch of Christian theology that offers modern defenses of the Christian religion

⬆ The Christian apologetic texts of G. K. Chesterton (here in 1909), such as *Orthodoxy* (1908) and *The Everlasting Man* (1925), were well received partly because they were so entertaining.

"It is idle to talk always of the alternative of reason and faith. Reason is itself a matter of faith. It is an act of faith to assert that our thoughts have any relation to reality at all."

G. K. Chesterton, *Orthodoxy* (1908)

The Renaissance and Enlightenment were largely Christian projects, advancing specifically Christian understandings of philosophy and science. Isaac Newton, for example, wrote more theology than physics, and in his physics he made sure that his model of the universe was an open one, allowing for supernatural causation (miracles) to take place. However, some of the immediate children of the Enlightenment, such as Karl Marx, Sigmund Freud, and Friedrich Nietzsche, attempted to divorce reason from religion, and then to either put down religion (Marx, Freud) or to put down both reason and religion (Nietzsche). In either case, subsequent centuries saw the gradual erosion of Christian influence in the academies of the West.

In the early twentieth century, however, a modern Christian apologetic renaissance began with Catholic polemist G. K. Chesterton (1874–1936), who published a classic text on the subject, *Orthodoxy*, in 1908. Chesterton's wit and repartee in the face of rising atheism quickly influenced another wave of Christian apologists, including C. S. Lewis (1898–1963). Lewis—an Oxford-trained philosopher, and atheist turned Christian—has been called the greatest Christian apologist of all time, and even if this is an exaggeration, he helped to release many Christians in the West from the belief that blind faith was their only option. One of these philosophers was Alvin Plantinga (b. 1932), who, with similar distinction, has been called the greatest living philosopher, and who *Time* magazine credits with the rebirth of Christian philosophy in North America.

The influence of modern Christian apologetics has been huge. Today nearly one in three philosophers, and even more scientists, in the West claim to be serious, miracle-believing Christians, and this number continues to rise. **AB**

Futurism
Filippo Marinetti

A short-lived movement that glorified the dynamism and power of the mechanized world

When the Italian poet and novelist Filippo Marinetti (1876–1944) published his "Futurist Manifesto" in the Paris newspaper *Le Figaro* on February 20, 1909, he hoped it would ignite a revolution and erase society's aging values—values perpetuated by what he called "cultural necrophiliacs." He implored his countrymen to throw off the "secondhand clothes" they had been wearing for far too long and argued that the time was ripe, at the start of a new and increasingly industrialized century, to create a new art and a new world representative of what was to come: speed, new technologies, and the glory of war.

Marinetti's manifesto found resonance within Italy's cultural and artistic circles, and its devotees included architects, musicians, artists, graphic and industrial designers, and filmmakers. Futuristic poetry dispensed entirely with verbs, adverbs, and punctuation—annoyances, the poets said, which only served to interrupt the new images seen in their use of only nouns. Futurist architects such as Antonio Sant'Elia (1888–1916) drew sketches of towering concrete cities that were devoid of Baroque curves and ornamentation. The artist Giacomo Balla's (1871–1958) painting *Dynamism of a Dog on a Leash* (1912) was a blur of legs, intended to depict the coming world in a state of rapid and inexorable change.

Initially, Futurism seemed like a breath of fresh air after decades of sentimental romanticism. Futurists appeared optimistic, even heroic; devotees of everything modern: automobiles, noise, speed, and burgeoning cities, as well as the industrialization that made it all possible. Violence and patriotism were also among their hallowed ideals (We will glorify war, the world's only hygiene . . .), and many enlisted when Italy entered World War I in 1915, which, due to the revealed horror of the trenches, ironically spelled the end of this ill-conceived movement. **BS**

⬆ Futurist architect Antonio Sant'Elia's drawing *Power Plant* from 1914 celebrates the advent of electricity. Although most of his designs were never built, they influenced architects and artists.

"It is from Italy that we launch through the world this violently upsetting incendiary manifesto of ours."

Filippo Marinetti, "Futurist Manifesto" (1909)

The Dozens
United States

Jazz Music
United States

An African game of insults that became a social pastime for black Americans

Blues and ragtime are fused to create a unique new form of improvised music

Trying to find a clear origin in time and place for The Dozens—a game of spoken words involving two contestants who take it in turns to hurl insults (or "snaps") at one another until one of them either surrenders or commits an act of violence against the other—is not easy. When the insults relate to sexual issues, the game is known as The Dirty Dozens. Also known as "woofing," "wolfing," "joning," "sounding," and "sigging," the game originated in West Africa, in countries such as Nigeria and Ghana, where it indicated a measure of each person's intelligence and social status. However, it first started to become a recognizable social phenomenon in the United States in the black districts of New Orleans in the early years of the twentieth century.

One of the United States' great cultural gifts to the world, jazz music most likely began in the early 1910s on the streets surrounding New Orleans's red light district of Storyville. Born out of a mix of African and European musical traditions, jazz features syncopation, improvisation, polyrhythms, and blue notes. There was no city like New Orleans in the early years of the twentieth century. Mass migration to the city after years of depressed cotton prices had given it a rare cosmopolitan mix, and musicians and brass bands were in high demand. There was no shortage of instruments; the city had been flooded with trumpets, trombones, cornets, and drum kits since the end of the Spanish-American War in 1898, when U.S. military bands disembarked in the city.

"We played The Dozens for recreation, like white folks play Scrabble."

H. Rap Brown, *Die Nigger Die!* (1969)

"Jazz is restless. It won't stay put and it never will."

J. J. Johnson, trombonist

Early examples of a Dozens contest would often involve twelve rounds of insults. In 1929 the hit song "The Dirty Dozen" by the African American songwriter and pianist Speckled Red conveyed the art of the insult in its lyrics: "Cause he's a rotten mistreater, robber, and a cheater; slip you with a dozen, yo pop ain't yo cousin; and you mama do the lordylord!" Speckled Red recalled playing The Dozens in his own community when he was a child, when men of words were looked up to. The game was also valued as a mechanism in the display of aggression, but never countenanced violence against whites. A Dozens game might begin with: "Now, first thing I'm gonna talk about is your ol' momma"; the first one to crack and throw a punch lost. Participants were overwhelmingly male, although females were known to play, too. **JMa**

Music became embedded in the daily lives of its citizens, while segregation formed African Americans into tight, insular communities—perfect ingredients, it turned out, for producing new forms of musical self-expression. Some claim this exotic new combination of blues, ragtime, and never-heard-before rhythms emerged spontaneously in cities across the United States, from Chicago to Kansas City, but evidence points to New Orleans as being the only city that possessed all of the factors necessary to create this new music, which thrived on improvisation and instrumental diversity.

The term "jazz" did not emerge until the 1920s and it was possibly a derivative of "jass," a reference to jasmine perfume, popular among the prostitutes of New Orleans. Incorporating Dixieland, swing, even funk and hip-hop, it is and always will be "America's music." **BS**

◄ Blues musician Speckled Red (pictured in 1960) was known for his recordings of "The Dirty Dozens."

The Oedipus Complex
Sigmund Freud

Drawing parallels between an ancient legend and an early developmental stage in boys, Freud launched a controversial psychoanalytic theory

⬆ Ingres's painting *Oedipus and the Sphinx* (*c.* 1808). When Oedipus solved the sphinx's riddle, he was made king of Thebes and wedded to Jocasta, who was later revealed to be his mother.

Oedipus is a character from ancient Greek mythology who, in unwitting fulfillment of an oracular prophecy, murders his father and goes on to marry his mother. Viennese psychologist Sigmund Freud (1856–1939), familiar with this legend through Sophocles's tragedy *Oedipus the King*, made connections between this myth and the material he claimed to have uncovered through dream interpretation, psychoanalysis of neurotic patients, and self-analysis. Freud first used the term "Oedipus complex" in print in 1910, by which time it had formed an integral part of his thinking on child development and the origin of neuroses.

Freud read the Oedipus myth as an expression of the repressed fantasies of every young male child. "It is the fate of all of us," he wrote, "to direct our first sexual impulse toward our mother and our first murderous wish against our father." According to Freud, at the age of three boys entered a stage of psychosexual development in which their genitals became the prime erogenous zone. In this "phallic stage," boys focused their desire upon their mothers; they violently resented and feared their fathers as more powerful rivals. He later extended the theory to female children in the "Electra complex"—girls desiring their fathers and feeling murderous toward their mothers.

Freud claimed that, in a normal individual, the Oedipal stage was left behind as the child learned to identify with the parent of its own gender and choose a sexual object outside the family. Those who remained fixated on their opposite-gender parent, however, developed neurotic symptoms and sexual deviance. Critics have pointed out that there is little in the way of solid evidence to support Freud's vision of the hidden psychosexual dramas of childhood. Nevertheless, the Oedipus complex has itself become a myth with great potency in modern culture. **RG**

"Freud … has not given an explanation of the ancient myth. What he has done is to propound a new myth."

Ludwig Wittgenstein, philosopher

Emergency Room
Louisville City Hospital, Kentucky

"Accident Services" herald a new generation of medical treatment

In the mid-1800s the Medical Institute of Louisville, Kentucky, was home to Samuel Gross (1805–84), one of the giants of nineteenth-century surgery. Gross pioneered new suturing techniques, set up one of the country's first surgical laboratories, and performed the first successful surgery on an abdominal stab wound. Gross is depicted performing surgery in Thomas Eakins's celebrated painting *The Gross Clinic* (1875) and he influenced future generations of medical students. Graduates from the University of Louisville established Kentucky's first clinic to educate students in clinical medicine and performed that state's first appendectomy. By the turn of the century Louisville was at the forefront of medical research in the United States, and it therefore came as no surprise when, in 1911, Louisville City Hospital opened the first "Accident Service," an early form of trauma care similar to services already being offered by railway companies and other workers' organizations in Europe. Louisville Hospital's emergency services were further expanded and improved with radical new approaches to trauma care instituted by the surgeon Dr. Arnold Griswold in 1935, and became a precursor of the modern emergency room, which began to take shape in the mid-1950s.

The advent of the Korean War in the early 1950s saw the approach to emergency care evolve further, with the realization that immediate treatment on the battlefield could save countless lives. This spurred the development of the emergency room; however, by the 1960s emergency room care in the United States was still uneven at best as doctors realized special training was required to properly equip doctors, surgeons, and nurses with the skills to cope with trauma. In 1968 the American College of Emergency Physicians was established to train a new breed of "emergency physicians." **BS**

Monetarism
Irving Fisher

The theory or practice of controlling the supply of money to stabilize the economy

Monetarism is a macroeconomic theory first considered by Martín de Azpilcueta, a Spanish theologian and early economist in the sixteenth century. It was only developed as a theory—the quantity theory of money—in the late 1800s and not fully unraveled until Irving Fisher (1867–1947), in *The Purchasing Power of Money* (1911), stressed the significance of the money supply as a primary factor in determining a nation's gross domestic product (GDP). The theory, a mix of core policies and dogmatic theoretical constructs, led to a belief that economies are at their most efficient when subject to only minimal government interference, and also that the growth rate of money in an economy should be fixed to the rate of GDP, thus limiting the Federal Reserve Bank's ability to "meddle."

"The rate of interest acts as a link between income-value and capital-value."
Irving Fisher

Many economists credit the rise of monetarism as an alternative to traditional Keynesian theory—which supports appropriate government regulation of the economy—to the U.S. economist Milton Friedman (1912–2006), who held that the growth of and quantity of money circulating in an economy directly affects rises in the cost of goods and services. Monetarism grew in the late 1970s after Keynesian theories failed in the face of stagflation: high inflation and high unemployment created by successive oil-price shocks.

However, monetarism was built on false assumptions: that central banks alone control the amount of money in circulation, and that inflation cannot be restricted by limiting the money supply. Even what constitutes "money" became difficult to define. Monetarism was fated to be an experiment that failed. **BS**

Blues Music
Southern African Americans

Music developed by African Americans in the rural southern United States

⬆ Unlike many rural bluesmen, W. C. Handy was an educated musician who encountered the blues at around age thirty. He remained passionate about the form until the end of his life.

Blues music, or, more simply, the blues, is a type of music original to the American Deep South, and one characterized by its scale structure, chord structure, notes, and lyrical themes. The blues also often features the use of "blue," or bent notes, caused by the musician raising or lowering notes after sounding them, as well as a three-line A-A-B verse form in which the first two verses repeat, and a twelve-bar, four/four-time stanza paired with a three-chord progression.

Along with jazz, the blues is considered one of the few original U.S. art forms, one that represents a merger between African and European musical traditions. Since Elizabethan times (1558–1603), the color blue had been associated with feelings of sadness and melancholy. Slaves working in southern fields often used a call-and-response style of singing as they worked, with many of these songs and spirituals expressing aspects of their lives of forced labor and servitude. This music, when blended with the structures of English ballads, developed into the style that became the blues.

In 1912, composer W. C. Handy (1873–1958), known as "the father of the blues," published the sheet music for a song, "Memphis Blues." Arguably the first blues song, it introduced Handy's style of twelve-bar blues. The first recording of instrumental blues music appeared the year after, in 1913, and blues music was gradually noticed before exploding in popularity in the 1920s; it was extremely popular for decades thereafter.

The history of the blues is an indelible part of modern music. Blues structures, particularly the twelve-bar blues form, are present in numerous contemporary popular songs, especially those of modern rock 'n' roll, R&B, and pop music. Its influence has also stretched to jazz, and country, and even modern classical music. Today, blues stars such as Eric Bibb and Robert Cray have enthusiastic followings. **MT**

"The blues tells a story. Every line of the blues has meaning."

John Lee Hooker, musician

Knowledge by Description / Knowledge by Acquaintance
Bertrand Russell

All knowledge is ultimately dependent on experience

The distinction between "knowledge by description" and "knowledge by acquaintance" can be applied to understand knowledge. There are at least two ways that we come to know truths about the world. One is through direct, "firsthand" experience of events and another is through description of these events. For example, a man, "John," who met Bertrand Russell (1872–1970) may know, by acquaintance, that Russell was a nice man. If John tells someone that Russell was nice, they know, by description, that "Bertrand Russell was a nice man." Our ability to distinguish between two different ways of learning about the world has profound impacts on philosophy.

Russell introduced the distinction in his seminal article "Knowledge by Acquaintance and Knowledge by Description" (1912). He was motivated to write about the distinction by the work of nineteenth-century philosopher John Grote. Russell, however, brought the idea to the contemporary philosophical world. He realized that the knowledge that we have by acquaintance is special because it is not really something that we put into sentences when we know it. For example, if a person met Russell and experienced his niceness, that experience is not really true or false; it is just an experience of niceness. It is not until they think about it and realize "Bertrand Russell is a nice man" that they can say whether the sentence is true or false. The amazing problem is the realization that our own thoughts about our experiences themselves are knowledge by description. The experience we have is by acquaintance, but as soon as we start making sentences about it, even to ourselves, we are engaging in description. Philosophers are still trying to figure out the nature of experience as it relates to knowledge. If knowledge requires that our sentences be true or false, then we cannot say our experience, our "knowledge by acquaintance," is really knowledge at all. **NM**

⬆ Philosopher Bertrand Russell, photographed in 1935. He was one of the founders of analytical philsophy, which remains the dominant philosophical tradition in the English-speaking world.

"Knowledge by acquaintance is always better than mere knowledge by description, and the first does not presuppose the second nor require it."

A. W. Tozer, Christian preacher

Gestalt Psychology
Max Wertheimer et al

A school of psychology stresses that the whole of anything is greater than its parts

The term "Gestalt" was first coined by the Austrian philosopher Christian von Ehrenfels, who in 1890 published *On Gestalt Qualities*, a critique of the prevailing Atomists who believed the natural world to be absolute without any regard to context. Von Ehrenfels challenged this through a musical example: play a song in the key of C and then in A flat. No two notes are the same, yet the listener will recognize the tunes as the same. In other words there are no absolutes and context matters. One of von Ehrenfels's students was Max Wertheimer (1880–1943); the publication of his "Experimental Studies of the Perception of Movement" in 1912 marked the foundation of the Gestalt school.

Gestalt psychology was formulated as a response to the inexorable accumulation of data through scientific

"A man is not only a part of his field, he is also one among other men."

Max Wertheimer

investigation and, in the opinion of its originators, the resultant total neglect of the phenomena that the scientific inquiry was supposed to be revealing. Much the same can be said for psychology and philosophy, pursuits replete with terms that seem full of potential, intuition, personality, and existentialism, but when we try and comprehend their meaning the terms fail us and we are left with a question: are these disciplines, in their present forms, equipped to deliver the enlightenment they proffer? Rather than ruminating over psychological hypothesis or scientific theorems, it was the hope of the founders of Gestalt psychology— Max Wertheimer and fellow psychologists Kurt Koffka (1886–1941) and Wolfgang Köhler (1887–1967)—to be able to determine the true nature of things without forever puzzling out unanswerable riddles. **BS**

Delusion
Karl Jaspers

The capacity for pathological beliefs is endemic to the human condition

Delusions are pathological beliefs that are adhered to with conviction despite there being a dearth of evidence to support them. Delusions are almost always pathological, and most occur as a result of impaired neurological function or mental illness. German philosopher Karl Jaspers (1883–1969) was the first to define the criteria for a belief to be considered delusional in his textbook *General Psychopathology* (1913).

Delusions can be broken down into four categories: bizarre (strange and implausible); nonbizarre (possible, though still false); mood-congruent (consistent with a depressive diagnosis); and mood-neutral (a belief that bears no relation to a person's emotional state). There are also a myriad of delusional "themes," such as poverty, in which the sufferer believes they are

"Might not [delusions] be imaginings that are mistaken for beliefs by the imaginer?"

Stanford Encyclopedia of Philosophy

impoverished; delusional parasitosis, a severe reaction against an imagined parasitic infestation; erotomania, thinking that someone is in love with you when they are not; and grandiose delusions, beliefs that usually revolve around a supernatural, religious, or science fiction theme that can be related to mental illnesses, such as bipolar disorders and schizophrenia.

Regardless of how many guises we attribute it, delusion does not have to be a destructive false assumption. Religious belief, for example, possesses many of the same attributes common to pathological delusions, and yet can be empowering. The fact is delusion remains an imagined contrivance, the product of intellectual thought, and in that sense it is a potential pitfall common to all. It is only the destructive, shared delusions referred to above that we tend to label. **BS**

The Cat (c. 1930), by Louis Wain, was possibly informed by the English artist's late-onset schizophrenia. ➡

Infinite Monkey Theorem
Émile Borel

A monkey typing at random for an infinite amount of time will type a given text

This completely implausible theorem, attributed to the French mathematician Émile Borel (1871–1956) in 1913 and popularized by astronomer Arthur Eddington (1882–1944) in his book *The Nature of the Physical World* (1928), asks us to believe that by taking an infinite number of monkeys and sitting them down at typewriters, eventually one of them will type a known work of literature, such as William Shakespeare's *Hamlet* (c. 1600). The raft of dilemmas that this illustration of the concepts of infinity and probability creates is self-evident. Philosophically, how can one calculate the probability of achieving a desired result if you cannot first demonstrate that the goal is feasible? The laws of probability also condemn it. A monkey has a one in twenty-six chance of typing the first letter of *Hamlet*.

"To be or not to be—that is thegrrdnm zsplkt."

Bob Newhart, comedian

Typing the second letter correctly sees that probability increase to one in 676. After just fifteen characters, the probability increases to a figure in the thousands of trillions, and there are still 130,000 correct letters to go.

In 2003 researchers at the University of Plymouth in the United Kingdom put six crested macaques in front of a computer. Occasionally, in between urinating on the keyboard and smashing it with a rock, the monkeys typed out a large number of "S"'s. The theorem, however, is not without its unintended uses. In his book *The Blind Watchmaker* (1986), the evolutionary biologist Richard Dawkins cited the theory to explain how complexity can arise from random mutations; that if any correct letters could somehow be "frozen" and the incorrect letters discarded then a Darwinian platform has been created for the monkey's descendants to improve on. **BS**

Behaviorism
John Watson

Our response to external stimuli becomes, for a time, a possible window to the mind

Psychological behaviorism can trace its beginning to the publication of the article "Psychology as a Behaviorist Views It" (1913) by John Watson (1878–1958), who believed behavior is acquired through conditioning. In the world of the behaviorist, the reason we do the things we do can be understood without the need to resort to complex psychological concepts that are too subjective and defy analysis. How we act is determined by external forces, not the machinations of our cognitive, emotional minds. Behaviorists such as Burrhus Frederic Skinner thought psychiatry need concern itself only with a subject's observable behavior in response to external physical stimuli. But can all the complexities of our behavior simply be attributed to the world around us, to mere "stimulus and effect?"

"Thinking is behavior. The mistake is in allocating the behavior to the mind."

B. F. Skinner, *About Behaviorism* (1974)

One of the proponents of this form of behaviorism was the Russian physiologist Ivan Pavlov, whose work with dogs led to him theorizing that behavior that is rewarded immediately is more likely to be repeated. Pavlov observed dogs salivating when about to be fed, but also noticed that after repeated feedings, the dogs began to salivate even when he entered the room without any food. Pavlov realized that the dogs had been conditioned to begin salivating; their behavior had been altered. What Pavlov had discovered, and Skinner after him, was that behavior, whether animal or human, can be "shaped." But to what extent?

Behaviorism was oft criticized for belittling psychiatry and did not stay long on the disciplinary landscape. It was too deterministic and left too little room for the expression of free will. **BS**

Gratuitous Act
André Gide

An act of crime or evil that defies classification and interpretation

In the existential novel *Lafcadio's Adventures* (1914) by French author André Gide (1869–1951), a young man named Amedee is pushed off the roof of a moving train by his half-brother Lafcadio, and is killed. Lafcadio, like Albert Camus's Meursault in *The Stranger* (1942), is oddly unmoved by his own actions, which are deemed a gratuitous act: an unmotivated crime committed without any apparent objective or subsequent remorse. There is no premeditation, only impulse—and the gaining of immediate gratification. Gide did more than anyone to evolve the idea of the unmotivated, unpremeditated, gratuitous act.

On a London street on April 1, 2009, a Scotland Yard policeman used a baton to beat a homeless man who had unwittingly and innocently wandered into the

"It is better to be hated for what you are than loved for what you are not."

André Gide

vicinity of a public protest. The homeless man's liver was injured in the assault, and fifty minutes later he died. The court described the incident as "a gratuitous act" by an officer who had "lost all self-control." The officer himself could offer no explanation for his actions.

The gratuitous act has always been used to argue against the existence of God. The argument is thus: if God exists, gratuitous evil would not exist; gratuitous evil exists, therefore God cannot exist. This, of course, presupposes that the gratuitous act actually exists and that there can indeed be effect without cause. Most, however, would scoff at such a suggestion. There cannot be an effect without a preceding cause, and perhaps the phrase is nothing more than a convenient label to describe acts that have no psychological explanation. **BS**

Postmodern Biblical Criticism
Great Britain

A postmodernist approach to theology and biblical studies

Postmodern biblical criticism came into fashion in the 1950s, but it originated much earlier. A British quarterly philosophical review, *The Hibbert Journal*, applied the term "postmodern" in a religious context in 1914, in an article titled "Post-Modernism." It used the phrase to describe the contemporary change in beliefs and attitudes in religious criticism: "The raison d'être of Post-Modernism is to escape from the double-mindedness of Modernism by being thorough in its criticism by extending it to religion as well as theology, to Catholic feeling as well as to Catholic tradition."

Postmodernist biblical criticism tackles issues of authorship, ethnicity, fantasy, gender, ideology, linguistics, and sexuality in the same way that postmodernism in general tackles topics. In philosophy, postmodernist thought is not one thing: it can refer to various types of thinking, such as deconstruction, structuralism, poststructuralism, and postcolonialism. Similarly, postmodernist biblical criticism does not refer to only one type of critical biblical analysis. It addresses issues regarding identity from the point of view of writers of the Bible and those whom they wrote about, as well as from readers in their interpretation of the Bible.

Postmodern biblical criticism remains very much alive as a discipline, and various philosophers and theologians continue to work in the field. French philosopher Jacques Derrida (1930–2004) famously used the example of the biblical Tower of Babel to explain multiple layers of meaning in his deconstructivist work *Des Tours de Babel* (Towers of Babel, 1985), in which he stressed the importance of reading the narrative in Hebrew. Contemporary writers engaged in postmodernist biblical criticism include the Jewish-American historian and Talmudic scholar Daniel Boyarin, the U.S. theologian and priest A. K. M. Adam, and the Australian theologian Mark G. Brett. **CK**

Dadaism
Artists of the Cabaret Voltaire

A nihilistic art movement that was opposed to war and traditional modes of artistic creation, favoring group collaboration, spontaneity, and chance

More a loosely knit group than an organized movement, Dadaism, which had its beginnings in Eastern Europe in the years prior to 1914, came to a head in Zurich, Switzerland, in 1916 as a protest against the barbarism of World War I (1914–18) among the artists and acolytes of the Cabaret Voltaire, a Zurich nightclub owned by the German poet Hugo Ball (1886–1927). After randomly placing a knife in a dictionary and it falling on the word "dada" meaning "hobby-horse," the group chose the word as the name for their anti-aesthetic activities. Considered a traitor in his own country for his opposition to the war, Ball wrote the "Dada Manifesto" (1916) and went on to become one of its leading proponents. His Cabaret Voltaire was the birthplace of Dada, safely ensconced as it was within neutral Switzerland while Europe was at war around them.

The Dadaists despised nationalism, materialism, and colonialism: anything that upheld the existing order and that had brought Europe to war was vilified, including its artistic traditions. Dadaists blamed the causes and continuing promulgation of the war on bourgeois and colonial interests, and used a new, deliberately irrational art to express their disgust at having been led into a conflict that nobody, aside from politicians and the military, seemed to want.

The art of Dada was whimsical, often sarcastic, vibrant, and occasionally silly. It did not adhere to any rules of form, although abstraction and Expressionism were never far away, and ready-made objects were a common theme, such as Marcel Duchamp's *Fountain* (1917), a porcelain urinal mounted on a pedestal, a statement that illustrated Dada's nonsensical nature. The movement in the United States was centered at Alfred Stieglitz's New York gallery "291." Dadaism proved resilient, only losing its relevance three decades after its birth in the face of post-World War II optimism. **BS**

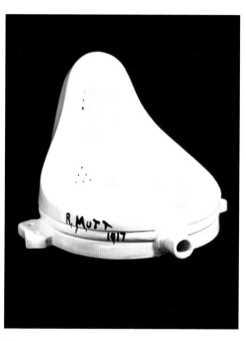

⬆ Dadaist ready-mades, such as Marcel Duchamp's *Fountain* (1917)—a porcelain urinal, which was signed "R. Mutt"—sparked heated debate about the meaning of art.

"For us, art is not an end in itself . . . but it is an opportunity for the true perception and the criticism of the times we live in."
Hugo Ball, Dadaist

Supermarket
Clarence Saunders

A large, self-service store that offers a wide variety of goods for purchase

Grocer Clarence Saunders (1881–1953) first developed the idea of self-service retail when he opened the Piggly Wiggly store in 1916 in Memphis, Tennessee. Customers entered the store via a turnstile, took a shopping basket, and viewed the merchandise available, which was displayed in elaborate aisles. By 1922, there were 1,200 Piggly Wiggly stores, and they became the model for the supermarket.

The first supermarket to incorporate the ideas of self-service, with separate product departments, discount pricing, and volume selling, was King Kullen, which opened in 1930 in New York City, with the slogan "Pile it high. Sell it low." Supermarkets took advantage of the wide-scale opulence in the United States and elsewhere that resulted from the economic growth in the decades after World War II (1939–45), which also saw increasing automobile ownership and suburban development. Self-service shopping took longer to catch on in the United Kingdom, and supermarkets only became established from the 1950s.

The rise of supermarkets and their later larger incarnation, the superstore, led to the decline of many smaller, local, family-owned shops. Many superstores, including Walmart in the United States, utilized novel purchasing and distribution logistics. This included buying in bulk and only building stores within a specific distribution radius so that transportation costs could be minimized. Businesses, such as Tesco in the United Kingdom, came to believe—with superior profits supplying abundant reasons—that, given the option, consumers would rather shop at one place with lower prices for all the items they required than shop at multiple locations. Supermarkets changed the way that people shopped in the latter portion of the twentieth century and have had a marked effect on the business culture of towns and cities. **CRD**

Customers discover a new way to shop for groceries at the Piggly Wiggly store in Memphis, USA, in 1918.

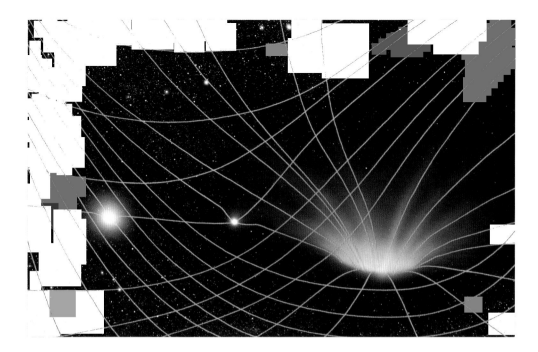

1916

General Relativity
Albert Einstein

The geometric theory of gravitation alters the fundamentals of the universe

One of the foundation stones of modern physics, general relativity (GR), or the general theory of relativity—the geometric theory of gravitation—was published by German-born physicist Albert Einstein (1879–1955) in 1916, and caused a scientific revolution.

With one sweeping theory, space and time were no longer absolute and passive; now they were dynamic, able to be bent, slowed down—the very matter that comprised them and surrounded them capable of altering their behavior. Even light itself could be shifted—general relativity predicted it could be curved by the gravitational pull generated by the interstellar objects it passed, a prediction confirmed by a solar eclipse just three years later. The universe had all of a sudden lost its static predictability. Physics, and the universe it was struggling to make sense of, had instantly become a lot more interesting.

GR was first and foremost a theory of gravity—one of the most fundamental forces in the universe—and turned on its ear the universally accepted gravitational laws of Isaac Newton, developed in the seventeenth century. No longer was gravity a straight line, an apple falling from a tree that continues straight down until it collides with the ground. In Einstein's universe, with planets and suns causing the space around them to be warped and altering the very fabric of spacetime, Newton's straight lines now had to bend to Einstein's curved, puckered universe. Orbits, in the words of U.S. astronomer and astrophysicist Carl Sagan, were really "tramlines in the sky," bent by gravity to take moons around planets and planets around suns—a predestined, endless loop along their otherwise straight, applelike trajectories. GR also illustrated a universe in a state of flux, a notion that so railed against Einstein's own view of a static universe that he tried to modify it but could not, unable to bend the laws of his own immutable theory. **BS**

⬆ An artwork shows the huge gravitational pull of a black hole (bottom right), which warps the fabric of space.

Wormholes
Hermann Weyl

Hypothetical tunnels in spacetime that would enable faster than light travel

First postulated by German theoretical physicist Hermann Weyl (1885–1955) as part of his book analyzing electromagnetic field energy, *Raum, Zeit, Materie* (Space, Time, Matter, 1918), wormholes are hypothetical constructs in spacetime (the merging of space and time into a single continuum). They are presumed theoretical shortcuts or tunnels through space, not unlike the rabbit hole Alice fell into only to emerge in the parallel, fantastical world of Wonderland. The name "wormhole" was given to them later, in 1957, by U.S. theoretical physicist John Wheeler (1911–2008).

Wormholes wholly lack any observational evidence. Their existence, however, is theoretically possible according to the laws of general relativity (1916) governing the universe of Albert Einstein (1879–1955). Einstein and his collaborator, Nathan Rosen (1909–95), saw them as tunnel-like pathways connecting disparate regions of spacetime. Their constructs were given a name: Einstein-Rosen bridges. The principle, however, did not sit well with many physicists who balked at the notion that such travel would, in effect, allow the transmission of data and objects at a speed greater than the speed of light, thus breaching one of the foundational aspects of special relativity (1905).

In 1962 Wheeler claimed that the wormhole of Weyl and Einstein/Rosen was inherently unstable and prone to closing at both ends moments after opening. Wheeler then divided wormholes into two categories: Lorenzian wormholes along the line of Einstein's standard model, and Euclidean wormholes, which exist only in "imaginary time" and the world of quantum mechanics. In 2010, British physicist Stephen Hawking (b. 1942) wrote that wormholes may be present not only in interstellar space, but also may be infinitely small and all around us here on Earth, winking in and out of existence unnoticed. He asserted that natural radiation would always rule out their use for time travel. **BS**

1918

Deflationary Theory of Truth
Gottlob Frege

The argument that there is no such thing as a truth beyond what is simply asserted

According to the deflationary theory of truth, the claim that a sentence is true means the same thing as simply asserting the sentence. The first notable defender of the deflationary theory was German philosopher and logician Gottlob Frege (1848–1925), who first presented the idea in 1918.

The central idea of the deflationary theory is that there is no deep nature to truth, and that adding the words "is true" to a sentence does not change the meaning of the sentence. The search for the nature of truth will always be frustrated, the deflationist says, because there is nothing there. So, if someone were to say that the sentence "there are 1001 ideas in this book" is true, they would have said simply that

there are 1001 ideas in this book. This minimalism is opposed to "inflationary" theories of truth, such as the correspondence theory or coherence theory, according to which truth requires correspondence with the facts or coherence with your beliefs, respectively. Early deflationary theorists such as Frege, Frank Ramsey (1903–30), and A. J. Ayer (1910–89) were motivated by a distrust of traditional philosophical metaphysical debates regarding the nature of truth, particularly because there seemed to be no hope of resolution. The theorists nevertheless recognized that the concept of truth was a useful one to have, as it allows people conveniently to affirm or deny whole sets of sentences, such as "everything that Einstein wrote is true" or "some things that Descartes said are true."

The deflationary theory has remained popular. Modern versions often claim that everything that there is to know about truth can be captured by an equivalence schema: <p> is true if and only if p. The "<>" element on the left-hand side of the schema indicates that the proposition, belief, or sentence is being mentioned rather than actually asserted. The right-hand side of the schema then uses it. **BSh**

⬆ Frege noted that "I smell the scent of violets" means the same as "It is true that I smell the scent of violets."

Modal Logic
Clarence Lewis

A form of logic intended to make sense of the ambiguities of everyday phrases

Modal logic was devised in 1918 by the U.S. academic philosopher Clarence Lewis (1883–1964), one of the founders of modern philosophical logic, in an attempt to circumvent the paradox of implication—that a false proposition was capable of implying any proposition. It has since developed into a mathematical tool for the study of description languages that discuss various types of relational structures.

Lewis was interested in looking at the reasoning behind everyday modalities (modes of truth), such as "It should be that . . . ," and "It ought to be the case that . . . ," and how their ambiguous phrasing seemed to allow for two kinds of truth, necessary and contingent. Consider the statement, "It is summer." But is it necessarily summer? Is it summer right now,

"Only the true statements are provable, and all the provable statements are true."

Joel McCance, "A Brief Introduction to Modal Logic"

or at some point in the future? Fly to the opposite hemisphere and it certainly would not be summer there. Logicians refer to such modifications to an initial assertion as "modalities" and examine the mode in which the statement could be considered to be true. The truth tables of basic logic cannot easily handle such ambiguities, and so Lewis promulgated "modal logic" to tease apart the contradictions in beliefs, possibilities, and the supposed truth of judgments.

Modal logic's principles are now used in linguistics, artificial intelligence, computer science, and game theory. Modal logic—given impetus by many logicians who have since expanded upon Lewis's original precepts—has come a long way since Lewis first propounded it, as the biannual Advances in Modal Logic conferences attest. **BS**

Prohibition
United States

Prevention of the sale of alcohol with the aim of obtaining partial or total abstinence

The temperance movement in the United States attributed society's ills to alcohol consumption. Progression toward national prohibition of the manufacture, sale, and distribution of alcoholic beverages was gradual, beginning with sporadic prohibitions arising from religious revivalism in the 1820s and 1830s. The Anti-Saloon League, founded in 1893, led state prohibition drives between 1906 and 1913, and during World War I a Wartime Prohibition Act was enacted to conserve grain for food production.

An amendment to the Constitution of the United States, championed by congressman Andrew Volstead (1860–1947), was passed by the U.S. Congress in December 1917 and ratified by the requisite three-fourths of the states in January 1919. The Eighteenth

"We have seen the evil of . . . liquors . . . let us see what [prohibition] will do for us."

Thomas Jordan Jarvis, U.S. congressman

Amendment (the National Prohibition Act, commonly referred to as the Volstead Act) was passed in October 1919 over the veto of President Woodrow Wilson.

By January 1920, prohibition was in effect in thirty-three states; however, the law was enforced only when and where the population was sympathetic to it. In December 1933, the Twenty-first Amendment repealed federal prohibition but allowed prohibition at the state and local levels; by 1966, all had abandoned it.

Prohibition gave impetus to entire illegal economies—bootlegging, speakeasies, and distilling operations. Criminal activity increased, and illegal manufacture and sales of liquor flourished, resulting in higher prices for liquor and beer. The Eighteenth Amendment is the only Constitutional amendment to have been ratified and later repealed. **BC**

Archetypes
Carl Jung

Universally recognized prototypes that inform our understanding and behavior

⬆ Carl Jung (pictured here in 1960) suggested the notion of unconscious archetypes in rejection of the idea that people must learn everything from birth.

"The concept of the archetype, which is an indispensable correlate of the idea of the collective unconscious, indicates the existence of definite forms in the psyche which seem to be present always and everywhere."

Carl Jung, *The Archetypes and the Collective Unconscious* (1934)

In the English language, the word "archetype" was first coined in the 1540s to describe something from which copies are made. It would not enter popular parlance until 1919, when Swiss psychiatrist Carl Jung (1875–1961) used it in an essay titled "Instinct and the Unconscious" to describe any type of behavior, symbol, term, or concept that was copied or emulated by others. In other words, it is a sort of universally recognized prototype. Jung asserted that archetypes are "ancient or archaic images that derive from the collective unconscious," the fragment of our unconscious mind that is passed down to us as an inherited gift. He also described archetypes as "primordial images" that have been expressed continuously throughout history in folklore and as far back as prehistoric rock art.

New archetypes are not so much created as discovered. They have always been within us, Jung claimed, hidden and waiting to be found as each of us journeys individually into our own psyche. Archetypal beings include the hero, the wise old man, and the fraud, while archetypal events include birth and death. According to Jung, these and countless other varieties of archetypes act as conduits for our experiences and emotions. Because they surface as recognizable patterns of behavior, archetypes can be studied in order to gain insights into human behavior.

Jung's five primary archetypes comprise: the self, which is the center of our psyche; the shadow, the opposite of our ego; the anima, which is the female aspect of man's psyche; the animus, the masculine image in women; and the persona, which equals the image that we as individuals present to those around us. Archetypes are all around us in literature, from the "ill-fated lovers" represented by Shakespeare's Romeo and Juliet, the "brooding antihero" of 1940s artist Bob Kane's Batman, to the "villain" Voldemort in author J. K. Rowling's *Harry Potter* series of novels. **BS**

Ponzi Scheme
Carlo Ponzi

A fraudulent investment operation promising significant returns on a risk-free investment

Carlo Ponzi (1882–1949), an Italian immigrant to the United States, scammed thousands of New Englanders out of millions of dollars with a get-rich-quick plan that involved investing in the conversion of European postage coupons into U.S. currency. In 1919, Ponzi formed the Securities Exchange Company, assuring investors that they would double their investments in ninety days. He ultimately defrauded thousands of investors out of approximately $15 million using only $30 worth of stamps. Ponzi was arrested in 1920 and charged with multiple counts of fraud and larceny and sentenced to prison. He was in and out of U.S. jails until 1934, when he was deported to Italy.

Variations of the Ponzi scheme, also known as a "pyramid scheme," had existed since the seventeenth century, and they all had but one objective: to make a fortune for the operator. First, the operator entices a small group of initial investors into the scheme. The early investors receive tremendous investment returns from funds secured from a second group of investors. The second group, in turn, receives funds obtained from a third group of investors, and so on until the operator absconds with the funds when the operation is about to collapse.

Ponzi was by no means the first or the last to profit from such a scheme. In 2008, Bernard Madoff, (*b.* 1938) a former chairman of the NASDAQ stock exchange, was charged with fraud for defrauding investors out of some $50 billion. Madoff orchestrated a multibillion-dollar scheme that swindled money from thousands of investors; although he did not promise spectacular short-term investment returns, his investors' phony account statements showed consistent positive returns even during turbulent market conditions. In March 2009, he pleaded guilty to eleven charges of fraud and money laundering, and in June he was sentenced to 150 years in prison. **BC**

⬆ Carlo Ponzi faces the police camera following arrest for forging a check in 1910. Ten years later, he received a five-year sentence for his pyramid scam as a warning to others.

"I landed in this country with $2.50 in cash and $1 million in hopes, and those hopes never left me."

Carlo Ponzi

Bauhaus
Walter Gropius

An integration of artist and craftsman that bridged the gap between art and industry

The Bauhaus approach to design originated in Weimar, Germany, with the foundation, in 1919, of a private architectural practice by Walter Gropius (1883–1969) and Adolph Meyer (1881–1929). It was a style born of the production lines of the new industrial age, which Gropius, after having witnessed firsthand the horrors of World War I (1914–18), was determined to harness for the betterment of society. In contrast to the skilled, romantic woodwork of the rural-based Arts and Crafts period, Bauhaus (German for "house of construction") would be an urban, city-bred movement with its roots firmly in modernism. When Gropius was appointed master of the Grand-Ducal Saxon School of Arts and Crafts, also in 1919, he transformed it into what would become known as the Bauhaus School.

> "A modern . . . lively architecture is the visible sign of an authentic democracy."

Walter Gropius

A Bauhaus building was almost always cube-shaped, replete with right angles and overwhelmingly asymmetrical. Ornamentation was shunned in favor of functionalism, open floor plans, and smooth facades. Advances in engineering allowed for walls to be built around skeletons of iron and steel for the first time, freeing them from the need to support the structure. Bauhaus colors were mostly gray, black, and white, roofs were flat, and industrial aestheticism meant a reduction of form to the barest of essentials. Rooms within Bauhaus buildings were sparsely furnished, too.

Bauhaus design extended to interior design, sculpture, painting, and even typography and poster art. Informing myriad disciplines, Bauhaus demonstrated the exhilarating idea that an individual's artistic spirit could exist in harmony with mass production. **BS**

Biblical Form Criticism
Martin Dibelius

Analysis that classifies the Bible according to the literary forms in which it is written

German theologian Hermann Gunkel (1862–1932) was the first to develop biblical form criticism, but it was German theologian Martin Dibelius (1883–1947) who pioneered the discipline's analytical method. Furthermore, it was Dibelius's work, *Die Formgeschichte des Evangeliums* (From Tradition to Gospel, 1919) that gave form criticism its name. Dibelius analyzed the gospels in terms of oral traditions and asserted that in their earliest forms they consisted of short sermons written for the early Christian community. Dibelius also demonstrated that the first-century CE gospel writer Luke had access to St. Paul's written records.

In biblical form criticism, the Bible is analyzed and classified into literary forms, such as elegies, parables, poems, and sayings. Critics then attempt to clarify

> "An original-original form never existed, or at least not in . . . missionary . . . Greek."

Martin Dibelius, *From Tradition to Gospel* (1919)

the history of their formation. Form criticism enables scholars to take into account the tradition behind the Gospels at the time of writing, and attempt to reconstruct the life of Jesus and his authentic sayings.

Dibelius's work was well received by his contemporaries. German theologian Rudolf Bultmann (1884–1976) developed form criticism, and in turn Bultmann's work revolutionized biblical scholarship, inspiring academics to further distinguish the sayings of Jesus from those of the authors of the Gospels.

Form criticism led to the foundation of the Jesus Seminar in 1985 in the United States. Consisting of some 150 scholars and laymen, it attempted to verify the historicity of Jesus's sayings and actions, going on to produce new translations of the apocrypha and New Testament for use as textual sources. **CK**

In 1925 the Bauhaus school moved from Weimar to these new premises in the German town of Dessau.

Le Monde entier parle du

MANIFESTE DU SURRÉALISME

POISSON SOLUBLE

par

ANDRÉ BRETON

Qu'est-ce que le Surréalisme?

KRA, ÉDITEUR
6, Rue Blanche

Le volume : 7 fr. 50

Nº 1 — Première année   1er Décembre 1924

LA RÉVOLUTION SURRÉALISTE

1919

Surrealism

André Breton

A movement giving artistic expression to dreams, imagination, and the unconscious

The Surrealist movement in art first emerged from within the Dada-esque artistic communities of Paris in the years after World War I (1914–18). An attempt to unlock the imagination through the channeling of the unconscious, its first artistic expression is generally ascribed to French writer and poet André Breton (1896–1966) who, in 1919, wrote what is considered the movement's first literary work, *Les Champs magnétiques* (The Magnetic Fields); he followed that, in 1924, with *Le Manifeste du surréalism* (The Surrealist Manifesto), later seen to be the movement's anthem.

Surrealists utilized dream imagery to uncover and comment on our deepest anxieties, often using collage and employing images from popular culture.

The movement proved enormously resilient to change, surviving challenges from existentialists and Abstract Expressionists as they sought to usurp its role as the preeminent artistic voice of the unconscious. However, it began to fracture when Breton tried to alter its primary focus from art to political activism, a move that split the movement into those who believed art to be inherently political and those who did not. Still, Surrealism would not die, and an exhibition of Surrealist art in New York in 1942, organized by art collector Penny Guggenheim, was an example of just how pervasive and universal the movement had become.

Influenced by Sigmund Freud's pioneering work in psychology, the Surrealists believed that the conscious mind, burdened as it was with all of society's accumulated cultural and religious taboos, needed to be freed, not only so that it could better express itself artistically, but also to help reveal society's multitude of destructive contradictions. Surrealism may not have gone on to achieve its lofty social objectives, but artistically it flourished, becoming arguably the most pervasive and influential art movement of the twentieth century. **BS**

The Surrealist Manifesto defined surrealism as "psychic automatism in its pure state."

Talkies
Lee de Forest

Motion pictures that featured the innovative addition of sound

The synchronization of motion pictures with sound, producing what were referred to at the time as "talkies," was first demonstrated at the Paris Exposition in 1900. Further demonstrations were occasionally held after that, but the technical difficulties involved in the process—which basically worked by crudely synchronizing the starting of the movie projector with an audio playback cylinder—made widespread commercial screenings all but impossible for two decades. However, in 1919, U.S. electrical engineer Lee de Forest (1873–1961) patented his Phonofilm sound on film process, which recorded sound directly onto the movie strip in the form of parallel lines of variable density. The lines recorded electrical waveforms from a microphone photographically, and were translated back into sound when the movie was projected.

The first commercial screening of talkies came on April 15, 1923, at the Rivoli Theater, New York City, with a set of short movies promoted by De Forest Phonofilms. The first commercial hit for talkies, *The Jazz Singer*, appeared four years later, in 1927, although its sound system was not de Forest's. The movie had fewer than 400 spoken words, but its success was undeniable, and within three years 95 percent of all new movies made used talkie technology. This proved a momentous change in the movie industry, simultaneously raising the cost of film production, which drove many smaller production companies out of business, and reducing the availability of jobs for many silent film stars, because the addition of sound to movies brought radical changes in the style of acting required. The bringing together of motion pictures and sound caused a revolution in film technology, the impact of which can be seen in the almost complete absence of professionally made silent films today. **JE**

↑ A huge crowd waits outside Warners' Theatre in New York City to see Al Jolson in *The Jazz Singer* in 1927.

Inferiority Complex
Alfred Adler

A psychological condition that is displayed through a lack of self-worth

The term "inferiority complex" was first used in passing by Sigmund Freud and Carl Jung, but assumed central importance in psychology during the 1920s on account of the work of Austrian psychotherapist, Alfred Adler (1870–1937). Adler had tired of Freud's emphasis on the unconscious as a factor in human behavior and believed that the reality of much behavior was relatively easy to explain. He believed that everyone begins life with feelings of inferiority simply because, as children, we lack many of the skills common to older people. This sense of inferiority—what Adler called inferiority feelings, not to be confused with a complex—is gradually overcome as people grow and develop. Thus, Adler's notion of the inferiority complex was one capable of being corrected.

"Exaggerated sensitiveness is an expression of the feeling of inferiority."

Alfred Adler

Sufferers of the inferiority complex feel inferior to those around them and believe they will never be able to compensate for their inadequacies. The complex develops first in childhood and is often the result of discrimination, bullying, physical disability, or some form of personal rejection. Later, as adults, when confronted with a challenge that cannot be overcome, a secondary inferiority complex can develop. Inferiority complexes can remain dormant, and associated feelings can include resentment, depression, and aggressive or irritable behavior. However, overcoming an inferiority complex can be relatively simple. If a person feels inferior because they do not fit into a particular group, studies indicate that changing groups and finding acceptance elsewhere are often all that is necessary to provide a way forward. **BS**

Country Music
United States

A form of popular music developed from U.S. rural folk and blues roots

Country music originated in the United States in the 1920s, in the folk culture of the rural South. In turn, U.S. folk had grown out of the folk music brought by successive waves of immigrants from Europe, especially the British Isles. Over time, such existing music was drawn upon by banjo players, hillbilly string bands, virtuoso fiddlers, blind balladeers, and gospel singers to generate a louder kind of music that could be heard above the hubbub of community functions. Some of this music came to be known as bluegrass. As southern musicians moved northward, their music came with them, and radio and recordings did much to popularize the style. With the likes of singers Gene Autry (1907–98), Roy Rogers (1911–98), and Tex Williams (1917–85), the music gained particular popularity in the 1940s, with

"I think there's enough room in country music for everybody."

Charley Pride, country musician

the label "country" replacing the slightly derogatory one "hillbilly" music.

Some of the earliest country music recordings emerged from Atlanta. The Grand Ole Opry, a concert hall in Nashville, Tennessee, itself considered the country music capital of the United States, provided radio performances for fans of country music from 1925. The Grand Ole Opry was housed in the Ryman Auditorium in 1943, where it remained until moving into the Grand Ole Opry House in 1974.

In the 1950s, the rise of rock 'n' roll challenged country music, but the latter evolved over time into a more pop-oriented form, and now has gained an international listenership. In recent years many rock acts—including Jon Bon Jovi and Kid Rock—have had crossover hits in the country music realm. **JE**

Country music duo the Delmore Brothers playing guitar in c. 1930. ➡

Autosuggestion
Émile Coué

The routine repetition of a formula that tricks people into feeling better

"Every day in every way I am getting better and better." This is the phrase the physician and psychologist Émile Coué (1857–1926) urged his patients to say to themselves twenty to thirty times every morning after waking and again at night before going to sleep. A former advocate of hypnotism, Coué abandoned that approach in favor of what he called "the laws of suggestion" as an adjunct to prescription medicines. As he explained in his book *Self-Mastery Through Conscious Autosuggestion* (1920), he thought autosuggestion to be much more than mere "positive thinking"—he believed a change in our unconscious thoughts actually had the potential to heal physical ailments. Rather than thinking of himself as a healer, Coué stressed that he merely provided his patients with the mental tools

> *"Autosuggestion is an instrument . . . with which we play unconsciously all our life."*
>
> Émile Coué

needed to heal themselves. Any idea implanted into the conscious mind, as long as it was within the realms of possibility, could become that person's reality.

Coué argued that walking along a plank of wood lying on the ground without falling off it is a relatively simple task. But take that plank and place it 100 feet (30 m) above the ground between two buildings, and suddenly crossing it becomes almost impossible. The plank has not changed, but now the mind is saying that crossing it cannot be done. A person accustomed to heights, however, could cross it with relative ease.

Coué himself defined autosuggestion as the influence of the imagination upon the moral and physical being of mankind. Whatever it was, people with all kinds of ailments came to him to be, at least in part, cured by what he called his "trick." **BS**

Bell Curve Grading
United States

A method of assigning grades according to a pre-determined distribution

The "bell curve" is a concept that states that the majority of things or events happen around the middle point and fewer things happen at the upper or lower end. In other words, the "mean" (average) is also the "mode" (most frequent). When this is plotted on a graph, the resulting shape resembles a bell. It is known in mathematics as the "de Moivre distribution," or the "Laplace-Gaussian curve" and is often used in education for grade distribution determinations.

The practice of bell curve grading, also known as grading on a curve, originated in the United States in the 1920s. It was developed in response to a study of 1912 by two Wisconsin researchers that found that high school English teachers in different schools assigned highly varied percentage grades to the same

> *"Grading on a curve is extremely distorting as a reference of mastery."*
>
> Rick Wormeli, *Fair Isn't Always Equal* (2006)

papers. By grading on the basis of "normal" probablility, as depicted by the bell curve, it was thought that a fairer distribution of grades could be ensured among teachers and the subjective nature of scoring could be brought into check.

When grading on an A = 100–90, B = 89–80, C = 79–70, D = 69–60, and F = 59–0 distribution, the top of the bell should be a middle C of 75 percent. If we assume that grade distribution should fit a "normal" curve then all grades must be normalized; overly low scores will be adjusted up and overly high ones will be adjusted down. It is a distortion of the original data for the sake of fulfilling the expectations of the statistical concept being used. There is some controversy over using the bell curve, especially in terms of modern concerns about grade inflation. **LW**

⬅ High-wire performers succeed mainly because, says Émile Coué, their minds tell them that they can.

Nuclear Fusion
Arthur Eddington

The means by which the sun emits energy, and a potential source of unlimited power

In 1920, while engaged in a search for neon isotopes, the British physicist Francis Aston (1877–1945) measured the mass of hydrogen and helium atoms and discovered that four hydrogen atoms weighed more than a single atom of helium. The significance of this was seen immediately by the British astrophysicist Arthur Eddington (1882–1944), who realized that the differential in mass of helium and hydrogen atoms as measured by Aston was the mechanism that allowed the sun, through the conversion of hydrogen into helium, to shine, producing heat and light.

Nuclear fusion—the conversion of matter into energy that occurs when atomic nuclei are brought together to create a larger, more stable nucleus—

occurs naturally within stars. Our sun fuses more than 600 million tonnes of hydrogen into helium every second. But replicating that "artificially" on Earth, on a large scale via a process that does not involve the detonation of a hydrogen bomb (the only process by which any meaningfully large amount of fusion has so far been achieved), is an entirely different proposition.

Research in nuclear fusion increased around the world after World War II (1939–45), although individual state-sponsored programs were oriented toward military uses and independent of each other. In 1958 this changed with the "Atoms for Peace" conference in Geneva, Switzerland. For the first time, research became coordinated and information was shared. It was agreed in Geneva that nuclear fusion was an achievable goal, but it was also acknowledged that inherent plasma instabilities meant that many hurdles would need to be overcome. The first fusion-generating devices, called "tokamaks," were designed and built in Russia in the late 1960s, and today the Joint European Torus tokamak near Oxford in the United Kingdom holds the record for fusion generation: it produced 16 megawatts of energy in a single second. **JMa**

Robotics
Karel Capek

Machines that reproduce human physical and/or mental capabilities

The idea of a mechanical device mimicking the form and functions of a human being, perhaps able to perform work for its creator, has long preoccupied mankind. Inventor and artist Leonardo da Vinci (1452–1519) sketched a humanoid robot in 1495, and in the eighteenth and nineteenth centuries innumerable life-sized automatons were built, including a mechanical duck, designed and constructed by inventor Jacques de Vaucanson (1709–82), that could move its wings and swallow food. Even so, it would not be until 1920 that Karel Capek (1890–1938), a Czech science fiction writer long before science fiction was considered a recognized genre, first used the word "robot" (a word suggested by his brother, Josef) in his play *Rossum's*

Universal Robots. The play describes a futuristic world of humanlike mechanical beings and takes place in a factory where "artificial people" are made.

Departing from the realm of fiction, engineer Joe Engleberger (*b.* 1925) and inventor George Devol (1912–2011) designed and built the world's first programmable robotic arm in 1954; named Unimate, it became in turn the first industrial robot, for General Motors in 1961. IBM produced its first commercial computer in 1964, and a swathe of advanced robotics accompanied Apollo 11 to the moon in 1969. In July 1994, an eight-legged tethered robot, Dante II, built by students at Pittsburgh's Carnegie Mellon University, descended into Alaska's Mount Spurr and collected fumarole gas samples, a major advance in the use of robotic explorers to access extreme terrain.

Traditionally robotics has promised more than it could deliver because computing power has always lagged behind the human imagination. But with the processing power of computer mainframes growing so fast, technicians predict that by 2050 robotic brains will be capable of executing 100 trillion commands per second, and will begin to rival human intelligence. **BS**

↑ A scene from *Rossum's Universal Robots* (1920), a play written by Karel Capek, who coined the term "robot."

Id, Ego, and Superego
Sigmund Freud

The view of our personalities as the product of three competing regions of our mind

The Id, Ego, and Superego are the three elements in Sigmund Freud's (1856–1939) psychoanalytic theory of personality. It is the interactions between them, he claimed in "Beyond the Pleasure Principle" (1920), that define our behavior. The Id contains our most basic and instinctual impulses, and acts according to Freud's so-called "pleasure principle." If the Id were all we possessed we would be at the same level as the animals. Hunger, anger, thirst, sex—these are the Id's insatiable needs. It is disorganized, incapable of judgment, and has no sense of morality or of good and evil. The Id exists solely for self-gratification. A human who acts solely on instincts derived from their Id would be akin to a sociopath. The Id gives us what we need to survive, but it is also the "devil on our shoulder."

"The poor Ego has a still harder time of it; it has to serve three harsh masters …"

Sigmund Freud, *New Introductory Lectures … (1932)*

Our conscience, our ability to moralize and criticize the rampant desires of the Id, is the realm of the Superego. It provides us with our sense of right and wrong. Freud referred to the Superego as the psyche's equivalent of the father figure, who raises us to be good citizens and disciplines us when we misbehave. It encourages us to remain within the boundaries of social expectations and cultural norms.

The Ego is now thought of as suppressing the Id's urges, and also of being a sort of organizer that takes the competing needs of the Id and Superego and turns them into something that is coherent and workable. Freud himself saw the Ego as more of a mediator in a strictly hierarchical structure, driven by the demands of the Id while at the same time confined within the boundaries of the Superego. **BS**

Death Drive
Sigmund Freud

The theory that everyone is subject to a subconscious impulse for self-destruction

In 1920, Austrian neurologist Sigmund Freud (1856–1939) published an essay, "Beyond the Pleasure Principle," about the struggles everyone has between two opposing impulses: Eros, the drive to creativity, pleasure, and sexual reproduction; and Thanatos, the Death Drive, an aggressive desire for self-destruction. Perhaps unsurprisingly, the theory—one of Freud's most obscure and enigmatic—was also his most poorly received. Nobody, neither psychologist nor layman, wanted to think of themselves as possessing an unstoppable drive to die.

Freud had always believed that every decision that people made was motivated by the pursuit of pleasure. Now he began seeking out alternate drives to explain an impetus toward destruction that he saw in the post-traumatic dreams of his patients. He also began to see death as part of the unfolding journey of life, a compulsion of the body—the organism—to return to its primordial inertia. This was, according to Freud, the body's most primitive, inhuman element.

Critics of the theory point to its coincidental emergence just months after the death of Freud's daughter, Sophie, who was a victim of the Spanish flu that ravaged Europe. Or maybe he was inspired by Friedrich Nietzsche's concept of the "eternal return," from death back to life? A "drive to death" did not please evolutionists, either; it was a theory that seemed to fly in the face of Darwinism and the survival of the fittest.

More likely, however, it was simply an outgrowth of Freud's own bewilderment at his troubled patients' resistance to treatment, and the persistent presence of depression and angst that he was unable to treat, particularly in veterans of World War I. The Death Drive seemed to fill Freud's own conceptual "gap," even as it left almost everyone else wondering just where it had come from. **BS**

Tractatus Logico-Philosophicus
Ludwig Wittgenstein

A philosophical treatise that sought to identify the nature of the relationship between language and reality

One of the twentieth century's most seminal philosophical works, the *Tractatus Logico-Philosophicus* (Logical-Philosophical Treatise) was published in 1921, three years after its author, Austrian-British philosopher Ludwig Wittgenstein (1889–1951), first developed its propositions while serving in the Austro-Hungarian army on the battlefields of Europe. He began writing it while held as a prisoner of war in an Italian prison camp, and completed it in the summer of 1918 at his family's summer house in Vienna.

Consisting almost entirely of a series of assumptions considered by the author to be self-evident, the treatise is virtually devoid of arguments as it attempts to explain the underlying logic of language, and how language represents the limits of what can be said and, therefore, of what can be reasoned. For Wittgenstein, the limitations of philosophy and the limitations of language are one and the same. By linking logic to metaphysics using language, he emptied philosophy of its circular reasoning, saying that, "If a question can be framed at all, it is also possible to answer it." The *Tractatus* provided new insights into the interconnectedness of language, of thought, and of the outside world, and supplied the everyday tools required to separate sense from nonsense.

Wittgenstein was admired by the Vienna Circle of philosophers at the University of Vienna, and British philosopher Bertrand Russell (1872–1970) described him as "the most perfect example I have ever known of genius." But he was a lonely and troubled man. He considered Russell his only peer, but that relationship soured to the point where he opposed Russell writing an introduction to the *Tractatus* (he did, even so). Tormented by thoughts of suicide, he regarded his professorial career as a "living death" and held many of his fellow philosophers in contempt. **BS**

⬆ Ludwig Wittgenstein was a member of one of the richest families in Austria, but also one of the most troubled. Three of his brothers committed suicide in differing circumstances.

"A man will be imprisoned in a room with a door that's unlocked and opens inward as long as it does not occur to him to pull rather than push."

Ludwig Wittgenstein

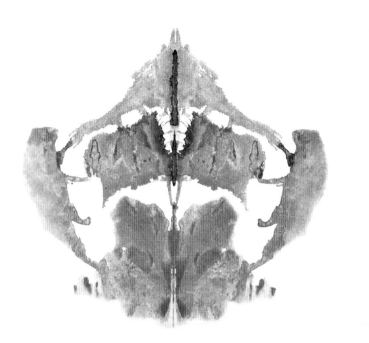

Rorschach Test
Hermann Rorschach

A subtle diagnostic tool that was derived from a childhood game

The use of ambiguous shapes and patterns to determine an individual's personality may first have been considered by prolific inventor and artist Leonardo da Vinci (1452–1519). But it would not be until 1921, in his book *Psychodiagnostik* (Psychodiagnostics), that Swiss psychiatrist Hermann Rorschach (1884–1922) would present the well-known inkblot test named after him. Rorschach's monograph contained ten cards, and the author believed that subjects invited to interpret these might reveal a tendency toward schizophrenia. The use of the cards as a personality test does not date until 1939.

Rorschach had taken Klecksography—a game popular among Swiss children that involved taking a random wet inkblot on a piece of paper and trying to fold it so that it made the shape of a bird or a butterfly—and transformed it into a science. As an adolescent he had always been torn between following a path in drawing or the natural sciences, and here he had devised for himself an ingenious compromise.

It was our ability to perceive, rather than to construct or imagine, that interested Rorschach most, and that is what the test was designed to measure. He was interested in our perceptions, what triggered them, and how they varied from person to person. He saw the inkblots as optical stimuli, put forward to harness our propensity to project our own interpretations onto ambiguous images, in the hope that analysts might be able to identify deeply buried traits and impulses.

Rorschach had trained with Carl Jung and was influenced by Sigmund Freud. Like many psychologists of his era, he was influenced by symbolism and symbolic associations. For example, in one paper he observed that neurotics were often obsessed with their watches, because the roundness of the faces symbolized for them their mother's breast, and the ticking, her heartbeat. His inkblots acted as symbols in a comparable way. **BS**

Rorschach inkblots serve as neutral yet suggestive stimuli for the purpose of psychological assessment.

Serialism
Arnold Schoenberg

An approach to composition involving the systematic organization of elements

Developed by Austrian composer Arnold Schoenberg (1874–1951), serialism is a method of composition whereby all twelve notes of the chromatic scale (or in later instances rhythms, dynamics, and other musical features) are systematically employed in comprehensive distribution, utilizing rows and sets as organizing principles. Embodied in his "twelve-tone technique," invented in 1921, serialism was envisioned as an attempt to distance composition from traditional tonality and melody. Schoenberg's phrase "emancipation of dissonance" related to his pursuit of atonality and his reframing of musicality.

Frequently, the serialist approach to composition institutes other constraints on organization beyond mere prescribed order, such as the use of elements equally and in similar proportion. Common intervals between tones may be established, or dynamic changes based on an inclusive pattern. While mathematical in its organization, the twelve-tone method was equally expressive as other approaches to composition, according to Schoenberg. He famously compared his music to all other forms of human work, with a skeleton and a circulatory and nervous system—"an honest and intelligent person who comes to us saying something he feels deeply and which is of significance to all of us."

Serialism can also be seen in a broader range of composition and production that extends to fields beyond music. It paralleled advances in mathematics, such as set theory, which deals with the properties of well-defined collections of objects, while also influencing the visual arts through the work of artists such as Josef Albers and Sol LeWitt. The structural understanding of sets and permutations in music also influenced scholars and critics, who returned to classical pieces in light of serialist principles to discover new features of their organization. **JD**

⬆ Composer Arnold Schoenberg was also one of the most influential teachers of the twentieth century.

Child Development
Jean Piaget

The theory that a child's intellectual development occurs in distinct stages

Jean Piaget (1896–1980) first came across psychoanalysis during a brief period of study at the University of Zurich, and in 1919 moved to Paris to work with the psychologist Alfred Binet (1857–1911), the inventor of the IQ test. Piaget became fascinated with young children who, in response to certain questions Binet would ask them, continually gave the same wrong answers. By 1921 Piaget had begun to publish his conclusions—that the cognitive processes of young children are very different to those of adults—marking the beginning of a lifetime of study that would make Piaget the undisputed pioneer of cognitive development in children.

Piaget saw a child's intellectual development as evolutionary, having certain points at which it simply "takes off." This is prompted by two ongoing

" … knowledge of the external world begins with an immediate utilization of things … "

Jean Piaget

processes: assimilation and accommodation. By sucking on everything around it as a reflex action, a baby is assimilating its world, transforming it to meet its individual needs. As the baby develops, it begins to engage in accommodation by picking things up and putting them in its mouth—a modification of the reflex response. Piaget came to believe that the conflict generated by these two opposing and ongoing actions creates the impetus for cognitive development.

Piaget's four stages of child development—the egocentric stage, the "magical thinking" stage, the development of logical thought, and the gaining of abstract reasoning—saw him labeled a "cognitive constructivist," as opposed to a "social constructivist," who believed that language and exposure to other people were equally influential. **BS**

Fixed-point Theorem
Stefan Banach

A mathematical principle demonstrating how a function can have a fixed point

First stated in 1922 and one of the great mathematical principles devised by Polish mathematician Stefan Banach (1892–1945), the Banach fixed-point theorem has become a vital ingredient in the theory of metric spaces (sets in which a notion of distance, called a metric, between elements of the sets is defined). The theorem has been used extensively in the field of topology and mapmaking. Explaining it without the aid of of graphs and algebra, however, is not easy.

Imagine somebody climbing a mountain. The climber begins at midday and reaches the summit six hours later. He or she stays on the summit overnight and the following day descends, beginning at midday again and taking just four hours to return to the starting point. Now imagine this depicted on a graph. There are two lines; one—the ascent—begins in the bottom left of the graph and heads to the top right, denoting time and height; the other line—the descent—starts at the top left of the graph, the summit's starting point, and goes down toward the bottom right. It is inevitable that at some point the two lines are going to have to intersect, and the point at which they do is an example of a mathematical "fixed point."

Variations in Banach's fixed-point theories are not restricted to mathematics, and also can be decidedly unfixed. For example, according to the Brouwer fixed-point theorem devised by Dutch mathematician Luitzen Brouwer (1881–1966), if a person stirs a cup of coffee, there will appear to be a point on the surface that is not moving. Due to the turbulence of the swirling coffee, however, it is fair to assume that the fixed point is in fact mobile and traverses the surface. Over the past fifty years, the fixed-point theorem has also been adapted for use in engineering, biology, and quantum mechanics. The Kakutani version (1941) is widely used in game theory and economics. **BS**

Etiquette in Society, in Business, in Politics, and at Home
Emily Post

A compendium of advice on how to negotiate the minefield of what, and what not, to say and do in social situations

Rules of etiquette first began to be formed in the court of Louis XIV (1638–1715), the so-called "Sun King" of France, with a series of elaborate social customs and protocols compiled by idle courtesans. Future first president of the United States, George Washington (1732–99), when still barely sixteen years of age, wrote his "Rules of Civility and Decent Behavior in Company and Conversation," comprising 110 rules, such as: "Every action done in company ought to be with some sign of respect to those that are present."

It would not be until 1922, however, that a book that virtually codified every minute aspect of etiquette in a single, all-encompassing volume was produced. Written by the U.S. author Emily Post (1872–1960), *Etiquette in Society, in Business, in Politics, and at Home* found a ready market and was a bestseller. In her book, Post referred to the "Best Society," not a fellowship of the wealthy but a Brotherhood "which spreads over the entire surface of the globe." Etiquette and good manners were not only for the few; they applied to everyone and went far beyond mere manners and deportment, extending into the realm of ethics.

Post leaves no stone unturned in her quest to reassure us about what we should say and do in every conceivable social situation. When do we shake hands, what do we say when introduced? When should a gentleman take off his hat, or merely raise it? When should one bow and, just as importantly, when should one not? And unless completely unavoidable, never call out someone's name in public. Being told to say "How do you do?" instead of "Charmed!" caused some to criticize *Etiquette* as a dated and irrelevant work. However, the book is currently in its eighteenth edition, proof that for those who consider manners to be the glue that holds society together, proper etiquette never goes out of fashion. **BS**

⬆ Emily Post (pictured in 1923) provided advice on etiquette to everyone from small boys to motorcar drivers, but her core market was young debutantes, suitors, and newly-weds.

"Manners are made up of trivialities of deportment which can be easily learned if one does not happen to know them; manner is personality . . ."

Emily Post

Copenhagen Interpretation
Niels Bohr

An explanation for the bizarre and random behavior of subatomic particles

Quantum mechanics takes a metaphysical approach toward understanding subatomic particles, providing physicists with tools to conduct experiments that might provide insights into their behavior. Yet quantum mechanics at times appears bizarre even to some physicists, and one of its most bizarre aspects is the so-called Many Worlds Theory, which suggests that, for each outcome of any given action, the universe can split it in two, allowing for the quantum particles in the event to behave in two entirely different ways.

Starting in 1924, at the University of Copenhagen, Danish physicist Niels Bohr (1885–1962) set out to try to explain this seeming contradictory duality. In what he called the Copenhagen Interpretation, he theorized that quantum particles do not exist solely in one state

"When it comes to atoms, language can be used only as in poetry."

Niels Bohr

or another, but in all of their possible states at the same time. This state is referred to by physicists as coherent superposition.

Moreover, every subatomic particle has two aspects, a wave aspect and a particle aspect, which may be compared to the two sides of the same coin. And just as a coin tossed in the air can land only on one side, so too a subatomic particle can behave as either a wave or a particle, though never both at the same time. Bohr's interpretation suggests that if a particle were to be observed in its natural state, the observer would see it only after it has been forced to "choose" which path to take—that path then becomes the "observed state." Consequently, electrons in identical experiments are capable of behaving differently, depending on which of their two aspects comes into play. **BS**

Art Deco
The Society of Decorator Artists

A visual arts design style characterized by geometric shapes and bold colors

The term "art deco" was first used to describe a new style of decorative arts seen at the art exhibition at the Musée des Arts Décoratifs in Paris in 1925. A showcase of French design, it included furniture, elements of interior design, botany, geometry, and naturalism. No object was spared its intervention: lamps, haircombs, footstools, lighting, automobiles, it was a philosophy of design that celebrated a new age of post-World War I exuberance, a prosperous era of style, fashion, skyscrapers, and the internal combustion engine.

It all began with La Société des artistes décorateurs (The Society of Decorator Artists), an artistic association formed in Paris after the city's Universal Exposition of 1900 with one purpose in mind: to show the world the beauty and form of French artistic and architectural

"… an assertively modern style … [that] responded to the demands of the machine."

Bevis Hillier, historian

expression. It was their work—pottery by Raoul Lachenal, graphic design by Eugène Grasset, luxury printed books by François-Louis Schmied, and humble bookbindings by Paul Bonet that ignited the art deco movement and took it from the exhibition halls of Paris to the rest of the world.

Art deco architecture featured stylized reliefs, geometric ornamentation, stepped lines, and machine-age chrome and Bakelite with a grandeur reminiscent of the Roman Republic (1509–27 BCE). Americans added the principles of streamlining, characterized by strong curves and clean lines, applied it to construction and automobiles and gave the world the Chrysler Building and the Buick Y-Job. Sadly, art deco came to an end in the mid-1940s, its perceived gaudiness not in keeping with the austerity of post-World War II economies. **BS**

Cultural Hegemony

Antonio Gramsci

A nonconfrontational approach to the overthrow of capitalist social structures

In the 1920s, Italian writer, political theorist, and cofounder and leader of the Communist Party of Italy Antonio Gramsci (1891–1937) coined the term "cultural hegemony" to describe how one single social class can slowly come to dominate the society of which it is a part. Believing that established capitalist societies were too entrenched to be taken over by force, Gramsci instead proposed a process of incremental change, of gaining a toehold within its hierarchical structures by influencing the leaders of churches, schools, and the bureaucracy to alter, over time, their thinking.

Gramsci compared capitalist social structures with defensive battlements. The state, he said, was an "outer ditch, behind which there stood a powerful system of fortresses and earthworks. The

"Gramsci's social thought contains some remarkably suggestive insights ..."

T. J. Jackson Lears, historian

superstructures of civil society are like the trench systems of modern warfare." The infiltration of society through cultural hegemony he believed, provided a way of gradually undermining these social foundations and effecting change. Gramsci's influence on evolving concepts within political science continued long after his death, with the publication in 1971 of *Selections from the Prison Notebooks*, which he wrote while imprisoned from 1926 to 1934. Hegemony, he said, is a constant struggle, its victories never final and always precarious.

Intent on loosening the rigid formulas of Marxism, cultural hegemony broadened the base of socialist ideology, and acknowledged the role of the state as a political reality and not just as a tool of the ruling class. It continues to aid historians striving to understand how an idea can undermine prevailing social hierarchies. **BS**

Television

Philo Taylor Farnsworth

An electronic communications system that transmits both images and sound

Television was not the product of a singular moment of scientific genius or technical insight, but rather a culmination of work by numerous engineers and inventors. Although Philo Taylor Farnsworth (1906–71) is credited with having produced the first successful electronic television in 1927, a mechanical television system had been invented as early as 1884 by German inventor Paul Gottlieb Nipkow (1860–1940). The first commercial television sets appeared in England and the United States in 1928. In 1937 Londoners purchased 9,000 television sets, allowing them to watch the coronation of King George VI.

The television is a device that can receive, decode, and display images and sounds sent over a great distance. Television images can be broadcast over radio

"It's the menace that everyone loves to hate but can't seem to live without."

Paddy Chayevsky, writer

frequencies and through closed-circuit television loops, as well as through satellite and cable transmissions. The earliest televisions could only display black-and-white analog images, although advances in technology led to color images, stereo sound, and digital signals.

By 1996, there were approximately one billion televisions in use around the world; a number that has continued to grow. The medium became synonymous with technological advances and significant moments of the twentieth century, and has had a profound impact on the way people communicate, interact socially, and spend their time. Its ubiquitous presence is an endless source of entertainment, news, information, and distraction, and it has played a pivotal role in social and political change around the world, used by both tyrant and liberator alike. **MT**

Hubble's Law
Georges Lemaître

A law that provides evidence for the expansion of the universe

↑ Albert Einstein talking to Georges Lemaître in Pasadena, California, in 1933. At a series of seminars held there, Lemaître detailed his theory and was applauded by Einstein.

Although misattributed to him, the idea that the universe is expanding did not originate with the astronomer Edwin Hubble (1889–1953), despite his paper of 1929 detailing his work at the Mount Wilson observatory in the hills outside Los Angeles. Using its 100-inch (250 cm) mirror, Hubble was able to detect redshifts in the light spectrum of galaxies and concluded that they were moving away from each other at an almost unfathomable rate. The further away a galaxy was, he said, the faster it was traveling. His discovery also enabled him to estimate the approximate point at which this expansion began, and so the Big Bang theory of the birth of the universe was born. The problem was, however, that two years earlier his conclusions had already been arrived at and published by the Belgian-born physicist and secular priest Georges Lemaître (1894–1966).

In 1927, while a part-time lecturer at the Catholic University of Louvain in Belgium, Lemaître published a paper with an exhausting title: "A Homogeneous Universe of Constant Mass and Growing Radius Accounting for the Radial Velocity of Extragalactic Nebulae." In it he postulated an expanding universe, and chided Albert Einstein for taking exception to his theory—"Your math is correct, but your physics is abominable." Lemaître even suggested a "rate of expansion," later called the Hubble Constant. Unfortunately Lemaître's conclusions were published in a little-known Belgian scientific journal and were largely overlooked by the worldwide astronomical fraternity.

In 1917 Einstein had allowed for an expanding universe in a model he created based upon his theory of general relativity, but later, in what he described as "the biggest blunder of my career," he revised and dismissed the theory. In 1931 Einstein paid Hubble, not Lemaître, a visit, and thanked him for his pioneering work, although he later acknowledged Lemaître's theory in 1933. **BS**

"Equipped with his five senses, man explores the universe around him and calls the adventure science."

Edwin Hubble, astronomer

The Question of Being

Martin Heidegger

An attempt to recover the true task of philosophy—the analysis of "being"

In his masterpiece *Sein und Zeit* (Being and Time), published in 1927, Martin Heidegger (1889–1976) reinvented the term *Dasein*, which is translated from the German as "being there" or "existence." Heidegger's term did not denote a static subject but a specific human and active consciousness that was fully engaged in the world. He remarked, "Dasein is ontically distinguished by the fact that, in its very Being, that Being is an issue for it." This means that Dasein is not only "existence" but it is also the choice to exist or not to exist. Human beings, unlike rocks, plants, and animals, not only exist but also have a purpose that they themselves define. Dasein was finally the fundamental philosophic category that could serve as the basis for all other fundamental philosophic discussions.

Heidegger's account of Dasein was substantially shaped by his reading of Aristotle, the ancient Greek philosopher who also devoted a great deal of time to discussions of being. While writing *Being and Time*, Heidegger rejected not only the traditional account of the separation between subject and object, which had existed in much of Western philosophy, especially after the seventeenth century, but also the philosophy of his time.

Being and Time is among the most important works produced in European philosophy in the twentieth century. It reinvigorated the study of ontology, the philosophic study of being and the nature of existence. Its publication made Heidegger a prominent public intellectual, but his sudden status had consequences. In 1933, Heidegger joined the Nazi Party and was elected the rector of Freiburg. Although he resigned a year later, numerous scholars have called attention to his support for the Nazi regime. This has presented a problem for posterity: are a philosopher's arguments tainted by his politics or may the two be evaluated independently? **CRD**

⬆ Despite the extremely dense and inaccessible nature of the text, Heidegger's *Sein und Zeit* (Being and Time, 1927) led to his recognition as one of the world's leading philosophers.

"Why are there beings at all instead of nothing? That is the question. Presumably it is not an arbitrary question, 'Why are there beings at all instead of nothing'— this is obviously the first of all questions."

Martin Heidegger

Uncertainty Principle
Werner Heisenberg

A challenge of measurement inherent in the quantum mechanical description of nature

Also called the principle of indeterminacy, the uncertainty principle was formulated in 1927 by Werner Heisenberg (1901–76) in the midst of debates between matrix and wave mechanic interpretations of quantum theory. Heisenberg showed that imprecision was unavoidable if a person tried to measure the position and momentum of a particle at the same time, and furthermore that the more accurately a person could determine the position of a particle, the less well known its momentum would be (and vice versa).

Heisenberg's insight is an observation relating to waves in general. While we can measure either the frequency of a wave or its position, we cannot measure both at the same time. The model of reality proposed by quantum physics, which invokes a wave-

"Not only is the universe stranger than we think, it is stranger than we can think."

Werner Heisenberg

particle duality, implies an inherent uncertainty and complementarity in the structure of the universe.

While uncertainty is present in any subatomic system, the principle is also related to the wider issue of how actual observation and measurement of the quantum world influences that world. Quantum particles themselves are affected by light, among other things, and through testing and measuring we inevitably disturb a given system. These insights in turn led Heisenberg back into the consideration of uncertainty as an ontological reality, not merely a result of observation. A superposition of states is resolved on observation (the "wave function" collapses). Heisenberg wrote, "I believe that one can formulate the emergence of the classical 'path' of a particle pregnantly as follows: the 'path' comes into being only because we observe it." **JD**

The Big Bang Theory
Georges Lemaître

The universe was originally a tiny, dense point that rapidly expanded into its current state

The Big Bang theory of cosmology states that the entire universe began its existence as a singular, incredibly hot point with infinite density and no volume. From this singularity, the universe rapidly expanded and cooled, eventually reaching the state it is in today. This rapid expansion was not merely that of the planets, nebulae, or galaxies, but actually of space itself along with all it contains.

Questions of how humanity and the universe originated are as old as human thought. At the start of the twentieth century, scientists made great strides in understanding the universe, although its origins remained largely a mystery. In 1929, astronomer Edwin Hubble observed that large bodies in the universe were moving away from the Earth. Not only that, but they also

". . . all the matter in the universe was created in one big bang."

Sir Fred Hoyle, astronomer

appeared to be moving away from one another at the same time. Two years prior to that, Belgian astronomer Georges Lemaître (1894–1966) proposed the idea that the universe originated from a primeval atom, expanding over time. After Hubble released his observations showing that the universe was expanding, and inferred a singular moment and point from which it all began, astronomer Fred Hoyle later referred to the idea as a "big bang" in order to differentiate it from the image of the universe he supported, the "solid state" theory.

The Big Bang theory is the widely accepted cosmological model for how the universe came to be. Its impact extends well beyond astronomy and physics. It has met with much objection from religious thinkers, while others have adopted it as evidence of a single solitary moment of creation. **MT**

An artwork showing the universe's evolution from the Big Bang (top) to the present day (bottom). ➡

Antibiotics
Alexander Fleming

The discovery of medication that destroys bacteria and prevents infection

Antibiotics are powerful medications or chemical compounds that do not allow bacteria to grow and spread. The human body is host to numerous types of bacteria that can cause harmful and potentially deadly infections. Antibiotics, often referred to today as antibacterials or antimicrobials, provide a way to fight these bacteria and prevent such complications.

Although humankind has used medicinal plants and concoctions for millennia, it was not until a purely accidental occurrence that the world of medicine had access to antibiotics. On September 3, 1928, Scottish bacteriologist Alexander Fleming (1881–1955) stumbled upon antibiotics when he discovered that one of his bacteria-coated glass plates contained a ring of fungus that was fending off the harmful bacteria surrounding it. That fungus was a species of the green mold *Penicillium notatum* and, following experiments to investigate the notion that it could be used to cure animals of infections without harm, penicillin became the first antibiotic.

It is inconceivable now to imagine modern medicine before the introduction of antibiotics, but prior to their widespread use beginning in the twentieth century, an infection of any kind could frequently prove fatal. Since Fleming's discovery of penicillin, numerous other antibiotics have been discovered, invented, and improved upon. These drugs form a cornerstone of modern medicine, and their discovery and the later discovery of how to produce them in large numbers have played a key role in the development of modern pharmaceutical sciences. Penicillin alone—heralded as a miracle drug after it was introduced during World War II—has been credited with saving more than 200 million lives. While some bacteria have since developed resistances to antibiotics, these drugs changed the way we look at medicine, single-handedly demonstrating the promise that pharmaceuticals could deliver. **MT**

Alexander Fleming, discoverer of penicillin, pictured in his laboratory in 1943.

Antimatter

Paul Dirac

Antiparticles that have the same mass as ordinary particles but have opposite charge

In 1928 the English theoretical physicist Paul Dirac (1902–84) constructed a quantum theory governing the behavior of electrons and electric and magnetic fields. Although he was unable to appreciate it at the time, his theory required the presence of another particle possessing the same mass as an opposing electron but having a positive, rather than a negative, charge. The theorized particle was the electron's undiscovered "antiparticle." Dirac's theory was soon proven in subsequent experiments by the U.S. physicist Carl Anderson (1905–91) in 1932, who photographed the curvature of particles as they passed through a magnetic field. It was Anderson who would rightly be credited with the discovery of the positron, the electron's antiparticle and the world's first undeniable proof of the existence of antimatter, and he was awarded a Nobel Prize, with Victor Francis Hess of Austria, for his work.

There is no inherent difference between matter and antimatter; the laws of physics apply almost equally to both. If they collide they annihilate one another and cease to exist. It was the start of the rewriting of an array of scientific textbooks. Since the beginning of physics everything everywhere was "matter—all that existed and all that we could see." With the addition of antimatter, the definition of what constituted matter required narrowing. Antimatter was made of antiparticles, such as antineutrons and antinuclei. Antiprotons were later discovered at the Lawrence Radiation Laboratory in California in the 1950s, antihydrogen was found in 1995, and antihelium in 2011. Dirac had opened a quantum Pandora's box, and although it was Anderson who found the positron, its discovery was foreseen in a paper published a year earlier, written by Dirac, in which he predicted an as yet unseen particle that he prophetically named the "antielectron." **BS**

⬆ Paul Dirac demonstrates a quantum mechanical model of the hydrogen molecule in 1933.

Well-formed Formula
David Hilbert and Wilhelm Ackermann

The appropriate and correct rendition of a word in a formal language

The concept of a "well-formed formula" (WFF) is a key element of modern logic, mathematics, and computer science. The idea of an appropriate and correct rendition of a word in a formal language is first explicitly mentioned in David Hilbert (1862–1943) and Wilhelm Ackermann's (1896–1962) *Grundzüge der Theoretischen Logik* (Principles of Mathematical Logic) in 1928. A formal language can be thought of as identical to the set of its WFFs, and the words or symbols in formal languages are governed by the rules of the formal language. The set of WFFs may be broadly divided into theorems (statements that have been proven on the basis of previously established statements) and non-theorems. Formal languages are, more specifically, artificial logical languages, governed by a highly regulated set of rules.

"Mathematics . . . is a conceptual system possessing internal necessity."

David Hilbert

In the formal language of symbolic logic (the logic of propositions), for example, one basic example of a WFF is called modus ponens and looks like this:

If P, then Q	or P → Q
P	or P
Therefore, Q	or Q

We can fill in the P and Q using philosopher René Descartes's well-known dictum: "If I think, then I am. I think. Therefore, I am."

All formal languages must have syntax, concrete definitions of not only the vocabulary of language's vocabulary but also the strings of vocabulary must count as WFFs. The concept of a WFF has become well known, for example, in the game WFF 'N PROOF: The Game of Modern Logic designed to teach symbolic logic to children. **JE**

A Room of One's Own
Virginia Woolf

A feminist text that urged women to seek their own independence

Penned by English novelist Virginia Woolf (1882–1941), one of the founders of modernism and one of the most influential of all English-speaking female authors, *A Room of One's Own* (1929) is an extended essay drawn from a series of lectures the author gave at Newnham and Girton colleges in Cambridge, England, in 1928, and it remains a landmark of twentieth-century feminism.

In it Woolf lamented the lack of legal rights for women from the Elizabethan period (1558–1603) onward. Mostly the essay is a critical history bemoaning the dearth of women writers—"It would have been impossible, completely and entirely, for any woman to have written the plays of Shakespeare in the age of Shakespeare"—while at the same time praising the work of Jane Austen and the Brontë sisters. Woolf asks

"A woman must have money and a room of her own if she is going to write."

Virginia Woolf

readers to accept the fact that women sometimes fall in love with women, and rails against society's embedded patriarchal and hierarchical structures. Where there are gaps in the factual records about women, Woolf draws upon fictional accounts to fill them in an attempt to give balance to a history written almost entirely by men.

The essay employs a fictional narrator, a woman named Mary, itself an oblique reference to a sixteenth-century figure who insisted on living outside of marriage, rejected the ideal of motherhood, and was eventually hung for her convictions. Woolf has been criticized by some for excluding colored women from her narrative, but her overriding concern was always the need for women writers—and by default all women of all colors and backgrounds—to have their own independence. **BS**

The first-edition cover of Virginia Woolf's seminal work, *A Room of One's Own* (1929). ➔

a room
of one's own

virginia woolf

Hays Code
Will H. Hays

A self-regulated code of ethics that limited free expression in the U.S. movie industry

In the first decades of the twentieth century there were more than forty separate censorship boards spread across the United States, all charged with the task of making sure the nation's filmmakers produced movies that did not stray beyond their myriad sets of moral boundaries. In 1922 the Motion Picture Association of America (MPAA) was formed and the first tentative steps toward self-regulation were taken—fueled by rising complaints regarding questionable content and high-profile scandals involving Hollywood personalities—with the establishment of the Movie Picture Production Code, also known as the Hays Code, in 1930. It was named for the MPAA's first president and chief censor, U.S. lawyer and political figure Will Hays (1879–1954), who was one of its authors along with other MPAA censors.

For the next thirty years, the Hays Code stipulated what was morally acceptable on the big screen. A cartoon might be banned because it made light of violent crime; nudity and overt sexual behavior were not permitted; the mocking of religions was banned, as was drug use unless essential to the plot. Homosexuals were unheard of, and sex symbols kept their clothes on.

The Hays Code did not apply to the theater, which meant playwrights could broach subjects that Hollywood could not. In the 1960s, when European cinema became increasingly popular, there was pressure for the code to be relaxed; Hollywood was also under pressure to compete with television for viewers. The code was eventually abandoned in the late 1960s and was replaced with the MPAA film rating system in 1968. The Hays Code has been criticized by some film critics for being unreasonably draconian. However, it should not be forgotten that despite its regulatory grip Orson Welles made *Citizen Kane* (1941) and Billy Wilder gave us *The Lost Weekend* (1945), the first Hollywood film on alcoholism. **BS**

Due to the Hays Code, married couples were often depicted in twin beds—as here in *The Thin Man* (1934).

Sex Reassignment Surgery

Kurt Warnekros

The development of surgical techniques to help transsexuals to be themselves

Sex reassignment surgery (SRS) is not a new concept. Operations were performed in ancient Greece and sexually permissive Rome. Also known as gender reassignment, SRS refers to a surgical procedure whereby a transsexual's gender appearance and/or genitalia are altered to mirror those of the opposing sex and of the person they inwardly feel themselves to be. The first recipient of male-to-female surgery in the twentieth century was a German, Lile Elbe, who was likely born intersexed (possessing a reproductive system not consistent with males or females). In Dresden in 1930 Elbe had her testicles removed by German gynecologist Dr. Kurt Warnekros (1882–1949). Four further operations followed over the next two years, including the removal of her penis and the transplanting of ovaries and a uterus, but Elbe died in September 1931 from complications shortly after the fifth procedure.

Contemporary SRS as we now know it, however, only began when new hormonal drugs and surgical procedures—including penile inversion surgery pioneered by French plastic surgeon Georges Burou—became available in the 1950s. Surgeons also began constructing vaginas using skin grafts obtained from patients' buttocks. In 1952 Christine Jorgensen became the United States' first nationally known transsexual after the *New York Daily News* printed her story on its front page under the banner headline: "Ex-GI Becomes Blonde Beauty."

In the 1960s finding surgeons capable of performing such complex, groundbreaking surgery was not easy and led to many transsexuals resorting to desperate measures. Some, such as the pioneer transsexual Aleshia Brevard, sliced off their own testicles. "In mid-operation I was left alone on a kitchen table," Brevard would later recount, "draped with Lysol-scented sheets. I sat up and finished my own castration." **BS**

Rastafarianism

Marcus Garvey

A religious movement combining Christianity and pan-African consciousness

Rastafarianism, often referred to as Rastafari, holds that the Judeo-Christian God, referred to as Jah, manifested in human form as both Jesus Christ and Emperor Haile Selassie I of Ethiopia. For Rastafari adherents there is no afterlife, but instead heaven exists on Earth in Africa, or Zion. Physical and spiritual immortality, or ever living, is possible for true believers, while resisting the power of white Europe and the United States (Babylon) is essential and accomplished by holding oneself as a humble, spiritual, and peaceful person.

Rastafarianism began in the 1930s in Kingston, Jamaica, when Marcus Garvey (1887–1940) started a black nationalist movement to teach Jamaicans about their origins as Africans and take pride in their roots. Garvey believed that the descendants of African slaves

> ## "Rastafari means to live in nature, to see the Creator in the wind, sea, and storm."
>
> **Jimmy Cliff, reggae musician**

who lived in Jamaica and other parts of the Western world were the true Israelites, and that a new, African messiah would arise. When Ras Tafari Makonnen (1892–1975), after whom the movement named itself, became emperor of Ethiopia in 1930, many of Garvey's followers believed that this was the sign of their impending return to Africa and that he, renamed Haile Selassie, was the physical embodiment of God.

Today there are fewer than an estimated one million Rastafarians worldwide. Followers are often associated with their use of marijuana, a plant that naturally grows in Jamaica and is used for medicinal and spiritual purposes. With no formal church, tenets, or dogma, Rastafarianism gave its followers a spiritual, peaceful ethos, one many nonadherents became familiar with through Jamaican music, such as ska and reggae. **MT**

Salsa

Cuban Dancers

A Latin American style of dancing with Afro-Cuban roots

Salsa (a Spanish word literally meaning "sauce") is a Latin American dance, usually performed to salsa music, a hybrid musical form. Salsa is a fusion of Caribbean and European elements and has its origins in the Cuban *son* and Afro-Cuban styles of dance. The *son* (which combines Spanish guitar playing with the call and response tradition of African music) originated in rural eastern Cuba and spread to Havana in the early twentieth century. Historians disagree about the exact beginnings of salsa, however, musicologist Max Salazar has traced the origin of the word "salsa" to the early 1930s, when Cuban musician Ignacio Piñeiro composed "Échale salsita," a Cuban *son* about tasteless food. Others suggest that the word was used as a cry to the band to up the tempo for the dancers

> ## "Salsa was an unmistakeable product of the pan-Caribbean."
>
> **Deborah Pacini Hernandez, anthropologist**

or as a cry of appreciation for a particular solo. Salsa dance is performed by couples in four/four time, with quick, fluid movements and rhythmic footwork. It has become internationally popular since the 1980s, and continues to evolve and incorporate elements of other styles of dance.

Western culture has gradually assimilated Cuban dance in general since the mid-1800s, including the conga, cha-cha, rumba, and various mambos. Cuban culture itself has absorbed a number of Iberian and African influences in its complex history, and such an interplay had produced the *son montuno* (a subgenre of *son Cubano*) style of dance, which became internationally popular in the 1930s (and was often mistakenly called rumba). This became one of the primary bases of contemporary salsa dance. **JE**

When he became emperor in 1930, Haile Selassie I was hailed as the new African messiah by Rastafarians.

Oscillating Universe
Albert Einstein

Cosmological theory of an eternally expanding and contracting universe

The oscillating universe theory, briefly considered and then reconsidered by Albert Einstein (1879–1955) in 1930, claims that the universe is in the midst of an endless cycle of expansion and contraction. The galaxies are expanding but will eventually reach a point of exhaustion whereby they will begin to collapse inward to a "Big Crunch" before exploding in another "Big Bang." The universe we currently exist in may be the first or it may be the latest in a series of collapses and rebirths.

There are a variety of cosmological hurdles to overcome for the adherent of the oscillating universe theory: there is not sufficient mass in the universe to generate the gravitational force to bring it all back for a "Big Crunch"; the speed at which galaxies are moving

"The universe is older and lighter weight than has previously been thought."

American Astronomical Society

is simply too great for their direction to be reversed; and reduced levels of nuclear fuel will result in a loss of mass that will reduce the gravitational pull of galaxies and make a reversal impossible, and ultimately all nuclear fuel in every galaxy will be exhausted and the universe will grow cold and die in a "Big Freeze."

Arguing the merits of an oscillating universe pits one against an array of impressive science. The American Astronomical Society says the universe is far lighter than previously supposed and that "galaxies and their stars are unlikely to stop expanding." Princeton University states: "There's simply not enough matter to close the universe," while the Harvard-Smithsonian Center for Astrophysics says it is "95 percent confident" there is nothing to keep the universe from continuing to balloon out forever. **BS**

Incompleteness Theorem
Kurt Gödel

A theory proving that there are limits to what can be ascertained by mathematics

After 2,000 years of being unable to prove Euclid's incontestable five postulates, including the idea that straight lines can be drawn infinitely in opposing directions (true but annoyingly difficult to demonstrate), the last thing mathematicians wanted published was a "theory of incompleteness." Obsessed with a need to prove everything and so dominate the world, the twentieth century had started in a wave of optimism—huge strides in mathematical theory were being taken and it seemed that, at last, the academic world was closing in on a unifying, all-encompassing "theory of everything." The Austrian mathematician Kurt Gödel (1906–78), however, put the brakes on that optimism when he proved his theorem in 1931. "Anything you can draw a circle around," he suggested, "cannot explain itself without referring to something outside the circle—something you have to assume, but cannot prove."

Gödel had taken the "I am a liar" paradox (if you are a liar then saying you are a liar is itself a lie) and transformed it into a mathematical formula. And if you accept that no equation has the capacity to prove itself, it must follow that there will always be more things in life that are true than we are able to prove. And, at a fundamental level, any conceivable equation will always have to be constructed over assumptions, at least some of which will be improvable.

According to Gödel's theory, if you draw a circle around the universe itself, then the universe cannot explain itself. To make sense of the universe, there must be something outside of it, something that we have to assume is there but whose existence we cannot prove. Gödel's circle may seem a simple construct but, as he acknowledged, it leaves the door open for the argument to turn decidedly theological. If God is not on the far side, then what is? **BS**

Swing Music
African American Musicians

A style of exuberant music that became the sound of a depression-hit generation of Americans

Taken from the phrase "swing feel," which was used to describe an off-beat or weak musical pulse, swing music began to take shape in the United States in the early 1920s when subtle, stylistic rhythm changes started to surface from within the established jazz repertoire, most notably among stride pianists. By the mid-1930s, swing had become a musical style all of its own with a sort of rhythmic "bouncing groove," providing a new kind of energetic intensity that was a welcome relief from the everyday tribulations of the Great Depression. Some historians have traced swing music's stage debut to 1931 and the music of the Chick Webb Orchestra, the house band of Harlem's Savoy Ballroom in New York City.

The small ensembles common to jazz, often including a single clarinet, trombone, trumpet, piano, bass, and drums, had to be expanded to accommodate swing music's more powerful and complex sounds: instruments were doubled, trebled, or more to give a section three or four trumpeters and a similar number of trombonists and saxophonists. All of a sudden there was more of everything; the era of the Big Band—of Duke Ellington's "It Don't Mean A Thing (If It Ain't Got That Swing)"—had arrived.

More a style of music than a genre, swing is more than the sum of its technical parts, more than just music comprised of "triplet note subdivisions." Its definition is more cultural than technical, with a sound that still makes people want to get up and dance, to move their bodies with energy and rhythm. Swing bands had strong rhythm sections with an emphasis on basses and drums, which were used as an anchor for the woodwinds, brass, and occasional stringed instruments such as violins or guitars. In the hands of later masters, such as Glenn Miller and Tommy Dorsey, it was loved by World War II's younger generation. **BS**

↑ Duke Ellington (center), pictured in 1939, had a big hit in the 1930s with "It Don't Mean a Thing (If It Aint Got That Swing)." It was probably the first song title to reference the musical style.

"Ah, swing, well we used to call it syncopation then they called it ragtime, then blues, then jazz. Now it's swing. White folks yo'all sho is a mess."

Louis Armstrong, musician

WORLD'S HIGHEST STANDARD OF LIVING

There's no way like the American Way

1931

The American Dream

James Truslow Adams

The idealistic belief that all individuals have the opportunity for prosperity and success

The phrase "the American Dream" may have only entered the popular lexicon with the publication in 1931 of *The Epic of America* by historian James Truslow Adams (1878–1949), but the idea was as old as the Declaration of Independence itself, embedded there in Thomas Jefferson's grand statement that "all men are created equal," and "endowed by their Creator with certain unalienable Rights, that among these are Life, Liberty, and the pursuit of Happiness." Abraham Lincoln then furthered the idea of a comfortable life for all in the 1860s by encouraging people to believe that through hard work and enterprise, everyone could achieve comfortable, middle-class lives. By the time Adams coined his well-known phrase, the United States

had long been puritan lawyer John Winthrop's "city upon a hill," the "rags-to-riches" land of nineteenth-century children's author Horatio Alger, and the land of opportunity for almost everyone else.

What Adams meant by "dream" was not the pursuit of wealth or status, despite finishing his manuscript in the midst of a "can-do" period, on the day President Herbert Hoover threw a switch in New York City to light up the just completed Empire State Building. Adams's dream was of a nation with an egalitarian social order, in which people were free to realize their individual potential and be accepted for what they were regardless of class, religion, or race: "that dream of a land in which life should be better and richer and fuller for everyone, with opportunity for each according to ability or achievement." Therein lay the problem. The idea was as diverse as the nation itself, and for African Americans for 200 years it was an unattainable goal created by whites for whites.

Keeping Adams's national ethos alive in the twenty-first century is proving difficult. Inequality is rife, and the gap between rich and poor in the United States is as great as ever. **BS**

Planned Obsolescence
Bernard London

The practice of deliberately designing products with a limited useful life

It is an idea as old as the Industrial Revolution (1760–1840): design a product with a built-in deficiency so that it becomes unusable or obsolete within a predetermined period of time. In effect, an item is "made to break" or "die." In the 1930s executives at General Electric investigated how they might be able to decrease the lifespan of their lightbulbs, and automobile makers began discussing how they might be able to build cars with approximate "use-by" dates.

The term "planned obsolescence" entered the lexicon for the first time in 1932 in a pamphlet titled "Ending the Depression through Planned Obsolescence" written by a Manhattan real estate broker, Bernard London, who advocated writing obsolescence into law in order to stimulate domestic consumption during the Great Depression.

Planned obsolescence decreased in popularity in the late 1950s, however, as ethics caused manufacturers to see themselves as con men, cheating workers out of their hard-earned money by selling them so-called "death-dated" products. Times have changed, however. Planned obsolescence is still with us, and it is becoming increasingly sophisticated. Toothbrush manufacturers, for example, now design their bristles with colorings to indicate when should be replaced, whether they need to be or not.

Obsolescence, though, is not always "planned." There is the obsolescence of function; for example, when the starter motor was introduced in 1913, all cars before it became obsolete overnight. There is also the obsolescence of desirability: when a product becomes dated and falls out of favor for aesthetic reasons. However, it is only planned obsolescence that brings with it ethical and moral considerations. Should products be intentionally made to fail so that businesses can sell more products and increase their profits at the expense of the hapless consumer? **BS**

Neoliberalism

Alexander Rüstow and Louis Rougier

A movement of free market economics that rose from the turmoil of the Great Depression

"Neoliberalism" entered the English language in 1932, when the German socialist and economist Alexander Rüstow (1885–1963) used it at a Dresden conference to describe a new generation of liberalism with beliefs that contrasted starkly to the civil libertarians and free marketeers of classical liberalism. Rüstow's neoliberalism developed out of the new economics of John Maynard Keynes, which were formed in the early 1930s in response to the failure of traditional economic theories to halt or correct the effects of the Great Depression.

The core principles of neoliberalism were the freeing of private enterprise from all government and bureaucratic shackles, the abolition of any regulation that might hinder the creation of profits, reduced public expenditure on social services and infrastructure, the

"The very design of neoliberal principles is a direct attack on democracy."

Noam Chomsky, *Hopes and Prospects* (2010)

selling-off of state-owned enterprises into private hands, and replacing the idea of "community" with that of individual responsibility. Although espoused by many leading economists in its heyday, by the 1960s neoliberalism was advocated by only a small minority.

Neoliberalism found its earliest organized expression in the Colloque Walter Lippman, a congress of twenty-six handpicked businessmen, economists, and civil servants who met in Paris in 1938 to push the neoliberal agenda. The movement was also given impetus by the failure of the French left-wing coalition, the Front Populaire, to transform France's existing social and economic structures. It was by no means a unified theory. Some called it, simply, "individualism," others "positive liberalism," with the term "neoliberalism" only emerging for reasons of strategy and commonality. **BS**

Dark Matter

Jan Hendrik Oort

A type of matter hypothesized to account for a large part of the universe's total mass

In 1932 the Dutch astronomer Jan Hendrik Oort (1900–92) turned his telescope toward visible stars in the disk of our Milky Way galaxy and began to observe the orbital velocities of stars within distant cluster galaxies. In each case the stars that Oort observed appeared to be traveling too fast considering the combined gravitational pull from the systems in which they were embedded. He concluded that there had to be some form of hidden gravitational force dragging them onward, some kind of hidden matter.

Simply put, dark matter is the unaccounted for, yet understood to be hidden, "stuff" of the universe, the presence of which can only be inferred by studying the gravitational effects it has on observable celestial bodies. Because it neither emits nor absorbs light or

" . . . the riddle is that the vast majority of the mass of the universe seems to be missing."

William J. Broad, *The New York Times* (1984)

radiation, it cannot be seen, and its precise nature is still only being guessed at.

The year after Oort's discovery, the Swiss astronomer and physicist Fritz Zwicky (1898–1974) correctly concluded, after examining the redshift in galaxies in the Coma cluster, that the universe seemed to be made up mostly of what he called "missing mass." Zwicky, who mapped thousands of galaxies that presently make up the Zwicky Galaxy Database, was the first to measure evidence of unseen mass using the virial theorem of kinetic energy.

A component of the universe, dark matter—currently thought to be a new kind of subatomic particle the discovery of which is the great quest of particle physics—is estimated to make up almost 85 percent of the matter in the universe. **BS**

Religious Humanism
The Chicago 34

A new philosophy dispenses with God and puts humankind in charge of its own fate

In the 1920s a new philosophy and assortment of ethical perspectives began to emerge among academics in the United States. It represented a radical challenge to established religious beliefs and attitudes that, it was thought, had lost their significance in the twentieth century and were no longer capable of solving many of the complexities and dilemmas of life. In 1933, thirty-four humanist scholars and academics at the University of Chicago put their signatures to, and then published, *A Humanist Manifesto*, outlining the tenets of this new worldview: the universe is self-existing and not created, man emerged from nature, self-realization should be everyone's ultimate goal, religion is little more than a mix of wishful thinking and sentimental hopes, and wealth needs to be evenly distributed to create

"Humanism is a philosophy of joyous service for the greater good of all humanity."

Linus Pauling, Nobel Prize-winning scientist

equitable societies and to foster the common good. It was man, with his free will, intelligence, and power, not God, who was solely responsible for the realization of his dreams and destiny. This new philosophy was called, ironically perhaps, religious humanism.

Religious humanism, like the religions it hoped to replace, had its own tenets, doctrines, and articles of faith (such as an unquestioning belief in evolution, and the separation of church and state), though many of its adherents would argue that it is more about perspectives and attitudes than dogma. Although humanist philosophies predate Socrates, the development of an organized school of thought has been surprisingly late in flowering. Today there are an estimated five million secular humanists throughout the world. **BS**

Falsifiability
Karl Popper

An argument that unless a theory has the capacity to be falsified, it cannot be science

In science, falsifiability means that if something has the capacity to be false, or to be disproved, then rigorous testing will, sooner or later, demonstrate it to be so. If a theory is not capable of being proven false, then scientists should place it in the category of pseudoscience. For example, the statement that you would be a lot happier if you were twenty years younger cannot be falsifiable because it is not possible to make ourselves younger and so test the hypothesis.

The influential Austrian-born philosopher Karl Popper (1902–94) first introduced his theory of potential falsifiability in *Logik der Forschung* (The Logic of Scientific Discovery, 1934). Popper held that in science first comes observation, then speculation, then falsification. Popper was uncompromising on the issue of falsifiability and

"Our theory of evolution . . . cannot be refuted by any possible observations."

L. C. Birch and P. R. Ehrlich, *Nature* (1967)

not even the giants of the scientific world escaped his scrutiny. Himself a "critical rationalist," Popper criticized neurologist Sigmund Freud (1856–1939) for what he considered his "unscientific methods," and even called to account Darwinism, saying that evolution was "not a testable scientific theory but a metaphysical research program," little more than a framework for future scientific inquiry.

Popper rejected confirmation as a means of theory proving, using his "white swan" concept as an example. No matter how many white swans are observed, it is unscientific to say that "all swans are white." To verify the statement, someone would have to travel the world and catalog and account for every swan in existence. Sheer logistics mean the statement cannot be falsified. Just one black swan is all a person needs to find. **BS**

Weak Force
Enrico Fermi

A fundamental force involved in the radioactive decay of subatomic particles

One of the four fundamental forces in nature, the existence of weak force was first hypothesized by Enrico Fermi (1901–54) in 1934. It is responsible for the decay of nuclear particles and is essential for the nuclear fusion that causes the sun's heat. It was also crucial in the process of nuclear synthesis that produced the heavy elements of which we are all composed.

The discovery of elementary particles and their interactions has often been triggered by difficulties in explaining the behavior of already observed particles. With the discovery of the neutron in 1932, the nucleus of the atom was known to consist of protons, neutrons, and electrons. Yet, it soon became apparent that the actions of these particles could not be adequately described by all the forces then known. Radioactivity occurs when the nucleus decays, and the process is

> "The weak force operates in a variety of radioactive transmutations . . ."
>
> Dr. Paul Davies, *New Scientist* (August 9, 1979)

explained by electromagnetic force; but that force could not account for a form of radiation called beta decay, in which a neutron is changed into a proton. As strong nuclear force was already known, this led Fermi to propose a weak form that would involve a particle called neutrinos, which was finally detected in 1956.

The weak force was still not fully described unless other particles could be found to mediate these weak interactions. The existence of these W and Z bosons was confirmed by particle accelerator experiments in 1983. These high energy experiments have also shown weak force to be remarkably powerful over very short distances, having a strength similar to the electromagnetic force. This led to a new theory that unifies these two forces as the electroweak force. **TJ**

Orgone Energy
Wilhelm Reich

A hypothetical life force composed of a massless, omnipresent substance

One of the more radical figures in psychiatry, the Austrian-born psychoanalyst Wilhelm Reich (1897–1957) put forward the notion that there was a secret, unseen energy present throughout the universe, which he called "orgone energy"—a combination of the words "orgasm" and "organism," hardly a surprise, perhaps, for a man who was a disciple of the Freudian idea that libidinal energy was the energy of life itself. Reich, however, carried Sigmund Freud's theory to bizarre extremes, isolating himself from mainstream psychiatry after massaging his disrobed patients in order to help dissolve their "muscular armor."

Orgone, which has never been proven to exist, is supposedly an omnipresent form of energy, a life force that is in constant motion and is, according to Reich, responsible for everything from the color of the sky

> "It is sexual energy which governs the structure of human feeling and thinking."
>
> Wilhelm Reich

and the presence of gravity to the failure of political revolutions and the satisfaction inherent in orgasm. He claimed he had seen transitional, microscopic beings that he called bions (which only staunch orgonomists can see). He claimed to have invented a new science, and felt that mainstream scientists only attacked his work because they felt it too "emotionally disturbing."

Reich also constructed what he called "orgone accumulators"—metal and organic-lined boxes that he said "trapped" orgone energy and harnessed it for use in biology, medicine, and even meteorology. Reich died in the Federal Penitentiary in Lewisburg, Pennsylvania, on November 3, 1957—imprisoned for criminal contempt when he refused to stop selling his discredited "orgone accumulators." **BS**

⬅ Enrico Fermi photographed in 1948 with equipment for the particle accelerator at the University of Chicago.

Impossible Object
Oscar Reutersvärd

Illusional drawings that challenge our perceptions as to what is real—while the eye accepts them as eminently feasible, the mind knows them to be impossible

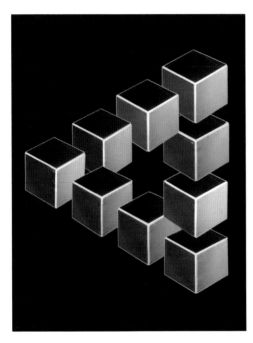

⬆ A concept derived by Swedish artist Oscar Reutersvärd, this figure has become known as the Penrose triangle, named for the mathematician, Roger Penrose, who popularized it.

"The impossibility of most impossible objects is not immediately registered, but requires scrutiny and thought before the inconsistency is detected . . ."

Irving Biederman, neuroscientist

An impossible object is an undecipherable figure, an optical illusion represented by a two-dimensional drawing that our brain immediately perceives as three-dimensional despite its existence being a geometric impossibility. Impossible objects can take many forms. They can include ambiguous line drawings, such as the Necker cube, possibly the world's first impossible object, which was drawn by the Swiss crystallographer Louis Necker in 1832. They can present false perspectives, such as parallel lines seeming to be parallel when they are in fact tilted, or depth ambiguity as seen in the well-known Penrose stairs, drawn by the English mathematical physicist Roger Penrose. Comprising a set of steps that connects back onto itself with four ninety-degree turns in a continuous loop, the drawing made it appear possible to infinitely either ascend or descend the staircase without, in the process, actually going up or down.

The "father of the impossible object," however, was the Swedish artist Oscar Reutersvärd (1915–2002), who drew his first object—the "impossible triangle"—during an idle moment in a Latin lecture at Stockholm University in 1934, and which Penrose would later describe as "impossibility in its purest form." Reutersvärd went on to produce more than 2,500 such drawings over his lifetime.

Impossible objects have garnered the attention of psychologists because they provide insights into the nature of perception. Computer scientists use them to develop models of our perceptive abilities, and mathematicians study their abstract structures. Moreover, they are whimsical conundrums, tricking our minds by initially giving us the impression of a known spatial object before their subtle geometry begins to confound us with images that at first seem possible, and yet are fundamentally and forever ambiguous. **BS**

Alcoholics Anonymous
Dr. Robert Smith and William B. Wilson

An organization established to assist alcoholics with their recovery

Alcoholics Anonymous (AA) is an organization whose fundamental intuition is that addicts require a conversion moment. This breakthrough is needed in order for them to recognize their own fallibility and relinquish control to God, a higher power, or whatever they conceive that to be. Recovery, one day at a time, involves the support of other members but with their identities protected. Former addicts can feel they are in a safe space to consider how to redress for past harm.

On June 10, 1935, Dr. Robert Smith (1879–1950), an alcoholic surgeon, finally succumbed to the urgings of his new friend and former alcoholic, William B. Wilson (1895–1971), to turn his fight with alcohol over to God. This became the founding day of the organization. Medical expertise had shrugged its shoulders, admitting that clinical treatment of alcoholics was doomed to failure and the only "cure" was a spiritual awakening. "Bill W." could personally testify to this when he experienced a flash of insight while attending the Oxford Group, a newly founded Christian sect. Both he and "Dr. Bob" acknowledged the need for a more ecumenical approach, and this led to Wilson developing his quasi-religious "Twelve Steps."

In 1939 Wilson wrote *Alcoholics Anonymous*, known as the "Big Book" by AA members. The Big Book's methods have been emulated by those seeking recovery from almost any potentially obsessive activity, from sex to shopping. How it works and who it works for, however, remain unanswered questions. Designed to be every bit as habit-forming as the initial addiction, its anonymity and "no dues or fees" rules keep it accessible and safe. A lack of hierarchical structure fosters a feeling of egalitarianism. The idea's success may have nothing to do with the steps, however. It may derive, instead, from the powerful sense of belonging that membership creates. **LW**

Keynesian Economics
John Maynard Keynes

A macroeconomic model that supports government intervention in fiscal policy

It is difficult to underestimate the significance of the economic theories of John Maynard Keynes (1883–1946). Finally, after 150 years of the laissez-faire economics of the eighteenth-century founder of contemporary economics Adam Smith, along came a set of principles, honed in the fires of the Great Depression, that turned traditional economics on its head. Keynes outlined his ideas in *The General Theory of Employment, Interest and Money* published in 1935–36. Instead of allowing the market to govern itself, Keynes argued that governments needed to get more involved in economic management. They needed to spend more, regulate more, and intervene more. In depressions or downturns, governments should inject their economies with cash so that spending can increase. More money

"All production is for the purpose of ultimately satisfying a consumer."

John Maynard Keynes

needed to be printed and pumped into society so that people would purchase and consume more. As far as Keynes was concerned, when spending increases so do earnings. In turn, higher earnings then lift demand and productivity, and pull economies out of recession. Once good times return, borrowed monies can be repaid.

U.S. President Franklin Roosevelt put Keynes's ideas into action in the mid-1930s with a massive public works program, but it was the United States' entry into World War II in 1941 that seemed to validate his theories, boosting productivity and laying the foundations for U.S. postwar economic prosperity. Keynes's theories are still debated today, and his approach of pump-priming the economy was returned to again during the recent global financial crisis. **BS**

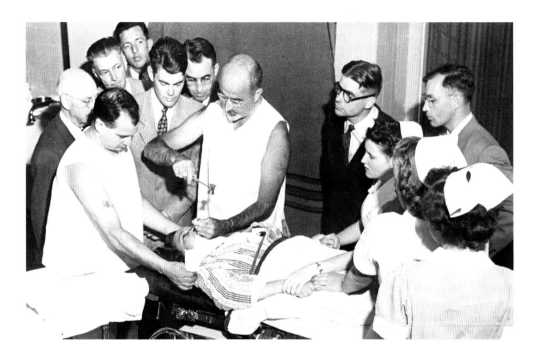

Lobotomy

António Moniz and Pedro Almeida Lima

A surgical procedure that severed the brain's neural pathways with serious side effects

A lobotomy, or prefrontal leukotomy, is a neurological procedure that involves severing the neural pathways that lead to and from the brain's prefrontal cortex. The world's first lobotomy on a human was performed in 1935 by the Portuguese neurophysicians António Moniz (1874–1955) and Pedro Almeida Lima (1903–85), who were inspired by a successful removal of tissue from a chimpanzee by two U.S. neuroscientists, John Fulton and Carlyle Jacobsen, earlier that same year. Moniz and Lima drilled two holes into the head of their patient, and injected ethanol into the prefrontal cortex. It was hoped the ethanol would interfere with the brain's neuronal tracts, which were believed to encourage the processing of irrational thoughts common to the mentally ill. The

paranoia and anxiety that the patient was suffering underwent a marked decrease after the groundbreaking operation, which would likely not have been possible were it not for Moniz's own work eight years earlier while at the University of Lisbon developing cerebral angiography, a technique allowing for visualization of the blood vessels surrounding the brain.

Moniz, convinced that patients who exhibited obsessive compulsive disorders were suffering from "fixed circuits" in their brains, later designed an instrument called a leukotome, which he used to remove brain matter and so disrupt the neuronal tracts more efficiently. The U.S. neurologist Walter Freeman, impressed by Moniz's work, performed the first lobotomy in the United States in 1936; he claimed that the debilitating effect the surgery had on patients needed to be weighed against a lifetime of padded cells and straitjackets. Freeman invented an ice pick-like instrument for performing the surgery. In 1949 Moniz shared a Nobel Prize for his pioneering work; however, the procedure began to fall out of favor in the 1950s with the introduction of a new generation of psychiatric (or antipsychotic) medicines. **BS**

Dr. Walter Freeman, who specialized in lobotomy in the United States, performs the procedure in 1949. ⬆

The Holocaust
Adolf Hitler

The state-sponsored killing of Jews and others by Nazi Germany

The Holocaust refers to the wholesale murder of six million European Jews and millions of others, including Gypsies, during World War II. The word was chosen (from the Greek meaning "sacrifice by fire") because the ultimate manifestation of the Nazi killing program was the extermination camps where victims' bodies were consumed in crematoria. The biblical word "Shoah" became the Hebrew term for the genocide in the 1940s.

Although the word "Holocaust" itself was only chosen later to describe the Nazi genocide, the ideology that led to it commenced with the Nürnberg Laws enacted on September 15, 1935. The Law for the Protection of German Blood and German Honor and the Law of the Reich Citizen were the centerpiece of anti-Semitic legislation and they were used to categorize Jews in all German-controlled lands. Categorization was the first stage of what the Nazis called "the final solution to the Jewish question." Besides Jews, trade unionists and social democrats were among the first to be arrested and incarcerated in concentration camps. Gypsies were the only other group that the Nazis systematically killed in gas chambers alongside the Jews. In 1939, the Nazis instituted the T4 Program, euphemistically a "euthanasia" program, to exterminate mentally retarded, physically disabled, and emotionally disturbed Germans who violated the Nazi ideal of Aryan supremacy. After the invasion of Poland in 1939, German occupation policy sought to systematically destroy the Polish nation and society.

In the immediate aftermath of the Holocaust, the International Military Tribunal in Nuremberg, Germany, was constituted. In October 1945, the defendants were formally indicted for crimes against peace, war crimes, crimes against humanity, and conspiracy to commit these crimes. The Nuremberg tribunal set precedents in seeking justice, however inadequate, for victims of atrocities. **BC**

 The arrival of a train transporting deported Jews at the Auschwitz death camp in Poland.

The Radiant City
Le Corbusier

A radical new vision for the skylines of our modern cities

In the 1920s the Swiss-born, modernist architect Le Corbusier (1887–1965) began formulating and refining his ideas on futuristic inner city living, with cruciform skyscrapers sheathed in glass, steel, and concrete that would, he believed, create a more efficient, classless society. In 1935 he published his ideas under the title *La Ville Radieuse* (The Radiant City).

Toronto in Canada embraced Le Corbusier's vision in a number of high-rise communities with appealing names such as Regent Park and Parkway Forest. Set well back from surrounding streets and footpaths, residents felt no connection to their environment, inhabiting structures separated by broad, mostly empty streets that were in fact just driveways devoid of pedestrian traffic, shops, or any other kind of "pulse."

"... To bring back the sky. To restore a clear vision of things. Air, light, joy."
Le Corbusier

Whereas most observers who looked at the skyline of 1930s Stockholm saw overwhelming beauty and grace, Le Corbusier saw only "frightening chaos and saddening monotony." In 1925 he had proposed bulldozing most of central Paris north of the Seine and replacing it with his cruciform towers. In the 1930s and 1940s he attempted to implement his vision of an ideal city by building a series of *unités*—the housing block unit of his *Radiant City*. The best-known example of these was the Unité d'Habitation (Housing Unit), constructed in 1952. Although Le Corbusier's designs were initially seen as utopian and geared to improving living conditions in urban areas, his work was later criticized for being soulless and totalitarian, and his vision has become associated with the alienating effects of modern urban planning and architecture. **BS**

Schrödinger's Cat
Erwin Schrödinger

A thought experiment used to question the status of subatomic particles

Schrödinger's cat is a paradoxical experiment in quantum mechanics devised in 1935 by the Austrian physicist Erwin Schrödinger (1887–1961). It is a thought experiment designed as a response to the Copenhagen interpretation, which implies that subatomic particles can exist in two distinct states up until the moment they are observed. To demonstrate his own skepticism of the Copenhagen interpretation, Schrödinger conducted a hypothetical experiment using a Geiger counter, a radioactive substance, a flask, a hammer, some acid, a steel chamber, and a cat.

The cat is placed inside the chamber so it cannot be seen, along with the aforementioned items. If the radioactive substance decays sufficiently over the course of the test period, the hammer shatters the

"When I hear about Schrödinger's cat, I reach for my gun."
Stephen Hawking, physicist

flask, which contains hydrocyanic acid (poisonous gas), and the cat dies. But has the flask been shattered? Is the cat dead? While the chamber remains sealed, it is impossible to know. According to superposition and the Copenhagen interpretation designed to explain it, particles can simultaneously exist in all their possible states, therefore, the cat inside the chamber is, until observed, both alive and dead. But how long is a superposition supposed to exist? At what point does the poor cat become either demonstrably alive or very dead? The Objective Collapse theory says superpositions end spontaneously, meaning the cat will be alive or dead long before the chamber is opened. In any case just because something may occur on the subatomic level hardly means it can be replicated with a cat. **BS**

◨ Le Corbusier photographed standing behind one of his high-rise architectural models in c. 1950.

The Work of Art in the Age of Mechanical Reproduction
Walter Benjamin

An assessment of the impact of mass reproduction on the unique work of art

↑ A photographic portrait of Walter Benjamin, taken in 1925. Tragically, he later committed suicide in 1940 while attempting to escape from the Nazis in France.

"For the first time in world history, mechanical reproduction emancipates the work of art from its parasitical dependence on ritual."

Walter Benjamin

It may have been written more than seventy-five years ago, but the German literary critic Walter Benjamin's (1892–1940) essay "The Work of Art in the Age of Mechanical Reproduction" (1936) remains a seminal and oft-debated work. Benjamin argued that the meaning of a piece of art alters as the means of creating it alter. Composed in an era of significant technological advancements, he saw the advent of mechanical (and therefore mass) reproduction as a progression from one-off pieces that had characterized art since its inception. Benjamin believed that greater production meant that more people could be introduced to art than ever before. Art, for the first time, would lose the "aura" it had acquired after centuries of depicting religious themes. No longer would it be there only for the privileged few; no longer would it be so authoritarian. It would, at last, be there for us all.

Benjamin felt it was important not to view reproductions, which could be mass-produced in books and other media, as possessing any less of the aura that was imparted to one-off masterworks by their inherent exclusivity. Consider photography, he told us. It makes no sense to make a single photograph from a photographic negative—there is no "original" photograph. Every identical image, no matter how many copies are made from that same negative, is as valid as the next. The same argument might be applied to film. People needed, in response to the new technological age in which they now found themselves, to alter how they saw and perceived art. In a time of extreme ideologies, such as fascism and communism, that used art as propaganda, Benjamin sought to de-politicize art, to make it beautiful—and truly universal. His arguments remain pertinent today, particularly in relation to contemporary debates about the opportunities for participation in art that are offered by electronic media. **BS**

Turing Machine
Alan Turing

A hypothetical machine that provided the basis for modern computers

The Turing machine was a theoretical construct first described by its inventor Alan Turing (1912–54) in his paper "On computable numbers, with an application to the Entscheidungsproblem" (1936–37) According to Turing's explanation, it showed that machines could provide calculations from "an unlimited memory capacity obtained in the form of an infinite tape marked out into squares, on each of which a symbol could be printed. At any moment there is one symbol in the machine; it is called the scanned symbol. The machine can alter the scanned symbol, and its behavior is in part determined by that symbol, but the symbols on the tape elsewhere do not affect the behavior of the machine." In other words, Turing's machine was able to read a paper tape and the symbols it contained, and carry out certain operations on the tape. The machine was also able to store a limited amount of information. This information enabled the machine to decide what to do as it scanned each symbol: change the information it had stored, write a new symbol onto the current tape cell, and/or move one cell left or right. The machine could also decide to halt; when solving a mathematical query, this was the point at which the answer had been reached.

Turing was a British mathematician and computer scientist who later worked at Britain's codebreaking cypher school at Bletchley Park during World War II (1939–45). He created his "theoretical computing machine" to act as a model for complex mathematical calculations. It could be set to run indefinitely, to operate in a loop, or to continue until it arrived at a given set of conditions. By the time that digital computers began to be developed in the 1940s, Turing's papers on how they would work were already ten years old. His machine was the first step in answering a fundamental question of computer science: what does it mean for a task to be computable? **BS**

⬆ The Digital Electronic Universal Computing Engine, pictured here in 1958, was a pioneering digital computer developed from earlier plans by Alan Turing.

"Everyone who taps at a keyboard . . . is working on an incarnation of a Turing machine."

Time magazine (March 29, 1999)

Sartre La nausée

folio

Texte intégral

Nausea
Jean-Paul Sartre

A novel that is one of the canonical works of existentialism

Set in 1930s France, *La Nausée* (Nausea, 1938)—the first novel by the existential philosopher Jean-Paul Sartre (1905–80)—is an account of the life of fictional historian Antoine Roquentin, who after years spent traveling the world returns to his native France. He settles down in a seaside town with the intention of continuing his research into the life of an eighteenth-century diplomat, Marquis de Rollebon. However, the Marquis ceases to be a historical figure as Roquentin brings him from the past into the present, and absorbs his subject slowly into himself: "I could feel him," Roquentin says, "like a slight glow in the pit of my stomach."

The "problem" with Roquentin is that he is compulsively introspective, to the point at which he observes even himself as little more than an object.

"Nausea gives us a few of the . . . most useful images of man in our time that we possess."

Hayden Carruth, poet

He strives to conform his consciousness to the world around him but fails. He becomes depressed, and a nauseous, "sweetish sickness" begins to descend upon him. In bringing the Marquis into the present in a quest for completeness, Roquentin—and Sartre—is rejecting, in true nihilist fashion, the psychoanalytic notion that to ignore the past is to annihilate one's own roots. Roquentin, however, triumphs over the world's indifference to man's aspirations, and commits to using his freedom to create his own meaning.

So, is *Nausea* a novel or a work of philosophy? French writer Albert Camus felt it an "uneasy marriage" of the two. The U.S. poet Hayden Carruth described it as a "proper work of art." Certainly it acknowledges that life can be meaningless, but also that it can be imbued with meaning through the choices we make. **BS**

People's War
Mao Zedong

An uprising of the peasantry in a struggle to overthrow an entrenched ruling class

The idea of a "people's war" emerged in its purest form in mid-1920s' China, when the young revolutionary Mao Tse-tung (1893–1976) began to comprehend the latent potential for rebellion among China's peasantry. It would not be until the late 1930s, however, that Mao's thoughts on precisely what a people's war should be, and how it should be fought, finally came together. His *On Protracted War* (1938) referred to three essential dogmas: first, that any rebellion would be rooted in the peasantry and promulgated from remote, rural bases; second, that the battles to be fought would be more political and ideological than military in nature; and third, that it would need to be a protracted war, with very clear stages and agreed long-term goals. Mao also believed people to be spiritual, strong,

"Weapons are . . . not the decisive factor; it is people, not things, that are decisive."

Mao Zedong

and resourceful beings, much more powerful than weapons, which he saw as lesser, "material" things

The primary goal of Mao's people's par was political mobilization, and the greatest challenge was to make his political objectives known to all. Mao was acutely aware that the peasantry yearned for a measure of economic prosperity, and so his economic reform program also had to be seen to offer the peasants a new sense of dignity and identity. It followed that the accomplishments of the leadership had to be made unambiguously clear to the people, as did its policies and objectives. The people were brought into the Communist Party fold by being made aware of, and being encouraged to identify with, the party's aims and ideals. Thus they could see that their fate and the fate of the party were one and the same. **BS**

The Birthday Problem
Richard von Mises

A mathematical problem with a solution that seems paradoxical

One of the best-known problems in the world of probability theory is what the U.S. mathematician Richard von Mises (1883–1953) called his birthday problem—calculating the likelihood of people in a given group sharing the same birthday. So what is the probability of two people sharing their special day, or three people, or four or more, and why does it matter? Prior to any analysis, assumptions need first be made. Leap years are ignored—the year in question is always 365 days long—and birthdays of the participants must be spread uniformly throughout the year. And so . . .

Person A has a birthday, and the chance that Person B shares that birthday is 1 in 365. To calculate this we multiply their separate probabilities (365/365) x (1/365), which equals 0.27 percent. Adding more people

" . . . we tend to mistake the question for one about ourselves. My birthday."

Steven Strogatz, *The New York Times* (October 1, 2012)

increases the chance that we will find two with the same birthday, but not by much. Even with five people, the likelihood of a shared birthday remains less than 1 percent. These low probabilities seem logical to us, but the confounding beauty of the birthday problem is that our logic is soon exponentially challenged when a lengthy equation confirms that only twenty-three subjects are needed to reach a 50 percent probability (50.73 percent, to be precise) that two people in a group will share the same birthday.

Only twenty-three, when one has 365 possibilities? And here is why we find the birthday problem so confounding. Our brains cannot cope with exponential increases or decreases in probabilities. And it is counterintuitive. It has the look of a paradox when in fact it is a demonstrable, hardwired equation. **BS**

MMPI
Starke Hathaway and John McKinley

A set of questions designed to provide revealing insights into our psyches

One of the most common personality assessment techniques in the world of mental health, the MMPI, or Minnesota Multiphasic Personality Inventory, was designed in 1940 to assess the psychopathology and personality traits of patients suspected of having various clinical and mental health issues and how they might benefit from possible treatments, including shock therapy. The original MMPI was based on more than 1,000 questions or "items" collected by its originators, psychologist Starke Hathaway (1903–84) and psychiatrist John McKinley (1891–1950) of the University of Minnesota, which they gleaned from psychology textbooks and clinical records of the time, before beginning on reducing them down to a "workable" 550.

*"1. I like mechanics magazines
2. I have a good appetite . . ."*

MMPI-2 true or false test questions

New scales to increase the accuracy in interpreting the data have since been added, and in 1989 the MMPI was revised as the MMPI-2 (comprising 567 items) to reflect our changing characteristics. The MMPI and its variants, though not perfect tools in the diagnosis of mental illness, nevertheless have retained their relevance. They have been used in court rooms, and as a screening technique in the selection of applicants for a variety of occupations, including airline pilots, police officers, and roles in the U.S. Secret Service. The application of MMPI-2 is widespread around the world, and it has been translated into more than thirty-four languages. A diagnosis should never be made on the strength of the MMPI alone, but it remains a key tool in determining a person's degree of social or personal maladjustment. **BS**

The MMPI-A test booklet, published in 1992, was the first MMPI test designed specifically for adolescents.

Softcover Test Booklet

MMPI-A

Minnesota Multiphasic Personality Inventory—ADOLESCENT™

James N. Butcher, John R. Graham, Carolyn L. Williams, and Beverly Kaemmer

S.R. Hathaway and J.C. McKinley

Product Number 25015

How to Read a Book: The Art of Getting a Liberal Education
Mortimer Adler

A guide to reading comprehension for the general reader

⬆ A photograph of Mortimer Adler in 1947, surrounded by his "Great Ideas"—a selection of 102 of the most important concepts in Western literature and thought.

U.S. philosopher and educator Mortimer Adler (1902–2001) received a scholarship to Columbia Univeristy in the 1920s; although he completed his undergraduate degree requirements in philosophy, he was never granted a BA. Nonetheless, he enrolled in the graduate program and was granted a PhD and became a philosophy of law professor at the University of Chicago. While teaching, Adler came to believe that students needed to be grounded in the "great ideas" embodied within the great classics. He was an advocate of reading and discussing great books in the pursuit of liberal education, and it was this that led him to publish his work, *How to Read a Book: The Art of Getting a Liberal Education* (1940).

How to Read a Book is divided into four parts. Part one includes what Adler termed the first two levels of reading: elementary and inspectional reading. Part two contains the third level of reading: analytical reading. Part three tells how to read different types of literature, including practical books, imaginative literature, stories, plays, poems, history, philosophy, science, mathematics, and social science. The final part of the book is dedicated to the ultimate goals of reading. The first goal is synoptical reading—the reading of different works on the same subject with a view to constituting a general view of a subject; the last goal of reading is to expand one's mind for further understanding.

Adler believed that, in a democracy, people must be enabled to discharge the responsibilities of free men and that liberal education is an indispensable means to that end. He wrote that the art of reading well is intimately related to the art of thinking clearly, critically, and freely. Adler described *How to Read a Book* as a book about reading in relation to life, liberty, and the pursuit of happiness. He went on to found the Great Books of the Western World series with Robert Hutchins in 1952. **BC**

> "In the case of good books, the point is not to see how many of them you can get through, but rather how many can get through to you."

Mortimer Adler

Three Laws of Robotics
Isaac Asimov

A fictional set of laws for governing the behavior of artificially intelligent beings

In 1941 the great science fiction writer Isaac Asimov (1920–92) wrote *Runaround*, the latest in a series of short stories on robots with positronic, humanlike brains in the era of space exploration. In *Runaround*, two astronauts and a robot, SPD-13, are sent to an abandoned mining station on Mercury. While there, a compound necessary to power the station's life-giving photo-cells, selenium, affects SPD-13 and causes him to become confused and unable to operate under the three Laws of Robotics. These laws are: 1) A robot must not injure a human being or allow a human to come to harm, 2) A robot must obeys orders given to it by a human, except if that order conflicts with the First Law, and 3) A robot must protect its own existence as long as that does not conflict with the First or Second Laws.

Over the course of his career, Asimov's position on the inviolability of the Three Laws varied, from seeing them as mere guidelines through to wholly uncompromising subroutines hotwired into the robot's brain. The Three Laws lifted robots from the mindless cadre of Frankenstein-like machines and creatures with no guiding principles that had characterized horror and science fiction for decades, and gave them the capacity to wrestle with moral dilemmas. In 1985 Asimov added a fourth law, known as the "Zeroth Law," to precede the First Law: a robot may not harm humanity, or, by inaction, allow humanity to come to harm.

Asimov's laws were so highly regarded that it was thought his Three Laws would, in the real age of robotics to come, be a foundational stone in a positronic Brave New World. The reality is that no computer or robot has so far had the Three Laws built into its network. They were, and remain, little more than imaginary literary devices, designed to further the plot of some of the finest science fiction novels ever written. **BS**

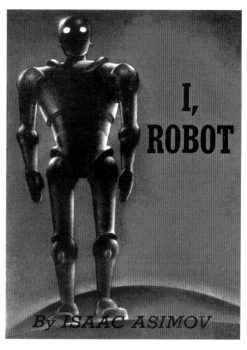

↑ *Runaround* (1941), the short story in which Isaac Asimov first introduced his Laws of Robotics, was one of nine science fiction short stories featured in his collection, *I, Robot* (1950).

"Many writers of robot stories, without actually quoting the Three Laws, take them for granted, and expect the readers to do the same."

Isaac Asimov

Epigenetics

C. H. Waddington

The study of modifications in genes that do not involve changes in DNA sequence

The biologist C. H. Waddington (1905–75) popularized the term "epigenetics" in 1942, calling it "biology which studies the causal interactions between genes and their products which bring the phenotype [an organism's observable characteristics] into being." Many geneticists at that time believed that there was a simple correspondence between an organism's genes and its characteristics; Waddington, however, argued that the phenotype of an organism was determined by the interaction of many genes with each other and with the environment.

The definition of epigenetics has since altered over time, but it is safe to say that the science of modern epigenetics is the study of alterations in gene activity not derived from changes to the genetic code. Or, to put it another way, epigenetics attempts to understand what can influence the development of an organism other than the usual DNA sequencing.

How genes develop is governed by the epigenone, which is located just outside and above the genome. Epigenones are like "tags" on our DNA, telling genes how to behave and passing down information crucial to the genome's development—information that is then passed down to following generations. For example, scientists know that if a pregnant woman eats poorly, her developing baby will suffer nutritional deficiencies after birth. However, could such transfers be carried a step further, to before pregnancy? How likely could the effects of a nutritional or dietary deficiency—say from a prolonged famine, for example—progress down through subsequent generations?

Epigenetics is helping us to understand how a parent's diet or illness can in effect switch on or off their child's genes long before the mother ever falls pregnant. Our genetic slates are no longer conveniently wiped clean with each successive generation. It is no longer a case of "you are what you eat." **BS**

A computer artwork of a U1 Adaptor (orange) silencing genes and disrupting DNA code. ⬆

1942   **Φ**

The Myth of Sisyphus
Albert Camus

The notion that hoping to gain a sense of meaning from the universe is absurd

In ancient Greek mythology, Sisyphus, a king of Ephyra (Corinth), was condemned to an eternity of futility and turmoil by the gods. He was forced forever to push a boulder up a steep hill, only to be compelled upon nearing the summit to roll it back down the hill; he therefore never completes his task. This endless repetitive toil that culminates only in failure summarizes everyone's life, according to French philosopher and novelist Albert Camus (1913–60). The universe in which we live offers no chance of a life of meaning or purpose, although by understanding this we can obtain whatever possible measure of meaning there is.

Camus published his essay, *The Myth of Sisyphus*, in 1942. In it, he described how mankind can best live in the light of what he calls "the absurd." Absurdity arises when humanity attempts to extract some meaning from a meaningless universe that offers only a life of endless toil followed by inevitable death. A life such as that, according to Camus, allows no purpose or meaning unless a person chooses to make an irrational leap of faith and adopt some religious credo. Any person who does not might otherwise conclude that the only real option is suicide.

In *The Myth of Sisyphus*, Camus argues that meaning can only come from accepting the toil and absurdity of life at face value. Yes, all life ends in death, and so it is only by being free to think and behave as we wish, pursuing our passions and rebelling against passive resignation to our certain fate, that human beings can achieve any true measure of happiness.

Camus's myth of Sisyphus is often included, fairly or not, with existential philosophy and its reflections on the quality of being, or ontology. For anyone struggling to find meaning in a world perceived as fundamentally meaningless, Camus suggested that defiance of meaninglessness could be the foundation on which meaning could be built. **MT**

⬆ Destined to forever push a boulder up a hill, Sisyphus represents man's futile search for life's meaning.

The Manhattan Project
Franklin D. Roosevelt

A scientific research program established to develop the first atomic weapon

The Manhattan Project was the codename given to the U.S. research and development program that created the first nuclear weapons. It lasted from 1942 to 1945, resulting in the detonation of the first atomic device on July 16, 1945, at a site near Alamogordo, New Mexico.

In the summer of 1939, before the outbreak of World War II, President Franklin D. Roosevelt (1882–1945) received the Einstein-Szilárd letter, a plea from physicists Albert Einstein, Leó Szilárd, and Eugene Wigner warning him of the possibility that Nazi Germany could develop an atomic bomb. Within a year, the United States was conducting research into the feasibility of such a weapon. The project grew steadily over time, and in 1942 President Roosevelt signed an order directing the creation of a nuclear weapon.

"Now I am become Death, the destroyer of worlds."

J. R. Oppenheimer, on witnessing the first nuclear test

Eventually falling under the direction of General Leslie Groves (1896–1970), the scientific research team that designed and built the device was led by physicist J. Robert Oppenheimer (1904–67).

The moment the Manhattan Project succeeded, it irrevocably altered human history and ushered in the Atomic Age. On August 6, 1945, the United States dropped an atomic weapon on Hiroshima, Japan, followed three days later by another weapon dropped on Nagasaki, Japan. Four years later, the Soviet Union developed its own atomic weapon, and the Cold War that followed lasted for decades. By its end, several nations possessed nuclear weapons that could reach across continents, threatening nuclear annihilation at the push of a button. Though the Cold War has ended, the threat nuclear weapons pose to humanity remains. **MT**

Carpooling
United States

The practice of sharing a car, usually for the daily commute to and from work

The concept of carpooling first arose in the United States in 1942. Oil was in short supply as a result of World War II, and so the U.S. government carried out a marketing campaign to encourage people to join car-sharing clubs as part of a general approach to rationing. Enthusiasm for carpooling waned after the end of the war, thanks to low fuel prices, but the practice was revived again in the 1970s following further fuel shortages. In response to the oil crisis of 1973, President Nixon's administration enacted a number of measures to provide funding for carpool initiatives. This was later added to by President Carter, who introduced a bill that sought to create a National Office of Ridesharing.

The idea has since spread to more than forty countries, and its benefits are plain: reduced travel

"Carpooling is often described as the 'invisible mode' [of transport] . . ."

Paul Minett, Trip Convergence Ltd.

expenses, forgoing the need to purchase a second car, less overall fuel consumption, and less congested roads. Some countries have even designated carpooling lanes to encourage the practice, while businesses, too, have designated parking spaces for carpoolers.

There were more than a billion automobiles in the world as of 2010, and in 2012, for the first time in history, the number of cars produced exceeded 60 million in a single year. This represents an inexorable upward trend that shows no sign of abating. Although carpooling does have its drawbacks, not least the issue of legal liability for the driver should passengers be injured in an accident, it still represents one of the more practical, immediate solutions to the problem of our dependence on fossil fuels, which reduce the quality of air in our congested cities. **BS**

Grandfather Paradox

René Barjavel

A hypothetical problem posed by the practicalities of time travel, which questions whether a time traveler can perform an action that eliminates the possibility of that action in the future

⬆ The Hollywood movie *Back to the Future II* (1989) was part of a franchise exploring plotlines in which a visitor from the future potentially affects present-day—and therefore future—events.

"In our version of time travel, paradoxical situations are censored. The grandfather is a tough guy to kill."

Seth Lloyd, professor of mechanical engineering

One of the great theorectical problems inherent in time travel, the grandfather paradox was first explored in René Barjavel's (1911–85) book *Le Voyageur Imprudent* (Future Times Three, 1943). It goes like this: you go back in time and kill your grandfather before he has children, thus making it impossible for your parents to have been born and, in turn, you. The conundrum is self-evident: how can killing your only chance of being born possibly result in you going on to exist? How could someone whose grandparents never conceived their own father or mother possibly come into existence?

The grandfather paradox has been used to argue that backward time travel must be impossible. One proposed solution involves there being two parallel timelines in which each reality is possible. Another, murkier theory is the Huggins Displacement Theory, which consigns a time traveler who goes back in time, say, three years, to also suffer being displaced by three light years, which in turn means being prevented by Albert Einstein's theory of relativity from doing anything that would tamper with his own timeline. And if you do not like those theories, there are plenty more. There is the Parallel Universe Theory, the Nonexistence Theory, and the Temporal Modification Negation Theory. Traveling back in time can be a confounding business.

Perhaps the best chance of rendering the paradox neutral comes from Seth Lloyd, a professor of mechanical engineering at the Massachusetts Institute of Technology. Lloyd's experiments with photons and a quantum mechanics principle called postselection (a cosmic facility that selects paradoxical situations and ensures they do not occur) suggest that if anyone did go back in time, the laws of probability would so conspire against them as to make their task of doing away with a grandparent nigh on impossible. **BS**

Hierarchy of Needs
Abraham Maslow

A pyramid of wellbeing intended to make the world a healthier place

Abraham Maslow (1908–70) was a U.S. psychologist who railed against the notion in psychiatry that people are simply "bags of symptoms." In 1943 he wrote a self-affirming paper that he titled "A Theory of Human Motivation," published in *Psychological Review*. In it, he stressed the importance of striving for self-actualization by pursuing love and a sense of belonging. He wanted to emphasize the positive aspects of being human, and believed that the study of "crippled, stunted, immature, and unhealthy specimens can yield only a crippled psychology." It was time to start affirming people again.

Maslow's model involved what he called a "hierarchical levels of needs." This hierarchy began with the most basic—our biological and physical need for air, food, shelter, sexual fulfilment, and sleep. Next came our need for safety in the form of law and order and protection from the elements; then the need for a sense of belonging, either in a family, in a group, or in relationships; followed by self-esteem, which involved the pursuit of cognitive growth, independence, prestige, and status; and finally the need to achieve self-actualization through realizing our own potential, personal growth, fulfilment, and peak experiences.

Maslow's well-known pyramid-shaped hierarchical diagram, with our basic needs at its foundation and self-actualization at its summit, was more than just a collection of labels; it was a comprehensive roadmap for a healthy, well-balanced life. Checks included keeping a proper pH balance, being active, building friendships, and finding a sweetheart. He took the homeostasis of the body—its evolved ability to crave food when undernourished, for example—and applied it to the whole of life in an attempt to keep the world healthy in body and in mind . . . and to free up the psychiatrist's couch. **BS**

Game Theory
J. von Neumann and O. Morganstern

An applied mathematical theory used to evaluate competitive situations

A branch of applied mathematics, game theory explores situations—called games—in which competing players have to make decisions knowing that the outcome of the game is also dependent upon the choices the others make. Such games require you to think about not only what is best for you, but also about what the other players are likely to do. Game theory studies such interactions in order to determine what choices each player should make.

In 1944, mathematician John von Neumann (1903–57) and economist Oskar Morgenstern (1902–77) published their book *Theory of Games and Economic Behavior*, in which they laid the foundations for modern game theory. Von Neumann and Morgenstern focused mostly on "zero-sum" games: situations in which one player can

"In terms of the game theory . . . the universe is so constituted as to maximize play."

George B. Leonard, writer and educator

win and another can lose but, when both outcomes are added together, no net positive is achieved. Other researchers, notably mathematician John Nash (b. 1928), developed the theory further, applying it to scenarios in which multiple players compete for shared goals, in which some players know more or less than others, or in which games take place over a series of steps or stages.

Though its name sometimes leads people to believe it is trivial or only useful for entertainment, game theory reaches across spectrums, influencing any scenario where people are engaged in competition, such as law, economics, politics, or even warfare. Game theory is abstract and often simplified in how it presents complex human behaviors, yet even in its simplified form it allows researchers the opportunity to analyze human activity with precision. **MT**

Hell Is Other People
Jean-Paul Sartre

Eternal torment comes from damaging relationships between people

In 1944, French existential philosopher and writer Jean-Paul Sartre (1905–80) wrote his play *Huis Clos*, often translated as "No Exit." In it, Sartre tells the story of three deceased people who must spend the afterlife confined in a room together. The relationships that develop between the three prove to be so acrimonious that one character concludes the play by saying that "hell is other people."

For Sartre, an atheist and existentialist, the promise of spending an afterlife exulted in heaven or condemned in hell was a fiction. Nevertheless, he wrote *No Exit* to describe what he saw as hell: a world where people must spend eternity with those they cannot get along with. True hell, for Sartre, is the pain and suffering endured from having to spend a life in bad relationships.

"There's no need for red-hot pokers. Hell is—other people!"

Jean-Paul Sartre, *Huis Clos* (1944)

The despair and bleakness present in *No Exit* led many to believe that Sartre intended the statement "hell is other people" as a descriptor of the realities of human existence in general, and that the only way to achieve true happiness was to live in isolation. Sartre himself later clarified his intention, saying that if people are in a spoiled or damaged relationship, their existence is hell, but that does not mean that all relationships are by nature hellish. To anyone concerned with their social relationships and the pursuit of a fulfilling or happy life, the notion that hell is other people is, at the very least, troubling. The idea forces us to ask questions about ourselves, about those with whom we share our lives, about how we affect one another, and about what, if anything, we can do to find happiness. **MT**

The Road to Serfdom
Friedrich von Hayek

A warning that state-controlled economies always lead to a loss of personal freedom

British economist Friedrich von Hayek's (1899–1992) book *The Road to Serfdom* (1944) was an ode to Liberalism: the ideology of freedom, equality, and small, noninterventionist governments. At the core of the work is a warning that any government that creates and fosters a planned, state-controlled economy will always gravitate to totalitarianism. For Hayek, economic plans always involved social objectives—but whose objectives? In such a regulated system, it is easy for special interests to be favored, but are these interests for the social good? However they are packaged, he warned, big, centrally controlled governments inevitably lead to a loss of freedom—and serfdom.

Hayek never expected his book to make much of an impact, but nonetheless felt writing it "a duty that

"In my opinion it is a grand book . . . I [am] . . . in agreement with virtually the whole of it."

John Maynard Keynes, economist

I must not evade." After struggling to find a publisher, the initial run of 2,000 copies sold in days. Another 30,000 followed, and when Reader's Digest serialized it in 1945 the book began to sell in millions. It went on to become recognized as one of the twentieth century's most expressive accounts of the nature of market libertarianism, and the threats that it faces.

Hayek felt that planning and intervention stifled spontaneous responses and initiatives by individuals to achieve economic outcomes, and believed that market forces alone could provide a populace with all of its needs. The free market, he claimed, would always win out over a socially planned economy because "it is the only method by which our activities can be adjusted . . . without the coercive or arbitrary intervention of authority." **BS**

United Nations
United States

An organization of world governments formed to prevent worldwide war

Founded in 1945 on the initial instigation of the United States, the United Nations is an international organization of member nations that serves to promote world peace, security, international cooperation, and economic development. As of 2011, when the Republic of South Sudan joined, there were 193 member states.

U.S. President Franklin D. Roosevelt (1882–1945) is credited with coining the name "United Nations," although the idea arguably first arose with German philosopher Immanuel Kant, who, in 1795, proposed an international organization allowing nations a way to promote peace and cooperate to expand commerce. The United Nations was intended to replace the League of Nations, the international organization formed in the wake of World War I (1914–18). Like its predecessor, the

"The United Nations system is still the best instrument for making the world less fragile."

Carlo Azeglio Ciampi, politician

United Nations was created to give countries a forum for resolving disagreements in order to avoid potential conflict. By 1939, after the obvious failure of the League of Nations in preventing a new war, talks had begun among the Allied nations to create a new international organization. On October 24, 1945, a majority of the original fifty signatory nations adopted the United Nations charter, and so it came into being.

While the League of Nations failed to prevent global conflict, the United Nations has, arguably, succeeded. Wars have not stopped since its formation, but neither has there been a worldwide conflict since 1945. And although coincidence does not a cause make, the United Nations has come to serve many additional purposes, and has maintained its place as the largest international organization of nations. **MT**

Passive-aggressive Behavior
William Menninger

The identification of a subtle form of below the surface aggression

While a colonel in the U.S. armed forces during World War II (1939–45), psychiatrist William Menninger (1899–1996) began to notice a pattern of behavior among enlisted men. They followed orders, but did so with a benign air bordering on disobedience. Menninger referred to this behavior as "below the surface hostility," and he gave it a label: passive-aggression.

There are now five commonly accepted levels of passive-aggressive behavior. The first, temporary compliance, is when someone complies with a request but delays acting on it. The second, intentional inefficiency, is doing something when asked but doing it in an unacceptable fashion. The third, escalation, is when a problem is allowed to escalate and pleasure is taken from the angst that follows. The fourth, hidden

"Denying feelings of anger is classic passive-aggressive behavior."

Psychology Today (November 23, 2010)

but conscious revenge, occurs when someone decides to "get back" at someone whom they feel has slighted them by, for example, stealing from them or damaging their property. The fifth level, self-depreciation, is where the passive-aggressive person goes to destructive lengths in the pursuit of vengeance.

Passivity and aggression are at opposite poles of our ability to communicate. The passive person allows their rights to be violated and does not speak out for fear of what might follow, while the aggressive person speaks out with no regard for the consequences or effect on others. Passive-aggressive behavior, however, does not alternate between the passive and the aggressive. It is a mix of the two, a combination of negativistic attitudes and a pattern of intentional inefficiencies that usually begin exhibiting in late adolescence. **BS**

The Intentional Fallacy
William Wimsatt and Monroe Beardsley

Knowing an artist's intent is irrelevant when considering an artistic work

In literary criticism it is not necessary or desirable to understand what an author intended, according to the intentional fallacy postulated by English critic William K. Wimsatt, Jr. (1907–75) and U.S. philosopher of art Monroe Beardsley (1915–85). Even if it were possible to understand what a writer, or any artist, intended when creating a work, the intentional fallacy disregards such intent and insists that focusing on what the work is, and what it accomplishes, is the best way to evaluate it.

Wimsatt and Beardsley published their paper "The Intentional Fallacy" in 1946. They rejected the view that if an artist creates something with a clear intention or meaning in mind, then the art necessarily reflects that meaning. Their position on criticism also opposed the neo-romantic idea that knowing an artist's

"Critical inquiries are not settled by consulting the Oracle."

William K. Wimsatt, Jr. and Monroe Beardsley

personal motivation is paramount to understanding a work. Understanding what an artist wanted to do, and whether the work accomplished that desire, was seen as irrelevant. Along with other critics who favored evaluating a work without considering outside factors, the authors of the intentional fallacy established a key element of what became known as New Criticism.

Although New Criticism and the intentional fallacy have faded in importance since the 1960s, they changed the way people view poetry, literature, and art. Looking at the *Mona Lisa* (1503–06), does it matter what Leonardo da Vinci intended? Reading the epic poem *Beowulf* (c. 850), does ignorance of the author make it less important or exciting? The intentional fallacy says "no," and states that we can, and should, measure art's meaning without the artist having to whisper in our ear. **MT**

Child-centered Child Rearing
Dr. Benjamin Spock

A revolutionary approach to child care that has continued to this day

Fluctuations in approaches to child rearing have been commonplace ever since the late 1700s, which is hardly surprising because raising children anywhere has always been governed by the cultural and historical norms of the time. The Great Depression was an era of survival-centered families, as parents fighting poverty and even malnutrition rightly worried for the wellbeing of themselves and their children. As the Depression eased, families became more parent-centered and children were seen as "self-regulating." Then, in the late 1940s, came a revolution in child-rearing—the publication of the Freudian pediatrician Dr. Benjamin Spock's (1903–98) best-selling book, *The Common Sense Book of Baby and Child Care* (1946). Child rearing in the United States would never be the same again.

"We believe that young children should be in bed by seven . . ."

Dr. Benjamin Spock, *Baby and Child Care* (1946)

One of the most influential pediatricians of all time, Spock was the first to use psychoanalysis to try and comprehend the needs of not only the child, but its parents, too. He wanted parents to be more affectionate, more considerate, to treat their children as people. Gone was the rigid, authoritarian approach to feeding and toilet training, the dearth of touching and outward displays of familial love. "Spock's Generation," as these children were sometimes called, would be kissed and cuddled, and encouraged to sit on their parents' laps. Critics, however, say he helped grow a generation of "molly-coddled" adolescents.

Nevertheless, by the time of his death in 1998 *Baby and Child Care* had sold more than fifty million copies and been translated into thirty-eight languages. Validation enough for his refreshing approach. **BS**

Dr. Benjamin Spock looks amused by the antics of two young patients in 1946. ➡

Pop Art

Eduardo Paolozzi

An art style that drew on elements of popular culture and reinterpreted them

Pop art developed in Britain and the United States in the mid- to late 1950s, but its first example was created in 1947. *I Was a Rich Man's Plaything* by printmaker Eduardo Paolozzi (1924–2005) was a collage of commercially printed papers mounted on a card support. It incorporated a cover of the magazine *Intimate Confessions* featuring a scantily-clad young woman, along with a World War II bomber, an advertisement for Coca-Cola, other small images, and—significantly—the word "Pop," torn from the pages of a comic book. The collage would become the movement's standard-bearer, even though the term "Pop art" would not be used until coined by the art critic Lawrence Alloway in 1954.

Pop art drew on the art that had grown up around everyone, intrinsic in everyday items such as movie

"[Paolozzi] cut and pasted the roots to what would become a . . . movement."

Kyuhee Baik, "The Creators' Project" website

posters, household appliances, advertising billboards, comic books, science fiction, and food packaging—all reflecting a growing economic prosperity. Pop art would blur the distinction between "high" art and the "low" art of popular culture.

After Paolozzi, the precursor of this avant-garde approach was The Independent Group, a British association of young artists and painters who first met as a group in 1952, determined to challenge prevailing modernist interpretations of fine art and discover the aesthetic beauty of the everyday "found object."

Examples of Pop art include images of Marilyn Monroe and Campbell's soup cans made by Andy Warhol (1928–87) in the 1960s. His repetition of common images lifted them into the realm of art, or, at least, into that of the coolly ambivalent and very curious. **BS**

Counterfactuals

Nelson Goodman

An explanation of causation expressed in terms of a conditional statement

A counterfactual is a statement of the form, "If P were true, then Q would be true," where P is actually false. U.S. philosopher Nelson Goodman (1906–98) launched the contemporary discussion of counterfactuals in an article in *Journal of Philosophy*, published in 1947.

In Goodman's seminal article, he noted that while counterfactuals are crucially important to reasoning in science, there was no account of how these sorts of statements could be true or false. The central problem was that counterfactuals made claims about the way things would be and not the way things actually were. Goodman proposed that a counterfactual was true only in the way that it was backed by the laws of nature that held in the actual world. While Goodman's account was highly influential, it was eventually eclipsed in

"There is a possible world in which kangaroos have no tails . . ."

David Lewis, *On the Plurality of Worlds* (1986)

popularity by the highly technical "possible-world semantics" for counterfactuals of U.S. philosopher David Lewis (1941–2001), according to which the truth of counterfactuals was determined by what happened in universes other than the actual one.

Counterfactuals have been studied extensively. Psychologists have investigated the role that counterfactuals play in reasoning and learning; economists, political scientists, and historians have proposed various methods for determining what "would have happened" on various counterfactual suppositions. In quantum computing, researchers have hypothesized that the output of a particular computer program could be determined by measuring the state of a quantum computer, even though the computer has not actually run the program. **BSh**

Critique of Everyday Life
Henri Lefebvre

A radical critique of modern life from a neo-Marxist viewpoint

Henri Lefebvre (1901–99) was one of the last great classical philosophers, and there was barely an aspect of everyday life that he did not either write about or comment on, although his work has been sadly neglected in the English-speaking world. A Marxist intellectual and renowned sociologist, he wrote *Critique of Everyday Life* (a work in three volumes, published in 1947, 1961, and 1981) as a scathing assault on modernism and all of the trivialities it produced, and of the entwined way in which these trivialities operate together to oppress and alienate. The trivial, he said, should not be beyond the scrutiny of the philosopher.

Lefebvre argued that what modernity gives us in terms of technology and rational understanding, it strips away from us in our reduced ability to socialize.

"The more needs a human being has, the more he exists."

Henri Lefebvre, *Critique of Everyday Life* (1947)

Work and leisure held no distinction either—both were regimented and lacking in spontaneity. *Publishers Weekly* called the book a "savage critique of our consumerist society," an attack on modernism that had nothing to do with a longing for the quaintness of some hypothetical "golden age," but was instead a rational clarion call to rebellion. "Man must be everyday, or he will not be at all," Lefebvre said in *Critique*'s opening pages. He must make himself free of alienation if he is to be the "total man," and the only way to do this is to rebel from the sameness of everyday life. He had no time for poets, or for most philosophers, too, both of whom he believed spent their time wavering between the familiar and the trivial. Art was not the answer, either. Action was what was needed, not poetry and paintings. **BS**

ISO
Switzerland

An organization established to standardize the world's goods and services

The International Organization for Standardization (ISO) was created in 1947 to facilitate the standardizing of the world's goods and services; it is headquartered in Geneva, Switzerland. A nongovernmental, voluntary organization comprised of more than 2,500 technical committees, it aims to promote global communication and collaboration, the development of worldwide standards in business and finance, and the growth of global trade. Draft standards are negotiated and, when developed, are shared with the ISO membership, who then comment and vote on them. Once a consensus is reached, the draft becomes an ISO standard. The ISO's three official languages are English, Russian, and French, and the standards it promulgates are intended to be applied worldwide by importers and exporters in both the public and private sectors, and throughout all stages of any product's design, engineering, manufacturing, and testing.

The ISO was initially founded to standardize the discipline of mechanical engineering in 1926, but the advent of World War II in 1939 forced it to be temporarily disbanded in 1942. It was reorganized in 1946 after a meeting of representatives from twenty-five nations at London's Institute of Civil Engineers; the new organization officially began its work in February 1947, working out of a private residence on Geneva's Route de Malagnou. Some 164 countries now have representatives within the ISO.

The ISO is a publishing juggernaut, producing technical reports and specifications, guidebooks, and amendments to existing standards. So far the ISO has published more than 19,000 international standards. ISO standards ensure that goods and services are well made, safe, and reliable. The ISO does not itself decide what should be standardized, but instead responds to requests from industry and consumer groups. **BS**

Alpha Male / Female
Rudolph Schenkel

A theory on human social behavior based on a flawed theory on wolves, regarding the hierarchical structure of a community

The concept of the alpha male and alpha female—that in every human social group, and also in some animal groups, there will emerge a dominant male or female—was first suggested by the Swiss animal behavioralist Rudolph Schenkel (1914–2003), in his well-known paper "Expression Studies on Wolves" (1947).

In the 1930s and 1940s, Schenkel observed what he believed to be purposefully aggressive behavior among wolves as they appeared to vie for dominance of their packs. There was only one problem, and it was a major one: Schenkel's subjects were all wolves held captive in zoos, and their behavior was not the same as that of wolves in the wild. Forcing wolves unrelated by family to cohabit a restricted space creates unnatural tensions and causes them to behave differently to familial packs in the wild. Nevertheless, the terms "alpha male" and "alpha female" took root, and in time they were applied to other animal species including, eventually and most commonly, humans. But, as U.S. wolf expert L. David Mech (b. 1937) pointed out, the theory had a fundamental flaw: studying wolf behavior in captivity and drawing generalized conclusions was analogous to basing our understanding of standard human behavior on what happens in refugee camps.

The term "alpha" was always a misleading one. Schenkel's alpha wolves did not possess the traits that we have come to expect them to have: they did not always lead the hunt, were not always the first to gorge on a kill, and were not always the largest. They were alphas through deference as much as through dominance, and it was not unusual for them to assume, and then lose, their alpha status.

And for all those controlling, dominating human beings to whom the term has been applied? Perhaps much the same kind of fleeting, transient authority should have been ascribed to them, too. **BS**

↑ A lower ranked wolf is reprimanded by an alpha of its pack. Most wolves who lead packs achieve their position simply by mating and producing pups, which then become their pack.

"Attempting to apply information about the behavior of assemblages of unrelated captive wolves to the familial structure of natural packs has resulted in considerable confusion."

L. David Mech, wildlife research biologist

and AP Science Writers' Review—

NSEY BOOK ON WOMEN

The Kinsey Reports
Dr. Alfred Kinsey and others

Revolutionary ideas on human male and female sexuality and sexual behavior

The Kinsey Reports were two studies by U.S. biologist and sexologist Dr. Alfred Kinsey (1894–1956) and fellow researchers that, based on 11,000 interviews, explored human sexuality and significantly changed established views of it in society at large. First came *Sexual Behavior in the Human Male*, in 1948, followed five years later by *Sexual Behavior in the Human Female* in 1953. Kinsey's findings placed human sexuality on the agenda as a legitimate object of study. Kinsey's object was to separate research on sex from moral judgment, at a time when sexuality was commonly discussed in terms of the "dangers" of masturbation, the "perversion" of any sexual activity conducted outside of the assumed norm, and even of sexually transmitted diseases being a "punishment" for sexual "wrongdoing."

"The only unnatural sex act is that which you cannot perform."
Dr. Alfred Kinsey

Such was society's refusal to discuss sexual matters at the time that many of Kinsey's findings seemed astounding: that women, too, were sexual beings, that masturbation and premarital intercourse were commonplace, and that more than a third of the interviewed adult males had had homosexual experiences at some point in their lives. The Kinsey Reports were particularly groundbreaking in their investigations of female sexuality and homosexuality, as discussion of both was still generally considered taboo. To a large degree, Western society's frankness in expressing sexual mores, its ability openly to discuss women's sexuality, masturbation, and homosexuality, and its readiness to distance research on sexuality from traditional Judeo-Christian moral biases, followed from widespread acceptance of Kinsey's research. **JE**

Feynman Diagram
Richard Feynman

A graphical representation of the interactions between subatomic particles

Feynman diagrams, named after their inventor, U.S. Nobel Laureate physicist Richard Feynman (1918–88), are visual depictions of how subatomic particles interact. They are composed of different types of lines, such as straight, wavy, solid, dotted, or looping, and drawn on charts of two axes, in which the vertical axis represents time and the horizontal one represents space.

Subatomic particles are notoriously difficult to observe, and equally hard to visualize. In order to describe accurately these incredibly small, fast, and invisible particles, theoretical physicists once had to work solely with formulas, relying on their understanding of mathematics to summarize the often very strange behaviors that occur at the quantum level. Then, in 1948, Feynman developed a method

"You can't say A is made of B or vice versa. All mass is interaction."
Richard Feynman

to translate the mathematical data into simple, visual depictions. With the aid of the diagrams, theoretical physicists could not only describe and explain what they were doing, but they also found the reverse to be true, that the diagrams aided in performing new calculations and opened up unfamiliar areas of research.

Originally devised by Feynman for his studies in quantum electrodynamics, the diagrams were soon found to be valuable in nuclear, particle, gravitational, and solid-state physics, too. Even learned physicists steeped in mathematics discovered that working with simple diagrams allowed them to better visualize scenarios that had once been purely mathematical. More than that, they now had a powerful new calculation tool: the Feynman diagram was a new light with which to investigate the darkness. **MT**

Three women react in exaggerated shock to a review of Alfred Kinsey's report on women in 1953.

Cybernetics
Norbert Wiener

Using feedback from a system to improve its ability to achieve its intended outcome

⬆ Norbert Wiener, founder of cybernetics, in a Massachusetts Institute of Technology classroom in 1949. Wiener was a child prodigy who earned his first degree at the age of fourteen.

" . . . the social system is an organization like the individual, that is bound together by a system of communication . . . in which circular processes of a feedback nature play an important part."

Norbert Wiener, *Cybernetics* (1948)

Named from the Greek word *kybernetes*, meaning "to steer" or "to navigate," the mathematical world of cybernetics developed at a time when huge strides were being made in computing and telecommunications. The theory was developed gradually throughout the 1940s by mathematicians such as Julian Bigelow (1913–2003), Alan Turing (1912–54) (the "father of artificial intelligence"), and notably Norbert Wiener (1894–1964), who published his book *Cybernetics, or Control and Communication in the Animal and the Machine* in 1948. In the book, Wiener defined cybernetics as the study of the structures and possibilities inherent in a system that exists within its own "closed loop," where any act within the system affects its own environment and produces information that allows the system to alter or modify its behavior. In other words, cybernetics is about systems that produce feedback, and how that feedback is used to improve the ability of that system to achieve its goal.

For example, imagine someone trying to steer a boat along a given course. The wind and tide will both act on the boat with the effect of driving it off course. However, by looking where he or she is going and using this feedback to steer the boat either left or right, the person steering is able to keep the boat (or system) on course.

The term "system" can refer to biological systems in humans and animals, and also to technological systems and systems such as the environment or the economy. Cybernetics touches on numerous academic disciplines, including electrical engineering, mathematics, biology, neurophysiology, anthropology, and psychology, and has been applied to fields such as business management and organizational learning. Although cybernetics is often thought to be linked to Artificial Intelligence, the two are distinct from one another. **BS**

Chemotherapy
Sidney Farber

The development of a new generation of drugs designed to fight cancer

A relatively unknown U.S. pediatric pathologist, Sidney Farber (1903–73), founded the Children's Cancer Research Foundation at Boston's Children's Hospital in 1947 and became its first full-time pathologist. Farber was a part of the postwar boom in medical research, and was convinced that the lack of sustained research was the only thing standing between cancers and their inevitable cure. Farber was at the same time exasperated by the seeming powerlessness of modern medicine when faced with cancer, and very much wanted to offer children and adults suffering from leukemia something more effective and lasting than a brief, cortisone-induced respite from an inevitable, and very painful, death.

Farber had been studying how folic acid accelerated the growth of bone marrow, and reasoned that if a drug capable of blocking folic acid could be synthesized, it might prevent the production of abnormal marrow common to leukemia. In 1947, he took the immunosuppressive drug aminopterin, which blocked chemical reactions necessary for DNA replication, and tested it on a group of sixteen young leukemia patients. Ten of the children entered temporary remission because the folic acid antagonists Farber used had inhibited the growth of their acute lymphoblastic leukemia cells. Farber published the results of his tests in the June 1948 issue of the *New England Journal of Medicine.*

His results were initially met with incredulity; it was, after all, the first time in medical history that nonsolid tumors, such as blood, had ever responded to drugs. Farber—a previously unheralded pathologist working from a basement laboratory—had effectively found a way to suppress the proliferation of cancer cells by denying them the ability to divide. In so doing, he had ushered in a new era of cancer chemotherapy, characterized by drug-induced remission. **BS**

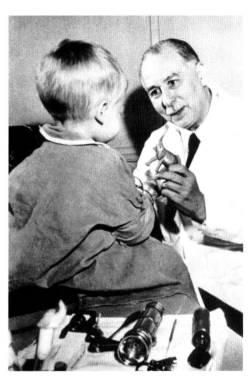

⬆ Sidney Farber with a young patient in 1960. Thanks to Farber's pioneering discovery, acute leukemia is today one of the most successfully treated nonsolid cancers in children.

"Dr. Farber would say that, in cancer, the child is the father to the man. Progress in cancer research at the clinical level almost always occurs in pediatrics first."

Dr. Emil Frei III, oncologist

Information Theory
Claude Shannon

A mathematical theory for processing and communicating information

In 1948, U.S. mathematician and electrical engineer Claude Shannon (1916–2001) published an article titled "A Mathematical Theory of Communication" in the *Bell System Technical Journal*. In the paper, Shannon set out the fundamental problem of communication: to reproduce, at one point in space, a message that has been created at another. He described what he saw as the basic components of communication: the presence of an information source that creates a message; a transmitter that takes the message and transforms it into a signal; a channel to carry the signal; a receiver to take the signal and convert it into the message; and a recipient—either human or machine— for which the message is intended. The paper also established an entirely new idea—that digital or

". . . semantic aspects of communication are irrelevant to the engineering problem."

Claude Shannon, "A Mathematical Theory . . ." (1948)

binary information could be treated like a measurable physical quantity, such as density or mass.

Known today as the "father of information theory," Shannon developed his theory while working for Bell Telephone Laboratories on the problem of how to most efficiently transmit information. "A Mathematical Theory of Communication" would prove to be a seminal piece of work, presenting a mathematical model for encoding information by attributing to it a value—either zero or one—and along the way proving that mathematics could be a tool to calculate the amount of information that a system could carry. To this day the paper provides guiding principles in the ongoing search for ever faster and more efficient communications systems, all the way from the Internet to Apple's iPod. **BS**

Binary Code
Claude Shannon

The conversion of information to strings of zeros and ones

Among the millions of ways in which human beings have found to communicate, the use of zeros and ones might be the farthest abstracted from lived experience. However, computers would still be languishing in the prehistory of information technology had not binary code—series of zeros and ones representing communicative symbols or computer functions— come into its own.

Binary numbers can be found in ancient Vedic manuscripts, where they were used as a memory aid. However, it was not until German mathematician Gottfied Leibniz (1646–1716), father of modern-day calculus, developed a system of logic that represented verbal utterances in mathematical code that the binary system was used for more complex applications.

". . . one can construct a fairly good coding of the message on a 0, 1 channel . . ."

Claude Shannon, "A Mathematical Theory . . ." (1948)

In 1948, building on English mathematician George Boole's (1815–64) algebraic system of Boolean logic, U.S. mathematican Claude Shannon (1916–2001) seized on binary code as the foundation for his groundbreaking paper "A Mathematical Theory of Communication." Information, he argued, can be reduced to the total of ones and zeros it takes to communicate it via machine. (Zeros and ones were selected because these two numbers served to express the flow and stoppage of electricity through a transistor: "one" means the transistor is on; "zero" means it is off.) Shannon's work was revelatory and formed the basis for the communication devices used in the twenty-first century. The theory makes it possible for communication devices to stream data and store vast amounts of visual and audio communication. **MK**

Binary code lies at the heart of computer and telecommunication systems. ➜

Self-fulfilling Prophecy
Robert K. Merton

A prediction that directly or indirectly causes itself to become true

The eminent U.S. sociologist Robert K. Merton (1910–2003) explained the term "self-fulfilling prophecy" (SFP) in 1948 as "a false definition of a situation evoking a new behavior which makes the original false conception come true." In other words, believing something strongly enough will make it come true because you are consciously and subconsciously acting in ways that will encourage it to happen. SFPs are not mere perceptions flowing from a belief; there must also be measurable consequences that conform to that belief.

The term has its roots in the Thomas theorem, devised in 1928 by another U.S. sociologist, William I. Thomas (1863–1947), who was of the opinion that, "If men define situations as real, they are real in their consequences." Even William Shakespeare was

"The Christian resolution to find the world ugly and bad has made [it] ugly and bad."

Friedrich Nietzsche, philosopher

aware of the powerful effects of belief: "There is nothing either good or bad," he wrote, "But thinking makes it so."

One of Merton's best-known examples of a self-fulfilling prophecy is his "run on a bank" theory; that if a few people believe their bank is about to run out of money, and if word gets around to that effect, in no time at all crowds will converge on the bank, withdraw their money, and the bank will be left with no cash when otherwise it would have remained solvent.

SFP has become an influential component of cognitive and self-perception theories, but perhaps more significant is that it is now such a part of our everyday collective consciousness. For a social science term to enter the general lexicon is not without precedent, but for something called a "sociological neologism" to do it? That is almost unheard of. **BS**

Holography
Dennis Gabor

The manipulation of light to create three-dimensional images

The world that we see around us is three-dimensional, but for most of history humans have been unable to realistically replicate that effect on a flat surface. Through the art of holography, the technique of making a three-dimensional image called a hologram, it became possible to bring a flat image to life.

The idea originated with the Hungarian-born scientist Dennis Gabor, who in 1948 came up with his theory of holography while working to improve the resolution of an electron microscope. Gabor's theory, for which he was awarded the Nobel Prize for Physics in 1971, centered on the interference patterns of light waves (created when two waves interact with each other). He posited that the crests and troughs of the light waves emitted from a source contain all the information of that source, and that if the wave pattern could be frozen for an instant and photographed then the pattern could be reconstructed to create an image with the same three-dimensional characteristics as the original source. Gabor had some success with putting his theory into practice, but light sources at the time were not sufficient to produce satisfactory results.

The invention of the low-cost, solid-state laser in the early 1960s changed this, however, as it provided a more coherent light source. A key breakthrough came in 1968 with the work of Stephen A. Benton, whose white-light transmission holography could be viewed in ordinary white light. Holograms made using this technique created a three-dimensional "rainbow" image from the seven colors that make up white light. Moreover, this form of hologram was able to be mass produced.

Holograms have since found a myriad of practical applications, from numerous security-related uses—such as the embossed holograms on credit cards—to employment in fields as diverse as computer technology, medicine, and art. **BS**

Universal Declaration of Human Rights

United Nations Member States

A document composed of thirty articles, which provided the first global expression of rights to which all human beings are inherently entitled

The Universal Declaration of Human Rights was adopted by the General Assembly of the United Nations (UN) on December 10, 1948. It was born out of a feeling that the existing UN Charter, laid out in 1945 following the horrors and atrocities of World War II, was insufficient in making plain the rights of people. Thus, a new document categorically stating the inalienable rights of every human being regardless of their status, color, or religion—rights to which we are all inherently entitled—was deemed necessary. It nevertheless maintained the principle of the original UN Charter, which "reaffirmed faith in fundamental human rights, and the dignity and worth of the human person."

The declaration's principal drafter was a Canadian, John Peter Humphrey (1905–80), a jurist, scholar, and long-time human rights activist. In 1946 Humphrey was appointed as the first director of the United Nations Division of Human Rights and he was also given the task of gathering and examining the documents that would inform and guide the commission in formulating the declaration. The former United States First Lady Eleanor Roosevelt (1884–1962) was appointed the commission's chairperson, and also played a prominent role in the drafting process.

The declaration was, however, in essence, merely a political document, not legally binding despite there being a vigorous argument on the subject. It has also been criticized for being decidedly pro-Western due to the hegemonic presence of the United States (U.S. delegates to the commission made it clear that they themselves were not in favor of its articles being legally binding). For the Americans it was more a statement of aspirations than facts, which perhaps explains the declaration's impotency in the face of countless global acts of genocide and state-sponsored terror in the years since its adoption. **BS**

⬆ A man studies a copy of the Universal Declaration of Human Rights, one of the first documents published by the United Nations.

"All human beings are born free and equal in dignity and rights. They are endowed with reason and conscience and should act toward one another in a spirit of brotherhood."

Article 1, Universal Declaration of Human Rights (1948)

GEORGE ORWELL

> 1984 <

ROMAN

Big Brother
George Orwell

A frightening picture of a bleak, dark, totalitarian, and very possible future

Big Brother is the omnipresent, public manifestation of "the Party," a totalitarian government in *Nineteen Eighty-Four* (1949), a novel by British writer George Orwell (1903–50). Accompanied by the slogan "Big Brother Is Watching You," the entity's gnarled face appears on innumerable hoardings throughout the city in which the novel is set. But is he real, or simply a psychological symbol used by the Party to maintain control and turn its incompetence into glorious victories?

The novel's central character, Winston Smith, is an employee in the Ministry of Truth who covertly loathes the party but can never decide if Big Brother is real or just a manufactured image. The novel never confirms Big Brother's existence, but whether he exists or not is hardly the point. The Party requires only that the

> *"You had to live . . . in the assumption that every sound you made was overheard . . ."*
>
> **George Orwell,** *Nineteen Eighty-Four* (1949)

populace believe that he exists so that it can benefit from the intimidation that the belief engenders.

Set in the mythical nation of Oceania, the novel is a bleak fable of state-controlled perpetual manipulation, propaganda, and mind control, set against the backdrop of an unending war (which may or may not be occurring) with the perhaps mythical, Party-generated enemies of Eurasia and Eastasia, used as a means to justify continuing repression.

The powerful science fiction novel was written in the midst of the Cold War between the United States and the Soviet Union. Having himself lived in Franco's Spain and Russia and witnessed their excesses, Orwell produced a dark vision of a totalitarian world as a warning to the West of what could happen if communism and fascism were left unchallenged. **BS**

Doublethink
George Orwell

Believing in two contradictory notions at the same time with equal conviction

Coined by British writer George Orwell (1903–50) in his novel *Nineteen Eighty-Four* (1949), the term "doublethink" refers to holding a belief in two or more contradictory ideas that cannot be true at the same time. "War is peace." "Freedom is slavery." "Your life is predetermined but you have free will." Such contradictory notions cannot be true at the same time, so those who believe that they are true are engaging in doublethink.

In the novel, the government, formed by a single ruling political party, controls the citizenry with a range of coercive tools, such as propaganda, secret police forces, torture, ever-present surveillance systems, and spies. The people may only hold a limited set of beliefs that support the regime's political goals. Sometimes, the government requires people to accept two beliefs

> *"To be conscious of complete truthfulness while telling carefully constructed lies . . . "*
>
> ***Yijing*** **(The Book of Changes,** *c.* **1000** BCE)

as true even though they contradict one another. So, through the miracle of doublethink, workers in the Ministry of Peace can engage in war, while those at the Ministry of Love feel at liberty to use torture for the purpose of extracting false confessions.

Doublethink has become widely used in popular discourse to describe a situation in which a person expounds or supports contradictory notions. In psychological terms, doublethink is known as cognitive dissonance, and occurs when contrary notions cause someone to alter their beliefs to better fit the contradictions. Political or social beliefs may be examined and criticized with reference to doublethink, and doing so helps to clarify why followers of an ideology, party, or doctrine often fervently pursue ideas that seem contrary to everyone else. **MT**

⬅ The cover of a German translation of *Nineteen Eighty-Four* (1949) depicts the all-seeing eyes of Big Brother.

Magical Realism
Alejo Carpentier

A Latin American writing style that mixes magic and urban grit

⬆ This rare hardcover edition of *One Hundred Years of Solitude* (1967) by Gabriel García Márquez hints at a moment in the novel when a Spanish galleon is found in the Colombian jungle.

"The existence of the marvelous real is what started magical realist literature, which some critics claim is the truly American literature."

Luis Leal, writer and literary critic

The first practitioner of magical realism was the Swiss-born, adopted Cuban author, essayist, and playwright Alejo Carpentier (1904–80). Carpentier introduced the world to the new genre with his novel *El reino de este mundo* (The Kingdom of This World, 1949), a fiction set around the Haitian Revolution in the early nineteenth century. In the novel, historical accuracy blended with themes of voodoo and timeless natural rhythms to produce a wholly original historical account.

However, Carpentier's examples of magical realism were not as stylized and implausible as those by authors he would subsequently influence, such as Colombian novelist Gabriel García Márquez (b. 1927). In what is still considered the style's pivotal work, *One Hundred Years of Solitude* (1967), García Márquez wrote of old men with angels' wings and raindrops falling as flowers—things that were a long way from the improbable though plausible magic of Carpentier.

The term "magical realism" had been coined in 1925 by German historian and art critic Franz Roh (1890–1965), although there it was couched in an essay on a new style of painting, the New Objectivity. What Roh saw as "magic" was simply the beauty of the world around him; the term had little in common with the work of Carpentier and García Márquez. In those authors' hands, magical realism is a mix of modern fiction, fantastical happenings, a layering of post-colonial ethnicities, multiple planes of reality, dreamlike states, ancient mythologies, and an age-old reliance on a sense of mystery, all in an effort to create a deeper, more authentic reality than conventional, realist approaches could ever hope to achieve. Distinct from the "fantasy" novel, which is set in fantastical though unfamiliar worlds, and often in the distant past or future, magical realism is rooted in the present day, among familiar images and themes, in a mix of mythical elements and fictional realism. **BS**

The Second Sex

Simone de Beauvoir

An epochal book about the place and role of women

A highly influential work of feminist philosophy, *Le Deuxième Sexe* (The Second Sex) was published in 1949 by French existentialist Simone de Beauvoir (1908–86). She began to write the book in 1946, only a year after French women were given the right to vote, and twenty-one years before they would legally be able to engage in birth control. Next door to France, in Switzerland, women would remain disenfranchised until 1971. Anyone wishing to understand where the fierce, almost wrathful strains in this tome came from would not have to look very far.

Published in two volumes, *The Second Sex* was one of literature's first attempts to view the sweep of human history from a strictly female perspective. In volume one, de Beauvoir delves into biology and psychoanalysis and the rise of the "superior" male from his beginnings as a nomadic hunter-gatherer, as she seeks to understand how women have come to be seen as the inferior "other" sex. In volume two, the writer follows the development of the female from childhood through adolescence to sexual maturity in an attempt to show that women are not created "feminine," but become feminine as the result of a multitude of external influences and processes.

Not everyone appreciated de Beauvoir's efforts. French existential author Albert Camus (1913–60) complained that it made Frenchmen look ridiculous. British poet Stevie Smith (1902–71) commented: "She has written an enormous book about women and it is soon clear that she does not like them . . ."

De Beauvoir refers to menstruation as a "curse" and to maternity as "servitude," and she exhibits an almost paranoid hostility toward marriage, which she derides as a "narcissistic compromise." No wonder, then, that the book qualified for the Vatican's Index of Forbidden Books—a badge of honor, some might think, for this seminal attempt to correct age-old assumptions. **BS**

⬆ Simone de Beauvoir, pictured here in 1945, identified herself as an author rather than a philosopher, but today she is viewed as having made lasting contributions to the field.

"One wonders if women still exist, if they will always exist, whether or not it is desirable that they should . . ."

Simone de Beauvoir, *The Second Sex* (1949)

Rhythm and Blues
Billboard magazine

A style of popular music of African American origin

"Rhythm and Blues" (R&B) was a term first used in 1949 by *Billboard* magazine. The phrase emerged as a result of the music industry's attempt after World War II to find a new way to describe the musical category they had long known as "race records," encompassing an amalgamation of predominantly gospel, jazz, and blues. In effect, record companies subsumed together and rebranded music assumed to be generally produced by black musicians for black audiences—and in that regard, R&B was more a marketing category than a specific musical genre. Marketing outside the African American community produced a distribution of R&B that deeply influenced U.S. musical culture.

A major influence on R&B music was jazz, which itself flourished in the 1920s and 1930s, and was

"Gospel, country, blues, rhythm and blues, jazz, rock 'n' roll are all really one thing."

Etta James, singer

a deep source of inspiration for R&B throughout its development until the 1950s. In the 1950s and 1960s, the relationship became more reciprocal, with R&B influencing jazz in turn. R&B was further influenced by vocal groups such as the Drifters and the Imperials, and also by the early recordings of gospel singers such as Sam Cooke (1931–64), Al Green (b. 1946), and Curtis Mayfield (1942–99).

R&B was very influential in the development of rock 'n' roll (which in the early 1950s was nearly identical to R&B), and was later influential in the development of soul and funk. R&B remains an important (though loosely defined) category in popular music, with electronic elements pushing it in the direction of urban music. Overall, it continues to be among the most influential genres in the United States. **JE**

Role Model
Robert K. Merton

The view that admiring and emulating certain people is a means of self-betterment

U.S. sociologist Robert K. Merton (1910–2003) spent almost his entire career, from 1941 to 1979, teaching at New York's Columbia University, and is renowned for his pioneering theoretical work in the analysis of social dynamics. One book, *Social Theory and Social Structure* (1949; later revised and expanded in 1957 and 1968), saw his addition to the study of sociology of new phrases such as "unintended consequences," the "self-fulfilling prophecy," and "role model." The latter is the idea that people exist in society whom others look toward as exhibiting a desired aspect of behavior, later emulating aspects of their mentality, behavior, and lifestyle. The concept arose from Merton's study of the socialization of medical students. He theorized that individuals will relate to an identified group of people and aspire to the social roles they occupy. Merton also noted that individuals may choose a succession of role models as they pass through life, emulating them in only restricted, specific ways rather than copying the totality of their lives.

Merton's pursuit of what he called his "middle-range" approach to analyzing social structures led him away from abstract or grand speculations, focusing instead on the grittiness of everyday life. Combine this with an uncommon love and respect for language, and here was a man with a unique ability to create phrases and terms that were so innately evocative and relevant that they lost no time is passing from the world of academia into everyday speech.

Merton became a model of academic inquiry. The author of more than 200 scholarly papers, he was the first sociologist ever to receive his nation's highest science award, the National Medal of Science—no mean feat for a young man born "into the slums of South Philadelphia," as he once said, who walked into his first sociology lecture "purely by chance." **BS**

Infomercial
Tico Bonomo

A combination of information and a commercial punchline in a long, leisurely broadcast that provides entertainment in itself and persuades buyers wary of a hard sell

When exactly the world's first modern infomercial series came into being is difficult to pin down, but as good a candidate as any was an hour-long real-estate program that ran every Sunday on television in San Diego, California, in the 1970s. The concept of using television shamelessly to sell a product, however, can be traced back to the NBC TV series *The Magic Clown* (1949), created by Tico Bonomo (1925–99) as a vehicle to sell his taffy-like candy bar, Turkish Taffy. Bonomo's program was followed by the development of direct marketing on U.S. television in the 1950s. One notable personality of that era was U.S. inventor and marketeer Ron Popeil (b. 1935), who invented numerous catchphrases while pitching kitchen gadgets, such as the Chop-O-Matic and the Veg-O-Matic, on television: "But wait, there's more!" is just one well-known example.

Infomercials, or Direct Response Television, commercials lasting anywhere from thirty to sixty minutes or more, began in earnest in the United States in 1984 when restrictions governing the number of advertising minutes permitted on broadcast television every hour were removed. Aimed at older audiences unresponsive to fast, high-pressure sales pitches, the infomercial had a more relaxed approach to selling. It took advantage of subtle production elements common to evening news programs, such as effective use of music, lighting, and flattering sets, all of which were integral to the delivery of the message.

Television stations favor infomercials because they reduce the need to purchase expensive "content." Advertisers like them because they can run in the early morning when advertising rates are low compared to daytime or prime time. And infomercials work. In 2009, Allstar Products Group used the infomercial to sell 20 million of its "Snuggies"—blankets with attached sleeves—and these now enjoy cult status. **BS**

↑ U.S. inventor and marketing personality Ron Popeil poses in front of a selection of the numerous gadgets that he designed and then sold using infomercials (1981).

"You can't ignore the Topsy Turvy Tomato Planter which grows tomatoes upside-down and has been snapped up by some ten million customers."

Scott Boilen, CEO Allstar Products Group

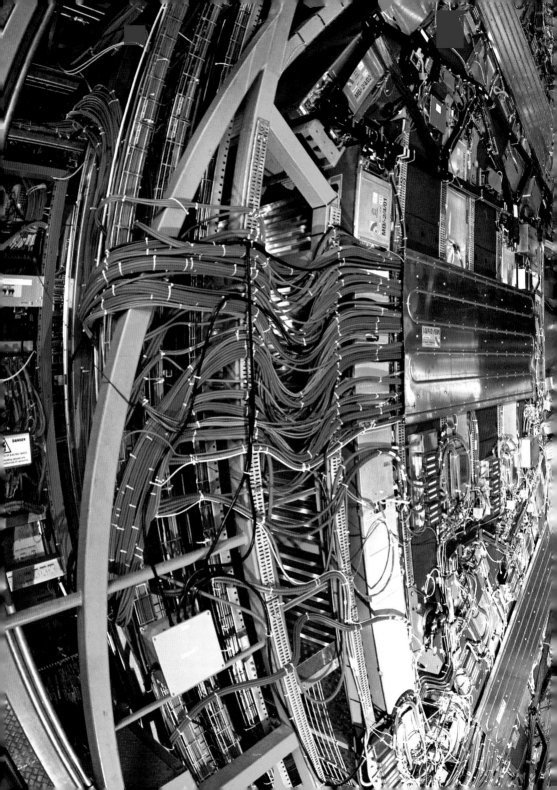

Contemporary
1950–Present

The ideas from this period reflect a rapidly changing world. The pursuit of greater equality provided the driving force for social movements that promoted ideas such as civil rights, feminism, and Fairtrade, while concern for the environment came to the fore with innovations such as recycling, Freecycling, and passive housing. Scientific and technological developments, such as cloning and commercial space flight, brought ideas from science fiction to life, and the phenomenal success of Tim Berners-Lee's concept to link the entire world together through shared data and information in a World Wide Web means that ideas both old and new can continue to be disseminated like at no other time in human history.

◄ Part of the CMS (Compact Muon Solenoid) detector at CERN, the European particle physics laboratory. It was used with the large hadron collider to search for the Higgs boson.

Pop Music
United Kingdom

A genre of music aimed at and enjoyed primarily by the young

The term "pop music" arose in the United Kingdom in the 1950s to describe popular music—rock 'n' roll music and other genres—that was recorded for commercial purposes and was specifically aimed at the mass youth market. "Pop" is a shortened form of the term "popular music," and as such it does not include such genres as jazz, folk, and world music. Pop songs generally tend to be around three minutes long, with lyrics on simple themes, and a catchy hook that draws in the listener.

By the early 1960s, British pop music had become distinct from rock 'n' roll and was identified with the Merseybeat sound that originated in Liverpool, England. Its acceptance was spearheaded by the popularity of British and also U.S. bands, in particular The Beatles, who greatly influenced fashion, fellow

"Come on, come on, come on, come on / Please, please me . . . like I please you."

The Beatles, "Please Please Me" (1963)

musicians, album concepts, music production, and the way that pop music was marketed. Later in the 1960s, pop came to refer to all kinds of popular music.

Pop music's association with Western, capitalist culture was such that it was banned in many communist countries. The Soviet Union regarded The Beatles as epitomizing a Western debauchery that could pervert Soviet youth. Nevertheless, young people in communist countries still managed to obtain copies of Beatles music, and some credit it and other pop music with helping to bring about the cultural revolution that brought about the fall of the Iron Curtain in 1989.

Pop music has since spawned a huge, global industry. British and U.S. artists continue to dominate the pop music scene; other specific genres, such as Europop, are valued more locally. **CK**

Sound Collage
Various

A method of combining preexisting sounds or excerpts into one musical work

In the visual arts, the idea of combining "found" elements from various media into an original work was popularized in the early twentieth century by Georges Braque and Pablo Picasso. In music also, a collage combines elements from different existing pieces.

A musical collage is not a medley, in which different songs are made to fit together; rather the individual parts should retain their distinct flavor, and the result could sound chaotic. Collage works, in which different strains by one composer are interlaced, have existed for centuries: *Battalia* (1673) by Bohemian-Austrian composer Franz Biber (1644–1704), for example, superimposes several tunes in different keys, and the *Second Symphony* (1910–16) by U.S. modernist composer Charles Ives (1874–1954) at times superimposes so many different tunes that two conductors are necessary. Collage emerged as a common technique among the avant-gardists of the 1950s and 1960s; one of the most prominent examples of that period is the third movement of *Sinfonia* (1968) by Italian composer Luciano Berio (1925–2003), in which many works appear over the steadily sounding third movement of Mahler's *Symphony No. 2*. In popular music, probably the most groundbreaking example is the song "Being for the Benefit of Mr. Kite" on the album *Sgt. Pepper's Lonely Hearts Club Band* (1967) by The Beatles, in which producer and arranger George Martin (b. 1926) spliced in cut-up snippets of fairground organ recordings to supply a circus atmosphere.

In electro-acoustic music, composers in the musique-concrète tradition, beginning in the early 1940s, would create collage works by combining sound objects from daily life. In hip-hop today, the sequencing of brief sampled sections from preexisting recordings to create new works is standard, although, the result is not as chaotic as an avant-garde collage. **PB**

Credit Cards
Frank McNamara

A small, usually plastic, card that authorizes the person named on it to charge goods or services to an account, for which the cardholder is billed periodically

During the 1920s, a number of different companies in the United States began to issue credit cards as a way of offering their regular customers an easier method to make payments. However, these cards, issued by individual businesses, could only be used at a very limited number of locations, such as at the gas stations owned by the issuing company. It was not until 1950, when businessman Frank McNamara invented the Diners Club card, that the potential of credit cards as a much broader form of payment was realized. McNamara had the idea when he discovered that he had no money with him to pay a restaurant bill. The Diners Club card allowed cardholders to visit any restaurant that accepted the card to use it to pay for their meal.

The fundamental idea of personal credit had existed since ancient times, but it was not until the widespread adoption of credit cards that immediate, nearly universal credit became available to the average consumer. Credit cards offered consumers the freedom to make everyday purchases that they could pay for at a later time; they also eliminated the need to always have cash on hand or to hope a seller would accept a personal check. The system worked because the card issuer, usually a bank or other financial institution, implicitly agreed to pay the seller for purchases made with the card. Consumers who use credit cards, therefore, essentially take out instantaneous loans each time they use the card to make a purchase.

The introduction of credit cards had a profound effect on the spending habits of many people. With credit cards, it became second nature to buy now and pay later, because consumers did not have to worry whether they had enough money for their purchases in their bank accounts. All they had to worry about was the bill, but that was a comfortable distance away. **MT**

⬆ A German credit card collector displays some of his collection in 1988, by which time many people were carrying wallets packed with various credit, debit, and store cards.

"Money is just the poor man's credit card."

Marshall McLuhan, philosopher of media theory

The Fermi Paradox
Enrico Fermi

Out of our vast universe, why has no one come to visit humanity on Earth?

The universe contains almost 100 billion observable galaxies far older than our own. With all that potential for life to evolve, and time for that life to develop interstellar travel, journey through space, and locate us via the radio waves we emit, it is extraordinary that we have not yet been visited by aliens. In 1950, Italian physicist Enrico Fermi (1901–54) was sitting with a group of friends who were pondering why we seem so alone. To Fermi, in whose mind the universe was surely teeming with advanced civilizations, it seemed a vexing paradox. "Where is everybody?" he asked.

Some academics have sought to answer the Fermi Paradox by citing the Rare Earth hypothesis, which argues that the possibility of conditions being right for life to arise anywhere are so infinitely small, even

"Civilizations rise . . . within their own solar systems, with no interstellar colonization."
Jennifer Ouellette, science writer

considering the innumerable stars in the universe, that it is very likely that we are the only life there is. Other solutions include the possibility that "they" are already here, or that they are signaling but we have not recognized their signals.

Fermi suggested that galactic colonization could be achieved quite easily, simply by inventing rocket ships and populating them with self-replicating robots. That may be a naive idea, but the ten-billion-year history of the universe certainly seems to allow enough time for a race to evolve and, by some estimates, explore a region of the galaxy 250 times over. However, if advanced life did evolve, why would they come here, to our obscure corner of our average-looking Milky Way galaxy? After all, as the great cosmologist Carl Sagan (1934–96) once said: "It is a very big cosmos." **BS**

Prisoner's Dilemma
Merrill Flood and Melvin Dresher

A model shows how human cooperation and conflict influence self-preservation

Consider this: two people rob a bank and are caught and placed in separate cells. Each is understandably more concerned about their own lot than that of their accomplice, and each is, unbeknown to the other, offered a deal—if you testify against your accomplice, the charges against you will be dropped. If both take the bait and confess, the prosecutor gets two convictions and neither goes free. And therein lays the dilemma. Should the prisoners take the chance that the other will not confess, and so confess and gain their own freedom, or steadfastly refuse to confess and risk being the one to remain imprisoned if the other confesses? Individually each is better off confessing if the other does not, yet if both confess, their situation worsens considerably.

"Can 'prisoners' . . . sustain cooperation when each has [an] incentive to cheat?"
Avinash Dixit, economist

The dilemma was formulated in 1950 by U.S. mathematicians Merrill Flood (1908–91) and Melvin Dresler (b. 1927) while working at the Rand Corporation on game theory—mathematical models examining conflict and cooperation between intelligent adversaries—and its application to nuclear strategy. The dilemma highlights the differences in rational thinking of the individual as opposed to the group. Members of a group who pursue individual self-interest could become worse off than group members who place the best interests of the group above their own. The dilemma assumes a bleak view of human nature, that we are inherently selfish and care little for what happens to others when our own self-interest is threatened, although this holds true more for large groups than small ones such as families. **BS**

Enneagram
Oscar Ichazo

A system of self-understanding based on the mystical properties of shapes

The enneagram is a geometrical figure comprising a triangle and an irregular hexagon overlapping to form a nine-pointed shape inside a circle. Armenian spiritual leader George Gurdjieff (1866–1949) was the first to suggest that the figure had mystical properties, and in the early 1950s it found a role at the heart of a personality profiling system developed principally by Bolivian self-development instructor Oscar Ichazo (*b.* 1931). Ichazo's Enneagram of Personality was based on a distinctive numbering of the nine points and an analysis of the relationships between them.

In 1971, Ichazo opened his first training school in northern Chile, dedicated to instructing others in the interpretation and use of the enneagram system. The success of the program meant that by the early 1990s

"All knowledge can be included in the enneagram and … it can be interpreted."

Marjorie Perloff, *The Encyclopedia of Aesthetics* (1998)

there were more than forty training centers located around the world. In these schools, practitioners are taught to recognize nine different "ego fixations" or personality types along with their associated basic fears, desires, and temptations. The system is intended as an exercise in attaining greater self-awareness and understanding, and enabling others to do the same.

The original Enneagram of Personality system has been adapted in a variety of ways. A Jesuit priest named Bob Ochs, for example, taught the system alongside religious doctrine in the early 1970s. However, the various manifestations of the enneagram system have been criticized by both religious and secular groups as having little or no scientific grounding. The profiles offered are claimed to be either somewhat arbitrarily assigned or too broad to be of use in meditation. **LW**

Musical Indeterminacy
John Cage

A compositional practice in which the musical outcome is not clearly defined

Indeterminacy is a term attributed to U.S. composer John Cage (1912–92), following the completion of his first indeterminate instrumental work, *Imaginary Landscape No. 4*, in 1951. It describes compositional practices in which the sounding outcome—either the length or the sound of individual parts, or both—of a work is not clearly defined. Thus the performer becomes a true co-creator of the work.

Cage's works extended the musical realm, as he drew inspirations from Eastern philosophy, the New York School of visual artists, and Fluxus, an avant-garde group of artists. While indeterminacy is related to improvisation, there are some fundamental differences: instead of the fixed harmonic or structural framework of a typical improvisatory composition, performance

"…the indeterminate score must be treated as … a process not a product."

Robert Zierolf, *Indeterminacy in Musical Form* (1983)

actions are described. In *Imaginary Landscape No. 4* a radio is used, with whatever program that is on becoming part of the piece. Indeterminacy reached the highest level with Cage's composition *4'33"* (1952), for which the descriptions and actions in the score are: three movements totaling the time four minutes and thirty-three seconds; at least one performer; no sound should be performed by the performer(s). A performance of the work thus consists of ambient noise, including sounds created by the audience.

Musical indeterminacy raised questions that are still relevant to musical discourse: Who is the creator of an indeterminate work? Which sounds are considered musical? What constitutes a good performance of an indeterminate work? and, perhaps the most intriguing question, What defines a musical work? **PB**

Televangelism
Fulton Sheen

A new breed of evangelists present their own versions of Christianity on television

⬆ Televangelist Dr. Robert H. Schuller poses in 1980 outside the newly constructed Crystal Cathedral in Garden Grove, California. Seating 2,736 people, it cost $18 million to build.

Televangelism—the use of the medium of television to evangelize or communicate the Christian gospel—started as a peculiarly U.S. phenomenon in the 1950s but has since spread to much of the Western world. Televangelism is lambasted by some critics as fraudulently misrepresenting the gospel, with as much time spent on fundraising as preaching; many preach the controversial "gospel of prosperity," which holds that God blesses those He favors most with material wealth. Televangelists operate in a medium—television—that has its own set of values and pressures, which, critics argue, are not always compatible with the message being preached.

Time magazine dubbed Roman Catholic archbishop Fulton Sheen (1895–1979) as the first U.S. televangelist after his weekly program *Life is Worth Living*, filmed at New York's Adelphi Theater, debuted on the DuMont Television Network in 1951. Sheen used a blackboard to help explain his themes. This debut was a long way from the shimmering reflections of the Crystal Cathedral in Los Angeles, built by televangelist Dr. Robert H. Schuller (*b.* 1926). Schuller began his ministry standing on the roof of his car at a drive-in theater and became the best-known U.S. televangelist with his own weekly show, *Hour of Power*, which began in 1970 and on which Schuller preached until 2006.

A common thread among televangelists is the relentless worldwide expansion of their ministries, with some preachers, such as Pastor Pat Robinson, being broadcast into as many as forty countries. Critics from within the church claim that the extreme fundamentalism of U.S. churches and society is a direct result of decades of televangelists promoting right-wing, politically-inspired messages that have altered the once-forgiving fabric of the U.S. church. Television is not just a source of news and current affairs. It is also a powerful tool for propaganda. **BS**

"We are all born with the power of speech, but we need grammar. Conscience, too, needs Revelation."

Fulton Sheen, *Life is Worth Living*, TV program

Peer Pressure
Solomon Asch

A study into how an individual is coerced into conforming with majority opinion

Early in the life of Polish-born U.S. psychologist Solomon Asch (1907–96), his Jewish parents left a glass of wine for the prophet Elijah at Passover. "Do you think he will take a sip?" the young Solomon asked. "Definitely," replied his uncle. And so with one suggestive comment that filled him with excitement and expectation, the boy stared at the glass of wine, and was sure he saw its level drop—just a little. It was remembering this experience that first prompted Asch's interest in investigating how individuals can be coerced by others into modifying their thoughts or behavior.

It was in 1951 that Asch, now working at Swarthmore College in Pennsylvania, staged his conformity experiments designed to demonstrate the human susceptibility to conforming to majority opinions. Asch selected 123 male subjects and secretly told a small percentage of them to provide obviously wrong answers to certain questions, in order to ascertain how many in the group would follow them by providing at least some of the same obviously incorrect answers. There were three trials, and in one, three-quarters of the participants repeated the deliberately wrong answers given by the few that Asch had set up. Over the course of the three trials, the overall level of conformity was 37 percent.

Asch explained the results in terms of peer group pressure. A peer group overwhelmingly comprises human beings of equal status and age who tend to inhabit the same social strata. The term "peer pressure" referred to the power and dynamics used within a peer group to influence the actions, attitudes, or values of someone within the group. Peer pressure is a pervasive psychological construct, particularly among the young who spend large amounts of time in school and various other structured groups, and tends to most affect those harboring low levels of self-esteem. **BS**

⬆ Asserting their maturity and independence, two boys light up cigarettes while an aghast younger companion looks on. Peer pressure dictates that he will probably attempt one, too.

"The ugly reality is that peer pressure reaches its greatest intensity at just the age when kids tend to be most insensitive and cruel."

Walt Mueller, authority on youth culture

Two Dogmas of Empiricism
Willard van Orman Quine

No truths can ever be accepted as fact without first being tested

"Two Dogmas of Empiricism," written by the U.S. philosopher and logician Willard van Orman Quine (1908–2000), first appeared in *The Philosophical Review* in 1951 and lost no time in becoming an object of controversy. Here was an attack on two of the pillars of the logical positivists: the analytic-synthetic distinction (the notion that there are both factual truths and logical truths), and the long-held belief that there are particular truths that no possible future experience will be able to cause us to consider false. In "Two Dogmas," Quine not only thought it unlikely that distinctions in the analytic-synthetic doctrine could ever be made, but he also cast doubt over whether or not absolute truths—those "hard core" truths capable of being tested and verified, which come to us primarily

"Analyticity can be defined only in terms of other equally suspect concepts . . ."

E. Sober and P. Hylton, *Quine's Two Dogmas* (2000)

through our sensory experiences of the world around us—could ever be abandoned in the face of any future events. He was, however, prepared to concede that some propositions could be jettisoned as a last resort.

The logical positivists had installed the "analytic–synthetic" as central to their philosophy. "Analytic" truths were those supposed innate truths grounded in meanings independent of facts, while "synthetic" refers to those facts that are grounded wholly in immutable facts. Both dogmas, Quine argued, are ill-founded. After explaining why, he went on to offer a theory of his own. Called epistemological holism, this holds that no theory can be tested in isolation but can be arrived at only after a thorough consideration of innumerable and largely undetermined factors; also, no truths are ever the result of *a priori* knowledge. **BS**

Munchausen Syndrome
Richard Asher

A mental disorder leading to self-harm and attention-seeking for imagined illnesses

Munchausen syndrome, named after Baron Hieronymus von Münchausen (1720–97), a German nobleman noted for telling fantastical stories of his own mythical exploits, was first observed and named in 1951 by British endocrinologist Richard Asher (1912–69), whose findings were published in the British medical journal *The Lancet* that same year. Munchausen's is a psychiatric condition in which a person fakes or simulates injury or illness in order to be hospitalized and treated as a patient, often changing doctors and hospitals in the hope of being the center of medical attention. Munchausen's is a chronic variant of a factitious disorder—an illness intentionally brought about solely for the purpose of gaining attention—and sufferers are often eager to undergo invasive surgery.

"They show pseudologia fantastica and travel widely for attention (wandering)."

D. A. Swanson, *The Munchausen Syndrome* (1981)

Like Baron von Münchausen, they are also known to make false and incredible claims about their own lives.

What triggers Munchausen syndrome is not known because sufferers insist their conditions are real. Symptoms include an often spectacular-looking medical history, a high degree of medical knowledge, inexplicable relapses, and new symptoms that appear after other tests prove negative. Munchausen sufferers have been known to poison themselves, interfere with diagnostic evaluations, contaminate urine samples, open up wounds, and fail to take prescribed medications.

Diagnosis is difficult and only confirmed after a careful study of the patient's behavior and responses to treatment. For cognitive behavior therapy to be effective, a person has first to admit to falsifying symptoms, which a Munchausen sufferer will never do. **BS**

Rock 'n' Roll
United States

A type of popular music characterized by a heavy beat and simple melodies

One of the earliest references to "rock" in a song title is found in "My Man Rocks Me," a blues ballad from the 1920s that had plenty of the overtly sexual overtones that would come to define rock 'n' roll almost three decades later. Early hints of what was to come could also be seen in the Boston Beat's "Big Band Boogie" (1939), and later Jimmy Preston's "Rock the Joint" (1949).

The five essential aspects of any rock 'n' roll song are a 4/4 beat, a strong back beat, an equally strong rolling rhythm, a blues-scale melody, and at least one electric guitar. Rock 'n' roll was beginning to emerge in the southern United States in the late 1940s and grew out of an amalgam of African rhythms and European instrumentation. Its immediate predecessor was the genre known as "jump blues," a 1940s offshoot

"Rock and roll music, if you like it, if you feel it, you can't help but move to it."

Elvis Presley, singer

of Rhythm and Blues (R&B) that was popular in black dance halls. Precisely when the transition occurred is difficult to say because the change was gradual rather than a paradigm shift. One characteristic of the new sound in its very early years was its syncopated rhythms (additional impulses in between the beats), similar to those found in swing and dance music.

In 1951, Pennsylvania-born radio disc jockey Alan "Moondog" Freed (1921–65) noticed that white teenagers were beginning to discover black R&B music. He gave it more air time and renamed it "rock 'n' roll," thinking that the black associations with "R&B" might dent its popularity with white audiences. He need not have worried. On April 12, 1954, Bill Haley and His Comets recorded "Rock Around the Clock," the song that brought rock 'n' roll into the mainstream. **BS**

Scientology
Lafayette Ronald Hubbard

A pseudo-scientific cult promising self-improvement through acts of auditing

Lafayette Ronald Hubbard (1911–86) entered the U.S. Navy in 1941 on the back of some impressive references. He never, however, achieved his apparent promise. Over the next two years Hubbard was involved in several incidents, including being sent home from a posting in Australia after a dispute with his superiors and mistakenly sailing his ship into Mexican waters and then conducting gunnery practice there. Hubbard was subsequently relieved of his command, and it was perhaps then that he first began thinking of founding the Church of Scientology.

First came his ideas about the relationship between mind and body, which he labeled "Dianetics." Hubbard saw everyone's goal to be subjugation of our "reactive minds," which prevent us from being more ethical,

"Scientology is evil … its practice is a serious threat to the community …"

Justice Anderson, Supreme Court of Australia

centered, and happy. Dianetics involved an act of auditing, the asking of questions designed to eliminate past experiences that encourage and feed the negative, reactive mind. Only by facing and answering these questions can our true potential be realized.

Hubbard incorporated these ideas into the body of beliefs and practices he called Scientology, established in 1952, teaching that the subconscious mind restricts us from being all that we can be, and that everyone needs to be freed from negative thoughts, which he called engrams. But over the years, the spirit of self-improvement in this pseudo-scientific cult has not attracted as much attention as the reports of adherents being brainwashed, bullied, and harassed to donate their money. Litigation is used aggressively to limit the damage caused by these reports. **BS**

The Urey-Miller Experiment
Stanley Miller and Harold Ure

An experiment to prove that life can arise from inorganic matter

In 1952 a chemistry graduate, Stanley Miller (1930–2007), and Nobel Laureate Harold Urey (1893–1981), who had proposed the idea of a "reducing atmosphere" (that Earth initially had a primitive atmosphere that became more complex over time), began a series of experiments designed to mimic that nascent atmosphere to see if it could be prompted through electrical discharges to generate organic compounds from inorganic matter, and so make possible the beginnings of life on Earth.

They constructed a series of three apparatuses—all of them closed systems in the form of a loop—into which was circulated a mix of hydrogen, methane, and ammonia. A container of boiling water added vapor to the gaseous soup, simulating a primitive vapor-heavy atmosphere, which was then subject to a high voltage

> ". . . significant in convincing scientists that life is likely to be abundant in the cosmos."

Carl Sagan, cosmologist

electrical charge before going through a condenser to cool and trickle back into the original vial, to begin the cycle again. After two weeks, Miller and Urey noted that 15 percent of the carbon within the system had formed into organic compounds, and that a tiny percentage of the carbon had gone on to form amino acids. There were also traces of hydroxyl acids and urea, all of which are the building blocks of life.

The results were published in an edition of *Science* magazine in 1953, and promptly ignited the public's imagination. In no time the term "prebiotic soup" entered popular culture. The experiment had significant shortcomings: neither oxygen nor nitrogen, both vital ingredients in Earth's atmospheric composition, was used, and many scientists now question the assumptions behind the reducing atmosphere theory. **BS**

Paralympic Games
Ludwig Guttmann

The apex of major international sports competitions for disabled athletes

The Paralympic Games evolved from a competition in the 1940s involving World War II veterans with spinal-cord injuries. Their organizer, neurologist Dr. Ludwig Guttmann (1899–1980), called them the paraplegic games. Guttmann believed that the therapeutic benefits of sports were not only important to improving his patients' physical rehabilitation but also helped to restore their confidence and self-respect.

During the war, Guttmann had organized wheelchair polo and basketball games for his patients at Stoke Mandeville Hospital in England and used the occasion of the 1948 London Summer Olympics to launch the first Stoke Mandeville Games. Those particular Games only involved sixteen patients competing in archery. Guttmann desired a truly

> "Without his efforts, they would have been condemned to the human scrapheap."

British Medical Journal (1980)

international experience and in 1952 he included Dutch ex-serviceman in the competition. This would lead, he hoped, to the worldwide recognition that sports should be integral to any rehabilitation program. In 1960, the International Stoke Mandeville Games (now officially named the first Paralympic Games) were held alongside the Rome Summer Olympics and involved 400 athletes from twenty-three countries competing in a variety of wheelchair sports. The first Winter Paralympics began in 1976. The competition has expanded slowly to include amputees, the blind, and athletes with cerebral palsy.

In recognition of its status in the Olympic Movement, the "para" is now intended in the sense of an event run in parallel with the Olympic Games. The aim is to "enable Paralympic athletes to achieve sporting excellence and inspire and excite the world." **TJ**

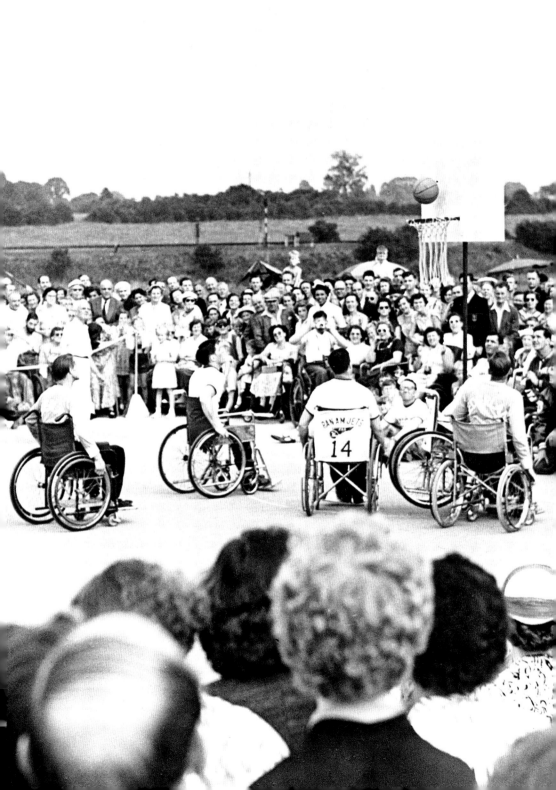

Performance Art
John Cage

A style of art that imbued the everyday with the potential to stimulate our senses

The origins of performance art lie in the Futurist and Dadaist movements of the early twentieth century. However, it did not come fully to life as an artistic style until 1952, when an untitled event was held at the Black Mountain College in North Carolina. Orchestrated by a group led by composer John Cage, it featured a number of performances from different disciplines that took place within a fixed time bracket, but did not hold any narrative or causal relation to each other.

From there, a new approach to art began to evolve, in which the idea behind the art took precedence over the aesthetic—it was the concept that made and justified the art. By the 1960s performances were no longer even referred to as performances: they were "happenings," "events"—involving impromptu

" … 'performance artist' … includes just about everything you might want to do."

Laurie Anderson, composer and performance artist

gatherings at unlikely venues. Artists rejected clear approaches and narratives, emphasizing instead the validity of the viewer's experience. Performers would come on stage for an evening of brushing their teeth or sitting reading a newspaper, or, as Yoko Ono did with John Lennon in 1969, laying in bed for a week. Performance art rarely resulted in a tangible object that could be purchased and displayed.

Art was being used in new and dynamic ways to comment on emerging social and ethical concerns in the politically charged era of civil rights and the anti-war movement. Female artists used their bodies to challenge attitudes to women. Within ten years performance art had gone global and direct to a new audience, eliminating the need for galleries, museums, and hierarchical interference. **BS**

Groupthink
William H. Whyte

A psychological phenomenon with potentially disastrous consequences

"Groupthink" is what occurs when a group of people makes a bad decision because its individual members give in to group pressures. For example, when group members' desire for harmony causes them to attempt to minimize conflict, they tend to conform their opinion to a decision that they believe will achieve consensus within the group. This desire means they fail to examine alternative ideas, solutions, or viewpoints that could be seen as controversial. The insistence on loyalty may lead to a prevailing, potentially fabricated, certainty that the chosen outcome was the best option. Groupthink can stifle creativity and independent thinking, and lead to irrational and flawed decisions.

The phrase "groupthink" was coined in 1952 by U.S. urbanist William H. Whyte (1917–99) in an article

"We are not talking about mere instinctive conformity … [but] rationalized conformity."

William H. Whyte, *Fortune* (1952)

in *Fortune* magazine, in which he examined how industrial society was attempting to master group skills. He argued that society was subject to groupthink in a negative fashion, and the individual had become "completely a creature of his environment, guided almost totally by the whims and prejudices of the group, and incapable of any real self-determination."

U.S. psychologist Irving Janis (1918–90) went on to develop the groupthink theory to describe systematic errors in collective decision making. He studied several U.S. military conflicts, and his books *Victims of Groupthink* (1972) and *Groupthink: Psychological Studies of Policy Decisions and Fiascoes* (1982) outline how he felt that groupthink had led to unwise decisions, such as the failure of the U.S. government to anticipate the Japanese attack on Pearl Harbor in 1941. **CK**

DSM

American Psychiatric Association

The creation of a standard criteria for classifying mental disorders

The publication in 1952 of the *Diagnostic and Statistical Manual of Mental Disorders* (DSM) was not the first time an attempt had been made to categorize known psychiatric conditions. In 1917 a manual containing twenty-two diagnoses was compiled by a group of psychiatrists and government bureaucrats, and by the 1920s almost every teaching center in the United States and many in Europe had their own individual system. In 1927 the New York Academy of Medicine began to move toward national nomenclature of disease, but it was not until the onset of World War II in 1939 that the need for a comprehensive reference book of mental disorders became apparent, as psychiatrists across the country became involved in the assessment and selection of tens of thousands of new recruits.

"DSM-1 ... was the first official manual of mental disorders to focus on clinical utility."

DSM fourth edition, text revision (2000)

By the late 1940s the call from psychiatrists across the United States for a renewed effort to categorize psychiatric conditions, especially personality disorders and stress-related illnesses, resulted in the publication of the first DSM. The manual was (and still is) a primary diagnostic tool, developed in conjunction with the American Psychiatric Association.

Despite most clinical diagnoses tending to be the result of intuitive thinking and observation on the part of the clinician, the fact remains that categorizing disorders based on medical theories rather than what is observable has always been considered scientifically prudent (cancers, too, are categorized according to their genetic characteristics). A uniform reference provides clinicians with a framework in which predictions, understanding, and, in time, cures can be realized. **BC**

DNA Double Helix

James Watson and Francis Crick

The unlocking of the structure of life's building blocks

As early as the 1940s scientists the world over knew that DNA was very likely life's building block. They also knew that it was composed of adenine, thymine, cytosine, and guanine. The only problem was that no one had the slightest idea what a strand of DNA might look like. A photograph of a DNA protein, now referred to as Photograph 51, taken in the early 1950s by Rosalind Franklin (1920–58), an X-ray diffraction expert at King's College, London, seemed to suggest the braided twist of a helix. But it was far from certain.

In 1951 James Watson (b. 1928) and Francis Crick (1916–2004), the helix's eventual co-discoverers, had theorized a triple helix, but their theory was flawed, as was that of chemist and Nobel Laureate Linus Pauling. Finally, in February 1953, realizing that

"The structure is an open one and its water content is rather high."

James Watson and Francis Crick, *Nature* (April 25, 1953)

the lack of a three-dimensional representation of the gene was the core problem confronting all molecular biology, Watson and Crick, with the benefit of the research of biochemist Erwin Chargaff (1905–2002), successfully calculated the pairing rules that led to the precise copying of molecules, the process essential for heredity, and in so doing uncovered the famed double-stranded helix.

Solving the pairing question was critical; DNA's four nitrogenous bases always pair the same way: thymine to adenine, and cytosine to guanine. These pairings fit neatly between the gene's two helical sugar-phosphate backbones and gave it its shape. Its form also meant it could "unzip" to both copy itself and carry genetic information. The world of biology would never be the same again. **BS**

James Watson (left) and Francis Crick with their model of part of a DNA molecule, May 1953. ➡

The Beetle in a Box
Ludwig Wittgenstein

Language must be shared if it is to have any meaning

Imagine that everyone owns a small box, and in that box there is something only the owner can see. When asked what is in the box, everyone provides the same answer: a beetle. Soon people are talking about beetles even though it is entirely possible that each person means something completely different.

When René Descartes (1596–1650) introduced the idea of mind-body dualism, he believed that it was possible to discount other people, other minds, and all outside concepts and build a system of knowledge based solely upon one's own thoughts. If this kind of Cartesian dualism is correct, it is possible for individuals to know what concepts and words mean simply by thinking about them. It is possible, therefore, for an individual mind to use a private language that no one

"The limits of my language means the limits of my world."

Ludwig Wittgenstein

else can ever know. Ludwig Wittgenstein (1889–1951) doubted this idea, and part of his book *Philosophical Investigations* (published posthumously in 1953) was devoted to debunking this notion of Cartesian dualism by showing that a private language is nonsensical. According to the beetle in the box hypothetical, all meaningful language must have some social basis and cannot exist solely in a person's mind. So, if a private language makes no sense, then referring to the idea of separate, inscrutable minds is meaningless.

Wittgenstein's beetle analogy, and his notion of private languages, became necessary reading for anyone studying or discussing the nature of human language. His observations on meaningful language necessarily being nonprivate are still widely discussed and debated today. **MT**

"If a Lion Could Speak . . ."
Ludwig Wittgenstein

A philosophical conundrum seemingly concerning shared consciousness

One of the most quoted and beguiling statements in the history of philosophical inquiry, "If a lion could speak, we couldn't understand him," was written by the Austrian-British philosopher Ludwig Wittgenstein (1889–1951) and published posthumously in 1953 in his book *Philosophical Investigations*. What he meant by the statement is still open to debate and it remains one of the discipline's great subjective teasers. Is it a comment on how we confront consciousness outside of our own? If a lion spoke in an audible language, why would we not be able to understand him? Why choose a lion? More to the point, would a talking lion even be a lion at all, and would his mind be a lion's mind?

Wittgenstein may have been trying to unravel a philosophical riddle, or perhaps just delighting in

"I don't know why we are here, but I'm pretty sure that it is not in order to enjoy ourselves."

Ludwig Wittgenstein

creating one, or he may simply have been unwittingly bowing to "compulsive anthropomorphism," the human need to give animals, and even innate objects, consciousness. The human race has done that for millennia: for example, in the Jewish Talmud, a dog drinks poison to save the life of its master. Humans have always been fooled by the apparent capacity of an animal to form conscious responses to inadvertent cues. So, our conditioned response to Wittgenstein's statement is, of course a lion can speak. And that leaves one further question: why would we not understand one if it did?

Another interpretation remains: was Wittgenstein only reminding us of humanity's gross neglect of the natural world, that before anyone can comprehend what is being said, we first need to better understand the creature that is saying it? **BS**

Value-added Tax
Maurice Lauré

A consumption-based tax that strives for a more equitable approach to taxation

A value-added tax (VAT) is a sales tax levied only on the "value that is added" at each point in the economic chain of supply of a particular product or service, and is ultimately paid for by the consumer at the point of sale. The first modern VAT was introduced in France on April 10, 1954, as an indirect taxation on consumption by the French economist Maurice Lauré (1917–2001), a joint director of the French taxation authority. Although a version of the idea had been suggested in Germany in 1918, it was Lauré's system that, for the first time in a modern economy, took the burden for collecting taxes away from the taxation authorities and retailers, and placed it in the hands of the taxpayer.

West Germany adopted the VAT in 1968, after which most other Western European countries followed suit.

"VAT has proved to be one of the EU's most enduring exports."

Adam Victor, *The Guardian* (December 31, 2010)

However, Lauré's tax was not the first time that the idea had been trialed. A consumption tax was introduced in the Netherlands by the duke of Alva in 1569, and in 1342 the first historical mention of a tax on goods and services occurred in Spain where a tax on each stage of production was initiated to help boost the state's dwindling coffers.

A VAT is now a prerequisite for any country seeking membership in the European Union and is an integral part of the taxation system of more than 145 nations. The only Organization for Economic Co-operation and Development nation that does not have a VAT is the United States. To limit the tax's regressive nature (meaning that the poor pay more), most countries impose smaller VAT rates for basic consumer items than they do for luxury items. **BS**

Warehouse Club
Sol Price

A retail store that sells discounted goods in bulk quantities to paying members

Warehouse clubs, also known as warehouse stores or wholesale clubs, were introduced by businessman Sol Price (1916–2009) in the United States. Unlike other retail stores, warehouse clubs require shoppers to buy a membership to shop there. In return, the clubs provide members with the chance to buy retail goods and services at discounted prices and in bulk quantities. Individual stores are large, expansive, and warehouse-like, hence the name.

Sol Price was an attorney in San Diego, California, in 1954 when he inherited an empty warehouse and decided to open a member-only retail store that limited goods to government employees, a store he called FedMart. The format quickly became successful, with Price expanding it to include a wider range of

"In the final analysis, you get what you pay for."

James Sinegal, Costco CEO and co-founder

items, including groceries and gasoline, as well as an in-store pharmacy and optical department. After opening multiple new stores and selling FedMart in the 1970s, Price opened a new warehouse club, Price Club, which later became Costco.

Warehouse clubs exposed the average consumer to something closer to a wholesale market, where they could, like large retailers, take advantage of the lower prices that come with buying larger quantities. Though the advantage of buying in bulk is well known, most consumers could not afford to—or did not have the ability to—buy large quantities of items at a wholesale discount prior to the introduction of warehouse clubs. As an added element, the warehouse clubs also provide the feeling of exclusivity that comes with having to pay for the privilege to shop. **MT**

Psychedelic Experience
Aldous Huxley

The use of psychedelic drugs to achieve a life-changing visionary experience

The term "psychedelic experience" is as vague as the state it is attempting to describe. Individual experiences of hallucinogenic drug taking vary, but most agree that perceptions are made brilliant, intense, and more immediate. Things that would not normally be noticed are seen, and achieve depths of significance and clarity beyond their everyday essence. It is an altered, ineffable state that has similarities with ritualistic, mystical traditions found in Eastern patterns of thought.

In 1954 the great science fiction author Aldous Huxley (1894–1963) published *The Doors of Perception*, a book that described his experience of being under the influence of the psychedelic drug mescaline. In taking the drug, Huxley wished to have a glimpse of the higher states that visionaries such as William Blake

"To be enlightened is to be aware, always, of total reality in its immanent otherness ..."
Aldous Huxley, *The Doors of Perception* (1954)

(1757–1827) had described (the title of his book is in fact taken from a line in Blake's work, *The Marriage of Heaven and Hell*, c. 1790). Huxley was profoundly affected by the experience, and concluded *The Doors of Perception* by arguing that mescaline (or something like it) should replace alcohol and other drugs because it provides the same sense of escapism and altered state of consciousness without the negative side effects.

The Doors of Perception received a mixed reception, but was nonetheless instrumental in paving the way for the psychedelic counterculture of the 1960s. Huxley continued to take psychedelic drugs for the remainder of his life, and was also influential in introducing other notable figures, such as poet Allen Ginsberg and psychologist and writer Timothy Leary, to the possibilities of psychedelic experimentation. **BS**

Wicca
Gerald Gardner

A duo-theistic neo-pagan witchcraft religion oriented toward nature

While witchcraft was traditionally practiced—and widely persecuted—in Europe for centuries, Wicca's relationship to pre-Christian forms of European witchcraft is largely based on rites or traditions adopted, and adapted, from a variety of pagan traditions, as opposed to a direct continuity over time. The Wicca religion became popular in England after English author Gerald Gardner (1884–1964) published *Witchcraft Today*, a guide to modern witchcraft, in 1954. The term "Wicca," though not used by Gardner, was coined in the 1960s to mean pagan witchcraft.

While Gardner is widely credited for the development of the modern Wicca religion, his beliefs and teachings are not universally accepted by all practitioners of the religion, or by those of other

"The first time I called myself a 'Witch' was the most magical moment of my life ..."
Margot Adler, author and Wiccan priestess

neo-pagan religions. There is no single organization or group that represents all practitioners, and followers hold a range of beliefs. Many Wiccans hold that a female goddess and a male horned god exist as equal co-deities; others venerate multiple gods or spirits. However, a belief in living in harmony with nature, the practice of magic, lunar and solar cycle rituals, and adherence to a moral code are common to all.

Wicca is relatively new, but it appears to be growing. There are about 1.2 million practitioners of witchcraft in the United States alone; numbers worldwide are difficult to assess. Wicca has influenced aspects of popular culture, with many novels, films, and television shows incorporating Wiccan ideas. It has also changed many of the negative associations that people had made with witchcraft and pagan religions. **MT**

◄ A woman dances in the glow of psychedelic light at the Avalon Ballroom in San Francisco in the 1960s.

Family Therapy
Murray Bowen

A suggestion for an entirely new approach to understanding how families work

Born into a family from Tennessee and the oldest of five children, Murray Bowen (1913–90) earned his medical degree in 1937. In 1946, after serving in the army during World War II, he began his psychiatric training. In 1954 he began a five-year study involving families at the National Institute of Mental Health in Bethesda, Maryland, and it was there that he developed his theories about family dynamics.

At the time, the concept of families sitting together to discuss their issues and inter-relations was largely unheard of. Bowen spent the late 1950s working with families that had an adult schizophrenic child living at home, and learned to observe the unfolding of family dramas. He became adept at observing human behavior and began what he called his Bowen Family

"The run away is as emotionally dependent as the person who never leaves home."

Murray Bowen

Systems Theory. Bowen regarded the family as a single emotional entity, each member of which is intimately connected with the other. His theory contained eight interlocking concepts, including the triangle, or three-person relationship; the differentiation of self where a person realizes their interdependence on others; the emotional cut-off that involves ignoring unresolved issues through avoidance; and sibling positioning, the idea that a child's position (middle child, etc.) can contribute to the development of particular traits.

Bowen was suspicious of psychoanalysis and instead used biological terms, sociology, and even anthropology to help make sense of human behavior. He was a pioneer who spent the rest of his life trying to understand how generations of family can shape us and help make us who we are. **BS**

American Civil Rights
Rosa Parks

A protest movement against racial discrimination in the United States

The American Civil Rights Movement of the 1950s and 1960s was a mass protest movement against racial segregation and discrimination in the United States. It aimed to raise public awareness of the plight of African Americans by nonviolent forms of protest. The movement monitored the activities of the racist organization the Ku Klux Klan and started a drive for voter registration; activists protested through sit-ins, marches, and rallies. Protestors sometimes suffered brutal treatment at the hands of the authorities.

The American Civil Rights Movement came into being in 1955. Although there had been some protests prior to then, 1955 was a pivotal year because it was when Rosa Parks (1913–2005), an African American woman who purported to be tired of the injustice,

"We can never be satisfied as long as a Negro . . . cannot vote."

Martin Luther King, Jr., Washington D.C., 1963

refused to give up her seat to a white man on a bus in Montgomery, Alabama. Parks was a member of the National Association for the Advancement of Colored People, an African American civil rights organization founded in 1909. She was arrested and thrown in jail for failing to follow the bus driver's instructions. Parks was found guilty and fined. Her actions ignited the Montgomery Bus Boycott led by an African American clergyman, Rev. Dr. Martin Luther King, Jr. (1929–68). African Americans boycotted buses and organized car pools. The Montgomery Bus Boycott attracted national attention and established King as the leader of the American Civil Rights Movement. In 1963, President Lyndon Johnson (1908–73) spearheaded the Civil Rights Act of 1964 and the Voting Rights Act of 1965, outlawing discriminatory voting practice. **CK**

Rosa Parks sits in the front of a bus in Alabama on December 21, 1956, after segregation was ruled illegal. ➔

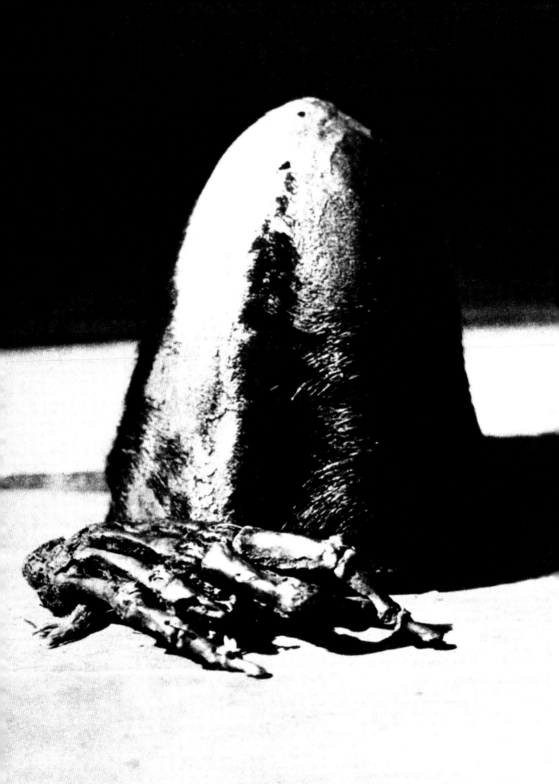

Cryptozoology
Bernard Heuvelmans

A pseudo-science devoted to discovering lost and mythical species

The term "cryptozoology" comes from the Greek *kryptos*, meaning "hidden," and refers to the "study of hidden animals." Cryptozoology is the search for cryptids—animals and plants that science does not recognize and whose existence relies on what at best can be called circumstantial evidence and unverifiable sightings—in a discipline that is perhaps best described as pseudo-scientific. Animals that are on the cryptozoologist's list may include extinct animals, such as dinosaurs or the flightless dodo, or animals that only exist in myth or legend, creatures such as the unicorn, griffin, Abominable Snowman (Yeti), and Loch Ness monster. Even proponents of cryptozoology acknowledge that evidence for almost everything on their list of creatures is weak.

"Until critical thought and good research are commonplace ... it will remain disrespected."

Ben Roesch, zoologist

The father of cryptozoology is Bernard Heuvelmans (1916–2001), whose book *On the Track of Unknown Animals* (1955) referred to the comparatively recent re-discovery of species thought to be extinct (at least by Europeans), such as the giant panda and the pygmy chimpanzee. Heuvelmans was often criticized for his belief in cryptids, especially after his attempt in the late 1960s to classify the so-called Minnesota Iceman, later revealed to be a hoax, as a new species of hominid, Homo pongoides. It is the nature of cryptozoologists, however, to become excited on spurious evidence. The carcass of a Megalodon, an extinct shark of the Cenozoic era, turned out to be that of a basking shark, but a species of sauropod dinosaur believed to live in the jungles of the Democratic Republic of Congo still remains elusive. The search goes on... **BS**

Bloom's Taxonomy
Benjamin Bloom and others

The classification of education and teaching into three domains of learning

In 1948, Dr. Benjamin Bloom (1913–99) met with other college and university examiners at the American Psychological Association annual meeting; this group of educators ultimately produced the *Taxonomy of Educational Objectives, The Classification of Educational Goals, Handbook I* in 1956. The hierarchical classification system in this handbook is commonly known as "Bloom's Taxonomy" and, more than fifty years after its publication, it is still used in teaching, curriculum writing, and learning theory disciplines. Bloom's Taxonomy is designed to focus educators on all three learning domains—cognitive, affective, and psychomotor—to create a more holistic form of education.

The cognitive domain involves knowledge and the development of intellectual skills. This includes

"What we are classifying is the intended behavior of students—to act, think, or feel."

Dr. Benjamin Bloom

the recall or recognition of specific facts, procedural patterns, and concepts that serve in the development of intellectual abilities and skills. There are six major categories within the domain, which can be thought of as degrees of difficulty that must be mastered progressively. The affective domain addresses people's feelings, values, appreciation, enthusiasms, motivations, and attitudes. The psychomotor domain includes physical movement, coordination, and use of the motor-skill areas to achieve speed, precision, distance, procedures, or techniques in execution.

Today, Bloom's Taxonomy is used to develop learning objectives. This is essential for teachers to plan and deliver instruction; design valid assessment tasks and strategies; and to ensure that instruction and assessment are aligned with the learning objectives. **BC**

Mind-brain Identity Theory
U. T. Place

A materialist theory proposing that mental states are identical to brain states

Mental states may consist of sensations, beliefs, desires, and other more complex thought patterns and the mind-brain identity theory attempts to explain these phenomena in materialist (or physical) terms. The earliest modern references to this theory appeared in 1933 by psychologist E. G. Boring (1886–1968). But its first explicit formulation was in 1956 in a journal article by philosopher and psychologist U. T. Place (1924–2000), whose ideas were further developed by philosopher J. J. C. Smart (1920–2012) in the 1950s.

Attempts to explain the mind in physical terms can be seen as a response to the dualism that emerged from René Descartes's philosophy in the seventeenth century. Place's and Smart's versions were both originally limited to arguing that all mental sensations

"[In science,] organisms are able to be seen as physicochemical mechanisms."

J. J. C. Smart, *Philosophical Review* (April 1959)

are reducible to physical correlates in the brain. For example, the experience of pain is correlated with a certain type of neural activity. However, this version of the identity theory could not adequately account for the fact that many sensations, such as pain, are specific mental events and therefore should be identical with equally specific neural activity. In order to resolve this, versions of the theory propose that even if similar mental states like pain may be exhibited in changeable brain states, this only shows that many different neurons may be more or less involved in the formation of any particular mental state. Sophisticated brain-imaging technologies and recent discoveries about the plasticity of the brain are rapidly advancing to the point at which neural correlates for the most individualized mental states may be discoverable. **TJ**

Cognitivism
H. Simon, N. Chomsky, and M. Minsky

A response to behaviorism whereby mental states are real, and can be evaluated

Cognition involves problem solving, decision making, memory, attention, comprehending linguistics, and our ability to process information. Behaviorists acknowledged the reality of cognitive thought but considered it only as a form of behavior. Cognitivism, however, rejected what it considered the simplistic "cause and effect" approach of behaviorism, arguing that behavior is largely determined by the way we think, and to study this is crucial to the understanding of psychology—and ourselves.

An early pioneer of cognitivism was the Swiss psychologist Jean Piaget (1896–1980), whose research on cognitive child development showed children's brains to have a far more refined mental structure than psychology had previously assumed. Piaget believed

"...certain aspects of our knowledge and understanding are innate..."

Noam Chomsky

cognitive development to be a maturing of mental processes as a result of our biological development. He showed that the "hidden black box of the mind" can be opened far earlier in life than anyone else thought possible, and that people are not the "programmed animals" of the behaviorists, capable of little more than responding to external stimuli. Our actions, say the cognitivists, are a consequence of our thoughts. At a meeting in 1956, Herbert Simon (1916–2001), Noam Chomsky (b. 1928), and Marvin Minsky (b. 1927) set the guidelines for the development of cognitive science.

Cognitive Behavioral Therapy, a recent amalgam of cognitivists and behavioralists, see mental disorders as the result of distorted outlooks (such as life being hopeless), perceptions that can be corrected if patients recognize and correct their errors in thinking. **BS**

U.S. writer, educator, linguist, and proponent of cognitivism, Noam Chomsky, at home in Boston in 1972. ➡

Objectivism
Ayn Rand

A novel philosophy disseminated by a provocative novelist

⬆ Ayn Rand at the National Book Awards in 1958. Her magnum opus, *Atlas Shrugged* (1957), encompassed her ideas of rationalism, individualism, and capitalism within a dystopian United States.

Frustrated with her intellectual climate, novelist and lay philosopher Ayn Rand (1905–82) collected ideas from a variety of philosophers and cobbled them into a unique view that she named Objectivism. She expounded on this personal worldview in her novel *Atlas Shrugged*, published in 1957. Rand defends Aristotle's ideas that reality exists objectively and authoritatively, that the laws of logic guide our understanding, and that consciousness is the seat of humans' ability to know. She defends the rationalist ideas that morality is objective and that conscious rationality bestows special moral significance. And she also defends the classical liberal idea that each person is obligated to respect every person's right to pursue her interests, so long as those pursuits do not interfere with another person's right to do so. Rand then argues that the only sociopolitical system consistent with these ideas is laissez-faire capitalism, that is, a free market economy.

One controversial implication is what Rand calls "the virtue of selfishness." Since each person is intrinsically valuable, one's primary moral obligation is to pursue one's own interests. This pursuit is limited only by the recognition that others are also valuable, and thus no one has the right to deceive or coerce others. Selfish interests cannot conflict because it cannot be in our interests to have something to which we have no right. Although some goods may result from collective action, such goods never justify the use of force.

Rand's philosophy continues to spark controversy, especially among those who argue that some "social goods" cannot be achieved by individuals and that unacceptable economic inequalities result from unregulated trade. Though not all capitalists would call themselves Objectivists, many cite Rand as a formative influence, including economist Walter Williams (*b.* 1936) and politician Ron Paul (*b.* 1935). **TJ**

> "1. 'Nature, to be commanded, must be obeyed' or 'Wishing won't make it so.'
> 2. 'You can't eat your cake and have it, too.'
> 3. 'Man is an end in himself.'
> 4. 'Give me liberty or give me death.'"
>
> Ayn Rand, sales conference at Random House, 1962

Mythologies
Roland Barthes

A philosophical account of how social values develop mythical meanings

Divided into two sections, Roland Barthes's (1915–80) *Mythologies* (1957) explains how commonly accepted social values are constructed into myths. The first section is a collection of essays, most of which were originally published in the Parisian magazine *Les Lettres Nouvelles*. Many of the essays use examples of reports and advertisements in newspapers and popular magazines in which certain words and images are used to convey stereotyped meanings—especially those associated with French middle-class values. Barthes discusses how wine, for example, is typically associated with all that is good in French society. But this creates a mythology that disguises the harmful implications of wine consumption and production. In the second section of the book, Barthes argues that since myths are essentially constructed through language, they are best analyzed by the methods used in the field of semiotics. By showing how words function as signs that can potentially carry many different meanings, semiotics can reveal the process that causes a particular symbolic meaning to become mythologized. Barthes then outlines seven main rhetorical techniques that are often used to construct and preserve these myths.

In describing his use of semiotics to expose the construction of various cultural myths, Barthes refers to the theory developed by linguist Ferdinand de Saussure (1857–1913). While adopting de Saussure's method, much of Barthes's analysis of middle-class myths is guided by a Marxist interpretation of consumer values. Likewise, he also notes how this method has much in common with that of psychoanalysis.

Ironically, Barthes's demystification of the use of myths to sell consumer products has given the advertising industry a firm foundation for their persuasive techniques. Nevertheless, the book's ideas have been just as seminal in setting the foundations for even more influential theories of social criticism. **TJ**

↑ Hertereau and Jourdan's wine poster (*c.* 1958) exemplifies Barthes's notion of the mythology surrounding wine's health and wellness properties.

"Myth does not deny things, on the contrary, its function is to talk about them; simply, it purifies them, it makes them innocent."

Roland Barthes, *Mythologies* (1957)

Tipping Point
Morton Grodzins

The critical point of accumulation that may cause a change, with major consequences

A tipping point describes an event where the concentration of certain elements in a system reaches a level that triggers a major change. It can be applied to the behavior of virtually any phenomenon in any field. Its effects can be sudden and quickly reversible, such as when a canoe capsizes. But it is more commonly associated with effects that are more durable, such as when the outbreak of a disease reaches a point at which an epidemic inevitably follows. The term was first used by political scientist Morton Grodzins (1917–64) in 1957 to describe the situation in urban areas of the United States where the black population would grow to a point that caused an exodus of whites.

While Grodzins used "tipping" and "tip point," the concept was already used by urban planners

". . . a place where radical change is more than a possibility. It is . . . a certainty."

Malcolm Gladwell, *The Tipping Point* (2000)

to describe this same sociological process. This metaphorical tipping point is derived from its literal meaning in physics, where a substance is tipped over, or into, a new state. That sense of disequilibrium is also captured in the metaphor's application to economics and to processes that are subject to cumulative feedback mechanisms, such as climate change.

More recently, author Malcolm Gladwell (*b.* 1963) recounted how the idea has been extremely fertile, especially in understanding sociological phenomena. He first noticed the term in its application to epidemiology, in which a large number of people contagiously adopt a type of behavior. In this sense, the idea of the tipping point has already reached a tipping point, and has proven itself a powerful means of reinterpreting everything from weather patterns to consumer habits. **TJ**

Happening
Allan Kaprow

An artistic interpretation of the everyday, which gave audiences and art new life

In the mind of Allan Kaprow (1927–2006), the U.S. painter, assembler of three-dimensional collages, and pioneer of performance art, a "happening" was "a game, an adventure, a number of activities engaged in by participants for the sake of playing." They were, he said, "events that, put simply, happen."

Kaprow may have coined the term in 1957 while attending some improvisational performances at the farm of sculptor George Segal (1924–2000), but what he witnessed had its roots in the challenge of the Futurists and Dadaists of the 1920s to traditional notions of what constitutes art, and how it is exhibited. Kaprow took the idea and applied it to his own art, which at first involved small scripted events where he encouraged his audience to make their own connections between

"The artist will discover out of ordinary things the meaning of ordinariness."

Allan Kaprow

themes and ideas. It soon grew to encompass many avant-garde artists who all brought their own perspectives and individual agendas. They were confronting the barrier between artist and audience by emphasizing the importance and involvement of the viewers, who would invariably be asked to add their own element so that no two acts were ever the same. They provoked interaction; they were "one-offs," temporary and ephemeral.

The movement peaked in 1963 with the Yam Festival held at Segal's farm, but declined in popularity thereafter. Less theatrical than the performance art with which it was often confused, happenings made artists out of all us, and did it in our world—on a farm, in a street, or an abandoned building. Art no longer was brought to the people; it was the people. **BS**

Allan Kaprow uses a lawnmower to shred paper before musicians and an audience on September 8, 1964. ➡

1957

Generative Grammar
Noam Chomsky

Rules determining sentence construction
by speakers of a particular language

In linguistics, generative grammar refers to the set of rules that produce sentences in a language. These rules of syntax determine how sentences are structured. For example, the English language is structured by rules specifying word order, as with the adjective "black" preceding the noun "cat." But other rules specify changes to the structure of words themselves such as the "ed" commonly added to a verb to indicate past tense. Noam Chomsky (b. 1928) first proposed a theory of generative grammar in 1957 and developed other versions that have come to dominate the field.

The original version—transformational grammar— was the idea that sentences are generated by formal rules that transform their structure. Before Chomsky's theories, the study of generative grammar had been largely concerned with providing a description of the generative rules specific to a particular language. The first systematic description of generative grammar was undertaken in the sixth century BCE by the Sanskrit grammarian Pāṇini. Central to Chomsky's theories was the much more ambitious and controversial idea that these generative grammars in different languages were the expression of what he called a universal grammar. This was the hypothesis that there must be inherited constraints on the range of possible grammars.

Many thinkers from centuries before Chomsky had noted the commonalities in the grammars of different languages and reasoned that they must be innate. However, Chomsky's theory can be seen as a response to theories such as behaviorism that had gained prominence in the 1950s and attempted to explain language learning as the product of repeated exposure to words and sounds in different contexts. While controversial, Chomsky's notion of a universal grammar quickly became dominant in understanding generative grammar, while also providing a source of insight into the human mind itself. **TJ**

Chomsky argued for an "innate" universal grammar rather than one learned from the environment.

Alien Abduction

Antonio Boas

An unexplained phenomenon that first arose in the science fiction obsessed 1950s

UFO sightings have been recorded since antiquity, but the first notable account of a human being abducted by aliens did not appear until 1957. Antonio Boas, a Brazilian farmer, claimed to have been taken aboard a spacecraft and coerced into having sex with a female humanoid creature, before being released.

The best-known tale of alien abduction, however, was revealed under hypnosis by Betty and Barney Hill, a married couple returning home after a holiday in Canada late in the evening on September 19, 1961. While driving along a heavily wooded road in central New Hampshire, they noticed a light in the sky that seemed to follow them for miles then landed on the road in front of them. They were taken aboard an alien

spacecraft, shown a star map detailing star patterns not observable from Earth, and physically examined before being released. There was not a shred of corroborating evidence to support their story, and the star map, which Betty later drew from memory, represented only random stars whose pattern and positions could easily be replicated by looking elsewhere in the universe.

Stories of contact with otherwordly beings (such as angels) have appeared throughout history and many cultures have believed in people being transported to other dimensions, so tales of alien abduction can perhaps be seen as a modern manifestation of this tradition. Scientifically, there is debate about whether abduction experiences relate to real physical events, psychological interaction, altered states of consciousness, or simply delusional fantasy. According to U.S. psychologist Stuart Appelle in his essay: "The Abduction Experience: A Critical Evaluation of Theory and Evidence" (1996), alien abductions are "subjectively real memories of being taken secretly against one's will by apparently nonhuman entities." The accounts of abductees are, for them, undoubtedly very real. But memories and recollections fall well short of proof. **BS**

⬆ Gene Barry, Ann Robinson, and townspeople approach a spacecraft in the film *The War of the Worlds* (1953).

Rational Ignorance

Anthony Downs

Ignorance is rational when the effort to acquire knowledge exceeds its benefit

According to the theory of rational ignorance, people can only spend so much of their day learning new information and so will ignore learning about that which will provide little reward. The cost-benefit analysis that individuals make when deciding what to learn about explains why so many people choose to remain ignorant about seemingly important topics.

Anthony Downs (b. 1930) coined the term "rational ignorance" in his book *An Economic Theory of Democracy* (1957). The phrase was used to explain why many voters knew very little about issues that seemed extremely important, such as nuclear proliferation. The threat of potential nuclear war affects everyone, but this does not mean that people will be interested in learning more about it. Even in the face of public

"... it is individually irrational to be well-informed ..."

A. Downs, *An Economic Theory of Democracy* (1957)

education programs or widely available information, people generally choose not to learn about important issues because there is little chance that their efforts will lead to a practical, personal benefit.

The economy is on shaky ground, political leaders are corrupt, and your roof has sprung a leak over your bed. Which problem will you devote hours of precious free time to investigating and trying to solve? The theory of rational ignorance knows the answer, and so do you. No matter how important something may seem, even the smallest problem is magnified when it directly affects you. It is why you spend time worrying about bills and your children instead of voting or learning about the super-volcano nearby that, though it has a small chance of erupting at some point within the next 100,000 years, will kill everyone you know. **MT**

↩ Rational ignorance is often cited as a cause of voter apathy.

Many Worlds Theory

Hugh Everett III

Our universe is only one of an infinite number of different universes

The many worlds theory, or many worlds interpretation, states that every quantum event that could result in two or more possible outcomes results in all outcomes taking place, each in a separate universe. All possible outcomes of every quantum event have effectively taken place, and all possible alternatives throughout history have actually occurred in some other universe.

At the quantum level, it is impossible to observe a particle without affecting its behavior, nor can we ever really be certain what a particle is doing at any given point. Quantum physicists can only predict the behavior of a particle by saying how likely an outcome is. This quantum uncertainty led physicist Niels Bohr (1885–1962) to propose that all particles exist in all states at the same time, an idea known as the Copenhagen

"[If an] amoeba had the same memories as its parent, it has not a life line, but a life tree."

Hugh Everett III

interpretation. However, physicist Hugh Everett III (1930–82) thought otherwise. For Everett, the observed event is the only one that happened in this universe. All the other possible outcomes also happened, but each in their own separate universe.

The idea of parallel dimensions or universes has long been a popular topic for fiction writers, but the many worlds theory was not intended as fiction. As an attempt to explain why the quantum world functions as it does, many worlds theory is one of several competitors, albeit with perhaps the most striking possibilities. The idea that every possible outcome of the choices you have made has, in reality, happened or taken place in a parallel universe is awe-inspiring and disturbing at the same time. Or perhaps aweinspiring in this universe and disturbing in another. **MT**

The Idea of Freedom
Mortimer J. Adler

A historical investigation of the major philosophical views on the meaning of freedom

⬆ Mortimer J. Adler (pictured in 1977) used a dialectical approach to examine the many philosophical avenues that the concept of freedom has taken over the years.

In 1952, Mortimer J. Adler (1902–2001) and his colleagues from the Institute of Philosophical Research began surveying the vast literature on the philosophical conceptions of freedom and attempted to distill the findings into some basic categories. In 1958, the results were published in *The Idea of Freedom: A Dialectical Examination of the Conceptions of Freedom*. This exhaustive research showed that the concept of freedom has essentially been understood as taking three distinct forms: circumstantial, acquired, and natural. However, when these more abstract conceptions are understood in terms of personal abilities, they reflect those of self-realization, self-perfection, and self-determination. The circumstantial freedom of self-realization consists in the person's ability to do as they wish, as far as circumstances allow; the acquired freedom of self-perfection involves learning how to act in accordance with some personal or moral ideal; the natural freedom of self-determination simply refers to the person's ability to control their own behavior. As many thinkers have also conceived freedom to have political and collective dimensions, Adler also regarded these as distinct conceptions—political freedom being an extension of the circumstantial freedom of self-realization; collective freedom as the social expression of the acquired freedom of self-perfection.

Philosophical attempts to describe the meaning of freedom have a long and varied history. Despite the many disagreements, Adler regarded philosophical inquiry itself as a historical dialog in which philosophers respond to the challenges raised in the work of other thinkers, past and present. As a result of this dialectical process, Adler believed that many of those philosophical notions would in fact come to agreement in certain respects. The research demonstrates how a dialectical view of an abstract concept can show how it has come to be understood. **TJ**

> *"A man is free who has in himself the ability or power whereby he can make what he does his own action and what he achieves his own property . . ."*
>
> Mortimer J. Adler, *The Idea of Freedom* (1958)

Two Concepts of Liberty
Isaiah Berlin

A vital distinction in understanding the political and personal value of freedom

Two Concepts of Liberty was originally composed as a lecture given at Oxford University in 1958 by the philosopher and political theorist Isaiah Berlin (1909–97). Berlin introduced the idea that liberty is nothing but the absence of constraints on personal action (negative liberty). This generally rules out any interference or coercion of citizens by political authorities, except for laws minimally required to defend that personal liberty. In contrast, positive liberty is expressed in the idea that people are not genuinely free unless they have the power to pursue their goals. Both concepts therefore agree that liberty requires freedom from unnecessary political and social constraints, but the positive version regards personal autonomy or self-determination as essential to the realization of that freedom.

Like many philosophical ideas, these two distinct interpretations of liberty had already been recognized by ancient Greek philosophers. However, Berlin's interest in the history of ideas enabled him to clearly observe how both concepts had developed as political ideals that would often come into conflict. Although the positive notion of liberty sought to enhance the opportunities for personal autonomy, if the concept was zealously adopted as a collective ideal it could easily have the opposite effect. The positive concept was most strongly promoted by Enlightenment philosopher Jean-Jacques Rousseau and was central to the ideology that inspired the French Revolution (1788–99).

As happened in the aftermath of that revolution and many since, the positive concept has often been used by totalitarian regimes to justify severe restrictions on personal liberty in order to realize goals identified with the common good of all citizens. Although liberal democracies are more firmly guided by an ideal of negative liberty, the positive concept is often represented in paternalistic laws governing health and safety. **TJ**

↑ The dual concepts of liberty proposed by Isaiah Berlin (pictured in 1992) differed according to whether the individual was allowed autonomy and the freedom of self-development.

"The fundamental sense of freedom is freedom from chains, from imprisonment, from enslavement by others. The rest is extension of this sense, or else metaphor."

Isaiah Berlin, *Four Essays on Liberty* (1969)

The Great Leap Forward
Mao Zedong

An attempt by China to rapidly modernize its industrial and agricultural production

The Great Leap Forward was a plan by China's communist government to accelerate the country's industrialization as part of its goal to become a self-sustaining economy. The scheme was devised by the founding father and leader of the communist government, Mao Zedong (1893–1976), and began in 1958. Industrialization was usually a process of gradual development made possible by capital investment in heavy machinery and new technologies. The Great Leap Forward was the ill-conceived idea that this gradual process could be skipped by developing numerous small-scale industries and increasing agricultural production at the same time.

The scheme began as a five-year plan and was conceived partly as a result of the apparent success of

". . . corpses often ended up in shallow graves or simply by the roadside."

Frank Dikötter, *Mao's Great Famine* (2010)

the government's initial five-year plan to build large-scale plants to increase the production of commodities such as coal, iron, and steel that would reduce the country's dependence on agriculture. That plan had succeeded with the aid of funds and technical expertise provided by the Soviet Union. Many farms had already been voluntarily organized into collectives as part of the first five-year plan, and under the Great Leap Forward collectives became large communes that now also included small-scale industries. Within a year, the Great Leap Forward had proven disastrous. With much of the labor force now diverted to work on these small industrial projects, agriculture was unable to supply enough food, and famine was the inevitable result. The idea was finally abandoned in 1961 only after the famine caused 20 to 40 million deaths. **TJ**

Meritocracy
Michael Young

A system that rewards individuals on the basis of their achievements or abilities

Any society that rewards individuals on the basis of certain desired talents may be described as a meritocracy. As a political principle, it applies to any system of government in which candidates are chosen for such qualities as general intelligence or diligence. Insofar as business organizations generally select and reward staff for their skills and achievements, they too are meritocracies. The term itself was coined in an ironic sense by British sociologist Michael Young (1915–2002), in his satire *The Rise of the Meritocracy, 1870–2033* (1958).

Meritocracy has become an established principle governing most modern democratic societies, and its popularity stems from the fact that it permits equality of opportunity. It rewards people for their own efforts and does not discriminate against anyone because of

"It is hard in a society that makes so much of merit to be judged as having none."

Michael Young, *The Guardian* (June 29, 2001)

their social status. Before the Age of Enlightenment it was a foreign concept in the history of European societies until the idea reached the British through contact with Confucianism. Confucius's philosophy placed a high value on a person's moral character rather than inherited advantages, so it was a laudable replacement for the old aristocratic European regimes. However, in *The Rise of Meritocracy*, Young described how this original ideal of merit had become corrupted, reduced to "intelligence plus effort," thereby creating a new social class that discriminated against anyone deemed to lack these capacities.

With its emphasis on equal opportunity, meritocracy has given modern democracies a strong moral basis. However, forms of social discrimination can be seen in practices such as psychometric tests used to hire staff. **TJ**

New Age
Various communities

A spiritual movement that draws on both Eastern and Western spiritual and metaphysical traditions in search of harmony and enlightenment

⬆ Nude couples on a balcony at the Esalen Institute in northern California in 1970. This residential community and retreat center still promotes a New Age philosophy today.

The phrase "New Age" was first used by William Blake in 1809 to describe what he saw as an approaching era of spiritual and artistic awareness. Elements of what we would recognize today as New Age continued to accumulate throughout the remainder of the nineteenth century, such as theosophy and various forms of spiritualism. In the 1960s the spiritual pioneers who established the Findhorn Community in Scotland and the Esalen Institute in California would, over many years, evolve into the very first contemporary New Age communities, helping people to find the "Christ within" or each person's "human potentialities" and culminating in the establishment of ongoing foundations to promote self-awareness.

To some, the New Age refers to the upcoming astrological age of Aquarius. Some New Age followers may believe in tarot cards, psychic readings, and other various occult practices; others might consult astrology for insights into their future, or crystals for healing; while still others seek the more benign pursuits of yoga and meditation. There is no obvious hierarchical structure within the New Age movement and no immutable doctrines, although in the 1970s the work of people such as David Spangler (*b.* 1945), the self-professed spiritual philosopher and clairvoyant, brought a sense of cohesion and provided hope for those who could not find answers to their questions in Christianity or Secular Humanism.

Fundamentally aligned to Hinduism, "New Age" covers a variety of groups who all share a common quest for harmony, enlightenment, a deeper sense of spiritual awareness, and personal healing and growth. It is not a cult, nor is it a religion. It has no recognized beginning or any particular founder. Rather it is a loose amalgam of worldviews, a philosophical approach to the world that is difficult to define. **BS**

"Life is not measured by the number of breaths we take, but by the moments that take our breath away."

George Carlin, comedian

Political Correctness
United States and United Kingdom

Using language that avoids potentially offensive or discriminatory terms

A person who is politically correct avoids using terms that hold potentially negative or offensive implications. The term, often abbreviated as "PC," can also mean policies that contain or rely upon such language, and behaviors or beliefs that are offensive, or potentially offensive, or presumptively exclusionary. For example, political correctness would replace the term "chairman" with "chairperson," and use "person with a disability" instead of "handicapped."

The term "political correctness" originated around the time of the Russian Revolution in 1917, when those who professed beliefs identical to those of the Communist Party were said to be politically correct in their thinking. The modern concept of political correctness, however, arose during the 1960s and 1970s. At that time, certain political activists who advocated for broad social reforms in the United States and the United Kingdom—a group broadly defined as the "new left"—began using the term to describe language that avoided having offensive connotations against groups that had been traditionally discriminated against. In the 1980s and 1990s many people on the political right began voicing widespread opposition to the PC movement. Today, the term is often used derisively to refer to any attempt to impose limitations on speech, belief, or thought.

Proponents of political correctness argue that changing language to be inoffensive to those who have traditionally been discriminated against is laudable, while opponents see the attempt to control language as a thinly veiled political strategy by those seeking to assert their own dominance over others. Yet despite the debate over its use, political correctness has been responsible for a significant change in language, behavior, and beliefs. Not only are some nonpolitically correct terms no longer widely used, but those who choose to use them can often be subject to condemnation. **MT**

Madness and Civilization
Michel Foucault

A seminal French work on how "madness" is a social construct

Michel Foucault (1926–84), a philosopher and clinical psychiatrist, argued in his first major work, *Madness and Civilization* (1961), that the Middle Ages accepted madness and visible deformity as a part of life. Madness was respected, even if it was also feared. This changed dramatically with the "Great Confinement," a movement of the seventeenth century that saw all sorts of people deemed "undesirable," as without reason and subject to detention by the state, physically chained to walls and floors. By the eighteenth century, lunatics were no longer chained but free to move about the asylum, now under the care of psychiatrists.

In the "Great Confinement" was the origin of modern notions of mental illness as the absence of reason and the beginnings of the psychiatric profession's scientific

> ## "Tamed, madness preserves all the appearances of its reign."
>
> Michel Foucault, *Madness and Civilization* (1961)

inquiry into its causes. The insane were no longer a part of everyday life; they were shut away, rendered invisible from society. Worse still, they were unwilling objects of probing scientific investigation. As civilization grew more complex, bureaucratic, and scientific, more types of behavior were considered unreasonable. Though psychiatrists professed to aid the insane, they were in fact imposing an insidious kind of social control.

For Foucault, there was no reality to mental illness; it was a social construct, a way for society to punish outlandish or odd behavior. His work was a boon to the 1960s counterculture, particularly to gay rights activists protesting the diagnosis of homosexuality as a mental disorder, and also to critics of psychiatry. To this day, psychologists assail Foucault's skepticism of the reality of mental illness, particularly schizophrenia. **CRD**

Liberating Violence
Frantz Fanon

Colonized people must use violent means to achieve liberation from a colonial power

In *The Wretched of the Earth* (1961), Frantz Fanon (1925–61) argues for the necessity of violence as the only means that can successfully liberate natives from colonial oppression. As this oppression is both physical and psychological, only complete liberation can restore independence. Without the use of violence, natives will remain dehumanized. Fanon essentially argues that the violence used by the colonizers only forces the natives themselves to resort to violent means of liberation.

As a native of the French colony Martinique, Fanon witnessed the abusive treatment of the native population by French soldiers stationed there during World War II (1939–45). He also voluntarily served with the French army and after qualifying in France as a psychiatrist, he wrote *Black Skin, White Masks* (1952)—a

"The starving peasant is the first of the exploited to discover that violence pays ..."
Frantz Fanon, *The Wretched of the Earth* (1961)

book that attempts to explain the sense of alienation felt by colonized natives. This led Fanon to confront the question of how a repressed and dispossessed native population could recover ownership and control over their nation. This diagnosis of alienation and the call for revolution were partly influenced by Marxist theory, but Fanon rejected the Marxist idea that an educated awareness of social class was needed to inspire native groups to revolt. He argued instead that those who are most motivated to lead such a violent revolt are the peasants, who are least dependent on the colonizers and therefore have no incentive to make compromises. Fanon's call for violent liberation has influenced many anti-colonial movements, and his understanding of racial and social oppression has also inspired its victims with the moral courage needed to assert their humanity. **TJ**

Rational Choice Theory
George Homans

A sociologist adapts economic theory to study human social interaction

Just as economic theories can play a significant role in studying the complexities of how the production and consumption of goods and services drives a nation's economy, so too can a set of principles—according to rational choice theory or RCT—be used to comprehend the elements of human to human interactions, to try and predict their intentional, goal-oriented behavior. The man who invented the theory, the U.S. sociologist George Homans (1910–89), based it upon the principles of behavioral psychology and deeply believed that psychology could provide explanations for sociological phenomena. He was particularly interested in reciprocal behavior and argued that new theories were not required to study this social interaction; all that was needed was to modify existing behavioral principles

"Human behavior ... is not free but shaped by rewards and punishments."
John Scott, sociologist

without forgetting that sociology always begins its analysis with the behavior, not of groups or institutions or structures, but of individuals.

RCT involves attempting to understand why and how we act to maximize rewards and weigh up costs and benefits before deciding on an action's expediency, the giving-up of individual control to a collective or group, and how we employ strategies designed to maintain our control over resources.

Homans followed the behavioralist model of social interaction that says we only enter into arrangements with others after already calculating possible rewards as opposed to the estimated costs of our actions. His theory is based on rationality, arguing that all our social actions are the result of rational choices, however irrational they may appear to be. **BS**

◄ An Algerian celebrates his country's independence from French rule in 1962.

The Drake Equation
Frank Drake

Estimating the number of detectable extraterrestrial cultures in the Milky Way

In 1961, astronomer and astrophysicist Frank Drake (b. 1930) devised an equation that was intended to guide the search for extraterrestrial intelligence by estimating the likely number of detectable civilizations within our own Milky Way galaxy.

The equation is: $N = R^* f_p n_e f_l f_i f_c L$, where the number of detectable civilizations, N, is the product of seven specific factors: R^* is the yearly rate of star formation in our galaxy; f_p is the fraction of those stars that have planetary systems; n_e is the number of habitable planets in each planetary system; f_l is the fraction of habitable planets that actually develop life; f_i is the fraction of those life-bearing planets where intelligence develops; f_c is the fraction of civilizations that develop detectable interstellar communication

"[P]robably only one in ten million stars has a detectable signal."

Frank Drake, *Cosmos Magazine* (2010)

technology; and L is the length of time that civilizations use such communication technology.

A decade before Drake's equation, physicist Enrico Fermi wondered why intelligent life had not been detected. Given the age of the universe, even if only a small fraction of planets were capable of communication, we should have evidence of it by now.

Though not formulated in response to Fermi, the idea that radio signals would be the most promising means of detecting intelligent life enabled Drake to see that communicative ability was a crucial factor in setting limits to the number of planets with potential civilizations. The two factors involving the development and continuing use of interstellar communications gave the equation a potentially fruitful way of answering Fermi's paradox. **TJ**

Milgram Experiments
Stanley Milgram

Experiments in social and moral psychology testing obedience to authority

The Milgram experiments were designed to investigate the extent to which individuals are willing to obey authority when instructed to perform apparently harmful acts against others. In the original and best-known experiment at Yale University in 1961, psychologist Stanley Milgram (1933–84) recruited forty men to participate in a study claiming to investigate memory and learning. Each man was assigned the role of "teacher" and asked to read a set of word pairs to a "learner" (an actor) in another room. The teacher had been falsely led to believe that the learner was connected to a machine capable of delivering electric shocks. A researcher instructed the teacher to administer a shock whenever the learner gave a wrong answer. The teacher was told to increase the strength

"... many subjects did, indeed, choose to reject the experimenter's commands ..."

Stanley Milgram

of each shock until the learner gave the correct answer. While some refused to continue after the learner began to shout in pain, 65 percent administered the strongest shock of 450 volts.

Milgram's experiments on obedience to authority emerged from his earlier studies on social conformity, but he was particularly troubled by the evidence at the Nuremberg trials that showed how willingly Nazi officers had committed atrocities and attempted to avoid any moral responsibility on the grounds that they were dutifully following the orders of their superiors. The original experiment raised many ethical objections. But variations of the experiment and attempts to replicate it decades later have consistently validated those initial findings, which show the moral conscience to be remarkably vulnerable to manipulation by authorities. **TJ**

The "teacher" subject of Milgram's experiment was asked to give electric shocks to an unseen "learner." ➡

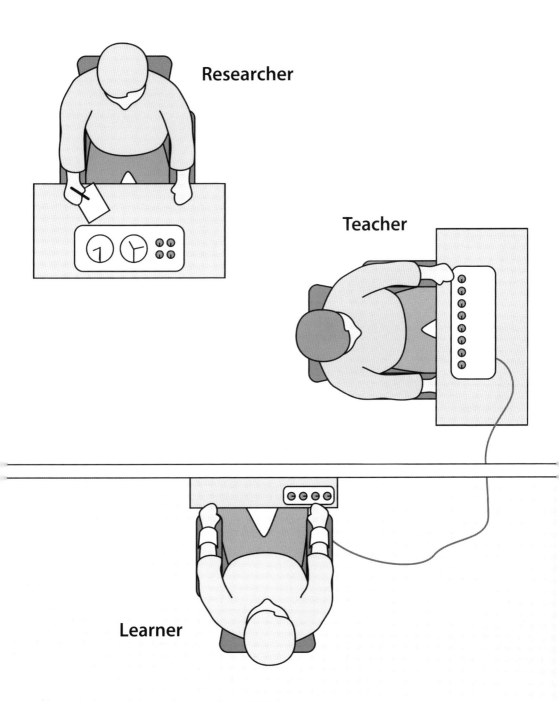

Researcher

Teacher

Learner

The Genesis Flood
John C. Whitcomb and Henry M. Morris

Revival of the creationist view that geological history is the result of a flood

Published in 1961, *The Genesis Flood: The Biblical Record and its Scientific Implications* proposed that geological history is best interpreted as resulting from the global flood described in Genesis 6:9. Young Earth creationists John C. Whitcomb (*b.* 1924) and Henry M. Morris (1918–2006) believed that the Book of Genesis provides a literal, factual, truthful account of Earth's creation and formation. By this interpretation Earth must be only about 6,000 to 10,000 years old, with the flood occurring less than 2,000 years later. To explain how this single deluge could be responsible for the layered fossil record, the authors contend that animals with the same bodily structures, behaviors, and local environments would be spread into the same locations by the action of the floodwaters.

"The evidence for divine inspiration is far weightier than the evidence for science."

John C. Whitcomb and Henry M. Morris

Also, the more mobile or buoyant would naturally be the last to survive the rising waters.

Early Christian thinkers had first spread the idea that the Genesis flood accounted for the range of fossils. However, once it became the subject of scientific inquiry in the eighteenth century, it became clear that Earth was formed not thousands but billions of years ago, and the depth and diversity of fossil layers showed they were built up long before humans appeared.

Modern geological science now provides a full account of the forces and events that produced the different fossil layers. Nevertheless, as creationism has since attempted to gain more respectability in the guise of Intelligent Design, the ideas in *The Genesis Flood* made it a best seller that retains its importance for fundamentalist Christians. **TJ**

Military-industrial Complex
Dwight D. Eisenhower

Relationship between producers of military goods and the officials who pay for them

As technology has become increasingly complicated, and modern weapons have become reliant upon large industries to produce them, the costs of military equipment have risen and given rise to an entire industry dedicated to providing governments with the materials. U.S. president Dwight D. Eisenhower (1890–1969) referred to the relationship between the military equipment producers and the government officials responsible for purchasing them as the military-industrial complex. The phrase describes the interconnected, and potentially corrupting, relationship between manufacturers and those in government who have the power to determine what the military needs and how much the government will spend to obtain it.

Humanity has engaged in warfare since before recorded history, but prior to the industrial age it was relatively rare for a nation to maintain a large standing army during peacetime. Serving as the supreme allied commander in Europe during World War II and as the president of the United States from 1953 to 1961, Eisenhower had extensive experience and knowledge about the relationship between the government and equipment manufacturers. He first used the phrase "military-industrial complex" in his farewell address to the nation in 1961. He warned that the size and scope of the nation's defense budget, and those interested in maintaining it, posed a distinct threat to the nation.

The idea that military material producers and government officials have a symbiotic relationship that benefits their own needs, and not necessarily those of the nation, has ingrained itself in popular U.S. discourse, and also spread to other nations. That idea may have also helped shape opinions about how large corporations—and not merely those involved in defense spending—depend on, and seek to influence, government spending and policy decisions. **MT**

Explanation, Reduction, and Empiricism
Paul Feyerabend

The idea of "incommensurability," or the thought that knowledge moves by great leaps and ruptures rather than simply replacing previously held notions

In the paper "Explanation, Reduction, and Empiricism" (1962) Paul Feyerabend (1924–94) challenged the notion that science is the objective, rational accumulation of facts and the gradual replacement of false or inconsistent theories with better, more robust ones. Instead, theory change in science was revolutionary in the sense that the terms used to describe the phenomena and the causal laws that govern them were fundamentally altered. Feyerabend concluded, "A theory is incommensurable with another if its ontological consequences are incompatible with the ontological consequences of the latter." This means that each subsequent theory used assumptions and vocabulary that represented a novel way of explaining and describing the fundamental characteristics of the universe, to such an extent that each subsequent manner of describing the world is mutually exclusive.

The problem presented in the paper came about through Feyerabend's criticism of existing accounts of theory change in science that could not account for the rapid changes in theoretical understanding that appeared to have taken place in the history of science, particularly in the physical sciences. Scientists and philosophers had held the belief that science was linear and conservative in its growth. Feyerabend countered that older theories were not merely modified but were rejected and replaced. Once a theory changed, the worldview of scientists changed, as did the ways in which they accumulate evidence for a theory.

Feyerabend's account of theories altered the way in which we view scientific method and the increase of knowledge in science. It allows us to compare better the relative merits of a theory and also to understand the assumptions of scientists at specific moments in historical time. **CRD**

⬆ Paul Feyerabend, pictured here in 1984, codified his anarchic thesis that scientific facts cannot be differentiated from myths in his seminal text, *Against Method* (1975).

"The interpretation of an observation is determined by the theories that we use to explain what we observe, and it changes as soon as those theories change."

Paul Feyerabend

Paradigm Shift
Thomas Kuhn

A change in how scientists approach and ask questions about a field of study

According to U.S. scientist, historian, and philosopher Thomas Kuhn (1922–96) in his book *The Structure of Scientific Revolutions* (1962), science does not progress in a linear fashion, building new knowledge from previously discovered truths. Instead, it proceeds in an ongoing process of periodic revolutions, in which a new way of thinking, known as a paradigm, overthrows the old way because the old way is perceived to be unable to explain problems adequately.

Kuhn focused his attention on understanding how scientific thought and knowledge progressed. In his studies of the history of science, he identified patterns in which the prevailing model, the paradigm, in a particular field would, periodically, be overturned by a new paradigm. This process is similar to the way in which political systems sometimes go through revolutions, where the old power is replaced by a new regime. This change from one way of thinking to a new way of thinking Kuhn dubbed a paradigm shift. When Copernicus (1473–1543) overturned the geocentric model with the new heliocentric model, not only did astronomers no longer think in terms of celestial spheres, but also the new questions they asked had nothing to do with the old model. This is one of the distinguishing features of a paradigm shift.

These periodic changes in the accepted paradigm portrayed a scientific process that was not, as many people had long believed, a linear progression from ignorance to knowledge. Instead, Kuhn proposed that most scientific progress was made by those who assume the validity of the current paradigm, and any inconsistencies or anomalies that arise to challenge the prevailing paradigm are viewed as erroneous or inconsequential by adherents. This view, widely held but still debated today, was radically different from the prevailing view of how science progresses. The idea of a paradigm shift was, in effect, a paradigm shift. **MT**

A multiple exposure portrait of historian Thomas Kuhn (1973), an exponent of scientific paradigms. ⬆

Silent Spring
Rachel Carson

The alarming idea that humankind was poisoning all life with pesticides

The term "silent spring" refers to the argument that uncontrolled and unexamined pesticides harm and kill animals, birds, and humans. It was argued that bird populations in the United States had declined in the 1950s, and this so-called "silencing of birds" was due to the overuse of pesticides. Humankind also was slowly being poisoned by the misuse of chemical pesticides that polluted the environment. Scientists, it was said, cannot accurately predict the long-term impact of the accumulation of chemicals on human health.

U.S. conservationist and marine biologist Rachel Carson (1907–64) began writing what came to be her book *Silent Spring* in 1958. It was serialized in *The New Yorker* in June 1962, and published as a book in September the same year. In it, she described how "chlorinated hydrocarbons and organic phosphorous insecticides altered the cellular processes of plants, animals, and, by implication, humans."

After *Silent Spring* was published, there was a public outcry, and the book was instrumental in launching the U.S. environmental movement. Investigations were launched into the validity of Carson's claims, resulting in changes to legislation regarding air, land, and water in the United States, including the banning of domestic production of DDT (a chlorinated organic insecticide) in 1972. *Silent Spring* remains a controversial work: its critics maintain that it stigmatizes DDT and fails to take into account DDT's advantages in controlling the transmission of malaria by killing the mosquitoes that carry the parasite. Some people claim that the decline in the use of DDT globally has led to the deaths of many people who might not otherwise have contracted malaria. A book of critical essays outlining errors in Carson's research, *Silent Spring at 50: The False Crises of Rachel Carson*, was published in 2012; it points out, for example, that bird populations were increasing in the United States at the time the work was published. **CK**

↑ A farmer sprays fruit trees with pesticide, a practice that was strongly criticized by Rachel Carson.

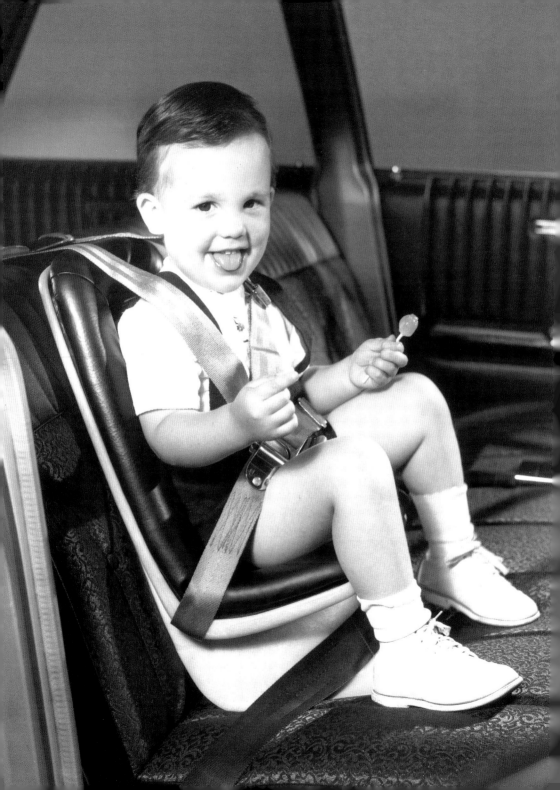

Automobile Child Safety Seat
Leonard Rivkin and Jean Ames

An innovation in recognition of the dangers to children of automobile travel

The invention of the child safety seat, which occurred simultaneously in the United States and the United Kingdom in 1962, denoted a shift from thinking of the automobile as simply a mode of transportation to recognizing it as a complex machine with inherent dangers for its passengers. Out of this belated recognition came the later installation of airbags, anti-lock brakes, and other auto safety measures.

From Denver, Colorado, Leonard Rivkin (b. 1926) designed a seat that restrained the child at the waist, while an Englishman, Jean Ames, produced a device consisting of a Y-shaped brace that came over the head and fell against the chest. Both had padded seats that elevated the child, and both were intended specifically to protect the child in the event of a crash.

"Car crashes are the No.1 killer of children 1 to 12 years old in the United States."

National Highway Traffic Safety Administration (2013)

Previous to the invention of the child safety seat, infants and small children had been placed in devices that sought to restrict movement and to elevate the child, rather than protect them. Infants were sometimes placed in canvas bags that were draped over seats. This had disastrous consequences in the event of an accident because at the time seats were designed to flip forward; the infant was catapulted into the windshield of the car. Rivkin invented his safety seat in response to the widespread installation of "bucket" seats designed for a single person to occupy, in contrast to the earlier bench seating in automobiles.

Child safety seats are now a ubiquitous feature of modern motoring. In many countries, including the United States, it is obligatory for parents to promote child safety in cars by using them. **CRD**

Personality Indicator
Katharine Briggs and Isabel Briggs Myers

A new template is created for evaluating why we act the way we do

During World War II, two U.S. women, Katharine Cook Briggs (1875–1968) and her daughter, author Isabel Briggs Myers (1897–1980), began to develop a simple questionnaire. Tens of thousands of women were entering their country's industrialized, wartime economy, and the questionnaire was intended to help them identify jobs that would best suit their individual personalities. The initial assessment of psychological preferences was based upon the four cognitive functions outlined by Swiss psychotherapist Carl Jung (1875–1961) in his book *Psychological Types* (1921), namely thinking, feeling, sensing, and intuition. The Briggs' questionnaire evolved over the years, and was eventually published, under the name of the Myers-Briggs Type Indicator (MBTI), in 1962.

"[It makes] the theory of psychological types . . . understandable and useful . . ."

Mary McCaulley, Myers-Briggs pioneer

Designed to unravel how we become aware of events and ideas and reach conclusions, the MBTI studied how our preferences grow out of the way we judge and perceive the things around us. It is made up of four key indices: extraversion–introversion—separating extraverts who focus outwardly on people and objects, from introverts whose perception is directed inwardly toward ideas and concepts; sensing–intuition—those who rely primarily on sensing observable facts, and those who intuit meanings and events outside of the mind; thinking–feeling—those who tend to think of consequences, and those who rely on feelings; and finally, judgment–perception—distinguishing between those who prefer to judge the world around them through thinking and feeling, and those who use perception, sensing, and intuiting. **BS**

◀ A child in the 1960s, secure in a commercially available safety seat suitable for bench-type seating.

1963

Φ

The Banality of Evil
Hannah Arendt

Acts of true evil are motivated not by hatred but by thoughtlessness

German-American political theorist Hannah Arendt (1906–75) first used the term "the banality of evil" in her work *Eichmann in Jerusalem: A Report on the Banality of Evil* (1963) to explain how a seemingly mild-mannered man, Nazi SS officer Otto Adolf Eichmann (1906–62), on trial for war crimes in Jerusalem in 1961, could have perpetrated such a monstrous crime against humanity, namely the organization of mass deportations of Jewish populations to concentration and extermination camps in Nazi-occupied Eastern Europe. For Arendt, Eichmann was neither a madman nor a monster. Rather, "The deeds were monstrous, but the doer . . . was quite ordinary, commonplace, and neither demonic nor monstrous."

Arendt formulated the term "the banality of evil" as part of a wider philosophic project to explain how a society as modern and, in her opinion, as cultured and refined as Germany could instigate and carry out such a thorough plan for mass murder as Adolf Hitler's Final Solution. Arendt decided that evil was not irrational, or born of hatred, but instead was the product of ordinary men wanting to be obedient to orders and who, above all, prized bureaucratic efficiency. What was most disturbing for Arendt was not that a man, group, or nation could think that it was necessary to exterminate all of the world's Jews for civilization to survive, but rather that acts required to achieve this could be undertaken without a second thought.

Although Arendt only used the phrase once, at the very end of her book, it has provided a generation of readers and writers with an entrée into her complex thought. *Eichmann in Jerusalem* catapulted Arendt to the status of a leading public intellectual. Before Arendt, the Nazis were portrayed as bloodthirsty killers, and the world has her to thank for providing a perhaps more troubling interpretation of events: that blind obedience leads to genocide. **CRD**

Nazi leader Adolf Eichmann stands in a prisoner's cage during his trial for war crimes in 1961. ⬆

1963

Φ

Gettier Problems
Edmund Gettier

Thought experiments that challenge our concept of what knowledge truly is

In his paper "Is Justified True Belief Knowledge?" (1963), U.S. philosopher Edmund Gettier (b. 1927) posed a challenge to "propositional knowledge," the knowledge of a true statement or *p* (ice is solid, no lizards have wings). Gettier argued that a belief supported by evidence may not be justified as knowledge. Philosophers before Gettier would have mounted a three-fold defense of propositional knowledge: first, a person believes *p*; second, *p* must be true or it is not knowledge; third, the belief must be justified or supported by evidence and clear reasoning. If these three conditions are satisfied, then it counts as knowledge and is a "justified true belief." Gettier would counter that by means of a "problem" or example

constructed according to his arguments: an individual may claim they own a car and have papers to prove it, but they may not in fact own the car. Or, an individual may see a barnlike shape next to a highway and believe that they have seen a barn, but the barn may be only a billboard, not an actual barn.

Philosophers have put forward forms of the "Gettier problem" of what justifies true knowledge from Plato's time onward. British philosopher Bertrand Russell (1872–1970) gave the example of an individual who believed the time was a certain hour but the clock had in fact stopped twelve hours earlier. But it was Gettier who demonstrated by simple logical analysis that belief can be mistaken in reality even when there is sufficient evidence for that belief.

Gettier's problem, for all of the philosophic literature it has generated, still has no definitive solution. This is unsurprising, but his conclusion is unsettling since it argues that just because we believe something to be true and have evidence for it, that does not mean that it is true in reality. The problem goes to the core of how we form beliefs, how we justify them, and whether those beliefs constitute true knowledge. **CRD**

↑ According to Gettier, viewers may believe that these are living cows in a field, but they cannot "know" that.

Chaos Theory
Edward Lorenz

Chaotic behaviors of complex phenomena have their own underlying order

U.S. meteorologist Edward Lorenz (1917–2008) is widely credited with having first experimentally verified what would be known as chaos theory when he published a paper titled "Deterministic Nonperiodic Flow" in 1963. In studying computerized simulations of weather conditions, Lorenz noticed that making miniscule changes in the initial data of an experiment had a significant impact on the final outcome. Even though the initial variables were measurable and knowable, complicated systems, such as weather patterns, were not predictable beyond a certain point. Randomness or imprecise measurements led to the complicated behavior and unpredictability of the chaotic systems.

Chaos theory is a mathematical explanation for how and why complicated systems act the way they do.

"… the pinball game is to chaos what the coin toss is to complete randomness …"

Flavio Lorenzelli, *The Essence of Chaos* (1993)

Chaotic systems appear random and ungoverned, but chaos theory explains these phenomena as anything but, showing how the unpredictable behavior is really the result of deterministic factors. Though the systems themselves are deterministic and follow the dictates of identifiable rules, their specific outcomes are unpredictable, and thus, chaotic.

With chaos theory, systems that were once unpredictable and chaotic became understandable, allowing for long-term predictions about the general character of the system, even if precise predictions were still impossible. It has been used in the study of epilepsy, economic systems, physics, politics, population growth, philosophy, electrical engineering, and numerous other fields to help understand complicated behaviors and what governs them. **MT**

Sexism
Betty Friedan

The practice of discriminating against people based on their gender

French author Simone de Beauvoir (1908–86) had promoted feminism with her book *The Second Sex* (1949), but by the 1960s women still had a long way to go to secure all the rights enjoyed by men. A second wave of feminist thought was sparked by another, equally influential work, *The Feminist Mystique* (1963) by U.S. writer and feminist Betty Friedan (1921–2006). Women, said Friedan, were expected to lead either a powerless and unfulfilling life as a homemaker or to sacrifice the possibility of having children in protection of their careers. She also noted that society's authority figures and media argued that women were unsuitable for many jobs simply because they were women.

A "sexist" argument is any that ascribes women's achievement, or lack of it, in a specific area to biology.

"The sexist myth is the … most pervasive myth the world has ever told itself …"

Sheldon Vanauken, author

Sexism, much like racism, is used by individuals or groups who possess power or influence in society to maintain their status. It is a linguistic instrument used by one person or group to impose their will upon another. Sexism can exist in any culture and be expressed by either gender.

Acknowledging the existence of sexism and underscoring its kinship with racism were essential to the feminist movement, which argued for equality of opportunity for men and women. Feminism contributed much to a larger critique of traditional society that occurred in the 1960s and 1970s. Civilization as defined by male hierarchy and domination was questioned, and discussions of sexism changed not only our view of world history but also how we speak and write about ourselves and the world. **CRD**

Betty Friedan railed against the traditional expectation for women to be full-time homemakers. ➡

The Global Village
Marshall McLuhan

The electronic media enable all people to be interconnected through technology

Canadian philosopher of communication theory Marshall McLuhan (1911–80) coined the phrase "the global village" in reference to how communications technologies—radio, television, and, in the present day, the Internet and wireless communications-allow individuals to experience events in "real time," even if they are separated from those events by time or distance. As he argued in his book *Understanding Media: The Extensions of Man* (1964), this was a positive development since it would engender a shared sense of community and responsibility for the actions and the fates of all the world's inhabitants. Everyone would then experience the closeness and intimacy known to successive generations of a small, rural village, but through the present-day medium of technology.

". . . we have extended our central nervous system itself in a global embrace . . ."

Marshall McLuhan, *Understanding Media* (1964)

McLuhan's turn of phrase perfectly captured how revolutionary the effects of the communications technologies of the twentieth century would become in defining human existence. McLuhan understood that any change in technology would affect the social life of individuals, nations, and cultures. He believed that cultures evolved and irrevocably changed through the discovery and widespread dissemination of technologies of communication, and so each new technology marked a new stage in a culture's development.

McLuhan was one of the most articulate theorists of the impact of globalization and the new forms of media that emerged after the advent of computing. His phrase is routinely used to describe the shared responsibility for the lives of others brought about by the sense of immediacy produced by electronic media. **CRD**

The Little Red Book
Mao Zedong

Core principles of the Communist Revolution in China, presented by Mao

The Little Red Book, or *Quotations from Chairman Mao Tse-tung*, first distributed in China in 1964, was a distillation of the thought of Mao Tse-tung (1893–1976), the leading theorist of Chinese Marxism or Maoism. Mao himself did not compile *The Little Red Book*; it was a selection of his speeches and writings spanning many years. Mao argued that nothing existed in the Chinese nation except for the masses and the Chinese Communist Party. All existence was war between social classes. His book instructed, "Everyone lives as a member of a particular class, and every kind of thinking, without exception, is stamped with the brand of a class." Revolutionary war was the "war of the masses, impossible for any force on earth to smash." *The Little Red Book* promised nothing but a bright future

"We must have faith in the masses and we must have faith in the Party."

Mao Zedong

for China, where the wealth of the country was created by "the workers, peasants, and working intellectuals."

Mao argued that conflict between social classes was the driving force behind history. The future of China lay in the ability of the nation to modernize its industry and agriculture. China was also to become an economically self-sufficient nation, capable of defending itself from capitalist countries bent on its destruction. China was finally to lead an international revolution in which capitalism and the enemies of socialism and equality were to be vanquished for good. This would lead to an era of prosperity and harmony.

The book was perhaps one of the most printed in history as it was required reading in communist China during Mao's lifetime. The work was very widely distributed, with many committing it to memory. **CRD**

◄ In a staged photograph of 1967, Marshall McLuhan poses with a television and televised images of himself.

1964

Hamilton's Rule / Kin Selection
W. D. Hamilton

Altruism within a family group makes sense in evolutionary terms

Although British evolutionary biologist W. D. Hamilton (1936–2000) did not coin the term "Hamilton's Rule," he gave it firm empirical backing in his two papers titled *The Genetical Evolution of Social Behavior* (1964). The rule refers to a definition by British evolutionary biologist John Maynard Smith (1920–2004): "By kin selection I mean the evolution of characteristics which favor the survival of close relatives of the affected individual." Hamilton's Rule argues that if an individual lays down his life for his fellows—say two brothers (though not one brother only) or four cousins—then, evolutionarily, it is a fair deal. If a behavior increases the fitness of related individuals, or if more members of the family survive due to the actions of one individual, then this would more than compensate the loss of fitness at the level of the individual, since all relatives carry a copy of the gene that might favor survival of the family.

Naturalist Charles Darwin (1809–82) had said: "No instinct has been produced for the exclusive good of other animals, but each animal takes advantage of the instincts of others." Later studies have demonstrated that animals frequently aid distressed relatives while ignoring the travails of unrelated individuals, even if the benefits of aiding those relatives outweigh the reproductive cost of aiding them.

Hamilton's Rule transformed our view of nature. After Darwin published his findings, people saw the natural world as a space of fierce competition between individuals in the struggle for resources. However, this view was unable to explain a number of animal behaviors, particularly human ones. The theory of kin selection explains the prevalence of altruism and sacrifice in animals, and also many of the cooperative behaviors that maintain law and order. It elucidates the basis of solidarity among families at the level of evolutionary fitness, and gives us a glimpse into how the first societies evolved. **CRD**

Hamilton's Rule explains the cooperative behavior of social insects such as the honey bee. ⬆

1964

Artworld Theory

Arthur Danto

"Art" is "art" only because its audience has a shared understanding of what art is

In the essay "The Artworld," first published in October 1964 in the *Journal of Philosophy*, U.S. art critic and philosopher Arthur Danto (*b*. 1924) argued that art was art only if the audience interpreted it as existing within the "Artworld." A work such as *Brillo Pad Box* by Andy Warhol (1928–87) was art—and not merely an item available at any store—because the audience that was viewing the work understood it as art. Danto argued that objects gained this recognition through the transformative power of "the theory of art," which set the rules for distinguishing art from non-art. The theory of art itself relied on specific norms and canons of interpretation that were supplied by what Danto termed the "Artworld."

The Artworld was a conception of art informed not merely by the past work of artists but also by the collective opinion of scholars, patrons, audiences, and journalists on the nature of art. It encompassed what museums had considered to be art through the ages. Importantly, art was not merely an imitation, as had been supposed in classical times, nor did it depend upon the opinion of a single individual. Danto's conception of the Artworld thus solved the problem of how discussions about art could be both a subjective appraisal and a conclusion commanding universal assent.

Danto's essay proved hugely influential, in particular on the Institutional Theory of Art that was put forward by U.S. philosopher of art George Dickie (*b*. 1926). Danto's conception of art as defined by culture, tradition, and audience interpretation allowed art criticism to take into account, for the first time, the social context of the reception of a work of art as well as the history of interpretations of what counted as art. It fused present and past in a novel way, allowing art criticism to emerge from "aesthetics" and into the broader realm of history and social life. **CRD**

⬆ *One and Three Chairs* (1965), a conceptual work by Joseph Kosuth, has full Artworld approval.

Higgs Boson
Peter Higgs

The most elementary type of particle explains how and why "mass" exists

The Higgs boson was first posited in 1964 by British theoretical physicist Peter Higgs (b. 1929). The existence of the particle type was tentatively verified on July 4, 2012, using measurements from the Large Hadron Collider (LHC) in Switzerland. The existence of the Higgs boson validates the "Standard Model" of particle physics and explains how and why elementary particles (electrons, protons, and neutrons) have mass. Just as important, this elementary particle explains why there are different forces, such as electromagnetic force, existing between particles in an atom.

By the 1960s, physicists had discovered a number of elementary particles and the forces that governed their interaction. The Standard Model described all the particles that make up matter and the interactions

"We open a new window ... into ... 95 percent of the unknown universe."
Rolf-Dieter Heuer, particle physicist

between them, including electrons, protons, and neutrons, and the particles that make up each of those. The Standard Model, due to a mathematical quirk, argued that all of the particles must be without mass. Mass must then emerge from interaction between the particles. Scientists assumed that the particles interacted with a "Higgs field" filled with Higgs bosons, which gave them mass by transferring energy to them.

The verification of the existence of the Higgs boson vindicated large-scale science projects funded by government, such as the LHC. With the Standard Model complete, there has been discussion of moving on to a "new physics" that could potentially lead to novel technologies, much in the same way that discoveries in physics paved the way for advances in electronics and computing technology. **CRD**

Identity Theft
United States

Stealing a person's identity for the purposes of espionage or financial gain

As the *Billings Montana Gazette* reported in 1964, "Four Americans who suffered a theft of their identities were listed on Tuesday as government witnesses at the Brooklyn spy trial of a Russian couple, who used their names." In the Cold War context, identity theft was defined as using a person's name to obscure or hide their actual identity as spies. More recently, identity theft has become associated with the assumption of a person's identity for the express purpose of financial gain through fraud. This change in definition points to a fundamental shift in U.S. culture.

Identity theft in the more contemporary sense has grown more common as ways of stealing personal, particularly financial, data have proliferated while the threat of Russian spies has diminished. Although the

"Surfing the Internet provides new frontiers for identity thieves."
San Diego Daily Transcript (1994)

Internet provides thieves with an inordinate number of ways to steal bank details, addresses, and telephone numbers in order to perpetrate fraud (including "phishing," posing as legitimate entities to obtain personal information), identity theft is also perpetrated using the regular mail.

In response to the methods used by criminals, banks have imposed protections such as encryption software for financial transactions. The United States Congress has passed a number of laws designed to protect its citizens against the worst effects of identity theft. An entire field of "fraud protection" has emerged in the United States in order to better define the laws concerning the definition and punishment of identity theft. Numerous U.S. federal agencies now prosecute identity thieves. **CRD**

A graphic of a proton-proton collision, one of many recorded during the search for the Higgs boson.

Democratic Peace Theory

Dean V. Babst

The notion that democratic governments do not fight each other

⬆ U.S. president John F. Kennedy poses with British prime minister Harold Wilson in c. 1960. Historically, their two countries have stood united against a number of totalitarian regimes.

In 1964, U.S. sociologist Dean V. Babst (1921–2006) published the first paper on democratic peace theory in the *Wisconsin Sociologist*. Drawing on *A Study of War* (1942) by U.S. political scientist Quincy Wright (1890–1970), Babst argued that since the emergence of the United States in 1789, not a single democratic nation had gone to war with another democratic nation until 1941. For Babst, this was extremely significant because democratically elected governments in the nineteenth and twentieth centuries "have grown greatly in number and size to become a world force." Babst believed that the continued proliferation of democratic governments would lead to a human future with far less bloodshed and armed conflict.

According to the democratic peace theory, democratically elected governments do not go to war with one another. Democracies have not gone to war with one another throughout history because individuals in democratic nations may choose whether to go to war or not, and, given the choice, will not do so. Factors characterizing a country having such a choice are freedom of speech and press, and also the establishment of decision-making capacities of government in freely elected institutions, such as the U.S. Congress or the British Parliament, rather than within the jurisdiction of a hereditary ruler or a dictatorial regime.

Democratic peace theory remains central to many assumptions of the United States' foreign policy. The administrations of George H. W. Bush (1989–93) and Bill Clinton (1993–2001) argued that a post-Soviet Russia would pose no military threat if it introduced democratic reforms. Democratic peace theory was also central to the George W. Bush administration's justification of the Iraq War in 2003 as a conflict waged to protect U.S. interests at home while promoting democracy abroad. **CRD**

> *"And the reason why I'm so strong on democracy is democracies don't go to war with each other. I've got great faith in democracies to promote peace."*
>
> George W. Bush, U.S. president 2001–09

SEALAB
U.S. Navy

Underwater habitats test the effects of isolation and deep-sea diving on humans

The ocean deeps offer more than the possibility of discovering new species in an unfamiliar habitat. There is also much to learn about the physiological and psychological effects of placing human beings for extended periods in the extremely isolated, artificial environment of a deep-sea station.

The United States Navy SEALAB program enabled human researchers, for the first time in history, to engage in research and salvage operations on the floor of the ocean. It was conceived as part of the navy's "Man in the Sea Program," which was tasked with understanding the physical effects on humans of increased barometric pressure, a majority helium atmosphere, and the physiological effects of prolonged isolation. All of the relatively small, steel SEALAB structures—comparable to submarines but without engines—were connected by a hose that supplied fresh water. There were three SEALAB submersible habitats, manned by so-called "aquanauts."

SEALAB I was lowered into the water off the coast of Bermuda in July of 1964, although the experiment was halted after only eleven days due to an impending tropical storm. SEALAB II was operational in 1965, and introduced a number of novelties not found in the first structure: showers, a laboratory to record conditions on the ocean floor, and a trained porpoise, Tuffy, who delivered supplies in response to a buzzer. SEALAB III, completed in 1969 and submerged at much greater depth than the previous two SEALABS, was scrapped after it developed a leak.

During the 1960s, SEALAB was a national sensation. It improved deep-sea salvage and rescue techniques, and provided psychiatrists and other medical professionals with a wealth of new information about effects of the deep-sea atmosphere. Discussions of human isolation pertaining to Mars missions now incorporate observations from SEALAB. **CRD**

⬆ Aquanaut Scott Carpenter stands atop SEALAB II and gives the signal for it to be lowered in 1965. Carpenter joined the SEALAB project after working as an astronaut for NASA.

"During the 1960s, new frontiers were being explored—space and sea."

Michelle Brown, *Santa Barbara Independent* (2012)

Repressive Tolerance
Herbert Marcuse

Repression of free thought under the guise of expression of free thought

The idea of repressive tolerance was launched in 1965 by an eponymous essay by German philosopher, sociologist, and political theorist Herbert Marcuse (1898–1979). Marcuse explained how liberal democracies inhibit constructive social change; affluence produces a surplus of consumer items, busyness, sexual provocations, and chatter, all paradoxically promoting a repressed and uncritical society. This is no historical accident, but a totalitarian, capitalist system seeking to maintain itself.

Marcuse specifically identified the promotion of tolerance as a powerful tool in suppressing alternative social developments. He characterized tolerance of repressive speech by the public as "inauthentic" since it doubly ensures that marginalized voices will never

> *"Liberating tolerance, then, would mean intolerance against . . . the Right . . ."*
>
> Herbert Marcuse, *Repressive Tolerance* (1965)

be heard. This apparent contradiction is pragmatically sensible: if the raison d'être of tolerance is to preserve the ground upon which free speech is to survive, anything that would undermine the significance and possibility of free speech must be resisted: "the ways should not be blocked on which a subversive majority could develop".

So, what is it that transmutes a policy of free speech into an instrument of repression? Rational discussion is no longer possible because various media have produced a common-sense totalitarian view. Any departure from the common-sense view is blocked. What no one should tolerate are linguistic blocks to free thought, such as so-called "political correctness." Until that is recognized, modern democracy will be barely distinguishable from fascism. **JC**

Cryonics and Cryogenics
Karl Werner

Preserving the deceased in anticipation of remarkable future medical advances

In 1965 a New York industrial designer named Karl Werner coined the word "cryonics"—derived from the Greek for "icy cold"—to refer to the science of low-temperature preservation of humans and animals whose lives cannot be sustained by contemporary medicine. The term "cryogenics" stems from the Greek for "the production of freezing cold," and is used today for a low-temperature state. The point on the temperature scale at which refrigeration ends and cryogenics begins is not well defined, but most scientists assume it to be -240 °F (-150 °C) or below.

The rationale for cryonics is that people who are considered dead by current legal or medical definitions may not necessarily be dead according to the more stringent "information-theoretic" definition

> *" . . . cryonics cannot be dismissed simply by calling its subjects 'dead.'"*
>
> Brian Wowk, "Medical Time Travel" (2004)

of death. Information-theoretic death describes the condition of a person whose recovery is theoretically impossible by any physical means. The concept arose in the 1990s in response to the problem that, as medical technology advances, conditions previously considered to be death, such as cardiac arrest, have become reversible.

Cryonics advocates say that current technology can preserve the fine cell structures of the brain in which memory and identity reside, and that demonstrably reversible cryopreservation is not necessary to achieve preservation of brain information that encodes memory and personal identity. They believe that the anatomical basis of mind can be preserved sufficiently to prevent information-theoretic death until future repairs might be possible. **JC**

A cryo-capsule containing the body of California psychology professor James Bedford (1967).

The Atkins Diet
Robert Atkins

A concerted approach to weight loss by choosing what to eat

The no-hunger, luxurious weight loss plan that really works!

'...the perfect diet for those who love food' **Nigella Lawson**

⬆ The Atkins diet involves limited intake of carbohydrates to switch the body's metabolism from metabolizing glucose as energy over to converting stored body fat to energy.

Whether our cave-dwelling ancestors ever worried about their diet of woolly mammoth is unrecorded. But throughout history, people—mainly women— have altered their diet in order to achieve some desired effect. It is therefore surprising that the first major book about dieting appeared as recently as 1972. Thanks to Dr. Robert Atkins (1930–2003), whose *Dr Atkins' Diet Revolution* was an instant best seller, we are now far more aware of the effects of what we eat, and are awash with such instructional manuals.

Atkins was a doctor with a medical degree from Cornell University Medical College and a private cardiology practice in New York. As a result of the stress of his work and poor eating habits, his weight ballooned to 224 pounds (100 kg). An article in the October 1963 issue of *The Journal of the American Medical Association* exploring the research of Dr. Alfred Pennington, who recommended removing all starch and sugar from meals and increasing fat and protein, prompted Atkins to try this restrictive diet, with immediate effect. He recommended the diet to his patients and, in 1965, appeared on "The Tonight Show" to promote his own dietary plan to lose weight. This regime was published in *Vogue* magazine in 1970 and was known for many years as "The Vogue Diet." The publication of Atkins's first book in 1972 opened the floodgates of his success.

Not everyone was convinced by the Atkins diet, arguing that his idea that carbohydrate is the bad guy oversimplifies the metabolic process and that his proposals for a low-fiber diet could have long-term medical consequences. For his part, Atkins acknowledged that he did not know how his diet worked, and never put the diet to peer review. His steady stream of books and articles, however, found a ready audience anxious to lose weight as their waistlines expanded. **SA**

"A revolution in our diet thinking is long overdue."

Dr. Robert Atkins, *Dr Atkins' Diet Revolution* (1972)

Less Is a Bore
Robert Venturi

A postmodern counter to Mies van der Rohe's well-known modernist dictum, "Less is more"

German-U.S. architect Ludwig Mies van der Rohe (1886–1969), like many of his post-World War I contemporaries, had wanted to establish an architectural style that expressed the modernist ethos of the twentieth century. The style he created celebrated extreme clarity and simplicity and was characterized by a minimal framework of structural order, balanced against an implied freedom of free-flowing open space. In his mature buildings he used modern materials, such as industrial steel and plate glass, to define interior spaces. He called his buildings "skin-and-bones" architecture.

During the 1950s, U.S. architect Robert Venturi (b. 1925) emerged as a prominent critic of the functionalist and symbolically empty architecture of corporate modernism. In 1966 he published what he called his "gentle manifesto," *Complexity and Contradiction in Architecture*, in which he made a case for the "difficult whole" rather than the diagrammatic forms popularized by van der Rohe. The manifesto demonstrated, through many examples, an approach to understanding architectural composition in terms of complexity, richness, and interest. Drawing from both vernacular and high-style sources, Venturi introduced fresh lessons to be learned from examining the buildings of architects as varied as Michelangelo, Alvar Aalto, Frank Furness, and Edwin Lutyens.

Venturi's own buildings typically juxtapose architectural systems and elements, and aim to acknowledge the conflicts often inherent in a project or site. This "inclusive" approach contrasted with the typical modernist effort to resolve and unify all factors in a complete and rigidly structured—and possibly less functional and more simplistic—work of art. Venturi's work arguably provided a key influence at important times in the careers of architects Robert Stern, Philip Johnson, Michael Graves, Graham Gund, and James Stirling, among others. **JDP**

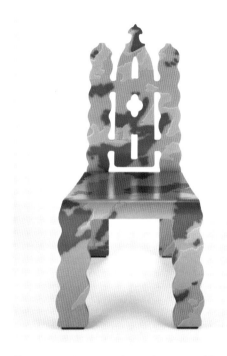

⬆ Architect Robert Venturi designed numerous articles of bespoke furniture, including this "Gothic Revival" chair (1984), painted by Philadelphia artist R. Michael Wommack.

"Each city is an archetype rather than a prototype, an exaggerated example from which to derive lessons for the typical."

Robert Venturi

LaVeyan Satanism
Anton LaVey

A religious philosophy based on individualism, self-control, and "eye for an eye" morality, rejecting the teaching of traditional religions such as Christianity

⬆ Anton LaVey poses in front of an inverted pentagram, a symbol of the Church of Satan, in 1967. The downward pointing vertices represent opposition to the Trinity.

"Blessed are the destroyers of false hope, for they are the true Messiahs."

Anton LaVey, *The Satanic Bible* (1969)

The Church of Satan was founded by Anton LaVey (1930–97) on April 30, 1966. In 1969 LaVey published *The Satanic Bible*, a collection of essays, observations, and rituals relating to the teachings of the church. Rather than advocating evil, LaVeyan Satanism (often referred to simply as "Satanism") promotes humanistic values such as self-assertion, rebellion against unjust authority, vital existence, and undefiled wisdom. Satanists regard *The Satanic Bible* as an authoritative text, and it has been referred to as "quasi-scripture."

Satanism asserts that the fundamental truth of the nature of reality is not known and that doubt is vital in the absence of proof. Satanism does not hold that "a life appropriate to a rational being" is the sole standard of moral right. If anything, Satanism holds that indulgence in life or "fun" is the highest standard of ethics. Satanists see reason as a means to knowledge but do not deem its possession as morally significant. Rather, the Satanic view sees as ethical the reality of domination of the weak by the strong. Believers have been described as "atheistic satanists" because they believe that God is not an external entity, but rather a projection of a person's own personality—a benevolent and stabilizing force in a person's life.

The Church of Satan proved popular with the media, thanks to tales of eccentric rituals at LaVey's home and its association with celebrities such as Jayne Mansfield and Sammy Davis, Jr., and by the time that *The Satanic Bible* was released in 1969 its membership had grown to well over 10,000 worldwide. Fractures in the organization appeared in the 1970s, leading to the formation of numerous alternative Satanist groups, but LaVey's ideas have continued to find followers. Since its publication there have been thirty printings of *The Satanic Bible* and more than a million copies have been sold. **JP**

Database
IBM

Electronic data should be organized for future use and ease of retrieval

Within any information storage unit, from a simple card index to a mainframe computer, a database is a collection of data designed and prearranged to aid its retrieval and use. The term "database" was first coined by workers attending to military computer systems and referred to information storage and retrieval techniques on "time-shared" computers, which were used by individual scientists to run specific programs for a limited amount of time, sharing the computing power of massive pieces of hardware.

In the 1960s, with the increase in data stored by computers and the lowering of average costs per unit moving the computer from the halls of government to private industry, two database system models were developed. The first was a hierarchical model known as IMS, introduced by IBM in 1966, which enabled the user to view the data as a hierarchical tree. A network model, in which different record types could be linked, was developed by CODASYL (Conference on Data Systems Languages) in 1969, based on a system invented by U.S. computer scientist Charles Bachman (b. 1924). In an effort to supersede both systems, English computer scientist Edgar F. Codd (1923–2003) proposed a "relational model" in 1970, which organized the data into simple tables and defined the relationship between them. This purely logical organization of data could be used with any data-processing machine and enabled large amounts of data to be efficiently organized and quickly retrieved.

With the advent of the Human Genome Project, global warming research, and numerous scientific and technological experiments, the amount of data that computers are expected to store and process is immense. The storage, organization, and retrieval of such immense quantities of data have been made possible with the aid of database software. **CRD**

Functionalism
David Lewis

A theory that mental states are constituted solely by their functional role

What is the mind, what role does it play in life, and how does it relate to consciousness and the physical body? The philosophical theory of functionalism was developed to address these issues.

At its core, functionalism is the idea that the mind is a function of the parts and processes of the brain. It states that what makes something a mental state depends not on its internal constitution but solely on its function, on the role it plays. Mental states—such as desire, distress, pain, belief, and so on—therefore have a purely functional role and are determined by sensory perceptions, behaviors, and other mental states. In his essay "An Argument for the Identity Theory" (1966), David Lewis (1941–2001) explored the meanings of these mental states in an approach often referred to as

"The definitive characteristic of any (sort of) experience as such is its causal role . . ."

D. Lewis, "An Argument for the Identity Theory" (1966)

analytic or conceptual functionalism. He proposed that while terms such as "belief" or "pain" get their meanings from our common sense approach to language, that meaning is not rigorous enough in theoretical terms. It is necessary to state that a mental state C is a state that is preconceived by B and causes D. Pain, for example, is caused by putting your hand on a hot cooker and produces a loud cry and anger at the person who left the hotplate on. These different stages are all necessary to explain the mental state of pain.

At a theoretical level, functionalism has developed as an alternative to the old Cartesian dualist ideas of the mind and body being two separate entities, and the more recent behaviorist ideas that allow only for a physical existence. While erudite, it allows us to better understand the nature of the human mind. **SA**

Kwanzaa
Maulana Karenga

A seven-day secular holiday celebrating African American culture and traditions

The Kwanzaa holiday, from December 26 to January 1, was introduced in 1966 by African American activist and author Maulana Karenga (b. 1941) as an annual observance designed to celebrate African American culture and traditions. Seven principles, the Kawaida—namely unity, self-determination, collective work and responsibility, cooperative economics, purpose, creativity, and faith—are promoted during the celebrations. The Kawaida are represented by seven candles in a holder called a "kinara," and celebrants light the candles during the week. Kwanzaa celebrants also wear traditional African clothing and discuss shared values during celebrations, and enjoy feasting and present-giving on the final day.

Karenga created Kwanzaa so that African Americans would have an alternative holiday to Christmas, one

> *"This is black power in its most lasting form. It's seen in the culture."*
>
> Keith Mayes, professor and author

that celebrated black culture, tradition, and history. The word *kwanza* means "first" in KiSwahili, but Karenga added an extra "a" to the word to give it seven letters, corresponding to the seven days and seven principles of the holiday. The holiday celebrates the first arrival of the yearly harvest, and although it focuses on African heritage and culture, it is not developed from any specific African tradition or holiday.

It is difficult to determine exactly how many people celebrate Kwanzaa every year, but estimates range widely, from about 500,000 to 5 million Americans, to as many as 30 million people or more around the world. The initial spread of Kwanzaa slowed after the Black Power movement of the 1960s and 1970s diminished in the United States, but it has retained its importance as a nonreligious holiday to many. **MT**

Black Power
Stokely Carmichael and Charles V. Hamilton

Radical assertion of black independence rather than black social integration

In 1966 black activists Stokely Carmichael (1941–98) and Charles V. Hamilton (b. 1929) published *Black Power*, stating that blacks must work together to achieve their cultural, economic, and political liberation. They called for the black people of the United States "to unite, to recognize their heritage, to build a sense of community . . . to define their own goals, to lead their own organizations."

Their approach was militant: "When you talk of black power, you talk of building a movement that will smash everything Western civilization has created." Images of young people singing "We Shall Overcome" were replaced in the media by new ones of militant black men and women wearing black berets, raising their fists, and carrying guns. Goals of social justice and integration

> *"I am black. I know that. I also know that while I am black I am a human being . . ."*
>
> Stokely Carmichael, "Black Power" speech (1966)

were replaced by ideas of black separatism and power, harking back to the Black Nationalism that had been preached in the 1920s by Marcus Garvey (1887–1940).

In 1966 and 1967, Carmichael lectured at campuses around the United States, North Vietnam, China, and Cuba. In 1967 he became honorary prime minister of the Black Panthers, the ultra-militant urban organization begun by Huey P. Newton (1942–89) and Bobby Seale (b. 1936). He moved to Guinea, West Africa, in 1969, calling on all black Americans to follow his example. In July 1969, he resigned from the Black Panther Party because of what he called "its dogmatic party line favoring alliances with white radicals." He advised, "dismiss the fallacious notion that white people can give anybody their freedom . . . Black power can only be realized when there exists a unified socialist Africa." **JDP**

Virtual Reality
Ivan Sutherland

A computer-generated environment able to simulate physical presence

The origin of the term "virtual reality" can be traced back to French playwright, poet, actor, and director Antonin Artaud (1896–1948) in his seminal book *The Theater and Its Double* (1938), in which he described theater as "la réalité virtuelle," in which "characters, objects, and images take on the phantasmagoric force of alchemy's visionary internal dramas," creating a "purely fictitious and illusory world in which the symbols of alchemy are evolved."

In 1965, U.S. computer scientist Ivan Sutherland (b. 1938) envisioned what he called the "ultimate display." Using this display, a person would look into a virtual world that appeared as real as the physical world. That world would be seen through a Head Mounted Display (HMD) and be augmented through three-dimensional

"[Virtual reality] is a looking glass into a mathematical wonderland."
Ivan Sutherland

sound and tactile stimuli. A computer would maintain the world model in real time, with users manipulating virtual objects in a realistic, intuitive way.

In 1966, Sutherland built the first computer-driven HMD; the computer system provided all the graphics for the display (previously, all HMDs had been linked to cameras). The HMD could display images in stereo, giving the illusion of depth, and it could also track the user's head movements, allowing the field of view to change appropriately as the user looked around.

Mychilo Cline, in his book *Power, Madness, and Immortality: The Future of Virtual Reality* (2009), predicts that, as we spend more and more time in virtual reality, there will be a gradual "migration to virtual space," resulting in unimagined changes in economics, worldview, and culture. **JDP**

Cultural Revolution
Mao Zedong

A proposed total break with traditional ideas and customs

Mao Zedong (1893–1976) took power in China in 1949 as leader of the Chinese Communist Party. With private enterprise and land ownership abolished, by the mid-1960s he was seeking to take the transformation of Chinese society to a whole new level. Communists had previously assumed their revolution would make the best of traditional culture and education available to the masses. Instead, Mao turned culture into a revolutionary battleground. In February 1964 he expressed contempt for formal education: "I do not approve of reading so many books." In 1965 his criticism spread to theater, with institutions such as the Beijing Opera being forced to stage revolutionary dramas.

In 1966 Mao formally launched the Great Proletarian Cultural Revolution, calling for an attack on four old

"Proletarian literature and art are part of the whole proletarian revolutionary cause ..."
Mao Zedong

elements in Chinese society: old customs, old habits, old culture, and old thinking. Chinese youth, organized into the Red Guards, was encouraged to denounce and humiliate its schoolteachers and university professors—especially shocking in a country where respect for elders was a fundamental Confucian value. Objects reflecting traditional Chinese culture were confiscated and destroyed, from chess sets to kites. University-educated intellectuals and officials were sent to work in factories and farms to learn from illiterate peasants and workers.

Mao's radical program for the erasure of the corrupt past and his extension of the revolutionary struggle into the cultural sphere found many admirers in the West, where Maoists formed an important element in the student revolts of the late 1960s. **RG**

◄ A researcher in the virtual-reality room at Tokyo University.

Deconstruction

Jacques Derrida

Confronting the metaphysical illusions embedded in Western thought

⬆ Jacques Derrida in 1987. He once wrote, "I believe in the value of the book, which keeps something irreplaceable, and in the necessity of fighting to secure its respect."

"The philosopher is interested only in the truth of meaning, beyond even signs and names ... the sophist manipulates empty signs ... the poet plays on the multiplicity of signifieds."

Jacques Derrida

Deconstruction is a school of textual analysis that originated in France in 1967 with the publication of a book, *Of Grammatology*, by French philosopher Jacques Derrida (1930–2004). This form of analysis is appropriate to texts in which binary oppositions can be detected in the construction of meaning and values; typically these texts structure experience in terms of antinomies, such as essence/appearance and freedom/determinism.

Events are conceived as alive, singular, and nonrepeatable. The living being undergoes a sensation, and this is inscribed in organic material. The idea of an inscription leads Derrida to the other pole. The machine that inscribes is based in repetition: "It is destined, that is, to reproduce impassively, imperceptibly." Derrida says: "To give up neither the event nor the machine, to subordinate neither one to the other ... this is perhaps a concern of thinking ..."

Derrida held that the function of oppositions should be studied, not to eliminate all oppositions (they are structurally necessary to produce sense) but to mark their "difference, undecidability, and eternal interplay." In order to recognize the antinomy of, for example, appearance and essence, the first step is to recognize that there is "a violent hierarchy"—in this case, essence is regarded as more significant. The second step of deconstruction is to identify "difference"—that is, to identify the basis for the binary opposition. The previously inferior term must be redefined in a new way and reinscribed as the "origin" of the opposition.

Reverse this by proposing that appearances give rise to essences, as existentialist Jean-Paul Sartre (1905–80) did when he claimed, "Existence precedes essence." Identify "difference," the being that makes a difference but which we cannot identify. It is undecidable, for example, whether "now" is in the past or the future; insofar as the difference is undecidable, it destabilizes the original decision that instituted the hierarchy. **JDP**

The Death of the Author
Roland Barthes

No single interpretation of a text can claim to be more authentic than any other

"The death of the author" is a postmodern theory of literary criticism formulated by French literary theorist and philosopher Roland Barthes (1915–80) in an essay of the same name (1967). The theory contends that a writer's intentions, and the context in which their work was created, do not need to be taken into account in interpreting a text for that interpretation to be valid. This is in stark contrast to the belief that art is a medium of communication between author and reader, and the meaning or message that the artist *intended* to communicate through their art is the only significant aspect of that work of art.

Barthes's idea was anticipated by the philosophical insights of W. K. Wimsatt and M. C. Beardsley who declared, in *The Intentional Fallacy* (1954), that a poem does not belong to its author, and to think otherwise is to commit the intentionalist fallacy; the implication is that objective and valid meaning can be extricated.

The popular criticism of Barthes's theory, and of aspects of postmodernism in general, is that denial of objective meaning in art and text means that every subjective interpretation of that art is equally valid. For example, a popular interpretation of Shakespeare's *Hamlet* is based on the Freudian concept of the "Oedipus Complex." A critic would point out that Shakespeare's text predates Freud's theories by several centuries, and therefore Shakespeare could not have intentionally embedded such meanings in his work. The postmodernist would counter that all meaning derived from the work of art exists only in the perceptions of the object's audience, and as such meaning is so subjective that attempting to distinguish these perceptions as more or less "real" or "valid" is a pointless practice. If that is the case, one question remains: how do we distinguish authentic interpretations from those that fail to reflect the viewer's or reader's response? **JDP**

⬆ Photographed in France in 1972, Roland Barthes preferred the term "scriptor" to "author" because the latter confers a perceived "authority" in determining a work's literary meaning.

"The birth of a reader must be at the cost of the death of an author."

Roland Barthes

Six Degrees of Separation
Stanley Milgram

Advances in travel and communication have greatly reduced social distance

If a person is one step away from each person he or she knows, and two steps away from each person known by one of the people he or she knows, then everyone is an average of six "steps" away from each person on Earth. This idea was originally set out in a short story, "Chain-Links" (1929) by Fryges Karinthy (1887–1938), and later popularized by a play, *Six Degrees of Separation* (1990), by John Guare (b. 1938).

In 1967 U.S. social psychologist Stanley Milgram (1933–84), designed the "Small World Experiment" to measure this connectedness empirically. He dispatched various packages to randomly selected people who were to deliver them to a specific person, who lived in Boston. Along with each forward of the package, a postcard was sent to Milgram's office so he could

"I am bound to everyone on this planet by a trail of six people."
John Guare, *Six Degrees of Separation* (1990)

record the relationship that existed between sender and receiver. After repeating the experiment many times using people from different cities, the results revealed that there were approximately five to six links connecting any two people. The research was groundbreaking in that it suggested that human society is a small-world network characterized by short path lengths. The experiments are often associated with the phrase "six degrees of separation," although Milgram did not use this term himself.

Milgram published the results of his research, and the article generated long-standing interest in the idea. However, detractors argue that Milgram's experiment did not demonstrate such a link, and the "six degrees" claim has been decried as an "academic urban myth," valid only in particular social contexts. **JDP**

Linguistic Turn
Richard Rorty

A new approach to the relationship between philosophy and language

The phrase "linguistic turn" was popularized with the publication in 1967 of an anthology, *The Linguistic Turn*, edited by U.S. philosopher Richard Rorty (1931–2007). The book contained studies of how philosophical paradoxes might be solved by learning how to increase our understanding of the language we use to describe them.

A linguistic turn is a proposition that argues, in part, that language in and of itself constructs its own reality. For example, in discussion of the attack on the World Trade Center in New York City in 2001, a person arguing the validity of the linguistic turn would say that we are not really talking about terrorism, aircraft, acts of heroism, or the collapse of buildings, we are really just analyzing the words we use in discussing the subject. Issues—social, political, ethical—have always been framed in terms of language, and proponents of the linguistic turn believe that we should try to understand the nature and structures of language as best we can.

The concept of the linguistic turn first surfaced in the early decades of the twentieth century and was used by thinkers such as British philosopher A. J. Ayer (1910–89), a proponent of logical positivism, who said in a paper in 1936: "The philosopher, as an analyst, is not directly concerned with the physical properties of things. He is concerned only with the way in which we speak about them. In other words, the propositions of philosophy are not factual, but linguistic in character."

Language, of all things, was suddenly being put forward as a central philosophical theme. Proponents of the linguistic turn, with their notion that language itself can constitute its own reality, often found themselves at odds with the broader philosophical movement. But they were asking interesting and important questions: How do words relate to everyday things? What makes a sentence true or false? **BS**

Atomic Model

Stephen Weinberg and Mohammad Abdus Salam

The nature of physical reality at its indivisible atomic level is proven mathematically after centuries of philosophical thought and scientific hypotheses

In 1803, English chemist and physicist John Dalton (1766–1844), built on the ancient Greek idea of the atom as an indivisible unit by putting forward the idea that gaseous elements are composed of "particles" that are indivisible and indestructible. Dalton even published a table of atomic weights relative to hydrogen.

The modern atomic model, however—showing electrons in constant motion in an electron "cloud" around a nucleus composed of neutrons and protons—did not arrive in one giant leap forward, or Eureka moment. The development of the atomic model evolved gradually, with each new version taking account of shortcomings of its predecessor. There was the "plum-pudding" model (1898), the cubic model (1902), the Saturnian model (1904), the Rutherford model (1911, in which Rutherford declared an atom to be 99.99 percent empty space), and the Bohr planetary model (1922), which had electrons moving in precise orbits around the nucleus in much the same way as planets circled the sun. The neutron was discovered in 1931, leading to the "gauge theory"—the basis for the standard model—in 1954. Antiprotons were first postulated in 1955, quarks in 1964, and on it went.

In 1960, U.S. theoretical physicist Sheldon Glashow (b. 1932) put forward his "electroweak theory," involving the unification of electromagnetism and "weak force," one of the four fundamental forces of nature responsible for the decay of subatomic particles. U.S. physicist Steven Weinberg (b. 1933) and Pakistani physicist Mohammad Abdus Salam (1926–96) took Glashow's work a step further by taking the Higgs mechanism, a process that imparts mass to elementary particles, and adding it to Glashow's electroweak theory. Abdus Salam proved the theory mathematically in 1967 and the modern atomic model was born. **BS**

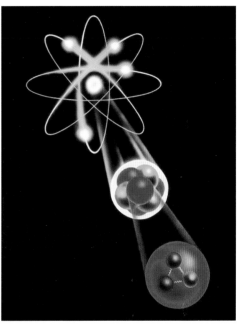

↑ Diagram of an atom. Electrons orbit the central nucleus, which consists of protons (red) and neutrons (blue). Each proton is made of two "up" quarks (dark blue) and one "down" quark (green).

"From time immemorial, man has desired to comprehend the complexity of nature in terms of as few elementary concepts as possible."

Mohammad Abdus Salam

Reggae
The Pioneers

A popular music style combining a slow beat with politically aware lyrics

Reggae is a form of popular music that came to the fore in the late 1960s in Kingston, Jamaica, developing out of rhythm and blues, rocksteady, and ska music. The earliest recorded example of the genre is thought to be "Long Shot (Bus' Me Bet)," made in 1967 by Jamaican vocal trio The Pioneers. Jamaica had gained its independence in 1962 and, initially, reggae lyrics were identified with raising black consciousness in the new country, in addition to attacking economic and social injustices from a black perspective.

The producers Duke Reid (1915–75) and Coxsone Dodd (1932–2004) were influential in creating the reggae sound. Early reggae artists include Toots and the Maytals, Bob Marley & The Wailers, and Desmond Dekker. Reggae is based on a dance beat, being played

"Play I some music: (dis a) reggae music! / Roots, rock, reggae: dis a reggae music!"

Bob Marley, "Roots, Rock, Reggae" (1976)

in either 4/4 or swing time, and it is notable for its offbeat rhythms and staccato chords played on the offbeats of the musical measure. The rhythm is driven by a variety of instruments: drums, electric and bass guitars, and sometimes "scrapers" consisting of a corrugated stick being rubbed by a plain stick.

In 1972, Jamaican reggae musician and actor Jimmy Cliff (b. 1948) starred in the film *The Harder They Come*, which helped reggae reach an international audience. The music spread to the United Kingdom and was adopted by bands such as UB40 and Aswad, as well as rock superstar Eric Clapton. Reggae has since become fused with local musical genres around the world and various reggae subgenres have developed over the years, with names such as roots reggae, dub, ragamuffin, and reggaeton. **CK**

Anti-psychiatry
David Cooper

Psychiatry labels behavior it does not support or understand as mental illness

The term "anti-psychiatry" was coined by South African psychiatrist David Cooper (1931–86) in his book *Psychiatry and Anti-Psychiatry* (1967). According to Cooper, mental illness was not illness at all, and what psychiatrists classified as "madness" was a form of self-expression that they deemed unacceptable.

The anti-psychiatry movement had its intellectual roots in the work of an earlier generation of sociologists and psychologists for whom mental illness was not the result of biology or genetic inheritance but a label imposed by society upon individuals who did not adhere to social norms. Cooper, himself a trained psychiatrist, considered traditional psychiatry to be antithetical to human growth and human potential. For Cooper and many others involved in the anti-

"Madness . . . is a movement . . . toward autonomy. This is [its] real 'danger' . . ."

David Cooper, *The Language of Madness* (1978)

psychiatry movement during its heyday in the 1960s and 1970s, traditional notions of mental illness and their associated treatments, especially shock therapy, were oppressive and unjustifiable. Mental illness was a "myth," a diagnosis primarily imposed upon individuals whom society considered eccentric or unmanageable. For anti-psychiatrists, even schizophrenia amounted to nothing but society's attempt to restrict the freedom of thought and expression of certain individuals.

Anti-psychiatrists were among the first to argue that homosexuality should not be classified as a mental illness, and were also among the strongest supporters for the "deinstitutionalization" of the mentally ill in the 1980s. Due to their efforts, the lay world is now more skeptical of the claims of psychiatrists and the efficacy of their treatments. **CRD**

Internationally renowned reggae singer and guitarist Bob Marley performs in Los Angeles in 1979.

Constructivist Epistemology
Jean Piaget

Knowledge is constructed by individuals from their own sensory experiences

⬆ Jean Piaget (here photographed in 1975) combined aspects of developmental psychology and constructivist epistemology to produce his influential doctrine of genetic epistemology.

The expression "constructivist epistemology" was first used in 1967 by Swiss psychologist and philosopher Jean Piaget (1896–1980) in the volume "Logical and Scientific Knowledge" of the Gallimard *Encyclopedia of the Pleiades*. Constructivism proposes new definitions for knowledge and truth based on inter-subjectivity instead of objectivity. Piaget argued that knowledge "does not reflect an objective ontological reality, but exclusively an ordering and organization of a world constituted by our experience" within the constraints of reality. Knowledge does not match reality: it organizes it. The philosophical forerunners of this view of knowledge are said to be Giambattista Vico (1678–1744) and George Berkeley (1685–1753).

Piaget asserted that children learn actively through an exploration of their environment. Piaget's learning theory looks through a developmental lens, and considers stages of knowledge acquisition to be directly linked to a child's developmental stage. Piaget's theory of "genetic epistemology" contributed greatly to the development of constructivist theory.

Constructivist epistemology asserts that the only tools available to a knower are the senses. It is through seeing, hearing, touching, smelling, and tasting that an individual interacts with the environment. The individual builds a picture of the world from this sensory data. Therefore, constructivism asserts that knowledge resides in individuals; that knowledge cannot be transferred intact from the head of a teacher to the heads of students. The student tries to make sense of what is taught by trying to fit it with their personal experience. On the other hand, meaning does not lie in words, which are based on the constructions of individuals. Communication is possible because individuals' meanings of words only have to be compatible with the meanings given by others. **JP**

> "Verum esse ipsum factum: *The true is precisely what is made.*"
>
> Giambattista Vico, political philosopher

Lateral Thinking
Edward de Bono

The attempt to override standard assumptions in order to access original ideas

Maltese physician and author Edward de Bono (b. 1933) invented the term "lateral thinking" (literally, sideways thinking) and it first appeared in print in his book, *The Use of Lateral Thinking* (1967). De Bono wrote of the importance of disrupting the dominant patterns preferred by the human brain in order to facilitate potential creative abilities. He explained that with logic a person starts out with certain ingredients, just as a chess player starts out with given pieces. But what are those pieces? In most real-life situations, the pieces—certain perceptions, concepts, and boundaries—are not given, they are just assumed. Lateral thinking is concerned, not with playing with the existing pieces, but with seeking to change those very pieces. It is concerned with perception and organization of the external world into new pieces that we can then "process."

Lateral thinkers use various acts of provocation to incite ideas that are free from prior assumptions. Random words, new stimuli, concept reversals, and other tricks are used deliberately to shift perceptional assumptions for the purpose of generating fresh observations and insights. The popular term for this creative activity is "thinking outside of the box."

Techniques for lateral thinking can be taught, and in 1974 de Bono put forward an education program named CoRT Thinking, which introduced some eighty different tools for thinking. CoRT helps the student to clearly differentiate lateral thinking skills from logical analyses (vertical thinking) and training in creativity/sensibility (horizontal thinking). Lateral thinking is a genuine alternative to training in other forms of thinking, but must be taught using a didactic and pedagogical approach. It has been successfully integrated into teacher-training programs and the school classroom since de Bono's book was published. **JP**

⬆ Edward de Bono demonstrates the logical way to tie a balloon. He is widely credited with expanding people's capacity to think, although critics call for evidence of his success.

"Removing the faults in a stage-coach may produce a perfect stage-coach, but it is unlikely to produce the first motor car."
Edward de Bono

The Society of the Spectacle
Guy Debord

In modern consumer society, imagery has become more significant than reality

La Société du spectacle (The Society of the Spectacle, 1967) is a work of philosophy and critical theory by French Marxist theorist Guy Debord (1931–94) that traces the development of a modern society in which authentic social life has been replaced with its representation. The work shares many of the assumptions of German critical theorists Theodor Adorno (1903–69) and Max Horkheimer (1895–1973), as presented in their book *Dialectic of Enlightenment* (1944).

Debord argues that, in a consumer society, "passive identification with the spectacle supplants genuine activity." Inevitably, social life moves away from "being" to "having," proceeding into a state of "appearing to have," or virtual living. "The spectacle" uses imagery to convey what people need and must have.

"All that once was directly lived has become mere representation."
Guy Debord, *The Society of the Spectacle* (1967)

In his social analysis, Debord sees the quality of life degraded into "repressive pseudo-enjoyment," which is progressively impoverished and lacking in authenticity. He compares the present-day role of mass-media marketing to that of religions in the past. Mass-media commodity images produce "waves of enthusiasm for a given product," resulting in "moments of fervent exaltation similar to the ecstasies of the convulsions and miracles of the old religious fetishism."

Debord's proposal is "to wake up the spectator who has been drugged by spectacular images." He encourages the use of *détournement*, which involves using spectacular images and language "to disrupt the flow of the spectacle." This radical action would encourage "a revolutionary reordering of life, politics, and art" and enable authentic being. **JP**

Reformed Epistemology
Alvin Plantinga

A philosophy of religion that seeks to defend faith as rational

Reformed epistemology originated in 1967 with the publication of *God and Other Minds* by analytic philosopher Alvin Plantinga (b. 1932), and was developed by him and others in the 1970s and 1980s. Reformed epistemology contends that belief in God is absolutely right, properly basic and logical, and that faith and belief can stand alone, justified in and of themselves—they are not something one needs to be "argued into." The term "epistemology" was originally coined in philosophy to refer to the study of the nature, scope, and limitations inherent in knowledge, and describes how what we know relates to our beliefs and notions of truth.

Reformed epistemology—essentially a body of apologetic arguments—is used in the hope of

" . . . belief in other minds and belief in God are in the same epistemological boat . . ."
Alvin Plantinga, *God and Other Minds* (1967)

demonstrating how traditional arguments against the existence of God are unreasonable and anti-intellectual. It is used to defend faith in a creator as being entirely rational, and explains how such a faith can be argued in the face of a complete lack of empirical evidence. It is a reaction against both evidentialism (that something can be believed only when there is sufficient evidence) and classic foundationalism (that beliefs can be inferred if drawn from earlier, more basic beliefs). It is also a response to the atheistic beliefs of secular society, challenging that it is simply improper for nonbelievers to assume that it is irrational to believe in God unless one can present evidence of His existence. And it is also a challenge to Christians, reminding them that it is improper to build a faith on the foundations of something as transitory as simply a good argument. **BS**

Biblical Rhetorical Criticism

James Muilenburg

Analysis of the stylistic devices used in the Judeo-Christian scriptures

⬆ A page from a thirteenth-century copy of the Hebrew Bible, with illustrations by Joseph Asarfati. "Hebrew Bible" is a term used by biblical scholars to refer to the Tanakh.

"What I am interested in, above all, is in understanding the nature of Hebrew literary composition, in exhibiting the structural patterns that are employed for the fashioning of a literary unit, whether in poetry or in prose ..."

James Muilenburg, "Form Criticism and Beyond" lecture (1968)

Biblical rhetorical criticism analyzes the Judeo-Christian scriptures to take into account their literary and theological dimensions. It examines the message of the authors by analyzing the stylistic devices, structures, and techniques they used to compose a narrative that would often be read aloud. Rhetorical criticism looks at the relationship between the text and its original intended audience. By reimagining the cultural setting, it examines how a text was used to achieve a particular effect—whether to inform, educate, persuade, or preach—and also considers the text's meaning. The critic can then communicate the message of the text to a contemporary audience faithfully.

Rhetorical criticism of the Bible can be first seen in the writings of the theologian and philosopher St. Augustine of Hippo (354–430). However, it did not become a formal analytical method until 1968, when U.S. theologian and professor of Hebrew Exegesis and Old Testament at San Francisco Theological Seminary, James Muilenburg (1896–1974), delivered his presidential address, "Form Criticism and Beyond," at the annual meeting of the Society of Biblical Literature at the University of California in Berkeley. In this lecture, he outlined the limitations of form criticism, which he regarded as too generalized. Muilenburg instead suggested a fresh approach to biblical study that he called "rhetorical criticism," which would consider what he believed to be the inextricable relationship between the form and content of a text.

Muilenburg's approach was highly influential, and rhetorical criticism went on to become a discipline. Notably, two of his students have become authorities on this method of biblical criticism: Phyllis Trible, author of works such as *God and the Rhetoric of Sexuality* (1978) and *Rhetorical Criticism: Context, Method, and the Book of Jonah* (1994), and Dale Patrick, author of *Rhetoric and Biblical Interpretation* (1990). **CK**

The Butterfly Effect

Edward Lorenz

A scientist's provocative insight into chaos and causality

U.S. mathematician Edward Lorenz (1917–2008)noticed, as many had before him, that the long-term weather forecasts of meteorologists were rarely accurate. He asked himself why major events such as hurricanes in the Atlantic should be so difficult for scientists to predict. His answer to this question has become known as "the butterfly effect."

Lorenz imagined a butterfly fluttering around in a rain forest. With each beat of its wings, the butterfly stirs the air, creating a minuscule but measurable change in the atmosphere. According to Lorenz, such a tiny input could make the difference between a storm gathering or not, because weather systems are extremely sensitive to small changes in input. A minute alteration in atmospheric conditions in May could result in a vast difference in the weather experienced in June, by tipping the evolution of the weather system in one direction or another. In a sense, a flap of a butterfly's wing could trigger a hurricane. And this was what made weather so difficult to predict. Since it was impossible to establish exactly the movements of every butterfly—the "butterfly" standing for any of the vast number of factors of all kinds influencing the system—it was impossible to accurately predict the outcome. Systems such as weather were labeled "chaotic" because, although not random, they could not be reduced to a clear chain of causes and effects.

The butterfly effect is a scientific version of an age-old paradox about trivial causes potentially having disproportionately large effects—as when the seventeenth-century French thinker Blaise Pascal argued that the shape of Cleopatra's nose may have radically altered the whole course of human history. It has been important scientifically as a stimulus to the development of novel techniques for describing the behavior of chaotic systems. **RG**

⬆ According to the butterfly effect theory, a butterfly flapping its wings in China can lead to unpredictable changes in U.S. weather a few days later.

"It used to be thought that the events that changed the world were things like big bombs, maniac politicians, huge earthquakes, or vast population movements . . . The things that really change the world, according to Chaos theory, are the tiny things."

Terry Pratchett and Neil Gaiman, *Good Omens* (1990)

Counterculture
Theodore Roszak

A critical subculture with values and mores subverting those of mainstream society

The term "counterculture" is attributed to U.S. historian Theodore Roszak (1933–2011), author of *The Making of a Counter Culture* (1969). Roszak identified common ground between student radicals and hippie dropouts in the 1960s, pointing to their mutual rejection of what he called "the technocracy," "the regime of corporate and technological expertise that dominates industrial society." Underpinned by the writings of Herbert Marcuse and Norman O. Brown, Allen Ginsberg, and Paul Goodman, Roszak's book was read widely by Vietnam War protesters, dropouts, and rebels.

A countercultural movement affects significant numbers of people and expresses the ethos, aspirations, and dreams of a specific population during a well-defined era. When oppositional forces

"Everything was called into question: family, work, education … sexuality …"
Theodore Roszak, *The Making of a Counter Culture* (1969)

reach critical mass, countercultures can trigger dramatic cultural changes. Examples of countercultural movements in the United States and Europe include Romanticism (1790–1840), Bohemianism (1850–1910), the more fragmentary counterculture of the Beat Generation (1944–64), and the hippie counterculture (1963–75). In each case, a "fringe culture" expanded and grew into a counterculture by defining its own values in opposition to mainstream norms.

The lifecycle includes phases of rejection, growth, partial acceptance, then absorption into the mainstream. Eventually each peaks and goes into decline, but leaves a lasting impact on mainstream cultural values. The "cultural shadows" left by the Romantics, Bohemians, Beats, and Hippies remain highly visible in contemporary Western culture. **JDP**

The Five Stages of Grief
Elisabeth Kübler-Ross

A crucial understanding of the human reaction to the imminence of death

While working with terminally ill patients in Chicago, the Swiss-American psychiatrist Elisabeth Kübler-Ross (1926–2004) became aware that the medical curriculum failed to address dying and death in any meaningful way. An instructor at the University of Chicago's Pritzker School of Medicine, she developed her ideas on the subject through interviews and a series of seminars, before publishing them in her book *On Death and Dying* (1969). A best seller, it revolutionized the way people thought about death and care for the dying.

Kübler-Ross's model proposed five stages of grief, popularly known by the acronym DABDA. After the initial Denial that it is happening, the patient then becomes Angry before attempting to Bargain their way out of trouble by trying to gain a little longer to live. The

"The process of grief always includes some qualities of anger."
Elisabeth Kübler-Ross, *On Death and Dying* (1969)

reality that this is impossible leads to Depression and then to the final stage of Acceptance. Kübler-Ross was always very clear that not everyone will pass through all five stages, nor do so in the same order. Reaction to death is always an intensely personal response.

At first the five-stage theory was applied only to those facing their own death, but it was soon expanded to other emotional experiences, such as bereavement or the end of a marriage. The wide range of applications to this theory brought it huge acceptance, but also criticism from clinical psychologists who argued that people experiencing loss are resilient, not grieving. Others felt the theory to be prescriptive, pushing people to rush through the stages rather than letting events unfold naturally. But its very simplicity and caring humanity has won the theory numerous admirers. **SA**

Young hippies turn their backs on mainstream society at the Isle of Wight Festival in 1969.

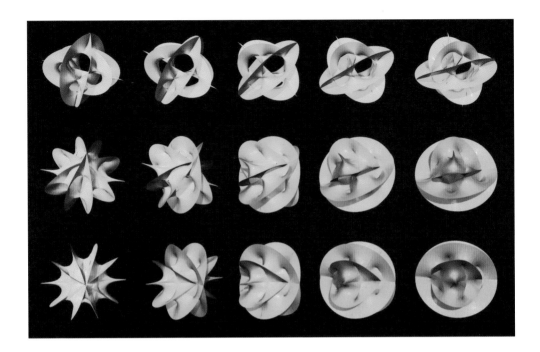

String Theory
Y. Nambu, H. B. Nielsen, and L. Susskind

A theory that seeks to reconcile general relativity with quantum mechanics

Physicists like their world to be unified and orderly, without contradictions or exceptions. There was thus a strong desire to unify the two great—and seemingly incompatible—theories of physics that explain the four fundamental forces of nature: the theory of general relativity, which relates gravity to space and time in the four-dimensional entity of spacetime; and the theory of quantum mechanics, which unites the three other forces of electromagnetism, strong nuclear force, and weak nuclear interaction. Work on this unified theory was advanced by Yoichiro Nambu (*b*. 1921), Holger Bech Nielsen (*b*. 1941) , and Leonard Susskind (*b*. 1940) in 1969.

For a unified theory to work, all four forces must be described in the same way. This means that gravity, and thus spacetime, must be packaged into discrete entities that can be measured. In comparison with the other three forces, gravity is very weak, implying that these packages must be miniscule. Finding a mathematic model for these packages provided the motivation behind string theory. In 1968 the Italian scientist Gabriele Veneziano (*b*. 1942) proposed that a model of strings might help. A year later, three scientists working independently of each other made the big leap. Nambu, Neilsen, and Susskind all proposed that Veneziano's model was actually a theory of strings, that the particles are not single mathematical points but tiny vibrating strings, each fundamental particle vibrating in a different way. At first these strings were thought to be in lines, but it is now realized that they form tiny loops. Crucially, the mathematical description of these loops also described gravity.

String theory, however, requires many more dimensions than the four of spacetime—perhaps ten—rolled up and shrunk inside each other so that only four are visible. Furthermore, there are six different string theories that have been suggested. The search for a unified theory of everything continues. **SA**

These Calabi-Yau manifolds are computer images of the extra six dimensions predicted by string theory.

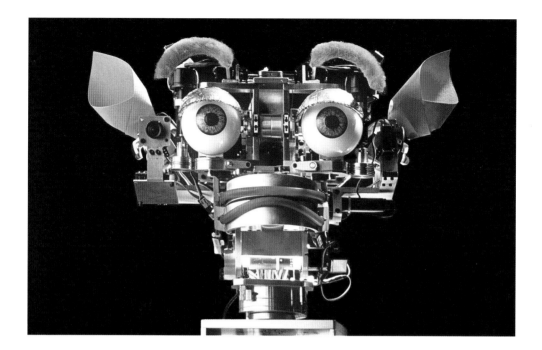

1969

The Frame Problem
John McCarthy and Patrick Hayes

The difficulty of specifying what is left unchanged when an action is performed

In the world of artificial intelligence (AI), the frame problem is the problem of describing the effects of actions or events using logic. It was a problem that first came to the attention of scientists in the AI world in 1969, when two computer scientists, John McCarthy (1927–2011) and Patrick Hayes (b. 1944), published a paper titled *Some Philosophical Problems from the Standpoint of Artificial Intelligence*.

There are generally agreed to be two main aims of AI: firstly, to engineer objects capable of performing tasks that, if performed by a human, would be said to require intelligence; and secondly, to reach a scientific understanding of the principles underlying such intelligent behavior. The frame problem arose in the early days of AI when even an uncomplicated task, such as moving a block, became complex, because when the block was moved it was necessary to update a vast amount of database information to explain why the block was no longer where it had been and why it had not been altered or changed. Humans are capable of selecting what is relevant (the block has been moved) and ignoring unnecessary complications (why the block is not where it was), but vast amounts of memory were needed to explain this to a computer. The frame problem, which began as little more than a technical annoyance, initially seemed to be almost endemic. Informing a database that an action has been altered fails, in the world of computer logic, to rule out a raft of other possible altered conditions.

In the 1980s a series of workable solutions were arrived at, and the frame problem is no longer thought of as an obstacle—though it has not been completely overcome. Solving it does not mean trying to process every conceivable implication of an action or event, and just as well. The day we are able to program human cognition, and the inherent solutions it will possess, has yet to come. **BS**

 Kismet, a robot designed to show facial expressions in response to events around it, showing fear.

Relational Database
Edgar F. Codd

The organized storage of data in tables that can be linked together

In a world awash with data, the importance of its management is crucial. Computer databases had first appeared in the 1960s, but the early systems were not without flaws. In 1970 a new model of database management was proposed by Edgar F. Codd (1923–2003), a British computer scientist who worked for IBM. He detailed its workings in a report titled "A Relational Model of Data for Large Shared Data Banks."

Codd's model worked by organizing data into tables, or "relations," that represented a single entity—for example, students. The rows of the table, known as tuples, each represented a particular instance of that entity—student A, student B, etc.—while the columns contained data for certain attributes of each tuple—student number, name, address, etc. The relational

". . . a means of describing data with its natural structure only . . ."

Edgar F. Codd, "A Relational Model of Data . . ." (1970)

database system would then allow you automatically to link together different tables by using a particular attribute as a "key," and so flexibly combine data in two or more of them (for example, the "student" table could be linked to a "course" table by using "student number" as a key; searching the database with a particular student number would then call up all information related to that student number from both tables).

Users of the database could specify the data it would contain, input that data, and then retrieve information from it later, all without knowing how the database program worked. The software system took care of the storage and retrieval of information. The effect of this was enormous, for Codd had created a system of infinite flexibility. One notable use has been in allocating products and issuing invoices to customers. **SA**

Ageism
Robert Neil Butler

A form of discrimination based on a person's age

First coined by physician and Pulitzer Prize-winning author Robert Neil Butler in 1969, the term "ageism" originally applied to negative prejudices people hold against seniors. Today, it is more broadly applicable to any act of discrimination based on a person's age.

Since prehistoric times, cultures around the world have regarded elderly people as repositories of knowledge and experience, holding them in high esteem. After the invention of the printing press made transmitting information easier and the Industrial Revolution (1760–1840) required workers to have the ability to quickly learn new skills, engage in longer hours of manual labor, as well as be able to move to where new jobs were relocated, the esteem in which old people were once held began to be replaced with

"Aging is not 'lost you' but a new stage of opportunity and strength."

Betty Friedan, author and feminist

negative associations. By 1969, when Butler identified ageism by name, prejudicial attitudes toward elderly people were widespread in many Western nations.

Ageism is not universally present, and significant differences in attitudes toward age exist across different cultures. Someone's age is one of those categories, such as race and gender, that is instantly apparent when we see them for the first time. Those instant observations can bring forth stereotypes that are applied to those categories, and lead to discrimination. Yet unlike other forms of discrimination, ageism is unique in that even though we may not be discriminated against today, we might suffer such treatment at a later time in life. As awareness of the issue has increased, many nations have adopted laws and policies that prohibit, and even criminalize, acts of ageism. **MT**

Speciesism
Richard D. Ryder

The practice of treating humans as superior to all other animals

Speciesism is the idea that being human gives one superior moral rights to nonhuman animals. Human speciesism is often compared with racism and sexism by animal rights advocates when applied to humans' disregard for animals' suffering.

The concept of animal rights has existed for centuries, as suggested by writers such as the English physician and physicist Thomas Young (1773–1829). However, the notion of "speciesism" did not arise until 1970, when British writer and psychologist Richard D. Ryder (b. 1940) used the term in a pamphlet that he distributed in Oxford, England, as part of a protest against experiments on animals.

Ryder received no response to his leaflet, so he reprinted it with an illustration of a chimpanzee

> *"Animals may be different from us, [but] this does not make them LESS than us."*
>
> Marc Bekoff, *Animals Matter* (2000)

experimentally infected with syphilis, and asked a colleague, David Wood (b. 1946), to add his name so that the leaflet would have a university address on it. Ryder sent the reprint to all the Oxford University colleges, and one of the recipients was Australian philosopher Peter Singer (b. 1946). Ryder used the term again in his essay "Experiments on Animals" in the book *Animals, Men and Morals: An Inquiry into the Maltreatment of Non-humans* (1971), which Singer reviewed in *The New York Review of Books* in 1973, describing it as a manifesto of animal liberation. Singer went on to write *Animal Liberation* (1975), in which he used and popularized the term "speciesism" to describe the exploitative treatment of animals. *Animal Liberation* is considered by many to be the founding philosophical statement of the animal rights movement. **CK**

Urgent Care Clinic
United States

Providing emergency medical treatment at locations other than hospitals

Urgent care clinics are walk-in centers where patients can receive certain limited forms of treatment for illnesses and injuries that require immediate attention, but which are not serious enough to warrant a visit to an emergency room. Unlike hospitals, which are generally open around the clock, urgent care clinics operate only at set times.

The concept of urgent care can be traced back to 1970, with the first clinics set up in the United States by physicians who wanted to relieve some of the burden on overstretched hospitals without reducing the availability of medicine and treatment. Now long established and numbering more than 10,000, these clinics had their powers and responsibilities codified in April 2009 when the Urgent Care Association of

> *"By definition, urgent care centers function as overflow valves for the public …"*
>
> Urgent Care Association of America

America began issuing certificates to practices that satisfied various criteria, including having on-site diagnostic services, such as phlebotomy and X-ray machines, and pharmacies that dispense medicines only to the clinic's own patients.

Urgent care clinics have since been opened in several other countries around the world, including Great Britain, Australia, Canada, Ireland, and Israel. In New Zealand, urgent care has been recognized as a medical specialty in its own right. Although critics point out the dangers of new patients attending the wrong type of facility for their needs through uncertainty about the exact nature of their problem, urgent care clinics have nonetheless carved out their own niche as informal but effective treatment centers. **GL**

Sexual Politics
Kate Millett

A groundbreaking attack on the subjugation of women

Are the sex scenes in the writings of authors such as D. H. Lawrence, Henry Miller, and Norman Mailer passages of literature or highly charged political acts and representations of the subjugation of women by men? Kate Millett (b. 1934) was in no doubt, and in a revolutionary book, *Sexual Politics*, first published in 1970, tackled this subjugation head-on.

Millett's best seller, developed from her Ph.D. thesis, is sometimes said to be the first book of academic feminist literary criticism. *Sexual Politics* is, in fact, much more than that. Defining politics as power-structured relationships in which one group of people is controlled by another, she focused on "the role which concepts of power and domination play in some contemporary literary descriptions of sexual activity itself." She then

" ... sex has a frequently neglected political aspect."
Kate Millett, *Sexual Politics* (1972)

widened her vision to analyze the social relationship between the sexes from a theoretical standpoint, elevating patriarchy into a political institution in its own right. This was groundbreaking stuff, for Lawrence was a then unchallengeable author and Mailer a widely revered modern master. Not every male author was so criticized: she praised Jean Genet, a gay outsider, as "the only living male writer of first-class literary gifts to have transcended the sexual myths of our era."

Millett's work produced a storm of protest, notably from Norman Mailer himself. Some feminists were also unsure. But in her attack on patriarchy masquerading as nature and its insidious effects on modern society, Millett produced a key feminist text that contributed to the second wave of feminism during the 1970s. It continues to influence feminist thinking today. **SA**

Biblical Canonical Criticism
Brevard Childs

Study of the Judeo-Christian scriptures, focusing on the text of the biblical canon

Biblical canonical criticism attempts to reconcile historical and sociological approaches to biblical criticism, approaching the Bible as a theologically valid document and examining the canonical presentation of biblical books and the theological implications of their final form. It is the shape of the scriptures that is important, rather than their content. Canonical criticism refutes the notion that the intention of the author is available and suggests that the text itself, and its position in the canon, is the only source of meaning.

Canonical criticism was pioneered by U.S. theologian Brevard Childs (1923–2007) in *Biblical Theology in Crisis* (1970), which focused on the text of the biblical canon as a finished product. Childs regarded biblical text as a witness to God and Jesus, rather than

" ... the emphasis should fall on the effect which the layering of tradition has had ... "
Brevard Childs

merely a source. The U.S. academic James A. Sanders (b. 1927) coined the term "canonical criticism" in his book *Torah and Canon* (1972), in which he examined why the Torah ends with Deuteronomy rather than Joshua, suggesting that its final canonical shape reinterprets Israel's story regarding the fulfillment of the idea of the Promised Land. Childs repudiated the term because he felt it described his approach as a historical-critical technique, rather than as a method of reading the Bible as sacred scripture.

Canonical criticism has spread via the work of scholars such as David S. Dockery (b. 1952). Critics argue that the shape of the canon has changed throughout history, so how can scholars decide which one should be used, and how can they be sure that the placing of the books of the Bible is part of its message. **CK**

Postmodern Music

Various

A genre of music that embraces the absence of one defining structure or ideology, as part of a general reaction to modernism and its scientific approach to artistic creation

⬆ John Zorn performs at a concert in 2000. Zorn's compositions, which juxtapose different styles and genres, have been described as "a sort of musical channel-surfing."

"Much of what might be called postmodern music requires of its listeners a certain theoretical sophistication and historical memory."

Linda Hutcheon, *The Politics of Postmodernism* (1989)

The term "postmodern" was used sporadically in the late nineteenth century, but did not receive today's meaning in the arts until architect Joseph Hudnut's essay "The Post-Modern House" (1945), in which he regretted some aspects of modern architecture and industrialized manufacturing techniques. As he argued, "We must remind ourselves that techniques have a strictly limited value as elements of expression." Hudnut instead advocated a spiritual and individualized approach to design and construction, and a harmonious architecture achieved with the help of arts. This understanding of postmodernism as an antithesis of modernism, the perceived science-driven approach to art, would later be complemented by a decentralized and value-relativistic understanding of histories and cultures, and increased skepticism toward technical and economic progress. Postmodernism made its way into musical discourses in the 1970s, as composers such as George Rochberg (1918–2005) and Alfred Schnittke (1934–98) embraced pluralistic approaches, incorporating stylistic elements or direct quotations from the past. Humor, considered antithetical to serious modernism, also became important, as did beauty and naiveté. Other approaches include those of composer and performer John Zorn's (*b.* 1953) genre juxtapositions, in which elements of jazz, pop, art music, and film music are contrasted, resulting in a funny and chaotic effect.

The "postmodern" label has also been applied retroactively to composers such as Gustav Mahler (1860–1911), thus casting the concept not as a late-twentieth-century musical style, but as an aesthetic approach to tradition. Postmodern works also raise the question of what constitutes modern music: could not works assembled from historical sources sound as new as a modernist work created through mathematical models? **PB**

Codependency
United States

The dependence on the needs of or control of another

Codependency, a psychological term that first came to prominence in the U.S. state of Minnesota in the 1970s, was originally coined to describe the unhealthy dynamics observed between spouses and family members who are either alcoholic or substance-dependent. Not easy to define, codependency often suffers from having as many definitions as there are experts capable of defining it. Broad in its implications, it was initially viewed as a personality characterized by low self-esteem, intense anxiety in interpersonal relationships, a tendency to go out of one's way to please others even when it means sacrificing one's own needs, possessing poorly-defined boundaries, a fear of being abandoned, and having difficulty in communicating feelings and needs. It has, in recent times, grown to include almost anyone with a pattern of dysfunctional relationships in which the needs of others have taken pre-eminence over the needs of the self. Even addictions are now increasingly being seen as having their roots in codependency, a trend that has led to claims that codependency is in fact the most widespread addiction ever faced by Western culture.

Inherent weaknesses in the psychology of codependent sufferers mean that those diagnosed often find themselves in harmful relationships, often with controlling and manipulative people, making the opportunities for seeking treatment difficult. Codependency is a progressive disorder that quickly can become habitual and does not go away easily. Group therapy, rather than self-help and individual psychotherapy, has statistically been proven to be the most effective recourse, hinging on the identification of failed coping strategies that have frequently persisted since childhood. A sad commentary on the condition can be seen in the joke: "When a codependent dies, someone else's life flashes before their eyes." **BS**

Recycling
United States

The reprocessing of discarded material for reuse

Human beings have recycled ever since they first manufactured tools, but the modern practice of recycling is associated with the first Earth Day—held in the United States on April 22, 1970—which prompted a movement that established thousands of community recycling centers in the United States and elsewhere.

The potential advantages of recycling are both economic and environmental, although it is not always easy to conduct a cost/benefit analysis. It is generally cheaper to reprocess discarded material than to process new material, but the costs of collecting and sorting recyclables are not negligible. Similarly, although recycling reduces the environmental impact of landfills and incineration, the collection and transport of recyclables contributes to air pollution, and

> "Recycling is a good thing to do. It makes people feel good to do it."
> Barry Commoner, biologist and educator

toxic recyclables can affect the health of people near recycling sites. Regulation at both the manufacturing and the consumption ends of production can improve the efficiency of recycling: for example, when manufacturers are required to use easily recyclable containers and packaging and when consumers are required to sort their recyclables prior to collection.

Recycling is already popular, both with the public and with government and industry. With a growing, urban and industrial world population, recycling will be increasingly important, although it is already feared that it will not be sufficient and that a shift to a closed-loop approach, in which every component of a manufactured product is either recyclable or biodegradable—or a comprehensive shift away from a consumer society—will be needed. **GB**

Breakdancing
Afrika Bambaataa

An energetic and acrobatic style of street dancing

Also known as "breaking," "b-boying," and "b-girling," breakdancing is a form of dance performed to hip-hop music. Breaking consists of several elements: toprock dance steps; downrock, in which a dancer uses their hands for support as well as their feet; power moves, involving acrobatic actions like a head spin; stylish poses to a strong beat in the music called "freezes"; and suicides, whereby a dancer holds a freeze to mark the end of a routine, perhaps by falling to the floor.

Hip-hop culture originated in the Bronx in New York in c. 1970. It was spearheaded by the DJs Afrika Bambaataa (b. 1957), Kool Herc (b. 1955), and Kool Moe Dee (b. 1962), who pioneered breakbeat deejaying. Bambaataa encouraged rival gangs among the African American and Latino communities to challenge each

"When I first learned about the dance in '77 it was called b-boying . . ."
Richard "Crazy Legs" Colón, *The Freshest Kids* (2002)

other to dance using acrobatic movements, back flips, and spins, rather than compete against one another by violent means. Bambaataa persuaded young men to leave gang culture behind—instead they became hip-hop aficionados and performed breakdance moves to the music at clubs and in the street.

By the 1980s, hip-hop had entered the mainstream and with it breakdancing, partly thanks to the success of the pioneering breakdancing group Rock Steady Crew. Pop star Michael Jackson incorporated breakdancing into his dance routines and one hundred breakdancers performed at the closing ceremony of the Summer Olympic Games at Los Angeles in 1984. From there, breakdancing spread to Europe, Asia, and Latin America, and it is still a popular form of street dance today. **CK**

The Original Position
John Rawls

A theory of justice that promotes fairness in lawmaking

The idea that laws result from a social contract between consenting citizens and their government dates back to the *Leviathan* of English philosopher Thomas Hobbes, published in 1651. It was U.S. philosopher John Rawls (1921–2002) who, in his book *A Theory of Justice* (1971), amended the thesis to include the idea of fairness.

A basic social contract requires individuals to consent to be governed because the collective benefits gained by that arrangement exceed the individual freedoms lost. But is that contract fair to all individuals? Might not some people coerce others into agreeing because they are stronger? Rawls thought they could, and that laws might be drawn up that were irrational or partial in their effects. He therefore proposed that such a contract be drawn up in what he called the original

"The original position is . . . a status quo in which any agreements reached are fair."
John Rawls, *A Theory of Justice* (1971)

position. In this hypothetical position, the negotiators of the contract operate behind "a veil of ignorance," having no information about the people they are negotiating for. They do not know, for example, what age they are, or gender, or ethnicity, or, crucially, what "conception of the good" each individual has to lead a good life. Behind this veil, the negotiators would then act rationally and impartially to determine two main principles of justice on which the new society would be based. Each citizen would enjoy the same basic liberties while, using the so-called "maximin" rule—maximizing the minimum—social and economic inequalities would be addressed to the benefit of the least advantaged. With his theory, Rawls created a benchmark of fairness against which to test our laws. The implications of "justice as fairness" are considerable. **SA**

6-febrero
2000

trazos
de historia
héroes y Mártires

13-10-2002

STRUCTURAS DE INJUSTICIA SOCIAL, SON LA
LENTA A NUESTROS POBRES." M

Liberation Theology
Gustavo Gutiérrez

A radical Christian response to poverty, oppression, and injustice

Faced with the social injustices they saw in their parishes, a number of Latin American Roman Catholic priests and theologians responded by developing a new interpretation of the teachings of Christ. Prominent among them was the Peruvian priest Gustavo Gutiérrez (b. 1928), whose book, *A Theology of Liberation* (1971), gave the movement its name.

Latin America in the 1950s and 1960s was a continent disfigured by military dictatorship, gross inequality, and extreme poverty. Formed in 1955, the Latin American Episcopal Conference of Bishops pushed the Roman Catholic Church to be more socially concerned, holding two major conferences to promote their ideas. Priests and theologians began to develop a new, liberation theology that was based on two principles. First, it

"[The] meaning of liberation is … a question about the very meaning of Christianity …"

Gustavo Gutiérrez, *A Theology of Liberation* (1971)

recognized the need for liberation from all forms of oppression, be they political, economic, social, racial, or sexual. Second, this new theology should grow out of the communities it represented, not be imposed by the Church from above. Solidarity with the poor would transform society, so every aspect of the Church and its teachings would be viewed from the angle of the poor.

In its portrayal of Christ as a political figure, liberation theology came under attack from conservatives within the Catholic Church. In 1979 Pope John Paul II cautioned against seeing Christ as a revolutionary, while in 1983 the Congregation for the Doctrine of the Faith criticized the theology as Marxist. Its main leaders ignored such criticisms, although at some cost. In 1980, the El Salvador archbishop Oscar Romero was assassinated while saying mass in a hospice. **SA**

Desert Versus Merit
John Rawls

The debate over what constitutes a fair basis for distributing rewards

The argument for distribution according to "desert" relies on thinking that distribution according to "merit" would involve injustice. It appeals to the notion that just distributions cannot be based on factors over which the recipients have no control. According to U.S. philosopher John Rawls (1921–2002), in his work *A Theory of Justice* (1971), the distribution of benefits according to race or gender, for example, seems unjust since neither factor is within a person's control. But what if the alleged bases for desert are also largely outside of a person's control? It would seem to follow that distributions based on guaranteed success are also unjust.

Claiming that individuals should be rewarded for factors under their control, but not for factors outside their control, Louis Pojman (1935–2005) argued that

"Justice is a constant and perpetual will to give every man his due."

Louis Pojman, "Equality and Desert" (1997)

desert is a species of merit that entails responsibility. According to this argument, individuals are free to choose their effort and thus may be held responsible for this choice, and so, on these grounds, should be rewarded for the strength of that effort. The position assumes that effort is within individual control and talent is beyond it, and that "effort" is clearly distinguishable from other factors and is measurable.

Joel Feinberg (1926–2004) called such meritorious qualities as intelligence, native athletic ability, and good upbringing "the bases of desert," meaning that while we may not deserve these traits, they can form the basis for reward. That is, while you may not deserve your superior intelligence or tendency to work hard, you do deserve the high grade on your essay, which is a product of your intelligence and effort. **JP**

◄ A mural of liberation theologist Oscar Romero in Suchitoto, El Salvador.

Gaia Hypothesis

James Lovelock

A new view of Earth and how conditions for life are sustained

⬆ James Lovelock stands in front of a statue of the Greek goddess of the Earth, Gaia, after whom his well-known theory is named, in August 1980.

It is generally always assumed that Earth is a solid object on which life flourishes. But what if Earth itself is alive, an organism in its own right? Such an insight occurred to James Lovelock (b. 1919), an independent British scientist, while looking for life somewhat farther afield.

In September 1965 Lovelock was working at the Jet Propulsion Laboratory in California on methods for detecting life on Mars, when he suddenly realized that there was no need to visit the planet to find the answer. Since life on Earth is responsible for its atmosphere, investigating the Martian atmosphere—or lack of it—through an infrared telescope would determine whether there was indeed life on the Red Planet. From this understanding, emerged the idea of Earth as a "living planet" and, in 1972, Lovelock's hypothesis that Earth is a single and self-regulating organism capable of maintaining life. The hypothesis—named Gaia after the ancient Greek personification of Earth (suggested by Lovelock's then neighbor, the novelist William Golding)—proposes that Earth is controlled by its community of interacting, living organisms in a self-regulating system. It looks after itself through the evolution of its biosphere, atmosphere, hydrosphere, and pedosphere. This system regulates salinity in the oceans and oxygen in the atmosphere. It achieves an environment that is optimal for life and is changed by that life. That does not mean that Gaia will necessarily look after and support human life. To the contrary, "Gaia will look after herself. And the best way for her to do that might well be to get rid of us," Lovelock warned in 1987.

From this hypothesis derives an entire philosophy of Earth as a living planet that has profound implications for the environment and the future of life itself. The full implications of this revolutionary hypothesis have yet to be explored. **SA**

"The Earth System behaves as a single, self-regulating system with physical, chemical, biological, and human components."

The Amsterdam Declaration of the International Humanist and Ethical Union (2001)

Gene Therapy
Theodore Friedmann and Richard Roblin

The use of DNA as a pharmaceutical agent to treat disease

Gene therapy is the treatment of diseases or disorders, especially those caused by genetic abnormalities, by the manipulation of genetic material. The term first came into wide use in the late 1960s and early 1970s, as various researchers began to investigate the possibility of altering DNA to treat disease. In 1972, Theodore Friedmann and Richard Roblin wrote an influential article titled "Gene Therapy for Human Genetic Disease?", which lay out the various technical and ethical challenges to be overcome before gene therapy could be considered a workable option for treating human disease.

The foundations for gene therapy were laid in the 1960s, as researchers began to make progress in understanding how genetic material, such as DNA and RNA, functioned at a molecular level. The idea that manipulating genetic material could cure disease was a natural one, and, by the time Friedmann and Roblin were writing in 1972, specific "vectors," such as the use of viruses with altered DNA, for changing a patient's DNA had already been proposed. Friedmann and Roblin argued that gene therapy would not be viable until researchers could describe with precision the effects of changing DNA in specific ways, and could develop vectors for doing this. The first experimental gene therapy treatment was approved by the U.S. Food and Drug Administration in 1990, for Ashanti DeSilva, a four-year-old suffering from an immune disorder.

Gene therapy has considerable promise for treating conditions such as cancer, cardiovascular disease, and autoimmune disorders. So far, however, it has been largely constrained to experimental trials, and has not yet led to the creation of widely available drugs or treatments. This may well change soon, as researchers continue to make progress toward developing safe, efficient, and reliable vectors for delivering gene therapy. **BSh**

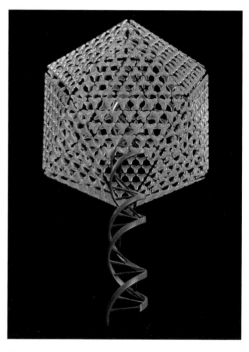

⬆ A computer artwork of a strand of DNA (deoxyribonucleic acid, red) being carried by a virus (blue), illustrating the concept of gene therapy using viruses.

"[We] feel that the irreversible and heritable nature of gene therapy means that the tolerable margin of risk and uncertainty in such therapy is reduced."

Theodore Friedmann and Richard Roblin, "Gene Therapy for Human Genetic Disease?" (1972)

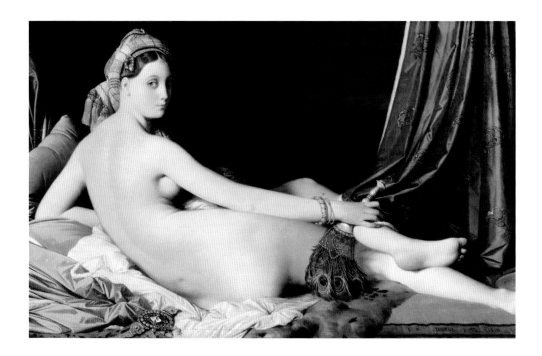

1972

Ways of Seeing
John Berger

A study of the hidden ideologies that affect how we view art

When we look at an old master painting, what is it we actually see? Are we looking at and understanding some classical scene or female nude, or are we viewing the painting through modern eyes? If the latter, what difference does that make? In John Berger's (b. 1926) view, it mattered greatly. In his four-part BBC television series *Ways of Seeing*, created with producer Mike Dibb (b. 1940) and first broadcast in 1972, and then in the succeeding book of the same name, he argued cogently that hidden ideologies affect how we view art.

John Berger is an English novelist and critic whose Marxist humanism informs his work: when he won the Booker Prize in 1972 for his novel *G.*, he donated half his winnings to the Black Panther Party. The ideas behind *Ways of Seeing* came from Walter Benjamin's (1892–1940) essay "The Work of Art in the Age of Mechanical Reproduction," published in 1936. Benjamin described a theory of art that would be "useful for the formulation of revolutionary demands in the politics of art," that art in the age of mechanical reproduction should be based on how politics was practiced. Berger agreed, arguing in the first program that constant reproduction of old masters has severed them from the context in which they were created. In discussing the female nude, he argued that only twenty or thirty such paintings depicted the woman herself, as opposed to a subject of male desire or idealization. He considered that the use of oil paint reflected the status of the patron who commissioned the painting and argued that color photography had taken over the role of painting.

Berger was deliberately polemical but his impact has been enormous. In criticizing traditional Western aesthetics he opened the door to feminist and other critics who read paintings with regard to the present day, rather than the purposes for which they were originally produced. **SA**

The Grande Odalisque (1814) by Ingres was used by Berger to examine the portrayal of women in art. ⬆

Gross National Happiness
King Jigme Singye Wangchuck

A holistic approach to assessing a country's social and economic progress

Gross national happiness is a nonquantitative measure of the overall quality of life of a nation's citizens that takes into account both economic and noneconomic criteria. All other things being equal, a nation with a high gross national happiness is more "developed" than a nation with a low gross national happiness. The concept was first articulated in 1972 by the king of Bhutan, Jigme Singye Wangchuck (b. 1955), and the government of Bhutan has used it ever since to assess their citizens' wellbeing and to analyze the effects of government policies.

The concept of gross national happiness was developed in response to the perceived shortcomings of purely economic measures of development, such as gross domestic product (GDP). In addition to economic criteria, a country's gross national happiness depends on factors such as the conservation of cultural heritage, equitable development, fair governance, and preservation of the natural environment. Proponents of gross national happiness often point out that once citizens' basic needs are met, further increases in income make relatively small differences to how happy citizens are. Moreover, there are certain ways of increasing GDP (such as exploiting natural resources) that may actually leave citizens worse off, and thus decrease gross national happiness.

The basic intuition behind gross national happiness—that wellbeing involves more than economic success, and that GDP is (at least by itself) an inadequate measure of citizens' quality of life—has seen increasing acceptance in recent years, especially among those interested in promoting sustainable development. More quantitative measures of wellbeing, such as the Index of Sustainable Economic Welfare (ISEW) and the Genuine Progress Indicator (GPI), can be seen as variations on this same basic idea. **BSh**

↑ King Jigme Singye Wangchuck of Bhutan (center) and attendants, pictured in 1976.

Punctuated Equilibrium
Niles Eldredge and Stephen Jay Gould

The theory that species evolve though periods of rapid change in between long periods of limited or no change

"Two outstanding facts of the fossil record —geologically 'sudden' origin of new species and failure to change thereafter (stasis)—reflect the predictions of evolutionary theory, not the imperfections of the fossil record."

Stephen Jay Gould

Species do not evolve through regular changes that occur gradually over time, according to the theory of punctuated equilibrium, but rather they arise through periodic episodes of rapid change. Those rapid interludes of change can arise for a variety of different reasons, but reactions to sudden changes in the environment or drastically advantageous mutations that naturally grant a species a significant edge are common causes.

Ever since Charles Darwin published *On the Origin of Species* in 1859, modern biology has largely been predicated on the theory that species gradually change over time. However, in 1972, U.S. paleontologists Niles Eldredge (b. 1943) and Stephen Jay Gould (1941–2002) published a paper titled "Punctuated equilibria: an alternative to phyletic gradualism," in which they proposed that the gradual model was incorrect, or at least incomplete. The two argued that the fossil record did not support the gradual change view, but instead showed that species tend to remain in the same state, known as stasis, for long periods of time. Evolutionary change occurred only in, geologically speaking, brief flashes of time.

Punctuated equilibrium proposes that at any given point in a species's history there will be little evidence for change. The evidence found in the fossil record has supported this claim, but it has also showed the opposite: that some species evolve gradually. The theory's influence is still somewhat controversial, with some believing it to be the dominant method of evolutionary change, and others believing that it is the exception to the rule of gradual change. Since its introduction, however, punctuated equilibrium has influenced other fields, such as linguistics and geo-political interactions, offering an alternate view to the idea of steady progress and adaptation. **MT**

The Limits to Growth
D. H. Meadows, D. L. Meadows, and others

A prediction of the exhaustion of the Earth's finite resources

It is now commonplace to discuss the world's waning natural resources—the fact that the Earth is running out of oil, rare minerals, and even water, for example. A mere forty or so years ago, such an idea was unthinkable, as economic growth was assumed to be inexorable. This change in thinking is due largely to *The Limits to Growth* (1972), a piece of work commissioned by the Club of Rome global economic think tank. With its detailed computer modeling, mathematical formulas, and dry text, *The Limits to Growth* made the apocalyptic statement that unchecked economic and population growth was harming the planet.

The authors of the book devised a computer model known as World3, which simulated the consequences of interactions between the Earth's resources and human exploitation. Five main variables were examined, covering world population, food production, industrialization, depletion of resources, and pollution. The model assumed that growth would be exponential but that the ability of technology to increase the availability of resources grew only linearly. Altering the growth trends in the five variables under three different scenarios produced an "overshoot and collapse" of the global economic system by the mid- to late twenty-first century in the first two scenarios, while the third resulted in a stabilized world.

Needless to say, the report attracted great interest and much criticism. Many economists attacked its methodology and rhetoric, arguing that technology could solve all problems providing growth continued. If it stopped, billions would be consigned to perpetual poverty. Yet twenty- and thirty-year updates by the original authors have confirmed their predictions, while others analyses carried out in Australia and elsewhere confirm the original report. There are indeed limits to growth. **SA**

Anthropic Principle
Brandon Carter

Observations of the universe must be compatible with the life-forms that observe it

The anthropic principle holds that the existence of intelligent observers, such as humans, provides evidence for physical facts about the universe, such as the precise values of the fundamental forces and the distribution of mass and energy. The concept was first posited by physicist Brandon Carter (*b.* 1942) in 1973.

Carter proposed the anthropic principle as a response to the "Copernican Principle," which states that the Earth (and the humans that live on it) does not occupy a privileged place in the universe. While he agreed with this principle, he noted that the existence of observers is privileged in a different sense: trivially, observers should always expect to find that the universe they observe is compatible with their own existence. Carter called this the weak anthropic

"I prefer to work with the simplest hypothesis compatible with the observational evidence."
Brandon Carter

principle. He also formulated, but did not endorse, a strong anthropic principle according to which the universe itself must be structured so as to admit the existence of intelligent observers.

Scientists and philosophers have applied versions of the anthropic principle to a variety of problems. For example, the principle is often brought up in discussions of "fine tuning" arguments for God's existence. Proponents of these arguments claim that the orderly nature of the universe, and the existence of intelligent life that this order allows, provides evidence of God's existence. In response, some critics have claimed that the weak anthropic principle can explain the orderly nature of the world equally well—if the universe were not "orderly," intelligent observers would simply not exist. **BSh**

Small Is Beautiful
E. F. Schumacher

An argument advocating a change of scale in economic activity

Small Is Beautiful: A Study of Economics as if People Mattered (1973) is a collection of essays by British economist E. F. Schumacher (1911–77). In the book, Schumacher criticizes several tenets of conventional economic thinking, particularly the assumption that increased economic productivity will increase human welfare.

Schumacher wrote *Small Is Beautiful* in response to what he felt was a false but widespread view: namely, that the best way to address problems such as poverty, starvation, and war was to increase the amount of goods and services that were being produced. Schumacher emphasized the frequently ignored "costs" of increased economic productivity, such as the consumption of finite natural resources, the pollution of the environment, and the happiness of workers

> "... if we squander the capital represented by living nature ... we threaten life itself."

E. F. Schumacher, *Small Is Beautiful* (1973)

who are made redundant by the deployment of advanced technology. As an alternative to maximizing productivity, Schumacher argued that we ought to focus our efforts on lowering consumption and on developing so-called "intermediate technology," which allows people (especially in developing countries) the opportunity to engage in meaningful work.

Schumacher's arguments in *Small Is Beautiful* have proved to be enormously influential, especially in relation to sustainable development, environmental ethics, and organizational theory. In particular, many scholars and policy makers have been influenced by his contention that things such as fossil fuels, the environment's tolerance for pollution, and workers' wellbeing are properly viewed as capital to be preserved, and should not be treated as income to be spent. **BSh**

Strong Force
D. Gross, F. Wilczek, and D. Politzer

A radical insight into the force that binds the smallest particles of matter

The four fundamental forces of physics are gravity, electromagnetism, and the weak and strong forces. The first two were discovered ahead of the others because they can be readily seen at work in the visible world; strong (like weak) force operates at a subatomic level, and was not known about until the twentieth century.

Scientists began hypothesizing the presence of a strong force in the mid-1930s, when they learned that atoms are made up of electrons orbiting a nucleus of protons and neutrons. Theorizing that electromagnetic repulsion between the protons should blow the nucleus apart, they posited the existence of another force many times stronger than electromagnetism to glue the nucleus together. In the 1960s, with the discovery of quarks (the subatomic particles that make

> "... without [strong force] every atom in the universe would spontaneously explode..."

David Evans, physicist

up the protons and neutrons), the argument shifted to how quarks stick together. In 1973, David Gross (b. 1941), Frank Wilczek (b. 1951), and David Politzer (b. 1949) published two papers solving a key part of the mystery. They realized that, unlike other forces, strong force appears to become stronger with distance; the force between two quarks in close proximity is so weak that they behave as if they are free particles, but as they move apart the force between them increases as if they are connected by an elastic band. The team won the Nobel Prize for Physics for this discovery in 2004.

Strong force may only act within a minuscule space, but it is now understood to be the most powerful of all forces. In fact, at these distances, scientists calculate that it is one hundred times greater than the next strongest force, electromagnetism. **JH**

An image of a three-jet event, which provides evidence of gluons, the carrier particles of strong force. ➡

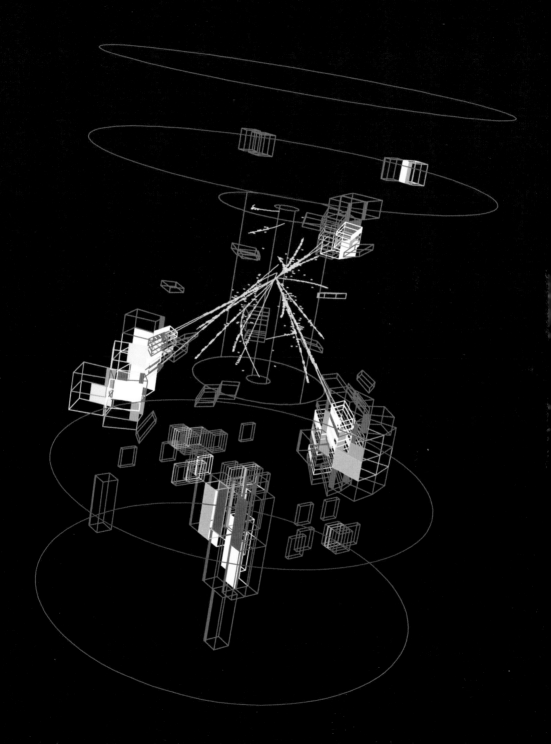

Stockholm Syndrome
Nils Bejerot

The tendency of a captive to identify with, bond, or sympathize with their captor

Stockholm syndrome (also known as terror bonding or traumatic bonding) is a complex psychological reaction experienced by persons in frightening situations. It has been identified in hostages, survivors of World War II concentration camps, members of religious cults, battered wives, and abused children. The term takes its name from a bank robbery that took place in Sweden in August 1973; robbers took three bank employees hostage for 131 hours. After their release, the employees seemed to have formed a paradoxical emotional bond with their captors. When freed, the victims hugged and kissed their captors and declared their loyalty to the kidnappers. The syndrome was named by Nils Bejerot (1921–88), who served as a psychiatric consultant to the Swedish police during the hostage standoff.

"It's hard to hate someone once you understand them."

Lucy Christopher, *Stolen: A Letter to My Captor* (2009)

There are no widely accepted diagnostic criteria for the Stockholm syndrome. When newspaper heiress Patty Hearst was abducted by the radical political group, the Symbionese Liberation Army (SLA), in 1974, she became their accomplice, adopted an assumed name, and abetted the SLA in a bank robbery. However, an FBI report has termed such close victim-captor relationships "over-emphasized, over-analyzed, over-psychologized, and over-publicized."

Study of Stockholm syndrome has influenced how law enforcement agencies handle hostage situations; crisis negotiators may try to encourage captor-hostage bonding by telling perpetrators about the victims' families or personal lives. Being viewed as a fellow human being, the theory holds, may be a victim's best hope for staying alive. **BC**

CCTV for Crime Prevention
United Kingdom and the United States

The use of cameras to produce images and recordings for crime surveillance purposes

Closed-circuit television (CCTV) works by sending a television signal to a limited number of predetermined monitors. A CCTV signal may be monitored by an onsite or remotely located security guard or police agency, or it may simply be recorded. CCTV is most commonly used to monitor high crime areas, such as parking lots, retail shops, airport terminals, and city centers.

The CCTV concept dates back to the 1930s, and by the 1950s it was being used to observe dangerous experiments, to deliver remote lectures, and to view live sporting events. However, it was not widely employed in crime prevention until the 1970s, when improved technology and reduced costs made it practical to deploy the technology on a large scale. In 1973, the British Home Office published an influential

"You [are] watched by a 'Teletector Synchroscan,' a caged [CCTV] camera."

Jack Rosenthal, *Life* magazine (July 11, 1969)

report that considered the possible benefits and drawbacks of CCTV as a deterrent against retail theft. In the years since this report, CCTV for crime prevention has been widely deployed in both the United Kingdom and other countries.

Advocates of CCTV argue that it is an effective method of situational crime prevention, insofar as it prevents crime by changing the physical environment. While studies have shown that CCTV is effective at reducing crime in certain contexts, some critics have alleged that it merely relocates crime, but does not prevent it. Others have argued that the widespread use of CCTV violates the privacy of those it records. The use of CCTV for crime prevention is likely to continue, especially if new technologies (such as facial recognition software) increase its effectiveness. **BSh**

◀ Patty Hearst, who joined the left-wing guerrilla group that kidnapped her, in a photograph from 1974.

Neoconservatism

Michael Harrington

A U.S. political ideology that merges traditional conservatism with political individualism

⬆ Jeane Kirkpatrick, an advocate of neoconservative foreign policy, speaking on U.S. television in 2003. As U.N. ambassador she played a prominent role in the Reagan administration.

The term "neoconservative" was first used in 1973 by U.S. democratic socialist leader and political theorist Michael Harrington (1928–89) to describe a group of former left-wing liberals who had adopted a variety of politically conservative views. The term has also been used to describe the variety of conservative thought defended by these thinkers, especially as it relates to foreign policy.

Some of the thinkers identified by Harrington as neoconservatives included the editor and journalist Irving Kristol, the sociologists Nathan Glazer and Daniel Bell, and the Democratic politician Daniel Patrick Moynihan. While these thinkers shared many of the values of the "New Left" of the 1960s, they differed in two significant ways. First, they advocated an interventionist U.S. foreign policy aimed at containing communism and promoting democracy. Second, they argued that the policies favored by the New Left (such as affirmative action, welfare, and changes to education policy) were unlikely to achieve their stated goals, and would instead have significant negative side effects. These commitments led some, but not all, of the neoconservatives to leave the Democratic Party and join the Republican Party.

Today, the term "neoconservative" is generally used to describe conservatives, such as author Charles Krauthammer and former Deputy Secretary of Defense Paul Wolfowitz, who advocate interventionist foreign policies aimed at promoting democracy. Neoconservativism is closely associated with ideas such as democratic peace theory, which holds that democracies will rarely or never go to war with each other, and with the thought of political philosopher Leo Strauss, who argued that the success of Western political institutions (such as representative democracy) depended crucially on many other aspects of Western culture. **BSh**

> *"[A neoconservative is a] liberal who has been mugged by reality."*
>
> Irving Kristol, journalist

Global Positioning System

Bradford Parkinson

A global navigation system using satellites to determine location, speed, and time

The Global Positioning System (GPS) is a global navigation system that uses Earth-orbiting satellites to determine location, speed, and time. The system consists of three segments: the space segment is the group of satellites themselves; the control segment involves ground-based tracking stations; and the user segment encompasses all those who use the system and the devices that receive the satellite signals. The abbreviation GPS is commonly used to refer to these receivers themselves, as they have become a standard feature in cell phones and cars. While the development of GPS was a collaborative effort, it was conceived by aeronautical engineer and U.S. Air Force officer Bradford Parkinson (b. 1935) in 1973.

The concept of a satellite navigation system emerged from a similar ground-based system that used radio signals between beacons to determine the position of ships and aircraft. Developed in the 1940s, many of these systems were used for military purposes, and the GPS was originally conceived as a missile guidance system. The first satellite was launched in 1978 and experimental military use of the system continued as more and more satellites were added. Put to major use during the Gulf War in 1990 to 1991, the system became fully operational in 1995 and was opened to civilian use the following year.

The GPS began with a constellation of twenty-four satellites, but by 2012 upgrades and expansions had taken that number to thirty-two. As these developments have improved the system's accuracy, its military applications have also expanded to enhance the performance of precision-guided weapons and to locate and monitor troop movements. The system's capacity to determine precise locations has been an invaluable aid for police and emergency services, and this extraordinary accuracy has made the GPS an indispensable asset that has many other applications. **TJ**

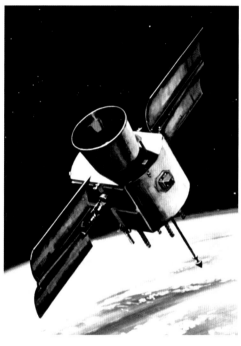

⬆ An artist's illustration of a Global Positioning System satellite in space. The user's position is worked out by calculating the time it takes for radio signals to reach the receiver from the satellite.

". . . anyone, anywhere in the world, can almost instantaneously determine his or her location in three dimensions to about the width of a street."

Bradford Parkinson

What Is it Like to Be a Bat?
Thomas Nagel

Another being's mental state can only be understood by experiencing it

According to philosopher Thomas Nagel (b. 1937), even if we can objectively describe all the physical qualities of existence, such as how a bat uses sonar, we will never be able to completely understand how it feels for the bat to be a bat because we are not bats. What is it like to be a bat? We can never truly know, because consciousness is more than just the physical process of sensation.

Nagel published his paper "What is it like to be a bat?" in 1974, largely in response to what he termed the "reductionist euphoria" that was dominant in the field at the time. Nagel offered his bat argument as a counter to the reductionist position that all mental phenomena, such as consciousness, could be explained in purely physical terms. Bats are so foreign

"... if I try to imagine this, I am restricted to the resources of my own mind ..."

Thomas Nagel, "What is it like to be a bat?" (1974)

to a human's experience, Nagel argued, that it is impossible for us to understand their concept of the world. Even with our grasp of the physical reality, our understanding of their personal reality is necessarily compromised if we lack first-hand experience of what it is to live as a bat lives.

Nagel's question gets to the heart of the experiential, subjective nature of consciousness, even if it is one that we can never really answer. For someone who has been completely blind since birth, does the word "color" have the same meaning as it does to the person who sees? How could it? And how could a person with sight ever understand what it is like to have always been without it? For Nagel, it is impossible, or nearly so, and is the reason why consciousness is more than an objective understanding. **MT**

Lifeboat Earth
Garrett Hardin

Rich nations should not risk their own safety by giving their finite resources to poor ones

Assume, for a moment, that after a terrible nautical calamity you and a small group of survivors have found yourself on a lifeboat in the middle of the ocean. Around you, in the water, are hundreds of other survivors begging to be let aboard. If you allow too many survivors onto your lifeboat, it will capsize and sink, dooming everyone. Do you allow any more people on? How many? And how do you choose who lives and who dies? Now imagine that the lifeboat is our planet, the people in the water are poor, developing nations, and the people in the lifeboat are rich nations. According to U.S. ecologist Garrett Hardin (1915–2003), this is why rich nations should not help poor nations.

The "lifeboat Earth" argument first appeared in Hardin's essay titled "Lifeboat Ethics: the Case

"Ruin is the destination toward which all men rush ..."

Garrett Hardin, "The Tragedy of the Commons" (1968)

Against Helping the Poor" (1974). He wrote it, in part, to counter the popularized notion that the Earth was a spaceship whose inhabitants relied upon it entirely for their survival. Those inhabitants, according to the "spaceship Earth" argument, had an equal duty to share and protect the ship. Hardin disagreed. The Earth was not a spaceship, he said, but a group of nations. Some nations possessed many resources while others had few, and the wealthy have no duty to assist the poor.

Hardin's essay puts everything from ethics to ecology, economics, and geo-politics under a stark canopy that has gained both critics and supporters. In its calculations, lifeboat Earth says that humans are not, by nature or effect, intrinsically equal. Some lives are worth more than others, and allowing everyone a chance at living merely guarantees a quicker end for all. **MT**

◄ Two fruit bats. According to Thomas Nagel, we will never be able to comprehend their experience of life.

The Standard Model of Particle Physics

Sheldon Glashow and Murray Gell-Mann

A comprehensive theory that attempts to explain and predict the interactions
of fundamental subatomic particles

⬆ Sheldon Glashow and Mohammad Abdus Salam, pictured
shortly before receiving the Nobel Prize for Physics 1979. They
were honored for their work on electroweak theory.

*". . . new particles were being found that
didn't seem to fit into any well-recognized
pattern, and one had no idea of what
was going on until the concept of the
standard model developed."*

Sheldon Glashow

What is the universe made of? The discovery of a single, unified theory of everything that answers that question is the ultimate goal of theoretical physics. So far, however, it has proved impossible to find one that accounts for the behavior of gravity. Nonetheless, since the 1970s, a theory that explains everything else has evolved: the Standard Model of Particle Physics.

The term "Standard Model" was first used at a conference in 1974 to summarize the combined research of many physicists. However, the model itself developed as a unification of the electroweak theory of Sheldon Glashow (b. 1932) and the strong nuclear force theory of quantum chromodynamics, which was pioneered by Murray Gell-Mann (b. 1929).

According to the Standard Model, all physical phenomena can ultimately be reduced to the interactions of two types of subatomic particles—quarks and leptons (both of which have six different varieties). These interactions are governed by three of the four fundamental forces of nature: the strong nuclear force, the weak nuclear force, and electromagnetism. The forces themselves are carried by their own intermediary particles known as bosons. This framework provides an explanation for the behavior of all matter and force in the universe (apart from gravity).

Much of the Standard Model's acceptance is due to the success of its predictions about the intermediary or "force-carrier" particles. While the photon had long been known as the force carrier for electromagnetism, observations later confirmed the model's predictions of the gluon as the particle at work in the strong nuclear force, and the exchange of W and Z bosons in the weak force. In 2012, experiments showed evidence for the existence of the Higgs boson. Although a transient particle, it is crucial to the Standard Model as it provides a means to explain how other particles acquire mass. **TJ**

Genetic Engineering
Rudolf Jaenisch

The manipulation of an organism's genome using biotechnology

Humans have been tampering with the gene pool of animals for thousands of years through the process of selective breeding. However, genetic engineering as we understand it today—the direct intervention and manipulation of DNA—only started in earnest in the 1970s.

Molecular cloning—the bringing together of genetic material from various sources—was first achieved by the U.S. biochemist Paul Berg in 1972, and the first genetically modified organisms were engineered in 1973. However, it was in 1974, when the pioneering biologist Rudolf Jaenisch (b. 1942) injected a DNA virus into a mouse embryo and created the world's first transgenic mammal, that it can be said the "Brave New World" of genetic engineering finally became an actual, physical reality. Genetic engineering was applied to tobacco plants in 1986 to make them resistant to herbicides, and in 1994 tomatoes became the world's first genetically modified crop. Transgenic, genetically modified crops, despite ethical and safety concerns, are now grown in more than thirty countries and are the subject of a vigorous debate between proponents of the new technology and those who designate it "Frankenstein food."

The term "genetic engineering" was actually first used in the science fiction novel *Dragon's Island*, by the U.S. author and "dean of sci-fi" Jack Williamson in 1951. This was just one year prior to the well-known Hershey–Chase experiments by geneticists Alfred Hershey and Martha Chase, which proved DNA to be the conveyor of hereditary genetic material, previously thought to have been carried by proteins. When molecular biologists James D. Watson and Francis Crick gave the world its first glimpse of our DNA's beautiful double-helix structure in 1953, the path to genetic engineering was well and truly defined. **BS**

Infotainment
U.S. broadcasters

News items that might be better classed as human interest stories

A news report gives information. A human interest story, such as a day in the life of a celebrity, provides entertainment. Traditionally, the two were separated in particular sections of a newspaper or on different radio and television programs. Today the distinction is blurred, giving rise to this portmanteau word for any program, website, or feature that contains something of both.

The variant word "infotainment" was first coined in 1974 as the title for a conference of the Intercollegiate Broadcasting System. The popularity of the term attests its usefulness as a description, but there is less certainty about that of the phenomenon it describes. Critics think that infotainment contains too little of the word's first two syllables. For example, in February of 2004 a CNN bulletin led with news of singer Janet Jackson

"Television is increasingly . . . 'infotainment,' not a credible source of information."

Richard Edelman, CEO of Edelman PR company

exposing her breast at the Super Bowl; the second item was the interception of a letter containing ricin addressed to the U.S. Senate majority leader. Defenders of this running order claimed that the nudity was of greater popular interest than a failed assassination; detractors regarded it as "dumbing down," which emphasizes trivial issues and sidelines important ones.

Although newsworthiness is subjective, there are certain criteria that have universal application: a hard news story should be serious and timely; with a soft news story there is no trigger event that demands it be reported immediately. Media analysts debate the merits of infotainment, but now that news is available online, on television, radio, and in print, broadcasters are under unprecedented pressure to catch audiences and hold onto them. **GL**

The Lives of a Cell
Lewis Thomas

The first popular science book suggests that the Earth is best understood as a cell

In *The Lives of a Cell: Notes of a Biology Watcher* (1974), a book written by U.S. immunologist, pathologist, and medical educator Lewis Thomas (1913–93), the author suggests that the Earth is perhaps best understood as a single cell. In a holistic conception of nature, he examines the relationship of the human race to nature and the universe, outlining the complex interdependence of all things. Thomas dismisses the idea of the self as a myth, suggesting that the human race is embedded in nature. He also suggests that society and language behave like organisms.

Furthermore, Thomas proposed that viruses, rather than being "single-minded agents of disease and death" are more like "mobile genes," which have played a key role in the evolution of species because

"I have been trying to think of the Earth as a kind of organism, but it is no go . . ."

Lewis Thomas, *The Lives of a Cell* (1974)

of their ability to move pieces of DNA from one individual, or species, to another.

The idea of the Earth as a single cell was formulated by Thomas in a collection of essays that were first published in the *New England Journal of Medicine*. Thomas's essays provide a basic foundation of biology explained from a philosophical and also a scientific perspective. He wrote in a poetic style that is rich in simile and metaphor, and which makes concepts easy to understand. The volume became a best seller and won a National Book Award in 1975.

The Lives of a Cell spearheaded a genre of writing devoted to popular science. It became a standard text studied in U.S. schools, colleges, and universities, and is still used as a text in contemporary times to help students develop a deeper understanding of biology. **CK**

Male Gaze
Laura Mulvey

A feminist theory analyzing how women can be objectified in visual culture

The feminist theory of the "male gaze" is applied to films, photographs, paintings, and advertisements in order to analyze how women are represented. It was originally conceived solely in regard to Hollywood movies. Film theorist Laura Mulvey (*b.* 1941) coined the term in 1975 in her essay "Visual Pleasure and Narrative Cinema" in the journal *Screen*. Her essay remains one of the most widely cited articles in film theory.

Psychoanalytic theory is instrumental to Mulvey's original concept of the male gaze. Referring to Sigmund Freud's notion of the pleasure involved in looking, or scopophilia, she argued, "In a world ordered by sexual imbalance, pleasure in looking has been split between the active/male and the passive/female. The determining male gaze projects its fantasy

"The gaze is male whenever it directs itself at, and takes pleasure in, women."

Laura Mulvey

onto the female form, which is styled accordingly." In Hollywood, where movies are made by and for men, Mulvey identified two roles for women: erotic object for the characters within the film and erotic object for the audience. Alfred Hitchcock's work was of particular interest because the audience and the film's protagonist are often embroiled in the same scopophilic experience, as she wrote, "In *Vertigo* (1958) . . . in *Marnie* (1964), and *Rear Window* (1954), the 'look' is central to the plot oscillating between voyeurism and fetishistic fascination."

In the early 1970s, feminists called for a revolutionary look at cinema: to turn it from an instrument of male gaze to female gaze. Some felt that the only way to change the way women were represented was to put theory into practice. This led Mulvey and other feminists to make their own movies. **JH**

Director Alfred Hitchcock sneaks a peek on set during the filming of *Vertigo* in 1958. ➡

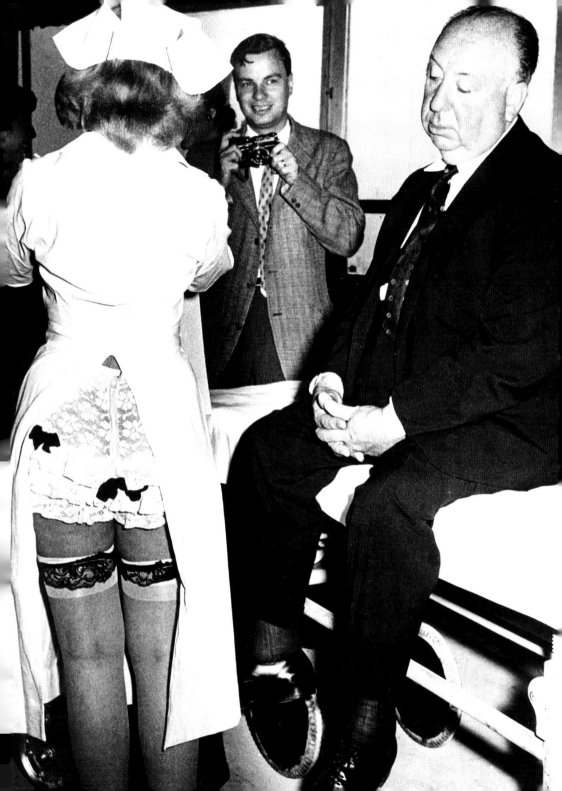

Fractals
Benoit Mandelbrot

Fractals and the concept of self-similarity take us into the world of the very small

⬆ A computer-generated image of a Mandelbrot fractal, derived from a Mandelbrot set—a group of complex numbers plotted using their real and imaginary parts as coordinates.

Difficult to fully explain even for mathematicians, fractals are objects or quantities that are self-similar, with the whole possessing the same shape as one or more of its constituent parts. There are no previously hidden, alternate structures that only appear under extreme magnification; the pattern of the larger object continues to copy itself down to the smallest observable particle—and beyond.

Virtually impossible to detect prior to the advent of the computer, the existence of fractals had been guessed at for centuries by scientists and academics with no means at their disposal to verify their suspicions. In the seventeenth century the German mathematician Gottfried Leibniz was the first to consider the likelihood of self-similarity, and in 1872 another German-born mathematician, Karl Weierstrass, produced his well-known Weierstrass function, a fractal-like graph with detail at every level. It was not until 1975, however, that Polish-born mathematician Benoit Mandelbrot (1924–2010), the father of fractal geometry, first used the word to describe what he called the Mandelbrot set—a collection of points with distinctive boundaries and having an obvious two-dimensional fractal appearance, a known shape but considered little more than a geometric curiosity by his predecessors. Mandelbrot coined the word "fractal" and published his ideas in 1975, which were later translated as *Fractals: Form, Chance, and Dimension* (1977).

Fractals have since appeared in algorithmic art—visual art using designs created from algorithms and made possible with the use of fractal-generating computer software. Not unlike photography, fractal art began as a subclass in the visual arts, but received a boost in its legitimacy when a fractal landscape was chosen for the August 1985 cover of *Scientific American*, which depicted a view of the Mandelbrot set in the form of a heavily inclined, mountainous plateau. **BS**

"If we talk about impact inside mathematics, and applications in the sciences, Mandelbrot is one of the most important figures of the last fifty years."

Heinz-Otto Peitgen, mathematician

Near-death Experience
Raymond Moody

A study of the sensations reported by people who have been on the threshold of death

Near death experiences (NDEs) encompass the broad range of sensations experienced by people who are either near death or believe themselves to be near death. While NDEs have been widely reported across many times and cultures, U.S. psychologist Raymond Moody's (b. 1944) book *Life After Life* (1975) sparked much of the current academic and popular interest in the topic.

In *Life After Life*, Moody examined more than one hundred case studies of people who had experienced "clinical death" and were subsequently revived. He argued that peoples' reports of NDEs were surprisingly uniform, and that the structure of the experiences could be broken into a number of discrete "stages." These stages included (1) feelings of serenity, (2) hearing noises, (3) becoming detached from one's body, (4) traveling through a "tunnel" of light, and (5) experiencing a "review" of one's life. Some people also reported meeting figures from various religious traditions, and many survivors of NDEs went on to experience significant changes in personality and outlook. Subsequent research into reports of NDEs has supported similar conclusions, though with some significant variations. For example, some people have reported NDEs that were dominated by feelings of fear and anxiety.

NDEs are sometimes taken to be evidence of an afterlife, and some survivors of NDEs have claimed to have seen or heard things that were in some way "miraculous." However, researchers in a number of fields have also explored the physiological and neurological bases of NDEs, and have made significant progress. While current research has not identified a single cause of NDEs, factors such as apoxia (the absence of oxygen to the brain), altered temporal lobe functioning, and the release of endorphins or other neurotransmitters have all been speculated to play some role. **BSh**

⬆ A drawing by English psychologist Dr. Susan Blackmore of a tunnel with light at the end, as seen by those who have undergone near-death experiences.

"If experiences of the type which I have discussed are real, they have very profound implications ... we cannot fully understand this life until we catch a glimpse of what lies beyond it."

Raymond Moody, *Life After Life* (1975)

⚗

Φ

Handicap Principle
Amotz Zahavi

A theory to explain why the peacock's tail is not contrary to Darwinian evolution

In 1975, in a paper titled "Mate Selection—A Selection for Handicap," the Israeli biologist Amotz Zahavi (b. 1928) announced an ingenious idea that shed light on a problem that had perplexed the best minds in evolutionary biology for more than a hundred years. He called it the Handicap Principle.

On April 3, 1860, the year after publishing *On the Origin of Species* (1859), Charles Darwin wrote to his colleague Asa Gray, "The sight of a feather in the peacock's tail, whenever I gaze at it, makes me sick." He worried that the peacock's tail did not fit with his theory of natural selection in which only the fittest creatures survive. How could a peacock's tail confer fitness? If anything, it appeared to handicap its owner. Zahavi, however, argued that the peacock's tail evolved

"It is possible to consider the handicap as a kind of test imposed on the individual."
Amotz Zahavi, "Mate Selection . . . " (1975)

precisely because it was a handicap, that a handicap might actually increase its owner's fitness. Talking about the ornate display of a cock pheasant's tail, he suggested that it displays to a female: "Look what a fine pheasant I must be, for I have survived in spite of this incapacitating burden behind me." The male succeeds in persuading the female because its handicap acts as a true fitness test; only the fittest are strong enough to survive it.

The idea was originally disputed by many academics, including Richard Dawkins, who argued that "the logical conclusion to it should be the evolution of males with only one leg and one eye." However, Dawkins and others were ultimately won over by a masterful piece of mathematical modeling by Alan Grafen in 1990, which revealed that natural selection could indeed favor males who evolve complex, costly displays or handicaps. **JH**

No-miracles Argument
Hilary Putnam

A philosophical theory that justifies scientific leaps into the unknown

Scientists can predict outcomes—for example, Sir Isaac Newton, from observations of Saturn, correctly predicted the existence of a then undiscovered planet. However, by speculating at all, Newton was departing from strict scientific precepts: his methods could be validated only retrospectively, once Neptune had been sighted. His hypothesis was based, to some extent, on faith: the belief that it is possible accurately to extrapolate (infer the unknown from data we already have). If the belief that scientific theories are at least approximately true were to be mistaken, the only remaining explanation would be that some things are miraculous. Since miracles are by definition inexplicable, they are therefore, again by definition, unscientific: that is the nub of the no-miracles argument, which was first posited by Hilary Putnam (b. 1926) in his book *Mathematics, Matter, and Method* (1975).

Despite its slight suggestion of circularity—the supposition that miracles are unscientific does not necessarily mean that they do not occur; it may simply mean that the current definition and purview of science are flawed—the no-miracles argument provides a philosophical justification for continued scientific research into areas where the premises are based on likelihood rather than on incontrovertible fact. As a simple illustration, when a stick is held half in and half out of water, we may observe that it appears to be bent at the point where it breaks the surface: but do we know for certain that that is the case with all sticks in all water? We do not and cannot, but we can assume that it is. Without such assumptions, research—and hence scientific advances—would be rendered, if not impossible, even harder than it already is. The no-miracles argument is thus both pragmatic and realistic. **GL**

Neuro-linguistic Programming
Richard Bandler and John Grinder

An approach to communication, personal development, and psychotherapy that argues that we can rid ourselves of inhibition through an effort of will

↑ Paul McKenna at a neuro-linguistic programming training seminar in 2006. The method is said to make business people more successful, fat people thinner, and to rid others of phobias.

Neuro-linguistic programming (NLP) was developed in the 1970s by two Americans, Richard Bandler (b. 1950) and John Grinder (b. 1940), whose collaboration began with their book *The Structure of Magic Vol. I* (1975). Based in part on some of the theories of Noam Chomsky—particularly the idea that every sentence has two structures: one superficial, the other underlying—NLP claimed to be an innovative method of treating phobias, depression, habit disorders (especially those on the obsessive-compulsive spectrum), psychosomatic illnesses, and learning difficulties.

The central tenet of NLP was that there is nothing anyone can do that we cannot not do ourselves. Thus inhibited, sick, and disabled people were encouraged by therapists to model their thoughts and words—and subsequently their actions—on those of people who were not so afflicted: failure would be turned into success simply through imitation of the successful. One of NLP's main marketing slogans was "finding ways to help people have better, fuller, and richer lives".

The theory of NLP was massively popular and soon came to be practiced by private therapists and hypnotherapists, as well as by management consultants worldwide. Bandler and Grinder quit their teaching jobs to devote their energies to NLP courses for students (who were charged $1,000 a head for a ten-day workshop) and then, even more lucratively, to best-selling books on the subject, such as *Frogs into Princes* (1979).

Meanwhile, skeptics cast doubt on the scientific basis of the concept. Gradually NLP came to be regarded as little more than a variant form of assertiveness training. However, although the credibility of certain aspects of NLP has been undermined, the practice has been highly influential and remains a major component of some business training courses. **GL**

"As long as you believe it is impossible, you will actually never find out if it is possible or not."

John Seymour, *Introducing Neuro-Linguistic Programming: The New Psychology of Personal Excellence* (1990)

The Selfish Gene
Richard Dawkins

The theory that genes are what drive the evolution of species

All organisms have, at the cellular level, strands of genetic material known as genes. These genes contain the basic information that life needs to grow, metabolize, and reproduce. In *The Selfish Gene*, published in 1976 while he was a lecturer at Oxford University, British biologist Richard Dawkins (*b*. 1941) proposed that it was these genes that actually propelled evolution. The organism in which the genes are found will strive not only to reproduce its own genetic material, but also to protect genetic material similar to itself.

Dawkins himself said that the ideas he expressed about evolution were not his alone, and that they had existed for quite some time, viewed by experts in the field as fairly standard. What was different about his idea was the way that he explained it, framing evolution

"We are all survival machines for the same kind of replicator—molecules called DNA."

Richard Dawkins, *The Selfish Gene* (1976)

as a mechanism through which self-replicating material made copies of itself. As part of his explanation he also drew an analogy with cultural phenomena, which he dubbed memes, that replicated themselves from person to person, growing or shrinking in popularity.

The Selfish Gene caused some controversy after its publication. Though some readers confused the title as implying that genes feel or express desires, the notion that life evolves because of the unconscious, blind goal that genes have for self-replication cast the very notion of evolution in a different light. The idea offered a new perspective on certain behaviors, such as altruism and attempts at reproduction that result in death soon after copulation. That view that genes are the fundamental unit of natural selection has since become widely accepted. **MT**

Meme
Richard Dawkins

An element that guides cultural evolution, as a gene guides genetic evolution

Memes are ideas, habits, tunes, skills, stories, fashions, catchphrases: any kind of behavior that can be copied from person to person through imitation. When these words or actions are heard or seen, they are selectively retained and then copied, sometimes with variation, and so they spread between people, within a culture.

British biologist Richard Dawkins (*b*. 1941) coined the term in his well-known book *The Selfish Gene* (1976); its last chapter was titled "Memes: the new replicators." Dawkins felt that "Darwinism is too big a theory to be confined to a narrow context of the gene," and so he introduced the idea of cultural evolution. To describe the self-replicating unit of cultural transmission, he took the Greek word *mimeme*, meaning "to copy," and shortened it to rhyme with the word "gene."

"Cultural transmission is analogous to genetic transmission . . ."

Richard Dawkins, *The Selfish Gene* (1976)

The word and idea were taken up enthusiastically, spawning a new discipline of memetics; indeed, they demonstrated how a successful evolutionary meme might actually spread. Dawkins was interested in the possibility of the meme being developed into a proper hypothesis of the human mind, which happened most notably in the hands of the intellectual heavyweights Daniel Dennett in *Consciousness Explained* (1991) and Susan Blackmore in *The Meme Machine* (1999). Dennett argued how "human consciousness is itself a huge complex of memes." Critics rebelled against the idea of selfish memes acting like mind-viruses, parasitizing their unwitting human hosts. But, as Dawkins said from the outset, our conscious foresight means "we have the power to defy the selfish genes of our birth and, if necessary, the selfish memes of our indoctrination." **JH**

A hypothetical "bait" meme lures other memes before propagating itself into people's minds.

Missing Letter Effect
Alice F. Healy

Research that shed new light on understanding the way that we read

In 1976 cognitive psychologist Alice F. Healy conducted experiments to determine the accuracy with which university students could identify every occurrence of certain letters in given passages of prose. Participants were asked to mark each target letter as they read silently at their normal speed. For example, in the sentence "Men who work very long hours pass too little time at home," they were asked to mark every letter "e." If they reached the end and found that they had missed one or more occurrences, they should not go back.

The results showed that recognition was much higher when the letters were sounded (for example, the "e" in "very") than when they were silent (the "h" in "hours"). Participants were more likely to notice the letters in words that gave the sentences their meaning

" . . . frequent words . . . show more detection errors than infrequent words . . ."

A. F. Healy, "Detection Errors on the Word *The*" (1976)

than in form words that were merely functional—more of them would mark the "t" in "time" than the "a" in "at."

Healy's work laid the foundation for further studies. One later experiment tasked participants to look for certain letters after previously having read the passage with no idea of what they would then be required to do: in such cases, the hit rate increased significantly.

Among the findings of this research was that fluent readers do not generally read every letter of every word, but rather assume what the word is from its general shape and the context. However, "fluent" is not necessarily accurate: witness, for example, the common confusion of "causal" and "casual." Study of the missing-letter effect has cast light on the workings of the human mind and enabled educationists better to help beginners and slow readers. **GL**

RSA Algorithm
R. L. Rivest, A. Shamir, and L. M. Adleman

A revolutionary method for coding data and maintaining privacy on the Internet

In 1977, a paper came out of the Laboratory for Computer Science at the Massachusetts Institute of Technology titled, "A Method for Obtaining Digital Signatures and Public-Key Cryptosystems." It had the presentience to forecast that "the era of 'electronic mail' may soon be upon us," adding, "we must ensure that two important properties of the current 'paper mail' system are preserved: (a) messages are private, and (b) messages can be signed." The proposed solution of the authors—Ronald Rivest (b. 1947), Adi Shamir (b. 1952), and Leonard Adleman (b. 1945)—was a type of cryptography that became known by the initials of their surnames: the RSA algorithm.

Two types of cryptosystem currently exist: secret-key (or symmetric) and public-key (or asymmetric). Secret-key relies on one key to code and decode the message. Public-key relies on two: a public (published) key that performs the encryption, and a private key (kept secret) used for decryption. Crucially, the sender of a message uses a different code to the recipient, so there is no need to transmit a code and risk interception. U.S. cryptographers Whitfield Diffie and Martin Hellman were the first to describe the concept of public-key cryptography in 1976 (although it now seems to have been invented a decade previously by the British Government Code Headquarters, but kept secret). However, Rivest, Shamir, and Adleman were the first to make it workable using prime numbers of about one hundred digits long.

Today the RSA system is the most popular form of public-key cryptography: it is found in most computer operating systems, is built into the main protocols for secure Internet communication, and is used by numerous institutions worldwide. In 2002, its inventors were given the Turing Award, perhaps the highest honor in computer science, for their ingenious idea. **GL**

Critique of Orientalism
Edward W. Said

A critical reassessment of Western scholarship of the "Orient," specifically in relation to the Arab Islamic world

Palestinian-American historian Edward W. Said (1935–2003) did not coin the word "Orientalism," but his choice of it as the title of his influential study in 1978 of relations between the Arab world and the West contributed greatly to subsequent understanding of the term.

According to Said, the West had consistently and chronically demeaned the Arab world in order to subjugate it. This view was received sympathetically by many who were anxious to re-evaluate history in the light of post-World War II political developments in the Middle East, notably the creation in 1948 of the state of Israel and the emergence of several Arab states as world powers because of their oil wealth.

Not everyone admired the work, however, and Said was criticized for a number of perceived flaws in his argument. One of the main objections was to his binary depiction of West and East as antagonistic monoliths, the former the oppressor, the latter the victim, whereas in truth there had been constant interplay between the two and exchanges of ideas and materials. Why, asked historian Bernard Lewis, if the British were so determined to suppress Egyptian national identity, as Said claimed, did they decipher the ancient language of the region? How, others asked, could a book titled *Orientalism* ignore as it did China and Japan? Some people thought that Said had ignored a complex symbiosis because it did not fit in with his pre-formed theories.

Orientalism may have been flawed (though Said responded trenchantly to these and many other criticisms) but it deeply influenced the development and content of postcolonial studies courses, not only as they relate to the Arabs but also to the whole world. Its impact has been felt around the globe, with editions in thirty-six different languages. **GL**

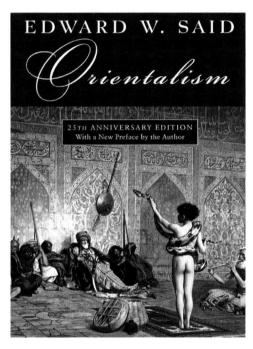

↑ *Orientalism* (1978) is Edward W. Said's best-known work, and has been referred to as one of the most influential scholarly books of the twentieth century.

"From the beginning of Western speculation about the Orient, the one thing the Orient could not do was to represent itself."

Edward W. Said, *Orientalism* (1978)

Rap Music
United States

A style in which rhythmic and/or rhyming speech is chanted to musical backing

Rap music is music with an insistent beat and accompanying lyrics, which may incorporate digital sampling (extracts from other recordings); it is alternatively known as hip-hop. The lyrics are spoken or chanted rather than sung. They may either rhyme in the conventional manner of verse or derive their rhythm from the beat. Many raps feature both types of lyric. The subject matter can range from traditional poetic themes, such as love and nature, to controversial "gangsta raps" that have been condemned for their misogyny and for glamorizing drugs and violence.

The use of repetitive drum beats to punctuate and dramatize spoken narratives is thought to have derived from West Africa, where it has been a common practice since precolonial times. The recitative—a style of singing

"… though the element of poetry is very strong, so is the element of the drum …"

Archie Shepp, jazz musician

that resembles (or is) speech—has a long tradition in the West, being used in opera and in musicals.

The use in English of the word "rap" as a verb or noun meaning "talk" dates from the sixteenth century, but its application to a form of music began among African Americans in the 1960s. One of the earliest exponents was Gil Scott-Heron (1949–2011), a jazz musician who became known as "the godfather of rap." The style came to prominence in 1979 when "Rapper's Delight" by the Sugarhill Gang, a New Jersey trio, became the first rap record to make the Top 40 singles chart. There followed a long line of rap stars, including Grandmaster Flash and the Furious Five, LL Cool J, Public Enemy, and the Beastie Boys. Later came a second wave ridden by, among others, P-Diddy, Snoop Dogg, Jay-Z, Eminem, and Kanye West. **GL**

Social Networking Service
United States

A platform to build social networks or social relations among people

The earliest services that enabled people to connect with each other via computer were e-mail and chat programs, which appeared in the early 1970s. The first social networking service in the modern sense of the term, however, was USENET, which began in 1979 as a messaging system between Duke University and the University of North Carolina. It spread rapidly into other U.S. universities and government agencies.

As the World Wide Web expanded in the 1990s, commercial companies began to set up online social networks that could be used by members of the public. The first of these, such as Classmates.com and SixDegrees.com, were generally intended as a means of reconnecting with old school, college, and work friends. Over time the purpose of social networking

"Social media is not about the exploitation of technology but service to community."

Simon Mainwaring, social media specialist

services was expanded to include dating services (such as Friendster), maintaining business contacts (LinkedIn), and enabling rock bands to connect with their fans (MySpace). Facebook, today the world's largest social network, was launched in 2004; it took the Classmates.com model and added improved profile pages, links, and other attractive features. It was joined online in 2006 by Twitter.

The benefits of social networking are numerous— it has made it easier for friends and family to stay in touch, enabled people to connect with others with similar interests, and has even proved a powerful tool for political activism, such as in the Arab Spring of 2011. However, many critics view social networking sites as simply an online form of popularity contest and important questions remain about users' privacy. **GL**

◄ U.S. rap star Grandmaster Flash, pictured here deejaying in 1980.

Sudoku
Howard Garns

Postmodernism
Jean-François Lyotard

A simple number game that became a worldwide phenomenon

A philosophy that challenged and deconstructed traditional beliefs

The name Sudoku is an abbreviation of the Japanese phrase "Only single numbers allowed," but the game itself, contrary to popular misconception, was not invented in Japan or by anyone of Japanese descent. Rather, it was created by a retired U.S. architect, Howard Garns (1905–89), in 1979.

Garns based his game on the "magic square" grid concepts of eighteenth-century Swiss mathematician Leonhard Euler, who himself had adapted them from early tenth-century Islamic medical journals. The original magic squares, attributed to the Persian-born chemist, astronomer, and physicist Jabir ibn Hayyan, were nine-celled squares featuring numbers one through to nine, with five in the middle and each row, column, and diagonal adding up to fifteen. It was

"Postmodernism" first emerged in the philosophical lexicon in 1979 in *The Postmodern Condition*, a work by the French philosopher and theorist Jean-François Lyotard (1924–98), and in no time cast a very wide and all-encompassing net: architecture, literature, the visual arts, religion, economics, science, ethics, and art. There was hardly a discipline or an idea that was not free of its influence, and its definitions are as broad as the areas of life it touches: it is the "drawing of fresh attention to established conventions," the "reintroduction of classical elements to past styles," and "any reaction to modernism that recalls traditional materials and forms, ideas and inquiries." The consensus is that it likely grew from a suspicion that science and understanding cannot answer all of life's questions, that reality is more

"Scientists have identified Sudoku as a classic meme . . ."

David Smith, *The Observer* (May 15, 2005)

"Simplifying . . . I define postmodern as incredulity toward metanarratives."

J.-F. Lyotard, *The Postmodern Condition* (1979)

known as the "buduh square," and became so popular that it doubled as a talisman. Magic squares then began to grow in size, from 4x4 to 6x6 and even 10x10 cells, which began appearing in the thirteenth century.

Grid-style number puzzles appeared for a time in late nineteenth-century French newspapers, but it was Garns's Sudoku puzzle that was the first attempt at the modern game so familiar to us today. It was originally referred to as Number Place and was published in *Dell Pencil Puzzles and Word Games* in May 1979. In Japan it was first published in the puzzle book *Monthly Nikolist* by the Japanese company Nikoli in 1984, as *Suuji Wa Dokushin Ni Kagiru*, "the numbers must occur only once." Two years later its grid was made symmetrical and fewer clues given, and when published in *The Times* of London in 2004, it became a phenomenon. **BS**

than the sum of our understanding. Postmodernism is skeptical of generalized conclusions that apply to us all —it is the individual experience and how we interpret it for ourselves that matters, not the collective universal law seen by others and applied to the collective.

The concept, however, is not without its detractors. Some have likened it to nothing more than a meaningless buzzword, used to describe everything from television commercials to the dread we feel at the prospect of nuclear war. And because of its inherent skepticism it denies too much and lacks the optimism that can come from scientific, philosophical, and religious truths.

But postmodernism may not be the successor to modernism it claims to be. Modernists queried religion, science, and concepts such as nationhood, too. So is postmodernism a new dynasty, or merely an heir? **BS**

Billiards (detail, 1985) by Gerhard Richter, a seminal figure in postmodern representational painting. ➡

Principles of Biomedical Ethics

Tom L. Beauchamp and James F. Childress

The development of a standard approach to biomedical ethics, which resolved ethical issues in terms of four ethical principles

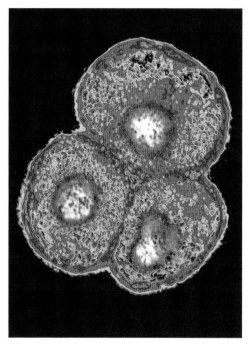

⬆ There are numerous ethical issues surrounding the medical use of human embryonic stem cells, which have the potential to develop into a variety of different cell types in the body.

Principles of Biomedical Ethics (*PBE*, 1979) is a book by philosophers Tom L. Beauchamp and James F. Childress (*b.* 1940). It was one of the first books to present a detailed, systematic treatment of ethical decision making in health care and biomedical research, and it laid the groundwork for contemporary research and teaching in this area.

Beauchamp and Childress began *PBE* by contrasting the utilitarian theory that an action's moral rightness is determined by its consequences with the deontological theory that there are "right-making" features of actions that have nothing to do with consequences. While the authors disagreed as to which theory is correct, they argued that both theories support a set of four "core" principles relevant to ethical decision making in medicine. These principles included duties to promote patients' wellbeing (beneficence), to avoid causing them harm (nonmalfeasance), to respect their decisions (autonomy), and to distribute health care goods and services in an equitable manner (justice). In the remainder of *PBE*, they applied these four principles to a variety of ethical problems that arise in medicine, such as the right of patients to refuse treatment, the problem of determining what counts as informed consent, and the appropriate way of conceptualizing professional-patient relationship.

Beauchamp and Childress have issued updated editions of *PBE* every few years, and it has been widely adopted in introductory courses on biomedical ethics at both the undergraduate and graduate level. More broadly, the book has played an important role in raising the academic profile of so-called "applied ethics," in which ethical theories are applied to particular issues that arise in discipline-specific contexts ("business ethics," "research ethics," "environmental ethics," and so on). **BSh**

"We understand 'biomedical ethics' . . . as the application of general ethical theories, principles, and rules to problems of therapeutic practice, health care delivery, and medical and biological research."

Tom L. Beauchamp and James F. Childress, *Principles of Biomedical Ethics* (1979)

The Expanding Circle
Peter Singer

The notion that morality should be based in utilitarianism

The expanding circle is a philosophical idea that the greatest good for the greatest number is the only measure of good or ethical behavior. It advocates that the "circle" of beings with rights and privileges should be expanded from humans to include many animal species that have "interests."

The Australian moral philosopher Peter Singer (b. 1946) used the phrase the "expanding circle of moral worth" in his book *Practical Ethics* (1979), which analyzes how ethics can be applied to difficult social questions, such as the use of animals for food and research, and the obligation of the wealthy to help the poor. He attempted to illustrate how contemporary controversies have philosophical roots and presented his own ethical theory to apply to practical cases. Many of Singer's ideas, such as his support for abortion, were controversial. In an attack on speciesism, he argued that differences between the species were morally irrelevant, and speciesism is akin to racism. Singer advocated redistributing wealth to alleviate poverty. He suggested that infanticide up to a month after birth is humane in the case in which a child may have an extreme disability. Singer argued that nonvoluntary euthanasia is neither good nor bad when the individual killed is in a coma.

Practical Ethics caused outrage in some quarters, leading Singer to make additions to later editions, outlining what he felt were misunderstandings that caused an adverse reaction to his ideas. He expanded on his theory further in his book *The Expanding Circle: Ethics and Sociobiology* (1981). Singer's views on the treatment of animals have been espoused by animal rights activists, but his idea of the expanding circle remains contentious among philosophers, advocates for the disabled, and pro-life supporters, and some assert that his stance on various issues can lead to eugenics. **CK**

Originalism
Paul Brest

A new reading of the U.S. Constitution as its authors (may have) intended

Originalism is any attempt to interpret and apply the U.S. Constitution as it would have been construed by contemporary eighteenth-century readers at the time of its inception in 1787. The word was coined in 1980 by U.S. academic Paul Brest (b. 1940) in an essay titled "The Misconceived Quest for Original Understanding."

Originalists may be divided into two main groups: those who want to keep faith with the intentions of those who drafted and ratified the Constitution; and those who subscribe to the original meaning theory, which requires that the Constitution be interpreted in the same way as reasonable persons living at the time of its creation would have interpreted it. At the root of all originalism is formalism—the belief that the judiciary is empowered only to uphold

"What in the world is a moderate interpretation of a constitutional text?"

Antonin Scalia, Supreme Court Justice

existing laws: creating, amending, and repealing them are the responsibilities of the legislature.

Originalists are generally regarded as politically conservative. One of the most prominent is Supreme Court Justice Antonin Scalia (b. 1936), who claimed that the Eighth Amendment (prohibiting cruel and unusual punishments) must be read, understood, and interpreted today according to what would have been regarded as cruel and unusual punishment in the 1790s. However, the theory has also been espoused by liberals such as Supreme Court Justice Hugo Black (1886–1971) and Yale lawyer Akhil Amar (b. 1958). Both groups represent a challenge to "Living Constitutionalists"— those who believe that the U.S. Constitution is open to interpretation in every succeeding age, and that it is flexible and dynamic, not rigid and moribund. **GL**

Naming and Necessity
Saul Kripke

A seminal work in the philosophy of language

Naming and Necessity (1980) is a book by U.S. philosopher and logician Saul Kripke (*b.* 1940), based on a series of lectures he gave at Princeton University in 1970. It is often considered one of the most important philosophical works of the twentieth century.

In *Naming and Necessity*, Kripke offers sustained arguments against several views about language and modality that were widely accepted at the time. The first view was descriptivism, which held that proper names referred to their targets in virtue of the descriptions speakers associate with them. The second view was the thesis of contingent identity, which held that the sorts of identities discovered by empirical investigation (such as "Mark Twain is Samuel Clemens") are not necessary, and are thus false in some "possible world." In contrast

"I will argue … that proper names are rigid designators…"

Saul Kripke, *Naming and Necessity* (1980)

to these views, Kripke argued that proper names were rigid designators that picked out the same target in every possible world and that identity claims involving these names were thus necessary. Kripke then used his account to argue against materialism, which held that mental events, such as a person's being in pain, were identical to physical events, such as the firing of neurons in that person's brain.

Kripke's thesis led some philosophers to abandon descriptivism and instead adopt a causal theory of reference, by which the meaning of a term is fixed by its causal history. His suggestion that necessary truths could be discovered by empirical investigation also renewed interest in philosophical metaphysics, as some felt that his arguments showed the importance of examining the natures of objects in the physical world. **BSh**

The Chinese Room Argument
John Searle

An argument against the possibility of true artificial intelligence

In the mid-twentieth century, a theory of consciousness known as functionalism developed. It explained the human mind in computational terms, rejecting the notion that there is something unique to human consciousness or the human brain. If a computer can pass a Turing Test by convincing an expert that it has a mind, then it actually does have a mind. In 1980, philosopher John Searle (*b.* 1932) responded to functionalism with his revolutionary article, "Minds, Brains, and Programs," in which he critiqued the possibility of artificial intelligence with his Chinese room argument.

Imagine that a man who does not speak Chinese is put in a windowless room with nothing but a Chinese dictionary that contains the appropriate responses for certain queries. A slip of paper is passed under the

"… the programmed computer understands… exactly nothing."

John Searle, "Minds, Brains, and Programs" (1980)

door with a Chinese phrase on it. The man looks up the appropriate response, writes it on the paper, and passes it under the door. Since he speaks no Chinese, he has no idea what he just said; he is only following the stimulus-response pattern indicated by the dictionary. To an observer outside the room, he seems to be a Chinese speaker, even though the phrases he reads and writes mean nothing to him. Similarly, a computer might pass a Turing Test, but it does so only by blindly following its programming. Though it has syntax (logical structure), it has no semantics (understanding of meaning). Thus, though computers may emulate human minds, they can never actually have minds.

Searle's article ignited a firestorm of debate in the fields of philosophy and artificial intelligence. His views are vital to dualistic explanations of consciousness. **JM**

Although a computer can play chess, that does not mean it has a mind that understands the game. →

Neocatastrophism
Luis Alvarez and Walter Alvarez

A theory arguing that asteroid impacts cause mass extinctions

Neocatastrophism is the new face of the discredited idea of catastrophism. It claims that our planet and its inhabitants have been shaped by cataclysmic events. The theory regained favor on June 6, 1980, with a publication in the journal *Science*. The paper, by the Nobel Prize winner Luis Alvarez (1911–88) and his son Walter (*b.* 1940), blamed the death of the dinosaurs, indeed the whole of the Cretaceous-Tertiary mass extinction, on an asteroid crashing into Earth.

The prevailing wisdom at the time was gradualism: a theory originated by the Victorian geologist Charles Lyell (1797–1875), which prescribed steady, creeping change. Charles Darwin (1809–82) seconded Lyell, and catastrophists were derided as standing against evolution. The Alvarezs' paper, however, was

"… the Cretaceous world is gone forever, and its ending was sudden and horrible."

Walter Alvarez, *T. rex and the Crater of Doom* (1997)

convincing. They had discovered that the Cretaceous-Tertiary boundary contained a clay layer with unusually high levels of an element rare in the Earth's crust, iridium. The isotopic ratio of iridium matched those found in asteroids. Moreover, the presence of shocked quartz granules, tektites, and glass spherules suggested an impact. The Alvarezs calculated that to account for the data the asteroid would have been about 6 miles (10 km) in diameter: large enough to kick enough dust into the sky to trigger a nuclear winter.

Ten years after the paper's publication, a suitable impact crater was discovered near Chicxulub, Mexico. The Alvarezs and their team precipitated a paradigm shift. Evolution is now thought to be able to occur in leaps and bounds, and neocatastrophism and asteroids are regarded as plausible agents for change. **JH**

Biblical Narrative Criticism
Robert Alter

A modern form of biblical criticism based in contemporary literary theory and practice

Biblical narrative criticism examines the scriptures from a literary perspective. It seeks to discover the role that literary art plays in shaping biblical narrative by painstaking analysis of the text, taking into account devices such as parallelism, details recorded, tempo, word order, sound, rhythm, syntax, repetition, characterization, and dialogue. Narrative criticism examines the Bible as a cohesive work of literature, rather than a collection of disparate documents, in order to find the interconnections in the text that highlight motifs and themes. It explores questions regarding authorial intent, the reliability of the narrator, and the ethical implications of multiple interpretations.

Narrative criticism began in 1981 with U.S. academic Robert Alter's (*b.* 1935) groundbreaking study of

"[The Bible] offers such splendid illustrations of the primary possibilities of narrative."

Robert Alter, *The Art of Biblical Narrative* (1981)

the Hebrew Bible, *The Art of Biblical Narrative*. Alter attempted to cast new light on the text by illuminating the subtlety of the narrative and its lexical nuances, and examining the Hebrew Bible as a document of religious history. He illustrated how the authors of the Hebrew Bible use wordplay, symmetry, and suchlike to create tension in a story, and so sustain the reader's interest.

Alter's radical study suggesting that the Bible is a work of literary art that merits studied criticism proved highly influential when it was published. As the 1980s progressed, narrative criticism became more popular via various publications, including Shimon Bar-Efrat's (*b.* 1929) *Narrative Art in the Bible* (1989). Narrative critics have since expanded the discipline to include the examination of issues such as plot development and the role of the omniscient narrator. **CK**

An artwork of an asteroid striking the Earth, similar to the one responsible for wiping out the dinosaurs.

Reaganomics
Ronald Reagan

The economic policies promoted by U.S. President Ronald Reagan during the 1980s

⬆ Ronald Reagan pictured preparing for his inaugural speech, following re-election for a second term in 1985. His election victory saw him win forty-nine out of fifty states.

"Reaganomics" is a term used to describe the economic policies of U.S. President Ronald Reagan (1911–2004), who held office from 1981 to 1989. The term was popularized by radio host Paul Harvey and was widely adopted by the news media and academics to discuss Reagan's policies, both during and after his presidency.

Throughout the 1970s, the United States had experienced high rates of both inflation and unemployment, and government deficits had been increasing. Reagan argued that these economic problems could be solved by cutting marginal tax rates and reducing regulation and nondefense government spending. He also endorsed the disinflationary monetary policy of Federal Reserve Chairman Paul Volker (b. 1927). Reagan's economic proposals were strongly influenced by the so-called "supply side" school of economics and the Laffer curve, which held that total government tax revenue might actually be increased if tax rates decreased. The thought was that a cut in tax rates might "pay for itself" if the resulting economic growth allowed for the government to collect the same amount in tax revenue.

Reagan implemented many of his proposals during his administration, most notably the one to sharply reduce marginal tax rates. Proponents of Reaganomics argue that these policies helped to lower unemployment, reduce the rate of inflation, and increase gross domestic product per capita and average productivity. Critics, meanwhile, argue that the effects of Reaganomics were largely negative. Among other things, they point to significant increases in government debt, consumer debt, the trade deficit, and income inequality. These debates have continued to the present day, with many conservatives (both in and outside of the United States) defending economic policies loosely based on Reaganomics, and many liberals arguing that these sorts of policies are likely to be ineffective. **BSh**

"In this present crisis, government is not the solution to our problem; government is the problem."

Ronald Reagan, Presidential Inaugural Address (1981)

The Theory of Communicative Action
Jürgen Habermas

An argument that the key to emancipation is to be found in communication

The Theory of Communicative Action is a two-volume work published in 1981 by German philosopher and sociologist Jürgen Habermas (*b.* 1929). The book's account of social theory has significantly influenced research in sociology and philosophy in both continental Europe and in English-speaking countries.

Habermas was a student of critical theorist Theodor Adorno (1903–69), and was influenced by Adorno's method of social criticism that blended aspects of Marxist historical materialism with psychoanalysis, phenomenology, and existentialism. In *The Theory of Communicative Action*, Habermas expanded this method of criticism even further to encompass research in sociology, linguistics, the philosophy of language, and the philosophy of science. He then used this methodology to provide a general account of rationality and social interaction, tied tightly to the ideal of "communicative action," which occurs when a group of actors enter a discussion with the purpose of reaching a jointly acceptable consensus. Habermas contrasted this with "strategic action," which occurs when actors treat each other as mere means to achieve individual ends. Habermas then discussed the ways that various types of communicative scenarios can be seen as approximating the ideal of communicative action.

Both *The Theory of Communicative Action*'s methodology and its conclusions have had significant scholarly and cultural impact. Many philosophers and sociologists have emulated Habermas's pluralistic methodology, which draws broadly from both the continental and analytic philosophical traditions, as well as from contemporary research in the social sciences. His emphasis on the importance of meaningful public discourse, and on the social structures that are needed to enable this, have influenced both scholars and policy makers. **BSh**

⬆ Jürgen Habermas speaks at the Jewish Museum in Berlin, Germany, during a ceremony to award the prize for "Understanding and Tolerance" on November 13, 2010.

"Communicative action refers to the interaction of . . . actors [who] seek to reach an understanding about the action situation and their plans of action in order to coordinate their actions by way of agreement"

Jürgen Habermas, *The Theory of Communicative Action* (1981)

1982

Holy Blood, Holy Grail
M. Baigent, R. Leigh, and H. Lincoln

A theory that Jesus Christ married Mary Magdalene and fathered a lineage of kings

The "Holy Blood, Holy Grail" hypothesis is a pseudo-historical conspiracy theory that claims that Jesus Christ survived his crucifixion and took Mary Magdalene as his wife, fathering one or more children with her. His bloodline later became the Merovingian dynasty of kings. Proponents of the theory believe that modern Christianity is based on a false account of the life of Christ and that a secret society called the Priory of Sion, which has existed for hundreds of years and included many of Europe's leading intellectuals, statesmen, and artists, will eventually restore the descendants of the Merovingians to power.

The groundwork for the theory began with a hoax perpetrated by Pierre de Plantard (1920–2000), a French draftsman and mystificator, in the 1950s. Plantard forged an elaborate hoax around a "historical" text called the *Dossiers Secrets d'Henri Lobineau* (Secret Files of Henri Lobineau), detailing the existence of the Priory of Sion, a shadow organization dedicated to installing the "Great Monarch" predicted by sixteenth-century French astrologer Nostradamus. In the 1980s, Henry Lincoln (*b.* 1930), an English television presenter, unaware that the *Dossiers Secrets* was a hoax, used it as the basis for a series of documentaries and a book, *The Holy Blood and the Holy Grail* (1982), co-authored with Michael Baigent (*b.* 1948) and Richard Leigh (1943–2007).

Elements of the Holy Blood, Holy Grail theory, especially the Priory of Sion, have enjoyed widespread popularity and become staples of both ongoing conspiracy theories, and conspiracy fiction—notably in Dan Brown's mystery detective novel *The Da Vinci Code* (2003). The theory has helped to popularize belief in "alternate history," the view that the modern world (of which Christianity is a major component) is based upon a falsehood that will eventually come to light—possibly with dire consequences for the current and supposedly false and oppressive world order. **BSh**

Rational Drug Design
Arvid Carlsson

Using information about the structure of a drug receptor to identify or create drugs

Most new drugs are, crudely, the result of trial and error, the result of testing a new chemical combination on cultured cells or lab rats and then matching the effects to treat a susceptible medical problem. But what if the process could be reversed? What if there could be rational drug design, starting by identifying the problem and then designing a drug to modulate or alter it therapeutically? Such was the thought that led to the development of selective serotonin reuptake inhibitors, some of the first drugs to be developed by rational drug design and now the most widely prescribed antidepressants in the world.

While employed by the Swedish pharmaceutical company Astra AB, the Swedish scientist Arvid Carlsson (b. 1923) worked on brompheniramine, an over the counter antihistamine drug used to treat symptoms of the common cold. The drug also had antidepressant properties, inhibiting the reuptake or reabsorption by cells of the neurotransmitter serotonin after it has performed its function of transmitting an impulse in the nervous system. Serotonin is thought to contribute to feelings of happiness and wellbeing, so by preventing it being reabsorbed, its effects are increased. Carlsson and his colleagues used their knowledge of how brompheniramine works to create from it a new rational drug, zimelidine, designed to work as a selective serotonin reuptake inhibitor. The drug went on sale to the public in 1982 but was later withdrawn and banned after serious side effects were observed.

Despite this setback, several more rational, antidepressant drugs were developed, most notably Prozac. Today, rational drug design is aided by powerful computer programs that can search through databases of chemical compounds and then select those compounds that are most likely to achieve the desired effect. **SA**

⬆ A computer artwork depicts the action of selective serotonin reuptake inhibitors at a chemical synapse.

Cell Phone
Motorola Corporation

A device that in time would transform the daily existence of billions of people

The idea of being able to make telephone calls while on the move first found fruition, in a limited sense, with the "walkie-talkie" two-way radio transceiver developed by the U.S. Motorola company during World War II (1939–45). Then, on June 17, 1946, a truck driver in St. Louis, Missouri, reached inside the cab of his truck for a handset, made a phone call, and ushered in the era of the wireless telephone. For more than a decade, technicians at AT&T and Bell Laboratories had been developing a wireless telephone service that would make and receive telephone calls from automobiles. The phone was predictably primitive. Only a few calls could be made at any one time, and there was only a single transmitter handling the calls of an entire urban region. Not only that, but each transmitting unit

"Marty called me . . . and said: 'We've got to build a portable cell phone.'"

Rudy Krolopp, product designer

(handset) weighed around 80 pounds (36 kg) and thus could hardly be considered truly mobile.

In the early 1970s, Marty Cooper, R&D chief at Motorola, gave product designer Rudy Krolopp the job of developing the world's first cellular telephone. Krolopp took his commission to his team—eight people in all—and said that if anybody present thought it could not be done, they should say so: nobody did. Within weeks they had developed a working model, but it would be another ten years and a hundred million dollars (mostly for building the necessary infrastructure) before Motorola was ready to launch its product. In 1983, the first cell phone to be offered commercially, the Motorola DynaTAC 8000X, or "The Brick" as it came to be affectionately called, initiated a revolution in telecommunications. **BS**

Multiple Intelligences
Howard Gardner

A theory that human intelligence is composed of several different capacities

The concept of multiple intelligences was first proposed by U.S. psychologist Howard Gardner (b. 1943) in his book *Frames of Mind: The Theory of Multiple Intelligences* (1983). Gardner argued that intelligence should be understood as a general capacity to solve particular sorts of problems or to produce services or goods valued by a person's peers. He suggested that there are multiple, distinct psychological capacities that count as intelligences, including the mastery of language, musical ability, logical or mathematical ability, and the ability to interact with others. Gardner originally proposed that there were seven intelligences, but later suggested that there may be more. He argued that each type of intelligence could be distinguished from the others by factors such as engaging different

"We all have these intelligences, that's what makes us human beings."

Howard Gardner, *Multiple Intelligences* (2011 edition)

areas of the brain and having different patterns of skill development. Importantly, each type of intelligence was supposed to be relatively independent from the others, and Gardner argued that people's performance on the tasks associated with one type of intelligence was only weakly relevant to predicting how they would do on tasks associated with another intelligence.

While Gardner's work has been influential, especially among educators, it has faced a number of criticisms. One concern has been the theory's vagueness and lack of testability. Another concern has been the purported lack of evidential support for the theory, since some studies have found that the sorts of capacities Gardner talks about are in fact highly correlated, and are not independent in the way that the theory of multiple intelligences would seem to predict. **BSh**

Downsizing
United States

Making a company or organization smaller by eliminating staff positions

To downsize is to make staff redundant from a job specifically for business reasons, such as improving efficiency or effectiveness. The term seems to have originated in the automotive industry in the 1970s, when cars were downsized by being built smaller and lighter to comply with new fuel economy standards. The concept of downsizing did not come to prominence until the 1980s, however, when U.S. companies sought a means to combat the combined effects of bloated managerial structures, recession, increased international competition, and new technology.

While the term was in vogue during the late 1980s and early 1990s, downsizing was regarded as ubiquitous. In fact, however, it was not as prevalent as it seemed: although it was common in the manufacturing sector—

"Personnel cutbacks have taken a heavy toll on employee loyalty ..."
Steven Prokesch, *The New York Times* (January 25, 1987)

then in the throes of a decades-long decline—it was not common in the retail and service sectors, which in fact were generally upsizing. Nor was downsizing as beneficial as it seemed: manufacturing firms that downsized reduced their labor costs per employee but also found their productivity decline; they increased their profitability but found their stock values declined. Interestingly, in the mid-1990s, a comparison of downsizing announcements with employment data revealed that a slim majority of announced downsizers were actual upsizers, restructuring their operations under the guise of downsizing.

Two of the main causes of downsizing are technological change and foreign competition. Since both are likely to continue, the practice of downsizing is likely to carry on, too. **GB**

Six Thinking Hats
Edward de Bono

Interchangeable approaches to getting good results in brainstorming sessions

In his book *Six Thinking Hats* (1985), author Edward de Bono (b. 1933) describes an innovative method of organizing ideas in order to reach the best conclusion in the fastest time. The approach may be used by individuals working alone but it is best suited to group discussions in which disparate and sometimes conflicting ideas may never be fully synthesized into plans of action: so-called "spaghetti thinking." Proceedings are chaired by a moderator or facilitator.

Users of the de Bono scheme take turns with the headwear (which may be literal or metaphorical). Each hat is a different color to indicate the type of thinking that they should concentrate on while wearing it. The white hat represents information: what do we actually know about the matter under discussion? The red

"[Having an] adequate way ... does not mean there cannot be a better way."
Edward de Bono, *Six Thinking Hats* (1985)

hat stands for emotion: what are our gut reactions to the matter in hand? While wearing the black hat, participants should focus on reasons for caution. The yellow hat represents optimistic responses: wearers should come up with best-case scenarios. Wearers of the green hat are encouraged to invent completely different approaches to the subject, to probe and to provoke. The blue hat, with which every sequence should begin and end, stands for what De Bono terms "meta thinking": at the start, blue hat wearers predict where the discussion might go; at the end of the session, they review where it has actually been and propose a plan of action. The Six Thinking Hats approach has been adopted by numerous companies, including Speedo, which used it while developing its swimsuit range. **GL**

Six Sigma
Motorola Corporation

A methodology for streamlining manufacturing and business processes

In 1986, U.S. telecommunications company Motorola Corporation established Six Sigma as part of the curriculum of its in-house Motorola Education and Training Center. Six Sigma was an employee enrichment program teaching a wide variety of subjects intended to improve employee productivity. Bill Smith, an engineer and quality control expert, joined Motorola in 1986 and worked with chief operating office John F. Mitchell on implementing Six Sigma. The system gained popularity after its enthusiastic adoption by General Electric's then chief executive officer, Jack Welch (b. 1935).

Six Sigma is a system of quality control in business. It seeks to standardize practices in manufacturing and other business processes with the goal of eliminating

"The worst experience I can imagine is being a casualty of process variation."

Six Sigma, "Variation—The Root of All Process Evil"

wasteful defects, such as nonconformity of a product or service to its original specifications. The primary assumption of Six Sigma is that manufacturing and business processes have features that can be measured, analyzed, improved, and controlled. The system is notable for its reliance on obscure nomenclature and its adherence to a rigid hierarchy, in which employees earn titles such as champion, master black belt, black belt, and green belt. By 2006, fifty-eight large companies had announced Six Sigma programs.

Business reaction to Six Sigma has been mixed; *Forbes* magazine pointed out that of the fifty-eight companies that had implemented Six Sigma programs by 2006, 91 percent regularly underperformed Standard & Poor's 500 (a stock market index based on the market capitalizations of 500 leading companies). **APT**

GM Food
United States

Altering the genetic makeup of plants and animals to increase their potential as foods

Genetically modified (GM) food is any edible product made from organisms whose DNA has been altered by scientists. After almost half a century of experimentation, in 1986 the U.S. Department of Agriculture approved genetic modification; since then, hundreds of patents have been awarded for GM plants.

The aim of genetic modification is to enhance organisms in commercial terms by reducing their flaws—for example, by removing material that may slow their rate of growth, or by introducing new material that will make them easier and cheaper to exploit. It can also be used to make food more nutritious—golden rice, for example, is normal rice that has been genetically modified to provide vitamin A to counter blindness and other diseases in children in the developing world.

"You are more likely to get hit by an asteroid than to get hurt by GM food."

Mark Lynas, writer and climate change specialist

At the time of writing, all GM foods are crop-derived, but work on GM salmon is also near completion.

GM food is highly controversial: opponents warn that interference with nature may reduce plants' resistance to pests and diseases or increase their production of toxins. There is also widespread concern that the long-term effects of GM on people and ecosystems are imperfectly understood.

Nevertheless, in 1995 the U.S. government approved GM foods for human consumption, and by the millennium nearly half of all the corn, cotton, and soybeans planted in the United States were GM. At the end of 2010, GM crops covered more than one-tenth of the world's farmland, and their extent continues to increase; GM food is now on sale almost everywhere, and indeed is helping to feed the world. **GL**

Kyōsei
Ryuzaburo Kaku

Businesses should practice symbiosis to promote mutual benefit and welfare

Kyōsei is a paradigm for business ethics that was implemented by Ryuzaburo Kaku (1926–2001), chairman of Canon Inc., in 1987. Kaku was a driving force behind the Caux Round Table, an international organization of business executives that first met in 1986 to promote ethical business practices throughout the world.

Kyōsei means "symbiosis" in the biological sense of species living together in mutually beneficial relationships. Kaku believed that businesses should harmonize profit and ethical principles and help to make the world a better place. He argued that business depends on a culture of responsibility and trust that can only be promoted by a commitment to ethical principles. *Kyōsei* is one of the cornerstones of stakeholder theory, a business philosophy that

"Kyōsei is living and working together for the common good of mankind."

Ryuzaburo Kaku

considers corporations to have moral obligations not only to their shareholders, but also to everyone with a stake in the company, such as employees, communities, customers, financiers, and suppliers. A business should strive to exist symbiotically with all of these stakeholders in order to promote the mutual welfare of all. Kaku believed that *kyōsei* also could be used to combat global imbalances in areas such as trade relations, employment, and the environment.

Kaku's leadership at Canon illustrated that a corporation could become more profitable by conducting business ethically to promote the long-term good of the global community. *Kyōsei* has been adapted as a core principle of environmental ethics, stressing that humans can thrive only if they learn to live symbiotically with the environment that sustains them. **JM**

Flynn Effect
James R. Flynn

The steady rise over time of standardized intelligence test scores

According to intelligent quotient (IQ) test scores, people are getting smarter: a phenomenon known as the Flynn effect. Named after James R. Flynn (b. 1934), the political studies professor who first observed it, the Flynn effect shows that test scores have risen dramatically in several nations around the world. Though IQ tests are regularly updated with new questions so that the average score across the test-taking population is 100, people given questions from prior tests tend to score higher than those who originally answered them.

Flynn published his findings in 1987 in a paper titled "Massive IQ Gains in 14 Nations: What IQ Tests Really Measure." The term the "Flynn effect" was later popularized by authors Charles Murray and Richard Hernstein in their book *The Bell Curve* (1994). Flynn's data

"… it struck me that … a phenomenon of great significance was being overlooked …"

James R. Flynn

showed an average rise in IQ of about 0.3 points per year. When measured against scores from tests from the 1930s, the Flynn effect implies that either people today are much smarter than the dullards of the past, or there is some other factor at work, such as IQ tests failing to measure intelligence accurately.

Flynn identified several possible causes for the increase in test scores, but the scientific community is still divided. Have we become smarter than our ancestors or are we better able to solve the kinds of questions posed in intelligence tests? If we are not more intelligent, do IQ tests measure what we think of as intelligence or do they measure something else? We do not know, but if one interpretation of the Flynn effect is right, it is only a matter of time before our intellectually superior descendants find out. **MT**

Mitochondrial Eve
R. Cann, M. Stoneking, and A. Wilson

All people descend from a single woman who lived 200,000 years ago

If we could travel back in time and trace the origins of each person from their mother, we could conceivably find a single mother from whom all modern humans descend. This single, hypothetical woman has been dubbed "mitochondrial Eve," in reference to the biblical story of Adam and Eve, and the DNA found in every human in the mitochondria organelles of their cells.

In the early 1980s, researchers discovered that samples of human mitochondrial DNA (mDNA)—DNA that is passed only from mother to offspring—were much more similar than samples taken from other primates. The closer the DNA of any two individuals, the more closely they are related, which means that humans, as a species, shared a common ancestor much more recently than other primates. In 1987, geneticists

"Adam named his wife Eve, because she would become the mother of all the living."

The Bible, Genesis 3:20

Rebecca Cann, Mark Stoneking (b. 1956), and Allan Wilson (1934–91) completed a study in which they sampled DNA from people across the world. They found that all modern humans shared mDNA from a single woman who, because the differences between samples were most pronounced in that region, probably lived in southern Africa about 200,000 years ago.

While the theory of mitochondrial Eve did not refer to the most recent common human ancestor, it created an alternative explanation to the idea of *Homo sapiens* humanity arising simultaneously in different parts of the world. Due in large part to the discovery of mitochondrial Eve, the more widely held belief today is that all modern humans are descended from a single African ancestor, which makes us more closely related than anyone thought previously. **MT**

Black Athena
Martin Bernal

An argument that European civilization sprang from Afro-Asian roots

The civilization of ancient Greece lies at the heart of Western culture. Most people take Greek culture to be quintessentially European, but what if its roots lay in the African and Asian societies of Egypt and Phoenicia?

In the three volumes of *Black Athena: The Afroasiatic Roots of Classical Civilization*, published between 1987 and 2006, British historian Martin Bernal (b. 1937) examined the evidence. A scholar of modern Chinese history, he began to examine his Jewish roots and soon realized that Hebrew and Phoenician—both dialects of a single Canaanite, Semitic language—were very similar to ancient Greek. The Greeks themselves had always identified themselves with Egypt and Phoenicia, but why had these roots been ignored over the centuries? As he read, Bernal realized that the idea of what he

"The political purpose of Black Athena is . . . to lessen European cultural arrogance."

Martin Bernal, *Black Athena* (1987)

called the Aryan model—that Greece had been settled by Aryans from central Europe—was wrong. In its place he suggested the ancient model, in which Egyptian and Phoenician influences were paramount. He was surprised to find that the shift between the two models had occurred quite recently, during the early nineteenth century, as Western anti-Semitism and racism gained academic credibility. The Aryan model became more racially acceptable, and thus Semitic and Egyptian influences on Greece were denied.

The impact of such thinking was extremely political. Saying that the African and Asian roots of Greece have been deliberately replaced by European roots was to accuse academia of racism. Not everyone concurred, but Bernal's theory has transformed thinking about the roots of Western civilization. **SA**

1988

Fairtrade
Solidaridad

A social movement that aims to improve the ethics of commerce

Fairtrade is an international initiative that was set up to protect the incomes of workers in developing countries, and also to establish and maintain sustainable environmental growth and regeneration policies. The concept underlying Fairtrade was developed after World War II (1939–45) in Europe and North America by religious groups and nongovernmental organizations that offered for sale inexpensive handicrafts imported from the developing world.

Subsequently, however, the cause gained momentum and influence. The first Fairtrade label was launched in 1988, when Dutch development agency Solidaridad sold fairly traded Mexican coffee in Dutch supermarkets under the "Max Havelaar" label. By the end of the twentieth century, official monitoring organizations, such as Fairtrade International, Fair Trade USA, and Eco-Social, were issuing certificates to importers who satisfied their principal requirement: that the developing world should receive a reasonable share of the profits generated by the sale of its products in the industrialized nations. The fairtrade movement focused on the terms of trade applied to bananas, chocolate, cocoa, coffee, tea, cotton, flowers, fresh fruit, gold, handicrafts, honey, sugar, and wine.

Since 2002, produce that meets Fairtrade International standards has been certified with labels bearing the Fair Trade Certified Mark. In order to earn this stamp of approval, goods must be reasonably priced and the profits distributed fairly; in addition, the producers must demonstrate that they aid social development and protect and conserve the environment. The goods must also be produced exclusively by individuals and companies that abide by United Nations and International Labor Organization requirements to ensure safety in the workplace, to guarantee the right to form unions, and to ban child labor and slave labor. **GL**

Fairtrade farmers in Kita, a cotton growing region of Mali. ⬆

Passive Housing
Bo Adamson and Wolfgang Feist

Building to a standard that dramatically reduces energy consumption

The *Passivhaus* (passive housing) concept was first discussed in 1988 by two professors, Bo Adamson of Lund University, Sweden, and Wolfgang Feist of the German Institute for Housing and Environment. The first development of the kind was a row of four terraced homes in Darmstadt, Germany, completed in 1990. It became Europe's first inhabited multi-family house to achieve a documented heating energy consumption of less than 12 kilowatt hours per square meter per year. In September 1996 the Passivhaus-Institut was founded, also in Darmstadt, to promote and control the standard of passive houses.

Passive houses—which can be offices, schools, or shops as well as homes—are structures intended to maximize energy efficiency. Most are purpose-built, but pre-existent buildings can also be refurbished into passive houses. They are airtight, or as close to airtight as possible: door and window frames are fitted with great care to eliminate drafts; walls are made from dense or lightweight materials. Windows are positioned to catch the sunshine, which powers a green heat-recovery ventilation system. Further warmth is derived from internal sources, such as the excess heat generated by refrigerators and washing machines and even the body heat of the inhabitants. If residents feel cold, they can light natural oil heaters; if they feel hot, they can open skylights. All artificial lighting comes from low-energy lamps powered by solar panels.

The building cost of a passive house is about 14 percent more than that of a conventional equivalent. However, the energy savings are immense: domestic power bills are reduced by at least 75 percent and sometimes by more than 90 percent. Passive housing is catching on: at the time of writing, there are around 30,000 certified structures of this type in Europe (mainly in Austria, Germany, and Scandinavia), and thus far the total has increased every year. **GL**

⬆ Passive housing in the Vauban quarter, Freiburg im Breisgau, Germany.

LGBT
United States

An acronym referring to the lesbian, gay, bisexual, and transgender community

Labels always present problems, particularly if they are affixed to people. One person's description can be another's offense, and nowhere is this truer than in the realm of human sexuality. As a result, it has taken years of negotiation and compromise to come up with the initialism "LGBT" to describe, in turn, the lesbian, gay, bisexual, and transgender community. No one person can claim credit for its first usage, and no single article or document can claim to be its founding manifesto, but from 1988 onward it gained increasing acceptance.

When differing sexual identities were first discussed in the late nineteenth century, the term "homosexual," or "of the same sex," was the preferred usage for gay people. But "lesbian" was preferred by some women because the "homo" of homosexual suggested it

"What is straight? A line can be straight, or a street, but the human heart, oh, no ..."

Tennessee Williams, *A Streetcar Named Desire* (1947)

referred to men only. Homosexual, however, had negative connotations, and was gradually replaced by "gay" during the 1970s. Feminists in search of equality with men insisted on using lesbian, and so the lesbian and gay community took wing. Both terms, however, are gender specific and thus ignore bisexuals and transgendered people. It became impossible to find one term that fitted all, and thus LGBT came into being.

While lesbians, gays, and bisexuals are primarily concerned with sexual orientation, transgendered and transsexual people are concerned with gender identity. Many argue that the term is divisive rather than inclusive, yet alternative generic terms are found wanting. "Queer" is negative to those who remember the word as an insult, and "rainbow" (embodied by the LGBT flag) is linked with the New Age movement. **SA**

European Single Currency
European Commission

The notion of a single currency that could be spent throughout Europe

Europe first enjoyed a common currency when it was part of the Roman Empire (27 BCE–476 CE). The first modern proposal was made in 1929 by German foreign minister Gustav Stresemann (1878–1929) as a way of ending post-World War I economic divisions. A second attempt was made in 1969, when the European Commission (EC) set out a plan for "greater coordination of economic policies and monetary cooperation." International economic turbulence soon sabotaged that idea, however.

The third and most successful attempt was initiated at a European summit meeting in Hannover in 1988, when the then president of the EC, Jacques Delors (b. 1925), was asked to draw up a timetable for economic and monetary union. In April 1989, Delors announced a

"Inspiration for the € symbol came from ... the first letter of the word Europe ..."

European Commission (October 30, 2010)

three-stage plan that eventually led to the introduction of new euro notes and coins in twelve European Union (EU) countries, on January 1, 2002. Five further EU countries later joined the currency, and it is also used in non-EU Montenegro and Kosovo, as well as in other EU-linked territories around the world.

Currently used by 326 million people, the euro has become the world's second most traded currency after the U.S. dollar. Its economic impact, however, has been disastrous. Common interest and exchange rates without the strengths of a full fiscal union have removed two crucial monetary levers from government control at a national level. What works for rich Germany does not work for poor Greece. The euro will survive because its politicians will it, but it has yet to prove its economic potential. **SA**

Restorative Justice
John Braithwaite

Doing justice by restoring the harm rather than punishing the offense

Restorative justice is a response to injustice, particularly crime, that involves a process of restitution, restoration, and reconciliation. In restorative justice, everybody affected by the crime is included in, and given a degree of authority over, the process; the participants are expected to attain a deliberative consensus; and the outcome is oriented toward reparation and reconciliation, rather than punishment. It is contrasted with retributive justice, according to which crime is primarily an offense to the state, not a harm to the victim, and a proportionate punishment is the best response. Proponents of restorative justice generally contend that it is deeply rooted in human history, but it emerged as a conscious theoretical alternative to retributive justice in the 1980s, most notably with the

> *"Restorative justice is about the idea that because crime hurts, justice should heal."*

John Braithwaite

publication of *Crime, Shame and Reintegration* in 1989 by Australian criminologist John Braithwaite (*b*. 1951).

As appealing as restorative justice may seem, critics have complained that it is formulated in unclear and conflicting ways, that it is really a view of punishment rather than of justice, that it is unsuccessful in reducing recidivism, that it is unjust in not ensuring equal treatment of similar offenders, and that it unduly focuses on individual offenders rather than on social conditions.

Restorative justice programs have become increasingly common since the 1990s, especially for cases involving youthful offenders and domestic violence. The South African Truth and Reconciliation Commission, established in 1995 to address the human rights violations of the apartheid era, is generally regarded as a mostly successful effort. **GB**

Outsourcing
Kodak Eastman Company

A logical consequence of the idea of the division of labor

To outsource, in business, is to obtain goods or services from external sources rather than to produce or perform them internally. When the sources are foreign, outsourcing is sometimes called offshoring. The term "outsource" appeared in English in *c*. 1980, with the term "offshoring" appearing shortly thereafter, although both practices clearly predate the terms. The first formal identification of outsourcing as a business strategy, however, occured in 1989, when the Kodak Eastman Company decided to outsource its IT systems to IBM.

Outsourcing is typically driven by considerations of efficiency. By specializing, the external source can avail itself of economies of scale or scope, thus providing its goods or services at a lower cost than the outsourcing company could manage. Meanwhile, the outsourcing company can benefit by concentrating on its core business. The external source may also not be subject to costs that the outsourcing company would be subject to, such as hiring and training specialized staff, dealing with a unionized workforce, and complying with government regulations regarding worker benefits or environmental practices. But outsourcing is not necessarily a panacea: for example, companies considering whether to outsource may have concerns about the quality of the goods or services provided by the external source, or their loss of control over the supply chain, or the possibility of the external source eventually becoming a rival.

It is likely that the recent interest in outsourcing and offshoring was driven by the advent of inexpensive telecommunications and then the Internet, enabling the extension of outsourcing to goods and services that previously would have been produced or performed internally. Outsourcing and offshoring are bound to continue—and they will continue to be a source of turbulence in the labor market. **GB**

World Wide Web / Internet

Tim Berners-Lee

The development of a worldwide interconnected data and information system that grew out of a Cold War-era defense program

The Internet is a system of interconnected computer networks that now uses the TCP/IP protocol suite to connect billions of users worldwide. However, its hugely influential present-day use was not envisaged at its inception. The Internet began as a Cold War-era initiative in the United States. Wary of Soviet technological supremacy after the launch of the Sputnik in 1957, and concerned that a single Soviet missile could obliterate the telephone network and cripple the nation, the U.S. government worked to develop a means to connect computers outside the telephone system. The result was the first file-sharing computer network, called ARPANET.

In the 1970s, U.S. computer scientists Vinton Cerf (b. 1943) and Bob Kahn (b. 1938) developed the TCP/IP protocol, which led to the National Science Foundation Network, or NSFNET, replacing ARPANET by the 1980s. However, it was a graduate of Oxford University, British computer scientist Tim Berners-Lee (b. 1955), who, in 1989, invented the World Wide Web, an Internet-based hypermedia initiative for global information sharing, while working at CERN, the European Particle Physics Laboratory. Berners-Lee created standards for hypertext documents (text documents with other data, such as images or links to other computers, embedded in them) shared across the NSFNET, and in 1990 wrote the first web client and server. The NSFNET was decommissioned in 1995, and the Internet was made available for private and commercial use.

Today the Internet is mainly used to access the World Wide Web's conglomerate of hypertext documents. Nearly a third of the world's 6.8 billion people frequently use the Internet. It enables personal enrichment, social connection, artistic development, economic development, commerce, and learning, and has shaped global politics and human society since the 1990s. **APT**

↑ This was the computer used at CERN by British scientist Tim Berners-Lee to devise the World Wide Web in the late 1980s and early 1990s.

"The Internet has made me very casual with a level of omniscience that was unthinkable a decade ago. I now wonder if God gets bored knowing the answer to everything."

Douglas Coupland, novelist

The End of History
Francis Fukuyama

Western liberal democracy is the last form that human society will take

"The end of history" is a theory about the final evolution of human society. According to this theory, humankind will eventually reach a state of socio-economic development at which there will be no further evolution but only refinements in the existing system. Contemporary proponents of the theory speculate that Western free market-based liberal democracy is the final socio-economic development.

Philosophers Georg Hegel (1770–1831) and Karl Marx (1818–83) speculated about the end of history. Marx believed that history would end in a communist utopian society, while Hegel thought it would end in a liberal state. The theory gained new prominence, however, when U.S. political scientist and economist Francis Fukuyama (b. 1952) expounded his version of

"Marx believed that the evolution of human societies was not open-ended . . ."
Francis Fukuyama

the theory in a paper, "The End of History?" (1989), which he subsequently developed into a best selling book, *The End of History and the Last Man* (1992).

The end of history theory does not claim that events will stop happening; it states that wholesale evolution of society will cease as all states converge on Western liberal democracy. The theory has important implications if true, since it controversially implies that communism, among other alternative forms of society, is retrogressive and unsustainable. This implication has been rejected by thinkers such as French philosopher Jacques Derrida (1930–2004), who likened the theory to a "New Gospel" reinforcing Christian eschatology, and British historian Perry Anderson (b. 1938), who points out that Western liberal democracies are still rife with poverty, suffering, and injustice. **APT**

Parental Advisory Label
Tipper Gore

A warning to parents on music products of content unsuitable for children

Introduced in 1990 on the instigation of author Tipper Gore (b. 1948), then wife of congressman Al Gore, parental advisory labels (PALs) originally took the form of square, nonremovable stickers with a dotted white line near the center and the legends "Explicit lyrics" at the top and "Parental advisory" at the bottom. The first album to carry a PAL was *Banned in the USA* (1990) by Luke featuring the 2 Live Crew. Two years later, PAL motifs began to be integrated into album cover artwork. In 1993, the logo was changed to a white box in a black rectangle, with "Explicit lyrics" becoming "Explicit content."

PALs warned prospective purchasers that the albums to which they were affixed contained profane language, sexual references, incitements to violence, or other material that the Recording Industry Association

"Kids have had to learn how to cover the Parental Advisory labels on their CDs . . ."
Tom Breihan, pitchfork.com

of America (RIAA) deemed inappropriate for people under the age of seventeen. But the effects of PALs were not always those intended by the RIAA. Some musicians regarded a PAL as a badge of honor and deliberately courted notoriety, though research indicates that controversial lyrics have little effect on sales. Since there was no consensus about what justified a PAL, there were numerous anomalies. Some material, such as the Geto Boys' self-titled album, was regarded as so extreme that it required additional warnings.

PALs have helped customers to sift out material that they regard as unsuitable. In the United States, Best Buy and other big retail chains have used their power in the marketplace to insist that record companies wanting products stocked in their stores produce "clean" alternative versions without the PAL label. **GL**

Anti-globalization
United States

A movement that seeks tighter controls over the powers of big international business

The second half of the twentieth century saw a vast increase in the number of big firms whose commercial activities transcended national boundaries and jurisdictions. Among the initiatives that facilitated this development was the "maquiladora program" in the 1960s, which enabled foreign companies to import parts and raw materials duty-free into Mexico, where they were assembled by low-paid workers before being re-exported, again without surcharge. The growth of this phenomenon—known as globalization—was accelerated in the 1980s by the deregulation of the Western world's financial markets.

This development had numerous benefits for industry but many potential disadvantages for individuals, not least because it was no longer clear which nation's laws governed the firms' activities.

The reaction against this trend took the form of what became known as the anti-globalization movement. It began as isolated murmurings of discontent, notably a demonstration on Wall Street, New York City, the day after Earth Day in 1990, but grew in the 1990s, mainly through the Internet, into a vocal and active pressure group. Supporters of anti-globalization oppose the unregulated economic and political power that has been rapidly acquired by multinational corporations, which have at the same time gained for themselves almost unrestricted liberty to maximize their profits, regardless of the interests or, in some cases, even the safety of their workers. Anti-globalists also object to the fact that big companies can cross borders and exploit natural resources almost at will, freedoms that are denied to most people.

Anti-globalization is to some extent a misnomer. Rather than oppose multinational and transnational businesses, supporters want to bring big firms under a new world authority that protects individuals and promotes sustainable development and fair trade. **GL**

1990

Godwin's Law

Michael Godwin

Glib comparisons to the Nazis are inuring people to the full horror of their acts

An early adopter of computers, U.S. attorney and author Michael Godwin (b. 1956) coined what has become known as "Godwin's Law" in 1990. After observing participants in Usenet newsgroups online discussion forums during the 1980s, he noticed that thoughtless comparisons to Hitler or the Nazis were abundant, and that people were losing perspective on what made the Nazis and the Holocaust so terrible.

Godwin came up with his Internet adage in an attempt to promote more considered dialogue: "I thought that if we continued to make trivial comparisons to Nazis or to Hitler or to the Holocaust, we in some ways were papering over how spiritually traumatic that period was for all of Western civilization,

and maybe for civilization generally." He decided to spread around his notion of Godwin's Law in various online forums. The law is a meme suggesting that the longer any online discussion goes on, whatever its scope or topic, it is inevitable that someone will make a comparison to Adolf Hitler or the Nazis. The law recognizes that heated debates usually proceed in predictable ways, with escalating rhetoric, and when participants want to call someone the worst thing they can think of, they suggest they are like Hitler or the Nazis; alternatively, people might also see fit to compare an unfortunate or undesirable event to the Holocaust. Godwin's Law is designed to point out that calling someone a Nazi on trivial grounds—for example, because they have mildly offensive views on healthcare policy—is inappropriate hyperbole.

Internet users began to quote and cite Godwin's Law in response to offending posts, and glib comparisons to Hitler and the Nazis became an Internet faux pas. Although Godwin originally framed his theory in criticism of online culture, it is also applied to traditional media culture and the wider world, and has thus entered into popular culture. **CK**

 A Cuban poster combines George W. Bush with Hitler to equal the terrorist Luis Posada Carriles.

Queer Theory
Teresa de Lauretis

A theory of "otherness" that challenges existing notions of gender and sexuality

Once considered as a pathological problem subject to the criminal code, homosexuality is now generally considered to be an acceptable sexuality alongside heterosexuality. But this model implies a duality that some critics argue is wrong. Sexuality is not a matter of either straight or gay, they say, and is too ambivalent to be thus confined. From these basic ideas have arisen the principles of queer theory.

The term "queer theory" was first used in 1990 by Teresa de Lauretis (b. 1938), an Italian-born academic working in the United States, at a working conference on lesbian and gay sexualities held at the University of California, Santa Cruz. She later formally introduced it in the article "Queer Theory, Lesbian and Gay Sexualities," published in a special issue of *A Journal of Feminist and*

> *"Queer is . . . whatever is at odds with the normal, the legitimate, the dominant."*
>
> David Halperin, gender theorist

Cultural Studies in 1991. As she put it, "Queer unsettles and questions the genderedness of sexuality." De Lauretis abandoned the term when it was adopted by those it had intended to subvert, but the idea stuck.

Queer theory arose out of feminist challenges to the idea that gender is part of our essential selves, and also from gay and lesbian studies of socially constructed ideas about sexuality. For queer theorists, sexual identities and gender itself are not fixed and cannot be labeled or categorized. The theory came of age in response to the AIDS crisis, when AIDS was termed a "gay disease" and homophobia dramatically increased. It has had a huge impact in film and literature, and in the Queercore movement of music, art, and magazines. The theory continues to challenge sexual stereotypes and celebrate the deviant and the different. **SA**

Generational Attitudes
William Strauss and Neil Howe

How and why attitudes change from generation to generation

The notion that every generation shares certain attitudes to life is not new, but it was partly codified by William Strauss (1947–2007) and Neil Howe (b. 1951), whose book *Generations* (1991) recounted the history of the United States from 1584 as a series of generational biographies. In *The Fourth Turning* (1997), the two U.S. academics further posited that generational attitudes are cyclic and complete a full revolution roughly once every eighty or ninety years.

Within each cycle are four phases, which Strauss and Howe likened to the seasons of the year. The high point of each cycle is a period during which new ideas—artistic, philosophical, religious, or scientific—inspire a surge of creativity: they call this point an "awakening" (corresponding to summer). The nadir is a major setback, such as a large-scale military conflict, which they term a "crisis" (corresponding to winter). Between these extremes are transitional periods analogous to spring and fall. The authors contend that such cycles have recurred throughout U.S. history: for example, the crisis of the Great Depression and World War II (1929–45) was followed, after a transitional period, by the revolution in consciousness of the 1960s, which represented an awakening.

What goes around comes around: each phase of the cycle lasts for approximately twenty years; at the conclusion of the fourth phase, attitudes and social norms have generally reverted to their original position. While only a construct, the theory has resonated and made it conventional for Westerners living at the start of the twenty-first century to identify themselves, depending upon their age, as "war children" (those born between roughly 1939 and 1945), "baby boomers" (1946–64), "Generation X" (mid-1960s to mid-1980s), or "Generation Y" (alternatively called "the Millennials," from around 1982 to 2000). **GL**

Ontology in Information Science
Tom Gruber

Developing a taxonomy of concepts to enable computers to reason more efficiently and communicate with one another more effectively

Ontology in its original sense, as expounded by philosophers, refers to the study of the categories of being. When someone reflects on the nature of existing things, how many there are, and what kinds of things there are, they engage in ontology in the traditional sense. In the twentieth century, however, the term took on a new meaning: an ontology became a domain-specific taxonomy of concepts designed to clarify thought by illuminating the relations between the various concepts residing in a specified domain, such as medicine, chess, architecture, or music.

Ontology in the information science sense began with the work of computer scientists in the late twentieth century, notably U.S. computer scientist Tom Gruber (b. 1959), in his paper "A Translation Approach to Portable Ontology Specifications," published in 1993 in the journal *Knowledge Acquisition*. Gruber and his peers realized that producing artificially intelligent machines that could reason in a manner analogous to humans required equipping those machines with detailed taxonomic information that allowed them to make correct inferences about the relations between their various concepts. The realization sparked a boom in research on various possible taxonomies, or ontologies.

Ontology has also enabled more efficient database communication in such diverse areas as biomedical informatics, library science, software engineering, warfare, and national security. For example, it has been suggested as a tool for resolving what British ontological scientist Barry Smith (b. 1952) has referred to as the "Database Tower of Babel Problem." This problem results from the idiosyncratic terminologies used by databases to organize their information. Databases constructed with shared ontologies can communicate more efficiently, with the result that less information is lost in the communication process. **APT**

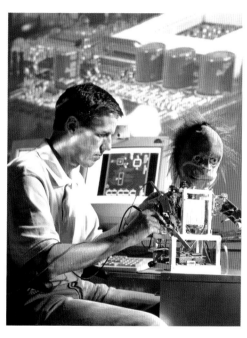

British artificial intelligence researcher Steve Grand with his robot, "Lucy," whose success depends on a common ontology shared by its internal circuits and computerized neural software.

"The key role of ontologies with respect to database systems is to specify a data modeling representation at a level of abstraction above specific database designs (logical or physical), so that data can be exported ... and unified."

Tom Gruber

McDonaldization
George Ritzer

The notion that the body politic aspires to the condition of a fast-food chain

In *The McDonaldization of Society* (1993), U.S. sociologist George Ritzer (b. 1940) analyzed the internal workings of the fast-food chain McDonald's and argued that they are symptomatic of developments in global society and economics. He examined five characteristics of the company, which he termed efficiency, calculability, predictability, control, and culture. Efficiency is the minimization of the time it takes to turn a hungry customer into a full one. Calculability is the principle that the only accurate measurement of success is sales; sales will hold up for as long as customers make no distinction between cheap, large quantities (which are measurable) and good quality (which is subjective). He further contended that McDonald's restaurants are predictable (the same all over the world) and

"McDonaldization has shown every sign of being an inexorable process . . ."

George Ritzer, *The McDonaldization of Society 6* (2011)

controlling (every member of staff performs a strictly defined and limited function). And, as the restaurant chain has proliferated, it has imposed its culture on indigenous dining traditions.

In Ritzer's view, McDonald's mirrors society, mainly in the United States but increasingly worldwide. He regards the introduction of monolithic systems in the name of efficiency as dehumanizing, because they deny individual freedom to think. This he calls the "iron cage" of bureaucracy, which creates "settings in which people cannot always behave as human beings."

Many people shared Ritzer's disapproval of these trends, and there was a consequent wave of hostility toward McDonald's. However, executives of the fast-food chain protested that Ritzer's account of their business practices was substantially inaccurate. **GL**

Metrosexuality
Mark Simpson

The rise of urban males with preoccupations that are traditionally taken to be female

"Metrosexual" is a term for an urban male who is concerned about his physical appearance and who spends a notable amount of time and money on personal grooming. The first recorded use of the word is in an article by British journalist Mark Simpson, published in November 1994. While Simpson is widely credited with having coined the term, he strenuously asserts that he picked it up from common parlance.

In addition to fastidious personal grooming, a metrosexual also enjoys devoting a conspicuous part of his (usually substantial) disposable income to the purchase of modish consumer products, such as designer-label clothing, sports cars, and fragrances. He typically lives in or within easy reach of a city ("metro" is a contraction of "metropolitan") and its supporting

"It represents a fundamental shift in what men are allowed to be and want."

Mark Simpson

infrastructure of gyms, manicurists, hairdressers, and stores. A metrosexual may be bisexual or gay, but the term is more significant if he is straight because his heterosexuality is offset by characteristics that may, in other contexts, be regarded as feminine or effeminate.

The popularization of the term served a useful purpose because it provided a way of describing a man who takes pride in his appearance without risking the pejorative overtones of words such as "dandy" or "narcissist." Among the celebrities to whom it has been applied are British soccer player David Beckham (b. 1975, who made it acceptable for straight Western men to wear sarongs) and U.S. movie star Brad Pitt (b. 1963), whose macho image is tempered by the softness of one who, like many metrosexuals, may be said to be "in touch with his feminine side." **GL**

A Pakistani metrosexual enjoys having a facial beauty treatment applied at a salon in Karachi in 2011. ➡

W3C
Tim Berners-Lee

A visionary computer scientist standardizes information sharing across the Internet

W3C, or the World Wide Web Consortium, is the primary international standards organization for the World Wide Web. Tim Berners-Lee (b. 1955), British computer scientist and architect of the modern Internet, working at the Massachusetts Institute of Technology Laboratory for Computer Science, founded the Consortium in 1994 in conjunction with DARPA, the U.S. Defense Advanced Research Projects Agency, and the European Commission. The Consortium works to maintain agreement among HTML content providers, such as businesses and government agencies, to ensure compatibility in the display of World Wide Web content. As of 2012 it had 351 member organizations.

The World Wide Web itself is a network of hypertext documents accessible via the Internet. Virtually all of an

"The Web does not just connect machines, it connects people."

Tim Berners-Lee

individual's interaction with the Internet occurs within the World Wide Web, which is accessed with a web browser. Globally, the volume of web user "traffic" is vast, and the standards upheld by W3C are essential in maintaining the World Wide Web and leading it to its full potential. W3C streamlines the international sharing of information, allowing computers in different geographic regions to "talk" to one another with optimal ease.

W3C is crucial for the viability of the World Wide Web—without it, information sharing on a global scale would be hugely problematic. Failure would have major consequences. For example, consider the events of the Arab Spring (2010–), in which Web-based social media such as Twitter and Facebook played a key role. Arguably, without W3C, and the social media that rely on it, this democratic movement would never have occurred. **APT**

Video on Demand
Cambridge Cable Network

A system allowing users to watch video content whenever they wish

Video on demand (VOD) is a technology that delivers video content that users can choose to watch and listen to when they want, irrespective of broadcast schedules. Upon receiving a user's request, with VOD, a centralized server streams online video data in real time to the viewer's set-top box, computer, or cell phone, so they can start watching the selected video almost immediately. The video remains on the transmitting server as compressed digital files. VOD is a convenient way for people to organize their television viewing to suit their own schedule and to watch movies at home, or on the move, rather than at a cinema. Often the paid-for video is available for a limited time.

The first successful experiments in VOD took place in Cambridge, England, in 1994 via the Cambridge

"Couch potatoes dislike wading through alphabetical lists of titles."

The Economist (2011)

Digital Interactive Television Trial conducted by academics and various companies. Video was streamed to homes and schools connected to the Cambridge Cable Network. The project, although successful, ended in 1996. In 1998, a fully commercial VOD service was launched that included broadcast television and Internet services.

Despite the success of early such experiments, VOD only took off in commercial terms in the 2000s when the cost of equipment dropped, the necessary bandwidth became available at a competitive price, and companies began to provide content that people actually wanted to watch. VOD grew throughout Europe, the United States, and the rest of the world to become the common way for users to consume entertainment that it is today. **CK**

← Tim Berners-Lee in 1995, holding the title of the consortium that he helped to found.

Amazon.com
Jeffrey P. Bezos

The online store that enabled consumers to buy books at the touch of a button

For hundreds of years, if readers wanted a book, they went to a bookstore; if the title was not in stock, they had to order it and wait for notification from the bookstore that it had come in. But the advent of the Internet in the 1990s gave U.S. businessman Jeffrey P. Bezos (b. 1964) the opportunity to make every book in existence—not just every title currently in print—available to anyone with a PC and a method of paying: the customer no longer had to leave home to shop.

Amazon.com (a name chosen principally because "A" is at the start of the alphabet) was founded in Washington State in 1994 and sold its first book in July of the following year. It later expanded into other markets, including CDs, DVDs, MP3 downloads, software, video games, clothing, domestic electronic appliances, food, toys, and jewelry. Meanwhile it spread its operations from the United States to other countries: the firm currently also has websites and warehouses in Canada, China, France, Germany, Italy, Japan, Spain, and the United Kingdom; by 2012, some 44 percent of its $12.8 billion sales were coming from outside the United States. At the time of writing, amazon.com is the biggest retailer in the world, with 69,000 employees fulfilling orders from 19.5 million customers a day, and the business is still growing.

With business booming, amazon.com has been able to reduce prices below a level that smaller competitors find economical, and, crucially, cut delivery times to the bone: for popular items, the time lag between receiving the order and making the delivery may be as little as twenty-four hours, at least in urban areas. Amazon.com has revolutionized the book world, challenging publishers to fulfill orders faster than ever before and confronting traditional main street retailers with a choice between streamlining and diversifying or closing forever. In the case of music, main street sellers have already all but disappeared in many areas. **GL**

The inside of the logistics center of amazon.de in Bad Hersfeld, Germany. ⬆

1994

Upcycling
Reiner Pilz

Recycling unwanted materials in ways that enhance their value

The limitation of some forms of recycling is that they reduce the already low value of the basic material. Expensive bricks end up as cheap aggregate that is used in the foundations of buildings and highways. Soda cans are flattened into sheets of aluminum that cost, ton for ton, less than the original drinks containers.

Many people believe that conservationists should set their sights higher than this. Instead of breaking up hardwood taken from refurbished buildings and reselling it as cheap firewood, environmentalists should mill it into flooring planks and thus increase its value.

This is not a new idea: laptop cases are made from old wetsuits; broken piano keys are turned into jewelry. However, the concept had no name until 1994, when

Reiner Pilz, whose German company manufactures electronic safety equipment for industrial machinery, remarked in an interview that "recycling" would be better termed "downcycling." "What we need," Pilz added, "is upcycling, where old products are given more value, not less."

Pilz's label stuck and was given wider currency by its use in books including *Upcycling* (1999) by Gunter Pauli and Johannes F. Hartkemeyer, and *Cradle to Cradle: Remaking the Way We Make Things* (2002) by Michael Braungart and William McDonough. The latter book also highlighted the ways in which reduction in the use of new raw materials can cause a corresponding decrease in energy usage, air and water pollution, and greenhouse gas emissions.

Once identifiable, the upcycling process became easier to promote. Upcycling first caught on in developing countries that could least afford new materials, but the new approach soon came westward. In 2010, Etsy, a U.S. e-commerce website selling handmade artifacts, offered just under 8,000 upcycled products; less than two years later, the number of products exceeded 150,000. **GL**

⬆ A market stall in Siem Reap, Cambodia, sells handbags made from upcycled rice sacks.

V-chip

Brett West and John P. Gardner

Technology to block television shows deemed inappropriate for children

In the late twentieth century there was growing concern worldwide that unsupervised children were being exposed to violent or sexually explicit television programs. To counter this, V-chip technology was developed by Canadian professor Tim Collings and patented in 1994 by two Americans, Brett West and John P. Gardner. The V-chip enables certain shows to be blocked on certain receivers (television sets). "V" originally stood for "viewer control," but, because the device is used mainly by adults wanting to protect children, it is more commonly taken to stand for "violence." Since 2000, all new televisions in the United States have had to have the chip installed by law.

The V-chip reads a code in the broadcast signal that gives any show a rating of between one and at least

> *"We're handing the TV remote control back to America's parents ..."*
>
> Bill Clinton, U.S. president 1993–2001

thirteen, depending on the amount of violence, sex, and foul language it contains. Ratings often appear on the screen at the start of programs. If the encoded number is higher than the number that has been set on a particular television, that show will not be accessible on that set. The encoded number is preset by the broadcaster according to strict guidelines, but those guidelines apply only to programs that are likely to be contentious: news bulletins and sports broadcasts do not have such ratings and are therefore unblockable.

The limitation of the V-chip is that it can be reset or deactivated by anyone who knows how to reset the television controls to 0000: hence it is reliably effective only with young children and technophobes. The device has also been criticized by Americans who believe that it violates the First Amendment. **GL**

Angie's List

Bill Oesterle and Angie Hicks

A dependable way to get good advice about prospective tradespeople

U.S. entrepreneur Angie Hicks launched the company that was to become Angie's List in suburban Columbus, Ohio, in 1995. The launch came in response to frustrations encountered by her cofounder, U.S. venture capitalist Bill Oesterle, who was trying to restore a 1920s home but had difficulty finding a reputable heating, ventilation, and air conditioning company. Knowing that Bill's problem was not unique, Bill and Angie decided to find a way to solve it that would benefit all homeowners.

The implementation of the idea fell to Angie, who went door to door recruiting members, collecting insights from homeowners, and signing them up for the new service. She also researched homeowners' issues and talked to service professionals, putting together a monthly newsletter designed to help homeowners find the right service professional for their needs. Within a year, Angie had enrolled more than 1,000 members to her neighborhood "grapevine group" and laid the foundation for what would become one of the fastest growing companies in the United States.

In 1999, the accumulated database of what was now known as Angie's List was transferred to the Internet. It then spread across North America, meanwhile broadening its scope to cover a wide range of services, including healthcare and automobile maintenance. At the time of writing, it has around 1.5 million subscribers, who post almost half a million reviews annually. Angie's List derives its revenue from two sources: individual subscriptions, the cost of which varies from region to region, and advertising. Companies are not allowed to join, and Angie's List staff monitor contributors to ensure that they do not receive payment for their comments. In an age when the opportunities to disseminate misinformation are greater than ever before, Angie's List is a boon to the consumer. **GL**

eBay
Pierre Omidyar

Originally set up to facilitate the purchase and sale of collectibles by auction, the eBay Internet site is now used by millions every day as a form of mass entertainment

In 1995, Iranian-U.S. entrepreneur Pierre Omidyar (b. 1967) set himself the task of writing a computer code on his personal web page that would enable people to bid in online auctions. In the same year, he launched the online service Auction Web, one of the first websites to link buyers and sellers via the Internet. Now called eBay and based in San Jose, California, it is a global online auction and trading company.

One key attraction of eBay is its trustworthiness, achieved through its use (and, since 2002, ownership) of PayPal, an automated online clearing house for the transfer of money. Also, in order to filter out unscrupulous or incompetent sellers, eBay solicits feedback that is posted online so that prospective purchasers can see how satisfied previous customers have been. However, one drawback is that low ratings are not always the fault of the seller, whose goods may be delayed or damaged in transit. After some vendors attempted to sabotage rivals by posting bad reviews in 2008, eBay removed the facility to post negative descriptions; the rating system now involves numerical scores only.

Although eBay strives to ensure that no offensive or illegal material is traded on the website, questions remain about its responsibility for transactions. The company has faced lawsuits for alleged complicity in the sale of counterfeit and damaged goods.

Although some items on eBay are advertised at a fixed price, most are open to offers for a certain period, at the end of which they are sold to the highest bidder. Many countries have their own eBay website: the original one covers the United States and Canada; most nations in Europe and many in Asia have their own; in Latin America, eBay operates in association with another e-commerce company, Mercado Libre. There are currently more than 300 million registered eBay users worldwide. **GL**

⬆ Pierre Omidyar, founder of eBay, photographed in 2002. His auction website was focused originally on collectibles such as soft toys, and innumerable items continue to be traded.

"eBay is a community anchored in commerce. It is a commerce site that built a community around it."

Meg Whitman, CEO Hewlett-Packard Co.

Ubuntu
Southern Africa

An African attitude to the world that has helped in the transition from apartheid

In 1995, the first democratically elected government of South Africa set up the Truth and Reconciliation Commission (TRC) with Desmond Tutu (b. 1931), first black archbishop of Cape Town, at its head. The commission investigated atrocities carried out under the previous apartheid regime. Although the TRC was not without its limitations, and was criticized by some for excessive leniency to those arraigned, it is nevertheless widely regarded as the greatest success of Nelson Mandela's presidency because it helped to end one period of enmity without starting another.

The TRC was strongly influenced by Ubuntu, a humanist philosophy that originated in southern Africa but came to the attention of the Western world in the late 1990s. The word came into English

"Ubuntu does not mean that people should not enrich themselves . . ."
Nelson Mandela, politician

from Swahili, one of more than 250 Bantu languages in which the word occurs. In common with other philosophies, Ubuntu cannot be easily summarized, but, according to Archbishop Tutu in his book *No Future Without Forgiveness* (1999), it is "about the fact that you can't exist as a human being in isolation . . . what you do affects the whole world." More specifically, Ubuntu counsels forgiveness rather than vengeance; conciliation rather than confrontation; tolerance, compassion, and respect for the humanity of others— all of them much easier to recite than to practice.

The word "Ubuntu" has been adopted as a pre-game chant by the Boston Celtics basketball team, and the Ubuntu axiom "I am because we are" became the title of a documentary about orphans in Malawi released in 2008 by popstar Madonna. **GL**

Craigslist
Craig Newmark

The Internet's leading contact network for music gigs, goods, and love

Craigslist is an online service that provides classified advertisements, community information, and community discussion forums. It is the brainchild of software engineer Craig Newmark (b. 1952), who, feeling lonely in California away from his native New Jersey, decided to set up a free e-mail service alerting like-minded people to forthcoming events in and around San Francisco. It was so successful after its launch in 1995 that it soon expanded into a website on which members could post information, initiate or participate in discussions, buy and sell goods, and find jobs. However, Craigslist became best known as a forum for people wishing to contact others for romance or sex.

What started as a hobby became in 1999 an incorporated, for-profit private company. In 2001,

"What works for us is the culture of trust our community has built with us."
Craig Newmark

Craigslist made its first foreign sortie, to Vancouver, Canada. By 2005, it had at least one website in every U.S. state, and it later expanded into seventy countries. There are now Craigslists available in French, German, Italian, Portuguese, and Spanish.

Worldwide, Craigslist now posts millions of advertisements each month. It is free to most private individuals, although following an agreement with forty U.S. state attorneys in 2008, charges were introduced for adverts for erotic services; in 2010 the "adult" category was withdrawn from both the U.S. and Canadian versions. Craigslist's chief sources of revenue are companies that place adverts for jobs and, in New York City, brokered apartment listings. Craigslist runs no paid-for banner adverts, a factor that has increased its perceived independence and trustworthiness. **GL**

A humorous portrait of Craigslist founder Craig Newmark in 2005, surrounded by tradeable artifacts. ➔

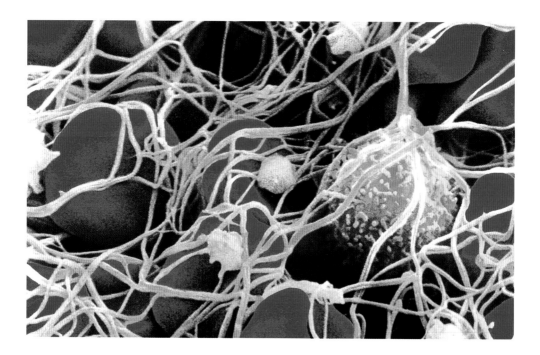

1996

Darwin's Black Box

Michael J. Behe

A scientist's challenge to the Darwinian assumption that there is no God

In his book *On the Origin of Species* (1859), naturalist Charles Darwin (1809–82) described his study of various creatures in South America and concluded that life on Earth evolves over time. Because Darwin argued that everything in the universe can be explained in evolutionary terms, other writers later used his findings to support the view that there is no God.

The publication in 1996 of *Darwin's Black Box: The Biochemical Challenge of Evolution* by U.S. biochemist Michael J. Behe (b. 1952) presented a new challenge to the Darwinian view by questioning the validity of its key assumption. The "black box" of the title refers to anything unproven that has to be taken on trust before a whole concept can be believed.

Among the things that Behe regarded as inexplicable in evolutionary terms are blood clotting and the immune system. These, he elaborated, are like components of a spring-loaded mousetrap: if one part of the whole is altered or removed, the whole contraption fails to work. Blood clotting and the immune system have not been proved to have evolved from something else, and it is unscientific to assume that they must have, just because evolution has been shown to apply to, for example, certain species of Galapagos chaffinch. Behe concluded that the essential quality of such things is what he termed their "irreducible complexity."

The content of Behe's book was essentially one scientist pointing out possible flaws in the findings of another. *Darwin's Black Box* received a cool reception from critics, who objected that its ideas were a rehash of the "watchmaker analogy"—that the world's apparently intelligent design requires an intelligent designer, God—first propounded by William Paley (1743–1805) and widely discredited post Darwin. Religious fundamentalists, however, cited Behe's theories as evidence that God could exist after all. **GL**

A colored microscopic image of a blood clot, which Behe states has no proven evolutionary origin. ↑

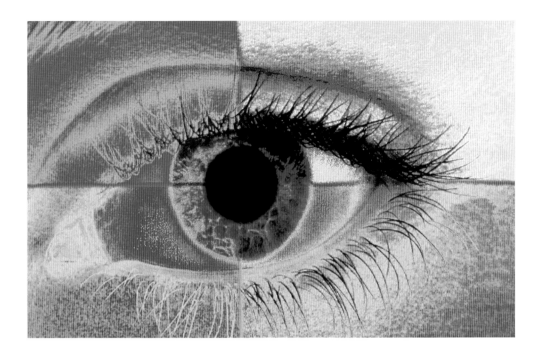

1996

Naturalistic Dualism
David Chalmers

Thought processes include ideas we can express and feelings that we cannot

Why are some thoughts and feelings easier to communicate than others? We can identify and tell each other the symptoms of a headache; we can recognize when we are awake; and know when we are hot or cold. But how do we put into words the feelings evoked in us by, for example, the color blue, the sound of a certain musical note, or the smell of charcoal?

According to Australian philosopher David Chalmers (b. 1966) in his book *The Conscious Mind* (1996), the former are examples of "easy problems" of consciousness, while the latter are "hard problems"—inexplicable but nevertheless real.

The distinction is important because, by acknowledging it, philosophy and science can move away from their traditional dependence on physicalism (the notion that things exist only insofar as they are perceived and describable) toward what Chalmers terms "naturalistic dualism"—an acceptance that consciousness has properties that are unquantifiable. Chalmers's theory is controversial because it posits a form of experience that cannot be explained in physical terms, and therefore implies that consciousness is ultimately more than just the individual's interpretation of neural processes in his or her brain.

Chalmers himself recognizes the difficulty: "It is widely agreed that experience arises from a physical basis, but we have no good explanation of why and how it so arises. Why should physical processing give rise to a rich inner life at all? It seems objectively unreasonable that it should, and yet it does."

The idea has its detractors, who say that as soon as we have defined consciousness, distinctions between hard and soft forms of it will dissipate. However, its supporters, foremost among whom is British philosopher Colin McGinn (b. 1950), have used it as the basis for a new mysterianism positing that parts of consciousness are beyond understanding. **GL**

AMBER Alert
Richard Hagerman

An initiative to thwart child abductors before they can do any harm

An AMBER Alert is a rapidly issued news bulletin to notify the public that a child may have been abducted. First used in the United States in 1996, the AMBER Alert was originally named in memory of nine-year-old Amber Hagerman, who was kidnapped and murdered in Arlington, Texas, that year. Amber's father, Richard Hagerman, was instrumental in setting up the broadcast alerts. Later, the term was incorrectly taken to be an acronym for "America's Missing: Broadcast Emergency Response."

AMBER Alerts are subject to strict guidelines: a law enforcement agency must confirm that an abduction has taken place; the child, who must be under the age of eighteen, must be at risk; descriptions of both the victim and, if possible, the suspected kidnapper should

"The goal of an AMBER Alert is to instantly galvanize the entire community . . ."
U.S. Department of Justice website

be provided. If these criteria are satisfied, the alerts are broadcast through all modern communications media—television, radio, and (since 2002) Internet, e-mail, and SMS messaging—as well as sometimes on road signs with LED displays. Most kidnapped children are murdered within three hours of their abduction, so rapid response to such events is crucial.

By 2006, the AMBER Alert had been adopted in twenty-six U.S. states, sometimes under other names. The system is not without its limitations; critics complain that too many notifications of this type are broadcast about children who have merely been taken out by a noncustodial parent. Nevertheless, similar schemes have now been introduced in Australia, Canada, France, Ireland, Malaysia, Mexico, Netherlands, and the United Kingdom. **GL**

Colonization of Mars
Robert Zubrin

Traveling to the Red Planet in order to escape overcrowding on Earth

The fear that the rapid increase in the human population of the Earth may continue until the whole planet is overcrowded, coupled with concerns that the global climate may be changing so much that it will make life insupportable, have inspired plans for colonizing another part of the solar system. Prominent among these is *The Case for Mars: The Plan to Settle the Red Planet and Why We Must*, published in 1996 by U.S. aerospace engineer Robert Zubrin (b. 1952).

Mars is the celestial body that is most suitable—or perhaps least unsuitable—for human habitation. It has enough atmosphere to protect settlers from solar and cosmic radiation, days that are less than one hour longer than those on Earth, similar (but longer) seasons (the Martian year is approximately two Earth years), and

"I believe that we will eventually establish self-sustaining colonies on Mars . . ."
Stephen Hawking, theoretical physicist

enough water (albeit frozen) and chemical elements to make it potentially conducive to human life.

One significant advantage of Mars is its relative proximity to Earth: at a minimum distance of 34 million miles (54.4 million km), it can be reached in nine months by modern spacecraft, and journey times may be reduced to as little as a fortnight by the introduction of nuclear rockets. Gravity is low (approximately one-third of that on Earth), as is the mean surface temperature (almost as low as the coldest day ever recorded in Antarctica). Nevertheless, several organizations are exploring the possibilities, including the Mars Society, which in association with NASA has set up analog research stations in Canada and Alaska, and Mars One, whose declared intention is to establish a permanent human colony on Mars by 2023. **GL**

A visualization by photographer and artist Victor Habbick of mining operations on the surface of Mars. ➜

Cognitive Fluidity
Steven Mithen

An explanation of how humans made the leap from barbarism to civilization

As far as anthropologists can tell, the minds of the earliest humans were focused exclusively on hunting, gathering, and staying alive. Then, no fewer than 30,000 years ago—suddenly in anthropological terms—there was a marked increase in enterprise and creativity; our human ancestors started to make tools and paint the walls of their caves, as well as to bury their dead instead of leaving them to decompose in the open air. Developments such as these laid the foundations of science, art, and religion.

The brains of our *Homo erectus* and Neanderthal forebears were the same size as those of today's humans and they had the same capacity for language, so what happened to make them turn some of their attention away from eking out their existence and toward imaginative and creative thinking?

The answer, according to British archaeologist Steven Mithen, is that, as a result of a genetic accident that rewired their primitive brains, cavemen developed a capacity to see likenesses in unlike things, to think laterally, and to apply experiences from certain particular parts of their lives to others. He named this newly acquired capacity "cognitive fluidity," and noted that, although it inspired the great leap forward from barbarism to civilization, it also had the disadvantage that it enabled people to entertain theories, such as parapsychology, that have no rational basis.

Mithen's account, first published in 1996 as *The Prehistory of the Mind: A Search for the Origins of Art, Religion, and Science*, was not without its limitations: in particular, it made no attempt to identify what might have caused this great change. Nevertheless, the work has provided a plausible account of the so-called "missing link"—the evolutionary bridge that humans crossed at some point in prehistory, thereby separating themselves from animals, particularly the apes that they most resemble in appearance and behavior. **GL**

A mixed group of anthropological models representing different stages of human evolution. ⬆

Cloning
Roslin Institute, Edinburgh

The first successful cloning of an animal from an adult cell, not an embryo

In 1996, English embryologist Ian Wilmut (b. 1944), Scottish biologist Keith Campbell (b. 1954), and researchers at the Roslin Institute near Edinburgh, Scotland, transplanted the nucleus from a mammary gland cell of a Dorset sheep into the extracted egg of a blackface ewe from Scotland. The egg was electrically stimulated to set off cell division, and when the cell began to divide it was placed within the uterus of a third ewe. The egg had been emptied of its own nucleus, and after seven days of being nurtured and cultured it was ready to begin reprogramming the introduced adult cell and develop it into an embryo.

When "Dolly," the world's first cloned mammal, was born 148 days later, she was a precise genetic copy of the first ewe. The fact that it took the researchers more than 270 attempts at fertilization using twenty-nine embryos implanted into thirteen surrogate mothers before success was achieved hardly seemed to matter.

Dolly was part of a program of experiments at the Roslin Institute designed to advance research into the production of medicines from the milk of farm animals. The ewe went on to give birth to six lambs, and lived out the remainder of her days at the Roslin Institute, enjoying a lifestyle that only can be described as pampered. After developing a lung tumor, the "world's most famous sheep" was euthanized on February 14, 2003, at the age of six and a half years.

Dolly had opened the door to a Brave New World of genetic engineering and all of the ethical minefields it would bring with it. In 2008, Samuel Wood, a biotech company executive with Stemagen, a privately held embryonic stem cell research company, became the first adult to witness a clone of himself mature into an embryo. Some DNA had been extracted from his skin cells and injected into a human egg, after which the multicelled embryo had developed. Dolly was just the beginning of an important chapter in science. **BS**

↑ Dolly the sheep (in foreground) was indistinguishable from sheep produced naturally.

Decentralized Energy
International Cogeneration Alliance

The generation of electricity from many small energy sources

The International Cogeneration Alliance was founded in 1997 when the United Nations Framework Convention on Climate Change called for cogeneration to be placed higher on the international agenda. In 2002, the organization changed its name to the World Alliance for Decentralized Energy and broadened its scope to include all forms of distributed generation, including renewable technologies such as solar photovoltaic panels and small-scale wind power.

Decentralized energy (DE) is the generating of electricity at a local level, not from massive centralized facilities such as gas and coal-powered plants and hydro-electric power stations, which involve huge inefficiencies and transmission losses due to the distances that energy is transmitted. Instead, compact

"The electricity system ... is going to change beyond recognition."

Walt Patterson, Royal Institute of International Affairs

wind, solar, and cogeneration units are placed close to where the power they generate will be consumed.

DE cuts carbon emissions and also reduces spending on infrastructure. DE technologies include small cogeneration units combining in the production of electricity and thermal energy; off-grid photovoltaic solar cells particularly suitable for remote locations; and wind turbines small enough to be mounted on urban rooftops. Small-scale local hydro-power units are proving popular in China, Tanzania, Indonesia, and Sri Lanka, and are able to deliver 90 kilowatts of power to 300 homes. Especially efficient are combined heat and power systems, which require 30 percent less fuel than traditional plants. The heat they produce as a by-product of generating electricity is converted to steam for use on site in various industrial processes. **BS**

Contactless Smart Card
Hong Kong Mass Transit Railway

A plastic card that allows for faster payments and reduces the need for cash

The contactless smart card looks like an ATM card or a credit card: a thin plastic sheet, typically measuring around 3 by 2 inches (8 x 5 cm). In it are embedded integrated electronic circuits that can store and process data, and communicate with a terminal by means of radio waves. The cards are used for identification, authentication, data storage, and as a fast and convenient method of paying for purchases that requires minimal human involvement.

The cards were first used in 1997 on the Hong Kong Mass Transit Railway (MTR), which introduced them to speed up ticketing: previously, passengers had to buy tickets at booking office windows; under the new system, known as Octopus, they could swipe in and out of stations by passing their cards over electronic

"Every day tens of millions of people safely use contactless technology ..."

Robert Siciliano, personal security expert

readers that would debit either their bank accounts or their prepaid credit by the appropriate fare. The success of the MTR scheme soon led to widespread adoption, first by numerous transportation systems—notably in Beijing, Shanghai, and London—and later by credit and debit card companies, including MasterCard, Visa, and American Express.

The advantages for the issuing organizations are clear: after the initial setup costs, cards are cheap to produce, administration requires minimal staffing, and receipt of payment is automatic and guaranteed. For users, the cards increase the speed of transactions but, if lost or stolen, they are easy to use dishonestly. Either way, such cards are the future: at the time of writing, an estimated two million passengers owned London's Oyster cards for use on the capital's transport alone. **GL**

⬅ Smaller wind turbines can be placed on site-specific green roofs.

Blog
Various

Online diaries that enable anyone with
an Internet connection to express a view

A blog is an online journal in which individuals or groups can record activities, thoughts, or beliefs. The term "web log" was coined in 1997 by Jorn Barger to describe his own website. In 1999, it was conflated to "blog" by Peter Merholz; the word rapidly acquired universal currency.

The identity of the first blogger is disputed, but among those with claims to the distinction is Tim Berners-Lee (b. 1955), widely credited as the creator of the Internet in 1992. Whatever the truth, by 1997 blogs had proliferated. At the start of 2013, the part of the Internet known as the blogosphere contained 2.5 billion sites that are accessed by visitors (a total of 376 million a day) plus an uncounted number of other blogs that are never viewed. The total is growing at

"So is blogging really a tool or a weapon? It depends on what way you take it …"

Aman Tiwari, Weird Blogger's Diaries website

the rate of one every second: this is partly due to the increasing number of languages on the Internet; the most prolific new entries are blogs in Chinese.

One reason for the success of blogs is the opportunity they provide for dialogue: online conversation in the form of comments and responses are often emphasized. The most popular blogs are news filters with brief comments and links to their sources. In some cases, they have spawned "superblogs," such as The Huffington Post, which publishes articles on politics and current affairs. At the other end of the spectrum are blogs that air grievances that the bloggers might hesitate to express via other methods. Some blogs raise revenue through sidebar advertisements; most, however, are produced without profit for the blogger's own amusement. **GL**

Dark Energy
Michael Turner

The mysterious force that makes the
universe expand at ever-increasing speed

At the start of the twentieth century, scientists believed that the universe was of a constant size and held in place by gravity. When Albert Einstein formulated the general theory of relativity he acknowledged it as "the cosmological constant" because his other findings contradicted the convention of a static universe.

In the 1920s U.S. astronomer Edwin Hubble discovered through observation of the red shift of light from distant galaxies that, far from being static, the universe is expanding. This prompted Einstein to declare the cosmological constant his "greatest blunder." It was then assumed that the rate of expansion would be slowing as gravity pulls galaxies toward each other. However, in 1998 three astrophysicists—Americans Adam Reiss and Saul

"Dark energy will govern expansion and determine the fate of the universe."

Eric Linder, physicist

Perlmutter and Australian Brian Schmidt—discovered that the expansion was accelerating. This necessitated the reintroduction of the cosmological constant into the theory of relativity: it was not a blunder after all.

U.S. cosmologist Michael Turner (b. 1949) coined the term "dark energy." Dark energy pushes galaxies apart and accounts for approximately 73 percent of the total mass energy of the universe. The remaining problem is that physicists who have tried to calculate the amount of it in space have come up with an answer that seems excessive by a factor of 10120. An explanation of this anomaly may lie in "inflationary theory," which suggests the possibility of more than one universe. The theory of multiple universes is supported by string theory, which has 10,500 possible solutions, one of which may account for the amount of dark energy in our universe. **GL**

Guideline Daily Amounts
United Kingdom

Labeling to help people work out whether their foods constitute a balanced diet

In the United States, the 1990 Nutrition Labeling and Education Act stipulated that packaged foods (excluding meat and poultry) should bear labels giving nutritional information about them, such as their fat and calorie content. Useful though these guidelines were, consumers still struggled to reassure themselves that they were eating the right foods, and in the right quantities, to best suit their personal needs.

An initiative to improve the usefulness of information provided on food labels, guideline daily amounts (GDAs) were first introduced in the United Kingdom in 1998 as a collaboration between government, the food industry, and consumer watchdog organizations. Each product was required to have two labels: one on the front, showing the number of calories, and the

"People can eat some of the foods they enjoy but still have a balanced diet."

Lindsay Farrar, Mirror Group Newspapers

other on the back, listing the percentage the food contained of the average person's daily requirement of each constituent and the total amount thereof in each package. Consumers then needed only to add up the percentages given on various foods to achieve the 100 percent that represented the optimum intake of that food element (energy, fat, salt) over one day.

The British lead was followed by the United States and much of Europe, but there were soon disputes about whether, for example, the calorie intake of men, women, and children could be standardized meaningfully. Neither do GDAs state that saturated fats are superfluous to anybody's requirements. Today, GDAs keep consumers' minds focused on the question of healthy eating, even if they cannot, at least in their present form, provide all the right answers. **GL**

Safe Haven Law
Geanie W. Morrison

Legislation that permits parents to put babies into care with no questions asked

Some people cannot cope with parenthood, and in extreme cases they may abandon their children. For years, such conduct was illegal and for fear of being caught desperate parents would leave their babies alone in locations where (in the best-case scenario) they hoped they would be found by someone who would care for them; the parents' main priority, however, was to avoid arrest.

In an effort to prevent small children from being thus endangered, in 1999, state representative Geanie W. Morrison of Texas filed legislation initially titled "the baby Moses law," under which adults (usually, but not necessarily, the parents) were permitted to leave unwanted newborn babies in safe places, such as a hospital or a police station. These locations were equipped with signs designating them as safe havens. The adults were not required to leave their names. The children would then be placed in the care of the state's child welfare department.

By 2008, every other U.S. state had enacted some form of what is now known as a "safe haven law." The upper-age limit for legal abandonment varies across the country: several states will not accept any child more than three days old; others will take babies for varying periods after birth up to one year; Nebraska, however, formed its legislation in such a way that it could be interpreted to mean anyone under the age of eighteen years (the Nebraska Supreme Court later reduced the age limit to thirty days).

Around twenty states have provisions for parents later to reclaim the infant, usually within a specified period. Five states permit a non-relinquishing parent to petition for custody of the child. Safe haven laws have definitely reduced the number of "baby dumpings" and possibly the number of terminations and infanticides. **GL**

GloFish
Dr. Gong Zhiyuan

Created to help in pollution studies, GloFish are now being marketed as the first genetically altered house pet

GloFish is the trade name of fish that have been genetically modified (GM) so that they are fluorescent (able to emit light that is brighter than that which they receive). They were patented in the United States by Yorktown Technologies of Austin, Texas, which started with black-and-white striped zebra fish (*Brachydanio rerio*; native to the rivers of India and Bangladesh) and now sells fluorescent fish in a wide range of colors— blue, green, orange, purple, red, and yellow—in the ornamental aquarium market. The company is today one of the leading sellers of ornamental and aquarium livestock.

The first fish of this type were created in 1999 by Dr. Gong Zhiyuan and his colleagues at the National University of Singapore. Taking a gene that naturally produces a green fluorescent protein in jellyfish, they inserted it into zebra fish embryos. Red zebra fish were then created by injecting them with a gene from a sea coral. Next, a team of researchers at the National Taiwan University created a GM rice fish (*Oryzias latipes*) that emitted a green light; other colors soon followed. The scientists' original aim had been to create fish that would give off warning lights on coming into contact with toxins, enabling the speedy detection of contamination in waterways. However, it quickly became apparent that they had created a potential marketing phenomenon.

In 2003, the U.S. Food and Drug Administration approved GloFish for sale because, although the creatures have been treated with drugs, they are inedible and will therefore not enter the human food chain. GloFish remain illegal in California, and are banned in Canada and throughout the European Union, but sales elsewhere are now in their billions: GloFish are found illuminating aquaria and ponds almost wherever they are permitted. **GL**

↑ Fluorescent fish have also been used by scientists to help with understanding cellular disease and development, as well as cancer and gene therapy.

"Very little is known about biotechnology. By understanding how we made the fish, people will understand the technology better and be less afraid."

Dr. Gong Zhiyuan

Krumping

Ceasare "Tight Eyez" Willis and Jo'Artis "Big Mijo" Ratti

A dance craze that spread across the world from its birthplace on the U.S. Pacific coast

⬆ A teenager dances in face paint, a still from the documentary *Krumped* (2004) by David LaChapelle; the filmmaker would return to the subject with *Rize* in 2005.

"The aggressive and visually stunning dance modernizes moves indigenous to African tribal rituals and features mind-blowing, athletic movement sped up to impossible speeds."

Sujit R. Varma, dance commentator

Krumping is a form of street dancing created by Ceasare "Tight Eyez" Willis and Jo'Artis "Big Mijo" Ratti in Los Angeles, California, in 2000. It is thought to have developed from "clowning," a dance devised in 1992 by Tommy Johnson and the Hip Hop Clowns, children's entertainers in South Central Los Angeles. Krumping was much wilder, but the link is demonstrated by krumpers who would paint their faces to look like circus performers; alternatively, they may make up like fierce warriors. Dropping the face paint by early 2001, groups of krumpers would do battle with rival groups as an alternative to violence and drug abuse in the inner city.

The etymology of "krump" is obscure, but after the word gained common currency it was said to stand for "Kingdom Radically Uplifted Mighty Praise." This explanation was evidently an attempt to give the dance religious connotations, but most people regard the acronym as too contrived to be anything other than a back formation.

Although difficult to codify, the dance broadly consists of free and exaggerated movements of all parts of the body in any direction to fast-paced music. In contrast to b-boying, in which dancers may lie on the floor, the main rule in krumping is that the dancer should remain upright at all times. Apart from that stipulation, krumping is entirely freestyle, never choreographed, and has been well described as "extreme hip-hop." According to the MTV website, if krumping "makes you look like Bozo [an incompetent person] having spasms, you're doing it right."

From its West Coast cradle, krumping quickly spread across the world, thanks partly to the publicity it gained from David LaChapelle's film documentary *Rize* (2005). Once the dance became mainstream, it was featured in several music videos, including "Hung Up" by Madonna and "Hey Mama" by The Black Eyed Peas, and retains its popularity today. **GL**

Evo-devo
National Academy of Sciences, United States

How life on Earth became so various in spite of its origins in a relatively small pool of genes

"Evo-devo" is a popular, informal term for the field of evolutionary developmental biology in general, and particularly its current efforts to resolve a problem that has puzzled researchers for hundreds of years. In 2000, a special section of the *Proceedings of the National Academy of Sciences* (PNAS) in the United States was devoted to "evo-devo," which saw the concept ushered into the mainstream.

Scientists have long wondered about the causes of radical changes in the appearance and characteristics of various species, such as the way in which the scales of prehistoric avians turned, over millions of years, into the feathers on modern birds. Some researchers maintain that the function of the creature dictates the creature's form—British naturalist Charles Darwin (1809–82) held that the finches of the Galapagos Islands evolved beaks of different shapes in order to access particular food sources.

Others have concluded that form precedes function—in other words, that the creature's characteristics are genetically predetermined and that it cuts its behavioral coat according to the cloth of its heredity. One of the early leaders of this school of thought was French zoologist Etienne Geffroy Saint-Hilaire (1722–1844), whose studies of invertebrates convinced him that the anatomical structure of a creature preordains its mode of existence.

The question is not whether evolution takes place—both schools agree that it does—but exactly what drives and influences the process. Genetic mutation is also a fact: evo-devo has demonstrated that a vast number of evolutionary changes have been driven by only a very small number of genes. What remains uncertain is exactly how mutations are preprogrammed at the embryonic stage and how an organism's phenotypes (observable traits) may be influenced by the organism's surroundings. **GL**

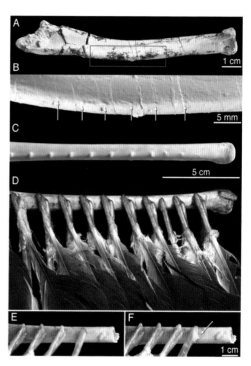

⬆ A selection of fossils, casts, and bones illustrates how quill knobs for feathers on a prehistoric velociraptor (A and B) show similarities to those of the modern turkey vulture (C–F).

"Evolution was in a strange mood when that creation came along ... It makes one wonder just where the plant world leaves off and the animal world begins."

John Colton, on flesh-eating plants

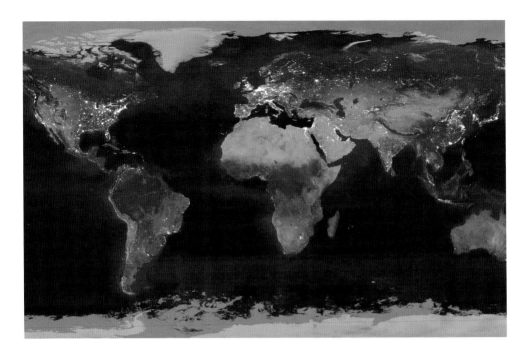

2000

The Anthropocene
Paul J. Crutzen

A new geological term for the modern age of human influence on Earth

The Anthropocene is a (currently unofficial) name for the most recent period of geological time, from the second half of the eighteenth century to the present day. The term, which is derived from the Greek meaning "recent age of man," was thought to be required because it is during this period, including the start of the Industrial Revolution in c. 1760, that the activities of humans have altered, more than ever before, Earth's surface, atmosphere, oceans, and systems of nutrient cycling. According to environmental journalist Elizabeth Kolbert, "Many stratigraphers [geologists who study rock layers] have come to believe that . . . human beings have so altered the planet in the past century or two that we've ushered in a new epoch." It was therefore thought appropriate to distinguish it from the Holocene Epoch, of which the past 200 years were formerly held to be a part, which covers approximately the previous 11,700 years, from the rise of modern humans at the start of the Stone Age.

The term "Anthropocene," coined by U.S. biologist Eugene F. Stoermer sometime in the late 1980s, was brought to public attention in 2000, when it was used in a speech and an article by Paul J. Crutzen, winner of the Nobel Prize in Chemistry in 1995.

In 2008, a motion was put before the Stratigraphy Commission of the Geological Society of London, England, proposing that the Anthropocene be formally adopted as an epoch on the geological time scale. At the time of writing, the matter was still under consideration. Opponents say that evidence of human impact on the Earth predates the 1750s by perhaps as many as 15,000 years, and that it would be redundant to distinguish the last two centuries from the rest of the Holocene. Nevertheless the term is in widespread use, notably by the Geological Society of America, which titled its annual meeting in 2011 "Archean to Anthropocene: The past is the key to the future." **GL**

Modern impact on the planet can be seen in the amount of light sources seen from space. ⬆

Virtual Workplace
Various

Computers have made it possible to run big companies without offices

By-products of the development of the Internet, virtual workplaces are offices without a physical location, but in which employees can collaborate regardless of where in the world they happen to be: residents of Sydney, Australia, can and do work for companies in London, England, not as field representatives but as fully functioning members of in-house teams.

A virtual workplace significantly reduces company overheads, most notably by saving the cost of premises that can accommodate all the staff. Tasks are distributed by email or other forms of electronic data transfer, performed by workers on or within reach of their own computers, and then returned to base or headquarters via the same media.

The system also has advantages for employees, saving them the cost of commuting and childcare, and enabling them (with the company's agreement) to work more flexible hours than are normally possible in a traditional office. According to a survey by Global Workplace Analytics, it is popular: 79 percent of respondents said they would rather work at home than in an office, and 39 percent of those said they would prefer a virtual workplace to a pay rise. However, some managers complain that virtual workplaces have restricted their ability to monitor their subordinates' working methods: they can now judge employees only on their performance.

Another of the problems associated with virtual workplaces is their inability to generate a sense of shared purpose, morale, or esprit de corps. The problem may be reduced by interactive systems such as teleconferencing and WYSIWIS ("what you see is what I see") technology, but even these do not entirely eliminate the difficulty: psychologists believe that tone of voice and gesture alone are insufficient to convey the finest nuances of meaning, which can be gathered only through physical proximity. **GL**

↑ Lack of a physical office may not hinder productivity.

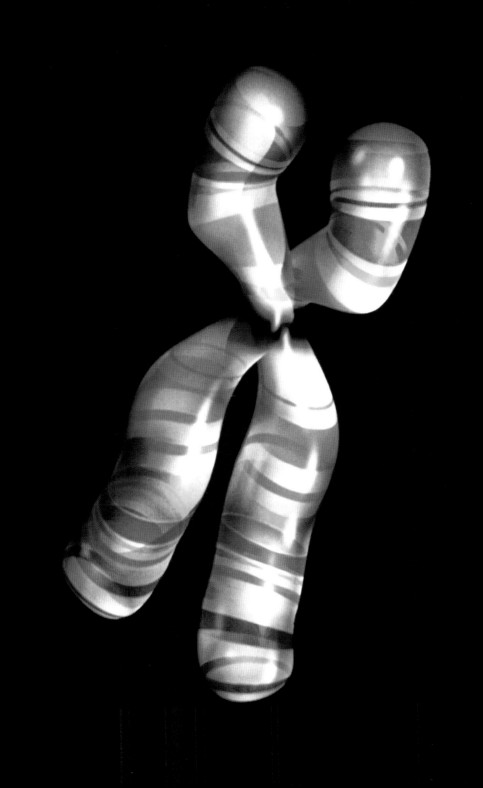

Y-chromosomal Adam
Peter Underhill

The identification of our most recent common male ancestor

The human Y chromosome does not recombine with the X chromosome but is transferred intact from father to son. Over time it may mutate, and mutations may be used to identify patrilineal descent. This gave molecular biologist Peter Underhill of Stanford University the basis for a research program that in 2000 revealed that the oldest common ancestor from whom all men alive today are descended lived around 59,000 years ago.

The news media had fun with the age gap between Y-chromosomal Adam and his female equivalent, mitochondrial Eve, who lived around 84,000 years earlier and had been identified a decade previously. Using the names of the first two humans in the Bible is potentially misleading: these were not the first people, merely the oldest that have been traced. Such red

> *"We are all Africans at the Y chromosome level and we are really all brothers."*
>
> Peter Underhill

herrings diverted attention from Underhill's most important findings, which concerned migration. From his study of 167 mutations in the Y chromosome of 1,062 men from twenty-one geographical regions, he determined that there had not been only one great exodus from Africa: some early humans had left the continent and later their descendants returned there; others went to Australia or India and Asia and then to Europe. Underhill also discovered that there are fewer Y chromosome lineages than mitochondrial, probably because the males were more promiscuous.

Although Y-chromosomal Adam is not expected to retain the title of our most recent common ancestor for long, his discovery represents a great advance in archaeogenetics—the reconstruction of human history from evidence contained in genes. **GL**

Six Green Principles
Global Green movement

Creation of a clear manifesto for ecologist political parties and environmentalists

At its inaugural convention in Canberra, Australia, in April 2001, the Global Green movement unveiled a charter that identified its aims and enabled environmentalists to focus their social and political ambitions more clearly than ever before. The document is known as the Six Green Principles and contains the following aspirations:

1) Ecological wisdom: based on the ecological philosophy formulated primarily by Norwegian Arne Naess (1912–2009), which emphasizes the need to protect "deep ecology"—the most fundamental things that sustain Earth—rather than waste effort combating minor abuses;

2) Social justice: the notion that everyone is equal and that people should all act in solidarity;

> *"The 'control of nature' is a phrase conceived in arrogance ..."*
>
> Rachel Carson, *Silent Spring* (1962)

3) Participatory democracy: every adult man and woman should have a vote, and their choices at the ballot box should be real and more diverse than is often reflected in many two-party systems;

4) Nonviolence: ending all forms of physical conflict;

5) Sustainability: ensuring that humans replace and replenish everything that they destroy in order to live;

6) Respect for diversity: the fair and equal treatment of minorities.

These desiderata are based on earlier manifestos produced by the Green movement, including their statement at the Rio Earth Summit in 1992 and the 2001 Accord between the Green Parties of the Americas and the Ecologist Parties of Africa. The Six Green Principles, however, are more codified than anything that preceded them. **GL**

◄ Computer-generated artwork showing the banding patterns on a male Y chromosome.

War on Terror
United States

Wikipedia
Jimmy Wales and Tim Shell

The military struggle to defeat Islamist and other terrorism

An online tool labeled as the world's most widely used reference source

The term "war on terror" is commonly used to refer to the military campaign launched by the United States in response to the events of 9/11. However, the phrase—introduced on September 20, 2001, when President George W. Bush made the unscripted remark that "This war on terrorism is going to take a while"—also encompasses the more general concept of a global war against terrorism.

The notion of a "war on terror" has proved deeply controversial since its introduction. For the Bush administration it provided justification for a national security policy that permitted the United States to engage in armed conflict against terrorist groups wherever they operate, with or without the support of the sovereign authority of a given country. Critics,

Wikipedia is an online encyclopedia that may be read for free by anyone with access to the Internet and that is potentially available to any writer who wants to make a new contribution or amend an existing entry.

Wikipedia was founded in 2001 by Jimmy Wales, a U.S. former bond trader, in succession to his Nupedia, another free online encyclopedia, which had become so bogged down in the verification process that it took around five years to clear the first twenty articles for publication. Contrastingly, in its first year of operation, Wikipedia—compiled by unpaid volunteers and unencumbered by an official advisory board—published 20,000 articles in eighteen languages. By its tenth anniversary, it had more than 3.5 million entries and appeared in 350 different language editions.

"Our nation's security and defeating terrorism trump all other priorities."

Arlen Specter, U.S. senator

"[With] Wikipedia . . . my childish idea of Heaven had been created here on Earth."

Victoria Pynchon, *Forbes* magazine

however, argue that it has done more harm than good, leading to the United States' isolation from Europe and increasing anti-American feeling abroad. Moreover, by regarding the fight against terrorism as a war, it has had the unintended effect of allowing terrorist groups to claim legitimacy for their actions—they are now "acts of war" and the perpetrators are viewed as soldiers rather than simply murderers.

The war on terror has dominated international politics for more than a decade and had far-reaching effects. In 2009 the then British Foreign Secretary David Miliband argued that the phrase gave "the impression of a unified, transnational enemy," when "the reality is that the motivations and identities of terrorist groups are disparate." Many politicians have since sought to distance themselves from the concept. **GL**

Ease of access is not without its problems: there have been several cases of people hacking into the entries and vandalizing them. However, trusted contributors are given access privileges that enable them to remove such material, and this self-correction process has produced a resource of unparalleled scope.

Although Wikipedia's authentication procedures do not satisfy the most rigorous academic requirements, footnote references in the fully developed entries provide links to independently verifiable source material. There are also "stubs" (the germs of entries that require expanding and developing); talk pages (discussions between contributors); and a related site called Wikipedia Commons, which is a repository of media files (photographs, maps, and so on) in use and usable in all Wikipedia material. **GL**

Jimmy Wales (left) has vowed to keep Wikipedia free and free from advertising. ➡

Big Crunch Theory

Andrei Linde

A proposal that dark energy will collapse the universe in a "big crunch"

As scientists struggled to understand the physics behind the big bang that led to the creation of the universe, they also pondered whether the universe would ever end. It has always been thought that the universe was constantly expanding; however, recent astronomical observations have led scientists, including Andrei Linde of Stanford University, to rethink their ideas about this end.

In 1998 astronomers concluded that the expansion of the universe was speeding up, rather than slowing down as previously assumed. The gravitational pull of matter that controlled the expansion of the universe was now being overruled by an anti-gravity force that was pushing the universe apart. As matter in the universe thinned out as the universe itself expanded,

"A few years ago, nobody would even seriously think about the end of the world."

Andrei Linde, *New Scientist* (September 6, 2002)

a repulsive force gained influence in its place. This suspect force, or dark energy, is an unknown, invisible substance distributed evenly throughout space and accounting for around 73 percent of the universe. Until this discovery, it was assumed that the universe would expand so much that it eventually fell apart in some big rip. Linde's insight, announced in 2002, is that this dark energy will not just drop to zero as the universe expands, but become negative. When it does, it will slow and then reverse the universe's expansion and cause space and time to collapse in a "big crunch."

Since the universe is already 14 billion years old, and if the collapse is dated to about 10 to 20 billions years' time, than we are currently living in its middle age. Whether Linde is right will never be known, for Earth will have collapsed into the Sun long before that. **SA**

Flash Mob

Bill Wasik

A publicity stunt that started a worldwide craze for spontaneous performances

The term "flash mob" was first recorded in 2003. It refers to a group of people who gather together suddenly in public, perform some kind of unusual, theatrical, or seemingly pointless act, and then disperse as quickly as they appeared.

The essence of a flash mob is its apparent spontaneity. It is a form of performance art. Although some flash mobs have been planned long in advance, they are more commonly spur of the moment conventions of people who have arranged to meet only shortly beforehand via cell phones or social media.

Flash mobs were the brainchild of Bill Wasik, senior editor of *Harper's Magazine* in New York City, who wanted to satirize people prepared to turn up at any event, no matter how trivial. His first attempt

"It is a new way to perform and find an audience . . . a new fun stage."

Bill Wasik

to create such a happening was thwarted when the management of the proposed location, a retail store in Manhattan, was tipped off in advance. Learning from this experience that leaks could ruin everything, Wasik next got a total of 130 participants to gather at four different bars: none of them was told the final destination or what they would do until they got to these preliminary staging posts. From there they proceeded to the ninth floor of Macy's, where they all briefly pretended to be shopping for a single "love rug."

The success of this flash mob, on June 3, 2003, started a trend that swept the world. Public enthusiasm for them diminished somewhat, however, after reports of "flash robs," in which large groups would congregate in a store and steal, overwhelming the staff by force of numbers. **GL**

Young people take part in a flash mob on the Moscow subway in 2011. ➡

The Freecycle Network
Deron Beal

A novel method of reducing waste by finding new homes for unwanted materials

The Freecycle Network (TFN) is an organization through which individuals and groups can acquire at no cost materials that are unwanted and that would otherwise be dumped in landfills. Its slogan is "Changing the world one gift at a time."

TFN originated in Tucson, Arizona, in 2003, when local resident Deron Beal compiled an inventory of what other homeowners were planning to throw away and emailed the list to friends and neighbors. In the process he proved that one person's trash is another person's treasure.

The idea soon caught on throughout the United States. Each local group operated independently, but first had to be approved by TFN's regional new group approvers. In 2005, TFN gained its first corporate

"The goal is to make it easier to give something away than to throw it away."

Deron Beal

sponsor, Waste Management Inc., which donated $130,000. In 2006, membership broke the 2 million mark and two years later TFN opened its own website, www.Freecycle.org. By the end of 2012, there were more than 5,000 groups in eighty-five countries with a total of more than 9 million members.

Meanwhile, Beal's control of TFN became controversial. In 2009, U.K. Freecycle members sought greater autonomy. Eventually, U.K. groups broke away and set up rival websites. TFN still has a presence in the United Kingdom, but now faces competition from Freecycle U.K. In 2010, Beal's claims to copyright in the term "freecycling" and his insistence on licencing all TFN groups in the United States were ruled unlawful. Nevertheless, no matter who controls freecycling, the practice is firmly established across the globe. **GL**

Sexting
Sunday Telegraph magazine

The practice of sending suggestive proposals by cell phone

People who send explicit erotic messages or images to one another by cell phone are said to be "sexting," which is a portmanteau of "sex" and "texting." The earliest recorded use of the term was in the British *Sunday Telegraph* magazine in 2005; seven years later, in 2012, "sexting" was officially recognized by Merriam-Webster's Collegiate Dictionary.

However, the prevalence of the practice remains uncertain: one survey reported that 59 percent of respondents had created, sent, or received a sexually explicit message or image by phone, while another received affirmative answers from only 2.5 percent of those questioned. The effectiveness of this research is restricted partly by the difficulty of verifying claims and partly by differing definitions of what constitutes "sexually explicit." Another difficulty is that, although indecent images of minors are unlawful, the age of majority is not the same in every state.

For people wishing to express an intimate desire or display an erotic image to another individual, sexting has the advantage of not requiring the participation of a third party—cell phones have built-in digital cameras that obviate the need for photographs or film clips to be developed. Conversely, such messages remain private only with the consent of sender and recipient, and there have been several cases in which their contents have been forwarded, accidentally or deliberately, to a wider audience. There is also the problem of bullying: sexting people who do not invite the messages and find receiving such material threatening and oppressive.

Although sexting is a contentious activity, it has increased the number of ways in which people can communicate their desires. It has also inspired a new tranche of text code initials, including "PiR" (parent in room) and "GNOC" (get naked on camera). **GL**

Church of the Flying Spaghetti Monster
Bobby Henderson

A satirical entity that was invented to challenge creationsim and the education policy of Middle America

In 2005, Bobby Henderson, a twenty-four-year-old physics graduate from Oregon State University, wrote to the Kansas State Board of Education in Topeka to ask whether, in view of the fact that they had just moved to allow intelligent design and creationism to be taught in public schools as an alternative to theories of evolution, they would consider giving equal classroom time to his own god, the Flying Spaghetti Monster (FSM), a supernatural being made of pasta and meatballs, who, he claimed to believe, had created the universe. Henderson also suggested that the first true believers in the FSM were pirates, and that the reduction in their number over the last 200 years was the direct cause of global warming.

Receiving no reply from Topeka, Henderson posted his letter online, and his website (www.venganza.org) soon became one of the most popular on the Internet, with millions of hits. He also received approximately 60,000 emails, 95 percent of whose authors clearly understood that his original intention had been to satirize the board's extraordinary willingness to rank belief and science equally.

Before long, Henderson's frivolous deity had garnered a vast number of followers, a development that moved its creator to style himself a prophet and found the Church of the Flying Spaghetti Monster. In 2006 he published *The Gospel of the Flying Spaghetti Monster*, which to date has reportedly sold more than 100,000 copies.

The Church of the Flying Spaghetti Monster may have been created as a satire, but like all satire it has a serious purpose. The ersatz institution has provided a rallying point for people who take the view that unverifiable assertions, such as the creation of the world in seven days and the divinity of Jesus Christ, should not be treated as facts. **GL**

⬆ Since its creation in 2005, the Flying Spaghetti Monster has replaced Christian iconography in many "believers" homes, appearing, for example, on top of their Christmas trees.

"The central belief is that an invisible and undetectable Flying Spaghetti Monster created the universe 'after drinking heavily.'"

thethinkingatheist.com

Equitrade
Malagasy Company

A scheme enabling poor countries to keep a bigger share of the wealth they generate

Equitrade goes one step further than Fairtrade, which ensures that growers and farmers in the developing world receive the correct market rate for their produce. Although Fairtrade helps to reduce exploitation of the poor, most of the value of their cash crops is added by processing, and most processing takes place in the developed world. Thus, for example, only 5 percent of the ultimate resale price of a bar of Fairtrade chocolate remains in the country that produced the cacao from which it is made. The balance goes to the wealthy nations in which the bar is made and sold.

Equitrade (short for "equitable trade") was set up in 2005 to enable poor nations to process and package their raw materials into finished products themselves, and thus to earn a greater share of the profits. Under

"Equitrade is . . . a standalone foundation and intends to extend to many products."

Neil Kelsall, Noetic Associates

a pilot Equitrade chocolate-producing scheme run by the Malagasy Company in Madagascar, just over half of the revenue remained in the country of origin, 40 percent of it going to the local manufacturer and packager, and 11 percent to the government in tax, which was then reinvested in the industry. The remaining 49 percent was divided between the exporter, the distributor, and the retailer.

According to Neil Kelsall of Noetic Associates, a British company pioneering this approach, "All it would take to end poverty in Madagascar is £750 million a year." The island's farms cannot generate that amount of money, but Equitrade aims to enable the nation to profit more substantially. To do that, it needs only equipment and a little expertise: by providing both, Equitrade could make poverty history. **GL**

Top-down Cosmology
Stephen Hawking and Thomas Hertog

A theory proposing that the origins of the universe depend upon an observer—us

The top-down theory of cosmology was proposed by British theoretical physicist and cosmologist Stephen Hawking (b. 1942) and Belgian cosmologist Thomas Hertog (b. 1975) to explain the origins of the universe. They collaborated to produce a paper outlining their theory, "Populating the landscape: A top-down approach" (2006). They drew on an interpretation of quantum mechanics, the paradox illustrated in the Austrian physicist Erwin Schrödinger's cat thought experiment, whereby an observer is required to decide if a particle is in a particular state.

Top-down cosmology posits that the universe had no unique, carefully fine-tuned initial state. (The bottom-up approach to cosmology includes the possibility of such a state being proscribed by an outside agency.) The top-down approach provides a framework that essentially traces histories backward, with the present time influencing the past. It asserts that the universe depends on what is being observed, contrary to the prevailing notion that the universe's history is independent of an observer. Thus, the universe emerges via observation and its history depends on the questions we ask today. Top-down cosmology envisions a set of alternative universes.

Hawking and Hertog's theory provides a possible resolution to the fine-tuning question, which is a topic of debate for theologians, philosophers, and cosmologists. The idea of a fine-tuned universe proposes that life in the universe exists because of a narrow range of fundamental physical constants. By claiming observation to be essential to the universe, top down-cosmology introduces ideas of metaphysics—intention, the mind, and so on—into how the universe is conceived. Top-down cosmology is one of several approaches to cosmology, including the Big Bang, multiverse, and eternal inflation theories. **CK**

Venture Philanthropy
Warren Buffett

Increasing the funds of charitable enterprises without expectation of significant profit, while actively influencing the ways in which the funds are used

Venture capital consists of money and other investments put in to new companies whose success cannot be assured because, although they may seem like good ideas, they do not conform to any established business model. Venture capitalism is high risk.

Venture philanthropy is a variation on that theme, which, though not in itself new, gained prominence in the first decade of the twenty-first century. In contrast to charitable donors, venture philanthropists advise on and may direct the ways in which funds are allocated, helping the schemes in which they have invested to increase their efficiency and grow. A leading example occurred in 2006 when U.S. billionaire Warren Buffett (b. 1930) pledged shares worth approximately $1.5 billion to the Bill & Melinda Gates Foundation on condition that income from the shares be distributed each year. Buffett's contribution effectively doubled the charity's annual financial and material backing for organizations, concepts, and techniques deemed to benefit society as a whole.

Most venture philanthropy investments are made in organizations funded mainly by charitable donations and staffed by professionals. Prominent examples include the Robin Hood Foundation and Tipping Point Community, which alleviate and aim to eradicate poverty in, respectively, New York City and the San Francisco Bay Area in the United States.

Naturally, the financial returns on venture philanthropy are small at best, and may be negligible. Nevertheless, this form of investment can be attractive to people who are wealthy enough or want to provide their services pro bono. Venture philanthropists may also use their donations to gain seats on the boards of corporate donors to the organization in which they have invested, thus diversifying their own business interests while benefiting society at large. **GL**

⬆ Warren Buffett addresses a press conference in New York, regarding his pledge of 10 million class B shares of the Berkshire Hathaway Corporation to the Bill & Melinda Gates Foundation.

"Venture philanthropy remains something of a Rorschach test. Depending on whom you ask, it is the future of philanthropy, a passing fad, good grantmaking, or misguided hubris."

Neil F. Carson, *Responsive Philanthropy* (2000)

UK Biobank
Wellcome Trust

A stockpile of human genes and tissue used to advance scientific research

A biobank is a store of human biological material that has been collected for research purposes. Historically, biological material gathered by scientists was kept in their own laboratories, seldom if ever contributing to any wider pool of knowledge. A cardiologist, for example, might have a collection of heart tissue of which gynecologists were completely unaware. For as long as it was believed that every genetic disease had a single cause, that situation was not seen as a problem, but by the 1990s it had become clear that most such diseases are caused by defects in multiple genes. It therefore became imperative to share information more widely than ever before.

Fortunately, this realization came at a time when computer technology had advanced to a state whereby

> *"Scientists are faced with a growing need for biospecimens: blood, saliva, plasma . . ."*

J. Sterling, *GEN* (2012)

the cost of making a genome-wide sweep of possible pathogens was no greater than that of examining a single gene. In 2006, the UK Biobank was established in Manchester, England, with initial volunteers being enrolled over the next four years. In addition to supplying biological samples, donors gave details of their medical histories, nutritional habits, and lifestyles so that researchers using their tissues would be fully informed of their medication taking and other factors.

Thereafter biobanks proliferated throughout the world. In the United States alone, by 2012 they stored nearly 400 million specimens; the total is increasing by around 20 million a year. The U.S. collections are linked by computer, enabling researchers to access information from any of them at any time. Biobanks represent a great leap forward in medicine. **GL**

Amortality
Catherine Mayer

Holding back the aging process by hiding most of its visible signs

"Amortality" was a word coined in 2009 by U.S. journalist Catherine Mayer to describe the increasing tendency of Western men and women to disguise and, to some limited extent, defer the normal aging process. Thus, fewer and fewer middle-aged and elderly people display the external signs of physical decline, which are hidden beneath perma-tans, disguised by Botox treatment and, in extreme cases, removed by nips and tucks and other forms of cosmetic surgery. No longer do the rich end their lives in the way that William Shakespeare proposed as a universal truth in his play *As You Like It* (c. 1599): "Sans teeth, sans eyes, sans taste, sans everything." Dentists give octogenarians teenagerlike smiles; laser surgery restores 20/20 vision to people who might otherwise be functionally blind;

> *"The important thing is . . . what you are able and willing to do"*

Nick Bostrom, Future of Humanity Institute

the drug Viagra sustains the libido of men long after they should have passed Shakespeare's Third Age. None of these interventions can stop people dying; they have become amortal, but not immortal.

Mayer wrote a detailed account of her observations in her book *Amortality: The Pleasures and Perils of Living Agelessly* (2011). She recalls, for example, Rolling Stone Mick Jagger saying in 1975, when he was thirty-two, that he "would rather be dead than singing 'Satisfaction' at forty-five," yet his band was still touring in the second decade of the twenty-first century, by which time its lead singer was approaching seventy years of age.

The defining characteristic of amortals is that they live the same way from the end of adolescence until death, continually fighting off external signs of decay. Mayer added a useful word to the language. **GL**

⬅ The interior of the UK Biobank holds a vast bank of medical data and material from volunteers.

World Anti-Piracy Observatory
United Nations

A website that coordinates and publicizes efforts to counter copyright infringement

The unauthorized use of people's intellectual property—a category that includes books they have written, movies they have directed, music they have recorded, computer software programs they have devised—is known to lawyers as copyright infringement, otherwise known as piracy. To help combat it, the United Nations Educational, Scientific and Cultural Organization (UNESCO) launched in 2010 the World Anti-Piracy Observatory (WAPO). This is a freely accessible website written in English, French, and Spanish that provides and can receive information about the efforts of all 200 UNESCO member states to stop such crimes and apprehend the culprits.

There are no universal copyright laws, and WAPO takes full account of regional differences. Its principal

"I applaud the plan to collect 150 copyright laws on the WAPO website."

Hartwig Thomas, Digitale Allmend

function is to collocate up-to-date information received from governments, authors' societies, cultural bodies, and private individuals throughout the world about legal, administrative, and nonlegislative anti-piracy policies. In addition to news, WAPO provides specimen contracts and the contact details of copyright authorities in each member nation, as well as best-practice case studies that may be used as templates for future action.

WAPO has attracted considerable online criticism for lack of scope and depth, but UNESCO is determined to develop the website further until it enables every national copyright enforcement authority to keep abreast of what its equivalents in other countries are doing, and hence assist the harmonization of international opposition to piracy. **GL**

Occupy Movement
Adbusters Media Foundation

Protests intended to inspire people to redistribute the world's wealth more evenly

The Occupy movement is a nonviolent international protest group opposing the control that, it believes, large corporations currently exercise over the global financial system. Its most commonly used slogan—"We are the 99 percent"—refers to what supporters regard as the iniquitous distribution of the world's wealth in favor of the remaining 1 percent. The name "Occupy" is taken from the movement's strategy of massing in a single building or confined public space and remaining there until its demands are addressed by the authorities.

The movement began in the United States in March of 2011 with Occupy Wall Street, which was well advertised in advance by the Canadian-based group Adbusters Media Foundation, and drew around 1,000 supporters to the financial district of New York City.

"We shouldn't go into debt for an education, medical care, or to put food on the table."

occupywallst.org

Over the following year, similar demonstrations were held in major cities worldwide, including Sydney, São Paulo, Paris, Berlin, Frankfurt, Hamburg, Leipzig, Tokyo, Auckland, Madrid, and Zurich. Numerous British cities also saw Occupy demonstrations; in London, around 3,000 protesters settled outside St. Paul's Cathedral after being barred access to the Stock Exchange.

Occupy's objectives are numerous but often ill-reported. They include the imposition on the largest multinational companies of a one-off levy, known as a Robin Hood tax because its objective is to take from the rich and give to the poor. The movement also demands the arraignment of fraudsters whom it holds responsible for the global financial crash in 2008, wide-ranging reforms of banking practices, and investigations into political corruption. **GL**

　　An Occupy protester wearing a Guy Fawkes mask presents an ironic message in London in 2011. ▶

Commercial Space Flight
Space X and Virgin Galactic

Private companies open up Earth's orbit to commerce and tourism

The era of commercial space travel dawned on October 7, 2012, with the first of twelve proposed cargo resupply missions to the International Space Station (ISS) by a Falcon 9 rocket and Dragon spacecraft, designed, built, and owned by the private, California-based company Space X. The launch, from Cape Canaveral in Florida, marked the beginning of a major resupply program and included the delivery of materials crucial to almost 170 ISS experiments in the fields of plant cell biology and human biotechnology.

The flight followed a successful demonstration mission in May when Space X became the world's first commercial company to rendezvous successfully with the orbiting station. At first, returning Dragon capsules will plunge into and be recovered from the Pacific Ocean, though Space X plans to fit subsequent capsules with deployable landing gear. Space X has ambitions far beyond hauling cargo, however. The company wants to colonize Mars, too, and to that end received, in August 2012, the Mars Pioneer Award.

Space X is not the only company intent on ending the monopoly on the cosmos previously enjoyed exclusively by the world's space agencies. Richard Branson's Virgin Galactic is also pioneering private space flight, backed by new Californian legislation designed to facilitate corporate investment in spaceflight technologies. Virgin's suborbital, air-launched SpaceShipTwo, a spaceplane designed for the purpose of space tourism, is part of a proposed fleet of five that will each begin to take eight passengers (six tourists and two pilots) into orbit from late 2013.

Spaceport America, the world's first purpose-built commercial spaceport, located in New Mexico, was declared open in October 2011. Its 10,000-foot-long (3,000 m) runway will take SpaceShipTwo into space and launch mankind into a new era of tourism, high above the surface of Earth. **BS**

Virgin Galactic's SpaceShipTwo, the world's first commercial spacecraft. ⬆

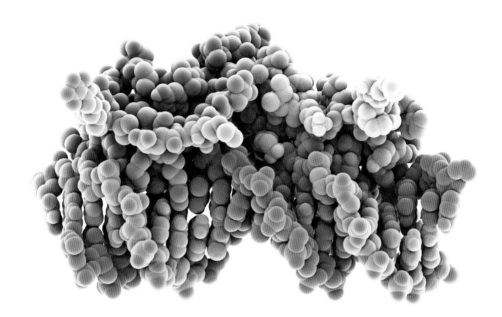

Not-junk DNA
ENCODE

Far more of the human genome has vital functions than was first realized

The ribbons of DNA (deoxyribonucleic acid) in our cells carry instructions for building proteins and thus continuing life, but it was long believed that stretches of them are useless. The idea of "junk DNA" was first formulated by the Japanese-American geneticist Susumu Ohno (1928–2000), writing in the *Brookhaven Symposium in Biology* in 1972. He argued that the human genome can only sustain a very limited number of genes and that, for the rest, "the importance of doing nothing" was crucial. In effect, he dismissed 98 percent of the total genetic sequence that lies between the 20,000 or so protein-coding genes.

Yet scientists always thought that such junk must have a purpose. And indeed, a breakthrough in 2012 revealed that this junk is in fact crucial to the way our human genome, that is the complete set of genetic information in our cells, actually works.

After mapping of the entire human genome was completed in 2003, scientists focused on the so-called junk DNA. Nine years later, in 2012, the international ENCODE (Encyclopedia of DNA Elements) project published the largest single genome update in *Nature* and other journals. It found that, far from useless, the so-called junk contained 10,000 genes—around 18 percent of the total—that help control how the protein-coding genes work. Also found were 4 million regulatory switches that turn genes on and off (it is the failure of these switches that leads to diseases such as type 2 diabetes and Crohn's disease). In total, ENCODE predicted that up to 80 percent of our DNA has some sort of biochemical function.

The discovery of these functioning genes will help scientists to understand common diseases and also to explain why diseases affect some people and not others. If that can be achieved, drugs can be devised to treat those diseases. Much work still needs to be done, but the breakthrough has been made. **SA**

⬆ Transcription factors (blue and green) regulate the flow of DNA (orange and pink) to RNA.

General Index

Page numbers in **bold** indicate main entries.

Breuil, Henri 33
Britten, Benjamin 326
Brookes, William Penny 496
Brunelleschi 168
Bruno, Giordano 336
Buddhism 59, 85, 86, 103, 104, 105, 107,
    108, 112
    arhat 148
    bodhisattva 235
    Four Noble Truths 146
    influence of Daoism 136
    influence of Zoroastrianism 109
    nirvana 103, 107, 145, 146
    Zen 275, 295
Buffet, Warren 935
Burckhardt, Jacob 517
Buridan, John 210
Burke, Edmund *Reflections on the*
    Revolution in France 444
bushidō 280
Butler, Robert Neil 830
butterfly effect 825
Byron, Lord George *Manfred* 141

C

Cage, John 744, 755
calculus 152
calendars 58
Caligula 94
Calvinism 328
Cambridge Cable Network 903
Camus, Albert *The Myth of Sisyphus* 709
Cann, Rebecca 887
cannibalism 22
Cantor, Georg 133, 542
Capek, Karel 663
capoeira 330
Carlsson, Arvid 879
Carmichael, Stokely 810
Carnot, Nicolas Léonard Sadi 467
Carpentier, Alejo 734
carpooling 710
Carrel, Alexis 615
Carson, Rachel *Silent Spring* 789
Carter, Brandon 845
cartoons 484
caste system, India 103, 104, 107
casuistry 173
catastrophism 79
categorical logic 207

causation 205, 305
Cayce, Edgar 112
Cayley, Arthur 229
Cayley, George 457, 485
CCTV for crime prevention 849
cell phones 881, 932
cells 370, 856
    cell theory 479
Cervantes, Miguel de *Don Quixote* 344
chakras 107
Chalmers, David *The Conscious Mind* 911
chance favors the prepared mind 501
chaos theory 794
Charles I 94
Chaucer, Geoffrey 285
Chekhov, Anton 140
chemical elements 441
chemical substance 368
chemotherapy 727
Cherbury, Lord Herbert 353
Chesterton, G. K. 632
chicken and egg conundrum 200
child development 668
child-centered child rearing 718
Childress, James F. *Principles of*
    Biomedical Ethics 870
Childs, Brevard 833
Chinese room argument 872
Chisholm, Roderick 227
Chomsky, Noam 532, 766, 772
Choron, Alexandre-Étienne 459
Christianity 56, 59, 65, 85, 86, 97, 99, 100,
    109, 112, 121, 157, 214, 255, 261
    Christian fundamentalism 595
    Christian universalism 258
    consubstantiation 289
    Crusades 221
    Easter 246
    Free Rein Defense (FRD) 248
    grace 239
    Holy Trinity 253
    Messiah 116
    millenialism 119
    missions 84
    modern Christian apologetics
        632
    original sin 251
    plainchant 240
    Protestantism 126, 260, 261, 323,
        324, 326, 328

Roman Catholicism 96, 126, 159,
    352, 505, 536, 549
Roman Empire 155
    scapegoat 117
    Second Coming 239
    Ten Commandments 122
    three theological virtues 241
    transubstantiation 283
Christmas 259, **260**
Chrysippus 207, 231
Church of England 326
Church of the Flying Spaghetti Monster
    933
Cicé, Jérôme Champion de 441
Cicero 166, 263
civil disobedience 495
Clark, John Bates 569
Classicism 168
Clausius, Rudolf 467, 505
Cleisthenes 151
Climacus, John *The Ladder of Divine*
    Ascent 273
clock, mechanical 306
cloning 915
clothing 24
    dyeing cloth 44
    ready-made clothing 474
Codd, Edgar F. 830
codependency 835
coffeehouses 319
cognitive fluidity 914
cognitivism 766
coherence theory of truth 627
colonialism 84
Columbus, Christopher 59
comedy 149
Comenius, John Amos *Orbis Pictus* 367
Communism 492
comparative psychology 538
compatibilism 412
Comte, Auguste 461, 470
Confucianism 136, 778, 813
    Confucian virtues 152
connectionism 597
conspicuous consumption 600
Constantine I 221
constructivism 617
constructivist epistemology 820
consubstantiation 289
consumerism 605

Contributors

Simon Adams (SA) is a historian and writer living and working in London. He studied history and politics at universities in London and Bristol and has written books for both adults and children for more than twenty years. He specializes in modern history, politics, and jazz.

Kimberly Baltzer-Jaray (KBJ), Ph.D., is a philosophy lecturer at the University of Guelph and King's University College (UWO), Ontario. She is president of the North American Society for Early Phenomenology, a writer for *Things & Ink Magazine*, and author of the blog *A Tattooed Philosopher's Blog: Discussion of the Type I Ink, Therefore I Am.*

Adam Barkman (AB), Ph.D. (Free University of Amsterdam), is associate professor of philosophy at Redeemer University College, Canada. He is the author of four books, including *Imitating the Saints* (2013) and *C. S. Lewis and Philosophy as a Way of Life* (2009), and is the coeditor of three books, most recently *The Philosophy of Ang Lee* (2013) and *The Philosophy and Culture of Ridley Scott* (2013).

Patricia Brace (PBr) is a professor of art history at Southwest Minnesota State University in Marshall, Minnesota. Her Ph.D. in comparative arts is from Ohio University. Her research interests include the aesthetic analysis of popular culture and her creative work is in jewelry design.

Glenn Branch (GB) studied philosophy at Brandeis University and the University of California, Los Angeles. He is the deputy director of the National Center for Science Education, a nonprofit organization that defends the teaching of evolution and climate change.

Per F. Broman (PB) is associate professor of music theory and the associate dean of the College of Musical Arts, Bowling Green State University. He was editor-in-chief of *What Kind of Theory Is Music Theory?* (2008). He recently completed a chapter on

Ingmar Bergman's use of music in his films (*Music, Sound and Filmmakers*; 2012) and a monograph on composer Sven-David Sandström (*Sven-David Sandström*; 2012).

Bob Cassella (BC) holds a BA in history from Norwich University and an MA in management from The George Washington University. He is the author of *Project Management Skills for Kids* (2003) and "Leader Development by Design" (2010).

Timothy Dale (TD) is an assistant professor of political science at the University of Wisconsin-La Crosse. He teaches in the area of political philosophy, and his research interests include democratic theory, political messaging in popular culture, and the scholarship of teaching and learning. He is coeditor of *Homer Simpson Marches on Washington: Dissent in American Popular Culture* (2010), and coauthor of *Political Thinking, Political Theory, and Civil Society* (2009) and the collection *Homer Simpson Ponders Politics: Popular Culture as Political Theory* (2013).

Christopher R. Donohue (CRD) received his doctorate in history from the University of Maryland, College Park, in 2013. He is the historian of the National Human Genome Research Institute at the National Institutes of Health. He is currently undertaking advanced research in public policy methodology at the National Research University Higher School of Economics in Moscow, Russia. He lives in Moscow and the United States.

Jeffrey Dueck (JD) is associate professor of philosophy at Nyack College. His teaching and writing focus on existentialism and pragmatism and how they intersect with issues in religion, ethics, and aesthetics.

George A. Dunn (GD) teaches in the philosophy and religion department of the University of Indianapolis and at the Ningbo Institute of Technology in

Zhejiang Province, China. He is the editor of several volumes in the Blackwell *Philosophy and Pop Culture* series.

Jeff Ewing (JE) is a freelance writer and a graduate student in sociology at the University of Oregon. Jeff has published a number of essays on popular culture and philosophy, including chapters in *Terminator and Philosophy* (2009) and *Arrested Development and Philosophy* (2011).

Janey Fisher (JF) is a freelance writer, copyeditor, and indexer working on both academic and educational books. She graduated in modern history from the University of Oxford in 1976 and taught secondary (high) school for four years before going into publishing. She is coauthor of *CSec Social Studies* (2nd edition, 2008) and author of its companion revision guide (2013), and has published two novels under her maiden name, Jane Anstey (see www.janeanstey.co.uk). She also writes an occasional current affairs blog (http://janeanstey.blogspot.com), where you can find any big ideas she might have from time to time.

Reg Grant (RG) is the author of more than fifty books on historical and military subjects, including *Flight: 100 Years of Aviation* (2004) and *Soldier: A Visual History of the Fighting Man* (2007).

Jackie Higgins (JH) was a staff producer and director at the BBC, where she made documentaries for the flagship science strand *Horizon* and the natural history strand *Natural World*. She has also made films for National Geographic and Discovery Channel.

Thomas Johnson (TJ) completed a Ph.D. in philosophy at the University of Melbourne, Australia, in 2005. Since then, he has taught philosophy and reviewed books in that area, and also continued researching many other areas in the humanities and sciences.

Carol King (CK) studied English literature at the University of Sussex, United Kingdom, and fine art at London's Central St Martin's. She is a freelance writer on art, travel, film, architecture, and photography.

Maria Kingsbury (MK) works as a librarian at Southwest Minnesota State University. She is currently a Ph.D. candidate in technical communication and rhetoric at Texas Tech University.

George Lewis (GL) graduated under another name from Oxford University and now writes encyclopedia entries and articles for a wide range of publications, from *Cosmopolitan* to *The Times* (London).

James McRae (JM) holds a Ph.D. in comparative philosophy from the University of Hawaii at Manoa, and currently serves as an associate professor of philosophy and religion and the coordinator for Asian studies at Westminster College in Fulton, Missouri. His books include *Environmental Philosophy in Asian Traditions of Thought* (with J. Baird Callicott, 1989) and *The Philosophy of Ang Lee* (with Robert Arp and Adam Barkman, 2013).

Nicolas Michaud (NM) is an assistant professor of philosophy at Florida State College, Jacksonville. He has contributed to many philosophy texts, including *Stephen Colbert and Philosophy* (2009), *Green Lantern and Philosophy* (2011), and *World of Warcraft and Philosophy* (2009). He recently edited *The Hunger Games and Philosophy* (2012) and is currently completing *Frankenstein and Philosophy* (2013).

Darryl J. Murphy (DM) is a scholar and writer. He has published numerous scholarly articles and reviews, including a chapter in *Breaking Bad and Philosophy* (2012). Darryl's first novel, *Samantha McTaggart and the Fellowship of Travellers, Volume 1: Morgan's DReAM*, was published in 2012. Darryl studied philosophy and then planning at the University of Guelph, and completed his Ph.D. in philosophy at Wilfrid Laurier University. You can follow Darryl on Twitter @DarrylJMurphy and find him on Facebook at http://goo.gl/keSS5.

Janette Poulton (JP), Ph.D. was awarded her doctorate for research on the development of philosophical dispositions in the middle years of schooling. She recently served her second term as president of the Federation of Australasian Philosophy in Schools Associations, is the education officer for the Victorian Association for Philosophy in Schools, and is on the International Council of Philosophical Inquiry with Children Executive for Philosophy in Schools. She is employed as the academic coordinator of the School of Education at MIT, Melbourne.

Brendan Shea (BSh), Ph.D., is currently visiting assistant professor of philosophy at Winona State University in Minnesota, United States. His research and teaching interests include the history and philosophy of science, logic, and inductive reasoning, and also the philosophy of popular culture.

John R. Shook (JSh), Ph.D., was a professor of philosophy at Oklahoma State University until 2006. Since then, he has been research associate in philosophy and a faculty member of the Science and the Public EdM online program at the University at Buffalo, New York. His latest book is *The God Debates: A 21st Century Guide for Atheists, Believers, and Everyone in Between* (2010).

Jeff Stephenson (JS) is a visiting assistant professor of philosophy at Montana State University, Bozeman, with research interests in contemporary virtue theory, akrasia, moral psychology, and political philosophy. He spends his spare time hiking with his wife and dog.

Barry Stone (BS) is an internationally published author of numerous general history titles, on topics ranging from religious hermits to modern architecture, who, in his alter ego as a travel writer, spends far too much time plotting future destinations. He lives with his family in Picton, a rural hamlet an hour's drive south of Sydney, Australia. His website is www.inscribedbystone.com.

Adam Patrick Taylor (APT) is a doctoral candidate in philosophy at the University at Buffalo in Buffalo, New York. He works primarily on the metaphysics of time and the human person and the philosophy of wellbeing.

Mark Theoharis (MT) is a writer and former attorney living in Kansas, United States. He writes about legal issues for law firms, businesses, and professionals who need to reach lay audiences.

Jamie Watson (JW) is assistant professor of philosophy at Young Harris College in Georgia, United States. He is coauthor of *Critical Thinking: An Introduction to Reasoning Well* (2011), *Philosophy Demystified* (2011), and *What's Good on TV? Understanding Ethics Through Television* (2011), all with Robert Arp, and is also coauthor of the forthcoming *Critical Thinker's Toolkit*, with Peter Fosl and Galen Foresman.

Lani Watson (LWa) is studying for a Ph.D. in philosophy at the University of Edinburgh. Her research topic is the philosophy of questions, with a focus on the role of questions in education. This is naturally guided by an insatiable inquisitiveness concerning the history of ideas and the thinking domain.

Lucy Weir (LW) is a Ph.D. candidate at University College Cork and is writing a thesis about evolutionary science, Zen, and the environmental crisis. The thesis illustrates the realization that philosophy as "practice-enlightenment" allows a person to see themself see and that this integrated, non-dualistic perspective is key to responding to the ecological emergency.

Picture Credits

Decoratifs, Paris, France/Archives Charmet/Bridgeman Art Library 610 Mondadori via Getty Images 612 © Everett Collection Historical/alamy images 614 The Granger Collection/TopFoto.co.uk 615 The Granger Collection/TopFoto.co.uk 616 © Pictorial Press/alamy images 618 Sofia Moro/Cover/Getty Images 619 TopFoto.co.uk 620 © ITAR-TASS Photo Agency/alamy images 621 © Michael Maslan Historic Photographs/Corbis 622 Topical press Agency/Hulton Archive/ Getty Images 623 Musée de Tesse, Le Mans, France/ Giraudon/Bridgeman Art Library 625 © Francois Werli/alamy images 626 © Hulton-Deutsch Collection/ Corbis 630 Museum of Modern Art, New York, USA/ Giraudon /Bridgeman Art Library/ © Succession Picasso/DACS, London 2013 632 Hulton Archive/Getty Images 633 De Agostini/akg images 634 JP Jazz Archive/ Redferns/Getty Images 636 Louvre, Paris/ © Photo Scala, Florence 638 © Bettmann/Corbis 639 © Pictorial Press Ltd/alamy images 641 courtesy Dr. W. S. Maclay and the Guttmann-Maclay Collection © D. Bayes/Lebrecht Music and Arts 642 NBC NewsWire/Getty Images 645 Corbis/ © Succession Marcel Duchamp/ADAGP, Paris and DACS, London 2013 646 Corbis 647 Julian Baum/Science Photo Library 648 Detlev van Ravenswaay/Science Photo Library 649 Anna Yu/Getty Images 651 akg images 652 Hulton Archive/Getty Images 653 © mugshot/alamy images 654 UIG via/Getty Images 656 Private Collection/Archives Charmet/ Bridgeman Art Library 657 © Bettmann/Corbis 659 Photo by Frank Driggs Collection/Getty Images 660 Tyler Stableford/Image Bank/Getty Images 662 RIA Novosti/Science Photo Library 663 © BBC/Corbis 665 © Pictorial Press Ltd/alamy images 666 Spencer Grant/Science Photo Library 667 © INTERFOTO/alamy images 669 © Bettmann/Corbis 671 Tarker/Lebrecht Music and Arts 673 © Bettmann/Corbis 674 akg images 675 Apic/Getty Images 677 Detlev van Ravenswaay/Science Photo Library 678 Popperfoto/Getty Images 679 American Institute of Physics/ Science Photo Library 681 Mortimer Rare Book Room, Smith College/ © Estate of Vanessa Bell, courtesy Henrietta Garnett 682 Moviestore Collection/Rex Features 683 © Bettmann/Corbis 684 © Hulton-Deutsch Collection/Corbis 687 Frank Driggs Collection/Getty Images 688 Photo by Margaret Bourke-White/ Time & Life Pictures/Getty Images 689 © Joshua Dalsimer/Corbis 692 University of Chicago/American Institute of Physics/Science Photo Library 694 Raul Gonzalez Perez/Science Photo Library 696 © Bettmann/Corbis 697 © World History Archive/alamy images 698 Corbis/ © FLC/ ADAGP, Paris and DACS, London 2013 700 Imagno/akg images 701 Photo by Walter Nurnberg/SSPL/Getty Images 702 La Nausée, Jean Paul Sartre, cover of folio edition, 1977, Illustration by Gourmelin © Editions Gallimard 705 Image courtesy of the University of Minnesota 706 Photo by George Skadding/Time Life Pictures/Getty Images 707 Private Collection/Photo © Christie's Images/The Bridgeman Art Library 708 Kenneth Eward/Science Photo Library 709 Alan E. Cober/ © Images.com/Corbis 711 Photo by Galerie Bilderwelt/Getty Images 712 Amblin/Universal/Courtesy Kobal Collection 715 Photo by Paul Popper/Popperfoto/Getty Images 716 Photo by Thomas D. Mcavoy/Time Life Pictures/Getty Images 719 Photo by Bob Gomel/Time Life Pictures/Getty Images 720 Derek Bayes/Lebrecht Music and Arts/ © Trustees of the Paolozzi Foundation, Licensed by DACS 2013 723 © Michael Weber/imagebroker/Corbis 724 © Bettmann/Corbis 726 Photo by Alfred Eisenstaedt/Pix Inc./ Time & Life Pictures/Getty Images 727 National Cancer Institute/Science Photo Library 729 Corbis 731 Getty Images 732 Design by Kurt Hilscher/akg images 734 Private Collection/Photo © Christie's Images/Bridgeman Art Library 735 Roger Viollet/Getty Images 737 © Tony Korody/Sygma/Corbis 738 Massimo Braga, The Lighthouse/Science Photo Library 741 Michael Urban/ © Reuters/Corbis 742 NASA/ESA/Getty Images 745 Photo by Herve GLOAGUEN/Gamma-Rapho/ Getty Images 746 Photo by Joan Adlen/Getty Images 747 © Keystone/Corbis 749 Prominent Features/Bellomo F/Courtesy Kobal Collection 750 Photo by Michael Ochs Archives/Getty Images 753 Photo by Keystone/Getty Images 754 AFP/Getty Images 757 A. Barrington Brown/Science Photo Library 760 © Ted Streshinsky/Corbis 763 © Bettmann/Corbis 764 Private Collection/Archives Charmet/Bridgeman Art Library 767 © JP Laffont/Sygma/Corbis 768 Photo by Alfred Eisenstaedt/Time Life Pictures/Getty Images 769 © Swim Ink 2, LLC/Corbis 771 Photo by Fred W. McDarrah/Getty Images 772 © Lucien Aigner/Corbis 773 Moviepix/Getty Images 774 Photo by John Dominis/Time Life Pictures/Getty Images 776 © Bettmann/Corbis 777 Corbis 779 Corbis 780 Photo: Arthur Ashatz/ Time Life/Getty Images 782 © Bettmann/Corbis 787 Fortean/ © 2006 TopFoto.co.uk 788 Photo by Bill Pierce/Time Life Pictures/Getty Images 789 David Nunnuk/Science Photo Library 790 Photo by Hulton Archive/Getty Images 792 Photo by Gjon Mili/Time & Life Pictures/Getty Images 793 Design Pics/The Irish Image Collection/Getty Images 795 Photo by Archive Photos/Getty Images 796 Photo by Bernard Gotfryd/Getty Images 798 Detini/F Bertola/Getty Images 799 Digital image, The Museum of Modern Art/ © Photo Scala, Florence/© ARS, NY and DACS, London 2013 800 Atlas Collaboration/CERN/Science Photo Library 802 Popperfoto/Getty Images 803 © Bettmann/Corbis 805 Photo by Henry Groskinsky/Time Life Pictures/Getty Images 807 Bridgeman Art Library London 808 © Bettmann/Corbis 811 Popperfoto/Getty Images 812 Yoshikazuy Tsuno/AFP/Getty Images 814 © Sophie Bassouls/Sygma/Corbis 815 Photo by Louis MONIER/Gamma-Rapho/Getty Images 817 Michael Gilbert/Science Photo Library 818 © Michael Ochs Archives/Getty Images 820 © Farrell Grehan/Corbis 821 © David Reed/Corbis 822 Photo by J. R. Eyerman/Time Life Pictures/Getty Images 824 Instituto da Biblioteca Nacional, Lisbon, Portugal/Giraudon/Bridgeman Art Library 825 Michael & Patricia Fogden/Getty Images 826 David Redfern/Getty Images 828 © Laguna Design/Science Photo Library/Corbis 829 Peter Menzel/Science Photo Library 832 Photo by Rolls Press/Popperfoto/Getty Images 834 Photo by Andrew Lepley/Redferns/Getty Images 836 © Michael Ochs Archives/Corbis 838 Margie Politzer/Getty Images 840 Anthony Howarth/Science Photo Library 841 Laguna Design/Science Photo Library 842 Louvre, Paris, France/Giraudon/ Bridgeman Art Library 843 Photo by John Scofield/National Geographic/Getty Images 847 Natural History Museum, London/Science Photo Library 848 © Mike Stewart/Sygma/Corbis 850 Photo by Alex Wong/Getty Images 851 Science Photo Library 852 Tim Flach/Getty Images 854 © Bettmann/Corbis 857 © Interfoto/ alamy images 858 Laguna Design/Science Photo Library 859 Fortean/TopFoto.co.uk 861 © Peter Dench/In Pictures/Corbis 863 Nemo Ramjet/Science Photo Library 865 © E. J. Camp/Corbis 866 Photo by David Corio/Michael Ochs Archives/Getty Images 869 Atelier Richter 870 James Cavallini/Science Photo Library 873 Photo by Andreas Feininger/Time & Life Pictures/Getty Images 874 David A. Hardy, Futures: 50 Years in Space Science Photo Library 876 Pete Souza/White House/Corbis 877 Odd Andersen/AFP/Getty Images 878 © EMPICS/TopFoto.co.uk 879 David Mack/Science Photo Library 880 Photo by NBC/NBCU Photo Bank/ Getty Images 882 JP Laffont/Sygma/Corbis 885 © Joerg Boethling/alamy images 888 © Simon Rawles/alamy images 889 Daniel Schoenen/Getty Images 890 © Levi Bianco/Getty Images 893 Photo by SSPL/Getty Images 894 © Reuters/Corbis 896 Tim Sloan/AFP/Getty Images 897 © Claudia Daut/Reuters/Corbis 899 Mark Thomas/Science Photo Library 901 Asif Hassan/AFP/Getty Images 902 Sam Ogden/Science Photo Library 904 © 2005 Keystone/TopFoto.co.uk 905 © Dan Herrick/alamy images 907 © Nathaniel Welch/Corbis 909 © Robyn Twomey/Corbis 910 CNRI/Science Photo Library 911 Pasieka/Science Photo Library 913 Victor Habbick Visions/Getty Images 914 P. Plailly/E. Daynes/Science Photo Library 915 Karen Kasmauski/Getty Images 916 © George Hammerstein/Corbis 919 Mehau Kulyk/Science Photo Library 921 Sam Yeh/AFP/Getty Images 922 © Jeff Minton/Corbis 923 © Mike Ellison 924 Felix Pharand-Deschenes, Globaia/ Science Photo Library 925 © Topic Photo Agency/Corbis 926 JJP/Eurelios/Science Photo Library 928 Simon Dawson/Bloomberg/Getty Images 931 © RIA Novosti/TopFoto.co.uk 933 Bobby Henderson 935 Nicholas Roberts/AFP/Getty Images 936 Wellcome Library, London 939 © Jenny Matthews/In Pictures/Corbis 940 Photo by David McNew/Getty Images 941 Laguna Design/Science Photo Library

Acknowledgments

Quintessence Editions would like to thank the following individuals for their assistance in the creation of this book:
Rebecca Gee, Helen Snaith, and Anna, Angelika, and Julia at akg-images.